Topic Tackler CD-ROM

The Topic Tackler CD is included FREE with each new copy of the text.

This software is a complete tutorial focusing on those concepts in managerial accounting that give students the most trouble. Help is provided for 2 key topics in every chapter using a step-by-step sequence of video clips, PowerPoint® slides, interactive exercises, and self-test quizzes. Help screens are provided that show the solution and explain why an answer is correct.

Concepts appearing in the text that receive additional treatment in Topic Tackler are marked by this unique icon in the margin.

Video Clips provide an engaging introduction to each concept and an enlightening, realworld perspective from a variety of professionals who rely on accounting for important business activities as well as accounting experts.

Slide Shows presented in PowerPoint offer step-by-step coverage of challenging topics, providing a great resource for review. Some feature animations and/or audio.

The **Practice** element includes a mixture of drag-and-drop and fill-in-the-blank exercises that reinforce chapter concepts by providing immediate feedback and explanation.

With **Self-Test**, students have an ideal vehicle for quizzing themselves on their comprehension of the material.

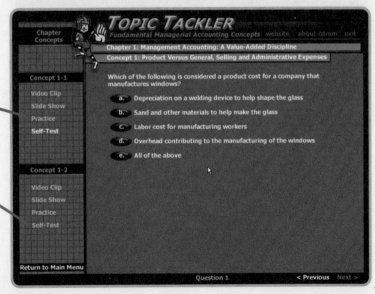

Fundamental Managerial
ACCOUNTING
Concepts

Second Edition

Fundamental Managerial

ACCOUNTING

Concepts

Thomas P. Edmonds

Cindy D. Edmonds

Bor-Yi Tsay
All of the University of Alabama-Birmingham

Nancy W. Schneider
Contributing Author Lynchburg College

McGraw-Hill
Irwin

Boston   Burr Ridge, IL   Dubuque, IA   Madison, WI   New York   San Francisco   St. Louis
Bangkok   Bogotá   Caracas   Kuala Lumpur   Lisbon   London   Madrid   Mexico City
Milan   Montreal   New Delhi   Santiago   Seoul   Singapore   Sydney   Taipei   Toronto

McGraw-Hill

A Division of The McGraw·Hill Companies

FUNDAMENTAL MANAGERIAL ACCOUNTING CONCEPTS

Published by McGraw-Hill/Irwin, a business unit of The McGraw-Hill Companies, Inc. 1221 Avenue of the Americas, New York, NY, 10020. Copyright © 2003, 2000 by The McGraw-Hill Companies, Inc. All rights reserved. No part of this publication may be reproduced or distributed in any form or by any means, or stored in a database or retrieval system, without the prior written consent of The McGraw-Hill Companies, Inc., including, but not limited to, in any network or other electronic storage or transmission, or broadcast for distance learning.

Some ancillaries, including electronic and print components, may not be available to customers outside the United States.

This book is printed on acid-free paper.

domestic   2 3 4 5 6 7 8 9 0 VNH/VNH 0 9 8 7 6 5 4 3 2
international 1 2 3 4 5 6 7 8 9 0 VNH/VNH 0 9 8 7 6 5 4 3 2 1

ISBN 0-07-247321-5

Publisher: *Brent Gordon*
Sponsoring editor: *Melody Marcus*
Managing developmental editor: *Gail Korosa*
Marketing manager: *Richard Kolasa*
Senior project manager: *Kimberly D. Hooker*
Production supervisor: *Debra Sylvester*
Media technology: *David Barrick*
Freelance design coordinator: *Laurie J. Entringer*
Supplement producer: *Cathy Tepper*
Photo research coordinator: *Jeremy Cheshareck*
Photo researcher: *Connie Gardner*
Cover design: *Ellen Pettengell Design*
Interior design: *Ellen Pettengell Design*
Typeface: *10/12 Times Roman*
Compositor: *GAC/Indianapolis*
Printer: *Von Hoffmann Press, Inc.*

Library of Congress Cataloging-in-Publication Data

Edmonds, Thomas P.
   Fundamental managerial accounting concepts / Thomas P. Edmonds, Cindy D. Edmonds, Bor-Yi Tsay.—2nd ed.
     p. cm.
   Includes index.
   ISBN 0-07-247321-5 (alk. paper)
   1. Managerial accounting. I. Edmonds, Cindy D. II. Tsay, Bor -Yi. III. Title.
HF5657.4.E35 2003
   658.15'11—dc21   2001044912

INTERNATIONAL EDITION ISBN 0-07-119916-0

www.mhhe.com

This book is dedicated to our students whose questions have so frequently caused us to reevaluate our method of presentation that they have, in fact, become major contributors to the development of this text

Thomas P. Edmonds

Thomas P. Edmonds, Ph.D., holds the Friends and Alumni Professorship in the Department of Accounting at the University of Alabama at Birmingham (UAB). He has been actively involved in teaching accounting principles throughout his academic career. Dr. Edmonds has coordinated the accounting principles courses at the University of Houston and UAB. He currently teaches introductory accounting in mass sections that frequently contain more than 180 students. He has received five prestigious teaching awards including the UAB President's Excellence in Teaching Award and the distinguished Ellen Gregg Ingalls Award for excellence in classroom teaching. He has written numerous articles that have appeared in many publications including *Issues in Accounting*, the *Journal of Accounting Education*, *Advances in Accounting Education*, *Accounting Education: A Journal of Theory, Practice and Research*, the *Accounting Review*, *Advances in Accounting*, the *Journal of Accountancy*, *Management Accounting*, the *Journal of Commercial Bank Lending*, the *Banker's Magazine*, and the *Journal of Accounting, Auditing, and Finance*. Dr. Edmonds is a member of the editorial board for *Advances in Accounting: Teaching and Curriculum Innovations* and *Issues in Accounting Education*. He has published four textbooks, five practice problems (including two computerized problems), and a variety of supplemental materials including study guides, work papers, and solutions manuals. Dr. Edmonds' writing is influenced by a wide range of business experience. He is a successful entrepreneur. He has worked as a management accountant for Refrigerated Transport, a trucking company. Dr. Edmonds also worked in the not-for-profit sector as a commercial lending officer for the Federal Home Loan Bank. In addition, he has acted as a consultant to major corporations including First City Bank of Houston, AmSouth Bank in Birmingham, Texaco, and Cortland Chemicals. Dr. Edmonds began his academic training at Young Harris Community College in Young Harris, Georgia. He received a B.B.A. degree with a major in finance from Georgia State University in Atlanta, Georgia. He obtained an M.B.A. degree with a concentration in finance from St. Mary's University in San Antonio, Texas. His Ph.D. degree with a major in accounting was awarded by Georgia State University. Dr. Edmonds' work experience and academic training have enabled him to bring a unique user perspective to this textbook.

Cindy D. Edmonds

Cindy D. Edmonds, Ph.D., is an Associate Professor of Accounting at the University of Alabama at Birmingham. She serves as the coordinator of the introductory accounting courses at UAB. Dr. Edmonds received the 2001 Loudell Ellis Robinson Excellence in Teaching Award. Also, in 2000 and 2001 she was one of two School of Business faculty members nominated for the Ellen Gregg Ingalls Award for excellence in classroom teaching. She has written a variety of supplemental text materials including practice problems, a study guide, work papers, and test banks. Dr. Edmonds' articles appear in numerous publications including *Advances in Accounting Education*, *Journal of Education for Business*, *Journal of Accounting Regulation*, *Advances in Accounting*, *Management Accounting*, *CMA Journal*, *Disclosures*, and *Business & Professional Ethics Journal*. Her manuscript "Running a City on a Shoe String" received a certificate of merit award from the Institute of Management Accountants. The manuscript was used by the City of Vestavia in its application for Moody's Municipal Bond Rating. Dr. Edmonds is heavily involved in service activities. She is the 2001 president of the Birmingham

Chapter of the American Society of Women Accountants. Dr. Edmonds has worked in the insurance industry, in a manufacturing company, and in a governmental agency. This work experience has enabled her to bring a real-world flavor to her writing. Dr. Edmonds holds a B.S. degree from Auburn University, an M.B.A degree from the University of Houston and a Ph.D. degree from the University of Alabama.

Bor-Yi Tsay

Bor-Yi Tsay, Ph.D., CPA is a Professor of Accounting at the University of Alabama at Birmingham (UAB) where he has taught since 1986. He has taught principles of accounting courses at the University of Houston and UAB. Currently, he teaches an undergraduate cost accounting course and an MBA accounting analysis course. Dr. Tsay received the 1996 Loudell Ellis Robinson Excellence in Teaching Award. He has also received numerous awards for his writing and publications including John L. Rhoads Manuscripts Award, John Pugsley Manuscripts Award, Van Pelt Manuscripts Award, and three certificates of merits from the Institute of Management Accountants. His articles appeared in *Journal of Accounting Education, Management Accounting, Journal of Managerial Issues, CPA Journal, CMA Magazine, Journal of Systems Management,* and *Journal of Medical Systems.* He currently serves as a member of the board of the Birmingham Chapter, Institute of Management Accountants. He is also a member of the American Institute of Certified Public Accountants and Alabama Society of Certified Public Accountants. Dr. Tsay received a B.S. in agricultural economics from National Taiwan University, an M.B.A. with a concentration in Accounting from Eastern Washington University, and a Ph.D. in Accounting from the University of Houston.

During the past decade, the effects of technology, globalization, and the concentration of power have acted to create a new business environment. This environment is characterized by rapid change and fierce competition. Managers are under extreme pressure to produce consistent earnings growth and employees are expected to make meaningful contributions to profitability early in their careers. To be able to succeed in this environment, students must develop critical thinking, communication, and computer skills as well as an understanding of accounting procedures and practices. The goal of this text is to better prepare students for entry into the new business environment by providing an appropriate balance between skill development and technical competence.

Traditionally, accounting education has emphasized a content-based approach. Specifically, skill development has been held at a relatively low level (focused primarily on comprehension and recall skills) and rigor has been measured by the quantity of content covered. More and more topics have been added to the curricula and textbooks grow ever larger. Unfortunately, this model provides little opportunity for professors to help students develop the skills that the new business environment demands. The number of classroom hours available is limited. With so much material to cover, there just is not time available to work on skill development.

This text offers you an opportunity to shift the traditional educational paradigm. Content is focused on essential concepts, thereby reducing the quantity of material that must be covered. As a result, you have more time to work on skill development. Indeed, the Instructors' Resource Manual provides step-by-step instructions for the implementation of innovative teaching methodologies such as active learning and group dynamics. It offers a rich set of short discovery learning cases which provide a forum for class-opening experiences that are highly effective in stimulating interest and developing critical thinking skills. In addition, the text itself contains many innovative features to better prepare students to face the challenges of a new business environment. These features are discussed next.

▌End-of-Chapter Materials

The balance between technical competence and other essential business skills is a delicate one that is best left to individual instructors. We offer an opportunity to shift the balance, the degree of which is up to you. The text offers a rich set of end-of-chapter materials that includes separate sections for conventional and innovative resources.

Conventional End-of-Chapter Materials

Conventional exercises and problems are presented in Set A and Set B series. The Set B represents a conceptual mirror image of the Set A exercises and problems. Names and numbers are changed and the context sometimes differs. However, if you have demonstrated concepts with Set A exercises or problems, you can rest assured that your students will be adequately prepared to work the mirror image Set B exercises or problems as a reinforcement experience. Instructors who choose to emphasize technical competence will find an abundant supply of conventional end-of-chapter materials.

Innovative End-of-Chapter Materials

An innovative activities section entitled Analyze, Think, Communicate, (ATC) is included in the end-of-chapter materials for each chapter. The ATC section includes business application cases, group exercises, research and writing assignments, and ethical dilemmas. Furthermore, each ATC section contains two Excel spreadsheet applications. The text is not designed to explain spreadsheet technicalities, but the Excel problems do include teaching tips that facilitate the student's ability to use spreadsheet software. The depth and diversity of the end-of-chapter materials allow you to select the degree of emphasis to place on business skill development (critical thinking, communication, research, writing, ethics, group dynamics, and computer technology) that you deem to be appropriate in the new business environment. Examples of the ATC materials are provided for your review.

WRITING ASSIGNMENT *Selection of the Appropriate Cost Driver* ATC 5–4

Bullions Enterprises, Inc. (BEI), makes gold, silver, and bronze medals used to recognize outstanding athletic performance in regional and national sporting events. The per unit direct costs of producing the medals follows.

	Gold	Silver	Bronze
Direct materials	$300	$130	$ 35
Labor	120	120	120

During 2002, BEI made 1,200 units of each type of medal for a total of 3,600 (1,200 × 3) medals. All medals are created through the same production process, and they are packaged and shipped in identical containers. Indirect overhead costs amounted to $324,000. BEI currently uses the number of units as the cost driver for the allocation of overhead cost. As a result, BEI allocated $90 ($324,000 ÷ 3,600 units) of overhead cost to each unit of medal produced.

Required

The president of the company has questioned the wisdom of assigning the same amount of overhead to each type of medal. He believes that overhead should be assigned on the basis of the cost to produce the medals. In other words, more overhead should be charged to expensive gold medals, less to silver, and even less to bronze. Assume that you are BEI's chief financial officer. Write a memo responding to the president's suggestion.

ETHICAL DILEMMA *Budget Games* ATC 8–5

Melody Lovelady is the most highly rewarded sales representative at Swift Corporation. Her secret to success is always to understate your abilities. Ms. Lovelady is assigned to a territory in which her customer base is increasing at approximately 25 percent per year. Each year she estimates that her budgeted sales will be 10 percent higher than her previous year's sales. With little effort, she is able to double her budgeted sales growth. At Swift's annual sales meeting, she receives an award and a large bonus. Of course, Ms. Lovelady does not disclose her secret to her colleagues. Indeed, she always talks about how hard it is to continue to top her previous performance. She tells herself if they are dumb enough to fall for this rubbish, I'll milk it for all it's worth.

Required
a. What is the name commonly given to the budget game Ms. Lovelady is playing?
b. Does Ms. Lovelady's behavior violate any of the standards of ethical conduct shown in Exhibit 1–13 of Chapter 1?
c. Recommend how Ms. Lovelady's budget game could be stopped.

...operating income? Explain...

GROUP ASSIGNMENT *Operating Leverage* ATC 2–2

The Parent Teacher Association (PTA) of Meadow High School is planning a fund-raising campaign. The PTA is considering the possibility of hiring Eric Logan, a world-renowned investment counselor, to address the public. Tickets would sell for $28 each. The school has agreed to let the PTA use Harville Auditorium at no cost. Mr. Logan is willing to accept one of two compensation arrangements. He will sign an agreement to receive a fixed fee of $10,000 regardless of the number of tickets sold. Alternatively, he will accept payment of $20 per ticket sold. In communities similar to that in which Meadow is located, Mr. Logan has drawn an audience of approximately 500 people.

Required

a. In front of the class, present a statement showing the expected net income assuming 500 people buy tickets.

b. The instructor will divide the class into groups and then organize the groups into four sections. The instructor will assign one of the following tasks to each section of groups.

Group Tasks

(1) Assume the PTA pays Mr. Logan a fixed fee of $10,000. Determine the amount of net income that the PTA will earn if ticket sales are 10 percent higher than expected. Calculate the percentage change in net income.

(2) Assume that the PTA pays Mr. Logan a fixed fee of $10,000. Determine the amount of net income that the PTA will earn if ticket sales are 10 percent lower than expected. Calculate the percentage change in net income.

(3) Assume that the PTA pays Mr. Logan $20 per ticket sold. Determine the amount of net income that the PTA will earn if ticket sales are 10 percent higher than expected. Calculate the percentage change in net income.

(4) Assume that the PTA pays Mr. Logan $20 per ticket sold. Determine the amount of net income that the PTA will earn if ticket sales are 10 percent lower than expected. Calculate the percentage change in net income.

c. Have each group select a spokesperson. Have one of the spokespersons in each section of groups go to the board and present the results of the analysis conducted in Part *b*. Resolve any discrepancies in the computations presented at the board and those developed by the other groups.

d. Draw conclusions regarding the risks and rewards associated with operating leverage. At a minimum, answer the following questions.

(1) Which type of cost structure (fixed or variable) produces the higher growth potential in profitability for a company?

(2) Which type of cost structure (fixed or variable) faces the higher risk of declining profitability for a company?

(3) Under what circumstances should a company seek to establish a fixed cost structure?

(4) Under what circumstances should a company seek to establish a variable cost structure?

...eatures of ethical misconduct ....ed in

ATC 4–6   SPREADSHEET ASSIGNMENT *Using Excel*

Dorina Company makes cases of canned dog food in batches of 1,000 cases and sells each case for $15. The plant capacity is 50,000 cases; the company currently makes 40,000 cases. DoggieMart has offered to buy 1,500 cases for $12 per case. Because product-level and facility-level costs are unaffected by a special order, they are omitted.

Required

a. Prepare a spreadsheet like the following one to calculate the contribution to income if the special order is accepted. Construct formulas so that the number of cases or the price could be changed and the new contribution would be automatically calculated.

b. Try different order sizes (such as 2,000) or different prices to see the effect on contribution to profit.

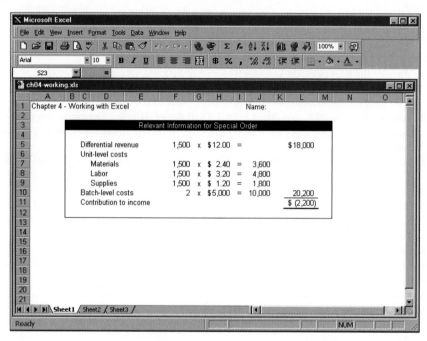

Spreadsheet Tips

1. The numbers in cells F7 to F9 should be formulas that refer to F5. This allows the number of cases to be changed in cell F5 with the other cells changing automatically.

2. The formula in cell F10 uses a function named ROUNDUP to calculate the even number of batches. The formula should be = ROUNDUP(F5/1000,0) where the zero refers to rounding up to the nearest whole number.

A variety of writing, group, technology, ethics, and Internet assignments is included. These problems are marked appropriately for easy identification.

Writing   **Group**   **Technology**   **Ethics**   **Internet**

Emphasis on Decision-Making Concepts

Traditional texts have emphasized accounting practices for manufacturing companies. The new business environment has resulted in a shift toward service companies, especially in the United States. The text recognizes this critical shift by emphasizing decision-making concepts applicable to both service and manufacturing companies. An examination of our brief table of contents (see page xxiv) shows that we introduce the topics such as operating leverage, cost-volume-profit analysis, relevance, and cost allocation early. We cover traditional topics such as manufacturing cost flow, job-order and process costing toward the end of the text. This placement is significant because it reflects the emphasis that we place on decision-making concepts throughout the text.

Isolating Concepts

How do you promote the understanding of concepts? We believe that concepts should be isolated and discussed within a decision-making context. The implementation of this strategy has caused us to deviate from the traditional approach in many respects. For example, notice that the traditional chapter covering cost terminology (i.e., usually Chapter 2) has been eliminated from this textbook. We believe that introducing a plethora of detached cost terms in a single chapter is an ineffective teaching strategy. At best, students tend to memorize a few definitions. Indeed, the primary theme of a *terms chapter* seems to be: "Here are some definitions. Memorize them now and you will use them later." This sets a bad precedent. The appropriate educational expectation is comprehension, not memorization.

In contrast, we isolate concepts and introduce them singly. For example, we separate the concept of *product costing* from the related issues of manufacturing cost flow and the corresponding recording procedures. We assume that all materials purchased are used during the accounting period and that all products started are completed during the accounting period. Accordingly, the only inventory account used is a finished goods account. Within this context, students can clearly see how depreciation on manufacturing equipment is accumulated in an inventory account while depreciation on administrative equipment is expensed. Similarly, differences between administrative salaries and production wages are readily apparent. We use a financial statements model to highlight these critical comparisons (See Exhibit 5 in Chapter 1 as an example). Manufacturing cost flow is discussed in a separate chapter after students have had time to digest the distinction between a product cost versus a general, selling, and administrative expense.

Interrelationships between Concepts

While isolating concepts facilitates the learning process, students must ultimately understand how the concepts are interrelated in business practice. The text has been written so that knowledge builds in a stepwise fashion to the point of full integration. For example, notice how the definitions of relevant costs are compared to those of cost behavior on page 141 of Chapter 4 and how the definitions of direct costs are contrasted to those of cost behavior and cost relevance on page 192 of Chapter 5. The commitment to integrated learning is evident not only in the text material but also in exercises and problems. The aim of this text is to develop a pedagogical format that facilitates the students' ability to apply accounting concepts to increasingly complex organizational environments.

Avoid Logical Inconsistencies

What is a period cost and how does it differ from a product cost? Traditionally, a period cost is defined as a cost that is expensed in the period in which it is incurred. This definition fails to distinguish period costs from product costs because product costs are also expensed in the period in which they are incurred (sold). Indeed, both period and product costs are accumulated in asset accounts until such time that the assets are used. More specifically, there is no conceptual difference in the way prepaids, supplies, depreciable assets, and inventory are treated in the financial statements. The fact is, the term "period" cost is a false identifier. We avoid this inconsistency by focusing on the true distinction, which is between product costs versus general, selling, and administrative costs. This is not an isolated incident but an example of a consistent commitment to avoid logical inconsistencies that thwart the comprehension of concepts.

Avoid Inconsistent Terminology

It is highly confusing when the same term is used to identify different concepts. Even so, many textbook authors have been careless in the use of terminology. For example, the term *fixed cost* is generally used to mean that a cost stays the same regardless of the volume of activity. However, within the context of a special order decision, the term fixed is used to imply that the cost stays the same regardless of whether the special order is accepted or rejected. Similarly, the term *direct cost* is frequently used interchangeably with the term *variable cost*. For example, books frequently compare "direct or variable" costing with full absorption costing. This terminology implies that direct and variable costing are the same thing. We have made every effort to avoid the use of conflicting terminology in this text.

Context-Sensitive Nature of Terminology

Students are frequently confused by the fact that the same exact cost can be classified as fixed, variable, direct, indirect, relevant, or not relevant. For example, the salary of a store manager is fixed regardless of the number of customers that enter the store. However, the same salary is variable relative to the number of stores operated by a company. The salary is directly traceable to a particular store but not to particular sales made in the store. The salary is relevant to a decision regarding whether to eliminate the store but not relevant to a decision as to whether a department within the store should be eliminated. Students must learn to identify the circumstances that determine the classification of costs. The chapter material, exercises, and problems in this text are designed to encourage students to analyze the decision-making

EXERCISE 2–1A *Identifying Cost Behavior*   **L.O. 1**

Sally's Kitchen, a fast-food restaurant company, operates a chain of restaurants across the nation. Each restaurant employs eight people; one is a manager paid a salary plus a bonus equal to 3 percent of sales. Other employees, two cooks, one dishwasher, and four waitresses, are paid salaries. Each manager is budgeted $2,000 per month for advertising cost.

Required
Classify each of the following costs incurred by Sally's Kitchen as fixed, variable, or mixed.
a. Manager's compensation relative to the number of customers.
b. Waitresses' salaries relative to the number of restaurants.
c. Advertising costs relative to the number of customers for a particular restaurant.
d. Rental costs relative to the number of restaurants.
e. Cooks' salaries at a particular location relative to the number of customers.
f. Cost of supplies (cups, plates, spoons, etc.) relative to the number of customers.

context rather than to memorize definitions. Exercise 2–1A in Chapter 2 provides an example of how the text teaches students to make appropriate interpretations of differential decision-making environments.

▌Excel Applications

Spreadsheet applications are an essential component of contemporary accounting practice. Students must be aware of the power of spreadsheet software and know how accounting data are presented in spreadsheet format. Toward this end, we have included a discussion of Microsoft Excel spreadsheet applications wherever appropriate in the text. In most instances, actual spreadsheets are shown in the text. Refer to Exhibit 1 in Chapter 8 and Exhibit 6 in Chapter 10 for examples. These exhibits are shown on the following pages for your review.

Also, end-of-chapter materials include problems that can be completed with spreadsheet software. These are indicated by an Excel logo, a sample of which is shown below.

Exhibit 8–1 *Static and Flexible Budgets in Excel Spreadsheet*

	Static Budget	Flexible Budgets				
Number of Units	18,000	16,000	17,000	18,000	19,000	20,000
Per Unit Standards						
Sales Revenue ($80.00)	$1,440,000	$1,280,000	$1,360,000	$1,440,000	$1,520,000	$1,600,000
Variable Manuf. Costs						
Materials ($12.00)	216000	192000	204000	216000	228000	240000
Labor ($16.80)	302400	268800	285600	302400	319200	336000
Overhead ($5.60)	100800	89600	95200	100800	106400	112000
Variable G,S,&A ($15.00)	270000	240000	255000	270000	285000	300000
Contribution Margin	550,800	489,600	520,200	550,800	581,400	612,000
Fixed Costs						
Manufacturing	201,600	201,600	201,600	201,600	201,600	201,600
G,S,&A	90,000	90,000	90,000	90,000	90,000	90,000
Net Income	$259,200	$198,000	$228,600	$259,200	$289,800	$320,400

PROBLEM 1–20A *Service Versus Manufacturing Companies*

L.O. 2, 3, 4, 5

Decker Company began operations on January 1, 2005, by issuing common stock for $30,000 cash. During 2005, Decker received $40,000 cash from revenue and incurred costs that required $60,000 of cash payments.

Required
Prepare an income statement, balance sheet, and statement of cash flows for Decker Company for 2005, under each of the following independent scenarios.

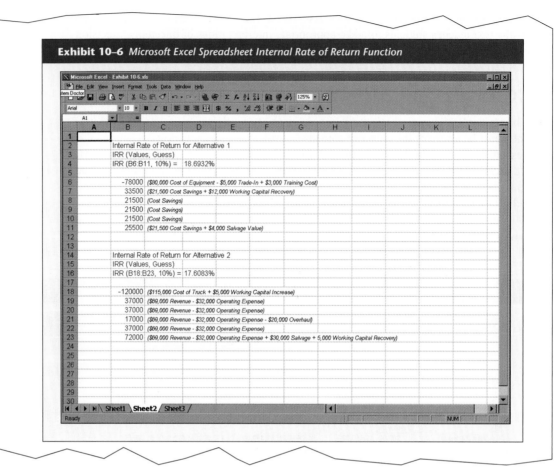

Exhibit 10–6 *Microsoft Excel Spreadsheet Internal Rate of Return Function*

▮ Interesting and Lively Writing Style

The text frequently conveys information through scenarios that permit students to view managers in action. In Chapter 3, a management team uses cost-volume-profit (CVP) analysis to evaluate the potential profitability of a new product. Along the way, the team confronts an ethical dilemma. Should substandard materials be used to accomplish a target-costing objective? In Chapter 5, a group of department heads advocates the use of allocation bases that serve their self-interests. Tempers fly and anger prevents one participant from reaching a compromise that would benefit his unit. The importance of the human side of the decision process becomes readily apparent. Interesting vignettes such as these are interspersed throughout the text. While this is not a novel, neither is it your typical dull textbook. Managerial accounting tools are introduced in a fashion that arouses and maintains student interest.

▮ Real-World Applications

Student interest is further piqued through the use of real-world illustrations. Each chapter opens with a feature titled *The Curious Accountant*. This feature poses an interesting question that relates to the general content of the chapter. The questions involve real-world companies and include pictures that stimulate student interest. The question is answered in a text box located a few pages after the page containing the question. Real-world applications that relate to specific topics covered within each chapter are introduced through a feature titled *Reality Bytes*. This feature may contain survey results, graphics, quotes from business leaders, and other information that relates the text material to accounting practice. The objective here is to stimulate student interest by demonstrating the usefulness of managerial accounting tools in the management of real-world organizations. Examples of **The Curious Accountant** and **Reality Bytes** are shown on the following page for your review.

the *curious* accountant

Most people would expect an increase in a company's revenues to cause an increase in its profits, but they may be surprised that a small percentage of change in revenue can generate a dramatic difference in profits. Consider the following data for Texaco.

Year	Revenues (in millions)	Percentage Increase From Previous Year	Operating Income Before Taxes (in millions)	Percentage Increase From Previous Year
2000	$50,100	43.5	$4,218	137.1
1999	34,925	13.0	1,779	153.8
1998	30,910	N/A	701	N/A

Note that the profitability numbers shown are for *operating income before taxes;* they do not include any unusual items that may have occurred at Texaco. Considering this, what could possibly explain how a relatively small increase in revenue (13%) could result in such a large increase in operating income (153.8%)?

reality bytes

Do real-world companies use *target pricing?* According to C. Michael Armstrong, CEO of AT&T, target costing is a very real business practice. Indeed, Mr. Armstrong suggests that an unreasonable target price is the chief cause of AT&T's decision to delay the widespread deployment of a new local phone service technology. The new "Project Angel" system uses radio technology to bypass the wires of the Baby Bell phone companies. Unfortunately, the cost of deploying the technology in a test site in Chicago averaged $1,100 per home. Although this cost is prohibitive, AT&T still plans to continue testing the project. According to Mr. Armstrong, "it'll probably take two more cycles of technology" before costs drop to a level that will enable AT&T to offer the system at a competitive price.

Source: Peter Elstrom, "AT&T's Fallen Angel," *Business Week,* April 13, 1998, p. 4.

▮ Managerial Orientation

This is not your typical cost accounting textbook approach. Service, financial, and not-for-profit entities are placed on equal footing with manufacturing companies. For example, a retail sales company is used as the background for the introduction of the budgeting chapter. A quick view of the table of contents reveals an early emphasis on decision making. In the first chapter, product costing is related to financing opportunities, managerial incentives, and income tax considerations. More traditional topics such as manufacturing cost flow and recording procedures are presented at the end of the text rather than at the beginning. Technical terminology is introduced within a decision-making context. For instance in Chapter 2, cost behavior is related to operating leverage through an example in which fixed cost structure is used to provide a competitive operating advantage. The interpretation rather than the computation of variances is emphasized in Chapter 8. The overall theme of the text is to introduce concepts in the context of decision making.

▮ Information Overload

The proposed table of contents reflects our efforts to address the information overload problem. We believe that existing managerial textbooks contain significantly more material than can be digested by the typical student. Education research suggests that information overload leads to memorization. Very little is accomplished when students are exposed to such a volume of material that they are unable to comprehend the basic concepts. This text seeks to emphasize the comprehension of concepts by reducing the volume of content. You will notice that we have limited the number of chapters to 14. This contrasts with traditional texts that normally contain between 18 and 20 chapters.

▮ Flexibility in Sequencing of Material

The arrangement of material in the table of contents represents only one of many alternatives for the sequence in which material can be covered. For example, after establishing a conceptual foundation by covering Chapters 1, 2, 4, and 5, you could proceed with coverage of Chapter 11 (product cost flow) followed by Chapter 12 (job-order and process costing). With the exception of the foundation chapters (1, 2, 4, and 5), all chapters stand alone. More specifically, you can skip around or omit Chapters 3 and 6 through 14 as you deem appropriate. Indeed, Chapters 7, 13, and 14 can be covered prior to Chapter 1. If your students do not cover cash flow concepts in their financial accounting course, we recommend that you begin your course by covering Chapter 14, Statement of Cash Flows. Several of the chapters in this text assume that students have had an exposure to cash flow concepts. Accordingly, it will be necessary to skip cash flow topics in certain chapters or to establish a foundation that will enable your students to identify cash flow concepts. Incidentally, we emphasize the direct method with the primary objective of having students identify events as financing, investing, or operating. Accordingly, gaining the exposure needed to cover the cash flow applications presented in the text is not a difficult task. Even so, if you choose to skip cash flow coverage, rest assured that you can do so without negative consequences. The text is designed to permit the maximum level of instructor flexibility.

Some instructors believe that management accounting begins with the budgeting process. Furthermore, they recognize the logical link between the coverage of financial statements in the financial accounting course and the coverage of pro forma statements in the budgeting chapter. Since our budgeting chapter is explained within the context of a retail establishment, you can start your managerial accounting course with Chapter 7 (planning for profit and cost control) if you are inclined to do so.

▌ Supplemental Materials

The text is supported by a complete package of supplements. Members of the author team have been heavily involved in the development of the supplement package. Accordingly, you can rest assured that the supplements match the text. The package includes the following items:

For Instructors

Instructor's Resource Manual: Prepared by Thomas P. Edmonds and Nancy Schneider (ISBN 0-07-247325-8) The text is suitable to new teaching approaches such as group dynamics and active pedagogy. The instructors' guide provides step-by-step explicit instructions as to how the text can be used to accomplish the implementation of these alternative teaching methodologies. Guidance is also provided for instructors who choose to use the traditional lecture method. The guide includes lesson plans, demonstration problems, student work papers for those problems, and solutions to the demonstration problems.

Solutions Manual: Prepared by Bor-Yi Tsay (ISBN 0-07-247324-X) The solutions manual has been prepared by the authors and contains complete answers to all questions, exercises, problems, and cases. The manual has been tested using a variety of quality control procedures to ensure accuracy. After the initial preparation of the solutions, the problems and exercises were reworked "blind." The second set of answers was then compared with the previous solutions by an independent reviewer. Any differences were reconciled. After this process, the solutions manual was again proofed and checked for accuracy by J. Russell Madray of Clemson University and the Madray Group, Inc. and Jed Ashley of Grossmont Community College. While the author team retains the responsibility for any errors that may occur, we express our appreciation for the individuals who have exhibited a zero tolerance attitude that is required to maintain the highest standards of excellence.

Solutions Transparencies (ISBN 0-07-247330-4): Prepared by Bor-Yi Tsay Transparencies are prepared in easy-to-read 14 point bold type. They are mirror images of the answers provided in the solutions manual and consistent with the forms contained in the working papers. This ensures congruence between your in-class presentations and the follow-up exposure that students attain when they view the solutions manual or use the working papers.

Test Bank: Prepared by J. Lowell Mooney (ISBN 0-07-247328-2) The test bank includes an expansive array of true/false, multiple-choice, short discussion questions, and open-ended problems.

Computest A computerized version of the test bank for more efficient use is available in a Windows platform available on the Presentation Manager CD-ROM.

Presentation Manager CD-ROM (ISBN 0-07-247333-9) This integrated CD allows instructors to customize their own classroom presentations. It contains key supplements such as PowerPoint slides, Test Bank, Instructor's Resource Manual, Solutions Manual, and videos. The Presentation Manager makes it easy for instructors to create multimedia presentations.

Managerial Accounting Video Library (ISBN 0-07-237617-1) These short videos developed by Dallas County Community College provide the impetus for lively classroom discussion. The focus is on the preparation, analysis, and use of accounting information for business decision making.

Web Page (http://www.mhhe.com/edmonds2003) Our Web page was created for both students and instructors. It includes the Online Learning Center that follows the text chapter by chapter. Students will find learning objectives and their explanations, key terms, Excel Templates, PowerPoint slides, and self-assessment quizzes. A secured Instructor Center includes text updates, sample syllabi, downloadable supplements, and much more.

For Students

Topic Tackler CD-ROM   A new key feature of this edition is our *free* Topic Tackler CD with the text. This software is a complete student tutorial focusing on those areas in the managerial accounting course that give students the most trouble. It offers help on two key topics for every chapter in the book, using video clips, PowerPoint slide shows, interactive exercises, and self-test quizzes. The key concepts are indicated in the text by a Topic Tackler logo that tells students they can refer to the CD for additional instruction.

Study Guide: Prepared by Cindy D. Edmonds (ISBN 0-07-247341-X)   Each chapter of the study guide includes a review and explanation of the chapter learning objectives as well as multiple-choice problems and short exercises. Completion of the study guide will enable the students to (1) review their comprehension of the text material, (2) prepare for examinations, and (3) obtain an additional perspective of the course material. The guide contains approximately 200 pages and includes appropriate work papers and a complete set of solutions.

Working Papers: Prepared by Bor-Yi Tsay (ISBN 0-07-247326-6)   The working papers provide forms that are useful in the completion of both exercises and problems. Working papers for the exercises provide headings and prerecorded example transactions that enable students to get started quickly and to work in an efficient manner. The forms provided for the problems can be used with either series A or B problems.

Excel Templates   This software is provided for use with selected problems in the text. The templates gradually become more complex, requiring students to build a variety of formulas. "What-if " questions are added to show the power of spreadsheets, and a simple tutorial is included. These templates were prepared by Jack Terry of ComSource Associates, Inc. and are available on the text Website.

Ramblewood Manufacturing, Inc., Windows-Based Practice Set on CD-ROM (Student ISBN 0072348151) Instructor's Manual (ISBN 0072346426)   This computerized practice set was prepared by Leland Mansuetti and Keith Weidkamp of Sierra College. It presents a simulation of business transactions for a corporation that manufactures metal fencing. It can be used to show job-order costing systems with JIT inventory in a realistic setting and takes about 10 to 14 hours to complete.

NetTutor   NetTutor is a live, online tutor that guides students through their accounting problems step-by-step. It allows students to communicate with live tutors in a variety of ways: through a Live Tutor Center, a Q&A Center, and an Archive Center. NetTutor is free with all new texts.

PowerWeb   Keeping your accounting course timely can be a job in itself, and now McGraw-Hill does that job for you. PowerWeb is a site from which you can access all of the latest news and developments pertinent to your course without all the clutter and dead links of a typical online search. Students can visit PowerWeb to take a self-grading quiz or check a daily news feed analyzed by an expert in management accounting.

■ Acknowledgments

Why do geese fly in a V-shape? Because the effort of the lead goose provides an uplifting draft that eases the burden of flight for the birds that follow. We are deeply indebted to the class testers and users of the first edition who have selflessly contributed their time and effort to the development of this book. Like the lead goose, their work has made the road of progress easier to travel for all who follow. We extend our deepest gratitude to those who have shared with us the frustrations and excitement associated with the development of innovative teaching materials. We are especially indebted to Tim Nygaard of Madisonville Community College, Bob Smith of Florida State University, Phil Olds of Virginia Commonwealth University, Mark Lawrence of the University of Alabama at Birmingham, Nancy Schneider of Lynchburg College, Walt Doehring and Bruce Lindsey of Genesee Community College, Jeffrey Galbreath of

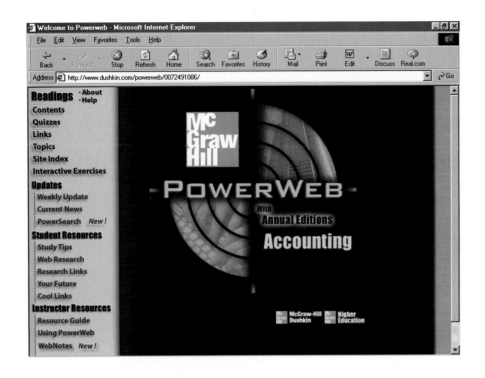

How's Your Math?

Do you have the math skills you need to succeed in this course?

*ALEKS is a registered trademark of ALEKS Corporation.

Log On for a
FREE 48-hour Trial
of **ALEKS®**

Why risk not succeeding in this course because you struggle with the prerequisite math skills?

Get access to a computer-based, personal math tutor:

- Available 24/7
- Driven by artificial intelligence
- Self-paced
- An entire month's subscription **for much less** than the cost of one hour with a human tutor

ALEKS is an inexpensive, private, infinitely patient math tutor that's accessible any time, anywhere you log on.

www.highedstudent.aleks.com

McGraw Hill

Greenfield Community College, Leonard Stokes of Siena College, Dorcas Berg of Wingate College, Pat McMahon of Palm Beach Community College, and Jed Ashley of Grossmont College.

The text underwent an extensive review process that included a diverse group of instructors located at schools across the country. The comments and suggestions of the reviewers have significantly influenced the writing of the text. Our efforts to establish a meaningful but manageable level of content was greatly influenced not only by their suggestions regarding what to include, but also by their opinions regarding what to leave out. Our grateful appreciation is extended to the following members of our review team:

We once again thank those individuals whose input over the last edition helped the book evolve to its present form:

James Bates,
  Mountain Empire Community College
Frank Beigbeder,
  Rancho Santiago College
Ashton Bishop,
  James Madison University
Amy Bourne,
  Tarrant County College
Eric Carlsen,
  Kean University
Sue Counte,
  Jefferson College
Jill D'Aquila,
  Iona College
Patricia Douglas,
  Loyola Marymount University
Dean Edmiston,
  Emporia State University
Robert Elmore,
  Tennessee Technological University
William Geary,
  College of William and Mary
Dinah Gottschalk,
  James Madison University
Donald Gribbin,
  Southern Illinois University
Larry Hegstad,
  Pacific Lutheran University
Fred Jex,
  Macomb Community College
Robert Landry,
  Massassoit Community College

Philip Little,
  Western Carolina University
Irvin Nelson,
  Utah State University
Bruce Neumann,
  University of Colorado
Hossein Nouri,
  College of New Jersey
Ashton Oravetz,
  Tyler Junior College
Thomas Phillips,
  Louisiana Tech University
Marjorie Platt,
  Northeastern University
Jane Reimers,
  Florida State University
Diane Riordan,
  James Madison University
Tom Robinson,
  University of Alaska
Kathryn Savage,
  Northern Arizona University
Nancy Schneider,
  Lynchburg College
Leonard Stokes,
  Siena College
Suneel Udpa,
  St. Mary's College
Sean Wright,
  DeVry Institute of Technology, Phoenix
Allan Young,
  DeVry Institute of Technology, Atlanta

Many others have contributed directly or indirectly to the development of the text. Participants in workshops and focus groups have provided useful feedback. Colleagues and friends have extended encouragement and support. Among these individuals our sincere appreciation is extended to Lowell Broom, University of Alabama at Birmingham; Bill Schwartz and Ed Spede of Virginia Commonwealth University; Doug Cloud, Pepperdine University—Malibu; Charles Bailey, University of Central Florida; Bob Holtfreter, Central Washington University; Kimberly Temme, Maryville University; Beth Vogel, Mount Mary College; Celia Renner, The University of Northern Iowa; Robert Minnear, Emory University; Larry Hegstad, Pacific Lutheran University; Shirish Seth, California State University at Fullerton; Richard Emery, Linfield College; Gail Hoover, Rockhurst; Bruce Robertson, Lock Haven University; Jeannie Folk, College of Dupage; Marvelyn Burnette, Wichita State University; Ron Mannino, University of Massachusetts; John Reisch, Florida Atlantic University; Rosalie Hallbauer, Florida International University; Lynne H. Shoaf, Belmont Abbey College; Jayne Maas, Towson University; Ahmed Goma, Manhattan College; John Rude, Bloomsburg University; Jack Paul, Lehigh University; Terri Gutierrez, University of Northern Colorado; Khondkar Karim, Monmouth University; Carol Lawrence, University of Richmond; Jeffrey Power, Saint Mary's University; Joanne Sheridan, Montana State University; and George Dow, Valencia Community College.

We are deeply indebted to our editor Melody Marcus. Her direction and guidance have added clarity and quality to the text. We are especially indebted to our developmental editor Gail Korosa. Gail has coordinated the exchange of ideas between our class testers, reviewers, copyeditor, and error checkers. She has done far more than simply pass along ideas. She has contributed numerous original suggestions that have enhanced the quality of the text. Our editors have certainly facilitated our efforts to prepare a book that will facilitate a meaningful understanding of accounting. Even so, their contributions are to no avail unless the text reaches its intended audience. We are most grateful to Rich Kolasa, Melissa Larmon, and the sales staff for providing the informative advertising that has so accurately communicated the unique features of the concepts approach to accounting educators. There are many others at McGraw-Hill/Irwin who at a moment's notice redirected their attention so as to focus their efforts on the development of this text. We extend our sincere appreciation to Kimberly Hooker, Debra Sylvester, Ed Przyzycki, David Barrick, Laurie Entringer, Jeremy Cheshareck, and Cathy Tepper. We deeply appreciate the long hours that you committed to the formation of a high-quality text.

Thomas P. Edmonds
Cindy D. Edmonds
Bor-Yi Tsay

Brief Contents

Contents

Chapter 6 — Cost Management in an Automated Business Environment: *ABC, ABM, and TQM*   232

Chapter 7 — Planning for Profit and Cost Control   278

Chapter 11 Product Costing in Service and Manufacturing Entities   444

Chapter 12 Job-Order, Process, and Hybrid Cost Systems   488

Chapter 13 Financial Statement Analysis   534

Chapter 14   Statement of Cash Flows   578

Fundamental Managerial
ACCOUNTING
Concepts

Management Accounting
A Value-Added Discipline

Learning Objectives

After completing this chapter, you should be able to:

1 Distinguish between managerial and financial accounting.

2 Identify the components of the cost of a product made by a manufacturing company including the cost of materials, labor, and overhead.

3 Understand the need to determine the average cost per unit of a product.

4 Understand the difference between a cost and an expense.

5 Explain how product versus general, selling, and administrative costs affects financial statements.

6 Understand how cost classification affects financial statements and managerial decisions.

7 Appreciate the need for a code of ethical conduct.

8 Distinguish product costs from upstream and downstream costs.

9 Understand how products provided by service companies differ from products made by manufacturing companies.

10 Explain how emerging trends including activity-based management, value-added assessment, and just-in-time inventory are affecting the managerial accounting discipline.

the *curious* accountant

Priceline.com began operations in April 1998 and first sold its stock to the public on March 30, 1999. By the end of 2000, the company had cumulative net losses of more than $1.4 billion. Even though its sales grew from $35 million in 1998 to more than $1 billion in 2000, it did not make a profit in any of those years. How can a company lose so much money and still be able to pay its bills?

*The statement of cash flows explains how a company obtained and used cash during some period. The sources of cash are known as **cash inflows,** and the uses are called **cash outflows.** The statement classifies cash receipts (inflows) and payments (outflows) into three categories: operating activities, investing activities, and financing activities. The following sections define these activities and outline the types of cash flows that are normally classified under each category.*

579

LO 1 Identify the types of business events that are reported in the three sections of the statement of cash flows.

Operating Activities

Operating activities include cash inflows and outflows generated by running (operating) the business. Some of the specific items that are shown under this section are as follows.

1. Cash receipts from sales, commissions, fees, and receipts from interest and dividends.
2. Cash payments for inventories, salaries, operating expenses, interest, and taxes.

Note that *gains* and *losses* are not included in this section. The total cash collected from the sale of assets is included in the investing activities section.

Investing Activities

Investing activities include cash flows that are generated through a company's purchase or sale of long-term operational assets, investments in other companies, and its lending activities. Some items included in this section follow.

1. Cash receipts from the sale of property, plant, equipment or of marketable securities as well as the collection of loans.
2. Cash payments used to purchase property, plant, equipment or marketable securities as well as loans made to others.

Financing Activities

Financing activities include cash inflows and outflows associated with the company's own equity transactions or its borrowing activities. The following are some items appearing under the financing activities section.

1. Cash receipts from the issue of stock and borrowed funds.
2. Cash payments for the purchase of treasury stock, repayment of debt, and payment of dividends.

When you are trying to classify transactions into one of the three categories, it is helpful to note that the identification of the proper category depends on the company's perspective rather than on the type of account being considered. For example, a transaction involving common stock is considered an investing activity if the company is purchasing or selling its investment in another company's common stock. In contrast, common stock transactions are classified as financing activities if the company is issuing its own stock or is buying back its own stock (treasury stock). Similarly, the receipt of dividends is classified as an operating activity, but the payment of dividends is classified as a financing activity. Furthermore, lending cash is considered to be an investing activity, and borrowing cash is a financing activity. Accordingly, proper classification centers on the behavior of the company involved rather than the type of instrument being used.

Noncash Investing and Financing Transactions

Occasionally, companies will engage in significant **noncash investing and financing transactions.** For example, a company may issue some of its common stock in exchange for the title to a plot of land. Similarly, a company could accept a mortgage obligation in exchange for the title of ownership to a building (a 100% owner-financed exchange). Since these types of transactions do not involve the exchange of cash, they cannot be included as cash receipts or payments on the statement of cash flows. However, the Financial Accounting Standards Board (FASB) has concluded that full and fair reporting requires the disclosure of all material investing and financing activities regardless of whether they involve the exchange of cash. Accordingly, the FASB requires that the statement of cash flows include a separate schedule for the disclosure of noncash investing and financing activities.

Exhibit 14–1

WESTERN COMPANY
Statement of Cash Flows
For the Year Ended December 31, 2001

Cash Flows from Operating Activities		
Plus: List of Individual Inflows	$XXX	
Less: List of Individual Outflows	(XXX)	
Net Increase (Decrease) from Operating Activities		$XXX
Cash Flows from Investing Activities		
Plus: List of Individual Inflows	XXX	
Less: List of Individual Outflows	(XXX)	
Net Increase (Decrease) from Investing Activities		XXX
Cash Flows from Financing Activities		
Plus: List of Individual Inflows	XXX	
Less: List of Individual Outflows	(XXX)	
Net Increase (Decrease) from Financing Activities		XXX
Net Increase (Decrease) in Cash		XXX
Plus: Beginning Cash Balance		XXX
Ending Cash Balance		$XXX
Schedule of Noncash Investing and Financing Activities		
List of Noncash Transactions		$XXX

■ Reporting Format for Statement of Cash Flows

The statement of cash flows is arranged with operating activities shown first, investing activities second, and financing activities last. Under each category, individual cash inflows are shown first, with cash outflows being subtracted and the net difference being carried forward. The schedule of noncash investing and financing activities is typically shown at the bottom of the statement. Exhibit 14–1 demonstrates this format of statement presentation.

With respect to the placement of the four primary financial statements, the statement of cash flows is usually presented last. However, a sizable number of companies show the statement of cash flows immediately after the income statement and balance sheet. A few companies show the statement of cash flows as the first statement. Exhibit 14–2 provides more details regarding the placement of the statement of cash flows relative to the other financial statements shown in annual reports.

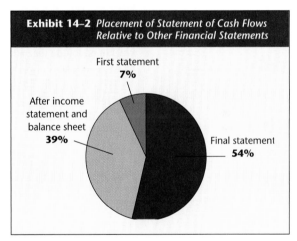

Exhibit 14–2 *Placement of Statement of Cash Flows Relative to Other Financial Statements*

First statement 7%
After income statement and balance sheet 39%
Final statement 54%

Data source: AICPA, *Accounting Trends and Techniques,* 2000.

■ Converting from Accrual to Cash-Basis Accounting

The operating activities section of the statement of cash flows is essentially a cash-basis income statement. Since accounting records are normally maintained on an accrual basis, it is necessary to convert data based on accruals and deferrals to cash equivalents to determine the amount of cash flow from operating activities. The following section discusses the conversion process.

LO2 Convert an accrual account balance to its cash equivalent.

Operating Activities

Converting Accruals to Cash

Accrual accounting is the process through which revenues and expenses are recognized in a period different from the one in which cash is exchanged. When accrual accounting is applied, revenue and expense items recognized in the current period may have cash consequences in a later period. Furthermore, revenue and expense items recognized in a past period may result in cash receipts or payments that materialize in the current period. Accordingly, the amount of cash receipts and payments realized during any particular accounting period may be larger or smaller than the amount of revenue and expense recognized during that period. The following section discusses the adjustments needed to convert accrual accounting to cash-basis accounting.

Revenue Transactions.   With regard to **revenue transactions,** the application of accrual accounting means that some revenue is likely to be reported on the income statement before or after the cash is received. Accordingly, the amount of revenue recognized is normally different from the amount of cash that the company realizes during any particular accounting period. Some customers purchase goods or services in the current accounting period but pay for them in a later period. Other customers may pay cash in the current period for goods or services purchased in a prior period. As a result, the cash received may be more or less than the amount of revenue recognized.

To convert revenue recognized to the corresponding amount of cash collected, it is necessary to analyze both the amount of revenue appearing on the income statement and the change in the balance of the accounts receivable account. For example, assume that a company reported $500 of revenue on its income statement. Furthermore, assume that during the accounting period under consideration, the beginning and ending balances in the company's Accounts Receivable account were $100 and $160, respectively. Accordingly, the balance in the receivables account increased by $60 ($160 − $100). Taking this fact into consideration, we can conclude that $60 of the $500 in sales was not collected in cash. Therefore, the amount of cash collected must have been $440 ($500 − $60).

The conclusion that $440 of cash was collected from the revenue transactions was derived through logic. This conclusion can be confirmed through a process commonly called the **T-account method.** The T-account method begins with the opening of the Accounts Receivable T-account with the appropriate beginning and ending balances displayed. In this case, the beginning balance is $100, and the ending balance is $160. Next a $500 debit is added to the account to record the recognition of the revenue. The resultant T-account appears as follows.

LO3 Prepare a statement of cash flows using the T-account method.

	Accounts Receivable	
Beginning Balance	100	
Debit to Record Sales	500	?
Ending Balance	160	

Mathematically adding $500 to a beginning balance of $100 does not result in an ending balance of $160. A $440 credit to the receivables account would be required to arrive at the $160 ending balance. Since cash collections result in credits to the Accounts Receivable account, it can be assumed that the Cash account was debited when the receivables account was credited. Accordingly, the analysis of the T-account also leads to the conclusion that $440 of cash was collected as a result of activities associated with the generation of revenue.

Expense Transactions.   Accrual accounting results in the recognition of **expense transactions** before the payment of cash occurs, which means that a liability is normally recorded at the time the expense is recognized. The liability is later reduced as cash payments are made. Accordingly, the amount of accrued expense displayed on the income statement must be analyzed in conjunction with any change in the balance of the related liability account in order to determine the amount of cash outflow associated with the expense recognition. For example, assume that a company reports $200 of utilities expense on its income statement. Furthermore,

answers to the *curious* accountant

First, it should be remembered that GAAP requires that earnings and losses be computed on an accrual basis. A company can have negative earnings and still have positive cash flows from operating activities. This was not the case at Priceline.com, however. From 1998 through 2000, the company's cash flows from operating activities totaled a negative $122.9 million. Although this is much less than the $1.4 billion cumulative losses the company incurred during the same period, it still does not pay the bills.

Priceline.com, like many new companies, was able to stay in business because of the cash it raised through financing activities. These cash flows were a positive $325.9 million for 1998 through 2000. The company also had some significant noncash transactions. Exhibit 14–3 presents Priceline.com's statement of cash flows from the first three years of its life.

Exhibit 14–3

PRICELINE.COM INCORPORATED
Statements of Cash Flows
(dollars in thousands)

	Year Ended December 31		
	2000	**1999**	**1998**
Operating Activities			
Net loss	$(315,145)	$(1,055,090)	$(112,243)
Adjustments to reconcile net loss to net cash used in operating activities			
Depreciation and amortization	17,385	5,348	1,860
Provision for uncollectible accounts	7,354	3,127	581
Warrant costs	8,595	1,189,111	67,866
Webhouse warrant	189,000	(189,000)	—
Net loss on disposal of fixed assets	12,398	—	—
Net loss on sale of equity investments	2,558	—	—
Asset impairment	4,886	—	—
Compensation expense arising from deferred stock awards	1,711	—	—
Changes in assets and liabilities			
Accounts receivable	7,401	(29,617)	(4,757)
Prepaid expenses and other current assets	1,194	(12,043)	(1,922)
Related party receivables	(3,484)	—	—
Accounts payable and accrued expenses	45,155	28,470	8,300
Other	1,276	(3,331)	112
Net cash used in operating activities	(19,716)	(63,025)	(40,203)
Investing Activities			
Additions to property and equipment	(37,320)	(27,416)	(6,607)
Purchase of convertible notes and warrants of licencees	(25,676)	(2,000)	
Proceeds from sales/maturities of investments	31,101	—	—
Funding of restricted cash and bank certificate of deposits	(4,779)	(8,789)	(680)
Investment in marketable securities	(5,000)	(38,771)	
Net cash used in investing activities	(41,674)	(76,976)	(7,287)
Financing Activities			
Related party payable	—	—	(1,072)
Issuance of long-term debt	—	—	1,000
Payment of long-term debt	—	(1,000)	
Principal payments under capital lease obligations	—	(25)	(22)
Issuance of common stock and subscription units	14,031	211,816	26,495
Payment received on stockholder note	—	—	250
Issuance of Series A convertible preferred stock	—	—	20,000
Issuance of Series B convertible preferred stock	—	—	54,415
Net cash provided by financing activities	14,031	210,791	101,066
Net increases in cash and cash equivalents	(47,359)	70,790	53,576
Cash and cash equivalents, beginning of period	124,383	53,593	17
Cash and cash equivalents, end of period	$ 77,024	$ 124,383	$ 53,593
Supplemental Cash Flow Information			
Cash paid during the period for interest	$ 4	$ 37	$ 61

assume that the beginning and ending balances in the Utilities Payable account are $70 and $40, respectively. This situation implies that the company not only made payments to cover the use of the utilities in the current period but also paid an additional $30 ($70 − $40) to reduce the obligations of prior periods. Accordingly, the amount of cash outflow associated with utility use is $230 ($200 + $30).

The T-account method can also be used to verify the $230 cash payment. A T-account for Utilities Payable is opened with beginning and ending balances placed into the account. Furthermore, a credit amounting to $200 is made to the account to reflect the recognition of the current period's utility expense. The resultant T-account appears as follows:

Utilities Payable

?	70	Beginning Balance
	200	Credit to Record Expense
	40	Ending Balance

Mathematical logic dictates that a $230 debit is required to arrive at the $40 ending balance ($70 + $200 − $230 = $40). Since debits to payable accounts are normally offset by credits to the Cash account, the T-account analysis indicates that cash outflows associated with utility expenses amounted to $230.

Check Yourself 14–1

Hammer, Inc., had a beginning balance of $22,400 in its Accounts Receivable account. During the accounting period, Hammer earned $234,700 of revenue on account. The ending balance in the Accounts Receivable account was $18,200. Based on this information alone, determine the amount of cash received from revenue transactions. In what section of the statement of cash flows would this cash flow appear?

Answer

Accounts Receivable

22,400	?
234,700	
18,200	

A $238,900 credit to accounts receivable is required to balance the account. This credit would be offset by a corresponding debit to cash. Cash received from revenue transactions appears in the operating activities section of the statement of cash flows.

Converting Deferrals to Cash

Deferral transactions are events in which cash receipts or payments occur before the associated revenue or expense is recognized. Since revenue and expense recognition occurs in one accounting period and the associated cash receipts and payments occur in a different accounting period, differences arise between income reported in the financial statements and the cash-basis income. The following section discusses the procedures necessary to convert deferrals to their cash-basis equivalents.

Revenue Transactions.   When cash is collected before the completion of the earnings process, a company incurs an obligation (liability) to provide goods or services at some future date. The revenue associated with the cash receipt is recognized in a later period when the work is accomplished. As a result, *the amount of revenue reported on the income statement and the amount of cash receipts normally differ.* The conversion of deferrals to cash requires an analysis of the amount of revenue reported and the change in the balance of the liability account, *Unearned Revenue.* For example, assume that the amount of revenue recognized was

$400 and that the Unearned Revenue account increased from a beginning balance of $80 to an ending balance of $110. The increase in the liability account implies that the company received cash in excess of the amount of the revenue recognized. Not only did the company earn the $400 of revenue reported on the income statement but also it received $30 ($110 − $80) for which it became obligated to provide goods and services in a future period. Accordingly, cash receipts associated with earnings activities amounted to $430 ($400 + $30).

An analysis of the T-account for unearned revenue confirms the receipt of $430 cash. The Unearned Revenue account is opened with the appropriate beginning and ending balances. A debit is made to the account to record the recognition of $400 of revenue. The resultant account appears as follows:

	Unearned Revenue	
		80	Beginning Balance
Debit to Recognize Revenue	400	?	
		110	Ending Balance

Clearly, $430 must have been added to the beginning balance of $80 so that when the $400 debit entry was subtracted, the resulting ending balance was $110. Since credit entries to the Unearned Revenue account are normally offset by corresponding debits to the Cash account, the analysis suggests that $430 of cash receipts was associated with revenue activities.

Expense Transactions. On many occasions, companies pay cash for goods or services that are not used immediately. The cost of the goods or services is normally capitalized in an asset account at the time the cash payment is made. The assets are then expensed in later periods when the goods or services are used in the process of earning revenue. Consequently, some items paid for in prior periods are expensed in the current period, while other items that are paid for in the current period are not expensed until later periods. *Accordingly, the amount of cash outflows normally differs from the amount of expense recognized for any given accounting period.*

To convert recognized expenses to cash flows, it is necessary to analyze the amount of change in the balance of certain asset accounts as well as the amount of corresponding expense that is recognized on the income statement. For example, assume that the beginning and ending balances in the Prepaid Rent account are $60 and $80, respectively, and that the amount of reported rent expense is $800. This situation suggests that the company not only paid enough cash to cover the $800 of recognized expense but also paid an additional $20 ($80 − $60). Therefore, the cash outflow associated with the rent payments amounted to $820 ($800 + $20).

The cash outflow of $820 for rent payments can be confirmed through T-account analysis. The beginning and ending balances are placed in a T-account for prepaid rent. The account is then credited to reflect the rent expense recognition of $800. The resultant T-account appears as follows:

	Prepaid Rent	
Beginning Balance	60		
	?	800	Credit to Recognize Expense
Ending Balance	80		

To have an ending balance of $80, there must have been an $820 debit to the account ($60 + $820 − $800 = $80). Since a debit to the Prepaid Rent account is normally offset by a credit to Cash, the analysis confirms that the cash outflow associated with rent payments is $820.

Investing Activities

Determining cash flow from investing activities may also require an analysis of changes in the beginning and ending account balances along with certain income statement data. For example, assume that the Land account had a beginning and ending balance of $900 and $300, respectively. Furthermore, assume that the income statement contained the recognition of a $200 gain on the sale of land. The $600 ($900 − $300) decline in the book value of the land suggests that the land was sold. The gain from the income statement implies that the land was sold for $200 more than its book value. Accordingly, the analysis suggests that the land was sold for $800 ($600 + $200) cash. Note that the amount of cash flow is different from the amount of gain appearing on the income statement. Indeed, the full $800 cash inflow appears in the investing activities section of the statement of cash flows. The operating activities section of the statement is not affected by the gain from the land sale.

The amount of cash inflow ($800) from investing activities can also be verified through the T-account method. An analysis of the beginning and ending balances in the Land account suggests that land costing $600 ($900 beginning balance − $300 ending balance) was sold. This amount, coupled with the $200 gain shown in the Retained Earnings account, suggests that $800 cash was collected from the sale. The appropriate T-accounts are as follows:

Cash			Land			Retained Earnings	
?			900	600			200
			300				

It is possible that the company could have received some resource other than cash when the land was sold. However, other alternative explanations would be discovered when the other balance sheet accounts were analyzed.

Financing Activities

Cash flow from financing activities can frequently be determined by simply analyzing the change in the balances of liability and stockholders' equity accounts. For example, an increase in bond liabilities from $500 to $800 implies that the company issued new bonds that resulted in the receipt of $300 cash. This conclusion can be supported by an analysis using the T-account method. A T-account is opened with the beginning and ending balances shown here.

Bonds Payable		
	500	Beginning Balance
	?	
	800	Ending Balance

A $300 credit must be added to the $500 opening balance in order to arrive at the $800 ending balance. Since cash is normally increased when bond liabilities increase, the analysis supports the conclusion that $300 of cash inflow was derived from the incurrence of debt.

Other explanations are also possible. Perhaps some of the company's stockholders decided to exchange their equity securities for debt securities. Or the company may have been willing to incur the obligation in exchange for some asset (property, plant, or equipment) other than cash. Such transactions would be reported in the schedule of noncash investing and financing transactions.

■ Comprehensive Example Using the T-Account Approach

LO3 Prepare a statement of cash flows using the T-account method.

The preceding discussion emphasized the need to analyze financial statements and supporting data in the process of preparing a statement of cash flows. The beginning and ending balances in the accounts being analyzed can be drawn from two successive balance sheets. The revenues, expenses, gains, and losses can be found on the income statement. Also, notes to the financial statements may contain information needed to identify noncash transactions. Exhibits 14–4 and 14–5 are the balance sheets, income statement, and additional information needed to prepare a statement of cash flows.

Exhibit 14–4

THE NEW SOUTH CORPORATION
Comparative Balance Sheets
As of December 31

	2004	2005
Current Assets		
Cash	$ 400	$ 900
Accounts Receivable	1,200	1,000
Interest Receivable	300	400
Inventory	8,200	8,900
Prepaid Insurance	1,400	1,100
Total Current Assets	11,500	12,300
Long-Term Assets		
Marketable Securities	3,500	5,100
Equipment	4,600	5,400
Less: Accumulated Depreciation	(1,200)	(900)
Land	6,000	8,500
Total Long-Term Assets	12,900	18,100
Total Assets	$24,400	$30,400
Current Liabilities		
Accounts Payable—Inventory Purchases	$ 1,100	$ 800
Salaries Payable	900	1,000
Other Operating Expenses Payable	1,300	1,500
Interest Payable	500	300
Unearned Rent Revenue	1,600	600
Total Current Liabilities	5,400	4,200
Long-Term Liabilities		
Mortgage Payable	0	2,500
Bonds Payable	4,000	1,000
Total Long-Term Liabilities	4,000	3,500
Stockholders' Equity		
Common Stock	8,000	10,000
Retained Earnings	7,000	12,700
Total Stockholders' Equity	15,000	22,700
Total Liabilities and Stockholders' Equity	$24,400	$30,400

Exhibit 14–5

THE NEW SOUTH CORPORATION
Income Statement
For the Year Ended December 31, 2005

Sales		$20,600
Cost of Goods Sold		(10,500)
Gross Margin		10,100
Operating Expenses		
Depreciation Expense	$ 800	
Salaries Expense	2,700	
Insurance Expense	600	
Other Operating Expenses	1,400	
Total Operating Expenses		(5,500)
Operating Income		4,600
Other Operating Income—Rent Revenue		2,400
Total Operating Income		7,000
Nonoperating Revenue and Expenses		
Interest Revenue	700	
Interest Expense	(400)	
Loss on Sale of Equipment	(100)	
Total Nonoperating Items		200
Net Income		$ 7,200

Additional information
1. The corporation sold equipment for $300 cash. This equipment had an original cost of $1,500 and accumulated depreciation of $1,100 at the time of the sale.
2. The corporation issued a $2,500 mortgage note in exchange for land.
3. There was a $1,500 cash dividend paid during the accounting period.

Preparation of Statement of Cash Flows

Begin the process of analyzing the financial statements by opening a T-account for each item on the balance sheets. Enter the beginning and ending balances for each item into the T-accounts. Use the 2004 balance sheet (see Exhibit 14–4) to determine the beginning balance of each account and the 2005 balance sheet to get the ending balances. The Cash account should be large enough to be divided into three components representing cash flows from operating, investing, and financing activities. Exhibit 14–6 contains a full set of T-accounts with all analytical transactions included. Each transaction is labeled with a lower-case letter. Since some analysis requires more than one entry, each letter is also followed by a number, which permits detailed labeling for each transaction. The following section explains each transaction in full detail.

Exhibit 14–6 *Balance Sheet T-Accounts*

Assets = Liabilities + Stockholders' Equity

Cash

Bal.	400		

Operating Activities

(a2)	20,800	11,500	(b3)
(g2)	1,400	2,600	(d2)
(h2)	600	300	(e2)
		1,200	(f2)
		600	(i2)

Investing Activities

| (k1) | 300 | 1,600 | (j1) |
| | | 2,300 | (l1) |

Financing Activities

(o1)	2,000	3,000	(n1)
		1,500	(p1)
Bal.	900		

Accounts Receivable

Bal.	1,200	20,800	(a2)
(a1)	20,600		
Bal.	1,000		

Interest Receivable

Bal.	300	600	(h2)
(h1)	700		
Bal.	400		

Inventory

Bal.	8,200	10,500	(b1)
(b2)	11,200		
Bal.	8,900		

Prepaid Insurance

Bal.	1,400	600	(e1)
(e2)	300		
Bal.	1,100		

Marketable Securities

Bal.	3,500		
(j1)	1,600		
Bal.	5,100		

Equipment

Bal.	4,600	1,500	(k1)
(l1)	2,300		
Bal.	5,400		

Accumulated Depreciation

(k1)	1,100	1,200	Bal.
		800	(c1)
		900	Bal.

Land

Bal.	6,000		
(m1)	2,500		
Bal.	8,500		

Accounts Payable—Inventory

(b3)	11,500	1,100	Bal.
		11,200	(b2)
		800	Bal.

Salaries Payable

(d2)	2,600	900	Bal.
		2,700	(d1)
		1,000	Bal.

Operating Exp. Payable

(f2)	1,200	1,300	Bal.
		1,400	(f1)
		1,500	Bal.

Interest Payable

(i2)	600	500	Bal.
		400	(i1)
		300	Bal.

Unearned Rent Revenue

(g1)	2,400	1,600	Bal.
		1,400	(g2)
		600	Bal.

Mortgage Payable

		0	Bal.
		2,500	(m1)
		2,500	Bal.

Bonds Payable

| (n1) | 3,000 | 4,000 | Bal. |
| | | 1,000 | Bal. |

Common Stock

		8,000	Bal.
		2,000	(o1)
		10,000	Bal.

Retained Earnings

(b1)	10,500	7,000	Bal.
(c1)	800	20,600	(a1)
(d1)	2,700	2,400	(g1)
(e1)	600	700	(h1)
(f1)	1,400		
(i1)	400		
(k1)	100		
(p1)	1,500		
		12,700	Bal.

Cash Flows from Operating Activities

Cash flow from operating activities is essentially a cash-basis income statement. Since accrual accounting is normally used in the preparation of formal financial statements, it is necessary to convert the income statement data to cash equivalents. Accordingly, each item on the income statement should be analyzed separately to assess its cash flow consequences.

Cash Receipts from Sales

The first item appearing on the income statement is $20,600 of sales revenue. Assuming that all sales transactions were on account, the entry to record sales would have required a debit to Accounts Receivable and a credit to Sales Revenue. Because the T-account analysis includes only balance sheet accounts and sales revenue acts to increase Retained Earnings, the entry to record sales in the T-accounts is shown as a debit to Accounts Receivable and a credit to Retained Earnings. This entry is labeled (a1) in Exhibit 14–6. After the sales revenue transaction is recorded, the cash inflow from sales can be determined by analyzing the Accounts Receivable T-account. Notice that the beginning balance of $1,200 plus the debit to receivables of $20,600 resulting from sales transactions suggests that $21,800 of receivables was available for collection. Since the ending balance in the receivables account amounts to $1,000, there must have been $20,800 ($21,800 − $1,000) of receivables collected. This cash inflow is recognized with a debit to the Cash account under the operating activities section and a credit to the Accounts Receivable account. This entry is labeled (a2) in Exhibit 14–6.

The preceding discussion introduces several practices that apply to the analysis of all cash flows from operating activities. First, note that all revenue, expense, gain, and loss transactions ultimately affect the Retained Earnings account. Accordingly, to reconcile the beginning and ending balances in Retained Earnings, all income statement items are posted directly to the Retained Earnings account. Second, the determination of when to stop the analysis depends on the reconciliation between the beginning and ending account balances. In this case, the analysis of Accounts Receivable stopped with the $20,800 credit because the beginning balance plus the debit and minus the credit equaled the ending balance. Accordingly, the analysis of the account is completed because the beginning and ending balances have been reconciled (the change in the account has been fully explained). The analysis for the entire statement is completed when the beginning and ending balances in all the balance sheet accounts are reconciled. Since many of the balance sheet accounts remain to be reconciled, the cash flow analysis in this case will continue.

Cash Payments for Inventory Purchases

It is helpful to make two simplifying assumptions in analyzing cash payments for inventory purchases. First, assume that the company employs the perpetual inventory method; second, assume that all purchases are made on account. Based on these assumptions, the entry to record the cost of goods sold ($10,500, as shown on the income statement in Exhibit 14–5) would have required a credit to the Inventory account and a debit to Retained Earnings (cost of goods sold). This entry is labeled (b1) in the exhibit. This entry only partly explains the change in the beginning and ending balances of the Inventory account. A closer analysis of this account suggests that some inventory must have been purchased. Given that the beginning balance in the Inventory account was $8,200 and that $10,500 of inventory cost was transferred to cost of goods sold, it is logical to assume that $11,200 of inventory was purchased to arrive at the ending Inventory balance of $8,900. The entry to record the inventory purchase, labeled (b2), includes a debit to Inventory and a credit to Accounts Payable. This entry completes the explanation of the change in the beginning and ending balances but only partly explains the change in the beginning and ending balances in the Accounts Payable account. Given a beginning balance in Accounts Payable of $1,100 and additional purchases on account amounting to $11,200, there must have been $12,300 of accounts payable available for payment. Since the ending balance in the Accounts Payable account amounted to $800, there must have been cash payments of $11,500 ($12,300 − $800). The entry to record this cash outflow, labeled (b3), includes a credit to the operating activities section of the Cash account and a debit to the Accounts Payable account.

Noncash Effects of Depreciation

The next item on the income statement is depreciation expense. Depreciation expense is a noncash charge against revenues. In other words, no cash changes hands at the time the depreciation expense is recorded. Indeed, the entry to record depreciation expense (c1) includes a debit to Retained Earnings (depreciation expense) and a credit to Accumulated Depreciation. This entry only partly explains the change in accumulated depreciation, indicating that further analysis is required. However, cash flow consequences associated with long-term assets and their respective contra accounts affect the investing activities section of the statement of cash flows. Accordingly, further analysis is delayed until investing activities are considered. At this stage, the analysis of cash flows from operating activities continues.

Cash Payments for Salaries

The entry to record $2,700 of salary expense includes a debit to Retained Earnings (salary expense) and a credit to Salaries Payable. This entry, labeled (d1), partly explains the change in beginning and ending balances in the Salaries Payable account. The beginning balance of $900 plus the $2,700 increase for the current period expense suggests that there were $3,600 of salaries available for payment during the period. Since the ending balance amounted to $1,000, there must have been a cash payment for salaries amounting to $2,600 ($3,600 − $1,000). The entry to record the cash payment for salaries includes a debit to the Salaries Payable account and a credit to the operating activities section of the Cash account. This entry is labeled (d2) in the exhibit.

Cash Payments for Insurance

The entry to record $600 of insurance expense requires a debit to Retained Earnings (insurance expense) and a credit to Prepaid Insurance. This entry, labeled (e1), partly explains the change in the beginning and ending balances in the Prepaid Insurance account. The beginning balance of $1,400 less the reduction of $600 associated with the recognition of insurance expense suggests an ending balance of $800. However, the balance sheet shows an actual ending balance of $1,100. Accordingly, a purchase of $300 ($1,100 − $800) of prepaid insurance must have been made during the accounting period. The cash outflow for the purchase of insurance is labeled (e2) and includes a debit to the Prepaid Insurance account and a credit to the operating activities section of the statement of cash flows.

Cash Payments for Other Operating Expenses

The $1,400 of other operating expenses appearing on the income statement is recorded in the T-accounts with a debit to Retained Earnings and a credit to the Operating Expenses Payable account. This entry, labeled (f1), partly explains the change in the beginning and ending balances in the Operating Expenses Payable account. Given a beginning balance of $1,300 and the $1,400 addition for current expenses, the total amount available for payment was $2,700 ($1,300 + $1,400). Since the ending balance amounted to $1,500, the cash payments must have amounted to $1,200 ($2,700 − $1,500). The entry to record the cash payment is labeled (f2) and includes a debit to the Operating Expenses Payable account and a credit to the operating activities section of the Cash account.

Cash Receipts for Rent

The entry to record $2,400 of rent revenue includes a debit to the Unearned Rent Revenue account and a credit to the Retained Earnings account. This entry, labeled (g1), partly explains the change in the beginning and ending balances in the Unearned Rent Revenue account. The beginning balance of $1,600 less the $2,400 reduction caused by the recognition of the rent revenue suggests that there must have been a credit (increase) in the account in order to arrive at an ending balance of $600. Since increases in the unearned account are offset by increases in cash, collections must have been equal to $1,400 ($1,600 + $1,400 − $2,400 = $600). The required entry for the cash receipt includes a credit to the Unearned Rent Revenue account and a debit to the operating activities section of the Cash account. This entry is labeled (g2) in Exhibit 14–6.

Cash Receipts from Interest

The entry to record $700 of interest revenue includes a debit to the Interest Receivable account and a credit to Retained Earnings (interest revenue). This entry, labeled (h1), partially explains the change in the beginning and ending balances in the Interest Receivable account. Given the beginning balance of $300 plus the $700 debit created through the recognition of interest revenue, the receivables account indicates that there was $1,000 ($300 + $700) of interest receivables available for collection. The ending balance of $400 implies that $600 ($1,000 − $400) of cash was collected. The entry to record this cash inflow is labeled (h2) and includes a credit to Interest Receivable and a debit to the operating activities section of the Cash account.

Cash Payments for Interest

The entry to record $400 of interest expense is labeled (i1) and includes a debit to Retained Earnings (interest expense) and a credit to Interest Payable. The entry partly explains the change in the beginning and ending balances in the Interest Payable account. The beginning balance of $500 plus the $400 that resulted from the recognition of interest expense suggests that there was $900 of interest obligations available for payment. The ending balance of $300 implies that $600 ($900 − $300) was paid in cash. The entry to recognize the cash outflow for this interest payment is labeled (i2) and includes a debit to the Interest Payable account and a credit to the operating activities section of the Cash account.

Noncash Effects of Loss

The loss on the sale of equipment does not affect cash flows from operating activities. The full proceeds from the sale constitute the amount of cash flow. The amount of any loss or gain is irrelevant. Indeed, the sale involves the disposal of an investment and therefore is shown under the investing activities section. Cash flow from operating activities is not affected by gains or losses on the disposal of long-term assets.

Completion of Analysis of Operating Activities

Since no other items appear on the income statement, the conversion process from accrual to cash is completed. The operating activities section of the Cash account contains all the cash receipts and payments necessary to determine the net cash flow from operations. This information is placed into the formal statement of cash flows (presented later in the chapter). With the completion of the assessment of cash flow from operating activities, the analysis proceeds to the cash flow effects associated with investing activities.

Check Yourself 14-2

Q Magazine, Inc., reported $234,800 of revenue for the month. At the beginning of the month, its Unearned Revenue account had a balance of $78,000. At the end of the month, the account had a balance of $67,000. Based on this information alone, determine the amount of cash received from revenue.

Answer The Unearned Revenue account decreased by $11,000 ($78,000 − $67,000). This decrease in unearned revenue would have coincided with an increase in revenue that did not involve receiving cash. As a result, $11,000 of the revenue earned had no effect on cash flow during this month. To determine the cash received from revenue, subtract the noncash increase from reported revenue. Cash received from revenue is $223,800 ($234,800 − $11,000).

Cash Flows from Investing Activities

Investing activities generally involve the acquisition (purchase) or disposal (sale) of long-term assets. Accordingly, the analysis of cash flows from investing activities centers on changes in the beginning and ending balances in long-term assets.

Cash Payments to Purchase Marketable Securities

The first long-term asset shown on the balance sheets is Marketable Securities. An analysis of this asset account indicates that the balance in the account increased from $3,500 at the beginning of the period to $5,100 at the end of the period. The most reasonable explanation for this increase is that the corporation purchased additional securities in the amount of $1,600 ($5,100 − $3,500). In the absence of information to the contrary, it is assumed that the purchase was made with cash. The entry to record the purchase includes a debit to the Marketable Securities account and a credit to the investing activities section of the Cash account. This entry is coded (j1) in Exhibit 14–6.

Cash Receipts from Sale of Equipment

The next asset on the balance sheets is Equipment. Our earlier review of the income statement disclosed a loss on the sale of equipment, which suggests that some equipment was sold during the period. This sale is expected to result in a cash inflow in the amount of the sales price. The additional information at the bottom of the income statement discloses that equipment costing $1,500 with accumulated depreciation of $1,100 was sold for $300. The difference between the $400 ($1,500 − $1,100) book value and the $300 sales price explains the $100 loss on the income statement. The cash receipt from the sale is $300. The original cost, accumulated depreciation, and loss do not affect cash flow. The entry to recognize the cash receipt includes a debit to the investing section of the Cash account, a debit to Retained Earnings (loss), a debit to the Accumulated Depreciation account, and a credit to the Equipment account. The entry is labeled (k1) in the exhibit.

Cash Payments to Purchase Equipment

The sale of equipment partially explains the change in the beginning and ending balances in the Equipment account. However, further analysis suggests that some equipment must have been purchased. A beginning balance of $4,600 less $1,500 for the equipment that was sold suggests that $2,300 of equipment must have been purchased in order to arrive at the ending balance of $5,400 ($4,600 − $1,500 + $2,300 = $5,400). The cash payment necessary to purchase the equipment is labeled (l1) and includes a debit to the Equipment account and a credit to the investing activities section of the Cash account.

Noncash Transaction for Land Acquisition

The Land account increased from a beginning balance of $6,000 to an ending balance of $8,500, thereby suggesting that $2,500 ($8,500 − $6,000) of land was acquired during the accounting

How did Florida Power and Lighting (FPL) acquire $501 million of property and equipment without spending any cash? Oddly enough, the answer can be found in the company's statement of cash flows. The supplemental schedule of noncash investing and financing activities section of FPL's cash statement shows that it acquired $81 million of equipment by accepting lease obligations and that it acquired $420 million of property by assuming debt. In other words, FPL acquired $501 million ($81 million + $420 million) in property and equipment by agreeing to pay for it later.

period. The additional information at the bottom of the income statement discloses the fact that the corporation acquired this land through the issuance of a mortgage. Accordingly, no cash consequences are associated with the transaction. The transaction recording this event is labeled (m1) in Exhibit 14–6. Since the transaction does not affect cash, it is shown in the separate schedule for noncash investing and financing transactions on the statement of cash flows.

Since all long-term asset accounts have been reconciled, the analysis of cash flows from investing activities is completed. The process continues with an assessment of cash flows associated with financing activities.

Cash Flows from Financing Activities

The long-term liability and stockholders' equity sections of the balance sheets are analyzed to assess the cash flows from financing activities. Note that the first long-term liability account on the balance sheet is Mortgage Payable. The change in this account was explained in the analysis of the land acquisition, discussed earlier in this chapter. As explained, this financing activity is shown along with the investing activity in the separate schedule for noncash transactions. Accordingly, the analysis of cash flows proceeds with the change in the Bond Liability account.

Cash Payment for Bonds

The balance in the Bonds Payable account decreased from $4,000 to $1,000. In the absence of information to the contrary, it is logical to assume that $3,000 ($4,000 − $1,000) was paid to reduce bond liabilities. The entry to record the cash outflow includes a debit to the Bonds Payable account and a credit to the financing activities section of the Cash account. This entry is coded (n1) in the exhibit.

Cash Receipt from Stock Issue

The balance in the Common Stock account increased from $8,000 to $10,000. In the absence of information to the contrary, it is logical to assume that $2,000 ($10,000 − $8,000) of cash was collected as proceeds from the issuance of common stock. The entry to record this cash inflow is labeled (o1) and includes a credit to Common Stock and a debit to the financing activities section of the Cash account.

Cash Payments for Dividends

Finally, additional information at the bottom of the income statement discloses a cash dividend of $1,500. The transaction to record this cash outflow includes a debit to the Retained Earnings account and a credit to the financing activities section of the Cash account. It is labeled (p1) in Exhibit 14–6.

▌Presenting Information in the Statement of Cash Flows

Since all income statement items have been analyzed, changes in balance sheet accounts have been explained, and all additional information has been considered, the analytical process is completed. The data in the T-account for cash must now be organized in appropriate financial statement format. Recall that cash flow from operations is presented first, cash flow from investing activities second, and cash flow from financing activities third. Noncash investing and financing activities are shown in a separate schedule or in the footnotes. Exhibit 14–7 is a statement of cash flows and a separate schedule for noncash activities.

▌Statement of Cash Flows Presented Under the Indirect Method

LO4 Explain how cash flow from operating activity reported under the indirect method differs from that reported under the direct method.

Up to now, the statement of cash flows has been presented in accordance with the **direct method.** The direct method is intuitively logical and is the method recommended by the Financial Accounting Standards Board. Even so, most companies use an alternative known as

Exhibit 14–7

THE NEW SOUTH CORPORATION Statement of Cash Flows For the Year Ended December 31, 2005			
Cash Flows from Operating Activities			
Cash Receipts from			
Sales	$20,800		
Rent	1,400		
Interest	600		
Total Cash Inflows		$22,800	
Cash Payments for			
Inventory Purchases	11,500		
Salaries	2,600		
Insurance	300		
Other Operating Expenses	1,200		
Interest	600		
Total Cash Outflows		(16,200)	
Net Cash Flow from Operating Activities			$ 6,600
Cash Flows from Investing Activities			
Inflow from Sale of Equipment		300	
Outflow to Purchase Marketable Securities		(1,600)	
Outflow to Purchase Equipment		(2,300)	
Net Cash Flow from Investing Activities			(3,600)
Cash Flows from Financing Activities			
Inflow from Stock Issue		2,000	
Outflow to Repay Debt		(3,000)	
Outflow for Dividends		(1,500)	
Net Cash Flow from Financing Activities			(2,500)
Net Increase in Cash			500
Plus: Beginning Cash Balance			400
Ending Cash Balance			$ 900
Schedule of Noncash Investing and Financing Activities			
Issue of Mortgage for Land			$ 2,500

the **indirect method.** The difference between the two methods is in the presentation of the operating activities section. The indirect method uses net income as reported on the income statement as the starting point. The method proceeds by showing the adjustments necessary to convert the accrual-based net income figure to a cash-basis equivalent. The conversion process can be accomplished by the application of three basic rules, which are discussed next.

An increase in the balance of the Accounts Receivable account would suggest that not all sales were collected in cash. Accordingly, the amount of revenue shown on the income statement would overstate the amount of cash collections. Therefore, it is necessary to subtract the amount of the increase in the receivables account from the amount of net income to convert the income figure to a cash-equivalent basis. Similarly, a decrease in the receivables balance has to be added to the net income figure. Extending this logic to all current asset accounts results in the first general rule of the conversion process. **Rule 1: Increases in current assets are deducted from net income, and decreases in current assets are added to net income.**

The opposite logic applies to current liabilities. For example, an increase in accounts payable suggests that not all expenses were paid in cash. Accordingly, it is necessary to add the increase in the payables account to the amount of net income to convert the income figure to a cash-equivalent basis. Conversely, decreases in payable accounts are deducted from net income. Extending the logic to all the current liability accounts produces the second general rule of the conversion process. **Rule 2: Increases in current liabilities are added to net income, and decreases in current liabilities are deducted from net income.**

The following account balances were drawn from the accounting records of Loeb, Inc.

Account Title	Beginning Balance	Ending Balance
Prepaid Rent	$4,200	$3,000
Interest Payable	$2,900	$2,650

Loeb reported $7,400 of net income during the accounting period. Based on this information alone, determine the amount of cash flow from operating activities.

Answer Based on Rule 1, the $1,200 decrease ($3,000 − $4,200) in Prepaid Rent (current asset) must be added to net income to determine the amount of cash flow from operating activities. Rule 2 requires that the $250 decrease ($2,650 − $2,900) in Interest Payable (current liability) must be deducted from net income. Accordingly, the cash flow from operating activities is $8,350 ($7,400 + $1,200 − $250). Note that paying interest is defined as an operating activity and should not be confused with dividend payments, which are classified as financing activities.

Finally, note that some expense and revenue transactions do not have cash consequences. For example, although depreciation is reported as an expense, it does not require the payment of cash. Similarly, losses and gains reported on the income statement do not have consequences that are reported in the operating activities section of the statement of cash flows. **Rule 3: All noncash expenses and losses are added to net income, and all noncash revenue and gains are subtracted from net income.**

Arley Company's income statement reported net income (in millions) of $326 for the year. The income statement included depreciation expense of $45 and a net loss on the sale of disposable assets of $22. Based on this information alone, determine the net cash flow from operating activities.

Answer Based on Rule 3, both the depreciation expense and the loss would have to be added to net income to determine cash flow from operating activities. Net cash flow from operating activities would be $393 ($326 + $45 + $22).

Exhibit 14–8

THE NEW SOUTH CORPORATION
Statement of Cash Flows (Indirect Method)
For the Year Ended December 31, 2005

Cash Flows from Operating Activities		
Net Income	$7,200	
Plus: Decreases in Current Assets		
and Increases in Current Liabilities		
Decrease in Accounts Receivable	200	
Decrease in Prepaid Insurance	300	
Increase in Salaries Payable	100	
Increase in Other Operating Expenses Payable	200	
Less: Increases in Current Assets		
and Decreases in Current Liabilities		
Increase in Interest Receivable	(100)	
Increase in Inventory	(700)	
Decrease in Accounts Payable for Inventory Purchases	(300)	
Decrease in Interest Payable	(200)	
Decrease in Unearned Revenue	(1,000)	
Plus: Noncash Charges		
Depreciation Expense	800	
Loss on Sale of Equipment	100	
Net Cash Flow from Operating Activities		$6,600
Cash Flows from Investing Activities		
Inflow from Sale of Equipment	300	
Outflow to Purchase Marketable Securities	(1,600)	
Outflow to Purchase Equipment	(2,300)	
Net Cash Flow from Investing Activities		(3,600)
Cash Flows from Financing Activities		
Inflow from Stock Issue	2,000	
Outflow to Repay Debt	(3,000)	
Outflow for Dividends	(1,500)	
Net Cash Flow from Financing Activities		(2,500)
Net Increase in Cash		500
Plus: Beginning Cash Balance		400
Ending Cash Balance		$ 900
Schedule of Noncash Investing and Financing Activities		
Issue of Mortgage for Land		$2,500

These three general rules apply only to items affecting operating activities. For example, Rule 2 does not apply to an increase or decrease in the current liability account for dividends because dividend payments are considered to be financing activities rather than operating activities. Accordingly, some degree of judgment must be exercised in applying the three general rules of conversion.

Exhibit 14–8 shows the presentation of a statement of cash flows under the indirect method. The statement was constructed by applying the three general rules of conversion to the data for The New South Corporation shown in Exhibits 14–4 and 14–5. Notice that the only difference between the statement presented under the indirect method (Exhibit 14–8) and the statement shown under the direct method (Exhibit 14–7) is the cash flow from operating activities section. Cash flows from investing and financing activities and the schedule of non-cash items are not affected by the alternative reporting format.

▌Consequences of Growth on Cash Flow

LO5 Explain how the classifications used on the statement of cash flows could provide misleading information to decision makers.

Why do decision makers in business need a statement of cash flows? Why is the information provided on the income statement not sufficient? Although it is true that the income statement shows how well a business is doing on an accrual basis, it does not show what is happening with cash. Understanding the cash flows of a business is extremely important because cash is used to pay the bills. A company, especially one that is growing rapidly, can have substantial earnings but be short of cash because it must buy goods before they are sold, and it may not receive cash payment until months after revenue is recognized on an accrual basis. To illustrate, assume that you want to go into the business of selling computers. You borrow $2,000 and use the money to purchase two computers that cost $1,000 each. Furthermore, assume that you sell one of the computers on account for $1,500. At this point, if you had a payment due on your loan, you would be unable to pay the amount due. Even though you had a net income of $500 (revenue of $1,500 − cost of goods sold of $1,000), you would have no cash until you collected the $1,500 cash due from the account receivable.

Real-World Data

The statement of cash flows frequently provides a picture of business activity that would otherwise be lost in the complexities of the application of accrual accounting. For example, consider the effects of restructuring charges on operating income versus cash flow experienced by IBM Corporation. For 1991, 1992, and 1993 combined, IBM reported operating *losses* (before taxes) of more than $17.9 *billion*. During this same period, it reported "restructuring charges" of more than $24 billion. Therefore, without the restructuring charges, IBM would have reported operating *profits* of about $6 billion (before taxes). Are restructuring charges an indication of something bad or something good? Who knows? Different financial analysts have different opinions about this issue. There is something about IBM's performance during these years that can be more easily understood. The company produced over $21 billion in positive cash flow from operating activities. It had no trouble paying its bills.

Investors consider cash flow information so important that they are willing to pay for it, even when the FASB discourages its use. Consider the following situation. The FASB *prohibits* companies from disclosing *cash flow per share* in audited financial statements. However, one very prominent stock analysis service, *Value Line Investment Survey,* has a significant customer base that continues to purchase its stock charts, which are prepared on the basis of cash flow per share rather than earnings per share. These investors obviously value information regarding cash flows.

Exhibit 14–9 is a comparison of the income from operations and the cash flow from operating activities for six real-world companies from three different industries for the 1998, 1999, and 2000 fiscal years.

Exhibit 14–9 *Operating Income versus Cash Flow From Operations (Amounts in $000)*				
	Company	**2000**	**1999**	**1998**
Alaska Airlines	Operating income	$ (7,400)	$ 119,400	$ 116,500
	Cash flow operations	197,700	294,500	272,400
Southwest Airlines	Operating income	625,224	474,378	433,431
	Cash flow operations	1,298,286	1,001,710	886,135
Boeing	Operating income	2,128,000	2,309,000	1,120,000
	Cash flow operations	5,942,000	6,224,000	2,415,000
Mattel	Operating income	170,177	108,387	328,253
	Cash flow operations	555,090	430,463	586,201
Sprint	Operating income	(576,000)	(745,000)	(585,000)
	Cash flow operations	4,315,000	1,952,000	4,199,000
Toll Brothers	Operating income	145,943	103,027	85,819
	Cash flow operations	(16,863)	(120,870)	(40,708)

Several things can be observed from Exhibit 14–9. First, notice that in most cases, other than Toll Brothers, cash flow from operating activities is higher than income from operations. This condition is true for many real-world companies because depreciation, a noncash expense, is usually significant. The most dramatic example of this is for Sprint in 2000. Even though Sprint reported a *net loss* from operations of $576 million, it generated *positive cash flow from operations* of more than $4 *billion*. This difference between cash flow from operations and operating income helps explain how some companies can have significant losses over a few years and continue to stay in business and pay their bills.

Next, the exhibit shows that the numbers for cash flow from operations can be more stable than the amounts for operating income. Results for Alaska Airlines demonstrate this clearly. Although the company's earnings changed from positive in 1998 and 1999 to negative in 2000, its cash flows from operations were always positive. Therefore, some financial statement analysts might prefer cash flow from operations as a more useful number for trend analysis than accrual-based earnings.

Finally, what could explain why Toll Brothers has *less* cash flow from operations than operating income? Does this mean that the company has a problem? Not necessarily. Toll Brothers is simply experiencing the same kind of growth described earlier for your computer sales business. Its cash is being used to support growth in the level of inventory. Toll Brothers is one of the nation's largest new-home construction companies. Its growth rates, based on the sales value of new homes closed, for the 2000, 1999, and 1998 fiscal years were 23 percent, 19 percent, and 25 percent, respectively. It is not the new acquisitions of property, plant, and equipment that affect cash flow from operations because these purchases are included in the investing activities section of the statement of cash flows. However, when Toll Brothers begins to build new homes, the company needs more inventory. Increases in inventory *do* affect cash flow from operations. Remember, increases in current assets decrease cash flow from operations. This fact alone might explain why the company has less cash flow from operations than operating income. Is this situation bad? Recall that in Chapter 8, the point was made that, *other things being equal*, it is better to have less inventory. At Toll Brothers, however, other things are not equal. The company has been growing rapidly.

The situation with Toll Brothers highlights what some accountants think is a weakness in the format of the statement of cash flows. Some think it misleading simply to classify all increases in long-term assets as *investing activities* and all changes in inventory as an adjustment to operating income to arrive at cash flow from operations. They argue that the increase in inventory at Toll Brothers that results from opening new stores should be classified as an investing activity, just as the cost of a new building is. Although it is true that inventory is classified as a current asset and buildings are classified as long-term assets, in reality there is a certain level of inventory that must be maintained permanently if a company is to remain in business. The GAAP format of the statement of cash flows penalizes cash flow from operations for increases in inventory that are really a permanent investment in assets.

Conversely, the same critics might argue that some purchases of long-term assets are not actually *investments* but merely replacements of old, existing property, plant, and equipment. In other words, the *investing activities* section of the statement of cash flows makes no distinction between expenditures that expand the business and those that simply replace old equipment (sometimes called *capital maintenance* expenditures).

Thus, the conclusion one must reach about using the statement of cash flows is the same as that for using the balance sheet or the earnings statement. Users cannot simply look at the numbers. They must analyze the numbers based on a knowledge of the particular business being examined.

Accounting alone cannot tell a businessperson how to make a decision. Making good business decisions requires an understanding of the business in question, the environmental and economic factors affecting the operation of that business, and the accounting concepts on which the financial statements of that business are based.

a look back

Throughout this course, you have been asked to consider many different accounting events that occur in the business world. In many cases, you were asked to consider the effects that these events have on a company's balance sheet, income statement, and statement of cash flows. By now, you should be aware that each of the financial statements shows a different, but equally important, view of the financial situation of the company in question.

This chapter provided a more detailed examination of only one financial statement, the statement of cash flows. The chapter presented a more comprehensive review of how an accrual accounting system relates to a cash-based accounting system. It is important that you understand not only both systems but also how the two systems relate to each other. This is the reason that a formal statement of cash flows begins with a reconciliation of net income, an accrual measurement, to net cash flow from operating activities, a cash measurement. Finally, this chapter explained how the idiosyncrasies of classifying cash events as operating, investing, or financing activities requires analysis and understanding of the financial information to reach correct conclusions.

This chapter probably completes your first course in accounting. We sincerely hope that this text has provided you a meaningful learning experience that will serve you well as you progress through your academic training and your ultimate career. Good luck and best wishes!

a look forward

SELF-STUDY REVIEW PROBLEM

The following financial statements pertain to Schlemmer Company.

BALANCE SHEETS As of December 31		
	2003	2004
Cash	$ 2,800	$48,400
Accounts Receivable	1,200	2,200
Inventory	6,000	5,600
Equipment	22,000	18,000
Accumulated Depreciation—Equip.	(17,400)	(13,650)
Land	10,400	17,200
Total Assets	$25,000	$77,750
Accounts Payable	$ 4,200	$ 5,200
Long-Term Debt	6,400	5,600
Common Stock	10,000	19,400
Retained Earnings	4,400	47,550
Total Liabilities and Equity	$25,000	$77,750

INCOME STATEMENT For the Year Ended December 31, 2004	
Sales Revenue	$67,300
Cost of Goods Sold	(24,100)
Gross Margin	43,200
Depreciation Expense	(1,250)
Operating Income	41,950
Gain on Sale of Equipment	2,900
Loss on Disposal of Land	(100)
Net Income	$44,750

Additional Data

1. During 2004 the company sold equipment for $8,900 that had originally cost $11,000. Accumulated depreciation on this equipment was $5,000 at the time of sale. Also, the company purchased equipment for $7,000.
2. The company sold for $2,500 land that had cost $2,600, resulting in the recognition of a $100 loss. Also, common stock was issued in exchange for land valued at $9,400 at the time of the exchange.
3. The company declared and paid dividends of $1,600.

Required

a. Use T-accounts to analyze the preceding data.
b. Using the direct method, prepare in good form a statement of cash flows for the year ended December 31, 2004.

Transactions Legend

a1. Revenue, $67,300.
a2. Collection of accounts receivable, $66,300 ($1,200 + $67,300 − $2,200).
b1. Cost of goods sold, $24,100.
b2. Inventory purchases, $23,700 ($5,600 + $24,100 − $6,000).
b3. Payments for inventory purchases, $22,700 ($4,200 + $23,700 − $5,200).
c1. Depreciation expense, $1,250 (noncash).
d1. Sale of equipment, $8,900; cost of equipment sold, $11,000; accumulated depreciation on equipment sold, $5,000.
d2. Purchase of equipment, $7,000.
e1. Sale of land, $2,500; cost of land sold, $2,600.
f1. Issue of stock in exchange for land, $9,400.
g1. Paid dividends, $1,600.
h1. Paid off portion of long-term debt. $800.

Solution to Requirement a

SCHLEMMER COMPANY
T-Accounts

| Assets | | = | Liabilities | + | Equity | |

Cash

Bal.	2,800	b3.	22,700
a2.	66,300	d2.	7,000
d1.	8,900	g1.	1,600
e1.	2,500	h1.	800
Bal.	48,400		

Accounts Payable

b3.	22,700	Bal.	4,200
		b2.	23,700
		Bal.	5,200

Common Stock

		Bal.	10,000
		f1.	9,400
		Bal.	19,400

Accounts Receivable

Bal.	1,200	a2.	66,300
a1.	67,300		
Bal.	2,200		

Long-Term Debt

| h1. | 800 | Bal. | 6,400 |
| | | Bal. | 5,600 |

Retained Earnings

b1.	24,100	Bal.	4,400
c1.	1,250	a1.	67,300
e1.	100	d1.	2,900
g1.	1,600		
		Bal.	47,550

Inventory

Bal.	6,000	b1.	24,100
b2.	23,700		
Bal.	5,600		

Equipment

Bal.	22,000	d1.	11,000
d2.	7,000		
Bal.	18,000		

Accumulated Depreciation

d1.	5,000	Bal.	17,400
		c1.	1,250
		Bal.	13,650

Land

Bal.	10,400	e1.	2,600
f1.	9,400		
Bal.	17,200		

Solution to Requirement b

SCHLEMMER COMPANY
Statement of Cash Flows
For the Year Ended December 31, 2004

Cash Flows from Operating Activities		
Cash Receipts from Customers	$66,300	
Cash Payments for Inventory Purchases	(22,700)	
Net Cash Flow Provided by Operating Activities		43,600
Cash Flows from Investing Activities		
Inflow from Sale of Equipment	8,900	
Inflow from Sale of Land	2,500	
Outflow to Purchase Equipment	(7,000)	
Net Cash Flow Provided by Investing Activities		4,400
Cash Flows from Financing Activities		
Outflow for Dividends	(1,600)	
Outflow for Repayment of Debt	(800)	
Net Cash Flow Used by Financing Activities		(2,400)
Net Increase in Cash		45,600
Plus: Beginning Cash Balance		2,800
Ending Cash Balance		$48,400
Schedule of Noncash Investing and Financing Activities		
Issued Common Stock for Land		$ 9,400

KEY TERMS

Accrual accounting *582*
Cash inflows *579*
Cash outflows *579*
Deferral transactions *584*

Direct method *594*
Expense transactions *582*
Financing activities *580*
Indirect method *595*

Investing activities *580*
Noncash investing and financing activities *580*
Operating activities *580*

Revenue transactions *582*
T-account method *582*

QUESTIONS

1. What is the purpose of the statement of cash flows?
2. What are the three categories of cash flows reported on the cash flow statement? Discuss each and give an example of an inflow and an outflow for each category.
3. What are noncash investing and financing activities? Provide an example. How are such transactions shown on the statement of cash flows?
4. Best Company had beginning accounts receivable of $12,000 and ending accounts receivable of $14,000. If total sales were $110,000, what amount of cash was collected?
5. Best Company's Utilities Payable account had a beginning balance of $3,300 and an ending balance of $5,200. Utilities expense reported on the income statement was $87,000. What was the amount of cash paid for utilities for the period?
6. Best Company had a balance in the Unearned Revenue account of $4,300 at the beginning of the period and an ending balance of $5,700. If the portion of unearned revenue Best recognized as earned during the period was $15,600, what amount of cash did Best collect?
7. Which of the following activities are financing activities?
   a. Payment of accounts payable.
   b. Payment of interest on bonds payable.
   c. Sale of common stock.
   d. Sale of preferred stock at a premium.
   e. Payment of a cash dividend.
8. Does depreciation expense affect net cash flow? Explain.
9. If Best Company sold land that cost $4,200 at a $500 gain, how much cash did it collect from the sale of land?
10. If Best Company sold office equipment that originally cost $7,500 and had $7,200 of accumulated depreciation at a $100 loss, what was the selling price for the office equipment?

11. In which section of the statement of cash flows would the following transactions be reported?
    a. Cash receipt of interest income.
    b. Cash purchase of marketable securities.
    c. Cash purchase of equipment.
    d. Cash sale of merchandise.
    e. Cash sale of common stock.
    f. Payment of interest expense.
    g. Cash proceeds from loan.
    h. Cash payment on bonds payable.
    i. Cash receipt from sale of old equipment.
    j. Cash payment for operating expenses.
12. What is the difference between preparing the statement of cash flows using the direct approach and using the indirect approach?
13. Which method (direct or indirect) of presenting the statement of cash flows is more intuitively logical? Why?
14. What is the major advantage of using the indirect method to present the statement of cash flows?
15. What is the advantage of using the direct method to present the statement of cash flows?
16. How would Best Company report the following transactions on the statement of cash flows?
    a. Purchased new equipment for $46,000 cash.
    b. Sold old equipment for $8,700 cash. The equipment had a book value of $4,900.
17. Can a company report negative net cash flows from operating activities for the year on the statement of cash flows but still have positive net income on the income statement? Explain.
18. Why does the FASB prohibit disclosing cash flow per share in audited financial statements?

EXERCISES—SERIES A

L.O. 1   EXERCISE 14–1A *Classifying Cash Flows Into Categories—Direct Method*

Required
Identify whether the cash flows in the following list should be classified as operating activities, investing activities, or financing activities on the statement of cash flows (assume the use of the direct method).
a. Acquired cash from issue of common stock.
b. Provided services for cash.
c. Acquired cash by issuing a note payable.
d. Paid cash for interest.
e. Paid cash dividends.
f. Paid cash to settle note payable.
g. Sold land for cash.
h. Paid cash to purchase a computer.
i. Paid cash for employee compensation.
j. Received cash interest from a bond investment.
k. Recognized depreciation expense.

L.O. 1   EXERCISE 14–2A *Cash Outflows From Operating Activities—Direct Method*

Required
Which of the following transactions produce cash outflows from operating activities (assume the use of the direct method)?
a. Cash payment to purchase inventory.
b. Cash payment for equipment.
c. Cash receipt from collecting accounts receivable.
d. Cash receipt from sale of land.
e. Cash payment for dividends.
f. Cash payment to settle an account payable.

L.O. 2   EXERCISE 14–3A *Using Account Balances to Determine Cash Flows From Operating Activities—Direct Method*

The following account balances are available for Pae Company for 2004.

Account Title	Beginning of Year	End of Year
Accounts Receivable	$23,000	$21,000
Interest Receivable	5,000	7,000
Accounts Payable	28,000	25,000
Salaries Payable	10,000	11,0000

Other Information for 2004

Sales on Account	$646,000
Interest Income	24,000
Operating Expenses	270,000
Salaries Expense for the Year	172,000

Required

(*Hint:* It may be helpful to assume that all revenues and expenses are on account.)

a. Compute the amount of cash *inflow* from operating activities.

b. Compute the amount of cash *outflow* from operating activities.

EXERCISE 14–4A *Using Account Balances to Determine Cash Flow From Operating Activities—Direct Method* **L.O. 2**

The following account balances were available for Jefferson Enterprises for 2002.

Account Title	Beginning of Year	End of Year
Unearned Revenue	$4,000	$6,000
Prepaid Rent	2,200	2,500

During the year, $65,000 of unearned revenue was recognized as having been earned. Rent expense for the period was $12,000. Jefferson Enterprises maintains its books on the accrual basis.

Required

Using T-accounts and the preceding information, determine the amount of cash inflow from revenue and cash outflow for rent.

EXERCISE 14–5A *Using Account Balances to Determine Cash Flow From Investing Activities* **L.O. 2**

The following account information pertains to Kallapur Company for 2005.

	Land				Marketable Securities	
Bal.	38,000	24,000		Bal.	78,000	49,000
	127,000				139,000	
Bal.	141,000			Bal.	168,000	

The income statement reported a $3,000 loss on the sale of land and a $2,500 gain on the sale of marketable securities.

Required

Prepare the investing activities section of the 2005 statement of cash flows.

EXERCISE 14–6A *Using Account Balances to Determine Cash Flow From Financing Activities* **L.O. 2, 3**

The following account balances pertain to Kilgore, Inc., for 2006.

	Bonds Payable				Common Stock				Paid-in Capital in Excess of Par Value	
		Bal.	245,000			Bal.	368,000			Bal.	90,000
150,000							200,000				60,000
		Bal.	95,000			Bal.	568,000			Bal.	150,000

Required

Prepare the financing activities section of the 2006 statement of cash flows.

L.O. 2, 3 **EXERCISE 14–7A** *Using Account Balances to Determine Cash Outflow for Inventory Purchases*

The following account information pertains to Gupta Company, which uses the perpetual inventory method and purchases all inventory on account.

Inventory				Accounts Payable		
Bal.	67,000				Bal.	49,000
	?	376,000		?		?
Bal.	72,000				Bal.	47,000

Required

Compute the amount of cash paid for the purchase of inventory.

L.O. 2, 4 **EXERCISE 14–8A** *Using Account Balances to Determine Cash Flow From Operating Activities—Indirect Method*

Altec Company presents its statement of cash flows using the indirect method. The following accounts and corresponding balances were drawn from Altec's accounting records for the period.

Account Titles	Beginning Balances	Ending Balances
Accounts Receivable	$24,000	$22,600
Prepaid Rent	1,650	1,950
Interest Receivable	900	700
Accounts Payable	10,200	8,850
Salaries Payable	2,700	2,950
Unearned Revenue	2,000	2,450

Net income for the period was $43,000.

Required

Using the preceding information, compute the net cash flow from operating activities using the indirect method.

L.O. 2, 3, 4 **EXERCISE 14–9A** *Using Account Balances to Determine Cash Flow From Operating Activities—Direct and Indirect Methods*

The following account balances are from Hutton Company's accounting records. Assume Hutton had no investing or financing transactions during 2002.

December 31	2001	2002
Cash	$65,000	$114,200
Accounts Receivable	75,000	77,000
Prepaid Rent	1,200	800
Accounts Payable	33,000	37,000
Utilities Payable	15,600	18,800
Sales Revenue		$272,000
Operating Expenses		(168,000)
Utilities Expense		(36,400)
Rent Expense		(24,000)
Net Income		$ 43,600

Required

a. Prepare the operating activities section of the 2002 statement of cash flows using the direct method.

b. Prepare the operating activities section of the 2002 statement of cash flows using the indirect method.

EXERCISE 14–10A *Interpreting Statement of Cash Flows Information* **L.O. 3, 5**

The following selected transactions pertain to Armstrong Corporation for 2004.

1. Paid $23,400 cash to purchase delivery equipment.
2. Sold delivery equipment for $2,900. The equipment had originally cost $15,000 and had accumulated depreciation of $13,000.
3. Borrowed $40,000 cash by issuing bonds at face value.
4. Purchased a building that cost $180,000. Paid $50,000 cash and issued a mortgage for the remaining $130,000.
5. Exchanged no-par common stock for machinery valued at $64,900.

Required

a. Prepare the appropriate sections of the 2004 statement of cash flows.
b. Explain how a company could spend more cash on investing activities than it collected from financing activities during the same accounting period.

PROBLEMS—SERIES A

PROBLEM 14–11A *Classifying Cash Flows* **L.O. 1**

Required

Classify each of the following as an operating activity (OA), an investing activity (IA), or a financing activity (FA) cash flow, or a noncash transaction (NT).

a. Bought land with cash.
b. Collected cash from accounts receivable.
c. Issued common stock for cash.
d. Repaid principal and interest on a note payable.
e. Declared a stock split.
f. Purchased inventory with cash.
g. Recorded amortization of goodwill.
h. Paid insurance with cash.
i. Issued a note payable in exchange for equipment.
j. Recorded depreciation expense.
k. Provided services for cash.
l. Purchased marketable securities with cash.
m. Paid cash for rent.
n. Received interest on note receivable.
o. Paid cash for salaries.
p. Received advance payment for services.
q. Paid a cash dividend.
r. Provided services on account.
s. Purchased office supplies on account.

PROBLEM 14–12A *Using Transaction Data to Prepare a Statement of Cash Flows* **L.O. 2, 3**

Store Company engaged in the following transactions during the 2002 accounting period. The beginning cash balance was $32,300.

1. Credit sales were $250,000. The beginning receivables balance was $95,000 and the ending balance was $103,000.
2. Salaries expense for the period was $56,000. The beginning salaries payable balance was $3,500 and the ending balance was $2,000.
3. Other operating expenses for the period were $125,000. The beginning operating expense payable balance was $4,500 and the ending balance was $9,600.
4. Recorded $19,500 of depreciation expense. The beginning and ending balances in the Accumulated Depreciation account were $14,000 and $33,500, respectively.
5. The Equipment account had beginning and ending balances of $210,000 and $240,000, respectively. The increase was caused by the cash purchase of equipment.
6. The beginning and ending balances in the Notes Payable account were $50,000 and $150,000, respectively. The decrease was caused by repaying bank loans.
7. There was $6,000 of interest expense reported on the income statement. The beginning and ending balances in the Interest Payable account were $1,200 and $1,000, respectively.

8. The beginning and ending Merchandise Inventory account balances were $90,000 and $108,000, respectively. The company sold merchandise with a cost of $156,000 (cost of goods sold for the period was $156,000). The beginning and ending balances of Accounts Payable were $9,500 and $11,500, respectively.

9. The beginning and ending balances of Notes Receivable were $2,500 and $10,000, respectively. The increase resulted from a cash loan to one of the company's employees.

10. The beginning and ending balances of the Common Stock account were $100,000 and $125,000, respectively. The increase was caused by the issue of common stock for cash.

11. Land had beginning and ending balances of $50,000 and $41,000, respectively. Land that cost $9,000 was sold for $14,700, resulting in a gain of $5,700.

12. The tax expense for the period was $7,700. The Tax Payable account had a $950 beginning balance and an $875 ending balance.

13. The Investments account had beginning and ending balances of $25,000 and $29,000, respectively. The company purchased investments for $18,000 cash during the period, and investments that cost $14,000 were sold for $9,000, resulting in a $5,000 loss.

Required

Convert the preceding information to cash-equivalent data and prepare a statement of cash flows.

L.O. 2, 3   PROBLEM 14–13A *Using Financial Statement Data to Determine Cash Flow from Operating Activities*

The following account information is available for Big Sky Company for 2004:

Account Title	Beginning of Year	End of Year
Accounts Receivable	$20,000	$24,000
Merchandise Inventory	58,000	56,000
Prepaid Insurance	24,000	2,000
Accounts Payable (Inventory)	20,000	21,000
Salaries Payable	4,200	2,800

Other Information
1. Sales for the period were $175,000.
2. Purchases of merchandise for the period were $85,000.
3. Insurance expense for the period was $42,000.
4. Other operating expenses (all cash) were $26,000.
5. Salary expense was $35,000.

Required
a. Compute the net cash flow from operating activities.
b. Prepare the cash flow from the operating activities section of the statement of cash flows.

L.O. 2, 3   PROBLEM 14–14A *Using Financial Statement Data to Determine Cash Flow from Investing Activities*

The following information pertaining to investing activities is available for Chico Company for 2005:

Account Title	Beginning of Year	End of Year
Machinery and Equipment	$425,000	$510,000
Marketable Securities	112,000	75,000
Land	90,000	110,000

Other Information for 2005
1. Marketable securities were sold at book value. No gain or loss was recognized.
2. Machinery was purchased for $110,000. Old machinery with a book value of $5,000 (cost of $25,000, accumulated depreciation of $20,000) was sold for $8,000.

Required
a. Compute the net cash flow from investing activities.
b. Prepare the cash flow from investing activities section of the statement of cash flows.

PROBLEM 14–15A *Using Financial Statement Data to Determine Cash Flow from Financing Activities*   **L.O. 2, 3**

The following information pertaining to financing activities is available for Tiger Company for 2004:

Account Title	Beginning of Year	End of Year
Bonds Payable	$300,000	$190,000
Common Stock	200,000	250,000
Paid-in Capital in Excess of Par	75,000	125,000

Other Information
1. Dividends paid during the period amounted to $45,000.
2. No new funds were borrowed during the period.

Required
a. Compute the net cash flow from financing activities for 2004.
b. Prepare the cash flow from the financing activities section of the statement of cash flows.

PROBLEM 14–16A *Using Financial Statements to Prepare a Statement of Cash Flows— Direct Method*   **L.O. 2, 3**

The following financial statements were drawn from the records of Pacific Company.

Balance Sheets as of December 31		
	2002	**2003**
Assets		
Cash	$ 2,800	$ 24,200
Accounts Receivable	1,200	2,000
Inventory	6,000	6,400
Equipment	42,000	19,000
Accumulated Depreciation—Equipment	(17,400)	(9,000)
Land	10,400	18,400
Total Assets	$45,000	$ 61,000
Liabilities and Equity		
Accounts Payable	$4,200	$2,600
Long-Term Debt	6,400	2,800
Common Stock	10,000	22,000
Retained Earnings	24,400	33,600
Total Liabilities and Equity	$45,000	$ 61,000

Income Statement for the Year Ended December 31, 2003	
Sales Revenue	$35,700
Cost of Goods Sold	(14,150)
Gross Margin	21,550
Depreciation Expense	(3,600)
Operating Income	17,950
Gain on Sale of Equipment	500
Loss on Disposal of Land	(50)
Net Income	$18,400

Additional Data
1. During 2003, the company sold equipment for $18,500; it had originally cost $30,000. Accumulated depreciation on this equipment was $12,000 at the time of the sale. Also, the company purchased equipment for $7,000 cash.
2. The company sold land that had cost $4,000. This land was sold for $3,950, resulting in the recognition of a $50 loss. Also, common stock was issued in exchange for title to land that was valued at $12,000 at the time of exchange.
3. Paid dividends of $9,200.

Required

Use the T-account method to analyze the data and prepare a statement of cash flows.

L.O. 2, 3　PROBLEM 14–17A *Using Financial Statements to Prepare a Statement of Cash Flows—Direct Method*

The following financial statements were drawn from the records of Raceway Sports:

Balance Sheets as of December 31		
	2001	**2002**
Assets		
Cash	$28,200	$123,600
Accounts Receivable	66,000	57,000
Inventory	114,000	126,000
Notes Receivable	30,000	0
Equipment	255,000	147,000
Accumulated Depreciation—Equipment	(141,000)	(74,740)
Land	52,500	82,500
Total Assets	$404,700	$461,360
Liabilities and Equity		
Accounts Payable	$48,600	42,000
Salaries Payable	24,000	30,000
Utilities Payable	1,200	600
Interest Payable	1,800	0
Note Payable	60,000	0
Common Stock	240,000	300,000
Retained Earnings	29,100	88,760
Total Liabilities and Equity	$404,700	$461,360

Income Statement for the Year Ended December 31, 2002	
Sales Revenue	$580,000
Cost of Goods Sold	(288,000)
Gross Margin	292,000
Operating Expenses	
Salary Expense	(184,000)
Depreciation Expense	(17,740)
Utilities Expense	(12,200)
Operating Income	78,060
Nonoperating Items	
Interest Expense	(3,000)
Gain or (Loss)	(1,800)
Net Income	$ 73,260

Additional Information

1. Sold equipment costing $108,000 with accumulated depreciation of $84,000 for $22,200 cash.
2. Paid a $13,600 cash dividend to owners.

Required

Use the T-account method to analyze the data and prepare a statement of cash flows.

L.O. 2, 4　PROBLEM 14–18A *Using Financial Statements to Prepare a Statement of Cash Flows—Indirect Method*

The comparative balance sheets for Redwood Corporation for 2003 and 2004 follow:

Balance Sheets as of December 31		
	2003	2004
Assets		
Cash	$ 40,600	$ 68,800
Accounts Receivable	22,000	30,000
Merchandise Inventory	176,000	160,000
Prepaid Rent	4,800	2,400
Equipment	288,000	256,000
Accumulated Depreciation	(236,000)	(146,800)
Land	80,000	192,000
Total Assets	$375,400	$562,400
Liabilities		
Accounts Payable (Inventory)	$ 76,000	$ 67,000
Salaries Payable	24,000	28,000
Stockholders' Equity		
Common Stock, $25 Par Value	200,000	250,000
Retained Earnings	75,400	217,400
Total Liabilities and Equity	$375,400	$562,400

Income Statement for the Year Ended December 31, 2004	
Sales	$1,500,000
Cost of Goods Sold	(797,200)
Gross Profit	702,800
Operating Expenses	
Depreciation Expense	(22,800)
Rent Expense	(24,000)
Salaries Expense	(256,000)
Other Operating Expenses	(258,000)
Net Income	$ 142,000

Other Information
1. Purchased land for $112,000.
2. Purchased new equipment for $100,000.
3. Sold old equipment that cost $132,000 with accumulated depreciation of $112,000 for $20,000 cash.
4. Issued common stock for $50,000.

Required
Prepare the statement of cash flows for 2004, using the indirect method.

EXERCISES—SERIES B

EXERCISE 14–1B *Classifying Cash Flows into Categories—Direct Method* **L.O. 1**

Required
Identify whether the cash flows in the following list should be classified as operating activities, investing activities, or financing activities on the statement of cash flows (assume the use of the direct method).
a. Sold merchandise on account.
b. Paid employee salary.
c. Received cash proceeds from bank loan.
d. Paid dividends.
e. Sold used equipment for cash.
f. Received interest income on a certificate of deposit.
g. Sold stock for cash.

h. Repaid bank loan.

i. Purchased equipment for cash.

j. Paid interest on loan.

L.O. 1   **EXERCISE 14–2B** *Cash Inflows from Operating Activities—Direct Method*

Required

Which of the following transactions produce cash inflows from operating activities (assume the use of the direct method)?

a. Cash payment for utilities expense.

b. Cash payment for equipment.

c. Cash receipt from interest.

d. Cash payment for dividends.

e. Collection of cash from accounts receivable.

f. Provide services for cash.

L.O. 2   **EXERCISE 14–3B** *Using Account Balances to Determine Cash Flow from Operating Activities—Direct Method*

The following account balances are available for Norstom Company for 2002.

Account Title	Beginning of Year	End of Year
Accounts Receivable	$40,000	$46,000
Interest Receivable	5,000	3,000
Accounts Payable	30,000	33,000
Salaries Payable	12,000	10,500

Other Information for 2002

Sales on Account	$275,000
Interest Income	25,000
Operating Expenses	196,000
Salaries Expense for the Year	75,000

Required

(*Hint:* It may be helpful to assume that all revenues and expenses are on account.)

a. Compute the amount of cash *inflow* from operating activities.

b. Compute the amount of cash *outflow* from operating activities.

L.O. 2   **EXERCISE 14–4B** *Using Account Balances to Determine Cash Flow from Operating Activities—Direct Method*

The following account balances were available for Earles Candy Company for 2001:

Account Title	Beginning of Year	End of Year
Unearned Revenue	$18,000	$8,000
Prepaid Rent	2,000	900

During the year, $41,000 of unearned revenue was recognized as having been earned. Rent expense for the period was $8,000. Earles Candy Company maintains its books on the accrual basis.

Required

Using T-accounts and the preceding information, determine the amount of cash inflow from revenue and cash outflow for rent.

L.O. 2   **EXERCISE 14–5B** *Using Account Balances to Determine Cash Flow from Investing Activities*

The following account information is available for McClung, Inc., for 2005:

	Land				Marketable Securities	
Bal.	20,000	50,000		Bal.	75,000	30,000
	100,000				40,000	
Bal.	70,000			Bal.	85,000	

The income statement reported a $9,000 gain on the sale of land and a $1,200 loss on the sale of marketable securities.

Required
Prepare the investing activities section of the statement of cash flows for 2005.

EXERCISE 14–6B *Using Account Balances to Determine Cash Flow from Financing Activities*　　**L.O. 2, 3**

The following account balances were available for Golden Company for 2007:

	Mortgage Payable			Capital Stock			Paid-in Capital in Excess of Par	
	148,000	Bal.		200,000	Bal.		65,000	Bal.
62,000				50,000			30,000	
	86,000	Bal.		250,000	Bal.		95,000	Bal.

Required
Prepare the financing activities section of the statement of cash flows for 2007.

EXERCISE 14–7B *Using Account Balances to Determine Cash Outflow for Inventory Purchases*　　**L.O. 2, 3**

The following account information is available for Sherman Company. The company uses the perpetual inventory method and makes all inventory purchases on account.

	Inventory				Accounts Payable	
Bal.	41,000				42,000	Bal.
	?	120,000		?	?	
Bal.	65,000				52,000	Bal.

Required
Compute the amount of cash paid for the purchase of inventory.

EXERCISE 14–8B *Using Account Balances to Determine Cash Flow from Operating Activities—Indirect Method*　　**L.O. 2, 4**

Maple Company presents its statement of cash flows using the indirect method. The following accounts and corresponding balances were drawn from Maple's accounting records.

Account Titles	Beginning Balances	Ending Balances
Accounts Receivable	$30,000	$35,000
Prepaid Rent	2,000	1,200
Interest Receivable	800	400
Accounts Payable	9,000	9,500
Salaries Payable	2,500	2,100
Unearned Revenue	1,200	2,200

Net income for the period was $45,000.

Required
Using the preceding information, compute the net cash flow from operating activities using the indirect method.

L.O. 2-4   **EXERCISE 14–9B** *Using Account Balances to Determine Cash Flow from Operating Activities—Direct and Indirect Methods*

The following information is from the accounting records of Mong Company:

	2000	2001
Cash	$ 42,000	$ 88,800
Accounts Receivable	158,000	159,800
Prepaid Rent	3,000	5,600
Accounts Payable	120,000	125,000
Utilities Payable	12,000	8,400
Sales Revenue		$212,000
Operating Expenses		(135,000)
Utilities Expense		(17,200)
Rent Expense		(10,000)
Net Income		$ 49,800

Required
a. Prepare the operating activities section of the 2001 statement of cash flows using the direct method.
b. Prepare the operating activities section of the 2001 statement of cash flows using the indirect method.

L.O. 3, 5   **EXERCISE 14–10B** *Interpreting Statement of Cash Flows Information*

The following selected transactions pertain to Johnston Company for 2003.
1. Purchased new office equipment for $9,800 cash.
2. Sold old office equipment for $2,000 that originally cost $12,000 and had accumulated depreciation of $11,000.
3. Borrowed $20,000 cash from the bank for six months.
4. Purchased land for $125,000 by paying $50,000 in cash and issuing a note for the balance.
5. Exchanged no-par common stock for an automobile valued at $26,500.

Required
a. Prepare the appropriate sections of the statement of cash flows for 2003.
b. What information does the noncash investing and financing activities section of the statement provide? If this information were omitted, could it affect a decision to invest in a company?

PROBLEMS—SERIES B

L.O. 1   **PROBLEM 14–11B** *Classifying Cash Flows*

Required
Classify each of the following as an operating activity (OA), an investing activity (IA), or a financing activity (FA) cash flow, or a noncash transaction (NT).
a. Paid cash for operating expenses.
b. Wrote off an uncollectible account receivable using the allowance method.
c. Wrote off an uncollectible account receivable using the direct write-off method.
d. Issued common stock for cash.
e. Declared a stock split.
f. Issued a mortgage to purchase a building
g. Purchased equipment with cash.
h. Repaid the principal balance on a note payable.
i. Made a cash payment for the balance due in the Dividends Payable account.
j. Received a cash dividend from investment in marketable securities.
k. Purchased supplies on account.
l. Collected cash from accounts receivable.
m. Accrued warranty expense.
n. Borrowed cash by issuing a bond.
o. Loaned cash to a business associate.
p. Paid cash for interest expense.
q. Incurred a loss on the sale of equipment.

r. Wrote down inventory because the year-end physical count was less than the balance in the Inventory account.

s. Paid cash to purchase inventory.

PROBLEM 14–12B *Using Transaction Data to Prepare a Statement of Cash Flows* **L.O. 2, 3**

Greenstein Company engaged in the following transactions during 2003. The beginning cash balance was $86,000.

1. Credit sales were $548,000. The beginning receivables balance was $128,000 and the ending balance was $90,000.
2. Salaries expense for 2003 was $232,000. The beginning salaries payable balance was $16,000 and the ending balance was $8,000.
3. Other operating expenses for 2003 were $236,000. The beginning operating Expense Payable balance was $16,000 and the ending balance was $10,000.
4. Recorded $30,000 of depreciation expense. The beginning and ending balances in the Accumulated Depreciation account were $12,000 and $42,000, respectively.
5. The Equipment account had beginning and ending balances of $44,000 and $56,000, respectively. The increase was caused by the cash purchase of equipment.
6. The beginning and ending balances in the Notes Payable account were $44,000 and $36,000, respectively. The decrease was caused by the cash repayment of debt.
7. There was $4,600 of interest expense reported on the income statement. The beginning and ending balances in the Interest Payable account were $8,400 and $7,500, respectively.
8. The beginning and ending Merchandise Inventory account balances were $22,000 and $29,400, respectively. The company sold merchandise with a cost of $83,600. The beginning and ending balances of Accounts Payable were $8,000 and $6,400, respectively.
9. The beginning and ending balances of Notes Receivable were $100,000 and $60,000, respectively. The decline resulted from the cash collection of a portion of the receivable.
10. The beginning and ending balances of the Common Stock account were $120,000 and $160,000, respectively. The increase was caused by the issue of common stock for cash.
11. Land had beginning and ending balances of $24,000 and $14,000, respectively. Land that cost $10,000 was sold for $6,000, resulting in a loss of $4,000.
12. The tax expense for 2003 was $6,600. The Tax Payable account had a $2,400 beginning balance and a $2,200 ending balance.
13. The Investments account had beginning and ending balances of $20,000 and $60,000, respectively. The company purchased investments for $50,000 cash during 2003, and investments that cost $10,000 were sold for $22,000, resulting in a $12,000 gain.

Required
Convert the preceding information to cash-equivalent data and prepare a statement of cash flows.

PROBLEM 14–13B *Using Financial Statement Data to Determine Cash Flow from Operating Activities* **L.O. 2, 3**

The following account information is available for Gables Auto Supplies for 2003:

Account Title	Beginning of Year	End of Year
Accounts Receivable	$ 17,800	$ 21,000
Merchandise Inventory	136,000	142,800
Prepaid Insurance	1,600	1,200
Accounts Payable (Inventory)	18,800	19,600
Salaries Payable	6,400	5,800

Other Information
1. Sales for the period were $248,000.
2. Purchases of merchandise for the period were $186,000.
3. Insurance expense for the period was $8,000.
4. Other operating expenses (all cash) were $27,400.
5. Salary expense was $42,600.

Required
a. Compute the net cash flow from operating activities.
b. Prepare the cash flow from the operating activities section of the statement of cash flows.

L.O. 2, 3   PROBLEM 14–14B *Using Financial Statement Data to Determine Cash Flow from Investing Activities*

The following information pertaining to investing activities is available for Tony's Flea Markets, Inc., for 2001.

Account Title	Beginning of Year	End of Year
Trucks and Equipment	$162,000	$170,000
Marketable Securities	66,000	51,200
Land	42,000	34,000

Other Information for 2001

1. Tony's sold marketable securities at book value. No gain or loss was recognized.
2. Trucks were purchased for $40,000. Old trucks with a cost of $32,000 and accumulated depreciation of $24,000 were sold for $11,000.
3. Land that cost $8,000 was sold for $10,000.

Required

a. Compute the net cash flow from investing activities.
b. Prepare the cash flow from the investing activities section of the statement of cash flows.

L.O. 2, 3   PROBLEM 14–15B *Using Financial Statement Data to Determine Cash Flow from Financing Activities*

The following information pertaining to financing activities is available for Engineered Components Company for 2002.

Account Title	Beginning of Year	End of Year
Bonds Payable	$170,000	$180,000
Common Stock	210,000	280,000
Paid-in Capital in Excess of Par	84,000	116,000

Other Information

1. Dividends paid during the period amounted to $28,000.
2. Additional funds of $40,000 were borrowed during the period by issuing bonds.

Required

a. Compute the net cash flow from financing activities for 2002.
b. Prepare the cash flow from the financing activities section of the statement of cash flows.

L.O. 2, 3   PROBLEM 14–16B *Using Financial Statements to Prepare a Statement of Cash Flows— Direct Method*

The following financial statements were drawn from the records of Healthy Products Co.

Balance Sheets as of December 31		
	2002	**2003**
Assets		
Cash	$ 1,940	$16,120
Accounts Receivable	2,000	2,400
Inventory	2,600	2,000
Equipment	17,100	13,700
Accumulated Depreciation—Equipment	(12,950)	(11,300)
Land	8,000	13,000
Total Assets	$18,690	$35,920
Liabilities and Equity		
Accounts Payable	$ 2,400	$ 3,600
Long-Term Debt	4,000	3,200
Common Stock	10,000	17,000
Retained Earnings	2,290	12,120
Total Liabilities and Stockholders' Equity	$18,690	$35,920

Income Statement for the Year Ended December 31, 2003

Sales Revenue	$17,480
Cost of Goods Sold	(6,200)
Gross Margin	11,280
Depreciation Expense	(1,750)
Operating Income	9,530
Gain on Sale of Equipment	1,800
Loss on Disposal of Land	(600)
Net Income	$10,730

Additional Data

1. During 2003, the company sold equipment for $6,800; it had originally cost $8,400. Accumulated depreciation on this equipment was $3,400 at the time of the sale. Also, the company purchased equipment for $5,000 cash.
2. The company sold land that had cost $2,000. This land was sold for $1,400, resulting in the recognition of a $600 loss. Also, common stock was issued in exchange for title to land that was valued at $7,000 at the time of exchange.
3. Paid dividends of $900.

Required

Use the T-account method to analyze the data and prepare a statement of cash flows.

PROBLEM 14–17B *Using Financial Statements to Prepare a Statement of Cash Flows—Direct Method*   L.O. 2, 3

The following financial statements were drawn from the records of Norton Materials, Inc.

Balance Sheets as of December 31

	2000	2001
Assets		
Cash	$ 14,100	$ 94,300
Accounts Receivable	40,000	36,000
Inventory	64,000	72,000
Notes Receivable	16,000	0
Equipment	170,000	98,000
Accumulated Depreciation—Equipment	(94,000)	(47,800)
Land	30,000	46,000
Total Assets	$240,100	$298,500
Liabilities and Equity		
Accounts Payable	$26,400	$24,000
Salaries Payable	10,000	15,000
Utilities Payable	1,400	800
Interest Payable	1,000	0
Note Payable	24,000	0
Common Stock	110,000	150,000
Retained Earnings	67,300	108,700
Total Liabilities and Equity	$240,100	$298,500

Income Statement for the Year Ended December 31, 2001

Sales Revenue	$300,000
Cost of Goods Sold	(144,000)
Gross Margin	156,000
Operating Expenses	
Salary Expense	(88,000)
Depreciation Expense	(9,800)
Utilities Expense	(6,400)
Operating Income	51,800
Nonoperating Items	
Interest Expense	(2,400)
Loss	(800)
Net Income	$ 48,600

Additional Information
1. Sold equipment costing $72,000 with accumulated depreciation of $56,000 for $15,200 cash.
2. Paid a $7,200 cash dividend to owners.

Required
Use the T-account method to analyze the data and prepare a statement of cash flows.

L.O. 2, 4   PROBLEM 14–18B *Using Financial Statements to Prepare a Statement of Cash Flows—Indirect Method*

The comparative balance sheets for Lind Beauty Products, Inc., for 2002 and 2003 follow:

Balance Sheets as of December 31		
	2002	2003
Assets		
Cash	$ 48,400	$ 6,300
Accounts Receivable	7,260	10,200
Merchandise Inventory	56,000	45,200
Prepaid Rent	2,140	700
Equipment	144,000	140,000
Accumulated Depreciation	(118,000)	(73,400)
Land	50,000	116,000
Total Assets	$189,800	$245,000
Liabilities and Equity		
Accounts Payable (Inventory)	$ 40,000	$ 37,200
Salaries Payable	10,600	12,200
Stockholders' Equity		
Common Stock, $50 Par Value	120,000	150,000
Retained Earnings	19,200	45,600
Total Liabilities and Equity	$189,800	$245,000

Income Statement for the Year Ended December 31, 2003	
Sales	$480,000
Cost of Goods Sold	(264,000)
Gross Profit	216,000
Operating Expenses	
Depreciation Expense	(11,400)
Rent Expense	(7,000)
Salaries Expense	(95,200)
Other Operating Expenses	(76,000)
Net Income	$ 26,400

Other Information
1. Purchased land for $66,000.
2. Purchased new equipment for $62,000.
3. Sold old equipment that cost $66,000 with accumulated depreciation of $56,000 for $10,000 cash.
4. Issued common stock for $30,000.

Required
Prepare the statement of cash flows for 2003 using the indirect method.

ANALYZE, THINK, COMMUNICATE

ATC 14–1   REAL-WORLD CASE *Following the Cash*

Panera Bread Company (Panera) was formerly known as Au Bon Pain Company (ABP). In May 1999, the ABP division of the company was sold to private investors for $72 million, and assumed the new name.
Panera operates retail bakery-cafes under the names Panera Bread and Saint Louis Bread Company. The following table shows the number of these cafes in operation for each of the past five years.

Year	Company Owned	Franchise Owned	Total
2000	90	172	262
1999	81	100	181
1998	70	45	115
1997	57	19	76
1996	52	10	62

Most of Panera's baked goods are distributed to the stores in the form of frozen dough. In March 1998, the company sold its frozen dough production facility to the Bunge Food Corporation for $13 million. Panera agreed to purchase its frozen dough from Bunge for at least the next five years.

Panera's statements of cash flows for 1998, 1999, and 2000 follow.

PANERA BREAD COMPANY
Consolidated Statements of Cash Flows
(Dollars in thousands)

	For the Fiscal Years Ended		
	December 30, 2000	December 25, 1999	December 26, 1998
Cash flows from operations			
Net income (loss)	$ 6,853	$ (629)	$(20,494)
Adjustments to reconcile net income (loss) to net cash provided by operating activities:			
Depreciation and amortization	8,412	6,379	12,667
Amortization of deferred financing costs	88	406	683
Provision for losses on accounts receivable	(111)	93	56
Minority interest	—	(25)	(127)
Tax benefit from exercise of stock options	4001	—	75
Deferred income taxes	664	42	(6,664)
Loss on early extinguishment of debt	—	382	—
Nonrecurring charge	494	5,545	26,236
Loss on disposal of assets	—	—	735
Changes in operating assets and liabilities:			
Accounts receivable	(308)	(1,596)	15
Inventories	(562)	(65)	212
Prepaid expenses	(543)	(3,560)	(535)
Refundable income taxes	(376)	—	480
Accounts payable	1,861	(3,037)	4,069
Accrued expenses	(645)	769	3,104
Deferred revenue	234	2,011	—
Net cash provided by operating activities	20,062	6,715	20,512
Cash flows from investing activities			
Additions to property and equipment	(20,089)	(15,306)	(21,706)
Proceeds from sale of assets	—	72,163	12,694
Change in cash included in net current liabilities held for sale	—	(466)	(1,305)
Payments received on notes receivable	35	114	240
Increase in intangible assets	—	(50)	(139)
Increase (decrease) in deposits and other	(771)	855	(956)
Increase in notes receivable	—	(30)	(45)
Net cash (used in) provided by investing activities	(20,825)	57,280	(11,217)
Cash flows from financing activities			
Exercise of employee stock options	8,206	96	1,203
Proceeds from long-term debt issuance	765	41,837	75,418
Principal payments on long-term debt	(391)	(106,073)	(84,253)
Purchase of treasury stock	(900)	—	—
Proceeds from issuance of common stock	182	148	268
Common stock issued for employee stock bonus	—	304	—
Increase in deferred financing costs	(24)	(110)	(506)
Decrease in minority interest	—	(121)	(418)
Net cash provided by (used in) financing activities	7,838	(63,919)	(8,288)
Net increase in cash and cash equivalents	7,075	76	1,007
Cash and cash equivalents at beginning of year	1,936	1,860	853
Cash and cash equivalents at end of year	$ 9,011	$ 1,936	$ 1,860
Supplemental cash flow information:			
Cash paid during the year for:			
Interest	$ 85	$ 4,250	$ 5,544
Income taxes	$ 512	$ 241	$ 268

Required

Using the information provided, including a careful analysis of Panera's statements of cash flows, answer the following questions. Be sure to explain the rationale for your answers and present any computations necessary to support them.

a. Was the sale of the frozen dough production facility for $13 million a cash sale? If so, what did Panera do with the cash it received?

b. Was the sale of the ABP division for $72 million a cash sale? If so, what did Panera do with the cash it received?

c. As shown in the preceding table, Panera has expanded its operations in each of the past five years. Approximately how much cash was spent on expansion in 1998, 1999, and 2000, and what were the sources of this cash for each year?

ATC 14–2 GROUP ASSIGNMENT *Preparing a Statement of Cash Flows*

The following financial statements and information are available for Blythe Industries, Inc.

Balance Sheets as of December 31

	2000	2001
Assets		
Cash	$120,600	$ 160,200
Accounts Receivable	85,000	103,200
Inventory	171,800	186,400
Marketable Securities (Available for Sale)	220,000	284,000
Equipment	490,000	650,000
Accumulated Depreciation	(240,000)	(310,000)
Land	120,000	80,000
Total Assets	$967,400	$1,153,800
Liabilities and Equity		
Liabilities		
Accounts Payable (Inventory)	$ 66,200	$36,400
Notes Payable—Long-Term	250,000	230,000
Bonds Payable	100,000	200,000
Total Liabilities	416,200	466,400
Stockholders' Equity		
Common Stock, No Par	200,000	240,000
Preferred Stock, $50 Par	100,000	110,000
Paid-in Capital in Excess of Par—Preferred Stock	26,800	34,400
Total Paid-In Capital	326,800	384,400
Retained Earnings	264,400	333,000
Less: Treasury Stock	(40,000)	(30,000)
Total Stockholders' Equity	$551,200	$ 687,400
Total Liabilities and Stockholders' Equity	$967,400	$1,153,800

Income Statement for 2001

Sales Revenue		$1,050,000
Cost of Goods Sold		(766,500)
Gross Profit		283,500
Operating Expenses		
Supplies Expense	$ 20,400	
Salaries Expense	92,000	
Depreciation Expense	90,000	
Total Operating Expenses		202,400
Operating Income		81,100
Nonoperating Items		
Interest Expense		(16,000)
Gain from the Sale of Marketable Securities		30,000
Gain from the Sale of Land and Equipment		12,000
Net Income		$ 107,100

Additional Information
1. Sold land that cost $40,000 for $44,000.
2. Sold equipment that cost $30,000 and had accumulated depreciation of $20,000 for $18,000.
3. Purchased new equipment for $190,000.
4. Sold marketable securities that cost $40,000 for $70,000.
5. Purchased new marketable securities for $104,000.
6. Paid $20,000 on the principal of the long-term note.
7. Paid off a $100,000 bond issue and issued new bonds for $200,000.
8. Sold 100 shares of treasury stock at its cost.
9. Issued some new common stock.
10. Issued some new $50 par preferred stock.
11. Paid dividends. (*Note:* The only transactions to affect retained earnings were net income and dividends.)

Required

Organize the class into three sections, and divide each section into groups of three to five students. Assign each section of groups an activity section of the statement of cash flows (operating activities, investing activities, or financing activities).

Group Task

Prepare your assigned portion of the statement of cash flows. Have a representative of your section put your activity section of the statement of cash flows on the board. As each adds its information on the board, the full statement of cash flows will be presented.

Class Discussion

Have the class finish the statement of cash flows by computing the net change in cash. Also have the class answer the following questions:
a. What is the cost per share of the treasury stock?
b. What was the issue price of the preferred stock?
c. What was the book value of the equipment sold?

BUSINESS APPLICATIONS CASE *Identifying Different Presentation Formats*

ATC 14–3

In *Statement of Financial Accounting Standards No. 95,* the Financial Accounting Standards Board (FASB) recommended but did not require that companies use the direct method. In Appendix B, Paragraphs 106–121, the FASB discussed its reasons for this recommendation.

Required
Obtain a copy of *Standard No. 95* and read Appendix B Paragraphs 106–21. Write a brief response summarizing the issues that the FASB considered and its specific reaction to those issues. Your response should draw heavily on paragraphs 119–21.

WRITING ASSIGNMENT *Explaining Discrepancies between Cash Flow and Operating Income*

ATC 14–4

The following selected information was drawn from the records of Fleming Company:

Assets	2002	2003
Accounts Receivable	$ 400,000	$ 840,200
Merchandise Inventory	720,000	1,480,000
Equipment	1,484,000	1,861,200
Accumulated Depreciation	(312,000)	(402,400)

Fleming is experiencing cash flow problems. Despite the fact that it reported significant increases in operating income, operating activities produced a net cash outflow. Recent financial forecasts predict that Fleming will have insufficient cash to pay its current liabilities within three months.

Required
Write a response explaining Fleming's cash shortage. Include a recommendation to remedy the problem.

ATC 14–5 **ETHICAL DILEMMA** *Would I Lie to You, Baby?*

Andy and Jean Crocket are involved in divorce proceedings. When discussing a property settlement, Andy told Jean that he should take over their investment in an apartment complex because she would be unable to absorb the loss that the apartments are generating. Jean was somewhat distrustful and asked Andy to support his contention. He produced the following income statement, which was supported by a CPA's unqualified opinion that the statement was prepared in accordance with generally accepted accounting principles.

CROCKET APARTMENTS
Income Statement
For the Year Ended December 31, 2003

Rent Revenue		$580,000
Less: Expenses		
Depreciation Expense	$280,000	
Interest Expense	184,000	
Operating Expense	88,000	
Management Fees	56,000	
Total Expenses		(608,000)
Net Loss		$ (28,000)

All revenue is earned on account. Interest and operating expenses are incurred on account. Management fees are paid in cash. The following accounts and balances were drawn from the 2002 and 2003 year-end balance sheets.

Account Title	2002	2003
Rent Receivable	$40,000	$44,000
Interest Payable	12,000	18,000
Accounts Payable (Oper. Exp.)	6,000	4,000

Jean is reluctant to give up the apartments but feels that she must because her present salary is only $40,000 per year. She says that if she takes the apartments, the $28,000 loss would absorb a significant portion of her salary, leaving her only $12,000 with which to support herself. She tells you that while the figures seem to support her husband's arguments, she believes that she is failing to see something. She knows that she and her husband collected a $20,000 distribution from the business on December 1, 2003. Also, $150,000 cash was paid in 2003 to reduce the principal balance on a mortgage that was taken out to finance the purchase of the apartments two years ago. Finally, $24,000 cash was paid during 2003 to purchase a computer system used in the business. She wonders, "If the apartments are losing money, where is my husband getting all the cash to make these payments?"

Required
a. Prepare a statement of cash flows for the 2003 accounting period.
b. Compare the cash flow statement prepared in Requirement *a* with the income statement and provide Jean Crocket with recommendations.
c. Comment on the value of an unqualified audit opinion when using financial statements for decision-making purposes.

ATC 14–6 **SPREADSHEET ANALYSIS** *Preparing a Statement of Cash Flows Using the Direct Method*

Refer to the information in Problem 14–18A. Solve for the statement of cash flows using the direct method. Instead of using the T-account method, set up the following spreadsheet to work through the analysis. The Debit/Credit entries are very similar to the T-account method except that they are entered onto a spreadsheet. Two distinct differences are as follows:
1. Instead of making entries on row 2 for Cash, cash entries are made beginning on row 24 under the heading Cash Transactions.
2. Entries for Retained Earnings are made on rows 15 through 20 since there are numerous revenue and expense entries to that account.

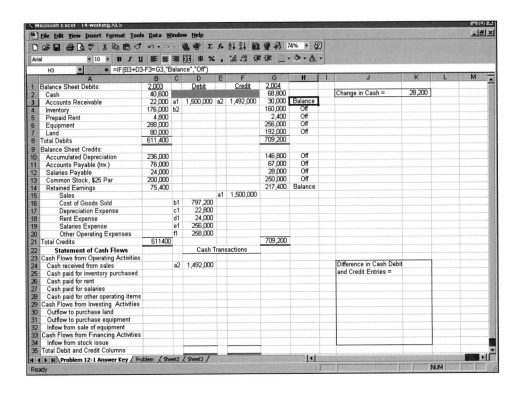

Required

a. Enter information in Column A.

b. Enter the beginning balance sheet amounts in Column B and ending balances in Column G. Total the debits and credits for each column.

c. To prevent erroneous entries to Cash in row 2, darken the area in Columns C through F.

d. In Columns C through F, record entries for the revenue and expenses and then the related conversions to cash flow. The first entry (a1) and (a2) converting Sales to Cash Received from Sales has been provided for you. So has the labeling for the expense entries (b1 through f1).

e. Record the four entries from the Other Information provided in Problem 14–18A. These are investing and financing activities.

f. In Column H, set up the IF function to determine whether the balance sheet accounts are in balance or not ("off"). Cell H3 for Accounts Receivable is provided for you. Cell H3 can be copied to all the balance sheet debit accounts. The balance sheet credit account formulas will differ given the different debit/credit rules for those accounts. The formula for Retained Earnings will need to include rows 14 through 20. *When the word "Balance" is reflected in every balance sheet cell in column H, the spreadsheet analysis is complete.* For more information about the IF function, refer to Spreadsheet Tips in ATC 11-9 of Chapter 11.

g. Total the Debit and Credit columns to ensure that the two columns are equal.

h. As a final check, beginning in cell J2, compute the change in the Cash account by subtracting the beginning balance from the ending balance. The difference will equal $28,200. Also beginning in cell J24, compute the difference in the debit and credit cash entries in rows 24 through 34. The difference should also equal $28,200.

Spreadsheet Tip

(1) Darken cells by highlighting the cells to be darkened. Select Format and then Cells. Click on the tab titled Patterns and choose a color.

SPREADSHEET ANALYSIS *Preparing a Statement of Cash Flows Using the Indirect Method*   ATC 14–7

(*Note:* If you completed ATC 14–6, that spreadsheet can be modified to complete this problem.)

Refer to the information in Problem 14–18A. Solve for the statement of cash flows using the indirect method. Instead of using the T-account method, set up the following spreadsheet to work through the analysis. The Debit/Credit entries are very similar to the T-account method except that they are entered onto a spreadsheet. Instead of making entries on row 2 for Cash, Cash Flow entries are made beginning on row 18.

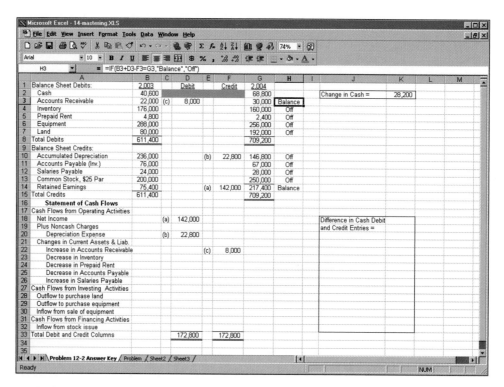

Required

a. Enter information in Column A.

b. Enter the beginning balance sheet amounts in Column B and ending balances in Column G. Total the debits and credits for each column.

c. To prevent erroneous entries to Cash in row 2, darken the area in Columns C through F.

d. Record the entry for Net Income. This is entry (a) provided.

e. Record the entry for Depreciation expense. This is entry (b) provided.

f. Record the entries for the changes in current assets and liabilities. The entry for the change in Accounts Receivable has been provided and is referenced as entry (c).

g. Record the four entries from the Other Information provided in Problem 14–18A. These are the investing and financing activities.

h. In Column H set up the IF function to determine whether the balance sheet accounts are in balance or not ("off"). Cell H3 for Accounts Receivable is provided for you. Cell H3 can be copied to all the balance sheet debit accounts. The balance sheet credit account formulas will differ given the different debit/credit rules for those accounts. *When the word "Balance" is reflected in every balance sheet cell in column H, the spreadsheet analysis is complete.* For more information on the IF function, refer to Spreadsheet Tips in ATC 11-9 of Chapter 11.

i. Total the Debit and Credit columns to ensure that the two columns are equal.

j. As a final check, beginning in cell J2, compute the change in the Cash account by subtracting the beginning balance from the ending balance. The difference will equal $28,200. Also beginning in cell J18, compute the difference in the debit and credit cash entries in rows 18 through 32. The difference should also equal $28,200.

absolute amounts Dollar totals reported in accounts on financial reports that can be misleading because they make no reference to the relative size of the company being analyzed. *p. 535*

absorption (full) costing Practice of capitalizing all product costs, including fixed manufacturing costs in inventory and expensing costs when goods are sold. *p. 459*

accounts receivable turnover Ratio measuring the quality of accounts receivable, calculated by dividing net sales by average net accounts receivable. *p. 540*

accrual accounting Accounting system that recognizes expenses or revenues before the associated cash payments or receipts occur. *p. 580*

accumulated conversion factors Factors used to convert a series of future cash inflows into their present value equivalent and that are applicable to cash inflows of equal amounts spread over equal interval time periods and that can be determined by computing the sum of the individual single factors used for each period. *p. 408*

acid-test ratio Measure of immediate debt-paying ability; calculated by dividing very liquid assets (cash, receivables, and marketable securities) by current liabilities. *p. 540*

activities The actions taken by an organization to accomplish its mission. *p. 22, 237*

activity base Factor that causes changes in variable cost; is usually some measure of volume when used to define cost behavior. *p. 62*

activity-based cost drivers Measures of the use and consumption of activities such as number of setups, percentage of use, and pounds of material delivered; used as allocation bases, the measures can improve the accuracy of allocations in technical and automated business environments in which overhead is no longer driven by volume. *p. 235*

activity-based costing (ABC) A two-stage allocation process that employs a variety of cost drivers. In the first stage, costs associated with specific business activities are allocated or assigned to activity cost pools. The second stage involves allocating these pooled costs to designated cost objects through the use of cost drivers. The cost drivers chosen for each cost pool are drivers that measure the demand placed on that cost pool by the cost object. *p. 237*

activity-based management (ABM) Management of the activities of an organization to add the greatest value by developing products that satisfy the needs of that organization's customers. *p. 22*

activity centers Cost centers organized around operating activities that have similar characteristics; reduce the costs of record keeping by pooling indirect costs in a manner that enables allocations through the use of a common cost driver. *p. 237*

allocation Process of dividing a total cost into parts and apportioning the parts among the relevant cost objects. *p. 193*

allocation base Cost driver that constitutes the basis for the allocation process. *p. 193*

allocation of scarce resource decisions Decisions that consider scarce resources in determining which products to produce and sell; found generally made by selecting the product that has the highest contribution margin per unit of scarce resource. *p. 159*

allocation rate Factor used to allocate or assign costs to a cost object; determined by taking the total cost to be allocated and dividing it by the appropriate cost driver. *p. 193*

annuity Equal series of cash flows received over equal intervals of time at a constant rate of return. *p. 409*

applied overhead Amount of overhead costs assigned during the period to work in process using the predetermined overhead rate. *p. 451*

appraisal costs Costs incurred to identify nonconforming products that were not avoided via the prevention cost expenditures. *p. 247*

average cost The total cost of making products divided by the total number of products made. *p. 8*

avoidable costs Future costs that can be avoided by taking a specified course of action. To be avoidable in a decision-making context, costs must differ among the alternatives. For example, if the cost of material used to make two different products is the same for both products, that cost could not be avoided by choosing to produce one product over the other. Therefore, the material's cost would not be an avoidable cost. *p. 141*

batch-level activities Activities (e.g., material handling, production setups) related to the production of groups of products, the cost of which is fixed regardless of the number of units produced; best allocated using cost drivers that measure activity consumption. *p. 240*

batch-level costs The costs associated with producing a batch of products. For example, the cost of setting up machinery to produce 1,000 products is a batch-level cost. The classification of batch-level costs is context sensitive. Postage for one product would be classified as a unit-level cost. In contrast, postage for a large number of products delivered in a single shipment would be classified as a batch-level cost. *p. 142*

benchmarking Identifying the best practices used by world-class competitors. *p. 21*

best practices Practices used by world-class companies. *p. 21*

book value per share Measure of a share of common stock; calculated by dividing stockholders' equity less preferred rights by the average number of common shares outstanding. *p. 547*

bottleneck A constraint limiting the capacity of a company to produce or sell its products. An example is a piece of equipment that cannot produce enough component parts to keep employees in the assembly department busy. *p. 160*

break-even point Point where total revenue equals total cost; can be expressed in units or sales dollars. *p. 101*

budget committee Group of individuals responsible for coordinating budgeting activities, normally consisting of upper-level managers including the president; vice presidents of marketing, production, purchasing, and finance; and the controller. *p. 279*

budgeting Form of planning that formalizes a company's goals and objectives in financial terms. *p. 279*

budget slack Difference between inflated and realistic standards. *p. 326*

by-products Products that share common inputs with other joint products but have relatively insignificant market values relative to the other joint products. *p. 204*

capital budget Budget that describes the company's plans regarding investments, new products, or lines of business for the coming year; is used as input to prepare many of the operating budgets and becomes a formal part of the master budget. *p. 283*

capital budgeting Financial planning activities that cover the intermediate range of time such as whether to buy or lease equipment, whether to purchase a particular investment, or whether to increase operating expenses to stimulate sales. *p. 280*

capital investments Expenditures for the purchase of operational assets that involve a long-term commitment of funds that can be critically important to the company's ultimate success; normally recovered through the use of the assets. *p. 406*

cash budget A budget that focuses on cash receipts and payments that are expected to occur in the future. *p. 289*

cash inflows Sources of cash. *p. 577*

cash outflows Uses of cash. *p. 577*

certified suppliers Suppliers who have gained the confidence of the buyer by providing quality goods and services at desirable prices and usually in accordance with strict delivery specifications; frequently provide the buyer with preferred customer status in exchange for guaranteed purchase quantities and prompt payment schedules. *p. 150*

companywide allocation rate Use of direct labor hours or some other measure of volume to allocate all overhead cost to the company's products or other cost objects. *p. 234*

constraints Factors that limit a business's ability to satisfy the demand for its products. *p. 159*

continuous improvement Total quality management (TQM) feature that refers to an ongoing process through which employees learn to eliminate waste, reduce response time, minimize defects, and simplify the design and delivery of products and services to customers. *p. 21*

contribution margin Difference between a company's sales revenue and total variable cost; represents the amount available to cover fixed cost and thereafter to provide a profit. *p. 57*

contribution margin per unit The contribution margin per unit is equal to the sales price per unit minus the variable cost per unit. *p. 100*

contribution margin ratio Result of dividing the contribution margin per unit by the sales price; can be used in cost-volume-profit analysis to determine the amount of the break-even sales volume expressed in dollars or to determine the dollar level of sales required to attain a desired profit. *p. 112*

controllability concept The practice that evaluates a manager only on the revenue and costs under his or her direct control. *p. 369*

cost Amount of resources used to acquire an asset or to produce revenue. *p. 189*

cost accumulation Process of determining the cost of a particular object by accumulating many individual costs into a single total cost. *p. 190*

cost allocation Process of dividing a total cost into parts and assigning the parts to relevant objects. *p. 13, 191*

cost averaging Method to determine the average cost per unit of a product or service by dividing the total cost by the activity base used in defining the cost; often is more relevant to decision making than actual costs. Pricing, performance evaluation, and control depend most often on average costs. *p. 62*

cost-based transfer price Transfer price based on the historical or standard cost incurred by the supplying segment. *p. 382*

cost behavior Way a cost reacts (goes up, down, or remains the same) relative to changes in some measure of activity (e.g., the behavior pattern of the cost of raw materials is to increase as the number of units of product made increases). *p. 60*

cost center Type of responsibility center in which the manager influences only costs and is held accountable for a specific output at a given level of cost. *p. 372*

cost driver Any factor, usually some measure of activity, that causes cost to be incurred, sometimes referred to as *activity base* or *allocation base*. Examples are labor hours, machine hours, or some other measure of activity whose change causes corresponding changes in the cost object. *p. 190*

cost objects Objects for which managers need to know the cost; can be products, processes, departments, services, activities, and so on. *p. 189*

cost of capital Return paid to investors and creditors for the use of their assets (capital); usually represents a company's minimum rate of return. *p. 407*

cost per equivalent unit Unit cost of product determined by dividing total production costs by the number of equivalent whole units. It is used to allocate product costs between processing departments (compute ending inventory and the amount of costs transferred to the subsequent department). *p. 503*

cost per unit of input Cost of one unit of material, labor, or overhead determined by multiplying the price paid for one unit of material, labor or overhead input by the usage of input for one unit of material, labor or overhead. *p. 330*

cost-plus pricing Pricing strategy that sets the price at cost plus a markup equal to a percentage of the cost. *p. 6, 100*

cost pool Many individual costs that have been accumulated into a single total for the purposes of allocation. *p. 202*

cost structure Company's cost mix (relative proportion of variable and fixed costs to total cost). When sales change, the size of the corresponding change in net income is directly related to the company's cost structure. Companies with a large percentage of fixed cost to variable costs have more fluctuation in net income with changes in sales. *p. 56*

cost tracing Relating specific costs to the objects that cause their incurrence. *p. 191*

cost-volume-profit (CVP) analysis Analysis that shows the interrelationships among sales prices, volume, fixed, and variable costs; an important tool in determining the break-even point or the most profitable combination of these variables. *p. 100*

current ratio Measure of liquidity; calculated by dividing current assets by current liabilities. *p. 539*

decentralization   Practice delegating authority and responsibility for the operation of business segments. *p. 368*

deferral transactions   Accounting transactions in which cash payments or receipts occur before the associated expense or revenue is recognized. *p. 582*

differential costs   Costs that differ among alternative business opportunities and are usually relevant information for decision making. Note, however, that not all are relevant. For example, although depreciation may differ between the alternatives, it is not avoidable because it is a sunk cost and therefore not relevant for decision making. *p. 141*

direct cost   Cost that is easily traceable to a cost object and for which the sacrifice to trace is small in relation to the information benefits attained. *p. 192*

direct labor   Wages paid to production workers whose efforts can be easily and conveniently traced to products. *p. 11*

direct method   (1) Allocation method that allocates service center costs directly to operating department cost pools. (2) Method of preparing the statement of cash flows that reports the total cash receipts and cash payments from each of the major categories of activities (collections from customers, payment to suppliers). *p. 210, 592*

direct raw materials   Costs of raw materials used to make products that can be easily and conveniently traced to those products. *p. 10*

dividend yield   Ratio for comparing stock dividends paid in relation to the market price; calculated as dividends per share divided by market price per share. *p. 548*

downstream costs   Costs, such as delivery costs and sales commissions, incurred after the manufacturing process is complete. *p. 19, 246*

earnings per share   Measure of the value of a share of common stock in terms of company earnings; calculated as net income available to common stockholders divided by the average number of outstanding common shares. *p. 546*

economies of scale   Concept by which the unit cost of production can be reduced by taking advantage of opportunities that become available when an operation's size is increased. Increased size usually results in an increased volume of activity that drives the per unit fixed cost down, resulting in a lower total cost of production. *p. 54*

efficient market hypothesis   The proposition that creditors and investors look to the substance of business events regardless of how those events are reported in financial reports. *p. 15*

equation method   Cost-volume-profit analysis technique that uses a basic mathematical relationship among sales, variable costs, fixed costs; desire net income before taxes and provides a solution in terms of units. *p. 113*

equipment replacement decisions   Decisions regarding whether existing equipment should be replaced with newer equipment based on identification and comparison of the avoidable costs of the old and new equipment to determine which equipment is more profitable to operate. *p. 153*

equivalent whole units   Result of expressing partially completed goods in an equivalent number of fully completed goods. *p. 503*

expense transactions   Transactions completed in the process of operating a business that decrease assets or increase liabilities. *p. 580*

external failure costs   Costs incurred when defective goods are delivered to customers. *p. 247*

facility-level activities   Activities (e.g., paying insurance on the facility, providing plant maintenance, and paying taxes) performed for the benefit of the production process as a whole and whose allocation is arbitrary. *p. 242*

facility-level costs   Costs incurred on behalf of the whole company or a segment of the company; not related to any specific product, batch, or unit of production or service and unavoidable unless the entire company or segment is eliminated. *p. 143*

failure costs   Costs incurred from the actual occurrence of nonconforming events. *p. 247*

favorable variance   Variance that occurs when actual costs are less than standard costs or when actual sales are higher than standard sales. *p. 323*

financial accounting   Field of accounting designed to meet the information needs of external users of business information (creditors, investors, governmental agencies, financial analysts, etc.); its objective is to classify and record business events and transactions to facilitate the production of external financial reports (income statement, balance sheet, statement of cash flows, and statement of changes in equity). *p. 4*

financial accounting standards board (FASB)   Private, independent board established by the accounting profession that has been delegated the authority by the SEC to establish most of the accounting rules and regulations for public financial reporting. *p. 6*

financial statement budgets (pro forma statements)   Projected financial statements found in the master budget that are based on information contained in the operating budgets. *p. 283*

financing activities   Cash inflows and outflows from transactions with investors and creditors (except interest). These cash flows include cash receipts from the issue of stock, borrowing activities and cash disbursements associated with dividends. *p. 580*

finished goods   End result of the manufacturing process measured by the accumulated cost of raw materials, labor, and overhead. *p. 7*

finished goods inventory   Asset account used to accumulate the product costs (direct materials, direct labor, and overhead) associated with completed products that have not sold. *p. 446*

first-in, first-out (FIFO) method   Method used to determine equivalent units when accuracy is deemed to be important; accounts for the degree of completion of both beginning and ending inventories but has a more complicated application. *p. 503*

fixed cost   Cost that in total remains constant when activity volume changes; varies per unit inversely with changes in the volume of activity. *p. 51*

flexible budgets   Budgets that show expected revenues and costs at a variety of different activity levels. *p. 320*

flexible budget variances   Differences between budgets based on standard amounts at the actual level of activity and actual results; caused by differences in standard and actual unit cost since the volume of activity is the same. *p. 324*

general, selling, and administrative costs   All costs not associated with obtaining or manufacturing a product; in practice are sometimes referred to as *period costs* because they are normally expensed in the period in which the economic sacrifice is incurred. *p. 12*

generally accepted accounting principles   Rules and regulations that accountants agree to follow when preparing financial reports for public distribution. *p. 6*

high-low method   Method of estimating the fixed and variable components of a mixed cost; determines the variable cost per unit by dividing the difference between the total cost of the high and low points by the difference in the corresponding high and low volumes. The fixed cost component is determined by subtracting the variable cost from the total cost at either the high or low volume. *p. 65*

horizontal analysis   Analysis technique that compares amounts of the same item over several time periods. *p. 535*

hybrid cost systems   Cost system that blends some of the features of a job-order costing system with some of the features of a process cost system. *p. 492*

ideal standard   Highest level of efficiency attainable, based on all input factors interacting perfectly under ideal or optimum conditions. *p. 327*

incremental revenue   Additional cash inflows from operations generated by using an additional capital asset. *p. 413*

indirect cost   Cost that cannot be easily traced to a cost object and for which the economic sacrifice to trace is not worth the informational benefits. *p. 12, 192*

indirect method   Method of preparing the statement of cash flows that uses the net income from the income statement as a starting point for reporting cash flow from operating activities; adjustments necessary to convert accrual-based net income to a cash-equivalent basis are shown in the operating activities section of the statement of cash flows. *p. 593*

information overload   Situation in which presentation of too much information confuses the user of the information. *p. 534*

inputs   The resources (material, labor, and overhead) used to make products. *p. 330*

interdepartmental service   Service performed by one service department for the benefit of another service department. *p. 211*

internal failure costs   Costs incurred when defects are corrected before goods reach the customer. *p. 247*

internal rate of return   Rate that will produce a present value of an investment's future cash inflows that equals cash outflows required to acquire the investments; alternatively, the rate that produces in a net present value of zero. *p. 412*

inventory holding costs   Costs associated with acquiring and retaining inventory including cost of storage space; lost, stolen, or damaged merchandise; insurance; personnel and management costs, and interest. *p. 23*

inventory turnover   Measurement of the volume of sales in relation to inventory levels; calculated as the cost of goods sold divided by average inventory. *p. 541*

investing activities   Cash inflows and outflows associated with buying or selling long-term assets including gains and losses. Also, cash inflows and outflows associated with lending activities (loans made to others—cash outflows or collections of loans made to others—cash inflows). *p. 580*

investment center   Type of responsibility center in which the manager can influence revenues, expenses, and capital investments. *p. 373*

job cost sheet   Document used in a job-order cost system to accumulate the materials, labor and overhead costs of a job through the various stages of production; at job completion, contains a summary of all costs that were incurred to complete that job; also known as *job-order cost sheet* or *job record. p. 492*

job-order cost system   System used to determine the costs of distinct, one-of-a-kind product that traces costs to products that are produced individually (i.e., custom designed building) or produced in batches (i.e., a special order for 100 wedding invitations). *p. 490*

joint costs   Common costs incurred in the process of making two or more products. *p. 203*

joint product   Products derived from joint cost. *p. 203*

just in time (JIT)   Inventory flow system that minimizes the amount of inventory on hand by making inventory available for customer consumption on demand, therefore eliminating the need to store inventory. The system reduces explicit holding costs including financing, warehouse storage, supervision, theft, damage, and obsolescence. It also eliminates hidden opportunity costs such as lost revenue due to the lack of availability of inventory. *p. 23*

labor efficiency variance   Variance occurring in a standard cost accounting system when the actual amount or quantity of direct labor used differs from the standard amount required. *p. 330*

labor rate variance   Variance that occurs when the actual pay rate differs from the standard pay rate for direct labor. *p. 330*

lax standards   Easily attainable goals that can be accomplished with minimal effort. *p. 327*

liquidity ratios   Measures of short-term debt-paying ability. *p. 539*

low-ball pricing   Pricing a product below competitors' price to lure customers away and then raising the price once customers depend on the supplier for the product. *p. 149*

making the numbers   Expression that indicates that marketing managers attained the sales volume indicated in the master budget. *p. 322*

management by exception   Use of management resources on areas that are not performing in accordance with expectations; a philosophy that directs management to concentrate on areas with significant variances. *p. 327, 369*

managerial accounting   Field of accounting designed to meet the information needs of managers and other individuals working inside the business. It is concerned with information gathering and reporting that adds value to the business. Managerial accounting information is not regulated or made available to the public. *p. 4*

manufacturing overhead   Production costs that cannot be traced directly to products. *p. 12*

manufacturing overhead account   Temporary account used during an accounting period to accumulate the actual overhead costs incurred and the total amount of overhead applied to the Work in Process account. At the end of the period, a debit balance in the account implies that overhead has been underapplied and a credit balance implies that overhead has been overapplied. The account is closed at year end in an adjusting entry to the inventory and Cost of Goods Sold accounts. If the balance is insignificant, it is closed only to Cost of Goods Sold. *p. 451*

margin of safety   Difference between break-even sales and budgeted sales expressed in units, dollars, or as a percentage; the amount by which actual sales can fall below budgeted sales before a loss is incurred. *p. 108*

market-based transfer price   Transfer price based on the external market price less any savings in cost; the closest approximation to an arm's-length transaction that segments can achieve. *p. 380*

master budget   Composition of the numerous separate but interdependent departmental budgets that cover a wide range of operating and financial factors such as sales, production, manufacturing expenses, and administrative expenses. *p. 283*

materiality   Characteristic that designates the point at which the knowledge of or lack of information would make a difference in a decision; can be measured in absolute, percentage, quantitative, or qualitative terms. *p. 535*

materials price variance   Variance that occurs when actual prices paid for raw materials differ from the standard prices. *p. 330*

materials quantity variance   Variance that occurs when the actual amounts of raw materials used to produce a good differ from the standard amounts required to produce that good. *p. 330*

materials requisition   A form used to request or order the materials needed to begin a designated job; can be a paper document or an electronic impulse delivered through a computer. Materials requisitioned for a job are summarized by the accounting department on a job cost sheet. *p. 492*

material variance   Variance that would affect decision making. *p. 328*

minimum rate of return   Minimum amount of profitability required to persuade a company to accept an investment opportunity; also known as *desired rate of return, required rate of return, hurdle rate, cutoff rate,* and *discount rate. p. 407*

mixed costs (semivariable costs)   Costs composed of a mixture of fixed and variable components. *p. 64*

most-favored customer status   Arrangement by which a supplier and customer achieve mutual benefit by providing each other with favorable treatment that is not extended to other associates. *p. 24*

negotiated transfer price   Transfer price established by agreement of both the selling and buying segments of the firm. *p. 381*

net margin   Profitability measurement that indicates the percentage of each sales dollar resulting in profit; calculated as net income divided by net sales. *p. 544*

net present value   Evaluation technique that uses a desired rate of return to discount future cash flows back to their present value equivalents and then subtracts the cost of the investment from the present value equivalents to determine the net present value. A zero or positive net present value (present value of cash inflows equals or exceeds the present value of cash outflows) implies that the investment opportunity provides an acceptable rate of return. *p. 412*

noncash investing and financing activities   Business transactions that do not directly affect cash, such as exchanging stock for land or purchasing property by using a mortgage; are reported as both an inflow and outflow in a separate section of the statement of cash flows. *p. 578*

nonvalue-added activities   Tasks undertaken that do not contribute to a product's ability to satisfy customer needs. *p. 22*

number of days' sales in inventory   Another way to look at the inventory turnover by converting the inventory turnover ratio into a number of days; calculated by dividing average inventory by the average cost of goods sold. *p. 541*

number of days' sales in receivables (average collection period)   Another way to look at the accounts receivable turnover by converting the turnover ratio into a number of days; calculated by dividing 365 days by the turnover ratio. *p. 540*

operating activities   Cash inflows and outflows associated with operating the business. These cash flows normally result from revenue and expense transactions including interest. However, cash flows associated with gains and losses are not included in operating activities. *p. 580*

operating budgets   Budgets prepared by different departments within a company that will become a part of the company's master budget; typically include a sales budget, an inventory purchases budget, a selling and administrative budget, and a cash budget. *p. 280*

operating departments   Departments assigned tasks leading to the accomplishment of the organization's objectives. *p. 210*

operating leverage   Operating condition in which a percentage change in revenue produces a proportionately larger percentage change in net income; measured by dividing the contribution margin by net income. The higher the proportion of fixed cost to total costs, the greater the operating leverage. *p. 53, 114*

opportunity cost   Cost of lost opportunities such as the failure to make sales due to an insufficient supply of inventory. *p. 25, 144*

ordinary annuity   Annuity whose cash inflows occur at the end of each accounting period. *p. 410*

outputs   Products that result from processing inputs. *p. 330*

outsourcing   The practice of buying goods and services from another company rather than producing them internally. *p. 148*

overapplied or underapplied overhead   Result of allocating more or less overhead costs to the Work in Process account than the amount of the actual overhead costs incurred. *p. 451*

overhead   Costs associated with producing products that cannot be cost effectively traced to products; includes indirect costs such as indirect materials, indirect labor, utilities, rent, depreciation on manufacturing facilities and equipment, and planning, design, and setup costs related to the manufacture of products. *p. 11*

overhead costs   Indirect costs of doing business that cannot be directly traced to a product, department, or process, such as depreciation. *p. 11*

participative budgeting   Budget technique that allows subordinates to participate with upper-level managers in setting budget objectives, thereby encouraging cooperation and support in the attainment of the company's goals. *p. 282*

payback method   Technique that evaluates investment opportunities by determining the length of time necessary to recover the initial net investment through incremental revenue or cost savings; the shorter the period, the better the investment opportunity. *p. 420*

percentage analysis Analysis of relationships between two different items to draw conclusions or make decisions. *p. 536*

period costs General, selling, and administrative costs that are expensed in the period in which the economic sacrifice is made. *p. 12*

perpetual (continuous) budgeting Continuous budgeting activity normally covering a 12-month time span by replacing the current month's budget at the end of each month with a new budget; keeps management constantly involved in the budget process so that changing conditions are incorporated on a timely bases. *p. 281*

postaudit Repeated calculation using the techniques originally employed to analyze an investment project; accomplished with the use of actual data available at the completion of the investment project so that the actual results can be compared with expected results based on estimated data at the beginning of the project. Its purpose is to provide feedback as to whether the expected results were actually accomplished in improving the accuracy of future analysis. *p. 423*

practical standard Level of efficiency in which the ideal standard has been modified to allow for normal tolerable inefficiencies. *p. 327*

predetermined overhead rate Rate determined by dividing the estimated overhead costs for the period by some measure of estimated total production activity for the period, such as the number of labor hours or machine hours. The base chosen should provide some logical measure of overhead use. The rate is determined before actual costs or activity are known. Throughout the accounting period, the rate is used to allocate overhead costs to the Work in Process Inventory account based on actual production activity. *p. 202, 450*

present value index Present value of cash inflows divided by the present value of cash outflows. Higher index numbers indicate higher rates of return. *p. 415*

present value table Table that consists of a list of factors to use in converting future values into their present value equivalents; composed of columns that represent different return rates and rows that depict different periods of time. *p. 408*

prestige pricing Pricing strategy that sets the price at a premium (above average markup above cost) under the assumption that people will pay more for the product because of its prestigious brand name, media attention, or some other reason that has piqued the interest of the public. *p. 110*

prevention costs Costs incurred to avoid nonconforming products. *p. 247*

price-earnings ratio Measurement used to compare the values of different stocks in terms of earnings; calculated as market price per share divided by earnings per share. *p. 547*

pro forma statements Budgeted financial statements prepared from the information in the master budget. *p. 283*

process cost system System used to determine the costs of homogeneous products, such as chemicals, foods or paints, that distributes costs evenly across total production; determines an average by dividing the total product costs of each production department by the number of units of product made in that department during some designated period of time. The total costs in the last production department include all costs incurred in preceding departments so that the unit cost determined for the last department reflects the final unit cost of the product. *p. 490*

product costs All costs related to obtaining or manufacturing a product intended for sale to customers; are accumulated in inventory accounts and expensed as cost of goods sold at the point of sale. For a manufacturing company, product costs include direct materials, direct labor, and manufacturing overhead. *p. 6*

product costing Classification and accumulation of individual inputs (materials, labor, and overhead) for determining the cost of making a good or providing a service. *p. 6*

product-level activities Activities (e.g., inventory holding cost, engineering developmental costs) that support a specific product or product line and whose allocation is based on the extent to which the activities are used in sustaining the product or product line. *p. 241*

product-level costs Costs incurred to support different kinds of products or services; can be avoided by the elimination of a product line or a type of service. *p. 142*

profit center Type of responsibility center in which the manager can influence both revenues and expenses for the center. *p. 372*

profitability ratios Measurements of a firm's ability to generate earnings. *p. 544*

qualitative characteristics Nonquantifiable features such as company reputation, welfare of employees, and customer satisfaction that can be affected by certain decisions. *p. 145*

quality The degree to which actual products or services conform to their design specifications. *p. 247*

quality cost report An accountant's report that typically lists the company's quality costs and provides a horizontal analysis showing each item as a percentage of total cost. *p. 248*

quantitative characteristics Numbers in decision making subject to mathematical manipulation, such as the dollar amounts of revenues and expenses. Opening a bottleneck to allow more products or services to be produced or sold. *p. 145*

quick ratio Same as acid-test ratio. *p. 540*

ratio analysis Same as percentage analysis. *p. 538*

raw materials Physical commodities (e.g., wood, metal, paint) used in the manufacturing process. *p. 10*

raw materials inventory Asset account used to accumulate the costs of materials such as lumber, metals, paints, chemicals that will be used to make the company's products. *p. 446*

reciprocal method Allocation method that considers two-way associations between/among service centers (service centers provide to as well as receive services from other service centers); uses simultaneous linear equations, but the resultant cost distributions are difficult to interpret. *p. 214*

reciprocal relationships Two-way associations in which departments provide services to and receive services from one another. *p. 213*

recovery of investment Recovery of the funds used to acquire the original investment. *p. 422*

reengineering Business practices designed by companies to make production and delivery systems more competitive in world markets by eliminating or minimizing waste, errors, and costs. *p. 21*

relevant costs Future-oriented costs that differ between business alternatives; also known as *avoidable costs. p. 141*

relevant information Decision-making information about costs, costs savings, or revenues that have these features: (1) future-oriented information and (2) the information differs between the alternatives; decision specific (information that is relevant in one decision may not be relevant in another decision). *Relevant costs* are referred to as *avoidable costs* and *relevant revenues* are referred to as *differential revenues. p. 140*

relevant range Range of activity over which the definitions of fixed and variable costs apply. *p. 61*

residual income Approach that evaluates managers on their ability to maximize the dollar value of earnings above some targeted level of earnings. *p. 377*

responsibility accounting Accounting system in which the accountability for results is assigned to a segment manager of the firm based on the amount of control or influence the manager possesses over those costs. *p. 367*

responsibility center Point in an organization where the control over revenue or expense items is located. *p. 372*

responsibility reports Reports of the performance of various responsibility centers of the firm with respect to controllable costs; show the variances that result from comparing budgeted and actual controllable costs. *p. 369*

retained earnings Equity account that is the culmination of all earnings retained in the business since inception (all revenues minus all expenses—including cost of goods sold—and distributions for the period added to all past retained earnings). *p. 453*

return on assets The ratio of net income divided by total assets. *p. 545*

return on equity Measure of the profitability of a firm based on earnings generated in relation to stockholders' equity; calculated as net income divided by stockholders' equity. *p. 546*

return on investment Measure of profitability based on the asset base of the firm. It is calculated as net income divided by total assets. ROI is a product of net margin and asset turnover. *p. 373, 545*

revenue transactions Transactions completed in the process of operating a business that increase assets or decrease liabilities. *p. 580*

sales activity (volume) variance Difference between sales based on a static budget (standard sales price times standard level of activity) and sales based on a flexible budget (standard sales price times actual level of activity). *p. 321*

sales price variance Difference between actual sales and expected sales based on the standard sales price per unit times the actual level of activity. *p. 324*

scattergraph method Method of estimating the variable and fixed components by which cost data are plotted on a graph and a regression line is visually drawn through the points so that the total distance between the data points and the line is minimized. *p. 66*

schedule of cost of goods manufactured and sold Schedule that summarizes the flow of manufacturing product costs; its result, cost of goods sold, is shown as a single line item on the company's income statement. *p. 457*

Securities and Exchange Commission (SEC) Government agency authorized by Congress to establish regulations regarding public reporting practices; requires companies that issue securities to the public to file annual audited financial statements with it. *p. 6*

segment Component part of an organization that is designated as a reporting entity. *p. 150*

sensitivity analysis Spreadsheet analysis that executes "what-if" questions to assess the sensitivity of profits to simultaneous changes in fixed cost, variable cost, and sales volume. *p. 109*

service departments Departments such as quality control, repair and maintenance, personnel, and accounting that provide support to the operating departments. *p. 210*

single-payment (lump-sum) Factors used to convert a lump-sum future cash inflow into a present value equivalent. *p. 408*

solvency ratios Measures of a firm's long-term debt-paying ability. *p. 542*

special order decisions Decisions of whether to accept orders from nonregular customers who want to buy goods or services significantly below the normal selling price. If the order's differential revenues exceed its avoidable costs, the order should be accepted. Qualitative features such as the order's effect on the existing customer base if accepted must also be considered. *p. 145*

spending variance Difference between actual fixed overhead costs and budgeted fixed overhead costs. *p. 335*

split-off point Point in the production process where products become separate and identifiable. *p. 203*

standards Per unit price or costs that "should be" based on a certain set of anticipated circumstances; per unit costs standards are composed of price and quantity standards that together provide the per unit cost standard. *p. 326*

start-up (setup) costs The costs associated with the activities of changing machinery, the production configuration, inspection, etc., to prepare for making a new product or a batch of a product. *p. 236*

statement of cash flows A financial statement that describes the sources and uses of cash that occurred during an accounting period. *p. 28*

static budgets Budgets such as the master budget based solely on the level of planned activity; remain constant even when volume of activity changes. *p. 320*

step method Two-step allocation method that considers one-way interdepartmental service center relationships by allocating costs from service centers to service centers as well as from service centers to operating departments; does not consider reciprocal relationships between service centers. *p. 211*

strategic cost management New management techniques that are designed to more accurately measure and control costs. The techniques have been implemented as a response to today's complex automated business environment. These new strategies include efforts to eliminate nonvalue-added activities, more efficient designs for the manufacturing process, and new ways to trace overhead costs to cost objects. *p. 246*

strategic planning Planning activities associated with long-range decisions such as defining the scope of the business, determining which products to develop, deciding whether to discontinue a business segment, and determining which market niche would be most profitable. *p. 280*

suboptimization Situation in which managers act in their own self-interests even though the organization as a whole suffers. *p. 377*

sunk costs Costs that have been incurred in past transactions and therefore are not relevant for decision making. In an equipment replacement decision, the cost of the old machine presently in use is a sunk cost and is not avoidable because it has already been incurred. *p. 140*

T-account method   Method of determining net cash flows by analyzing beginning and ending balances on the balance sheet and inferring the periods transactions from the income statement. *p. 580*

target pricing   The practice of controlling cost factors so as to make products that can be sold at the price customers are willing to pay. *p. 245*

target pricing (target costing)   Pricing strategy that begins with the determination of a price at which a product will sell and then focuses on the development of that product with a cost structure that will satisfy market demands. *p. 103–104*

theory of constraints (TOC)   Practice used by many businesses to increase profitability by managing bottlenecks or constrained resources by identifying the bottlenecks restricting the operations of the business and then opening them by relaxing the constraints. *p. 160*

time value of money   Concept that recognizes the fact that the present value of an opportunity to receive one dollar in the future is less than one dollar because of interest, risk, and inflation factors. *p. 406*

total quality management (TQM)   Management philosophy that includes: (1) a continuous systematic problem solving philosophy that engages personnel at all levels of the organization to eliminate waste, defects and nonvalue-added activities and (2) a continuous organizational commitment to the accomplishment of customer satisfaction of quality costs in a manner that leads to the highest level of customer satisfaction. *p. 21, 248*

transferred-in costs   Costs transferred from one department to the next; combined with the materials, labor, and overhead costs incurred in the department so that when goods are complete, the total product cost of all departments is transferred to the Finished Goods Inventory account. *p. 491*

transfer price   Price at which products or services are transferred between divisions or other subunits of an organization. *p. 380*

trend analysis   Study of the performance of ratios over a period of time. *p. 536*

turnover of assets   Measure of sales in relation to assets; calculated as net sales divided by total assets. *p. 544*

unadjusted rate of return   Measure of profitability computed by dividing the average incremental increase in annual net income by the average cost of the original investment (original cost ÷ 2). *p. 421*

unfavorable variance   Variance that occurs when actual costs exceed standard costs or when actual sales are less than standard sales. *p. 330*

unit-level activities   Activities that occur each time a unit of product is made; the costs associated with these activities exhibit a variable cost behavior pattern. *p. 239*

unit-level costs   Costs incurred each time a company makes a single product or performs a single service and that can be avoided by eliminating a unit of product or service. Likewise, unit-level costs increase with each additional product produced or service provided. *p. 142*

upstream costs   Costs incurred before the manufacturing process begins, for example, research and development costs. *p. 19, 246*

value-added activity   Any unit of work that contributes to a product's ability to satisfy customer needs. *p. 22*

value-added principle   The benefits attained (value added) by the accounting process should exceed the cost of the process. *p. 6*

value chain   Linked sequence of activities that create value for the customer. *p. 22*

variable cost   Cost that in total changes in direct proportion to changes in volume of activity; remains constant per unit when volume of activity changes. *p. 52*

variable costing   Product costing system that capitalizes only variable cost in inventory; its income statement subtracts variable costs from revenue to determine contribution margin. Fixed costs, including product cost, are subtracted from the contribution margin to determine net income. In this format the amount of net income is not affected by the volume of production. *p. 459*

variances   Differences between standard and actual amounts. *p. 321*

vertical analysis   Analysis technique that compares items on financial statements to significant totals. *p. 537*

vertical integration   Attainment of control over the entire spectrum of business activity from production to sales; as an example a grocery store that owns farms. *p. 149*

visual fit line   Line drawn by visual inspection to minimize the total distance between the data points and the line; used to estimate fixed and variable cost. *p. 67*

volume-based cost drivers   Measures of volume such as labor hours, machine hours, or amounts of materials that have a strong correlation with unit-level overhead cost and that make appropriate allocation bases for the allocation of unit-level overhead costs. *p. 235*

volume variance   Difference between the budgeted fixed cost and the amount of fixed costs allocated to production. *p. 335*

voluntary costs   Prevention and appraisal costs that are a function of managerial discretion. *p. 247*

weighted average method   Method often used in a process cost system for determining equivalent units; ignores the state of completion of items in beginning inventory and assumes that items in beginning inventory are complete. *p. 503*

work ticket   Mechanism (paper or electronic) used to accumulate the time spent on a job by each employee; sent to the accounting department where wage rates are recorded and labor costs are determined. The amount of labor costs for each ticket is summarized on the appropriate job-order cost sheet; sometimes called a *time card*. *p. 493*

working capital   Current assets minus current liabilities. *p. 414, 539*

working capital ratio   Another term for the current ratio; calculated by dividing current assets by current liabilities. *p. 539*

Work in Process Inventory   Asset account used to accumulate all product costs (direct materials, direct labor, and overhead) associated with incomplete products in production. *p. 446*

Photo Credits

Chapter 1

p. 3 AP Photo/Laura Rauch. **p. 5** Tony Freeman/PhotoEdit.
p. 18 Associate Press. **p. 21** Charles Gupton/Stock Boston.
p. 23 Courtesy of Ford Motor Company.

Chapter 2

p. 51 AP Photo/Barry Sweet. **p. 53** Photo Disc.
p. 63 Richard Levine. **p. 67** Susan Van Etten/PhotoEdit.

Chapter 3

p. 99 SuperStock. **p. 104** Courtesy of AT&T
p. 105 Photo Disc. **p. 116** GE Information Services, Inc.

Chapter 4

p. 139 Courtesy APL. **p. 141** Barbara Alper/Stock Boston.
p. 143 Tim Wright/CORBIS. **p. 149** No Credit Required.

Chapter 5

p. 189 Charles Gupton/Stock Boston. **p. 190** Cele Seldon.
p. 194 Courtesy Southwest Airlines. **p. 200** Edward Miller/
Stock Boston.

Chapter 6

p. 233 Bob Daemmrich/Stock Boston. **p. 234** Spencer Grant/
Photo Edit. **p. 238** Benjamin F. Fink Jr./Getty Images.
p. 249 Jon Riley/Tony Stone Images.

Chapter 7

p. 279 AP Photo/Mark J. Terrill, File. **p. 281** Spencer Grant/
Photo Edit. **p. 286** GoldEyewire/Getty Images. **p. 291** CORBIS.

Chapter 8

p. 319 Eyewire/Getty Images. **p. 322** Richard Pasley/
Stock Boston. **p. 333** Rob Crandall/Stock Boston.
p. 338 Bob Daemmrich/Stock Boston.

Chapter 9

p. 367 Tony Freeman/Photo Edit. **p. 370** AP Photo/Kalamazoo Gazette,
Wayne Anderson. **p. 378** Charles Gupton/Stock Boston.
p. 379 Myrleen Ferguson/PhotoEdit.

Chapter 10

p. 405 Liaison/Getty Images. **p. 407** Photo Disc.
p. 413 Robert Brenner/PhotoEdit. **p. 418** McLaughlin/The Image Works.

Chapter 11

p. 445 Charles Gupton/Stock Boston.
p. 447 Michael Newman/PhotoEdit. **p. 450** Griffin/The Image Works.

Chapter 12

p. 489 Charels and O and apos; Rear/CORBIS. **p. 490** Bill Aaron/PhotoEdit.
p. 493 Spencer Grant/PhotoEdit.
p. 510 David Young Wolff/PhotoEdit.

Chapter 13

p. 535 Bonnie Kamin/PhotoEdit. **p. 536** CORBIS.
p. 552 David Young Wolff/PhotoEdit.

Chapter 14

p. 579 AP Photo/Lisa Poole. **p. 590** Bonnie Kamin/PhotoEdit.
p. 593 Peter Menzel/Stock Boston.

Index

C

Capacity to control, 328
Capital budget, 283, 294, 295
Capital budgeting, 280, 294, 295
Capital investments, 405–424
    defined, 406
    internal rate of return and, 412–413, 416–418, 424
    net present value and, 412, 415–416, 424
    payback method and, 420–421, 424
    postaudits and, 423
    techniques for comparing, 414–415
    time value of money and, 406–411, 424
        relevance and, 418–422
    unadjusted rate of return and, 421–422, 424
Capital maintenance expenditures, 598
Cash-basis accounting, 581–586, 599
Cash budget, 283, 289–292, 294, 295
Cash inflows, 28, 406, 413–414, 423, 424, 579
    conversion of, into present values, 407–411
    unequal, 421
Cash outflows, 28, 406, 409, 414, 423, 579
Cash payments, 287–291, 589–594
Cash receipts, 285, 290, 589, 591–593
Certified suppliers, 150
Characteristics of items being considered, 328
Companywide allocation rate, 234, 249
Compounding, 411
Conservatism, 553
Constraints, 159
    relaxing, 160
Context-sensitive relevance, 144–145
Continuous (perpetual) budgeting, 281
Continuous improvement, 21
Contribution margin, 57, 68, 100, 115
    CVP variables and, 110–111
    fixed costs and, 106–107, 116
    measurement of operating leverage using, 58
    sales price and, 103–104, 116
    target profit and, 102–103, 116
    variable costs and, 104–106, 116
Contribution margin per unit, 100, 101, 115, 116
Contribution margin ratio, 112, 117
Controllability concept, 369
Coordination, 281, 294
Corporate-level facility costs, 143
Corrective action, 282, 294
Cost(s):
    allocation of, to solve timing problems, 201–202
    applied fixed, 335
    appraisal, 247

Cost(s)—(cont.)
    average; see Cost averaging
    avoidable; see Relevant costs
    batch-level, 142, 146, 155
    classification of, 8–9, 13–16
    defined, 189
    differential, 141, 155–156
    direct, 191–192, 207–208
    downstream, 19, 26, 246, 250
    external failure, 247
    facility-level, 143, 146, 155
        relevance of allocated, 245
    failure, 247
    fixed; see Fixed costs
    general, selling, and administrative, 12, 26, 336
    historical, 375, 553
    indirect, 12, 156, 191–192, 207–208
        allocation of, to objects, 193–194
    internal failure, 247
    joint, 203, 208
        allocation of, 203–204
    labor, 10–11
    material, 10
    mixed (semivariable), 64, 68
    opportunity, 25, 144, 146–148, 153–155
    overhead; see Overhead costs
    period, 12
    prevention, 247
    product, 6, 26
        in manufacturing companies, 7–13, 26
        in service companies, 19–20, 26
    product-level, 142–143, 146, 155
    relevant; see Relevant costs
    replacement, 375
    segment-level facility, 143
    standard, 320, 327, 328
    start-up (setup), 236
    sunk, 140–141, 144, 151, 155, 204, 415
    total, 52, 60–61, 101
    transferred-in, 491
    unit-level, 142, 146, 155
    upstream, 19, 26, 246, 250
    variable; see Variable cost
    voluntary, 247
Cost accumulation, 190
Cost allocation, 13, 26, 151, 156, 191, 193, 208
    approaches to: direct method, 210–211
        reciprocal method, 213–214
        step method, 211–213
    comparison of, with activity-based costing, 238
    human factor in, 205–207
    use of, in budgeting decision, 205–206

EXERCISE 12–11A *Process Cost System*   L.O. 3

Sensation, Inc., is a cosmetics manufacturer. Its assembly department receives raw cosmetics from the molding department. The assembly department places the raw cosmetics into decorative containers and transfers them to the packaging department. The assembly department's Work in Process Inventory account had a $118,000 balance as of August 1. During August, the department incurred raw materials, labor, and overhead costs amounting to $144,000, $170,000, and $160,000, respectively. The department transferred products that cost $684,000 to the packaging department. The balance in the assembly department's Work in Process Inventory account as of August 31 was $82,000.

Required
Determine the cost of raw cosmetics transferred from the molding department to the assembly department during August.

EXERCISE 12–12A *Selecting the Appropriate Cost System*   L.O. 5

Alberto's Car Wash (ACW) offers customers three cleaning options. Under Option 1, only the exterior is cleaned. With Option 2, the exterior and interior are cleaned. Option 3 provides exterior waxing as well as exterior and interior cleaning. ACW completed 3,400 Option 1 cleanings, 4,800 Option 2 cleanings, and 2,100 Option 3 cleanings during 2001. The average cost of completing each cleaning option and the price charged for it are shown here.

	Option 1	Option 2	Option 3
Price charged	$7	$11	$18
Costs of completing task	3	4	13

Required
a. Is ACW a manufacturing or a service company? Explain.
b. Which cost system, job-order or process, is most appropriate for ACW? Why?
c. What is the balance in ACW's Work in Process and Finished Goods Inventory accounts on the December 31 balance sheet?
d. Speculate as to the major costs that ACW incurs to complete a cleaning job.

PROBLEMS—SERIES A

PROBLEM 12–13A *Job-Order Cost System*   L.O. 2, 7

Patinkin Manufacturing Corporation was started with the issuance of common stock for $10,000. It purchased $7,000 of raw materials and worked on three job orders during 2001 for which data follow. (Assume that all transactions are for cash unless otherwise indicated.)

	Direct Raw Materials Used	Direct Labor
Job 1	$1,000	$2,000
Job 2	2,000	4,000
Job 3	3,000	2,000
Total	$6,000	$8,000

Factory overhead is applied using a predetermined overhead rate of $0.50 per direct labor dollar. Jobs 2 and 3 were completed during the period and Job 3 was sold for $9,000. Patinkin paid $400 for selling and administrative expenses. Actual factory overhead was $3,500.

Required
a. Record the preceding events in a horizontal statements model. In the Cash Flow column, designate the cash flows as operating activities (OA), investing activities (IA), or financing activities (FA). The first event for 2001 has been recorded as an example.

Assets					=	Equity			Rev.	−	Exp.	=	Net Inc.	Cash Flow
Cash	+ Raw M.	+ MOH	+ WIP	+ F. Goods	= C. Stk.	+ Ret. Ear.			Rev.	−	Exp.	=	Net Inc.	Cash Flow
10,000 +	NA	+ NA	+ NA	+ NA	= 10,000	+ NA			NA	−	NA	=	NA	10,000 FA

b. Reconcile all subsidiary accounts with their respective control accounts.

c. Record the closing entry for over- or underapplied manufacturing overhead, assuming that the amount is insignificant. Close revenue and expense accounts.

d. Prepare a schedule of cost of goods manufactured and sold, an income statement, a balance sheet, and a statement of cash flows for 2001.

L.O. 2, 7   PROBLEM 12–14A Job-Order Cost System

Wald Construction Company began operations on January 1, 2001, when it acquired $8,000 cash from the issuance of common stock. During the year, Wald purchased $5,200 of direct raw materials and used $4,800 of the direct materials. There were 108 hours of direct labor worked at an average rate of $8 per hour paid in cash. The predetermined overhead rate was $5 per direct labor hour. The company started construction on three prefabricated buildings. The job cost sheets reflected the following allocations of costs to each building.

	Direct Materials	Direct Labor Hours
Job 1	$1,200	30
Job 2	2,000	50
Job 3	1,600	28

The company paid $160 cash for indirect labor costs. Actual overhead cost paid in cash other than indirect labor was $420. Wald completed Jobs 1 and 2 and sold Job 1 for $2,100 cash. The company incurred $200 of selling and administrative expenses that were paid in cash. Over- or underapplied overhead is closed to Cost of Goods Sold.

Required

a. Record the preceding events in a horizontal statements model. In the Cash Flow column, designate the cash flows as operating activities (OA), investing activities (IA), or financing activities (FA). The first event for 2001 has been recorded as an example.

Assets					=	Equity			Rev.	−	Exp.	=	Net Inc.	Cash Flow
Cash	+ Raw M.	+ MOH	+ WIP	+ F. Goods	= C. Stk.	+ Ret. Ear.			Rev.	−	Exp.	=	Net Inc.	Cash Flow
8,000 +	NA	+ NA	+ NA	+ NA	= 8,000	+ NA			NA	−	NA	=	NA	8,000 FA

b. Reconcile all subsidiary accounts with their respective control accounts.

c. Record the closing entry for over- or underapplied manufacturing overhead, assuming that the amount is insignificant. Close revenue and expense accounts.

d. Prepare a schedule of cost of goods manufactured and sold, an income statement, a balance sheet, and a statement of cash flows for 2001.

L.O. 3, 8   PROBLEM 12–15A Process Cost System

Carpenters, Inc., makes rocking chairs. The chairs move through two departments during production. Lumber is cut into chair parts in the cutting department, which transfers the parts to the assembly department for completion. The company sells the unfinished chairs to hobby shops. The following transactions apply to Carpenters' operations for its first year, 2001. (Assume that all transactions are for cash unless otherwise stated.)

1. The company was started when it acquired a $100,000 cash contribution from the owners.

2. The company purchased $30,000 of direct raw materials and $800 of indirect materials. Indirect materials are capitalized in the Production Supplies account.

3. Direct materials totaling $12,000 were issued to the cutting department.

4. Labor cost was $56,400. Direct labor for the cutting and assembly departments was $20,000 and $26,000, respectively. Indirect labor costs were $10,400.

5. The predetermined overhead rate was $0.50 per direct labor dollar.

6. Actual overhead costs other than indirect materials and indirect labor were $12,800 for the year.
7. The cutting department transferred $24,000 of inventory to the assembly department.
8. The assembly department transferred $40,000 of inventory to finished goods.
9. The company sold inventory costing $36,000 for $60,000.
10. Selling and administrative expenses were $6,000.
11. A physical count revealed $200 of production supplies on hand at the end of 2001.
12. Assume that over- or underapplied overhead is insignificant.

Required
a. Record the data in T-accounts.
b. Record the closing entry for over- or underapplied manufacturing overhead, assuming that the amount is insignificant.
c. Close the revenue and expense accounts.
d. Prepare a schedule of cost of goods manufactured and sold, an income statement, a balance sheet, and a statement of cash flows for 2001.

PROBLEM 12–16A *Process Cost System*

L.O. 3, 4, 8

Use the ending balances from Problem 12–15A as the beginning balances for this problem. The transactions for the second year of operation (2002) are described here. (Assume that all transactions are cash transactions unless otherwise indicated.)
1. The company purchased $40,000 of direct raw materials and $1,300 of indirect materials.
2. Materials totaling $13,400 were issued to the cutting department.
3. Labor cost was $47,000. Direct labor for the cutting and assembly departments was $22,000 and $20,000, respectively. Indirect labor costs were $5,000. (*Note:* Assume that sufficient cash is available when periodic payments are made. These amounts represent summary data for the entire year and are not presented in exact order of collection and payment.)
4. The predetermined overhead rate was $0.50 per direct labor dollar.
5. Actual overhead costs other than indirect materials and indirect labor for the month were $14,600.
6. The cutting department transferred $30,000 of inventory to the assembly department.
7. The assembly department transferred $60,000 of inventory to finished goods.
8. The company sold inventory costing $34,000 for $64,000.
9. Selling and administrative expenses were $8,400.
10. At the end of 2002, $300 of production supplies was on hand.
11. Assume that over- or underapplied overhead is insignificant.

Required
a. Record the data in T-accounts.
b. Record the closing entry for over- or underapplied manufacturing overhead, assuming that the amount is insignificant.
c. Close the revenue and expense accounts.
d. Prepare a schedule of cost of goods manufactured and sold, an income statement, a balance sheet, and a statement of cash flows for 2002.

PROBLEM 12–17A *Process Cost System Cost of Production Report*

L.O. 3

Rowan Company had 250 units of product in its work in process inventory at the beginning of the period and started 2,000 additional units during the period. At the end of the period, 750 units were in work in process inventory. The ending work in process inventory was estimated to be 60 percent complete. The cost of work in process inventory at the beginning of the period was $4,560, and $36,000 of product costs was added during the period.

Required
Prepare a cost of production report showing the following.
a. The number of equivalent units of production.
b. The product cost per equivalent unit.
c. The total cost allocated between the ending Work in Process Inventory and Finished Goods Inventory accounts.

PROBLEM 12–18A *Determining Inventory Cost Using a Process Cost System*

L.O. 3

Borg Company had 200 units of product in work in process inventory at the beginning of the period. It started 1,400 units during the period and transferred 1,200 units to finished goods inventory. The ending work in process inventory was estimated to be 80 percent complete. Cost data for the period follow.

Product Costs	
Beginning balance	$ 7,900
Added during period	14,520
	$22,420

Required

Prepare a cost of production report showing the following.

a. The number of equivalent units of production.

b. The product cost per equivalent unit.

c. The total cost allocated between ending work in process inventory and finished goods inventory.

L.O. 3   **PROBLEM 12–19A** *Process Cost System*

Ryan Plastic Products, Inc., makes a plastic toy using two departments, parts and assembly. The following data pertain to the parts department's transactions in 2003.

1. The beginning balance in the Work in Process Inventory account was $5,700. This inventory consisted of parts for 1,000 toys. The beginning balances in the Raw Materials Inventory, Production Supplies, and Cash accounts were $64,000, $1,000, and $200,000, respectively.

2. Direct materials costing $52,000 were issued to the parts department. The materials were sufficient to make 5,000 additional toys.

3. Direct labor cost was $47,000, and indirect labor costs are $4,600. All labor costs were paid in cash.

4. The predetermined overhead rate was $0.30 per direct labor dollar.

5. Actual overhead costs other than indirect materials and indirect labor for the year were $9,500, which was paid in cash.

6. The department completed parts work for 4,500 toys. The remaining toy parts were 60 percent complete. The completed parts were transferred to the assembly department.

7. All of the production supplies had been used by the end of 2003.

8. Over- or underapplied overhead was closed to the Cost of Goods Sold account.

Required

a. Determine the number of equivalent units of production.

b. Determine the product cost per equivalent unit.

c. Allocate the total cost between the ending work in process inventory and parts transferred to the assembly department.

d. Record the transactions in a partial set of T-accounts.

L.O. 3   **PROBLEM 12–20A** *Process Cost System*

Pepper Cola Corporation produces a new soft drink brand, Spicy Icy, using two production departments, mixing and bottling. Pepper's beginning balances and data pertinent to the mixing department's activities for 2002 follow.

Accounts	Beginning Balances
Cash	$ 39,000
Raw Materials Inventory	18,500
Production Supplies	500
Work in Process Inventory (400,000 units)	50,000
Common Stock	108,000

1. Pepper Cola issued additional common stock for $50,000 cash.

2. The company purchased raw materials and production supplies for $37,000 and $1,000, respectively, in cash.

3. The company issued $50,000 of raw materials to the mixing department for the production of 500,000 units of Spicy Icy that were started in 2002. A unit of soft drink is the amount needed to fill a bottle.

4. The mixing department used 2,700 hours of labor during 2002, consisting of 2,500 hours for direct labor and 200 hours for indirect labor. The average wage was $12 per hour. All wages were paid in 2002 in cash.

5. The predetermined overhead rate was $2 per direct labor hour.

6. Actual overhead costs other than indirect materials and indirect labor for the year amounted to $1,800, which was paid in cash.
7. The mixing department completed 600,000 units of Spicy Icy. The remaining inventory was 50 percent complete.
8. The completed soft drink was transferred to the bottling department.
9. The ending balance in the Production Supplies account was $700.

Required
a. Determine the number of equivalent units of production.
b. Determine the product cost per equivalent unit.
c. Allocate the total cost between the ending work in process inventory and units transferred to the bottling department.
d. Record the transactions in T-accounts.

PROBLEM 12–21A *Process Cost System*   L.O. 3, 8

Zapp Corporation makes a health beverage named Zapp that is manufactured in a two-stage production prcoess. The drink is first created in the Conversion Department where material ingredients (natural juices, supplements, preservatives, etc.) are combined. On July 1, 2005 the company had a sufficient quantity of partially completed beverage mix in the Conversion Department to make 50,000 containers of Zapp. This beginning inventory had a cost of $30,000. During July, the company added ingredients necessary to make 200,000 containers of Zapp. The cost of these ingredients was $154,000. During July, liquid mix representing 225,000 containers of the beverage was transferred to the Finishing Department. The beverage mix is poured into containers and packaged for shipment in the Finishing Department. Beverage that remained in the Conversion Department at the end of July was 20 percent complete. At the beginning of July the Finishing Department had 20,000 containers of beverage mix. The cost of this mix was $24,000. The department added $44,050 of manufacturing costs (materials, labor and overhead) during July. During July 219,000 containers of Zapp were completed. The ending inventory for this department was 25 percent complete at the end of July.

Required
a. Prepare a Cost of Production Report for the Conversion Department for July.
b. Prepare a Cost of Production Report for the Finishing Department for July.
c. If 218,000 containers of Zapp are sold in July for $327,000, determine the company's gross margin for July.

EXERCISES—SERIES B

EXERCISE 12–1B *Matching Products with Appropriate Cost Systems*   L.O. 1

Required
Indicate which cost system (job-order, process, or hybrid) would be most appropriate for the type of product listed in the left-hand column. The first item is shown as an example.

Type of Product	Type of Cost System
a. House	Job-Order
b. Oil	
c. Luxury yacht	
d. Special-order personal computer	
e. Over-the-counter personal computer	
f. Mouse pad for a computer	
g. Aircraft carrier	
h. Makeup sponge	
i. Handheld video game player	
j. Generic coffee mug	
k. Personalized coffee mug	
l. Surgery	
m. Audit engagement	
n. Shoes	
o. Treadmill	
p. Textbook	

L.O. 1   **EXERCISE 12–2B** *Identifying the Appropriate Cost System*

Sorenson Corporation's Riverside Plant in Twin City, Minnesota, produces the company's weed-control chemical solution, Weed Vanish. Production begins with pure water from a controlled stream to which the plant adds different chemicals in the production process. Finally, the plant bottles the resulting chemical solution. The process is highly automated with different computer-controlled maneuvers and testing to ensure the quality of the end product. With only 20 employees, the plant can produce up to 6,400 bottles per day.

Required

Recommend the type of cost system (job-order, process, or hybrid) Riverside Plant should use. Explain your recommendation.

L.O. 1, 2   **EXERCISE 12–3B** *Job-Order or Process Costing*

Vivian Barker, an artist, plans to make her living drawing customer portraits at a stand in Underground Atlanta. She will carry her drawing equipment and supplies to work each day in bags. By displaying two of her best hand-drawn portraits on either side of her stand, she expects to attract tourists' attention. Ms. Barker can usually draw a customer's portrait in 30 minutes. Her materials cost is minimal, about $2 for a portrait. Her most significant cost will be leasing the stand for $1,200 per month. She estimates she can replace supplies and worn out equipment for $50 per month. She plans to work 20 days each month from noon to 9:00 P.M. After surveying her planned work environment before beginning the business, she observed that six other artists were providing customer portraits in that section of Underground Atlanta. Their portrait prices ranged from $25 to $45 per portrait. They also offered to frame portraits for customers at $15 per frame. Ms. Barker found that she could obtain comparable frames for $5 each and that properly framing a portrait takes about 10 minutes. The biggest challenge, Ms. Barker observed, was attracting tourists' interest. If she could draw portraits continuously during her workdays, she could earn quite a respectable income. But she noticed several of the artists were reading magazines as she walked by.

Required

a. Should Ms. Barker use a job-order or process cost system for her art business?
b. List the individual types of costs Ms. Barker will likely incur in providing portraits.
c. How could Ms. Barker estimate her overhead rate per portrait when she does not know the number of portraits she will draw in a month?
d. Ms. Barker will not hire any employees. Will she have labor cost? Explain.

L.O. 2, 7   **EXERCISE 12–4B** *Job-Order Costing in a Manufacturing Company*

Ingle Drapery, Inc., specializes in making custom draperies for both commercial and residential customers. It began business on August 1, 2001, by acquiring $40,000 cash through issuing common stock. In August 2001, Ingle accepted drapery orders, Jobs 801 and 802, for two new commercial buildings. The company paid cash for the following costs related to the orders:

Job 801	
Raw materials	$ 9,200
Direct labor (512 hours at $25 per hour)	12,800
Job 802	
Raw materials	6,500
Direct labor (340 hours at $25 per hour)	8,500

During the same month, Ingle paid $18,000 for various indirect costs such as utilities, equipment leases, and factory-related insurance. The company estimated its annual manufacturing overhead cost would be $300,000 and expected to use 20,000 direct labor hours in its first year of operation. It planned to allocate overhead based on direct labor hours. On August 31, 2001, Ingle completed Job 801 and collected the contract price of $35,000. Job 802 was still in process.

Ingle uses a just-in-time inventory management system. Consequently, it has no raw materials inventory. Raw materials purchases are recorded directly in the Work in Process Inventory account.

Required

a. Use a horizontal financial statements model as follows to record Ingle's accounting events for August 2001. The first event is shown as an example.

Assets					=	Equity							
Cash	+	Work in Process	+	Finished Goods	+	Manuf. Overhead	=	Com. Stock	+	Ret. Ear.	Rev. − Exp. = Net Inc.		Cash Flow
40,000	+	NA	+	NA	+	NA	=	40,000	+	NA	NA − NA = NA		40,000 FA

b. What was Ingle's ending inventory on August 31, 2001? Is this amount the actual or the estimated inventory cost?

c. When is it appropriate to use estimated inventory cost on a year-end balance sheet?

EXERCISE 12–5B *Job-Order Costing in a Manufacturing Company*   **L.O. 2, 7**

Lagoon Advertisements, Inc., designs and produces television commercials for clients. On March 1, 2002, the company issued common stock for $57,000 cash. During March, Lagoon worked on three jobs. Pertinent data follow.

Special Orders	Materials	Labor
Job 301	$4,500	450 hours @ $40 per hour
Job 302	8,100	360 hours @ $75 per hour
Job 303	7,300	680 hours @ $35 per hour

Actual production overhead cost: $30,100
Predetermined overhead rate: $20 per direct labor hour

Lagoon paid these costs in cash. Jobs 301 and 302 were completed and sold for cash to customers during March. Job 303 was incomplete at month end. Job 301 sold for $38,000, and Job 302 sold for $54,000. Lagoon also paid $10,000 cash in March for selling and administrative expenses.

Lagoon uses a just-in-time inventory management system. Consequently, it has no raw materials inventory. Raw materials purchases are recorded directly in the Work in Process Inventory account.

Required

a. Use a horizontal financial statements model, as follows, to record Lagoon's accounting events for March 2002. The first event is shown as an example.

Assets					=	Equity							
Cash	+	Work in Process	+	Finished Goods	+	Manuf. Overhead	=	Com. Stock	+	Ret. Ear.	Rev. − Exp. = Net Inc.		Cash Flow
57,000	+	NA	+	NA	+	NA	=	57,000	+	NA	NA − NA = NA		57,000 FA

b. Record the entry to close the amount of underapplied or overapplied manufacturing overhead to Cost of Goods Sold (in the expense category) in the horizontal financial statements model.

c. Determine the gross margin for March.

EXERCISE 12–6B *Job-Order Costing in a Service Company*   **L.O. 2, 7**

Tang Consulting, Inc., provides financial and estate planning services on a retainer basis for the executive officers of its corporate clients. It incurred the following labor costs on services for three corporate clients during March 2003:

	Direct Labor
Contract 1	$15,000
Contract 2	9,000
Contract 3	36,000
Total	$60,000

Tang allocated March overhead costs of $27,000 to the contracts based on the amount of direct labor costs incurred on each contract.

Required

a. Assuming the revenue from Contract 3 was $82,000, what amount of income did Tang earn from this contract?

b. Based on the preceding information, will Tang report finished goods inventory on its balance sheet for Contract 1? If so, what is the amount of this inventory? If not, explain why not.

L.O. 2　**EXERCISE 12–7B** *Determine Missing Information for a Job Order*

The following information pertains to Job 593 that Decatur Manufacturing Company completed during January 2001. Materials and labor costs for the job were $31,000 and $19,000, respectively. Applied overhead costs were $22,000. Decatur completed and delivered the job to its customer and earned a $25,000 gross profit.

Required

Determine the contract price for the job.

L.O. 3　**EXERCISE 12–8B** *Process Costing: Determining Equivalent Units*

In March 2002, Lengthy Corporation's battery plant had 2,000 units in its beginning work in process inventory. During March, the company added 24,000 units to production. At the end of the month, 8,000 units of product were in process.

Required

(Each requirement is independent of the other.)

a. Assuming the ending inventory units were 40 percent complete, determine the total number of equivalent units (number transferred out plus number in ending inventory) processed by the battery plant.

b. Assuming the total number of equivalent units (number transferred out plus number in ending inventory) processed by the battery plant was 20,000, what was the ending inventory percentage of completion?

L.O. 3　**EXERCISE 12–9B** *Allocating Costs in a Process Costing System*

Acton Corporation, a manufacturer of diabetic testing kits, started November production with $75,000 in beginning inventory. During the month, the company incurred $420,000 of materials cost and $240,000 of labor cost. It applied $165,000 of overhead cost to inventory. The company processed 18,000 total equivalent units of product.

Required

(Each requirement is independent of the other.)

a. Assuming 3,000 equivalent units of product were in ending work in process inventory, determine the amount of cost transferred from the Work in Process Inventory account to the Finished Goods Inventory account. What was the cost of the ending work in process inventory?

b. Assuming 14,000 equivalent units of product were transferred from work in process inventory to finished goods inventory, determine the cost of the ending work in process inventory. What was the cost of the finished goods inventory transferred from work in process?

L.O. 3　**EXERCISE 12–10B** *Process Costing: Determining Equivalent Units and Allocating Costs*

Hastert Corporation, which makes suitcases, completed 42,000 suitcases in August 2001. At the end of August, work in process inventory consisted of 6,000 suitcases estimated to be 40 percent complete. Total product costs for August amounted to $1,554,000.

Required

a. Determine the cost per equivalent unit.

b. Determine the cost of the goods transferred to finished goods.

c. Determine the cost of the ending work in process inventory.

L.O. 3　**EXERCISE 12–11B** *Process Costing: Supply Missing Information*

Salvation Publications, Inc., produces Bibles in volume. It printed and sold 120,000 Bibles last year. Demand is sufficient to support producing a particular edition continuously throughout the year. For this operation, Salvation uses two departments, printing and binding. The printing department prints all pages and transfers them to the binding department, where it binds the pages into books. The binding department's Work in Process Inventory account had a $30,000 balance on September 1. During September, the binding department incurred raw materials, labor, and overhead costs of $11,000, $38,000, and $71,000, respectively. During the month, the binding department transferred Bibles that cost $360,000 to finished goods. The balance in the binding department's Work in Process Inventory account as of September 30 was $53,000.

Required

Determine the cost of pages transferred from the printing department to the binding department during the month of September.

EXERCISE 12–12B *Selecting the Appropriate Costing System*

L.O. 5

Eagan Automotive Specialties, Inc., has a successful market niche. It customizes automobile interiors to fit the various needs of disabled customers. Some customers need special equipment to accommodate disabled drivers. Others need modified entrance and seating arrangements for disabled passengers. Customer vehicles vary according to different brands and models of sedans, minivans, sport utility vehicles, and full-size vans. Eagan's engineers interview customers directly to ascertain their special needs. The engineers then propose a design, explaining it and its cost for the customer's approval. Customers have the opportunity to request changes. Once the company and customer agree on an engineering design and its price, they sign a contract, and the customer's vehicle is delivered to Eagan's factory. The factory manager directs mechanics to customize the vehicle according to the engineering design.

Required

a. Is Eagan a manufacturing company or a service company? Explain.
b. Which cost system, job-order or process, would be most appropriate for Eagan? Why?
c. Does Eagan have work in process and finished goods inventories?
d. Should Eagan classify engineering design costs as materials, labor, or overhead? Why?

PROBLEMS—SERIES B

PROBLEM 12–13B *Job-Order Cost System*

L.O. 2, 7

Navajo Corporation was created on January 1, 2003, when it received a stockholder's contribution of $40,000. It purchased $7,900 of raw materials and worked on three job orders during the year. Data about these jobs follow. (Assume all transactions are for cash unless otherwise indicated.)

	Direct Raw Materials Used	Direct Labor
Job 1	$2,100	$ 3,200
Job 2	1,700	4,800
Job 3	3,200	4,480
Total	$7,000	$12,480

The average wage rate is $16 per hour. Manufacturing overhead is applied using a predetermined overhead rate of $7.50 per direct labor hour. Jobs 1 and 3 were completed during the year, and Job 1 was sold for $9,800. Navajo paid $1,400 for selling and administrative expenses. Actual factory overhead was $6,000.

Required

a. Record the preceding events in a horizontal statements model. In the Cash Flow column, designate the cash flows as operating activities (OA), investing activities (IA), or financing activities (FA). The first event for 2003 has been recorded as an example.

Assets					=	Equity					
Cash	+ Raw M.	+ MOH	+ WIP	+ F. Goods	=	C. Stk.	+ Ret. Ear.	Rev. − Exp. = Net Inc.	Cash Flow
4,000 +	NA	+ NA	+ NA	+ NA	=	4,000	+ NA	NA − NA = NA	4,000 FA

b. Reconcile all subsidiary accounts with their respective control accounts.
c. Record the closing entry for over- or underapplied manufacturing overhead, assuming that the amount is insignificant. Close revenue and expense accounts.
d. Prepare a schedule of cost of goods manufactured and sold, an income statement, a balance sheet, and a statement of cash flows for 2003.

PROBLEM 12–14B *Job-Order Cost System*

L.O. 2, 7

Gerald Roofing Corporation was founded on January 1, 2002, when stockholders contributed $3,500 for common stock. During the year, Gerald purchased $3,000 of direct raw materials and used $2,700 of

direct materials. There were 80 hours of direct labor worked at an average rate of $10 per hour paid in cash. The predetermined overhead rate was $8 per direct labor hour. The company started three custom roofing jobs. The job cost sheets reflected the following allocations of costs to each.

	Direct Materials	Direct Labor Hours
Roof 1	$1,000	20
Roof 2	500	12
Roof 3	1,200	48

The company paid $220 cash for indirect labor costs and $300 cash for production supplies, which were all used during 2002. Actual overhead cost paid in cash other than indirect materials and indirect labor was $180. Gerald completed Roofs 1 and 2 and collected the contract price for Roof 1 of $2,700 cash. The company incurred $620 of selling and administrative expenses that were paid with cash. Over- or underapplied overhead is closed to Cost of Goods Sold.

Required

a. Record the preceding events in a horizontal statements model. In the Cash Flow column, designate the cash flows as operating activities (OA), investing activities (IA), or financing activities (FA). The first event for 2002 has been recorded as an example.

Assets					=	Equity						Cash Flow
Cash +	Raw M. +	MOH +	WIP +	F. Goods	=	C. Stk. +	Ret. Ear.		Rev. −	Exp. =	Net Inc.	
3,500 +	NA +	NA +	NA +	NA	=	3,500 +	NA		NA −	NA =	NA	3,500 FA

b. Reconcile all subsidiary accounts with their respective control accounts.

c. Record the closing entry for over- or underapplied manufacturing overhead, assuming that the amount is insignificant. Close revenue and expense accounts.

d. Prepare a schedule of cost of goods manufactured and sold, an income statement, a balance sheet, and a statement of cash flows for 2002.

L.O. 3, 8   PROBLEM 12–15B *Process Cost System*

Gonzales Food Company makes frozen vegetables. Production involves two departments, processing and packaging. Raw materials are cleaned and cut in the processing department and then transferred to the packaging department where they are packaged and frozen. The following transactions apply to Gonzales' first year (2001) of operations. (Assume that all transactions are for cash unless otherwise stated.)

1. The company was started when it acquired $80,000 cash from the issue of common stock.
2. Gonzales purchased $42,000 of direct raw materials and $7,500 of indirect materials. Indirect materials are capitalized in the Production Supplies account.
3. Direct materials totaling $38,000 were issued to the processing department.
4. Labor cost was $77,000. Direct labor for the processing and packaging departments was $32,500 and $25,500, respectively. Indirect labor costs were $19,000.
5. The predetermined overhead rate was $0.80 per direct labor dollar.
6. Actual overhead costs other than indirect materials and indirect labor were $22,500 for the year.
7. The processing department transferred $60,500 of inventory to the packaging department.
8. The packaging department transferred $70,000 of inventory to finished goods.
9. The company sold inventory costing $63,000 for $117,500.
10. Selling and administrative expenses were $23,500.
11. A physical count revealed $3,000 of production supplies on hand at the end of 2001.
12. Assume that over- or underapplied overhead is insignificant.

Required

a. Record the data in T-accounts.

b. Record the closing entry for over- or underapplied manufacturing overhead, assuming that the amount is insignificant.

c. Close the revenue and expense accounts.

d. Prepare a schedule of cost of goods manufactured and sold, an income statement, a balance sheet, and a statement of cash flows for 2001.

PROBLEM 12–16B *Process Cost System*

L.O. 3, 4, 8

Use the ending balances from Problem 12–15B as the beginning balances for this problem. The transactions for the second year of operation (2002) are described here. (Assume that all transactions are cash transactions unless otherwise indicated.)

1. The company purchased $51,000 of direct raw materials and $9,000 of indirect materials.
2. Materials costing $41,000 were issued to the processing department.
3. Labor cost was $89,500. Direct labor for the processing and packaging departments was $36,000 and $29,500, respectively. Indirect labor costs were $24,000. (*Note:* Assume that sufficient cash is available when periodic payments are made. These amounts represent summary data for the entire year and are not presented in exact order of collection and payment.)
4. The predetermined overhead rate was $0.80 per direct labor dollar.
5. Actual overhead costs other than indirect materials and indirect labor for the year was $25,000.
6. The processing department transferred $125,000 of inventory to the packaging department.
7. The packaging department transferred $175,000 of inventory to finished goods.
8. The company sold inventory costing $171,000 for $325,000.
9. Selling and administrative expenses amounted to $32,000.
10. At the end of the year, $2,000 of production supplies was on hand.
11. Assume that over- or underapplied overhead is insignificant.

Required
a. Record the data in T-accounts.
b. Record the closing entry for over- or underapplied manufacturing overhead, assuming that the amount is insignificant.
c. Close the revenue and expense accounts.
d. Prepare a schedule of cost of goods manufactured and sold, an income statement, a balance sheet, and a statement of cash flows for 2002.

PROBLEM 12–17B *Process Cost System Cost of Production Report*

L.O. 3

At the beginning of 2000, Udall Company had 3,600 units of product in its work in process inventory, and it started 38,400 additional units of product during the year. At the end of the year, 12,000 units of product were in the work in process inventory. The ending work in process inventory was estimated to be 50 percent complete. The cost of work in process inventory at the beginning of the period was $9,000, and $108,000 of product costs was added during the period.

Required
Prepare a cost of production report showing the following.
a. The number of equivalent units of production.
b. The product cost per equivalent unit.
c. The total cost allocated between the ending Work in Process Inventory and Finished Goods Inventory accounts.

PROBLEM 12–18B *Determining Inventory Cost Using Process Costing*

L.O. 3

Caston Company's beginning work in process inventory consisted of 4,500 units of product on January 1, 2003. During 2003, the company started 24,000 units of product and transferred 23,500 units to finished goods inventory. The ending work in process inventory was estimated to be 30 percent complete. Cost data for 2003 follow.

	Product Costs
Beginning balance	$ 57,000
Added during period	453,000
	$510,000

Required
Prepare a cost of production report showing the following.
a. The number of equivalent units of production.
b. The product cost per equivalent unit.
c. The total cost allocated between ending work in process inventory and finished goods inventory.

L.O. 3, 8　**PROBLEM 12–19B** *Process Cost System*

Sosa Corporation makes blue jeans. Its process involves two departments, cutting and sewing. The following data pertain to the cutting department's transactions in 2006.

1. The beginning balance in work in process inventory was $17,544. This inventory consisted of fabric for 6,000 pairs of jeans. The beginning balances in raw materials inventory, production supplies, and cash were $90,000, $4,200 and $271,200, respectively.
2. Direct materials costing $56,136 were issued to the cutting department; this amount of materials was sufficient to start work on 15,000 pairs of jeans.
3. Direct labor cost was $67,200, and indirect labor cost was $5,400. All labor costs were paid in cash.
4. The predetermined overhead rate was $0.25 per direct labor dollar.
5. Actual overhead costs other than indirect materials and indirect labor for the year amounted to $7,680, which was paid in cash.
6. The cutting department completed cutting 16,000 pairs of jeans. The remaining jeans were 40 percent complete.
7. The completed units of cut fabric were transferred to the sewing department.
8. All of the production supplies had been used by the end of the year.
9. Over- or underapplied overhead was closed to the Cost of Goods Sold account.

Required
a. Determine the number of equivalent units of production.
b. Determine the product cost per equivalent unit.
c. Allocate the total cost between ending work in process inventory and units transferred to the sewing department.
d. Record the transactions in a partial set of T-accounts.

L.O. 3, 8　**PROBLEM 12–20B** *Process Cost System*

Felton Paper Products Corporation produces paper cups using two production departments, printing and forming. Beginning balances and printing department data for 2003 follow.

Accounts	Beginning Balances
Cash	$ 91,000
Raw Materials	41,000
Production Supplies	3,000
Work in Process Inventory (300,000 units)	36,000
Common Stock	171,000

1. Felton Paper Products issued additional common stock for $220,000 cash.
2. The company purchased raw materials and production supplies for $80,000 and $7,000, respectively, in cash.
3. The company issued $114,000 of raw materials and $7,200 of production supplies to the printing department for the production of 800,000 paper cups.
4. The printing department used 6,200 hours of labor during 2003, consisting of 5,600 hours for direct labor and 600 hours for indirect labor. The average wage was $10 per hour. All the wages were paid in 2003 in cash.
5. The predetermined overhead rate was $0.50 per direct labor dollar.
6. Actual overhead costs other than indirect materials and indirect labor for the year amounted to $14,800, which was paid in cash.
7. The printing department completed 700,000 paper cups. The remaining cups were 50 percent complete.
8. The completed paper cups were transferred to the forming department.
9. The ending balance in the Production Supplies account was $2,800.

Required
a. Determine the number of equivalent units of production.
b. Determine the product cost per equivalent unit.
c. Allocate the total cost between the ending work in process inventory and units transferred to the forming department.
d. Record the transactions in T-accounts.

PROBLEM 12-21B *Process Cost System* L.O. 3, 8

Novelty Gifts makes unique western gifts that are sold at souvenir shops. One of the company's more popular products is a ceramic Eagle that is produced in a mass production process that entails two manufacturing stages. In the first production stage ceramic glass is heated and molded into the shape of the Eagle by the Compression Department. Finally, color and artistic detail is applied to the Eagle by the Finishing Department. The company has just hired a new accountant who will be responsible for preparing the Cost of Production Report for June 2003. The accountant is given the following information from which to prepare his report.

Departmental Cost Information for June

	Compression	Finishing
Costs in beginning inventory	$ 3,000	$14,400
Costs added during June:		
Materials	$42,000	$18,120
Labor	$20,000	$13,200
Overhead	$90,000	$62,000

Departmental Product Information for June

	Compression	Finishing
Units in beginning inventory	5,000	1,800
Units started	26,000	23,000
Units in ending inventory	8,000 (25% complete)	4,800 (80% complete)

Required
a. Prepare a Cost of Production Report for the Conversion Department for June.
b. Prepare a Cost of Production Report for the Finishing Department for June.
c. If 12,000 units are sold in July for $160,000, determine the company's gross margin for June.

ANALYZE, THINK, COMMUNICATE

BUSINESS APPLICATIONS CASE *Supplying Missing Information* ATC 12-1

Brad Hoff, who was recently employed by Tennant Corporation, has discovered that the accounting records for the past month are incomplete. His search of the records and supporting documents revealed the following fragments of information.

	March 1	March 31
Raw materials inventory	$ 42,600	$ 39,000
Work in process inventory	52,200	56,700
Finished goods inventory	100,300	93,850
Raw materials purchased		(h) = ?
Raw materials available		(g) = ?
Raw materials used		(f) = ?
Labor (overhead is 150% of labor cost)		(e) = ?
Manufacturing overhead		225,000
Total manufacturing costs		(d) = ?
Total work in process		(c) = ?
Cost of goods manufactured		(b) = ?
Cost of goods available for sale		(a) = ?
Cost of goods sold		443,000

Required
a. Compute the missing amounts.
b. If a physical count of the ending raw materials inventory revealed that the balance shown in the table was understated by $1,000, how would this error have affected the income statement?

ATC 12–2   GROUP ASSIGNMENT *Job-Order Cost System*

Bowen Bridge Company constructs bridges for the State of Kentucky. During 2003, Bowen started work on three bridges. The cost of materials and labor for each bridge follows.

Special Orders	Materials	Labor
Bridge 305	$407,200	$352,700
Bridge 306	362,300	375,000
Bridge 307	801,700	922,800

The predetermined overhead rate is $1.20 per direct labor dollar. Actual overhead costs were $2,170,800. Bridge 306 was completed for a contract price of $1,357,000 and was turned over to the state. Construction on Bridge 305 was also completed but the state had not yet finished its inspection process. General selling and administrative expenses amounted to $210,000. Over- or underapplied overhead is closed directly to the Cost of Goods Sold account. The company recognizes revenue when it turns over a completed bridge to a customer.

Required
a. Divide the class into groups of four or five students each and organize the groups into three sections. Assign Task 1 to the first section of groups, Task 2 to the second section, and Task 3 to the third section.

Group Tasks

(1) Determine the cost of construction for Bridge 305.
(2) Determine the cost of construction for Bridge 306.
(3) Determine the cost of construction for Bridge 307.

b. Select a spokesperson from each section. Use input from the three spokespersons to prepare an income statement and the asset section of the balance sheet.
c. Does the net income accurately reflect the profitability associated with Bridge 306? Explain.
d. Would converting to a process cost system improve the accuracy of the amount of reported net income? Explain.

ATC 12–3   RESEARCH ASSIGNMENT *Job-Order or Process Cost System?*

The article "Lights! Cameras! . . . Accountants!" (*Management Accounting,* June 1996) describes the product cost system used by Buena Vista Visual Effects (BVVE), which produces special effects used in movies. Some of its credits include the lifelike dinosaurs in *Jurassic Park* and the rapid-fire ping-pong match in *Forrest Gump*. Read this article and complete the following requirements.

Required
a. Does BVVE use a job-order or a process cost system?
b. What type of costs does BVVE include in overhead? Name some of the specific costs included.
c. What predetermined overhead rate does BVVE use?
d. Does BVVE use estimated or actual costs in its product costing system?
e. How often does BVVE prepare variance cost reports? Provide a logical explanation as to why this time span is used.

ATC 12–4   WRITING ASSIGNMENT *Determining the Proper Cost System*

Professor Julia Silverman received the following E-mail message.

"I don't know if you remember me. I am Tim Wallace. I was in your introductory accounting class a couple of years ago. I recently graduated and have just started my first real job. I remember your talking about job-order and process cost systems. I even looked the subject up in the textbook you wrote. In that book, you say that a process cost system is used when a company produces a single, homogeneous, high-volume, low-cost product. Well, the company I am working for makes T-shirts. All of the shirts are the same. They don't cost much, and we make nearly a million of them every year. The only difference in any of the shirts is the label we sew in them. We make the shirts for about 20 different companies. It seems to me that we should be using a process costing system. Even so, our accounting people are using

a job-order cost system. Unfortunately, you didn't tell us what to do when the company we work for is screwed up. I need some advice. Should I tell them they are using the wrong accounting system? I know I am new around here, and I don't want to offend anybody, but if your book is right, the company would be better off if it started using a process cost system. Some of these people around here didn't go to college, and I'm afraid they don't know what they are doing. I guess that's why they hired someone with a degree. Am I right about this or what?"

Required

Assume that you are Professor Silverman. Write a return E-mail responding to Mr. Wallace's inquiry.

ETHICAL DILEMMA *Amount of Equivalent Units*   ATC 12–5

René Alverez knew she was in over her head soon after she took the job. Even so, the opportunity for promotion comes along rarely and she believed that she would grow into it. Ms. Alverez is the cost accounting specialist assigned to the finishing department of Standard Tool Company. Bill Sawyer, the manager of the finishing department, knows exactly what he is doing. In each of the three years he has managed the department, the cost per unit of product transferred out of his Work in Process Inventory account has declined. His ability to control cost is highly valued, and it is widely believed that he will be the successor to the plant manager, who is being promoted to manufacturing vice president. One more good year would surely seal the deal for Mr. Sawyer. It was little wonder that Ms. Alverez was uncomfortable in challenging Mr. Sawyer's estimate of the percentage of completion of the department's ending inventory. He contended that the inventory was 60 percent complete, but she believed that it was only about 40 percent complete.

After a brief altercation, Ms. Alverez agreed to sign off on Mr. Sawyer's estimate. The truth was that although she believed she was right, she did not know how to support her position. Besides, Mr. Sawyer was about to be named plant manager, and she felt it unwise to challenge such an important person.

The department had beginning inventory of 5,500 units of product and it started 94,500 units during the period. It transferred out 90,000 units during the period. Total transferred-in and production cost for the period was $902,400. This amount included the cost in beginning inventory plus additional costs incurred during the period. The target (standard) cost per unit is $9.45.

Required

a. Determine the equivalent cost per unit, assuming that the ending inventory is considered to be 40 percent complete.

b. Determine the equivalent cost per unit, assuming that the ending inventory is considered to be 60 percent complete.

c. Comment on Mr. Sawyer's motives for establishing the percentage of completion at 60 percent rather than 40 percent.

d. Assuming that Ms. Alverez is a certified management accountant, would informing the chief accountant of her dispute with Mr. Sawyer violate the confidentiality standards of ethical conduct in Exhibit 1–13 of Chapter 1?

e. Did Ms. Alverez violate any of the standards of ethical conduct in Exhibit 1–13 of Chapter 1? If so, which ones?

SPREADSHEET ASSIGNMENT *Using Excel*   ATC 12–6

Lewis Company had 8,000 units of product in work in process inventory at the beginning of the period and started 16,000 units during the period. At the end of the period, 4,000 units remained in work in process. The ending work in process inventory was estimated to be 40 percent complete. The cost of the units in beginning work in process inventory was $22,080. During the period, $38,400 of product costs were added.

Required

a. Construct a spreadsheet that incorporates the preceding data into a table. The following screen capture is an example.

b. Insert a section into the spreadsheet to calculate total manufacturing costs.

c. Insert a section into the spreadsheet to calculate equivalent units and cost per equivalent unit.

d. Insert a section into the spreadsheet to allocate the manufacturing costs between finished goods and ending work in process.

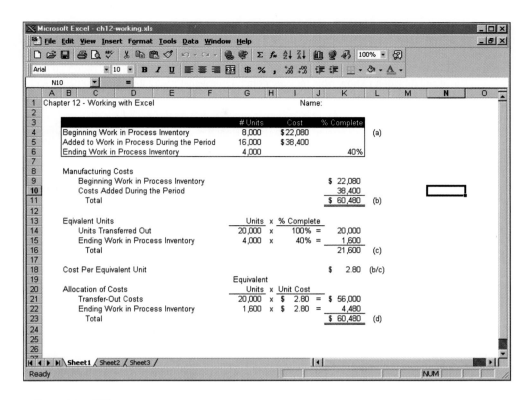

Spreadsheet Tip

(1) The cells that contain numbers below row 7 should all be formulas to allow changes to the data in rows 3 to 6 that will automatically be reflected in the rest of the spreadsheet.

ATC 12–7   SPREADSHEET ASSIGNMENT *Mastering Excel*

Refer to the job cost sheet in Exhibit 12–3.

Required

Construct a spreadsheet that recreates the job cost sheet in Exhibit 12–3. Use formulas wherever possible, such as in the total row.

Spreadsheet Tips

(1) Center the headings for direct materials, direct labor, and applied overhead across two or three columns by choosing Format and Cells and checking the Merge box under the alignment tab. A shortcut to center these is to click on the Merge and Center icon in the formatting tool bar.

(2) All lines in the job cost sheet can be drawn using Format and Cells and then choosing the border tab.

13

Financial Statement Analysis

Learning Objectives

After completing this chapter, you should be able to:

1 Describe the factors associated with the communication of useful information.

2 Differentiate between horizontal and vertical analysis.

3 Understand what the term *ratio analysis* means.

4 Calculate the ratios that facilitate the assessment of a company's debt-paying ability.

5 Calculate the ratios that facilitate the assessment of a company's solvency.

6 Calculate the ratios that facilitate the assessment of a company's managerial effectiveness.

7 Calculate the ratios that facilitate the assessment of a company's position in the stock market.

8 Identify different forms for presenting analytical data.

9 Understand the limitations of financial statement analysis.

the *curious* accountant

Sears' annual report indicated that in 2000 the company had net income amounting to $1,343 million. In comparison, Lands' End reported approximately $48 million in net income for its 2000 accounting period. Does this suggest that Sears' financial performance is better than Lands' End? The answer is no. What the comparison says more than anything else is that Sears is a much larger company than Lands' End. How could you compare the performance of companies of such vastly different size?

The utility of financial statement information can be enhanced when it is expressed in the form of ratios that permit comparisons across time and among companies. Accordingly, both internal and external users can benefit from a knowledge of common techniques to analyze these statements. Before we begin a detailed explanation of numerous ratios and percentages, however, we look at the factors involved in communicating useful information.

Factors in Communicating Useful Information

LO1 Describe the factors associated with the communication of useful information.

The primary objective of accounting is to provide information that is useful for decision making. To prepare information that will meet this objective, accountants must give consideration to the intended users, the purpose for which the information is being prepared, and the process by which the information is analyzed.

The Users

The users of financial information include managers, creditors, stockholders, potential investors, and regulatory agencies. Each of these groups represents many strata of individuals and organizations, all with different purposes and varying levels of sophistication concerning the activities of the business world. For example, an investor may be the individual who knows little about financial statements, a large investment house whose expertise in analysis includes the use of complex statistical procedures, or someone whose expertise falls between that of these individuals. One financial reporting issue concerns the level of knowledge to which the information should be aimed. Condensing the complexities of business to a level easily understood by the uninformed investor has become increasingly difficult. It is generally recognized that the user should be considered to be a person with a reasonable knowledge of business or one who has the capacity and willingness to achieve a reasonable knowledge. Terms such as "reasonable, average, prudent, informed, and sophisticated" are often used in trying to describe the users of information, yet such ambiguous qualities are difficult to define.

The Purpose of the Desired Information

Just as each potential user possesses a different level of knowledge, each also requires different information, depending on the decision at hand. Financial statements are general-purpose statements, meaning that they are prepared to be used by a wide variety of parties rather than being aimed at one specific group. For this reason, some disclosed information may be irrelevant to some users but vital to others. Different forms of analysis are necessary to identify the information that is most relevant to a particular decision.

Financial statements can be only synopses of economic information. The costs of providing all information about a firm would be prohibitive to the business. **Information overload** is also a consideration. When too much information is presented, the important pieces of information can often be obscured by trivialities. The user confronted with reams of data may become so frustrated in attempting to isolate desired information that the value of what *is* provided may be lost.

Information Analysis

Because of the many categories of users, the different levels of knowledge, the varying needs of decision makers, and the general nature of financial statements, a number of techniques are used in analysis. In the following sections, we consider a number of the methods of analysis commonly employed. No method of analysis is right or wrong; the choice depends on which tool appears to provide information that is most relevant to an individual situation.

Methods of Analysis

LO2 Differentiate between horizontal and vertical analysis.

Analysis of financial statements should focus primarily on isolating those pieces of information that will provide the desired input to a decision. The information required can take many forms but usually involves some form of comparison. This may entail comparing changes in

the same item over a number of years, key relationships within the same year, or the operations of several firms in the same industry. Although many of these comparisons overlap, this chapter discusses methods of analysis in three categories: horizontal, vertical, and ratio. Exhibits 13–1 and 13–2 represent comparative financial statements for Milavec Company and will be referred to in the examples of analysis techniques.

Exhibit 13–1

MILAVEC COMPANY
Income Statements and Statements of Retained Earnings
For the Years Ending December 31

	2004	2003
Sales	$900,000	$800,000
Cost of Goods Sold		
Beginning Inventory	43,000	40,000
Purchases	637,000	483,000
Goods Available for Sale	680,000	523,000
Ending Inventory	70,000	43,000
Cost of Goods Sold	610,000	480,000
Gross Margin from Sales	290,000	320,000
Operating Expenses	248,000	280,000
Income before Taxes	42,000	40,000
Income Taxes	17,000	18,000
Net Income	25,000	22,000
Plus: Retained Earnings,		
Beginning Balance	137,000	130,000
Less: Dividends	0	15,000
Retained Earnings,		
Ending Balance	$162,000	$137,000

Exhibit 13–2

MILAVEC COMPANY
Balance Sheets
As of December 31

	2004	2003
Assets		
Cash	$ 20,000	$ 17,000
Marketable Securities	20,000	22,000
Notes Receivable	4,000	3,000
Accounts Receivable	50,000	56,000
Merchandise Inventory	70,000	43,000
Prepaid Expenses	4,000	4,000
Property, Plant, and		
Equipment (net)	340,000	310,000
Total Assets	$508,000	$455,000
Equities		
Accounts Payable	$ 40,000	$ 38,000
Salaries Payable	2,000	3,000
Taxes Payable	4,000	2,000
Bonds Payable, 8%	100,000	100,000
Preferred Stock, 6%,		
$100 par, cumulative	50,000	50,000
Common Stock, $10 Par	150,000	125,000
Retained Earnings	162,000	137,000
Total Equities	$508,000	$455,000

Horizontal Analysis

Horizontal analysis refers to the study of an individual item over a period of time. This period of time may be only the current operating period or may be many years. Several approaches may be taken in reviewing one account: study of absolute amounts, percentages, and trends.

Absolute Amounts

Financial statement users are interested in the **absolute amounts** of various accounts for many reasons. Economic statistics are built on totals of absolute amounts as reported by businesses. These include gross national product figures and the amount spent to replace productive capacity. Financial statement users with expertise in particular industries can look at costs such as research and development and know whether a company is spending excessively or conservatively.

Simply using absolute amounts has many drawbacks, however. The major problem is that the **materiality** level differs from firm to firm. *Materiality* is a term that is difficult to define but nevertheless is used constantly in accounting. Firms are not required to account strictly for *immaterial* items, yet it is very difficult to look at an absolute amount and fully appreciate its significance without considering the size of other accounts of the business. Exxon Corporation's financial statements are presented in millions of dollars, indicating that amounts are rounded to the nearest million for reporting purposes. In that case, a $400,000 account may be considered immaterial and may be omitted altogether. This $400,000 amount, however, could represent total sales to a much smaller firm and therefore is material for it. No comparisons would be possible between the two companies' operating performance using only absolute amounts.

Exhibit 13–3

MILAVEC COMPANY
Comparative Income Statements
For the Years Ending December 31

	2004	2003	Percentage Difference
Sales	$900,000	$800,000	+12.5%*
Cost of Goods Sold	610,000	480,000	+27.1
Gross Margin from Sales	290,000	320,000	−9.4
Operating Expenses	248,000	280,000	−11.4
Income before Taxes	42,000	40,000	+5.0
Income Taxes	17,000	18,000	−5.6
Net Income	$ 25,000	$ 22,000	+13.6

(900,000 − 800,000); all changes expressed as percentages of previous totals.

Percentage Analysis

Percentage analysis involves establishing the relationship of one amount to another. In horizontal analysis, an account is expressed as a percentage of the previous balance of the same account. This type of analysis attempts to eliminate the materiality problems of comparing firms of different sizes by putting each on the same basis: 100 percent. Exhibit 13–3 presents a condensed version of Milavec's income statement showing horizontal percentages of each item.

The percentage changes reveal some interesting features. Even though Milavec's net income has increased slightly more than total sales, it may be pricing its products too low. The cost of goods sold increased much more than sales, resulting in a lower gross margin. A more detailed analysis would also investigate the substantial decrease in operating expenses despite the increase in volume.

In any analysis, whether of percentages, absolute amounts, or ratios, you must be careful to avoid making simplistic conclusions about the resulting information. Numerical relationships should be used to identify areas requiring further study. Recall from Chapter 8 that a change in what may appear to be a favorable direction may not necessarily be a good sign. The underlying reasons must be considered.

Check Yourself 13–1

The following information was drawn from the annual reports of two retail companies (amounts are shown in millions). One company is an upscale department store; the other is a discount store. Based on this limited information, identify which company is the upscale department store.

	Company A	Company B
Sales	$325	$680
Cost of goods sold	130	408
Gross margin	$195	$272

Answer Company A's gross margin represents 60 percent ($195 ÷ $325) of sales. Company B's gross margin represents 40 percent ($272 ÷ $680) of sales. Since an upscale department store would have higher margins than a discount store, the data suggest that Company A is the upscale department store.

Trend Analysis

Trend analysis is simply an extension of percentage analysis to cover several periods of time. When more than two figures are studied, two basic approaches could be used: choosing one base year on which to base increases or decreases or calculating the percentage of change from each preceding figure. For example, assume that Milavec's sales for 2001 and 2002 had been $600,000 and $750,000, respectively.

	2004	2003	2002	2001
Sales	$900,000	$800,000	$750,000	$600,000
Increase over 2001 sales	50.0%	33.3%	25.0%	—
Increase over preceding year	12.5%	6.7%	25.0%	—

answers to the *curious* accountant

Percentages and ratios provide a common base that facilitates comparisons among companies of divergent sizes. For example, horizontal analysis reveals that Sears' 2000 earnings were approximately 7.6 percent lower than its 1999 earnings. In contrast, Lands' End experienced an approximate 54 percent earnings increase during the same period. Although Sears is a much larger company, Lands' End's earnings performance was certainly more impressive. Be aware that percentage computations also suffer from limitations that must be considered. For example, a high growth rate in 2000 may be due to the fact that a company's 1999 performance was weak. Indeed, a lower sustained growth rate may be far more impressive than a financial roller coaster ride. Being a good financial analyst involves much more than simply calculating ratios. It is important that you learn to interpret the ratios as well as to calculate them.

From this analysis, Milavec's 2004 sales represent a 50 percent increase over 2001 sales, and a very large increase (25 percent) occurred in 2002. From 2002 and 2003, sales increased only 6.7 percent but in the following year increased much more (12.5 percent).

Vertical Analysis

Vertical analysis is a procedure that uses percentages to compare each of the parts of an individual statement to the whole. Horizontal analysis considers one item over many time periods, and vertical analysis considers many items in the same interval of time.

Vertical Analysis of the Income Statement

In this type of analysis, each item is generally shown as a percentage of sales. Even though vertical analysis pertains to one statement, its usefulness is enhanced when vertical analysis of several years is performed. Exhibit 13–4 presents Milavec's income statements for 2004 and 2003. From this analysis, interesting relationships or changes in relationships can be identified. For example, the cost of goods sold has increased significantly as a percentage of sales. However, operating expenses and income taxes have decreased in relation to sales. Each of these points bears more analysis as to the trends they may be exhibiting for future profits.

Exhibit 13–4

MILAVEC COMPANY
Vertical Analysis of Comparative Income Statements

	2004		2003	
	Amount	Percentage of Sales	Amount	Percentage of Sales
Sales	$900,000	100.0%	$800,000	100.0%
Cost of Goods Sold	610,000	67.7	480,000	60.0
Gross Margin from Sales	290,000	32.3	320,000	40.0
Operating Expenses	248,000	27.6	280,000	35.0
Income before Taxes	42,000	4.7	40,000	5.0
Income Taxes	17,000	1.9	18,000	2.3
Net Income	$ 25,000	2.8%	$ 22,000	2.7%

Vertical Analysis of the Balance Sheet

When vertical analysis of the balance sheet is performed, each asset is presented as a percentage of total assets and each equity account is presented as a percentage of total equity. The vertical analysis of Milavec's balance sheets in Exhibit 13–5 reveals few large changes in percentages from the preceding year; however, when percentages are analyzed, small changes may represent a substantial increase in current assets, and because inventory is one of the less

Exhibit 13-5

MILAVEC COMPANY
Vertical Analysis of Corporation Balance Sheets

	2004	Percentage of Total	2003	Percentage of Total
Assets				
Cash	$ 20,000	3.9%	$ 17,000	3.7%
Marketable Securities	20,000	3.9	22,000	4.8
Notes Receivable	4,000	0.8	3,000	0.7
Accounts Receivable	50,000	9.8	56,000	12.3
Merchandise Inventory	70,000	13.8	43,000	9.5
Prepaid Expenses	4,000	0.8	4,000	0.9
Total Current Assets	168,000	33.0	145,000	31.9
Property, Plant, and Equipment	340,000	67.0	310,000	68.1
Total Assets	$508,000	100.0%	$455,000	100.0%
Equities				
Accounts Payable	$ 40,000	7.9%	$ 38,000	8.3%
Salaries Payable	2,000	0.4	3,000	0.7
Taxes Payable	4,000	0.8	2,000	0.4
Total Current Liabilities	46,000	9.1	43,000	9.4
Bonds Payable, 8%	100,000	19.7	100,000	22.0
Total Liabilities	146,000	28.8	143,000	31.4
Preferred Stock 6%, $100 par	50,000	9.8	50,000	11.0
Common Stock, $10 par	150,000	29.5	125,000	27.5
Retained Earnings	162,000	31.9	137,000	30.1
Total Stockholders' Equity	362,000	71.2	312,000	68.6
Total Equities	$508,000	100.0%	$455,000	100.0%

liquid current assets, this change may have significant consequences. Another pitfall to avoid in this analysis is the temptation to perceive that the decrease in the percentages of the non-changing accounts indicates decreasing absolute amounts. Bonds payable and preferred stock have not changed, although their percentages of the total have decreased.

Ratio Analysis

LO3 Understand what the term *ratio analysis* means.

Ratio analysis is a form of vertical analysis in that it involves comparisons among different accounts in the same set of statements. It differs in that individual ratios indicate relationships between specific accounts rather than between an account and the designated total on the statement. Numerous ratios are used for a wide variety of purposes, and the remainder of this chapter will be devoted to a discussion of some of the more commonly used ones.

Objectives of Ratio Analysis

As stated earlier, the various users of financial statements approach analysis with many different objectives. Although managers often use internally generated data to analyze operations, much information prepared for external purposes can be quite useful in examining past operation and determining future policies. Creditors are interested in assurances that the firm will be able to repay its debts on a timely basis. Both creditors and stockholders are concerned with the various means used to finance the company, whether through debt, equity transactions, or earnings. Stockholders and potential investors desire indicators of the future value of their investments and look to past performance of earnings and dividend policy to provide information that they hope will provide clues to the future. Although it is difficult to draw strictly defined lines among all of these objectives, we study debt-paying ratios grouped into three specific categories: liquidity ratios, solvency ratios, and profitability ratios.

▋Measures of Debt-Paying Ability

Liquidity Ratios

Liquidity ratios as defined in this context are those that indicate a firm's short-term debt-paying ability. As such, they deal primarily with current assets and liabilities. The examples in the following section are taken from information presented in the financial statements of Milavec Company.

LO4 Calculate the ratios that facilitate the assessment of a company's debt-paying ability.

Working Capital

Working capital is defined as current assets minus current liabilities. Because current liabilities represent debts that must be satisfied in the current operating period and current assets are those assets that can be most easily converted into funds in the current period, working capital theoretically represents the funds that the company will have remaining to operate. Another way to look at working capital is to think of it as the cushion against short-term debt-paying problems. The amount of working capital at the end of 2004 and 2003 for Milavec Company is the following.

	2004	2003
Current assets	$168,000	$145,000
– Current liabilities	46,000	43,000
Working capital	$122,000	$102,000

Milavec's working capital experienced a dramatic increase from 2003 to 2004, but the numbers themselves tell us little. Whether $122,000 is a sufficient amount or not depends on many factors, among them the industry in which Milavec operates, its size, and the maturity dates of its current obligations. We can see, however, that the increase in working capital is primarily due to the increase in inventories.

Current Ratio

Working capital is an absolute amount and suffers from the difficulties of comparison that were mentioned earlier. It would be very difficult to compare Milavec's $122,000 with working capital from another firm of $122,000 and come to meaningful conclusions. However, by expressing the same information as a ratio, we have a better measure of the strength of the company's debt-paying ability in relation to other firms. The **current ratio**, also frequently called the **working capital ratio**, is calculated as follows.

$$\text{Current ratio} = \frac{\text{Current assets}}{\text{Current liabilities}}$$

To illustrate the usefulness of the current ratio, consider Milavec's position in relation to a larger firm with current assets of $500,000 and current liabilities of $378,000.

	Milavec	Other Firm
Current assets (a)	$168,000	$500,000
– Current liabilities (b)	46,000	378,000
Working capital	$122,000	$122,000
Current ratio (a ÷ b)	3.65:1	1.32:1

The current ratio is expressed as the number of dollars of current assets to one dollar of current liabilities. In our example, despite the identical amount of working capital, Milavec appears to be in a much stronger working capital position. Any conclusions to be drawn from

this analysis must consider the particular circumstances of the firm; there is no "good" current ratio for which to strive. Many financial statement users consider 2:1 to be an acceptable level; however, some industries may require more or less. A current ratio could also be too high, indicating poor management of investment opportunities in relation to current operational requirements.

Quick Ratio

The **quick ratio,** also known as the **acid-test ratio**, is a more conservative form of the current ratio. The quick ratio considers the fact that some accounts classified as current assets are less liquid than others. For example, inventories may take several months to sell; also, prepaid expenses serve only to offset otherwise necessary expenditures as time elapses. The quick ratio attempts to measure the firm's *immediate* debt-paying ability by considering only cash, receivables, and current marketable securities (known as *quick assets*) in relation to current liabilities.

$$\text{Quick ratio} = \frac{\text{Quick assets}}{\text{Current liabilities}}$$

The current ratios and quick ratios for 2004 and 2003 for Milavec Company follow.

	2004	2003
Current ratio	168,000 ÷ 46,000	145,000 ÷ 43,000
	3.65:1	3.37:1
Quick ratio	94,000 ÷ 46,000	78,000 ÷ 43,000
	2.04:1	1.81:1

The decreasing quick ratio from 2003 to 2004 mainly reflects the larger investment in inventory in 2004.

Accounts Receivable Ratios

In an era when credit plays an enormous role in defining purchasing power, it is imperative for a company to manage its receivables in an effective manner. Two relationships are often examined to indicate a firm's collection record: **accounts receivable turnover** and **number of days' sales in receivables.**

1. *Turnover.* Accounts receivable turnover is calculated as follows.

$$\text{Accounts receivable turnover} = \frac{\text{Net credit sales}}{\text{Average accounts receivable}}$$

Net credit sales refers to sales on account after discounts and returns. When credit sales make up the bulk of sales or when the sales figure is not divided into cash and credit sales, the total sales figure must be used. *Net accounts receivable* refers to receivables after subtracting the allowance for bad debts, and it is preferable to use an average figure when available. With comparative statements, a beginning and ending balance can be used, but it is even better if monthly data are available. Milavec Company's accounts receivable turnover is computed as follows:

	2004	2003
Net sales (assume all on account) (a)	$900,000	$800,000
Beginning receivables	$ 56,000	$ 55,000*
Ending receivables	50,000	56,000
Average receivables (b)	$ 53,000	$ 55,500
Turnover (a ÷ b)	16.98	14.41

*Additional data are not in illustration.

The 16.98 turnover figure for 2004 indicates that the company collects its average receivables almost 17 times a year. The higher the number, the faster the collections. A company can have a cash flow problem and lose substantial purchasing power if sales are tied up in receivables for long periods of time.

2. *Average collection period.* This ratio is sometimes called *number of days' sales in receivables.* Another way to look at the turnover figure is to determine the number of days, on average, it takes to collect a receivable. If receivables are collected 16.98 times in 2004*, the average is 366 ÷ 16.98 (the number of days in the year divided by turnover), in this case 22 days. For 2003, it took 25 days to collect the average receivable (365 ÷ 14.41). In summary, the *average collection period* can be calculated as follows.

$$\text{Average collection period} = \frac{\text{Number of days in the year}}{\text{Accounts receivable turnover}}$$

Although the time required for collection improved, no other conclusions can be reached without an analysis of the industry, Milavec's past performance, and the general economic environment.

Inventory Ratios

A fine line exists between having too much and too little inventory in stock. Insufficient inventory can lead to lost sales and time-consuming delays. Too much inventory can use needed space, cost extra insurance coverage, and become obsolete. In analyzing the funds tied up in inventory, the same two ratios are used as in accounts receivable analysis.

1. **Inventory turnover** indicates the number of times, on the average, that total inventory is replaced during the year. The relationship is computed as follows.

$$\text{Inventory turnover} = \frac{\text{Cost of goods sold}}{\text{Average inventory}}$$

Again, it is preferable to use as many figures as are available for the average calculation. Inventory turnover for Milavec is as follows.

	2004	2003
Cost of goods sold (a)	$610,000	$480,000
Beginning inventory	43,000	40,000
Ending inventory	70,000	43,000
Average inventory (b)	$ 56,500	$ 41,500
Inventory turnover (a ÷ b)	10.80	11.57

Generally, a higher turnover indicates that merchandise is being handled more efficiently. However, trying to compare firms in different industries can be dangerous. Grocery stores and many retail outlets have high turnover while appliance and jewelry stores have much lower turnover due to the nature of the goods being sold. We will look at this issue in more detail when we discuss return on investment.

2. **Number of days' sales in inventory** is determined by dividing the number of days in the year by inventory turnover to identify the number of days required to sell inventory, a figure that approximates the number of days the firm could sell inventory without purchasing more. For Milavec, this figure was 34 days in 2004 (366 ÷ 10.80) and 32 days in 2003 (365 ÷ 11.57). In summary, the number of days' sales that remain in inventory can be computed as follows.

$$\text{Number of days' sales in inventory} = \frac{\text{Number of days in the year}}{\text{Inventory turnover}}$$

*Note that 2004 is a leap year containing 366 days; otherwise 365 days would have been used in the computations.

Solvency Ratios

LO5 Calculate the ratios that facilitate the assessment of a company's solvency.

Solvency ratios are used to analyze a firm's long-term debt-paying ability and the composition of its financing structure. These ratios measure the relationships between different portions of the equity section of the balance sheet. Creditors are concerned about the firm's ability to satisfy outstanding obligations. The larger the percentage of liabilities, the greater is the risk that the company could fall behind or default on payments. Stockholders, too, are concerned about the firm's ability to pay debts; their interest is in the company's ability to maintain high earnings per share and dividend payments. Each group desires that financing be undertaken in such a way to minimize the risk of its investment, whether that investment is in debt or stockholders' equity.

Debt/Equity Ratios

The following ratios are simply three ways to express the same relationship; however, each is frequently used. You should be familiar with all three.

1. *Ratio of liabilities to total equity.* This ratio is presented as a percentage. It simply notes the percentage of the company that is financed by debt. Often you will see this ratio presented as a percentage of liabilities to total assets.
2. *Stockholders' equity ratio.* This ratio, also a percentage, is the difference between the debt/equity ratio and 100 percent. It is the percentage of total equities (or total assets) represented by stockholders' equity.
3. *Debt/equity ratio.* In this ratio, *equity* is a shortened form of stockholders' equity. The previous two ratios considered parts of equity in relation to total equity; this ratio examines the parts in relation to each other, resulting in a dollar amount of liabilities for every dollar of stockholder's equity.

The calculations for these three common ratios can be summarized as follows

$$\text{Liabilities to total equity} = \frac{\text{Total liabilities}}{\text{Total equities (liabilities + stockholders' equity)}}$$

$$\text{Stockholders' equity ratio} = \frac{\text{Total stockholders' equity}}{\text{Total equities (liabilities + stockholders' equity)}}$$

$$\text{Debt/equity ratio} = \frac{\text{Total liabilities}}{\text{Total stockholders' equity}}$$

Usin g these formulas for Milavec Company produces the following.

	2004	2003
Total liabilities (a)	$146,000	$143,000
Total stockholders' equity (b)	362,000	312,000
Total equities (liabilities + stockholders' equity) (c)	$508,000	$455,000
Liabilities to total equity (a ÷ c)	29%	31%
Total stockholders' equity ratio (b ÷ c)	71%	69%
Debt to equity ratio (a ÷ b)	0.40:1	0.46:1

Each year the company's liabilities accounted for slightly less than one-third of total equity. The amount of liabilities per dollar of stockholders' equity declined by 0.06. It is impossible to say whether this slight reduction in the percentage of liabilities is a favorable trend. Perhaps the company is in a strong enough position to incur more liabilities. However, a lower level of liabilities generally suggests greater security because the likelihood of foreclosure is lessened.

Number of Times Bond Interest Is Earned

This ratio provides a quick look at the burden that long-term debt interest payments pose for the company. This is often calculated with the debt/equity ratios.

$$\frac{\text{Number of times bond}}{\text{interest is earned}} = \frac{\text{Income before taxes and bond interest expense}}{\text{Bond interest expense}}$$

The result of dividing the numerator by bond interest expense indicates how often the interest obligation could be satisfied. Obviously, interest will be paid only once, but the more often it *could* be paid, the stronger is the company's ability to meet its obligations. For Milavec, this calculation is as follows.

	2004	2003
Income before taxes	$42,000	$40,000
Bond Interest (100,000 × 0.08) (b)	8,000	8,000
Income before taxes and interest (a)	$50,000	$48,000
Times interest earned (a ÷ b)	6.25 times	6 times

This type of analysis can be done with any expense or dividend payment. The other calculation most frequently seen is the number of times the preferred dividend is earned. The ratio takes much the same form except that the numerator is net income (after taxes) and the denominator, naturally, is the preferred dividend.

Check Yourself 13–2

Selected data for Riverside Corporation and Academy Company follow (amounts are shown in millions).

	Riverside Corporation	Academy Company
Total liabilities (a)	$650	$450
Stockholders' equity (b)	300	400
Total equities (liabilities + stockholders' equity) (c)	$950	$850
Interest expense on bonds (d)	$ 65	$ 45
Income before taxes (e)	140	130
Income before taxes and interest (f)	$205	$175

Based on this information alone, which company would likely obtain the less favorable interest rate on additional debt financing?

Answer Interest rates vary with risk levels. Companies with less solvency (long-term debt-paying ability) generally must pay higher interest rates to obtain financing. Two solvency measures for the two companies follow.

	Riverside Corporation	Academy Company
Debt to total equities ratio (a ÷ c)	68.4%	52.9%
Times interest earned (f ÷ d)	3.15 times	3.89 times

Since Riverside has a higher percentage of debt and a lower times interest earned ratio, the data suggest that Riverside is less solvent than Academy. Riverside would therefore likely have to pay a higher interest rate to obtain additional financing.

Plant Assets to Long-Term Liabilities

Often a company secures its long-term liabilities by indenture. Financial statement users are interested in analyzing a firm's long-term ability to borrow funds on the strength of its asset base. This ratio provides such a measure and is calculated as follows.

$$\text{Plant assets to long-term liabilities} = \frac{\text{Net plant assets}}{\text{Long-term liabilities}}$$

For Milavec Company, these ratios follow.

	2004	2003
Net plant assets (a)	$340,000	$310,000
Bonds payable (b)	100,000	100,000
Plant assets to long-term liabilities (a ÷ b)	3.4:1	3.1:1

▎Measures of Profitability

LO6 Calculate the ratios that facilitate the assessment of a company's managerial effectiveness.

Profitability refers to the company's ability to generate earnings. Numerous ratios can be used to measure different aspects of profitability. Both management and external users desire information about how a firm is succeeding in generating profits and how these profits are being used to reward investors. The following two sections discuss ratios designed to measure managerial effectiveness and ratios frequently used by investors to measure return. This is simply a convenient way to categorize **profitability ratios** because investors often use measures of managerial effectiveness to predict future returns.

Measures of Managerial Effectiveness

The most common ratios used to evaluate managerial effectiveness involve measurement of how the assets are generating sales and what percentage of these sales result in earnings. It is important to remember that an *absolute amount* of sales or earnings has little meaning unless the size of the company is considered.

Net Margin

You are probably familiar with the terms *gross margin* and *gross profit,* which refer to the amount of sales dollars remaining after a major expense, cost of goods sold, is subtracted. **Net margin** refers to the amount of the sales dollar remaining after all expenses are subtracted. Net margin can be calculated in several ways; some of the most common methods limit the expenses to normal operating expenses or expenses other than tax expense. For our purposes, however, we will use all expenses for simplicity. By dividing net income by net sales, we arrive at net margin expressed as a percentage of sales.

$$\text{Net margin} = \frac{\text{Net income}}{\text{Net sales}}$$

For Milavec Company, the net margins for the two years presented are as follows.

	2004	2003
Net income (a)	$ 25,000	$ 22,000
Net sales (b)	900,000	800,000
Net margin (a ÷ b)	2.78%	2.75%

Milavec is maintaining approximately the same net margin. Obviously, the larger the percentage, the better; however, it is difficult to analyze whether the net margin is adequate without considering factors such as the particular industry and the history of the company.

Turnover of Assets

Turnover of assets (frequently called "asset turnover" ratio) is a ratio that measures how many sales dollars are being generated for each dollar of assets. Like the margin calculation, the parts of this ratio can be defined in several different ways. Assets may be limited to operating assets,

or a total assets figure may be desired. Also, when the amount of assets changes significantly during the year, it is desirable to use the average asset base rather than the year-end balance. We use the latter to promote simplicity.

$$\text{Turnover of assets} = \frac{\text{Net sales}}{\text{Total assets}}$$

For Milavec, the turnover of assets calculations are as follows.

	2004	2003
Net sales (a)	$900,000	$800,000
Total assets (b)	508,000	455,000
Asset turnover (a ÷ b)	1.77	1.76

Analysis of asset turnover is also subject to other considerations. The particular industry may have high turnover if only minimal investment is required to operate the business. On the other hand, industries that require large amounts of machinery may be characterized by lower asset turnover.

Return on Investment

Return on investment combines the two preceding ratios (net margin and turnover of assets) to produce a measure that is easier to use in comparing different industries. Return on investment (ROI), often called **return on assets** or *earning power,* is calculated as follows.

$$\text{ROI} = \text{Net margin} \times \text{Asset turnover}$$

Remember that these two ratios consist of the following parts.

$$\frac{\text{Net income}}{\text{Net sales}} \times \frac{\text{Net sales}}{\text{Total assets}}$$

By canceling net sales from both fractions, ROI can also be expressed as follows.

$$\text{ROI} = \frac{\text{Net income}}{\text{Total assets}}$$

When the amount of assets changes significantly during the year, it is desirable to use the average asset base rather than the year-end balance. Although it may seem easier to think of ROI simply as the last fraction, it is very important to understand that it is a result of two considerations: how earnings are generated from sales and how sales are generated from assets. For Milavec, the calculation of ROI is as follows.

2004
$2.78\% \times 1.77 = 4.92\%$

2003
$2.75\% \times 1.76 = 4.84\%$

Using the fraction approach produces the same result. To understand how ROI can be used to compare different industries, consider the following figures for a retail clothing store and an appliance store.

	Margin		Turnover		ROI
Clothing store	2%	×	3.0	=	6%
Appliance store	4	×	1.5	=	6

Each has the same ROI, but it is arrived at in a different manner. The appliance store must earn a higher percentage of sales because its turnover is lower. Grocery stores often have net margins far less than 1 percent, yet the extremely high turnover results in significant profitability.

Return on Equity

Return on equity (ROE) is often used to measure the profitability of the firm in relation to the amount invested by stockholders. ROE is higher than ROI simply because the ratio does not consider that part of the business that is financed by debt. This ratio is really another way to look at leverage, much like the debt/equity ratios discussed earlier. ROE is computed as follows.

$$ROE = \frac{\text{Net income}}{\text{Total stockholders' equity}}$$

When the amount of stockholders' equity changes significantly during the year, it is desirable to use the average equity base rather than the year-end balance. The preceding formula produces the following ROE figures for Milavec Company.

	2004	2003
Net income (a)	$ 25,000	$ 22,000
Preferred stock, 6%, $100 par, cumulative	50,000	50,000
Common stock, $10 par	150,000	125,000
Retained earnings	162,000	137,000
Total stockholders' equity (b)	$362,000	$312,000
ROE (a ÷ b)	6.9%	7.1%

The slight decrease in ROE is due primarily to the increase in common stock from 2003. Although earnings were higher, the increase in total stockholders' equity offsets this. From the information provided, we do not know whether Milavec had the use of these additional funds all or part of the year. If these data are available, it is best to calculate a weighted average amount of stockholders' equity.

Stock Market Ratios

LO7 Calculate the ratios that facilitate the assessment of a company's position in the stock market.

Present and potential investors in a company's stock employ many common ratios. The ratios are primarily used in analyzing companies of different sizes and different industries in relation to their earnings and dividends. Remember that a purchaser of stock can profit in two ways: the dividends paid and the increase in the value of the stock. Thus, although investors consider dividends to be important, they are also interested in the overall earnings performance of the company as an indication of the value of the stock they own.

Earnings per Share

Perhaps the most frequently quoted ratio of earnings performance is **earnings per share** (EPS), which attempts to measure the value of a share of stock by attributing to it a portion of the company's earnings. Do not confuse EPS with *dividends per share*. Rarely would a company distribute all the year's earnings to the stockholders. EPS calculations are among the most complex in accounting, and more advanced textbooks devote entire chapters to their calculation. At this level, we deal with the following basic formula.

$$\text{Earnings per share} = \frac{\text{Net earnings available for common stock}}{\text{Average number of outstanding common shares}}$$

By limiting the net earnings figure to earnings available for common stock, we eliminate the amount of the preferred dividend ($0.06 \times \$50,000 = \$3,000$) from consideration. Note that Exhibit 13–1 indicates that preferred dividends were not paid in 2004. However, since the preferred stock is cumulative, the preferred dividend is in arrears and not available to the common stockholders. The number of common shares outstanding is determined by dividing the book value of the stock by the par value per share ($\$150,000 \div \$10 = 15,000$ for 2004 and $\$125,000 \div \$10 = 12,500$ for 2003). With these considerations in mind, the 2004 EPS figure for Milavec is as follows.

$$\frac{\$25,000 \text{ (net income)} - \$3,000 \text{ (preferred dividend)}}{(15,000 + 12,500)/2 \text{ (average outstanding common shares)}} = \$1.60 \text{ per share}$$

A great deal of importance is attached to EPS figures, so it is important to understand the many limitations involved. Numerous variables are involved in calculating income, including different methods for depreciation, inventory cost flow, and revenue recognition, to name only a few. The denominator is also very much in question because various factors affect the number of shares to include. Numerous opportunities exist for manipulation of the EPS figure, and the prudent investor must consider all these in deciding how much weight to attach to earnings per share.

Book Value

Book value per share is another frequently quoted measure of a share of stock. It is calculated as follows.

$$\text{Book value per share} = \frac{\text{Stockholders' equity} - \text{Preferred rights}}{\text{Average outstanding common shares}}$$

Instead of using stockholders' equity as the numerator, we could have easily used assets minus liabilities, which is the formula for determining a company's "net worth." Net worth is a misnomer because a company's worth is not reflected in the accounts. Because assets are recorded at historical costs and different methods are used to transfer their costs to expense, the book value of assets remaining after liabilities have been deducted really means little if anything. Nevertheless, because the term *book value per share* is used frequently, you should be aware of its definition.

Preferred rights refers to the amount of money that would be required to satisfy the claims of preferred stockholders. If a call premium exists, that must also be considered. In our example, we assume that the preferred stock can be retired at par; thus, book value per share for 2004 is as follows.

$$\frac{\$362,000 - \$50,000}{(15,000 + 12,500)/2} = \$22.69 \text{ per share}$$

Price-Earnings Ratio

The **price-earnings ratio,** often called the *PE ratio,* is a measure that weighs the earnings per share of each firm by the price of a share of stock. Assume that Firms A and B have an EPS of $3.60 and Firm C has an EPS of $4.10. Based on these data alone, you may prefer the higher EPS of Firm C. However, your decision may change when you consider that the price of one share of stock in each firm is $43.20, $36.00, and $51.25, respectively. Now which share of stock should you buy? The price of Firm C's stock is higher, but then, its EPS is higher, too. Using the PE ratio can reduce all three firms to the same comparison basis:

$$\text{Price-earnings ratio} = \frac{\text{Market price per share}}{\text{Earnings per share}}$$

Thus, the PE ratios for the three firms are as follows:

A	B	C
12.0	10.0	12.5

An immediate reaction to this might be to consider Firm B to be the best buy for your money. On the other hand, there must be some reason that Firm C's stock is selling at 12½ times earnings. Perhaps technology or expert management is keeping the price high. It is difficult, therefore, to use these ratios in a naive manner to make stock decisions as the reasons behind the ratios must be examined as well.

Dividend Yield

The **dividend yield** is a measure of the profitability of particular interest to those investors who are primarily investing to receive short-term returns in the form of dividends. Dividend yield gives a measure of the dividends received as a percentage of the market price of the stock.

$$\text{Dividend yield} = \frac{\text{Dividends per share}}{\text{Market price per share}}$$

As an example, consider Firms D and E. The information required to calculate dividend yield is as follows:

	Firm D	Firm E
Dividends per share (a)	$ 1.80	$ 3.00
Market price per share (b)	40.00	75.00
Dividend yield (a ÷ b)	4.5%	4.0%

Even though the actual dividend per share is higher for Firm E ($3.00 versus $1.80), the yield is lower (4.5 percent versus 4.0 percent) because the price of the stock is so high.

Other Ratios

In actuality, a wide array of other ratios may be used to analyze profitability. Most of these ratios follow the logic of many of the ratios presented. For example, you should be able to calculate the *yield* of a number of factors. Yield can be simply expressed as what is received as a percentage of what is given up. We calculated the dividend yield, which could be either for common or preferred stock. The earnings yield would be earnings per share as a percentage of market price. Yield on a bond can be calculated in much the same way (interest received divided by the price of the bond).

Another category of ratios includes those used to calculate the number of times a particular item is earned as a measure of the safety of that item. Although the most commonly calculated measures involve bond interest and the preferred dividend, the same format can be used for any expense or other payout. The specific ratios presented in this chapter are summarized in Exhibit 13–6.

Exhibit 13–6 *Summary of Key Relationships*

Liquidity Ratios	1. Working capital	Current assets − Current liabilities
	2. Current ratio	Current assets ÷ Current liabilities
	3. Quick (acid-test) ratio	(Current assets − Inventory − Prepaids) ÷ Current liabilities
	4. Accounts receivable turnover	Net credit sales ÷ Average net receivables
	5. Average collection period	Days in year ÷ Accounts receivable turnover
	6. Inventory turnover	Cost of goods sold ÷ Average inventory
	7. Number of days required to sell inventory	Days in year ÷ Inventory turnover
Solvency Ratios	8. Liabilities to total equities	Total liabilities ÷ Total equities
	9. Stockholders' equity ratio	Total stockholders' equity ÷ Total equities
	10. Debt/equity ratio	Total liabilities ÷ Total stockholders' equity
	11. Number of times bond interest earned	Income before taxes and bond interest expense ÷ Bond interest expense
	12. Plant assets to long-term liabilities	Net plant assets ÷ Long-term liabilities
Profitability Ratios	13. Net margin	Net income ÷ Net sales
	14. Turnover of assets	Net sales ÷ Total assets
	15. Return on investment (also: return on assets)	Net income ÷ Total assets
	16. Return on equity	Net income ÷ Total stockholders' equity
Stock Market Ratios	17. Earnings per share	Net earnings available for common stock ÷ Average outstanding common shares
	18. Book value per share	(Stockholders' equity − Preferred rights) ÷ Average outstanding common shares
	19. Price-earnings ratio	Market price per share ÷ Earnings per share
	20. Dividend yield	Dividends per share ÷ Market price per share

The last category we discuss consists simply of other percentages. A *ratio* is, by definition, a percentage. It is a measure of one item (the numerator) in terms of another (the denominator). In this chapter, we have discussed the major percentages, but different circumstances could call for the calculation of less common ratios. You should be able to calculate a ratio of *any* two items that are of interest in your analysis. In the Milavec example, you may be interested in the percentage of its operating expenses that are prepaid at the end of the year. The answer is 1.6 percent (2004 prepaid expenses ÷ 2004 total operating expenses).

LO8 Identify different forms for presenting analytical data.

Presentation of Analytical Relationships

Analytical information can be presented in endless ways in annual reports; the only limits are the creativity of the individual firm and the costs involved. Although most of the information included in annual reports is not required, companies often aid the user of the statements by preparing and presenting the information in a manner that can be more easily understood than simple numbers. Some of the more common forms of presentation are bar charts, pie charts, and graphs. Examples of these three forms are presented in Exhibits 13–7, 13–8, and 13–9.

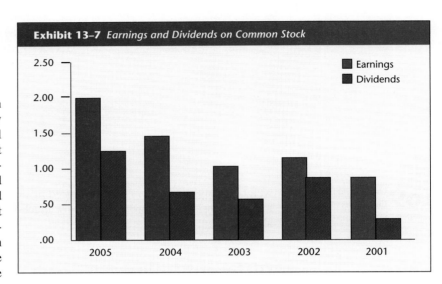

Exhibit 13–7 *Earnings and Dividends on Common Stock*

Limitations of Financial Statement Analysis

Analyzing financial statements is much like buying a new car. Each car is different, and each one has applicable statistics to be considered: gas mileage, size of engine, reputation of maker, color, accessories, and price, to name a few. Just as it is difficult to compare a Toyota station wagon to a Ferrari sports car, so it is difficult to compare a small

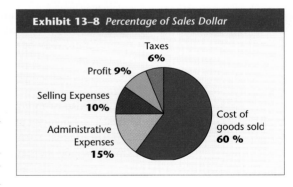

Exhibit 13–8 *Percentage of Sales Dollar*

textile firm to a giant oil company. This is the classic situation of comparing apples and oranges. The only way the potential buyer can compare the two cars is to focus on key pieces of data expressed on the same basis for each car. Gas mileage is a comparable factor. The superior gas mileage of the station wagon may pale in comparison to the thrill of driving the sports car, yet the price of the latter may prove to be the statistic that determines the ultimate choice.

An investor, or any other external user, can use ratios only as a general guide or set of clues to the potential of the business. It is very easy to place too much

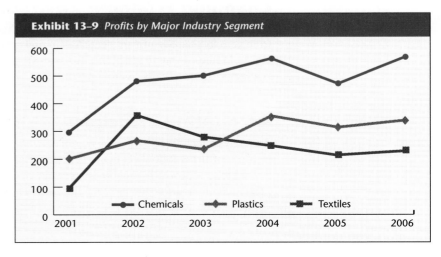

Exhibit 13–9 *Profits by Major Industry Segment*

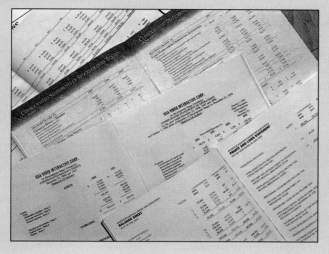

reality bytes

The most widely recognized source of financial information is a company's annual report. Most companies provide copies of their annual report free of charge. Normally, a person can obtain a copy of the annual report simply by calling the corporate office and asking the receptionist to direct the call to the appropriate department. Another source for public companies registered with the Securities and Exchange Commission is the Edgar database, which can be accessed through the Internet address www.sec.org. Also, many brokerage houses offer free financial information through their Web pages. As an example, we suggest that you try the Internet address www.schwab.com.

LO9 Understand the limitations of financial statement analysis.

weight on any one figure. From the preceding discussion, you should realize that many factors must be considered before deciding how much faith to place in a ratio and what the ratio really means.

Different Industries

Different industries may be affected by unique social policies, special accounting procedures, or other individual industry attributes. Before the ratios of the companies in different industries can be compared, these factors must be considered. For some industries, a high debt/equity ratio may be common and much more acceptable than in other industries. A particular line of business may require more or less working capital than some average. In this case, the working capital and quick ratios would have little meaning when compared to those of other firms.

Because of industry-specific factors, most professional analysts specialize in certain industries. Financial analysts for brokerage houses, banks, insurance funds, and so on may specialize in areas such as mineral or oil extraction, chemicals, banking, retail, insurance, bond markets, and international markets.

Changing Economic Environment

When comparing firms, an analyst must realize that the general state of the economy changes from year to year. Significant decreases in fuel costs and drops in interest rates in recent years make old rule-of-thumb guidelines for analysis of these factors obsolete. In addition, inflation is a factor whose effects cannot be ignored.

Accounting Principles

An analysis technique is only as reliable as the data on which it is based. Although the great majority of firms follow generally accepted accounting principles, a wide variety of methods is available from which to choose in certain categories, including different inventory and depreciation methods, different schedules for recognizing revenue on construction projects, and different ways to account for oil and gas exploration costs. Companies that may otherwise be identical may use different accounting methods and therefore produce noncomparable ratios.

For this reason, many analysts try to recast statements by estimating what the results would have been under the same methods.

Accrual accounting requires the use of many estimates; bad debt expense, warranty expense, asset lives, and salvage value are just a few. The reliability of the resulting income figures depends on the expertise and the integrity of the persons responsible for the estimates.

Specific characteristics of accounting model affect the numbers that are produced. Two underlying concepts in particular, *conservatism* and *historical cost,* have a tremendous impact on financial reporting. By accruing estimated losses and deferring gains until realization, conservatism biases financial statements in a downward direction. There are persuasive reasons for the conservatism principle, but it does distort the use of accounting figures as indicators of the potential for future gains.

The historical cost concept is probably the greatest single culprit in distorting the results of financial statement analysis. The historical cost of an asset does not represent its value in the present. To make matters worse, the $10,000 asset purchased in 1960 cannot even be compared to the $10,000 asset purchased in 1975 because of the difference in the value of the dollar. Because of historical cost, financial statements are full of dollars of different sizes. By adding and subtracting these dollars, the result is much like adding miles to kilometers.

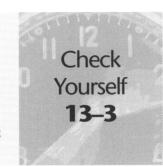

The return on equity for Gup Company is 23.4 percent and for Hunn Company is 17 percent. Does this mean Gup Company is better managed than Hunn Company?

Answer No single ratio can adequately measure management performance. Even analyzing a wide range of ratios provides only limited insight. Any useful interpretation requires the analyst to recognize the limitations of ratio analysis. For example, ratio norms typically differ between industries and may be affected by temporary economic factors. In addition, companies' use of different accounting practices and procedures produces different ratio results even when underlying circumstances are comparable.

Check Yourself 13–3

a look
back

Financial statement analysis involves many factors, among them the characteristics of the users, what information is desired, and how the information is to be used. Three general methods of analysis are *horizontal, vertical,* and *ratio analysis.* The ratios that are commonly calculated can be analyzed in terms of their ability to measure a firm's liquidity, solvency, and profitability. The specific ratios presented in this chapter are summarized in Exhibit 13–6. Despite the ease of calculation and the apparent insights provided by ratios, they have limitations involving differing industry characteristics, differing economic conditions, and the fundamental principles of the accounting system used to produce the numbers.

a look
forward

The next chapter covers the statement of cash flows. In that chapter, you will learn how to classify cash transactions into one of three categories, including financing activities, investing activities, and operating activities. In addition, the chapter explains how to prepare a statement of cash flows using the T-account method and how to distinguish the direct method of presentation from the indirect method. The level and timing of coverage of the statement of cash flows differ among schools. Accordingly, your instructor may or may not cover this chapter.

SELF-STUDY REVIEW PROBLEM

Financial statements for Stallings Company follow.

INCOME STATEMENTS
for the Years Ended December 31

	2005	2004
Revenues		
Net Sales	$315,000	$259,000
Expenses		
Cost of Goods Sold	(189,000)	(154,000)
General, Selling, and Administrative Expenses	(54,000)	(46,000)
Interest Expense	(4,000)	(4,500)
Income Before Taxes	68,000	54,500
Income Tax Expense (40%)	(27,200)	(21,800)
Net Earnings	$ 40,800	$ 32,700

BALANCE SHEETS AS OF DECEMBER 31

	2005	2004
Assets		
Current Assets		
Cash	$ 6,500	$ 11,500
Accounts Receivable	51,000	49,000
Inventories	155,000	147,500
Total Current Assets	212,500	208,000
Plant and Equipment (net)	187,500	177,000
Total Assets	$400,000	$385,000
Equities		
Liabilities		
Current Liabilities		
Accounts Payable	$ 60,000	$ 81,500
Other	25,000	22,500
Total Current Liabilities	85,000	104,000
Bonds Payable	100,000	100,000
Total Liabilities	185,000	204,000
Stockholders' Equity		
Common Stock (50,000 shares, $3 par)	150,000	150,000
Paid-In Capital in Excess of Par	20,000	20,000
Retained Earnings	45,000	11,000
Total Stockholders' Equity	215,000	181,000
Total Equities	$400,000	$385,000

Required

a. Use horizontal analysis to determine which expense item increased by the highest percentage from 2004 to 2005.

b. Use vertical analysis to determine whether the inventory balance is a higher percentage of total assets in 2004 or 2005.

c. Calculate the following ratios for 2004 and 2005. When data limitations prohibit computing averages, use year-end balances in your calculations.

(1) Net margin

(2) Return on investment

(3) Return on equity

(4) Earnings per share

(5) Price-earnings ratio (market price per share at the end of 2005 and 2004 was $12.04 and $8.86, respectively)

(6) Book value per share of common stock

(7) Times interest earned

(8) Working capital

(9) Current ratio

(10) Acid-test ratio
(11) Accounts receivable turnover
(12) Inventory turnover
(13) Stockholders' equity ratio
(14) Total liabilities to total stockholders' equity

Solution to Requirement a

Income tax expense increased by the greatest percentage. Computations follow.

Cost of goods sold ($189,000 − $154,000) ÷ $154,000 = 22.73%
General, selling, and administrative ($54,000 − $46,000) ÷ $46,000 = 17.39%
Interest expense decreased.
Income tax expense ($27,200 − $21,800) ÷ $21,800 = 24.77%

Solution to Requirement b

2004: $147,500 ÷ $385,000 = 38.31%
2005: $155,000 ÷ $400,000 = 38.75%
Inventory is slightly larger relative to total assets in 2005.

Solution to Requirement c

		2005	2004
1.	$\dfrac{\text{Net income}}{\text{Net sales}}$	$\dfrac{\$40,800}{\$315,000} = 12.95\%$	$\dfrac{\$32,700}{\$259,000} = 12.63\%$
2.	$\dfrac{\text{Net income}}{\text{Average total assets}}$	$\dfrac{\$40,800}{\$392,500} = 10.39\%$	$\dfrac{\$32,700}{\$385,000} = 8.49\%$
3.	$\dfrac{\text{Net income}}{\text{Average total stockholders' equity}}$	$\dfrac{\$40,800}{\$198,000} = 20.61\%$	$\dfrac{\$32,700}{\$181,000} = 18.07\%$
4.	$\dfrac{\text{Net income}}{\text{Average common shares outstanding}}$	$\dfrac{\$40,800}{50,000} = \$0.816$	$\dfrac{\$32,700}{50,000} = \$0.654$
5.	$\dfrac{\text{Market price per share}}{\text{Earnings per share}}$	$\dfrac{\$12.04}{\$0.816} = 14.75 \text{ times}$	$\dfrac{\$8.86}{\$0.654} = 13.55 \text{ times}$
6.	$\dfrac{\text{Stockholders' equity − Preferred rights}}{\text{Average outstanding common shares}}$	$\dfrac{\$215,000}{50,000} = \$4.30$	$\dfrac{\$181,000}{50,000} = \$3.62$
7.	$\dfrac{\text{Net income + Taxes + Interest expense}}{\text{Interest expense}}$	$\dfrac{\$40,800 + \$27,200 + \$4,000}{\$4,000} = 18 \text{ times}$	$\dfrac{\$32,700 + \$21,800 + \$4,500}{\$4,500} = 13.1 \text{ times}$
8.	Current assets − Current liabilities	$\$212,500 − \$85,000 = \$127,500$	$\$208,000 − \$104,000 = \$104,000$
9.	$\dfrac{\text{Current assets}}{\text{Current liabilities}}$	$\dfrac{\$212,500}{\$85,000} = 2.5{:}1$	$\dfrac{\$208,000}{\$104,000} = 2{:}1$
10.	$\dfrac{\text{Quick assets}}{\text{Current liabilities}}$	$\dfrac{\$57,500}{\$85,000} = 0.68{:}1$	$\dfrac{\$60,500}{\$104,000} = 0.58{:}1$
11.	$\dfrac{\text{Net credit sales}}{\text{Average net accounts receivable}}$	$\dfrac{\$315,000}{\$50,000} = 6.3 \text{ times}$	$\dfrac{\$259,000}{\$49,000} = 5.29 \text{ times}$
12.	$\dfrac{\text{Cost of goods sold}}{\text{Average inventory}}$	$\dfrac{\$189,000}{\$151,250} = 1.25 \text{ times}$	$\dfrac{\$154,000}{\$147,500} = 1.04 \text{ times}$
13.	$\dfrac{\text{Stockholders' equity}}{\text{Total equities}}$	$\dfrac{\$215,000}{\$400,000} = 53.75\%$	$\dfrac{\$181,000}{\$385,000} = 47.01\%$
14.	$\dfrac{\text{Total liabilities}}{\text{Stockholders' equity}}$	$\dfrac{\$185,000}{\$215,000} = 86.05\%$	$\dfrac{\$204,000}{\$181,000} = 112.71\%$

KEY TERMS

Absolute amounts *537*
Accounts receivable turnover *542*
Acid-test ratio *542*
Book value per share *549*
Current ratio *541*
Dividend yield *550*
Earnings per share *548*

Horizontal analysis *537*
Information overload *536*
Inventory turnover *543*
Liquidity ratios *541*
Materiality *537*
Net margin *546*
Number of days' sales in inventory *543*

Number of days' sales in receivables *542*
Percentage analysis *538*
Price-earnings ratio *549*
Profitability ratios *546*
Quick ratio *542*
Ratio analysis *540*
Return on assets *547*

Return on equity *548*
Return on investment *547*
Solvency ratios *544*
Trend analysis *538*
Turnover of assets *546*
Vertical analysis *539*
Working capital *541*
Working capital ratio *541*

QUESTIONS

1. Why are ratios and trends used in financial analysis?
2. What do the terms *liquidity* and *solvency* mean?
3. What is apparent from a horizontal presentation of financial statement information? A vertical presentation?
4. What is the significance of inventory turnover, and how is it calculated?
5. What is the difference between the current ratio and the quick ratio? What does each measure?
6. Why are absolute amounts of limited use when comparing firms?
7. What is the difference between return on investment and return on equity?
8. Which ratios are used to measure long-term debt-paying ability? How is each calculated?
9. What are some limitations of the earnings per share figure?
10. What are the components of return on investment? What does each measure?
11. What is information overload?
12. What is the price-earnings ratio? Explain the difference between it and the dividend yield.
13. What environmental factors must be considered in analyzing firms?
14. How do accounting principles affect financial statement analysis?

EXERCISES—SERIES A

L.O. 4 **EXERCISE 13–1A** *Inventory Turnover*

Selected financial information for Collins Company for 2004 follows.

Sales	$1,500,000
Cost of Goods Sold	1,100,000
Merchandise Inventory	
Beginning of Year	250,000
End of Year	300,000

Required

Assuming that the merchandise inventory buildup was relatively constant, how many times did the merchandise inventory turn over during 2004?

L.O. 5 **EXERCISE 13–2A** *Number of Times Bond Interest Earned*

The following data come from the financial records of Haddin Corporation for 2002.

Sales	$1,800,000
Bond Interest Expense	60,000
Income Tax Expense	300,000
Net Income	400,000

Required

How many times was bond interest earned in 2002?

L.O. 4 **EXERCISE 13–3A** *Current Ratio*

Inaya Corporation wrote off a $700 uncollectible account receivable against the $8,400 balance in its allowance account.

Required

Explain the effect of the write-off on Inaya's current ratio.

L.O. 4 **EXERCISE 13–4A** *Working Capital and Current Ratio*

On June 30, 2003, Alpha Company's total current assets were $200,000 and its total current liabilities were $100,000. On July 1, 2003, Alpha issued a short-term note to a bank for $25,000 cash.

Required

a. Compute Alpha's working capital before and after issuing the note.
b. Compute Alpha's current ratio before and after issuing the note.

EXERCISE 13–5A *Working Capital and Current Ratio*

On June 30, 2003, Alpha Company's total current assets were $200,000 and its total current liabilities were $100,000. On July 1, 2003, Alpha issued a long-term note to a bank for $25,000 cash.

Required
a. Compute Alpha's working capital before and after issuing the note.
b. Compute Alpha's current ratio before and after issuing the note.

EXERCISE 13–6A *Horizontal Analysis*

Yoshi Corporation reported the following operating results for two consecutive years.

	2002	2001	Percentage Change
Sales	$1,000,000	$900,000	
Cost of Goods Sold	750,000	600,000	
Gross Margin	250,000	$300,000	
Operating Expenses	205,000	225,000	
Income before Taxes	45,000	$ 75,000	
Income Taxes	17,100	30,000	
Net Income	$ 27,900	$ 45,000	

Required
a. Compute the percentage changes in Yoshi Corporation's income statement components between the two years.
b. Comment on apparent trends revealed by the percentage changes computed in Requirement *a.*

EXERCISE 13–7A *Vertical Analysis*

Kirby Company reported the following operating results for two consecutive years.

2000	Amount	Percent of Sales
Sales	$600,000	
Cost of Goods Sold	400,000	
Gross Margin on Sales	200,000	
Operating Expenses	130,000	
Income before Taxes	70,000	
Income Taxes	30,000	
Net Income	$ 40,000	
2001	**Amount**	**Percent of Sales**
Sales	$580,000	
Cost of Goods Sold	377,000	
Gross Margin on Sales	203,000	
Operating Expenses	150,000	
Income before Taxes	53,000	
Income Taxes	23,000	
Net Income	$ 30,000	

Required
Express each income statement component for each of the two years as a percent of sales.

EXERCISE 13–8A *Ratio Analysis*

The balance sheet for Sims Corporation follows.

Current Assets	$ 500,000
Long-Term Assets (net)	3,180,000
Total Assets	$3,680,000

Current Liabilities	$ 350,000
Long-Term Liabilities	1,960,000
Total Liabilities	$2,310,000
Capital Stock and Retained Earnings	1,370,000
Total Liabilities and Capital	$3,680,000

Required

Compute the following.

Working capital	_____
Current ratio	_____
Liabilities to total assets	_____
Stockholders' equity ratio	_____
Debt/equity ratio	_____

L.O. 7   **EXERCISE 13–9A** *Ratio Analysis*

During 2003, Wooden Corporation reported after-tax net income of $4,737,000. During the year, the number of shares of stock outstanding remained constant at 10,000 of $100 par, 9 percent preferred stock and 400,000 shares of common stock. The company's total stockholders' equity is $23,000,000 at December 31, 2003. Wooden Corporation's common stock was selling at $52 per share at the end of its fiscal year. All dividends for the year have been paid, including $4.80 per share to common stockholders.

Required

Compute the following:

a. Earnings per share

b. Book value per share of common stock

c. Price-earnings ratio

d. Dividend yield

L.O. 2, 3, 4, 5, 6, 7   **EXERCISE 13–10A** *Ratio Analysis*

Required

Match each of the following ratios with the formula used to compute it.

_____	1. Working capital	a.	Net income ÷ Total stockholders' equity
_____	2. Current ratio	b.	Cost of goods sold ÷ Average inventory
_____	3. Quick ratio	c.	Current assets − Current liabilities
_____	4. Accounts receivable turnover	d.	Days in year ÷ Inventory turnover
_____	5. Average collection period	e.	Net income ÷ Total assets
_____	6. Inventory turnover	f.	(Net income − Preferred dividends) ÷ Average outstanding common shares
_____	7. Number of days' sales in inventory	g.	(Current assets − Inventory − Prepaid expenses) ÷ Current liabilities
_____	8. Liabilities to total equity	h.	Total liabilities ÷ Total equity
_____	9. Stockholders' equity ratio	i.	Days in year ÷ Accounts receivable turnover
_____	10. Return on investment	j.	Total stockholders' equity ÷ Total equity
_____	11. Return on equity	k.	Net credit sales ÷ Average net receivables
_____	12. Earnings per share	l.	Current assets ÷ Current liabilities

L.O. 2   **EXERCISE 13–11A** *Horizontal and Vertical Analysis*

Income statements for Posey Company for 2002 and 2003 follow.

	2003	2002
Sales	$242,000	$184,000
Cost of Goods Sold	$150,000	$102,000
Selling Expenses	40,000	22,000
Administrative Expenses	24,000	28,000
Interest Expense	6,000	10,000
Total Expenses	$220,000	$162,000
Income before Taxes	$ 22,000	$ 22,000
Income Taxes Expense	6,000	4,000
Net Income	$ 16,000	$ 18,000

Required

a. Perform a horizontal analysis, showing the percentage change in each income statement component between 2002 and 2003.

b. Perform a vertical analysis, showing each income statement component as a percent of sales for each year.

EXERCISE 13–12A *Ratio Analysis*   **L.O. 2, 3, 4, 5, 6, 7**

Compute the specified ratios using Victor Company's balance sheet for 2001.

Assets	
Cash	$ 7,500
Marketable Securities	4,000
Accounts Receivable	6,500
Inventory	5,500
Property and Equipment	85,000
Accumulated Depreciation	(6,250)
Total Assets	**$102,250**

Equities	
Accounts Payable	$ 4,250
Current Notes Payable	1,750
Mortgage Payable	2,250
Bonds Payable	10,750
Common Stock, $50 Par	55,000
Paid-In Capital in Excess of Par	2,000
Retained Earnings	26,250
Total Equities	**$102,250**

The average number of common stock shares outstanding during 2001 was 880 shares. Net income for the year was $7,500.

Required

Compute each of the following:

a. Current ratio.

b. Earnings per share.

c. Quick (acid-test) ratio.

d. Return on investment.

e. Return on equity.

f. Debt/equity ratio.

EXERCISE 13–13A *Comprehensive Analysis*   **L.O. 4, 5, 6, 7**

Required

Indicate the effect of each of the following transactions on (1) the current ratio, (2) working capital, (3) stockholders' equity, (4) book value per share of common stock, (5) retained earnings.

a. Collected account receivable.

b. Wrote off account receivable.

c. Purchased treasury stock.

d. Purchased inventory on account.

e. Declared cash dividend.

f. Sold merchandise on account at a profit.

g. Issued stock dividend.

h. Paid account payable.

i. Sold building at a loss.

EXERCISE 13–14A *Accounts Receivable Turnover, Inventory Turnover, and Net Margin*   **L.O. 4, 7**

Selected data from Olson Company follow.

Balance Sheet As of December 31		
	2000	1999
Accounts Receivable	$600,000	$564,000
Allowance for Doubtful Accounts	(30,000)	(24,000)
Net Accounts Receivable	$570,000	$540,000
Inventories, Lower of Cost or Market	$720,000	$660,000

Income Statement For the Year Ended December 31		
	2000	1999
Net Credit Sales	$3,000,000	$2,640,000
Net Cash Sales	600,000	480,000
Net Sales	$3,600,000	$3,120,000
Cost of Goods Sold	$2,400,000	$2,160,000
Selling, General, & Administrative Expenses	360,000	324,000
Other Expenses	60,000	36,000
Total Operating Expenses	$2,820,000	$2,520,000

Required

Compute the following.

a. The accounts receivable turnover for 2000.

b. The inventory turnover for 2000.

c. The net margin for 1999.

L.O. 4, 5   EXERCISE 13–15A *Comprehensive Analysis*

The December 31, 2002, balance sheet for Stevenson, Inc., is presented here. These are the only accounts on Stevenson's balance sheet. Amounts indicated by question marks (?) can be calculated using the following additional information.

Assets	
Cash	$ 50,000
Accounts Receivable (net)	?
Inventory	?
Property, Plant, and Equipment (net)	588,000
	$864,000
Liabilities and Stockholders' Equity	
Accounts Payable (trade)	$?
Income Taxes Payable (current)	50,000
Long-Term Debt	?
Common Stock	600,000
Retained Earnings	?
	$?
Additional Information	
Current Ratio (at year end)	1.5 to 1.0
Total Liabilities ÷ Total Stockholders' Equity	0.8
Gross Margin Percent	30%
Inventory Turnover (Cost of Goods Sold ÷ Ending Inventory)	10.5 times
Gross Margin for 2002	$630,000

Required

Determine the following.

a. The balance in trade accounts payable as of December 31, 2002.

b. The balance in retained earnings as of December 31, 2002.

c. The balance in the inventory account as of December 31, 2002.

PROBLEM 13–16A *Vertical Analysis*   L.O. 2

The following percentages apply to Ziff Company for 2002 and 2003.

	2003	2002
Sales	100.0%	100.0%
Cost of Goods Sold	61.0	64.0
Gross Margin	39.0%	36.0%
Selling and Administrative Expense	26.5%	20.5%
Interest Expense	2.5	2.0
Total Expenses	29.0%	22.5%
Income before Taxes	10.0%	13.5%
Income Tax Expense	5.5	7.0
Net Income	4.5%	6.5%

Required
Assuming that sales were $700,000 in 2002 and $900,000 in 2003, prepare income statements for the two years.

PROBLEM 13–17A *Ratio Analysis*   L.O. 5, 6, 7

Lakeshore Company's income statement information follows.

	2000	1999
Net Sales	$630,000	$390,000
Income before Interest and Taxes	165,000	127,500
Net Income after Taxes	83,250	94,500
Bond Interest Expense	13,500	12,000
Stockholders' Equity, December 31 (1998: $300,000)	457,500	352,500
Common Stock, par $50, December 31	390,000	345,000

The average number of shares outstanding was 7,800 for 2000 and 6,900 for 1999.

Required
Compute the following ratios for Lakeshore for 2000 and 1999.
a. Number of times bond interest was earned.
b. Earnings per share based on the average number of shares outstanding.
c. Price-earnings ratio (market prices: 2000, $96 per share; 1999, $116 per share).
d. Return on average equity.
e. Net margin.

PROBLEM 13–18A *Effect of Transactions on Current Ratio and Working Capital*   L.O. 4

Fondren Manufacturing has a current ratio of 3:1 on December 31, 2000. Indicate whether each of the following transactions would increase ($+$), decrease ($-$), or not affect (NA) Fondren's current ratio and its working capital.

Required
a. Paid cash for a trademark.
b. Wrote off an uncollectible account receivable.
c. Sold equipment for cash.
d. Sold merchandise at a profit (cash).
e. Declared a cash dividend.
f. Purchased inventory on account.
g. Scrapped a fully depreciated machine (no gain or loss).
h. Issued a stock dividend.
i. Purchased a machine with a long-term note.
j. Paid a previously declared cash dividend.
k. Collected accounts receivable.
l. Invested in current marketable securities.

L.O. 7   PROBLEM 13–19A *Ratio Analysis*

Selected data for Gillock Company for 2002 and additional information on industry averages follow.

Earnings (net income)		$ 261,000
Preferred Stock (19,800 shares at $50 par, 4%)		$ 990,000
Common Stock (45,000 shares at $1 par, market value $56)		45,000
Paid-in Capital in Excess of Par—Common		720,000
Retained Earnings		843,750
		$2,598,750
Less: Treasury Stock		
Preferred (1,800 shares)	$81,000	
Common (1,800 shares)	36,000	117,000
Total Stockholders' Equity		$2,481,750

Note: Dividends in arrears on preferred stock: $36,000. The preferred stock can be called for $51 per share.

Industry averages	
Earnings per share	$ 5.20
Price-earnings ratio	9.5
Return on equity	11.2%

Required
a. Calculate and compare Gillock Company's ratios with the industry averages.
b. Discuss factors you would consider in deciding whether to invest in the company.

L.O. 2   PROBLEM 13–20A *Supply Missing Balance Sheet Numbers*

The bookkeeper for Pengo's Country Music Bar went insane and left this incomplete balance sheet. Pengo's working capital is $120,000 and its stockholders' equity ratio is 60 percent.

Assets		
Current Assets		
Cash		$ 28,000
Accounts Receivable		56,000
Inventory		(A)
Prepaid Expenses		12,000
Total Current Assets		$ (B)
Long-Term Assets		
Building		$ (C)
Less: Accumulated Depreciation		(52,000)
Total Long-Term Assets		280,000
Total Assets		$ (D)
Equities		
Liabilities		
Current Liabilities		
Accounts Payable		$ (E)
Notes Payable		16,000
Income Tax Payable		14,000
Total Current Liabilities		$50,000
Long-Term Liabilities		
Mortgage Payable		(F)
Total Liabilities		$ (G)
Stockholders' Equity		
Common Stock		140,000
Retained Earnings		(H)
Total Stockholders' Equity		(I)
Total Equities		$ (J)

Required
Complete the balance sheet by supplying the missing amounts.

PROBLEM 13–21A *Ratio Analysis*

L.O. 2, 3, 4, 5, 6, 7

The following financial statements apply to Hayden Company.

	2002	2001
Revenues		
Net Sales	$630,000	$525,000
Other Revenues	12,000	14,000
Total Revenues	$642,000	$539,000
Expenses		
Cost of Goods Sold	$378,000	$309,750
Selling Expenses	64,000	58,000
General and Administrative Expenses	32,000	30,000
Interest Expense	8,000	9,000
Income Tax Expense (40%)	64,000	52,900
Total Expenses	$546,000	$459,650
Earnings from Continuing Operations before Extraordinary Items	96,000	79,350
Extraordinary Gain (net of $8,000 tax)	12,000	0
Net Earnings	$108,000	$ 79,350
Assets		
Current Assets		
Cash	$ 13,000	$ 23,000
Marketable Securities	2,000	3,000
Accounts Receivable	100,000	95,000
Inventories	300,000	290,000
Prepaid Expenses	10,000	5,000
Total Current Assets	$425,000	$416,000
Plant and Equipment (net)	314,000	314,000
Intangibles	61,000	0
Total Assets	$800,000	$730,000
Equities		
Liabilities		
Current Liabilities		
Accounts Payable	$120,000	$163,000
Other	50,000	45,000
Total Current Liabilities	$170,000	$208,000
Bonds Payable	200,000	200,000
Total Liabilities	$370,000	$408,000
Stockholders' Equity		
Common Stock ($3 par)	300,000	300,000
Paid-In Capital in Excess of Par	40,000	40,000
Retained Earnings	90,000	(18,000)
Total Stockholders' Equity	$430,000	$322,000
Total Equities	$800,000	$730,000

Required

Calculate the following ratios for 2001 and 2002. When data limitations prohibit computing averages, use year-end balances in your calculations.

a. Net margin
b. Return on investment
c. Return on equity
d. Earnings per share
e. Price-earnings ratio (market prices at the end of 2002 and 2001 were $5.94 and $4.77, respectively)
f. Book value per share of common stock
g. Times bond interest earned
h. Working capital
i. Current ratio
j. Quick (acid-test) ratio
k. Accounts receivable turnover
l. Inventory turnover
m. Stockholders' equity ratio
n. Total liabilities to total stockholders' equity

L.O. 2   **PROBLEM 13–22A** *Horizontal Analysis*

Financial statements for Kapowski Company follow.

KAPOWSKI COMPANY
Balance Sheets
As of December 31

	2003	2002
Assets		
Current Assets		
Cash	$ 47,000	$ 36,000
Marketable Securities	62,000	18,000
Accounts Receivable (net)	160,000	140,000
Inventories	400,000	430,000
Prepaid Items	80,000	30,000
Total Current Assets	$ 749,000	$ 654,000
Investments	$ 80,000	$ 60,000
Plant (net)	800,000	765,000
Land	86,000	73,000
Total Assets	$1,715,000	$1,552,000
Equities		
Liabilities		
Current Liabilities		
Notes Payable	$ 50,000	$ 20,000
Accounts Payable	320,000	300,000
Salaries Payable	62,000	49,000
Total Current Liabilities	$ 432,000	$ 369,000
Noncurrent Liabilities		
Bonds Payable	$ 300,000	$ 300,000
Other	100,000	80,000
Total Noncurrent Liabilities	$400,000	$380,000
Total Liabilities	$832,000	$749,000
Stockholders' Equity		
Preferred Stock, (par value $100, 5% cumulative, non-participating; 2,000 shares authorized and issued no dividends in arrears)	$ 200,000	$ 200,000
Common Stock ($5 par; 50,000 shares authorized; 30,000 shares issued)	150,000	150,000
Paid-In Capital in excess of par—Preferred	30,000	30,000
Paid-In Capital in excess of par—Common	100,000	100,000
Retained Earnings	403,000	323,000
Total Stockholders' Equity	$ 883,000	$ 803,000
Total Equities	$1,715,000	$1,552,000

KAPOWSKI COMPANY
Statements of Income and Retained Earnings
For the Years Ended December 31

	2003	2002
Revenues		
Sales (net)	$700,000	$630,000
Other Revenues	13,000	15,000
Total Revenues	$713,000	$645,000
Expenses		
Cost of Goods Sold	$350,000	$308,700
Selling, General, and Administrative	165,000	150,000
Interest Expense	23,000	21,500
Income Tax Expense (40%)	70,000	65,920
Total Expenses	$608,000	$546,120
Net Earnings (Net Income)	$105,000	$98,880
Retained Earnings, January 1	323,000	249,120
Less: Preferred Stock Dividends	10,000	10,000
Common Stock Dividends	15,000	15,000
Retained Earnings, December 31	$403,000	$323,000

Required
Prepare a horizontal analysis of both the balance sheet and income statement.

PROBLEM 13–23A *Ratio Analysis*

L.O. 2, 3, 4, 5, 6, 7

Required
Use the financial statements for Kapowski Company from Problem 13–22A to calculate the following ratios for 2003 and 2002.
a. Working capital
b. Current ratio
c. Quick ratio
d. Receivables turnover (beginning receivables at January 1, 2002, were $140,000.)
e. Number of days' sales in receivables (average collection period)
f. Inventory turnover (beginning inventory at January 1, 2002, was $420,000.)
g. Number of days' sales in inventory
h. Stockholders' equity ratio
i. Debt/equity ratio
j. Number of times bond interest earned
k. Plant assets to long-term debt
l. Net margin
m. Turnover of assets
n. Return on investment
o. Return on equity
p. Earnings per share
q. Book value per share of common stock
r. Price-earnings ratio (market price per share: 2002, $35.25; 2003, $37.50)
s. Dividend yield on common stock

PROBLEM 13–24A *Vertical Analysis*

L.O. 2

Required
Use the financial statements for Kapowski Company from Problem 13–22A to perform a vertical analysis of both the balance sheets and income statements for 2003 and 2002.

EXERCISES—SERIES B

EXERCISE 13–1B *Inventory Turnover*

L.O. 4

Selected financial information for Zeller Company for 2003 follows.

Sales	$2,750,000
Cost of Goods Sold	2,400,000
Merchandise Inventory	
Beginning of Year	340,000
End of Year	620,000

Required
Assuming that the merchandise inventory buildup was relatively constant, how many times did the merchandise inventory turn over during 2003?

EXERCISE 13–2B *Number of Times Bond Interest Earned*

L.O. 5

The following data come from the financial records of the Sharit Corporation for 2002.

Sales	$5,000,000
Bond Interest Expense	250,000
Income Tax	700,000
Net Income	1,300,000

Required

How many times was bond interest earned in 2002?

L.O. 4   **EXERCISE 13–3B** *Current Ratio*

Hargrove Corporation purchased $500 of merchandise on account.

Required

Explain the effect of the purchase on Hargrove's current ratio.

L.O. 4   **EXERCISE 13–4B** *Working Capital and Current Ratio*

On October 31, 2003, Westside Company's total current assets were $250,000 and its total current liabilities were $100,000. On November 1, 2003, Westside purchased marketable securities for $50,000 cash.

Required

a. Compute Westside's working capital before and after the securities purchase.
b. Compute Westside's current ratio before and after the securities purchase.

L.O. 4   **EXERCISE 13–5B** *Working Capital and Current Ratio*

On October 31, 2003, Westside Company's total current assets were $250,000 and its total current liabilities were $100,000. On November 1, 2003, Westside bought manufacturing equipment for $50,000 cash.

Required

a. Compute Westside's working capital before and after the equipment purchase.
b. Compute Westside's current ratio before and after the equipment purchase.

L.O. 2   **EXERCISE 13–6B** *Horizontal Analysis*

Nagoya Corporation reported the following operating results for two consecutive years.

	2003	2002	Percentage Change
Sales	$2,200,000	$2,000,000	
Cost of Goods Sold	1,320,000	1,270,000	
Gross Margin	880,000	730,000	
Operating Expenses	375,000	325,000	
Income before Taxes	505,000	405,000	
Income Taxes	225,000	158,000	
Net Income	$ 280,000	$ 247,000	

Required

a. Compute the percentage changes in Nagoya Corporation's income statement components for the two years.
b. Comment on apparent trends revealed by the percentage changes computed in Requirement *a*.

L.O. 2   **EXERCISE 13–7B** *Vertical Analysis*

Bangui Company reported the following operating results for two consecutive years.

2000	Amount	Percentage of Sales
Sales	$500,000	
Cost of Goods Sold	320,000	
Gross Margin	180,000	
Operating Expenses	95,000	
Income before Taxes	85,000	
Income Taxes	27,000	
Net Income	$ 58,000	

2001	Amount	Percentage of Sales
Sales	$640,000	
Cost of Goods Sold	408,000	
Gross Margin	232,000	
Operating Expenses	115,000	
Income before Taxes	117,000	
Income Taxes	31,000	
Net Income	$ 86,000	

Required

Express each income statement component for each of the two years as a percentage of sales.

EXERCISE 13–8B *Ratio Analysis*

L.O. 2

Balance sheet data for the Condrey Corporation follows.

Current Assets	$100,000
Long-Term Assets (Net)	700,000
Total Assets	$800,000
Current Liabilities	$ 75,000
Long-Term Liabilities	225,000
Total Liabilities	300,000
Common Stock and Retained Earnings	500,000
Total Liabilities and Stockholders' Equity	$800,000

Required

Compute the following:
a. Working capital
b. Current ratio
c. Liabilities to total assets
d. Stockholders' equity ratio
e. Debt/equity ratio

EXERCISE 13–9B *Ratio Analysis*

L.O. 7

During 2001, Markus Corporation reported net income after taxes of $960,000. During the year, the number of shares of stock outstanding remained constant at 20,000 shares of $100 par 8 percent preferred stock and 200,000 shares of common stock. The company's total equities at December 31, 2001, were $3,500,000, which included $640,000 of liabilities. The common stock was selling for $40 per share at the end of the year. All dividends for the year were declared and paid, including $3.60 per share to common stockholders.

Required

Compute the following.
a. Earnings per share
b. Book value per share
c. Price-Earnings ratio
d. Dividend yield

EXERCISE 13–10B *Ratio Analysis*

L.O. 2, 3, 4, 5, 6, 7

Match each of the following ratios with its formula.

_____ 1. Price-Earnings ratio		a. Total liabilities ÷ Total stockholders' equity
_____ 2. Dividend yield		b. Current assets ÷ Current liabilities
_____ 3. Book value per share		c. Days in the year ÷ Accounts receivable turnover
_____ 4. Plant assets to long-term liabilities		d. (Net income − Preferred dividends) ÷ Average outstanding common shares
_____ 5. Number of times bond interest is earned		e. (Stockholders' equity − Preferred rights) ÷ Average outstanding common shares
_____ 6. Earnings per share		f. Days in the year ÷ Inventory turnover
_____ 7. Net margin		g. Dividends per share ÷ Market price per share
_____ 8. Debt/equity ratio		h. Net plant assets ÷ Long-term liabilities
_____ 9. Current ratio		i. Market price per share ÷ Earnings per share
_____ 10. Turnover of assets		j. Net income ÷ Net sales
_____ 11. Average collection period		k. Net sales ÷ Total assets
_____ 12. Number of days' sales in inventory		l. Income before taxes and bond interest expense ÷ Bond interest expense

L.O. 2   **EXERCISE 13–11B** *Horizontal and Vertical Analysis*

Sathos Company reported the following operating results for 2002 and 2003.

	2003	2002
Sales	$240,000	$216,000
Cost of Goods Sold	126,000	114,000
Selling Expenses	15,000	12,000
Administrative Expenses	27,000	25,000
Interest Expense	4,000	5,000
Total Expenses	172,000	156,000
Income before Taxes	68,000	60,000
Income Taxes Expense	14,000	12,000
Net Income	$ 54,000	$ 48,000

Required

a. Perform a horizontal analysis, showing the percentage change in each income statement component between 2002 and 2003.

b. Perform a vertical analysis, showing each income statement component as a percent of sales for each year.

L.O. 2, 3, 4, 5, 6, 7   **EXERCISE 13–12B** *Ratio Analysis*

Compute the specified ratios using the following December 31, 2003, statement of financial position for Ensley Company.

Assets	
Cash	$ 16,000
Marketable Securities	4,500
Accounts Receivable	36,400
Inventory	56,100
Property and Equipment	75,000
Accumulated Depreciation	(12,000)
Total Assets	$176,000

Equities	
Accounts Payable	$19,600
Current Notes Payable	3,400
Mortgage Payable	31,000
Bonds Payable	21,000
Common Stock	64,000
Retained Earnings	37,000
Total Equities	$176,000

The average number of common shares outstanding during 2003 was 1,500. Net earnings for the year were $24,000.

Required

Compute each of the following:

a. Current ratio
b. Earnings per share
c. Acid-test ratio
d. Return on investment
e. Return on equity
f. Debt/equity ratio

EXERCISE 13–13B *Comprehensive Analysis*

L.O. 4, 5, 6, 7

The following is a list of transactions.

a. Paid cash for short-term marketable securities.
b. Purchased a computer, issuing a short-term note for the purchase price.
c. Purchased factory equipment, issuing a long-term note for the purchase price.
d. Sold merchandise on account at a profit.
e. Paid cash on accounts payable.
f. Received cash from issuing common stock.
g. Sold a factory for cash at a profit.
h. Purchased raw materials on account.
i. Paid cash for property taxes on administrative buildings.

Required

Indicate the effect of each of the preceding transactions on (a) the quick ratio, (b) working capital, (c) stockholders' equity, (d) the debt/equity ratio, (e) retained earnings.

EXERCISE 13–14B *Accounts Receivable Turnover, Inventory Turnover, and Net Margin*

L.O. 4, 7

Selected data from Farrel Company follow.

Balance Sheet Data As of December 31		
	2001	2000
Accounts Receivable	$320,000	$300,000
Allowance for Doubtful Accounts	(16,000)	(14,000)
Net Accounts Receivable	$304,000	$286,000
Inventories, Lower of Cost or Market	$200,000	$210,000

Income Statement Data Year Ended December 31		
	2001	2000
Net Credit Sales	$2,000,000	$1,500,000
Net Cash Sales	400,000	300,000
Net Sales	$2,400,000	$1,800,000
Cost of Goods Sold	$1,400,000	$1,100,000
Selling, General, and Administrative Expenses	200,000	140,000
Other Expenses	100,000	80,000
Total Operating Expenses	$1,700,000	$1,320,000

Required

Compute the following.

a. The accounts receivable turnover for 2001.
b. The inventory turnover for 2001.
c. The net margin for 2000.

L.O. 4, 5   EXERCISE 13–15B *Comprehensive Analysis*

December 31, 2002, balance sheet data for Lehman Company follow. All accounts are represented. Amounts indicated by question marks (?) can be calculated using the following additional information.

Assets	
Cash	$ 15,000
Accounts Receivable (net)	?
Inventory	?
Property, Plant, and Equipment (net)	278,000
	$?
Liabilities and Stockholders' Equity	
Accounts Payable (trade)	$ 26,000
Income Taxes Payable (current)	14,000
Long-Term Debt	?
Common Stock	160,000
Retained Earnings	?
	$?
Additional Information	
Quick ratio (at year end)	1.3 to 1
Working Capital	$42,000
Inventory Turnover (Cost of goods sold ÷ Ending Inventory)	12 times
Debt/Equity Ratio	0.8
Gross Margin for 2002	$126,000

Required

Determine the following.

a. The balance in accounts receivable as of December 31, 2002.
b. The turnover of assets for 2002.
c. The balance of long-term debt as of December 31, 2002.
d. The balance in retained earnings as of December 2002.

PROBLEMS—SERIES B

L.O. 2   PROBLEM 13–16B *Vertical Analysis*

Giodano Corporation's controller has prepared the following vertical analysis for the president.

	2003	2002
Sales	100.0%	100.0%
Cost of Goods Sold	57.0	54.0
Gross Margin	43.0%	46.0%
Selling and Administrative Expense	18.0%	20.0%
Interest Expense	2.8	4.0
Total Expenses	20.8%	24.0%
Income before Taxes	22.2%	22.0%
Income Tax Expense	10.0	8.0
Net Income	12.2%	14.0%

Required

Sales were $600,000 in 2002 and $960,000 in 2003. Convert the analysis to income statements for the two years.

L.O. 5, 6, 7   PROBLEM 13–17B *Ratio Analysis*

Information from Taylor Company's financial statements follows.

	2001	2000
Net Sales	$1,800,000	$1,250,000
Income before Interest and Taxes	400,000	325,000
Net Income after Taxes	175,000	120,000
Bond Interest Expense	45,000	30,000
Stockholders' Equity, December 31 (1999: $600,000)	900,000	750,000
Common Stock, Par $30, December 31	525,000	450,000

Average number of shares outstanding was 16,000 for 2001 and 15,000 for 2000.

Required

Compute the following ratios for Taylor Company for 2001 and 2000.

a. Number of times bond interest was earned.

b. Earnings per share based on the average number of shares outstanding.

c. Price-earnings ratio (market prices: 2001, $75 per share; 2000, $60 per share).

d. Return on average equity.

e. Net margin.

PROBLEM 13–18B *Effect of Transactions on Current Ratio and Working Capital*   **L.O. 4**

Bowden Company has a current ratio of 2:1 on June 30, 2003. Indicate whether each of the following transactions would increase (+), decrease (−), or not affect (NA) Bowden's current ratio and its working capital.

Required

a. Issued 10-year bonds for $100,000 cash.

b. Paid cash to settle an account payable.

c. Sold merchandise for more than cost.

d. Recognized depreciation on plant equipment.

e. Purchased a machine by issuing a long-term note payable.

f. Purchased merchandise inventory on account.

g. Received customer payment on accounts receivable.

h. Paid cash for federal income tax expense (assume that the expense has not been previously accrued).

i. Declared cash dividend payable in one month.

j. Received cash for interest on a long-term note receivable (assume that interest has not been previously accrued).

k. Received cash from issuing a short-term note payable.

l. Traded a truck for a sedan.

PROBLEM 13–19B *Ratio Analysis*   **L.O. 7**

Selected data for Higgins Company for 1999 and additional information on industry averages follow.

Earnings (net income)		$ 210,000
Preferred Stock (20,000 shares at $35 par, 6%)		$ 700,000
Common Stock (40,500 shares at $10 par, market value $38)		405,000
Paid-in Capital in Excess of par—common		450,000
Retained Earnings		600,000
		$2,155,000
Less: Treasury Stock		
Preferred (1,000 shares)	$36,000	
Common (500 shares)	16,000	52,000
Total Stockholders' Equity		$2,103,000

Note: Dividends in arrears on preferred stock: $39,900. The preferred stock can be called for $46 per share.

Industry averages	
Earnings per share	$2.50
Price-earnings ratio	8
Return on equity	7.3%

Required

a. Calculate and compare Higgins Company's ratios with the industry averages.

b. Discuss factors you would consider in deciding whether to invest in the company.

L.O. 2   PROBLEM 13–20B *Supply Missing Balance Sheet Numbers*

Candace Lanier discovered a piece of wet and partially burned balance sheet after her office was destroyed by fire. She could recall a current ratio of 1.75 and a stockholders' equity ratio of 55 percent.

Assets	
Current Assets	
Cash	$ 50,000
Accounts Receivable	(A)
Inventory	84,000
Prepaid Expenses	18,000
Total Current Assets	$ (B)
Long-Term Assets	
Building	$ (C)
Less: Accumulated Depreciation	(60,000)
Total Long-Term Assets	$360,000
Total Assets	$ (D)
Equities	
Liabilities	
Current Liabilities	
Accounts Payable	$ 84,000
Notes Payable	(E)
Income Tax Payable	36,000
Total Current Liabilities	$160,000
Long-Term Liabilities	
Bonds Payable	90,000
Mortgage Payable	(F)
Total Liabilities	$ (G)
Stockholders' Equity	
Common Stock	$180,000
Retained Earnings	(H)
Total Stockholders' Equity	(I)
Total Equities	$ (J)

Required

Complete the balance sheet by supplying the missing amounts.

L.O. 2, 3, 4, 5, 6, 7   PROBLEM 13–21B *Ratio Analysis*

The following financial statements apply to Arichbald Appliances, Inc.

ARICHBALD APPLIANCES, INC. Balance Sheets As of December 31		
	2002	2001
Assets		
Current Assets		
Cash	$ 196,100	$ 152,000
Marketable Securities	40,000	30,000
Accounts Receivable (net)	186,000	180,000
Inventories	300,000	320,000
Prepaid Expenses	45,000	23,000
Total Current Assets	$ 767,100	$ 705,000
Investments	200,000	200,000
Plant (net)	400,000	390,000
Other	100,000	90,000
Total Assets	$1,467,100	$1,385,000

continued

Equities		
Liabilities		
Current Liabilities		
Notes Payable	$ 10,000	$ 15,000
Accounts Payable	165,000	150,000
Other	60,000	30,000
Total Current Liabilities	$ 235,000	$ 195,000
Noncurrent Liabilities		
Bonds Payable	250,000	250,000
Other	60,000	30,000
Total Noncurrent Liabilities	$ 310,000	$ 280,000
Total Liabilities	$ 545,000	$ 475,000
Stockholders' Equity		
Preferred Stock ($100 par, 7% cumulative, non-participating; $100 liquidating value; 1,000 shares authorized and issued; no dividends in arrears)	$ 100,000	$ 100,000
Common Stock ($10 par; 50,000 shares authorized; 20,000 shares issued)	200,000	200,000
Paid-In Capital in excess of par—Preferred	60,000	6,000
Paid-In Capital in excess of par—Common	200,000	200,000
Retained Earnings	362,100	404,000
Total Stockholders' Equity	$ 922,100	$ 910,000
Total Equities	$1,467,100	$1,385,000

ARCHIBALD APPLIANCES, INC.

Statements of Income and Retained Earnings

For the Years Ended December 31

	2002	2001
Revenues		
Sales (net)	$400,000	$380,000
Other Revenues	12,000	7,000
Total Revenues	$412,000	$387,000
Expenses		
Cost of Goods Sold	$232,000	$216,600
Selling, General, and Administrative	115,000	96,000
Bond Interest Expense	16,500	16,000
Income Tax Expense (40%)	19,400	23,360
Total Expenses	$382,900	$351,960
Net Earnings (net income)	$ 29,100	$ 35,040
Retained Earnings, January 1	350,000	331,960
Less: Preferred Stock Dividends	7,000	7,000
Common Stock Dividends	10,000	10,000
Retained Earnings, December 31	$362,100	$350,000

Required

Calculate the following ratios for 2002.

a. Working capital

b. Current ratio

c. Quick ratio

d. Accounts receivable turnover

e. Average collection period

f. Inventory turnover

g. Number of days' sales in inventory

h. Stockholders' equity ratio

i. Debt/equity ratio

j. Times bond interest earned

k. Plant assets to long-term debt

l. Net margin
m. Turnover of assets
n. Return on investment
o. Return on equity
p. Earnings per share
q. Book value
r. Price-earnings ratio (market price: $13.26)
s. Dividend yield on common stock

L.O. 2, 3, 4, 5, 6, 7   **PROBLEM 13–22B** *Ratio Analysis*

Berger Company's stock is quoted at $16 per share at December 31, 2003 and 2002. Berger's financial statements follow.

BERGER COMPANY Balance Sheets As of December 31 (In thousands)		
	2003	**2002**
Assets		
Current Assets		
Cash	$ 1,750	$ 1,800
Marketable Securities at cost which approximates market	6,500	5,500
Accounts Receivable, net of allowance for doubtful accounts	52,500	47,500
Inventories, lower of cost or market	63,000	77,000
Prepaid Expenses	1,250	1,200
Total Current Assets	$125,000	$133,000
Property, Plant, and Equipment, net of accumulated depreciation	155,500	154,000
Investments	1,000	1,500
Long-Term Receivables	7,000	8,000
Goodwill and Patents, net of accumulated amortization	3,000	3,250
Other Assets	3,500	4,250
Total Assets	$295,000	$304,000
Liabilities and Stockholders' Equity		
Current Liabilities		
Notes Payable	$ 2,500	$ 7,500
Accounts Payable	19,000	24,000
Accrued Expenses	12,250	13,500
Income Taxes Payable	500	500
Payments Due within one year	3,250	3,500
Total Current Liabilities	$ 37,500	$ 49,000
Long-Term Debt	84,500	90,000
Deferred Income Taxes	37,000	33,500
Other Liabilities	4,500	4,000
Total Liabilities	$163,500	$176,500
Stockholders' Equity		
Common Stock, $1 par value; 10,000,000 shares authorized and 5,000,000 shares issued and outstanding	$ 5,000	$ 5,000
5% Cumulative Preferred Stock, par value $100 per share; $100 liquidating value; authorized 25,000 shares; issued and outstanding 20,000 shares	2,000	2,000
Additional Paid-In Capital, common	53,500	53,500
Retained Earnings	71,000	67,000
Total Stockholders' Equity	$131,500	$127,500
Total Liabilities and Stockholders' Equity	$295,000	$304,000

Required
Based on the preceding information, compute the following for 2003 only.
a. Current ratio
b. Quick (acid-test) ratio
c. Number of days' sales in average receivables (average collection period), assuming a business year consisting of 300 days and all sales on account
d. Inventory turnover
e. Book value per share of common stock

BERGER COMPANY
Statements of Income and Retained Earnings
For the Years Ended December 31
(in thousands)

	2003	2002
Net Sales	$300,000	$250,000
Costs and Expenses		
Cost of Goods Sold	245,000	200,000
Selling, General, and Administrative Expenses	33,000	30,000
Other	3,500	3,000
Total Costs and Expenses	$281,500	$233,000
Income Before Income Taxes	$ 18,500	$ 17,000
Income Taxes	8,400	7,900
Net Income	$ 10,100	$ 9,100
Retained Earnings at Beginning of Period	67,000	63,000
Less: Dividends on Common Stock	6,000	5,000
Dividends on Preferred Stock	100	100
Retained Earnings at End of Period	$ 71,000	$ 67,000

f. Earnings per share on common stock
g. Price-earnings ratio on common stock
h. Stockholders' equity ratio
i. Return on investment
j. Return on equity

PROBLEM 13–23B *Horizontal Analysis*   **L.O. 2**

Required
Use the financial statements for Berger Company from Problem 13–22B to perform a horizontal analysis of both the balance sheet and income statement for 2003 and 2002.

PROBLEM 13–24B *Vertical Analysis*   **L.O. 2**

Required
Use the financial statements for Berger Company from Problem 13–22B to perform a vertical analysis (based on total assets, total equities, and sales) of both the balance sheets and income statements for 2003 and 2002.

ANALYZE, THINK, COMMUNICATE

BUSINESS APPLICATIONS CASE *Horizontal Analysis*   **ATC 13–1**

During 1997, the Philip Morris Company reached agreements with the states of Mississippi, Florida, and Texas to make current and future payments related to health care costs that these states had incurred to treat certain illnesses of smokers. As a result, on its 1997 income statement, Philip Morris recognized the expense settlement charges for $1.457 billion. This type of expense had not been recognized in 1995 or 1996. The settlement charges were included in operating income; they were *not* classified as extraordinary. Philip Morris's operating incomes, before subtracting income taxes, for 1995, 1996, and 1997 were as follows.

1995	1996	1997
$9.347 billion	$10.683 billion	$10.611 billion

Required
a. Compute the percentage growth in Philip Morris's operating income before taxes from 1995 to 1996 and from 1996 to 1997.
b. Determine what Philip Morris's operating income before taxes would have been in 1997 if there had been no settlement charges expense. Using this revised number, compute the percentage growth in operating income before taxes from 1996 to 1997.

c. Assuming Philip Morris experiences the same average growth rate in earnings from 1997 to 1998 that it did from 1995 to 1996 to 1997, develop a rough estimate of its 1998 operating income before taxes under two separate assumptions:
   (1) No settlement charges were shown in 1998.
   (2) The settlement charges in 1998 are the same amount as they were in 1997.

ATC 13–2 GROUP ASSIGNMENT *Ratio Analysis and Logic*

Presented here are selected data from the 10-K reports of four companies for the 1997 fiscal year. The four companies, in alphabetical order, are

BellSouth Corporation, a telephone company that operates in the southeastern United States.
Caterpillar, Inc., a manufacturer of heavy machinery.
Dollar General Corporation, a company that owns Dollar General Stores discount stores.
Tiffany & Company, a company that operates high-end jewelry stores.

The data, presented in the order of the amount of sales, are as follows. Dollar amounts are in millions.

	A	B	C	D
Sales	$20,561	$18,110	$2,627.3	$1,017.6
Cost of goods sold	6,254	13,374	1,885.2	453.4
Net earnings	3,261	1,665	144.6	72.8
Inventory or	NA	2,603	632.0	386.4
Materials and supplies	398	NA	NA	NA
Accounts receivable	4,750	3,331	0	99.5
Total assets	36,301	20,756	914.8	827.1

Required

a. Divide the class into groups of four or five students per group and then organize the groups into four sections. Assign Task 1 to the first section of groups, Task 2 to the second section, Task 3 to the third section, and Task 4 to the fourth section.

Group Tasks

(1) Assume that you represent BellSouth Corporation. Identify the set of financial data (Column A, B, C, or D) that relates to your company.
(2) Assume that you represent Caterpillar, Inc. Identify the set of financial data (Column A, B, C, or D) that relates to your company.
(3) Assume that you represent Dollar General Corporation. Identify the set of financial data (Column A, B, C, or D) that relates to your company.
(4) Assume that you represent Tiffany & Company. Identify the set of financial data (Column A, B, C, or D) that relates to your company.

Hint: Use a gross margin ratio (gross margin ÷ sales), a net margin ratio (net income ÷ sales), and return on assets (net income ÷ total assets) to facilitate identifying the financial data related to your particular company.

b. Select a representative from each section. Have the representatives explain the rationale for the group's selection. The explanation should include a set of ratios that support the group's conclusion.

ATC 13–3 RESEARCH ASSIGNMENT *Different Presentation Formats*

The August 10, 1998, issue of *Business Week* includes the article "Nokia" (p. 54). Read this article and complete the following requirements.

Required

a. Comment on the various ways that financial statement information is presented in this article.
b. Does the article focus on horizontal or vertical analysis? Explain why you think the article chose the focus you have identified.
c. Provide some examples of information presented in absolute dollar amounts and in percentages. Explain why a reader may be interested in data that are presented in both absolute and percentage values.

ATC 13–4 WRITING ASSIGNMENT *Interpreting Ratios*

Following are the debt to assets, return on assets, and return on equity ratios for four companies from two different industries. The range of interest rates each company was paying on its long-term debt is provided. Each of these public companies is a leader in its particular industry, and the data are for the fiscal years ending in 1997. All numbers are percentages.

	Debt to Assets*	Return on Assets	Return on Equity	Interest Rates
Banking Industry				
Wachovia Corporation	92	1.0	11.5	5.7–7.0
Wells Fargo & Co.	87	1.2	9.0	6.1–11.0
Home Construction Industry				
Pulte Corporation	62	2.5	6.5	7.0–10.1
Toll Brothers, Inc.	66	5.8	16.9	7.8–10.5

*Debt to assets ratio is defined as total liabilities divided by total assets.

Required

a. Based only on the debt to assets ratios, the banking companies appear to have the most financial risk. Generally, companies that have more financial risk are charged higher interest rates. Write a brief explanation of why the banking companies can borrow money at lower interest rates than the construction companies.

b. Explain why the return on equity ratio for Wachovia is more than 10 times higher than its return on assets ratio, and Pulte's return on equity ratio is less than 3 times higher than its return on assets ratio.

ETHICAL DILEMMA *Making the Ratios Look Good*

ATC 13–5

J. Talbot is the accounting manager for Kolla Waste Disposal Corporation. Kolla is having its worst financial year since its inception. The company is expected to report a net loss. In the midst of such bad news, Ms. Talbot surprised the company president, Mr. Winston, by suggesting that the company write off approximately 25 percent of its garbage trucks. Mr. Winston responded by noting that the trucks could still be operated for another two or three years. Ms. Talbot replied, "We may use them for two or three more years, but you couldn't sell them on the street if you had to. Who wants to buy a bunch of old garbage trucks and besides, it will make next year's financials so sweet. No one will care about the additional write-off this year. We are already showing a loss. Who will care if we lose a little bit more?"

Required

a. How will the write-off affect the following year's return on assets ratio?

b. How will the write-off affect the asset and income growth percentages?

c. Would writing off the garbage trucks violate any of the standards of ethical conduct shown in Exhibit 1–13 of Chapter 1?

SPREADSHEET ASSIGNMENT *Using Excel*

ATC 13–6

Tomkung Corporation's 2003 income statements are presented in the following spreadsheet.

Required
Construct a spreadsheet to conduct horizontal analysis of the income statements for 2003 and 2002.

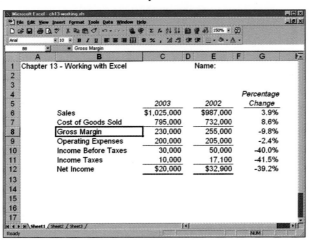

SPREADSHEET ASSIGNMENT *Mastering Excel*

ATC 13–7

Refer to the data in ATC 13–6.

Required
Construct a spreadsheet to conduct vertical analysis for both years, 2003 and 2002.

Statement of Cash Flows

Learning Objectives

After completing this chapter, you should be able to:

1 Identify the types of business events that are reported in the three sections of the statement of cash flows.

2 Convert an accrual account balance to its cash equivalent.

3 Prepare a statement of cash flows using the T-account method.

4 Explain how cash flow from operating activity reported under the indirect method differs from that reported under the direct method.

5 Explain how the classifications used on the statement of cash flows could provide misleading information to decision makers.

the *curious* accountant

A vendor's acceptance of credit and debit cards is expensive. Normally, the credit card company charges a fee by discounting the amount paid to the vendor for each charge. For example, suppose that the U.S. Postal Service (USPS) accepts a charge card as payment for $100 of stamps. When the USPS presents the credit card receipt to the credit card company for payment, the company pays USPS less than $100, perhaps $96. The actual discount rate depends on individual agreements between credit card companies and their customers. In this case, the USPS receives only $96 for $100 worth of stamps. Even so, the credit card customer must pay the bank $100. The $4 difference between the amount that the bank gave USPS and the amount that the customer paid the USPS is the fee that the bank charges for providing credit services. Incidentally, the credit card customer usually is required to pay the bank interest if the credit balance remains outstanding after the payment due date and may pay an annual fee. At a minimum, the USPS must pay a fee to enable its customers to pay for purchases with their charge cards. Because the USPS has a virtual monopoly on regular delivery mail, why is it willing to pay fees to permit customers to use credit cards? Why doesn't the agency accept only cash or checks?

Worldwide growth in capitalism has created a highly competitive, global business environment. Managers have responded by using technology to increase productivity. They employ sophisticated techniques to more accurately measure and control cost. Accordingly, they are able to identify and eliminate nonprofitable products and to promote those products that maximize profitability. Accounting managers work with engineers to develop designs to make the manufacturing process more efficient. Managers seek to identify and eliminate nonvalue-added

233

activities, and they direct attention to the development of quality control procedures that reduce cost and enhance customer satisfaction. This chapter focuses on the new and emerging business practices employed by world-class companies.

■ Development of a Single Companywide Cost Driver

LO 1 Understand the limitations associated with using direct labor hours as a single companywide overhead allocation rate.

Traditional cost systems were created when the manufacturing process was labor intensive. In most cases, indirect manufacturing costs were relatively small and highly correlated with the use of labor. In other words, products using a high level of labor consumed a high amount of overhead. Given this correlation, the number of labor hours constituted an effective cost driver for the allocation of overhead costs. To illustrate, suppose that production workers spent an eight-hour day working on two jobs. Job 1 required two hours to complete, and Job 2 required six hours. Now suppose that $120 of utilities were consumed during the day. How much of the $120 should be assigned to each job? The utility cost cannot be directly traced to each specific job, but it is likely that the job that required more labor also consumed a larger part of the utility cost. For example, workers consume more heat, lights, water, and so on the longer they work on a job. Using this line of reasoning, it is rational to allocate the utility cost to the two jobs on the basis of *direct labor hours*. Specifically, the utility cost could be allocated at the rate of $15 per hour ($120 ÷ 8 hours). Job 1 could be assigned $30 of the total cost ($15 per hour × 2 hours), and the remaining $90 of cost ($15 × 6 hours) could be assigned to Job 2.

Just as direct labor drives the cost of utilities, it also drives many other indirect costs. Consider the depreciation charges on the tools used in the process of completing the jobs. The more time worked, the more the tools are used. Accordingly, direct labor hours could be an effective cost driver (i.e., allocation base) for the depreciation expense associated with tool usage. Similar arguments could be made for supervisory salaries, supplies, manufacturing rent expense, and so forth. Indeed, many companies invoked this rationale to justify the use of direct labor hours as the *sole basis* for the establishment of a **companywide allocation rate.** These companies used the labor-based, companywide overhead rate to allocate all overhead costs to their products or other cost objects. Clearly, using one base for all overhead costs caused some degree of inaccuracy in the measurement of some cost objects. Remember, however, that in the labor-intensive environment that spawned the use of a companywide allocation rate, overhead costs were relatively small compared to the costs of labor and materials. Accordingly, to the extent that inaccurate allocations did occur, they were relatively insignificant as to amount.

Automation has changed the nature of the manufacturing process to the extent that the number of direct labor hours no longer constitutes an effective allocation base in many modern manufacturing companies. Indeed, machines have largely replaced human labor. The workers that remain operate technically complex equipment. They are highly skilled and not easily replaced. As a result, workers are seldom laid off when production declines. Likewise, increasing the number of units produced does not require the addition of employees. Production control is accomplished by simply turning additional machines on or off. Under these circumstances, labor is not related to the volume of production and therefore loses its effectiveness as a rational basis for the allocation of overhead costs. Accordingly, labor-intensive companies that become automated usually find it necessary to develop more refined and sophisticated ways to allocate overhead costs.

As machines have replaced people, overhead costs have become a larger part of total manufacturing cost. In highly automated companies, overhead costs may be larger than the cost of

labor or materials combined. Although the misallocation of an insignificant amount of overhead does little harm, inaccurate distributions of major costs can destroy the integrity of accounting information. Accordingly, understanding how automation affects the allocation of overhead costs is critical.

Effects of Automation on the Selection of a Cost Driver

In an automated manufacturing company, robots and sophisticated machinery have replaced the human labor that traditionally transformed raw materials into finished goods. To understand how these changes affect the selection of a cost driver, we will return to the previous example. Suppose the production process for Job 2 is automated. Now instead of using six hours of labor, it requires only one hour of direct labor and four hours of mechanical processing. Assume that the use of the new machinery causes utility consumption to increase. Furthermore, total overhead costs increase as a result of the additional depreciation charges on the new machinery. Suppose that these changes cause the amount of daily overhead to increase from $120 to $420. Because Job 1 requires two hours of direct labor and Job 2 requires one hour of direct labor, the allocation rate becomes $140 per direct labor hour ($420 ÷ 3 hours). As a result, $280 ($140 × 2 hours) of the total overhead cost is allocated to Job 1 and $140 ($140 × 1 hour) is allocated to Job 2. The pre- and postautomation allocations are compared here.

LO2 Understand how automation has affected the selection of cost drivers.

Product	Preautomation Cost Distribution	Postautomation Cost Distribution
Job 1	$30	$280
Job 2	90	140
Total	$120	$420

Clearly, the postautomation use of direct labor hours as the cost driver distorts the allocation of the overhead cost. Although the actual processing of Job 1 was not affected by the automation, it received a $250 ($280 − $30) increase in its share of the allocated overhead cost. This increase should have been assigned to Job 2 because the automation of that job caused overhead costs to increase. The problem results from the fact that the automation caused the consumption of labor for Job 2 to decrease. Notice that prior to automation, Job 2 represented six of a total of eight hours of labor. Accordingly, Job 2 was allocated 75 percent (6 ÷ 8) of the overhead cost with the remaining 25 percent being allocated to Job 1. After automation, Job 2 consumed only one of a total of three hours of labor, thereby receiving only 33 percent of the allocated overhead, leaving 67 percent of the allocation for Job 1. These changes in the allocation base coupled with the increase in total overhead cost cause the postautomation cost of Job 1 to be significantly overstated and of Job 2 to be significantly understated.

One way to solve the misallocation problem is to select a more effective volume-based cost driver. For example, instead of using labor hours, machine hours could be used to allocate the utility cost. Indeed, we demonstrated the use of many different **volume-based cost drivers** (e.g., material dollars, material quantities, machine hours, labor dollars) in Chapter 5. Unfortunately, many of the automated processes generate costs that have no cause-and-effect relationship with volume-based cost drivers. To accomplish more meaningful allocations, many companies have begun to use **activity-based cost drivers** to improve the accuracy of product costing. To illustrate, consider the case of Carver Soup Company.

Activity-Based Cost Drivers

Carver Soup Company (CSC) makes vegetable and tomato soup in batches. Each time the company changes from a batch of vegetable soup to a batch of tomato soup or vice versa, it incurs certain costs. For example, the mixing, blending, and cooking equipment must be cleaned.

LO3 Distinguish between volume-based versus activity-based cost drivers.

Settings on the equipment must be changed to the specifications required for the particular soup being made. Quality testing must be conducted to ensure that the recipe has been applied correctly. Because these costs are incurred each time a new batch is started, they are called **start-up** or **setup costs.** CSC plans to make 180 batches of each type of soup during the accounting period. Expected production information is summarized in the following table.

	Vegetable	Tomato	Total
Number of cans	954,000	234,000	1,188,000
Number of setups	180	180	360

CSC expects that each setup will cost $264. Accordingly, the total expected setup cost is $95,040 ($264 × 360 setups). Using the number of cans as the cost driver (i.e., volume-based driver) produces an allocation rate of $0.08 per can ($95,040 ÷ 1,188,000 cans). Multiplying the allocation rate times the weight of the base (i.e., number of cans) produces the following allocation.

Product	Allocation Rate	×	Number of Cans Produced	=	Allocated Product Cost
Vegetable	$0.08	×	954,000	=	$76,320
Tomato	0.08	×	234,000	=	18,720

As expected, the volume-based (number of cans) allocation rate assigns more cost to the high-volume vegetable soup product; however, this allocation is misleading. Assigning more setup cost to the vegetable soup makes little sense because both products required the *same number of setups.* Given that the setup cost should be distributed equally between the two products, the volume-based cost driver is *overcosting the high-volume product* (vegetable soup) and undercosting the low-volume product (tomato soup). In other words, some of the cost that should be assigned to tomato soup is being allocated to vegetable soup.

The factor that is causing the setup cost to be incurred is the number of times the setup activity is conducted. The more setups undertaken, the higher the total setup cost. Accordingly, an *activity-based cost driver* (number of setups) is a more appropriate base for the allocation of the setup costs. Indeed, the activity-based cost driver does allocate an equal portion of the setup cost to both products. Specifically, the allocation rate is $264 ($95,040 ÷ 360 setups) per setup. Multiplying the allocation rate times the weight of the base (number of setups) produces the following allocation.

Product	Allocation Rate	×	Number of Setups	=	Allocated Product Cost
Vegetable	$264	×	180	=	$47,520
Tomato	264	×	180	=	47,520

Activity-Based Cost Drivers Enhance Relevance

The *activity-based cost driver* produces a better allocation because it distributes the *relevant costs* to the appropriate products. If CSC were to stop producing tomato soup, it could *avoid* 180 setups costing $47,520. We are, of course, assuming that the employees currently performing the setup activities could be discharged. Likewise, we assume that the supplies and other resources used in the setup process could be saved. This *avoidable cost is relevant* to decision making. Indeed, the volume-based product cost data provide misleading information for decision-making purposes. Suppose that CSC has an opportunity to outsource the setup activity for tomato soup. A company specializing in the performance of setup activities offers to provide 180 setups for $40,000. A manager considering the volume-based allocated cost of $18,720 would reject the offer because the cost of performing the setup activities appears to be less than the cost of outsourcing them. In fact, CSC should accept the offer because it could avoid $47,520 of cost if the outside company performs the setup activity. In a highly automated

environment in which companies produce many different products with varying levels of production, it is little wonder that many companies have turned to activity-based costing to improve the accuracy of their allocations and the effectiveness of their decisions.

Professional Training Services, Inc. (PTSI), offers professional exam review courses for both the certified public accountant (CPA) and the certified management accountant (CMA) exams. Many more students take the CPA review courses than the CMA review courses. PTSI uses the same size and number of classrooms to teach both courses; its CMA courses simply have more empty seats. PTSI is trying to determine the cost of offering the two courses. The company's accountant has decided to allocate classroom rental cost based on the number of students enrolled in the courses. Explain why this allocation base will likely result in an inappropriate assignment of cost to the two cost objects. Identify a more appropriate allocation base.

Answer Using the number of students as the allocation base will assign more of the rental cost to the CPA review courses because those courses have higher enrollments. This allocation is inappropriate because the number of classrooms, not the number of students, drives the amount of rental cost. Since both courses require the same number of classrooms, the rental cost should be allocated equally between them. Several allocation bases would produce an equal allocation, such as the number of classrooms, the number of courses, or a 50/50 percentage split.

Check Yourself 6–1

▌Activity-Based Costing

Activity-based costing (ABC) is a two-stage allocation process that employs a variety of cost drivers. In the first stage, ABC assigns costs to pools according to the activities that cause the costs to be incurred. In the second stage, the costs in the activity cost pools are allocated to products. Accordingly, the first step in developing an ABC system is to identify the essential activities and the costs required to perform those activities.

Activities are the actions taken by an organization to accomplish its mission. Typical activities include acquiring raw materials, transforming materials into completed products, and delivering products to customers. These general categories of activities can be subdivided into more detailed subclassifications. For example, the activity of acquiring raw materials can be separated into subcategory activities such as identifying suppliers, obtaining price quotes, evaluating product specifications, completing purchase orders, confirming the receipt of goods purchased, and so on. Each of these categories can be subdivided into more detailed classifications. For instance, the identification of suppliers may include activities such as reviewing advertisements, making Internet searches, and obtaining recommendations from business associates. Additional subdivisions are obviously possible. Indeed, companies typically perform thousands of activities in the process of accomplishing their goals.

Identification of Activity Centers

Maintaining the records necessary to determine the cost of performing thousands of activities is expensive. To reduce record-keeping costs, companies organize related activities into hubs called **activity centers.** Overhead costs associated with performing the related activities are combined into cost pools. Pooling costs according to activity centers reduces the number of allocations and the record keeping required to make those allocations. Because the activities assigned to each center are related, rational cost allocations can be accomplished through the use of a common cost driver. The number of activity centers used by a company depends on a *cost/benefit analysis.* Companies are willing to incur higher record-keeping costs only to the extent that such record keeping pays for itself through improved decision making. Accordingly, the number of cost centers established by a company depends on management's judgment as to whether the additional accuracy is worth the cost that must be incurred to attain that accuracy.

LO4 Identify and use activity cost centers and related cost drivers in an activity-based cost system.

Comparison of ABC with Traditional Two-Stage Cost Allocation

How does an ABC system differ from the traditional two-stage allocation systems discussed in the appendix of Chapter 5? Traditional two-stage allocation systems pool costs according to departments. Costs in the departmental cost pools are then allocated to cost objects by using some form of volume-based cost driver. In contrast, an ABC system pools costs by activity centers and then uses a variety of volume- and activity-based cost drivers to allocate costs to cost objects. Typically, an ABC system has many more activity centers than the number of departments in a traditional two-stage allocation system. Indeed, ABC improves cost tracing by increasing the number of cause-and-effect relationships employed in the assignment of indirect costs. Instead of assigning costs to a few departments, ABC assigns costs to numerous activity centers. The primary differences between a traditional two-stage allocation system and the ABC system are depicted graphically in Exhibit 6–1. Both allocation systems shown in the exhibit could be drawn with more cost pools. In other words, businesses can have more than two departments or three activity centers. The exhibit is designed to show the typical case in which an ABC system incorporates more cost pools than does a traditional two-stage allocation plan.

LO5 Classify activities into one of four hierarchical categories including unit-level, batch-level, product-level, and facility-level activities.

Types of Production Activities

Many companies have found that organizing activities into four hierarchical categories facilitates cost tracing. These categories are (1) unit-level activities, (2) batch-level activities,

focus on International Issues

Eliminating Nonvalue-Added Activities in a Sushi Bar

Identifying and eliminating activities that do not add value can lead to increased customer satisfaction and profitability. An emerging trend in Japanese sushi bars validates this point. Sushi delivered via conveyor belt leads to significant cost savings that are passed on to customers. A moving belt, not a waiter, delivers sushi directly to the customers. Cooks fill the merry-go-round conveyor belt, instead of patron orders. The savings associated with the elimination of nonvalue-added activities such as taking orders, delivering food, and avoiding waste have enabled conveyor belt shops to offer customers quality sushi at economy prices—two pieces for $1 vs. $3 to $4 at standard sushi shops. Customers are so wowed by the deal that they are braving waits of up to an hour. Owners are benefiting, too, because diners get their fill and move on faster, thereby increasing turnover and sales volume. The increased volume produced is highly profitable because fixed costs are not affected by the soaring sales. When insights gained through activity-based costing (ABC) lead to the changes in the way a business is managed, the process is known as *activity-based management* (ABM).

Source: Miki Tanikawa, "Sushi Bars: What Comes Around," *Business Week*, November 9, 1998, p. 8.

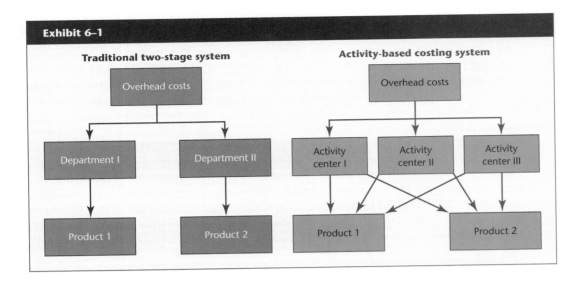

Exhibit 6–1

(3) product-level activities, and (4) facility-level activities.[1] The overhead costs associated with each category are pooled together and allocated to products according to the way those products benefit from the activities. *The primary objective is to trace the cost of performing activities to the products that are causing the activities to be performed.* To illustrate, we discuss the classification of the overhead costs incurred by Unterman Shirt Company.

Unterman has two different product lines, dress shirts and casual shirts. The company expects to produce 680,000 dress shirts and 120,000 casual shirts during 2003 and expects overhead costs to total $5,730,000. Currently, Unterman assigns an equal amount of overhead to each shirt. Under these conditions, determining the overhead cost per shirt is easily accomplished by dividing the total expected overhead cost by the total expected production ($5,730,000 ÷ 800,000 units = $7.16 per shirt rounded to the nearest whole cent). Dress shirts and casual shirts require approximately the same amount of direct materials and labor. Direct materials cost approximately $8.20 per shirt, and direct labor costs approximately $6.80. Accordingly, the total cost per shirt is $22.16 ($7.16 + $8.20 + $6.80). Unterman sells shirts for $31 each, thereby yielding a gross margin of $8.84 per shirt ($31 − $22.16).

Bob Unterman, president and owner of the company, is convinced that although the allocation computation is easy, it is also inaccurate. The direct materials and labor costs seem reasonable, but he is sure that the overhead costs are not the same for both product lines. Accordingly, Mr. Unterman decides to hire a consultant, Rebecca Lynch, to trace the overhead costs to the two product lines. Ms. Lynch decides to use an *activity-based cost* system. She begins by identifying the activities necessary to make shirts and categorizes the activities into the following four activity cost centers.

Unit-Level Activity Center

Unit-level activities occur each time a unit of product is made. For example, every time a shirt is made, Unterman incurs inspection costs, machine-related utility costs, and costs for production supplies. Accordingly, total unit-level cost increases each time a product is made and decreases each time the volume of production is reduced. Some costs that are not purely unit-level costs exhibit behavior patterns that justify treating them as such. For example, suppose that machinery is lubricated after every eight hours of continuous operation. Although the cost of lubrication is not incurred each time a shirt is produced, the cost behavior pattern is so closely tied to the level of production that it may be treated as a unit-level cost even though it does not meet a strict interpretation of that categorization.

---

[1]The cost associated with these activities was discussed in Chapter 4. It may be helpful to review the definitions of these costs prior to continuing your study of this chapter.

Ms. Lynch identifies the following unit-level overhead costs: (1) $300,000 for machine-related utilities, (2) $50,000 for machine maintenance, (3) $450,000 for indirect labor and materials, (4) $200,000 for inspection and quality control, and (5) $296,000 for miscellaneous unit-level costs. She combines these costs into a single cost pool containing $1,296,000 of overhead cost and assigns this cost to a *unit-level activity center.* This assignment constitutes the first stage of the two-stage ABC allocation system. In other words, $1,296,000 of the total $5,730,000 overhead cost has now been allocated to one of the four activity centers. The remaining balance of the overhead cost will be allocated among the three other activity centers.

The second-stage cost assignment involves allocating the $1,296,000 unit-level cost pool between the two product lines. Because unit-level costs are incurred each time a shirt is produced, they should be allocated with a base that is correlated with the level of production. Assume that Ms. Lynch chooses to use direct labor hours as the allocation base. Past performance suggests that 272,000 direct labor hours are required to make the dress shirts and 48,000 direct labor hours are required to make the casual shirts. Based on this information, Ms. Lynch allocates the unit-level overhead costs and computes the cost per unit as indicated in Exhibit 6–2.

Exhibit 6–2 *Allocation of Unit-Level Overhead Costs*

	Product Lines		
	Dress Shirts	Casual Shirts	Total
Number of direct labor hours (a)	272,000	48,000	320,000
Cost per labor hour ($1,296,000 ÷ 320,000 hours) (b)	$4.05	$4.05	NA
Total allocated overhead cost (c = a × b)	$1,101,600	$194,400	$1,296,000
Number of shirts (d)	680,000	120,000	800,000
Cost per shirt (c ÷ d)	$1.62	$1.62	

Notice that the unit-level costs follow a variable cost behavior pattern. Total cost changes in direct proportion to the number of units produced. Cost per unit is constant regardless of the number of units produced. Because cost per unit is not affected by the volume of activity, the pricing structure of dress versus casual shirts should not be affected by the fact that the company makes more dress shirts than casual shirts.

Batch-Level Activity Center

Batch-level activities are related to the production of groups of products. Costs associated with a batch of products are fixed regardless of the number of units of product included in the batch of work. For example, the costs associated with setting up machinery to cut material for a certain size shirt are the same regardless of how many are cut with that particular machine setting. Similarly, the cost of a first-item batch test is the same regardless of whether 200 or 2,000 shirts are made in the batch. Another cost commonly classified as a batch-level cost is materials handling. This classification applies because materials are usually transferred from one department to another in batches. For example, all of the small dress shirts are cut in the sizing department. Then the entire batch of cut material is transferred to the sewing department. Because the equipment used to transfer materials makes a single delivery of all of the work-in-process inventory in any size batch, the cost of materials handling is the same regardless of whether the batch load is large or small.

Because total batch costs depend on the number of batch runs performed, more costs should be allocated to products that require more batch runs. Assume that Ms. Lynch estimates total batch-level overhead costs to be $690,000. Accordingly, the first-stage allocation places this amount in a batch-level cost pool.

With respect to the second-stage allocation, Ms. Lynch determines that the casual shirt line requires considerably more setups than the dress shirt line because the casual shirts are subject to frequent style changes. Because customers are willing to buy only small amounts of items with limited shelf life, Unterman is forced to produce casual shirts in small batches. Based on this information, Ms. Lynch decides that more of the batch-level costs should be

allocated to the casual shirt line than to the dress shirt line. She believes that the number of setups constitutes the most rational allocation base. Because 1,280 setups are performed for casual shirts and 1,020 setups are required to make the dress shirts, Ms. Lynch allocates the batch-level costs as indicated in Exhibit 6–3.

Exhibit 6–3 *Allocation of Batch-Level Overhead Costs*

	Product Lines		
	Dress Shirts	Casual Shirts	Total
Number of setups performed (a)	1,020	1,280	2,300
Cost per setup ($690,000 ÷ 2,300 setups) (b)	$300	$300	NA
Total allocated overhead cost (c = a × b)	$306,000	$384,000	$690,000
Number of shirts (d)	680,000	120,000	800,000
Cost per shirt (c ÷ d)	$0.45	$3.20	

Notice that the per shirt batch-level cost for casual shirts is considerably larger than the per shirt cost for dress shirts. This occurs for two reasons. First, as indicated, more batch-level costs are assigned to the casual shirt line ($384,000 versus $306,000). Second, the number of casual shirts made is significantly smaller than the number of dress shirts made (120,000 units versus 680,000). Recall that batch-level costs follow a fixed cost behavior pattern relative to the number of units in a particular batch. This means that the cost per unit increases as the number of units in a batch decreases. For example, if setup costs amount to $300, the cost per unit for a batch of 100 units is $3 ($300 ÷ 100 units). The cost per unit rises to $30 if the batch contains only 10 units ($300 ÷ 10 units). This explains why the average batch cost per shirt is considerably higher for casual shirts ($3.20 per shirt) than for dress shirts ($0.45). Accordingly, when batch-level costs are significant, companies should pursue products with high volume. As demonstrated in this case, low-volume products are more expensive to make because the fixed costs must be spread over fewer shirts. To the extent that cost affects pricing, the casual shirts should be priced higher than the dress shirts.

Product-Level Activity Center

Product-level activities support a specific product or product line made by a company. Examples include materials inventory holding costs, engineering development costs, and legal fees to obtain and protect patents, copyrights, trademarks, and brand names. Unterman Shirt Company prides itself on being the fashion leader with respect to contemporary trends in style. It incurs considerable fashion design costs to ensure that it remains the trend setter. The company also incurs engineering costs of continually improving the quality of materials used in its products. In addition, it incurs legal fees to protect the brand names of the company's products. After a careful review of Unterman's operations, Ms. Lynch concludes that $1,800,000 of the total overhead cost could be traced to the product-level activity center.

The second-stage allocation requires assessing the extent to which these activities focus on sustaining the dress shirt line versus the casual shirt line. Interviews with fashion design personnel disclose that more of their time is spent on casual shirts because the styles of these shirts change so frequently. Similarly, the engineers spend more of their time developing new fabric, buttons, and zippers for casual shirts. The materials used in dress shirts are fairly stable. Although some work is performed to improve the quality of dress shirt materials, the time spent is significantly less than that spent on the more unusual materials used in the casual shirts. Similarly, the legal department spends more time developing and protecting the newer patents, trademarks, and brand names of the casual line of shirts. Based on these interviews, Ms. Lynch concludes that 70 percent of the product-level cost pool should be allocated to the casual line of shirts, leaving 30 percent of the pool to be allocated to the dress shirt line. Based on this information, she allocates product-level costs to the two product lines as indicated in Exhibit 6–4.

As indicated, product-level costs are frequently distributed unevenly for the different product lines. In the case of Unterman Shirts, considerably more costs are incurred to sustain the casual

Exhibit 6–4 *Allocation of Product-Level Overhead Costs*

	Product Lines		
	Dress Shirts	Casual Shirts	Total
Percent of product-level activity utilization (a)	30%	70%	100%
Total allocated overhead cost (b = a × $1,800,000)	$540,000	$1,260,000	$1,800,000
Total units produced (c)	680,000	120,000	800,000
Cost per unit (b ÷ c)	$0.79*	$10.50	

*Rounded to the nearest whole cent.

shirt line than the dress shirt line. If differential costs are distributed evenly over all products as is the case using a single companywide overhead rate, distortions in cost measurement occur. These distortions can lead to negative consequences such as irrational pricing policies and reward structures that motivate inappropriate behavior. The use of ABC reduces the likelihood of measurement distortions by more accurately tracing costs to the products that cause their incurrence. In this case, more of the overhead cost is assigned to the casual shirt product line.

Facility-Level Activity Center

Facility-level activities are performed to benefit the production process as a whole and therefore are not related to any specific product, batch, or unit of production. For example, the fire insurance on the manufacturing facility does not benefit any particular product or product line. Other examples of facility-level costs include depreciation for the manufacturing facility and the costs of security, landscaping and plant maintenance, general utilities, and taxes. With respect to Unterman Shirt Company, Ms. Lynch identifies $1,944,000 of facility-level overhead costs. Because no logical relationship exists between these facility-level manufacturing costs and the two product lines, she is forced to allocate these costs on an arbitrary basis. Assuming that the facility-level costs are arbitrarily allocated equally over the total number of units produced, Ms. Lynch allocates 85 percent (680,000 ÷ 800,000) of the facility-level cost pool to the dress shirt product line and 15 percent (120,000 ÷ 800,000) to the casual shirt line. The allocation schedule and computation of cost per unit are shown in Exhibit 6–5.

Exhibit 6–5 *Allocation of Facility-Level Overhead Costs*

	Product Lines		
	Dress Shirts	Casual Shirts	Total
Percent of total units (a)	85%	15%	100%
Total allocated overhead cost (b = a × $1,944,000)	$1,652,400	$291,600	$1,944,000
Total units produced (c)	680,000	120,000	800,000
Cost per unit (b ÷ c)	$2.43	$2.43	

Classification of Activities Not Limited to Four Categories

As previously indicated, the number of activity centers used in business practice depends on cost/benefit analysis. The four categories used here frequently constitute a starting point. Any of the four categories could be further subdivided into more detailed activity centers. For example, an activity cost center for unit-level labor-related activities and a different center for unit-level machine-related activities could be established. Indeed, identifying the list of activity centers to use in a real-world company can be quite tedious. Paulette Bennett describes the process used in the Material Control Department at Compumotor, Inc., as follows:

> Recognizing that ordinarily the two biggest problems with an ABC project are knowing where to start and how deep to go, we began by analyzing the activities that take place in our procurement process. As the old saying goes, to find the biggest alligators you usually have to wade into the

weeds; therefore, we started by writing down all the procurement activities. Creating a real world picture of costs by activity was our aim. But had we used our initial list we would have designed a spreadsheet so large that no human could ever have emerged alive at the other end.[2]

Ms. Bennett's abbreviated list still contained 83 separate activities. Even so, this list represents the activity centers for only one department of a very large company. Although we limit our discussion for instructional purposes to four general categories, be aware that the real-world equivalent is far more complicated.

Under what circumstances would the number of units produced be an inappropriate allocation base for batch-level costs?

Answer Using the number of units produced as the allocation base would allocate more of the batch-level costs to high-volume products and less of the costs to low-volume products. Since batch-level costs are normally related to the number of batches rather than the number of units made in each batch, allocation of batch-level costs based on units produced would result in poor product cost estimates; the costing system would overcost high-volume products and undercost low-volume products. It would be appropriate to use the number of units produced only when each batch consists of the same number of product units. Even under these circumstances, the number of units merely serves as a proxy for the number of batches. It would still be more appropriate to use the number of batches to allocate batch-level costs.

Context-Sensitive Classification of Activities

Note that a particular type of activity could be classified as belonging to any of the four hierarchical categories. For example, inspections conducted on a piecemeal basis is a unit-level activity. Inspecting the first item of each batch to determine whether the setup was accomplished properly is a batch-level activity. Inspections established for a specific product or product line are product-level activities. Finally, inspections of the factory building are facility-level activities. You cannot memorize a list of activities as belonging to any particular category. You must learn instead to analyze the context within which the activity takes place to classify it properly.

Cost Driver Selection

As noted, activity-based costing uses *volume-based cost drivers* and *activity-based cost drivers.* Volume-based drivers are appropriate for indirect costs that increase or decrease relative to the volume of activity. Accordingly, the use of cost drivers such as units, labor hours, or machine hours is appropriate for unit-level activities. The problem with traditional costing systems is that they use a volume-based measure (usually labor hours) for the allocation of all indirect costs. In contrast, the more sophisticated ABC approach uses activity drivers such as number of setups or percentage of utilization for overhead costs that are not affected by volume. Accordingly, ABC improves the accuracy of allocations by using a combination of volume- and activity-based cost drivers.

Use of the Information to Trace Costs to Product Lines

A summary of the ABC allocation plan prepared by Ms. Lynch is shown in Exhibit 6–6. Mr. Unterman was shocked to see that the overhead costs for casual shirts line is virtually three times the cost for dress shirts. For comparative purposes, he asked Ms. Lynch to prepare the

[2]Paulette Bennett, "ABM and the Procurement Cost Model," *Management Accounting,* March 1996, pp. 28–32.

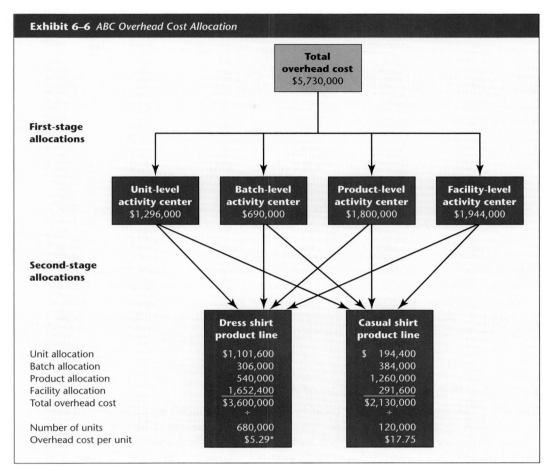

Exhibit 6–6 *ABC Overhead Cost Allocation*

Total overhead cost $5,730,000

First-stage allocations

| Unit-level activity center $1,296,000 | Batch-level activity center $690,000 | Product-level activity center $1,800,000 | Facility-level activity center $1,944,000 |

Second-stage allocations

	Dress shirt product line	Casual shirt product line
Unit allocation	$1,101,600	$ 194,400
Batch allocation	306,000	384,000
Product allocation	540,000	1,260,000
Facility allocation	1,652,400	291,600
Total overhead cost	$3,600,000	$2,130,000
	÷	÷
Number of units	680,000	120,000
Overhead cost per unit	$5.29*	$17.75

*Rounded to the nearest whole cent.

Exhibit 6–7 *Allocation of Facility-Level Overhead Costs*

	Gross Margins Product Lines		ABC Margins Product Lines	
	Dress Shirts	Casual Shirts	Dress Shirts	Casual Shirts
Sales price	$31.00	$31.00	$31.00	$31.00
Cost of goods sold				
Materials cost	(8.20)	(8.20)	(8.20)	(8.20)
Labor cost	(6.80)	(6.80)	(6.80)	(6.80)
Overhead	(7.16)	(7.16)	(5.29)	(17.75)
Margin	$ 8.84	$ 8.84	$10.71	$ (1.75)

information shown in Exhibit 6–7. This table shows the computation of traditional per unit gross margins versus the ABC margins for the two product lines. Recall that direct materials and direct labor costs for dress and casual shirts are $8.20 and $6.80, respectively. The difference in the margins is attributable to the overhead allocation. Using a traditional companywide overhead rate results in the allocation of an equal amount of overhead to each shirt ($5,730,000 ÷ 800,000 units = $7.16 per shirt). In contrast, the ABC approach assigns $5.29 to each dress shirt and $17.75 to each casual shirt. These differential rates reflect the cost of activities used to make the shirts. Total overhead cost is $5,730,000 under both approaches. It is the *assignment of* rather than the *amount of* the total cost that differs for the two approaches. ABC makes clear the fact that making a casual shirt costs more than making a dress shirt.

After reviewing the data in Exhibit 6–7, Mr. Unterman remarked, "I knew that the overhead wasn't being allocated on a rational basis, but I had no idea we were incurring losses on the casual shirt line. Something must be done. What are our options?"

Under- and Overcosting

Clearly, the single companywide overhead rate has resulted in undercosting Unterman Shirt Company's casual line. Indeed, the understated overhead cost has caused Unterman to price its product below cost. The most obvious response to the ABC margin data shown in Exhibit 6–7 is to raise the price of casual shirts. Unfortunately, the market may not be willing to co-operate. If other companies are selling casual shirts at prices near $31, Unterman's customers may buy from the company's competitors instead of paying a higher price for Unterman's shirts. In a market-driven economy, raising prices may not be a viable option. Accordingly, Unterman may be forced to establish a target-pricing strategy.

LO6 Understand the effect that under- or overcosting can have on profitability.

Target pricing requires management to determine the price that customers are willing to pay. The company then controls cost factors to produce the product at a cost that will enable it to sell at the price that customers demand. The data in Exhibits 6–3 and 6–4 indicate that batch-level and product-level costs are significantly higher for casual shirts than for dress shirts. Unterman may be too fashion conscious with respect to its casual shirt line. Perhaps the company would be better off to relinquish its trend-setting position. It could adopt the strategy of focusing on a few traditional styles. This would enable the company to reduce fashion de-sign costs. Furthermore, because following established trends provides more security than set-ting new ones, the traditional designs may increase customer confidence in the marketability of the casual shirt line, which will likely lead them to place larger orders, which would enable Unterman to reduce its per unit batch costs.

Note that the single companywide overhead rate not only undercosts the casual shirt line but also overcosts the dress shirt line. To the extent that price is affected by the overstated overhead cost, the dress shirt line is overpriced. Overpricing can place the dress shirt business at a competitive disadvantage, which can lead to the loss of market share, which in turn can have a snowballing effect. If volume declines, Unterman's fixed costs will be spread over fewer units, resulting in a higher cost per unit. Higher costs encourage price increases, which further aggravate the competitive disadvantage. To avoid this condition, it is as important for Unterman to consider lowering the price of its dress shirts as it is to consider raising the price of its casual shirts.

Examining the Relevance of Allocated Facility-Level Costs

If Unterman is unable to raise the price or lower the cost of its casual shirts, management should consider eliminating that product line. As indicated in Chapter 4, evaluating the elim-ination of a product line requires an assessment of the *relevant costs*. Recall that the relevant costs are those costs that can be *avoided* by eliminating a product line. So which of the ABC–allocated overhead costs can be avoided by eliminating the casual shirt product line? Generally, the unit-level, batch-level, and product-level costs can be eliminated or substan-tially reduced when a product line is eliminated. On the other hand, *facility-level costs are usu-ally not affected by product elimination and are therefore unavoidable.* Depreciation on the manufacturing building and the cost of security, insurance, taxes, and so forth will remain the same regardless of whether Unterman makes casual shirts. Indeed, *many companies do not al-locate facility-level costs directly to products for decision-making purposes.* With respect to Unterman, the avoidable overhead costs amount to $15.32 (unit-level $1.62 + batch-level $3.20 + product-level $10.50) see Exhibits 6–2, 6–3, and 6–4. Assuming that direct labor and materials costs can be avoided, the total avoidable cost is $30.32 ($8.20 materials + $6.80 labor + $15.32 overhead). Because the avoidable cost is less than the sales price of $31, the analysis suggests the casual shirt product line should not be eliminated.

answers to the *curious* accountant

In 1994, the USPS commissioned Coopers & Lybrand (C&L), a large accounting firm, to conduct activity-based cost (ABC) studies of its key revenue collection processes. C&L developed an ABC model for USPS's existing cash and check revenue collection and a similar ABC model for debit and credit card activities. The ABC model identified costs associated with unit, batch, and product activities. *Unit-level activity* was defined as the acceptance and processing of a payment by item. *Batch-level activities* involved the closeout at the end of the day, consolidation, and supervisory review. *Product-level activities* included maintenance for bank accounts and deposit reconciliation for the cash and checks model and terminal maintenance and training for the credit and debit card system. A comparison of the cost of the two activity models revealed that a significant cost savings could be achieved in the long term by implementing a debit and credit card system. Some examples of expected cost savings included a decrease in the per unit transaction cost due to the fact that credit card customers tend to spend more per transaction than do cash customers. In addition, the cost of activities associated with the collection of bad debts falls to virtually zero when debit or credit cards are used and the cost of cash management activities declines. Funds are collected earlier (no check collection float occurs), thereby reducing the need for financing and the resultant interest cost. In summary, C&L projected a negative benefit for a debit and credit card system (due largely to high initial implementation costs) through 1997. Projections showed that from 1998 through 2000, the net benefits of card acceptance would be $5.2 million, $15.6 million, and $28.8 million, respectively. So the USPS started accepting plastic because ABC analysis revealed that implementing a debit and credit card program would save money!

Source: Terrel L. Carter, Ali M. Sedghat, and Thomas D. Williams, "How ABC Changed the Post Office," *Management Accounting,* February 1998, pp. 28–36.

Downstream Costs and Upstream Costs

LO7 Distinguish between manufacturing costs, upstream costs, and downstream costs.

The analysis in the preceding paragraph is incomplete because it considers only product costs. Businesses incur **upstream costs** that occur before or **downstream costs** that occur after goods are manufactured. These costs may be relevant to decisions regarding the elimination of a product or product line. For example, suppose that Unterman pays sales personnel a $2 commission on each shirt sold. Although these commissions are selling and administrative costs, they are relevant to a decision regarding whether to eliminate the casual shirt line. Indeed, the commission expense could be avoided if Unterman sells no casual shirts. As a result, the total avoidable cost is $32.32 ($30.32 product costs + $2.00 sales commissions). Under these circumstances, the total avoidable cost ($32.32) is above the sales price of $31 per unit, leading to the conclusion that Unterman should abandon the casual shirt product line. Likewise, upstream costs such as research and development must be considered in decision making. Ultimately, products must be sold at a price that exceeds the total cost to develop, make, and sell them. Anything less than this amount will lead to the eventual demise of the business.

Employee Attitudes and the Availability of Data

LO8 Appreciate the limitations of activity-based costing including the effects of employee attitudes and the availability of data.

As the preceding scenarios indicate, ABC costing can bring insights that lead to the implementation of cost-cutting measures, including the elimination of products and product lines. Because these measures can result in the loss of jobs, it is little wonder that employees are sometimes reluctant to cooperate with the implementation of an ABC system. It is important to make employees aware that ABC and other **strategic cost management** techniques frequently result in a redirection of the workforce rather than the displacement of workers. Ultimately, the benefits of employment depend on the employer's competitive health. Accordingly, actions that benefit a company usually benefit its employees as well. The implementation of an ABC system is more likely to succeed when key managers and their personnel are convinced that their fate as well as that of the company will be affected positively.

Even when employees are cooperative, data can be difficult to collect. Frequently, the necessary data are not being collected. For example, suppose that a manager wants to allocate inspection costs on the basis of the number of hours an inspector spends on each job.

Unfortunately, the inspector may not maintain records regarding the time spent on individual jobs. Accordingly, making the allocation requires a policy change requiring inspectors to maintain records regarding time spent on individual jobs. The accuracy of the allocation then depends on how conscientious the inspectors were in maintaining their time reports. As this example indicates, gaining personnel support and obtaining accurate data are two of the more challenging obstacles to the implementation of a successful ABC system.

▮ Total Quality Management

Quality is widely recognized as a key ingredient in a company's ability to obtain and retain customers. Even so, *quality* is an elusive term. It does not always mean "the very best." A silver spoon is of a higher quality than a plastic spoon, but customers are perfectly willing to accept plastic spoons when they eat at fast-food restaurants. So what do we mean when we say that a business must produce quality products to be competitive? **Quality** refers to the degree with which actual products or services *conform* to their design specifications. The costs that companies incur to ensure quality conformance can be classified into four categories: prevention, appraisal, internal failure, and external failure.

LO9 Categorize quality costs into one of four categories including prevention costs, appraisal cost, internal failure cost, and external failure cost.

Prevention and appraisal costs are incurred because of the potential lack of conformance with quality standards. **Prevention costs** are incurred to avoid nonconforming products. **Appraisal costs** are incurred to identify nonconforming products that were not avoided via the prevention cost expenditures. **Failure costs** result from the actual occurrence of nonconforming products. **Internal failure costs** are incurred when defects are corrected before the goods reach the customer. **External failure costs** result from defective goods being delivered to customers.

The four components can be summarized into two broad categories. Because prevention and appraisal costs are a function of managerial discretion, they are often called **voluntary costs.** Management makes direct decisions as to the amount of funds to be expended for these voluntary costs. In contrast, failure costs are not directly controllable by management. For example, the cost of customer dissatisfaction may not be measurable, much less controllable. Even though failure costs may not be directly controllable, they are definitely related to voluntary costs. When additional funds are allocated for prevention and appraisal activities, failure costs tend to decline. The logic is obvious; as the level of control increases, quality conformance increases, thereby lowering failure costs. When control activities are reduced, quality conformance decreases and failure cost increases. Accordingly, *voluntary costs and failure costs move in opposite directions.*

LO10 Understand relationships among the components of quality cost.

Minimization of Total Quality Cost

Total quality control cost is defined as the sum of voluntary costs plus failure costs. Because voluntary costs and failure costs are negatively correlated, the minimum amount of total quality cost is located at the point on a graph where the marginal voluntary expenditures equal the marginal savings on failure cost. This relationship is depicted in Exhibit 6–8.

The data in Exhibit 6–8 clearly indicate that the minimum total quality cost per unit is located at a level of quality assurance that is less than 100 percent. At very low levels of assurance, significant failure costs outweigh any cost savings that would be attained by avoiding voluntary costs. In contrast, extremely high levels of quality assurance result in voluntary cost expenditures that are not offset by failure cost savings. Although the "zero defects" concept sounds great, it does not represent a cost-effective strategy. Realistic managers seek to minimize total quality cost rather than to eliminate all defects.

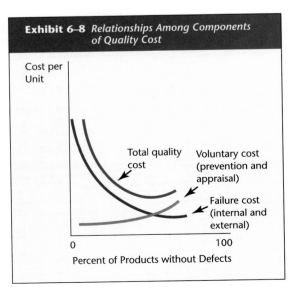

Exhibit 6–8 *Relationships Among Components of Quality Cost*

Check Yourself 6–3

Is it wiser to spend money on preventing defects or on correcting failures?

Answer The answer depends on where a company's product falls on the "total quality cost" line (see Exhibit 6–8). If the product falls left of the cost minimization point, spending more on preventing defects would produce proportionately greater failure cost savings. In other words, a company would spend less in total by reducing failure costs through increasing prevention costs. Under these circumstances, it would be wise to incur prevention costs. On the other hand, if the product falls right of the "total quality cost" line, the company would spend more to prevent additional defects than it would save by reducing failure costs. Under these circumstances, it makes more sense to pay the failure costs than attempt to avoid them by incurring prevention costs.

Quality Cost Reports

LO11 Prepare and interpret information contained in quality cost reports.

Management of quality costs in a manner that leads to the highest level of customer satisfaction is known as **total quality management (TQM).** To facilitate TQM, accountants are frequently asked to prepare a **quality cost report,** which typically lists the company's quality costs and provides a horizontal analysis showing each item as a percentage of the total cost. Data are normally shown for two or more accounting periods to reveal the effects of changes over time. Exhibit 6–9 is a quality cost report for Unterman Shirt Company. The company's accountant prepared the report to assess the effects of a quality control campaign that the company recently initiated. Review the information in Exhibit 6–9 and attempt to determine Unterman's quality control strategy and the degree of the campaign's success or failure.

The data in Exhibit 6–9 suggest that Unterman is seeking to control quality by focusing on appraisal activities. The total expenditures for prevention activities remained unchanged,

Exhibit 6–9 *Quality Cost Report for Unterman Shirt Company*

	2002		2001	
	Amount	Percentage*	Amount	Percentage*
Prevention costs				
Product design	$ 50,000	6.54%	$ 52,000	6.60%
Preventive equipment (depreciation)	7,000	0.92	7,000	0.89
Training costs	27,000	3.53	25,000	3.17
Promotion and awards	22,000	2.88	22,000	2.79
Total prevention	106,000	13.87	106,000	13.45
Appraisal costs				
Inventory inspection	75,000	9.82	25,000	3.17
Reliability testing	43,000	5.63	15,000	1.90
Testing equipment (depreciation)	20,000	2.62	12,000	1.52
Supplies	12,000	1.57	8,000	1.02
Total appraisal	150,000	19.63	60,000	7.61
Internal failure costs				
Scrap	90,000	11.78	40,000	5.08
Repair and rework	140,000	18.32	110,000	13.96
Downtime	38,000	4.97	20,000	2.54
Reinspection	30,000	3.93	12,000	1.52
Total internal failure	298,000	39.01	182,000	23.10
External failure costs				
Warranty repairs and replacement	120,000	15.71	260,000	32.99
Freight	20,000	2.62	50,000	6.35
Customer relations	40,000	5.24	60,000	7.61
Restocking and packaging	30,000	3.93	70,000	8.88
Total external failure	210,000	27.49	440,000	55.84
Grand total	$764,000	100.00%	$788,000	100.00%

*Percentages do not add exactly because of rounding.

Does quality pay? It definitely does, according to returns provided in the stock market. The Baldridge Index, which is composed of companies that have received the Malcolm Baldridge National Quality Award, outperformed the Standard & Poor's (S&P) 500 stock index by almost 3 to 1. As indicated in Exhibit 6–10, the Baldridge Index provided a 362 percent four-year return as compared to a 148 percent return provided by S&P 500 index. Because stock prices reflect investor beliefs regarding companies' present and future earnings, these returns provide a clear indication that investors believe that quality enhances profitability.

Exhibit 6–10 *Real-World Reporting Practices*

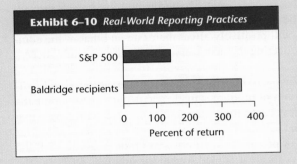

Source: "Quality Claims Its Own Bull Market," *Business Week*, March 16, 1998, p. 113.

but expenditures for appraisal activities increased significantly. The results of this strategy are also apparent in the failure cost data. Notice that internal failure costs increased significantly while external failure cost decreased dramatically. The strategy was successful in lowering total quality costs. Even so, the data suggest that more improvement is possible. Notice that 86.13 percent (appraisal 19.63 percent + internal failure 39.01 percent + external failure 27.49 percent) of total quality cost is associated with finding and correcting mistakes. You have probably heard the adage that "an ounce of prevention is worth a pound of cure." If Unterman were to concentrate more on prevention, perhaps it could avoid many of the appraisal and failure costs.

a look
back

Many traditional cost systems used direct labor hours as the sole basis for the allocation of overhead costs. Labor hours served as an effective *companywide allocation base* because labor was highly correlated with the incurrence of overhead costs. In other words, more labor resulted in the production of more products and the incurrence of more overhead cost. Accordingly, it made sense to assign more overhead to cost objects that required more labor. Because labor was related to the volume of production, it was frequently called a *volume-based cost driver*. Other volume-based cost drivers included machine hours, number of units, and labor dollars. Companywide, volume-based cost drivers were never perfect measures of overhead consumption. However, misallocation was not a serious problem because overhead costs were relatively small. If a manager misallocates an insignificant cost, it does not matter.

Automation has changed the nature of the manufacturing process. This change may cause significant distortions in the allocation of overhead costs when a companywide, volume-based cost driver is used as the allocation base. There are two primary reasons for distortions. First, in an automated environment, the same amount of labor (i.e., a flip of a switch) may be required to produce a large or a small volume of products. Under these circumstances, labor use

is not related to the incurrence of overhead and cannot be used as a rational allocation base. Second, the distortions may be significant because overhead costs are much higher relative to the cost of labor and materials. For example, when robots replace people in the production process, depreciation becomes a larger portion of the total product cost and labor becomes a smaller portion of the total.

To improve the accuracy of allocations, managerial accountants began to study the wide array of activities required to make a product. Such activities may include acquiring raw materials, materials handling and storage activities, product design activities, legal activities, and traditional production labor activities. Various measures of these activities can be used as a basis for making numerous allocations related to the determination of product cost. The process of using activity measures to allocate overhead costs has become known as *activity-based costing (ABC)*. In an ABC system, costs are allocated in a two-stage process. First, activities are organized into *activity centers* and the related costs of performing these activities are combined into *cost pools*. Second, the pooled costs are allocated to designated cost objects through the use of activity-based cost drivers. The implementation of ABC is most likely to succeed when employees are made aware that it will positively affect their fate and that of the company. Without employee cooperation, collecting the necessary data for the system's success may be difficult.

Many ABC systems begin by organizing activities into one of four categories. Total *unit-level activity cost* increases each time a unit of product is made and decreases each time the volume of production is reduced. Unit-level activity costs can be allocated with a base that is correlated with the level of production (volume-based cost drivers). *Batch-level activities* are related to the production of groups of products. Their costs are fixed regardless of the number of units in a batch. Batch-level costs are assigned so that the products requiring the most batches are assigned the most batch costs. *Product-level activities* support a specific product or specific product line. Product-level cost are frequently assigned to products based on the product's percentage use of product-level activities. *Facility-level activities* are performed for the benefit of the production process as a whole. The allocation of these costs is often arbitrary.

Accurate allocations are important because distortions can cause products to be over- or undercosted. Overcosting can cause a product line to be overpriced, and overpriced products may cause a company to lose market share, and the decline in sales revenue will cause profits to fall. When products are underpriced, revenue is less than it should be, and profitability suffers.

Product costs are frequently distinguished from upstream and downstream costs. *Upstream costs* result from activities that occur *before* goods are manufactured. Examples include research and development, product design, and legal development. *Downstream costs* result from activities that occur *after* the goods are manufactured. Examples of downstream costs include selling and administrative expenses. The treatment of upstream and downstream costs is important in making pricing decisions and decisions regarding the elimination of a product or product line.

a look forward

The next chapter introduces the topics of planning and cost control. You will learn how to prepare budgets and projected (i.e., pro forma) financial statements. Finally, you will learn the importance of considering human factors as well as the quantitative aspects of the budgeting process.

SELF-STUDY REVIEW PROBLEM

Adventure Luggage Company makes two types of airline carry-on bags. One bag type designed to meet mass market needs is constructed of durable polyester. The other bag type aimed at the high-end luxury market is made of genuine leather. Sales of the polyester bag have declined recently because of stiff price competition. Indeed, Adventure would have to sell this bag at less than production cost to match the competition. Adventure's president suspects that something is wrong with how the company estimates

the bag's cost. He has asked the company's accountant to investigate that possibility. The accountant gathered the following information relevant to estimating the cost of the company's two bag types.

Both bags require the same amount of direct labor. The leather bags have significantly higher materials costs, and they require more inspections and rework because of higher quality standards. Since the leather bags are produced in smaller batches of different colors, they require significantly more setups. Finally, the leather bags generate more legal costs due to patents and more promotion costs because Adventure advertises them more aggressively. Specific cost and activity data follow.

	Polyester Bags	Leather Bags
Per unit direct materials cost	$30	$90
Per unit direct labor cost	2 hours @ $14 per hour	2 hours @ $14 per hour
Annual sales volume	7,000 units	3,000 units

Total annual overhead costs are $872,000. Adventure currently allocates overhead costs using a traditional costing system based on direct labor hours.

To reassess the overhead allocation policy and the resulting product cost estimates, the accountant subdivided the overhead into four categories and gathered information about these cost categories and the activities that caused the company to incur the costs. These data follow.

			Amount of Cost Driver		
Category	Estimated Cost	Cost Driver	Polyester	Leather	Total
Unit level	$480,000	Number of machine hours	20,000	60,000	80,000
Batch level	190,000	Number of machine setups	1,500	3,500	5,000
Product level	152,000	Number of inspections	200	600	800
Facility level	50,000	Equal percentage	50%	50%	100%
Total	$872,000				

Required

a. Determine the total cost and cost per unit for each product line, assuming that Adventure allocates overhead costs to each product line using direct labor hours as a companywide allocation base. Also determine the combined cost of the two product lines.

b. Determine the total cost and cost per unit for each product line, assuming that Adventure allocates overhead costs using an ABC system. Determine the combined cost of the two product lines.

c. Explain why the total combined cost computed in Requirements *a* and *b* is the same. Given that the combined cost is the same using either system, why is an ABC system with many different allocation rates better than a traditional system with a single companywide overhead rate?

Solution to Requirement a

Predetermined Overhead Rate

Polyester		Leather		
2 hr. × 7,000 Units	+	2 hr. × 3,000 Units		
14,000 direct labor hours		6,000 direct labor hours	=	20,000 Hours

Allocation rate = $872,000 ÷ 20,000 hours = $43.60 per direct labor hour

Allocated Overhead Costs

Type of Bag	Allocation Rate	×	Number of Hours	=	Allocated Cost
Polyester	$43.60	×	14,000	=	$610,400
Leather	43.60	×	6,000	=	261,600
Total			20,000		$872,000

Total Cost of Each Product Line and Combined Cost

Type of Bag	Direct Materials*	+	Direct Labor†	+	Allocated Overhead	=	Total
Polyester	$210,000	+	$196,000	+	$610,400	=	$1,016,400
Leather	270,000	+	84,000	+	261,600	=	615,600
Combined totals	$480,000	+	$280,000	+	$872,000	=	$1,632,000

*Direct materials
Polyester $30 × 7,000 units = $210,000
Leather   90 × 3,000 units = 270,000

†Direct labor
Polyester $14 × 14,000 hours = 196,000
Leather   14 × 6,000 hours = 84,000

Cost per Unit Computations Using Traditional Cost System

Type of bag	Total Cost	÷	Units	=	Cost per Unit
Polyester	$1,016,400	÷	7,000	=	$145.20
Leather	615,600	÷	3,000	=	205.20
Combined total	$1,632,000				

Solution to Requirement b

Overhead Cost Allocation Using ABC

	Unit	Batch	Product	Facility	Total
Cost pool	$480,000	$190,000	$152,000	$50,000	$872,000
÷ Cost drivers	Number of machine hours 80,000	Number of setups 5,000	Number of inspections 800	Equally 50%	
= Rate	$6 per machine hour	$38 per setup	$190 per inspection	$25,000	

Overhead Allocation for Polyester Bags

	Unit	Batch	Product	Facility	Total
Weight	20,000	1,500	200	1	
× Rate	$6	$38	$190	$25,000	
Allocation	$120,000	$57,000	$38,000	$25,000	$240,000

Overhead Allocation for Leather Bags

	Unit	Batch	Product	Facility	Total
Weight	60,000	3,500	600	1	
× Rate	$ 6	$ 38	$ 190	$25,000	
Allocation	$360,000	$133,000	$114,000	$25,000	$632,000

Total Cost of Each Product Line and Combined Cost

Type of Bag	Direct Materials	+	Direct Labor	+	Allocated Overhead	=	Total
Polyester	$210,000	+	$196,000	+	$240,000	=	$ 646,000
Leather	270,000	+	84,000	+	632,000	=	986,000
Combined totals	$480,000	+	$280,000	+	$872,000	=	$1,632,000

Cost per Unit Computations Under ABC System

Type of bag	Total Cost	÷	Units	=	Cost per Unit
Polyester	$ 646,000	÷	7,000	=	$ 92.29
Leather	986,000	÷	3,000	=	328.67
Combined total	$1,632,000				

Solution to Requirement c

The allocation method (ABC versus traditional costing) does not affect the total amount of cost to be allocated. Therefore, the total cost is the same using either method. However, the allocation method (ABC versus traditional costing) does affect the cost assigned to each product line. Since the ABC system more accurately traces costs to the products that cause the costs to be incurred, it provides a more accurate estimate of the true cost of making the products. The difference in the cost per unit using ABC versus traditional costing is significant. For example, the cost of the polyester bag was determined to be $145.20 using the traditional allocation method and $92.29 using ABC. This difference could have led Adventure to overprice the polyester bag, thereby causing the decline in sales volume. To the extent that ABC is more accurate, using it will improve pricing and other strategic decisions that significantly affect profitability.

KEY TERMS

Activities *237*
Activity-based cost drivers *235*
Activity-based costing (ABC) *237*
Activity centers *237*
Appraisal costs *247*
Batch-level activities *240*

Companywide allocation rate *234*
Downstream costs *246*
External failure costs *247*
Facility-level activities *242*
Failure costs *247*
Internal failure costs *247*
Prevention costs *247*

Product-level activities *241*
Quality *247*
Quality cost report *248*
Start-up (setup) costs *236*
Strategic cost management *246*
Total quality management (TQM) *248*

Target pricing *245*
Unit-level activities *239*
Upstream costs *246*
Volume-based cost drivers *235*
Voluntary costs *247*

QUESTIONS

1. Why did traditional cost systems base allocations on a single companywide cost driver?
2. Why are labor hours ineffective as a companywide allocation base in many industries today?
3. What is the difference between volume-based cost drivers and activity-based cost drivers?
4. Why do activity-based cost drivers provide more accurate allocations of overhead in an automated manufacturing environment?
5. When would it be appropriate to use volume-based cost drivers in an activity-based cost system?
6. Martinez Manufacturing makes two products, one of which is produced at a significantly higher volume than the other. The low-volume product consumes more of the company's engineering resources because it is technologically complex. Even so, the company's cost accountant chose to allocate engineering department costs based on the number of units produced. How could selecting this allocation base affect a decision about outsourcing engineering services for the low-volume product?
7. Briefly describe the activity-based costing allocation process.
8. Tom Rehr made the following comment: "Facility-level costs should not be allocated to products because they are irrelevant for decision-making purposes." Do you agree or disagree with this statement? Justify your response.
9. To facilitate cost tracing, a company's activities can be subdivided into four hierarchical categories. What are these four categories? Describe them and give at least two examples of each category.
10. Beth Nelson, who owns and runs a small sporting goods store, buys most of her merchandise directly from manufacturers. Ms. Nelson was shocked at the $7.50 charge for a container of three ping-pong balls. She found it hard to believe that it could have cost more than $1.00 to make the balls. When she complained to Jim Wilson, the marketing manager of the manufacturing company, he tried to explain that the cost also included companywide overhead costs. How could companywide overhead affect the cost of ping-pong balls?
11. If each patient in a hospital is considered a cost object, what are examples of unit-, batch-, product-, and facility-level costs that would be allocated to this object using an activity-based cost system?

12. Milken Manufacturing has three product lines. The company's new accountant, Marvin LaSance, is responsible for allocating facility-level costs to these product lines. Mr. LaSance is finding the allocation assignment a daunting task. He knows there have been disagreements among the product managers over the allocation of facility costs, and he fears being asked to defend his method of allocation. Why would the allocation of facility-level costs be subject to disagreements?

13. Why would machine hours be an inappropriate allocation base for batch-level costs?

14. Alisa Kamuf's company has reported losses from operations for several years. Industry standards indicate that prices are normally set at 30 percent above manufacturing cost, which Ms. Kamuf has done. Assuming that her other costs are in line with industry norms, how could she continue to lose money while her competitors earn a profit?

15. Issacs Corporation produces two lines of pocket knives. The Arrowsmith product line involves very complex engineering designs; the Starscore product line involves relatively simple designs. Since its introduction, the low-volume Arrowsmith products have gained market share at the expense of the high-volume Starscore products. This pattern of sales has been accompanied by an overall decline in company profits. Why may the existing cost system be inadequate?

16. What is the relationship between activity-based management and just-in-time inventory?

EXERCISES—SERIES A

L.O. 5   **EXERCISE 6–1A** *Classifying the Costs of Unit-, Batch-, Product-, or Facility-Level Activities*

Meadowbrook Manufacturing is developing an activity-based costing system to improve overhead cost allocation. One of the first steps in developing the system is to classify the costs of performing production activities into activity cost pools.

Required

Using your knowledge of the four categories of activities, classify the cost of each activity in the following list into unit-, batch-, product-, or facility-level cost pools.

Cost Activity	Cost Pool
a. Wages of maintenance staff	
b. Labeling and packaging	
c. Plant security	
d. Ordering materials for a specific type of product	
e. Wages of workers moving units of work between work stations	
f. Factorywide electricity	
g. Salary of a manager in charge of a product line	
h. Sales commissions	
i. Engineering product design	
j. Supplies	

L.O. 4   **EXERCISE 6–2A** *Identifying Appropriate Cost Drivers*

Required

Provide at least one example of an appropriate cost driver (allocation base) for each of the following activities.

a. Products are labeled, packaged, and shipped.

b. Machinists are trained on new computer-controlled machinery.

c. Lighting is used for production facilities.

d. Materials are unloaded and stored for production.

e. Maintenance is performed on manufacturing equipment.

f. Sales commissions are paid.

g. Direct labor is used to change machine configurations.

h. Production equipment is set up for new production runs.

i. Engineering drawings are produced for design changes.

j. Purchase orders are issued.

L.O. 4, 5   **EXERCISE 6–3A** *Classifying Costs and Identifying the Appropriate Cost Driver*

Chenco Manufacturing incurred the following costs during 2005 to produce its high-quality precision instruments. The company used an activity-based costing system and identified the following activities.

1. Materials handling.
2. Inventory storage.

3. Inspection of each batch produced.
4. Salaries of receiving clerks.
5. Setup for each batch produced.
6. Insurance on production facilities.
7. Depreciation on manufacturing equipment.

Required
a. Classify each activity as a unit-level, batch-level, product-level, or facility-level activity.
b. Identify an appropriate cost driver (allocation base) for each activity.

EXERCISE 6–4A *Context-Sensitive Nature of Activity Classification*

L.O. 5

Required
Describe a set of circumstances in which the cost of painting could be classified as a unit-level, a batch-level, a product-level, or a facility-level cost.

EXERCISE 6–5A *Context-Sensitive Nature of Activity Classification*

L.O. 5

Yuri Company makes two types of circuit boards. One is a high-caliber board designed to accomplish the most demanding tasks; the other is a low-caliber board designed to provide limited service at an affordable price. During its most recent accounting period, Yuri incurred $80,000 of inspection cost. When Yuri recently established an activity-based costing system, its activities were classified into four categories. Each of the categories and appropriate cost drivers follow.

	Direct Labor Hours	Number of Batches	Number of Inspectors	Number of Square Feet
High caliber	4,000	25	3	40,000
Low caliber	16,000	15	2	60,000
Totals	20,000	40	5	100,000

Required
Allocate the inspection cost between the two products assuming that it is driven by (a) unit-level activities, (b) batch-level activities, (c) product-level activities, or (d) facility-level activities.

EXERCISE 6–6A *Computing Overhead Rates Based on Different Cost Drivers*

L.O. 4

Luke Industries produces two electronic decoders, P and Q. Decoder P is more sophisticated and requires more programming and testing than does Decoder Q. Because of these product differences, the company wants to use activity-based costing to allocate overhead costs. It has identified four activity pools. Relevant information follows.

Activity Pools	Cost Pool Total	Cost Driver
Repair and maintenance on assembly machine	$180,000	Number of units produced
Programming cost	399,000	Number of programming hours
Software inspections	30,000	Number of inspections
Product testing	40,000	Number of tests
Total overhead cost	$649,000	

Expected activity for each product follows.

	Number of Units	Number of Programming Hours	Number of Inspections	Number of Tests
Decoder P	20,000	2,000	190	1,400
Decoder Q	30,000	1,500	60	1,100
Totals	50,000	3,500	250	2,500

Required
a. Compute the overhead rate for each activity pool.
b. Determine the overhead cost allocated to each product.

L.O. 1, 3

EXERCISE 6–7A *Comparing an ABC System With a Traditional Cost System*

Use the information in Exercise 6–6A to complete the following requirements. Assume that before shifting to activity-based costing, Luke Industries allocated all overhead costs based on direct labor hours. Direct labor data pertaining to the two decoders follow.

	Direct Labor Hours
Decoder P	10,000
Decoder Q	15,000
Total	25,000

Required

a. Compute the amount of overhead cost allocated to each decoder when using direct labor hours as the allocation base.

b. Determine the cost per unit for overhead when using direct labor hours as the allocation base and when using ABC.

c. Explain why the per unit overhead cost is lower for the high-volume product when using ABC.

L.O. 1, 3 **EXERCISE 6–8A** *Allocating Costs With Different Cost Drivers*

Sunshine Company produces commercial gardening equipment. Since production is highly automated, the company allocates its overhead costs to product lines using activity-based costing. The costs and cost drivers associated with the four overhead activity cost pools follow.

	Activities			
	Unit Level	**Batch Level**	**Product Level**	**Facility Level**
Cost	$50,000	$20,000	$10,000	$120,000
Cost driver	2,000 labor hrs.	40 setups	Percentage of use	12,000 units

Production of 800 sets of cutting shears, one of the company's 20 products, took 200 labor hours and six setups and consumed 15 percent of the product-sustaining activities.

Required

a. Had the company used labor hours as a companywide allocation base, how much overhead would it have allocated to the cutting shears?

b. How much overhead is allocated to the cutting shears using activity-based costing?

c. Compute the overhead cost per unit for cutting shears using first activity-based costing and then using direct labor hours for allocation if 800 units are produced. If direct product costs are $50 and the product is priced at 30 percent above cost (rounded to the nearest whole dollar), for what price would the product sell under each allocation system?

d. Assuming that activity-based costing provides a more accurate estimate of cost, indicate whether the cutting shears would be over- or underpriced if direct labor hours are used as an allocation base. Explain how over- or undercosting can affect Sunshine's profitability.

e. Comment on the validity of using the allocated facility-level cost in the pricing decision. Should other costs be considered in a cost-plus-pricing decision? If so, which ones? What costs would you include if you were trying to decide whether to accept a special order?

L.O. 1, 3 **EXERCISE 6–9A** *Allocating Costs With Different Cost Drivers*

Hokaido Publishing identified the following overhead activities, their respective costs, and their cost drivers to produce the three types of textbooks the company publishes.

Activity (Cost)	Cost Driver	Type of Textbook		
		Deluxe	**Moderate**	**Economy**
Machine maintenance ($240,000)	Number of machine hours	250	750	1,000
Setups ($420,000)	Number of setups	30	15	5
Packing ($108,000)	Number of cartons	10	30	50
Photo development ($336,000)	Number of pictures	4,000	2,000	1,000

Deluxe textbooks are made with the finest-quality paper, six-color printing, and many photographs. Moderate texts are made with three colors and a few photographs spread throughout each chapter. Economy books are printed in black and white and include pictures only in chapter openings.

Required

a. Hokaido currently allocates all overhead costs based on machine hours. The company produced the following number of books during the prior year.

Deluxe	Moderate	Economy
50,000	150,000	200,000

Determine the overhead cost per book for each book type.

b. Determine the overhead cost per book, assuming that the volume-based allocation system described in Requirement *a* is replaced with an activity-based costing system.

c. Explain why the per unit overhead costs determined in Requirements *a* and *b* differ.

EXERCISE 6–10A *Computing Product Cost With Given Activity Allocation Rates*   L.O. 4

Neil Manufacturing produces two modems, one for laptop computers and the other for desktop computers. The production process is automated, and the company has found activity-based costing useful in assigning overhead costs to its products. The company has identified five major activities involved in producing the modems.

Activity	Allocation Base	Allocation Rate
Materials receiving & handling	Cost of material	2% of material cost
Production setup	Number of setups	$150.00 per setup
Assembly	Number of parts	$6.00 per part
Quality inspection	Inspection time	$1.50 per minute
Packing and shipping	Number of orders	$10.00 per order

Activity measures for the two kinds of modems follow.

	Labor Cost	Material Cost	Number of Setups	Number of Parts	Inspection Time	Number of Orders
Laptops	$2,398	$10,000	30	42	7,200 min.	65
Desktops	2,206	15,000	12	24	5,100 min.	20

Required

a. Compute the cost per unit of laptop and desktop modems, assuming that Neil made 300 units of each type of modem.

b. Explain why laptop modems cost more to make even though they have less material cost and are smaller than desktop modems.

EXERCISE 6–11A *Allocating Facility-Level Cost and a Product Elimination Decision*   L.O. 4

Maples Boards produces two kinds of skate boards. Selected unit data for the two boards for the last quarter follow.

	Basco Boards	Shimano Boards
Production costs		
Direct materials	$54	$72
Direct labor	$78	$102
Allocated overhead	$30	$36
Total units produced and sold	4,000	8,000
Total sales revenue	$672,000	$1,776,000

Maples allocates production overhead using activity-based costing. It allocates delivery expense and sales commissions, which amount to $108,000 per quarter, to the two products equally.

Required
a. Compute the net profit for each product.
b. Assuming that the overhead allocation for Basco boards includes $24,000 of facility-level cost, would you advise Maples to eliminate these boards? (*Hint:* Consider the method used to allocate the delivery and selling expense.)

L.O. 10   EXERCISE 6–12A *Quality Cost Components and Relationships*

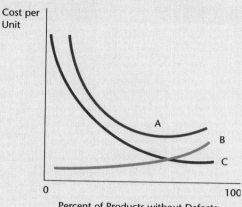

Required
The preceding graph depicts the relationships among the components of total quality cost.
a. Label the lines identified as A, B, and C.
b. Explain the relationships depicted in the graph.

PROBLEMS—SERIES A

L.O. 1, 3   PROBLEM 6–13A *Comparing an ABC System With a Traditional Cost System*

Nikki Electronics produces video games in three market categories, commercial, home, and miniature. Nikki has traditionally allocated overhead costs to the three products using the companywide allocation base of direct labor hours. The company recently implemented an ABC system when it installed computer-controlled assembly stations that rendered the traditional costing system ineffective. In implementing the ABC system, the company identified the following activity cost pools and cost drivers.

Category	Total Pooled Cost	Types of Costs	Cost Driver
Unit	$720,000	Indirect labor wages, supplies, depreciation, machine maintenance	Machine hours
Batch	388,800	Materials handling, inventory storage, labor for setups, packaging, labeling and shipping, scheduling	Number of production orders
Product	211,200	Research and development	Time spent by research department
Facility	600,000	Rent, utilities, maintenance, admin. salaries, security	Square footage

Additional data for each of the product lines follow.

	Commercial	Home	Miniature	Total
Direct materials cost	$36.00/unit	$24.00/unit	$30.00/unit	—
Direct labor cost	$14.40/hour	$14.40/hour	$18.00/hour	—
Number of labor hours	6,000	12,000	2,000	20,000
Number of machine hours	10,000	45,000	25,000	80,000
Number of production orders	200	2,000	800	3,000
Research and development time	10%	20%	70%	100%
Number of units	15,000	45,000	14,000	74,000
Square footage	20,000	50,000	30,000	100,000

Required
a. Determine the total cost and cost per unit for each product line, assuming that overhead costs are allocated to each product line using direct labor hours as a companywide allocation base. Also determine the combined cost of all three product lines.

b. Determine the total cost and cost per unit for each product line, assuming that an ABC system is used to allocate overhead costs. Determine the combined cost of all three product lines.

c. Explain why the combined total cost computed in Requirements *a* and *b* is the same amount. Given that the combined cost is the same using either allocation method, why is an ABC system with many different allocation rates more accurate than a traditional system with a single companywide overhead rate?

PROBLEM 6–14A *Effect of Automation on Overhead Allocation*   L.O. 2

Oriental Rug Company makes two types of rugs, seasonal and all purpose. Both types of rugs are handmade, but the seasonal rugs require significantly more labor because of their decorative designs. The annual number of rugs made and the labor hours required to make each type of rug follow.

	Seasonal	All Purpose	Totals
Number of rugs	1,200	2,800	4,000
Number of direct labor hours	120,000	168,000	288,000

Required

a. Assume that annual overhead costs total $144,000. Select the appropriate cost driver and determine the amount of overhead to allocate to each type of rug.

b. Oriental automates the seasonal rug line resulting in a dramatic decline in labor usage, to make 1,200 rugs in only 12,000 hours. Oriental continues to make the all-purpose rugs the same way as before. The number of rugs made and the labor hours required to make them after automation follow.

	Seasonal	All Purpose	Totals
Number of rugs	1,200	2,800	4,000
Number of direct labor hours	12,000	168,000	180,000

Overhead costs are expected to increase to $180,000 as a result of the automation. Allocate the increased overhead cost to the two types of rugs using direct labor hours as the allocation base and comment on the appropriateness of the allocation.

PROBLEM 6–15A *Using Activity-Based Costing to Improve Allocation Accuracy*   L.O. 3, 4

This problem is an extension of Problem 6–14A, which must be completed first.
Oriental's accounting staff has disaggregated the $180,000 of overhead costs into the following items.

(1) Inspection costs	$ 16,000
(2) Setup costs	10,800
(3) Engineering costs	16,000
(4) Legal costs related to products	6,000
(5) Materials movement cost per batch	2,400
(6) Salaries of production supervisors	40,000
(7) Fringe benefit costs	8,000
(8) Utilities costs	4,000
(9) Plant manager's salary	24,000
(10) Depreciation on production equipment	36,000
(11) Depreciation on building	8,000
(12) Miscellaneous costs	5,000
(13) Indirect materials costs	2,800
(14) Production employee incentive costs	1,000
Total	$180,000

Required

a. Each of Oriental's rug lines operates as a department. The all-purpose department occupies 6,000 square feet of floor space, and the seasonal department occupies 12,000 square feet of space. Comment on the validity of allocating the overhead costs by square footage.

b. Assume that the following additional information is available.
   (1) Rugs are individually inspected.
   (2) Oriental incurs setup costs each time a new style of seasonal rug is produced. The seasonal rugs were altered nine times during the year. The manual equipment for all-purpose rugs is reset twice

each year to ensure accurate weaving. The setup for the technical equipment used to weave seasonal rugs requires more highly skilled workers, but the all-purpose rugs require more manual equipment, thereby resulting in a *per setup* charge that is roughly equal for both types of rugs. Oriental undertook 22 setups during the year, 18 of which applied to seasonal rugs and 4 that applied to all-purpose rugs.

(3) Ninety percent of the product-level costs can be traced to producing seasonal rugs.

(4) Six supervisors oversee the production of all-purpose rugs. Because seasonal rugs are made in an automated department, only two production supervisors are needed.

(5) Each rug requires an equal amount of indirect materials.

(6) Costs associated with production activities are assigned to six activity cost pools: (1) labor-related activities, (2) unit-level activities, (3) batch-level activities, (4) product-level supervisory activities, (5) other product-level activities, and (6) facility-level activities.

Organize the $180,000 of overhead costs into activity center cost pools and allocate the costs to the two types of rugs.

c. Assuming that 90 seasonal and 240 all-purpose rugs were made in January, determine the overhead costs that would be assigned to each of the two rug types for the month of January.

L.O. 4   PROBLEM 6–16A *Using Activity-Based Costing to Improve Allocation Accuracy*

The Scholars' Paradise, Inc. (SPI), is a profit-oriented education business. SPI provides remedial training for high school students who have fallen behind in their classroom studies. It charges its students $300 per course. During the previous year, SPI provided instruction for 2,000 students. The income statement for the company follows.

Revenue	$600,000
Cost of Instructors	(238,000)
Overhead Costs	(170,000)
Net Income	$192,000

The company president, Kim Donavan, indicated in a discussion with the accountant, Victor Singh, that she was extremely pleased with the growth in the area of computer-assisted instruction. She observed that this department served 400 students using only one part-time instructor. In contrast, the classroom-based instructional department required 32 instructors to teach 1,600 students. Ms. Donavan noted that the per student cost of instruction was dramatically lower for the computer-assisted department. She based her conclusion on the following information.

SPI pays its part-time instructors an average of $7,000 per year. The total cost of instruction and the cost per student are computed as follows.

Type of Instruction	Computer-Assisted	Classroom
Number of instructors (a)	2	32
Number of students (b)	400	1,600
Total cost (c = a × $7,000)	$14,000	$224,000
Cost per student (c ÷ b)	$35	$140

Assuming that overhead costs were distributed equally across the student population, Ms. Donavan concluded that the cost of instructors was the critical variable in the company's capacity to generate profits. Based on her analysis, her strategic plan called for heavily increased use of computer-assisted instruction.

Mr. Singh was not so sure that computer-assisted instruction should be stressed. After attending a seminar on activity-based costing (ABC), he believed that the allocation of overhead cost could be more closely traced to the different types of learning activities. To facilitate an activity-based analysis, he developed the following information about the costs associated with computer-assisted versus classroom instructional activities. He identified $96,000 of overhead costs that were directly traceable to computer-assisted activities, including the costs of computer hardware, software, and technical assistance. He believed the remaining $74,000 of overhead costs should be allocated to the two instructional activities based on the number of students enrolled in each program.

Required

a. Based on the preceding information, determine the total cost and the cost per student to provide courses through computer-assisted instruction versus classroom instruction.

b. Comment on the validity of stressing growth in the area of computer-assisted instruction.

PROBLEM 6–17A *Key Activity-Based Costing Concepts*   **L.O. 6**

Williams Paint Company makes paint in many different colors; it charges the same price for all of its paint regardless of the color. Recently, Williams' chief competitor cut the price of its white paint, which normally outsells any other color by a margin of 4 to 1. Williams' marketing manager requested permission to match the competitor's price. When Gene Taylor, Williams' president, discussed the matter with Kay Spencer, the chief accountant, he was told that the competitor's price was below Williams' cost. Mr. Taylor responded, "If that's the case, then there is something wrong with our accounting system. I know the competition wouldn't sell below cost. Prepare a report showing me how you determine our paint cost and get back to me as soon as possible."

The next day, Ms. Spencer returned to Mr. Taylor's office and began by saying, "Determining the cost per gallon is a pretty simple computation. It includes $1.10 of labor, $3.10 of materials, and $4.00 of overhead for a total cost of $8.20 per gallon. The problem is that the competition is selling the stuff for $7.99 per gallon. They've got to be losing money."

Mr. Taylor then asked Ms. Spencer how she determined the overhead cost. She replied, "We take total overhead cost and divide it by total labor hours and then assign it to the products based on the direct labor hours required to make the paint." Mr. Taylor then asked what kinds of costs are included in the total overhead cost. Ms. Spencer said, "It includes the depreciation on the building and equipment, the cost of utilities, supervisory salaries, interest. Just how detailed do you want me to go with this list?"

Mr. Taylor responded, "Keep going, I'll tell you when I've heard enough."

Ms. Spencer continued, "There is the cost of setups. Every time a color is changed, the machines have to be cleaned, the color release valves reset, a trial batch prepared, and color quality tested. Sometimes mistakes occur and the machines must be reset. In addition, purchasing and handling the color ingredients must be accounted for as well as adjustments in the packaging department to change the paint cans and to mark the boxes to show the color change. Then . . ."

Mr. Taylor interrupted, "I think I've heard enough. We sell so much white paint that we run it through a separate production process. White paint is produced continuously. There are no shutdowns and setups. White uses no color ingredients. So why are these costs being assigned to our white paint production?"

Ms. Spencer replied, "Well, sir, these costs are just a part of the big total that is allocated to all of the paint, no matter what color it happens to be."

Mr. Taylor looked disgusted and said, "As I told you yesterday, Ms. Spencer, something is wrong with our accounting system!"

Required

a. Explain what the terms *overcost* and *undercost* mean. Is Williams' white paint over- or undercosted?

b. Explain what the term *companywide overhead rate* means. Is Williams using a companywide overhead rate?

c. Explain how Williams could improve the accuracy of its overhead cost allocations.

PROBLEM 6–18A *Pricing Decisions Made With ABC System Cost Data*   **L.O. 4, 7**

Ivan Sporting Goods Corporation makes two types of racquets, tennis and badminton. The company uses the same facility to make both products even though the processes are quite different. The company has recently converted its cost accounting system to activity-based costing. The following are the cost data that Sam Cooper, the cost accountant, prepared for the third quarter of 2002 (during which Ivan made 70,000 tennis racquets and 30,000 badminton racquets):

Direct Cost	Tennis Racquet (TR)	Badminton Racquet (BR)
Direct materials	$14 per unit	$10 per unit
Direct labor	38 per unit	28 per unit

Category	Estimated Cost	Cost Driver	Amount of Cost Driver
Unit level	$ 750,000	Number of inspection hours	TR: 15,000 hours; BR: 10,000 hours
Batch level	250,000	Number of setups	TR: 80 setups; BR: 45 setups
Product level	150,000	Number of TV commercials	TR: 4; BR: 1
Facility level	650,000	Number of machine hours	TR: 30,000 hours; BR: 35,000 hours
Total	$1,800,000		

Inspectors are paid according to the number of actual hours worked, which is determined by the number of racquets inspected. Engineers who set up equipment for both products are paid monthly salaries.

TV commercial fees are paid at the beginning of the quarter. Facility-level cost includes depreciation of all production equipment.

Required

a. Compute the cost per unit for each product.

b. If management wants to price badminton racquets 30 percent above cost, what price should the company set?

c. The market price of tennis racquets has declined substantially because of new competitors entering the market. Management asks you to determine the minimum cost of producing tennis racquets in the short term. Provide that information.

L.O. 4, 7 **PROBLEM 6–19A** *Target Pricing and Target Costing With ABC*

Hardy Cameras, Inc., manufactures two models of cameras. Model ZM has a zoom lens; Model DS has a fixed lens. Hardy uses an activity-based costing system. The following are the relevant cost data for the previous month.

Direct Cost per Unit	Model ZM	Model DS
Direct materials	$30	$15
Direct labor	33	12

Category	Estimated Cost	Cost Driver	Use of Cost Driver
Unit level	$ 27,000	Number of units	ZM: 2,400 units; DS: 9,600 units
Batch level	50,000	Number of setups	ZM: 25 setups; DS: 25 setups
Product level	90,000	Number of TV commercials	ZM: 15; DS: 10
Facility level	300,000	Number of machine hours	ZM: 500 hours; DS: 1,000 hours
Total	$467,000		

Hardy's facility has the capacity to operate 4,500 machine hours per month.

Required

a. Compute the cost per unit for each product.

b. The current market price for products comparable to Model ZM is $146 and for DS is $54. If Hardy sold all of its products at the market prices, what was its profit or loss for the previous month?

c. A market expert believes that Hardy can sell as many cameras as it can produce by pricing Model ZM at $140 and Model DS at $50. Hardy would like to use those estimates as its target prices and have a profit margin of 20 percent of target prices. What is the target cost for each product?

d. Is there any way for the company to reach its target costs?

L.O. 4 **PROBLEM 6–20A** *Cost Management With an ABC System*

Percy Chairs, Inc., makes two types of chairs. Model Diamond is a high-end product designed for professional offices. Model Gold is an economical product designed for family use. Judith Percy, the president, is worried about cut-throat price competition in the chairs market. Her company suffered a loss last quarter, an unprecedented event in its history. The company's accountant prepared the following cost data for Ms. Percy.

Direct Cost per Unit	Model Diamond (D)	Model Gold (G)
Direct materials	$20 per unit	$10 per unit
Direct labor	$24/hour × 2 hours production time	$24/hour × 1 hour production time

Category	Estimated Cost	Cost Driver	Use of Cost Driver
Unit level	$ 300,000	Number of units	D: 15,000 units; G: 35,000 units
Batch level	750,000	Number of setups	D: 104 setups; G: 146 setups
Product level	450,000	Number of TV commercials	D: 5; G: 10
Facility level	500,000	Number of machine hours	D: 1,500 hours; G: 3,500 hours
Total	$2,000,000		

The market price for office chairs comparable to Model Diamond is $112 and to Model Gold is $68.

Required

a. Compute the cost per unit for both products.

b. Andrew Ryan, the chief engineer, told Ms. Percy that the company is currently making 150 units of Model Diamond per batch and 245 units of Model Gold per batch. He suggests doubling the batch sizes to cut the number of setups in half, thereby reducing the setup cost by 50 percent. Compute the cost per unit for each product if Ms. Percy adopts his suggestion.

c. Is there any side effect if Ms. Percy increases the production batch size by 100 percent?

PROBLEM 6–21A *Assessing a Quality Control Strategy*   L.O. 10, 11

The following quality cost report came from the records of Rios Company.

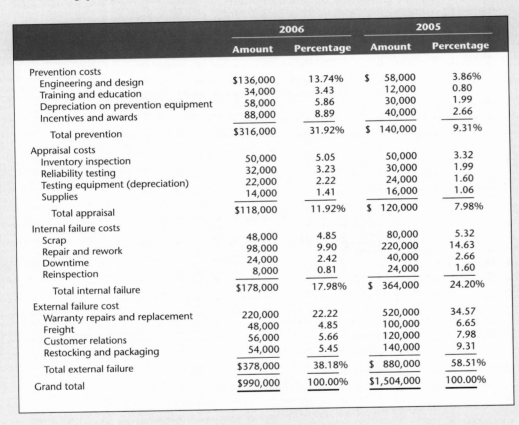

	2006		2005	
	Amount	Percentage	Amount	Percentage
Prevention costs				
Engineering and design	$136,000	13.74%	$ 58,000	3.86%
Training and education	34,000	3.43	12,000	0.80
Depreciation on prevention equipment	58,000	5.86	30,000	1.99
Incentives and awards	88,000	8.89	40,000	2.66
Total prevention	$316,000	31.92%	$ 140,000	9.31%
Appraisal costs				
Inventory inspection	50,000	5.05	50,000	3.32
Reliability testing	32,000	3.23	30,000	1.99
Testing equipment (depreciation)	22,000	2.22	24,000	1.60
Supplies	14,000	1.41	16,000	1.06
Total appraisal	$118,000	11.92%	$ 120,000	7.98%
Internal failure costs				
Scrap	48,000	4.85	80,000	5.32
Repair and rework	98,000	9.90	220,000	14.63
Downtime	24,000	2.42	40,000	2.66
Reinspection	8,000	0.81	24,000	1.60
Total internal failure	$178,000	17.98%	$ 364,000	24.20%
External failure cost				
Warranty repairs and replacement	220,000	22.22	520,000	34.57
Freight	48,000	4.85	100,000	6.65
Customer relations	56,000	5.66	120,000	7.98
Restocking and packaging	54,000	5.45	140,000	9.31
Total external failure	$378,000	38.18%	$ 880,000	58.51%
Grand total	$990,000	100.00%	$1,504,000	100.00%

Required

a. Explain the strategy that Rios Company initiated to control its quality costs.

b. Indicate whether the strategy was successful or unsuccessful in reducing quality costs.

c. Explain how the strategy likely affected customer satisfaction.

EXERCISES—SERIES B

EXERCISE 6–1B *Classifying the Costs of Unit-, Batch-, Product-, or Facility-Level Activities*   L.O. 5

Uptown Manufacturing is developing an activity-based costing system to improve overhead cost allocation. One of the first steps in developing the system is to classify the costs of performing production activities into activity cost pools.

Required

Using the four-tier cost hierarchy described in the chapter, classify each of the following costs into unit-level, batch-level, product-level, or facility-level cost pools.

Cost Activity	Cost Pool
a. Lubricant for machines	
b. Parts used to make a particular product	
c. Machine setup cost	
d. Salary of the plant manager's secretary	
e. Factory depreciation	
f. Advertising costs for a particular product	
g. Wages of assembly line workers	
h. Product design costs	
i. Materials requisition costs for a particular work order	
j. Security guard wages	

L.O. 4   **EXERCISE 6–2B** *Identifying Appropriate Cost Drivers*

Required

Provide at least one example of an appropriate cost driver (allocation base) for each of the following activities.

a. The production supervisor completes the paperwork initiating a work order.

b. The production manager prepares materials requisition forms.

c. Workers move materials from the warehouse to the factory floor.

d. Assembly line machines are operated.

e. Workers count completed goods before moving them to a warehouse.

f. A logistics manager runs a computer program to determine the materials release schedule.

g. Janitors clean the factory floor after workers have left.

h. Mechanics apply lubricant to machines.

i. Engineers design a product production layout.

j. Engineers set up machines to produce a product.

L.O. 4, 5   **EXERCISE 6–3B** *Classifying Costs and Identifying the Appropriate Cost Driver*

Gurosky Corporation, a furniture manufacturer, uses an activity-based costing system. It has identified the following selected activities:

1. Inspecting wood prior to using it in production.

2. Packaging completed furniture in boxes for shipment.

3. Inspecting completed furniture for quality control.

4. Purchasing TV time to advertise a particular product.

5. Incurring property taxes on factory buildings.

6. Incurring paint cost for furniture produced.

7. Setting up machines for a particular batch of production.

Required

a. Classify each activity as a unit-level, batch-level, product-level, or facility-level activity.

b. Identify an appropriate cost driver (allocation base) for each of the activities.

L.O. 5   **EXERCISE 6–4B** *Understanding the Context-Sensitive Nature of Classifying Activities*

Required

Describe a set of circumstances in which labor cost could be classified as a unit-level, batch-level, product-level, or facility-level cost.

L.O. 5   **EXERCISE 6–5B** *Understanding the Context-Sensitive Nature of Classifying Activities*

Merriam Company makes two types of cell phones. Handy is a thin, pocket-size cell phone that is easy to carry around. Action is a palm-size phone convenient to hold while the user is talking. During its most recent accounting period, Merriam incurred $150,000 of quality-control costs. Recently Merriam established an activity-based costing system, which involved classifying its activities into four categories. Each of the categories and appropriate cost drivers follow.

	Direct Labor Hours	Number of Batches	Number of Inspectors	Number of Square Feet
Handy	26,000	38	10	37,000
Action	24,000	22	5	83,000
Totals	50,000	60	15	120,000

Merriam uses direct labors hours to allocate unit-level activities, number of batches to allocate batch-level activities, number of inspectors to allocate product-level activities, and number of square feet to allocate facility-level activities.

Required

Allocate the quality-control cost between the two products, assuming that it is driven by (a) unit-level activities, (b) batch-level activities, (c) product-level activities, and (d) facility-level activities.

EXERCISE 6–6B *Computing Overhead Rates Based on Different Cost Drivers*   **L.O. 4**

Ballentine Industries produces two surge protectors: VC620 with six outlets and PH630 with eight outlets and two telephone line connections. Because of these product differences, the company plans to use activity-based costing to allocate overhead costs. The company has identified four activity pools. Relevant information follows.

Activity Pools	Cost Pool Total	Cost Driver
Machine setup	$120,000	Number of setups
Machine operation	300,000	Number of machine hours
Quality control	48,000	Number of inspections
Packaging	32,000	Number of units
Total overhead cost	$500,000	

Expected activity for each product follows.

	Number of Setups	Number of Machine Hours	Number of Inspections	Number of Units
VC620	48	1,400	78	25,000
PH630	72	2,600	172	15,000
Total	120	4,000	250	40,000

Required

a. Compute the overhead rate for each activity pool.
b. Determine the overhead cost allocated to each product.

EXERCISE 6–7B *Comparing an ABC System With a Traditional Cost System*   **L.O. 1, 3**

Use the information in Exercise 6–6B to complete the following requirements. Assume that before shifting to activity-based costing, Ballentine Industries allocated all overhead costs based on direct labor hours. Direct labor data pertaining to the two surge protectors follow.

	Direct Labor Hours
VC620	16,000
PH630	9,000
Total	25,000

Required:

a. Compute the amount of overhead cost allocated to each surge protector when using direct labor hours as the allocation base.
b. Determine the cost per unit for overhead when using direct labor hours as the allocation base and when using ABC.
c. Explain why the per unit overhead cost is lower for the higher-volume product when using ABC.

EXERCISE 6–8B *Allocating Costs With Different Cost Drivers*   **L.O. 1, 3**

Sandmon Sporting Goods, Inc., produces indoor treadmills. The company allocates its overhead costs using activity-based costing. The costs and cost drivers associated with the four overhead activity cost pools follow.

Activities	Unit Level	Batch Level	Product Level	Facility Level
Cost	$750,000	$300,000	$150,000	$900,000
Cost driver	12,500 labor hours	50 setups	Percentage of use	15,000 units

Producing 5,000 units of PFT200, one of the company's five products, took 4,000 labor hours, 25 setups, and consumed 30 percent of the product-sustaining activities.

Required

a. Had the company used labor hours as a companywide allocation base, how much overhead would it have allocated to the 5,000 units of PFT200?

b. How much overhead is allocated to the 5,000 PFT200 units using activity-based costing?

c. Compute the overhead cost per unit for PFT200 using activity-based costing and direct labor hours if 5,000 units are produced. If direct product costs are $337 and PFT200 is priced at 20 percent above cost (rounded to the nearest whole dollar), compute the product's selling price under each allocation system.

d. Assuming that activity-based costing provides a more accurate estimate of cost, indicate whether PFT200 would be over- or underpriced if Sandmon uses direct labor hours as the allocation base. Explain how over- or undercosting can affect Sandmon's profitability.

e. Comment on the validity of using the allocated facility-level cost in the pricing decision. Should other costs be considered in a cost-plus pricing decision? If so, which ones? What costs would you include if you were trying to decide whether to accept a special order?

L.O. 1, 3   **EXERCISE 6–9B** *Allocating Costs With Different Cost Drivers*

Burns Shoes Corporation produces three brands of shoes, Brisk, Pro, and Runner. Relevant information about Burns' overhead activities, their respective costs, and their cost drivers follows.

Overhead Costs	Cost Driver	Brisk	Pro	Runner
Fringe benefits ($360,000)	Labor hours	10,000	20,000	20,000
Setups ($200,000)	Number of setups	15	25	10
Packing costs ($40,000)	Number of cartons	200	300	300
Quality control ($300,000)	Number of tests	120	200	80

Required

a. Burns currently allocates all overhead costs based on labor hours. The company produced the following numbers of pairs of shoes during the prior year.

Brisk	Pro	Runner
10,000	15,000	20,000

Determine the overhead cost per pair of shoes for each brand.

b. Determine the overhead cost per pair of shoes for each brand, assuming that the volume-based allocation system described in Requirement *a* is replaced with an activity-based costing system.

c. Explain why the per pair overhead costs determined in Requirements *a* and *b* differ.

L.O. 4   **EXERCISE 6–10B** *Computing Product Cost With Given Activity Allocation Rates*

Using automated production processes, Gutner Videos produces two kinds of camcorders: N100 is an analog recorder and D200 is a digital recorder. The company has found activity-based costing useful in assigning overhead costs to its products. It has identified the following five major activities involved in producing the camcorders.

Activity	Allocation Base	Allocation Rate
Materials receiving and handling	Cost of materials	3% of materials cost
Production setup	Number of setups	$1,500 per setup
Assembly	Number of parts	$8 per part
Quality inspection	Inspection time	$25 per minute
Packing and shipping	Number of orders	$80 per order

Activity measures for the two kinds of camcorders follow.

	Labor Cost*	Materials Cost*	Number of Setups	Number of Parts	Inspection Time	Number of Orders
N100	$450,000	$250,000	10	10,000	800 min.	25
D200	300,000	300,000	25	10,000	4,800 min.	50

*Both are direct costs.

Required
a. Compute the cost per unit of N100 and D200, assuming that Gutner made 1,000 units of each type of camcorder.
b. Explain why the D200 digital camcorders cost more to make although their direct costs are less than those for the N100 analog camcorders.

EXERCISE 6–11B Allocating Facility-Level Cost and a Product Elimination Decision L.O. 4

Bagsley Corporation produces two types of juice that it packages in cases of 24 cans per case. Selected per case data for the two products for the last month follow.

	Orange Juice	Tomato Juice
Production costs		
Direct material	$3	$2
Direct labor	$2	$3
Allocated overhead	$3	$4
Total cases produced and sold	25,000	15,000
Total sales revenue	$280,000	$170,000

Bagsley allocates production overhead using activity-based costing but allocates monthly packaging expense, which amounted to $80,000 last month, to the two products equally.

Required
a. Compute the net profit for each product.
b. Assuming that the overhead allocation for the tomato juice includes $30,000 of facility-level cost, would you advise Bagsley to eliminate this product? (*Hint:* Consider the method used to allocate the monthly packaging expense.)

EXERCISE 6–12B Applying Concepts of Quality Cost Management L.O. 10

Jocelyn Vince, the president of Grayson Industries, Inc., was beaming when she was reviewing the company's quality cost report. After she had implemented a quality-control program for three years, the company's defect rate had declined from 20 percent to 3 percent. Mrs. Vince patted Julian Marbury, the production manager, on his back and said: "You have done a great job! I plan to reward you for your hard work. However, I want the defects to disappear completely before I promote you to the position of executive vice president. So, zero-defect is going to be your personal goal for the coming year." Mr. Marbury responded wearily, "I'm not sure that's really a good idea."

Required
Write a memorandum to the president explaining that zero defect is not a practical policy.

PROBLEMS—SERIES B

PROBLEM 6–13B Comparing an ABC System With a Traditional Costing System L.O. 1, 3

Since its inception, Pioneer Laboratory, Inc., has produced a single product, Product S109. With the advent of automation, the company added the technological capability to begin producing a second product, Product N227. Because of the success of Product N227, manufacturing has been shifting toward its production. Sales of Product N227 are now 50 percent of the total annual sales of 20,000 units, and the company is optimistic about the new product's future sales growth. One reason the company is excited

about the sales potential of its new product is that the new product's gross profit margin is higher than that of Product S109. Management is thrilled with the new product's initial success but concerned about the company's declining profits since the product's introduction. Suspecting a problem with the company's costing system, management hires you to investigate.

In reviewing the company's records, product specifications, and manufacturing processes, you discover the following information.

1. The company is in an extremely competitive industry in which markups are low and accurate estimates of cost are critical to success.
2. Product N227 has complex parts that require more labor, machine time, setups, and inspections than Product S109.
3. Budgeted costs for direct materials and labor follow.

Direct Cost per Unit	Product S109	Product N227
Direct materials	$24	$24
Direct labor	$15/hour × 2 hours production time	$15/hour × 2.8 hours production time

4. The company presently allocates overhead costs to its products based on direct labor hours. After carefully studying the company's overhead, you identify four different categories of overhead costs. Using your knowledge of this company and similar companies in the same industry, you estimate the total costs for each of these categories and identify the most appropriate cost driver for measuring each product's overhead consumption. Detailed information for each cost category follows.

Category	Estimated Cost	Cost Driver	Use of Cost Driver
Unit level	$ 540,000	Number of machine hours	S109: 20,000 hours; N227: 60,000 hours
Batch level	228,000	Number of machine setups	S109: 1,500; N227: 3,500
Product level	180,000	Number of inspections	S109: 200; N227: 600
Facility level	60,000	Equal percentage for products	S109: 50%; N227: 50%
Total	$1,008,000		

Required

a. Determine the predetermined overhead rate the company is using.
b. Compute the amount of overhead the company assigns to each product using this rate.
c. Determine the cost per unit and total cost of each product when overhead is assigned based on direct labor hours.
d. To remain competitive, the company prices its products at only 20 percent above cost. Compute the price for each product with this markup.
e. Compute the overhead rate for each category of activity.
f. Determine the amount of overhead cost, both in total and per unit, that would be assigned to each product if the company switched to activity-based costing.
g. Assuming that prices are adjusted to reflect activity-based costs, determine the revised price for each product.
h. Based on your results for Requirements f and g, explain why Product N227 costs more to make than previously apparent and why sales prices therefore need to be adjusted.

L.O. 1, 3   PROBLEM 6–14B *Using Activity-Based Costing to Improve Allocation Accuracy*

Vivian's Commemoratives makes and sells two types of decorative plates. One plate displays a hand-painted image of Princess Diana; the other plate displays a machine-pressed image of Marilyn Monroe. The Diana plates require 25,000 hours of direct labor to make; the Monroe plates require only 5,000 hours of direct labor. Overhead costs are composed of (1) $70,000 machine-related activity costs including indirect labor, utilities, and depreciation and (2) $50,000 labor-related activity costs including overtime pay, fringe benefits, and payroll taxes.

Required

a. Assuming that Vivian's uses direct labor hours as the allocation base, determine the amount of the total $120,000 overhead cost that would be allocated to each type of plate.
b. Explain why using direct labor hours may distort the allocation of overhead cost to the two products.
c. Explain how activity-based costing could improve the accuracy of the overhead cost allocation.

PROBLEM 6–15B *Using Activity-Based Costing to Improve Allocation Accuracy*   L.O. 4

This problem is an extension of Problem 6–14B, which must be completed first.

Assume the same data as in Problem 6–14B with the following additional information. The hours of machine time for processing plates are 1,000 for Diana plates and 2,500 for Monroe plates.

Required

a. Establish two activity centers, one for machine-related activities and the second for labor-related activities. Assign the total overhead costs to the two activity centers.

b. Allocate the machine-related overhead costs to each product based on machine hours.

c. Allocate the labor-related overhead costs to each product based on direct labor hours.

d. Draw a diagram that compares the one-stage allocation method used in Problem 6–14B with the two-stage activity-based costing approach used in this problem.

PROBLEM 6–16B *Using Activity-Based Costing to Improve Business Decisions*   L.O. 4

Kassick CPA and Associates is a local accounting firm specializing in bookkeeping and tax services. The firm has four certified public accountants who supervise 20 clerks. The clerks handle basic bookkeeping jobs and prepare tax return drafts. The CPAs review and approve the bookkeeping jobs and tax returns. Each CPA receives a fixed salary of $8,000 per month; the clerks earn an hourly rate of $15. Because the clerks are paid by the hour and their work hours can be directly traced to individual jobs, their wages are considered direct costs. The CPAs' salaries are not traced to individual jobs and are therefore treated as indirect costs. The firm allocates overhead based on direct labor hours. The following is Kassick's income statement for the previous month.

	Bookkeeping	Tax	Total
Revenues	$50,000	$50,000	$100,000
Direct Expenses	(18,000)*	(18,000)*	(36,000)
Indirect Supervisory Expenses	(16,000)	(16,000)	(32,000)
Net Income	$16,000	$16,000	$ 32,000

*1,200 clerical hours were used in each category during the previous month.

Carla Kassick, CPA and chief executive officer, is not sure that the two operations are equally profitable as the income statement indicates. First, she believes that most of the CPAs' time was spent instructing clerks in tax return preparation. The bookkeeping jobs appear to be routine, and most of the clerks can handle them with little supervision. After attending a recent professional development seminar on activity-based costing (ABC), Ms. Kassick believes that the allocation of indirect costs can be more closely traced to different types of services. To facilitate an activity-based analysis, she asked the CPAs to document their work hours on individual jobs for the last week. The results indicate that, on average, 25 percent of the CPAs' hours was spent supervising bookkeeping activities and the remaining 75 percent was spent supervising tax activities.

Required

a. Based on the preceding information, reconstruct the income statement for bookkeeping services, tax services, and the total, assuming that Kassick revises its allocation of indirect supervisory costs based on ABC.

b. Comment on the results and recommend a new business strategy.

PROBLEM 6–17B *Key Activity-Based Costing Concepts*   L.O. 6

Gulf Boot and Shoe Company makes hand-sewn boots and shoes. Gulf uses a companywide overhead rate based on direct labor hours to allocate indirect manufacturing costs to its products. Making a pair of boots normally requires 2.4 hours of direct labor, and making a pair of shoes requires 1.8 hours. The company's shoe division, facing increased competition from international companies that have access to cheap labor, has responded by automating its shoe production. The reengineering process was expensive, requiring the purchase of manufacturing equipment and the restructuring of the plant layout. In addition, utility and maintenance costs increased significantly for operating the new equipment. Even so, labor costs decreased significantly. Now making a pair of shoes requires only 18 minutes of direct labor. As predicted, the labor savings more than offset the increase in overhead cost, thereby reducing the total cost to make a pair of shoes. The company experienced an unexpected side effect, however; according to the company's accounting records, the cost to make a pair of boots increased although the manufacturing

process in the boot division was not affected by the reengineering of the shoe division. In other words, the cost of boots increased although Gulf did not change anything about the way it makes them.

Required
a. Explain why the accounting records reflected an increase in the cost to make a pair of boots.
b. Explain how the companywide overhead rate could result in the underpricing of shoes.
c. Explain how activity-based costing could improve the accuracy of overhead cost allocations.

L.O. 4   PROBLEM 6–18B *Pricing Decisions Made With ABC System Cost Data*

Schaffer Furniture Corporation makes two types of dining tables, Elegance for formal dining and Comfort for casual dining, at its single factory. With the economy beginning to experience a recession, Ken Schaffer, the president, is concerned about whether the company can stay in business as market prices fall. At Mr. Schaffer's request, Amy Chang, the controller, prepared cost data for analysis.

Inspectors are paid according to the number of actual hours worked, determined by the number of tables inspected. Engineers who set up equipment for both products are paid monthly salaries. TV commercial fees are paid at the beginning of the quarter.

Direct Cost	Elegance (E)	Comfort (C)
Direct materials	$60 per unit	$33 per unit
Direct labor	$36 per hour × 1.5 hours production time	$36 per hour × 1 hour production time

Category	Estimated Cost	Cost Driver	Use of Cost Driver
Product inspection	$120,000	Number of units	E: 2,500 units; C: 7,500 units
Machine setups	75,000	Number of setups	E: 23 setups; C: 27 setups
Product advertising	210,000	Number of TV commercials	E: 5; C: 9
Facility depreciation	405,000	Number of machine hours	E: 5,000 hours; C: 5,000 hours
Total	$810,000		

Required
a. Compute the cost per unit for each product.
b. If management wants to make 30 percent of cost as a profit margin for Elegance, what price should the company set?
c. The market price of tables in the Comfort class has declined because of the recession. Management asks you to determine the minimum cost of producing Comfort tables in the short term. Provide that information.

L.O. 4, 7   PROBLEM 6–19B *Target Pricing and Target Costing With ABC*

Vicaro Corporation manufactures two models of watches. Model Wonder displays cartoon characters and has simple features designed for kids. Model Marvel has sophisticated features such as dual time zones and an attached calculator. Vicaro's product design team has worked with a cost accountant to prepare a budget for the two products for the next fiscal year as follows.

Direct Cost	Wonder (W)	Marvel (M)
Direct materials	$8 per unit	$20 per unit
Direct labor	$40/hour × 0.2 hour production time	$40/hour × 0.6 hour production time

Category	Estimated Cost	Cost Driver	Use of Cost Driver
Materials handling	$366,000	Number of parts	W: 700,000; M: 520,000
Machine setups	180,000	Number of setups	W: 50; M: 40
Product testing	28,000	Number of units tested	W: 1,000; M: 400
Facility depreciation	360,000	Number of machine hours	W: 3,200; M: 4,000
Total	$934,000		

Wonder watches have 35 parts, and Marvel watches have 65 parts. The budget calls for producing 20,000 units of Wonder and 8,000 units of Marvel. Vicaro tests 5 percent of its products for quality assurance. It sells all its products at market prices.

Required

a. Compute the cost per unit for each product.

b. The current market price for products comparable to Wonder is $36 and for products comparable to Marvel is $110. What will Vicaro's profit or loss for the next year be?

c. Vicaro likes to have a 25 percent profit margin based on the current market price for each product. What is the target cost for each product? What is the total target profit?

d. The president of Vicaro has asked the design team to refine the production design to bring down the product cost. After a series of redesigns, the team recommends a new process that requires purchasing a new machine that costs $400,000 and has five years of useful life and no salvage value. With the new process and the new machine, Vicaro can decrease the number of machine setups to four for each product and cut the cost of materials handling in half. The machine hours used will be 4,500 for Wonder and 6,500 for Marvel. Does this new process enable Vicaro to achieve its target costs?

PROBLEM 6–20B *Cost Management With an ABC System*   **L.O. 4, 7**

Yates Corporation manufactures two different coffee makers, Professional for commercial use and Home for family use. Alan Winfrey, the president, recently received complaints from some members of the board of directors about the company's failure to reach the expected profit of $400,000 per month. Mr. Winfrey is, therefore, under great pressure to improve the company's bottom line. Under his direction, Becky Hall, the controller, prepared the following monthly cost data for Mr. Winfrey.

Direct Cost	Professional (P)	Home (H)
Direct materials	$42 per unit	$14 per unit
Direct labor	$36 per hour × 0.8 hour production time	$36 per hour × 0.3 hour production time

Category	Estimated Cost	Cost Driver	Use of Cost Driver
Product inspection	$ 120,000	Number of units	P: 15,000 units; H: 45,000 units
Machine setups	30,000	Number of setups	P: 30 setups; H: 45 setups
Product promotion	400,000	Number of TV commercials	P: 10; H: 10
Facility depreciation	590,000	Number of machine hours	P: 7,160 hours; H: 4,640 hours
Total	$1,140,000		

The market price for coffee makers comparable to Professional is $130 and to Home is $44. The company's administrative expenses amount to $390,000.

Required

a. Compute the cost per unit for both products.

b. Determine the company's profit or loss.

c. April Loren, the marketing manager, recommends that the company implement a focused marketing strategy. She argues that advertisements in trade journals would be more effective for the commercial market than on TV. In addition, the cost of journal ads would be only $42,000. She also proposes sending discount coupons to targeted households to reach a broad market base. The coupons program would cost $144,000. Compute the new cost of each product, assuming that Mr. Winfrey replaces TV advertising with Ms. Loren's suggestions.

d. Determine the company's profit or loss using the information in Requirement *c*.

PROBLEM 6–21B *Assessing a Quality Control Strategy*   **L.O. 10, 11**

Kofi Mensah, the president of Wilson Plastic Company, is a famous cost cutter in the plastics industry. Two years ago, he accepted an offer from Wilson's board of directors to help the company cut costs quickly. In fact, Mr. Mensah's compensation package included a year-end bonus tied to the percentage of cost decrease over the preceding year. On February 12, 2002, Mr. Mensah received comparative financial information for the two preceding years. He was especially interested in the results of his cost-cutting measures on quality control. The quality report shown on page 272 was extracted from the company's financial information:

Required

a. Explain the strategy that Mr. Mensah initiated to control Wilson's costs.

b. Indicate whether the strategy was successful or unsuccessful in reducing quality costs.

c. Explain how the strategy will likely affect the company's business in the long term.

	2001		2000	
	Amount	Percentage	Amount	Percentage
Prevention costs				
Engineering and design	$ 65,000	6.57%	$ 69,000	7.39%
Training and education	26,000	2.63	76,000	8.14
Depreciation on prevention equipment	15,000	1.51	15,000	1.60
Incentives and awards	20,000	2.02	20,000	2.14
Total prevention	$126,000	12.73%	$180,000	19.27%
Appraisal costs				
Product and materials inspection	33,000	3.33	73,000	7.82
Reliability testing	27,000	2.73	67,000	7.17
Testing equipment (depreciation)	38,000	3.83	38,000	4.07
Supplies	10,000	1.01	16,000	1.71
Total appraisal	$108,000	10.90%	$194,000	20.77%
Internal failure costs				
Scrap	52,000	5.25	120,000	12.85
Repair and rework	46,000	4.65	150,000	16.06
Downtime	64,000	6.46	40,000	4.28
Reinspection	8,000	0.81	24,000	2.57
Total internal failure	$170,000	17.17%	$334,000	35.76%
External failure cost				
Warranty repairs and replacement	347,000	35.05	125,000	13.38
Freight	75,000	7.58	31,000	3.32
Customer relations	45,000	4.55	28,000	3.00
Restocking and packaging	119,000	12.02	42,000	4.50
Total external failure	$586,000	59.20%	$226,000	24.20%
Grand total	$990,000	100.00%	$934,000	100.00%

ANALYZE, THINK, COMMUNICATE

ATC 6–1   BUSINESS APPLICATION CASE *Using ABC to Improve Product Costing*

Dayton Technologies produces component parts for vinyl window manufacturers. The component parts consist of strips of material priced and sold by the linear foot. The material comes in different grades and colors. Dayton recently implemented an ABC system. To evaluate the effectiveness of the new system, Dayton's managerial accountants prepared reports comparing cost data based on ABC allocations and cost data based on traditional costing methods. The traditional costing approach used a single driver (material dollars) as the basis for product costing allocations. The ABC system uses a variety of cost drivers related to the activities required to produce the vinyl materials. The following data about three specific products were included in the reports.

Product	Selling Price per Foot	Feet Produced	ABC Cost per Foot	Traditional Cost per Foot
X	$1.25	425,000	$1.10	$0.81
Y	0.95	400,000	0.87	0.67
Z	0.89	350,000	0.74	0.53

Data Source: N. R. Pemberton, L. Arumugam, and N. Hassan, "From Obstacles to Opportunities," *Management Accounting,* March 1996, pp. 20–27. To facilitate the development of the case, it was necessary to rename the products and to mathematically manipulate some of the original data included in the article, but these changes are cosmetic in nature and do not compromise the results of the comparison.

Required
a. Determine the ABC margin ([selling price − ABC cost] × feet produced) for each product.
b. Determine the traditional margin ([selling price − traditional cost] × feet produced) for each product.
c. Explain why the ABC margins are lower than the traditional margins.

d. Based on the information provided, has traditional costing resulted in over- or undercosting of products X, Y, and Z? Suggest how the over- or undercosting has affected Dayton's profitability.

e. Suggest what action management should take with respect to the discoveries brought to light by the ABC cost analysis. Assume that Dayton normally expects a product to produce a margin of at least 25 percent of the sales price.

GROUP ASSIGNMENT *Using ABC in a Service Business*

ATC 6–2

A dialysis clinic provides two types of treatment for its patients. Hemodialysis (HD), an in-house treatment, requires that patients visit the clinic three times each week for dialysis treatments. Peritoneal dialysis (PD) permits patients to self-administer their treatments at home on a daily basis. On average, the clinic serves 102 HD patients and 62 PD patients. A recent development caused clinic administrators to develop a keen interest in cost measurement for the two separate services. Managed care plans such as HMOs began to pay treatment providers a fixed payment per insured participant regardless of the level of services provided by the clinic. With fixed fee revenues, the clinic was forced to control costs to ensure profitability. As a result, knowing the cost to provide HD versus PD services was critically important for the clinic. It needed accurate cost measurements to answer the following questions. Were both services profitable, or was one service carrying the burden of the other service? Should advertising be directed toward acquiring HD or PD patients? Should the clinic eliminate HMO service?

Management suspected the existing cost allocation system was inaccurate in measuring the true cost of providing the respective services; it had been developed in response to Medicare reporting requirements. It allocated costs between HD and PD based on the ratio of cost to charges (RCC). In other words, RRC allocates indirect costs in proportion to revenues. To illustrate, consider the allocation of $883,280 of indirect nursing services costs, which are allocated to the two treatment groups in relation to the revenue generated by each group. Given that the clinic generated total revenue of $3,006,775, an allocation rate of 0.2937633 per revenue dollar was established ($883,280 ÷ $3,006,775). This rate was multiplied by the proportionate share of revenue generated by each service category to produce the following allocation.

Type of Service	Service Revenue	×	Allocation Rate	=	Allocated Cost
HD	$1,860,287	×	0.2937633	=	$546,484
PD	1,146,488	×	0.2937633	=	336,796
Total	$3,006,775	×	0.2937633	=	$883,280

To better assess the cost of providing each type of service, the clinic initiated an activity-based costing (ABC) system. The ABC approach divided the nursing service cost into four separate cost pools. A separate cost driver (allocation base) was identified for each cost pool. The cost pools and their respective cost drivers follow.

	Total	HD	PD
Nursing services cost pool categories			
RNs	$239,120	?	?
LPNs	404,064	?	?
Nursing administration and support staff	115,168	?	?
Dialysis machine operations (tech. salaries)	124,928	?	?
Total	$883,280	?	?

	Total	HD	PD
Activity cost drivers (corresponding to cost pools)			
Number of RNs	7	5	2
Number of LPNs	19	15	4
Number of treatments (nursing administration)	34,967	14,343	20,624
Number of dialyzer treatments (machine operations)	14,343	14,343	0

Data Source: T. D. West and D. A. West, "Applying ABC to Healthcare," *Management Accounting,* February 1999, pp. 22–33.

Required

a. Organize the class into four sections and divide the sections into groups of four or five students each. Assign Task 1 to the first section of groups, Task 2 to the second section, Task 3 to the third section, and Task 4 to the fourth section.

Group Tasks

(1) Allocate the RN cost pool between the HD and PD service centers.

(2) Allocate the LPN cost pool between the HD and PD service centers.

(3) Allocate the nursing administration and support staff cost pool between the HD and PD service centers.

(4) Allocate the dialysis machine operations cost pool between the HD and PD service centers.

b. Have the class determine the total cost to allocate to the two service centers in the following manner. Select a representative from each section and have the selected person go to the board. Each representative should supply the allocated cost for the cost pool assigned by her respective section. The instructor should total the amounts and compare the ABC cost allocations with those developed through the traditional RCC system.

c. The instructor should lead the class in a discussion that addresses the following questions.

(1) Assuming that the ABC system provides a more accurate measure of cost, which service center (HD or PD) is overcosted by the traditional allocation system and which is undercosted?

(2) What is the potential impact on pricing and profitability for both service centers?

(3) How could management respond to the conditions described in the problem?

ATC 6–3 RESEARCH ASSIGNMENT *When ABC Does Not Work Well*

Is ABC the silver bullet? Does it always provide better estimates of product cost? Are ABC results always superior? Does it always improve the fairness of allocation? Will ABC always identify the non-value-added activities? The answer to all of these questions is, unfortunately, a definitive no! Read the article "Can ABC Bring Mixed Results?" by S. P. Landry, L. M. Wood, and T. M. Lindquist in the March 1997 edition of *Management Accounting* (pp. 28–33) and complete the following requirements.

Required

a. The article compares the results of implementing an ABC system at two divisions of Hewlett-Packard (HP). Identify the division that reported success with its ABC system.

b. Why was an ABC system established at the Colorado Springs Division?

c. What is the primary difference between the operations of the Colorado Springs Division and the Boise Division? How could this difference impact the implementation of ABC?

d. The article identifies four conditions that caused the failure of ABC at the Colorado Springs Division. What were these conditions?

e. Based on this article, do you believe that its authors have a positive or negative opinion of the capacity of ABC to more accurately measure cost than a traditional system?

ATC 6–4 WRITING ASSIGNMENT *Assessing a Strategy to Control Quality Cost*

Lucy Sawyer, who owns and operates Sawyer Toy Company, is a perfectionist. She believes literally in the "zero-defects" approach to quality control. Her favorite saying is, "You can't spend too much on quality." Even so, in 2001 her company experienced an embarrassing breach of quality that required the national recall of a defective product. She vowed never to repeat the experience and instructed her staff to spend whatever it takes to ensure that products are delivered free of defects in 2002. She was somewhat disappointed with the 2002 year-end quality cost report shown here.

	2001	2002
Prevention costs	$120,000	$ 80,000
Appraisal costs	240,000	430,000
Internal failure costs	140,000	560,000
External failure cost	320,000	210,000
Grand total	$820,000	$1,280,000

Although external failure costs had declined, they remained much higher than expected. The increased inspections had identified defects that were corrected, thereby avoiding another recall; however,

the external failure costs were still too high. Ms. Sawyer responded by saying, "We will have to double our efforts." She authorized hiring additional inspectors and instructed her production supervisors to become more vigilant in identifying and correcting errors.

Required

Assume that you are the chief financial officer (CFO) of Sawyer Company. Ms. Sawyer has asked you to review the company's approach to quality control. Prepare a memo to her that evaluates the existing approach, and recommend changes in expenditure patterns that can improve profitability as well as increase the effectiveness of the quality control system.

ETHICAL DILEMMA *Conflicts Between Controlling Cost and Providing Social Responsibility to Patients*

ATC 6–5

This case examines potential ethical issues faced by the dialysis clinic described in ATC 6–2. It is, however, an independent case that students may study in conjunction with or separately from ATC 6–2. The dialysis clinic provides two types of treatment for its patients. Hemodialysis (HD), an in-house treatment, requires patients to visit the clinic three times each week. Peritoneal dialysis (PD) permits patients to self-administer their treatments at home on a daily basis. The clinic serves a number of HMO patients under a contract that limits collections from the HMO insurer to a fixed amount per patient. As a result, the clinic's profitability is directly related to its ability to control costs. To illustrate, assume that the clinic is paid a fixed annual fee of $15,000 per HMO patient served. Also assume that the current cost to provide health care averages $14,000 a year per patient, resulting in an average profitability of $1,000 per patient ($15,000 − $14,000). Because the revenue base is fixed, the only way the clinic can increase profitability is to lower its average cost of providing services. If the clinic fails to control costs and the average cost of patient care increases, profitability will decline. A recent ABC study suggests that the cost to provide HD service exceeds the amount of revenue generated from providing that service. The clinic is profitable because PD services generate enough profit to more than make up for losses on HD services.

Required

Respond to each potential scenario described here. Each scenario is independent of the others.

a. Suppose that as a result of the ABC analysis, the chief accountant, a certified management accountant (CMA), recommends that the clinic discontinue treating HD patients referred by the HMO provider. Based on this assumption, answer the following questions.

   (1) Assume that the clinic is located in a small town. If it discontinues treating the HD patients, they will be forced to drive 50 miles to the nearest alternative treatment center. Does the clinic have a moral obligation to society to continue to provide HD service although it is not profitable to do so?

   (2) The accountant's recommendation places profitability above the needs of HD patients. Does this recommendation violate any of the standards of ethical conduct described in Chapter 1, Exhibit 1–13?

b. Assume that the clinic continues to treat HD patients referred by HMOs. However, to compensate for the loss incurred on these patients, the clinic raises prices charged to non-HMO patients. Is it fair to require non-HMO patients to subsidize services provided to the HMO patients?

c. Suppose that the clinic administrators respond to the ABC data by cutting costs. The clinic overbooks HMO patients to ensure that downtime is avoided when cancellations occur. It reduces the RN nursing staff and assigns some of the technical work to less qualified assistants. Ultimately, an overworked, underqualified nurse's aide makes a mistake, and a patient dies. Who is at fault—the HMO, the accountant who conducted the ABC analysis, or the clinic administrators who responded to the ABC information?

SPREADSHEET ASSIGNMENT *Using Excel*

ATC 6–6

Tameron Corporation produces video games in three market categories: commercial, home video, and miniature handheld. Tameron has traditionally allocated overhead costs to the three product categories using the companywide base of direct labor hours. The company recently switched to an ABC system when it installed computer-controlled assembly stations that rendered the traditional costing system ineffective. In implementing the ABC system, the company identified the cost pools and drivers shown in the following spreadsheet. The activity in each of the three product lines appears in rows 3 to 9. The pooled costs are shown in cells E11 to E15.

Required

a. Construct a spreadsheet like the following one to compute the total cost and cost per unit for each product line. Cells K4 to K9, G12 to I15, E19 to E28, G19 to G28, I19 to I28, and K26 should all be formulas.

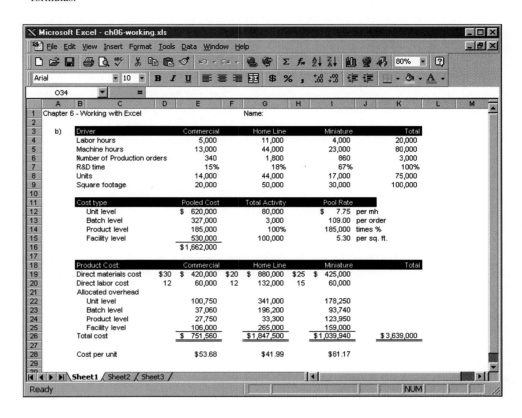

ATC 6–7   SPREADSHEET ASSIGNMENT *Mastering Excel*

Beasley Company makes three types of exercise machines. Data have been accumulated for four possible overhead drivers. Data for these four possible drivers are shown in rows 3 to 7 of the following spreadsheet.

Required

a. Construct a spreadsheet that will allocate overhead and calculate unit cost for each of these alternative drivers. A screen capture of the spreadsheet and data follows.

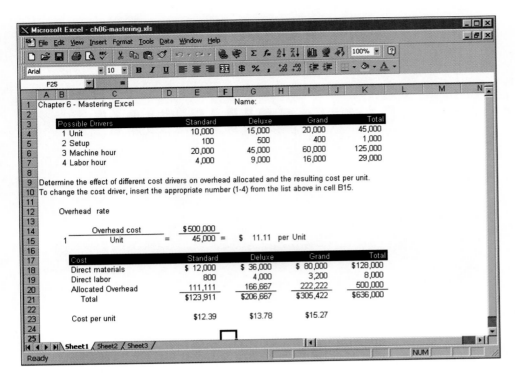

Spreadsheet Tips

1. This spreadsheet uses a function called *vertical lookup*. This function can pull the appropriate values from a table. The form of this function is =VLOOKUP (value, table, column#). In this example, the table is in cells B4 to K7. Three examples of the use of VLOOKUP follow.
2. Cell C15 is =VLOOKUP (B15, B4:K7, 2). This function operates by using the one (1) in cell B15 to look up a value in the table. Notice that the table is defined as B4: K7 and that the function is looking up the value in the second column, which is Unit.
3. Cell E15 is =VLOOKUP (B15, B4:K7, 10). In this case, the function is looking up the value in the tenth column, which is 45,000. Be sure to count empty columns.
4. Cell E20 is =VLOOKUP (B15, B4:K7, 4)*G15. In this case, the function is looking up the value in the fourth column, which is $10,000. Be sure to count empty columns.
5. Cells I15, G20, and I20 also use the VLOOKUP function.
6. After completing the spreadsheet, you can change the value in cell B15 (1-4) to see the effect of choosing a different driver for overhead.

Planning for Profit and Cost Control

Learning Objectives

After completing this chapter, you should be able to:

1 Understand budgeting as a planning process.

2 Identify and describe the three levels of planning for business activity.

3 Understand the advantages of budgeting.

4 Appreciate the human factor in the budget process.

5 Identify the primary components of a master budget.

6 Prepare a sales budget and associated schedule of cash receipts.

7 Prepare a purchases budget and associated schedule of cash payments.

8 Prepare a selling and administrative expense budget and associated schedule of cash payments.

9 Prepare a cash budget.

10 Prepare a set of pro forma financial statements including an income statement, balance sheet, and statement of cash flows.

the *curious* accountant

How much money will you need next week, next month, or next year? How will you get that money? Will you need to borrow, or will your earnings cover your needs? These questions apply to companies as well as individuals. Indeed, think about trying to determine how much money Capital Records will need next year. Will cash flows from sales of records by stars such as Faith Hill and Tim McGraw cover the costs of promoting artists who do not sell? How much money will be needed to pay the back-up studio artists, cover designers, attorneys, executives, and other employees? Will money be available for ordinary expenses such as rent, utilities, and postage? How do really large companies know what the future will bring?

*Planning is critical to the operation of a profitable business. The area of planning that is associated with financial matters is commonly called **budgeting,** which is a process that involves coordinating the finances of all areas of the business. For example, the production department cannot formulate its manufacturing plan until it knows how many units of product to produce. The level of production depends on the sales projection, which the marketing department normally develops. The marketing department cannot project sales volume until it knows the type of products that the company will sell. This information comes from the research and development department. The scenario could be continued, but the point should be clear now. A company's* master budget *results from the combination of numerous specific budgets that have been prepared by different departments within the business.*

*The responsibility for the coordination of budgeting activities normally rests with a **budgeting committee.** This committee supervises the preparation of the master budget and is responsible for settling disputes among various departments over budget matters. The*

committee also receives reports on how various segments are progressing toward the attainment of their budget standards. The budgeting committee is not an accounting committee. Indeed, its membership—the president; vice presidents of marketing, production, purchasing, finance; and the controller—attests to the importance and comprehensive nature of the budgeting process.

▌The Planning Process

LO1 Understand budgeting as a planning process.

The nature of planning changes according to the length of the time period being considered. Generally, the shorter the time period, the more specific the plans. Consider your decision to enter college as an example. A well-organized decision could be subdivided into three distinct planning phases. First, there are the long-range plans. To make these plans, a student must consider a number of questions. Should he go to college? What does he intend to gain from the experience? Does he want a broader base of understanding, or is he seeking to attain specific job skills? In what area does he want to concentrate his studies? Unfortunately, many students go to college to find answers to these questions rather than to accomplish preplanned goals, and many of them learn the misfortunes of poor planning the hard way. While their friends are graduating, they find themselves starting over with a new major.

The second planning phase involves planning for time periods of intermediate length, usually defined as three to five years. In this stage, the potential student must decide which school to attend, how to support himself while in school, and whether to live on or off campus.

In the final phase, the student plans for the short term, deciding which courses to take in the coming year, which instructors to choose, how to schedule part-time employment, and whether to join a study group. At this stage, the plans become specific, and details are important. The work may seem tedious, but careful planning generally leads to the efficient use of resources and to high levels of productivity. A word of caution is in order, however; plans are only as good as the intentions that support them. Making a careful plan for entering dental school is a waste of time for the individual who truly desires to build homes.

▌Three Levels of Planning for Business Activity

LO2 Identify and describe the three levels of planning for business activity.

When applied to business activity, the three levels of planning are called *strategic planning, capital budgeting,* and *operations budgeting.* **Strategic planning** involves making long-term decisions such as defining the scope of the business, determining which products to develop, deciding whether to discontinue a product, and determining which market niche should be most profitable. Upper-level management is responsible for these decisions. Strategic plans are stated in descriptive rather than quantified terms. Objectives such as "to be the largest firm" or "to be the best-quality producer" result from strategic planning. Although strategic planning is an interesting area, an in-depth discussion of the subject is beyond the scope of this text.

Capital budgeting deals with intermediate range planning. It involves making decisions such as whether to buy or lease equipment, to stimulate sales, or to increase the company's asset base. Capital budgeting will be discussed in detail in a later chapter.

The **operating budget** constitutes the central focus of this chapter. It involves the establishment of a *master budget* that will direct the firm's activities over the short term. The master budget states objectives in specific quantities and includes sales targets, production objectives, and financing plans. The master budget constitutes a specific statement of management's short-term plans and represents a description of how management intends to achieve its objectives.

The master budget normally covers a one-year time span. It is frequently subdivided into quarterly projections and often includes quarterly data subdivided by month. Obviously, management does not want to wait until year end to know whether it will meet its budget. Monthly data provide the timely feedback necessary to take corrective action.

Many companies use a technique known as **perpetual** or **continuous budgeting** that utilizes a 12-month reporting period. At the completion of the current month, a new month is added to the end of the budget period, resulting in a continuous 12-month budget. The advantage of the perpetual budget is that it keeps management involved in the budget process. The traditional approach too often leads to a frenzied stop-and-go mentality. The annual budget is prepared in a year-end rush, and the assumptions underlying its formation are forgotten shortly thereafter. Changing conditions are not likely to be discussed until the next year-end review cycle. The perpetual budget corrects these shortcomings by keeping management continuously involved with the budget. Adding a new monthly budget each month to replace the preceding month's budget forces management into a constant 12-month think-ahead process.

■ Advantages of Budgeting

Budgeting is a costly, time-consuming activity; however, the sacrifices are more than offset by the benefits. Budgeting encourages planning, coordination, performance measurement, and corrective action.

LO3 Understand the advantages of budgeting.

Planning

Almost everyone makes plans. Shortly after waking up each morning, most people think about what they will do during the day. This thinking ahead is a form of planning. Likewise, most business managers naturally think ahead about how they will conduct their business. Unfortunately, the planning is frequently as informal as making a few mental notes. The problem with this type of planning is that it lacks the capacity for effective communication. The business manager knows what she wants to accomplish, but her superiors and subordinates have no knowledge of these objectives. If a manager's plans are inconsistent with her superior's plans, considerable amounts of time and effort will likely be wasted before the disagreement is discovered. Similarly, subordinates must wait until the manager tells them what to do; they have no way to exercise self-initiative because they do not know what is expected of them. Budgeting attempts to solve these problems by acting as a communication vehicle. The budget formalizes the manager's plans in a document that clearly communicates objectives to both superiors and subordinates.

Coordination

In certain situations, an action that is beneficial to one department may be detrimental to another department. For example, the purchasing agent may desire to order large amounts of raw materials to obtain discounts from suppliers. In doing so, the purchasing agent poses a storage problem for the inventory manager who must contend with excessive warehousing costs. The budgeting process forces departments to coordinate their activities to ensure the attainment of the objectives of the firm as a whole.

Performance Measurement

Budgets represent a specific, quantitative statement of management's objectives. As such, budgets represent standards that can be used to evaluate performance. For example, if a company

budgets for $10 million in sales volume, this figure can be treated as a benchmark for measuring the performance of the sales department. If actual sales exceed the budgeted figure, the sales department should be recognized for superior performance. If the actual figure falls below the budgeted amount, the sales manager should be called on to explain the unsatisfactory sales volume.

Corrective Action

Budgeting provides advance notice of shortages, bottlenecks, or other weaknesses in operating plans. For example, a cash flow budget advises management when the company can expect to experience cash shortages during the coming year. Based on this information, the company can establish an organized borrowing plan with its creditors. Without such information, management would be forced to rush to the bank at the last minute to cover shortages as they arise. If the shortages occur during periods of tight credit, the company may be unable to find the necessary financing, or it may have to pay excessively high rates of interest to obtain the funds it needs. Budgeting provides an early warning system that advises managers of potential trouble spots in time for them to react in a calm and rational manner.

▌Consideration of the Human Factor

LO4 Appreciate the human factor in the budget process.

Proper handling of human relations is essential to the establishment of an effective budget system. People have a natural tendency to be uncomfortable with budgets because budgets often have a constraining effect. The freedom to follow an individual's own whim is certainly more appealing than the rigor of sticking to an established plan. Furthermore, evaluation related to budgeted expectations frightens many people. Most students experience a similar fear about being tested. As with an examination, the budget represents a standard by which performance is evaluated. Employees are put in the position of wondering whether they will be able to attain the expected level of performance. For many people, this is an unsettling experience.

The attitudes of upper-level management have a significant impact on the effectiveness of a budget. Subordinates develop a keen awareness of management's expectations; if upper-level managers degrade, make fun of, or ignore the budget, subordinates will follow suit. If management uses budgets to humiliate or embarrass subordinates, they will resent the treatment and the budgeting process. To be effective, upper-level management must consider the budget as a sincere effort to express realistic goals that employees will be expected to accomplish, and their behavior must demonstrate this. The proper atmosphere is essential to budgeting success.

One technique, which has frequently proven successful in creating a healthy atmosphere, is known as **participative budgeting.** As the name implies, this technique encourages participation in the budget process by personnel at all levels of the organization, not just upper-level managers. Information flows from the bottom up as well as from the top down during the budget preparation. Because they are directly responsible for accomplishing the budget objectives, subordinates are able to make more realistic estimates of what can be attained. Their participation in budget preparation is likely to result in the development of a team mentality. Participation encourages subordinates to be more cooperative, less fearful, and more highly motivated. Under participative budgeting, subordinates should no longer look at budgets as representations of self-imposed constraints; they have no one to blame but themselves if they fail to accomplish the budget objectives.

Upper management participates in the process to ensure that the employee-generated objectives are consistent with the company's objectives. Furthermore, if subordinates were granted complete freedom to establish budget standards, they might be tempted to set lax standards to ensure that they will meet the budget goals. A sincere effort is required by both managers and subordinates if the participatory process is to generate an effective budget.

If handled properly, budgets can help motivate employees to achieve superior performance. Natural human fears must be overcome, and management must strive to create an effective

budget atmosphere. If these conditions are satisfied, the budget will represent realistic goals that employees will be encouraged to attain.

▌The Master Budget

The **master budget** consists of a series of detailed schedules and budgets that describe the company's overall financial plans for the coming accounting period. The three major budget categories are (1) *operating budgets,* (2) *capital budgets,* (3) *financial statement budgets.* The budgeting process normally begins with the preparation of the operating budgets. An *operating budget* is prepared by individual departments within a company and becomes part of the company's master budget. The number of operating budgets depends on the nature of the business entity. For example, budgeting for the inventory needs of a manufacturing entity requires the preparation of a raw materials budget, a labor budget, and an overhead budget. In contrast, a retail company needs only an inventory purchases budget. The next section of this chapter focuses on Hampton Hams Company, a retail sales company that uses four operating budgets: (1) a sales budget, (2) an inventory purchases budget, (3) a selling and administrative (S&A) budget, and (4) a cash budget.

LO5 Identify the primary components of a master budget.

The sales, inventory, and S&A budgets contain schedules that identify the cash consequences associated with the various business activities. For example, the sales budget includes a schedule of cash receipts from customers. Similarly, the inventory and S&A budgets contain schedules of cash payments associated with acquiring inventory and paying expenses. Preparation of the master budget begins with the sales forecast. The detailed budgets for inventory purchases and operating expenses are developed on the basis of projected sales. The information in the schedules of cash receipts and payments is used in the preparation of the cash budget.

The **capital budget** describes the company's intermediate-range plans regarding investments in facilities, equipment, new products, store outlets, and lines of business. The information from the capital budget is input to several operating budgets. For example, acquisitions of equipment result in the recognition of depreciation expense that appears on the S&A budget. In addition, the cash flows associated with capital investments appear on the cash budget.

Information contained in the operating budgets is used to prepare the **financial statement budgets.** Again, the number of financial statement budgets, also called **pro forma statements,** depends on the nature and needs of the budget entity. The company analyzed in this chapter, Hampton Hams, prepares three pro forma statements including an income statement, a balance sheet, and a statement of cash flows. Specific operating budgets provide data related to particular financial statements; for example, the sales, inventory, and S&A budgets contain information used to prepare the income statement and balance sheet. The sales budget, for example, contains information regarding the amount of sales revenue shown in the income statement and accounts receivable balances. Similarly, the inventory and the S&A expense budgets contain expense and liability information that appears on the income statement and balance sheet. The cash budget contains (1) the amount of interest expense appearing on the income statement, (2) the ending cash balance and capital acquisitions that appear on the balance sheet, and (3) the bulk of information that is included in the statement of cash flows. Exhibit 7–1 is a graphic presentation of the information flows in a master budget.

▌Hampton Hams Budgeting Illustration

To illustrate the budgeting process, we describe the budgeting activities of the Hampton Hams Company. Hampton Hams (HH) is a major corporation with retail outlets located in shopping malls throughout the United States. As its name implies, the company sells cured hams. By focusing on a single product, the company has been able to standardize its operations, and the high degree of standardization has enabled the company to exercise stringent cost control procedures, which have allowed it to offer high-quality hams at competitive prices.

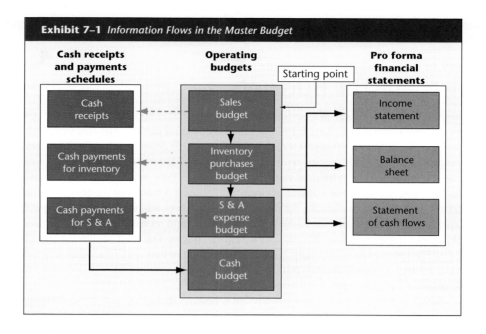

Exhibit 7–1 *Information Flows in the Master Budget*

Hampton Hams has experienced phenomenal growth during the past five years, adding an average of five new stores each month. Within the past month, HH opened two new stores in Indianapolis, Indiana, and plans to open a third in the near future. It finances new stores with debt. The company has a line of credit with National Bank, whose lending officer has asked for a monthly budget for each of the first three months of the new store's operations. HH plans to open the store in October, and the accountant began to prepare a master budget for the months of October, November, and December. The first step in the budgeting process was to develop a sales budget.

Sales Budget

LO6 Prepare a sales budget and associated schedule of cash receipts.

The preparation of the master budget begins with the sales forecast. The accuracy of the sales forecast is critical because it acts as the data source for all of the other budgets. If the sales figures are unreliable, the entire budgeting process is a waste of time. Thus, it is easy to understand why every available effort is made to obtain reliable estimates of projected sales.

The marketing department normally coordinates the effort to establish the sales forecast. Frequently, the information flows from the bottom up to the higher management levels. Sales personnel are asked to prepare estimates of sales projections for their designated products and territories and then to pass them up the line where they are combined with the estimates of other sales personnel to form the regional and national estimates. Using a variety of information sources, upper-level sales managers make appropriate adjustments to the estimates generated by the salespersons. Some of the more common inputs to the adjustment process include information gathered from industry periodicals and trade journals, analysis of general economic conditions, marketing surveys, historical sales figures, and assessments of changes in competitive forces. The information may be assimilated through a sophisticated system of computer programs, statistical techniques, and quantitative methods, or it may simply be subjected to the professional judgment of the upper-level sales managers. Regardless of the technique, the senior vice president of sales ultimately formulates a sales forecast for which she is held responsible.

To initiate the budgeting process for HH's new store, the sales manager reviewed the sales history of stores operating in locations similar to the proposed site. He then made adjustments for start-up conditions. October was considered an opportune time to start a new store because customers would have time to become familiar with the store's location during October before the holiday season. He expected significant sales growth in November and December and envisioned the company's hams as the centerpiece of many Thanksgiving and Christmas dinner

tables. Specifically, he expected the new store's sales to start in October at $160,000. Cash versus credit sales (i.e., sales on account) were projected at $40,000 and $120,000, respectively, and sales were expected to increase 20 percent per month during November and December. Based on these estimates, the sales manager prepared the sales budget (see Exhibit 7–2).

Notice that the sales budget is subdivided into two panels, the first of which describes the projected sales for each month. The sales forecast for November is computed by adding a 20 percent increase to the amount of October sales. For example, *cash sales* for November are calculated as $48,000 ($40,000 + [$40,000 × 0.20]) and for December as $57,600 ($48,000 + [$48,000 × 0.20]). *Sales on account* are computed using the same mathematical procedures.

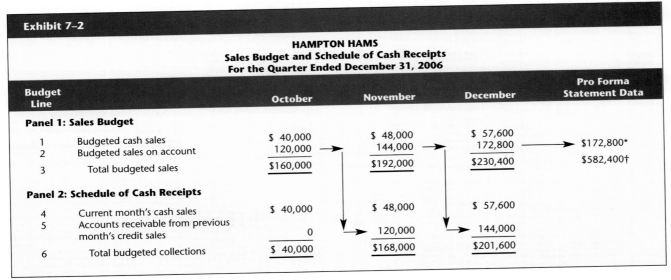

Exhibit 7–2

HAMPTON HAMS
Sales Budget and Schedule of Cash Receipts
For the Quarter Ended December 31, 2006

Budget Line		October	November	December	Pro Forma Statement Data
Panel 1: Sales Budget					
1	Budgeted cash sales	$ 40,000	$ 48,000	$ 57,600	
2	Budgeted sales on account	120,000	144,000	172,800	$172,800*
3	Total budgeted sales	$160,000	$192,000	$230,400	$582,400†
Panel 2: Schedule of Cash Receipts					
4	Current month's cash sales	$ 40,000	$ 48,000	$ 57,600	
5	Accounts receivable from previous month's credit sales	0	120,000	144,000	
6	Total budgeted collections	$ 40,000	$168,000	$201,600	

*Ending accounts receivable balance appearing on the balance sheet.
†Sales revenue appearing on income statement (sum of monthly amounts: $160,000 + $192,000 + $230,400).

Schedule of Cash Receipts

Panel 2 in Exhibit 7–2 contains a schedule of the cash receipts associated with the expected sales. This information is used to prepare the cash budget in a later section of this chapter. The accountant has prepared the schedule under the assumption that accounts receivable from credit sales are collected *in full* in the month following the sale. In practice, collections may be somewhat more complicated, perhaps spread over several months, and some receivables may become bad debts that are never collected. Service charges for credit card sales may also reduce the amount collected. Regardless of the level of complication associated with making the estimates, the objective is to determine the amount and timing of expected cash collections. In the HH case, *total cash receipts* are determined by adding the *accounts receivable balance* from the previous month's *credit sales* to the current month's *cash sales*. Because the business will begin in October, no accounts receivable balance from September (i.e., previous month's credit sales) is available. Accordingly, cash receipts for October equal the amount of October's *cash sales*. November collections equal November's *cash sales* plus the *accounts receivable balance* generated from October's *credit sales* ($48,000 + $120,000 = $168,000). December's receipts equal December's *cash sales* and the *accounts receivable balance* generated from November's *credit sales* ($57,600 + $144,000 = $201,600). The amounts in the Pro Forma Statement Data column are discussed next.

Pro Forma Financial Statement Data

The column Pro Forma Statement Data contains two items that will appear on the end-of-quarter (i.e., December 31) budgeted financial statements. The first item ($172,800) represents

the amount of the ending *accounts receivable balance* on the pro forma balance sheet. Since December's credit sales will be collected in January, the receivables account will have a $172,800 balance as of December 31, 2006. The pro forma balance sheet is shown later in Exhibit 7–7. We suggest you trace the accounts receivable balance from the sales budget to the pro forma statements before continuing.

The second item in the Pro Forma Statement Data column ($582,400) is the amount of *sales revenue* reported on the company's budgeted income statement. This amount was determined by summing the amounts of the monthly sales. In other words, sales for the quarter equal the total sales for each month of the quarter ($160,000 + $192,000 + $230,400 = $582,400). The pro forma income statement is shown later in Exhibit 7–6. Again, we encourage you to trace the data from the operating budget to the financial statement budget.

Inventory Purchases Budget

LO7 Prepare a purchases budget and associated schedule of cash payments.

After the amount of projected sales has been established, HH's accountant focuses on the amount of inventory needed to satisfy the sales demand. Meeting the sales demand requires having enough inventory to cover expected sales and future sales between reorder points. Accordingly, the *total amount of inventory needed* for each month equals the amount of *budgeted sales* plus the desired *ending inventory*. The total amount of inventory needed can be obtained from two sources. First, the company can use existing stock. In other words,

focus on International Issues

Buyer Beware: An Appropriate Caveat in International Markets

What happens when budget preparers cross the line to become fraud perpetrators? Perhaps nothing happens when international boundaries are interjected into the equation. Take the case of Bre-X Minerals as an example. The value of Bre-X's stock, which trades on the Vancouver Stock Exchange, soared when the company announced a gold find in Indonesia said to be worth billions. The company's estimates of the size of the find increased steadily from 40 million ounces to 57 million to 71 million. The final estimate announced by Bre-X's vice chairman suggested that the real size of the find might be 200 million ounces, making it one of the largest in recent history. The stock price followed the upward spiral, ultimately reaching a market capitalization of $4.5 billion. When an independent review concluded that the original tests had been falsified, Bre-X's stock collapsed.

The Bre-X fraud bilked billions from international investors. Even so, Canadian regulators continue to express a laissez-faire attitude toward the regulation of their markets. Why? There is little motive for eliminating the transfer of billions from U.S., European, and Asian investors to Canadian rogues. Clearly, companies operating in foreign environments must learn to adopt a buyer beware operating style.

Source: Kevin Whitlaw, "Fool's Gold and Other Goodies from Canada," *U.S. News & World Report* (May 19, 1997), pp. 50–51.

customer demand can be satisfied with goods that are in *beginning inventory*. The difference between the amount of *goods needed* and the *beginning inventory* is the amount of *goods to be purchased*. Accordingly, the purchases budget follows a logical format that is summarized here.

Cost of budgeted sales	XXX
Plus: Desired ending inventory	XXX
Inventory needed	XXX
Less: Beginning inventory	(XXX)
Amount to purchase	XXX

Assume that HH's *cost of budgeted sales* equals 70 percent of *total budgeted sales*. In addition, HH has the policy of maintaining an ending inventory that equals 20 percent of the current month's *cost of budgeted sales*. Based on this information and the data contained in the sales budget, the accountant prepared the purchases budget shown in Panel 1 of Exhibit 7–3. The *budgeted cost of sales* for October was determined by multiplying October's *budgeted sales* times 70 percent ($160,000 \times 0.70 = $112,000$). *Budgeted cost of sales* for November and December were computed in a similar fashion. The *desired ending inventory* for October was computed by multiplying October's *budgeted cost of goods sold* times 20 percent ($112,000 \times 0.20 = $22,400$). Desired ending inventory for November and December is computed in a similar fashion. The inventory purchases budget for HH is shown in Panel 1 of Exhibit 7–3.

Exhibit 7–3

HAMPTON HAMS
Inventory Purchases Budget and Schedule of Cash Payments for Inventory
For the Quarter Ended December 31, 2006

Budget Line	October	November	December	Pro Forma Statement Data
Panel 1: Purchases Budget				
1 Budgeted cost of goods sold	$112,000	$134,400	$161,280	407,680*
2 Plus: Desired end inventory (line 1 × 0.20)	22,400	26,880	32,256	32,256†
3 Inventory needed	$134,400	$161,280	$193,536	
4 Less: Beginning inventory	0	(22,400)	(26,880)	
5 Total required purchases	$134,400	$138,880	$166,656	33,331‡
Panel 2: Schedule of Cash Payments for Inventory Purchases				
6 Current purchases at 80%	$107,520	$111,104	$133,325	
7 Prior month's purchases at 20%	0	26,880	27,776	
8 Total budgeted payments for inventory	$107,520	$137,984	$161,101	

*Cost of goods sold appearing on pro forma income statement (sum of monthly amounts $112,000 + $134,400 + $161,280).
†Ending inventory balance appearing on pro forma balance sheet.
‡Ending accounts payable balance appearing on pro forma balance sheet ($166,656 × 0.20).

Schedule of Cash Payments for Inventory Purchases

Panel 2 of Exhibit 7–3 contains the cash payments budget. All merchandise is purchased on account. Because the hams are perishable, the supplier demands that a significant portion of the accounts payable be settled within the month of purchase. Specifically, 80 percent of the current payables balance must be paid in the month goods are purchased. The remaining 20 percent is paid during the following month. Because the store opens in October, no September balance exists. Accordingly, *cash payments* for October are 80 percent of October's *required purchases* ($134,400 \times 0.80 = $107,520$). *Cash payments* for November amount to 80 percent

of November purchases plus 20 percent of October purchases ([$138,880 $\times$ 0.80 = $111,104] + [$134,400 $\times$ 0.20 = $26,880] = $137,984). Similarly, *cash payments* for December amount to 80 percent of December purchases plus 20 percent of November purchases ([$166,656 $\times$ 0.80 = 133,325] + [$138,880 $\times$ 0.20 = $27,776] = $161,101).

Pro Forma Financial Statement Data

The purchases budget contains three items that are relevant to the preparation of the pro forma financial statements. First, the amount of cost of goods sold (see Exhibit 7–3, Budget Line 1) will be shown on the budgeted income statements. The amount of the *cost of goods sold* for the quarter equals the total of the monthly amounts ($112,000 + $134,400 + $161,280 = $407,680). The *ending inventory* balance for December 31 also represents the ending inventory balance for the quarter. Accordingly, the $32,256 ending inventory balance is shown in the pro forma balance sheet. Finally, the assumed payments schedule results in a year-end balance in the *accounts payable account*. Because 20 percent of December credit purchases will be paid in January, the payables account will have a balance of $33,331 (from Line 5, December column, $166,656 $\times$ 0.20 = $33,331) as of December 31, 2006. In the previous and all future computations, we round the numbers to the nearest whole dollar amount. We suggest that you trace these amounts to the pro forma statements shown in Exhibits 7–6 and 7–7.

Check
Yourself
7–1

Main Street Sales Company purchased $80,000 of inventory during June. Purchases are expected to increase by 2 percent per month in each of the next three months. Main Street makes all purchases on account. It normally pays cash to settle 70 percent of its accounts payable during the month of purchase and settles the remaining 30 percent in the month following purchase. Based on this information, determine the accounts payable balance Main Street would report on its July 31 balance sheet.

Answer Purchases for the month of July are expected to be $81,600 ($80,000 $\times$ 1.02). Main Street will pay 70 percent of the resulting accounts payable in cash during July. The remaining 30 percent represents the expected balance in accounts payable as of July 31. Therefore, the balance would be $24,480 ($81,600 $\times$ 0.3).

Selling and Administrative Expense Budget

LO8 Prepare a selling and administrative expense budget and associated schedule of cash payments.

The selling and administrative (S&A) expense budget for Hampton Hams' new store is shown in Exhibit 7–4. Most items in Panel 1 are self-explanatory; however, two of them merit some explanation. The depreciation expense (see Line 5 in Exhibit 7–4) was based on information contained in the *capital expenditures budget*. Although detailed capital budgets are not presented in this chapter, you can assume that the budget indicates that opening the new store will require a significant investment in store fixtures including refrigeration equipment. Each of HH's stores is furnished with an identical equipment package. Total investment in fixtures, which are expected to have an average useful life of 10 years and a $10,000 salvage value, is expected to be $130,000. Depreciation expense is determined on a straight-line basis resulting in an annual charge of $12,000 ([$130,000 − $10,000] $\div$ 10). Monthly depreciation expense is $1,000 ($12,000 annual charge $\div$ 12 months). Notice that the S&A expense budget does not contain a provision for interest expense; the amount of interest expense cannot be determined until the amount of expected borrowing has been established through the preparation of the *cash budget*. Accordingly, the interest component will be determined at a later point in the budgeting process.

Schedule of Cash Payments for Selling and Administrative Expenses

Panel 2 of Exhibit 7–4 contains the schedule of cash payments associated with S&A expenses. Differences between expense recognition and cash flow result from several conditions. First,

Exhibit 7–4

HAMPTON HAMS
S&A Expense Budget and Schedule of Cash Payments for S&A Expense
For the Quarter Ended December 31, 2006

Budget Line		October	November	December	Pro Forma Statement Data
Panel 1: Selling and Administrative Expense Budget					
1	Salary expense	$24,000	$24,000	$24,000	
2	Sales commissions (2% of sales)	3,200	3,840	4,608 ⟶	$ 4,608*
3	Supplies expense (1% of sales)	1,600	1,920	2,304	
4	Utilities	1,400	1,400	1,400 ⟶	1,400†
5	Depreciation on store equipment	1,000	1,000	1,000	3,000‡
6	Rent	3,600	3,600	3,600	
7	Miscellaneous	900	900	900	
8	Total S&A expenses before interest	$35,700	$36,660	$37,812	110,172§
Panel 2: Schedule of Cash Payments for Selling and Administrative Expenses					
9	Salary expense paid monthly as incurred	$24,000	$24,000	$24,000	
10	Prior month's sales commissions, 100%	0	3,200	3,840	
11	Supplies expense paid monthly as incurred	1,600	1,920	2,304	
12	Prior month's utilities, 100%	0	1,400	1,400	
13	Rent paid monthly as incurred	3,600	3,600	3,600	
14	Miscellaneous paid monthly as incurred	900	900	900	
15	Total cash payments for S&A expenses	$30,100	$35,020	$36,044	

*Ending Sales Commissions Payable account balance shown on pro forma balance sheet.
†Ending Utilities Payable account balance shown on pro forma balance sheet.
‡Accumulated depreciation appears on the pro forma balance sheet (sum of monthly amounts: $1,000 + $1,000 + $1,000).
§S&A expense appearing on pro forma income statement (sum of monthly amounts: $35,700 + $36,660 + $37,812).

cash payments for sales commissions and utilities are expected to be paid in the month following their incurrence. Notice that depreciation expense is not included in the cash payments budget. Recall that the cash outflow for equipment is shown as an investing activity at the time cash is paid to purchase the equipment. Accordingly, this item will be shown as a separate line item on the cash budget.

Pro Forma Financial Statement Data

The assumed payments schedule results in a year-end *balance in the sales commissions and utilities payable accounts.* Because December's payments for commissions and utilities will be paid in January, the commissions and utilities payable accounts will have balances of $4,608 and $1,400, respectively, as of December 31 (see Pro Forma Statement Data column amounts for Budget Lines 2 and 4, Exhibit 7–4). The items will appear on the pro forma balance sheet. The total amount of S&A expenses before interest is determined by summing the monthly amounts ($35,700 + $36,660 + 37,812 = $110,172). This amount appears on Budget Line 8 under the Pro Forma Statement column. The S&A expense is shown on the pro forma income statement. We suggest that you trace the accumulated depreciation, utilities and commissions payable and the total S&A expense to the pro forma statements shown later in Exhibits 7–6 and 7–7.

Cash Budget

Few things are more important to the success of a company than the effective management of cash. If excess cash is permitted to accumulate, the business will lose the opportunity to earn investment income or to repay debt, thereby reducing interest costs. On the other hand, if cash shortages occur, the business will be unable to pay its debts and may be forced into bankruptcy. A **cash budget** is prepared to advise management of anticipated cash shortages or excessive cash balances. Management uses this information to plan its financing activities. It

LO9 Prepare a cash budget.

makes arrangements with creditors to ensure that anticipated shortages can be covered by borrowing. It also plans to repay past borrowings and to make appropriate investments in the periods in which excess amounts of cash are expected.

The cash budget is composed of three major components including (1) a cash receipts section, (2) a cash payments section, and (3) a financing section. Most of the raw data needed to prepare the cash budget are included in the cash receipts and payments schedules that were discussed earlier; however, further refinements of these data are sometimes necessary. The complete cash budget is shown in Exhibit 7–5.

Exhibit 7–5

HAMPTON HAMS
Cash Budget
For the Quarter Ended December 31, 2006

Budget Line		October	November	December	Pro Forma Statement Data
Cash Receipts					
1	Beginning cash balance	$ 0	$ 7,624	$ 7,550	
2	Add cash receipts (Exhibit 7–2)	40,000	168,000	201,600	$409,600*
3	Total cash available	40,000	175,624	209,150	
Less: Cash Payments					
4	For inventory purchases (Exhibit 7–3)	107,520	137,984	161,101	406,605†
5	For S&A expenses (Exhibit 7–4)	30,100	35,020	36,044	101,164‡
6	To purchase store fixtures	130,000	0	0	130,000§
7	Total cash payments	267,620	173,004	197,145	
Cash Needs					
8	Shortage (surplus) of cash: (Line 7−Line 3)	227,620	(2,620)	(12,005)	
9	Plus desired cash cushion	10,000	10,000	10,000	
Financing Activity					
10	Amount borrowed (repaid)	237,620	7,380	(2,005)	242,995‡‡
11	Interest expense at 1% per month	(2,376)	(2,450)	(2,430)	7,256**
12	Ending cash balance (Line 3 − 7 + 10 + 11)	$ 7,624	$ 7,550	$ 7,570 ⟶	$ 7,570††

*Operating Activities section of pro forma statement of cash flows (sum of monthly amounts $40,000 + $168,000 + $201,600).
†Operating Activities section of pro forma statement of cash flows (sum of monthly amounts $107,520 + $137,984 + $161,101).
‡Operating Activities section of pro forma statement of cash flows (sum of monthly amounts $30,100 + $35,020 + $36,044).
§Investing Activities section of pro forma statement of cash flows (sum of monthly amounts $130,000 + $0 + $0). The investment in store fixtures also appears on the pro forma balance sheet.
‡‡Financing Activities section of pro forma statement of cash flows (sum of monthly amounts $237,620 + $7,380 − $2,005).
**Operating Activities section of pro forma statement of cash flows (sum of monthly amounts $2,376 + $2,450 + $2,430).
††The ending cash balance appears on the pro forma balance sheet (Exhibit 7–7) and as the last item in the statement of cash flows (Exhibit 7–8).

Cash Receipts Section

The cash receipts for HH is shown in the *schedule of cash receipts* (refer to Budget Line 6 in Panel 2 of Exhibit 7–2). The amounts in this schedule are transferred to Budget Line 2 of the cash budget (Exhibit 7–5). The expected cash receipts are added to the beginning cash balance to determine the amount of cash available for use (Budget Line 3 in Exhibit 7–5).

Cash Payments Section

Cash payments include expected cash outflows for inventory purchases, S&A expenses, and investments. The cash payments for inventory purchases are shown in the *schedule of cash*

Budgets are used by those outside as well as those inside the company. A person who wants to borrow money from a bank may be required to produce a cash budget that shows his ability to repay principal and interest. Similarly, investors use earnings projections to decide which company's stock to buy. Indeed, budgeting is an essential ingredient in the effective operation of the U.S. capital markets.

payments for inventory purchases (Budget Line 8 in Panel 2 of Exhibit 7–3). The amounts in the inventory payments schedule have been transferred to Budget Line 4 of the cash budget (Exhibit 7–5). The cash payments for S&A expenses shown in the *schedule of cash payments for S&A expenses* (Budget Line 15 in Panel 2 of Exhibit 7–4). The amounts in the receipts schedule are transferred to Budget Line 5 of the cash budget (Exhibit 7–5). Also recall that the *capital expenditures budget* (the detail of which is not shown in this chapter) indicated that HH would spend $130,000 to equip the new store with the standard fixtures package. This amount is shown on Budget Line 6 on the cash budget (Exhibit 7–5), and the total of expected cash payments is displayed on Budget Line 7.

Financing Section

In October, HH expects to have a cash deficit of $227,620 (Budget Line 8, October column, Exhibit 7–5). Accordingly, HH will need to borrow money to finance the establishment and operation of the new store. If the company were to borrow only $227,620, it would have an insufficient amount of funds available to pay interest and to maintain a reasonable minimum ending cash balance. For this reason, HH decided to borrow a *cash cushion* amounting to $10,000 more than the amount of the expected cash shortage. This amount is shown on Budget Line 9 of Exhibit 7–5. The total amount borrowed is $237,620 ($227,620 cash shortage + $10,000 cash cushion), shown on Budget Line 10.

In practice, borrowing and repayment activities occur on a daily basis. For firms managing millions of dollars, one day's interest is a large amount of money. However, for illustrative purposes, the computation of daily interest is too cumbersome. As a result, for the purpose of computing interest, we assume that HH borrows and repays on the first day of each month. Furthermore, we assume that it pays interest in cash on the last day of each month. The interest rate on the line of credit is 1 percent per month. Accordingly, interest expense (Budget Line 11, Exhibit 7–5) for October is $2,376 ($237,620 amount borrowed × 0.01). The ending cash balance is determined by adding the cash available (Budget Line 3) plus the funds borrowed (Budget Line 10) minus total cash payments for S&A expense (Budget Line 7) minus cash paid for interest expense (Budget Line 11). The result appears on Budget Line 12. The ending cash balance becomes the beginning cash balance for the following month.

The computation for the amount borrowed in November begins with the cash surplus of $2,620 (Budget Line 8). This surplus is insufficient to maintain the $10,000 desired cash cushion. Accordingly, HH must borrow an additional $7,380 ($10,000 − $2,620). Interest expense is calculated as 1 percent of the outstanding debt ([$237,620 October borrowings + $7,380 November borrowings] × 0.01 = $2,450).

291

In December, the company produces enough surplus cash to make a partial repayment of the principal balance. The amount available for repayment is $2,005 ($12,005 surplus − $10,000 cash cushion). The interest expense for December is $2,430 ([$237,620 + $7,380 − $2,005] × 0.01).

Pro Forma Financial Statement Data

The *pro forma statement of cash flows* is shown in Exhibit 7–8. The total of the cash receipts and the totals of the cash payments for inventory and S&A expenses are shown in the Cash Flow from Operating Activities section of the pro forma statement of cash flows. The totals of the cash receipts and payments are determined by summing the monthly amounts. For example, the total cash receipts ($409,600) shown on the cash budget (Exhibit 7–5, Budget Line 2) is computed by adding the amounts for October, November, and December. Totals for the cash payment items on Budget Lines 4 and 5 are computed in a similar fashion. The $130,000 purchase price of the store fixtures appears in the Cash Flow from Investing Activities section of the statement of cash flows and in the Assets section of the pro forma balance sheet. The amount borrowed ($242,995, Budget Line 10) is determined by adding the borrowings in October and November minus the repayment made in December ($237,620 + $7,380 − $2,005 = $242,995) and is shown in the Cash Flow from Financing Activities section of the pro forma statement of cash flows (Exhibit 7–8) and in the Liabilities section of the pro forma balance sheet (Exhibit 7–7). The total amount of interest expense shown in Exhibit 7–6 is also determined by summing the monthly amounts on Line 11 of Exhibit 7–5 ($2,376 + $2,450 + $2,430 = $7,256). Because the interest is paid in cash, the interest expense is shown in the Cash Flow from Operating Activities section of the pro forma statement of cash flows (Exhibit 7–8) and on the pro forma income statement (Exhibit 7–6). Finally, the ending cash balance ($7,570) for December also constitutes the ending balance for the quarter. This amount is shown on the pro forma balance sheet and as the last item on the pro forma statement of cash flows.

Exhibit 7–6

HAMPTON HAMS
Pro Forma Income Statement
For the Quarter Ended December 31, 2006

		Data Source
Sales Revenue	$582,400	Exhibit 7–2
Cost of Goods Sold	(407,680)	Exhibit 7–3
Gross Margin	174,720	
Selling and Administrative Expenses	(110,172)	Exhibit 7–4
Operating Income	64,548	
Interest Expense	(7,256)	Exhibit 7–5
Net Income	$ 57,292	

Check Yourself 7–2

Astor Company expects to incur the following operating expenses during September: Salary Expense, $25,000; Utility Expense, $1,200; Depreciation Expense, $5,400; and Selling Expense, $14,000. In general, it pays operating expenses in cash in the month in which it incurs them. Based on this information alone, determine the total amount of cash outflow Astor would report in the Operating Activities section of the pro forma statement of cash flows.

Answer Depreciation is not included in cash outflows because companies do not pay cash when they recognize depreciation expense. The total cash outflow is $40,200 ($25,000 + $1,200 + $14,000).

Pro Forma Income Statement

LO10 Prepare a set of pro forma financial statements.

The budgeted income statement for Hampton Hams is shown in Exhibit 7–6. The information needed to prepare this statement is contained in Exhibits 7–2, 7–3, 7–4, and 7–5. The budgeted income statement provides insight into the new store's expected profitability. If expected profitability is unsatisfactory, management may decide to abandon the project or to alter planned activity. Perhaps the owners of the shopping center would be willing to lease space for less, employees might accept lower pay, or the number of employees could be

reduced. Likewise, the pricing strategy could be scrutinized for possible changes. Indeed, budgets are usually prepared on spreadsheets or computerized mathematical models that enable managers to easily perform "what-if" analysis. Managers change some variable on the spreadsheet, and the software instantly presents a revised set of budgets. Although computer technology can provide instant access to a wide array of budgeted data, the manager remains responsible for data analysis and decision making. The proper interpretation of budget data requires an understanding of the origins and limitations of the budget amounts. For this reason, we recommend that you retrace the data in the financial statements back to the source data in the referenced exhibits.

Exhibit 7–7

HAMPTON HAMS
Pro Forma Balance Sheet
As of the Quarter Ended December 31, 2006

			Data Source
Assets			
Cash		$ 7,570	Exhibit 7–5
Accounts Receivable		172,800	Exhibit 7–2
Inventory		32,256	Exhibit 7–3
Store Fixtures and Equipment	$130,000		Exhibit 7–4 Discussion
Accumulated Depreciation	(3,000)		Exhibit 7–4 Discussion
Book Value of Equipment		127,000	
Total Assets		$339,626	
Liabilities			
Accounts Payable		$ 33,331	Exhibit 7–3
Utilities Payable		1,400	Exhibit 7–4
Sales Commissions Payable		4,608	Exhibit 7–4
Line of Credit Borrowings		242,995	Exhibit 7–5
Equity			
Retained Earnings		57,292	
Total Liabilities and Equity		$339,626	

Pro Forma Balance Sheet

Most of the items shown on the pro forma balance sheet in Exhibit 7–7 have been explained in the previous exhibits. The new store has no contributed capital because its operations are fully financed through debt and retained earnings. The amount of the retained earnings equals the amount of net income because no distributions were made and because no earnings from prior periods exist. Again, you are encouraged to trace the amounts shown in the financial statement to the source data contained in Exhibits 7–2 through 7–5.

Pro Forma Statement of Cash Flows

The pro forma statement of cash flows is shown in Exhibit 7–8. All information used to prepare this statement was drawn from the cash budget

Exhibit 7–8

HAMPTON HAMS
Pro Forma Statement of Cash Flows
For the Quarter Ended December 31, 2006

Cash Flow from Operating Activities		
Cash Receipts from Customers	$409,600	
Cash Payments for Inventory	(406,605)	
Cash Payments for S&A Expenses	(101,164)	
Cash Payments for Interest Expense	(7,256)	
Net Cash Flow from Operations		$(105,425)
Cash Flow from Investing Activities		
Cash Outflow to Purchase Fixtures		(130,000)
Cash Flow from Financing Activities		
Inflow from Borrowing on Line of Credit		242,995
Net Change in Cash		7,570
Plus Beginning Cash Balance		0
Ending Cash Balance		$ 7,570

answers to the *curious* accountant

Capital Records, like almost all companies, engages in a sophisticated budgeting process. Complications due merely to the size of today's major companies require extensive planning to ensure that they remain solvent.

shown in Exhibit 7–5. The individual items have been discussed in previous sections of the chapter. However, to reinforce your understanding, we suggest that you trace the amounts shown in the statement of cash flows to their source in the cash budget. If you have trouble tracing any of the information, you should reread the section titled Pro Forma Financial Statement Data in the discussion of the cash budget.

Check Yourself 7–3

How do pro forma financial statements differ from the financial statements presented in a company's annual report to stockholders?

Answer Pro forma financial statements are based on estimates and projections about business events that a company expects to occur in the future. The financial statements presented in a company's annual report to stockholders are based on historical events that occurred prior to the preparation of the statements.

a look back

The planning of financial matters is called *budgeting.* The degree of detail included in a company's budget depends on the time period considered. Generally, the shorter the time period, the more specific the plans. *Strategic planning* involves long-term plans, such as the overall objectives of the business. Examples of strategic planning include which products to manufacture and sell and which market niches to pursue. Strategic plans are stated in descriptive terms and are very broad. Capital budgeting deals with intermediate investment planning. *Operations budgeting* deals with short-term plans and is used in creating the master budget.

The budgeting committee has the responsibility of incorporating numerous departmental budgets into a master budget for the whole company. The *master budget* is very detailed with objectives stated in specific amounts; it represents a description of how management intends to achieve its objectives. It usually covers a one-year period of time. Budgeting encourages planning, coordination, performance measurement, and corrective action.

Employees may feel uncomfortable with budgets, which can have constraining effects and can serve as standards by which performance is evaluated. Therefore, the human factor should be considered in establishing an effective budget system. Upper-level management must set the proper atmosphere by taking budgets seriously and avoiding using them to humiliate subordinates. One way to create the proper atmosphere is to encourage subordinates' participation in the budgeting process; *participative budgeting* can help to set goals that are more realistic about what can be accomplished and to establish a team mentality in trying to reach those goals.

The primary components of the master budget are the *operating budgets,* the *capital budgets,* and the *financial statement budgets.* The budgeting process begins with the preparation of the operating budgets, which consist of detailed schedules and budgets prepared by the company's departments. The first operating budget to be prepared is the sales budget. The detailed operating budgets for inventory purchases and S&A expenses are based on the projected sales indicated in the sales budget. The information in the schedules of cash receipts (prepared in conjunction with the sales budget) and of cash payments (prepared in conjunction with the inventory and S&A budgets) is used in preparing the cash budget. The cash budget subtracts cash receipts from cash payments; the resultant cash surplus or shortage determines the company's financing activities.

The capital budget describes the company's long-term plans regarding investments in facilities, equipment, new products, or other lines of business. The information from the capital budget is used as input to several of the operating budgets.

The financial statements budgets (pro forma financial statements) are prepared from information contained in the operating budgets. The operating budgets for sales, inventory, and S&A expenses contain information that is used to prepare the income statement and balance sheet. The cash budget includes the amount of interest expense appearing on the income statement, the ending cash balance, the capital acquisitions that appear on the balance sheet, and most of the information included in the statement of cash flows.

Once a company has completed its budget, it has determined what it plans to do. Then the plan must be followed. The next chapter investigates the techniques associated with performance evaluation. You will learn to compare actual results to budgets, to calculate variances, and to identify the parties who are normally held accountable for creating the deviations from expectations. Finally, you will learn to appreciate the human factors that must be considered in taking corrective action when employees fail to accomplish budget goals.

a look
forward

SELF-STUDY REVIEW PROBLEM

The Getaway Gift Company operates a chain of small gift shops that are located in prime vacation towns. Getaway is considering opening a new store on January 1, 2003. Getaway's president recently attended a business seminar that explained how formal budgets could be useful in judging the new store's likelihood of succeeding. Assume you are the company's accountant. The president has asked you to explain the budgeting process and to provide sample reports that show the new store's operating expectations for the first three months (January, February, and March). Respond to the following specific requirements:

Required

a. List the operating budgets and schedules included in a master budget.

b. Explain the difference between pro forma financial statements and the financial statements presented in a company's annual reports to shareholders.

c. Prepare a sample sales budget and a schedule of expected cash receipts using the following assumptions. Getaway estimates January sales will be $400,000 of which $100,000 will be cash and $300,000 will be credit. The ratio of cash sales to sales on account is expected to remain constant over the three-month period. The company expects sales to increase 10 percent per month. The company expects to collect 100 percent of the accounts receivable generated by credit sales in the month following the sale. Use this information to determine the amount of accounts receivable that Getaway would report on the March 31 pro forma balance sheet and the amount of sales it would report on the first quarter pro forma income statement.

d. Prepare a sample inventory purchases budget using the following assumptions. Cost of goods sold is 60 percent of sales. The company desires to maintain a minimum ending inventory equal to 25 percent of the current month's cost of goods sold. Getaway makes all inventory purchases on account. The company pays 70 percent of accounts payable in the month of purchase. It pays the remaining 30 percent in the following month. Prepare a schedule of expected cash payments for inventory purchases. Use this information to determine the amount of cost of goods sold Getaway would report on the first quarter pro forma income statement and the amounts of ending inventory and accounts payable it would report on the March 31 pro forma balance sheet.

Solution to Requirement a

A master budget would include (1) a sales budget and schedule of cash receipts, (2) an inventory purchases budget and schedule of cash payments for inventory, (3) a general, selling, and administrative expenses budget and a schedule of cash payments related to these expenses, and (4) a cash budget.

Solution to Requirement b

Pro forma statements result from the operating budgets listed in the response to Requirement *a*. Pro forma statements describe the results of expected future events. In contrast, the financial statements presented in a company's annual report reflect the results of events that have actually occurred in the past.

Solution to Requirement c

General Information				
Sales growth rate		10%		**Pro Forma Statement Data**
Sales Budget	**January**	**February**	**March**	
Sales				
Cash sales	$100,000	$110,000	$121,000	
Sales on account	300,000	330,000	363,000	$ 363,000*
Total sales	$400,000	$440,000	$484,000	$1,324,000†
Schedule of Cash Receipts				
Current cash sales	$100,000	$110,000	$121,000	
Plus 100% of previous month's credit sales	0	300,000	330,000	
Total budgeted collections	$100,000	$410,000	$451,000	

*Ending accounts receivable balance reported on March 31 pro forma balance sheet.
†Sales revenue reported on first quarter pro forma income statement (sum of monthly sales).

Solution to Requirement d

General information				
Cost of goods sold percentage		60%		**Pro Forma Statement Data**
Desired ending inventory percentage of CGS		25%		
Inventory Purchases Budget	**January**	**February**	**March**	
Budgeted cost of goods sold	$240,000	$264,000	$290,400	$794,400*
Plus: Desired ending inventory	60,000	66,000	72,600	72,600†
Inventory needed	300,000	330,000	363,000	
Less: Beginning inventory	0	(60,000)	(66,000)	
Required purchases	$300,000	$270,000	$297,000	89,100‡
Schedule of Cash Payments for Inventory Purchases				
70% of current purchases	$210,000	$189,000	$207,900	
30% of prior month's purchases	0	90,000	81,000	
Total budgeted payments for inventory	$210,000	$279,000	$288,900	

*Cost of goods sold reported on first quarter pro forma income statement (sum of monthly amounts).
†Ending inventory balance reported on March 31 pro forma balance sheet.
‡Ending accounts payable balance reported on pro forma balance sheet ($297,000 × 0.3).

KEY TERMS

Budget committee 279
Budgeting 279
Capital budget 283
Capital budgeting 280

Cash budget 289
Financial statement budgets (pro forma statements) 283
Master budget 283

Operating budgets 280
Participative budgeting 282
Perpetual (continuous) budgeting 281

Pro forma statements 283
Strategic planning 280

QUESTIONS

1. Budgets are useful only for small companies that can estimate sales with accuracy. Do you agree with this statement?
2. Why does preparing the master budget require a committee?
3. What are the three levels of planning? Explain each briefly.
4. What is the primary factor that distinguishes the three different levels of planning from each other?

5. What is the advantage of using a perpetual budget instead of the traditional annual budget?

6. What are the advantages of budgeting?

7. How may budgets be used as a measure of performance?

8. Ken Shilov, manager of the marketing department, tells you that "budgeting simply does not work." He says that he made budgets for his employees and when he reprimanded them for failing to accomplish budget goals, he got unfounded excuses. Suggest how Mr. Shilov could encourage employee cooperation.

9. What is a master budget?

10. What is the normal starting point in developing the master budget?

11. How does the level of inventory affect the production budget? Why is it important to manage the level of inventory?

12. What are the components of the cash budget? Describe each.

13. The primary reason for preparing a cash budget is to determine the amount of cash to include on the budgeted balance sheet. Do you agree or disagree with this statement? Explain.

14. What information does the pro forma income statement provide? How does its preparation depend on the operating budgets?

15. How does the pro forma statement of cash flows differ from the cash budget?

EXERCISES—SERIES A

EXERCISE 7–1A *Budget Responsibility*

L.O. 1, 4

Wendy Wexler, the accountant, is a perfectionist. No one can do the job as well as she can. Indeed, she has found budget information provided by the various departments to be worthless. She must change everything they give her. She has to admit that her estimates have not always been accurate, but she shudders to think of what would happen if she used the information supplied by the marketing and operating departments. No one seems to care about accuracy. Indeed, some of the marketing staff have even become insulting. When Ms. Wexler confronted one of the salesmen with the fact that he was behind in meeting his budgeted sales forecast, he responded by saying, "They're your numbers. Why don't you go out and make the sales? It's a heck of a lot easier to sit there in your office and make up numbers than it is to get out and get the real work done." Ms. Wexler reported the incident, but, of course, nothing was done about it.

Required
Write a short report suggesting how the budgeting process could be improved.

EXERCISE 7–2A *Preparing the Sales Budget*

L.O. 6, 10

Speedy Shoes, which expects to start operations on January 1, 2005, will sell sports shoes in shopping malls. Speedy Shoes has budgeted sales as indicated in the following table. The company expects a 20 percent increase in sales per month for May and June. The ratio of cash sales to sales on account will remain stable from April through June.

Sales	April	May	June
Cash sales	$ 30,000	?	?
Sales on account	90,000	?	?
Total budgeted sales	$120,000	?	?

Required
a. Complete the sales budget by filling in the missing amounts.
b. Determine the amount of sales revenue Speedy Shoes will report on its second quarter pro forma income statement.

EXERCISE 7–3A *Preparing a Schedule of Cash Receipts*

L.O. 6, 10

Scotty Beds, Inc., sells brass beds. Its budget director has prepared the following sales budget. The company had $120,000 in accounts receivable on July 1. Scotty Beds normally collects 100 percent of accounts receivable in the month following the month of sale.

Sales	July	August	September
Sales Budget			
Cash sales	$ 40,000	$ 44,000	$ 48,400
Sales on account	90,000	99,000	108,900
Total budgeted sales	$130,000	$143,000	$157,300
Schedule of Cash Receipts			
Current cash sales	?	?	?
Plus collections from accounts receivable	?	?	?
Total budgeted collections	$160,000	$134,000	$147,400

Required

a. Complete the schedule of cash receipts by filling in the missing amounts.

b. Determine the amount of accounts receivable the company will report on its third quarter pro forma balance sheet.

L.O. 6   EXERCISE 7–4A *Preparing Sales Budgets With Different Assumptions*

Camen Corporation, which has three divisions, is preparing its sales budget. Each division expects a different growth rate because economic conditions vary in different regions of the country. The growth expectations per quarter are 2 percent for East Division, 3 percent for West Division, and 5 percent for South Division.

Division	First Quarter	Second Quarter	Third Quarter	Fourth Quarter
East Division	$260,000	?	?	?
West Division	370,000	?	?	?
South Division	170,000	?	?	?

Required

a. Complete the sales budget by filling in the missing amounts. (Round figures to the nearest dollar.)

b. Determine the amount of sales revenue that the company will report on its quarterly pro forma income statements.

L.O. 6   EXERCISE 7–5A *Determining Cash Receipts From Accounts Receivable*

Happy Wishes operates a mail-order business that sells clothes designed for frequent travelers. It had sales of $580,000 in December. Because Happy Wishes is in the mail-order business, all sales are made on account. The company expects a 30 percent drop in sales for January. The balance in the Accounts Receivable account on December 31 was $90,400 and is budgeted to be $67,600 as of January 31. Happy Wishes normally collects accounts receivable in the month following the month of sale.

Required

a. Determine the amount of cash Happy Wishes expects to collect from accounts receivable during January.

b. Is it reasonable to assume that sales will decline in January for this type of business? Why or why not?

L.O. 6   EXERCISE 7–6A *Using Judgment in Making a Sales Forecast*

Stars, Inc., is a candy store located in a large shopping mall.

Required

Write a brief memo describing the sales pattern that you would expect Stars to experience during the year. In which months will sales likely be high? In which months will sales likely be low? Explain why.

L.O. 7   EXERCISE 7–7A *Preparing an Inventory Purchases Budget*

Bright Nights Company sells lamps and other lighting fixtures. The purchasing department manager prepared the following inventory purchases budget. Bright Nights' policy is to maintain an ending inventory balance equal to 10 percent of that month's cost of goods sold.

	January	February	March
Budgeted cost of goods sold	$84,500	$92,950	$102,245
Plus: Desired ending inventory	8,450	?	?
Inventory needed	92,950	?	?
Less: Beginning inventory	20,000	?	?
Required purchases (on account)	$72,950	$93,795	$103,175

Required

a. Complete the inventory purchases budget by filling in the missing amounts.
b. Determine the amount of cost of goods sold the company will report on its first quarter pro forma income statement.
c. Determine the amount of ending inventory the company will report on its pro forma balance sheet at the end of the first quarter.

EXERCISE 7–8A *Preparing a Schedule of Cash Payments for Inventory Purchases*   **L.O. 7**

Dale Wholesale Books buys books and magazines directly from publishers and distributes them to grocery stores. The wholesaler expects to purchase the following inventory.

	April	May	June
Required purchases (on account)	$80,000	$100,000	$120,000

Dale's accountant prepared the following schedule of cash payments for inventory purchases. Dale's suppliers require that 95 percent of purchases on account be paid in the month of purchase; the remaining 5 percent are paid in the month following the month of purchase.

Schedule of Cash Payments for Inventory Purchases			
	April	May	June
Payment for current accounts payable	$76,000	?	?
Payment for previous accounts payable	4,800	?	?
Total budgeted payments for inventory	$80,800	$99,000	$119,000

Required

a. Complete the schedule of cash payments for inventory purchases by filling in the missing amounts.
b. Determine the amount of accounts payable the company will report on its pro forma balance sheet at the end of the second quarter.

EXERCISE 7–9A *Determining the Amount of Expected Inventory Purchases and Cash Payments*   **L.O. 7**

Henderson Company, which sells electric razors, had $356,000 of cost of goods sold during the month of June. The company projects a 5 percent increase in cost of goods sold during July. The inventory balance as of June 30 is $36,800, and the desired ending inventory balance for July is $31,800. Henderson pays cash to settle 80 percent of its purchases on account during the month of purchase and pays the remaining 20 percent in the month following the purchase. The accounts payable balance as of June 30 was $44,000.

Required

a. Determine the amount of purchases budgeted for July.
b. Determine the amount of cash payments budgeted for inventory purchases in July.

EXERCISE 7–10A *Preparing a Schedule of Cash Payments for Selling and Administrative Expenses*   **L.O. 8**

The budget director for Loehman Window Cleaning Services prepared the following list of expected operating expenses. All expenses requiring cash payments are paid for in the month incurred except salary

expense and insurance. Salary is paid in the month following the month in which it is incurred. The insurance premium for six months is paid on October 1. October is the first month of operations; accordingly, there are no beginning account balances.

	October	November	December
Budgeted Operating Expenses			
Equipment lease expense	$ 8,000	$ 8,000	$ 8,000
Salary expense	6,500	7,150	7,866
Cleaning supplies	2,600	2,860	3,146
Insurance expense	1,000	1,000	1,000
Depreciation on computer	1,600	1,600	1,600
Rent	1,800	1,800	1,800
Miscellaneous expenses	500	500	500
Total operating expenses	$22,000	$22,910	$23,912
Schedule of Cash Payments for Operating Expenses			
Equipment lease expense	?	?	?
Prior month's salary expense, 100%	?	?	?
Cleaning supplies	?	?	?
Insurance premium	?	?	?
Depreciation on computer	?	?	?
Rent	?	?	?
Miscellaneous expenses	?	?	?
Total disbursements for operating expenses	$18,900	$19,660	$20,596

Required

a. Complete the schedule of cash payments for operating expenses by filling in the missing amounts.

b. Determine the amount of salaries payable the company will report on its pro forma balance sheet at the end of the fourth quarter.

c. Determine the amount of prepaid insurance the company will report on its pro forma balance sheet at the end of the fourth quarter.

L.O. 7   **EXERCISE 7–11A** *Preparing Inventory Purchases Budgets With Different Assumptions*

Executive officers of Ramos Company are wrestling with their budget for the next year. The following are two different sales estimates provided by two difference sources.

Source of Estimate	First Quarter	Second Quarter	Third Quarter	Fourth Quarter
Sales manager	$500,000	$400,000	$360,000	$640,000
Marketing consultant	$550,000	$480,000	$400,000	$600,000

Ramos' past experience indicates that cost of goods sold is about 70 percent of sales revenue. The company tries to maintain 10 percent of the next quarter's expected cost of goods sold as the current quarter's ending inventory. This year's ending inventory is $30,000. Next year's ending inventory is budgeted to be $32,000.

Required

a. Prepare an inventory purchases budget using the sales manager's estimate.

b. Prepare an inventory purchases budget using the marketing consultant's estimate.

L.O. 8, 10   **EXERCISE 7–12A** *Determining the Amount of Cash Payments and Pro Forma Statement Data for Selling and Administrative Expenses*

January budgeted selling and administrative expenses for the retail shoe store that Abdul Ali plans to open on January 1, 2003, are as follows: sales commissions, $13,000; rent, $10,000; utilities, $6,000; depreciation, $4,800; and miscellaneous, $1,600. Utilities are paid in the month following their incursion. Other expenses are expected to be paid in cash in the month in which they are incurred.

Required

a. Determine the amount of budgeted cash payments for January selling and administrative expenses.
b. Determine the amount of utilities payable the store will report on the January 31st pro forma balance sheet.
c. Determine the amount of depreciation expense the store will report on the income statement for the year 2003, assuming that monthly depreciation remains the same for the entire year.

EXERCISE 7–13A *Preparing a Cash Budget*   L.O. 9, 10

The accountant for Nelly's Dress Shop prepared the following cash budget. Nelly's desires to maintain a cash cushion of $14,000 before the interest payment at the end of each month. Funds are assumed to be borrowed on the first day and repaid on the last day of each month. Interest is charged at the rate of 2 percent per month. The company had a beginning balance in its line-of-credit loan of $40,000.

Cash Budget	July	August	September
Beginning cash balance	$ 18,000	?	?
Add: Cash receipts	160,000	$188,000	$225,600
Cash available before current financing activity (a)	$178,000	?	?
Less: Disbursements			
For inventory purchases	$153,526	$134,230	$164,152
For S&A expenses	44,500	54,560	56,432
Total budgeted disbursements (b)	$198,026	?	?
Payments minus receipts			
Shortage (surplus)	$ 20,026	?	?
Plus: Cash cushion	14,000	?	?
Financing activity			
Borrowing (repayment) (c)	34,026	?	?
Interest expense at 2 percent per month (d)	1,481	?	?
Ending cash balance (a − b + c − d)	$ 12,519	$ 12,474	$ 12,544

Required

a. Complete the cash budget by filling in the missing amounts. Round all computations to the nearest whole dollar.
b. Determine the amount of net cash flows from operating activities Nelly's will report on the third quarter pro forma statement of cash flows.
c. Determine the amount of net cash flows from financing activities Nelly's will report on the third quarter pro forma statement of cash flows.

EXERCISE 7–14A *Determining Amount to Borrow and Pro Forma Statement Balances*   L.O. 9, 10

Doris Ferraro owns a small restaurant in New York City. Ms. Ferraro provided her accountant with the following summary information regarding expectations for the month of June. The balance in accounts receivable as of May 31 is $48,000. Budgeted cash and credit sales for June are $88,000 and $460,000, respectively. Credit sales are made through Visa and MasterCard and are collected rapidly. Ninety percent of credit sales is collected in the month of sale, and the remainder is collected in the following month. Ms. Ferraro's suppliers do not extend credit. Cash payments for June are expected to be $620,000. Ms. Ferraro has a line of credit that enables the restaurant to borrow funds on demand; however, they must be borrowed on the first day of the month. Interest is paid in cash on the last day of the month. Ms. Ferraro desires to maintain a $20,000 cash balance before the interest payment. Her annual interest rate is 9 percent.

Required

a. Compute the amount of funds Ms. Ferraro needs to borrow for June.
b. Determine the amount of interest expense the restaurant will report on the June pro forma income statement.
c. What amount will the restaurant report as interest payable on the June 30 pro forma balance sheet?

EXERCISE 7–15A *Preparing Pro Forma Income Statements With Different Assumptions*   L.O. 10

Jim Pullman, the controller of Swanson Corporation, is trying to prepare a sales budget for the coming year. The income statements for the last four quarters follow.

	First Quarter	Second Quarter	Third Quarter	Fourth Quarter	Total
Sales revenue	$125,000	$120,000	$132,000	$223,000	$600,000
Cost of goods sold	75,000	72,000	79,200	133,800	360,000
Gross profit	50,000	48,000	52,800	89,200	240,000
Selling & admin. expense	25,000	24,000	26,400	44,600	120,000
Net income	$ 25,000	$ 24,000	$ 26,400	$ 44,600	$120,000

Historically, cost of goods sold is about 60 percent of sales revenue. Selling and administrative expenses are about 20 percent of sales revenue.

Lou Swanson, the chief executive officer, told Mr. Pullman that he expected sales next year to be 10 percent above last year's level. However, Mindy Pell, the vice president of sales, told Mr. Pullman that she believed sales growth would be only 5 percent.

Required

a. Prepare a pro forma income statement including quarterly budgets for the coming year using Mr. Swanson's estimate.

b. Prepare a pro forma income statement including quarterly budgets for the coming year using Ms. Pell's estimate.

c. Explain why two executive officers in the same company could have different estimates of future growth.

PROBLEMS—SERIES A

L.O. 6   PROBLEM 7–16A *Preparing a Sales Budget and Schedule of Cash Receipts*

Mankato Pointers, Inc., expects to begin operations on January 1, 2004; it will operate as a specialty sales company that sells laser pointers over the Internet. Mankato expects sales in January 2004 to total $50,000 and to increase 10 percent per month in February and March. All sales are on account. Mankato expects to collect 60 percent of accounts receivable in the month of sale, 30 percent in the month following the sale, and 10 percent in the second month following the sale.

Required

a. Prepare a sales budget for the first quarter of 2004.

b. Determine the amount of sales revenue Mankato will report on the first 2004 quarterly pro forma income statement.

c. Prepare a cash receipts schedule for the first quarter of 2004.

d. Determine the amount of accounts receivable as of March 31, 2004.

L.O. 7, 10   PROBLEM 7–17A *Preparing the Inventory Purchases Budget and Schedule of Cash Payments*

Celebration, Inc., sells fire works. The company's marketing director developed the following cost of goods sold budget for April, May, and June.

	April	May	June
Budgeted cost of goods sold	$40,000	$50,000	$80,000

Celebration had a beginning inventory balance of $3,600 on April 1 and a beginning balance in accounts payable of $14,800. The company desires to maintain an ending inventory balance equal to 10 percent of the current period's cost of goods sold. Celebration makes all purchases on account. The company pays 60 percent of accounts payable in the month of purchase and the remaining 40 percent in the month following purchase.

Required

a. Prepare an inventory purchases budget for April, May, and June.

b. Determine the amount of ending inventory Celebration will report on the end-of-quarter pro forma balance sheet.
c. Prepare a schedule of cash payments for inventory for April, May, and June.
d. Determine the balance in accounts payable Celebration will report on the end-of-quarter pro forma balance sheet.

PROBLEM 7–18A *Preparing Pro Forma Income Statements With Different Assumptions*   **L.O. 10**

Top executive officers of Posan Company, a merchandising firm, are preparing the next year's budget. The controller has provided everyone with the current year's projected income statement.

	Current Year
Sales Revenue	$1,600,000
Cost of Goods Sold	960,000
Gross Profit	640,000
Selling & Admin. Expenses	520,000
Net Income	$ 120,000

Cost of goods sold is usually 60 percent of sales revenue, and selling and administrative expenses are usually 20 percent of sales plus a fixed cost of $200,000. The president has announced that the company's goal is to increase net income by 15 percent.

Required
The following items are independent of each other.
a. What percentage increase in sales would enable the company to reach its goal? Support your answer with a pro forma income statement.
b. The market may become stagnant next year, and the company does not expect an increase in sales revenue. The production manager believes that an improved production procedure can cut cost of goods sold by 2 percent. What else can the company do to reach its goal? Prepare a pro forma income statement illustrating your proposal.
c. The company decides to escalate its advertising campaign to boost consumer recognition, which will increase selling and administrative expenses to $640,000. With the increased advertising, the company expects sales revenue to increase by 15 percent. Assume that cost of goods sold remains a constant proportion of sales. Can the company reach its goal?

PROBLEM 7–19A *Preparing a Schedule of Cash Payments for Selling and Administrative Expenses*   **L.O. 8, 9**

Summit is a retail company specializing in men's hats. Its budget director prepared the list of expected operating expenses that follows. All items are paid when incurred except sales commissions and utilities, which are paid in the month following their incursion. July is the first month of operations, so there are no beginning account balances.

	July	August	September
Salary expense	$10,000	$10,000	$10,000
Sales commissions (4 percent of sales)	1,440	1,600	1,760
Supplies expense	360	400	440
Utilities	1,200	1,200	1,200
Depreciation on store equipment	2,600	2,600	2,600
Rent	6,600	6,600	6,600
Miscellaneous	720	720	720
Total S&A expenses before interest	$22,920	$23,120	$23,320

Required
a. Prepare a schedule of cash payments for selling and administrative expenses.
b. Determine the amount of utilities payable as of September 30.
c. Determine the amount of sales commissions payable as of September 30.

L.O. 9   **PROBLEM 7–20A** *Preparing a Cash Budget*

Schroeder Medical Clinic has budgeted the following cash flows.

	January	February	March
Cash receipts	$96,000	$102,000	$120,000
Cash payments			
For inventory purchases	86,300	68,000	82,000
For S&A expenses	31,000	32,000	27,000

Schroeder Medical had a cash balance of $8,000 on January 1. The company desires to maintain a cash cushion of $5,000 before making a monthly interest payment. Funds are assumed to be borrowed on the first day of each month and repaid on the last day of each month; the interest rate is 1 percent per month. The company had a $40,000 beginning balance in its line of credit liability account.

Required

Prepare a cash budget. (Round all computations to the nearest whole dollar.)

L.O. 6, 7, 8   **PROBLEM 7–21A** *Preparing Budgets With Multiple Products*

DeFoor Fruits Corporation wholesales peaches and oranges. Anne DeFoor is working with the company's accountant to prepare next year's budget. Ms. DeFoor estimates that sales will increase 5 percent annually for peaches and 10 percent for oranges. The current year's sales revenue data follow.

	First Quarter	Second Quarter	Third Quarter	Fourth Quarter	Total
Peaches	$240,000	$250,000	$300,000	$250,000	$1,040,000
Oranges	400,000	450,000	570,000	380,000	1,800,000
Total	$640,000	$700,000	$870,000	$630,000	$2,840,000

Based on the company's past experience, cost of goods sold is usually 60 percent of sales revenue. Company policy is to keep 20 percent of the next period's estimated cost of goods sold as the current period's ending inventory. (*Hint:* Use the cost of goods sold for the first quarter to determine the beginning inventory for the first quarter.)

Required

a. Prepare the company's sales budget for the next year for each quarter by individual product.

b. If the selling and administrative expenses are estimated to be $700,000, prepare the company's budgeted annual income statement.

c. Ms. DeFoor estimates next year's ending inventory will be $34,000 for peaches and $56,000 for oranges. Prepare the company's inventory purchases budgets for the next year showing quarterly figures by product.

L.O. 6, 7, 8   **PROBLEM 7–22A** *Preparing a Master Budget for Retail Company With No Beginning Account Balances*

Canyon Company is a retail company that specializes in selling outdoor camping equipment. The company is considering opening a new store on October 1, 2003. The company president formed a planning committee to prepare a master budget for the first three months of operation. As budget coordinator, you have been assigned the following tasks.

Required

a. October sales are estimated to be $100,000 of which 40 percent will be cash and 60 percent will be credit. The company expects sales to increase at the rate of 25 percent per month. Prepare a sales budget.

b. The company expects to collect 100 percent of the accounts receivable generated by credit sales in the month following the sale. Prepare a schedule of cash receipts.

c. The cost of goods sold is 60 percent of sales. The company desires to maintain a minimum ending inventory equal to 10 percent of the current month's cost of goods sold. Assume that all purchases are made on account. Prepare an inventory purchases budget.

d. The company pays 70 percent of accounts payable in the month of purchase and the remaining 30 percent in the following month. Prepare a cash payments budget for inventory purchases.

e. Budgeted selling and administrative expenses per month follow.

Salary expense (fixed)	$16,000
Sales commissions	5 percent of Sales
Supplies expense	2 percent of Sales
Utilities (fixed)	$1,400
Depreciation on store equipment (fixed)*	$4,000
Rent (fixed)	$4,800
Miscellaneous (fixed)	$1,200

*The capital expenditures budget indicates that Canyon will spend
$164,000 on October 1 for store fixtures, which are expected to have
a $20,000 salvage value and a three-year (36-month) useful life.

Use this information to prepare a selling and administrative expenses budget.

f. Utilities and sales commissions are paid the month after they are incurred; all other expenses are paid in the month in which they are incurred. Prepare a cash payments budget for selling and administrative expenses.

g. Canyon borrows funds and repays them on the first day of the month. It pays interest of 1 percent per month in cash on the last day of the month. To be prudent, the company desires to maintain a $12,000 cash cushion before paying interest. Prepare a cash budget.

h. Prepare a pro forma income statement for the quarter.

i. Prepare a pro forma balance sheet at the end of the quarter.

j. Prepare a pro forma statement of cash flows for the quarter.

PROBLEM 7–23A *Behavioral Impact of Budgeting*   L.O. 4

Sweet Grove Corporation has three divisions, each operating as a responsibility center. To provide an incentive for divisional executive officers, the company gives divisional management a bonus equal to 20 percent of the excess of actual net income over budgeted net income. The following is Greer Division's current year's performance.

	Current Year
Sales revenue	$3,600,000
Cost of goods sold	2,160,000
Gross profit	$1,440,000
Selling & admin. expenses	720,000
Net income	$ 720,000

The president has just received next year's budget proposal from the vice president in charge of Greer Division. The proposal budgets a 5 percent increase in sales revenue with an extensive explanation about stiff market competition. The president is puzzled. Greer has enjoyed revenue growth of around 10 percent for each of the past five years. The president had consistently approved the division's budget proposals based on 5 percent growth in the past. This time, the president wants to show that he is not a fool. "I will impose a 15 percent revenue increase to teach them a lesson!" the president says to himself smugly.

Assume that cost of goods sold and selling and administrative expenses remain stable in proportion to sales.

Required

a. Prepare the budgeted income statement based on Greer Division's proposal of a 5 percent increase.

b. If growth is actually 10 percent as usual, how much bonus would Greer Division's executive officers receive if the president had approved the division's proposal?

c. Prepare the budgeted income statement based on the 15 percent increase the president imposed.

d. If the actual results turn out to be a 10 percent increase as usual, how much bonus would Greer Division's executive officers receive since the president imposed a 15 percent increase?

e. Propose a better budgeting procedure for Sweet Grove.

EXERCISES—SERIES B

EXERCISE 7–1B *Budget Responsibility*   L.O. 1, 4

Tom Lapinski, the controller of Moore Industries, Inc., is very popular. He is easygoing and does not offend anybody. To develop the company's most recent budget, Mr. Lapinski first asked all department

managers to prepare their own budgets. He then added together the totals from the department budgets to produce the company budget. When Jane Samford, Moore's president, reviewed the company budget, she sighed and asked, "Is our company a charitable organization?"

Required

Write a brief memo describing deficiencies in the budgeting process and suggesting improvements.

L.O. 6, 10   EXERCISE 7–2B *Preparing a Sales Budget*

Antonio's Restaurant is opening for business in a new shopping center. Tony Warren, the owner, is preparing a sales budget for the next three months. After consulting friends in the same business. Ms. Warren estimated July revenues as shown in the following table. She expects revenues to increase 5 percent per month in August and September.

Revenues Budget	July	August	September
Food sales	$12,000	?	?
Beverage and liquor sales	8,000	?	?
Total budgeted revenues	$20,000	?	?

Required

a. Complete the sales budget by filling in the missing amounts.
b. Determine the total amount of revenue Antonio's Restaurant will report on its quarterly pro forma income statement.

L.O. 6, 10   EXERCISE 7–3B *Preparing a Schedule of Cash Receipts*

Waddle Imports, Inc., sells goods imported from the Far East. Using the second quarter's sales budget, Suzy Ho is trying to complete the schedule of cash receipts for the quarter. The company had accounts receivable of $430,000 on April 1. Waddle Imports normally collects 100 percent of accounts receivable in the month following the month of sale.

Sales	April	May	June
Sales Budget			
Cash sales	$120,000	$132,000	$124,000
Sales on account	480,000	568,000	500,000
Total budgeted sales	$600,000	$700,000	$624,000
Schedule of Cash Receipts			
Current cash sales	?	?	?
Plus: Collections from accounts receivable	?	?	?
Total budgeted collections	$550,000	$612,000	$692,000

Required

a. Help Ms. Ho complete the schedule of cash receipts by filling in the missing amounts.
b. Determine the amount of accounts receivable the company will report on the quarterly pro forma balance sheet.

L.O. 6   EXERCISE 7–4B *Preparing Sales Budgets With Different Assumptions*

Hulsey International, Inc., has three subsidiaries, Wendall Trading Company, Camden Medical Supplies Company, and Gulf Shipping Company. Because the subsidiaries operate in different industries, Hulsey's corporate budget for the coming year must reflect the different growth potentials of the individual industries. The growth expectations per quarter for the subsidiaries are 4 percent for Wendall, 1 percent for Camden, and 3 percent for Gulf.

Subsidiary	Current Quarter Sales	First Quarter	Second Quarter	Third Quarter	Fourth Quarter
Wendall	$200,000	?	?	?	?
Camden	300,000	?	?	?	?
Gulf	400,000	?	?	?	?

Required

a. Complete the sales budget by filling in the missing amounts. (Round the figures to the nearest dollar.)

b. Determine the amount of sales revenue Hulsey will report on the quarterly pro forma income statements.

EXERCISE 7–5B *Determining Cash Receipts From Accounts Receivable*

L.O. 6

Batson Corporation is about to start a business as an agricultural products distributor. Because its customers will all be retailers, Batson will sell its products solely on account. The company expects to collect 50 percent of accounts receivable in the month of sale and the remaining 50 percent in the following month. Batson expects sales revenues of $100,000 in July, the first month of operation, and $120,000 in August.

Required

a. Determine the amount of cash Batson expects to collect in July.

b. Determine the amount of cash Batson expects to collect in August.

EXERCISE 7–6B *Using Judgment in Making a Sales Forecast*

L.O. 6

Angel's Greetings Corporation sells greeting cards for various occasions.

Required

Write a brief memo describing the sales pattern that you would expect Angel's Greetings to experience during the year. In which months will sales likely be high? Explain why.

EXERCISE 7–7B *Preparing an Inventory Purchases Budget*

L.O. 7

GetWell Drugstores, Inc., sells prescription drugs, over-the-counter drugs, and some groceries. The purchasing manager prepared the following inventory purchases budget. GetWell desires to maintain an ending inventory balance equal to 20 percent of that month's cost of goods sold.

Inventory Purchases Budget	January	February	March
Budgeted cost of goods sold	$35,000	$30,000	$40,000
Plus: Desired ending inventory	7,000	?	?
Inventory needed	42,000	?	?
Less: Beginning inventory	8,000	?	?
Required purchases (on account)	$34,000	?	?

Required

a. Complete the inventory purchases budget by filling in the missing amounts.

b. Determine the amount of cost of goods sold the company will report on the first quarter pro forma income statement.

c. Determine the amount of ending inventory the company will report on the first quarter pro forma balance sheet.

EXERCISE 7–8B *Preparing a Schedule of Cash Payments for Inventory Purchases*

L.O. 7

Neighborhood Grocery buys and sells groceries in a community far from any major city. Justin Romer, the owner, budgeted the store's purchases as follows:

	October	November	December
Required purchases (on account)	$25,000	$24,000	$31,000

Neighborhood's suppliers require that 70 percent of accounts payable be paid in the month of purchase. The remaining 30 percent is paid in the month following the month of purchase.

Schedule of Cash Payments for Inventory Purchases			
	October	November	December
Payment for current accounts payable	$17,500	?	?
Payment for previous accounts payable	6,000	?	?
Total budgeted payments for inventory	$23,500	?	?

Required

a. Complete the schedule of cash payments for inventory purchases by filling in the missing amounts.

b. Determine the amount of accounts payable Neighborhood will report on the store's quarterly pro forma balance sheet.

L.O. 7   **EXERCISE 7–9B** *Determining the Amount of Inventory Purchases and Cash Payments*

Tanner Oil Corporation, which distributes gasoline products to independent gasoline stations, had $400,000 of cost of goods sold in January. The company expects a 2.5 percent increase in cost of goods sold during February. The ending inventory balance for January is $22,000, and the desired ending inventory for February is $25,000. Tanner pays cash to settle 60 percent of its purchases on account during the month of purchase and pays the remaining 40 percent in the month following the purchase. The accounts payable balance as of January 31 was $30,000.

Required

a. Determine the amount of purchases budgeted for February.

b. Determine the amount of cash payments budgeted for inventory purchases in February.

L.O. 8   **EXERCISE 7–10B** *Preparing a Schedule of Cash Payments for Selling and Administrative Expenses*

The controller for Central Laundry Services prepared the following list of expected operating expenses. All expenses requiring cash payments except salary expense and insurance are paid for in the month incurred. Salary is paid in the month following its incursion. The annual insurance premium is paid in advance on January 1. January is the first month of operations. Accordingly, there are no beginning account balances.

	January	February	March
Budgeted Selling and Administrative Expenses			
Equipment depreciation	$ 5,600	$ 5,600	$ 5,600
Salary expense	2,700	2,500	2,850
Cleaning supplies	1,000	940	1,100
Insurance expense	600	600	600
Equipment maintenance expense	500	500	500
Leases expense	1,600	1,600	1,600
Miscellaneous expenses	400	400	400
Total S&A expenses	$12,400	$12,140	$12,650
Schedule of Cash Payments for Selling and Administrative Expenses			
Equipment depreciation	?	?	?
Prior month's salary expense, 100%	?	?	?
Cleaning supplies	?	?	?
Insurance premium	?	?	?
Equipment maintenance expense	?	?	?
Leases expense	?	?	?
Miscellaneous expenses	?	?	?
Total Payments for S&A expenses	$10,700	$ 6,140	$ 6,100

Required

a. Complete the schedule of cash payments for selling and administrative expenses by filling in the missing amounts.

b. Determine the amount of salaries payable the company will report on its quarterly pro forma balance sheet.

c. Determine the amount of prepaid insurance the company will report on its quarterly pro forma balance sheet.

L.O. 7   **EXERCISE 7–11B** *Preparing Inventory Purchases Budgets With Different Assumptions*

Sophia Callie has been at odds with her brother and business partner, Justin, since childhood. The sibling rivalry is not all bad, however; their garden shop, Callie Gardens and Gifts, has been very successful. When the partners met to prepare the coming year's budget, their forecasts were different, naturally. Their sales revenue estimates follow.

Source of Estimate	First Quarter	Second Quarter	Third Quarter	Fourth Quarter
Sophia	$320,000	$400,000	$280,000	$360,000
Justin	280,000	300,000	320,000	400,000

Past experience indicates that cost of goods sold is about 60 percent of sales revenue. The company tries to maintain 15 percent of the next quarter's expected cost of goods sold as the current quarter's ending inventory. The ending inventory this year is $25,000. Next year's ending inventory is budgeted to be $35,000.

Required

a. Prepare an inventory purchases budget using Sophia's estimate.

b. Prepare an inventory purchases budget using Justin's estimate.

EXERCISE 7–12B *Determining the Amount of Cash Payments for Selling and Administrative Expenses*

L.O. 8, 10

Andy Ramirez, managing partner of Ramirez Business Consulting, is preparing a budget for January 2004, the first month of business operations. Andy estimates the following monthly selling and administrative expenses: office lease, $4,000; utilities, $1,400; office supplies, $2,200; depreciation, $12,000; referral fees, $5,000; and miscellaneous, $1,000. Referral fees will be paid in the month following the month they are incurred. Other expenses will be paid in the month in which they are incurred.

Required

a. Determine the amount of budgeted cash payments for January selling and administrative expenses.

b. Determine the amount of referral fees payable the firm will report on the January 31 pro forma balance sheet.

c. Determine the amount of office lease expense the company will report on its 2004 pro forma income statement, assuming that the monthly lease expense remains the same throughout the whole year.

EXERCISE 7–13B *Preparing a Cash Budget*

L.O. 9, 10

Percy Emerson, the accounting manager of Pyramid Antique Company, is preparing his company's cash budget for the next quarter. Pyramid desires to maintain a cash cushion of $4,000 before making the interest payment at the end of each month. As cash flows fluctuate, the company either borrows funds on the first day of a month or repays them at the end of a month. It pays interest on borrowed funds at the rate of 1.5 percent per month. On April 1, Pyramid owed $30,000 on its line of credit loan.

Cash Budget	April	May	June
Beginning cash balance	$ 11,000	?	?
Add: Cash receipts from customers	160,000	$189,000	$205,000
Cash available before current financing activity (a)	$171,000	?	?
Less: Disbursements			
For inventory purchases	155,000	150,000	158,000
For S&A expenses	35,000	36,000	34,000
Total Budgeted Disbursements (b)	190,000	?	?
Payments Minus Receipts			
Shortage (Surplus)	19,000	?	?
Plus: Cash cushion	4,000	?	?
Financing activity			
Borrowing (repayment) (c)	23,000	?	?
Interest Expense at 1.5% per month (d)	795	?	?
Ending cash balance (a − b + c − d)	$ 3,205	$ 3,205	$ 3,238

Required

a. Complete the cash budget by filling in the missing amounts. Round all computations to the nearest whole dollar.

b. Determine the amount of net cash flows from operating activities Pyramid will report on its quarterly pro forma statement of cash flows.

c. Determine the amount of net cash flows from financing activities Pyramid will report on its quarterly pro forma statement of cash flows.

L.O. 9, 10   **EXERCISE 7–14B** *Determining Amount to Borrow and Pro Forma Statement Balances*

Yuri Andropov, the president of Yuri's Flowers, Inc., has been working with his controller to manage the company's cash position. The controller provided Yuri the following data.

Balance of accounts receivable, June 30	$ 31,000
Balance of line of credit, June 30	0
Budgeted cash sales for July	70,000
Budgeted credit sales for July	340,000
Budgeted cash payments for July	390,000

The company typically collects 75 percent of credit sales in the month of sale and the remainder in the month following the sale. Yuri's line of credit enables the company to borrow funds readily, with the stipulation that any borrowing must take place on the first day of the month. Mr. Andropov likes to maintain a $15,000 cash balance before any interest payments. The annual interest rate is 12 percent.

Required
a. Compute the amount of funds Mr. Andropov needs to borrow on July 1.
b. Determine the amount of interest the company will report on the July pro forma income statement.

L.O. 10   **EXERCISE 7–15B** *Preparing Pro Forma Income Statements With Different Assumptions*

Wirthlin Corporation's budget planning meeting is like a zoo. Barry Sulkas, the credit manager, is naturally conservative and Sherry Smith, the marketing manager, is the opposite. They have argued back and forth about the effect of various factors that influence the sales growth rate, such as credit policies and market potential. Based on the following current year data provided by Jenny Denton, the controller, Barry expects Wirthlin's revenues to grow 4 percent each quarter above last year's level; Sherry insists the growth rate will be 12 percent per quarter.

Current Year	First Quarter	Second Quarter	Third Quarter	Fourth Quarter	Total
Sales revenue	$240,000	$200,000	$216,000	$314,000	$970,000
Cost of goods sold	122,000	101,000	106,000	156,000	485,000
Gross margin	118,000	99,000	110,000	158,000	485,000
Selling & admin. expenses	32,000	26,000	26,400	40,600	125,000
Net income	$ 86,000	$ 73,000	$ 83,600	$117,400	$360,000

Historically, cost of goods sold has been about 50 percent of sales revenue. Selling and administrative expenses have been about 12.5 percent of sales revenue.

Required
a. Prepare a pro forma income statement for the coming year using the credit manager's growth estimate.
b. Prepare a pro forma income statement for the coming year using the marketing manager's growth estimate.
c. Explain why two executives in the same company could have different estimates of future growth.

PROBLEMS—SERIES B

L.O. 6   **PROBLEM 7–16B** *Preparing a Sales Budget and Schedule of Cash Receipts*

Porta Corporation sells mail-order computers. In December 2002, it has generated $700,000 of sales revenue; the company expects a 20 percent increase in sales in January and 10 percent in February. All sales are on account. Porta normally collects 80 percent of accounts receivable in the month of sale and 20 percent in the next month.

Required
a. Prepare a sales budget for January and February 2003.
b. Determine the amount of sales revenue Porta would report on the bimonthly pro forma income statement for January and February 2003.

c. Prepare a cash receipts schedule for January and February 2003.
d. Determine the amount of accounts receivable as of February 28, 2003.

PROBLEM 7–17B *Preparing the Inventory Purchases Budget and Schedule of Cash Payments* **L.O. 7, 10**

Amber Company's purchasing manager, Wayne Kenmore, is preparing a purchases budget for the next quarter. At his request, Allen Kahn, the manager of the sales department, forwarded him the following preliminary sales budget.

	October	November	December
Budgeted sales	$640,000	$768,000	$960,000

For budgeting purposes, Amber estimates that cost of goods sold is 75 percent of sales. The company desires to maintain an ending inventory balance equal to 20 percent of the current period's cost of goods sold. The September ending inventory is $120,000. Amber makes all purchases on account and pays 70 percent of accounts payable in the month of purchase and the remaining 30 percent in the following month. The balance of accounts payable at the end of September is $90,000.

Required
a. Prepare an inventory purchases budget for October, November, and December.
b. Determine the amount of ending inventory Amber will report on the end-of-quarter pro forma balance sheet.
c. Prepare a schedule of cash payments for inventory for October, November, and December.
d. Determine the balance in accounts payable Amber will report on the end-of-quarter pro forma balance sheet.

PROBLEM 7–18B *Preparing Pro Forma Income Statements With Different Assumptions* **L.O. 10**

Ross Horn, a successful entrepreneur, is reviewing the results of his first year in business. His accountant delivered the following income statement just five minutes ago.

	Current Year
Sales Revenue	$600,000
Cost of Goods Sold	384,000
Gross Profit	$216,000
Selling & Admin. Expenses	132,000
Net Income	$ 84,000

Mr. Horn would like net income to increase 20 percent in the next year. This first year, selling and administrative expenses were 10 percent of sales revenue plus $72,000 of fixed expenses.

Required
The following questions are independent of each other.
a. Mr. Horn expects that cost of goods sold and variable selling and administrative expenses will remain stable in proportion to sales next year. The fixed selling and administrative expenses will increase to $86,400. What percentage increase in sales would enable the company to reach Mr. Horn's goal? Prepare a pro forma income statement to illustrate.
b. Market competition may become serious next year, and Mr. Horn does not expect an increase in sales revenue. However, he has developed a good relationship with his supplier, who is willing to give him a volume discount that will decrease cost of goods sold by 3 percent. What else can the company do to reach Mr. Horn's goal? Prepare a pro forma income statement illustrating your proposal.
c. If the company escalates its advertising campaign to boost consumer recognition, the selling and administrative expenses will increase to $240,000. With the increased advertising, the company expects sales revenue to increase by 25 percent. Assume that cost of goods sold remains constant in proportion to sales. Can the company reach Mr. Horn's goal?

PROBLEM 7–19B *Preparing a Schedule of Cash Payments for Selling and Administrative Expenses* **L.O. 8**

Burgen Travel Services, Inc., has prepared its selling and administrative expenses budget for the next quarter. It pays all expenses when they are incurred except sales commissions, advertising expense, and

telephone expense. These three items are paid in the month following the one in which they are incurred. January is the first month of operations, so there are no beginning account balances.

	January	February	March
Salary expense	$ 8,000	$ 8,000	$ 8,000
Sales commissions	600	640	800
Advertising expense	500	500	600
Telephone expense	1,000	1,080	1,100
Depreciation on store equipment	4,000	4,000	4,000
Rent	10,000	10,000	10,000
Miscellaneous	800	800	800
Total S&A expenses before interest	$24,900	$25,020	$25,300

Required

a. Prepare a schedule of cash payments for selling and administrative expenses.
b. Determine the amount of telephone payable as of March 31.
c. Determine the amount of sales commissions payable as of February 28.

L.O. 9   PROBLEM 7–20B *Preparing a Cash Budget*

Doran Company has budgeted the following cash flows:

	April	May	June
Cash receipts	$300,000	$450,000	$604,000
Cash payments			
For inventory purchases	390,000	400,000	440,000
For S&A expenses	80,000	106,000	132,000

Doran had a $36,000 cash balance on April 1. The company desires to maintain a $60,000 cash cushion before paying interest. Funds are assumed to be borrowed on the first day of each month and repaid on the last day of each month; the interest rate is 1.50 percent per month. The company had a $150,000 beginning balance in its line of credit liability account.

Required

Prepare a cash budget. (Round all computations to the nearest whole dollar.)

L.O. 6, 7, 8   PROBLEM 7–21B *Preparing Budgets With Multiple Products*

Kohl Enterprises, Inc., has two products, palm-size computers and programmable calculators. Tracie Mann, the chief executive officer, is working with her staff to prepare next year's budget. Ms. Mann estimates that sales will increase at an annual rate of 20 percent for palm-size computers and 5 percent for programmable calculators. The current year sales revenue data follow.

	First Quarter	Second Quarter	Third Quarter	Fourth Quarter	Total
Palm-size computers	$500,000	$550,000	$620,000	$730,000	$2,400,000
Programmable calculators	250,000	275,000	290,000	325,000	1,140,000
Total	$750,000	$825,000	$910,000	$1,055,000	$3,540,000

Based on the company's past experience, cost of goods sold is usually 75 percent of sales revenue. Company policy is to keep 10 percent of the next period's estimated cost of goods sold as the current period ending inventory.

Required

a. Prepare the company's sales budget for the next year for each quarter by individual products.
b. If the selling and administrative expenses are estimated to be $600,000, prepare the company's budgeted annual income statement for the next year.

c. Ms. Mann estimates the current year's ending inventory will be $78,000 for computers and $32,000 for calculators and the ending inventory next year will be $88,000 for computers and $42,000 for calculators. Prepare the company's inventory purchases budget for the next year showing quarterly figures by product.

PROBLEM 7–22B *Preparing a Master Budget for Retail Company With No Beginning Account Balances*

L.O. 6, 7, 8

King Gifts Corporation begins business today, December 31, 2001. Angel Ma, the president, is trying to prepare the company's master budget for the first three months (January, February, and March) of 2002. Since you are her good friend and an accounting student, Ms. Ma asks you to prepare the budget based on the following specifications.

Required
a. January sales are estimated to be $200,000 of which 30 percent will be cash and 70 percent will be credit. The company expects sales to increase at the rate of 10 percent per month. Prepare a sales budget.
b. The company expects to collect 100 percent of the accounts receivable generated by credit sales in the month following the sale. Prepare a schedule of cash receipts.
c. The cost of goods sold is 50 percent of sales. The company desires to maintain a minimum ending inventory equal to 20 percent of the current month cost of goods sold. Assume that all purchases are made on account. Prepare an inventory purchases budget.
d. The company pays 60 percent of accounts payable in the month of purchase and the remaining 40 percent in the following month. Prepare a cash payments budget for inventory purchases.
e. Budgeted selling and administrative expenses per month follow.

Salary expense (fixed)	$20,000
Sales commissions	8 percent of Sales
Supplies expense	4 percent of Sales
Utilities (fixed)	$1,800
Depreciation on store equipment (fixed)*	$5,000
Rent (fixed)	$7,200
Miscellaneous (fixed)	$2,000

*The capital expenditures budget indicates that King will spend $350,000 on January 1 for store fixtures. The fixtures are expected to have a $50,000 salvage value and a five-year (60-month) useful life.

Use this information to prepare a selling and administrative expenses budget.
f. Utilities and sales commissions are paid the month after they are incurred; all other expenses are paid in the month in which they are incurred. Prepare a cash payments budget for selling and administrative expenses.
g. The company borrows funds and repays them on the first day of the month. It pays interest of 1.5 percent per month in cash on the last day of the month. For safety, the company desires to maintain a $50,000 cash cushion before paying interest. Prepare a cash budget.
h. Prepare a pro forma income statement for the quarter.
i. Prepare a pro forma balance sheet at the end of the quarter.
j. Prepare a pro forma statement of cash flows for the quarter.

PROBLEM 7–23B *Behavioral Impact of Budgeting*

L.O. 4

Candice Karr, the director of Sakura Corporation's Mail-Order Division, is preparing the division's budget proposal for next year. The company's president will review the proposal for approval. Ms. Karr estimates the current year final operating results will be as follows.

	Current Year
Sales revenue	$9,600,000
Cost of goods sold	5,280,000
Gross profit	4,320,000
Selling & admin. expenses	1,920,000
Net income	$2,400,000

Ms. Karr believes that the cost of goods sold as well as selling and administrative expenses will continue to be stable in proportion to sales revenue.

Sakura has an incentive policy to reward division managers whose performance exceeds their budget. Division directors receive a 10 percent bonus based on the excess of actual net income over the division's budget. For the last two years, Ms. Karr has proposed a 4 percent rate of increase, which proved accurate. However, her honesty and accuracy in forecasting caused her to receive no year-end bonus at all. She is pondering whether she should do something differently this time. If she continues to be honest, she should propose an 8 percent growth rate because of robust market demand. Alternatively, she can propose a 4 percent growth rate as usual and thereby expect to receive some bonus at year end.

Required

a. Prepare a pro forma income statement, assuming a 4 percent estimated increase.

b. Prepare a pro forma income statement, assuming an 8 percent increase.

c. Assume the president eventually approves the division's proposal with the 4 percent growth rate. If growth actually is 8 percent, how much bonus would Ms. Karr receive?

d. Propose a better budgeting procedure for Sakura Corporation.

ANALYZE, THINK, COMMUNICATE

ATC 7–1   BUSINESS APPLICATIONS CASE *Preparing and Using Pro Forma Statements*

Lance Coleman, a student at Lake State University, plans to subsidize his education by starting a company that rents computer equipment to fellow students. Mr. Coleman has negotiated a line of credit with the National Bank of Glen Grove. The credit line permits Mr. Coleman to borrow up to $3,000 at 10 percent interest, which is payable in cash on December 31 of each year. Mr. Coleman plans to borrow the entire $3,000 amount on January 1, 2003. He plans to use the money to purchase a computer expected to have a useful life of two years and a $750 salvage value. Rent revenue is projected to be $150 cash per month. At December 31, 2004, Mr. Coleman plans to sell the computer and repay the bank loan.

Required

a. Based on the information provided, prepare a pro forma income statement, balance sheet, and statement of cash flows for 2003 and 2004.

b. Review the pro forma statements and recommend how Mr. Coleman could improve profitability. Your recommendation(s) should result in real profit improvement. Accounting manipulation such as extending the life of the asset or increasing its salvage value is not acceptable. Furthermore, Mr. Coleman cannot increase the amount borrowed, reduce the interest rate, or raise revenues.

ATC 7–2   GROUP ASSIGNMENT *Master Budget and Pro Forma Statements*

The following trial balance was drawn from the records of Havel Company as of October 1, 2002.

Cash	16,000	
Accounts receivable	60,000	
Inventory	40,000	
Stare equipment	200,000	
Accumulated depreciation		76,800
Accounts payable		72,000
Line of credit loan		100,000
Common stock		50,000
Retained earnings		17,200
Totals	316,000	316,000

Required

a. Divide the class into groups, each with 4 or 5 students. Organize the groups into three sections. Assign Task 1 to the first section, Task 2 to the second section, and Task 3 to the third section.

Group Tasks

(1) Based on the following information, prepare a sales budget and a schedule of cash receipts for October, November, and December. Sales for October are expected to be $180,000, consisting of $40,000 in cash and $140,000 on credit. The company expects sales to increase at the rate of 10 percent per month. All of accounts receivable is collected in the month following the sale.

(2) Based on the following information, prepare a purchases budget and a schedule of cash payments for inventory purchases for October, November, and December. The inventory balance as of October 1 was $40,000. Cost of goods sold for October is expected to be $72,000. Cost of goods sold is expected to increase by 10 percent per month. The company desires to maintain a minimum ending inventory equal to 20 percent of the current month cost of goods sold. Seventy-five percent of accounts payable is paid in the month that the purchase occurs; the remaining 25 percent is paid in the following month.

(3) Based on the following selling and administrative expenses budgeted for October, prepare a selling and administrative expenses budget for October, November, and December.

Sales commissions (10% increase per month)	$ 7,200
Supplies expense (10% increase per month)	1,800
Utilities (fixed)	2,200
Depreciation on store equipment (fixed)	1,600
Salary expense (fixed)	34,000
Rent (fixed)	6,000
Miscellaneous (fixed)	1,000

Cash payments for sales commissions and utilities are made in the month following the one in which the expense is incurred. Supplies and other operating expenses are paid in cash in the month in which they are incurred.

b. Select a representative from each section. Have the representatives supply the missing information in the following pro forma income statement and balance sheet for the fourth quarter of 2002. The statements are prepared as of December 31, 2002.

Income Statement

Sales Revenue	$?
Cost of Goods Sold	?
Gross Margin	357,480
Operating Expenses	?
Operating Income	193,290
Interest Expense	(2,530)
Net Income	$190,760

Balance Sheet

Assets		
Cash		$ 9,760
Accounts Receivable		?
Inventory		?
Store Equipment	$200,000	
Accumulated Depreciation Store Equipment	?	
Book Value of Equipment		118,400
Total Assets		$314,984
Liabilities		
Accounts Payable		?
Utilities Payable		?
Sales Commissions Payable		?
Line of Credit		23,936
Equity		
Common Stock		50,000
Retained Earnings		?
Total Liabilities and Equity		$314,984

c. Indicate whether Havel will need to borrow money during October.

ATC 7-3   RESEARCH ASSIGNMENT *Establishing a Budget System*

Read the article "How to Set Up a Budgeting and Planning System" in the January 1997 issue of *Management Accounting*. The article describes the initiation of a budget system for Penn Fuel Gas, Inc. (PFG). PFG is a medium-size public utility holding company. The budget manager discusses the real-world challenges encountered during the initiation process. Satisfy the following requirements.

Required

a. Identify the user groups that motivated establishing a budgeting system for PFG.

b. Describe the considerations given to hiring and training the budget staff.

c. Discuss the shortcomings of the existing accounting information system that complicated implementing the budget system. How were these shortcomings overcome?

d. The benefits of budgeting can be thwarted by negative behavioral reactions such as low-balling revenues or padding expenses. How did PFG avoid these pitfalls?

e. Describe the benefits that PFG obtained from its budget system.

ATC 7-4   WRITING ASSIGNMENT *Continuous Budgeting*

HON Company is the largest maker of mid-priced office furniture in the United States and Canada. Its management has expressed dissatisfaction with its *annual* budget system. Fierce competition requires businesses to be flexible and innovative. Unfortunately, building the effects of innovation into an annual budget is difficult because actions and outcomes often are evolutionary. Innovation unfolds as the year progresses. Consequently, HON's management team reached the conclusion that "when production processes undergo continuous change, standards developed annually for static conditions no longer offer meaningful targets for gauging their success."

Required

Assume that you are HON Company's budget director. Write a memo to the management team explaining how the practice of continuous budgeting could overcome the shortcomings of an annual budget process. (For insight, read the article "Continuous Budgeting at the HON Company," *Management Accounting,* January 1996. This article describes HON's real-world experience with a continuous budget system.)

ATC 7-5   ETHICAL DILEMMA *Bad Budget System or Unethical Behavior?*

Clarence Cleaver is the budget director for the Harris County School District. Mr. Cleaver recently sent an urgent E-mail message to Sally Simmons, principal of West Harris County High. The message severely reprimanded Ms. Simmons for failing to spend the funds allocated to her to purchase computer equipment. Ms. Simmons responded that her school already has a sufficient supply of computers; indeed, the computer lab is never filled to capacity and usually is less than half filled. Ms. Simmons suggested that she would rather use the funds for teacher training. She argued that the reason the existing computers are not fully utilized is that the teachers lack sufficient computer literacy necessary to make assignments for their students.

Mr. Cleaver responded that it is not Ms. Simmons' job to decide how the money is to be spent; that is the school board's job. It is the principal's job to spend the money as the board directed. He informed Ms. Simmons that if the money is not spent by the fiscal closing date, the school board would likely reduce next year's budget allotment. To avoid a potential budget cut, Mr. Cleaver reallocated Ms. Simmons' computer funds to Jules Carrington, principal of East Harris County High. Mr. Carrington knows how to buy computers regardless of whether they are needed. Mr. Cleaver's final words were, "Don't blame me if parents of West High students complain that East High has more equipment. If anybody comes to me, I'm telling them that you turned down the money."

Required

a. Do Mr. Cleaver's actions violate the standards of ethical conduct shown in Exhibit 1-13 of Chapter 1?

b. Explain how participative budgeting could improve the allocation of resources for the Harris County School District.

ATC 7-6   SPREADSHEET ASSIGNMENT *Using Excel*

The accountant for Nelly's Dress Shop prepared the fourth quarter, 2004, cash budget that appears on the following spreadsheet. Nelly's has a policy to maintain a minimum cash balance of $14,000 before the interest payment at the end of each month. The shop borrows and repays funds on the first day of the month. The interest rate is 2 percent per month.

Required

a. Construct a spreadsheet to model the cash budget as in the following screen capture. Be sure to use formulas where possible so that any changes to the estimates will be automatically reflected in the spreadsheet.

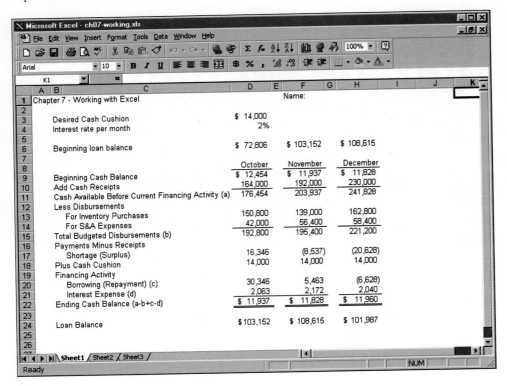

Spreadsheet Tips

(1) Rows 11, 15, 17, 18, 20 to 22, and 24 should be based on formulas.

(2) Cells F6, H6, F9, and H9 should be based on formulas also. For example, cell F6 should be =D24.

SPREADSHEET ASSIGNMENT *Mastering Excel*

ATC 7–7

Spitzer Company has collected sales forecasts for next year from three people.

Sources of Sales Estimate	First Quarter	Second Quarter	Third Quarter	Fourth Quarter
a. Sales manager	$520,000	$410,000	$370,000	$610,000
b. Marketing consultant	540,000	480,000	400,000	630,000
c. Production manager	460,000	360,000	350,000	580,000

They have estimated that the cost of goods sold is 70 percent of sales. The company tries to maintain 10 percent of next quarter's expected cost of goods sold as the current quarter's ending inventory. The ending inventory of this year is $25,000. For budgeting, the ending inventory of the next year is expected to be $28,000.

Required

a. Construct a spreadsheet that allows the inventory purchases budget to be prepared for each of the preceding estimates.

Spreadsheet Tip

The VLOOKUP function can be used to choose one line of the preceding estimates. See the spreadsheet tips in Chapter 6 for an explanation of VLOOKUP.

Performance Evaluation

Learning Objectives

After completing this chapter, you should be able to:

1 Distinguish between flexible and static budgets.

2 Understand how spreadsheet software can be used to prepare flexible budgets.

3 Compute revenue and cost variances and interpret those variances as indicating favorable or unfavorable performance.

4 Compute sales activity variances (differences between static and flexible budgets) and explain how the volume variance affects fixed and variable costs.

5 Compute and interpret flexible budget variances (differences between a flexible budget and actual results).

6 Appreciate the human response to flexible budget variances.

7 Appreciate the process of setting standards.

8 Understand the criteria for selecting the most appropriate variances for investigation.

9 Calculate price and usage variances.

10 Identify the responsible parties for price and usage variances.

the *curious* accountant

Memorial Hospital spent significantly more than it budgeted in serving its patients. Even so, the hospital administrators were congratulated for a job well done. What phenomenon could explain this apparent contradiction?

Suppose that you are a carpenter who makes picnic tables. You are normally expected to make 200 tables per year (the planned volume of activity), *but because of unexpected customer demand, you have been asked to make 225 tables* (the actual volume of activity). *You work hard and make the tables. Should you be criticized for using more materials, labor, or overhead than you normally use? Should the sales staff be criticized for selling more tables than expected? Obviously, the answer to both of these questions is an emphatic no! Performance evaluation must be based on the* actual volume *of activity rather than the* planned volume *of activity. To facilitate planning and performance evaluation, managerial accountants frequently prepare budgets that are based on different levels of activity. These budgets are called* flexible budgets. *Their name is derived from the fact that the budget flexes or changes when the volume of activity changes.*

▮ Preparation of Flexible Budgets

LO1 Distinguish between flexible and static budgets.

A **flexible budget** can be seen as an extension of the *master budget* that we discussed in Chapter 7. Recall that the master budget is based solely on the level of planned activity. Because of its rigid dependency on a single estimate of volume, the master budget is frequently called a **static budget.** In other words, the master budget remains static or stays the same when the volume of activity changes. Flexible budgets differ from static budgets in that they show the estimated amount of revenues and costs that are expected at a variety of levels of activity.

To illustrate the differences between static and flexible budgets, assume that Melrose Manufacturing Company makes small, high-quality statues that are used in award ceremonies. Melrose plans to make and sell 18,000 statues during its 2001 accounting period. Management's best estimates of the expected sales price and per unit costs for the statues are called *standard prices and costs.* The standard price and costs for the 18,000 statues follow.

Per unit sales price and variable costs	
Expected sales price	$80.00
Standard materials cost	12.00
Standard labor cost	16.80
Standard overhead cost	5.60
Standard general, selling, and administrative cost	15.00
Fixed costs	
Manufacturing cost	$201,600
General, selling, and administrative cost	90,000

LO2 Understand how spreadsheet software can be used to prepare flexible budgets.

Static and flexible budgets are based on the same per unit *standard* amounts and the same fixed costs. The difference between the two budgets stems solely from the different volumes used to compute the budget amounts. Melrose Manufacturing's static budget is shown in Column D of the Excel spreadsheet in Exhibit 8–1. The amount of sales revenue and the amounts of the variable costs in Column D are determined by multiplying the per unit standards shown

Exhibit 8–1 *Static and Flexible Budgets in Excel Spreadsheet*

		Per Unit Standards	Static Budget		Flexible Budgets				
Number of Units			18,000		16,000	17,000	18,000	19,000	20,000
Sales Revenue		$80.00	$1,440,000		$1,280,000	$1,360,000	$1,440,000	$1,520,000	$1,600,000
Variable Manuf. Costs									
Materials		$12.00	216,000		192,000	204,000	216,000	228,000	240,000
Labor		$16.80	302,400		268,800	285,600	302,400	319,200	336,000
Overhead		$5.60	100,800		89,600	95,200	100,800	106,400	112,000
Variable G,S,&A		$15.00	270,000		240,000	255,000	270,000	285,000	300,000
Contribution Margin			550,800		489,600	520,200	550,800	581,400	612,000
Fixed Costs									
Manufacturing			201,600		201,600	201,600	201,600	201,600	201,600
G,S,&A			90,000		90,000	90,000	90,000	90,000	90,000
Net Income			$259,200		$198,000	$228,600	$259,200	$289,800	$320,400

in Column C by the number of units shown in Cell D4 (planned activity). For example, the amount of sales revenue shown in Cell D7 is determined by multiplying the per unit sales price in Cell C7 by the number of units shown in Cell D4 ($80 × 18,000 units = $1,440,000). The variable cost amounts are computed in a similar fashion. In each case, the cost per unit amount shown in Column C is multiplied by the planned activity shown in Cell D4.

Suppose that management wants to know what will happen to net income *if* actual volume is 16,000, 17,000, 18,000, 19,000, or 20,000 units. In other words, management wants to see a series of *flexible budgets*. This *what-if* information can be easily determined by using the computational power of the Excel spreadsheet. The formulas used to determine the static budget amounts in Column D can simply be copied to Columns F through J. Then by changing the input variable to reflect the alternative levels of activity shown in Row 4, the appropriate amounts are calculated instantaneously. The result is the series of flexible budgets shown in Columns F through J.

The flexible budgets can be used for planning and performance evaluation. For example, managers may be able to evaluate the adequacy of the company's cash position by assuming different levels of activity. Similarly, the number of employees, the amounts of materials, and the necessary equipment and storage facilities can be evaluated for a variety of different potential activity levels. In addition to facilitating the planning activities, flexible budgets are critical to the implementation of an effective performance evaluation system.

The master budget of Parcel, Inc., called for a production and sales volume of 25,000 units. At that volume, total budgeted fixed costs were $150,000 and total budgeted variable costs were $200,000. Prepare a flexible budget for an expected volume of 26,000 units.

Answer Budgeted fixed costs would remain unchanged at $150,000 because changes in the volume of activity do not affect budgeted fixed costs. Budgeted variable costs would increase to $208,000, computed as follows: Calculate the budgeted variable cost per unit ($200,000 ÷ 25,000 units = $8) and then multiply that variable cost per unit by the expected volume ($8 × 26,000 units = $208,000).

Check Yourself 8–1

■ Determination of Variances for Performance Evaluation

One means of evaluating managerial performance is to compare *standard* amounts with the *actual* results. The differences between the standard and actual amounts are called **variances;** they can be either *favorable* or *unfavorable.* Because managers seek to maximize revenue, a *favorable sales variance* occurs when actual sales revenue is higher than expected (standard) revenue. An *unfavorable sales variance* occurs when actual sales are lower than expected. Because managers try to minimize costs, *favorable cost variances* occur when actual costs are *lower than* standard costs. *Unfavorable cost variances* occur when actual costs are *higher* than standard costs. These relationships are summarized below.

LO3 Compute revenue and cost variances and interpret those variances as indicating favorable or unfavorable performance.

- When actual sales are higher than expected sales, variances are favorable.
- When actual sales are lower than expected sales, variances are unfavorable.
- When actual costs are higher than standard costs, variances are unfavorable.
- When actual costs are lower than standard costs, variances are favorable.

Sales Activity (Volume) Variances

The amount of a **sales activity (volume) variance** is calculated by determining the difference between the static budget, which is based on the planned volume, and a flexible budget prepared for the actual volume. This variance provides a measure of how effective managers have

LO4 Compute sales activity variances and explain how the volume variance affects fixed and variable costs.

been in attaining the planned volume of activity. To illustrate, we assume that Melrose Manufacturing Company actually makes and sells 19,000 statues during 2001. Recall that the planned volume of activity was 18,000 statues. Melrose's static budget, flexible budget, and activity variances are shown in Exhibit 8–2.

Exhibit 8–2 *Melrose Manufacturing Company's Sales Volume Variances*

	Static Budget	Flexible Budget	Activity Variances	
Number of units	18,000	19,000	1,000	Favorable
Sales revenue	$1,440,000	$1,520,000	$80,000	Favorable
Variable manufacturing costs				
Materials	216,000	228,000	12,000	Unfavorable
Labor	302,400	319,200	16,800	Unfavorable
Overhead	100,800	106,400	5,600	Unfavorable
Variable G, S, & A	270,000	285,000	15,000	Unfavorable
Contribution margin	550,800	581,400	30,600	Favorable
Fixed costs				
Manufacturing	201,600	201,600	0	
G, S, & A	90,000	90,000	0	
Net income	$ 259,200	$ 289,800	$30,600	Favorable

Interpretation of the Sales and Variable Cost Variances

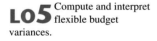

LO5 Compute and interpret flexible budget variances.

Because the static and flexible budgets are based on the same standard sales price and per unit variable costs, the variances are solely attributable to the differences between the planned and actual volume of activity. Marketing managers are usually held responsible for the volume variance. Because the volume of sales drives the level of production, production managers have little control over volume, although exceptions do occur. For example, the production manager is responsible for poor quality control in the production process that could lead to goods of low quality that are difficult to sell. Likewise, the production manager is responsible for delays in the production process that could affect the availability of products, which may restrict the volume of sales activity. Under normal circumstances, however, the marketing campaign controls the volume of sales. Upper-level marketing managers are on the front lines of the promotional program; they create the sales plan and are in the best position to explain why sales goals are or are not attained. When marketing managers talk about **making the numbers,** they are usually referring to their ability to attain the sales volume indicated in the master budget.

In the case of Melrose Manufacturing Company, the marketing manager not only made his numbers but also exceeded the planned volume of sales by 1,000 units. At the standard price, the additional volume produces a favorable revenue variance of $80,000 (1,000 units × $80 per unit). The increase in volume also produces unfavorable variable cost variances as indicated in

Exhibit 8–2. The net result of producing and selling the additional 1,000 units is an increase of $30,600 in the contribution margin, indeed a favorable condition. These preliminary results suggest that the marketing manager is to be congratulated for a job well done. In practice, however, more analysis is necessary. For example, a closer look at market share could reveal whether the manager was able to win customers from the company's competitors or whether the manager simply reaped the benefit of a wave of unexpected industrywide consumer demand. Furthermore, the increase in sales volume could have been attained by lowering the sales price, the success of which depends on the relationship between the magnitude of the change in the sales price versus the magnitude of the increase in sales volume. This possibility will be analyzed further in a later section of this chapter.

The unfavorable variable cost variances in Exhibit 8–2 are somewhat misleading because variable costs are, by definition, expected to increase as volume increases. Indeed, as previously stated, the unfavorable cost variances are more than offset by the favorable revenue variance, thereby resulting in a higher contribution margin. As a result, the variable cost volume variances could be more appropriately considered expected than unfavorable.

Fixed Cost Considerations

Notice that the total amount of fixed costs is the same in both the static and flexible budgets. By definition, the budgeted amount of fixed costs remains the same regardless of the volume of activity. Because fixed costs are the same in both budgets, what can be gained by analyzing these costs? To answer this question, consider what you have learned about fixed cost behavior. Based on our previous discussions regarding *operating leverage,* you should recall that a small increase in sales volume can have a dramatic impact on profitability. Indeed, notice that although the 1,000 unit activity variance produces a 5.6 percent increase in revenue ($80,000 variance ÷ $1,440,000 static budget sales base), it results in an 11.8 percent increase in profitability ($30,600 variance ÷ $259,200 static budget net income base). In this case, the favorable sales activity variance has an even larger beneficial effect on profitability. If management is trying to understand why profitability increased so dramatically, it should consider the higher than expected sales volume.

Companies using a cost-plus-pricing strategy must be concerned with differences between the planned and actual volume of activity. Because actual activity is unknown until the end of the accounting period, prices that must be maintained currently are based on planned (estimated) activity. At the *planned volume* of activity of 18,000 units, Melrose's total fixed cost per unit is expected to be as follows.

Fixed manufacturing cost	$201,600	
Fixed G, S, & A cost	90,000	
Total fixed cost	$291,600 ÷ 18,000 units = $16.20 per statue	

At the *actual volume* of 19,000 units, the fixed cost per unit drops to $15.35 per statue ($291,600 ÷ 19,000 units). Because Melrose's prices were established on the $16.20 budgeted cost rather than the actual cost of $15.35, the statues would have been overpriced. This condition could provide a price advantage for competitors that may limit Melrose's sales growth. Do not be deceived by the increase in sales volume. Perhaps sales volume could have been even higher if the statues had been competitively priced.

Although it appears that Melrose did not encounter this problem, you should note that underpricing can also have detrimental consequences. If planned activity is overstated, the estimated cost per unit will be understated and prices will be set too low. When the higher amount of actual costs is subtracted from revenues, actual profits will be lower than expected. To avoid these negative consequences, companies that consider unit cost in pricing decisions must monitor activity variances closely.

The activity variance is considered *unfavorable* if actual volume is less than planned because this produces a higher cost per unit than expected. A **favorable variance** occurs if the actual volume is higher than planned because this produces a lower cost per unit than expected. As this discussion implies, however, both favorable and unfavorable variances can lead to negative consequences. The ideal condition is to achieve the greatest possible degree of accuracy.

Flexible Budget Variances

For purposes of performance evaluation, a flexible budget prepared at the actual volume of activity is compared to actual results. Because the volume of activity is the same for the flexible budget and the actual results, any reported variances result from differences between the standard and actual per unit amounts. To illustrate the determination and analysis of flexible

budget variances, we assume that Melrose Manufacturing Company experienced the following *actual* per unit amounts during its 2001 accounting period. The 2001 per unit *standard* amounts that were listed earlier are repeated here for your convenience.

	Standard	Actual
Sales price	$80.00	$78.00
Variable materials cost	12.00	11.78
Variable labor cost	16.80	17.25
Variable overhead cost	5.60	5.75
Variable general, selling, and administrative (G, S, & A) cost	15.00	14.90

Actual and budgeted fixed costs are shown in Exhibit 8–3.

The flexible budget, actual results, and flexible budget variances for Melrose Manufacturing Company's 2001 accounting period are shown in Exhibit 8–3. The flexible budget data are the same as those shown in Exhibit 8–2. Recall that the flexible budget amounts are determined by multiplying the standard per unit amounts by the actual volume of production. For example, the sales revenue in the *flexible budget is determined by multiplying the standard sales price by the actual volume* ($80 × 19,000). The variable cost data are computed in a similar manner. The *actual results are calculated by multiplying the actual per unit sales price and cost figures shown in the preceding table by the actual volume of activity.* For example, the sales revenue in the Actual column is determined by multiplying the actual sales price by the actual volume ($78 × 19,000 = $1,482,000). The actual cost figures are computed in a similar manner. The **flexible budget variances** represent the difference between the flexible budget amounts and the actual results.

Exhibit 8–3 *Flexible Budget Variances for Melrose Manufacturing Company*

	Flexible Budget	Actual Results	Total Variances	
Number of units	19,000	19,000	0	
Sales revenue	$1,520,000	$1,482,000	$38,000	Unfavorable
Variable manufacturing costs				
Materials	228,000	223,820	4,180	Favorable
Labor	319,200	327,750	8,550	Unfavorable
Overhead	106,400	109,250	2,850	Unfavorable
Variable G, S, & A	285,000	283,100	1,900	Favorable
Contribution margin	581,400	538,080	43,320	Unfavorable
Fixed costs				
Manufacturing	201,600	210,000	8,400	Unfavorable
G, S, & A	90,000	85,000	5,000	Favorable
Net income	$ 289,800	$ 243,080	$46,720	Unfavorable

Calculating Sales Price Variance

Because the volume of activity used in the flexible budget equals the level of activity actually experienced, the price variance must be attributable to the sales price rather than to the sales volume. In this case, the actual sales price of $78 per unit is less than the standard price of $80 per unit. Because Melrose sold its product for less than the standard sales price, the **sales price variance** is classified as *unfavorable*. The unfavorable designation in this case is misleading, however; recall that sales volume was 1,000 units higher than expected. The additional volume may have been attributable to the fact that Melrose's marketing manager lowered the sales price. Whether the combination of factors (lower sales price and higher sales volume) is favorable or unfavorable depends on the magnitude of the sales price variance versus the magnitude of the volume variance. In this case, the total sales variance (i.e., price and volume) can be computed as follows:

Actual sales (19,000 units × $78 per unit)	$1,482,000	
Expected sales (18,000 units × $80 per unit)	1,440,000	
Total sales variance	$ 42,000	Favorable

Alternatively,

Activity variance (i.e., volume)	$ 80,000	Favorable
Sales price variance	(38,000)	Unfavorable
Total sales variance	$ 42,000	Favorable

This analysis suggests that lowering prices had a favorable impact on the generation of total revenue. Accordingly, the unfavorable label on the sales price variance is indeed misleading. This condition highlights the fact that favorable variances cannot automatically be interpreted as good and unfavorable variances as bad. All variances should be considered signals for the need to conduct a rational investigation as to their cause.

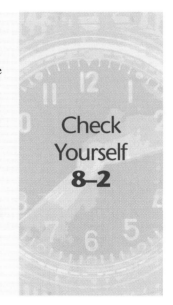

Scott Company's master budget called for an expected sales volume of 30,000 units. Budgeted direct materials cost was $4 per unit. Scott actually produced and sold 32,000 units with an actual materials cost of $131,000. Determine the materials activity (volume) variance and identify the organizational unit most likely responsible for this variance. Determine the flexible budget variance and identify the organizational unit most likely responsible for this variance.

Answer The activity variance is the difference between the expected materials usage at the planned volume of activity and the expected materials usage at the actual volume of activity ([$4 × 30,000 units] − [$4 × 32,000] = $8,000). The variance is unfavorable because expected direct materials cost at actual volume was higher than budgeted direct materials cost at planned volume. The unfavorable variance might not be a bad thing. The variance is due to increased volume, which could be a good thing. The organizational unit most likely responsible for the activity variance is the marketing department.

The flexible budget variance is the difference between the expected materials cost at the actual volume ($4 × 32,000 units = $128,000) and the actual materials cost of $131,000. The $3,000 ($128,000 − $131,000) variance is unfavorable because it cost more than expected to make the 32,000 units. Either the production department or the purchasing department is most likely responsible for this variance.

Check Yourself 8–2

■ The Human Factor Associated With Flexible Budget Variances

The flexible budget cost variances provide insight into how efficiently managers have operated the business. For example, Melrose Manufacturing Company's favorable materials variance could indicate that managers were shrewd in negotiating price concessions, discounts, or delivery terms that reduced the price the company paid for materials. Similarly, managers may have used materials efficiently, thereby reducing the amount used. In contrast, the unfavorable labor variance could indicate that managers have been lax in controlling employee wages or have failed to motivate their employees to work hard. As with sales variances, cost variances must be analyzed carefully. What appears to be favorable on the surface may, in fact, be unfavorable. For example, the favorable materials variance might have been obtained by paying low prices for inferior goods. The substandard materials could have required additional labor in the production process, which would explain the unfavorable labor variance. Again, we caution that variances, whether favorable or unfavorable, should be treated as signals for the need for investigation.

In general, variances should not be used to single out managers for praise or punishment. The purpose of variances is to provide information that facilitates efficiency and improves

LO6 Appreciate the human response to flexible budget variances.

The administrators of Memorial Hospital may deserve to be congratulated even if actual costs exceed the expected (i.e., standard) costs of serving patients. Perhaps the number of patients served is considerably higher than expected. Under these circumstances, variable costs are expected to increase because the volume of activity has increased. If the increase in cost is less than the standard necessary to serve the additional customers, the flexible budget variances are favorable. This indicates that the administrators were diligent in the use of the resources required to serve the unexpected patient load. In this case, the administrators would, in fact, deserve to be congratulated.

productivity. If they are misused as a means of assigning rewards and punishment, managers are likely to respond by withholding or manipulating information. For example, a manager might manipulate the determination of the standard cost by deliberately overstating the amount of materials and/or labor that is expected to be required to complete a job. Later, the manager's performance will be evaluated as positive when the actual cost of materials and/or labor is lower than the inflated standard. Indeed, this practice has become so common that it has been given a name. The difference between inflated and realistic standards is called **budget slack.** A similar game played with respect to revenue is called *low-balling.* In this case, the sales staff deliberately underestimates the amount of expected sales. Later when actual sales exceed expected sales, personnel are rewarded for exceeding the budget.

The motive for gamesmanship can be reduced by having superiors and subordinates participate in the standard-setting process with a sincere intent to attain agreed-upon, reasonable expectations. Once standards have been established, they must be incorporated into an evaluation system that promotes long-term respect among superiors and their subordinates. If standards are used solely for punitive purposes, gamesmanship will rapidly degrade the standard costing system.

▎Establishment of Standards

LO7 Appreciate the process of setting standards.

Establishing standards is probably the most difficult task required in the development of a standard cost system. A **standard** represents what *should be* based on a certain set of anticipated circumstances. Think for a moment of the complexity of the standard-setting task. Suppose that you are charged with establishing the standard cost of a pair of blue jeans. A partial list of the things you would need to know would include where you can get the best price for materials, who will pay transportation costs, whether cash or volume discounts are available, whether the suppliers with the lowest price are reliable, and whether they can supply the amount needed on a timely basis, how the material should be cut to conserve time and labor, in what order the pieces of material should be sewn together, what the wage rates of the persons who will provide the labor are, whether overtime will be necessary, and how many pairs of jeans need to be produced. Obtaining this information is obviously too large a task for one person. Effective standard setting requires the combined experience, judgment, and predictive capacity of all personnel who have responsibility for price and quantity decisions. Even when a multitalented group of experienced persons is involved in standard setting, the process requires significant amounts of trial and error. Revising standards is a common occurrence even in established systems.

Historical data provide a good starting point for the establishment of standards. These data must be updated for changes in technology, plant layout, new methods of production, worker productivity, and so on. Indeed, changes of this nature frequently result from the initiation of a standard cost system. Remember that a *standard* represents what *should be* rather than what *is* or *was.* Frequently, engineers are consulted to establish standards, which represent the most efficient way to perform the required tasks. The engineers perform time and motion studies

and review material utilization in the process of developing standards. Established practices and policies are frequently changed in response to the engineers' reports.

Behavioral implications must also be considered when developing standards. Managers, supervisors, purchasing agents, and other associated personnel should be consulted for two reasons: (1) their experience and expertise enable them to provide invaluable input to standard development and (2) persons who are involved in the standard-setting process are more likely to accept the resulting standards and to be motivated by them.

Management should also consider the desired level of difficulty necessary to achieve standard performance. The ranges of difficulty can be subdivided into three logical categories: (1) ideal standards, (2) practical standards, and (3) lax standards.

Ideal standards represent perfection; they show what costs should be under ideal circumstances. They ignore allowances for normal materials waste and spoilage. They do not consider ordinary labor inefficiencies due to machine down time, cleanup, breaks, or personal needs. Ideal standards are beyond the capabilities of most, if not all, employees. Such standards may motivate some individuals to constantly strive for improvement, but unattainable standards tend to discourage the majority of people. When confronted with consistent failure, most people will become demotivated and reduce their efforts to succeed. In addition, the variances associated with ideal standards lose significance. They tend to reflect deviations that are largely beyond the control of the participants, and they obscure true measures of superior or inferior performance, thereby reducing the capacity for control.

Practical standards can be accomplished with a reasonable degree of effort; they constitute attainable goals for employees. They allow for normal levels of inefficiency in materials and labor usage. An average worker performing in a diligent manner would be able to achieve standard performance. Practical standards have motivational appeal for most employees; the feeling of accomplishment that they attain through earnest effort tends to encourage them to do their best. Practical standards also produce meaningful variances. Deviations from the standard usually result from factors that the worker controls. Positive variances normally represent superior performance, and negative variances indicate inferior performance.

Lax standards represent easily attainable goals. Standard performance can be accomplished with minimal effort. Lax standards lack motivational appeal for most people; constant success attained by minimal effort tends to create boredom and low performance. In addition, variances lose meaningful content. Deviations caused by superior or inferior performance are obscured by the built-in slack.

The employee's level of ability must be considered when establishing standards. Standards that are attainable for a seasoned workforce may represent ideal standards to an inexperienced workforce. To be effective, standards should be constantly monitored and adjusted appropriately as the need arises.

Need for Standard Costs

As the previous discussion suggests, standard costs constitute the building blocks for the preparation of the master and flexible budgets. Accordingly, they facilitate the planning process. Standard costs also establish benchmarks by which actual performance can be judged. By highlighting differences between expected (i.e., standard) and actual performance, standard costing permits management to focus attention on the areas of greatest need. Because management talent is a valuable and expensive resource, businesses cannot afford to have managers devote large amounts of time to operations that are functioning normally. Instead, managers should concentrate on areas that are not performing in accordance with expectations. In other words, management should attend to the exceptions; indeed, this management philosophy has become known as the **management by exception** doctrine.

Standard costing facilitates the use of the exception principle. By reviewing performance reports that show differences between actual and standard costs, management is able to concentrate on the items that show significant variances. Areas that show only minor variances are subject to a cursory review or are ignored, as management deems appropriate.

Selecting Variances to Investigate

LO8 Understand the criteria for selecting the most appropriate variances to investigate.

Judgment, based on experience, plays a significant role in deciding which variances merit investigation. However, we can identify several factors that influence the decision. These include the *materiality concept, frequency of occurrence, capacity to control,* and the *characteristics of the item being considered.*

Standard costs are by nature estimated figures and therefore cannot be perfect predictors of actual costs. Slight variances will emerge in the normal course of business. These slight variances should not be investigated because they are not likely to produce useful information. In recognition of this fact, many companies follow the materiality concept by establishing guidelines for selecting variances to analyze. For example, a company may set a dollar or a percentage limit and instruct managers to ignore variances that fall below these limits. Only variances that qualify as material will be investigated. A **material variance** is one that would affect decision making. The need to analyze material variances applies to favorable as well as unfavorable variances. As mentioned earlier, purchasing substandard materials can create favorable variances, resulting in what may seem to be a positive price variance; however, the company's products will ultimately reflect the fact that they were constructed with substandard materials and sales will fall.

The concept of *frequency of occurrence* is closely related to the materiality concept. An immaterial variance that amounts to $20,000 during one month can become a material variance amounting to $240,000 if the monthly performance is repeated throughout the year. Variance reports should highlight frequent as well as large variations.

The *capacity to control* refers to management's ability to take corrective action. If utility rates cause variances between actual and standard overhead cost, management has little control over these variances. Conversely, if actual labor costs exceed standard costs because a supervisor is unable to motivate employees, management can control this variance. Managers should concentrate on controllable variances to maximize their utility to the firm.

The *characteristics of the items being considered* may permit management abuse. For example, managers can reduce actual costs in the short term by delaying expenditures for maintenance, research and development, advertising, and so on. Although cost reductions in these areas may produce favorable variances and immediate gratification, they will have a long-term detrimental impact on profitability. Unfortunately, managers under stress may yield to the temptations of the short-term benefits. As a result, variances associated with these critical items should be closely scrutinized.

As previously indicated, the primary advantage of using a standard cost system is that it efficiently uses management talent to control costs. Secondary benefits include the following.

1. Standard cost systems provide immediate feedback that permits rapid response to troubled areas. For example, a standard amount of materials may be issued for a particular job. Requisitions of additional materials may require supervisory approval indicated by the use of specially marked requisition forms. Each time a supervisor is forced to use one of these forms, she is immediately aware that excess materials are being used and has time to act before the excessive material usage becomes unmanageable.

2. If established and maintained properly, standard cost systems can boost morale and motivate employees. Reward systems can be linked to accomplishments that exceed the established performance standards. Under such circumstances, employees become extremely conscious of the time and materials they use, minimizing waste and reducing costs.

3. Standard cost systems encourage proper planning. The failure to plan properly results in overbuying, excessive inventory, wasted time, and so on. A standard cost system forces planning, resulting in a more efficient operation with less waste.

Manufacturing Cost Variances

The *manufacturing costs* incurred by Melrose Manufacturing Company are summarized here for your convenience.

	Standard	Actual
Variable materials cost per unit	$ 12.00	$ 11.78
Variable labor cost per unit	16.80	17.25
Variable overhead cost per unit	5.60	5.75
Total per unit variable manufacturing cost (a)	$ 34.40	$ 34.78
Total units produced (b)	19,000	19,000
Total variable manufacturing cost (a × b)	$653,600	$660,820
Fixed manufacturing cost	201,600	210,000
Total manufacturing cost	$855,200	$870,820

Based on this information, we can determine that the total manufacturing cost variance is $15,620 ($870,820 − $855,200), which is unfavorable because Melrose actually incurred more cost than expected.

What caused Melrose to spend more money than expected? Did it spend more or less than expected on materials, labor, or overhead? Did it spend more or less than expected for fixed costs? To answer these questions, it is necessary to subdivide the total manufacturing cost variance into four logical subcomponents. Specifically, the total manufacturing cost variance ($15,620) can be subdivided into three variable cost variances (materials, labor, and overhead) and one fixed cost variance. Indeed, these individual variances were listed in Exhibit 8–3. Recall that the standard variable cost amounts in Exhibit 8–3 were determined by multiplying the standard cost per unit by the actual number of units produced. Similarly, the actual variable cost amounts were determined by multiplying the actual cost per unit by the actual number of units produced. These relationships can be expressed as follows:

Actual Costs	**Standard Costs**
Actual quantity	Actual quantity
×	×
Actual cost per unit	Standard cost per unit

Total variance

Algebraically, the variance can be expressed as follows.

$$\left| \begin{array}{cc} \text{Actual variable} & \text{Standard variable} \\ \text{cost per unit} & \text{cost per unit} \end{array} \right| \times \begin{array}{c} \text{Actual number} \\ \text{of units} \end{array} = \begin{array}{c} \text{Variable cost} \\ \text{variance} \end{array}$$

Notice that the differences between actual and standard amounts are shown as an absolute value. This indicates that the mathematical sign is not useful in interpreting the condition of the variance. To determine the condition of the variance, use the same rules as previously discussed, which are repeated here for your convenience.

- When actual costs are higher than standard costs, variances are unfavorable.
- When actual costs are lower than standard costs, variances are favorable.

Using the algebraic equations and the classification rules, we can reconstruct the product cost variances in Exhibit 8–3. The formulas and their results are shown in Exhibit 8–4. To confirm your understanding that the algebraic formulas are merely an alternative way to accomplish the same result, you should compare the manufacturing cost variances in Exhibit 8–3 with those in Exhibit 8–4.

The information in Exhibit 8–4 suggests that Melrose spent less than expected for materials and more than expected for labor and overhead. Fixed manufacturing costs were also higher than expected. This information is useful, but more detailed information is necessary to facilitate cost control. For example, we know that Melrose paid more for labor than expected,

Exhibit 8–4 *Total Manufacturing Cost Variances for Melrose Manufacturing Company*

Variable manufacturing costs	
Materials cost variance	
lActual cost − Standard costl × Actual units = l$11.78 − $12.00l × 19,000 =	$ 4,180 Favorable
Total labor cost variance	
lActual cost − Standard costl × Actual units = l$17.25 − $16.80l × 19,000 =	8,550 Unfavorable
Total overhead cost variance	
lActual cost − Standard costl × Actual units = l$ 5.75 − $ 5.60l × 19,000 =	2,850 Unfavorable
Total variable costs variances	$ 7,220 Unfavorable
Fixed manufacturing cost	8,400 Unfavorable
Total manufacturing cost variance	$15,620 Unfavorable

but we do not know whether the employees were paid higher wages or worked more hours. To obtain this information, analyzing the price and amount of each resource used in the production process is necessary.

Price and Usage Variances

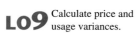

LO9 Calculate price and usage variances.

The resources used in the manufacturing process are frequently called **inputs** (i.e., materials, labor, and overhead). The purpose of the manufacturing process is to transform the set of *inputs* into **outputs** (i.e., products). As previously indicated, managers establish standards to exercise control over the consumption of the inputs. A *standard* represents the amount of input that management *expects* to be consumed in the manufacturing process. The **cost per unit of input** is composed of two factors: price and usage. A *favorable variance* occurs when production costs are less than expected (i.e., the standard price). An **unfavorable variance** occurs when production costs are more than expected. Likewise, favorable and unfavorable *usage variances* occur when production consumes more or less of an input than the standard amount. Price and usage variances are computed for each input factor in the production process including materials, labor, and variable overhead. The specific names of the variances change to reflect the nature of the input being analyzed. For example, a variance for materials may be called a **materials price variance** and a **materials quantity variance;** the equivalent labor variances are called a **labor rate variance** and a **labor efficiency variance.** Regardless of the names used, the underlying concepts and computational procedures are the same for all variable price and usage variances.

Calculating Materials Price and Usage Variances

To illustrate the determination of the materials price and usage variances, return to the case of Melrose Manufacturing Company. Recall that performance evaluation is based on a flexible budget. Accordingly, the total materials variance is computed on the basis of the actual level of production of 19,000 statues. As shown in Exhibit 8–4, the total materials variance is computed as follows.

$$\left| \begin{array}{c} \text{Actual} \\ \text{cost} \end{array} - \begin{array}{c} \text{Standard} \\ \text{cost} \end{array} \right| \times \begin{array}{c} \text{Actual} \\ \text{quantity} \end{array} = |\$11.78 - \$12.00| \times 19,000 = \$4,180 \text{ Favorable}$$

Why is the variance favorable? Because *actual cost* is lower than *standard cost.* In other words, Melrose spent less on materials than it expected to pay to make 19,000 statues. What caused the company to spend less than planned? The price of the materials may have been less than expected, or the company may have used fewer materials than expected. To determine which or what combination of these two components caused the total favorable variance, we must first separate the cost per unit data into quantity and price components. To illustrate, assume that the materials cost per unit data are composed of the following amounts.

	Actual Data	Standard Data
Quantity of materials per unit	6.2 pounds	6.0 pounds
Price per pound	× $1.90	× $2.00
Cost per unit	$11.78	$12.00

Based on this breakdown, we can determine the total quantity of materials as follows.

	Actual Data	**Standard Data**
Actual production volume	19,000 units	19,000 units
Quantity of materials per unit	× 6.2 pounds	× 6.0 pounds
Total quantity of materials	117,800 pounds	114,000 pounds

We can now validate the fact that the total variance is composed of price and quantity components. Specifically, the total variance can be recalculated as follows.

Actual Costs		**Standard Costs**	
Actual quantity	117,800	Standard quantity	114,000
×	×	×	×
Actual price	$1.90	Standard price	$2.00
	$223,820		$228,000
		Total variance: $4,180 Favorable	

To isolate the price and usage variances, we insert a Variance-Dividing Data column between the Actual Cost and Standard columns. The Variance-Dividing Data column is composed of a combination of standard and actual data. Specifically, the *standard price* is multiplied by the *actual quantity* of materials purchased and used.[1] The result is shown in Exhibit 8–5.

Exhibit 8–5 *Materials Price and Usage Variances for Melrose Manufacturing Company*

Actual Cost		**Variance Dividing Data**		**Standard Cost**	
Actual quantity	117,800	Actual quantity	117,800	Standard quantity	114,000
×	×	×	×	×	×
Actual price	$1.90	Standard price	$2.00	Standard price	$2.00
	$223,820		$235,600		$228,000
		Price variance		Quantity variance	
		$11,780 Favorable		$7,600 Unfavorable	
		Total variance: $4,180 Favorable			

Algebraic Notation. The amount of the price variance (i.e., difference between the *Actual Cost column* and the *Variance-Dividing Data column*) can be determined by multiplying the difference between the actual and standard price by the actual quantity. This relationship can be written algebraically as follows.

$$\text{Price variance} = |\text{Actual price} - \text{Standard price}| \times \text{Actual quantity}$$
$$= |\$1.90 - \$2.00| \times 117,800$$
$$= \$0.10 \times 117,800$$
$$= \$11,780 \text{ Favorable}$$

As with the previous variance formulas, the difference between the actual price and the standard amounts is expressed as an *absolute value*. This mathematical notation suggests that the mathematical sign is not useful in interpreting the condition of the variance. To assess the

---

[1] In practice, raw materials are frequently stored in inventory prior to being used. Accordingly, differences may exist between the amount of materials purchased and the amount of materials used. When this condition occurs, the price variance is determined on the basis of the quantity of materials *purchased,* and the quantity variance is determined on the basis of the quantity of materials *used.* This text makes the simplifying assumption that the amount of materials purchased equals the amount of materials used during the period.

condition of the variance, you must consider the type of variance being analyzed. With respect to cost variances, managers seek to attain actual prices that are lower than expected (standard) prices. In the case of Melrose Manufacturing Company, the actual price ($1.90) is less than the standard price ($2.00). Accordingly, the price variance is classified as favorable.

The materials usage variance also can be expressed in an algebraic formula. Specifically, the amount of the usage variance (difference between the *Variance-Dividing Data column* and the *Standard Cost column*) can be determined by multiplying the difference between the actual and standard quantity by the standard price. This relationship can be written algebraically as follows.

$$\text{Quantity variance} = |\text{Actual quantity} - \text{Standard quantity}| \times \text{Standard price}$$
$$= |117,800 - 114,000| \times \$2.00$$
$$= 3,800 \times \$2.00$$
$$= \$7,600 \text{ Unfavorable}$$

LO10 Identify the responsible parties for price and usage variances.

Responsibility for Materials Variances. A purchasing agent is normally considered to be responsible for a *favorable price variance*. The standard materials price is established for a particular grade of material. The standard assumes that the material will be purchased in a manner that will give the company favorable trade terms including volume discounts, cash discounts, transportation savings, and supplier services. Due diligence in placing orders enables the purchasing agent to take advantage of positive trading terms. Under these circumstances, the company pays less than standard prices, which is reflected in the form of a favorable price variance. An investigation of the favorable price variance could result in the identification of purchasing strategies that can be shared with other purchasing agents. The analysis of favorable as well as unfavorable variances can result in the development of efficiencies that benefit the entire production process.

Certain factors limit the purchasing agent's control of the price variance. The agent may exercise his duties with diligence and still be confronted with an unfavorable price variance for many reasons. Suppliers may raise prices, rush orders may be necessary because of poor scheduling by the production department, or a truckers' strike may force the use of a more expensive delivery system. These and other factors are beyond the control of the purchasing agent. Care must be taken to ensure the identification of the proper causes of unfavorable variances. False accusations and overreactions lead only to resentment that will ultimately destroy the productive potential of the standard costing system.

The condition of the *materials usage variance* can be determined by simply looking at the quantity data. Because the actual quantity used is higher than the standard quantity, the variance is unfavorable. In other words, using more materials than expected increases the cost of production. If management is trying to minimize cost, using more materials than expected is an unfavorable condition. The materials quantity variance is largely under the control of the production department. Unfavorable variances reflect materials waste that may be caused by inexperienced workers, faulty machinery, negligent application, or poor planning. Unfavorable variances may also be caused by factors that are beyond the control of the production department, such as the purchasing agent's purchase of substandard materials. The lower-quality material may result in more scrap (waste) in the production process that would be reflected in an unfavorable usage variance.

Calculating Labor Variances

LO9 Calculate price and usage variances.

Labor variances are calculated using the same general formulas as those used to compute the materials price and usage variances. Accordingly, the total labor variance shown in Exhibit 8–4 is computed as follows.

$$\left| \frac{\text{Actual}}{\text{cost}} - \frac{\text{Standard}}{\text{cost}} \right| \times \frac{\text{Actual}}{\text{units}} = |\$17.25 - \$16.80| \times 19,000 = \$8,550$$

Assume that Melrose's accountant determined that the labor cost per unit data are composed of the following amounts:

Do purchasing agents really make a difference? They certainly do—at least that is the opinion of Inspector General Eleanor Hill, who is in charge of policing waste and fraud at the Department of Defense. Explaining preposterous costs such as a $76 screw, Ms. Hill told a Senate Armed Services subcommittee that Pentagon buyers failed to obtain volume discounts, neglected to compare prices with competitors, or otherwise failed to pursue aggressive purchasing strategies. Specifically, Ms. Hill said, "Department of Defense procurement approaches were poorly conceived, badly coordinated, and did not result in the government getting good value for the prices paid both for commercial and noncommercial items. We found considerable evidence that the Department of Defense had not yet learned how to be an astute buyer in the commercial marketplace."

Source: John Diamond, "Audits Say Pentagon Continues to Overpay," *USA Today*, March 19, 1998, p. 2A.

	Actual Data	Standard Data
Quantity of labor per unit	1.5 hours	1.4 hours
Price per hour	× $11.50	× $12.00
Cost per unit	$17.25	$16.80

Based on this breakdown, we can determine the total quantity of labor as follows.

	Actual Data	Standard Data
Actual production volume	19,000 units	19,000 units
Quantity of labor per unit	× 1.5 hours	× 1.4 hours
Total quantity of labor	28,500 hours	26,600 hours

Using the price and quantity information described here, the labor price and usage variances can be computed as shown in Exhibit 8–6.

Exhibit 8–6 *Labor Price and Usage Variances for Melrose Manufacturing Company*

Actual Cost		Variance Dividing Data		Standard Cost	
Actual hours	28,500	Actual hours (AHrs)	28,500	Standard hours (SHrs)	26,600
×	×	×	×	×	×
Actual price (AP)	$11.50	Standard price (SP)	$12.00	Standard price (SP)	$12.00
	$327,750		$342,000		$319,200

Labor price variance
$14,250 Favorable

Labor usage variance
$22,800 Unfavorable

Algebraic solution: |AP − SP| × AHrs
|$11.50 − $12.00| × 28,500 = $14,250

Algebraic solution: |AHrs − SHrs| × SP
|28,500 − 26,600| × $12.00 = $22,800

Total variance: 8,550 Unfavorable

Responsibility for Labor Variances. A quick glance at the price of labor indicates that the *labor price variance* is favorable because the actual amount paid for labor is less than the

LO10 Identify the responsible parties for price and usage variances.

333

standard rate. The production supervisor is usually responsible for the labor price variance because price variances normally result from the use of labor rather than from an underpayment or overpayment of the hourly rate. Labor price rates are frequently fixed by contracts. Accordingly, rates below or above established rates are not likely; however, the use of semiskilled labor to perform highly skilled tasks or vice versa will produce rate variances. Similarly, the use of unanticipated overtime will cause unfavorable variances. Production department supervisors are in the best position to control the assignment of labor and are therefore held accountable for the resultant labor price variances.

Labor usage variances measure the productive use of the labor force. Because Melrose used more labor than expected, the labor usage variance will be unfavorable. Unsatisfactory labor performance has many causes; low morale or poor supervision are possibilities. Furthermore, machine breakdowns, inferior materials, and poor planning can cause interruptions that waste labor and reduce productivity. Because these factors are generally under the control of the production department supervisors, these individuals are normally held responsible for labor usage variances.

Price and usage variances may be interrelated. The favorable labor price variance may have been obtained by using less skilled employees who may require more time to do the job, thereby causing an unfavorable labor usage variance. Once again, the variances must be investigated with due diligence before drawing conclusions as to who should be held responsible for them.

Check Yourself 8-3

DogHouse, Inc., expected to build 200 dog houses during July. Each dog house was expected to require 2 hours of direct labor. Labor cost was expected to be $10 per hour. The company actually built 220 dog houses using an average of 2.1 labor hours per dog house at an actual labor rate averaging $9.80 per hour. Determine the labor rate and usage variances.

Answer

Labor rate variance = (Actual rate − Standard rate) × Actual quantity
Labor rate variance = ($9.80 − $10.00) × (220 units × 2.1 hours) = $92.40 Favorable

Labor usage variance = (Actual quantity − Standard quantity) × Standard rate
Labor usage variance = ([220 × 2.1] − [220 × 2.0]) × $10 = $220.00 Unfavorable

Variable Overhead Variances

Variable overhead variances utilize the same general formulas as used to compute the other price and usage variances. However, unique characteristics that require special attention are associated with variable overhead costs. First, variable overhead is composed of a variety of inputs including supplies, utilities, indirect labor, and so on. The variable overhead cost pool is normally assigned to products on the basis of a predetermined variable overhead allocation rate. The use of a single rate to represent a mixture of different costs complicates the interpretation of variances. Suppose the actual overhead rate is higher than the predetermined rate. Does this mean that the company paid more than it should have paid for supplies, utilities, maintenance, or some other input variable? Indeed, the cost of some overhead inputs may have been higher than expected while others were lower than expected. Similarly, an overall usage variance provides no clue as to which overhead inputs were over- or underused. Due to the difficulty of interpreting the results, many companies do not calculate price and usage variances for variable overhead costs. For this reason, we limit our coverage of this subject to the total flexible budget variances shown in Exhibit 8–3.

Fixed Overhead Variances

It should be clear from the previous discussion that *variable costs* have price and usage variances and that *fixed overhead costs* can also have price variances. Remember that *fixed*

means that it stays the same relative to changes in the volume of production; it does not mean that it stays the same as expected. You may certainly pay more or less than you expected to pay for a fixed cost. For example, a supervisor may receive an unexpected raise, thereby causing actual salary costs to be higher than expected. Similarly, a manager may be able to negotiate a reduction in the rental cost for the manufacturing equipment, causing the actual rental costs to be lower than expected. The difference between the *actual fixed overhead costs* and the *budgeted fixed overhead costs* is called a **spending variance.** The spending variance is favorable if the amount spent is less than that expected (i.e., actual cost is less than the budgeted cost). The variance is unfavorable if more than expected is spent (i.e., actual is more than budgeted).

The analysis of fixed overhead costs differs from that of variable costs because no potential usage variance exists. If Melrose pays $25,000 to rent its manufacturing facility, the company cannot use more or less of this rent no matter how many units of product it makes. Because the rent cost is fixed, however, the *cost per unit* of product will differ depending on the number of units of product made. The more products made, the lower the cost per unit. The fewer products made, the higher the cost per unit. Because the volume of activity affects the cost per unit, a variance between the expected and actual volume of activity is important. Accordingly, it is common practice to calculate a volume variance for fixed overhead costs. The **volume variance** is the difference between the *budgeted fixed cost* and the *amount of fixed costs allocated to production.* The amount of *allocated cost* is frequently called the *applied fixed cost.*

To illustrate the computation of the fixed overhead variances, we return to the case of Melrose Manufacturing Company. First, the overhead spending variance is shown in Exhibit 8–3. Specifically, the spending variance is the difference between the budgeted fixed overhead and the actual fixed overhead (|$201,600 budgeted − $210,000 actual| = $8,400 spending variance). The variance is considered unfavorable because Melrose actually spent more than it expected to spend for fixed overhead costs. Recall that there is no fixed overhead usage variance.

Calculation of the overhead volume variance involves first calculating the fixed cost predetermined overhead rate. Given budgeted fixed costs of $201,600 and planned activity of 18,000 statues, the predetermined fixed overhead rate is $11.20 per statue ($201,600 ÷ 18,000 statues). Based on actual production of 19,000 statues, $212,800 ($11.20 × 19,000 units) of fixed overhead costs would be applied (i.e., allocated) to production. The difference between the budgeted fixed overhead and the applied fixed overhead produces a volume variance of $11,200 (|$201,600 budgeted − $212,800 applied| = $11,200 variance). A summary of the fixed overhead variances is shown in Exhibit 8–7.

Exhibit 8–7 *Fixed Overhead Spending and Volume Variances for Melrose Manufacturing Company*

Actual Fixed Overhead Cost		Variance-Dividing Data		Standard Fixed Overhead Cost	
Actual fixed cost	$210,000	Budgeted fixed cost	$201,600	Applied fixed cost	$212,800
		Overhead spending variance		Overhead volume variance	
		$8,400 Unfavorable		$11,200 Favorable	

Responsibility for Fixed Overhead Cost Variances

There is no way to know who is responsible for the unfavorable fixed overhead spending variance because all of the fixed overhead costs have been pooled together. To improve accountability, significant fixed overhead costs that are controllable such as supervisory salaries should be tagged for individual analysis. Fixed overhead costs that are not controllable may still be reported as informational items for management. Fixed costs that are not controllable in the short term may be manageable in the long term. Accordingly, staying abreast of differences between the expected and actual costs of fixed overhead is important for management.

LO10 Identify the responsible parties for price and usage variances.

The fixed overhead volume variance is favorable because the actual volume of production was higher than the planned volume. This condition caused a decrease in the cost per unit of product. Note that the lower cost per unit does not result from a reduction in spending. Indeed, as indicated earlier, Melrose actually spent more than it expected to spend on fixed overhead costs. The variance is caused by a higher utilization of the company's manufacturing facilities. Specifically, Melrose has taken greater advantage of the *economies of scale.* Because the overhead costs are fixed, a higher volume of production results in a lower cost per unit of product. As a rule, a company with high fixed costs should utilize its facilities to produce as high a volume as possible, thereby lowering its cost per unit of production. Of course, this rule assumes that products produced can be sold at prevailing prices. The underutilization of manufacturing facilities causes a higher cost per unit; an unfavorable volume variance should alert management to this condition. In summary, a volume variance signifies the over- or underutilization of facilities rather than over- or underspending.

As previously discussed, production managers are not usually responsible for volume variances. The level of production is normally determined by the sales volume that is under the control of upper-level marketing managers. Although the volume variance does provide a measure of the effective utilization of facilities, the marketing department is primarily responsible for establishing the volume of activity. Accordingly, marketing managers should be held accountable for volume variances.

Summary of Manufacturing Cost Variances

As indicated, the total variable manufacturing cost variance can be subdivided into materials, labor, and overhead variances. These variances can be further subdivided into price and usage variances. Manufacturing fixed cost can be subdivided into spending and volume variances. As its name implies, *volume variance* is not a cost variance; volume variance shows how volume affects fixed cost *per unit,* but it does not provide any indication of a difference between the *total* amount of actual and expected costs. The relationships between the cost variances computed for Melrose Manufacturing Company are summarized in Exhibit 8–8.

We have discussed a number of variable and fixed manufacturing cost variances. The algebraic formulas used to compute these variances are summarized in Exhibit 8–9.

■ General, Selling, and Administrative Cost Variances

LO9 Calculate price and usage variances.

Variable general, selling, and administrative (G, S, & A) costs can have *price and usage variances.* For example, suppose that Melrose decides to attach a promotional advertising brochure to each statue it sells. Melrose may pay more or less for each brochure (i.e., incur a price variance). Melrose also could use more or fewer of the brochures than it expected to use (i.e., incur a usage variance). Indeed, businesses frequently compute variances for many G, S, & A costs such as sales commissions, food and entertainment, postage, and supplies. The algebraic formulas used to compute variances for variable manufacturing costs apply equally to the computation of variable G, S, & A cost variances.

Fixed G, S, & A costs are also subject to variance analysis. As indicated in Exhibit 8–3, Melrose Manufacturing incurred a favorable $5,000 G, S, & A fixed cost *spending variance.* This means that Melrose actually had spent lower fixed G, S, & A costs than was expected. A fixed cost *volume variance* could also be computed. Certainly, changes in the volume of sales activity affect the per unit amounts of fixed G, S, & A costs.

A number of individuals are responsible for G, S, & A cost variances. For example, lower-level sales personnel can be responsible for controlling the price and usage of promotional items. In contrast, upper-level administrative officers are responsible for fixed salary expenses. Due to the variety of personnel and types of costs involved, a full discussion of G, S, & A cost variances is beyond the scope of this text.

Exhibit 8-8 *Relationships Between Manufacturing Cost Variances for Melrose Manufacturing Company*

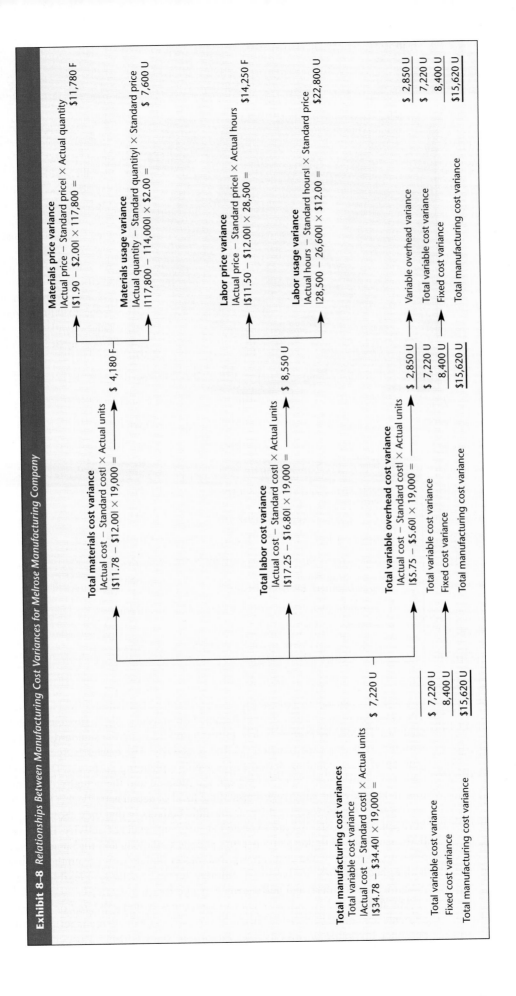

Materials price variance
|Actual price − Standard price| × Actual quantity
|$1.90 − $2.00| × 117,800 = $11,780 F

Materials usage variance
|Actual quantity − Standard quantity| × Standard price
|117,800 − 114,000| × $2.00 = $ 7,600 U

Total materials cost variance
|Actual cost − Standard cost| × Actual units
|$11.78 − $12.00| × 19,000 = ⟶ $ 4,180 F

Labor price variance
|Actual price − Standard price| × Actual hours
|$11.50 − $12.00| × 28,500 = $14,250 F

Labor usage variance
|Actual hours − Standard hours| × Standard price
|28,500 − 26,600| × $12.00 = $22,800 U

Total labor cost variance
|Actual cost − Standard cost| × Actual units
|$17.25 − $16.80| × 19,000 = ⟶ $ 8,550 U

Variable overhead variance $ 2,850 U
Total variable cost variance $ 7,220 U
Fixed cost variance   8,400 U
Total manufacturing cost variance $15,620 U

Total variable overhead cost variance
|Actual cost − Standard cost| × Actual units
|$5.75 − $5.60| × 19,000 = ⟶ $ 2,850 U
Total variable cost variance $ 7,220 U
Fixed cost variance   8,400 U
Total manufacturing cost variance $15,620 U

Total manufacturing cost variances
Total variable cost variance
|Actual cost − Standard cost| × Actual units
|$34.78 − $34.40| × 19,000 = $ 7,220 U

Total variable cost variance $ 7,220 U
Fixed cost variance   8,400 U
Total manufacturing cost variance $15,620 U

Does variance analysis apply to service companies as well as manufacturers? The answer is a definite yes! Express Oil Change could establish standard rates and times for the labor required to perform specific auto maintenance functions. Similarly, it could establish standards for materials such as oil, filters, and transmission fluid. Also, fixed overhead costs and measures of volume (i.e., number of vehicles serviced) exist. Accordingly, a full range of variances could be computed for the services provided.

Exhibit 8–9 *Algebraic Formulas for Variances*

1. Variable cost variances (materials, labor, and overhead)
   a. Price variance

   |Actual price − Standard price| × Actual quantity

   b. Usage variance

   |Actual quantity − Standard quantity| × Standard price

2. Fixed overhead variances
   a. Fixed overhead spending variance

   |Actual fixed overhead costs − Budgeted fixed overhead costs|

   b. Fixed overhead volume variance

   |Applied fixed overhead costs − Budgeted fixed overhead costs|

a look back

The essential topics in this chapter included the master budget, flexible budgets, and variance analysis. The *master budget* is determined by multiplying the standard sales price and per unit variable costs times the planned volume of activity. The master budget is prepared at the beginning of the accounting period and is used for planning purposes. The master budget is not adjusted to reflect differences between the planned and the actual volume of activity. Since this budget stays the same regardless of the level of actual activity, it is sometimes called a *static budget. Flexible budgets* differ from static budgets in that they show the estimated amount of revenue and costs that are expected at different levels of activity. Both static and flexible budgets are based on the same per unit standard amounts and the same fixed costs. The total amounts of revenue and costs shown in a master budget differ from those shown in a flexible budget because they are based on different levels of activity. Flexible budgets are used for planning, cost control, and performance evaluation.

The differences between standard (sometimes called *expected* or *estimated*) and actual amounts are called *variances*. Variances are used to evaluate managerial performance and can be either favorable or unfavorable. *Favorable sales variances* occur when actual sales are

338

greater than expected sales. *Unfavorable sales variances* occur when actual sales are less than expected sales. *Favorable cost variances* occur when actual costs are less than expected costs. *Unfavorable cost variances* occur when actual costs are more than expected costs.

Activity variances are determined by the difference between the static budget and a flexible budget. Since both static and flexible budgets are based on the same standard sales price and costs per unit, the activity variances are attributable solely to differences between the planned and the actual volume of activity. Favorable sales activity variances suggest that the marketing manager has performed positively by selling more than was expected. Unfavorable sales activity variances suggest the inverse. Favorable or unfavorable variable cost activity variances are not meaningful for performance evaluation because variable costs are expected to change in proportion to changes in the volume of activity.

Flexible budget variances are computed by taking the difference between the amounts of revenue and variable costs that are expected at the actual volume of activity and the actual amounts of revenue and variable costs incurred at the actual volume of activity. Since the volume of activity is the same for the flexible budget and the actual results, variances are caused by the differences between the standard and actual sales price and per unit costs. Flexible budget variances are used for cost control and performance evaluation.

Flexible budget variances can be subdivided into *price and usage variances.* Price and usage variances for materials and labor can be computed with the following formulas. Variable overhead variances are calculated with the same general formulas; however, the interpretation of the results is more difficult due to the variety of inputs in variable overhead.

Price variance = |Actual price − Standard price| × Actual Quantity
Quality variance = |Actual quantity − Standard quantity| × Standard Price

The purchasing agent is normally held accountable for the material price variance. The production department supervisor is usually held responsible for the materials usage variance and the labor price and usage variances.

The fixed overhead cost variance is made up of a spending variance and a volume variance computed as follows:

Spending OH variance = Actual fixed OH costs − Budgeted fixed OH costs
OH volume variance = Budgeted fixed cost − Applied (allocated) fixed costs

The overhead spending variance is similar to a price variance. While fixed costs stay the same relative to changes in production volume, they may be more or less than they are expected to be. For example, a production supervisor's salary will stay the same regardless of the level of activity, but the supervisor may receive a raise resulting in higher than expected fixed costs. The fixed overhead volume variance is favorable if the actual volume of production is higher than the expected volume. A higher volume of production results in a lower cost per unit. The volume variance measures how effectively production facilities are being utilized.

Care must be taken when interpreting variances. For example, a purchasing agent may produce a favorable price variance by buying low-quality materials at a low price. However, an unfavorable labor usage variance may occur because the employees have difficulty using the substandard materials. In this case, the production supervisor is faced with an unfavorable usage variance for which she is not responsible. In addition, the purchasing agent's undesirable behavior produced a favorable price variance. Accordingly, favorable variances cannot be assumed to indicate favorable performance. Likewise, unfavorable variances do not always suggest poor performance. All variances must be carefully investigated before responsibility is assigned.

Chapter 9 introduces other techniques that are used to evaluate managerial performance. The concept of decentralization and its relationship to responsibility accounting will be covered. You will learn how to calculate and interpret the return on investment and residual income. Finally, you will study the approaches used to establish the price of products that are transferred between divisions of the same company.

SELF-STUDY REVIEW PROBLEM

Bugout Pesticides, Inc., established the following standard price and costs for a termite control product that it sells to exterminators.

Variable price and cost data (per unit)	Standard	Actual
Sales price	$52.00	$49.00
Materials cost	10.00	10.66
Labor cost	12.00	11.90
Overhead cost	7.00	7.05
General, selling, and administrative (G, S, & A) cost	8.00	7.92
Expected fixed costs (in total)		
Manufacturing	$150,000	$140,000
General, selling, and administrative	60,000	64,000

The 2002 master budget was established at an expected volume of 25,000 units. Actual production and sales volume for the year was 26,000 units.

Required

a. Prepare the pro forma income statement for Bugout's 2002 master budget.

b. Prepare a flexible budget income statement at the actual volume.

c. Determine the sales activity (volume) variances and indicate whether they are favorable or unfavorable. Comment on how Bugout would use the variances to evaluate performance.

d. Determine the flexible budget variances and indicate whether they are favorable or unfavorable.

e. Identify the two variances Bugout is most likely to analyze further. Explain why you chose these two variances. Who is normally responsible for the variances you chose to investigate?

f. Each unit of product was expected to require 4 pounds of material, which has a standard cost of $2.50 per pound. Actual materials usage was 4.1 pounds per unit at an actual cost of $2.60 per pound. Determine the materials price and usage variances.

Solution to Requirements a, b, and c

Number of units		25,000	26,000	
	Per Unit Standards	Master Budget	Flexible Budget	Activity Variances
Sales revenue	$52	$1,300,000	$1,352,000	$52,000 F
Variable manufacturing costs				
Materials	$10	(250,000)	(260,000)	10,000 U
Labor	$12	(300,000)	(312,000)	12,000 U
Overhead	$7	(175,000)	(182,000)	7,000 U
Variable G, S, & A	$8	(200,000)	(208,000)	8,000 U
Contribution margin		375,000	390,000	15,000 F
Fixed costs				
Manufacturing		(150,000)	(150,000)	0
G, S, & A		(60,000)	(60,000)	0
Net income		$ 165,000	$ 180,000	$15,000 F

The sales activity variances are useful in determining how changes in sales volume affect revenues and costs. Since the flexible budget is based on standard prices and costs, the variances do not provide insight into differences between standard prices and costs versus actual prices and costs.

Solution to Requirement d

Number of units		26,000	26,000	
	Actual Unit Price/Cost	Flexible Budget*	Actual Results	Variances
Sales revenue	$49.00	$1,352,000	$1,274,000	$78,000 U
Variable manuf. costs				
Materials	$10.66	(260,000)	(277,160)	17,160 U
Labor	$11.90	(312,000)	(309,400)	2,600 F
Overhead	$7.05	(182,000)	(183,300)	1,300 U
Variable G, S, & A	$7.92	(208,000)	(205,920)	2,080 F
Contribution margin		390,000	298,220	91,780 U
Fixed costs				
Manufacturing		(150,000)	(140,000)	10,000 F
G, S, & A		(60,000)	(64,000)	4,000 U
Net income		$ 180,000	$ 94,220	$85,780 U

*The price and cost data for the flexible budget come from the previous table.

Solution to Requirement e

The management by exception doctrine focuses attention on the sales price variance and the materials variance. The two variances are material in size and are generally under the control of management. Upper-level marketing managers are responsible for the sales price variance. These managers are normally responsible for establishing the sale price. In this case, the actual sales price is less than the planned sales price, resulting in an unfavorable flexible budget variance. Mid-level production supervisors and purchasing agents are normally responsible for the materials cost variance. This variance could have been caused by waste or by paying more for materials than the standard price. Further analysis of the materials cost variance follows in Requirement f.

Solution to Requirement f

$$\text{(Actual cost} - \text{Standard cost)} \times \quad \text{Actual quantity} \quad = \text{Price variance}$$
$$(\$2.60 - \$2.50) \quad \times (4.1 \text{ pounds} \times 26,000 \text{ units}) = \quad \$10,660 \text{ U}$$

$$\text{(Actual quantity} - \text{Standard quantity)} \times \text{Standard price} = \text{Usage variance}$$
$$[(4.1 \times 26,000) - (4.0 \times \$26,000)] \quad \times \quad \$2.50 \quad = \quad \$6,500 \text{ U}$$

The total of the price and usage variances ([$10,660 + $6,500] = $17,160) equals the total materials flexible budget variance computed in Requirement d.

KEY TERMS

Budget slack *326*
Cost per unit of input *330*
Favorable variance *323*
Flexible budget *320*
Flexible budget variance *324*
Ideal standard *327*
Inputs *330*
Labor efficiency variance *330*

Labor rate variance *330*
Lax standard *327*
Making the numbers *322*
Management by exception *327*
Materials price variance *330*
Materials quantity variance *330*

Material variance *328*
Outputs *330*
Practical standard *327*
Sales price variance *324*
Sales activity (volume) variance *321*
Spending variance *335*

Standard *326*
Static budget *320*
Unfavorable variance *330*
Variances *321*
Volume variance *335*

QUESTIONS

1. What is the difference between a static budget and a flexible budget? When is each used?
2. When the operating costs for Bill Smith's production department were released, he was sure that he would be getting a raise. His costs were $20,000 less than the planned cost in the master budget. His

supervisor informed him that the results look good but that a more in-depth analysis is necessary before raises can be assigned. What other considerations could Mr. Smith's supervisor be interested in before she rates his performance?

3. When are sales and cost variances favorable and unfavorable?

4. Joan Mason, the marketing manager for a large manufacturing company, believes her unfavorable sales volume variance is the responsibility of the production department. What production circumstances that she does not control could have been responsible for her poor performance?

5. When would variable cost volume variances be expected to be unfavorable? How should unfavorable variable cost volume variances be interpreted?

6. What factors could lead to an increase in sales revenues that would not merit congratulations to the marketing manager?

7. With respect to fixed costs, what are the consequences of the actual volume of activity exceeding the planned volume?

8. How are flexible budget variances determined? What causes these variances?

9. Minnie Divers, the manager of the marketing department for one of the industry's leading retail businesses, has been notified by the accounting department that her department experienced an unfavorable sales volume variance in the preceding period but a favorable sales price variance. Based on these contradictory results, how would you interpret her overall performance as suggested by her variances?

10. What three attributes are necessary for establishing the best standards? What information and considerations should be taken into account when establishing standards?

11. What are the three ranges of difficulty in standard setting? What level of difficulty normally results in superior employee motivation?

12. "So many variances," exclaimed Carl, a production manager with Bonnyville Manufacturing. "How do I determine the variances that need investigation? I can't possibly investigate all of them." Which variances will lead to useful information?

13. What is the primary benefit associated with using a standard cost system?

14. A processing department of Carmine Corporation experienced a high unfavorable materials quantity variance. The plant manager initially commented, "The best way to solve this problem is to fire the supervisor of the processing department." Do you agree? Explain.

15. Sara Anderson says that she is a busy woman with no time to look at favorable variances. Instead, she concentrates solely on the unfavorable ones. She says that favorable variances imply that employees are doing better than expected and need only quick congratulations. In contrast, unfavorable variances indicate that change is needed to get the substandard performance up to par. Do you agree? Explain.

16. What two factors affect the total materials and labor variances?

17. Who is normally responsible for a materials price variance? Identify two factors that may be beyond this individual's control that could cause an unfavorable price variance.

18. John Jamail says that he doesn't understand why companies have labor price variances because most union contracts or other binding agreements set wage rates that do not normally change in the short term. How could rate variances occur even when binding commitments hold the dollar per hour rate constant?

19. Which individuals are normally held responsible for labor efficiency variances?

20. What is the primary cause of an unfavorable overhead volume variance?

21. What is the primary cause of a favorable overhead spending variance?

22. Explain how to record an unfavorable material price variance in the ledger accounts, assuming the variance is immaterial. How is this variance account closed at the end of the accounting period? What would be the effect on net income if the closing entry were omitted?

EXERCISES—SERIES A

L.O. 3   **EXERCISE 8–1A** *Classifying Variances as Favorable or Unfavorable*

Required

Indicate whether each of the following variances is favorable or unfavorable. The first one has been done as an example.

Item to Classify	Standard	Actual	Type of Variance
Sale volume	30,600 units	30,200 units	Unfavorable
Sales price	$3.60 per unit	$3.63 per unit	
Materials cost	$2.90 per pound	$3.00 per pound	
Materials usage	91,000 pounds	90,000 pounds	
Labor cost	$10.00 per hour	$9.60 per hour	
Labor usage	61,000 hours	61,800 hours	
Fixed cost spending	$400,000	$390,000	
Fixed cost per unit (volume)	$3.20 per unit	$3.16 per unit	

EXERCISE 8–2A *Determining Amount and Type (Favorable vs. Unfavorable) of Variance*   **L.O. 3**

Required

Compute variances for the following items and indicate whether each variance is favorable (F) or unfavorable (U).

Item	Budget	Actual	Variance	F or U
Sales revenue	$500,000	$489,000		
Cost of goods sold	$385,000	$360,000		
Material purchases at 5,000 pounds	$275,000	$280,000		
Materials usage	$180,000	$178,000		
Sales price	$500	$489		
Production volume	950 units	900 units		
Wages at 4,000 hours	$60,000	$58,700		
Labor usage at $16 per hour	$96,000	$97,000		
Research and development expense	$22,000	$25,000		
Selling and administrative expenses	$49,000	$40,000		

EXERCISE 8–3A *Preparing Master and Flexible Budgets*   **L.O. 1**

Annapolis Manufacturing Company established the following standard price and cost data.

Sales price	$10 per unit
Variable manufacturing cost	$4 per unit
Fixed manufacturing cost	$4,000 total
Fixed selling and administrative cost	$1,600 total

Annapolis planned to produce and sell 1,100 units. Actual production and sales amounted to 1,200 units.

Required

a. Prepare the pro forma income statement in contribution format that would appear in a master budget.

b. Prepare the pro forma income statement in contribution format that would appear in a flexible budget.

EXERCISE 8–4A *Determining Sales Activity (Volume) Variances*   **L.O. 4**

Required

Use the information provided in Exercise 8–3A.

a. Determine the sales activity variances.

b. Classify the variances as favorable (F) or unfavorable (U).

c. Comment on the usefulness of the variances with respect to performance evaluation and identify the member of the management team most likely to be responsible for these variances.

d. Explain why the fixed cost variances are zero.

e. Determine the fixed cost per unit based on planned activity and the fixed cost per unit based on actual activity. Assuming Annapolis uses information in the master budget to price the company's product, comment on how the activity (volume) variance could affect the company's profitability.

EXERCISE 8–5A *Determining Flexible Budget Variances*   **L.O. 5**

Use the standard price and cost data provided in Exercise 8–3A. Assume that the actual sales price is $9.60 per unit and that the actual variable cost is $4.10 per unit. The actual fixed manufacturing cost is $3,800, and the actual selling and administrative expenses are $1,700.

Required
a. Determine the flexible budget variances.
b. Classify the variances as favorable (F) or unfavorable (U).
c. Comment on the usefulness of the variances with respect to performance evaluation and identify the member(s) of the management team who is (are) most likely to be responsible for these variances.

L.O. 5   EXERCISE 8–6A *Using a Flexible Budget to Accommodate Market Uncertainty*

According to its original plan, Manchester Consulting Services Company would charge its customers for service at $180 per hour in 2003. The company president expects consulting services provided to customers to reach 40,000 hours at that rate. The marketing manager, however, argues that actual results may range from 35,000 hours to 45,000 hours because of market uncertainty. Manchester's standard variable cost is $70 per hour, and its standard fixed cost is $3,000,000.

Required
Develop flexible budgets based on the assumptions of service levels at 35,000 hours, 40,000 hours, and 45,000 hours.

L.O. 4, 5   EXERCISE 8–7A *Evaluating a Decision to Increase Sales Volume by Lowering Sales Price*

Davis Educational Services had budgeted its training service charge at $100 per hour. The company planned to provide 40,000 hours of training services during 2004. By lowering the service charge to $90 per hour, the company was able to increase the actual number of hours to 42,000.

Required
a. Determine the sales activity variance, and indicate whether it is favorable (F) or unfavorable (U).
b. Determine the flexible budget variance, and indicate whether it is favorable (F) or unfavorable (U).
c. Did lowering the price of training services increase profitability? Explain.

L.O. 4   EXERCISE 8–8A *Responsibility for Sales Volume (Activity) Variance*

Solarite Company expected to sell 350,000 of its four-function calculators during 2003. It set the standard sales price for the calculators at $17.00 each. During June, it became obvious that the company would be unable to attain the expected volume of sales. Solarite's chief competitor, Cackle, Inc., had lowered prices and was pulling market share from Solarite. To be competitive, Solarite matched Cackle's price, lowering its sales price to $16.00 per calculator. Cackle responded by lowering its price even further to $12.00 per calculator. In an emergency meeting of key personnel, Solarite's accountant, Saline Raul, stated, "Our cost structure simply won't support a sales price in the $12 range." The production manager, Josephine Daniels, said, "I don't understand why I'm here. The only unfavorable variance on my report is a fixed cost volume variance and that one is not my fault. We can't be making the product if the marketing department isn't selling it."

Required
a. Describe a scenario in which the production manager is responsible for the fixed cost volume variance.
b. Describe a scenario in which the marketing manager is responsible for the fixed cost volume variance.
c. Explain how a decline in sales volume would affect Solarite's ability to lower its sales price.

L.O. 5   EXERCISE 8–9A *Responsibility for Variable Manufacturing Cost Variance*

Sanchez Manufacturing Company set its standard variable manufacturing cost at $24 per unit of product. The company planned to make and sell 4,000 units of product during 2002. More specifically, the master budget called for total variable manufacturing cost to be $96,000. Actual production during 2002 was 4,200 units, and actual variable manufacturing costs amounted to $101,640. The production supervisor was asked to explain the variance between budgeted and actual cost ($101,640 − $96,000 = $5,640). The supervisor responded that she was not responsible for the variance that was caused solely by the increase in sales volume controlled by the marketing department.

Required
Do you agree with the production supervisor? Explain.

L.O. 9, 10   EXERCISE 8–10A *Calculating the Materials Usage Variance*

Martha Winters is the manager of the Center Point Bagel Shop. The corporate office had budgeted her store to sell 5,400 ham sandwiches during the week beginning July 17. Each sandwich was expected to contain

6 ounces of ham. During the week of July 17, the store actually sold 5,842 sandwiches and used 35,636 ounces of ham. The standard cost of ham is $0.84 per ounce. The variance report from company headquarters showed an unfavorable materials usage variance of $2,718.24. Ms. Winters thought the variance was too high, but she had no accounting background and did not know how to register a proper objection.

Required
a. Is the variance calculated properly? If not, recalculate it.
b. Provide three independent explanations as to what could have caused the materials price variance that you determined in Requirement *a*.

EXERCISE 8–11A *Determining Materials Price and Usage Variances*

L.O. 9

Love Link produced a special Mother's Day arrangement that included six roses. The standard and actual costs of the roses used in each arrangement follow.

	Standard	Actual
Average number of roses per arrangement	6.0	6.1
Price per rose	× $0.32	× $0.30
Cost of roses per arrangement	$1.92	$1.83

Love Link planned to make 760 arrangements but actually made 800.

Required
a. Determine the total flexible budget materials variance and indicate whether it is favorable (F) or unfavorable (U).
b. Determine the materials price variance and indicate whether it is favorable (F) or unfavorable (U).
c. Determine the materials usage variance and indicate whether it is favorable (F) or unfavorable (U).
d. Confirm the accuracy of Requirements *a*, *b*, and *c* by showing that the sum of the price and usage variances equals the total variance.

EXERCISE 8–12A *Responsibility for Materials Usage Variance*

L.O. 9, 10

Tampa Fruit Basket Company makes baskets of assorted fruit. The standard and actual costs of oranges used in each basket of fruit follow.

	Standard	Actual
Average number of oranges per basket	3.00	3.80
Price per orange	× $0.30	× $0.25
Cost of oranges per basket	$0.90	$0.95

Tampa actually produced 25,000 baskets.

Required
a. Determine the materials price variance and indicate whether it is favorable (F) or unfavorable (U).
b. Determine the materials usage variance and indicate whether it is favorable (F) or unfavorable. (U)
c. Explain why the purchasing agent may have been responsible for the usage variance.

EXERCISE 8–13A *Responsibility for Labor Rate and Usage Variances*

L.O. 10

Erie Manufacturing Company incurred a favorable labor rate variance and an unfavorable labor usage variance.

Required
a. Describe a scenario in which the personnel manager is responsible for the unfavorable usage variance.
b. Describe a scenario in which the production manager is responsible for the unfavorable usage variance.

EXERCISE 8–14A *Calculating and Explaining Labor Price and Usage Variances*

L.O. 9, 10

Friedman and Sons, a CPA firm, established the following standard labor cost data for completing what the firm referred to as a Class 2 tax return. Friedman expected each Class 2 return to require 3.6 hours of

labor at a cost of $42 per hour. The firm actually completed 600 returns. Actual labor hours averaged 3.9 hours per return and actual labor cost amounted to $38.40 per hour.

Required

a. Determine the total labor variance and indicate whether it is favorable (F) or unfavorable (U).
b. Determine the labor price variance and indicate whether it is favorable (F) or unfavorable (U).
c. Determine the labor usage variance and indicate whether it is favorable (F) or unfavorable (U).
d. Explain what could have caused these variances.

L.O. 9   EXERCISE 8–15A *Determining the Standard Labor Rate*

Gilmore Car Wash, Inc., expected to wash 900 cars during the month of August. Washing each car was expected to require 0.25 hours of labor. The company actually used 252 hours of labor to wash 840 cars. The labor usage variance was $336 unfavorable.

Required

a. Determine the standard labor rate.
b. If the actual labor rate is $7.50, indicate whether the labor rate variance would be favorable (F) or unfavorable (U).

L.O. 9, 10   EXERCISE 8–16A *Calculating the Variable Overhead Variance*

Deaver Company established a predetermined variable overhead cost rate at $7.00 per direct labor hour. The actual variable overhead cost rate was $6.80 per hour. The planned level of labor activity was 75,000 hours of labor. The company actually used 77,000 hours of labor.

Required

a. Determine the total flexible budget variable overhead cost variance.
b. Like many companies, Deaver has decided not to separate the total variable overhead cost variance into price and usage components. Explain why Deaver made this choice.

L.O. 9, 10   EXERCISE 8–17A *Determining and Interpreting Fixed Overhead Variances*

Rommel Company established a predetermined fixed overhead cost rate of $24 per unit of product. The company planned to make 9,000 units of product but actually produced only 8,000 units. Actual fixed overhead costs were $228,000.

Required

a. Determine the fixed overhead cost spending variance and indicate whether it is favorable or unfavorable. Explain what this variance means. Identify the manager(s) who is (are) responsible for the variance.
b. Determine the fixed overhead cost volume variance and indicate whether it is favorable or unfavorable. Explain why this variance is important. Identify the manager(s) who is (are) responsible for the variance.

PROBLEMS—SERIES A

L.O. 1, 4   PROBLEM 8–18A *Determining Sales Activity Variances*

Irvine Publications established the following standard price and costs for a hard cover picture book that the company produces.

Standard price and variable costs	
Sales price	$48.00
Materials cost	12.00
Labor cost	6.00
Overhead cost	8.40
General, selling, and administrative costs	9.60
Expected fixed costs	
Manufacturing	$180,000
General, selling, and administrative	72,000

Irvine planned to make and sell 30,000 copies of the book.

Required
a. Prepare the pro forma income statement that would appear in the master budget.
b. Prepare flexible budget income statements, assuming production volumes of 29,000 and 31,000 units.
c. Determine the sales activity variances, assuming production and sales volume are actually 31,000 units.
d. Indicate whether the variances are favorable (F) or unfavorable (U).
e. Comment on how Irvine could use the variances to evaluate performance.

PROBLEM 8–19A *Determining and Interpreting Flexible Budget Variances*

L.O. 5

Use the standard price and cost data supplied in Problem 8–18A. Assume that Irvine actually produced and sold 31,000 books. The actual sales price and costs incurred follow.

Actual price and variable costs	
Sales price	$47.00
Materials cost	12.24
Labor cost	5.88
Overhead cost	8.46
General, selling, and administrative costs	9.50
Actual fixed costs	
Manufacturing	$168,000
General, selling, and administrative	76,800

Required
a. Determine the flexible budget variances.
b. Indicate whether each variance is favorable (F) or unfavorable (U).
c. Identify the management position responsible for each variance. Explain what could have caused the variance.

PROBLEM 8–20A *Flexible Budget Planning*

L.O. 1

Rick Tong, the president of Aker Computer Services, needs your help. He wonders about the potential effects on the firm's net income if he changes the service rate that the firm charges its customers. The following basic data pertain to fiscal year 2005.

Standard rate and variable costs	
Service rate per hour	$90.00
Labor cost	48.00
Overhead cost	7.50
General, selling, and administrative cost	4.50
Expected fixed costs	
Facility repair	$525,000.00
General, selling, and administrative	150,000.00

Required
a. Prepare the pro forma income statement that would appear in the master budget if the firm expects to provide 25,000 hours of services in 2005.
b. A marketing consultant suggests to Mr. Tong that the service rate may affect the number of service hours that the firm can achieve. According to the consultant's analysis, if Aker charges customers $85 per hour, the firm can achieve 32,000 hours of services. Prepare a flexible budget using the consultant's assumption.
c. The same consultant also suggests that if the firm raises its rate to $95 per hour, the number of service hours will decline to 21,000. Prepare a flexible budget using the new assumption.
d. Evaluate the three possible outcomes you determined in Requirements *a, b,* and *c* and recommend a pricing strategy.

PROBLEM 8–21A *Determining Materials Price and Usage Variances*

L.O. 9

Wilkin Fruit Drink Company planned to make 400,000 containers of apple juice. It expected to use two cups of frozen apple concentrate to make each container of juice, thus using 800,000 cups (400,000 containers × 2 cups) of frozen concentrate. The standard price of one cup of apple concentrate is $0.25.

Wilkin actually paid $220,336.20 to purchase 816,060 cups of concentrate, which was used to make 402,000 containers of apple juice.

Required

a. Are flexible budget materials variances based on the planned volume of activity (400,000 containers) or actual volume of activity (402,000 containers)?
b. Compute the actual price per cup of concentrate.
c. Compute the standard quantity (number of cups of concentrate) required to produce the containers.
d. Compute the materials price variance and indicate whether it is favorable (F) or unfavorable (U).
e. Compute the materials usage variance and indicate whether it is favorable (F) or unfavorable (U).

L.O. 9   **PROBLEM 8–22A** *Determining Labor Price and Efficiency Variances*

Julia's Doll Company produces handmade dolls. The standard amount of time spent on each doll is 1.5 hours. The standard cost of labor is $8 per hour. The company planned to make 20,000 dolls during the year but actually used 30,800 hours of labor to make 22,000 dolls. The payroll amounted to $247,632.

Required

a. Should labor variances be based on the planned volume of 20,000 dolls or the actual volume of 22,000 dolls?
b. Prepare a table that shows the standard labor price, the actual labor price, the standard labor hours, and the actual labor hours.
c. Compute the labor price variance and indicate whether it is favorable (F) or unfavorable (U).
d. Compute the labor efficiency variance and indicate whether it is favorable (F) or unfavorable (U).

L.O. 9   **PROBLEM 8–23A** *Computing Fixed Overhead Variances*

In addition to other costs, Northwestern Phone Company planned to incur $425,000 of fixed manufacturing overhead in making 340,000 telephones. Northwestern actually produced 348,000 telephones, incurring actual overhead costs of $427,000. Northwestern establishes its predetermined overhead rate based on the planned volume of production (expected number of telephones).

Required

a. Calculate the predetermined overhead rate.
b. Determine the overhead spending variance and indicate whether it is favorable (F) or unfavorable (U).
c. Determine the overhead volume variance and indicate whether it is favorable (F) or unfavorable (U).

L.O. 9   **PROBLEM 8–24A** *Computing Materials, Labor, and Overhead Variances*

The following data were drawn from the records of Wells Corporation.

Planned volume for year (static budget)	8,000 units
Standard direct materials cost per unit	3 lbs. @ $2.00 per pound
Standard direct labor cost per unit	2 hours @ $4.00 per hour
Total expected fixed overhead costs	$36,000
Actual volume for the year (flexible budget)	8,400 units
Actual direct materials cost per unit	2.9 lbs. @ $2.10 per pound
Actual direct labor cost per unit	2.2 hrs. @ $3.80 per hour
Total actual fixed overhead costs	$35,200

Required

a. Prepare a materials variance information table showing the standard price, the actual price, the standard quantity, and the actual quantity.
b. Calculate the materials price and quantity variances. Indicate whether the variances are favorable (F) or unfavorable (U).
c. Prepare a labor variance information table showing the standard rate, the actual rate, the standard hours, and the actual hours.
d. Calculate the labor price and efficiency variances. Indicate whether the variances are favorable (F) or unfavorable (U).
e. Calculate the predetermined overhead rate, assuming that Wells uses the number of units as the allocation base.

f. Calculate the overhead spending variance. Indicate whether the variance is favorable (F) or unfavorable (U).

g. Calculate the overhead volume variance. Indicate whether the variance is favorable (F) or unfavorable (U).

PROBLEM 8–25A *Computing Materials, Labor, and Overhead Variances* **L.O. 9**

Carlos Manufacturing Company produces a component part of a top secret military communication device. Standard production and cost data for the part, Product X, follow.

Planned production	40,000 units
Per unit direct materials	2 lbs. @ $1.80 per lb.
Per unit direct labor	3 hrs. @ $8.00 per hr.
Total estimated fixed overhead costs	$936,000

Carlos purchased and used 84,460 pounds of material at an average cost of $1.85 per pound. Labor usage amounted to 119,480 hours at an average of $8.10 per hour. Actual production amounted to 41,200 units. Actual fixed overhead costs amounted to $984,000. The company completed and sold all inventory for $2,400,000.

Required

a. Prepare a materials variance information table showing the standard price, the actual price, the standard quantity, and the actual quantity.

b. Calculate the materials price and usage variances. Indicate whether the variances are favorable (F) or unfavorable (U).

c. Prepare a labor variance information table showing the standard rate, the actual rate, the standard hours, and the actual hours.

d. Calculate the labor price and efficiency variances. Indicate whether the variances are favorable (F) or unfavorable (U).

e. Calculate the predetermined overhead rate, assuming that Carlos uses the number of units as the allocation base.

f. Calculate the overhead spending and volume variances and indicate whether they are favorable (F) or unfavorable (U).

g. Determine the amount of gross margin Carlos would report on the year-end income statement.

PROBLEM 8–26A *Computing Variances* **L.O. 9**

Nagoya Manufacturing Company produces a single product. The following data apply to the standard cost of materials and labor associated with making the product.

Materials quantity per unit	1 pound
Materials price	$2.50 per pound
Labor quantity per unit	2 hours
Labor price	$4.50 per hour

During the year, the company made 1,800 units of product. At the end of the year, the variance accounts had the following balances.

Materials Usage Variance account	$100 Favorable
Materials Price Variance account	$88 Unfavorable
Labor Usage Variance account	$450 Unfavorable
Labor Price Variance account	$740 Favorable

Required

a. Determine the actual amount of materials used.

b. Determine the actual price paid per pound for materials.

c. Determine the actual labor hours used.

d. Determine the actual labor price per hour.

L.O. 9   PROBLEM 8–27A *Computing Standard Cost and Analyzing Variances*

Legend Company manufactures molded candles that are finished by hand. The company developed the following standards for a new line of drip candles.

Amount of direct materials per candle	1.6 pounds
Price of direct materials per pound	$0.75
Quantity of labor per unit	2 hours
Price of direct labor per hour	$6.00/hour
Total budgeted fixed overhead	$126,000

During 2003, Legend expected to produce 30,000 drip candles. Production lagged behind expectations, and it actually produced only 24,000 drip candles. At year-end, direct materials purchased and used amounted to 37,000 pounds at a unit price of $0.60 per pound. Direct labor costs were actually $5.75 per hour and 46,000 actual hours were worked to produce the drip candles. Overhead for the year actually amounted to $130,000. Overhead is applied to products using a predetermined overhead rate based on estimated units.

Required

(Round all computations to two decimal places.)

a. Compute the standard cost per candle for direct materials, direct labor, and overhead.
b. Determine the total standard cost for one drip candle.
c. Compute the actual cost per candle for direct materials, direct labor, and overhead.
d. Compute the total actual cost per candle.
e. Compute the price and usage variances for direct materials and direct labor. Identify any variances that Legend should investigate. Offer possible cause(s) for the variances.
f. Compute the fixed overhead spending and volume variances. Explain your findings.
g. Although the individual variances (price, usage, and overhead) were large, the standard cost per unit and the actual cost per unit differed by only a few cents. Explain why.

L.O. 1, 3   PROBLEM 8–28A *Analyzing Not-for-Profit Entity Variances*

The Southeast Accounting Association held its annual public relations luncheon in April 2008. Based on the previous year's results, the organization allocated $21,150 of its operating budget to cover the cost of the luncheon. To ensure that costs would be appropriately controlled, Jane Trudeau, the treasurer, prepared the following budget for the 2008 luncheon.

The budget for the luncheon was based on the following expectations.

1. The meal cost per person was expected to be $11.80. The cost driver for meals was attendance, which was expected to be 1,400 individuals.
2. Postage was based on $0.37 per invitation and 3,000 invitations were expected to be mailed. The cost driver for postage was number of invitations mailed.
3. The facility charge is $1,000 for a room that will accommodate up to 1,600 people; the charge for one to hold more than 1,600 people is $1,500.
4. A fixed amount was designated for printing, decorations, the speaker's gift, and publicity.

SOUTHEAST ACCOUNTING ASSOCIATION
Public Relations Luncheon Budget
April 2008

Operating funds allocated	$21,150
Expenses	
Variable costs	
Meals (1,400 × $11.80)	$16,520
Postage (3,000 × 0.37)	1,110
Fixed costs	
Facility	1,000
Printing	950
Decorations	840
Speaker's gift	130
Publicity	600
Total expenses	21,150
Budget surplus (deficit)	$ 0

Actual results for the luncheon follow.

SOUTHEAST ACCOUNTING ASSOCIATION	
Actual Results for Public Relations Luncheon	
April 2008	
Operating funds allocated	$21,150
Expenses	
Variable costs	
Meals (1,620 × $12.50)	$20,250
Postage (4,000 × 0.37)	1,480
Fixed costs	
Facility	1,500
Printing	950
Decorations	840
Speaker's gift	130
Publicity	600
Total expenses	$25,750
Budget deficit	$ (4,600)

Reasons for the differences between the budgeted and actual data follow.

1. The president of the organization, Jean Coburn, increased the invitation list to include 1,000 former members. As a result, 4,000 invitations were mailed.
2. Attendance was 1,620 individuals. Because of higher than expected attendance, the luncheon was moved to a larger room, thereby increasing the facility charge to $1,500.
3. At the last minute, Ms. Trudeau decided to add a dessert to the menu, which increased the meal cost to $12.50 per person.
4. Printing, decorations, the speaker's gift, and publicity costs were as budgeted.

Required

a. Prepare a flexible budget and compute the activity variances based on a comparison between the master budget and the flexible budget.
b. Compute flexible budget variances by comparing the flexible budget with the actual results.
c. Ms. Coburn was extremely upset with the budget deficit. She immediately called Ms. Trudeau to complain about the budget variance for the meal cost. She told Ms. Trudeau that the added dessert caused the meal cost to be $3,730 ($20,250 − $16,520) over budget. She added, "I could expect a couple hundred dollars one way or the other, but a couple thousand is totally unacceptable. At the next meeting of the budget committee, I want you to explain what happened." Assume that you are Ms. Trudeau. What would you tell the members of the budget committee?
d. Since this is a not-for-profit organization, why should anyone be concerned with meeting the budget?

EXERCISES—SERIES B

EXERCISE 8–1B *Classifying Variances as Favorable or Unfavorable*

L.O. 3

Required
Indicate whether each of the following variances is favorable (F) or unfavorable (U). The first one has been done as an example.

Item to Classify	Standard	Actual	Type of Variance
Sales volume	26,900 units	27,300 units	Favorable
Sales price	$4.72 per unit	$4.60 per unit	
Materials cost	$1.68 per pound	$1.72 per pound	
Materials usage	102,400 pounds	103,700 pounds	
Labor cost	$8.25 per hour	$8.80 per hour	
Labor usage	56,980 hours	55,790 hours	
Fixed cost spending	$249,000	$244,000	
Fixed cost per unit (volume)	$2.51 per unit	$3.22 per unit	

L.O. 3   **EXERCISE 8–2B** *Recognizing Favorable vs. Unfavorable Variances*

Compute variances for the following items and indicate whether each variance is favorable (F) or unfavorable (U).

Item	Budget	Actual	Variance	F or U
Sales revenue	$310,000	$325,000		
Cost of goods sold	$225,000	$200,000		
Materials purchases at 5,000 pounds	$130,000	$145,000		
Materials usage	$135,000	$130,000		
Sales price	$550	$560		
Production volume	890 units	900 units		
Wages at 3,800 hours	$55,936	$55,822		
Labor usage at $17 per hour	$91,800	$92,340		
Research and development expense	$33,000	$36,000		
Selling and administrative expenses	$58,000	$56,000		

L.O. 1   **EXERCISE 8–3B** *Preparing Master and Flexible Budgets*

Gosselin Manufacturing Company established the following standard price and cost data.

Sales price	$12 per unit
Variable manufacturing cost	$8 per unit
Fixed manufacturing cost	$20,000 total
Fixed selling and administrative cost	$18,000 total

Gosselin planned to produce and sell 18,000 units. It actually produced and sold 19,000 units.

Required
a. Prepare the pro forma income statement that would appear in a master budget. Use the contribution margin format.
b. Prepare the pro forma income statement that would appear in a flexible budget. Use the contribution margin format.

L.O. 4   **EXERCISE 8–4B** *Determining Sales Activity (Volume) Variances*

Required
Use the information provided in Exercise 8–3B.
a. Determine the sales activity variances.
b. Classify the variances as favorable or unfavorable.
c. Comment on the usefulness of the variances with respect to performance evaluation and identify the member of the management team most likely to be responsible for these variances.
d. Explain why the fixed cost variances are zero.
e. Determine the fixed cost per unit based on planned activity and the fixed cost per unit based on actual activity. Assuming Gosselin uses information in the master budget to price its product, explain how the activity (volume) variance could affect the company's profitability.

L.O. 5   **EXERCISE 8–5B** *Determining Flexible Budget Variances*

Use the standard price and cost data provided in Exercise 8–3B. Assume the actual sales price was $11.90 per unit and the actual variable cost was $7.95 per unit. The actual fixed manufacturing cost was $21,000, and the actual selling and administrative expenses were $17,300.

Required
a. Determine the flexible budget variances.
b. Classify the variances as favorable or unfavorable.
c. Comment on the usefulness of the variances with respect to performance evaluation and identify the member(s) of the management team that is (are) most likely to be responsible for these variances.

L.O. 5   **EXERCISE 8–6B** *Using a Flexible Budget to Accommodate Market Uncertainty*

Stancil Cable Installation Services, Inc., is planning to open a new regional office. Based on a market survey Stancil commissioned, the company expects services demand for the new office to be between 60,000 and 70,000 hours annually. The firm normally charges customers $40 per hour for its installation

services. Stancil's expects the new office to have a standard variable cost of $25 per hour and standard fixed cost of $1,000,000 per year.

Required
a. Develop flexible budgets based on 60,000 hours, 65,000 hours, and 70,000 hours of services.
b. Based on the results for Requirement *a,* comment on the likely success of Stancil's new office.

EXERCISE 8–7B *Evaluating a Decision to Increase Sales Volume by Reducing Sales Price*   **L.O. 4, 5**

At the beginning of its most recent accounting period, Roof Renew had planned to clean 400 house roofs at an average price of $420 per roof. By reducing the service charge to $390 per roof, the company was able to increase the actual number of roofs cleaned to 450.

Required
a. Determine the sales activity variance and indicate whether it is favorable (F) or unfavorable (U).
b. Determine the flexible budget variance and indicate whether it is favorable (F) or unfavorable (U).
c. Did reducing the price charged for cleaning roofs increase profitability? Explain.

EXERCISE 8–8B *Responsibility for Sales Volume (Activity) Variance*   **L.O. 4**

Creighton Manufacturing Company had an excellent year. The company had hired a new marketing director in January. The new director's great motivational appeal had inspired the sales staff, and, as a result, sales were 20 percent higher than expected. In a recent management meeting, the company president, Jerry Selden, congratulated the marketing director and then criticized Mr. Colson, the company's production manager, because of an unfavorable fixed cost spending variance. Mr. Colson countered that the favorable fixed cost volume variance more than offset the unfavorable fixed cost spending variance. He argued that Mr. Selden should evaluate the two variances in total and that he should be rewarded rather than criticized.

Required
Do you agree with Mr. Colson's defense of the unfavorable fixed cost spending variance? Explain.

EXERCISE 8–9B *Assessing Responsibility for a Labor Cost Variance*   **L.O. 5**

Martindale Technologies Company's 2003 master budget called for using 60,000 hours of labor to produce 180,000 units of software. The standard labor rate for the company's employees is $19 per direct labor hour. Demand exceeded expectations, resulting in production and sales of 210,000 software units. Actual direct labor costs were $1,323,000. The year-end variance report showed a total unfavorable labor variance of $183,000.

Required
Assume you are the vice president of manufacturing. Should you criticize or praise the production supervisor's performance? Explain

EXERCISE 8–10B *Calculating the Materials Usage Variance*   **L.O. 9, 10**

Linda Feeney manages the Little Candy Shop, which was expected to sell 4,000 servings of its trademark candy during July. Each serving was expected to contain 6 ounces of candy. The standard cost of the candy was $0.10 per ounce. The shop actually sold 3,800 servings and actually used 22,100 ounces of candy.

Required
a. Compute the materials usage variance.
b. Explain what could have caused the variance that you computed in Requirement *a.*

EXERCISE 8–11B *Determining Materials Price and Usage Variances*   **L.O. 9**

Color It, Inc., makes paint that it sells in 1-gallon containers to retail home improvement stores. During 2004, the company planned to make 190,000 gallons of paint. It actually produced 198,000 gallons. The standard and actual quantity and cost of the color pigment for 1 gallon of paint follow.

	Standard	Actual
Quantity of materials per gallon	2.4 ounces	2.5 ounces
Price per ounce	× $0.30	× $0.32
Cost per gallon	$0.72	$0.80

Required

a. Determine the total flexible budget materials variance for pigment. Indicate whether the variance is favorable or unfavorable.

b. Determine the materials price variance and indicate whether the variance is favorable (F) or unfavorable (U).

c. Determine the materials usage variance and indicate whether the variance is favorable (F) or unfavorable (U).

d. Confirm your answers to Requirements *a, b,* and *c* by showing that the sum of the price and usage variances equals the total variance.

L.O. 9   **EXERCISE 8–12B** *Responsibility for Materials Price Variance*

Soft Treats, Inc., makes ice cream that it sells in 5 gallon containers to retail ice cream parlors. During 2002, the company planned to make 100,000 containers of ice cream. It actually produced 97,000 containers. The actual and standard quantity and cost of sugar per container follow.

	Standard	Actual
Quantity of materials per container	2 pounds	2.1 pounds
Price per pound	× $0.29	× $0.30
Cost per container	$0.58	$0.63

Required

a. Determine the materials price variance and indicate whether the variance is favorable (F) or unfavorable (U).

b. Determine the materials usage variance and indicate whether the variance is favorable (F) or unfavorable (U).

c. Explain how the production manager could have been responsible for the price variance.

L.O. 9, 10   **EXERCISE 8–13B** *Responsibility for Labor Rate and Usage Variance*

Brown Manufacturing Company incurred an unfavorable labor rate variance.

Required

a. Describe a scenario in which the personnel manager is responsible for the unfavorable rate variance.

b. Describe a scenario in which the production manager is responsible for the unfavorable rate variance.

L.O. 9, 10   **EXERCISE 8–14B** *Calculating and Explaining Labor Price and Usage Variances*

Bayou Landscaping Company established the following standard labor cost data to provide complete lawn care service (cutting, edging, trimming, and blowing) for a small lawn. Bayou expected each lawn to require 2 hours of labor at a cost of $12 per hour. The company actually serviced 400 lawns using an average of 1.75 labor hours per lawn. Actual labor costs were $14 per hour.

Required

a. Determine the total labor variance and indicate whether the variance is favorable (F) or unfavorable (U).

b. Determine the labor price variance and indicate whether the variance is favorable (F) or unfavorable (U).

c. Determine the labor usage variance and indicate whether the variance is favorable (F) or unfavorable (U).

d. Explain what could have caused the variances computed in Requirements *b* and *c.*

L.O. 9   **EXERCISE 8–15B** *Determining Standard Labor Hours*

Cutting Up, Inc., is a hair salon. It expected to provide 120 hair color treatments during December. Each treatment was expected to require 0.5 hours of labor at the standard labor rate of $15 per hour. The salon actually provided 125 treatments. The actual labor rate averaged $14.80. The labor price variance was $15 favorable.

Required

a. Determine the actual number of labor hours used per treatment.

b. Indicate whether the labor usage variance would be favorable (F) or unfavorable (U).

EXERCISE 8–16B *Calculating a Variable Overhead Variance*

L.O. 9, 10

Gupta Manufacturing Company established a predetermined variable overhead cost rate of $9.10 per direct labor hour. The actual variable overhead cost rate was $9.40 per direct labor hour. Gupta planned to use 150,000 hours of direct labor. It actually used 152,000 hours of direct labor.

Required
a. Determine the total flexible budget variable overhead cost variance.
b. Many companies do not subdivide the total variable overhead cost variance into price and usage components. Under what circumstances would it be appropriate to distinguish between the price and usage components of a variable overhead cost variance? What would be required to accomplish this type of analysis?

EXERCISE 8–17B *Determining and Interpreting Fixed Overhead Variances*

L.O. 9, 10

Khun Manufacturing Company established a predetermined fixed overhead cost rate of $135 per unit of product. The company planned to make 19,000 units of product but actually produced 20,000 units. Actual fixed overhead costs were $2,750,000.

Required
a. Determine the fixed overhead cost spending variance. Indicate whether the variance is favorable (F) or unfavorable (U). Explain what this variance means. Identify the manager(s) who is (are) responsible for the variance.
b. Determine the fixed overhead cost volume variance. Indicate whether the variance is favorable (F) or unfavorable (U). Explain what the designations *favorable* and *unfavorable* mean with respect to the fixed overhead volume variance.

PROBLEMS—SERIES B

PROBLEM 8–18B *Determining Sales Activity Variances*

L.O. 1, 4

Keelan Food Corporation developed the following standard price and costs for a refrigerated TV dinner that the company produces.

Standard price and variable costs	
Sales price	$12.98
Materials cost	4.50
Labor cost	1.30
Overhead cost	0.28
General, selling, and administrative costs	2.10
Expected fixed costs	
Manufacturing cost	$250,000
General, selling, and administrative costs	180,000

Keelan plans to make and sell 200,000 TV dinners.

Required
a. Prepare the pro forma income statement that would appear in the master budget.
b. Prepare flexible budget income statements, assuming production and sales volumes of 180,000 and 220,000 units.
c. Determine the sales activity variances, assuming production and sales volume are actually 190,000 units.
d. Indicate whether the variances are favorable (F) or unfavorable (U).
e. Comment on how Keelan could use the variances to evaluate performance.

PROBLEM 8–19B *Determining and Interpreting Flexible Budget Variances*

L.O. 5

Use the standard price and cost data supplied in Problem 8–18B. Assume that Keelan actually produced and sold 216,000 units. The actual sales price and costs incurred follow.

Actual price and variable costs	
Sales price	$12.90
Materials cost	4.40
Labor cost	1.34
Overhead cost	0.28
General, selling, and administrative costs	2.20
Actual fixed costs	
Manufacturing cost	$256,000.00
General, selling, and administrative costs	178,000.00

Required

a. Determine the flexible budget variances.

b. Indicate whether each variance is favorable (F) or unfavorable (U).

c. Identify the management position responsible for each variance. Explain what could have caused the variance.

L.O. 1   PROBLEM 8–20B *Flexible Budget Planning*

Executive officers of Pusan Seafood Processing Company are holding a planning session for fiscal year 2005. They have already established the following standard price and costs for their canned seafood product.

Standard price and variable costs	
Price per can	$6.00
Materials cost	2.10
Labor cost	1.28
Overhead cost	0.20
General, selling, and administrative costs	0.50
Expected fixed costs	
Production facility costs	$430,000.00
General, selling, and administrative costs	360,000.00

Required

a. Prepare the pro forma income statement that would appear in the master budget if the company expects to produce 600,000 cans of seafood in 2005.

b. A marketing consultant suggests to Pusan's president that the product's price may affect the number of cans the company can sell. According to the consultant's analysis, if the firm sets its price at $5.40, it could sell 810,000 cans of seafood. Prepare a flexible budget based on the consultant's suggestion.

c. The same consultant also suggests that if the company raises its price to $6.50 per can, the volume of sales would decline to 400,000. Prepare a flexible budget based on this suggestion.

d. Evaluate the three possible outcomes developed in Requirements *a, b,* and *c* and recommend a pricing strategy.

L.O. 9   PROBLEM 8–21B *Determining Materials Price and Usage Variances*

Baxton Swimsuit Specialties, Inc., makes fashionable women's swimsuits. Its most popular swimsuit, with the Sarong trade name, uses a standard fabric amount of 6 yards of raw material with a standard price of $2.50 per yard. The company planned to produce 100,000 Sarong swimsuits in 2004. At the end of 2004, the company's cost accountant reported that Baxton had used 636,000 square feet of fabric to make 102,000 swimsuits. Actual cost for the raw material was $1,653,600.

Required

a. Are flexible budget material variances based on the planned volume of 100,000 swimsuits or actual volume of 102,000 swimsuits?

b. Compute the actual price per yard of fabric.

c. Compute the standard quantity (yards of fabric) required to produce the swimsuits.

d. Compute the materials price variance and indicate whether it is favorable (F) or unfavorable (U).

e. Compute the materials usage variance and indicate whether it is favorable (F) or unfavorable (U).

L.O. 9   PROBLEM 8–22B *Determining Labor Price and Efficiency Variances*

As noted in Problem 8–21B, Baxton Swimsuit makes swimsuits. In 2004, Baxton produced its most popular swimsuit, the Sarong, for a standard labor price of $15 per hour. The standard amount of labor was

1.0 hour per swimsuit. The company had planned to produce 100,000 Sarong swimsuits. At the end of 2004, the company's cost accountant reported that Baxton had used 107,000 hours of labor to make 102,000 swimsuits. The total labor cost was $1,647,800.

Required

a. Should the labor variances be based on the planned volume of 100,000 swimsuits or on the actual volume of 102,000 swimsuits?

b. Prepare a table that shows the standard labor price, the actual labor price, the standard labor hours, and the actual labor hours.

c. Compute the labor price variance and indicate whether it is favorable (F) or unfavorable (U).

d. Compute the labor efficiency variance and indicate whether it is favorable (F) or unfavorable (U).

PROBLEM 8–23B *Computing Fixed Overhead Variances*   L.O. 9

Ryan Sporting Goods Co. manufactures baseballs. According to Ryan's 2002 budget, the company planned to incur $600,000 of fixed manufacturing overhead costs to make 200,000 baseballs. Ryan actually produced 187,000 balls, incurring $592,000 of actual fixed manufacturing overhead costs. Ryan establishes its predetermined overhead rate on the basis of the planned volume of production (expected number of baseballs).

Required

a. Calculate the predetermined overhead rate.

b. Determine the overhead spending variance and indicate whether it is favorable (F) or unfavorable (U).

c. Determine the overhead volume variance and indicate whether it is favorable (F) or unfavorable (U).

PROBLEM 8–24B *Computing Materials, Labor, and Overhead Variances*   L.O. 9

Ken Winslow was a new cost accountant at Winslow Plastics, Inc. He was assigned to analyze the following data that his predecessor left him.

Planned volume for year (static budget)	5,000 units
Standard direct materials cost per unit	2 lbs. @ $1.50 per pound
Standard direct labor cost per unit	0.5 hours @ $10.00 per hour
Total expected fixed overhead costs	$6,000
Actual volume for the year (flexible budget)	5,400 units
Actual direct materials cost per unit	1.9 lbs. @ $1.60 per pound
Actual direct labor cost per unit	0.6 hrs. @ $8.00 per hour
Total actual fixed overhead costs	$6,200

Required

a. Prepare a materials variance information table showing the standard price, the actual price, the standard quantity, and the actual quantity.

b. Calculate the materials price and quantity variances and indicate whether they are favorable (F) or unfavorable (U).

c. Prepare a labor variance information table showing the standard price, the actual price, the standard hours, and the actual hours.

d. Calculate the labor price and efficiency variances and indicate whether they are favorable (F) or unfavorable (U).

e. Calculate the predetermined overhead rate, assuming that Winslow Plastics uses the number of units as the allocation base.

f. Calculate the overhead spending variance and indicate whether it is favorable (F) or unfavorable (U).

g. Calculate the overhead volume variance and indicate whether it is favorable (F) or unfavorable (U).

PROBLEM 8–25B *Computing Materials, Labor, and Overhead Variances*   L.O. 9

Alderman Corporation makes mouse pads for computer users. After the first year of operation, Chelsea Alderman, the president and chief executive officer, was eager to determine the efficiency of the company's operation. In her analysis, she used the following standards provided by her assistant.

Units of planned production	200,000
Per unit direct materials	1 square foot @ $0.25 per square foot
Per unit direct labor	0.2 hrs. @ $7.00 per hr.
Total estimated fixed overhead costs	$100,000

Alderman purchased and used 230,000 square feet of material at an average cost of $0.24 per square foot. Labor usage amounted to 39,600 hours at an average of $6.90 per hour. Actual production amounted to 208,000 units. Actual fixed overhead costs amounted to $102,000. The company completed and sold all inventory for $707,200.

Required

a. Prepare a materials variance information table showing the standard price, the actual price, the standard quantity, and the actual quantity.

b. Calculate the materials price and usage variances and indicate whether they are favorable (F) or unfavorable (U).

c. Prepare a labor variance information table showing the standard price, the actual price, the standard hours, and the actual hours.

d. Calculate the labor price and efficiency variances and indicate whether they are favorable (F) or unfavorable (U).

e. Calculate the predetermined overhead rate, assuming that Alderman uses the number of units as the allocation base.

f. Calculate the overhead spending and volume variances and indicate whether they are favorable (F) or unfavorable (U).

g. Determine the amount of gross margin Alderman would report on the year-end income statement.

L.O. 9 PROBLEM 8–26B *Computing Variances*

A fire destroyed most of Medhat Products Corporation's records. Lucy Hines, the company's accountant, is trying to piece together the company's operating results from salvaged documents. She discovered the following data.

Standard materials quantity per unit	2.5 pounds
Standard materials price	$2 per pound
Standard labor quantity per unit	0.6 hour
Standard labor price	$12 per hour
Actual number of products produced	4,000 units
Materials price variance	$396 favorable
Materials quantity variance	$200 favorable
Labor price variance	$976 unfavorable
Labor usage variance	$480 unfavorable

Required

a. Determine the actual amount of materials used.

b. Determine the actual price per pound paid for materials.

c. Determine the actual labor hours used.

d. Determine the actual labor price per hour.

L.O. 9 PROBLEM 8–27B *Computing Standard Cost and Analyzing Variances*

Norton Manufacturing Company, which makes aluminum alloy wheels for automobiles, recently introduced a new luxury wheel that fits small sports cars. The company developed the following standards for its new product.

Amount of direct materials per wheel	2 pounds
Price of direct materials per pound	$5.50
Quantity of labor per wheel	2.5 hours
Price of direct labor per hour	$8.00/hour
Total budgeted fixed overhead	$168,000

In its first year of operation, Norton expected to produce 3,000 sets of wheels (four wheels per set). Because of unexpected demand, it actually produced 3,600 sets of wheels. By year-end direct materials purchased and used amounted to 30,000 pounds of aluminum at a cost of $175,500. Direct labor costs were actually $8.40 per hour. Actual hours worked were 2.2 hours per wheel. Overhead for the year actually amounted to $180,000. Overhead is applied to products using a predetermined overhead rate based on the total estimated number of wheels to be produced.

Required

(Round all computations to two decimal places.)

a. Compute the standard cost per wheel for direct materials, direct labor, and overhead.
b. Determine the total standard cost per wheel.
c. Compute the actual cost per wheel for direct materials, direct labor, and overhead.
d. Compute the actual cost per wheel.
e. Compute the price and usage variances for direct materials and direct labor. Identify any variances that Norton should investigate. Based on your results, offer a possible explanation for the labor usage variance.
f. Compute the fixed overhead spending and volume variances. Explain your findings.

PROBLEM 8–28B *Analyzing Not-for-Profit Organization Variances*

L.O. 3, 4, 5

The Finance Department of Eastern State University planned to hold its annual distinguished visiting lecturer (DVL) presentation in October 2005. The secretary of the department prepared the following budget based on costs that had been incurred in the past for the DVL presentation.

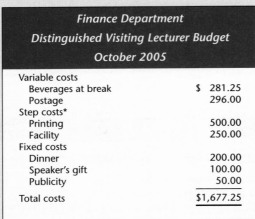

Finance Department Distinguished Visiting Lecturer Budget October 2005	
Variable costs	
Beverages at break	$ 281.25
Postage	296.00
Step costs*	
Printing	500.00
Facility	250.00
Fixed costs	
Dinner	200.00
Speaker's gift	100.00
Publicity	50.00
Total costs	$1,677.25

*Step costs are costs that change abruptly after a defined range of volume (attendance). They do not change proportionately with unit volume increases (i.e., the cost is fixed within a range of activity but changes to a different fixed cost when the volume changes to a new range). For instance, the facility charge is $250 for from 1 to 400 attendees. From 401 to 500 attendees, the next larger room is needed, and the charge is $350. If more than 500 attended, the room size and cost would increase again.

The budget for the presentation was based on the following expectations:
1. Attendance was estimated at 50 faculty from Eastern State and neighboring schools, 125 invited guests from the business community, and 200 students. Beverage charge per attendee would be $0.75. The cost driver for beverages is the number of attendees.
2. Postage was based on $0.37 per invitation; 800 invitations were expected to be mailed to faculty and finance business executives. The cost driver for postage is the number of invitations mailed.
3. Printing cost was expected to be $500 for 800 invitations and envelopes. Additional invitations and envelopes could be purchased in batches of 100 units with each batch costing $50.
4. The DVL presentation was scheduled at a downtown convention center. The facility charge was $250 for a room that has a capacity of 400 persons; the charge for one to hold more than 400 people was $350. The convention center provided refreshments at break except beverages.
5. After the presentation, three Eastern State faculty members planned to take the speaker to dinner. The dinner had been prearranged at a local restaurant for $200 for a three-course dinner.
6. A gift for the speaker was budgeted at $100.
7. Publicity would consist of flyers and posters placed at strategic locations around campus and business offices, articles in the business section of the local newspapers, and announcements made in business classes and school newspapers. Printing for the posters and flyers had been prearranged for $50.
8. The speaker lives in the adjoining state and had agreed to drive to the presentation at his own expense.

The actual results of the presentation follow.
1. Attendance consisted of 450 faculty, business executives, and students.
2. An additional 100 invitations were printed and mailed when the Finance Department decided that selected alumni should also be invited.

3. Based on RSVP responses, the department rented the next size larger room at a cost of $350 for the presentation.
4. The speaker's gift cost was as budgeted.
5. The department chairperson decided to have a four-course dinner, which cost $230.
6. Because of poor planning, the posters and flyers were not distributed as widely as expected. It was decided at the last minute to hire a temporary assistant to make phone calls to alumni. The actual publicity cost was $75.

Required

a. Prepare a flexible budget and compute activity variances based on a comparison between the master budget and the flexible budget. Briefly explain the meaning of the activity variances.
b. Compute flexible budget variances by comparing the flexible budget with the actual results. Briefly explain the meaning of the variable cost flexible budget variances. Discuss the fixed cost variances.
c. Calculate the expected and actual fixed cost per attendee. Discuss the significance of the difference in these amounts.
d. Since the department is a not-for-profit entity, why is it important for it to control the cost of sponsoring the distinguished visiting lecturer presentation?

ANALYZE, THINK, COMMUNICATE

ATC 8–1   BUSINESS APPLICATIONS CASE *Static Versus Flexible Budget Variances*

Ken Juneau is the manufacturing production supervisor for Pacific Lamp Company. Trying to explain why he did not get the year-end bonus that he had expected, he told his wife, "This is the dumbest place I ever worked. Last year the company set up this budget assuming it would sell 150,000 lamps. Well, it sold only 140,000. The company lost money and gave me a bonus for not using as much materials and labor as was called for in the budget. This year, the company has the same 150,000 goal and it sells 160,000. The company's making all kinds of money. You'd think I'd get this big fat bonus. Instead, management tells me I used more materials and labor than was budgeted. They say the company would have made a lot more money if I'd stayed within my budget. I guess I gotta wait for another bad year before I get a bonus. Like I said, this is the dumbest place I ever worked."

Pacific Lamp Company's master budget and the actual results for the most recent year of operating activity follow.

	Master Budget	Actual Results	Variances	F or U
Number of units	150,000	160,000	10,000	
Sales revenue	$33,000,000	$35,520,000	$2,520,000	F
Variable manufacturing costs				
Materials	4,800,000	5,300,000	500,000	U
Labor	4,200,000	4,400,000	200,000	U
Overhead	2,100,000	2,290,000	190,000	U
Variable G, S, & A	5,250,000	6,180,000	930,000	U
Contribution margin	$16,650,000	$17,350,000	$ 700,000	F
Fixed costs				
Manufacturing	7,830,000	7,830,000	0	
G, S, & A	6,980,000	6,980,000	0	
Net income	$ 1,840,000	$ 2,540,000	$ 700,000	F

Required

a. Did the marketing department increase sales by lowering prices or by using some other strategy?
b. Is Mr. Juneau correct in his conclusion that something is wrong with Pacific Lamp Company's performance evaluation system? If so, make suggestions for improving the system.
c. Prepare a flexible budget and determine the amount of the flexible budget variances.
d. With respect to the flexible budget variances, assume that the materials price variance was favorable and the usage variance was unfavorable. Explain why Mr. Juneau may not have been responsible for the usage variance. Explain why he may have been responsible for the usage variance.

e. With respect to the flexible budget variances, assume that the labor price variance is unfavorable. Was the labor usage variance favorable (F) or unfavorable (U)?

f. Is the fixed cost volume variance favorable (F) or unfavorable (U)? Explain its effect on the cost per lamp.

GROUP ASSIGNMENT *Variable Price and Usage Variances and Fixed Cost Variances*

ATC 8–2

Kemp Tables, Inc. (KTI), makes picnic tables of 2 × 4 planks of treated pine. It sells the tables to large retail discount stores such as Wal-Mart. After reviewing the following data generated by KTI's chief accountant, Arianne Darwin, the company president, expressed concern that the total manufacturing cost was more than $0.5 million above budget ($7,084,800 − $6,520,000 = $564,800).

	Actual Results	Master Budget
Cost of planks per table	$ 44.10	$ 40.00
Cost of labor per table	26.10	25.50
Total variable manufacturing cost per table (a)	$ 70.20	$ 65.50
Total number of tables produced (b)	82,000	80,000
Total variable manufacturing cost (a × b)	$5,756,400	$5,240,000
Total fixed manufacturing cost	1,328,400	1,280,000
Total manufacturing cost	$7,084,800	$6,520,000

Ms. Darwin asked Conrad Pearson, KTI's chief accountant, to explain what caused the increase in cost. Mr. Pearson responded that things were not as bad as they seemed. He noted that part of the cost variance resulted from making and selling more tables than had been expected. Making more tables naturally causes the cost of materials and labor to be higher. He explained that the flexible budget cost variance was less than $0.5 million. Specifically, he provided the following comparison.

	Actual Results	Flexible Budget
Cost of planks per table	$ 44.10	$ 40.00
Cost of labor per table	26.10	25.50
Total variable manufacturing cost per table (a)	$ 70.20	$ 65.50
Total number of tables produced (b)	82,000	82,000
Total variable manufacturing cost (a × b)	$5,756,400	$5,371,000
Total fixed manufacturing cost	1,328,400	1,280,000
Total manufacturing cost	$7,084,800	$6,651,000

Based on this information, he argued that the relevant variance for performance evaluation was only $433,800 ($7,084,800 − $6,651,000). Ms. Darwin responded, "*Only* $433,800! I consider that a very significant number. By the end of the day, I want a full explanation as to what is causing our costs to increase."

Required

a. Divide the class into groups of four or five students and divide the groups into three sections. Assign Task 1 to the first section, Task 2 to the second section, and Task 3 to the third section.

Group Tasks

1. Based on the following information, determine the total materials cost variance and the price and usage variances. Assuming that the variances are an appropriate indicator of cause, explain what could have caused the variances. Identify the management position responsible.

	Actual Data	Standard Data
Number of planks per table	21	20
Price per plank	× $2.10	× $2.00
Material cost per table	$44.10	$40.00

2. Based on the following information, determine the total labor cost variance and the price and usage variances. Assuming that the variances are an appropriate indicator of cause, explain what could have caused each variance. Identify the management position responsible.

	Actual Data	Standard Data
Number of hours per table	2.9	3.0
Price per hour	× $9.00	× $8.50
Labor cost per table	$26.10	$25.50

3. Determine the amount of the fixed cost spending and volume variances. Explain what could have caused these variances. Based on the volume variance, indicate whether the actual fixed cost per unit would be higher or lower than the budgeted fixed cost per unit.

b. Select a spokesperson from each section to report the amount of the variances computed by the group. Reconcile any differences in the variances reported by the sections. Reconcile the individual variances with the total variance. Specifically, show that the total of the materials, labor, and overhead variances equals the total flexible budget variance ($433,800).

c. Discuss how Ms. Darwin should react to the variance information.

ATC 8–3　RESEARCH ASSIGNMENT　*Nonfinancial Performance Measures*

The article "How Nonfinancial Performance Measures Are Used" (*Management Accounting*, February 1998) describes several emerging performance measures that do not rely on financial data. Read this article and complete the following requirements.

Required

a. What are nonfinancial performance measures? Provide several examples.

b. The article describes five categories of nonfinancial performance measures. Identify these categories. Which category do executives consider most important?

c. Can you compute variances for nonfinancial performance measures? Explain.

d. Comment on the extent to which executives use nonfinancial measures.

e. The authors indicate that their study identified three red flags that executives need to address to use nonfinancial performance measures more effectively. Identify and briefly discuss these three red flags.

ATC 8–4　WRITING ASSIGNMENT　*Standard Costing—The Human Factor*

Kemp Corporation makes a protein supplement called Power Punch™. Its principal competitor for Power Punch is the protein supplement Superior Strength™, made by Jim Adams Company (JAC). Mr. Adams, a world-renowned weight-lifting champion, founded JAC. The primary market for both products is athletes. Kemp sells Power Punch to wellness stores, which sell it, other supplements, and health foods to the public. In contrast, Superior Strength is advertised in sports magazines and sold through orders generated by the ads.

Mr. Adams's fame is an essential factor in his company's advertising program. He is a dynamic character whose personality motivates people to strive for superior achievement. His demeanor not only stimulates sales but also provides a strong inspirational force for company employees. He is a kind, understanding individual with high expectations who is fond of saying that "mistakes are just opportunities for improvement." Mr. Adams is a strong believer in total quality management.

Mr. Quayle, president of Kemp Corporation, is a stern disciplinarian who believes in teamwork. He takes pride in his company's standard costing system. Managers work as a team to establish standards and then are held accountable for meeting them. Managers who fail to meet expectations are severely chastised, and continued failure leads to dismissal. After several years of rigorous enforcement, managers have fallen in line. Indeed, during the last two years, all managers have met their budget goals.

Even so, costs have risen steadily. These cost increases have been passed on to customers through higher prices. As a result, Power Punch is now priced significantly higher than Superior Strength. In fact, Superior Strength is selling directly to the public at a price that is below the wholesale price that Kemp is charging the wellness stores. The situation has reached a critical juncture. Sales of Power Punch are falling while Superior Strength is experiencing significant growth. Given that industry sales have remained relatively stable, it is obvious that customers are shifting from Power Punch to Superior Strength. Mr. Quayle is perplexed. He wonders how a company with direct market expenses can price its products so low.

Required
a. Explain why JAC has been able to gain a pricing advantage over Kemp.
b. Assume that you are a consultant whom Kemp's board of directors has asked to recommend how to halt the decline in sales of Power Punch. Provide appropriate recommendations.

ETHICAL DILEMMA *Budget Games*

ATC 8–5

Melody Lovelady is the most highly rewarded sales representative at Swift Corporation. Her secret to success is always to understate your abilities. Ms. Lovelady is assigned to a territory in which her customer base is increasing at approximately 25 percent per year. Each year she estimates that her budgeted sales will be 10 percent higher than her previous year's sales. With little effort, she is able to double her budgeted sales growth. At Swift's annual sales meeting, she receives an award and a large bonus. Of course, Ms. Lovelady does not disclose her secret to her colleagues. Indeed, she always talks about how hard it is to continue to top her previous performance. She tells herself if they are dumb enough to fall for this rubbish, I'll milk it for all it's worth.

Required
a. What is the name commonly given to the budget game Ms. Lovelady is playing?
b. Does Ms. Lovelady's behavior violate any of the standards of ethical conduct shown in Exhibit 1–13 of Chapter 1?
c. Recommend how Ms. Lovelady's budget game could be stopped.

SPREADSHEET ASSIGNMENT *Using Excel*

ATC 8–6

Irvine Publications established the following standard price and costs for a hard cover picture book that the company produces.

Standard price and variable costs	
Sales price	$48.00
Materials cost	12.00
Labor cost	6.00
Overhead cost	8.40
General, selling, and administrative costs	9.60
Expected fixed costs	
Manufacturing	$180,000
General, selling, and administrative	72,000

Irvine planned to make and sell 30,000 copies of the book.

Required
Construct a spreadsheet like the one shown in Exhibit 8–1 to illustrate a static budget and a flexible budget for production volumes of 28,000, 29,000, 30,000, 31,000, and 32,000.

SPREADSHEET ASSIGNMENT *Mastering Excel*

ATC 8–7

Wilkin Fruit Drink Company planned to make 400,000 containers of apple juice. It expected to use two cups of frozen apple concentrate to make each container of juice, thus using 800,000 cups (400,000 containers $\times$ 2 cups) of frozen concentrate. The standard price of one cup of apple concentrate is $0.25. Actually, Wilkin produced 404,000 containers of apple juice and purchased and used 820,000 cups of concentrate at $0.26 per cup.

Required
a. Construct a spreadsheet template that could be used to calculate price and usage variances. The template should be constructed so that it could be used for any problem in the chapter that refers to price and usage variances by changing the data in the spreadsheet. The screen capture on page 364 represents a template for price and usage variances.

Spreadsheet Tip
(1) The shaded cells can be changed according to the data in each problem. All other cells are formulas based on the numbers in the shaded cells.
(2) The cells that label the variances as F or U (favorable (F) or unfavorable (U)) are based on a function called IF. The IF function is needed because the variance can be either favorable or

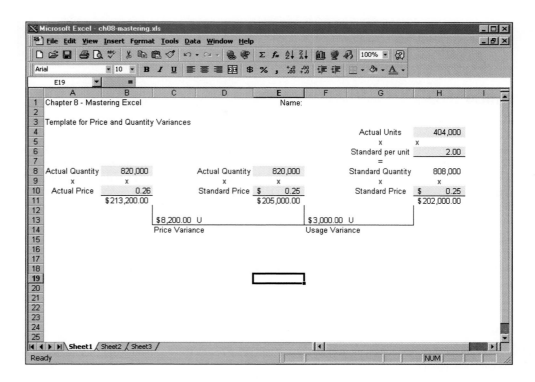

unfavorable. The formula must determine whether actual expenditures exceed budgeted expenditures to determine whether the variance is unfavorable or favorable. As an example, the formula in cell D13 is =IF(B11>E11,'U','F'). The formula evaluates the expression B11>E11. If this expression is true (B11 is greater than E11), the text U is inserted in cell D13. The IF function can also be used to place formulas or numbers in a cell based on whether an expression is true or false. For example, the formula =IF(B11>E11,B11−E11,E11−B11) would calculate the amount of the variance as a positive number regardless of which amount is larger.

(3) An easier way to make the variance a positive number regardless of whether it is favorable or unfavorable is to use the absolute value function. The format of the formula in cells C13 and F13 would be =ABS(left number − right number).

(4) The lines around the variances are produced by using the borders in Excel (Format, Cells, Border).

Chapter

9

Responsibility Accounting

Learning Objectives

After completing this chapter, you should be able to:

1 Understand the concept of decentralization and describe its relationship to responsibility accounting.

2 Prepare and use responsibility reports.

3 Understand the controllability concept.

4 Explain how the management by exception doctrine relates to responsibility reports.

5 Understand the differences in cost, profit, and investment centers.

6 Evaluate investment opportunities by using the return on investment technique.

7 Evaluate investment opportunities by using the residual income technique.

8 Understand the three common approaches used to establish transfer prices.

the *curious* accountant

Donald V. Fites is the chief executive officer of Caterpillar Inc. (Cat), a giant corporation with worldwide operations. Indeed, in 1998 more than 51 percent of its sales came from overseas. Mr. Fites hopes to increase that percentage to more than 75 percent by the end of the next decade. Accordingly, he spends a considerable amount of time analyzing the impact of foreign economies on Cat sales. When not involved in international issues, Mr. Fites is speaking to improve the company's fragile relationship with the United Autoworkers. In the 1990s, Mr. Fites spearheaded a $2 billion investment to modernize his company's U.S. plants. With things such as these on his agenda, how does Mr. Fites know that the company's purchasing agent is not paying too much for the paint used to color and protect its equipment?

Walter Keller is a production manager for Evans Corporation. His budget includes a monthly allowance of $20,000 for labor costs. During April, his employees became unusually lethargic, everyone just seemed to slow down. They spoke of spring fever, beautiful weather, and a desire to be outside. The result was a decline in productivity, higher labor costs, and an unfavorable budget variance. Does this mean that the budget failed to control the labor costs? The answer is no. People, not budgets, control costs. In this case, Mr. Keller is responsible for the cost overrun.

*Budgeting is merely a tool that is used in the process of cost control. The actual control of cost is the responsibility of management. **Responsibility accounting** focuses reporting on individual managers; its objective is to increase productivity by providing information that is helpful in evaluating managerial performance. For example, expense items that the production department manager controls are presented in one report and the items that the marketing department manager controls are presented in a different report. This chapter discusses the development and utilization of a responsibility accounting system.*

▌Decentralization Concept

LO1 Understand the concept of decentralization and describe its relationship to responsibility accounting.

Clear lines of authority and responsibility are essential in establishing a responsibility accounting system. Divisions of authority and responsibility normally occur as a natural consequence of the management function. In a small business, it is possible for one person to control the entire operation. This person is able to perform all of the necessary functions such as marketing, management, production, and accounting because of the simplicity of the business structure. In contrast, the level of complexity in large corporations is so great that it precludes using a single decision maker.

Consider as an example the decision to hire employees. In a small business, the owner/operator works in the business and is familiar with the job requirements, level of skill required, and local wage rates. She is, therefore, in a position to make a decision as to whom to offer a job. A major corporation, however, may have thousands of different jobs that require different skill levels. These jobs must be performed in a variety of locations that have different wage rate structures. Obviously, the president of the corporation cannot know all that is necessary to make informed hiring decisions for the entire company. Instead, he delegates that responsibility to individuals who are knowledgeable about the particular circumstances associated with the hiring decisions. Accordingly, a personnel department may be established to handle employment practices and policies.

Similarly, other departments or divisions will be established to delegate the decision-making authority to the individuals who are best suited to making the decision. The practice of delegating authority and responsibility is referred to as **decentralization.** Some of the advantages of decentralization include the following.

1. *Encourages upper-level management to concentrate on strategic decisions.* Because local management makes routine decisions, upper-level management has more time to concentrate on long-term planning, goal setting, and performance evaluation.
2. *Promotes improvements in decision making.* Local managers are usually better informed about local issues. Furthermore, their proximity to these issues permits them to react more rapidly to developing events. As a result, local managers are generally able to make better decisions.
3. *Motivates managers to improve productivity.* The freedom to act coupled with responsibility for the actions taken results in an environment that encourages most individuals to perform at high levels.
4. *Trains lower-level managers to accept greater responsibilities.* Decision making is a general skill. Managers who are accustomed to making decisions regarding local issues are generally able to apply their decision-making skills to broader issues when they are promoted to upper management positions.
5. *Improves performance evaluation.* When lines of authority and responsibility are clearly drawn, credit or blame can be more easily assigned based on the results achieved.

Decentralization can also have detrimental effects. If authority is too widely disbursed, the cohesiveness of the overall organization may suffer. Five people working independently on a project will accomplish less than five people who put forth a team effort. For example, if each player on a basketball team were interested only in maximizing the number of points she scored personally, the total team score would suffer. Instead of passing the ball to a teammate who was in a good position to score, players would take poor shots to improve their personal scores. Managers in decentralized organizations must be encouraged to develop a team mentality; the benefit to the firm as a whole must take priority over personal successes or failures of any particular manager. Authority and responsibility should be delegated in a manner that promotes achieving the goals of the total firm.

▌Organization Chart

Exhibit 9–1 is a partial organization chart showing the lines of authority and responsibility of a decentralized business. The chart includes five levels of responsibility. Other companies may

have more or fewer responsibility levels, depending on their respective needs to decentralize. The responsibility levels are arranged in a hierarchical order with responsibility reports moving from the bottom upward. The information contained in the responsibility reports is cumulative; in other words, each manager receives detailed information about his or her particular responsibility level plus summary information about all responsibility centers that are under his chain of authority.

▌ Responsibility Reports

A **responsibility report** is prepared for each individual who has control over revenue or expense items. It normally includes a list of the items under that person's control, the budgeted amount for each item, the actual amount spent for each item, and the difference between the budgeted and actual amounts (the variance). The report shows the manager what was expected of her and how her actual performance compared to those expectations.

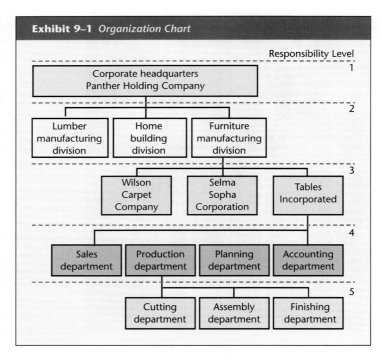

Exhibit 9–1 *Organization Chart*

LO2 Prepare and use responsibility reports.

Controllability Concept

The **controllability concept** is crucial to an effective responsibility accounting system. Each manager's evaluation should be based on only the revenue or cost items that he controls. Motivation is lost when a manager is rewarded or punished for actions that are beyond the scope of his control. Unfortunately, control may be shared rather than absolute. An actual case may serve to illustrate this point.

LO3 Understand the controllability concept.

Dorothy Pasework, a buyer for a large department store chain, was held responsible for the retail sales of the goods that she purchased from wholesalers because it is the buyer's responsibility to purchase goods that can be resold. She purchased a large inventory of copper cookware that she thought would sell rapidly during the Christmas season. The expected sales failed to materialize, and upper management criticized Ms. Pasework's purchase. She complained that she was not at fault because the sales staff had not marketed the cookware properly, citing two instances in which she had personally visited stores that were not displaying the cookware in accordance with her instructions. The sales staff charged that the potential for selling the cookware was insufficient to merit the effort necessary to set up a proper display.

The exercise of control is frequently clouded as the preceding case illustrates. Accordingly, managers are usually held responsible for items over which they exercise *predominant* rather than *absolute* control. This practice can lead to motivational problems. Business operates in an imperfect world, however, and certain compromises must be accepted to continue operating activity. At times responsibility accounting may not be completely fair, but it has proven to be an effective means of motivation in most situations. It is management's job to ensure that the numbers generated in a responsibility accounting system are properly interpreted and that rewards and punishments are administered fairly.

Management by Exception and Degree of Summarization

Responsibility reports are arranged in a manner that promotes the use of the **management by exception** doctrine. As noted earlier, the reports of a particular manager contain detailed

LO4 Explain how the management by exception doctrine relates to responsibility reports.

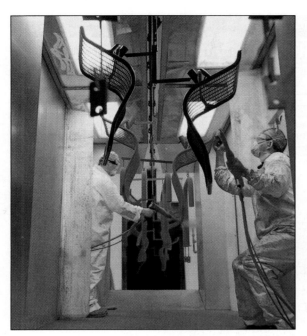

information about revenue and cost items that are directly under his control, as well as summary data with regard to the activities of the responsibility centers that fall under his authority. We will use the chain of command as shown in Exhibit 9–1 as an example.

Starting with the Finishing department at the fifth level of responsibility, the supervisor's report would contain all of the cost and revenue items under her control. For example, the report would include the salary expenses of the employees who work in the Finishing department; the expenses associated with the direct materials such as paint, supplies, and small tools used in the department; and any other expenses over which the supervisor had control. The report for the manager of the Production department (the fourth level) would include the *total* of the items shown in the Finishing department's report. It would also include the report *totals* of the other departments under the production manager's chain of authority (i.e., Cutting and Assembly departments). In addition, the production manager's report would include a detailed account of the individual items for which he was personally responsible. These items may include administrative staff expenses and supervisory salaries.

The responsibility report for the manager of Tables Incorporated (third level) would include summary totals from the reports of the fourth-level managers (Sales, Production, Planning and Accounting departments) and a detailed analysis of the items under her direct control. This method of summarization continues up the chain of command.

Ultimately, headquarters personnel would receive summary data from the division managers and would add their particular revenue and expense items to those data. The data at headquarters level (first level) would include all revenue and expense items because full responsibility rests at the top of the organization. Accordingly, headquarters personnel usually prepare year-to-date financial statements to gain an understanding of the current financial condition.

Note that each manager receives only *summary* information regarding the performance of the responsibility centers that are under his supervision. For example, the production manager will be advised as to the amount of the *total* budget variance incurred by the Finishing department but is not informed as to the cause of the variance. That information is reported only to the supervisor of the Finishing department. At first glance, the lack of detailed information may appear to hinder the production manager's ability to control costs. In fact, it has the opposite effect. Be aware that managers are normally very busy individuals who must ration their time carefully. The supervisor of the Finishing department should look at her responsibility report and take the necessary corrective action without bothering the production manager. The production manager should become concerned only when one of his supervisors loses control. The summary data in the production manager's report will be sufficient to advise him of such situations. Accordingly, managers will concentrate only on the exceptional items (management by exception), which will be automatically highlighted in their responsibility reports.

Qualitative Reporting Features

Responsibility reports should be stated in simple terms. If they are too complex, managers will ignore them. The reports should show clearly the budgeted and actual amounts of controllable revenue and expense items. Variances should be highlighted to promote the management by exception doctrine. Regular communication between the report preparer and the report user should be maintained to ensure the relevance of the information. Furthermore, reports must be issued on a timely basis. A report that describes yesterday's problem is not nearly as useful as one that reports today's problem. The utility of information tends to decrease with the passage of time.

Responsibility Reports Illustrated

Exhibit 9–2 is a partial set of responsibility reports for the second through fifth levels of Panther Holding Company. Before analyzing these reports, you may find it useful to review Panther's organization chart in Exhibit 9–1. From the lower level upward, each successive report contains summary data from the preceding report. For example, the total $150 unfavorable variance in the Finishing department's report is a single line item in the Production department's report.

The illustration demonstrates how the summary data are useful in employing the management by exception doctrine. For example, a cursory review of the Furniture Manufacturing

Exhibit 9–2 *Responsibility Reports*

PANTHER HOLDING COMPANY
Second Level: Furniture Manufacturing Division
For the Month Ended January 31, 2004

	Budget	Actual	Variance	
Controllable expenses				
Administrative Division expense	$ 20,400	$ 31,100	$(10,700)	U
Company president's salary	9,600	9,200	400	F
Wilson Carpet Company	82,100	78,400	3,700	F
Selma Sopha Corporation	87,200	116,700	(29,500)	U
Tables Incorporated	48,600	51,250	(2,650)	U
Total	$247,900	$286,650	$(38,750)	U

PANTHER HOLDING COMPANY
Third Level: Tables Incorporated
For the Month Ended January 31, 2004

	Budget	Actual	Variance	
Controllable expenses				
Administrative Division expense	$ 3,000	$ 2,800	$ 200	F
Department managers' salaries	10,000	11,200	(1,200)	U
Sales Department costs	9,100	8,600	500	F
Production Department costs	13,500	13,750	(250)	U
Planning Department costs	4,800	7,000	(2,200)	U
Accounting Department costs	8,200	7,900	300	F
Total	$ 48,600	$ 51,250	$ (2,650)	U

PANTHER HOLDING COMPANY
Fourth Level: Production Department
For the Month Ended January 31, 2004

	Budget	Actual	Variance	
Controllable expenses				
Administrative Staff expense	$ 900	$ 1,100	$ (200)	U
Supervisory salaries	2,800	2,800	0	
Cutting Department costs	1,400	1,200	200	F
Assembly Department costs	2,800	2,900	(100)	U
Finishing Department costs	5,600	5,750	(150)	U
Total	$ 13,500	$ 13,750	$ (250)	U

PANTHER HOLDING COMPANY
Fifth Level: Finishing Department
For the Month Ended January 31, 2004

	Budget	Actual	Variance	
Controllable expenses				
Wages expenses	$ 3,200	$ 3,000	$ 200	F
Direct materials	1,100	1,400	(300)	U
Supplies	400	500	(100)	U
Small tools	600	650	(50)	U
Other expenses	300	200	100	F
Total	$ 5,600	$ 5,750	$ (150)	U

Division's report indicates that the division manager should concentrate her efforts on two areas. First, Selma Sopha Corporation's expenditures are out of line as evidenced by the $29,500 unfavorable variance. Furthermore, the Furniture Manufacturing Division manager's administrative expenses are well above the budget expectations. Based on this information, the manager should ask for detailed reports covering these two areas. Management's attention is automatically directed to the areas that need the most supervision. The other areas seem to be operating within reasonable bounds and can be left to the direction of their respective managers.

A responsibility report would also be prepared for the first responsibility level, corporate headquarters. The report would be similar to those shown in Exhibit 9–2. Furthermore, at least at the headquarters level, year-to-date earnings statements would be prepared to inform management of the company's over-all performance. Many times divisions or companies operating within divisions also prepare year-to-date earnings statements that are used for managerial purposes and therefore are normally prepared in a contribution margin format. The January 2004 earnings statement for the Panther Holding Company is shown in Exhibit 9–3.

Exhibit 9–3 *Panther Earnings Statement*

PANTHER HOLDING COMPANY
Earnings Statement for Internal Use
For the Month Ended January 31, 2004

	Budget	Actual	Variance	
Sales	$984,300	$962,300	$(22,000)	U
Variable expenses				
Variable product costs	343,100	352,250	(9,150)	U
Variable selling expenses	105,000	98,000	7,000	F
Other variable expenses	42,200	51,100	(8,900)	U
Total variable expenses	490,300	501,350	(11,050)	U
Contribution margin	494,000	460,950	(33,050)	U
Fixed expenses				
Fixed product cost	54,100	62,050	(7,950)	U
Fixed selling expense	148,000	146,100	1,900	F
Other fixed expenses	23,000	25,250	(2,250)	U
Total fixed expenses	225,100	233,400	(8,300)	U
Net income	$268,900	$227,550	$(41,350)	U

■ Responsibility Centers

LO5 Understand the differences in cost, profit, and investment centers.

A **responsibility center** is the point in an organization where the control over revenue or expense items is located. The point of control may be a division, a department, a subdepartment, or even a single machine. For example, a transportation company may identify a semitrailer truck as a responsibility center. The company holds the driver of the truck responsible for the revenue and expense items associated with operating the truck. Responsibility centers may be divided into three categories: cost, profit, and investment.

A **cost center** is a business segment that incurs expenses but does not generate revenue. Managers of cost centers can only influence costs; they cannot control them. In the Panther organization chart (see Exhibit 9–1), the Finishing Department and the Production Department are representative cost centers. As the illustration implies, cost centers normally exist at the lower levels of the organization chart.

A **profit center** differs from a cost center in that it not only incurs costs but also generates income. In other words, this responsibility center can influence both revenue and expense items. The manager of a cost center is judged on his ability to control costs within a budget range, but the manager of a profit center is judged on her ability to produce revenue in excess of expenses. In the Panther organization chart, the companies at the third-level (Wilson

In fact, Mr. Fites does not need to know whether too much is being spent for paint. Such operational details are assigned to lower-level managers. Caterpillar's operations are so complex that a single person cannot possibly supervise its activities directly. Instead, authority and responsibility are delegated to competent managers under whose direction the functions are performed. Organizations such as Caterpillar could not function without the implementation of the principles of decentralization.

Carpet Company, Selma Sopha Corporation, and Tables Incorporated) are considered profit centers.

Investment center managers are responsible for revenue and expense items and for the investment of capital. Accordingly, these managers are held accountable for assets and liabilities as well as earnings. Investment centers are normally located at the upper-levels of the organization chart. The second-level division managers in the Panther organization are in charge of investment centers (managers of the lumber, home, and furniture divisions).

Managerial Performance Measurement

One of the primary purposes of a responsibility accounting system is to facilitate the measurement of managerial performance. Managers are assigned responsibility for certain cost, profit, or investment centers. Managerial performance can be measured by comparing the operating results of the assigned responsibility center with established standards or with the results of other responsibility centers within the organization.

In general, managers of cost centers are evaluated on the basis of their ability to attain preestablished standards by comparing actual costs with standard costs. Favorable variances indicate good performance and unfavorable variances suggest poor performance. In contrast, the results of profit centers are normally evaluated on the basis of earnings that are reported in a contribution format. The actual earnings may be compared with budgeted amounts, previous results, or the earnings of other profit centers. The results of investment centers must be evaluated on the basis of assets invested as well as revenue and expense measures. The measurement techniques (standard cost and contribution margin format income reporting) used for cost and profit centers have been discussed in previous chapters. The remainder of this chapter is devoted to discussing performance measures that are applicable to investment centers.

Return on Investment

Businesses use assets to obtain more assets. For example, a grocery store uses cash to purchase inventory. The inventory is converted back to cash when it is sold to customers. If the business is profitable, the amount of cash received from the sale of the inventory will exceed the amount of cash that was used to purchase the inventory. Performance can be measured by the ability to increase the ratio of the assets returned to the amount of assets used. This measure is commonly referred to as the **return on investment** (ROI). It can be expressed in a simple equation.

LO6 Evaluate investment opportunities by using the return on investment technique.

$$ROI = \frac{\text{Net income}}{\text{Investment}}$$

To illustrate the use of ROI as an evaluation technique, assume that two managers are given $1,000 each to invest. The first manager invests in a certificate of deposit that earns $110 per year. The second manager invests in inventory that is sold at a $120 profit. The two managers' respective ROIs are computed as follows.

First Manager

$$ROI = \frac{\text{Net income}}{\text{Investment}} = \frac{\$110}{\$1,000} = 11\%$$

Second Manager

$$ROI = \frac{\text{Net income}}{\text{Investment}} = \frac{\$120}{\$1,000} = 12\%$$

Based on *quantitative* information alone, the second manager's performance is superior to the performance of the first manager. In other words, a higher ROI indicates better performance.

Check Yourself 9–1

Green View is a lawn services company whose operations are divided into two districts. The District 1 manager controls $12,600,000 of assets. District 1 produced $1,512,000 of net income during the year. The District 2 manager controls $14,200,000 of assets. District 2 reported $1,988,000 of net income for the same period. Use return on investment to determine which manager is performing better.

Answer

District 1

$$ROI = \text{Net income} \div \text{Investment} = \$1,512,000 \div \$12,600,000 = 12\%$$

District 2

$$ROI = \text{Net income} \div \text{Investment} = \$1,988,000 \div \$14,200,000 = 14\%$$

Because the higher ROI indicates the better performance, the District 2 manager is the superior performer. This conclusion is based solely on quantitative results. In real-world practice, companies also consider qualitative factors.

Qualitative Considerations

Using ROI as an evaluation technique may be complicated by certain qualitative characteristics. For example, assume that Panther Holding Company decides to use ROI to evaluate the performance of Renata Zupanic, the manager of the Furniture Manufacturing Division. What items should be included in the earnings and investment figures? Suppose that one year ago Panther decided to close a furniture plant because recessionary conditions had caused a decline in the demand for furniture. Panther considered the situation to be temporary and planned to reopen the plant when demand returned to normal levels. Should this plant be included in Ms. Zupanic's investment base when computing the ROI for her division? It would be unfair to hold her responsible for such nonoperating assets. Accordingly, most companies do not use net income and total assets in the ROI formula. Instead, they normally use *operating income* divided by *operating assets.*

Some companies refine the computation even further by using only *controllable items* in the formula. This practice has appeal for motivational purposes, but it is usually difficult at the investment center level to segregate controllable from noncontrollable items. As discussed earlier, when controllable versus noncontrollable criteria are used, the concept of predominant control as opposed to absolute control must be employed. Regardless of the definition used for earnings and investment, management must exercise judgment in deciding which specific items to include in the computation.

Measurement Basis

The ROI computation is further complicated by the question of what *value* to use for the assets included in the investment base. Suppose that three machines, A, B and C, are assigned to different investment centers. Each machine originally cost $5,000 and is currently rented to customers by its respective investment center. Net rental income for each machine is approximately $1,000. Machine A was purchased first and has a current book value (cost minus accumulated depreciation) of $2,000. Machine B was purchased second and has a book value of

$4,000. Machine C was purchased last but was depreciated on an accelerated basis that resulted in a more rapid decline in book value. Machine C's current book value is $2,500. See Exhibit 9–4 for the computation of ROI for each machine using book value as the valuation basis.

Do the data in Exhibit 9–4 imply that the manager of the investment center to which Machine A is assigned is outperforming the managers of the other investment centers? Obviously, the answer is no. The only difference is that Machine A is older and therefore has a lower book value. Machine C is newer, but it still has a reduced book value because it was depreciated on an accelerated basis.

Exhibit 9–4 *Comparison of ROIs*

$$ROI = \frac{\text{Net income}}{\text{Investment}}$$

$$\text{Machine A} = \frac{1,000}{2,000} = 50\%$$

$$\text{Machine B} = \frac{1,000}{4,000} = 25\%$$

$$\text{Machine C} = \frac{1,000}{2,500} = 40\%$$

Clearly, when book value is used as the valuation basis, the ROI is affected by the age of the asset and the method of depreciation. Accordingly, the use of book value can cause severe motivational problems. Managers will believe that comparisons of the ROIs of different investment centers are unfair because the numbers do not accurately reflect performance. Furthermore, managers may be tempted to use obsolete equipment because its replacement would increase the amount of their investment base for the ROI computation.

The problems described here may be reduced by using original cost instead of book value in the denominator of the ROI formula. In this example, each of the machines had an original cost of $5,000. Accordingly, the ROI for each machine is 20 percent ($1,000 ÷ $5,000). Note, however, that this practice may not entirely solve the valuation problem. As a result of inflation and technological advances, comparable equipment purchased at different times will have different costs. To counter this problem, some accountants advocate the use of *replacement cost* rather than *historical cost* as the valuation base. Although this practice is frequently suggested, it is seldom used because of the difficulty of determining the amount that it would cost to replace particular assets. For example, imagine the difficulty of determining the replacement cost of all of the assets in a factory such as a steel mill that has been operating for years.

As this discussion implies, the selection of the valuation basis is a complicated matter. In spite of its shortcomings, most companies continue to use book value as the valuation basis. Accordingly, it is important for management to consider those shortcomings when using ROI as a technique for performance evaluation.

Factors Affecting Return on Investment

The ROI formula can be subdivided into two ratios. It is often helpful to make this subdivision to encourage managers to further analyze factors that affect the firm's profitability. Profitability is affected by the *margin earned* on sales and by the number of times that the margin is collected during the accounting period (the *turnover rate*). For example, an item that can be purchased for $1 and sold for $1.20 may be more profitable than an item that is purchased for $1 and sold for $1.50. Perhaps during the accounting period 75 units of the item with the $0.20 margin could be sold but only 25 units of the item with the $0.50 margin could be sold. Under these circumstances, the first item would produce $15 (75 × $0.20) of profit during the accounting period while the second item would produce only $12.50 (25 × $0.50) of profit. Clearly, both margin and turnover affect profitability. If we express both of the factors as separate ratios, the following expanded version of the ROI formula can be developed.

Step 1

$$\text{Margin} = \frac{\text{Net income}}{\text{Sales}}$$

Step 2

$$\text{Turnover} = \frac{\text{Sales}}{\text{Investment}}$$

Step 3
$$ROI = Margin \times Turnover$$

Step 4
$$ROI = \frac{Net\ income}{Sales} \times \frac{Sales}{Investment}$$

To illustrate, assume that Gamma Company produced $15,000 of net earnings from $200,000 of sales. Furthermore, Gamma had invested $100,000 in assets to produce the sales. Based on this information, Gamma's ROI can be computed as follows.

$$
\begin{aligned}
ROI &= Margin \times Turnover \\
&= \frac{\$15,000}{\$200,000} \times \frac{\$200,000}{\$100,000} \\
&= 7.5\% \times 2 \\
&= 15\%
\end{aligned}
$$

It may be helpful to verify that this is the same ROI figure that would result from using our original ROI formula. Recall that the original formula was as follows.

$$ROI = \frac{Net\ income}{Investment}$$

In this case

$$ROI = \frac{\$15,000}{\$100,000} = 15\%$$

Although the expanded formula looks more complicated, it is generally more useful because it encourages managers to concentrate on all of the factors that affect ROI. By analyzing the expanded formula, we can see that profitability and the resultant ROI can be improved in one of three ways. Specifically, *increased sales, lowered expenses,* or *reduced investment base* will increase ROI. Each of these possibilities is demonstrated using the Gamma Company illustration.

1. *Increase ROI by increasing sales.* Suppose that Gamma Company increases sales from $200,000 to $240,000, thereby resulting in an increase in net income from $15,000 to $19,500. The ROI becomes

$$
\begin{aligned}
ROI &= Margin \times Turnover \\
&= \frac{\$19,500}{\$240,000} \times \frac{\$240,000}{\$100,000} \\
&= 8.125\% \times 2.4 \\
&= 19.5\%
\end{aligned}
$$

2. *Increase ROI by reducing expenses.* Assume that Gamma Company embarks on a campaign to lower expenses without affecting sales or the investment base. It is successful in its effort to control expenses to the point that earnings increase from $15,000 to $20,000. Accordingly, ROI becomes

$$
\begin{aligned}
ROI &= Margin \times Turnover \\
&= \frac{\$20,000}{\$200,000} \times \frac{\$200,000}{\$100,000} \\
&= 10\% \times 2 \\
&= 20\%
\end{aligned}
$$

3. *Increase ROI by reducing the investment base.* Managers who become too income oriented frequently overlook this possibility. By reducing the amount of funds invested in operating assets such as inventory or accounts receivable, they can increase profitability because the funds released from current operations can be reinvested in other assets that produce new earnings. This effect is reflected in the ROI computation. For example, assume that through

efficient operations, Gamma Company is able to reduce the carrying value of its inventory so that the required investment to produce the same amount of sales drops from $100,000 to $80,000. As a result, ROI becomes

$$ROI = Margin \times Turnover$$
$$= \frac{\$15,000}{\$200,000} \times \frac{\$200,000}{\$80,000}$$
$$= 7.50\% \times 2.5$$
$$= 18.75\%$$

In each case, the ROI increased from the original 15 percent to some higher percentage. The use of the expanded ROI formula and the Gamma illustration emphasize that ROI is affected by sales, net earnings, and the level of investment. The prudent manager will consider all three components when trying to improve the company's profitability.

What three actions can a manager take to improve ROI?

Answer
1. Increase sales
2. Reduce expenses
3. Reduce the investment base

Check Yourself 9-2

Residual Income

Suppose that you are the manager of an investment center that operates within a large corporation. You are evaluated based on your ability to maximize your ROI. The corporation's overall ROI is 15 percent. However, your particular investment center has consistently outperformed other investment centers. Its current ROI is 20 percent. You have an opportunity to invest funds in a project that promises to earn an 18 percent ROI. Would you accept the investment opportunity?

LO7 Evaluate investment opportunities by using the residual income technique.

These circumstances place you in an awkward position. The corporation would benefit from having you accept the project because the expected ROI of 18 percent is higher than the corporate average ROI of 15 percent. However, you personally would suffer from a decision to accept the project because it would result in a decline in the level of your investment center's current ROI of 20 percent. Accordingly, you are forced to choose between your personal benefit and that of the corporation. When faced with decisions such as these, many managers choose to benefit themselves at the expense of their corporations. The term used to describe this situation is **suboptimization.**

To avoid *suboptimization,* many businesses use an evaluation technique known as **residual income.** This approach evaluates a manager on his ability to maximize the dollar value of earnings above some targeted level of earnings. The targeted level of earnings is established by multiplying the amount of investment by a desired ROI. Expressed as a formula, *residual income* is defined as follows.

$$Residual\ income = Earned\ income - (Investment \times Desired\ ROI)$$

To illustrate, assume that Bender Division is defined as an investment center of Amcom Corporation. Noel Ducote, Bender's manager, controls $5,000,000 of assets that were used to produce net income of $900,000. Amcom has established a desired ROI of 12 percent based on the corporation's average ROI. Based on this information, the residual income associated with the Bender Division is computed in Exhibit 9–5.

Notice that Bender Division's current ROI is 18 percent ($900,000 ÷ $5,000,000). If Mr. Ducote discovers an opportunity to invest an additional $1,000,000 in a project that is expected to provide a 14 percent ROI, would he be motivated to accept it under a residual

Exhibit 9–5 *Computation of Residual Income*

Residual income = Earned income − (Investment × Desired ROI)
              = $900,000 − ($5,000,000 × 0.12)
              = $900,000 − $600,000
              = $300,000

Exhibit 9–6 *Computation of Residual Income After Additional Investment*

Residual income = Earned income − (Investment × Desired ROI)
              = $1,040,000* − ($6,000,000† × 0.12)
              = $1,040,000 − $720,000
              = $320,000

*Earned income: $900,000 + $140,000 = $1,040,000
†Investment: $5,000,000 + $1,000,000 = $6,000,000

income evaluation system? The answer is yes because the new investment would result in an increase in the total dollar value of the residual income. This fact is verified by the computations in Exhibit 9–6. Notice that the amount of investment is increased by the $1,000,000 additional funding and earned income is increased by $140,000 ($1,000,000 × 0.14).

Accepting the new project would add $20,000 to Bender's residual income ($320,000 − $300,000). Because Mr. Ducote is evaluated on his ability to maximize residual income, he would benefit by the decision to accept any investment project that returns an ROI in excess of the desired 12 percent. The fact that Bender's ROI will fall does not enter into the decision. Accordingly, the residual income approach eliminates the problem of goal incongruence between management and the company.

Numerous comparisons are possible when using the residual income approach. The level of residual income in the current year can be compared with the level earned in previous years, with some target level, or with the amount generated by other investment centers. When making comparisons between different investment centers, however, care must be taken to ensure that the managers have equal access to investment funds because managers with larger investment bases would produce higher levels of residual income simply as a result of the size of their operations but not of superior performance. Here, as with any other evaluation techniques, fair and accurate assessments are possible only if upper management exercises due care when interpreting the results.

focus on International Issues

Do Managers in Different Countries Stress the Same Performance Measures?

Companies operating in different countries frequently choose different performance measures to evaluate their managers.

For example, although U.S. companies tend to favor some form of return on investment (ROI), Japanese companies tend to emphasize return on sales (ROS) as a primary measure of financial performance.* In general, the Japanese assume a constant sales price, thereby requiring a reduction in cost or an increase in volume to generate an increase in ROS. This approach is consistent with the Japanese orientation toward long-term growth and profitability. In contrast, the majority of U.S. companies focus on ROI, which encourages and emphasizes short-term profitability. U.S. firms were at one time criticized for their emphasis on short-term profitability, but the more entrenched style of Japanese companies has hindered their ability to adapt to changing times. As a result, many Japanese companies have begun to reevaluate their management philosophy and the corresponding measures of performance. Even so, in a world filled with diversity, managers will likely continue to stress performance measures that reflect a variety of social customs.

*Robert S. Kaplan, "Measures for Manufacturing Excellence," *Emerging Practices in Cost Management* in WG&L Corporate Finance Network Database, 1998.

Young Company's desired rate of return is 14 percent. Christina Fallin, manager of Young's northeastern investment center, controls $12,600,000 of assets. During the most recent year, Fallin's district produced net earnings of $1,839,600. Determine the amount of the northeastern investment center's residual income.

Answer

Residual income = Earned income − (Investment × Desired ROI)
Residual income = $1,839,600 − ($12,600,000 × 0.14) = $75,600

Check Yourself 9–3

Transfer Pricing

In vertically integrated companies, one division commonly sells goods or services to another division. For example, in the case of Panther Holding Company in Exhibit 9–1, the Lumber Manufacturing Division may sell lumber to the Home Building and Furniture Manufacturing Divisions. When such intercompany sales occur, the price to charge is likely to become a heated issue.

LO8 Understand the three common approaches used to establish transfer prices.

reality bytes

The Volkswagen Beetle assembly plant purchases some of the parts used to make the car from independent third-party companies. Other parts are produced internally. Determining the cost of the parts purchased from outsiders is fairly easy by locating the price paid listed on the invoice. Determining the price of the goods that are transferred from one division to another division of the same company is a bit more difficult. To maintain motivation, Volkswagen's managers are required to establish transfer prices that are deemed to be fair to both the division sending and the division receiving the transferred parts.

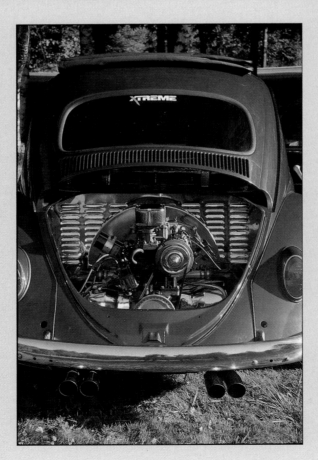

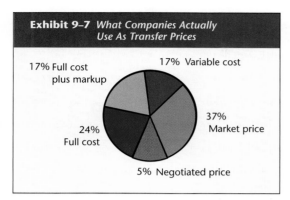

Exhibit 9–7 *What Companies Actually Use As Transfer Prices*

- 17% Full cost plus markup
- 17% Variable cost
- 37% Market price
- 24% Full cost
- 5% Negotiated price

Source: R. Tang, "Transfer Pricing in the 1990s," *Management Accounting,* pp. 22–26.

In a decentralized organization, each division is likely to be defined as an investment center with the division manager being held responsible for profitability. When goods are transferred internally, the sales price of one division becomes a cost to the other division. Accordingly, the amount of profit included in the **transfer price** will increase the selling division's earnings and decrease the purchasing division's earnings (via increased expenses). It is to the advantage of the selling division to obtain the highest price while the purchasing division seeks the lowest price possible. When a competitive evaluation system based on profitability measures is imposed on this situation, it is easy to understand why the transfer price is subject to considerable controversy.

Three common approaches are used to establish transfer prices. They are (1) price based on market forces, (2) price based on negotiation, and (3) price based on cost. Some specific measures and the frequency of their use are shown Exhibit 9–7.

Market-Based Transfer Prices

The preferred method for establishing transfer prices is to base them on some form of competitive market price. Ideally, the selling division should have the authority to sell its merchandise to outsiders as well as, or in preference to, its other divisions. Likewise, the purchasing divisions should have the option to buy goods from outsiders if they are able to obtain favorable prices. However, both selling and purchasing divisions would be motivated to deal with each other because of savings in selling, administrative, and transportation costs that arise as a natural result of internal transactions.

Market-based transfer prices are preferred because they promote efficiency and fairness. Market forces coupled with the responsibility for profitability motivate managers to utilize their resources effectively. For example, Jerry Lowe, the manager of the lumber division, may stop producing high-quality woods that the furniture division uses if he finds that it is more profitable to produce low-quality lumber. The furniture division can buy its needed material from outside companies that have chosen to operate in the less-profitable, high-quality market sector. Accordingly, the company as a whole benefits from Mr. Lowe's insight. An additional advantage of using market prices is the sense of fairness associated with them. It is difficult for a manager to complain that the price that she is being charged is too high when she has the opportunity to seek a lower price elsewhere. The natural justice of the competitive marketplace is firmly implanted in the psyche of most modern managers.

Negotiated Transfer Prices

Unfortunately, in many instances, a necessary product may not be available elsewhere or the market price may not be in the best interest of the company as a whole. Sometimes a division makes a unique product that only one of its company's other divisions uses. When this occurs, the external market cannot be used as a deciding factor in determining the transfer price. At other times, market-based transfer prices may lead to suboptimization, discussed earlier.

Consider the case of Garms Industries. It operates several divisions that function in a relatively autonomous fashion. One division, TrueTrust Motors, Inc., makes small electric motors used in appliances such as refrigerators, washing machines, fans, and so on. Garms has another division, CleanCo, that makes and sells vacuum cleaners. CleanCo produces approximately 30,000 vacuum cleaners per year. It currently purchases the motors used in its vacuums from a company that is not part of the Garms organization. The president of Garms asked the TrueTrust division manager to establish a price at which it could make and sell motors to CleanCo. The manager submitted the following cost and price data.

Variable (unit-level) costs	$45
Per unit fixed cost at a volume of 30,000 units	15
Allocated corporate-level facility sustaining costs	20
Total cost	$80

*TrueTrust has enough excess capacity that its existing business will not be affected by a decision to make motors for CleanCo. However, TrueTrust would be required to buy additional equipment and hire a supervisor to make the motors that CleanCo requires.

Adding a profit margin of $10 per unit, the manager of TrueTrust concluded that his division could provide the motors that CleanCo needs at a price of $90 per unit. When the proposal was presented to the division manager of CleanCo, she rejected the offer, stating that her division was currently buying motors in the open market at a price of $70 each. Existing competitive pressures in the vacuum cleaning market would not permit an increase in the sales price of her product. She explained that accepting TrueTrust's offer would increase CleanCo's costs significantly, thereby negatively impacting the division's profitability.

After studying the cost data, Garms' president quickly concluded that the company as a whole would suffer from suboptimization if CleanCo were to continue to purchase motors from a third-party vendor. He noted that the allocated corporate-level facility-sustaining costs were not relevant to the transfer pricing decision because they would be incurred regardless of whether TrueTrust made the motors for CleanCo. He recognized that both the variable and fixed costs were relevant because they could be avoided if TrueTrust did not make the motors. Since TrueTrust's avoidable cost of $60 ($45 variable cost + $15 fixed cost) per unit was below the $70 price per unit that CleanCo was currently paying, Garms would save $10 per motor, thereby increasing overall company profitability by $300,000 ($10 cost savings per unit × 30,000 units). He proceeded to establish a reasonable range for a negotiated transfer price.

If the market price were less than the avoidable cost of production, the supplying division (TrueTrust) and the company as a whole (Garms) would be better off to buy the product than to make it. Accordingly, it would be unreasonable to expect the TrueTrust division to produce and sell a product at a price that is below its avoidable cost, thereby establishing the avoidable cost as the bottom point of the reasonable range for the transfer price. On the topside, it would be unreasonable to expect an acquiring division (CleanCo) to pay more than the price it is currently paying for motors. As a result, the market price becomes the top point of the reasonable range for the transfer price. Accordingly, the reasonable transfer price range can be expressed mathematically as follows:

Market price $\geq$ Reasonable transfer price $\geq$ Avoidable product cost

In summary, the reasonable range for the transfer price is between the market price necessary to buy a product and the avoidable cost of making it. In the case of the Garms Industries, the reasonable range of the transfer price for vacuum cleaner motors would be between the market price of $70 per unit and the avoidable cost of production of $60.[1] Garms' president noted that any transfer price within this range would benefit both divisions and the company as a whole. He then encouraged the two division managers to negotiate a transfer price within the reasonable range that would be fair to both parties.

As this scenario suggests, a **negotiated transfer price** can be more beneficial than a market-based transfer price under the right set of circumstances. When the managers involved

---

[1]This discussion recognizes that the supplying division (TrueTrust) has excess capacity. When the supplying division is operating at full capacity with external buyers, the minimum price for the reasonable transfer price range would include not only the avoidable cost but also an opportunity cost. Specifically, an opportunity cost exists when the supplying division is forced to forgo the opportunity to profit from sales it could otherwise make to external buyers. On the other hand, if the supplying division has excess capacity to cover both existing orders and the additional orders on which the transfer price is negotiated, the opportunity cost is zero. In other words, the supplying division does not have to give up anything to accept an order from another division. While a full discussion of the treatment of the opportunity cost would be insightful, it would also be complicated. As a result, we will defer further coverage of this topic to more advanced courses.

agree to a negotiated price, the concept of fairness is preserved. Furthermore, the element of profit remains intact; and the evaluation concepts discussed in this chapter can be applied. Although negotiated prices are not as good as market prices, they are able to offer many of the same advantages. Accordingly, they should act as the first possible alternative when a company is unable to use market-based transfer prices.

Suppose that Mr. Lutz and Ms. Everhart are unable to agree on a negotiated transfer price. Should the president of TrueTrust establish a reasonable price and force the managers to accept it? There is no definitive answer to this question. However, most senior-level executives recognize the motivational importance of maintaining autonomy in a decentralized organization. So long as the negative consequences are not significant, divisional managers are usually permitted to exercise their own judgment. In other words, the long-term benefits derived from autonomous management outweigh the short-term detriments of suboptimization.

Cost-Based Transfer Prices

The least desirable strategy is a **cost-based transfer price.** When cost is used, the amount of cost must first be determined. Some companies base the transfer price on *variable cost* (proxy for avoidable cost). Other companies use the *full cost* (variable cost plus an allocated portion of fixed cost) as the transfer price. In either case, using cost as the basis for transfer prices acts to remove the profit motive. Without profitability as a guide, the incentive to control cost is diminished. One department's inefficiency is simply passed on to the next department. The result is low companywide profitability. Despite this potential detrimental effect, many companies continue to use cost as the basis for transfer prices because cost represents an objective number that is easy to compute. When a company chooses to use cost-based transfer prices, *it should use standard rather than actual costs.* With this approach, departments are at least held responsible for the variances that they generate and some degree of cost control is encouraged.

a look back

The practice of delegating authority and responsibility is referred to as *decentralization.* Clear lines of authority and responsibility are essential in establishing a responsibility accounting system. In a responsibility accounting system, segment managers are held accountable for profits based on the amount of control they have over the profits in their segment.

Responsibility reports are used to compare actual results with budgets. The reports should be simple with variances highlighted to promote the *management by exception* doctrine. Individual managers should be held responsible only for those revenue or cost items that they control. Each manager should receive only summary information regarding the performance of the responsibility centers that are under her supervision.

A *responsibility center* is the point in an organization where control over revenue or expense is located. *Cost centers* are segments that incur costs but do not generate revenues. *Profit centers* generate revenues as well as incur costs, thus allowing for the calculation of profit. *Investment centers* generate revenues and incur expenses and can influence capital investment decisions.

One of the primary purposes of responsibility accounting is to evaluate managerial performance. Comparison of actual results with standards and budgets and calculation of *return on investment* are used for this purpose. Because return on investment uses revenues, expenses, and investment, problems of measuring these parameters must be considered. The return on investment can be analyzed in terms of the margin earned on sales as well as the turnover (number of times the margin is collected) during the period. The *residual income approach* is sometimes used to avoid *suboptimization,* which occurs when managers choose to reject investment projects that would benefit their company's ROI but would reduce their investment center's ROI. The residual income approach evaluates managers on their ability to generate earnings above some targeted level of earnings.

Transfer pricing can affect a division's profitability. A transfer price must be determined when one division sells goods or services to another division within the same company. It is to the advantage of the selling division to obtain the highest price while the purchasing divi-

sion seeks the lowest price possible. The three most common bases used to establish transfer prices are *market forces, negotiation,* and *cost.*

The next chapter expands on the concepts you learned in this chapter. You will see how managers select investment opportunities that will affect their future ROIs. You will learn to use present value techniques that consider the time value of money; specifically, you will learn to compute the net present value and the internal rate of return for potential investment opportunities. You will also learn to use less-sophisticated analytical techniques such as payback and the unadjusted rate of return.

a look
forward

SELF-STUDY REVIEW PROBLEM

The September Health Corporation (SHC) operates four divisions. Sarah Simmons is the district manager of the Western Division. Ms. Simmons manages $20,000,000 of assets on which she produces a return on investment (ROI) of 20 percent. Given that the companywide desired rate of return is 16 percent, Simmons' track record is impressive. SHC's upper managers are so impressed with her performance that they have agreed to transfer $4,000,000 of additional capital to the Western Division. The best additional investment opportunity that Ms. Simmons has been able to locate is expected to produce an 18 percent return on investment.

Required

a. How would accepting the investment opportunity affect Western Division's ROI?
b. Would SHC Corporation benefit if Ms. Simmons accepts the investment opportunity she has identified?
c. What effect will accepting the proposed investment opportunity have on the Western Division's residual income (RI)? Show computations.
d. Would ROI or RI be the better measure for Ms. Simmons performance? Explain.

Solution to Requirement a
Western Division's ROI if Ms. Simmons accepts the proposed investment opportunity:

	Investment	×	ROI	=	Net Income
Current	$20,000,000	×	0.20	=	$4,000,000
Proposed	4,000,000	×	0.18	=	720,000
Total	$24,000,000				$4,720,000

The revised ROI = $4,720,000 ÷ $24,000,000 = 19.666667%

Accepting the proposed investment opportunity would cause the Western Division's ROI to decline from 20 percent to 19.666667 percent.

Solution to Requirement b
Because the expected ROI (18 percent) on the proposed investment is higher than SHC's desired ROI (16 percent), SHC would benefit if the Western Division accepted the project.

Solution to Requirement c
Residual income if Ms. Simmons accepts the investment opportunity:

$$\text{Earnings} - (\text{Investment} \times \text{Desired ROI}) = \text{RI}$$
$$(\$24,000,000 \times 0.19666667) - (\$24,000,000 \times 0.16) = \$880,000$$

Residual income if Ms. Simmons rejects the investment opportunity:

$$\text{Earnings} - (\text{Investment} \times \text{Desired ROI}) = \text{RI}$$
$$(\$20,000,000 \times 0.20) - (\$20,000,000 \times 0.16) = \$800,000$$

Accepting the proposed investment would cause the Western Division's residual income to increase by $80,000 ($880,000 − $800,000).

Solution to Requirement d
In this case, using ROI for performance evaluation may result in suboptimization. Specifically, Ms. Simmons would have to choose between reducing the performance measure (ROI) of her division or

benefiting the company as a whole. The RI approach would avoid this conflict and therefore appears to be the better approach.

KEY TERMS

Controllability concept *369*
Cost-based transfer price *382*
Cost center *372*
Decentralization *368*
Investment center *373*

Management by exception *369*
Market-based transfer price *380*
Negotiated transfer price *381*

Profit center *372*
Residual income *377*
Responsibility accounting *367*
Responsibility center *372*

Responsibility reports *369*
Return on investment *373*
Suboptimization *377*
Transfer price *380*

QUESTIONS

1. Pam Kelly says she has no faith in budgets. Her company, Kelly Manufacturing Corporation, spent thousands of dollars to install a sophisticated budget system. One year later the company's expenses are still out of control. She believes budgets simply do not work. How would you respond to Ms. Kelly's beliefs?
2. All travel expenses incurred by Pure Water Pump Corporation are reported only to John Daniels, the company president. Pure Water is a multinational company with five divisions. Are travel expenses reported following the responsibility accounting concept? Explain.
3. What are five potential advantages of decentralization?
4. Who receives responsibility reports? What do the reports include?
5. How does the concept of predominant as opposed to that of absolute control apply to responsibility accounting?
6. How do responsibility reports promote the management by exception doctrine?
7. What is a responsibility center?
8. What are the three types of responsibility centers? Explain how each differs from the others.
9. Carmen Douglas claims that her company's performance evaluation system is unfair. Her company uses return on investment (ROI) to evaluate performance. Ms. Douglas says that even though her ROI is lower than another manager's, her performance is far superior. Is it possible that Ms. Douglas is correct? Explain your position.
10. What two factors affect the computation of return on investment?
11. What three ways can a manager increase the return on investment?
12. How can a residual income approach to performance evaluation reduce the likelihood of suboptimization?
13. Is it true that the manager with the highest residual income is always the best performer?
14. Why are transfer prices important to managers who are evaluated based on profitability criteria?
15. What are three approaches to establishing transfer prices? List the most desirable approach first and the least desirable last.
16. If cost is the basis for transfer pricing, should actual or standard cost be used? Why?

EXERCISES—SERIES A

L.O. 1 **EXERCISE 9–1A** *Organization Chart and Responsibilities*

The production manager is responsible for the assembly, cleaning, and finishing departments. The executive vice president reports directly to the president but is responsible for the activities of the production department, the finance department, and the sales department. The sales manager is responsible for the advertising department.

Required
Arrange this information into an organization chart and indicate the responsibility levels involved.

L.O. 3 **EXERCISE 9–2A** *Responsibility Report*

Bonn Department Store is divided into three major departments: Men's Clothing, Women's Clothing, and Home Furnishings. Each of these three departments is supervised by a manager who reports to the general manager. The departments are subdivided into different sections managed by floor supervisors.

The Home Furnishings Department has three floor supervisors, one for furniture, one for lamps, and one for housewares. The following items were included in the company's most recent responsibility report.

Travel expenses for the housewares buyer
Seasonal decorations for the furniture section
Revenues for the Home Furnishings Department
Administrative expenses for the Men's Clothing Department
Utility cost allocated to the Home Furnishings Department
Cost of part-time Christmas help for the Women's Department
Delivery expenses for furniture purchases
Salaries for the sales staff in the lamp section
Storewide revenues
Salary of the general manager
Salary of the Men's Clothing Department manager
Allocated companywide advertising expense
Depreciation on the facility

Required
Which items are likely to be the responsibility of the Home Furnishings Department manager?

EXERCISE 9–3A *Organization Chart and Controllable Costs*

L.O. 1, 3

Cracker Company has employees with the following job titles.

President of the company
Vice president of marketing
Product manager
Controller
Vice president of manufacturing
Treasurer
Regional sales manager
Personnel manager
Cashier
Vice president of finance
Fringe benefits manager
Board of directors
Production supervisors
Vice president of administration
Sales office manager

Required
a. Design an organization chart using these job titles.
b. Identify some possible controllable costs for the person holding each job title.

EXERCISE 9–4A *Income Statement for Internal Use*

L.O. 1, 2

Richardson Company has provided the following 2002 data.

Budget	
Sales	$204,000
Variable product costs	82,000
Variable selling expense	24,000
Other variable expenses	2,000
Fixed product costs	8,400
Fixed selling expense	12,600
Other fixed expenses	1,200
Variances	
Sales	4,400 U
Variable product costs	2,000 F
Variable selling expense	1,200 U
Other variable expense	600 U
Fixed product costs	120 F
Fixed selling expense	200 F
Other fixed expenses	80 U

Required

Prepare in good form a budgeted and actual income statement for internal use.

L.O. 1, 2   EXERCISE 9–5A *Evaluating a Cost Center Including Flexible Budgeting Concepts*

Merryton Medical Equipment Company makes a blood pressure measuring kit. Lou Seles is the production manager. The production department's static budget and actual results for 2002 follow.

	Static Budget	Actual Results
	20,000 kits	*21,000 kits*
Direct materials	$ 300,000	$ 323,400
Direct labor	270,000	277,200
Variable manufacturing overhead	70,000	89,200
Total variable costs	640,000	689,800
Fixed manufacturing cost	360,000	356,000
Total manufacturing cost	$1,000,000	$1,045,800

Required

a. Convert the static budget into a flexible budget.
b. Use the flexible budget to evaluate Mr. Seles' performance.
c. Explain why Mr. Seles' performance evaluation does not include sales revenue and net income.

L.O. 3, 5   EXERCISE 9–6A *Evaluating a Profit Center*

Cathy Craig, the president of Children's Best Corporation, is trying to determine this year's pay raises for the store managers. Children's Best has seven stores in the southwestern United States. Corporate headquarters purchases all toys from different manufacturers globally and distributes them to individual stores. Additionally, headquarters makes decisions regarding location and size of stores. These practices allow Children's Best to receive volume discounts from vendors and to implement coherent marketing strategies. Within a set of general guidelines, store managers have the flexibility to adjust product prices and hire local employees. Ms. Craig is considering three possible performance measures for evaluating the individual stores: cost of goods sold, return on sales (net income divided by sales), and return on investment.

Required

Using the concept of controllability, advise Ms. Craig about the best performance measure.

L.O. 6   EXERCISE 9–7A *Return on Investment*

An investment center of Tannihill Corporation shows a net income of $3,600 on an investment of $15,000.

Required

Compute the return on investment.

L.O. 6   EXERCISE 9–8A *Return on Investment*

Strauss Company calculated its return on investment as 15 percent. Sales are now $90,000, and the investment base is $150,000.

Required

a. If expenses are reduced by $9,000 and sales remain unchanged, what return on investment will result?
b. If both sales and expenses cannot be changed, what change in the investment base is required to achieve the same result?

L.O. 7   EXERCISE 9–9A *Residual Income*

Bissonnet Corporation has a desired rate of return of 10 percent. Wayne Chu is in charge of one of Bissonnet's three investment centers. His center controlled operating assets of $9,000,000 that were used to earn $1,170,000.

Required

Compute Mr. Chu's residual income.

EXERCISE 9–10A *Residual Income* L.O. 7

Wellstone Cough Drops operates two divisions. The following information pertains to each division for 2002.

	Division A	Division B
Sales	$90,000	$30,000
Operating income	$ 9,000	$ 4,800
Average operating assets	$36,000	$24,000
Company's desired rate of return	20%	20%

Required
a. Compute each division's residual income.
b. Which division increased the company's profitability more?

EXERCISE 9–11A *Return on Investment and Residual Income* L.O. 6, 7

Required
Supply the missing information in the following table for Carmen Company.

Sales	$600,000
ROI	?
Investment in operating assets	?
Operating income	?
Turnover	2
Residual income	?
Margin	0.10
Desired rate of return	18%

EXERCISE 9–12A *Comparing Return on Investment with Residual Income* L.O. 6, 7

The San Diego Division of Cascade, Inc., has a current ROI of 20 percent. The company target ROI is 15 percent. The San Diego Division has an opportunity to invest $2,000,000 at 18 percent but is reluctant to do so because its ROI will fall to 19.2 percent. The present investment base for the division is $3,000,000.

Required
Demonstrate how Cascade can motivate the San Diego Division to make the investment by using the residual income method.

EXERCISE 9–13A *Transfer Pricing* L.O. 8

Porter Company has two divisions, A and B. Division A manufactures 6,000 units of product per month. The cost per unit is calculated as follows.

Variable costs	$ 6
Fixed costs	20
Total cost	$26

Division B uses the product created by Division A. No outside market for Division A's product exists. The fixed costs incurred by Division A are allocated headquarters-level facility-sustaining costs. The manager of Division A suggests that the product be transferred to Division B at a price of at least $26 per unit. The manager of Division B argues that the same product can be purchased from another company for $16 per unit and requests permission to do so.

Required
a. Should Porter allow the manager of Division B to purchase the product from the outside company for $16 per unit? Explain.
b. Assume you are the president of the company. Write a brief paragraph recommending a resolution of the conflict between the two divisional managers.

L.O. 8   **EXERCISE 9–14A** *Transfer Pricing and Avoidable Cost*

The Tire Division of Reliable Way Company (RWC) produces a radial all-purpose tire for trucks that it sells wholesale to automotive manufacturers. Per unit sales and cost data for this tire follow.

Selling price	$108
Unit-level variable cost	$ 72
Corporate-level fixed cost	$ 30
Manufacturing capacity	30,000 units
Average sales	25,000 units

RWC also has a Trucking Division that provides delivery service for outside independent businesses as well as divisions of RWC. The Trucking Division, which uses approximately 4,000 tires a year, presently buys tires for its trucks from an outside supplier for $102 per tire.

Required

Recommend a transfer price range for the truck tires that would be profitable for both divisions if the Trucking Division purchased the tires internally. Assume that both divisions operate as investment centers.

L.O. 8   **EXERCISE 9–15A** *Transfer Pricing and Fixed Cost per Unit*

The Precision Parts Division of Portal Company plans to set up a facility with the capacity to make 5,000 units annually of an electronic computer part. The avoidable cost of making the part is as follows.

Costs	Total	Cost per Unit
Variable cost	$300,000	$60
Fixed cost	$ 80,000	$16 (at capacity)

Required

a. Assume that Portal's Assembly Division is currently purchasing 3,000 of the electronic parts each year from an outside supplier at a market price of $100. What would be the financial consequence to Portal if the Precision Parts Division makes the part and sells it to the Assembly Division? What range of transfer prices would increase the financial performance of both divisions?

b. Suppose that the Assembly Division increases production so that it could use 5,000 units of the part made by the Precision Parts Division. How would the change in volume affect the range of transfer prices that would financially benefit both divisions?

PROBLEMS—SERIES A

L.O. 3   **PROBLEM 9–16A** *Determining Controllable Costs*

Kyle Dannon is the manager of the production department of Chambliss Corporation. Chambliss incurred the following costs during 2001.

Production department supplies	$ 7,600
Administrative salaries	280,000
Production wages	652,000
Materials used	529,200
Depreciation on manufacturing equipment	361,600
Corporate-level rental expense	240,000
Property taxes	68,600
Sales salaries	286,800

Required

Prepare a list of expenditures that Mr. Dannon controls.

L.O. 2, 3   **PROBLEM 9–17A** *Comparing Controllability and Responsibility*

Eureka Lambardo manages the production division of Yates Corporation. Ms. Lambardo's responsibility report for the month of August follows.

	Budget	Actual	Variance	
Controllable costs				
Raw materials	$30,000	$37,500	$ 7,500	U
Labor	15,000	20,700	5,700	U
Maintenance	3,000	3,600	600	U
Supplies	2,550	1,800	750	F
Total	$50,550	$63,600	$13,050	U

The budget had called for 7,500 pounds of raw materials at $4 per pound, and 7,500 pounds were used during August; however, the purchasing department paid $5 per pound for the materials. The wage rate used to establish the budget was $15 per hour. On August 1, however, it increased to $18 as the result of an inflation index provision in the union contract. Furthermore, the purchasing department did not provide the materials needed in accordance with the production schedule, which forced Ms. Lambardo to use 100 hours of overtime at a $27 rate. The projected 1,000 hours of labor in the budget would have been sufficient had it not been for the 100 hours of overtime. In other words, 1,100 hours of labor were used in August.

Required

a. When confronted with the unfavorable variances in her responsibility report, Ms. Lambardo argued that the report was unfair because it held her accountable for materials and labor variances that she did *not* control. Is she correct? Comment specifically on the materials and labor variances.

b. Prepare a responsibility report that reflects the cost items that Ms. Lambardo controlled during August.

c. Will the changes in the revised responsibility report require corresponding changes in the financial statements? Explain.

PROBLEM 9–18A *Performance Reports and Evaluation*

L.O. 2, 3, 4

Ford Corporation has four divisions: the assembly division, the processing division, the machining division, and the packing division. All four divisions are under the control of the vice president of manufacturing. Each division has a manager and several departments that are directed by supervisors. The chain of command runs downward from vice president to division manager to supervisor. The processing division is composed of the paint and finishing departments. The May responsibility reports for the supervisors of these departments follow.

	Budgeted*	Actual	Variance	
Paint Department				
Controllable costs				
Raw materials	$21,600	$22,500	$ 900	U
Labor	45,000	49,500	4,500	U
Repairs	3,600	2,880	720	F
Maintenance	1,800	1,710	90	F
Total	$72,000	$76,590	$4,590	U
Finishing Department				
Controllable costs				
Raw materials	$17,100	$16,920	$ 180	F
Labor	32,400	29,700	2,700	F
Repairs	2,160	2,430	270	U
Maintenance	1,260	1,530	270	U
Total	$52,920	$50,580	$2,340	F

*Ford uses flexible budgets for performance evaluation.

Other pertinent cost data for May follow.

	Budgeted*	Actual
Cost data of other divisions		
Assembly	$243,000	$238,680
Machining	211,500	216,360
Packing	316,080	309,690
Other costs associated with		
Processing division manager	180,000	178,200
Vice president of manufacturing	99,000	102,780

*Ford uses flexible budgets for performance evaluation.

Required

a. Prepare a responsibility report for the manager of the processing division.
b. Prepare a responsibility report for the vice president of manufacturing.
c. Explain where the $4,500 unfavorable labor variance in the paint department supervisor's report is included in the vice president's report.
d. Based on the responsibility report prepared in Requirement *a,* explain where the processing division manager should concentrate his attention.

L.O. 5

PROBLEM 9–19A *Different Types of Responsibility Centers*

Cullman Bank is a large municipal bank with several branch offices. The bank's computer department handles all data processing for bank operations. In addition, the bank sells the computer department's expertise in systems development and excess machine time to several small business firms, serving them as a service bureau.

The bank currently treats the computer department as a cost center. The manager of the computer department prepares a cost budget annually for senior bank officials to approve. Monthly operating reports compare actual and budgeted expenses. Revenues from the department's service bureau activities are treated as other income by the bank and are not reflected on the computer department's operating reports. The costs of serving these clients are included in the computer department reports, however.

The manager of the computer department has proposed that bank management convert the computer department to a profit or investment center.

Required

a. Describe the characteristics that differentiate a cost center, a profit center, and an investment center from each other.
b. Would the manager of the computer department be likely to conduct the operations of the department differently if the department were classified as a profit center or an investment center rather than as a cost center? Explain.

L.O. 2

PROBLEM 9–20A *Evaluating a Profit Center*

Cummings, Akers, and Associates is a CPA firm specializing in tax services. The firm has five branch offices in various communities. Justin Cummings, the managing partner, makes all decisions regarding personnel and facility acquisitions for the entire firm. Each branch manager determines employee work hours and compensation. Mr. Cummings emphasized to his branch managers that profit is their number one responsibility. Jenny Lanky manages the Reno Branch, which has the following static budget and actual results for 2002.

	Static Budget 10,000 Service Hours @$50 per Hour	Actual Results 9,600 Service Hours @$56 per Hour
Service revenue	$500,000	$537,600
Less: Variable costs		
Direct labor	(240,000)	(258,800)
Variable office overhead	(40,000)	(40,320)
Contribution margin	$220,000	$228,480
Less: Fixed costs		
Office rent	(40,000)	(40,000)
Other administrative expenses	(120,000)	(116,000)
Net income for the branch	$ 60,000	$ 72,480

Required

a. Convert the static budget into a flexible budget.
b. Determine the activity variances between the static budget and the flexible budget.
c. Compute the flexible budget variances.
d. Did Ms. Lanky do a good job as a branch manager? Support your answer with the information derived from Requirements *a, b,* and *c.*
e. Would you use return on investment to evaluate Ms. Lanky's performance? Explain.

L.O. 6 **PROBLEM 9–21A** *Return on Investment*

Baltic Corporation's balance sheet indicates that the company has $400,000 invested in operating assets. During 2003, Baltic earned income of $60,000 on $800,000 of sales.

Required
a. Compute Baltic's margin for 2003.
b. Compute Baltic's turnover for 2003.
c. Compute Baltic's return on investment for 2003.
d. Recompute Baltic's ROI under each of the following independent assumptions.
   (1) Sales increase from $800,000 to $1,000,000, thereby resulting in an increase in income from $60,000 to $80,000.
   (2) Sales remain constant, but Baltic reduces expenses resulting in an increase in income from $60,000 to $64,000.
   (3) Baltic is able to reduce its invested capital from $400,000 to $320,000 without affecting income.

PROBLEM 9–22A *Comparing Return on Investment and Residual Income*

L.O. 6, 7

The manager of the Shocco Division of Trussville Manufacturing Corporation is currently producing a 20 percent return on invested capital. Trussville's desired rate of return is 16 percent. The Shocco Division has $8,000,000 of capital invested and access to additional funds as needed. The manager is considering a new investment that will require a $2,000,000 capital commitment and promises an 18 percent return.

Required
a. Would it be advantageous for Trussville Manufacturing Corporation if the Shocco Division makes the investment under consideration?
b. What effect would the proposed investment have on the Shocco Division's return on investment? Show computations.
c. What effect would the proposed investment have on the Shocco Division's residual income? Show computations.
d. Would return on investment or residual income be the better performance measure for the Shocco Division's manager? Explain.

PROBLEM 9–23A *Transfer Pricing*

L.O. 8

Bolton Radio Corporation is a subsidiary of Wolenski Companies. Bolton makes car radios that it sells to retail outlets. It purchases speakers for the radios from outside suppliers for $28 each. Recently, Wolenski acquired the Amper Speaker Corporation, which makes car radio speakers that it sells to manufacturers. Amper produces and sells approximately 200,000 speakers per year which represents 70 percent of its operating capacity. At the present volume of activity, each speaker costs $24 to produce. This cost consists of a $16 variable cost component and an $8 fixed cost component. Amper sells the speakers for $30 each. The managers of Bolton and Amper have been asked to consider using Amper's excess capacity to supply Bolton with some of the speakers that it currently purchases from unrelated companies. Both managers are evaluated based on return on investment. Amper's manager suggests that the speakers be supplied at a transfer price of $30 each (the current selling price). On the other hand, Bolton's manager suggests a $24 transfer price, noting that this amount covers total cost and provides Amper a healthy contribution margin.

Required
a. What transfer price would you recommend?
b. Discuss the effect of the intercompany sales on each manager's return on investment.
c. Should Amper be required to use more than excess capacity to provide speakers to Bolton? In other words, should it sell to Bolton some of the 200,000 units that it is currently selling to unrelated companies? Why or why not?

EXERCISES—SERIES B

EXERCISE 9–1B *Organizational Chart and Responsibilities*

L.O. 1

Yesterday Solomon Corporation's board of directors appointed Jacqueline Cooper as the new president and chief executive officer. This morning, Ms. Cooper presented to the board a list of her management team members. The vice presidents are Andy Cranston, regional operations; Tom Ivanisevic, research and development; and Fanny Ewell, chief financial officer. Reporting to Mr. Cranston are the directors of American, European, and Asian operations. Reporting to Mr. Ivanisevic are the directors of the Houston, Seattle, and Charlotte laboratories. Reporting to Ms. Ewell are the controller and the treasurer.

Required

Arrange the preceding information into an organization chart and indicate the responsibility levels involved.

L.O. 3   EXERCISE 9–2B *Responsibility Report*

Solomon Corporation divides its operations into three regions: American, European, and Asian. The following items appear in the company's responsibility report.

European director's salary
Revenues of the French branch
Office expenses of the Japanese branch
Corporation president's salary
Asian director's salary
Revenues of the Taiwanese branch
Revenues of the British branch
Office expenses of the French branch
Revenues of the U.S. branch
Administrative expenses of the corporate headquarters
Office expenses of the Taiwanese branch
Office expenses of the Canadian branch
Revenues of the Japanese branch
Revenues of the Canadian branch
Office expenses of the British branch
Office expenses of the U.S. branch
American director's salary

Required

Which items should Solomon include in the responsibility report for the director of Asian operations?

L.O. 1, 3   EXERCISE 9–3B *Organizational Chart and Controllable Cost*

Tom Ivanisevic, Solomon Corporation vice president of research and development, has overall responsibility for employees with the following positions:

Directors of the Houston, Seattle, and Charlotte laboratories
Senior researchers reporting to laboratory directors
A personnel manager in each laboratory
An accounting manager in each laboratory
Research assistants working for senior researchers
Recruiters reporting to a personnel manager
Bookkeepers reporting to an accounting manager

Required

a. Design an organization chart using these job positions.
b. Identify some possible controllable costs for persons holding each of the job positions.

L.O. 1, 2   EXERCISE 9–4B *Income Statement for Internal Use*

Weaver Company has provided the following data for 2003:

Budget	
Sales	$387,000
Variable product costs	112,000
Variable selling expense	39,000
Other variable expenses	8,000
Fixed product costs	56,000
Fixed selling expense	21,000
Other fixed expenses	2,000
Actual results	
Sales	394,000
Variable product costs	113,000
Variable selling expense	42,000
Other variable expenses	7,000
Fixed product costs	60,000
Fixed selling expense	19,200
Other fixed expenses	10,000

Required
a. Prepare in good form a budgeted and actual income statement for internal use.
b. Calculate variances and identify them as favorable (F) or unfavorable (U).

EXERCISE 9–5B *Evaluating a Cost Center (including flexible budgeting concepts)*

L.O. 1, 2

Ronnie Dodson, president of Dodson Door Products Company, is evaluating the performance of Sam Pendleton, the plant manager, for 2002, the last fiscal year. Mr. Dodson is concerned that production costs exceeded budget by nearly $21,000. He has available the 2002 static budget for the production plant, as well as the actual results, both of which follow:

	Static Budget:	Actual Results:
	5,000 Doors	5,250 Doors
Direct materials	$225,000	$231,000
Direct labor	110,000	126,000
Variable manufacturing overhead	60,000	60,900
Total variable costs	395,000	417,900
Fixed manufacturing overhead	205,000	203,000
Total manufacturing cost	$600,000	$620,900

Required
a. Convert the static budget into a flexible budget.
b. Use the flexible budget to evaluate Mr. Pendleton's performance.
c. Explain why Mr. Pendleton's performance evaluation doesn't include sales revenue and net income.

EXERCISE 9–6B *Evaluating a Profit Center*

L.O. 3, 5

Cindy Juneau, president of World Travel Company, a travel agency, is seeking a method of evaluating her seven branches. Each branch vice president is authorized to hire employees and devise competitive strategies for the branch territory. Ms. Juneau wonders which of the following three different measures would be most suitable: return on investment, net income, or return on sales (net income divided by sales).

Required
Using the concept of controllability, advise Ms. Juneau about the best performance measure.

EXERCISE 9–7B *Computing Return on Investment*

L.O. 7

A Midfield Corporation investment center shows a profit of $60,000 and an investment of $480,000.

Required
Compute the return on investment.

EXERCISE 9–8B *Return on Investment*

L.O. 6

With annual sales of $6,000,000 and an investment base of $3,000,000, Melton Company achieved a 10 percent ROI.

Required
a. If Melton reduces expenses by $75,000 and sales remain unchanged, what ROI will result?
b. If Melton cannot change either sales or expenses, what change in the investment base is required to achieve the same result you calculated for Requirement *a*?

EXERCISE 9–9B *Computing Residual Income*

L.O. 7

Daylon Corporation's desired rate of return is 15 percent. Southeast Division, one of Daylon's five investment centers, earned a profit of $3,600,000 last year. The division controlled $20,000,000 of operational assets.

Required
Compute Southeast Division's residual income.

EXERCISE 9–10B *Computing Residual Income*

L.O. 7

Fast Oil Change operates two divisions. The following pertains to each division for 2003:

	St. Louis Division	Kansas City Division
Sales	$960,000	$720,000
Operating income	$ 75,000	$ 48,200
Average operating assets	$300,000	$240,000
Company's desired rate of return	15%	15%

Required

a. Compute each division's residual income.

b. Which division increased the company's profitability more?

L.O. 6, 7 **EXERCISE 9–11B** *Supply Missing Information Regarding Return on Investment and Residual Income*

Required

Supply the missing information in the following table for Saso Company.

Sales	?
ROI	12%
Investment in operating assets	$600,000
Operating income	?
Turnover	?
Residual income	?
Margin	0.08
Desired rate of return	11%

L.O. 6, 7 **EXERCISE 9–12B** *Contrasting Return on Investment with Residual Income*

The Baton Rouge Division of Louisiana Garage Doors, Inc., is currently achieving a 16 percent ROI. The company's target ROI is 10 percent. The division has an opportunity to invest an additional $500,000 at 13 percent but is reluctant to do so because its ROI will fall to 15.5 percent. The division's present investment base is $2,500,000.

Required

Explain how management can use the residual income method to motivate the Baton Rouge Division to make the investment.

L.O. 8 **EXERCISE 9–13B** *Transfer Pricing*

Aquatech Company makes household water filtration equipment. The Pure Blue Division manufactures filters. The Sweet Water Division then uses the filters as a component of the final product Aquatech sells to consumers. The Pure Blue Division has the capacity to produce 8,000 filters per month at the following cost per unit:

Variable costs	$12
Division fixed costs	10
Allocated corporate-level facility-sustaining costs	8
Total cost per filter	$30

Sweet Water currently uses 6,000 Pure Blue filters per month. Larry Proctor, Sweet Water's manager, is not happy with the $30 transfer price charged by Pure Blue. He points out that Sweet Water could purchase the same filters from outside vendors for a market price of only $24. Loudell Fletcher, Pure Blue's manager, refuses to sell the filters to Sweet Water below cost. Mr. Proctor counters that he would be happy to purchase the filters elsewhere. Because Pure Blue does not have other customers for its filters, Ms. Fletcher appeals to Mark Bibbs, the president of Aquatech, for arbitration.

Required

a. Should the president of Aquatech allow Mr. Proctor to purchase filters from outside vendors for $24 per unit? Explain.

b. Write a brief paragraph describing what Mr. Bibbs should do to resolve the conflict between the two division managers.

EXERCISE 9–14B *Transfer Pricing and Avoidable Cost* **L.O. 8**

Lopez Household Equipment Corporation recently acquired two new divisions. The Southlake Division manufactures vacuum cleaner motors. The Red Mountain Division makes household vacuum cleaners. Each division was formerly an independent company and continues to maintain its own customer base. Southlake Division data pertaining to vacuum cleaner motors follow:

Selling price per motor	$34
Unit-level variable costs per motor	$18
Division-level fixed costs per motor	$ 6
Corporate-level fixed costs per motor	$ 4
Manufacturing capacity	54,000 units per year
Average sales	32,000 units per year

The Red Mountain Division currently buys motors for its vacuum cleaners from an outside supplier at a price of $27 per unit. Red Mountain uses approximately 20,000 motors per year.

Required
Recommend a transfer price range for the motors that would be profitable for both divisions if the Red Mountain Division purchased the motors internally. Assume both divisions operate as investment centers.

EXERCISE 9–15B *Transfer Pricing and Fixed Cost per Unit* **L.O. 8**

The Singleton Division of Jaybro Company currently produces electric fans that desktop computer manufacturers use as cooling components. The Ezekiel Division, which makes laptop computers, has asked the Singleton Division to design and supply 20,000 fans per year for its laptop computers. Ezekiel currently purchases laptop fans from an outside vendor at the price of $18 each. However, Ezekiel is not happy with the vendor's unstable delivery pattern. To accept Ezekiel's order, Singleton would have to purchase additional equipment and modify its plant layout. The additional equipment would enable the company to add 35,000 laptop fans to its annual production. Singleton's avoidable cost of making 20,000 laptop fans follows:

Costs	Total	Per Unit
Variable costs	$120,000	$6
Fixed cost	140,000	7

Required
a. What would be the financial consequence to Jaybro Company if the Singleton Division makes the laptop fans and sells them to the Ezekiel Division? What range of transfer prices would increase the financial performance of both divisions?
b. Suppose the Ezekiel Division increases production so that it could use 35,000 Singleton Division laptop fans. How would the change in volume affect the range of transfer prices that would financially benefit both divisions?

PROBLEMS—SERIES B

PROBLEM 9–16B *Determining Controllable Costs* **L.O. 3**

At a professional conference just a few days ago, Marlon Angelo, the president of Weiss Corporation, learned how the concept of controllability relates to performance evaluation. In preparing to put this new knowledge into practice, he reviewed the financial data of the company's sales department.

Salaries of salespeople	$ 450,000
Cost of goods sold	48,000,000
Facility-level corporate costs	820,000
Travel expenses	64,000
Depreciation on equipment	200,000
Salary of the sales manager	120,000
Property taxes	8,000
Telephone expenses	78,000

Required
Help Mr. Angelo prepare a list of expenditures that the sales manager controls.

L.O. 3   **PROBLEM 9–17B** *Controllability and Responsibility*

Barry Conroy, president of Ruseiski Corporation, evaluated the performance report of the company's production department. Mr. Conroy was confused by some arguments presented by Amy Berger, the production manager. Some relevant data follow.

Variances	Amount	
Materials quantity variance	$400,000	U
Materials price variance	240,000	F
Labor rate variance	76,000	F
Labor efficiency variance	276,000	U
Volume variance	600,000	U

Ms. Berger argues that she had done a great job, noting the favorable materials price variance and labor rate variance. She argued that she had had no control over factors causing the unfavorable variances. For example, she argued that the unfavorable materials quantity variance was caused by the purchasing department's decision to buy substandard materials that resulted in a substantial amount of spoilage. Moreover, she argued that the unfavorable labor efficiency variance resulted from the substantial materials spoilage which in turn wasted many labor hours, as did the hiring of underqualified workers by the manager of the personnel department. Finally, she said that the sales department's failure to obtain a sufficient number of customer orders really caused the unfavorable volume variance.

Required
a. What would you do first if you were Barry Conroy?
b. Did Ms. Berger deserve the credit she claimed for the favorable variances? Explain.
c. Was Ms. Berger responsible for the unfavorable variances? Explain.

L.O. 2, 3, 4   **PROBLEM 9–18B** *Performance Reports and Evaluation*

The mortgage division of Jacobs Financial Services, Inc., is managed by a vice president who supervises three regional operations. Each regional operation has a general manager and several branches directed by branch managers.

The eastern region has two branches, Jefferson and Vincent. The March responsibility reports for the managers of these branches follow.

	Budgeted*	Actual	Variance	
Jefferson Branch				
Controllable costs				
Employee compensation	$144,000	$150,400	$ 6,400	U
Office supplies	36,000	35,000	1,000	F
Promotions	76,000	64,000	12,000	F
Maintenance	8,000	10,600	2,600	U
Total	$264,000	$260,000	$ 4,000	F
Vincent Branch				
Controllable costs				
Employee compensation	$130,000	$125,000	$ 5,000	F
Office supplies	38,000	42,000	4,000	U
Promotions	72,000	75,000	3,000	U
Maintenance	10,000	9,600	400	F
Total	$250,000	$251,600	$ 1,600	U

*Jacobs uses flexible budgets for performance evaluation.

Other pertinent cost data for March follow.

	Budgeted*	Actual
Cost data of other regions		
Southern	$700,000	$726,000
Western	860,000	844,000
Other costs controllable by		
Eastern region general manager	140,000	146,000
Vice president of mortgage	192,000	196,000

*Jacobs uses flexible budgets for performance evaluation.

Required
a. Prepare a responsibility report for the general manager of the eastern region.
b. Prepare a responsibility report for the vice president of the mortgage division.
c. Explain where the $12,000 favorable promotions variance in the Jefferson branch manager's report is included in the vice president's report.
d. Based on the responsibility report prepared in Requirement *a*, explain where the eastern region's general manager should concentrate her attention.

PROBLEM 9–19B *Different Types of Responsibility Center*

L.O. 5

Olympus Industries, Inc., has five different divisions; each is responsible for producing and marketing a particular product line. The electronic division makes cellular telephones, pagers, and modems. The division also buys and sells other electronic products made by outside companies. Each division maintains sufficient working capital for its own operations. The corporate headquarters, however, makes decisions about long-term capital investments.

Required
a. For purposes of performance evaluation, should Olympus classify its electronic division as a cost center, a profit center, or an investment center? Why?
b. Would the manager of the electronic division be likely to conduct the operations of the division differently if the division were classified as a different type of responsibility center than the one you designated in Requirement *a*? Explain.

PROBLEM 9–20B *Evaluating a Profit Center*

L.O. 2

Larson Fruits Corporation, a fruit wholesaler, has four divisions, each specializing in a particular fruit. Although the four divisions negotiate with their suppliers about prices and quantities of their fruits, the corporate office retains the authority to make decisions about long-term investments. The following data reflect the Orange Division's budgeted and actual operations in 2004.

	Static Budget 2,500,000 Boxes @$15 per Box	Actual Results 2,325,000 Boxes @$14.50 per Box
Sales revenue	$37,500,000	$33,712,500
Less: Variable costs		
Cost of goods sold	(27,500,000)	(25,528,750)
Shipping expenses	(325,000)	(306,250)
Selling expenses	(625,000)	(500,000)
Contribution margin	9,050,000	8,377,500
Less: Fixed costs		
Personnel expenses	(1,500,000)	(1,600,000)
Other administrative expenses	(750,000)	(737,500)
Net income for the division	$ 6,800,000	$ 6,040,000

Required
a. Convert the static budget into a flexible budget.
b. Determine the activity variances between the static budget and the flexible budget.
c. Compute the flexible budget variances.
d. Did the manager of the Orange Division do a good job as a branch manager? Support your answer with the information derived from Requirements *a*, *b*, and *c*.
e. Would you use return on investment to evaluate the division's performance? Explain.

L.O. 6   PROBLEM 9–21B *Return on Investment*

Essex Corporation's balance sheet indicates that the company has $600,000 invested in operating assets. During 2003, Essex earned $96,000 of income on $1,920,000 of sales.

Required
a. Compute Essex's margin for 2003.
b. Compute Essex's turnover for 2003.
c. Compute Essex's return on investment for 2003.
d. Recompute Essex's ROI under each of the following independent assumptions.
   (1) Sales increase from $1,920,000 to $2,160,000, thereby resulting in an increase in income from $96,000 to $113,400.
   (2) Sales remain constant, but Essex reduces expenses, thereby resulting in an increase in income from $96,000 to $100,800.
   (3) Essex is able to reduce its invested capital from $600,000 to $576,000 without affecting income.

L.O. 6, 7   PROBLEM 9–22B *Comparing Return on Investment and Residual Income*

Amber Crayton, the manager of Triden Division, Valley Corporation, has enjoyed success. Her division's return on investment (ROI) has consistently been 16 percent on a total investment of $25,000,000. Valley evaluates its division managers based on ROI. The company's desired ROI is 12 percent. Ms. Crayton is evaluating an investment opportunity that will require a $5,000,000 capital investment and is expected to result in a 13 percent return.

Required
a. Would it be advantageous for Valley Corporation if Ms. Crayton makes the investment under consideration?
b. What effect will making the proposed investment have on Triden Division's ROI? Show computations.
c. What effect will making the proposed investment have on Triden Division's residual income (RI)? Show computations.
d. Would ROI or RI be the better performance measure for Ms. Crayton? Explain.

L.O. 8   PROBLEM 9–23B *Transfer Pricing*

Southwood Electronics Corporation makes a modem that it sells to retail stores for $150 each. The variable cost to produce a modem is $70 each; the total fixed cost is $10,000,000. Southwood is operating at 80 percent of capacity and is producing 200,000 modems annually. Southwood's parent company, Creekview Corporation, notified Southwood's president that another subsidiary company, Ridge Technologies, Inc., has begun making computers and can use Southwood's modem as a part. Ridge needs 40,000 modems annually and is able to acquire similar modems in the market for $144 each.

Under instruction from the parent company, the presidents of Southwood and Ridge meet to negotiate a price for the modem. Southwood insists that its market price is $150 each and will stand firm on that price. Ridge, on the other hand, wonders why it should even talk to Southwood when Ridge can get modems at a lower price.

Required
a. What transfer price would you recommend?
b. Discuss the effect of the intercompany sales on each president's return on investment.
c. Should Southwood be required to use more than excess capacity to provide modems to Ridge if Ridge's demand increases to 60,000 modems? In other words, should it sell some of the 200,000 modems that it currently sells to unrelated companies to Ridge instead? Why or why not?

ANALYZE, THINK, COMMUNICATE

ATC 9–1   BUSINESS APPLICATIONS CASE *Responsibility Accounting*

Jethro Brothers Metal Products, Inc., produces fabricated steel products on a contract basis. Profits based on annual sales volume averaging about $20,000,000 have been modest as compared to industry averages for the past several years. The firm has operated with decentralized management for many years with the president, Dave Jethro, being able to keep a fairly good sense of all aspects of the business.

Two project managers work with Mr. Jethro in supervising each project from the bidding stage through production and delivery. However, they do not have complete authority with respect to production decisions, materials purchases, or labor negotiations. Many of these tasks are frequently performed by individuals who have had experience in these fields. For instance, Twyla Pugh, the purchasing agent, makes many independent buying decisions. She analyzes some of the signed contracts and production schedules and orders the necessary materials. Indirect materials are ordered from time to time by Seth Gattis, the part-time production supervisor. Mr. Gattis is frequently in charge of production to the extent that he schedules some projects and often assigns workers to the various jobs. He also has many years of experience as a welder and often works in this capacity.

Jessica Liu, the accountant, has suggested to Mr. Jethro that some reorganization might be in order since continued efforts to control costs and improve profits under the present organization have not been effective. Mr. Jethro doesn't see much advantage to reorganization, especially if it involves more administrative people; he is proud of the relatively low general and administrative expenses that his firm incurs. He admits that factory overhead could use some monitoring; this is evident from the fact that the predetermined overhead rate has increased rather steadily over time.

The sales manager, Trent Hook, is very much interested in what the accountant is saying. He believes that lower bids would result in more contracts, which should help profits since the company is operating at less than 75 percent capacity, but lower bids are possible only by reducing costs.

Mr. Jethro has conceded that the accountant may have a point and asks: "Jessica, do you believe that a change in organization could improve profits?"

Required
If you were Ms. Liu, how would you organize this company? Is it possible to apply the principles of responsibility accounting?

GROUP ASSIGNMENT *Return on Investment versus Residual Income*

ATC 9–2

Bellco, a division of Becker International Corporation, is operated under the direction of Antoin Sedatt. Bellco is an independent investment center with approximately $72,000,000 of assets that generate approximately $8,640,000 in annual net income. Becker International has additional investment capital of $12,000,000 that is available for the division managers to invest. Mr. Sedatt is aware of an investment opportunity that will provide an 11 percent annual net return. Becker International's desired rate of return is 10 percent.

Required
Divide the class into groups of four or five students and then organize the groups into two sections. Assign Task 1 to the first section and Task 2 to the second section.

Group Tasks

1. Assume that Mr. Sedatt's performance is evaluated based on his ability to maximize return on investment (ROI). Compute ROI using the following two assumptions: Bellco retains its current asset size and Bellco accepts and invests the additional $12,000,000 of assets. Determine whether Mr. Sedatt should accept the opportunity to invest additional funds. Select a spokesperson to present the decision made by the group.
2. Assume that Mr. Sedatt's performance is evaluated based on his ability to maximize residual income. Compute residual income using the following two assumptions: Bellco retains its current asset base and Bellco accepts and invests the additional $12,000,000 of assets. Determine whether Mr. Sedatt should accept the opportunity to invest additional funds. Select a spokesperson to present the decision made by the group.
3. Have a spokesperson from one of the groups in the first section report the two ROIs and the group's recommendation for Mr. Sedatt. Have the groups in this section reach consensus on the ROI and the recommendation.
4. Have a spokesperson from the second section report the two amounts of residual income and disclose the group's recommendation for Mr. Sedatt. Have this section reach consensus on amounts of residual income.
5. Which technique (ROI or residual income) is more likely to result in suboptimization?

RESEARCH ASSIGNMENT *Responsibility for Profit*

ATC 9–3

The October 5, 1998, issue of *Business Week* contains the article "The Pall over Toyland" by Kathleen Morris (p. 50). The article suggests that changes in social attitudes may have permanently changed the

demand for toys. Growth in toy sales for 1998 was expected to be a mere 2 percent although the number of kids is increasing at a far more rapid pace. According to the article, research suggests that "kids are junking their toys sooner these days, putting aside Barbie in favor of Spice Girls CDs, clothes, and video games. Kids' interest in traditional toys is peaking one or two years earlier than 10 years ago." Read this article and complete the following requirements.

Required

a. How will declining sales affect performance measures such as the ROI and residual income of a toy company?

b. Changes in social attitudes are beyond management's control. Therefore, managers cannot be held responsible for the decline in toy sales. Performance measures should be developed to reward managers who are doing a good job if companies are hit by unfavorable general economic trends. Do you agree with this line of reasoning? Explain your position.

c. How are toy manufacturers responding to the apparent changes in social attitudes?

d. How does Adam Klein, head of marketing and strategy for Hasbro, describe his company? Do you believe the new attitude will improve profitability? Given Klein's new vision for Hasbro, would you be willing to invest money in the company? Should Klein be rewarded for the work he did to develop a new business strategy, or should his reward be based on how net income is affected?

ATC 9–4　　WRITING ASSIGNMENT *Transfer Pricing*

Green Lawn Mower, Inc., recently acquired Hallit Engines, a small engine manufacturing company. Green's president believes in decentralization and intends to permit Hallit to continue to operate as an independent entity. However, she has instructed the manager of Green's lawn mower assembly division to investigate the possibility of purchasing engines from Hallit instead of using the current third-party supplier. Hallit has excess capacity. The current full cost to produce each engine is $96. The avoidable cost of making engines is $78 per unit. The assembly division, which currently pays the third party supplier $90 per engine, offers to purchase engines from Hallit at the $90 price. Hallit's president refuses the offer, stating that his company's engines are superior to those the third party supplier provides. Hallit's president believes that the transfer price should be based on the market price for independent customers which is $132 per engine. The manager of the assembly division agrees that Hallit's engines are higher quality than those currently being used but notes that Green's customer base is in the low-end, discount market. Putting more expensive engines on Green mowers would raise the price above the competition and would hurt sales. Green's president tries to negotiate a settlement between the assembly manager and Hallit's president, but the parties are unable to agree on a transfer price.

Required

a. Assuming that Green makes and sells 40,000 lawn mowers per year, what is the cost of suboptimization resulting from the failure to establish a transfer price?

b. Assume that you are a consultant asked by the president of Green to recommend whether a transfer price should be arbitrarily imposed. Write a brief memo that includes your recommendation and your justification for making it.

ATC 9–5　　ETHICAL DILEMMA *Manipulating Return on Investment and Residual Income*

The October 5, 1998, issue of *Business Week* includes the article "Who Can You Trust?" authored by Sarah Bartlett. Among other dubious accounting practices, the article describes a trick known as the "big bath," which occurs when a company makes huge unwarranted asset write-offs that drastically overstate expenses. Outside auditors (CPAs) permit companies to engage in the practice because the assets being written off are of questionable value. Because the true value of the assets cannot be validated, auditors have little recourse but to accept the valuations suggested by management. Recent examples of questionable write-offs include Motorola's $1.8 billion restructuring charge and the multibillion-dollar write-offs for "in-process" research taken by high-tech companies such as Compaq Computer Corp. and WorldCom, Inc.

Required

a. Why would managers want their companies to take a big bath? (*Hint:* Consider how a big bath affects return on investment and residual income in the years following the write-off.)

b. Annual reports are financial reports issued to the public. The reports are the responsibility of auditors who are CPAs who operate under the ethical standards promulgated by the American Institute

of Certified Public Accountants. As a result, attempts to manipulate annual report data are not restricted by the Institute of Management Accountants Standards of Ethical Conduct shown in Exhibit 1-13 of Chapter 1. Do you agree or disagree with this conclusion? Explain your position.

SPREADSHEET ASSIGNMENT *Using Excel*

ATC 9–6

Waldon Corporation's balance sheet shows that the company has $600,000 invested in operating assets. During 2001, Waldon earned $120,000 on $960,000 of sales. The company's desired return on investment (ROI) is 12 percent.

Required
a. Construct a spreadsheet to calculate ROI and residual income using these data. Build the spreadsheet using formulas so that the spreadsheet could be used as a template for any ROI or residual income problem. The following screen capture shows how to construct the template.

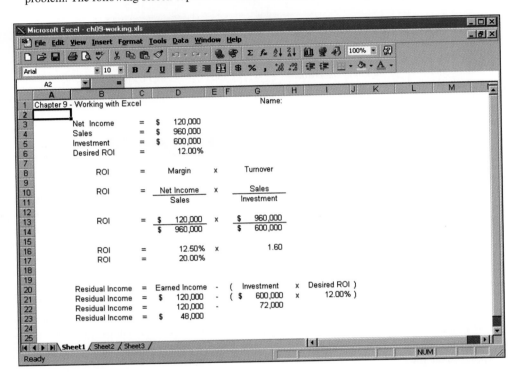

Spreadsheet Tips

(1) The cells below row 12 that show numbers should all be based on formulas. This allows changes in the data rows 3 to 6 to be automatically recalculated.

(2) The parentheses in columns F and J have been entered as text in columns that have a column width of 1.

SPREADSHEET ASSIGNMENT *Mastering Excel*

ATC 9–7

The Pillar Manufacturing Company has three identified levels of authority and responsibility. The organization chart as of December 31, 2004 appears as follows:

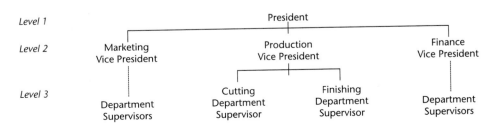

Pertinent expenses for Level 3 follow:

	Budget	Actual
Finishing Department		
Wages expense	$6,240	$6,000
Direct materials	2,300	2,400
Supplies	840	980
Small tools	1,300	1,140
Other	700	820

Pertinent expenses for Level 2 follow:

	Budget	Actual
Production Department		
Administrative expenses	$ 1,200	$1,400
Supervisory salaries	5,800	5,200
Cutting Department	6,800	6,420
Finishing Department	11,380	11,340

Pertinent expenses for Level 1 follow:

	Budget	Actual
President's Office Expense		
Supervisory salaries	$ 4,900	$ 5,100
Clerical staff	800	400
Other expenses	600	700
Production Department	25,180	24,360
Marketing Department	8,850	8,300
Finance Department	5,900	6,220

Required

a. Construct a spreadsheet that shows responsibility reports for the finishing department supervisor, the production vice president, and the president.

b. Include formulas in the responsibility reports that illustrate the interrelationships between these reports. For example, changes in the finishing department report should be automatically reflected in the production department report.

Spreadsheet Tip

(1) Use the absolute value function [=ABS(value)] in the formulas that calculate the variances.

Chapter

10

Planning for Capital Investments

Learning Objectives

After completing this chapter, you should be able to:

1 Distinguish between capital investments and investments in stocks and bonds.

2 Understand and apply the concept of time value of money to capital investment decisions.

3 Distinguish between return on investment and recovery of investment.

4 Explain why the cost of capital constitutes the minimum acceptable rate of return for a capital investment.

5 Use present value tables to determine the present value of future cash flows.

6 Distinguish between lump-sum payments and ordinary annuities.

7 Appreciate the power of computer software in determining present values.

8 Understand the reinvestment assumption implicit in the interest tables and computer software.

9 Determine and interpret the net present value of an investment opportunity.

10 Determine the internal rate of return of an investment opportunity.

11 Identify the typical cash inflows and outflows associated with capital investments.

12 Determine the payback period for an investment opportunity.

13 Determine the unadjusted rate of return for an investment opportunity.

14 Conduct a postaudit of an investment that has been exercised.

the *curious* accountant

Universal Studios in Florida unveiled plans to build Islands of Adventure, a $1.5 billion theme park. Universal believes it can attract customers with high-technology, futuristic thrill rides. The company's chief rival, Disney World, has opted out of the high-tech option. Just how many visitors will be needed to recapture a $1.5 billion investment? How long will it take Universal to recoup its investment? What techniques do companies use to help them justify such vast investments?

The president of EZ Rentals (EZ) is considering the possibility of expanding the company's rental service business. EZ's customers have made numerous requests for LCD projectors that can be used with notebook computers. Indeed, forecasts based on a recent marketing study indicate that the rental of projectors could generate revenue of approximately $200,000 per year. The possibility of increasing revenue is alluring, but EZ's president has a number of unanswered questions. How much do the projectors cost? What is their expected useful life? Will they have a salvage value? Do we have the money it takes to buy them? Do we have the technical expertise to support the product? How much will training cost? How long can we expect customer demand to last? What if we buy the projectors and they become technologically obsolete? How quickly will we be able to recover our investment? Are there other more profitable ways to invest our funds?

Most managers get a bit nervous about making decisions to spend large sums of money that will have long-term effects on their company's profitability. What if Company A spends millions of dollars to build a factory in the United States while its competitors locate their manufacturing facilities in countries that provide cheap labor? Company A's products will become overpriced, but it cannot move the facility because it cannot find a buyer for the factory. What if a pharmaceutical company spends millions of dollars to develop a drug that fails to attain

405

FDA approval? What if another company installs underground cable wire but satellite transmission steals its market? What if a company buys computer equipment that rapidly becomes technologically obsolete? Although these possibilities may be considered remote, they can be very expensive when they do occur. For example, Wachovia Bank's 1997 annual report shows a $70 million dollar write-off of computer equipment. This chapter discusses some of the analytical techniques companies use to evaluate major investment opportunities.

▌Capital Investment Decisions

LO1 Distinguish between capital investments and investments in stocks and bonds.

The purchases of long-term operational assets are **capital investments.** Capital investments differ from investments in stocks and bonds in one important respect. Investments in stocks and bonds can be sold in organized free markets such as the New York Stock Exchange. In contrast, investments in capital assets normally can be recovered only by using those assets. Once a company purchases a capital asset, it is committed to that investment for an extended period of time. If its market turns sour, it is stuck with the consequences. Likewise, the company may be unable to take advantage of new opportunities because its capital is committed. The ultimate profitability of an enterprise hinges, to a large extent, on the quality of a few critically important capital investment decisions.

A capital investment decision is essentially a decision to exchange current cash outflows for the promise of receiving future cash inflows. In the case of EZ Rentals, investing in projection equipment, a cash outflow today, provides an opportunity to collect $200,000 per year in rental revenue, a future cash inflow. Assuming that the projectors have a useful life of four years and no salvage value, how much should EZ be willing to pay for the future cash inflows? If you were EZ's president, would you spend $700,000 today to receive $200,000 per year for the next four years? You would be giving up $700,000 today for the opportunity to receive $800,000 (4 × $200,000) in the future. What happens if the future expectation fails to materialize? What if you collect less than $200,000 per year? If revenue is only $160,000 per year, you would lose $60,000 ($700,000 − [4 × $160,000]). Is $700,000 too much to pay for an opportunity to get $200,000 per year for four years? If $700,000 were too high, would you spend $600,000? If this figure is still too high, how about $500,000? There is no correct answer to these questions. However, an understanding of the *time value of money* concept can help you formulate a rational response.

Time Value of Money

LO2 Understand and apply the concept of time value of money to capital investment decisions.

The **time value of money** concept recognizes the fact that *the present value of a dollar received in the future is less than a dollar.* For example, you may be willing to pay only $0.90 today to receive a promise to collect $1.00 one year from today. The further into the future the receipt is expected to occur, the smaller is its present value. In other words, one dollar to be received two years from today is worth less than one dollar to be received one year from today. Likewise, one dollar to be received three years from today is less valuable than one dollar to be received two years from today, and so on.

The present value of cash inflows diminishes as the time until expected receipt increases for several reasons. First, today's dollar could be deposited in a savings account to earn *interest* that increases its total value. If you wait for your money, you lose the opportunity to earn interest. Second, an element of *risk* is associated with the future dollar. Conditions may change resulting in the failure to collect. Finally, *inflation* diminishes the buying power of the dollar. In other words, the longer you must wait to receive a dollar, the less you will be able to buy with it.

When a company invests in capital assets, it gives present dollars in exchange for the opportunity to receive future dollars. Given the negative consequences associated with trading

current dollars for future dollars, companies must be compensated to encourage them to invest in capital assets. The compensation a company receives is called a *return on investment,* which, as discussed in Chapter 9, is normally expressed as a percentage of the amount of the investment. For example, a $1,000 investment that earns annual income of $100 provides a 10 percent rate of return ($100 ÷ $1,000 = 10%).

Determining the Minimum Rate of Return

What is the minimum *return on investment* that will persuade a company to accept an investment opportunity? To answer this question, most companies consider their cost of capital. To attract capital, a company must provide a benefit to its creditors and owners. For example, the company pays interest to creditors and dividends to owners. Companies that earn a return that is lower than their cost of capital eventually go bankrupt. In other words, they cannot continuously pay out more than they collect. Accordingly, *the* **cost of capital** *represents the* **minimum rate of return** *on investments.* Calculating the cost of capital is a relatively complicated task covered in finance courses. Accordingly, we will not attempt to cover that topic in this text. Instead, we proceed to the subject of how management accounting uses the cost of capital to evaluate investment opportunities. Before we begin, it may be helpful to note that the cost of capital is referred to by a number of terms. In practice, it is sometimes called the *minimum rate of return, the desired rate of return, the required rate of return, the hurdle rate, the cutoff rate,* or the *discount rate.* These terms will be used interchangeably throughout this chapter.

LO3 Distinguish between return on investment and recovery of investment.

LO4 Explain why the cost of capital constitutes the minimum acceptable rate of return for a capital investment.

Study the following cash inflow streams expected from two different potential investments.

	Year 1	Year 2	Year 3	Total
Alternative 1	$2,000	$3,000	$4,000	$9,000
Alternative 2	4,000	3,000	2,000	9,000

Based on visual observation alone, which alternative has the higher present value? Why?

Answer Alternative 2 has the higher present value. The size of the discount increases as the length of the time period increases. In other words, a dollar received in year 3 has a lower present value than a dollar received in year 1. Since most of the expected cash inflows from Alternative 2 are received earlier than those from Alternative 1, Alternative 2 has a higher present value even though the total expected cash inflows are the same.

Check
Yourself
10–1

Converting Future Cash Inflows into Their Equivalent Present Values

Given a desired rate of return and the amount of the future cash flow, simple algebra can be used to determine the present value. To illustrate, we examine the $200,000 that EZ expects to earn during the first year that it leases the projectors. Assuming that EZ desires to earn a 12 percent rate of return, what amount of cash should it invest today (present value outflow) to obtain the $200,000 cash inflow at the end of the year (future value)? The answer can be determined as follows.[1]

$$\text{Investment} + (0.12 \times \text{Investment}) = \text{Future cash inflow}$$
$$1.12 \text{ Investment} = \$200,000$$
$$\text{Investment} = \$200,000 \div 1.12$$
$$\text{Investment} = \$178,571$$

---

[1] All computations in this chapter are rounded to the nearest whole dollar.

The computations indicate that if EZ invests $178,571 cash on January 1 and earns a 12 percent return on the investment, it will have $200,000 on December 31. Stated differently, an investor who is able to earn a 12 percent return on investment is indifferent as to the choice of having $178,571 now or receiving $200,000 one year from now. The investor views the two options as being equal. The following mathematical proof supports this equality.

$$\text{Investment} + (0.12 \times \text{Investment}) = \$200,000$$
$$\$178,571 + (0.12 \times \$178,571) = \$200,000$$
$$\$178,571 + 21,429 = \$200,000$$
$$\$200,000 = \$200,000$$

LO5 Use present value tables to determine the present value of future cash flows.

Present Value Table for Single-Amount Cash Inflows. The algebraic process described above is used to convert a onetime receipt of cash at some time in the future into a present value. Onetime receipts of cash are frequently called **single-payment** or **lump sum** cash flows. Because EZ desires to earn a 12 percent rate of return, the previous computations suggest that the present value of the first cash inflow is $178,571. We now determine the present value of receiving a single amount (lump sum) of $200,000 in the second, third, and fourth years. Using algebra to convert these future values into their present value equivalents requires a considerable amount of mathematical manipulation. To simplify such computation, financial analysts frequently use tables that contain factors to use to convert future values into their present value equivalents. The table of conversion factors is used to transform future values into present values; therefore, it is commonly called a **present value table.**[2] A present value table is normally composed of columns that represent different return rates and rows that represent different periods of time. A typical present value table is shown as Table 1 in Appendix A.

To illustrate the use of the present value table, locate the conversion factor in Table 1 at the intersection of the 12% column and the row representing one period. At this location, you will find the conversion factor 0.892857. Multiplying this factor by the $200,000 expected cash inflow yields the result $178,571 ($200,000 × 0.892857). Notice that this is the same value that was determined algebraically in the previous section of this chapter. The conversion factors in the present value tables reduce the mathematical manipulation required to convert future values to present values.

The conversion factors for the second, third, and fourth periods are 0.797194, 0.711780, and 0.635518, respectively. These factors are located under the 12% column at rows 2, 3, and 4, respectively. Validate your understanding of the present value table by locating these factors in Table 1 of Appendix A. Multiplying the conversion factors by the future cash inflow for each period produces their present value equivalents. The conversion process is shown in Exhibit 10–1.

Exhibit 10–1	Present Value of a $200,000 Cash Inflow to be Received for Four Years					
	PV	=	FV	×	Present Value Table Factor =	Present Value Equivalent
Period 1	PV	=	$200,000	×	0.892857 =	$178,571
Period 2	PV	=	200,000	×	0.797194 =	159,439
Period 3	PV	=	200,000	×	0.711780 =	142,356
Period 4	PV	=	200,000	×	0.635518 =	127,104
					Total	$607,470

The information in Exhibit 10–1 indicates that investing $607,470 today at a 12 percent rate of return is equivalent to receiving $200,000 per year for four years. Stated differently, because EZ Rentals desires to earn a 12 percent rate of return, the company should be willing to pay $607,470 to purchase the projectors.

LO6 Distinguish between lump-sum payments and ordinary annuities.

Present Value Table for Annuities. The mathematical manipulation required to convert the lump-sum cash inflows just described into their present value equivalents can be simplified even further by accumulating the present value table factors prior to multiplying them by the cash inflows. For example, the total of the present value table factors shown in Exhibit 10–1 is 3.037349 (0.892857 + 0.797194 + 0.711780 + 0.635518). By multiplying this **accumulated conversion factor** by the expected annual cash inflow, we determine the present value

[2]The present value table is constructed from the mathematical formula $(1 \div [1 + r]^n)$ where r equals the rate of return and n equals the number of periods.

equivalent of $607,470 ($200,000 $\times$ 3.037349). As with lump-sum conversion factors, accumulated conversion factors can be precalculated and organized in a table format with *columns* that represent different rates of return and *rows* that represent different periods of time. A present value table showing accumulated conversion factors is shown in Table 2 of Appendix A. To confirm your understanding of this present value table, locate the conversion factor at the intersection of the 12% column and the row representing the fourth time period. At this intersection, you will find the value 3.037349, confirming that the accumulated conversion factors are merely the sum of the individual conversion factors.

The conversion factors shown in Table 2 apply to an **annuity,** which is a series of cash flows that meets three criteria: (1) equal payment amounts, (2) equal time intervals, and (3) a constant rate of return. In the case of EZ Rentals, all cash inflows were for equivalent amounts ($200,000); the interval between cash inflows was an equal length of time (one year); and the rate of return applied to each inflow was held constant at 12 percent. Accordingly, the series of expected cash inflows from renting the projectors is classified as an annuity. The present value annuity table cannot be used if any of these conditions is not satisfied.

The purpose of the present value annuity tables is to reduce the amount of mathematical computations necessary to convert future cash inflows into their present value equivalents. In the case of EZ Rentals, you can convert the cash inflows as shown in Exhibit 10–1. This process requires you to locate four conversion factors, to multiply each conversion factor by the annual cash inflow (four multiplications), and to sum the products of the multiplications. In contrast, you can treat the series of payments as an annuity. This requires a single multiplication of a conversion factor drawn from Table 2 by the amount of the annuity payment. Regardless of which conversion approach you choose to use, you obtain the same result (a present value of $607,470). Recall also that the conversion can be accomplished by applying an algebraic formula. Indeed, the table values are derivations of algebraic formulas. The purpose of the present value tables is to reduce the computations necessary to convert future values to present values.

Software Programs That Determine Present Values. Software programs offer an even more efficient means of converting future values into present value equivalents. These programs are frequently built into handheld calculators and computer spreadsheet programs. Different software developers use a variety of input formats. As an example, we demonstrate the procedures used in a Microsoft Excel spreadsheet.

LO7 Appreciate the power of computer software in determining present values.

An Excel spreadsheet contains a variety of financial functions, one of which is designed to convert a future value annuity into its present value equivalent. This present value function uses the syntax *PV(rate,nper,pmt)* in which *rate* is the desired rate of return, *nper* is the number of periods, and *pmt* is the amount of the payment (periodic cash inflow). To convert a future value annuity into its present value equivalent, you provide the function with the appropriate amounts for the rate, number of periods, and amount of the annuity (cash inflows) into a spreadsheet cell. When you press the Enter key, the present value equivalent appears in the spreadsheet cell.

The instantaneous conversion power of the spreadsheet is extremely useful for answering what-if questions. Exhibit 10–2 demonstrates this power by providing spreadsheet conversions for three different scenarios. The first scenario includes the cash flow annuity assumptions used in the EZ Rentals case. Specifically, the spreadsheet provides the present value equivalent ($607,470) for an annuity at a 12 percent rate of interest with a four-year term and a $200,000 per year cash inflow. Notice that the present value is shown as a *negative* number. This format is used to indicate that a $607,470 *cash outflow* would be required to obtain the cash inflow annuity. The present value equivalent shown under Scenario 2 answers the question, What if we change the annuity assumptions under Scenario 1 to reflect a 14 percent desired rate of return? The present value equivalent shown under Scenario 3 answers the question, What if we change the annuity assumptions under Scenario 1 to reflect a $300,000 annual cash inflow? Similarly, a wide range of scenarios could be examined rapidly by changing the variables included in the spreadsheet function. In each case, the computer would do the

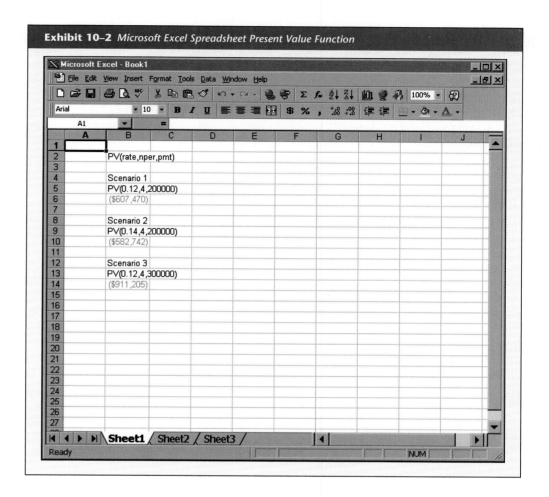

Exhibit 10–2 *Microsoft Excel Spreadsheet Present Value Function*

calculations, leaving the manager more time to spend on the analysis of the data rather than its mathematical manipulation.

Although the software approach is widely used in business practice, the diversity of interfaces used in different calculators and spreadsheet programs makes it an inappropriate approach for textbook presentations. Accordingly, this text uses the present value tables in Appendix A in the demonstration problems in the text and in the end-of-chapter exercises and problems. If you use software to solve these problems, you will obtain the same answers. All approaches including formulas, conversion tables, and software are based on the same mathematical principles and will therefore produce the same results.

Ordinary Annuity Assumption. You may have noticed that all of the conversion methods we have described assumed that the cash inflows occurred at the end of each accounting period. This distribution pattern is called an **ordinary annuity**.[3] In practice, cash inflows are likely to be spread evenly over the period. For example, EZ Rentals is likely to collect cash revenue from the rental of its projectors on a monthly basis rather than collecting a single lump-sum receipt at the end of each of the four years. Even so, the ordinary annuity assumption is frequently used in practice because it simplifies the computations associated with accounting for the time value of money. Recall that capital investment projections are based on

---

[3]When cash inflows occur at the beginning of each accounting period, the distribution is called an *annuity due.* Although this distribution pattern is applicable to some business transactions, its application is less common than the ordinary annuity. This text focuses on the more common practice of using an ordinary annuity assumption.

many estimates because pinpoint accuracy about the future is impossible to obtain. The anticipated cash inflows, the life of the investment, and the rate of return involve future expectations that are subject to many uncertainties. The compromise between accuracy and simplicity associated with the ordinary annuity assumption is just one more factor requiring human judgment in the decision-making process.

Reinvestment Assumption. The present value computations in the previous sections indicate that investing $607,470 today at a 12 percent rate of return is equivalent to receiving $200,000 per year for four years. Stated differently, a $200,000 cash inflow per year is equivalent to earning a 12 percent rate of return on a $607,470 investment. Exhibit 10–3 illustrates this relationship.[4]

LO8 Understand the reinvestment assumption implicit in the interest tables and computer software.

The information in Exhibit 10–3 indicates that an investment in the projection equipment does yield a 12 percent return. It is customary practice to assume that the desired rate of return includes the effects of *compounding*.[5] Accordingly, when we say an investment is "earning the desired rate of return," we are making the assumption that the cash inflows generated by the investment are reinvested at the desired rate of return. In this case, we are assuming that EZ will reinvest the $200,000 annual cash inflows in other investments that will earn a 12 percent return.

Exhibit 10–3 *Cash Flow Classifications for EZ's Investment in Projectors*

Time Period	(a) Investment Balance During the Year	(b) Annual Cash Inflow	(c) Return on Investment (a × 0.12)	(d) Recovered Investment (b − c)	(e) Year-End Investment Balance (a − d)
1	$607,470	$200,000	$72,896	$127,104	$480,366
2	480,366	200,000	57,644	142,356	338,010
3	338,010	200,000	40,561	159,439	178,571
4	178,571	200,000	21,429	178,571	(0)
Totals		$800,000	$192,530	$607,470	

▌Techniques for Analyzing Capital Investment Proposals

Numerous analytical tools and techniques may be used to facilitate capital investment decisions. Each of the procedures has certain advantages and disadvantages. Management may choose to apply more than one technique to a particular proposal to take full advantage of the information at its disposal. Although it may seem that the application of different techniques to the same proposal is expensive, this is not the case. Most companies have access to computer facilities that include a variety of standard capital budgeting programs. Accordingly, applying different techniques to the same proposal normally requires little extra effort. In

---

[4]Exhibit 10–3 is analogous to an amortization table for a long-term note with equal payments.

[5]*Compounding* refers to reinvesting the proceeds from an investment so that the total amount of invested capital increases, thereby resulting in even higher returns. For example, assume that $100 is invested at a 10 percent compounded annual rate of return. At the end of the first year, the investment yields a $10 return ($100 × 0.10). The $10 return plus any recovered investment is reinvested so that the total amount of invested capital at the beginning of the second year is $110. The return for the second year is $11 ($110 × 0.10). All funds are reinvested so that the return for the third year is $12.10 ([$110 + $11] × 0.10).

contrast, the benefits of obtaining a perspective that is not biased by selecting only one particular analytical procedure are substantial.

Net Present Value

LO9 Determine and interpret the net present value of an investment opportunity.

By using the present value conversion techniques just described, EZ Rentals management was able to determine that it would be willing to make a $607,470 present value investment to obtain a four-year, $200,000 future value annuity cash inflow. Note carefully that the $607,470 investment is *not* the cost of the projection equipment but is the amount that EZ is willing to pay for the equipment. The cost of the equipment may be more or less than its present value to EZ Rentals. To determine whether EZ should invest in the equipment, the present value of the future cash inflows ($607,470) must be compared to the cost of the equipment (the current cash outflow required to purchase the equipment). Specifically, the cost of the investment is subtracted from the present value of the future cash inflows to determine the **net present value** of the investment opportunity. A positive net present value indicates that the investment will yield a rate of return that is higher than 12 percent. In contrast, a negative net present value suggests the return is less than 12 percent.

To illustrate, assume that the projection equipment can be purchased for $582,742. Should EZ accept the capital investment opportunity? Based on the assumption of a desired rate of return of 12 percent, the answer is yes. The net present value of the investment opportunity is computed as follows.

Present value of future cash inflows	$607,470
Cost of investment (required cash outflow)	(582,742)
Net present value	$ 24,728

The positive net present value suggests that the investment will earn a rate of return in excess of 12 percent. Because the projected rate of return is higher than the desired rate of return, the analysis suggests that the investment opportunity should be accepted.

Check Yourself 10–2

To increase productivity, Wald Corporation is considering the purchase of a new machine that costs $50,000. Wald expects using the machine to increase annual net cash inflows by $12,500 for each of the next five years. Wald desires a minimum annual rate of return of 10 percent on the investment. Determine the net present value of the investment opportunity and recommend whether Wald should acquire the machine.

Answer

Present value of future cash flows = Future cash flow × Table 2 factor ($n = 5, r = 10\%$)
Present value of future cash flows = $12,500 × 3.790787 = $47,385
Net present value = PV of future cash flow − Cost of machine
Net present value = $47,385 − $50,000 = ($2,615)

The negative net present value indicates the investment will yield a rate of return below the desired rate of return. Wald should not acquire the new machine.

Internal Rate of Return

LO10 Determine the internal rate of return of an investment opportunity.

The net present value method indicates that EZ's investment in the projection equipment will provide a return in excess of the desired rate, but it does not compute the actual rate of return to expect from the investment. If EZ's management team wants to know the rate of return to expect from the investment in the projectors, it must use the *internal rate of return method.*

The **internal rate of return** is defined as the rate that equates the present value of cash inflows and outflows. In other words, it is the rate that will produce a zero net present value. In

the case of EZ Rentals, the internal rate of return can be determined as follows. First, compute the *present value table factor* for a $200,000 annuity that would yield a $582,742 present value cash outflow (cost of investment).

Present value table factor $\times$ $200,000 = $582,742
Present value table factor = $582,742 $\div$ $200,000
Present value table factor = 2.91371

Second, since the expected annual cash inflows constitute a four-year annuity, scan Table 2 in Appendix A at period $n = 4$. Try to locate the table factor just computed. The rate that is listed at the top of the column in which the factor is located is the internal rate of return. We suggest that you turn to Table 2 and determine the internal rate of return for this case before you read further. The correct answer is located in the 14 percent column. The difference in the table value (2.913712) and the value computed here (2.91371) is due to truncation. Accordingly, if EZ invests $582,742 in the projectors and the equipment produces a $200,000 annual cash flow for four years, EZ will earn a 14 percent rate of return on its investment.

The *internal rate of return* may be compared with a *desired rate of return* to determine whether to accept or reject a particular investment project. Assuming that EZ desires to earn a minimum rate of return of 12 percent, the preceding analysis suggests that it should accept the investment opportunity. More specifically, because the internal rate of return (14 percent) is higher than the desired rate of return (12 percent), the investment alternative should be accepted. An internal rate of return that is below the desired rate would suggest that a particular proposal should be rejected. Because the desired rate of return constitutes the line of demarcation for the acceptance or rejection of investment alternatives, it is sometimes called the *cutoff rate* or the *hurdle rate*. In other words, to be accepted, an investment proposal must provide an internal rate of return that is higher than the hurdle rate, cutoff rate, or desired rate of return. Recall that these terms are merely alternative expressions for the firm's *cost of capital*. Ultimately, to be accepted, an investment must provide an internal rate of return that is higher than the company's cost of capital.

▌Techniques for Measuring Investment Cash Flows

LO11 Identify the typical cash inflows and outflows associated with capital investments.

EZ Rentals' analysis of the option to purchase projection equipment represents a simple capital investment scenario. The project included only one cash outflow and a single annuity inflow. Many investment decisions involve a variety of cash outflows and inflows. The following section of this chapter discusses the different types of cash flows encountered in business practice.

Cash Inflows

Cash inflows generated from capital investments come from *four basic sources*. As suggested in the case of EZ Rentals, the most common source of cash inflows is incremental revenue. **Incremental revenue** refers to the *additional* cash inflows from operations generated by using an additional capital asset. For example, a taxi company expects revenues from taxi fares to increase if it purchases additional automobiles. Similarly, investments in new apartments should result in rent revenue; the opening of a new store should result in incremental sales revenue.

The second type of cash inflow results from *cost savings*. More specifically, decreases in cash outflows have the same overall effect as increases in cash inflows. Either way, the firm's

cash position is improved. For example, purchasing an automated computer system may enable a company to reduce cash outflows associated with salaries. Similarly, relocating a manufacturing facility near the source of its raw materials can reduce cash outflows associated with transportation costs. Ben Franklin recognized the value of cost savings in his famous observation, "A penny saved is a penny earned."

An investment's *salvage value* is a third source of cash inflow. Even when one company has fully used an asset, it may still be useful to another company. Accordingly, many assets are sold after some company no longer considers them to be useful. The salvage value represents a one-time cash inflow obtained at the termination of the investment.

A cash inflow can also be obtained through a *reduction in the amount of* **working capital** that is necessary to support an investment. A certain level of working capital is required to support most business investments. For example, a new retail outlet store requires cash, inventory, receivables, and so on to accomplish its sales function. When an investment is terminated, the decrease in the working capital commitment associated with the investment normally results in a cash inflow.

Cash Outflows

Cash outflows can be categorized into *three primary groups.* The first group includes the outflows associated with the *initial investment.* Care must be taken to identify all cash outflows that are connected with the purchase of a capital asset. The purchase price, transportation costs, installation costs, and training costs are examples of typical cash outflows related to the initial investment.

Second, cash outflows may result from *increases in operating expenses.* If a company increases its output capacity by investing in additional equipment, it may experience higher utility bills, labor costs, maintenance expenses, and so on when the machinery is placed into service. These expenditures cause cash outflows to increase.

Third, *increases in working capital* commitments result in cash outflows. Frequently, investments in new assets must be supported by a certain level of working capital. For example, investing in a copy machine requires that cash be spent to buy and maintain a supply of paper, toner, and other supplies. An increase in the amount of working capital commitment should be treated as a cash outflow in the period that the commitment is required.

Exhibit 10–4 summarizes the cash inflow and outflow items discussed. The illustration does not contain an exhaustive list but provides a summary of the most common cash flow items found in business practice.

Exhibit 10–4 *Typical Cash Flows Associated With Capital Investments*

Inflow Items	Outflow Items
1. Incremental revenue	1. Initial investment
2. Cost savings	2. Incremental expenses
3. Salvage values	3. Working capital commitments
4. Recovery of working capital	

■ Techniques for Comparing Alternative Capital Investment Opportunities

The management of Torres Transfer Company is considering two investment opportunities. The first opportunity, which would enable Torres to modernize its maintenance facility, would require the purchase of $80,000 of new equipment. The equipment would have an expected useful life of five years and a $4,000 salvage value and would replace existing equipment that had originally cost $45,000. The old equipment has a current book value of $15,000 and a trade-in value of $5,000. The old equipment is technologically obsolete, but it can operate for an additional five years. Torres expects to incur $3,000 of training cost to teach employees to operate the new equipment. Training is provided by the manufacturer of the equipment and must be paid for on the day the equipment is purchased. Two primary advantages are associated with the modernization. First, it will permit the company to better manage its inventory

of small parts. Indeed, the company's accountant believes that by the end of the first year after its implementation, the carrying value of small parts inventory can be reduced by $12,000. Second, the modernization is expected to increase efficiency, resulting in a $21,500 reduction in annual operating expenses.

The second investment alternative available to Torres is the purchase of a truck that would enable Torres to expand its delivery area and thereby increase revenue. The truck is expected to cost $115,000. It will have a useful life of five years and a $30,000 salvage value. Operating the truck will require the company to increase its inventory of supplies, its petty cash account, and its accounts receivable and payable balances. As a result of these changes, an investment in the truck is expected to add $5,000 to the company's working capital base immediately. The working capital cash outflow is expected to be recovered at the end of the truck's useful life. The truck is expected to produce $69,000 per year in additional revenues. The driver's salary and other operating expenses are expected to be $32,000 per year. A major overhaul costing $20,000 is expected to be required at the end of the third year of operation. Assuming that Torres desires to earn a rate of return of 14 percent, which of the two investment alternatives should it choose?

Net Present Value

We begin our analysis by calculating the net present value of the two investment alternatives. The results of these computations are shown in Exhibit 10–5. Study this exhibit carefully before reading further. Note the three-step approach used to determine the net present value of each investment alternative. Step 1 requires the identification of all cash inflows; some may be annuities, and others may be lump-sum receipts. In the case of Alternative 1, the cost saving is an annuity, and the inflow from the salvage value is a lump-sum receipt. Once the cash flows have been identified, the appropriate conversion factors are identified and the cash flows are converted to their equivalent present values. Step 2 follows the same process to determine the present value of the cash outflows. Step 3 subtracts the present value of the outflows from the present value of the inflows to determine the net present value. The same three-step approach is used to determine the net present value of Alternative 2.

LO9 Determine and interpret the net present value of an investment opportunity.

Most of the items in Exhibit 10–5 are self-explanatory. However, note that with respect to Alternative 1, the original cost and the book value of the old equipment have been ignored. As indicated in a previous chapter, these cost measures represent *sunk costs* and are not relevant to the decision-making process. The concept of relevance applies to long-term capital investment decisions just as it applies to the short-term special decisions that were discussed in Chapter 4. To be relevant to a capital investment decision, costs or revenues must involve a different present and future cash flow for each alternative. The historical cost of the old equipment does not differ between the alternatives and therefore, is not relevant.

The fact that both investment alternatives produce a *positive net present value* indicates that both investments will generate a return in excess of 14 percent. Although this information is useful, it does not indicate which investment is the more favorable. Indeed, the data may even mislead an uninformed manager. One is tempted to identify Alternative 2 as the better choice because its present value ($11,703) is higher than that produced by Alternative 1 ($8,414). However, net present value is expressed in *absolute dollar* amounts. This means that a large investment project can have a net present value that is higher than that of a small project even though the smaller project is earning a higher rate of return.

To make reasonable comparisons among investment alternatives, management should consider the size of the investment in the present value analysis. This can be accomplished by computing a **present value index.** This index is computed by dividing the present value of cash inflows by the present value of cash outflows. *The higher the ratio, the higher the rate of return per dollar invested in the proposed project.* The present value index for the two alternatives available to Torres Transfer Company are as follows.

Exhibit 10–5 *Net Present Value Analysis*

	Amount	×	Conversion Factor	=	Present Value
Alternative 1: Modernize Maintenance Facility					
Step 1: Cash inflows					
1. Cost savings	$21,500	×	3.433081*	=	$73,811
2. Salvage value	4,000	×	0.519369†	=	2,077
3. Working capital recovery	12,000	×	0.877193‡	=	10,526
Total					$86,414
Step 2: Cash outflows					
1. Cost of equipment					
($80,000 cost—$5,000 trade-in)	$75,000	×	1.000000§	=	$75,000
2. Training costs	3,000	×	1.000000§	=	3,000
Total					$78,000
Step 3: Net present value					
Total present value of cash inflows	$86,414				
Total present value of cash outflows	(78,000)				
Net present value	$ 8,414				
Alternative 2: Purchase Delivery Truck					
Step 1: Cash inflows					
1. Incremental revenue	$ 69,000	×	3.433081*	=	$236,883
2. Salvage value	30,000	×	0.519369†	=	15,581
2. Working capital recovery	5,000	×	0.519369†	=	2,597
Total					$255,061
Step 2: Cash outflows					
1. Cost of truck	$115,000	×	1.000000§	=	$115,000
2. Working capital increase	5,000	×	1.000000§	=	5,000
3. Increased operating expense	32,000	×	3.433081*	=	109,859
4. Major overhaul	20,000	×	0.674972∓	=	13,499
Total					$243,358
Step 3: Net present value					
Total present value of cash inflows	$255,061				
Total present value of cash outflows	(243,358)				
Net present value	$ 11,703				

*Present value of annuity table 2, $n = 5$, $r = 14\%$.
†Present value of single payment table 1, $n = 5$, $r = 14\%$.
‡Present value of single payment table 1, $n = 1$, $r = 14\%$.
§Present value at beginning of period 1.
∓Present value of single payment table 1, $n = 3$, $r = 14\%$.

$$\text{Present value index for Alternative 1} = \frac{\text{Present value of cash inflows}}{\text{Present value of cash outflows}} = \frac{\$86,415.04}{\$78,000.00} = 1.108$$

$$\text{Present value index for Alternative 2} = \frac{\text{Present value of cash inflows}}{\text{Present value of cash outflows}} = \frac{\$255,060.51}{\$243,358.03} = 1.048$$

The present value index can be used to rank order investment alternatives. In this case, the indices reveal that Alternative 1 would yield a higher return than Alternative 2.

Internal Rate of Return

LO10 Determine the internal rate of return of an investment opportunity.

Investment alternatives can also be rank ordered by calculating the internal rate of return for each investment. Generally, *the higher the rate, the better the investment.* We previously demonstrated the calculation of the internal rate of return for an investment that generates a simple cash inflow annuity. Unfortunately, the computations are significantly more complicated for investments with uneven cash flows. Recall that the internal rate of return is the rate that produces a zero net present value. The manual computation of the rate that produces a

zero net present value may require a tedious trial-and-error process. First, estimate the rate of return for a particular investment and proceed by calculating the net present value. If the calculation produces a negative net present value, reduce the estimated rate of return and recalculate. If this calculation produces a positive net present value, the actual internal rate of return lies between the first and second estimates. Proceed by making a third estimate and once again recalculate the net present value. Continue in this fashion until you locate the rate of return that produces a net present value of zero. Fortunately, many calculators and spreadsheet programs are designed to make these computations. To illustrate, we show the process used in a Microsoft Excel spreadsheet. Excel uses the syntax *IRR(values, guess)* in which *values* is a reference to cells that contain the cash flows for which you want to calculate the internal rate of return and *guess* is a number that you guess is close to the internal rate of return (IRR) result. The IRRs for the two investment alternatives available to Torres Transfer Company are shown in Exhibit 10–6. When reviewing this exhibit, be aware that the Excel approach requires you to net cash outflows against cash inflows for any period that contains both. We have labeled the net cash flows in the spreadsheet for your convenience. This labeling process is not necessary to execute the IRR function. Indeed, the entire function, including values and guess, can be entered into a single cell of the spreadsheet. Accordingly, for a person who is familiar with spreadsheet programs, the input required can be significantly simplified.

Exhibit 10–6 *Microsoft Excel Spreadsheet Internal Rate of Return Function*

The IRR results in Exhibit 10–6 validate the rank ordering that was accomplished through the present value index. Again, Alternative 1 (modernize maintenance facility) with an internal rate of return of 18.69 percent ranks above Alternative 2 (purchase a truck) with an internal rate of return of 17.61 percent. Recall that this result occurs even though Alternative 2 produced a higher net present value (see Exhibit 10–5). However, it must also be noted that Alternative 2 still may be the better investment option, depending on the amount of funds available for investment. Suppose that Torres has $120,000 of available funds to invest. Because Alternative 1 requires only a $78,000 initial investment, $42,000 ($120,000

McDonald's knows that some locations are better than others. Locations in high traffic areas bring more customers with more cash than do low traffic areas. Unfortunately, high traffic locations usually cost more. Rent is higher and demand for employees increases salaries, taxes and other charges in highly populated areas. Accordingly, cash flows vary for McDonald's restaurants located in different types of areas. Fortunately, McDonald's can use discounted cash flow techniques such as net present value and internal rate of return to compare investment opportunities at different locations. These techniques enable the company to select the most profitable locations for new restaurants.

− $78,000) of capital will not be invested. If Torres has no other investment opportunities for this $42,000, the company would be better off to invest the entire $120,000 in Alternative 2 ($115,000 cost of truck + $5,000 working capital increase). In other words, earning 17.61 percent on a $120,000 investment is better than earning 18.69 percent on a $78,000 investment with no return on the remaining $42,000. Again, this discussion emphasizes the fact that management accounting requires the exercise of judgment in the decision-making process.

■ Relevance and the Time Value of Money

Suppose that you have the opportunity to invest in one of two capital projects. Both projects require an immediate cash outflow of $6,000 and will produce future cash inflows of $8,000. The only difference between the two projects is the timing of the receipt of the inflows. The receipt schedule for both projects follows.

	Project 1	Project 2
2001	$3,500	$2,000
2002	3,000	2,000
2003	1,000	2,000
2004	500	2,000
Total	$8,000	$8,000

Because both projects cost the same and produce the same total cash inflows, they may appear to be equal. In other words, regardless of whether you select Project 1 or Project 2, you pay $6,000 and receive $8,000. When consideration is given to the time value of money, however, Project 1 is clearly preferable to Project 2. To validate this point, we determine the net present value of both projects, assuming a 10 percent desired rate of return.

Net Present Value for Project 1

Period	Cash Inflow	×	Conversion Factor Table 1, $r = 10\%$	=	Present Value
1	$3,500	×	0.909091	=	$3,182
2	3,000	×	0.826446	=	2,479
3	1,000	×	0.751315	=	751
4	500	×	0.683013	=	342
Present value of future cash inflows					$6,754
Present value of cash outflow					(6,000)
Net present value Project 1					$ 754

Net Present Value for Project 2

	Cash Inflow Annuity	×	Conversion Factor Table 2, $r = 10\%$, $n = 4$		Present Value
Present value of cash outflow	$2,000	×	3.169865		$6,340
Cost of Project					(6,000)
Net present value Project 2					$ 340

Clearly, the net present value of Project 1 ($754) is preferable to the net present value of Project 2 ($340). As this case illustrates, it is important to recognize that the timing as well as the amount of cash flows has a significant impact on capital investment decisions. Recall that costs or revenues must be different for the alternatives to be considered relevant. Cash flows that differ with respect to the timing of payment or receipt are relevant for decision-making purposes.

Tax Considerations

To this point, we have ignored the effect of taxes on capital investment decisions. Taxes are important because they affect the amount of cash flows generated by investments. To illustrate, assume that Wu Company purchases an asset that costs $240,000. The asset has a four-year useful life and no salvage value and is depreciated on a straight-line basis. The asset generates cash revenue of $90,000 per year. Finally, assume that Wu's income tax rate is 40 percent. What is the net present value of the asset, assuming that Wu's management desires to earn a 10 percent rate of return after taxes? The first step in answering this question is to calculate the amount of annual cash flow generated by the asset. The appropriate computations are shown in Exhibit 10–7.

Because the depreciation did not require a cash payment (cash is paid at the time of purchase rather than when depreciation is recognized), it must be added back to after-tax income to determine the amount of annual cash inflow. Once the amount of the cash flow has been determined, the net present value can be determined as indicated here.

$$\begin{array}{ccccccc} \text{Cash flow} \\ \text{annuity} \end{array} \times \begin{array}{c} \text{Conversion factor} \\ \text{Table 2, } r = 10\%, n = 4 \end{array} = \begin{array}{c} \text{Present Value} \\ \text{Cash Inflows} \end{array} - \begin{array}{c} \text{Present Value} \\ \text{Cash Outflows} \end{array} = \begin{array}{c} \text{Net Present} \\ \text{Value} \end{array}$$

$$\$78,000 \times 3.169865 = \$247,249 - \$240,000 = \$7,249$$

Exhibit 10–7 *Determining Cash Flow from Investment*

	Period 1	Period 2	Period 3	Period 4
Cash revenue	$90,000	$90,000	$90,000	$90,000
Depreciation expense (noncash)	(60,000)	(60,000)	(60,000)	(60,000)
Income before taxes	$30,000	$30,000	$30,000	$30,000
Income tax at 40%	(12,000)	(12,000)	(12,000)	(12,000)
Income after tax	$18,000	$18,000	$18,000	$18,000
Depreciation add back	60,000	60,000	60,000	60,000
Annual cash inflow	$78,000	$78,000	$78,000	$78,000

Companies such as Universal Studios use a variety of sophisticated analytical techniques to help them evaluate the worthiness of different investment opportunities. Two of these include net present value and internal rate of return. However, it is important to recognize that these techniques are merely mathematical manipulations of estimated cash flows. The adage "garbage in, garbage out" applies here. The appearance of mathematical precision must not be permitted to obscure the underlying economic uncertainty. The final result— no matter how precise it looks—is still just a rough estimate.

Notice that the depreciation sheltered some of the income from taxation. In other words, the tax rate is applied to income after depreciation has been deducted. Without depreciation, the income tax would have been $36,000 ($90,000 × 0.40) instead of $12,000 ($30,000 × 0.40). The $24,000 differential ($36,000 − $12,000) is known as a *depreciation tax shield.* The amount of the depreciation tax shield can also be computed by multiplying the tax rate by the depreciation expense ($60,000 × 0.40 = $24,000).

Because of the time value of money concept, companies desire to maximize the depreciation tax shield early in the life of an asset. In other words, companies want to delay paying taxes as long as possible. For this reason, most companies calculate depreciation according to the *modified accelerated cost recovery system (MACRS)* as permitted in the tax law. As its name implies, MACRS recognizes depreciation on an accelerated basis, thereby recognizing larger amounts of depreciation in the early years of an asset's useful life. The higher depreciation charges mean lower amounts of taxable income and thereby lower taxes. In the later years of an asset's useful life, this condition reverses itself. Specifically, lower depreciation charges result in higher taxes. Accordingly, accelerated depreciation does not allow companies to avoid taxes but to delay them. Given what you now know about the time value of money, however, you can easily understand why a company would desire to delay making cash payments as long as possible.

Techniques That Ignore the Time Value of Money

Several techniques for evaluating capital investment proposals ignore the time value of money. Although these techniques sacrifice accuracy, they provide a quick and simple means of evaluation. When investments are small or the returns are realized within a short time frame, these techniques are likely to lead to the same decisions that would result if more sophisticated techniques were employed.

Payback Method

LO12 Determine the payback period for an investment opportunity.

The **payback method** is simple to apply and easy to understand. It provides information regarding how long it will take to recover the initial cash outflow (the cost) of the investment. The formula for computing the payback period, measured in years, is as follows.

Payback period = Net cost of investment ÷ Annual net cash inflow

To illustrate, assume that Winston Cleaners can purchase a new machine that will press shirts in half the time of the one currently used. The new machine costs $100,000 and will reduce labor cost by $40,000 per year over a four-year useful life. The payback period is computed as follows.

Payback period = $100,000 ÷ $40,000 = 2.5 years

Interpreting Payback. Generally, investments with shorter payback periods are considered to be better. However, this conclusion can be invalid because the method considers only the recovery of the investment. It provides no measurement of the profitability of different investment alternatives. To illustrate, assume that we extend the Winston Cleaners illustration to include an opportunity to purchase a different machine that also costs $100,000 and provides an annual labor savings of $40,000. However, the second machine will last for five instead of

420

four years. The payback period remains at 2.5 years ($100,000 ÷ $40,000), but the second machine is obviously a better investment because it improves profitability by providing an additional year of cost savings. The payback analysis does not reflect this fact.

Unequal Cash Flows. The preceding illustration assumed that the cash savings accrued equally over the life of the asset. The payback method may be complicated when cash inflows are collected on an unequal basis. Suppose that a company purchases a machine for $6,000. The machine will be used erratically and is expected to provide incremental income over the next five years as follows.

2001	2002	2003	2004	2005
$3,000	$1,000	$2,000	$1,000	$500

Based on this cash inflow pattern, what is the payback period? The problem can be solved in two acceptable ways. First, the incremental revenue can be accumulated to the point at which the sum equals the amount of the original investment.

Year	Annual Amount	Cumulative Total
2001	$3,000	$3,000
2002	1,000	4,000
2003	2,000	6,000

This approach reveals that payback would be accomplished at the end of three years.

The second alternative uses an averaging concept. The specific payments are used to determine an average annual cash inflow. This figure is then used in the denominator of the payback equation. Using the preceding data, the payback period is computed as follows.

1. Compute the average annual cash inflow.

$$2001 + 2002 + 2003 + 2004 + 2005 = \text{Total} \div 5 = \text{Average}$$
$$\$3,000 + \$1,000 + \$2,000 + \$1,000 + \$500 = \$7,500 \div 5 = \$1,500$$

2. Compute the payback period.

$$\frac{\text{Net cost of}}{\text{investment}} \div \frac{\text{Average annual}}{\text{net cash inflow}} = 6,000 \div 1,500 = 4 \text{ years}$$

The average method is useful when a company purchases a number of similar assets with differing cash return patterns.

Unadjusted Rate of Return

The **unadjusted rate of return** method is another commonly used evaluation technique. It derives its name from the fact that it does not adjust the cash flows to reflect the time value of money. It is sometimes called the *simple rate of return*. The unadjusted rate of return is computed as follows.

LO13 Determine the unadjusted rate of return for an investment opportunity.

$$\frac{\text{Unadjusted}}{\text{rate of return}} = \frac{\text{Average incremental increase in annual net income}}{\text{Net cost of original investment}}$$

To illustrate the computation of the unadjusted rate of return, assume that The Dining Table, Inc., is considering the establishment of a new restaurant that will require a $2,000,000 original investment. Management anticipates operating the restaurant for 10 years before significant renovations will be required. The restaurant is expected to provide an average after-tax return of $280,000 per year. The unadjusted rate of return is computed as follows.

$$\text{Unadjusted rate of return} = \$280,000 \div \$2,000,000 = 14\% \text{ per year}$$

The accuracy of the unadjusted rate of return suffers from its failure to recognize the recovery of invested capital. With respect to a depreciable asset, the capital investment is normally recovered through revenue over the life of the asset. To illustrate, assume that we purchase a $1,000 asset with a two-year life and a zero salvage value. For simplicity, we ignore income taxes. We assume that the asset produces $600 of cash revenue per year. The income statement for the first year of operation appears as follows.

Revenue	$600
Depreciation Expense	(500)
Net Income	$100

Based on this information, what is the amount of invested capital during the first year? To answer this question, let us examine the cash flows. First, $1,000 in cash outflow was used to purchase the asset (the original investment). Next, we collected $600 of cash revenue of which $100 was a *return on investment* (net income) and $500 of which was a **recovery of investment.** As a result, $1,000 was invested in the asset at the beginning of the year and $500 was invested at the end of the year ($500 was recovered during the year). Similarly, we will recover an additional $500 of capital during the second year of operation, thereby leaving a zero balance of invested capital at the end of the second year. Given that the cash inflows from revenue are collected somewhat evenly over the life of the investment, the amount of invested capital will range from a beginning balance of $1,000 to an ending balance of zero. On average, we will have $500 invested in the asset (the midpoint between $1,000 and zero). As this discussion implies, the average investment can be determined by dividing the total original investment by 2 ($1,000 ÷ 2 = $500). The unadjusted rate of return based on average invested capital can be calculated as follows.

$$\text{Unadjusted rate of return (Based on average investment)} = \frac{\text{Average incremental increase in annual net income}}{\text{Net cost of original investment} \div 2}$$

$$= \frac{\$100}{\$1,000 \div 2} = 20\%$$

To avoid distortions caused by the failure to recognize the recovery of invested capital, it is recommended that you use the unadjusted rate of return based on the *average investment* when working with investments in depreciable assets.

Check Yourself 10–3

EZ Rentals can purchase a van that costs $24,000. The van has an expected useful life of three years and no salvage value. EZ expects rental revenue from the van to be $12,000 per year. Determine the payback period and the unadjusted rate of return.

Answer

Payback = Cost of the investment ÷ Annual cash inflow
Payback = $24,000 ÷ $12,000 = 2 years
Unadjusted rate of return = Net income ÷ Average cost of the investment

Revenue	$12,000	
Depreciation expense	(8,000)	[$24,000 ÷ 3 years]
Net income	$ 4,000	

Unadjusted rate of return = $4,000 ÷ (24,000 ÷ 2) = 33.33%

■ Real-World Reporting Practices

In a recent study, researchers found that companies in the forestry industry use discounted cash flow techniques more frequently when the investment being considered is in long-term

timber investments. The use of techniques that ignore the time value of money increased when other shorter-term capital investment projects were being considered. The researchers' findings are summarized in Exhibit 10–8.

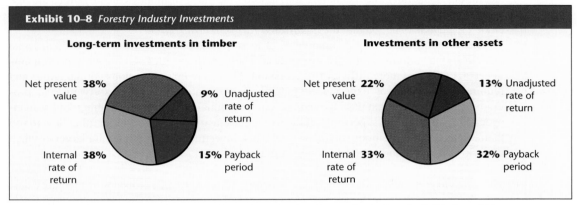

Exhibit 10–8 *Forestry Industry Investments*

Long-term investments in timber

Net present value **38%** — **9%** Unadjusted rate of return

Internal rate of return **38%** — **15%** Payback period

Investments in other assets

Net present value **22%** — **13%** Unadjusted rate of return

Internal rate of return **33%** — **32%** Payback period

Data Source: J. Bailes, J. Nielsen, and S. Lawton, "How Forest Product Companies Analyze Capital Budgets," *Management Accounting,* October 1998, pp. 24–30.

▌Postaudits

The analytical techniques for evaluating capital investment proposals are highly dependent on the estimates of future cash flows. Although no one can be expected to predict the future with perfect accuracy, gross errors can lead to the demise of an organization. For example, optimistic projections of future cash inflows that do not materialize will lead to investments that do not return the cost of capital. Accordingly, managers must take their projections seriously. A postaudit is one way to ensure that managers closely scrutinize their capital investment decisions. A **postaudit** is conducted at the end of a capital investment project; it repeats the analytical technique that was used to justify the original investment. For example, if an internal rate of return was used as the basis for approving an investment project, an internal rate of return computation should be used in the postaudit. The difference between the original computation and the postaudit computation is that *actual* rather than estimated cash flows are used in the postaudit. This practice provides an opportunity to determine whether the expected results were actually accomplished.

LO14 Conduct a postaudit for an investment that has been exercised.

The purpose of the postaudit should be continuous improvement rather than punishment. Managers who are chastised for failing to attain expected results might become overly cautious when asked to provide estimates for future projects. Being overly conservative can create problems as serious as those caused by being too optimistic. Two types of errors can be made with respect to a capital investment decision. First, a manager might accept a project that should have been rejected. This result usually stems from being too optimistic in the projection of future cash flows. Second, the manager might reject a project that should have been accepted. These missed opportunities are usually the result of underestimating future cash flows. Indeed, a manager can become so cautious that she is unable to locate enough projects to fully invest the firm's funds. Remember that idle cash earns no return. If projects continue to outperform expectations, managers are probably being too conservative in their estimations of future cash flows. If projects consistently fail to live up to their expectations, managers are probably being too optimistic in their projections of future cash flows. Either way, the company suffers. The goal of a postaudit is to provide feedback that enables managers to improve the accuracy of the projections of future cash flows, thereby maximizing the quality of the firm's capital investments.

Capital expenditures have a significant, long-term effect on profitability. They usually involve major cash outflows that are recovered through future cash inflows. The most common cash inflow items include incremental revenue, savings of operating cost, salvage value, and working capital releases. The most common outflow items are the initial investment, increases in operating expenses, and working capital commitments.

a look
back

Several techniques for analyzing the cash flow items associated with capital investments are available. The techniques can be divided into two categories: (1) techniques that include time value of money considerations and (2) techniques that ignore time value of money considerations. Generally, the techniques that ignore time value of money considerations are less accurate but offer the benefits of simplicity and ease of understanding. These techniques include the *payback method* and the *unadjusted rate of return method*.

The techniques that include time value of money considerations are the *net present value method* and the *internal rate of return method*. These methods offer significant improvements in accuracy but are more difficult to understand. They may involve tedious computations and require the exercise of experienced judgment. Fortunately, computer software and programmed calculators that ease the tedious computational burden are available to most managers. Furthermore, the superiority of the techniques justifies the effort of learning how to use them. Indeed, these methods should be used when investment expenditures are larger or when cash flow items extend over a prolonged time period.

a look forward

The next chapter moves into unexplored territory. It introduces the concept of inventory cost flow. It discusses how costs move through a series of inventory accounts including raw materials, work in process, and finished goods. It presents techniques that enable overhead costs to be assigned to inventory as it is being produced. It identifies the differences in product costing for service and manufacturing companies. Finally, it introduces two approaches used to value inventory, variable versus full-absorption costing.

SELF-STUDY REVIEW PROBLEM

The CFO of Advo Corporation is considering two investment opportunities. The expected future cash inflows for each opportunity follow:

	Year 1	Year 2	Year 3	Year 4
Project 1	$144,000	$147,000	$160,000	$178,000
Project 2	204,000	199,000	114,000	112,000

Both investments require an initial payment of $400,000. Advo's desired rate of return is 16 percent.

Required

a. Compute the net present value of each project. Which project should Advo adopt based on the net present value approach?

b. Use the summation method to compute the payback period for each project. Which project should Advo adopt based on the payback approach?

Solution to Requirement a

Project 1					
Cash Inflows			Table Factor*		Present Value
Year 1	$144,000	$\times$	0.862069	$=$	$124,138
Year 2	147,000	$\times$	0.743163	$=$	109,245
Year 3	160,000	$\times$	0.640658	$=$	102,505
Year 4	178,000	$\times$	0.552291	$=$	98,308
PV of cash inflows					434,196
Cost of investment					(400,000)
Net present value					$ 34,196

*Table 1, $n = 1$ through 4, $r = 16\%$

Project 2				
Cash Inflows		**Table Factor***		**Present Value**
Year 1	$204,000	× 0.862069	=	$175,862
Year 2	199,000	× 0.743163	=	147,889
Year 3	114,000	× 0.640658	=	73,035
Year 4	112,000	× 0.552291	=	61,857
PV of cash inflows				458,643
Cost of investment				(400,000)
Net present value				$ 58,643

*Table 1, n = 1 through 4, r = 16%

Advo should adopt Project 2 since it has a greater net present value.

Solution to Requirement b

Cash Inflows	Project 1	Project 2
Year 1	$144,000	$204,000
Year 2	147,000	199,000
Total	$291,000	$403,000

By the end of the second year, Project 2's cash inflows have more than paid for the cost of the investment. In contrast, Project 1 still falls short of investment recovery by $109,000 ($400,000 − $291,000). Advo should adopt Project 2 since it has a shorter payback period.

APPENDIX

Table 1 *Present Value of $1*

n	4%	5%	6%	7%	8%	9%	10%	12%	14%	16%	20%
1	0.961538	0.952381	0.943396	0.934579	0.925926	0.917431	0.909091	0.892857	0.877193	0.862069	0.833333
2	0.924556	0.907029	0.889996	0.873439	0.857339	0.841680	0.826446	0.797194	0.769468	0.743163	0.694444
3	0.888996	0.863838	0.839619	0.816298	0.793832	0.772183	0.751315	0.711780	0.674972	0.640658	0.578704
4	0.854804	0.822702	0.792094	0.762895	0.735030	0.708425	0.683013	0.635518	0.592080	0.552291	0.482253
5	0.821927	0.783526	0.747258	0.712986	0.680583	0.649931	0.620921	0.567427	0.519369	0.476113	0.401878
6	0.790315	0.746215	0.704961	0.666342	0.630170	0.596267	0.564474	0.506631	0.455587	0.410442	0.334898
7	0.759918	0.710681	0.665057	0.622750	0.583490	0.547034	0.513158	0.452349	0.399637	0.353830	0.279082
8	0.730690	0.676839	0.627412	0.582009	0.540269	0.501866	0.466507	0.403883	0.350559	0.305025	0.232568
9	0.702587	0.644609	0.591898	0.543934	0.500249	0.460428	0.424098	0.360610	0.307508	0.262953	0.193807
10	0.675564	0.613913	0.558395	0.508349	0.463193	0.422411	0.385543	0.321973	0.269744	0.226684	0.161506
11	0.649581	0.584679	0.526788	0.475093	0.428883	0.387533	0.350494	0.287476	0.236617	0.195417	0.134588
12	0.624597	0.556837	0.496969	0.444012	0.397114	0.355535	0.318631	0.256675	0.207559	0.168463	0.112157
13	0.600574	0.530321	0.468839	0.414964	0.367698	0.326179	0.289664	0.229174	0.182069	0.145227	0.093464
14	0.577475	0.505068	0.442301	0.387817	0.340461	0.299246	0.263331	0.204620	0.159710	0.125195	0.077887
15	0.555265	0.481017	0.417265	0.362446	0.315242	0.274538	0.239392	0.182696	0.140096	0.107927	0.064905
16	0.533908	0.458112	0.393646	0.338735	0.291890	0.251870	0.217629	0.163122	0.122892	0.093041	0.054088
17	0.513373	0.436297	0.371364	0.316574	0.270269	0.231073	0.197845	0.145644	0.107800	0.080207	0.045073
18	0.493628	0.415521	0.350344	0.295864	0.250249	0.211994	0.179859	0.130040	0.094561	0.069144	0.037561
19	0.474642	0.395734	0.330513	0.276508	0.231712	0.194490	0.163508	0.116107	0.082948	0.059607	0.031301
20	0.456387	0.376889	0.311805	0.258419	0.214548	0.178431	0.148644	0.103667	0.072762	0.051385	0.026084

Table 2 *Present Value of an Annuity of $1*

n	4%	5%	6%	7%	8%	9%	10%	12%	14%	16%	20%
1	0.961538	0.952381	0.943396	0.934579	0.925926	0.917431	0.909091	0.892857	0.877193	0.862069	0.833333
2	1.886095	1.859410	1.83393	1.808018	1.783265	1.759111	1.735537	1.690051	1.646661	1.605232	1.527778
3	2.775091	2.723248	2.673012	2.624316	2.577097	2.531295	2.486852	2.401831	2.321632	2.245890	2.106481
4	3.629895	3.545951	3.465106	3.387211	3.312127	3.239720	3.169865	3.037349	2.913712	2.798181	2.588735
5	4.451822	4.329477	4.212364	4.100197	3.992710	3.889651	3.790787	3.604776	3.433081	3.274294	2.990612
6	5.242137	5.075692	4.917324	4.766540	4.622880	4.485919	4.355261	4.111407	3.888668	3.684736	3.325510
7	6.002055	5.786373	5.582381	5.389289	5.206370	5.032953	4.868419	4.563757	4.288305	4.038565	3.604592
8	6.732745	6.463213	6.209794	5.971299	5.746639	5.534819	5.334926	4.967640	4.638864	4.343591	3.837160
9	7.435332	7.107822	6.801692	6.515232	6.246888	5.995247	5.759024	5.328250	4.946372	4.606544	4.030967
10	8.110896	7.721735	7.360087	7.023582	6.710081	6.417658	6.144567	5.650223	5.216116	4.833227	4.192472
11	8.760477	8.306414	7.886875	7.498674	7.138964	6.805191	6.495061	5.937699	5.452733	5.028644	4.327060
12	9.385074	8.863252	8.383844	7.942686	7.536078	7.160725	6.813692	6.194374	5.660292	5.197107	4.439217
13	9.985648	9.393573	8.852683	8.357651	7.903776	7.486904	7.103356	6.423548	5.842362	5.342334	4.532681
14	10.563123	9.898641	9.294984	8.745468	8.244237	7.786150	7.366687	6.628168	6.002072	5.467529	4.610567
15	11.118387	10.379658	9.712249	9.107914	8.559479	8.060688	7.606080	6.810864	6.142168	5.575456	4.675473
16	11.652296	10.837770	10.105895	9.446649	8.851369	8.312558	7.823709	6.973986	6.265060	5.668497	4.729561
17	12.165669	11.274066	10.477260	9.763223	9.121638	8.543631	8.021553	7.119630	6.372859	5.748704	4.774634
18	12.659297	11.689587	10.827603	10.059087	9.371887	8.755625	8.201412	7.249670	6.467420	5.817848	4.812195
19	13.133939	12.085321	11.158116	10.335595	9.603599	8.905115	8.364920	7.365777	6.550369	5.877455	4.843496
20	13.590326	12.462210	11.469921	10.594014	9.818147	9.128546	8.513564	7.469444	6.623131	5.928841	4.869580

KEY TERMS

Accumulated conversion factors *408*
Annuity *409*
Capital investments *406*
Cost of capital *407*

Incremental revenue *413*
Internal rate of return *412*
Minimum rate of return *407*
Net present value *412*
Ordinary annuity *410*

Payback method *420*
Postaudit *423*
Present value index *415*
Present value table *408*
Recovery of investment *422*

Single-payment (lump-sum) *408*
Time value of money *406*
Unadjusted rate of return *421*
Working capital *414*

QUESTIONS

1. What is a capital investment? How does it differ from an investment in stocks or bonds?
2. What are three reasons that cash is worth more today than cash to be received in the future?
3. "A dollar today is worth more than a dollar in the future." "The present value of a future dollar is worth less than one dollar." Are these two statements synonymous? Explain.
4. Define the term *return on investment.* How is the return normally expressed? Give an example of a capital investment return.
5. How does a company establish its minimum acceptable rate of return on investments?
6. If you wanted to have $500,000 one year from today and desired to earn a 10 percent return, what amount would you need to invest today? Which amount has more value, the amount today or the $500,000 a year from today?
7. Why are present value tables frequently used to convert future values to present values?
8. Define the term *annuity.* What is one example of an annuity receipt?
9. How can present value "what-if" analysis be enhanced by using software programs?
10. Receiving $100,000 per year for five years is equivalent to investing what amount today at 14 percent? Provide a mathematical formula to solve this problem, assuming use of a present value annuity table to convert the future cash flows to their present value equivalents. Provide the expression for the Excel spreadsheet function that would perform the present value conversion.
11. Maria Espinosa borrowed $15,000 from the bank and agreed to repay the loan at 8 percent annual interest over four years, making payments of $4,529 per year. Because part of the bank's payment from Ms. Espinosa is a recovery of the original investment, what assumption must the bank make to earn its desired 8 percent compounded annual return?

12. Two investment opportunities have positive net present values. Investment A's net present value amounts to $40,000 while B's is only $30,000. Does this mean that A is the better investment opportunity? Explain.
13. What criteria determine whether a project is acceptable under the net present value method?
14. Does the net present value method provide a measure of the rate of return on capital investments?
15. Which is the best capital investment evaluation technique for ranking investment opportunities?
16. Paul Henderson is a manager for Spark Company. He tells you that his company always maximizes profitability by accepting the investment opportunity with the highest internal rate of return. Explain to Mr. Henderson how his company may improve profitability by sometimes selecting investment opportunities with lower internal rates of return.
17. What is the relationship between desired rate of return and internal rate of return?
18. What typical cash inflow and outflow items are associated with capital investments?
19. "I always go for the investment with the shortest payback period." Is this a sound strategy? Why or why not?
20. "The payback method cannot be used if the cash inflows occur in unequal patterns." Do you agree or disagree? Explain.
21. What are the advantages and disadvantages associated with the unadjusted rate of return method for evaluating capital investments?
22. How do capital investments affect profitability?
23. What is a postaudit? How is it useful in capital budgeting?

EXERCISES—SERIES A

EXERCISE 10–1A *Identifying Cash Inflows and Outflows*

L.O. 2

Required
Indicate which of the following items will result in cash inflows and which will result in cash outflows. The first one is shown as an example.

Item	Type of Cash Flow
a. Incremental revenue	Inflow
b. Initial investment	
c. Salvage values	
d. Recovery of working capital	
e. Incremental expenses	
f. Working capital commitments	
g. Cost savings	

EXERCISE 10–2A *Determining the Present Value of a Lump-Sum Future Cash Receipt*

L.O. 2, 5

Jim Hanke turned 20 years old today. His grandfather established a trust fund that will pay Mr. Hanke $40,000 on his next birthday. Unfortunately, Mr. Hanke needs money today to start his college education, and his father is willing to help. He has agreed to give Mr. Hanke the present value of the future cash inflow, assuming a 10 percent rate of return.

Required
a. Use a present value table to determine the amount of cash that Mr. Hanke's father should give him.
b. Use an algebraic formula to prove that the present value of the trust fund (the amount of cash computed in Requirement *a*) is equal to its $40,000 future value.

EXERCISE 10–3A *Determining the Present Value of a Lump-Sum Future Cash Receipt*

L.O. 2, 5

Tracy Plum expects to receive a $600,000 cash benefit when she retires five years from today. Ms. Plum's employer has offered an early retirement incentive by agreeing to pay her $360,000 today if she agrees to retire immediately. Ms. Plum desires to earn a rate of return of 12 percent.

Required
a. Assuming that the retirement benefit is the only consideration in making the retirement decision, should Ms. Plum accept her employer's offer?
b. Identify the factors that cause the present value of the retirement benefit to be less than $600,000.

L.O. 2, 5   **EXERCISE 10–4A** *Determining the Present Value of an Annuity*

The dean of the School of Business is trying to decide whether to purchase a copy machine to place in the lobby of the building. The machine would add to student convenience, but the dean feels compelled to earn an 8 percent return on the investment of funds. Estimates of cash inflows from copy machines that have been placed in other university buildings indicate that the copy machine would probably produce incremental cash inflows of approximately $6,000 per year. The machine is expected to have a three-year useful life with a zero salvage value.

Required

a. Use Present Value Table 1 in Appendix A to determine the maximum amount of cash the dean should be willing to pay for a copy machine.

b. Use Present Value Table 2 in Appendix A to determine the maximum amount of cash the dean should be willing to pay for a copy machine.

c. Explain the consistency or lack of consistency in the answers to Requirements *a* and *b*.

L.O. 2, 5, 9   **EXERCISE 10–5A** *Determining Net Present Value*

Value Ride, Inc., is considering investing in two new vans that are expected to generate cash inflows of $16,000 per year. The vans' purchase price is $52,000. Their expected life and salvage value of each are four years and $12,000, respectively. Value Ride has an average cost of capital of 14 percent.

Required

a. Calculate the net present value of the investment opportunity.

b. Indicate whether the investment opportunity is expected to earn a return that is above or below the cost of capital and whether it should be accepted.

L.O. 2, 5, 9   **EXERCISE 10–6A** *Determining Net Present Value*

Luke Calahon is seeking part-time employment while he attends school. He is considering purchasing technical equipment that will enable him to start a small training services company that will offer tutorial services over the Internet. Luke expects demand for the service to grow rapidly in the first two years of operation as customers learn about the availability of the Internet assistance. Thereafter, he expects demand to stabilize. The following table presents the expected cash flows.

Year of Operation	Cash Inflow	Cash Outflow
2003	$4,500	$3,000
2004	6,500	4,000
2005	7,000	4,200
2006	7,000	4,200

In addition to these cash flows, Mr. Calahon expects to pay $7,000 for the equipment. He also expects to pay $1,200 for a major overhaul and updating of the equipment at the end of the second year of operation. The equipment is expected to have a $500 salvage value and a four-year useful life. Mr. Calahon desires to earn a rate of return of 8 percent.

Required

(Round computations to the nearest whole penny.)

a. Calculate the net present value of the investment opportunity.

b. Indicate whether the investment opportunity is expected to earn a return that is above or below the desired rate of return and whether it should be accepted.

L.O. 2, 5, 9   **EXERCISE 10–7A** *Using Present Value Index*

Pell Company has a choice of two investment alternatives. The present value of cash inflows and outflows for the first alternative is $90,000 and 84,000, respectively. The present value of cash inflows and outflows for the second alternative is $220,000 and $213,000, respectively.

Required

a. Calculate the net present value of each investment opportunity.

b. Calculate the present value index for each investment opportunity.

c. Indicate which investment will produce the higher rate of return.

EXERCISE 10–8A *Determining the Internal Rate of Return*

L.O. 2, 10

Larson Manufacturing Company has an opportunity to purchase some technologically advanced equipment that will reduce the company's cash outflow for operating expenses by $640,000 per year. The cost of the equipment is $3,093,265.28. Larson expects it to have a 10-year useful life and a zero salvage value. The company has established an investment opportunity hurdle rate of 15 percent and uses the straight-line method for depreciation.

Required
a. Calculate the internal rate of return of the investment opportunity.
b. Indicate whether the investment opportunity should be accepted.

EXERCISE 10–9A *Using the Internal Rate of Return to Compare Investment Opportunities*

L.O. 2, 10

Marvin and Kasick (M&K) is a partnership that owns a small company. It is considering two alternative investment opportunities. The first investment opportunity will have a five-year useful life, will cost $9,335.16, and will generate expected cash inflows of $2,400 per year. The second investment is expected to have a useful life of three years, will cost $6,217.13, and will generate expected cash inflows of $2,500 per year. Assume that M&K has the funds available to accept only one of the opportunities.

Required
a. Calculate the internal rate of return of each investment opportunity.
b. Based on the internal rates of return, which opportunity should M&K select?
c. Discuss other factors that M&K should consider in the investment decision.

EXERCISE 10–10A *Determining the Cash Flow Annuity With Income Tax Considerations*

L.O. 2, 11

To open a new store, Drexler Tire Company plans to invest $320,000 in equipment expected to have a four-year useful life and no salvage value. Drexler expects the new store to generate annual cash revenues of $420,000 and to incur annual cash operating expenses of $260,000. Drexler's average income tax rate is 30 percent. The company uses straight-line depreciation.

Required
Determine the expected annual net cash inflow from operations for each of the first four years after Drexler opens the new store.

EXERCISE 10–11A *Evaluating Discounted Cash Flow Techniques*

L.O. 11

Ashley Posey is angry with Bob Quinn. He is behind schedule developing supporting material for tomorrow's capital budget committee meeting. When she approached him about his apparent lackadaisical attitude in general and his tardiness in particular, he responded, "I don't see why we do this stuff in the first place. It's all a bunch of estimates. Who knows what future cash flows will really be? I certainly don't. I've been doing this job for five years, and no one has ever checked to see if I even came close at these guesses. I've been waiting for marketing to provide the estimated cash inflows on the projects being considered tomorrow. But, if you want my report now, I'll have it in a couple of hours. I can make up the marketing data as well as they can."

Required
Does Mr. Quinn have a point? Is there something wrong with the company's capital budgeting system? Write a brief response explaining how to improve the investment evaluation system.

EXERCISE 10–12A *Determining the Payback Period*

L.O. 12

Regions Airline Company is considering expanding its territory. The company has the opportunity to purchase one of two different used airplanes. The first airplane is expected to cost $900,000; it will enable the company to increase its annual cash inflow by $300,000 per year. The plane is expected to have a useful life of five years and no salvage value. The second plane costs $1,800,000; it will enable the company to increase annual cash flow by $450,000 per year. This plane has an eight-year useful life and a zero salvage value.

Required
a. Determine the payback period for each investment alternative and identify the alternative Regions should accept if the decision is based on the payback approach.
b. Discuss the shortcomings of using the payback method to evaluate investment opportunities.

L.O. 12 **EXERCISE 10–13A** *Determining the Payback Period With Uneven Cash Flows*

Avondale Company has an opportunity to purchase a forklift to use in its heavy equipment rental business. The forklift would be leased on an annual basis during its first two years of operation. Thereafter, it would be leased to the general public on demand. Avondale would sell it at the end of the fifth year of its useful life. The expected cash inflows and outflows follow.

Year	Nature of Item	Cash Inflow	Cash Outflow
2004	Purchase price		$24,000
2004	Revenue	$10,000	
2005	Revenue	10,000	
2006	Revenue	7,000	
2006	Major overhaul		3,000
2007	Revenue	6,000	
2008	Revenue	4,800	
2008	Salvage value	3,200	

Required
a. Determine the payback period using the accumulated cash flows approach.
b. Determine the payback period using the average cash flows approach.

L.O. 13 **EXERCISE 10–14A** *Determining the Unadjusted Rate of Return*

Harmick Painting Company is considering whether to purchase a new spray paint machine that costs $6,000. The machine is expected to save labor, increasing net income by $900 per year. The effective life of the machine is 15 years according to the manufacturer's estimate.

Required
a. Determine the unadjusted rate of return based on the average cost of the investment.
b. Discuss the shortcomings of using the unadjusted rate of return to evaluate investment opportunities.

L.O. 12, 13 **EXERCISE 10–15A** *Computing the Payback Period and Unadjusted Rate of Return for One Investment Opportunity*

Chaw Rentals can purchase a van that costs $24,000; it has an expected useful life of three years and no salvage value. Chaw uses straight-line depreciation. Expected revenue is $12,000 per year.

Required
a. Determine the payback period.
b. Determine the unadjusted rate of return based on the average cost of the investment.

PROBLEMS—SERIES A

L.O. 5, 9 **PROBLEM 10–16A** *Using Present Value Techniques to Evaluate Alternative Investment Opportunities*

ASAP Delivery is a small company that transports business packages between San Francisco and Los Angeles. It operates a fleet of small vans that moves packages to and from a central depot within each city and uses a common carrier to deliver the packages between the depots in the two cities. ASAP recently acquired approximately $4 million of cash capital from its owners, and its president, Alex Cade, is trying to identify the most profitable way to invest these funds.

Phil Duvall, the company's operations manager, believes that the money should be used to expand the fleet of city vans at a cost of $3,600,000. He argues that more vans would enable the company to expand its services into new markets, thereby increasing the revenue base. More specifically, he expects cash inflows to increase by $1,400,000 per year. The additional vans are expected to have an average useful life of four years and a combined salvage value of $500,000. Operating the vans will require additional working capital of $200,000, which will be recovered at the end of the fourth year.

In contrast, Amber Gomez, the company's chief accountant, believes that the funds should be used to purchase large trucks to deliver the packages between the depots in the two cities. The conversion process would produce continuing improvement in operating savings with reductions in cash outflows as the following:

Year 1	Year 2	Year 3	Year 4
$800,000	$1,600,000	$2,000,000	$2,200,000

The large trucks are expected to cost $4,000,000 and to have a four-year useful life and a $400,000 salvage value. In addition to the purchase price of the trucks, up-front training costs are expected to amount to $80,000. ASAP Delivery's management has established a 16 percent desired rate of return.

Required
a. Determine the net present value of the two investment alternatives.
b. Calculate the present value index for each alternative.
c. Indicate which investment alternative you would recommend. Explain your choice.

PROBLEM 10–17A *Using the Payback Period and Unadjusted Rate of Return to Evaluate Alternative Investment Opportunities* **L.O. 12, 13**

Eric Horton owns a small retail ice cream parlor. He is considering expanding the business and has identified two attractive alternatives. One involves purchasing a machine that would enable Mr. Horton to offer frozen yogurt to customers. The machine would cost $5,400 and has an expected useful life of three years with no salvage value. Additional annual cash revenues and cash operating expenses associated with selling yogurt are expected to be $3,960 and $600, respectively.

Alternatively, Mr. Horton could purchase for $6,720 the equipment necessary to serve cappuccino. That equipment has an expected useful life of four years and no salvage value. Additional annual cash revenues and cash operating expenses associated with selling cappuccino are expected to be $5,520 and $1,620, respectively.

Income before taxes earned by the ice cream parlor is taxed at an effective rate of 20 percent.

Required
a. Determine the payback period and unadjusted rate of return (use average investment) for each alternative.
b. Indicate which investment alternative you would recommend. Explain your choice.

PROBLEM 10–18A *Using Net Present Value and Internal Rate of Return to Evaluate Investment Opportunities* **L.O. 9, 10**

Tonia Owusu, the president of Owusu Enterprises, is considering two investment opportunities. Because of limited resources, she will be able to invest in only one of them. Project A is to purchase a machine that will enable factory automation; the machine is expected to have a useful life of four years and no salvage value. Project B supports a training program that will improve the skills of employees operating the current equipment. Initial cash expenditures for Project A are $200,000 and for Project B are $80,000. The annual expected cash inflows are $63,094 for Project A and $26,338 for Project B. Both investments are expected to provide cash flow benefits for the next four years. Owusu Enterprise's cost of capital is 8 percent.

Required
a. Compute the net present value of each project. Which project should be adopted based on the net present value approach?
b. Compute the approximate internal rate of return of each project. Which one should be adopted based on the internal rate of return approach?
c. Compare the net present value approach with the internal rate of return approach. Which method is better in the given circumstances? Why?

PROBLEM 10–19A *Using Net Present Value and Payback Period to Evaluate Investment Opportunities* **L.O. 9, 12**

Patric Spradley saved $400,000 during the 25 years that he worked for a major corporation. Now he has retired at the age of 50 and has begun to draw a comfortable pension check every month. He wants to ensure the financial security of his retirement by investing his savings wisely and is currently considering two investment opportunities. Both investments require an initial payment of $300,000. The following table presents the estimated cash inflows for the two alternatives.

	Year 1	Year 2	Year 3	Year 4
Opportunity #1	$ 89,000	$ 94,000	$126,000	$162,000
Opportunity #2	164,000	174,000	28,000	24,000

Mr. Spradley decides to use his past average return on mutual fund investments as the discount rate; it is 8 percent.

Required

a. Compute the net present value of each opportunity. Which should Mr. Spradley adopt based on the net present value approach?

b. Compute the payback period for each project. Which should Mr. Spradley adopt based on the payback approach?

c. Compare the net present value approach with the payback approach. Which method is better in the given circumstances?

L.O. 9, 12, 13 **PROBLEM 10–20A** *Effects of Straight-Line Versus Accelerated Depreciation on an Investment Decision*

Magby Electronics is considering investing in manufacturing equipment expected to cost $92,000. The equipment has an estimated useful life of four years and a salvage value of $12,000. It is expected to produce incremental cash revenues of $48,000 per year. Magby has an effective income tax rate of 30 percent and a desired rate of return of 12 percent.

Required

a. Determine the net present value and the present value index of the investment, assuming that Magby uses straight-line depreciation for financial and income tax reporting.

b. Determine the net present value and the present value index of the investment, assuming that Magby uses double-declining-balance depreciation for financial and income tax reporting.

c. Why do the net present values computed in Requirements *a* and *b* differ?

d. Determine the payback period and unadjusted rate of return (use average investment), assuming that Magby uses straight-line depreciation.

e. Determine the payback period and unadjusted rate of return (use average investment), assuming that Magby uses double-declining-balance depreciation. (*Note:* Use average annual cash flow when computing the payback period and average annual income when determining the unadjusted rate of return.)

f. Why are there no differences in the payback periods or unadjusted rates of return computed in Requirements *d* and *e?*

L.O. 9 **PROBLEM 10–21A** *Applying the Net Present Value Approach With and Without Tax Considerations*

Martin Keeton, the chief executive officer of Keeton Corporation, has assembled his top advisers to evaluate an investment opportunity. The advisers expect the company to pay $200,000 cash at the beginning of the investment and the cash inflow for each of the following four years to be the following.

Year 1	Year 2	Year 3	Year 4
$42,000	$48,000	$60,000	$92,000

Mr. Keeton agrees with his advisers that the company should use the discount rate (required rate of return) of 12 percent to compute net present value to evaluate the viability of the proposed project.

Required

a. Compute the net present value of the proposed project. Should Mr. Keeton approve the project?

b. Jane Lilly, one of the advisers, is wary of the cash flow forecast and she points out that the advisers failed to consider that the depreciation on equipment used in this project will be tax deductible. The depreciation is expected to be $40,000 per year for the four-year period. The company's income tax rate is 30 percent per year. Use this information to revise the company's expected cash flow from this project.

c. Compute the net present value of the project based on the revised cash flow forecast. Should Mr. Keeton approve the project?

L.O. 10, 13 **PROBLEM 10–22A** *Comparing Internal Rate of Return With Unadjusted Rate of Return*

Mueller Auto Repair, Inc., is evaluating a project to purchase equipment that will not only expand the company's capacity but also improve the quality of its repair services. The board of directors requires all capital investments to meet or exceed the minimum requirement of a 10 percent rate of return. However,

the board has not clearly defined the rate of return. The president and controller are pondering two different rates of return: unadjusted rate of return and internal rate of return. The equipment, which costs $200,000, has a life expectancy of five years. The increased net profit per year will be approximately $14,000, and the increased cash inflow per year will be approximately $55,400.

Required
a. If it uses the unadjusted rate of return (use average investment) to evaluate this project, should the company invest in the equipment?
b. If it uses the internal rate of return to evaluate this project, should the company invest in the equipment?
c. Which method is better for this capital investment decision?

PROBLEM 10–23A *Postaudit Evaluation*

L.O. 14

Dennis Reddy is reviewing his company's investment in a cement plant. The company paid $30,000,000 five years ago to acquire the plant. Now top management is considering an opportunity to sell it. The president wants to know whether the plant has met original expectations before he decides its fate. The company's discount rate for present value computations is 8 percent. Expected and actual cash flows follow.

	Year 1	Year 2	Year 3	Year 4	Year 5
Expected	$6,600,000	$9,840,000	$9,120,000	$9,960,000	$8,400,000
Actual	5,400,000	6,120,000	9,840,000	7,800,000	7,200,000

Required
a. Compute the net present value of the expected cash flows as of the beginning of the investment.
b. Compute the net present value of the actual cash flows as of the beginning of the investment.
c. What do you conclude from this postaudit?

EXERCISES—SERIES B

EXERCISE 10–1B *Identifying Cash Inflows and Outflows*

L.O. 2

Required
Bill Armstrong is considering whether to invest in a dump truck. Mr. Armstrong would hire a driver and use the truck to haul trash for customers. He wants to use present value techniques to evaluate the investment opportunity. List sources of potential cash inflows and cash outflows Mr. Armstrong could expect if he invests in the truck.

EXERCISE 10–2B *Determining the Present Value of a Lump-Sum Future Cash Receipt*

L.O. 2, 5

One year from today Kay Hopkins is scheduled to receive a $50,000 payment from a trust fund her father established. She wants to buy a car today but does not have the money. A friend has agreed to give Kay the present value of the $50,000 today if she agrees to give him the full $50,000 when she collects it one year from now. They agree that 8 percent reflects a fair discount rate.

Required
a. You have been asked to determine the present value of the future cash flow. Use a present value table to determine the amount of cash that Kay's friend should give her.
b. Use an algebraic formula to verify the result you determined in Requirement *a*.

EXERCISE 10–3B *Determining the Present Value of a Lump-Sum Future Cash Receipt*

L.O. 2, 5

Paul Hughes has a terminal illness. His doctors have estimated his remaining life expectancy as three years. Paul has a $1,000,000 life insurance policy but no close relative to list as the beneficiary. He is considering canceling the policy because he needs the money he is currently paying for the premiums to buy medical supplies. A wealthy close friend has advised Paul not to cancel the policy. The friend has proposed instead giving Paul half a million dollars to use for his medical needs while keeping the policy in force. In exchange, Paul would designate the friend as the policy beneficiary. Paul is reluctant to take the $500,000 because he believes that his friend is offering charity. His friend has tried to convince Paul that the offer is a legitimate business deal.

Required

a. Determine the present value of the $1,000,000 life insurance benefit. Assume a 10 percent discount rate.

b. Assuming 10 percent represents a fair rate of return, is Paul's friend offering charity or is he seeking to profit financially from Paul's misfortune?

L.O. 2, 5 **EXERCISE 10–4B** *Determining the Present Value of an Annuity*

Marilyn Boulware is considering whether to install a drink machine at the gas station she owns. Marilyn is convinced that providing a drink machine at the station would increase customer convenience. However, she is not convinced that buying the machine would be a profitable investment. Friends who have installed drink machines at their stations have estimated that she could expect to receive net cash inflows of approximately $2,000 per year from the machine. Marilyn believes that she should earn 10 percent on her investments. The drink machine is expected to have a two-year life and zero salvage value.

Required

a. Use Present Value Table 1 to determine the maximum amount of cash Marilyn should be willing to pay for a drink machine.

b. Use Present Value Table 2 to determine the maximum amount of cash Marilyn should be willing to pay for a drink machine.

c. Explain the consistency or lack of consistency in the answers to Requirement *a* versus Requirement *b*.

L.O. 2, 5, 9 **EXERCISE 10–5B** *Determining the Net Present Value*

Linda Potter, manager of the Great Music Hall, is considering the opportunity to expand the company's concession revenues. Specifically, she is considering whether to install a popcorn machine. Based on market research, she believes that the machine could produce incremental cash inflows of $1,500 per year. The purchase price of the machine is $4,300. It is expected to have a useful life of three years and a $1,000 salvage value. Ms. Potter has established a desired rate of return of 16 percent.

Required

a. Calculate the net present value of the investment opportunity.

b. Should the company buy the popcorn machine?

L.O. 2, 5, 9 **EXERCISE 10–6B** *Determining the Net Present Value*

John Moreau has decided to start a small delivery business to help support himself while attending school. Mr. Moreau expects demand for delivery services to grow steadily as customers discover their availability. Annual cash outflows are expected to increase only slightly because many of the business operating costs are fixed. Cash inflows and outflows expected from operating the delivery business follow:

Year of Operation	Cash Inflow	Cash Outflow
2003	$ 8,500	$4,000
2004	9,500	4,500
2005	10,500	4,800
2006	11,500	5,000

The used delivery van Mr. Moreau plans to buy is expected to cost $16,500. It has an expected useful life of four years and a salvage value of $3,000. At the end of 2004, Mr. Moreau expects to pay additional costs of approximately $800 for maintenance and new tires. Mr. Moreau's desired rate of return is 12 percent.

Required

(Round computations to the nearest whole penny.)

a. Calculate the net present value of the investment opportunity.

b. Indicate whether the investment opportunity is expected to earn a return above or below the desired rate of return. Should Mr. Moreau start the delivery business?

L.O. 2, 5, 9 **EXERCISE 10–7B** *Using the Present Value Index*

Two alternative investment opportunities are available to John Kuhn, president of Kuhn Enterprises. For the first alternative, the present value of cash inflows is $133,000, and the present value of cash outflows

is $127,000. For the second alternative, the present value of cash inflows is $230,000, and the present value of cash outflows is $223,000.

Required
a. Calculate the net present value of each investment opportunity.
b. Calculate the present value index for each investment opportunity.
c. Indicate which investment will produce the higher rate of return.

EXERCISE 10–8B *Determining the Internal Rate of Return* L.O. 2, 10

Tommy Putman, CFO of Greystone Enterprises, is evaluating an opportunity to invest in additional manufacturing equipment that will enable the company to increase its net cash inflows by $400,000 per year. The equipment costs $1,196,244.80. It is expected to have a five-year useful life and a zero salvage value. Greystone's cost of capital is 18 percent.

Required
a. Calculate the internal rate of return of the investment opportunity.
b. Indicate whether Greystone should purchase the equipment.

EXERCISE 10–9B *Using the Internal Rate of Return to Compare Investment Opportunities* L.O. 2, 10

Laura Perrier has two alternative investment opportunities to evaluate. The first opportunity would cost $99,674.82 and generate expected cash inflows of $14,000 per year for 17 years. The second opportunity would cost $91,272.96 and generate expected cash inflows of $12,000 per year for 15 years. Ms. Perrier has sufficient funds available to accept only one opportunity.

Required
a. Calculate the internal rate of return of each investment opportunity.
b. Based on the internal rate of return criteria, which opportunity should Ms. Perrier select?
c. Identify two other evaluation techniques Ms. Perrier could use to compare the investment opportunities.

EXERCISE 10–10B *Determining a Cash Flow Annuity With Income Tax Considerations* L.O. 2, 11

David Bess is considering whether to invest in a computer game machine that he would place in a hotel his brother owns. The machine would cost $7,000 and has an expected useful life of three years and a salvage value of $1,000. Mr. Bess estimates the machine would generate revenue of $3,500 per year and cost $600 per year to operate. He uses the straight-line method for depreciation. His income tax rate is 30 percent.

Required
What amount of net cash inflow from operations would Mr. Bess expect for the first year if he invests in the machine?

EXERCISE 10–11B *Evaluating Discounted Cash Flow Techniques* L.O. 11

Four years ago Judy Lowe decided to invest in a project. At that time she had projected annual net cash inflows would be $48,000. Over its expected four-year useful life, the project had produced significantly higher cash inflows than anticipated. The actual average annual cash inflow from the project was $56,000. Lowe breathed a sigh of relief. She always worried that projects would not live up to expectations. To avoid this potential disappointment she tried always to underestimate the projected cash inflows of potential investments. She commented, "I prefer pleasant rather than unpleasant surprises." Indeed, no investment approved by Ms. Lowe had ever failed a postaudit review. Her investments consistently exceeded expectations.

Required
Explain the purpose of a postaudit and comment on Ms. Lowe's investment record.

EXERCISE 10–12B *Determining the Payback Period* L.O. 12

The management team at Kazenski Manufacturing Company has decided to modernize the manufacturing facility. The company can replace an existing, outdated machine with one of two technologically advanced machines. One replacement machine would cost $400,000. Management estimates that it would reduce cash outflows for manufacturing expenses by $160,000 per year. This machine is expected to have an eight-year useful life and a $10,000 salvage value. The other replacement machine would cost $504,000 and would reduce annual cash outflows by an estimated $180,000. This machine has an expected 10–year useful life and a $50,000 salvage value.

Required

a. Determine the payback period for each investment alternative and identify which replacement machine Kazenski should buy if it bases the decision on the payback approach.

b. Discuss the shortcomings of the payback method of evaluating investment opportunities.

L.O. 12   **EXERCISE 10–13B** *Determining the Payback Period With Uneven Cash Flows*

High Country Snowmobile Company is considering whether to invest in a particular new snowmobile model. The model is top-of-the-line equipment for which High Country expects high demand during the first year it is available for rent. However, as the snowmobile ages, it will become less desirable and its rental revenues are expected to decline. The expected cash inflows and outflows follow.

Year	Nature of Cash Flow	Cash Inflow	Cash Outflow
2003	Purchase price	—	$14,000
2003	Revenue	$8,000	—
2004	Revenue	6,000	—
2005	Revenue	5,500	—
2005	Major overhaul	—	2,000
2006	Revenue	3,000	—
2007	Revenue	2,000	—
2007	Salvage value	1,600	—

Required

a. Determine the payback period using the accumulated cash flows approach.

b. Determine the payback period using the average cash flows approach.

L.O. 13   **EXERCISE 10–14B** *Determining the Unadjusted Rate of Return*

Fast Shuttle Service, Inc., is considering whether to purchase an additional shuttle van. The van would cost $18,000 and have a zero salvage value. It would enable the company to increase net income by $1,350 per year. The manufacturer estimates the van's effective life as five years.

Required

a. Determine the unadjusted rate of return based on the average cost of the investment.

b. What is the shortcoming of using the unadjusted rate of return to evaluate investment opportunities.

L.O. 12, 13   **EXERCISE 10–15B** *Computing the Payback Period and Unadjusted Rate of Return for the Same Investment Opportunity*

Lake Shore Marina (LSM) rents pontoon boats to customers. It has the opportunity to purchase an additional pontoon boat for $30,000; it has an expected useful life of four years and no salvage value. LSM uses straight-line depreciation. Expected rental revenue for the boat is $9,000 per year.

Required

a. Determine the payback period.

b. Determine the unadjusted rate of return based on the average cost of the investment.

c. Assume that the company's desired rate of return is 30 percent. Should LSM purchase the additional boat?

PROBLEMS—SERIES B

L.O. 5, 9   **PROBLEM 10–16B** *Using Present Value Techniques to Evaluate Alternative Investment Opportunities*

Stagg Automobile Repair, Inc., currently has three repair shops in Atlanta. Norman Stagg, the president and chief executive officer, is facing a pleasant dilemma: the business has continued to grow rapidly and major shareholders are arguing about different ways to capture more business opportunities. The company requires a 12 percent rate of return for its investment projects and uses the straight-line method of depreciation for all fixed assets.

One group of shareholders wants to open another shop in a newly developed suburban community. This project would require an initial investment of $240,000 to acquire all the necessary equipment,

which has a useful life of five years with a salvage value of $80,000. Once the shop begins to operate, another $60,000 of working capital would be required; it would be recovered at the end of the fifth year. The expected net cash inflow from the new shop follows.

Year 1	Year 2	Year 3	Year 4	Year 5
$24,000	$48,000	$76,000	$96,000	$120,000

A second group of shareholders prefers to invest $200,000 to acquire new computerized diagnostic equipment for the existing shops. The equipment is expected to have a useful life of five years with a salvage value of $40,000. Using this state-of-the-art equipment, mechanics would be able to pinpoint automobile problems more quickly and accurately. Consequently, it would allow the existing shops to increase their service capacity and revenue by $60,000 per year. The company would need to train mechanics to use the equipment, which would cost $20,000 at the beginning of the first year.

Required
a. Determine the net present value of the two investment alternatives.
b. Calculate the present value index for each alternative.
c. Indicate which investment alternative you would recommend. Explain your choice.

PROBLEM 10–17B *Using the Payback Period and Unadjusted Rate of Return to Evaluate Alternative Investment Opportunities*

L.O. 12, 13

Laquisha and Muriel Services is planning a new business venture. With $200,000 of available funds to invest, it is investigating two options. One is to acquire an exclusive contract to operate vending machines in civic and recreation centers in a small suburban city for four years. The contract requires the firm to pay the city $80,000 cash at the beginning. The firm expects the cash revenue from the operation to be $100,000 per year and the cash expenses to be $56,000 per year.

The second option is to operate a printing shop in an office complex. This option would require the company to spend $144,000 for printing equipment that has a useful life of four years with a zero salvage value. The cash revenue is expected to be $170,000 per year and cash expenses are expected to be $94,000 per year.

The firm uses the straight-line method of depreciation. Its effective income tax rate is expected to be 20 percent.

Required
a. Determine the payback period and unadjusted rate of return (use average investment) for each alternative.
b. Indicate which investment alternative you would recommend. Explain your choice.

PROBLEM 10–18B *Using Net Present Value and Internal Rate of Return to Evaluate Investment Opportunities*

L.O. 9, 10

Mark Hayes' rich uncle gave him $200,000 cash as a birthday gift for his 40th birthday. Unlike his spoiled cousins who spend money carelessly, Mr. Hayes wants to invest the money for his future retirement. After an extensive search, he is considering one of two investment opportunities. Project 1 would require an immediate cash payment of $176,000; Project 2 needs only a $80,000 cash payment at the beginning. The expected cash inflows are $57,600 per year for Project 1 and $28,000 per year for Project 2. Both projects are expected to provide cash flow benefits for the next four years. Mr. Hayes found that the interest rate for a four-year certificate of deposit is about 7 percent. He decided that this is his required rate of return.

Required
a. Compute the net present value of each project. Which project should Mr. Hayes adopt based on the net present value approach?
b. Compute the approximate internal rate of return of each project. Which project should Mr. Hayes adopt based on the internal rate of return approach?
c. Compare the net present value approach with the internal rate of return approach. Which method is better in the given circumstances?

PROBLEM 10–19B *Using Net Present Value and Payback Period to Evaluate Investment Opportunities*

L.O. 9, 12

Belinda Patel just won a lottery and received a cash award of $400,000 net of tax. She is 61 years old and would like to retire in four years. Weighing this important fact, she has found two possible investments,

both of which require an immediate cash payment of $320,000. The expected cash inflows from the two investment opportunities are as follows.

	Year 1	Year 2	Year 3	Year 4
Opportunity A	$182,400	$104,000	$ 59,200	$ 67,200
Opportunity B	45,600	53,600	118,400	270,400

Ms. Patel decided that her required rate of return should be 10 percent.

Required

a. Compute the net present value of each opportunity. Which should Ms. Patel choose based on the net present value approach?

b. Compute the payback period for each opportunity. Which should Ms. Patel choose based on the payback approach?

c. Compare the net present value approach with the payback approach. Which method is better in the given circumstances?

L.O. 9, 12, 13   **PROBLEM 10–20B** *Effects of Straight-Line Versus Accelerated Depreciation on an Investment Decision*

Tulsa Pipe, Inc., decided to spend $40,000 to purchase new state-of-the-art equipment for its manufacturing plant. The equipment has a five-year useful life and a salvage value of $10,000. It is expected to generate additional cash revenue of $16,000 per year. Tulsa Pipe's required rate of return is 10 percent; its effective income tax rate is 25 percent.

Required

a. Determine the net present value and the present value index of the investment, assuming that Tulsa Pipe uses straight-line depreciation for financial and income tax reporting.

b. Determine the net present value and the present value index of the investment, assuming that Tulsa Pipe uses double-declining-balance depreciation for financial and income tax reporting.

c. Why are there differences in the net present values computed in Requirements *a* and *b*?

d. Determine the payback period and unadjusted rate of return (use average investment), assuming that Tulsa Pipe uses straight-line depreciation.

e. Determine the payback period and unadjusted rate of return (use average investment), assuming that Tulsa Pipe uses double-declining-balance depreciation. (*Note:* Use average annual cash flow when computing the payback period and average annual income when computing the unadjusted rate of return.)

f. Why are there no differences in the payback period or unadjusted rate of return computed in Requirements *d* and *e*?

L.O. 9   **PROBLEM 10–21B** *Applying the Net Present Value Approach With and Without Tax Considerations*

Kenneth Fultz, the president of Kenny's Moving Services, Inc., is planning to spend $250,000 for new trucks. He expects the trucks to increase the company's cash inflow as follows.

Year 1	Year 2	Year 3	Year 4
$65,400	$71,286	$77,702	$84,694

The company's policy stipulates that all investments must earn a minimum rate of return of 10 percent.

Required

a. Compute the net present value of the proposed purchase. Should Mr. Fultz purchase the trucks?

b. Wilma Rooney, the controller, is wary of the cash flow forecast and points out that Mr. Fultz failed to consider that the depreciation on trucks used in this project will be tax deductible. The depreciation is expected to be $60,000 per year for the four-year period. The company's income tax rate is 30 percent per year. Use this information to revise the company's expected cash flow from this purchase.

c. Compute the net present value of the purchase based on the revised cash flow forecast. Should Mr. Fultz purchase the trucks?

PROBLEM 10–22B *Comparing Internal Rate of Return With Unadjusted Rate of Return* **L.O. 10, 13**

Walsh Computers, Inc., faces stiff market competition. Top management is considering the replacement of its current production facility. The board of directors requires all capital investments to meet or exceed a 9 percent rate of return. However, the board has not clearly defined the rate of return. The president and controller are pondering two different rates of return: unadjusted rate of return and internal rate of return. To purchase a new facility with a life expectancy of four years, the company must pay $720,000. The increased net profit per year resulting from improved conditions would be approximately $80,000; the increased cash inflow per year would be approximately $220,000.

Required
a. If it uses the unadjusted rate of return (use average investment) to evaluate this project, should the company invest in the new facility?
b. If it uses the internal rate of return to evaluate this project, should the company invest in the new facility?
c. Which method is better for this capital investment decision?

PROBLEM 10–23B *Postaudit Evaluation* **L.O. 14**

Bradley Zeigler is wondering whether he made the right decision four years ago. As the president of Zeigler Health Care Services, he acquired a hospital specializing in elder care with an initial cash investment of $5,600,000. Mr. Zeigler would like to know whether the hospital's financial performance has met the original investment objective. The company's discount rate (required rate of return) for present value computations is 14 percent. Expected and actual cash flows follow.

	Year 1	Year 2	Year 3	Year 4
Expected	$1,840,000	$1,920,000	$2,000,000	$2,400,000
Actual	1,600,000	1,520,000	2,560,000	2,800,000

Required
a. Compute the net present value of the expected cash flows as of the beginning of the investment.
b. Compute the net present value of the actual cash flows as of the beginning of the investment.
c. What do you conclude from this postaudit?

ANALYZE, THINK, COMMUNICATE

BUSINESS APPLICATIONS CASE *Payback and Net Present Value* **ATC 10–1**

Acker Steel Company (ASC) is a steel-processing firm with sales approximating 24,000 tons per year. It purchases large coils of hot rolled prime steel from several steel mills, including U.S. Steel. Each coil weighs between 30 and 35 thousand pounds. ASC flattens or levels the coils into rectangular pieces (sheets) in sizes ranging up to 144 inches by 36 inches. Customers then use these sheets in stamping machines to punch out various steel parts.

A number of ASC's customers need steel sheets with a width of 48 inches but ASC's current leveling machines have the capability to cut pieces only up to 36 inches wide. The marketing department predicts that ASC could increase its sales by 4,000 tons in the first year if it purchases a new 48-inch leveling machine. The wider steel would sell at an average price of $415 per ton in the first two years. The following is a five-year sales volume and price forecast for the wider steel.

Year	Volume in Tons	Sales Price
1	4,000	$415
2	4,160	415
3	4,400	455
4	4,800	455
5	5,120	460

ASC can purchase a machine to produce 48-inch wide sheets for $460,000. The machine has an expected useful life of five years and a salvage value of $80,000. In addition to depreciation, the expected operating expenses for the machine are as follows.

	Years	
	1, 2	3, 4, 5
Expected operating expenses		
Variable cost per ton of output		
Materials cost	$ 240	$ 270
Labor cost	60	75
Overhead	45	50
Fixed cost per year		
Supervision	100,000	112,000
Maintenance	44,000	48,000
Miscellaneous (excluding depreciation)	16,000	20,000

These operating expenses would be paid in cash in the year they are incurred. The cost of capital is 10 percent. Depreciation is computed using the straight-line method. The effective income tax rate is 35 percent. Tax expense is paid in cash in the year in which it is incurred. All revenues are collected in cash in the year revenue is recognized.

Required

a. Prepare income statements using the contribution margin approach for each of the five years.
b. Compute the payback period for the investment. Use the incremental accumulation method.
c. Determine the net present value of the investment opportunity.
d. Indicate whether you would recommend accepting or rejecting the investment.
e. Comment on factors involving uncertainty.

ATC 10–2   GROUP ASSIGNMENT *Net Present Value*

Espada Real Estate Investment Company (EREIC) purchases new apartment complexes, establishes a stable group of residents, and then sells the complexes to apartment management companies. The average holding time is three years. EREIC is currently investigating two alternatives.

1. EREIC can purchase Harding Properties for $4,500,000. The complex is expected to produce net cash inflows of $360,000, $502,500, and $865,000 for the first, second, and third years of operation, respectively. The market value of the complex at the end of the third year is expected to be $5,175,000.
2. EREIC can purchase Summit Apartments for $3,450,000. The complex is expected to produce net cash inflows of $290,000, $435,000, and $600,000 for the first, second, and third years of operation, respectively. The market value of the complex at the end of the third year is expected to be $4,050,000.

EREIC has a desired rate of return of 12 percent.

Required

a. Divide the class into groups of four or five students per group and then divide the groups into two sections. Assign Task 1 to the first section and Task 2 to the second section.

Group Tasks

   (1) Calculate the net present value and the present value index for Harding Properties.
   (2) Calculate the net present value and the present value index for Summit Apartments.

b. Have a spokesperson from one group in the first section report the amounts calculated by the group. Make sure that all groups in the section have the same result. Repeat the process for the second section. Have the class as a whole select the investment opportunity that EREIC should accept given that the objective is to produce the higher rate of return.
c. Assume that EREIC has $4,500,000 to invest and that any funds not invested in real estate properties must be invested in a certificate of deposit earning a 5 percent return. Would this information alter the decision made in Requirement *b*?
d. This requirement is independent of Requirement *c*. Assume there is a 10 percent chance that the Harding project will be annexed by the city of Hoover, which has an outstanding school district. The annexation would likely increase net cash flows by $37,500 per year and would increase the market value at the end of year 3 by $300,000. Would this information change the decision reached in Requirement *b*?

RESEARCH ASSIGNMENT *Which Capital Budgeting Techniques Are Used in Practice ?*

ATC 10–3

The October 1998 issue of *Management Accounting* includes the article "How Forest Product Companies Analyze Capital Budgets" written by Bailes, Nielsen, and Lawton (pp. 24–30). The article describes a study that investigates changes in the capital budgeting techniques used by companies in the forestry industry from 1977 to 1997. Read this article and complete the following requirements.

Required

a. The survey asked executives to indicate their use of four capital budgeting techniques. Name these techniques.

b. What percentage of the companies surveyed used discounted cash flow techniques (internal rate of return and net present value) in 1977? What percentage used these techniques in 1997?

c. Was company size related to the type of technique used? If so, describe the relationship.

d. An extended time horizon increases the level of risk inherent in capital investment projects in the forestry industry. How do forestry companies adjust for this heightened level of risk?

WRITING ASSIGNMENT *Limitations of Capital Investment Techniques*

ATC 10–4

Webb Publishing Company is evaluating two investment opportunities. One is to purchase an Internet company with the capacity to open new marketing channels through which Webb can sell its books. This opportunity offers a high potential for growth but involves significant risk. Indeed, losses are projected for the first three years of operation. The second opportunity is to purchase a printing company that would enable Webb to better control costs by printing its own books. The potential savings are clearly predictable but would make a significant change in the company's long-term profitability.

Required

Write a response discussing the usefulness of capital investment techniques (net present value, internal rate of return, payback, and unadjusted rate of return) in making a choice between these two alternative investment opportunities. Your response should discuss the strengths and weaknesses of capital budgeting techniques in general. Furthermore, it should include a comparison between techniques based on the time value of money versus those that are not.

ETHICAL DILEMMA *Postaudit*

ATC 10–5

Gaines Company recently initiated a postaudit program. To motivate employees to take the program seriously, Gaines established a bonus program. Managers receive a bonus equal to 10 percent of the amount by which actual net present value exceeds the projected net present value. Victor Holt, manager of the North Western Division, had an investment proposal on his desk when the new system was implemented. The investment opportunity required a $250,000 initial cash outflow and was expected to return cash inflows of $90,000 per year for the next five years. Gaines' desired rate of return is 10 percent. Mr. Holt immediately reduced the estimated cash inflows to $70,000 per year and recommended accepting the project.

Required

a. Assume that actual cash inflows turn out to be $91,000 per year. Determine the amount of Mr. Holt's bonus if the original computation of net present value were based on $90,000 versus $70,000.

b. Is Mr. Holt's behavior in violation of any of the standards of ethical conduct in Exhibit 1-13 of Chapter 1?

c. Speculate about the long-term effect the bonus plan is likely to have on the company.

d. Recommend how to compensate managers in a way that discourages gamesmanship.

SPREADSHEET ASSIGNMENT *Using Excel*

ATC 10–6

Kilby Company is considering the purchase of new automated manufacturing equipment that would cost $150,000. The equipment would save $42,500 in labor costs per year over its six-year life. At the end of the fourth year, the equipment would require an overhaul that would cost $25,000. The equipment would have a $7,500 salvage value at the end of its life. Kilby's cost of capital is 12 percent.

Required

a. Prepare a spreadsheet similar to the one following to calculate net present value, the present value index, and the internal rate of return.

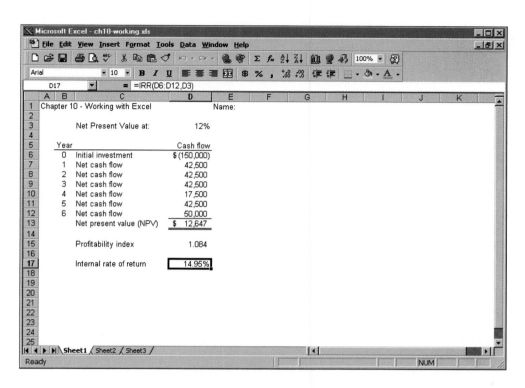

Spreadsheet Tips

Spreadsheets have built-in financial functions that make net present value and internal rate of return calculations very easy. The formats of these formulas are as follows.

1. *Net Present Value:* = NPV(rate,value1,value2,value3…value29) where up to 29 values are allowed. The values must be at the end of the period, and each period must be equal in time (one year, for example). The formula is = NPV(D3,D7,D8,D9,D10,D11,D12) + D6.

2. *Internal Rate of Return:* = IRR(values,guess) where *values* is the range that includes the cash flows (D6 to D12) and *guess* is an estimate of the rate. Use the cost of capital as the guess.

3. *Percentage:* Rather than entering 12% in the formulas, refer to cell D3. This will allow you to change the rate and see the effect on the NPV and present value index.

4. *Present Value Index:* You must construct a formula because no built-in function calculates it.

ATC 10–7   SPREADSHEET ASSIGNMENT *Mastering Excel*

ASAP Delivery is a small company that transports business packages between San Francisco and Los Angeles. It operates a fleet of small vans that moves packages to and from a central depot within each city and uses a common carrier to deliver the packages between the depots in the two cities. ASAP recently acquired approximately $4 million of cash capital from its owners, and its president, Alex Cade, is trying to identify the most profitable way to invest these funds.

Phil Duvall, the company's operations manager, believes that the money should be used to expand the fleet of city vans at a cost of $3,600,000. He argues that more vans would enable the company to expand its services into new markets, thereby increasing the revenue base. More specifically, he expects cash inflows to increase by $1,400,000 per year. The additional vans are expected to have an average useful life of four years and a combined salvage value of $500,000. Operating the vans will require additional working capital of $200,000, which will be recovered at the end of the fourth year.

In contrast, Amber Gomez, the company's chief accountant, believes that the funds should be used to purchase large trucks to deliver the packages between the depots in the two cities. The conversion process would produce continuing improvement in operating savings with reductions in cash outflows as the following:

Year 1	Year 2	Year 3	Year 4
$800,000	$1,600,000	$2,000,000	$2,200,000

The large trucks are expected to cost $4,000,000 and to have a four-year useful life and a $400,000 salvage value. In addition to the purchase price of the trucks, up-front training costs are expected to amount to $80,000. ASAP Delivery's management has established a 16 percent desired rate of return.

Required

a. Prepare a spreadsheet similar to the preceding one that calculates the net present value and the present value index for the two investments.

b. Include formulas in your spreadsheet to calculate the internal rate of return for each investment alternative.

Chapter

11

Product Costing in Service and Manufacturing Entities

Learning Objectives

After completing this chapter, you should be able to:

1 Understand the need for service and product cost information.

2 Understand how product costs flow from raw materials, to Work in Process, to Finished Goods, and ultimately to Cost of Goods Sold accounts.

3 Distinguish between costing for service versus manufacturing entities.

4 Demonstrate how product cost flow affects financial statements through a horizontal financial statements model.

5 Understand the necessity of assigning estimated overhead costs to the inventory and cost of goods sold accounts during an accounting period.

6 Record applied and actual overhead costs in a manufacturing overhead account.

7 Record product costs in T-accounts.

8 Understand the cyclical nature of product cost flows.

9 Comprehend the relationship between over- or underapplied overhead and variance analysis.

10 Prepare a schedule of cost of goods manufactured and sold.

11 Prepare a set of financial statements for a manufacturing entity.

12 Distinguish between absorption and variable costing.

the *curious* accountant

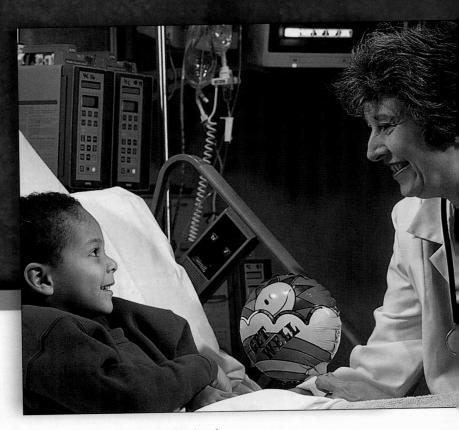

Many of the costs of providing services to a hospital patient are unknown when the patient is being treated. For example, the cost of the salaries of the physician and nurses may not be known until year end. Similarly, the actual cost of rental fees, janitorial services, billing charges, bad debts, and many other items will not be known until long after the patient has been treated. How can hospital administrators know what to charge a patient today if they do not know the cost of providing services until later?

The purpose of service and product costing systems is to supply information regarding the cost of providing services or making products. Product and service cost information is used in financial reporting, managerial accounting, and contract negotiations. Indeed, it is difficult to imagine an organization that could effectively conduct its operations without knowing the cost of providing services or making products.

Companies are required by generally accepted accounting principles (GAAP) to show service and product costs in their public financial reports. For example, product costs for manufacturing companies must be allocated between inventory (shown on the balance sheet) and cost of goods sold (shown on the income statement). Similarly, service companies must match the costs of providing services with the revenues generated from the services provided on their income statements. Accordingly, product and service costing is required for financial reporting.

Product and service cost information is also used for managerial accounting purposes. Companies need to know the cost of providing services or making products so they can plan their operations. For example, the budgeting process could not be accomplished without knowing the cost of services or products. Service and product costing is also needed for cost control. Corrective action may be taken if expected costs are inconsistent with actual costs. Finally, service and product cost information may be used in pricing and other short-term

decision making. For example, the cost of a service or product may be used in special order, outsourcing, or product elimination decisions.

Service and product costing information may be used by governmental agencies to regulate rates for public service entities such as utility companies or hospitals. Service and product costs are also used in determining the amount due on contracts that compensate companies for the costs they incur plus a reasonable profit (cost-plus contracts). For example, many governmental defense contracts are established on a cost-plus basis. Cost-plus pricing may also be used in private companies; for example, many builders of custom homes are compensated on the basis of cost-plus contracts. Thus, costing information is necessary for contract negotiations. *This chapter shows you how manufacturing companies determine the cost of the products they make.*

■ Cost Flow in Manufacturing Companies

LO1 Understand the need for service and product cost information.

In the previous chapters, we assumed that all inventory started during an accounting period was also completed during that accounting period. Accordingly, all product costs were included in the account Finished Goods Inventory or were expensed as Cost of Goods Sold. Most real-world companies have raw materials on hand at the end of the accounting period, and most manufacturing companies are likely to have inventory items that have been started but have not been completed. Indeed, most manufacturing companies accumulate their product costs in three distinct inventory accounts: (1) **Raw Materials Inventory**, which includes lumber, metals, paints, and chemicals that will be used to make the company's products; (2) **Work in Process Inventory**, which includes partially completed products; and (3) **Finished Goods Inventory**, which includes fully processed products that are ready for sale.

The cost of materials is first recorded in the Raw Materials Inventory account. The cost of the materials placed in production is then transferred from the Raw Materials Inventory account to the Work in Process Inventory account. The cost of labor and overhead are added to the Work in Process Inventory account. The cost of the goods completed during the period is transferred from the Work in Process Inventory account to the Finished Goods Inventory account. The cost of the goods that are sold during the accounting period is transferred from the Finished Goods Inventory account to the Cost of Goods Sold account. The balances that remain in the Raw Materials, Work in Process, and Finished Goods Inventory accounts appear on the balance sheet. The amount of product cost transferred to the Cost of Goods Sold account is expensed on the income statement. The flow of manufacturing costs is shown in Exhibit 11–1.

■ Cost Flow in Service Companies

LO2 Understand how product costs flow from Raw Materials, to Work in Process, to Finished Goods, and ultimately to Cost of Goods Sold accounts.

LO3 Distinguish between costing for service versus manufacturing entities.

Like manufacturing companies, many service companies have costs that begin with raw materials and pass through production stages such as work in process, finished goods, and cost of goods sold. For example, a hamburger from McDonald's starts with raw materials (meat, bun, and condiments), goes through work in process (is cooked, assembled, and wrapped), becomes a finished product, and is sold to a customer. Given this scenario, why is McDonald's classified as a *service* rather than a *manufacturing* company? The distinguishing feature is that the product from McDonald's is consumed immediately. In general, services cannot be stored and sold at a later time. As a result, service companies do not have Work in Process and Finished Goods Inventory accounts in which to store costs before transferring them to a Cost of Goods Sold account. At the end of the day, McDonald's has no work in process or finished goods inventory.

Is a retail company such as Toys-R-Us a service or manufacturing company? Because wholesale and retail companies have large inventory accounts, it may seem odd to think of

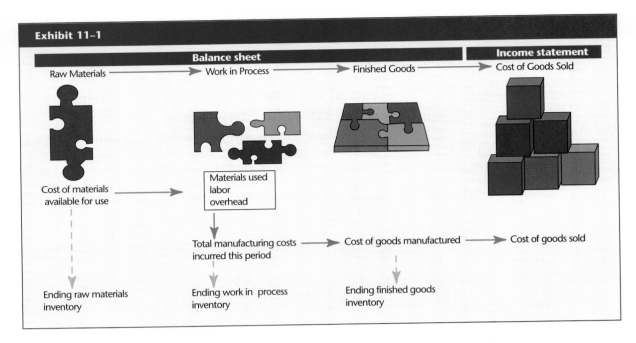

Exhibit 11–1

them as service companies. Even so, wholesale and retail companies are traditionally classified this way. To understand this classification, think about what the employees of a wholesale or retail company do. Clearly, the actions of the employees cannot be stored and used at a later time. The services of a salesperson are consumed as the customer is being assisted. Other organizations that provide services include insurance companies, banks, cleaning establishments, airlines, law firms, hospitals, hotels, and governmental agencies.

Even though service companies do not store their costs in inventory accounts for financial reporting purposes, they do accumulate cost information to facilitate decision making. For example, a hotel needs to know the cost of providing a room to assess whether its pricing policy is appropriate. A private school may compare the expected and actual cost of offering a course to ensure that costs are controlled. An airline needs to know the cost of providing service for a specific route to decide whether to maintain or eliminate the route. Understanding the cost of providing services is just as important as knowing the cost of making a product regardless of whether the cost is stored in an inventory balance sheet account or charged directly to the income statement.

■ Manufacturing Cost Flow Illustrated

To illustrate how manufacturing costs flow through ledger accounts, we consider the case of Ventra Manufacturing Company, which makes mahogany jewelry boxes that it sells to department stores. The account balances shown in Exhibit 11–2 were drawn from the company's accounting records as of January 1, 2002.

Ventra Manufacturing's 2002 accounting events are introduced here. The effects of the events are summarized in the T-accounts shown in Exhibit 11–4 page 454. We strongly suggest that you study Exhibit 11–4 carefully as you read the description of the events provided in the following

LO4 Demonstrate how product costs flow affects financial statements through a horizontal financial statement model.

Exhibit 11–2 *Trial Balance as of January 1, 2002*

Cash	$ 64,500	
Raw Materials Inventory	500	
Work in Process Inventory	0	
Finished Goods Inventory	836	
Manufacturing Equipment	40,000	
Accumulated Depreciation		$ 10,000
Common Stock		76,000
Retained Earnings		19,836
Totals	$105,836	$105,836

section of this chapter. The illustration assumes that Ventra determines the cost of making its product on a monthly basis. Accounting events for January are described here.

Events Affecting Manufacturing Cost Flow in January

Event 1
Raw Materials Purchased

Ventra Manufacturing pays $26,500 cash to purchase raw materials. For the sake of simplicity, we assume that all raw materials are purchased one time at the beginning of the accounting period. In practice, materials are usually purchased on a more frequent basis. The effects of the materials purchase on the company's financial statements are shown in the following horizontal financial statements model[1].

Assets			= Liabilities + Equity	Revenue − Expenses = Net Income	Cash Flow
Cash	+	**Raw Materials Inventory**			
(26,500)	+	26,500	= NA + NA	NA − NA = NA	(26,500) OA

This event is an asset exchange event; neither the income statement nor the total assets shown on the balance sheet are affected. One asset account, Cash, decreases, and another asset account, Raw Materials Inventory, increases. Costs of raw materials are only one component of the company's total manufacturing costs. The materials costs will be included as part of the cost of goods sold expense that will be recognized when the inventory is sold to customers. Because cash is spent for a current asset that will be used in the operation of the business, the cash outflow is shown in the operating activities (OA) section of the statement of cash flows.

Event 2
Raw Materials Placed into Production

Ventra places $1,100 of raw materials into production in the process of making jewelry boxes. This event is also an asset exchange event; total assets shown on the balance sheet are not affected. One asset account, Raw Materials Inventory, decreases, and another asset account, Work in Process Inventory, increases. Neither the income statement nor the statement of cash flows is affected. The effects of the material usage on the company's financial statements follow.

Assets			= Liabilities + Equity	Revenue − Expenses = Net Income	Cash Flow
Raw Materials Inventory	+	**Work in Process Inventory**			
(1,100)	+	1,100	= NA + NA	NA − NA = NA	NA

Raw materials represent *direct* inputs to the production process that are accounted for under the *perpetual inventory method.* Because the materials are traced directly to products, it is easy to match the cost flow with the physical flow. Every time direct materials are moved from storage to work in process, the cost of materials is transferred in the accounting records as well.

Event 3
Production Supplies Purchased

Ventra pays $2,000 cash to purchase production supplies. This event is also an asset exchange event; total assets shown on the balance sheet are not affected. One asset account, Cash, decreases, and another asset account, Production Supplies, increases. Net income is not affected. However, the cash flow associated with the purchase of supplies is shown in the operating section of the statement of cash flows. The effects of this event on the company's financial statements follow.

---

[1]The horizontal model derives its name from the fact that it arranges the major elements from the financial statements horizontally across a single page. Reading from left to right, elements of the balance sheet are presented first, followed by those of the income statement, and then the statement of cash flows. The types of activities recognized in the cash statement are identified by the letters OA for operating activities, IA for investing activities, and FA for financing activities.

Assets			=	Liabilities	+	Equity	Revenue	−	Expenses	=	Net Income	Cash Flow
Cash	+	Production Supplies										
(2,000)	+	2,000	=	NA	+	NA	NA	−	NA	=	NA	(2,000) OA

The production supplies are recorded in a separate asset account because practicality dictates that they be maintained under the *periodic inventory method*. Production supplies are *indirect* inputs. Such small quantities are used on each unit that it is not worth the trouble to track the actual costs as the materials are being used. Nobody wants to stop to make a journal entry every time several drops of glue are used. *Instead of recognizing supply usage as it occurs (perpetually), the amount of usage is determined at the end of the accounting period (periodically)*. The record-keeping procedures used to include the cost of production supplies in the flow of manufacturing costs are described in the explanation of the treatment of overhead costs (see Event 5).

Ventra pays production workers $1,400 cash. Note carefully that these wages are *not* treated as salary expense. Because the labor was used to make jewelry boxes, the cost is included in the Work in Process Inventory account. In other words, this is an asset exchange event. Cash was exchanged for the value added by making the inventory. Accordingly, one asset, *Cash*, decreases, and another asset, *Work in Process Inventory*, increases. Total assets as shown on the balance sheet are not affected nor is the income statement. The cash outflow is shown in the operating activities section of the statement of cash flows. The effects of the labor usage on the company's financial statements follow.

Event 4
Production Workers Paid

Assets			=	Liabilities	+	Equity	Revenue	−	Expenses	=	Net Income	Cash Flow
Cash	+	Work in Process Inventory										
(1,400)	+	1,400	=	NA	+	NA	NA	−	NA	=	NA	(1,400) OA

Flow of Overhead Costs

Assume that Ventra made 500 jewelry boxes during January. What is the cost per jewelry box? Why does management need this information? To the extent that Ventra uses a cost-plus-pricing strategy, it is necessary to know the cost per jewelry box to determine the price to charge for each one. Product cost information is also needed to accomplish control and performance evaluation. By comparing the current cost of production with historical or standard cost data, management can evaluate performance and take appropriate action to ensure that the company will accomplish its goals. Accordingly, Ventra has an immediate need to know the cost of products made in January for many reasons.

LO5 Understand the necessity of assigning estimated overhead costs to the inventory and cost of goods sold accounts during an accounting period.

The *direct costs* of making the 500 jewelry boxes in January include $1,100 for materials and $1,400 for labor. The *actual indirect overhead costs* are unknown. Indeed, some of these costs will not be known until the end of the year. For example, Ventra uses the periodic inventory method to determine the cost of production supplies. Accordingly, the amount of supplies used will not be known until the year-end count of supplies is completed. Similarly, the actual cost of taxes, insurance, landscaping, supervisory bonuses, and other indirect costs may be unknown in January. Even so, Ventra cannot delay important managerial decisions until actual cost data become available. In summary, Ventra needs information on January 31 that will not be available until December 31. This condition is depicted in the following graphic.

Like manufacturing companies, service companies use predetermined overhead rates to obtain timely information for decision-making purposes. For example, the Marriott Corporation cannot wait until the end of the year to price its rooms or banquet services. Customers want price information before actual cost data can be determined. Accordingly, Marriott's management team must base decisions on estimated (predetermined) rather than actual costs.

To resolve the conflict between the need for information and the availability of information, Ventra is forced to use *estimated costs* in its accounting system *during the accounting period*. To illustrate, assume that Ventra's accountant estimates that $40,320 of indirect overhead costs will be incurred during the entire year. This *estimate* of overhead cost includes $1,600 for the cost of production supplies, $10,000 of depreciation cost, and $28,720 of other costs such as supervisory salaries, rent on the manufacturing facility, utilities, and maintenance. How much of the $40,320 *estimated* overhead cost should be allocated to the units produced in January? To answer this question, it is necessary to identify the most appropriate allocation base. Assuming that the goods (jewelry boxes) are homogeneous (each box is exactly the same as every other box), it makes sense to assign the same amount of overhead cost to each box. This assignment is accomplished by using the number of units as the allocation base.

Suppose that Ventra's accountant expects that 12,000 jewelry boxes will be made during the year. Based on this estimate, the allocation rate is $3.36 per unit ($40,320 expected cost ÷ 12,000 units). Because the overhead allocation rate is determined before the actual overhead costs are known, it is called a **predetermined overhead rate**. Based on a $3.36 predetermined overhead rate, $1,680 of overhead cost is allocated to the 500 jewelry boxes made in January ($3.36 × 500 boxes).

Manufacturing Overhead Account

LO6 Record applied and actual overhead costs in a Manufacturing Overhead account.

How are overhead costs recorded in the accounting records? Estimated overhead costs are *applied* (assigned) to Work in Process Inventory *at the time goods are produced*. In the case of Ventra Manufacturing, $1,680 of overhead cost would be applied (transferred) to the Work in Process account during the month of January. However, actual overhead costs may be incurred at a different time than the time when goods are being made. For example, Ventra may recognize depreciation or the use of supplies at the end of the year. As a result, actual and estimated overhead costs are recorded at different times during the accounting period.

At the time estimated overhead is transferred to the Work in Process Inventory account, a corresponding amount of estimated overhead is accumulated in a *temporary* account called *Manufacturing Overhead.* The amount of overhead placed in the credit side of the manufacturing overhead account is called **applied overhead.** It may be helpful to think of the **Manufacturing Overhead account** as a temporary asset account. The recognition of estimated overhead can then be viewed as an asset exchange transaction. At the time estimated overhead is recognized, the temporary account, Manufacturing Overhead, decreases and the Work in Process Inventory account increases. Actual overhead costs are recorded as increases in the Manufacturing Overhead account at the time they are incurred. For example, at the end of the accounting period, the amount of supplies used is removed from the Supplies account and placed into the Manufacturing Overhead account. In this case, the balance in the Supplies account decreases and the balance in the Manufacturing Overhead account increases.

Because differences normally exist between estimated and actual overhead costs, the Manufacturing Overhead account is likely to contain a balance at the end of the accounting period. If more overhead has been applied than was actually incurred, the account balance represents the amount of **overapplied overhead**. If less overhead was applied than was incurred, the account balance will be classified as **underapplied overhead**. Overapplied overhead means that the amount of estimated overhead cost recorded in the Work in Process Inventory account was more than the amount of actual overhead cost incurred. Underapplied overhead means that the amount of estimated overhead cost recorded in the Work in Process Inventory account was less than the amount of actual overhead cost incurred. Because costs flow from Work in Process Inventory to Finished Goods Inventory and then to Cost of Goods Sold, these accounts will also be overstated or understated relative to actual costs. If the amount of the overapplied or underapplied overhead is significant, it must be allocated proportionately to the Work in Process Inventory, Finished Goods Inventory, and Cost of Goods Sold accounts.

In most cases, over- and underapplied overhead is not significant. When the amounts are insignificant, companies may correct the misapplied overhead in any manner they deem expedient. Under these circumstances, companies normally avoid the complication associated with allocating the over- or underapplied overhead among the inventory accounts and Cost of Goods Sold. Instead, the total amount of the overhead correction is assigned directly to Cost of Goods Sold. We have adopted this simplifying practice throughout the text and in the end-of-chapter exercises and problems. The flow of product cost including actual and applied overhead is shown in Exhibit 11–3. To illustrate the use of a Manufacturing Overhead account, we return to the case of Ventra Manufacturing Company.

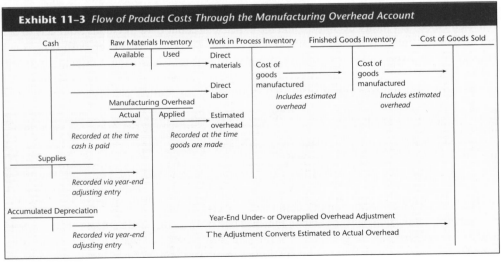

Exhibit 11–3 *Flow of Product Costs Through the Manufacturing Overhead Account*

Ventra recognizes $1,680 of estimated manufacturing overhead costs at the end of January (see previous section entitled Flow of Overhead Costs to review the computation of this amount). This event is another asset exchange event. Total assets shown on the balance sheet, net income, and cash flow are not affected. The temporary asset account Manufacturing Overhead

Event 5
Overhead Costs Recognized

decreases, and the asset account Work in Process Inventory increases. The effects of this event on the company's financial statements follow.

Assets			= Liabilities	+ Equity	Revenue	− Expenses	= Net Income	Cash Flow
Manufacturing Overhead	+	Work in Process Inventory						
(1,680)	+	1,680	= NA	+ NA	NA	− NA	= NA	NA

Event 6
Work in Process Completed and Cost Transferred to Finished Goods

Ventra transfers the total cost of the 500 jewelry boxes made in January ($1,100 materi-als + $1,400 labor + $1,680 estimated overhead = $4,180 cost of goods manufactured) from Work in Process to Finished Goods. This event is an asset exchange event. Total assets shown on the balance sheet, net income, and cash flow are not affected. The asset account Work in Process Inventory decreases, and the asset account Finished Goods Inventory increases. The effects of this event on the company's financial statements follow.

Assets			= Liabilities	+ Equity	Revenue	− Expenses	= Net Income	Cash Flow
Work in Process Inventory	+	Finished Goods Inventory						
(4,180)	+	4,180	= NA	+ NA	NA	− NA	= NA	NA

Event 7
Cost of Goods Sold Expense Recognized

Ventra transfers the cost of 400 jewelry boxes from the Finished Goods Inventory account to the Cost of Goods Sold account. Remember that a total of 500 jewelry boxes cost-ing $4,180 were made during January. Also, the Finished Goods Inventory account had a be-ginning balance of $836. Assume that this cost represented 100 units of inventory. As a result, 600 units (100 + 500) of finished goods costing $5,016 ($836 + $4,180) were available for sale. If 400 units are sold, 200 units remain in the Finished Goods Inventory account. Ac-cordingly, the cost of the 600 boxes ($5,016) must be allocated between the Finished Goods Inventory account and the Cost of Goods Sold account. The amount of the allocation is com-puted by first determining the cost per unit of jewelry boxes. Given 600 boxes at a cost of $5,016, the cost per unit is $8.36 ($5,016 ÷ 600). Based on this cost per unit, $3,344 ($8.36 × 400 boxes) is transferred from Finished Goods Inventory to Cost of Goods Sold. This leaves an ending balance of $1,672 in the Finished Goods Inventory account.

The transfer of cost from Finished Goods Inventory to Cost of Goods Sold is an asset use event. Total assets and owners' equity shown on the balance sheet decrease. The asset account Finished Goods Inventory decreases, and the expense account Cost of Goods Sold acts to de-crease owners' equity (retained earnings). Net income decreases. However, cash flow is not affected by the expense recognition. Be aware that the sales transaction is composed of two events. The following shows the effects of the expense recognition. The effects of the corre-sponding revenue recognition are discussed in the following section as a separate event.

Assets	= Liabilities	+ Equity	Revenues	− Expenses	= Net Income	Cash Flow
Finished Goods Inventory		Retained Earnings				
(3,344)	= NA	+ (3,344)	NA	− 3,344	= (3.344)	NA

The cost per unit information just computed is useful for many purposes. For example, the amount of the allocation between ending Finished Goods Inventory and the Cost of Goods Sold accounts is necessary for the preparation of financial statements. Accordingly, Ventra must com-pute the cost per unit data if the company desires to prepare interim (monthly or quarterly) fi-nancial reports. The cost per unit for the month of January also could be compared to the cost per unit for the previous accounting period or to standard cost data to evaluate cost control and per-formance. Finally, the cost per unit data are useful in setting the price under a cost-plus-pricing strategy. To illustrate, assume that Ventra desires to earn a gross margin of $5.64 per jewelry box. Under these circumstances, it would charge $14 ($8.36 cost + $5.64 gross profit) per unit for

each jewelry box. Indeed, when recording the effects of the revenue recognition for the 400 boxes sold, we assume that Ventra does, in fact, charge its customers $14 per unit.

Ventra recognizes $5,600 ($14 per unit × 400 units) of sales revenue. This is an asset source transaction. The asset account Cash increases and the owners' equity account **Retained Earnings** increases. Net income increases as does the operating activities section of the statement of cash flows. The effects of the revenue recognition follow.

Event 8
Revenue Recognized on Jewelry Boxes Sold

Assets	=	Liabilities	+	Equity		Revenues	−	Expenses	=	Net Income		Cash Flow
5,600	=	NA	+	5,600		5,600	−	NA	=	5,600		5,600 OA

Ventra pays $1,200 cash for manufacturing overhead costs including indirect labor, utilities, and rent. The amount of actual overhead is an asset exchange event. The event acts to transfer cost from the asset account, Cash to the temporary asset account, Manufacturing overhead. Total assets on the balance sheet are unaffected as is net income. However, the cash outflow reduces the operating activities section of the statement of cash flows. These effects follow.

Event 9
Actual Cash Overhead Costs Incurred

	Assets			=	Liabilities	+	Equity		Revenue	−	Expenses	=	Net Income		Cash Flow
Cash	+	Manufacturing Overhead													
(1,200)	+	1,200		=	NA	+	NA		NA	−	NA	=	NA		(1,200) OA

Recall that $1,680 of overhead was applied to the Work in Process Inventory account. This amount is significantly more than the $1,200 of actual overhead. The difference occurs because the estimated overhead includes several costs that have not yet been recognized. For example, the amount of supplies used and depreciation expense are not recognized until an adjusting entry is made on December 31. Although these costs are recognized in December, an appropriate portion of the cost must be included in the measurement of the cost of products made in January. Otherwise, all of the cost of supplies and depreciation would be assigned to the products made in December. Because the manufacturing equipment and supplies are actually used throughout the accounting period, assigning all of the cost of these resources to December alone overstates the cost of December production and understates the cost of production during other months. Such distortions in the measurement of product cost could mislead management in the decision-making process. By using *estimated* overhead costs during the accounting period, management is able to reduce the distortions that occur if actual costs are used. The difference between actual and estimated overhead is rectified through a *year-end adjusting entry*. No attempt is made to reconcile differences on an interim basis.

Candy Manufacturing Company had a beginning balance of $24,850 in its Work in Process Inventory account. Candy added the following costs to work in process during the accounting period: direct materials, $32,000; direct labor, $46,000; manufacturing overhead, $39,900. If the ending balance in the Work in Process Inventory account was $22,100, what was the amount of the Cost of Goods Manufactured (cost of goods transferred to Finished Goods Inventory)?

Answer

Beginning work in process inventory	$ 24,850
Manufacturing costs added	
Direct materials	32,000
Direct labor	46,000
Manufacturing overhead	39,900
Total work in process	142,750
Less: Ending work in process inventory	(22,100)
Cost of goods manufactured	$120,650

Check Yourself 11–1

answers to the *curious* accountant

As with manufacturing companies, service companies such as hospitals must use estimated costs for decision-making purposes. Hospital administrators must estimate all of the overhead costs associated with treating a patient. The estimated costs are then allocated to the cost objects (i.e., patients) to accomplish pricing and other managerial decisions.

Summary of Events Occurring in January

LO7 Record product costs in T-accounts.

Refer to Exhibit 11–4, which summarizes the events that occurred during January. The top section of the exhibit provides a graphic illustration of the *physical flow* of the resources used to make the jewelry boxes. The bottom section shows the effects of product *cost flow* through Ventra's ledger accounts. Events 1 through 7 are described in the exhibit. Event 8 recognizes the sales revenue, and Event 9 reflects the actual overhead cost incurred in January. As indicated, the January balances in the Finished Goods Inventory and Cost of Goods Sold accounts include the cost of materials, labor, and an *estimated* amount of overhead. Estimated overhead cost continues to be applied to the Work in Process Inventory account throughout the year. Actual overhead costs are accumulated in the Manufacturing Overhead account as they are incurred. The accounts are adjusted at year end to reconcile the difference between the estimated and actual overhead costs.

Exhibit 11–4 *Flow of Product Cost for Ventra Manufacturing Company's January Production*

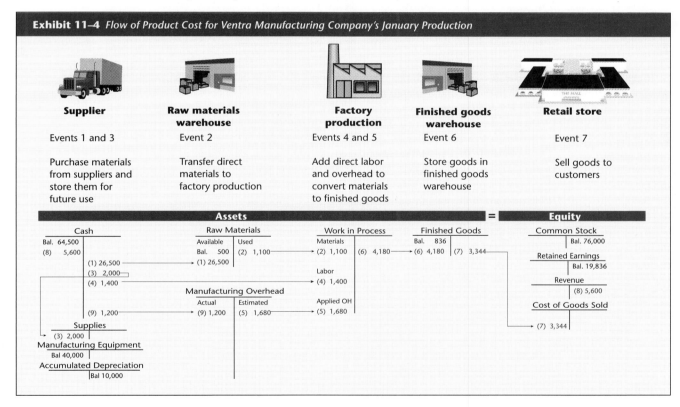

Events Affecting Manufacturing Cost Flow for February Through December

LO8 Understand the cyclical nature of product cost flows.

The events affecting Ventra Manufacturing Company for the months of February through December are summarized here. The sequence of events is numbered in a manner that reflects a continuation of the activity that occurred in January. Because nine events occurred in January, the first event, which represents activity from February through December, is Event 10. The list includes the following.

10. Ventra uses $24,860 of raw materials.
11. The company pays production workers $31,640 cash.

454

12. Because production is started on an additional 11,300 jewelry boxes, \$37,968 (11,300 units $\times$ the predetermined overhead rate of \$3.36 per unit) of overhead is applied to the Work in Process Inventory account.

13. The company completes work on 10,300 units of product and transfers \$86,108 of cost of goods manufactured from the Work in Process Inventory account to the Finished Goods Inventory account.

14. Ventra sells 9,600 units of product and records \$80,256 of cost of goods sold.

15. The company recognizes \$134,400 of cash revenue for the products sold in Event 14.

16. The company pays \$30,500 cash for overhead costs including indirect labor, rent, and utilities.

17. The year-end count of production supplies indicates that \$300 of supplies are on hand as of December 31. Accordingly, \$1,700 (\$2,000 supplies available − \$300 ending balance) of indirect materials cost is recognized as being used during the accounting period. Notice that this is a year-end recognition of actual overhead cost.

18. Ventra recognizes \$10,000 of actual overhead cost for depreciation of manufacturing equipment.

19. The company pays \$31,400 cash for general, selling, and administrative expenses.

20. A year-end review of the Manufacturing Overhead account reveals that overhead cost is underapplied by \$3,752. In other words, actual overhead (\$43,400) is higher than the estimated amount of overhead (\$39,648). Because estimated overhead cost passes through the ledger accounts (from Work in Process Inventory, to Finished Goods Inventory, and ultimately to Cost of Goods Sold), the balance in the Cost of Goods Sold account is understated. The adjusting entry to close the Manufacturing Overhead account and to increase the balance in the Cost of Goods Sold account is made.

The flow of these costs through the ledger accounts is shown in Exhibit 11–5. The exhibit includes the effects of the January events as well as those described for February through December. The January data are shown in blue to distinguish them from the data for the remainder of the year. The flow of product costs are highlighted with black arrows to facilitate your review of the exhibit. Carefully trace the effects of each transaction to ensure that you understand how product costs flow in a manufacturing entity.

LO7 Record product costs in T-accounts.

Analyses of Underapplied Overhead

What caused the overhead to be underapplied by \$3,752? Recall that the predetermined overhead rate is based on two estimates including the estimated overhead cost and the estimated volume of production. At the beginning of the accounting period, Ventra estimated that total overhead cost would be \$40,320, but actual overhead costs were \$43,400. Accordingly, Ventra spent \$3,080 more than it expected to spend for overhead cost. Having identified the *spending variance*, a \$672 portion of the underapplied overhead (\$3,752 − \$3,080) remains unexplained. This variance is the result of the difference between the actual and estimated volume of activity and is appropriately called a *volume variance*. Recall that Ventra estimated production volume to be 12,000 units, but actual volume was only 11,800 units (500 units made in January + 11,300 units made from February through December). As a result, the predetermined overhead rate of \$3.36 per unit was applied to 200 fewer units (12,000 units − 11,800 units) than expected. This results in a volume variance of \$672 (\$3.36 predetermined overhead rate $\times$ 200 units). The combination of the spending and volume variances[2] explains the total amount of the underapplied overhead (\$3,080 + \$672 = \$3,752).

Because the actual cost is higher than the expected cost, the spending variance is unfavorable. In addition, the volume variance is unfavorable because the actual volume is less than expected, thereby implying that the manufacturing facilities were not utilized to the extent

LO9 Comprehend the relationship between over- or underapplied overhead and variance analysis.

---

[2]The predetermined overhead rate used in this chapter represents the standard cost and quantity of both variable and fixed inputs. As discussed in Chapter 8, separate standards can be established for variable versus fixed costs. In this chapter, we assume that the variable cost variances are insignificant. Accordingly, the discussion focuses on the effects associated with fixed cost variances.

Exhibit 11–5 *Product Cost Flow for Ventra Manufacturing Company's 2002 Accounting Period*

Cash

Bal.	64,500	
(8)	5,600	(1) 26,500 →
(15)	134,400	
		(3) 2,000
Bal.	79,860	

Supplies

(3)	2,000	(17) 1,700 →
Bal.	300	

Manufacturing Equip.

Bal.	40,000

Accumulated Depreciation

		Bal. 10,000
(18)	10,000 →	(18) 10,000 →
		Bal. 20,000

Raw Materials Inventory

Available		Used	
Bal.	500	(2)	1,100 →
(1)	26,500	(10)	24,860 →
Bal.	1,040		

Manufacturing Overhead

Actual		Estimated		Applied OH	
(9)	1,200 →	(5)	1,680 →	(5)	1,680
(16)	30,500 →	(12)	37,968 →	(12)	37,968 →
(17)	1,700 →				
(18)	10,000 →				
(20)	3,752			Bal.	8,360
Bal.	0				

Work in Process Inventory

Materials		
(2)	1,100	
(10)	24,860	(6) 4,180 →
Labor		(13) 86,108 →
(4)	1,400	
(11)	31,640	
Applied OH		
(5)	1,680	
(12)	37,968 →	
Bal.	8,360	

(4) 1,400 →
(11) 31,640

(9) 1,200 →
(16) 30,500 →

(19) 31,400

Finished Goods Inventory

Bal.	836	
(6)	4,180 →	(7) 3,344 →
(13)	86,108 →	(14) 80,256 →
Bal.	7,524	

Cost of Goods Sold

(7)	3,344	
(14)	80,256	
		→ (20) 3,752
Bal.	87,352	

Common Stock

Bal.	76,000

Retained Earnings

Bal.	19,836

Revenue

(8)	5,600
(15)	134,400

G,S&A Expense

(19)	31,400

456

anticipated. In other words, fixed costs such as depreciation, rent, and supervisory salaries were spread over fewer units of product than expected, thereby increasing the cost per unit of product. If the variances are significant, estimated product costs would have been understated by an amount that could have distorted the decision-making process. For example, products could have been underpriced, thereby adversely affecting profitability. Accordingly, making estimates as accurately as possible is critically important. Even so, some minimal degree of inaccuracy is inevitable. No one knows exactly what the future will bring. Remember that managers are seeking to improve decision making. Although perfection is unattainable, responsible estimation will certainly provide timely information that is useful for decision making.

Check Yourself 11–2

At the beginning of the accounting period, Nutrient Manufacturing Company estimated its total manufacturing overhead cost for the coming year would be $124,000. Furthermore, the company expected to use 15,500 direct labor hours during the year. Nutrient actually incurred overhead costs of $128,500 for the year and actually used 15,800 direct labor hours. Nutrient allocates overhead costs to production based on direct labor hours. Would overhead costs be overapplied or underapplied? What effect will closing the overhead account have on cost of goods sold?

Answer

Predetermined overhead rate = Total expected overhead cost ÷ Allocation base
Predetermined overhead rate = $124,000 ÷ 15,500 hours = $8 per direct labor hour

Applied overhead = Predetermined overhead rate × Actual direct labor hours
Applied overhead = $8 × 15,800 = $126,400

Since the applied overhead ($126,400) is less than the actual overhead ($128,500), the overhead is underapplied. Closing the overhead account will increase Cost of Goods Sold by $2,100 ($128,500 − $126,400).

■ Preparation of Schedule of Cost of Goods Manufactured and Sold

LO10 Prepare a schedule of cost of goods manufactured and sold.

In practice, the general ledger system depicted in Exhibit 11–5 may include millions of events. The vast amount of data makes analysis exceedingly difficult. To facilitate the analytical process, the information in the ledger accounts is summarized in a *schedule* that explains the determination of the cost of goods manufactured and sold. The schedule is an internal document that does not appear in a company's published financial statements. However, the result of the schedule (cost of goods sold) does appear in the income statement. Exhibit 11–6 illustrates a **schedule of cost of goods manufactured and sold** for Ventra's 2002 accounting period.

The information in the schedule in Exhibit 11–6 mirrors the transaction data included in the ledger accounts. To verify this fact, compare the information in the Raw Materials Inventory account in Exhibit 11–5 with the computation of the cost of direct raw materials used in the schedule in Exhibit 11–6. The beginning raw materials balance, amount of purchases, and ending materials balance are identical in the ledger account and the schedule. However, the information in the schedule is presented in summary form. For example,

Exhibit 11–6 *Ventra Manufacturing Company*

Schedule of Cost of Goods Manufactured and Sold
For the Year Ended December 31, 2002

Beginning raw materials inventory	$ 500
Plus: Purchases	26,500
Raw materials available for use	27,000
Less: Ending raw materials inventory	(1,040)
Direct raw materials used	25,960
Direct labor	33,040
Overhead (actual overhead cost)	43,400
Total manufacturing costs	102,400
Plus: Beginning work in process inventory	0
Total work in process inventory	102,400
Less: Ending work in process inventory	(8,360)
Cost of goods manufactured	94,040
Plus: Beginning finished goods inventory	836
Cost of goods available for sale	94,876
Less: Ending finished goods inventory	(7,524)
Cost of goods sold	$ 87,352

LO11 Prepare a set of financial statements for a manufacturing entity.

the amount of direct materials used is shown as $25,960 in the schedule. This same amount is shown as two separate events ($1,100 + $24,860) in the T-account in Exhibit 11–5. Similarly, the $33,040 amount shown as direct labor in the schedule represents the total of the two amounts ($1,400 + $31,640) of labor cost shown in the Work in Process Inventory account in Exhibit 11–5. In practice, one number in the schedule may represent thousands of individual events that are captured in the ledger accounts. Accordingly, the schedule simplifies the process of analyzing manufacturing cost flow data for decision-making purposes.

It is important to note that the *actual* amount of overhead cost is shown in the schedule of cost of goods manufactured and sold. Remember that financial statement data are gathered at the end of the accounting period when actual cost data are available. Although the estimated cost data are used for internal decision making, actual historical cost data are presented in the schedule.

Exhibit 11–7

VENTRA MANUFACTURING COMPANY
Income Statement
For the Year Ended December 31, 2005

Sales Revenue	$140,000
Cost of Goods Sold	(87,352)
Gross Margin	52,648
Selling and Administrative Expenses	(31,400)
Net Income	$ 21,248

Exhibit 11–8

VENTRA MANUFACTURING COMPANY
Balance Sheet
As of December 31, 2005

Assets	
Cash	$ 79,860
Raw Materials Inventory	1,040
Work in Process Inventory	8,360
Finished Goods Inventory	7,524
Production Supplies	300
Manufacturing Equipment	40,000
Accumulated Depreciation—Manufac. Equip.	(20,000)
Total Assets	$117,084
Stockholders' Equity	
Common Stock	$ 76,000
Retained Earnings	41,084
Total Stockholders' Equity	$117,084

Exhibit 11–9

VENTRA MANUFACTURING COMPANY
Statement of Cash Flows
For the Year Ended December 31, 2005

Cash Flows from Operations	
Inflow from Customers	$140,000
Outflow for Production of Inventory*	(93,240)
Outflow for Selling and Administrative Expenses	(31,400)
Net Inflow from Operating Activities	15,360
Cash Flow from Investing Activities	0
Cash Flow from Financing Activities	0
Net Change in Cash	15,360
Plus: Beginning Cash Balance	64,500
Ending Cash Balance	$79,860

*See Cash account in Exhibit 11–5:$26,500 + $2,000 + $1,400 + $31,640 + $1,200 + $30,500 = $93,240.

▮ Financial Statements

The result of schedule of the cost of goods manufactured and sold is shown as the single line item *cost of goods sold* on the company's income statement. The amount of cost of goods sold is subtracted from the sales revenue to determine the gross margin. Selling and administrative expenses are subtracted from gross margin to calculate the amount of net income. Ventra Manufacturing's income statement is shown in Exhibit 11–7, and its balance sheet is shown in Exhibit 11–8. For demonstration purposes in Exhibit 11–8, we show the three inventory accounts (Raw Materials, Work in Process, and Finished Goods) separately. In practice, these accounts are frequently combined and shown as a single amount on the balance sheet. The statement of cash flows is shown in Exhibit 11–9. Review these statements carefully to ensure that you understand how the information shown in the T-accounts in Exhibit 11–5 is ultimately presented in a company's public financial reports.

▮ Motive to Overproduce

Absorption Costing Versus Variable Costing

As discussed previously, the cost of manufacturing products can be divided into fixed and variable cost categories. For example, the cost of materials, labor, and supplies frequently increases and decreases in direct proportion to the number of units produced. Other costs incurred to make products are fixed costs. The cost of rent, depreciation, and supervisory salaries remains constant regardless of the number of products made. Generally accepted accounting principles require that *all* product costs, both fixed and variable, be accumulated in the inventory accounts until

the products are sold. The product costs are expensed as cost of goods sold when the goods are sold. This practice is called **absorption (full) costing**.[3] To illustrate, assume that Hokai Manufacturing Company incurs the following costs to produce 2,000 units of inventory.

LO12 Distinguish between absorption and variable costing.

Inventory Costs	Cost per Unit	×	Units	=	Total
Variable manufacturing costs	$9	×	2,000	=	$18,000
Fixed overhead				=	12,000
Total (full absorption product cost)				=	$30,000

Suppose that Hokai sells all 2,000 units of inventory for $20 per unit (sales = 2,000 × $20 = $40,000). Under these circumstances, gross margin amounts to $10,000 ($40,000 sales − $30,000 cost of goods sold). What happens to profitability if Hokai increases production while holding sales constant? Profitability increases because cost of goods sold decreases. More specifically, overpro-

Exhibit 11–10 *Cost per Unit*

Inventory Costs

Fixed overhead (a)	$12,000	$12,000	$12,000
Number of units (b)	2,000	3,000	4,000
Fixed overhead per unit (a ÷ b)	$ 6	$ 4	$ 3
Variable manufacturing costs	9	9	9
Full absorption product cost per unit	$ 15	$ 13	$ 12

ducing spreads the fixed cost over more units, thereby reducing the cost per unit and the amount charged to cost of goods sold. Exhibit 11–10 illustrates this phenomenon; it shows the cost per unit at production levels of 2,000, 3,000, and 4,000 units.

Exhibit 11–11 is Hokai's income statements assuming a sales volume of 2,000 units and production levels of 2,000, 3,000, and 4,000 units.

Exhibit 11–11 *Absorption Income Statements at Different Levels of Production With Sales Held Constant at 2,000 Units*

Level of Production	2,000		3,000		4,000
Sales ($20 per unit × 2,000 units)	$40,000		$40,000		$40,000
Cost of goods sold ($15 × 2,000) =	30,000	($13 × 2,000) =	26,000	($12 × 2,000) =	24,000
Gross margin	$10,000		$14,000		$16,000

Suppose that management is under pressure to increase profitability. Management cannot control sales because the purchaser makes the decision to buy. Under these conditions, management may be tempted to increase profitability by increasing production. You may wonder what is so wrong about increasing production. The problem lies in inventory accumulation. Notice that the level of inventory increases by 1,000 units when 3,000 units are produced but only 2,000 are sold. Likewise, the inventory rises to 2,000 units when 4,000 are produced but 2,000 are sold. Considerable risks and costs are associated with holding excess inventory. The inventory may become obsolete, damaged, stolen, or destroyed by fire, weather, or other disasters. Furthermore, holding inventory requires warehouse space, employee handling, financing, and insurance costs. In the long term, these risks and costs reduce the company's profitability. Accordingly, the overproduction of inventory is a poor business practice. To motivate managers to increase profitability without motivating them to overproduce, many companies use an internal reporting format known as *variable costing*.

Variable Costing

Under **variable costing**, only the *variable* product costs are accumulated in an inventory account. The income statement is prepared under the contribution margin approach, and variable product costs are subtracted from the revenue to determine the contribution margin. Fixed costs are then subtracted from the contribution margin to determine the amount of net income.

LO12 Distinguish between absorption and variable costing.

[3]Since absorption costing includes all product costs including manufacturing costs, it is sometimes called *full costing*.

Accordingly, fixed manufacturing costs are expensed in the period in which they are incurred (the period in which the resource is used) regardless of when the inventory is sold. Under these circumstances, the amount of reported profit is not affected by increases in productivity. This point is illustrated in the variable cost income statements presented in Exhibit 11–12.

Exhibit 11–12 *Variable Income Statements at Different Levels of Production With Sales Held Constant at 2,000 Units*

Level of Production	2,000		3,000		4,000
Sales ($20 per unit × 2,000 units)	$40,000		$40,000		$40,000
Variable cost of goods sold ($9 × 2,000) =	(18,000)	($9 × 2,000) =	(18,000)	($9 × 2,000) =	(18,000)
Contribution margin	22,000		22,000		22,000
Fixed manufacturing costs	(12,000)		(12,000)		(12,000)
Net income	$10,000		$10,000		$10,000

Although managers may still overproduce under variable costing, at least they are not tempted to do so by the lure of reporting higher profits. Accordingly, the variable reporting format encourages management to make business decisions that have a more favorable impact on long-term profitability. Variable costing can be used only for internal reporting because generally accepted accounting principles prohibit its use in external financial statements.

Check Yourself 11–3

If production exceeds sales, will absorption or variable costing produce the higher amount of net income? Which method (absorption or variable costing) is required for external financial reporting?

Answer Absorption costing produces a higher amount of net income when production exceeds sales. With absorption costing, fixed manufacturing costs are treated as inventory and remain in inventory accounts until the inventory is sold. In contrast, all fixed manufacturing costs are expensed with variable costing. Therefore, with absorption costing, some fixed manufacturing costs will be in inventory rather than in expense accounts, so expenses will be lower and net income will be higher than with variable costing (when production exceeds sales). Generally accepted accounting principles require companies to use absorption costing for external financial reporting purposes.

a look back

Most manufacturing companies accumulate product costs in three inventory accounts. The *Raw Materials Inventory account* is used to accumulate the cost of direct *raw materials* purchased for use in production. The *Work in Process Inventory account* includes the cost of partially completed products. Finally, the *Finished Goods Inventory account* contains the costs of fully completed products that are ready for sale. When direct materials are purchased, their costs are first placed in the Raw Materials Inventory account. The costs of the materials used in production are transferred from this account to the Work in Process Inventory account. The cost of direct labor and overhead are added to the Work in Process Inventory account. As goods are completed, their costs are transferred from Work in Process Inventory to Finished Goods Inventory. When goods are sold, their cost is transferred from Finished Goods Inventory to Cost of Goods Sold. The ending balances in the Raw Materials, Work in Process, and Finished Goods Inventory accounts appear on the balance sheet. The product cost in the Cost of Goods Sold account is subtracted from revenue on the income statement to determine the gross margin.

Many of the actual indirect overhead costs incurred to make products are unknown until the end of the accounting period. Examples of such costs may include the cost of rent, supplies, utilities, indirect materials, and labor. Because many managerial decisions require product cost information before year end, companies frequently estimate the amount of overhead cost. The estimated overhead costs are assigned to products through the use of a *predetermined overhead rate*.

Actual and applied overhead costs are accumulated in the temporary account *Manufacturing Overhead*. Differences between actual and applied overhead result in a balance in the Manufacturing Overhead account at the end of the accounting period. If actual overhead is higher than applied overhead, the balance represents *underapplied overhead*. If actual overhead is lower than applied overhead, the balance represents *overapplied overhead*. If the amount of over- or underapplied overhead is insignificant, it is charged directly to cost of goods sold through a year-end adjusting entry.

Manufacturing cost information is summarized in a report known as a *schedule of cost of goods manufactured and sold*. This schedule explains the determination of the amount of cost of goods sold that appears on the income statement. The actual amount of overhead cost is used in the schedule.

Generally accepted accounting principles require all product costs (fixed and variable) to be accumulated in inventory accounts until the products are sold. This practice is called *absorption costing*. Under absorption costing, management may be tempted to increase profitability by producing more units than can be sold (overproducing). Overproducing spreads the fixed cost over more units, thereby reducing the cost per unit and the amount charged to cost of goods sold. The unfortunate effect is, however, that the extra units must be held in inventory. In the long term, the risks and costs associated with inventory accumulation will reduce profitability. To eliminate the costs of inventory accumulation associated with overproduction, many companies use *variable costing* for determining product cost for internal reporting purposes. Under variable costing, only the variable product costs are accumulated in inventory accounts. Fixed product costs are expensed in the period they are incurred, not when products are sold. As a result, overproduction does not decrease the product cost per unit and managers are not tempted to overproduce to increase profitability.

Would you use the same product cost system to determine the cost of a bottle of Pepsi as you use to determine the cost of a stealth bomber? You will find the answer to this question in the next chapter, which expands on the basic cost flow concepts introduced in this chapter. You will be introduced to job-order, process, and hybrid cost systems. You will learn to identify the types of services and products that are most appropriate for each type of cost system.

a look forward

SELF-STUDY REVIEW PROBLEM

Tavia Manufacturing Company's first year of operation is summarized in the following list. All transactions are cash transactions unless otherwise indicated.

1. Acquired cash by issuing common stock.
2. Purchased administrative equipment.
3. Purchased manufacturing equipment.
4. Purchased direct raw materials.
5. Purchased indirect materials (production supplies).
6. Used direct raw materials in making products.
7. Paid direct labor wages to manufacturing workers.
8. Applied overhead costs to Work in Process Inventory.
9. Paid indirect labor salaries (production supervisors).
10. Paid administrative and sales staff salaries.
11. Paid rent and utilities on the manufacturing facilities.
12. Completed work on products.
13. Sold completed inventory for cash. (revenue event only)
14. Recognized cost of goods sold.
15. Recognized depreciation on manufacturing equipment.
16. Recognized depreciation on administrative equipment.
17. Recognized the amount of production supplies that had been used during the year.
18. Closed the Manufacturing Overhead account. Overhead had been underapplied during the year.

Required

a. Use the horizontal statements model to show how each event affects the balance sheet, income statement, and statement of cash flows. Indicate whether the event increases (+), decreases (−), or does not affect (NA) each element of the financial statements. Also designate the classification of cash flows using the letters OA for operating activity, IA for investing activity, and FA for financing activity.
b. Identify the accounts affected by each event and indicate whether they increased or decreased as a result of the event.

Solution to Requirement a

Event No.	Assets	= Liab.	+ Equity	Rev.	− Exp.	= Net Inc.	Cash Flow
1	+	n/a	+	n/a	n/a	n/a	+ FA
2	− +	n/a	n/a	n/a	n/a	n/a	− IA
3	− +	n/a	n/a	n/a	n/a	n/a	− IA
4	− +	n/a	n/a	n/a	n/a	n/a	− OA
5	− +	n/a	n/a	n/a	n/a	n/a	− OA
6	− +	n/a	n/a	n/a	n/a	n/a	n/a
7	− +	n/a	n/a	n/a	n/a	n/a	− OA
8	− +	n/a	n/a	n/a	n/a	n/a	n/a
9	− +	n/a	n/a	n/a	n/a	n/a	− OA
10	−	n/a	−	n/a	+	−	− OA
11	− +	n/a	n/a	n/a	n/a	n/a	− OA
12	− +	n/a	n/a	n/a	n/a	n/a	n/a
13	+	n/a	+	+	n/a	+	+ OA
14	−	n/a	−	n/a	+	−	n/a
15	− +	n/a	n/a	n/a	n/a	n/a	n/a
16	−	n/a	−	n/a	+	−	n/a
17	− +	n/a	n/a	n/a	n/a	n/a	n/a
18	−	n/a	−	n/a	+	−	n/a

Solution to Requirement b

Event No.	Account Title	Increase/Decrease	Account Title	Increase/Decrease
1	Cash	+	Common Stock	+
2	Administrative Equipment	+	Cash	−
3	Manufacturing Equipment	+	Cash	−
4	Raw Materials Inventory	+	Cash	−
5	Production Supplies	+	Cash	−
6	Work in Process Inventory	+	Raw Materials Inventory	−
7	Work in Process Inventory	+	Cash	−
8	Work in Process Inventory	+	Manufacturing Overhead	−
9	Manufacturing Overhead	+	Cash	−
10	Salary Expense	+	Cash	−
11	Manufacturing Overhead	+	Cash	−
12	Finished Goods Inventory	+	Work in Process Inventory	−
13	Cash	+	Sales Revenue	+
14	Cost of Goods Sold	+	Finished Goods Inventory	−
15	Manufacturing Overhead	+	Accumulated Depreciation	+
16	Depreciation Expense	+	Accumulated Depreciation	+
17	Manufacturing Overhead	+	Production Supplies	−
18	Cost of Goods Sold	+	Manufacturing Overhead	−

KEY TERMS

Absorption (full) costing *459*
Applied overhead *451*
Finished Goods Inventory *446*

Manufacturing Overhead
  account *451*
Overapplied or underapplied
  overhead *451*

Predetermined overhead
  rate *450*
Raw Materials Inventory *446*
Retained Earnings *453*

Schedule of cost of goods
  manufactured and sold *457*
Variable costing *459*
Work in Process Inventory *446*

QUESTIONS

1. What is the difference between direct and indirect raw materials costs?
2. Direct raw materials were purchased on account, and the costs were subsequently transferred to Work in Process Inventory. How would the transfer affect assets, liabilities, equity, and cash flows? What is the effect on the income statement? Would your answers change if the materials had originally been purchased for cash?
3. How do manufacturing costs flow through inventory accounts?
4. Goods that cost $2,000 to make were sold for $3,000 on account. How does their sale affect assets, liabilities, and equity? What is the effect on the income statement? What is the effect on the cash flow statement?
5. At the end of the accounting period, an adjusting entry is made for the accrued wages of production workers. How would this entry affect assets, liabilities, and equity? What is the effect on the income statement? What is the effect on the cash flow statement?
6. X Company recorded the payment for utilities used by the manufacturing facility by crediting Cash and debiting Manufacturing Overhead. Why was the debit made to Manufacturing Overhead instead of Work in Process Inventory?
7. Why is the salary of a production worker capitalized while the salary of a marketing manager expensed?
8. Al Carmon says that his company has a difficult time establishing a predetermined overhead rate because the number of units of product produced during a period is difficult to measure. What are two measures of production other than the number of units of product that Mr. Carmon could use to establish a predetermined overhead rate?
9. What do the terms *overapplied overhead* and *underapplied overhead mean?*
10. What are *product costs* and *selling, general, and administrative costs?* Give examples of product costs and of selling, general, and administrative costs.
11. How does the entry to close an insignificant amount of overapplied overhead to the Cost of Goods Sold account affect net income?
12. Why are actual overhead costs not used in determining periodic product cost?
13. Because of seasonal fluctuations, Buresch Corporation has a problem determining the unit cost of its products. For example, high heating costs during the winter months cause the cost per unit to be higher than the per unit cost in the summer months even when the same number of units of product is produced. Suggest how Buresch can improve the computation of per unit cost.
14. What is the purpose of the Manufacturing Overhead account?
15. For what purpose is the schedule of cost of goods manufactured and sold prepared? Do all companies use the statement?
16. How does the variable costing approach differ from the absorption costing approach? Explain the different income statement formats used with each approach.
17. How is profitability affected by increases in productivity under the variable and absorption costing approaches?
18. Under what circumstance is a variable costing statement format used? What potential problem could it eliminate?

EXERCISES—SERIES A

EXERCISE 11–1A *Product Cost Flow and Financial Statements*

L.O. 2, 4, 10, 11

Cameron Manufacturing Company was started on January 1, 2005. The company was affected by the following events during its first year of operation.

1. Acquired $1,600 cash from the issue of common stock.

2. Paid $500 cash for direct raw materials.
3. Transferred $400 of direct raw materials to work in process.
4. Paid production employees $600 cash.
5. Paid $300 cash for manufacturing overhead costs.
6. Applied $245 of manufacturing overhead costs to work in process.
7. Completed work on products that cost $1,000.
8. Sold products that cost $800 for $1,400 cash.
9. Paid $400 cash for selling and administrative expenses.
10. Made a $50 cash distribution to the owners.
11. Closed the Manufacturing Overhead account.

Required

a. Record these events in a horizontal statements model. Also designate the classification of cash flows using the letters OA for operating activities, IA for investing activities, and FA for financing activities. The first event is shown as an example.

Assets					=	Equity					
Cash +	MOH +	Raw M. +	WIP +	F. Goods	= C. Stk. +	Ret. Ear.	Rev. −	Exp. =	Net Inc.	Cash Flow
1,600 +	NA +	NA +	NA +	NA	= 1,600 +	NA	NA −	NA =	NA	1,600 FA

b. Prepare a schedule of cost of goods manufactured and sold.

L.O. 2, 7, 10, 11   **EXERCISE 11–2A** *Recording Events in T-Accounts and Preparing Financial Statements*

Reeves Manufacturing Company was started on January 1, 2001, when it acquired $1,000 cash from the issue of common stock. During the first year of operation, $400 of direct raw materials was purchased with cash, and $300 of the materials was used to make products. Direct labor costs of $500 were paid in cash. Reeves applied $320 of overhead cost to the Work in Process account. Cash payments of $350 were made for actual overhead costs. The company completed products that cost $800 and sold goods that had cost $600 for $1,000 cash. Selling and administrative expenses of $240 were paid in cash.

Required

a. Open T-accounts and record the events affecting Reeves Manufacturing. Include closing entries.
b. Prepare a schedule of cost of goods manufactured and sold, an income statement, a balance sheet, and a statement of cash flows.
c. Explain the difference between net income and cash flow from operating activities.

L.O. 4   **EXERCISE 11–3A** *Effect of Accounting Events on Financial Statements*

Required

Use a horizontal statements model to indicate how each of the following independent accounting events affects the elements of the balance sheet, income statement, and statement of cash flows. Indicate whether the event increases (I), decreases (D), or does not affect (NA) each element of the financial statements. Also designate the classification of cash flows using the letters OA for operating activities, IA for investing activities, and FA for financing activities. The first two transactions are shown as examples.

a. Paid cash to purchase raw materials.
b. Recorded cash sales revenue.
c. Paid cash for actual manufacturing overhead cost.
d. Closed the Manufacturing Overhead account when overhead was overapplied.
e. Transferred cost of completed inventory to finished goods.
f. Paid cash for wages of production workers.
g. Paid cash for salaries of selling and administrative personnel.
h. Recorded adjusting entry to recognize amount of manufacturing supplies used (the company uses the periodic inventory method to account for manufacturing supplies).

Event No.	Balance Sheet				Income Statement			Statement of Cash Flow
	Assets =	Liab. +	C. Stk +	Ret Ear.	Rev. −	Exp. =	Net Inc.	
a.	I D	NA	NA	NA	NA	NA	NA	D OA
b.	I	NA	NA	I	I	NA	I	I OA

EXERCISE 11–4A *Preparing Financial Statements*

L.O. 2, 10, 11

Dominion Corporation began fiscal year 2001 with the following balances in its inventory accounts.

Raw Materials	$ 84,000
Work in Process	126,000
Finished Goods	42,000

During the accounting period, Dominion purchased $360,000 of raw materials and issued $372,000 of materials to the production department. Direct labor costs for the period amounted to $486,000, and factory overhead of $72,000 was applied to Work in Process Inventory. Assume that there was no over- or underapplied overhead. Goods costing $918,000 to produce were completed and transferred to Finished Goods Inventory. Goods costing $904,000 were sold for $1,200,000 during the period. Selling and administrative expenses amounted to $108,000.

Required
a. Determine the ending balance of each of the three inventory accounts that would appear on the year-end balance sheet.
b. Prepare a schedule of cost of goods manufactured and sold and an income statement.

EXERCISE 11–5A *Missing Information in a Schedule of Cost of Goods Manufactured*

L.O. 10

Required
Supply the missing information on the following schedule of cost of goods manufactured.

AMIGO CORPORATION
Schedule of Cost of Goods Manufactured
For the Year Ended December 31, 2005

Raw Materials		
Beginning Inventory	$?	
Plus: Purchases	180,000	
Raw Materials Available for Use	222,000	
Minus: Ending Raw Materials Inventory	?	
Cost of Direct Raw Materials Used		$186,000
Direct Labor		?
Manufacturing Overhead		36,000
Total Manufacturing Costs		$465,000
Plus: Beginning Work in Process Inventory		?
Total Work in Process during the Period		$?
Minus: Ending Work in Process Inventory		69,000
Cost of Goods Manufactured		$459,000

EXERCISE 11–6A *Cost of Goods Manufactured and Sold*

L.O. 10

The following information pertains to Bullard Manufacturing Company for March 2005. Assume actual overhead equaled applied overhead.

March 1	
Inventory balances	
Raw materials	$ 80,000
Work in process	130,000
Finished goods	86,000
March 31	
Inventory balances	
Raw materials	$ 75,000
Work in process	120,000
Finished goods	71,000
During March	
Costs of raw materials purchased	$ 24,000
Costs of direct labor	20,000
Costs of manufacturing overhead	32,000
Sales revenues	155,000

Required
a. Prepare a schedule of cost of goods manufactured and sold.
b. Calculate the amount of gross margin on the income statement.

L.O. 6, 9 EXERCISE 11–7A *Calculating Applied Overhead*

Cobb Inc. estimates manufacturing overhead costs for the 2002 accounting period as follows.

Equipment depreciation	$192,000
Supplies	21,000
Materials handling	34,000
Property taxes	15,000
Production setup	21,000
Rent	45,000
Maintenance	40,000
Supervisory salaries	132,000

The company uses a predetermined overhead rate based on machine hours. Estimated hours for labor in 2002 were 200,000 and for machines were 125,000.

Required
a. Calculate the predetermined overhead rate.
b. Determine the amount of manufacturing overhead applied to Work in Process Inventory during the 2002 period if actual machine hours were 140,000.

L.O. 5, 9 EXERCISE 11–8A *Treatment of Over- or Underapplied Overhead*

Foster Company estimates that its overhead costs for 2004 will be $900,000 and output in units of product will be 300,000 units.

Required
a. Calculate Foster's predetermined overhead rate based on expected production.
b. If 24,000 units of product were made in March 2004, how much overhead cost would be allocated to the Work in Process Inventory account during the month?
c. If actual overhead costs in March were $70,000, would overhead be overapplied or underapplied and by how much?

L.O. 6, 9 EXERCISE 11–9A *Recording Overhead Costs in T-Accounts*

Minghs Company and Sathe Company both apply overhead to the Work in Process Inventory account using direct labor hours. The following information is available for both companies for the year.

	Minghs Company	Sathe Company
Actual manufacturing overhead	$40,000	$80,000
Actual direct labor hours	10,000	12,000
Underapplied overhead		4,000
Overapplied overhead	8,000	

Required
a. Compute the predetermined overhead rate for each company.
b. Using T-accounts, record the entry to close the overapplied or underapplied overhead at the end of the accounting period for each company, assuming the amounts are immaterial.

L.O. 6, 9 EXERCISE 11–10A *Treatment of Over- or Underapplied Overhead*

Jerris Company and Frankel Company assign manufacturing overhead to the Work in Process Inventory using direct labor cost. The following information is available for the companies for the year:

	Jerris Company	Frankel Company
Actual direct labor cost	$290,000	$240,000
Estimated direct labor cost	300,000	200,000
Actual manufacturing overhead cost	112,000	184,000
Estimated manufacturing overhead cost	120,000	160,000

Required
a. Compute the predetermined overhead rate for each company.
b. Determine the amount of overhead cost that would be applied to Work in Process Inventory for each company.
c. Compute the amount of overapplied or underapplied manufacturing overhead cost for each company.

EXERCISE 11–11A *Recording Manufacturing Overhead Costs in T-Accounts*

L.O. 6

Wang Corporation manufactures model airplanes. The company purchased for $425,000 automated production equipment that can make the model parts. The equipment has a $25,000 salvage value and a 10-year useful life.

Required
a. Assuming that the equipment was purchased on March 1, record in T-accounts the adjusting entry that the company would make on December 31 to record depreciation on equipment.
b. In which month would the depreciation costs be assigned to units produced?

EXERCISE 11–12A *Missing Information in T-Accounts*

L.O. 2, 6, 9

Marble Manufacturing recorded the following amounts in its inventory accounts in 2004.

Raw Materials Inventory		
75,000	(a)	
20,000		

Work in Process Inventory		
	20,000	
40,000		
30,000		
(c)		

Finished Goods Inventory		
20,000	(d)	
2,500		

Cost of Goods Sold		
(e)		

Manufacturing Overhead		
(b)	30,000	
2,500		

Required
Determine the dollar amounts for (a), (b), (c), (d), and (e). Assume that underapplied and overapplied overhead is closed to Cost of Goods Sold.

EXERCISE 11–13A *Variable Costing Versus Absorption Costing*

L.O. 12

North Park Company incurred manufacturing overhead cost for the year as follows.

Direct materials	$20/unit
Direct labor	$14/unit
Manufacturing overhead	
Variable	$6/unit
Fixed	$15,000 ($10/unit for 1,500 units)
Variable selling & admin. expenses	$4,000
Fixed selling & admin. expenses	$8,000

The company produced 1,500 units and sold 1,000 of them at $90 per unit. Assume that the production manager is paid a 2 percent bonus based on the company's net income.

Required
a. Prepare an income statement using absorption costing.
b. Prepare an income statement using variable costing.
c. Determine the manager's bonus using each approach. Which approach would you recommend for internal reporting and why?

L.O. 5   EXERCISE 11–14A *Smoothed Unit Cost*

Vacakes Manufacturing estimated its product costs and volume of production for 2005 by quarter as follows.

	First Quarter	Second Quarter	Third Quarter	Fourth Quarter
Direct raw materials	$100,000	$ 50,000	$150,000	$ 75,000
Direct labor	60,000	30,000	90,000	45,000
Manufacturing overhead	100,000	155,000	200,000	115,000
Total production costs	$260,000	$235,000	$440,000	$235,000
Expected units produced	20,000	10,000	30,000	15,000

Vacakes Company sells a souvenir item at various resorts across the country. Its management uses the product's estimated quarterly cost to determine the selling price of its product. The company expects a large variance in demand for the product between quarters due to its seasonal nature. The company does not expect overhead costs, which are predominately fixed, to vary significantly as to production volume or with amounts for previous years. Prices are established by using a cost-plus-pricing strategy. The company finds variations in short-term unit cost confusing to use. Unit cost variations complicate pricing decisions and many other decisions for which cost is a consideration.

Required

a. Based on estimated total production cost, determine the expected quarterly cost per unit for Vacakes' product.

b. How could overhead costs be estimated each quarter to solve the company's unit cost problem? Calculate the unit cost per quarter based on your recommendation.

PROBLEMS—SERIES A

L.O. 2, 4, 8, 10, 11   PROBLEM 11–15A *Manufacturing Cost Flow Across Three Accounting Cycles*

The following accounting events affected Barber Manufacturing Company during its first three years of operation. Assume that all transactions are cash transactions.

Transactions for 2001

1. Started manufacturing company by issuing common stock for $2,000.
2. Purchased $1,000 of direct raw materials.
3. Used $800 of direct raw materials to produce inventory.
4. Paid $400 of direct labor wages to employees to make inventory.
5. Applied $250 of manufacturing overhead cost to Work in Process Inventory.
6. Finished work on inventory that cost $900.
7. Sold goods that cost $600 for $1,100.
8. Paid $370 for selling and administrative expenses.
9. Actual manufacturing cost amounted to $228 for the year.

Transactions for 2002

1. Acquired additional $400 of cash from common stock.
2. Purchased $1,200 of direct raw materials.
3. Used $1,300 of direct raw materials to produce inventory.
4. Paid $600 of direct labor wages to employees to make inventory.
5. Applied $320 of manufacturing overhead cost to Work in Process Inventory.
6. Finished work on inventory that cost $1,800.
7. Sold goods that cost $1,600 for $2,800.
8. Paid $500 for selling and administrative expenses.
9. Actual manufacturing overhead cost amounted to $330 for the year.

Transactions for 2003

1. Paid a cash dividend of $500.
2. Purchased $1,400 of direct raw materials.
3. Used $1,200 of direct raw materials to produce inventory.
4. Paid $440 of direct labor wages to employees to make inventory.
5. Applied $290 of manufacturing overhead cost to work in process.

6. Finished work on inventory that cost $2,000.
7. Sold goods that cost $2,200 for $3,500.
8. Paid $710 for selling and administrative expenses.
9. Annual manufacturing overhead costs were $280 for the year.

Required

a. Record the preceding events in a horizontal statements model. Close overapplied or underapplied overhead to Cost of Goods Sold. Also designate the classification of cash flows using the letters OA for operating activities, IA for investing activities, and FA for financing activities. The first event is shown as an example.

Assets					=	Equity			Rev.	–	Exp.	=	Net Inc.	Cash Flow
Cash	+ MOH	+ Raw M.	+ WIP	+ F. Goods	=	C. Stk.	+	Ret. Ear.						
2,000	+ NA	+ NA	+ NA	+ NA	=	2,000	+	NA	NA	–	NA	=	NA	2,000 FA

b. Prepare a schedule of cost of goods manufactured and sold, an income statement, a balance sheet, and a statement of cash flows as of the close of business on December 31, 2001.
c. Close appropriate accounts.
d. Repeat Requirements *a* through *c* for years 2002 and 2003.

PROBLEM 11–16A *Manufacturing Cost Flow for Monthly and Annual Accounting Periods*   **L.O. 2, 6, 8, 9, 10, 11**

Leslie Laney started Etowah Manufacturing Company to make a universal television remote control device that she had invented. The company's labor force consisted of part-time employees. The following accounting events affected Etowah Manufacturing Company during its first year of operation. (Assume that all transactions are cash transactions unless otherwise stated.)

Transactions for January 2001, First Month of Operation

1. Issued common stock for $2,500.
2. Purchased $350 of direct raw materials and $50 of production supplies.
3. Used $200 of direct raw materials.
4. Used 80 direct labor hours; production workers were paid $8 per hour.
5. Expected total overhead costs for the year to be $2,750, and direct labor hours used during the year to be 1,000. Calculate an overhead rate and apply the appropriate amount of overhead costs to Work in Process Inventory.
6. Paid $120 for salaries to administrative and sales staff.
7. Paid $20 for indirect manufacturing labor.
8. Paid $175 for rent and utilities on the manufacturing facilities.
9. Started and completed 100 remote controls; all costs were transferred from the Work in Process Inventory account to the Finished Goods Inventory account.
10. Sold 90 remote controls at a price of $18 each.

Transactions for Remainder of 2001

11. Acquired an additional $10,000 by issuing common stock.
12. Purchased $3,250 of direct raw materials and $750 of production supplies.
13. Used $2,500 of direct raw materials.
14. Paid production workers $8 per hour for 900 hours of work.
15. Applied the appropriate overhead cost to Work in Process Inventory.
16. Paid $1,300 for salaries of administrative and sales staff.
17. Paid $200 of indirect manufacturing labor cost.
18. Paid $2,000 for rental and utility costs on the manufacturing facilities.
19. Transferred 950 additional remote controls that cost $10.60 each from the Work in Process Inventory account to the Finished Goods Inventory account.
20. Determined that $140 of production supplies was on hand at the end of the accounting period.
21. Sold 850 remote controls for $18 each.
22. Determine whether the overhead is over- or underapplied. Close the Manufacturing Overhead account to the Cost of Goods Sold account.
23. Close the revenue and expense accounts.

Required

a. Open T-accounts and post transactions to the accounts.
b. Prepare a schedule of cost of goods manufactured and sold, an income statement, a balance sheet, and a statement of cash flows for 2001.

L.O. 2, 4, 9, 10, 11   **PROBLEM 11–17A** *Manufacturing Cost Flow for One-Year Period*

Grob Manufacturing started 2004 with the following account balances.

Cash	$1,000
Common Stock	2,000
Retained Earnings	3,000
Raw Materials Inventory	1,200
Work in Process Inventory	800
Finished Goods Inventory (320 units @$6.25)	2,000

Transactions during 2004

1. Purchased $2,880 of raw materials with cash.
2. Transferred $3,750 of raw materials to the production department.
3. Incurred and paid cash for 180 hours of direct labor @$16 per hour.
4. Applied overhead costs to the Work in Process Inventory account. The predetermined overhead rate is $16.50 per direct labor hour.
5. Incurred actual overhead costs of $3,000 cash.
6. Completed work on 1,200 units for $6.40 per unit.
7. Paid $1,400 in selling and administrative expenses in cash.
8. Sold 1,200 units for $9,600 cash revenue (assume FIFO cost flow).

Grob charges overapplied or underapplied overhead directly to Cost of Goods Sold.

Required

a. Record the preceding events in a horizontal statements model. Also designate the classification of cash flows using the letters OA for operating activities, IA for investing activities, and FA for financing activities. The beginning balances are shown as an example.

Assets					=	Equity							
Cash	+	Raw M.	+ MOH +	WIP	+ F. Goods	= C. Stk.	+ Ret. Ear.	Rev.	− Exp.	= Net Inc.	Cash Flow
1,000	+	1,200	+ NA +	800	+ 2,000	= 2,000	+ 3,000	NA	− NA	= NA	NA

b. Prepare a schedule of cost of goods manufactured and sold, an income statement, a balance sheet, and a statement of cash flows for 2004.

L.O. 2, 6, 7, 10, 11   **PROBLEM 11–18A** *Manufacturing Cost for One Accounting Cycle*

The following trial balance was taken from the records of Stan Manufacturing Company at the beginning of 2001.

Cash	$ 4,000	
Raw Materials Inventory	1,000	
Work in Process Inventory	1,600	
Finished Goods Inventory	2,800	
Property, Plant, and Equipment	10,000	
Accumulated Depreciation		$ 4,000
Common Stock		7,200
Retained Earnings		8,200
Total	$19,400	$19,400

Transactions for the Accounting Period

1. Stan purchased $7,600 of direct raw materials and $400 of indirect raw materials on account. The indirect materials are capitalized in the Production Supplies account. Materials requisitions showed that $7,200 of direct raw materials had been used for production during the period. The use of indirect materials is determined at the end of the year by physically counting the supplies on hand.
2. By the end of the year, $7,000 of the accounts payable had been paid in cash.
3. During the year, direct labor amounted to 950 hours recorded in the Wages Payable account at $14 per hour.
4. By the end of the year, $12,000 of wages payable had been paid in cash.

5. At the beginning of the year, the company expected overhead cost for the period to be $8,400 and 1,000 direct labor hours to be worked. Overhead is allocated based on direct labor hours, which, as indicated in Event 3, amounted to 950 for the year.
6. Administrative and sales expenses for the year amounted to $1,200 paid in cash.
7. Utilities and rent for production facilities amounted to $6,200 paid in cash.
8. Depreciation on the plant and equipment used in production amounted to $2,000.
9. Assume that $16,000 of goods were completed during the year.
10. Assume that $17,000 of finished goods inventory was sold for $24,000 cash.
11. A count of the production supplies revealed a balance of $118 on hand at the end of the year.
12. Any over- or underapplied overhead is considered to be insignificant.

Required

a. Open T-accounts with the beginning balances shown in the preceding list and record all transactions for the year including closing entries in the T-accounts. (*Note:* Open new T-accounts as needed.)
b. Prepare a schedule of cost of goods manufactured and sold, an income statement, a balance sheet, and a statement of cash flows.

PROBLEM 11–19A *Manufacturing Cost Flow for Multiple Accounting Cycles*   **L.O. 2, 6, 7, 8, 9, 10, 11**

The following events apply to Chateau Manufacturing Company. Assume that all transactions are cash transactions unless otherwise indicated.

Transactions for the 2004 Accounting Period

1. The company was started on January 1, 2004, when it acquired $216,000 cash by issuing common stock.
2. The company purchased $48,000 of direct raw materials with cash and used $3,240 of these materials to make its products in January.
3. Employees provided 900 hours of labor at $7.60 per hour during January. Wages are paid in cash.
4. The estimated manufacturing overhead costs for 2004 were $86,400. Overhead is applied on the basis of direct labor hours. The company expected to use 12,000 direct labor hours during 2004. Calculate an overhead rate and apply the overhead for January to work in process inventory.
5. The employees completed work on all inventory items started in January. The cost of this production was transferred to the Finished Goods Inventory account. Determine the cost per unit of product produced in January, assuming that a total of 1,800 units of product were started and completed during the month.
6. The company used an additional $41,400 of direct raw materials and 11,500 hours of direct labor at $7.60 per hour during the remainder of 2004. Overhead was allocated on the basis of direct labor hours.
7. The company completed work on inventory items started between February 1 and December 31, and the cost of the completed inventory was transferred to the Finished Goods Inventory account. Determine the cost per unit for goods produced between February 1 and December 31, assuming that 23,000 units of inventory were produced. If the company desires to earn a gross profit of $3.60 per unit, what price per unit must it charge for the merchandise sold?
8. The company sold 22,000 units of inventory for cash at $12.80 per unit. Determine the number of units in ending inventory and the cost per unit incurred for this inventory.
9. Actual manufacturing overhead costs paid in cash were $87,600.
10. The company paid $50,400 cash for selling and administrative expenses.
11. Close the Manufacturing Overhead account.
12. Close the revenue and expense accounts.

Transactions for the 2005 Accounting Period

1. The company purchased $54,000 of direct raw materials with cash and used $3,420 of these materials to make products in January.
2. Employees provided 950 hours of labor at $7.60 per hour during January.
3. On January 1, 2005, Chateau hired a production supervisor at an expected cost of $1,440 cash per month. The company paid cash to purchase $6,000 of manufacturing supplies; it anticipated that $5,520 of these supplies would be used by year end. Other manufacturing overhead costs were expected to total $86,400. Overhead is applied on the basis of direct labor hours. Chateau expected to use 14,000 hours of direct labor during 2005. Based on this information, determine the total expected overhead cost for 2005. Calculate the predetermined overhead rate and apply the overhead cost for the January production.
4. The company recorded a $1,440 cash payment to the production supervisor.
5. The employees completed work on all inventory items started in January. The cost of this production was transferred to the Finished Goods Inventory account. Determine the cost per unit of

product produced in January, assuming that 1,900 units of product were started and completed during the month.

6. During February 2005, the company used $3,600 of raw materials and 1,000 hours of labor at $7.60 per hour. Overhead was allocated on the basis of direct labor hours.

7. The company recorded a $1,440 cash payment to the production supervisor for February.

8. The employees completed work on all inventory items started in February; the cost of this production was transferred to the Finished Goods Inventory account. Determine the cost per unit of product produced in February, assuming that 2,000 units of product were started and completed during the month.

9. The company used an additional $43,200 of direct raw materials and 12,000 hours of direct labor at $7.60 per hour during the remainder of 2005. Overhead was allocated on the basis of direct labor hours.

10. The company recorded $14,400 of cash payments to the production supervisor for work performed between March 1 and December 31.

11. The company completed work on inventory items started between March 1 and December 31. The cost of the completed goods was transferred to the Finished Goods Inventory account. Compute the cost per unit of this inventory, assuming that there were 24,000 units of inventory produced.

12. The company sold 26,000 units of product for $13.20 cash per unit. Assume that the company uses the FIFO inventory cost flow method to determine the cost of goods sold.

13. The company paid $51,600 cash for selling and administrative expenses.

14. As of December 31, 2005, $600 of production supplies was on hand.

15. Actual cost of other manufacturing overhead was $85,200 cash.

16. Close the manufacturing overhead account.

17. Close the revenue and expense accounts.

Required

a. Open T-accounts and record the effects of the preceding events.

b. Prepare a schedule of cost of goods manufactured and sold, an income statement, a balance sheet, and a statement of cash flows for both years.

L.O. 10   **PROBLEM 11–20A** *Comprehensive Review Problem*

During their senior year at Heath College, two business students, Wayne Manning and Monica Cassey, began a part-time business making personal computers. They bought the various components from a local supplier and assembled the machines in the basement of a friend's house. Their only cost was $480 for parts; they sold each computer for $840. They were able to make three machines per week and to sell them to fellow students. The activity was appropriately called Manning Cassey Computers (MCC). The product quality was good, and as graduation approached, orders were coming in much faster than MCC could fill them.

A national CPA firm made Ms. Cassey an attractive offer of employment, and a large electronic company was ready to hire Mr. Manning. Students and faculty at Heath College, however, encouraged the two to make MCC a full-time venture. The college administration had decided to require all students in the schools of business and engineering to buy their own computers beginning in the coming fall term. It was believed that the quality and price of the MCC machines would attract the college bookstore to sign a contract to buy a minimum of 1,000 units the first year for $720 each. The bookstore sales were likely to reach 2,000 units per year, but the manager would not make an initial commitment beyond 1,000.

The prospect of $720,000 in annual sales for MCC caused the two young entrepreneurs to wonder about the wisdom of accepting their job offers. Before making a decision, they decided to investigate the implications of making MCC a full-time operation. Their study provided the following information relating to the production of their computers.

Components from wholesaler	$ 480 per computer
Assembly labor	15 per hour
Manufacturing space rent	3,000 per month
Utilities	600 per month
Janitorial services	480 per month
Depreciation of equipment	3,840 per year
Labor	2 hours per computer

The two owners expected to devote their time to the sales and administrative aspects of the business.

Required
a. Classify each cost item into the categories of direct materials, direct labor, and manufacturing overhead.
b. Classify each cost item as either variable or fixed.
c. What is the cost per computer if MCC produces 1,000 units per year? What is the cost per unit if MCC produces 2,000 units per year?
d. If the job offers for Mr. Manning and Ms. Cassey totaled $96,000, would you recommend that they accept the offers or proceed with plans to make MCC a full-time venture?

PROBLEM 11–21A *Absorption Versus Variable Costing*

L.O. 12

Huff Manufacturing Company makes a product that sells for $36 per unit. Manufacturing costs for the product amount to $14 per unit variable, and $40,000 fixed. During the current accounting period, Huff made 4,000 units of the product and sold 3,500 units.

Required
a. Prepare an absorption costing income statement.
b. Prepare a variable costing income statement.
c. Explain why the amount of net income on the absorption costing income statement differs from the amount of net income on the variable costing income statement. Your answer should include the amount of the inventory balance that would exist under the two costing approaches.

PROBLEM 11–22A *Absorption Versus Variable Costing*

L.O. 12

Windom Glass Company makes stained glass lamps. Each lamp that it sells for $420 per lamp requires $24 of direct materials and $96 of direct labor. Fixed overhead costs are expected to be $270,000 per year. Windom Glass expects to sell 1,000 lamps during the coming year.

Required
a. Prepare income statements using absorption costing, assuming that Windom Glass makes 1,000, 1,250, and 1,500 lamps during the year.
b. Prepare income statements using variable costing, assuming that Windom Glass makes 1,000, 1,250, and 1,500 lamps during the year.
c. Explain why Windom Glass may produce income statements under both absorption and variable costing formats. Your answer should include an explanation of the advantages and disadvantages associated with the use of the two reporting formats.

PROBLEM 11–23A *Absorption and Variable Costing*

L.O. 12

Vicaro Manufacturing pays its production managers a bonus based on the company's profitability. During the two most recent years, the company maintained the same cost structure to manufacture its products.

Year	Units Produced	Units Sold
Production and Sales		
2001	4,000	4,000
2002	6,000	4,000
Cost Data		
Direct materials		$10 per unit
Direct labor		$16 per unit
Manufacturing overhead—variable		$8 per unit
Manufacturing overhead—fixed		$72,000
Variable selling & administrative expenses		$6 per unit sold
Fixed selling & administrative expenses		$40,000

(Assume that selling & administrative expenses are associated with goods sold.)

Vicaro sells its products for $36 a unit.

Required
a. Prepare income statements based on absorption costing for 2001 and 2002.

b. Since Vicaro sold the same number of units in 2001 and 2002, why did net income increase in 2002?

c. Discuss management's possible motivation for increasing production in 2002.

d. Determine the costs of ending inventory for 2002. Comment on the risks and costs associated with the accumulation of inventory.

e. Based on your answers to Requirements *b* and *c*, suggest a different income statement format. Prepare income statements for 2001 and 2002 using your suggested format.

EXERCISES—SERIES B

L.O. 2, 4　　**EXERCISE 11–1B** *Product Cost Flow and Financial Statements*

McQueen Manufacturing began business on January 1, 2004. The following events pertain to its first year of operation.

1. Acquired $1,800 cash by issuing common stock.
2. Paid $600 cash for direct raw materials.
3. Transferred $500 of direct raw materials to Work in Process Inventory.
4. Paid production employees $700 cash.
5. Applied $325 of manufacturing overhead costs to Work in Process Inventory.
6. Completed work on products that cost $1,100.
7. Sold products for $1,600 cash.
8. Recognized cost of goods sold from Event No. 7 of $875.
9. Paid $450 cash for selling and administrative expenses.
10. Paid $350 cash for actual manufacturing overhead costs.
11. Made a $100 cash distribution to owners.
12. Closed the manufacturing overhead account.

Required

a. Record the preceding events in a horizontal statements model. Also designate the classification of cash flows using the letters OA for operating activities, IA for investing activities, and FA for financing activities. The first event is shown as an example.

Assets					=	Equity						
Cash	+ MOH	+ Raw M.	+ WIP	+ F. Goods	= C. Stk.	+ Ret. Ear.		Rev.	− Exp.	= Net Inc.		Cash Flow
1,800	+ NA	+ NA	+ NA	+ NA	= 1,800	+ NA		NA	− NA	= NA		1,800　FA

b. Prepare a schedule of cost of goods manufactured and sold.

L.O. 2, 7, 10, 11　　**EXERCISE 11–2B** *Recording Events in T-Accounts and Preparing Financial Statements*

Sudol Manufacturing Company was started on January 1, 2002, when it acquired $2,000 cash by issuing common stock. During its first year of operation, it purchased $600 of direct raw materials with cash and used $450 of the materials to make products. Sudol paid $800 of direct labor costs in cash. The company applied $580 of overhead costs to Work in Process Inventory. It made cash payments of $550 for actual overhead costs. The company completed products that cost $1,300 to make. It sold goods that had cost $1,030 to make for $1,700 cash. It paid $400 of selling and administrative expenses in cash.

Required

a. Open the necessary T-accounts and record the 2002 events in the accounts. Include closing entries.

b. Prepare a schedule of cost of goods manufactured and sold, an income statement, a balance sheet, and a statement of cash flows.

L.O. 4　　**EXERCISE 11–3B** *Effect of Accounting Events on Financial Statements*

Required

Use a horizontal statements model to show how each of the following independent accounting events affects the elements of the balance sheet, income statement, and statement of cash flows. Indicate whether the event increases (I), decreases (D), or does not affect (NA) each element of the financial statements. Also designate the classification of cash flows using the letters OA for operating activities, IA for investing activities, and FA for financing activities. The first two transactions are shown as examples.

a. Paid cash to purchase raw materials.
b. Recorded cash sales revenue.
c. Applied overhead to Work in Process Inventory based on the predetermined overhead rate.
d. Closed the manufacturing overhead account when overhead was underapplied.
e. Recognized cost of goods sold.
f. Recognized depreciation expense on manufacturing equipment.
g. Purchased manufacturing supplies on account.
h. Sold fully depreciated manufacturing equipment for the exact amount of its salvage value.

Event No.	Balance Sheet				Income Statement			Statement of Cash Flows
	Assets =	Liab. +	C. Stk +	Ret Ear.	Rev. −	Exp. =	Net Inc.	
a.	I D	NA	NA	NA	NA	NA	NA	D OA
b.	I	NA	NA	I	I	NA	I	I OA

EXERCISE 11–4B *Preparing Financial Statements* L.O. 2, 10, 11

Mull Manufacturing Company started 2004 with the following balances in its inventory accounts: Raw Materials, $27,000; Work in Process, $28,000; Finished Goods, $33,000. During 2004 Mull purchased $170,000 of raw materials and issued $165,000 of materials to the production department. It incurred $190,000 of direct labor costs and applied manufacturing overhead of $187,000 to Work in Process Inventory. Assume there was no over- or underapplied overhead at the end of the year. Mull completed goods costing $525,000 to produce and transferred them to finished goods inventory. During the year, Mull sold goods costing $507,000 for $769,000. Selling and administrative expenses for 2004 were $180,000.

Required
a. Using T-accounts, determine the ending balance Mull would report for each of the three inventory accounts that would appear on the December 31, 2004, balance sheet.
b. Prepare the 2004 schedule of cost of goods manufactured and the 2004 income statement.

EXERCISE 11–5B *Missing Information in a Schedule of Cost of Goods Manufactured and Sold* L.O. 10

Required
Supply the missing information on the following schedule of cost of goods manufactured and sold.

SCHEINER CORPORATION
Statement of Cost of Goods Manufactured and Sold
For the Year Ended December 31, 2005

Raw Materials		
Beginning Inventory	$ 40,000	
Plus: Purchases	?	
Raw Materials Available for Use	320,000	
Minus: Ending Raw Materials Inventory	$?	
Cost of Direct Raw Materials Used		$290,000
Direct Labor		240,000
Manufacturing Overhead		?
Total Manufacturing Costs		$750,000
Plus: Beginning Work in Process Inventory		?
Total Work in Process during the Year		$786,000
Minus: Ending Work in Process Inventory		(41,000)
Cost of Goods Manufactured		$?
Plus: Beginning Finished Goods Inventory		?
Finished Goods Available For Sale		$798,000
Minus: Ending Finished Goods Inventory		?
Cost of Goods Sold		$756,000

EXERCISE 11–6B *Cost of Goods Manufactured and Sold* L.O. 10

The following information was drawn from the accounting records of Barrett Manufacturing Company.

	Beginning	Ending
Raw materials inventory	$2,000	$2,300
Work in process inventory	3,100	2,500
Finished goods inventory	3,400	2,900

During the accounting period, Barrett paid $8,000 to purchase raw materials, $7,500 for direct labor, and $5,500 for overhead costs. Assume that actual overhead equaled applied overhead.

Required

a. Determine the amount of raw materials used.

b. Determine the amount of cost of goods manufactured (the amount transferred from Work in Process Inventory to Finished Goods Inventory).

c. Assuming sales revenue of $38,400, determine the amount of gross margin.

L.O. 6, 9   EXERCISE 11–7B *Calculating Applied Overhead*

Ludden Enterprises' budget included the following estimated costs for the 2003 accounting period.

Depreciation on manufacturing equipment	$ 86,000
Cost of manufacturing supplies	15,000
Direct labor cost	432,000
Rent on manufacturing facility	38,000
Direct materials cost	370,000
Manufacturing utilities cost	30,000
Maintenance cost for manufacturing facility	26,000
Administrative salaries cost	152,500

The company uses a predetermined overhead rate based on machine hours. It estimated machine hour usage for 2003 would be 30,000 hours.

Required

a. Identify the manufacturing overhead costs Ludden would use to calculate the predetermined overhead rate.

b. Calculate the predetermined overhead rate.

c. Explain why the rate is called "predetermined."

d. Assuming Ludden actually used 29,200 machine hours during 2003, determine the amount of manufacturing overhead it would have applied to Work in Process Inventory during the period.

L.O. 5, 9   EXERCISE 11–8B *Treatment of Over- or Underapplied Overhead*

On January 1, 2004, Bushong Company estimated that its total overhead costs for the coming year would be $278,800 and that it would make 34,000 units of product. Bushong actually produced 34,600 units of product and incurred actual overhead costs of $281,000 during 2004.

Required

a. Calculate Bushong's predetermined overhead rate based on expected costs and production.

b. Determine whether overhead was overapplied or underapplied during 2004.

c. Explain how the entry to close the manufacturing overhead account will affect the Cost of Goods Sold account.

L.O. 6, 9   EXERCISE 11–9B *Recording Overhead Costs in a T-Account*

Kankakee Manufacturing Company incurred actual overhead costs of $59,600 during 2002. It uses direct labor dollars as the allocation base for overhead costs. In 2002, actual direct labor costs were $84,000, and overhead costs were underapplied by $800.

Required

a. Calculate the predetermined overhead rate for 2002.

b. Open T-accounts for Manufacturing Overhead and Cost of Goods Sold. Record the overhead costs and the adjusting entry to close Manufacturing Overhead in these accounts.

c. Explain how the entry to close the Manufacturing Overhead account at the end of 2002 would affect the amount of net income reported on the 2002 income statement.

EXERCISE 11–10B *Treatment of Over- or Underapplied Overhead* L.O. 6, 9

Hamilton Company and Griffin Company base their predetermined overhead rates on machine hours. The following information pertains to the companies' most recent accounting periods.

	Hamilton	Griffin
Actual machine hours	12,300	19,500
Estimated machine hours	12,000	20,000
Actual manufacturing overhead costs	$50,400	$115,000
Estimated manufacturing overhead costs	$49,800	$116,000

Required
a. Compute the predetermined overhead rate for each company.
b. Determine the amount of overhead cost that would be applied to work in process for each company and compute the amount of overapplied or underapplied manufacturing overhead cost for each company.
c. Explain how closing the Manufacturing Overhead account would affect the Cost of Goods Sold account for each company.

EXERCISE 11–11B *Recording Manufacturing Overhead Costs* L.O. 6, 9

Curfman Manufacturing Company incurred the following actual manufacturing overhead costs: (1) cash paid for plant supervisor's salary, $58,000, (2) depreciation on manufacturing equipment, $27,000, and (3) manufacturing supplies used, $2,300 (Curfman uses the periodic inventory method for manufacturing supplies). Applied overhead amounted to $88,000.

Required
a. Open the appropriate T-accounts and record the manufacturing overhead costs described.
b. Record the entry Curfman would make to close the Manufacturing Overhead account to Cost of Goods Sold.

EXERCISE 11–12B *Missing Information in Inventory T-Accounts* L.O. 6, 9

The following incomplete T-accounts were drawn from the records of Schlinder Manufacturing Company:

Raw Materials Inventory

125,000	(a)
6,000	

Work in Process Inventory

	260,000
78,000	
(b)	

Finished Goods Inventory

(c)	
25,000	

Cost of Goods Sold

(d)	

Manufacturing Overhead

85,000	(e)
4,000	

Required
Determine the dollar amounts for (a), (b), (c), (d), and (e). Assume that underapplied and overapplied overhead is closed to Cost of Goods Sold.

EXERCISE 11–13B *Variable Costing Versus Absorption Costing* L.O. 12

The following information was drawn from the records of Cayse Company:

Variable costs (per unit)			Fixed costs (in total)	
Direct materials	$ 8		Manufacturing overhead	$24,000
Direct labor	10		Selling and administrative	24,800
Manufacturing overhead	3			
Selling and administrative	7			

During the most recent month Cayse produced 4,000 units of product and sold 3,800 units of product at a sales price of $49 per unit.

Required

a. Prepare an income statement for the month using absorption costing.

b. Prepare an income statement for the month using variable costing.

c. Explain why a company might use one type of income statement for external reporting and a different type for internal reporting.

L.O. 5   **EXERCISE 11–14B** *Smoothing Unit Cost*

Unit-level (variable) manufacturing costs for Preston Manufacturing Company amount to $8. Fixed manufacturing costs are $9,000 per month. Production workers provided 800 hours of direct labor in January and 1,400 hours in February. Preston expects to use 12,000 hours of labor during the year. It actually produced 1,200 units of product in January and 2,100 units of product in February.

Required

a. For each month, determine the total product cost and the per unit product cost, assuming that actual fixed overhead costs are charged to monthly production.

b. Use a predetermined overhead rate based on direct labor hours to allocate the fixed overhead costs to each month's production. For each month, calculate the total product cost and the per unit product cost.

c. Preston employs a cost-plus-pricing strategy. Would you recommend charging production with actual or allocated fixed overhead costs? Explain.

PROBLEMS—SERIES B

L.O. 2, 4, 6, 8, 10, 11   **PROBLEM 11–15B** *Manufacturing Cost Flow Across Three Accounting Cycles*

The following accounting events affected Billano Manufacturing Company during its first three years of operation. Assume that all transactions are cash transactions.

Transactions for 2001

1. Started manufacturing company by issuing common stock for $2,400.
2. Purchased $960 of direct raw materials.
3. Used $720 of direct raw materials to produce inventory.
4. Paid $600 of direct labor wages to employees to make inventory.
5. Applied $600 of manufacturing overhead to Work in Process Inventory.
6. Actual manufacturing overhead costs amounted to $610.
7. Finished work on inventory that cost $1,080.
8. Sold goods that cost $720 for $960.
9. Paid $60 for selling and administrative expenses.

Transactions for 2002

1. Acquired additional $1,200 of cash from issuance of common stock.
2. Purchased $960 of direct raw materials.
3. Used $840 of direct raw materials to produce inventory.
4. Paid $720 of direct labor wages to employees to make inventory.
5. Applied $640 of manufacturing overhead to Work in Process Inventory.
6. Actual manufacturing overhead costs amounted to $630.
7. Finished work on inventory that cost $1,800.
8. Sold goods that cost $1,680 for $1,920.
9. Paid $120 for selling and administrative expenses.

Transactions for 2003

1. Purchased $600 of direct raw materials.
2. Used $960 of direct raw materials to produce inventory.

3. Paid $360 of direct labor wages to employees to make inventory.
4. Applied $500 of manufacturing overhead to Work in Process Inventory.
5. Actual manufacturing overhead costs amounted to $520.
6. Finished work on inventory that cost $1,980.
7. Sold goods that cost $2,160 for $2,640.
8. Paid $240 for selling and administrative expenses.
9. Paid a cash dividend of $480.

Required

a. Record the preceding events in a horizontal statements model. Close overapplied or underapplied overhead to Cost of Goods Sold. Also designate the classification of cash flows using the letters OA for operating activities, IA for investing activities, and FA for financing activities. The first event is shown as an example.

Assets					=	Equity		Rev.	−	Exp.	=	Net Inc.	Cash Flow
Cash + MOH + Raw M. + WIP + F. Goods					=	C. Stk. +	Ret. Ear.	Rev.	−	Exp.	=	Net Inc.	Cash Flow
2,400 + NA + NA + NA + NA					=	2,400 +	NA	NA	−	NA	=	NA	2,400 FA

b. Prepare a schedule of cost of goods manufactured and sold, an income statement, a balance sheet, and a statement of cash flows as of the close of business on December 31, 2001.
c. Close appropriate accounts to the Retained Earnings account.
d. Repeat Requirements *a* through *c* for years 2002 and 2003.

PROBLEM 11–16B *Manufacturing Cost for One Accounting Cycle*   L.O. 2, 6, 7, 10, 11

The following trial balance was taken from the records of Corey Manufacturing Company at the beginning of 2001.

Cash	$ 5,600	
Raw Materials Inventory	400	
Work in Process Inventory	1,200	
Finished Goods Inventory	800	
Property, Plant, & Equipment	14,000	
Accumulated Depreciation		$ 4,000
Common Stock		8,400
Retained Earnings		9,600
Total	$22,000	$22,000

Transactions for the Accounting Period

1. Corey purchased $9,200 of direct raw materials and $1,000 of indirect raw materials on account. The indirect materials are capitalized in the Production Supplies account. Materials requisitions showed that $8,000 of direct raw materials had been used for production during the period. The use of indirect materials is determined at the end of the period by physically counting the supplies on hand at the end of the year.
2. By the end of the accounting period, $7,000 of the accounts payable had been paid in cash.
3. During the year, direct labor amounted to 1,200 hours recorded in the Wages Payable account at $12 per hour.
4. By the end of the accounting period, $13,000 of the Wages Payable account had been paid in cash.
5. At the beginning of the accounting period, the company expected overhead cost for the period to be $11,000 and 1,250 direct labor hours to be worked. Overhead is applied based on direct labor hours, which, as indicated in Event 3, amounted to 1,200 for the year.
6. Administrative and sales expenses for the period amounted to $2,800 paid in cash.
7. Utilities and rent for production facilities amounted to $6,000 paid in cash.
8. Depreciation on the plant and equipment used in production amounted to $4,000.
9. Assume that $30,000 of goods were completed during the period.
10. Assume that $20,000 of finished goods inventory was sold for $28,000 cash.
11. A count of the production supplies revealed a balance of $300 on hand at the end of the accounting period.
12. Any over- or underapplied overhead is considered to be insignificant.

Required

a. Open T-accounts with the beginning balances shown in the preceding list and record all transactions for the period including closing entries in the T-accounts. (*Note:* Open new T-accounts as needed.)

b. Prepare a schedule of cost of goods manufactured and sold, an income statement, a balance sheet, and a statement of cash flows.

L.O. 2, 4, 6, 10, 11   PROBLEM 11–17B *Manufacturing Cost Flow for One-Year Period*

Markus Manufacturing started 2005 with the following account balances.

Cash	$2,250
Common Stock	2,000
Retained Earnings	750
Raw Materials Inventory	100
Work in Process Inventory	220
Finished Goods Inventory (50 units @ $3.60/unit)	180

Transactions during 2005

1. Purchased $750 of raw materials with cash.
2. Transferred $500 of raw materials to the production department.
3. Incurred and paid cash for 80 hours of direct labor was at $7.50 per hour.
4. Applied overhead costs to the working process inventory. The predetermined overhead rate is $7.50 per direct labor hour.
5. Incurred actual overhead costs of $650 cash.
6. Completed work was on 300 units for $3.60 per unit.
7. Paid $200 in selling and administrative expenses in cash.
8. Sold 200 units for $1,250 cash revenues.

Markus charges overapplied or underapplied overhead directly to Cost of Goods Sold.

Required

a. Record the preceding events in a horizontal statements model. Also designate the classification of cash flows using the letters OA for operating activities, IA for investing activities, and FA for financing activities. The beginning balances are shown as an example.

Assets					=	Equity						
Cash	+ Raw M.	+ MOH	+ WIP	+ F. Goods	= C. Stk.	+ Ret. Ear.		Rev.	− Exp.	= Net Inc.		Cash Flow
2,250	+ 100	+ NA	+ 250	+ 150	= 2,000	+ 750		NA	− NA	= NA		NA

b. Prepare a schedule of cost of goods manufactured and sold, an income statement, a balance sheet, and a statement of cash flows for 2005.

L.O. 2, 6, 7, 10, 11   PROBLEM 11–18B *Manufacturing Cost Flow for Monthly and Annual Accounting Periods*

Huffman Manufacturing Company manufactures puzzles that depict the works of famous artists. The company rents a small factory and uses local labor on a part-time basis. The following accounting events affected Huffman during its first year of operation. (Assume that all transactions are cash transactions unless otherwise stated.)

Transactions for First Month of Operation 2001

1. Issued common stock for $30,000.
2. Purchased $8,000 of direct raw materials and $600 of indirect raw materials. Indirect materials are recorded in a Production Supplies account.
3. Used $7,792 of direct raw materials.
4. Used 700 direct labor hours; production workers were paid $12 per hour.
5. Expected total overhead costs for the year to be $33,600 and direct labor hours used during the year to be 9,600. Calculate an overhead rate and apply the appropriate amount of overhead costs to Work in Process.
6. Paid $1,600 for salaries to administrative and sales staff.
7. Paid $1,400 for indirect manufacturing labor.
8. Paid $1,200 for rent and utilities on the manufacturing facilities.
9. Started and completed 956 puzzles; all costs were transferred from the Work in Process Inventory account to the Finished Goods Inventory account.
10. Sold 800 puzzles at a price of $24 each.

Transactions for Remainder of 2001

11. Acquired an additional $300,000 by issuing common stock.
12. Purchased $92,000 of direct raw materials and $8,000 of indirect raw materials.
13. Used $82,100 of direct raw materials.
14. Paid production workers $12 per hour for 9,800 hours of work.
15. Applied the appropriate overhead cost to Work in Process Inventory.
16. Paid $17,600 for salaries of administrative and sales staff.
17. Paid $15,400 for the salary of the production supervisor.
18. Paid $13,200 for rental and utility costs on the manufacturing facilities.
19. Transferred 12,000 additional puzzles that cost $19.50 each from Work in Process Inventory to Finished Goods Inventory accounts.
20. Determined that $5,800 of production supplies was on hand at the end of the accounting period.
21. Sold 8,000 puzzles for $24 each.
22. Determine whether overhead is over- or underapplied. Close the manufacturing overhead account to cost of goods sold.
23. Close the revenue and expense accounts.

Required

a. Open T-accounts and post transactions to the accounts.
b. Prepare a schedule of cost of goods manufactured and sold, an income statement, a balance sheet, and a statement of cash flows for 2001.

PROBLEM 11–19B *Manufacturing Cost Flow for Multiple Accounting Cycles*

L.O. 2, 6, 7, 8, 9, 10, 11

The following events apply to Dixie Manufacturing Company. Assume that all transactions are cash transactions unless otherwise indicated.

Transactions for the 2001 Accounting Period

1. The company was started on January 1, 2001, when it acquired $1,000,000 cash by issuing common stock.
2. The company purchased $600,000 of direct raw materials with cash and used $52,000 of these materials to make its products in January.
3. Employees provided 1,500 hours of labor at $16 per hour during January. Wages are paid in cash.
4. The estimated manufacturing overhead costs for 2001 are $1,300,000. Overhead is applied on the basis of direct labor costs. The company expected $260,000 of direct labor costs during 2001. Record applied overhead for January.
5. By the end of January, the employees completed work on all inventory items started in January. The cost of this production was transferred to the Finished Goods Inventory account. Determine the cost per unit of product produced in January, assuming that a total of 10,000 units of product were started and completed during the month.
6. The company used an additional $468,000 of direct raw materials and 13,500 hours of direct labor at $16 per hour during the remainder of 2001. Overhead was allocated on the basis of direct labor cost.
7. The company completed work on inventory items started between February 1 and December 31, and the cost of the completed inventory was transferred to the Finished Goods Inventory account. Determine the cost per unit for goods produced between February 1 and December 31, assuming that 90,000 units of inventory were produced. If the company desires to earn a gross profit of $6 per unit, what price per unit must it charge for the merchandise sold?
8. The company sold 60,000 units of inventory for cash at $25.60 per unit. Determine the number of units in ending inventory and the cost per unit of this inventory.
9. Actual manufacturing overhead costs paid in cash were $1,220,000.
10. The company paid $300,000 cash for selling and administrative expenses.
11. Close the Manufacturing Overhead account.
12. Close the revenue and expense accounts.

Transactions for the 2002 Accounting Period

1. The company acquired $600,000 cash from the owners.
2. The company purchased $400,000 of direct raw materials with cash and used $41,600 of these materials to make products in January.
3. Employees provided 1,200 hours of labor at $16 per hour during January.
4. On January 1, 2002, Dixie expected the production facilities to cost $3,000 cash per month. The company paid cash to purchase $14,000 of manufacturing supplies, and it anticipated that $14,000 of these supplies would be used by year end. Other manufacturing overhead costs were expected to total $910,000. Overhead is applied on the basis of direct labor costs. Dixie expects direct labor

costs of $160,000 during 2002. Based on this information, determine the total expected overhead cost for 2002. Calculate the predetermined overhead rate and apply the overhead cost for the January production. Also, record the purchase of manufacturing supplies.

5. The company recorded a $3,000 cash payment for production facilities in January.

6. In January, the employees completed work on all inventory items started in January. The cost of this production was transferred to the Finished Goods Inventory account. Determine the cost per unit of product produced in January assuming that a total of 8,000 units of product was started and completed during the month.

7. During February 2002, the company used $31,200 of raw materials and 900 hours of labor at $16 per hour. Overhead was allocated on the basis of direct labor cost.

8. The company recorded a $3,000 cash payment for production facilities in February.

9. In February, the employees completed work on all inventory items started in February; the cost of this production was transferred to the Finished Goods Inventory account. Determine the cost per unit of product produced in February, assuming that 6,000 units of product were started and completed during the month.

10. The company used an additional $286,000 of direct raw materials and 8,250 hours of direct labor at $16 per hour during the remainder of 2002. Overhead was allocated on the basis of direct labor cost.

11. The company recorded $30,000 of cash payments for production facilities for the period between March 1 and December 31.

12. The company completed work on inventory items started between March 1 and December 31. The cost of the completed goods was transferred to the Finished Goods Inventory account. Compute the cost per unit of this inventory, assuming that 55,000 units of inventory were produced.

13. The company sold 90,000 units of product for $28 per unit cash. Assume that the company uses the FIFO inventory cost flow method to determine the cost of goods sold.

14. The company paid $260,000 cash for selling and administrative expenses.

15. As of December 31, 2002, $2,400 of production supplies was on hand.

16. Actual cost of other manufacturing overhead was $922,000 cash.

17. Close the manufacturing overhead account.

18. Close the revenue and expense accounts.

Required

a. Open T-accounts and record the effects of the preceding events.

b. Prepare a schedule of cost of goods manufactured and sold, an income statement, a balance sheet, and a statement of cash flows for both years.

L.O. 10   PROBLEM 11–20B *Comprehensive Review Problem*

Martha Chandler has worked as the plant manager of Morris Corporation, a large manufacturing company, for 10 years. The company produces stereo CD players for automotive vehicles and sells them to some of the largest car manufacturers in the country. Ms. Chandler has always toyed with the idea of starting her own car stereo manufacturing business. With her experience and knowledge, she is certain that she can produce a superior stereo at a low cost. Ms. Chandler's business strategy would be to market the product to smaller, more specialized car manufacturers. Her potential market is car manufacturers who sell at a lower volume to discriminating customers. She is confident that she could compete in this market that values low-cost quality production. She would not compete with Morris or the other large stereo producers that dominate the market made up of the largest automotive producers.

Ms. Chandler already has firm orders for 800 stereos from several automotive producers. Based on the contacts that she has made working for Morris, Ms. Chandler is confident that she can make and sell 2,000 stereos during the first year of operation. However, before making a final decision, she decides to investigate the profitability of starting her own business. Relevant information follows.

Components from wholesaler	$54.00 per stereo
Assembly labor	$12.60 per hour
Rent of manufacturing buildings	$14,400.00 per year
Utilities	$360.00 per month
Sales salaries	$720.00 per month
Depreciation of equipment	$2,400.00 per year
Labor	3 hours per stereo

During the first year, Ms. Chandler expects to be able to produce the stereos with only two production workers and a part-time salesperson to market the product. Ms. Chandler expects to devote her time

to the administrative aspects of the business and to provide back-up support in the production work. She has decided not to pay herself a salary but to live off the profits of the business.

Required

a. Classify each cost item into the categories of direct materials, direct labor, and manufacturing overhead.

b. Classify each cost item as either variable or fixed.

c. What is the cost per stereo if Ms. Chandler's company produces 800 units per year? What is the unit cost if the company produces 2,000 units per year?

d. If Ms. Chandler's job presently pays her $18,000 a year, would you recommend that she proceed with the plans to start the new company if she could sell stereos for $144 each?

PROBLEM 11–21B *Absorption versus Variable Costing*

L.O. 12

Balogh Manufacturing Company makes a product that sells for $50 per unit. Manufacturing costs for the product amount to $24 per unit variable, and $160,000 fixed. During the current accounting period, Balogh made 8,000 units of the product and sold 7,600 units.

Required

a. Prepare an absorption costing income statement.

b. Prepare a variable costing income statement.

c. Explain why the amount of net income on the absorption costing income statement differs from the amount of net income on the variable costing income statement. Your answer should include the amount of the inventory balance that would exist under the two costing approaches.

PROBLEM 11–22B *Absorption versus Variable Costing*

L.O. 12

Stoll Company makes ladderback chairs that it sells for $300 per chair. Each chair requires $42 of direct materials and $108 of direct labor. Fixed overhead costs are expected to be $180,000 per year. Stoll expects to sell 1,500 chairs during the coming year.

Required

a. Prepare income statements using absorption costing, assuming that Stoll makes 1,500, 2,000, and 2,500 chairs during the year.

b. Prepare income statements using variable costing, assuming that Stoll makes 1,500, 2,000, and 2,500 chairs during the year.

c. Explain why Stoll may produce income statements under both absorption and variable costing formats. Your answer should include an explanation of the advantages or disadvantages associated with the use of the two reporting formats.

PROBLEM 11–23B *Absorption and Variable Costing*

L.O. 12

Smith Manufacturing pays its production managers a bonus based on the company's profitability. During the two most recent years, the company maintained the same cost structure to manufacture its products.

Year	Units Produced	Units Sold
Production and Sales		
2001	5,000	5,000
2002	7,000	5,000
Cost Data		
Direct materials		$8 per unit
Direct labor		$12 per unit
Manufacturing overhead—variable		$4 per unit
Manufacturing overhead—fixed		$91,000
Variable selling & administrative expenses		$4 per unit sold
Fixed selling & administrative expenses		$30,000

(Assume that selling & administrative expenses are associated with goods sold.)

Smith's sales revenue for both years was $280,000.

Required

a. Prepare income statements based on absorption costing for the years 2001 and 2002.

b. Since Smith sold the same amount in 2001 and 2002, why did net income increase in 2002?

c. Discuss management's possible motivation for increasing production in 2002.
d. Determine the costs of ending inventory for 2002. Comment on the risks and costs associated with the accumulation of inventory.
e. Based on your answers to Requirements *b* and *c*, suggest a different income statement format and prepare income statements for 2001 and 2002 using your suggested format.

ANALYZE, THINK, COMMUNICATE

ATC 11–1   BUSINESS APPLICATIONS CASE *Predetermined Overhead Rate*

Pacini Company makes frozen dinners that it sells to airline companies. The average materials cost per meal is $2.60, and the average labor cost is $1.60. Pacini incurs approximately $480,000 of fixed manufacturing overhead costs annually. The marketing department estimated that Pacini would sell approximately 240,000 meals during the coming year. Unfortunately, Pacini has experienced a steady decline in sales even though the airline industry has had a steady increase in the number of passengers. The chief accountant, Stella Edwards, was overheard saying that when she calculated the predetermined overhead rate, she deliberately lowered the estimated number of meals expected to be sold because she had lost faith in the marketing department's ability to deliver on its estimated sales numbers. Ms. Edwards explained, "This way, our actual cost is always below the estimated cost. It is about the only way we continue to make a profit." Indeed, the company had a significant amount of overapplied overhead at the end of each year.

Required
a. Explain how the overapplied overhead affects the determination of year-end net income.
b. Assume that Ms. Edwards used 200,000 meals as the estimated sales to calculate the predetermined overhead rate. Determine the difference in expected cost per meal she calculated and the cost per meal that would result if the marketing department's estimate (240,000 units) had been used.
c. Assuming that Pacini uses a cost-plus pricing policy, speculate how Ms. Edwards' behavior could be contributing to the decline in sales.

ATC 11–2   GROUP ASSIGNMENT *Schedule of Cost of Goods Manufactured and Sold*

The following information is from the accounts of Depree Manufacturing Company for 2002.

Required
a. Divide the class into groups of four or five students per group and organize the groups into three sections. Assign Task 1 to the first section of groups, Task 2 to the second section, and Task 3 to the third section.

Group Tasks

(1) The ending balance in the Raw Materials Inventory account was $208,000. During the accounting period, Depree used $2,348,900 of raw materials inventory and purchased $2,200,000 of raw materials. Determine the beginning raw materials inventory balance.
(2) During the accounting period, Depree used $2,348,900 of raw materials inventory and $2,780,200 of direct labor. Actual overhead costs were $3,300,000. Ending work in process inventory amounted to $450,000, and cost of goods manufactured amounted to $8,389,100. Determine the beginning balance in the Work in Process Inventory account.
(3) The cost of goods manufactured was $8,389,100, and the cost of goods sold was $8,419,100. Ending finished goods inventory amounted to $360,000. Determine the beginning balance in the Finished Goods Inventory account.
b. Select a spokesperson from each section. Use input from the three spokespersons to prepare a schedule of cost of goods manufactured and sold. The spokesperson from the first section should provide information for the computation of the cost of raw materials used. The spokesperson from the second section should provide information for the determination of the cost of goods manufactured. The spokesperson from the third section should provide information for the determination of the cost of goods sold.

ATC 11–3   RESEARCH ASSIGNMENT *Distinction Between Service and Manufacturing Companies*

Broadcast.com is an Internet-based company that was highlighted in an article written by Steven V. Brull, which appeared on page 142 of the November 9, 1998, issue of *Business Week*. Read this article and complete the following requirements.

Required

a. Is broadcast.com a service or a manufacturing company? Explain.

b. What type of inventory accounts would you expect broadcast.com to maintain?

c. Identify some cost drivers that would be appropriate for broadcast.com to use when calculating a pre-determined overhead rate.

WRITING ASSIGNMENT *Inventory Cost Flow in Manufacturing Environment*   ATC 11–4

Barret Cameron, a student in Professor Wagner's managerial accounting course, asked the following question. "In the first accounting course, the teacher said inventory costs flow on a FIFO, LIFO, or weighted average pattern. Now you are telling us inventory costs flow through raw materials, to work in process, and then to finished goods. Is this manufacturing stuff a new cost flow method or what?"

Required

Assume that you are Professor Wagner. Write a brief memo responding to Mr. Cameron's question.

ETHICAL DILEMMA *Absorption Costing*   ATC 11–5

Cliff Dennis may become a rich man. He is the creative force behind Amazing Drives, a new company. Amazing makes external drives that permit computer users to store large amounts of information on small floppy diskettes. Amazing has experienced tremendous growth since its inception three years ago. Investors have recognized the company's potential, and its stock is currently selling at 60 times projected earnings. More specifically, the company's 2004 earnings forecast shows estimated income to be $0.30 per share and the current market price is $18 per share ($0.30 $\times$ 60). Mr. Dennis has stock options permitting him to buy 2,000,000 shares of stock for $12 per share on January 1, 2005. This means that he could earn $6 per share on the options. In other words, he would buy the stock at $12 per share and sell it at $18 per share. As a result, Mr. Dennis would earn $12,000,000 ($6 $\times$ 2,000,000 shares).

Unfortunately, weak economies in foreign countries have caused low demand for Amazing's products in international markets. Company insiders are painfully aware that Amazing Drives is going to be unable to meet its projected income numbers. If actual earnings fall short of the projected earnings, the market will manifest its disappointment by discounting the stock price. Mr. Dennis is concerned that the value of his stock options could plummet.

At its inception three years ago, Amazing invested heavily in manufacturing equipment. Indeed, expecting dramatic growth, the company purchased a significant amount of excess capacity. As a result, the company incurs approximately $28,800,000 in fixed manufacturing costs annually. If Amazing continues to produce at its current level, it will make and sell approximately 800,000 drives during 2004. In the face of declining sales, Mr. Dennis has issued a puzzling order to his production manager. Specifically, he has told the production manager to increase production so that 1,200,000 drives will be completed during 2004. Mr. Dennis explained that he believes the economies in foreign countries will surge ahead in 2005 and that he wants Amazing to have the inventory necessary to satisfy the demand.

Required

a. Suppose that actual earnings for 2004 are $0.18 per share. The market becomes disappointed, and the price-earnings ratio falls to 40 times earnings. What is the value of Mr. Dennis' stock options under these circumstances?

b. Determine the impact on income reported in 2004 if production is 800,000 units versus 1,200,000 units.

c. Why would Mr. Dennis order the increase in production?

d. Does Mr. Dennis' behavior violate any of the standards of ethical conduct in Exhibit 1-13 of Chapter 1?

e. Identify the features described in this case that could motivate criminal and ethical misconduct. (It may be helpful to reread the ethics material in Chapter 1 before attempting to satisfy this requirement.)

SPREADSHEET ASSIGNMENT *Using Excel*   ATC 11–6

Manning Cassey Computers (MCC) plans to produce and sell 1,600 computers for $720 each in the next fiscal year. The company's cost data follow.

Components from wholesaler	$480 per computer
Assembly labor	$15 per hour
Manufacturing space rent	$3,000 per month
Utilities	$600 per month
Janitorial services	$480 per month
Depreciation of equipment	$3,840 per year
Labor time per computer	2 hours

Required

a. Construct a spreadsheet to calculate the cost of goods manufactured and the cost per unit for MCC. Use formulas in the schedule so that the cost of goods manufactured will automatically be calculated as you change the number of units sold.

b. Add an abbreviated income statement to your spreadsheet that incorporates the cost from Requirement *a*.

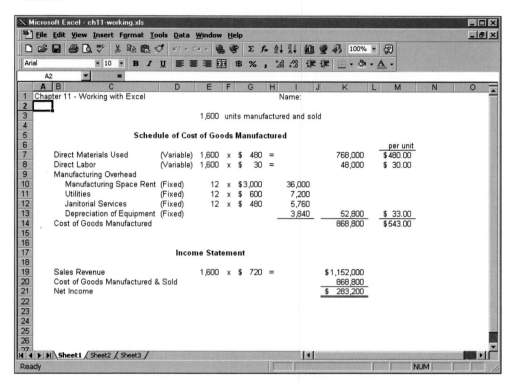

Spreadsheet Tip

1. Build the spreadsheet so that the number of units in cell E3 can be changed and cost of goods manufactured and net income will be recalculated automatically.

SPREADSHEET ASSIGNMENT *Mastering Excel*

ATC 11–7

Stanley Manufacturing Company, which sold 16,000 units of product at $20 per unit, collected the following information regarding three different levels of production.

Inventory Costs			
Fixed overhead	$100,000	$100,000	$100,000
Number of units produced	16,000	20,000	25,000
Fixed overhead per unit	$6.25	$5.00	$4.00
Variable manufacturing costs	$12.00	$12.00	$12.00
Full absorption cost per unit	$18.25	$17.00	$16.00

Required

a. Construct a spreadsheet that includes the preceding data in the top of the spreadsheet. The rows for fixed overhead per unit and full absorption cost per unit should be based on formulas.

b. Include absorption costing income statements at these three levels of production like those in Exhibit 11–11. Use formulas so that the number of units produced in the preceding table can be changed and net income will be recalculated automatically.

c. Include variable costing income statements at these three levels of production like those in Exhibit 11–12. Use formulas so that the number of units produced in the preceding table can be changed and net income will be recalculated automatically.

Job-Order, Process, and Hybrid Cost Systems

Learning Objectives

After completing this chapter, you should be able to:

1 Distinguish between job-order and process cost systems.

2 Identify product cost flows through a job-order cost system.

3 Identify product cost flows through a process cost system.

4 Distinguish between raw materials cost and transferred-in cost.

5 Understand how hybrid accounting systems can be created by combining different components of job-order and process cost systems.

6 Identify the various forms of documentation used in a job-order cost system.

7 Understand how accounting events in a job-order system affect financial statements.

8 Understand how accounting events in a process cost system affect financial statements.

9 Convert partially completed units into equivalent whole units.

the *curious* accountant

Suppose that a division of Ford Motor Company incurred approximately $76,500,000 of production cost in the process of making vehicles during the month of August. Assume that the division completed construction on 5,000 vehicles during the month and that 200 vehicles were in different stages of production at month's end. How would Ford managers decide the amount of the total production cost that should be charged to the partially completed vehicles? On what financial statement should the cost of these partially completed vehicles be shown?

Benchmore Boat Company made five boats during the current year, and Janis Juice Company made 500,000 cans of apple juice during the same year. Determining the cost of a boat made by Benchmore requires a different cost system than the one Janis used to determine the cost of a can of juice. Each boat has unique characteristics that affect its cost. For example, making an 80-foot yacht requires more labor and materials than making a 30-foot sailboat. Benchmore needs a system that traces product costs to individual inventory items (specific boats). Different boats should have different costs. In contrast, one can of juice is virtually identical to another. Accordingly, each can of juice should have the same cost. Unfortunately, costs are frequently distributed unevenly over the units of production. Suppose that Janis pays $2,000 per month to rent its manufacturing facility. In a month when Janis makes 40,000 cans of juice, the rent cost is $0.05 per can ($2,000 ÷ 40,000 cans). However, if Janis makes 20,000 cans, the cost per can increases to $0.10 ($2,000 ÷ 20,000 cans). Unlike Benchmore, Janis needs a cost system that distributes costs evenly across its total production (number of cans of juice made during an accounting period).

489

■ Cost Systems

As the preceding paragraph suggests, the type of product affects the accounting system used to determine product cost. The two most common types of costing systems are a job-order cost system and a process cost system. Some companies use a hybrid costing system that incorporates some combination of the procedures used in job-order and process systems. The following section of the text will discuss the types of products most suited to each costing system. In addition, the accounting procedures used in each type of costing system will be explained.

Cost Systems and Type of Product

LO1 Distinguish between job-order and process cost systems.

A cost accounting system designed to accumulate costs by individual products is a **job-order cost system**. The boats made by Benchmore represent only one example of the products that are suited to job-order costing. Other examples include movies made by Walt Disney Productions, office buildings constructed by Rust Engineering, and airplanes made by Boeing. Job-order cost systems apply not only to individual inventory items but also to groups or batches of inventory items. For example, Hernandes Shirt Company may account for the production of a special order of 20,000 shirts sold to the United States Army as a single job. Accordingly, job-order cost systems are employed when costs are accumulated by individual products or batches of products.

A cost system designed to distribute costs evenly over a homogeneous product line is a **process cost system.** In addition to beverage companies such as Janis, oil companies such as Texaco, chemical companies such as Dow Chemical, food processors such as General Mills, and paint manufacturers such as Sherwin-Williams frequently use process costing. The products made by these companies are normally produced in mass quantities through a continuous process that provides similar inputs to each unit produced. Under these circumstances, the *per unit product cost* is normally determined by dividing the total product cost by the number of units of product made during some designated span of time. Accordingly, process cost systems *average* product costs across the total number of items made.

To a lesser extent, cost averaging is also used in a job-order costing system. In all situations, some costs cannot be directly traced to particular jobs. Items such as indirect materials, indirect labor, utilities, rent, depreciation, and so on are not cost effectively traceable and so these costs are normally added together and averaged across some common measure of production such as labor hours, machine hours, square footage, and so forth to determine an overhead rate that is used to allocate the total cost to individual products. Furthermore, when jobs are organized in batches of a number of similar products, the cost per unit is determined by dividing the total cost of the job by the number of units of product in the batch. Although more effort is made to trace cost to specific products under a job-order system, *both* job-order and process costing require *some form of cost averaging.*

Job-Order Cost Flow

LO2 Identify product cost flows through a job-order cost system.

The accounting systems used for job-order and process costing have been patterned after the physical flow of products as they move through the production process. For example, Benchmore Boat Company builds its boats on a custom basis. It starts each boat as a separate project when it requisitions raw materials from the materials supply center. Designated workers are assigned to work on specific boats. Finally, indirect (overhead) costs are assigned to each boat on the basis of the size of the project as measured by the hours of labor required to build the boat.

Benchmore uses a *job-order cost system* to accumulate cost in a manner that is consistent with the way the boats are made; for example, each boat is given a specific job identification number. The inventory accounts are maintained on a perpetual basis. Product costs are

accumulated separately by designated job identification number. The costs of each boat move through the Work in Process Inventory to the Finished Goods Inventory accounts and out to Cost of Goods Sold parallel to actual production flow. Exhibit 12–1 depicts the flow of product costs for five boats that Benchmore plans to construct and sell. Notice carefully that the Work in Process Inventory is composed of distinct jobs, each of which contains the costs of materials, labor, and overhead uniquely associated with a specific inventory item. In other words, one Work in Process Inventory control account has numerous subsidiary accounts. Likewise, Finished Goods Inventory contains subsidiary accounts that show the separate cost of each boat.

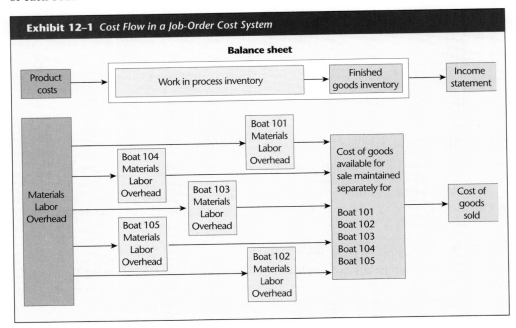

Exhibit 12–1 *Cost Flow in a Job-Order Cost System*

Process Cost Flow

Process cost systems utilize the same general ledger accounts as those used by job-order cost systems. Product costs flow from Raw Materials Inventory to Work in Process Inventory on to Finished Goods Inventory and then out to Cost of Goods Sold. The primary difference between the two systems centers on accounting for the work in process inventory. Instead of accumulating product costs by jobs in a single Work in Process Inventory control account, a process cost system accumulates these costs by departments, each of which has its own separate Work in Process Inventory account. Products normally move through a series of work centers on a continuous basis. For example, Janis Juice Company uses three distinct processes to produce its cans of apple juice. Raw materials enter the extraction department where juice concentrate is collected from whole fruit. The juice extract then passes to the mixing department where water, sugar, food coloring, and preservatives are added. The juice mixture then moves to the packaging department where it is poured into cans and boxed for shipment. The cost of all goods that move through a processing center (department) is charged to that center's Work in Process Inventory account.

LO3 Identify product cost flows through a process cost system.

Parallel to the pattern of the physical flow, cost accumulations are passed from one department to the next. In essence, the finished products of one department become the raw materials of the next department. The costs transferred from one department to the next are **transferred-in costs**. Transferred-in costs are combined with the additional materials, labor, and overhead costs incurred by each succeeding department. Accordingly, when goods are complete, the total product cost of all departments is transferred to Finished Goods Inventory. Exhibit 12–2 illustrates the cost flow for the process costing system used by Janis Juice

LO4 Distinguish between raw materials cost and transferred-in cost.

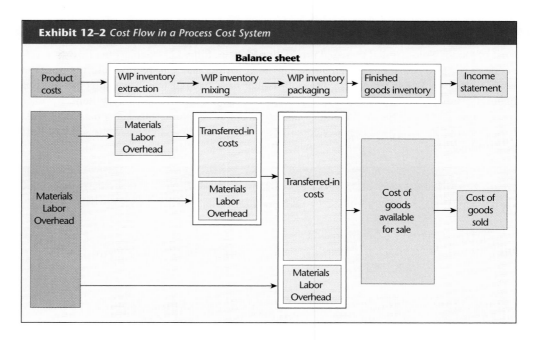

Exhibit 12-2 *Cost Flow in a Process Cost System*

<table>
<tr><td colspan="5" align="center">**Balance sheet**</td></tr>
<tr><td>Product costs</td><td>WIP inventory extraction → WIP inventory mixing → WIP inventory packaging</td><td>Finished goods inventory</td><td>Income statement</td></tr>
</table>

LO5 Understand how hybrid accounting systems can be created by combining different components of job-order and process cost systems.

Company. To understand the distinction between job-order and process cost systems, you should carefully compare the cost flow patterns depicted in Exhibits 12–1 and 12–2.

Hybrid Accounting Systems

In practice, many companies use a **hybrid cost system** that blends some of the features of a job-order cost system with some of the features of a process cost system. For example, Gateway 2000 makes hundreds of thousands of computers with standard features. It produces these computers through a continuous flow assembly line process that is compatible with process costing. Each unit requires the same amount of labor to assemble the same standard set of parts into finished products (computers) that are ready made for immediate delivery. However, Gateway also accepts orders for customized products that have unique features. For example, some customers may want a larger monitor, more memory, or a faster processor than the standard model has. Gateway accommodates these requests by customizing the products as they move through the production process. The customized features require cost-tracing features commonly associated with job-order costing. Accordingly, Gateway uses a hybrid cost system that combines some of the features of both process and job-order cost systems.

LO6 Identify the various forms of documentation used in a job-order cost system.

Documentation in a Job-Order Cost System

In a job-order cost system, product costs are accumulated on a **job cost sheet,** also called a *job-order cost sheet* or a *job record*. A separate job cost sheet is prepared for each individual job. As each job moves through the various stages of production, detailed information regarding the cost of materials, labor, and overhead is added to the job cost sheet. Accordingly, when a particular job is finished, the accompanying job cost sheet contains a summary of all costs incurred to complete that job.

The information recorded on the job cost sheet has two primary source documents. The first is a **materials requisition** form. Before a designated job can be started, the job supervisor prepares a list of materials that are needed to begin work. The mechanism used to requisition the necessary materials from the materials supply center depends on the level of technology present in the manufacturing environment. Some companies create a paper trail by delivering hard-copy documents to and from the different departments, but most modern businesses deliver requests electronically through a network of computers. Regardless of whether

Job-order, process, and hybrid cost systems apply to service companies as well as manufacturing entities. Indeed, one institution frequently maintains different cost systems. For example, a hospital cafeteria may maintain food cost data under a process cost system while the billing department maintains and bills cost data for each particular patient under a job-order system.

the information is maintained on paper documents or stored electronically, the information regarding material requisitions for each job is communicated to the accounting department where it is summarized on the job cost sheet.

The second source document for the job cost sheet is a **work ticket**, sometimes called a *time card*. The work ticket includes space for the job number, employee identification, and work description. The amount of time spent on each job is recorded on the work ticket, which is forwarded to the accounting department where the wage rates are recorded and the amount of labor cost is computed on the job cost sheet. Again, information gathering can be accomplished manually or electronically. Regardless of the form used, information regarding direct labor costs is collected for each individual job and added to that job's cost sheet.

Finally, each job cost sheet provides space for the inclusion of the amount of applied overhead. The job cost sheets are maintained perpetually with new cost data being added as work on the job progresses. Accordingly, a prorated share of the estimated overhead cost is systematically added to the cost sheet through the use of a predetermined overhead rate. Exhibit 12–3 shows a job cost sheet with accompanying materials requisition forms and work tickets for Benchmore Boat Company's job-order identification number for Boat 101.

Job-Order Cost System Illustrated

To illustrate the use of a job-order cost system by a business, we analyze the operations of Benchmore Boat Company during its 2003 accounting period. The company's beginning account balances for 2003 are shown in Exhibit 12–4.

LO7 Understand how accounting events in a job-order system affect financial statements.

Benchmore's 2003 accounting events are described next. The events have been recorded in ledger T-accounts shown in Exhibit 12–5 on page 499. You may find it helpful to trace each event to the T-accounts. The events have been numbered sequentially and cross-referenced in Exhibit 12–5. The effect of each event on the financial statements is shown individually and discussed in the following sections of this chapter.

Benchmore paid cash to purchase $14,000 of raw materials. The effects of this event on the company's financial statements follow.

Event 1
Raw Materials Purchased

Assets			= Liabilities + Equity			Revenue − Expenses = Net Income			Cash Flow
Cash	+	Raw Materials Inventory							
(14,000)	+	14,000	= NA	+	NA	NA − NA	=	NA	(14,000) OA

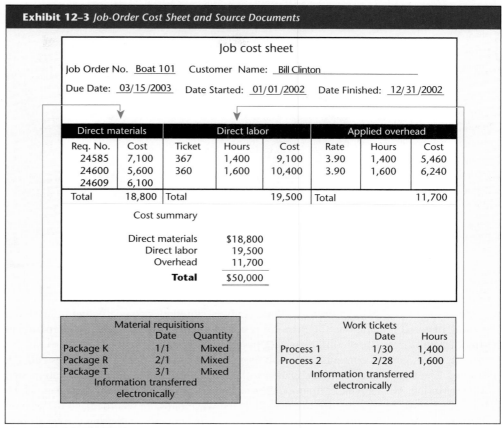

Exhibit 12–3 *Job-Order Cost Sheet and Source Documents*

Job cost sheet

Job Order No. __Boat 101__   Customer Name: __Bill Clinton__

Due Date: __03/15/2003__   Date Started: __01/01/2002__   Date Finished: __12/31/2002__

Direct materials		Direct labor			Applied overhead		
Req. No.	Cost	Ticket	Hours	Cost	Rate	Hours	Cost
24585	7,100	367	1,400	9,100	3.90	1,400	5,460
24600	5,600	360	1,600	10,400	3.90	1,600	6,240
24609	6,100						
Total	18,800	Total		19,500	Total		11,700

Cost summary

Direct materials	$18,800
Direct labor	19,500
Overhead	11,700
Total	$50,000

Material requisitions

	Date	Quantity
Package K	1/1	Mixed
Package R	2/1	Mixed
Package T	3/1	Mixed

Information transferred electronically

Work tickets

	Date	Hours
Process 1	1/30	1,400
Process 2	2/28	1,600

Information transferred electronically

Exhibit 12–4

BENCHMORE BOAT COMPANY
Trial Balance
As of January 1, 2003

	Debit	Credit
Cash	$ 73,000	
Production Supplies	300	
Raw Materials Inventory	7,000	
Work in Process Inventory	34,000	
Finished Goods Inventory	85,000	
Manufacturing Equipment	90,000	
Accumulated Depreciation		$ 32,000
Common Stock		200,000
Retained Earnings		57,300
Total	$289,300	$289,300

Exhibit 2–4 *continued*

Subsidiary Account Balances

Work in Process		Finished Goods	
Boat 103	$14,000	Boat 101	$50,000
Boat 104	8,000	Boat 102	35,000
Boat 105	12,000		
Total	$34,000	Total	$85,000

Event 1 is an asset exchange event; it does not affect total assets shown on the balance sheet. One asset account, Cash, decreases, and another asset account, Raw Materials Inventory, increases. The income statement is not affected. The cash outflow is shown in the operating activities section of the statement of cash flows.

Event 2
Raw Materials Used

Benchmore used $17,000 of direct raw materials in the process of making boats. The amount used for each job was $8,000, $3,400, and $5,600 for Boat 103, Boat 104, and Boat 105, respectively. The effects of this event on the company's financial statements follow.

Assets				= Liabilities + Equity			Revenue − Expenses = Net Income			Cash Flow
Raw Materials Inventory	+	Work in Process Inventory								
(17,000)	+	17,000	=	NA	+	NA	NA − NA = NA			NA

This event is an asset exchange event that does not affect total assets shown on the balance sheet. One asset account, Raw Materials Inventory, decreases, and another asset account, Work in Process Inventory, increases. The income statement and the statement of cash flows are not affected. In addition to the effects on the Work in Process Inventory control account, the individual job cost sheets are adjusted to reflect the material used on each job. Exhibit 12–5 illustrates these effects.

Benchmore paid $1,200 cash to purchase production supplies. The effects of this event on the company's financial statements follow.

Event 3
Production Supplies Purchased

Assets			= Liabilities	+ Equity	Revenue	− Expenses	= Net Income	Cash Flow
Cash	+	Production Supplies						
(1,200)	+	1,200	= NA	+ NA	NA	− NA	= NA	(1,200) OA

This event is an asset exchange event that does not affect total assets shown on the balance sheet. One asset account, Cash, decreases, and another asset account, Production Supplies, increases. The purchase of production supplies does not affect the income statement. The cost of supplies is allocated to the Work in Process Inventory account via the predetermined overhead rate and is expensed as part of cost of goods sold. However, the cash flow associated with the purchase of supplies is shown in the operating section of the statement of cash flows.

Benchmore paid $8,000 cash to production workers who worked on Boat 103. The effects of this event on the company's financial statements follow.

Event 4
Production Workers Paid

Assets			= Liabilities	+ Equity	Revenue	− Expenses	= Net Income	Cash Flow
Cash	+	Work in Process Inventory						
(8,000)	+	8,000	= NA	+ NA	NA	− NA	= NA	(8,000) OA

Note that these wages are *not* treated as salary expense. Because the labor was used to make inventory, the cost is included in the Work in Process Inventory account. In other words, this is an asset exchange event. One asset, Cash, decreases, and another asset, Work in Process Inventory, increases. Neither the total assets shown on the balance sheet nor the income statement is affected. The cash outflow is shown in the operating activities section of the statement of cash flows. In addition to the effects on the Work in Process Inventory control account, the individual job cost sheet would be adjusted to reflect the labor used on each job. Exhibit 12–5 illustrates this effect. Notice that the $8,000 labor cost is shown both in the Work in Process Inventory control account and on the job cost sheet for Boat 103.

Benchmore applied estimated manufacturing overhead costs to the job identified as Boat 103. Work on Boat 103 is complete. Even so, many of the costs associated with making it may not be known. Indeed, the boat may even be sold before all of the costs associated with making it are known. Although a proportionate share of the total production supplies, depreciation, supervisory salaries, rental cost, utilities, and so on were used during the early part of the year, the actual cost of these resources will not be known until the end of the year. To obtain the information needed to make decisions (e.g., the price to charge for the boat), Benchmore must estimate the overhead costs associated with making Boat 103.

Event 5
Overhead Costs Applied

To obtain as accurate an estimate as possible, Benchmore began by reviewing the overhead costs incurred during the previous year. Adjustments were made for expected changes. Assume that Benchmore's estimate of total overhead costs included the following items: production supplies, $900; depreciation, $8,000; and utilities and other indirect costs, $7,090. Accordingly, the total estimated overhead is $15,990 ($900 + $8,000 + $7,090). Because boats that require more labor also require more overhead inputs, a logical relationship exists between the number of labor hours used to make a boat and the consumption of indirect overhead costs. For example, the longer people work, the more supplies they use. Similarly, more work translates into more use of the equipment, thereby causing an increase in the consumption of utilities and

depreciation. Based on the link between the amount of labor used and the consumption of indirect costs, Benchmore decided to use *direct labor hours* as the base for the allocation of overhead costs. Benchmore estimated that a total of 4,100 labor hours would be used during 2003 and established a *predetermined overhead rate* as shown:

$$\text{Predetermined overhead rate} = \text{Total estimated overhead costs} \div \text{Total estimated direct labor hours}$$

$$\text{Predetermined overhead rate} = \$15,990 \div 4,100$$
$$= \$3.90 \text{ per direct labor hour}$$

Assuming that 1,600 actual direct hours of labor were used on Boat 103, Benchmore applies $6,240 (1,600 hours $\times$ $3.90) of overhead to that job. The effects of this application on the company's financial statements follow.

Assets			= Liabilities	+ Equity	Revenue	− Expenses	= Net Income	Cash Flow
Manufacturing Overhead	+	Work in Process Inventory						
(6,240)	+	6,240	= NA	+ NA	NA	− NA	= NA	NA

The event is an asset exchange transaction. One asset account, Work in Process Inventory, increases and another temporary asset account, Manufacturing Overhead, decreases. Overhead costs do not affect the income statement at the time they are applied to the Work in Process Inventory account. However, they do affect the income statement through the recognition of cost of goods sold at the time goods are sold. Likewise, the overhead application does not affect cash flow. Cash flow is affected when the indirect costs are paid, not when they are applied to Work in Process Inventory. The job cost sheet for Boat 103 reflects the increase in the cost associated with the application of the estimated overhead cost. The account balances in Exhibit 12–5 illustrate this.

Event 6
Product Costs for Boat 103 Transferred to Finished Goods Inventory

Benchmore finished work on Job 103 and transferred $36,240 of product costs from Work in Process Inventory to Finished Goods Inventory. The effects of this transfer on the company's financial statements follow.

Assets			= Liabilities	+ Equity	Revenue	− Expenses	= Net Income	Cash Flow
Work in Process Inventory	+	Finished Goods Inventory						
(36,240)	+	36,240	= NA	+ NA	NA	− NA	= NA	NA

This event is an asset exchange event. Costs are transferred from the Work in Process Inventory control account to the Finished Goods Inventory control account. Total assets shown on the balance sheet are unaffected as are the income statement and the statement of cash flow. The job cost sheet is transferred to the finished goods file folder. These effects are illustrated in Exhibit 12–5.

Event 7
Selling and Administrative Expense Paid

Benchmore paid $24,500 cash for selling and administrative expenses. The effects of this transaction on the company's financial statements follow.

Assets	= Liabilities	+ Equity	Revenue	− Expenses	= Net Income	Cash Flow
(24,500) =	NA	+ (24,500)	NA	− 24,500	= (24,500)	(24,500) OA

This is an asset use transaction. Cash and retained earnings decrease as a result of the expense recognition. Net income decreases as a result of the expense recognition. Likewise, the cash outflow reduces the net cash flow from operating activities.

Event 8
Production Workers Paid

Benchmore paid production workers $12,000 cash for work performed on Jobs 104 and 105. The amount of direct labor used on each job was $5,000 and $7,000 for Boat 104 and

Boat 105, respectively. These jobs were still under construction at the end of 2003. The effects of this event on the company's financial statements follow.

Assets			= Liabilities	+ Equity	Revenue	− Expenses	= Net Income	Cash Flow
Cash	+	Work in Process Inventory						
(12,000)	+	12,000	= NA	+ NA	NA	− NA	= NA	(12,000) OA

This is an asset exchange event. It does not affect total assets as shown on the balance sheet or the income statement The cash outflow is shown in the operating activities section of the statement of cash flows. In addition to the effects on the Work in Process Inventory control account, the individual job cost sheets are adjusted to reflect the labor used on each job. Exhibit 12–5 illustrates these effects.

Benchmore applied estimated manufacturing overhead costs to the jobs for Boats 104 and 105. The predetermined overhead rate was previously computed to be $3.90 per direct labor hour (see Event 5). Assume that the work described in Event 8 required 1,000 direct labor hours for Boat 104 and 1,400 direct labor hours for Boat 105. Based on this information, the amount of estimated overhead cost that should be applied to the two jobs is calculated.

Event 9
Overhead Costs Applied

Job Number	Predetermined Overhead Rate	×	Actual Labor Hours Used	=	Amount of Applied Overhead
Boat 104	$3.90	×	1,000	=	$3,900
Boat 105	$3.90	×	1,400	=	5,460
Total					$9,360

The effects of applying the overhead on the company's financial statements follow.

Assets			= Liabilities	+ Equity	Revenue	− Expenses	= Net Income	Cash Flow
Manufacturing Overhead	+	Work in Process Inventory						
(9,360)	+	9,360	= NA	+ NA	NA	− NA	= NA	NA

The overhead application is an asset exchange event. Total assets, net income, and cash flow are not affected. The job cost sheets for Boats 104 and 105 reflect an increase in overhead cost of $3,900 and $5,460, respectively. You should trace these allocations to the accounts shown in Exhibit 12–5.

Benchmore paid $6,100 cash for utilities and other indirect product costs. The effects of this event on the company's financial statements follow.

Event 10
Cash for Overhead Costs Paid

Assets			= Liabilities	+ Equity	Revenue	− Expenses	= Net Income	Cash Flow
Cash	+	Manufacturing Overhead						
(6,100)	+	6,100	= NA	+ NA	NA	− NA	= NA	(6,100) OA

The incurrence of the *actual overhead costs* is an asset exchange transaction. Total assets, net income, and job cost sheets are not affected. The cash outflow is shown in the operating activities section of the statement of cash flows. Remember that estimated overhead costs have already been recorded in the job cost sheets.

Benchmore recognized $8,000 of depreciation on manufacturing equipment. The original cost of the equipment was $90,000. It had a 10-year useful life and an estimated salvage value of $10,000. The annual depreciation charge is $8,000 ([$90,000 − $10,000] ÷ 10 = $8,000). The effects of this event on the company's financial statements follow.

Event 11
Depreciation on Manufacturing Equipment Recognized

Assets			= Liabilities	+ Equity	Revenue	− Expenses	= Net Income	Cash Flow
Book Value of Equipment	+	Manufacturing Overhead						
(8,000)	+	8,000	= NA	+ NA	NA	− NA	= NA	NA

This depreciation represents an *actual* indirect product cost (overhead), *not* an expense. Accordingly, this transaction is an asset exchange. The book value of the manufacturing equipment decreases and the Manufacturing Overhead account increases. The total amount of assets shown on the balance sheet is not affected, nor are the income statement and the statement of cash flows. Finally, notice that the job cost sheets are not affected by the *actual* overhead cost (depreciation). Remember that *estimated* overhead flows through the inventory accounts and the associated job cost sheets.

Event 12
Actual Cost of Production Supplies Recognized as Overhead

Benchmore made the year-end count of supplies and recognized actual overhead cost for the amount of supplies used. During the accounting period, $1,500 of production supplies were available for use ($300 beginning balance + $1,200 supplies purchased). Assuming that a physical count reveals that $400 of supplies is on hand at the end of the accounting period, $1,100 of supplies must have been used ($1,500 − $400). The effects of recognizing supplies used on the company's financial statements follow:

Assets			= Liabilities	+ Equity	Revenue	− Expenses	= Net Income	Cash Flow
Supplies	+	Manufacturing Overhead						
(1,100)	+	1,100	= NA	+ NA	NA	− NA	= NA	NA

The event is an asset exchange transaction. Total assets, net income, and cash flow are not affected, nor are the job cost sheets. Remember that estimated overhead costs have already been recorded in the job cost sheets.

Event 13
Sales Revenue Recognized

Benchmore sold Boat 101 for $91,000 cash. The effects of this event on the company's financial statements follow.

Assets	= Liabilities	+ Equity	Revenue	− Expenses	= Net Income	Cash Flow
91,000 =	NA	+ 91,000	91,000	− NA	= 91,000	91,000 OA

The revenue recognition from the sale of inventory is an asset source event. The asset account, Cash, and the equity account, Retained Earnings, increase. The recognition of revenue also increases the amount of net income shown on the income statement. In addition, the operating activities section of the statement of cash flows increases.

Event 14
Cost of Goods Sold Recognized

Benchmore recognized cost of goods sold for Boat 101. The effects of this event on the company's financial statements follow.

Assets	= Liabilities	+ Equity	Revenue	− Expenses	= Net Income	Cash Flow
(50,000) =	NA	+ (50,000)	NA	− 50,000	= (50,000)	NA

The recognition of cost of goods sold is an asset use transaction. It acts to decrease an asset account, Finished Goods Inventory, and an equity account, Retained Earnings. The recognition of the expense decreases net income, but cash flow is not affected by the recognition of cost of goods sold. Recall that the impact on cash flow was recognized when cash was spent in the process of making the inventory. The job cost sheet for Boat 101 is transferred to the permanent files. The cost sheet is not discarded at the time of sale because it contains information that could be valuable in estimating the cost of similar special order jobs in the future.

Event 15
Cost of Goods Sold Adjusted for Overapplied Overhead

Benchmore closed the Manufacturing Overhead account and reduced the cost of goods sold by $400. Actual overhead costs amounted to $15,200 although $15,600 of overhead cost had

Exhibit 12-5 *Ledger T-Accounts for Benchmore Boat Company*

Cash

Bal.	73,000	(1)	14,000
(13)	91,000	(3)	1,200
		(4)	8,000
		(7)	24,500
		(8)	12,000
		(10)	6,100
Bal.	98,200		

Supplies

Bal.	300	(12)	1,100
(3)	1,200		
Bal.	400		

Equipment

Bal.	90,000	

Accumulated Dep.

		Bal.	32,000
		(11)	8,000
		Bal.	40,000

Raw Materials Inventory

Bal.	7,000	(2)	17,000
(1)	14,000		
Bal.	4,000		

Manufacturing Overhead

(10)	6,100	(5)	6,240
(11)	8,000	(9)	9,360
(12)	1,100		
(15)	400		
Bal.	0		

Work in Process Inventory

Bal.	34,000	(6)	36,240
(2)	17,000		
(4)	8,000		
(5)	6,240		
(8)	12,000		
(9)	9,360		
Bal.	50,360		

Finished Goods Inventory

Bal.	85,000	(14)	50,000
(6)	36,240		
Bal.	71,240		

Common Stock

	Bal.	200,000

Retained Earnings

	Bal.	57,300

Revenue

	(13)	91,000

Cost of Goods Sold

(14)	50,000	(15)	400

Selling and Admin. Exp.

(7)	24,500	

Job Cost Sheets (Subsidiary accounts)

Boat 101

Beg. Bal.	50,000
Sold	(50,000)
End Bal.	0

Boat 102

Beg. Bal.	35,000
Cost Added	0
End Bal.	35,000

Boat 103

Beg. Bal.	0
Cost Added	36,240
End Bal.	36,240

Boat 103

Beg. Bal.	14,000
Mat.	8,000
Lab.	8,000
O.H.	6,240
Product Cost	36,240
To Finish Goods	(36,240)
End Bal.	0

Boat 104

Beg. Bal.	8,000
Mat.	3,400
Lab.	5,000
O.H.	3,900
End Bal.	20,300

Boat 105

Beg. Bal.	12,000
Mat.	5,600
Lab.	7,000
O.H.	5,460
End Bal.	30,060

Boat 101

Cost Sheet Data Transferred to Permanent Storage

been applied. Accordingly, the overhead has been overapplied by $400 ($15,600 − $15,200). This means that too much overhead has been transferred to the Work in Process, Finished Goods Inventory, and Cost of Goods Sold Inventory accounts. If the amount were significant, it would have to be allocated proportionately among the inventory accounts and the Cost of Goods Sold accounts. In this case, the amount is assumed to be insignificant and is assigned exclusively to cost of goods sold. The effects of this event on the company's financial statements follow.

Assets	=	Liabilities	+	Equity	Revenue	−	Expenses	=	Net Income	Cash Flow
400	=	NA	+	400	NA	−	(400)	=	400	NA

Exhibit 12–6

BENCHMORE BOAT COMPANY
Trial Balance
As of December 31, 2003

	Debit	Credit
Cash	$ 98,200	
Raw Materials	4,000	
Work in Process	50,360	
Finished Goods	71,240	
Supplies	400	
Equipment	90,000	
Accumulated Depreciation		$ 40,000
Common Stock		200,000
Retained Earnings		57,300
Revenue		91,000
Cost of Goods Sold	49,600	
Selling and Administrative Expense	24,500	
Total	$388,300	$388,300

Overapplied overhead means that too much estimated cost was transferred from the asset accounts to Cost of Goods Sold. The preceding entry corrects this misstatement. When $400 is placed in the overhead account, total assets increase. The increase in assets is offset by a corresponding decrease in the Cost of Goods Sold account. This reduces expenses and increases net income, thereby resulting in an increase in the Retained Earnings equity account. Cash flow is unaffected. After this adjustment, the total increases in the overhead account (actual costs) equal the total decreases (estimated costs). Accordingly, the Manufacturing Overhead account has an ending balance of zero and does not appear on any financial statement.

The ending trial balance for Benchmore Boat Company is show in Exhibit 12–6.

Check Yourself 12–1

Wilson Cabinets makes custom cabinets for home builders. It incurred the following costs during the most recent month.

Inventory	Materials	Labor
Job 1	$4,200	$2,700
Job 2	2,300	5,000
Job 3	1,700	800

Wilson's predetermined overhead rate is $0.80 per direct labor dollar. Actual overhead costs were $7,100. Wilson completed and sold Jobs 1 and 2 during the month, but Job 3 was not complete at month end. The selling prices for Jobs 1 and 2 were $14,900 and $16,600, respectively. What amount of gross margin would Wilson report on the income statement for the month?

Answer Cost accumulated in the Work in Process account:

Inventory	Materials	Labor	Overhead*	Total
Job 1	$4,200	$2,700	$2,160	$ 9,060
Job 2	2,300	5,000	4,000	11,300
Job 3	1,700	800	640	3,140

*80% of direct labor cost.

Total allocated overhead is $6,800 ($2,160 + $4,000 + $640). Since actual overhead is $7,100, overhead is underapplied by $300 ($7,100 − $6,800).

Sales revenue ($14,900 + $16,600)	$31,500
Cost of Goods Sold (Job 1, $9,060 + Job 2, $11,300 + Underapplied overhead, $300)	(20,660)
Gross margin	$10,840

Process Cost System Illustrated

A process cost system utilizes the same general ledger accounts as those described for the job-order cost system. Product costs flow through Raw Materials Inventory, Work in Process Inventory, Finished Goods Inventory, and out to Cost of Goods Sold. The primary difference between the two systems centers on accounting for Work in Process Inventory. Instead of accumulating work in process costs by job, a process cost system accumulates these costs by department for a specific period of time. The cost of all goods that move through a processing center is charged to that center. Because production is not divided into jobs or job lots, the need for the work in process subsidiary documents (job cost sheets) is eliminated. Accordingly, a process cost system is simpler and easier to maintain; although it offers simplicity, it does not distinguish the cost of one product from that of another. Accordingly, a process system is not appropriate for companies that manufacture products that are distinctly different from one another; it is suited to manufacturing operations characterized by the continuous production of a uniform product. In a process cost system, all products are considered to have the same cost per unit.

LO8 Understand how accounting events in a process cost system affect financial statements.

To illustrate the use of a process cost system by a business, we analyze the operations of Janis Juice Company during its 2003 accounting year. Recall that Janis uses three distinct processes to produce its cans of apple juice. Raw materials enter the *extraction department* where juice concentrate is collected from whole fruit. The juice extract then passes to the *mixing department* where water, sugar, food coloring, and preservatives are added. The juice mixture then moves to the *packaging department* where it is poured into cans and boxed for shipment. The company's beginning account balances for 2003 are shown in Exhibit 12–7.

The 2003 accounting events for Janis are discussed individually in the following sections. The events, which are recorded in ledger T-accounts in Exhibit 12–9 on page 505, have been numbered sequentially and cross-referenced for your convenience. Trace each event to the T-accounts.

Exhibit 12–7

JANIS JUICE COMPANY
Trial Balance
As of January 1, 2003

	Debit	Credit
Cash	$320,000	
Raw Materials—Fruit	7,800	
Raw Materials—Additives	3,100	
Raw Materials—Containers	9,500	
Work in Process—Extraction	22,360	
Work in Process—Mixing	7,960	
Work in Process—Packaging	21,130	
Finished Goods	20,700	
Common Stock		$180,000
Retained Earnings		232,550
Total	$412,550	$412,550

Janis paid cash to purchase $84,000 of raw materials. The effects of this event on the company's financial statements follow.

Event 1
Raw Materials Purchased

Assets			= Liabilities + Equity		Revenue − Expenses = Net Income			Cash Flow
Cash	+	Raw Materials Inventory						
(84,000)	+	84,000	= NA	+ NA	NA	− NA	= NA	(84,000) OA

This event is an asset exchange event. Total assets and net income are not affected. The cash outflow is shown in the operating activities section of the statement of cash flows. The total materials cost was divided into three categories: $25,000 for whole fruit, $30,000 for additives, and $29,000 for containers. A separate inventory account is maintained for each category. Trace this event to the ledger accounts in Exhibit 12–9.

Janis used $26,720 of whole fruit to obtain extract used to make juice. The effects of this event on the company's financial statements follow.

Event 2
Raw Materials Used in Extraction Department

Assets			= Liabilities + Equity		Revenue − Expenses = Net Income			Cash Flow
Raw Materials—Fruit	+	WIP—Extraction						
(26,720)	+	26,720	= NA	+ NA	NA	− NA	= NA	NA

This event is an asset exchange event. It does not affect total assets, net income, or cash flow. Notice carefully that the cost of the materials used is not assigned to any particular product or batch of products but to the extraction department, which provides virtually the same value-added service to each can of juice.

Event 3
Production Workers in
Extraction Department Paid

Janis paid $38,000 cash to production workers who worked in the extraction department. The effects of this event on the company's financial statements follow.

Assets			= Liabilities	+ Equity	Revenue	− Expenses	= Net Income	Cash Flow
Cash	+	WIP—Extraction						
(38,000)	+	38,000	= NA	+ NA	NA	− NA	= NA	(38,000) OA

This is an asset exchange event. Total assets and net income are not affected. The cash outflow is shown in the operating activities section of the statement of cash flows. Again, this cost is assigned to the department rather than to individual products.

Event 4
Overhead Costs Applied to
Extraction Department

Janis applied estimated manufacturing overhead costs to work in process in the extraction department. Janis has identified a logical relationship between the number of labor dollars and the consumption of indirect overhead costs. The more dollars paid for labor, the higher the consumption of indirect resources. Janis estimated that in 2003, $96,000 of indirect cost would be incurred and that $120,000 would be paid to production workers. Based on these estimates, Janis established a *predetermined overhead* rate as follows.

$$\text{Predetermined overhead rate} = \text{Total estimated overhead costs} \div \text{Total estimated direct labor hours}$$

$$\text{Predetermined overhead rate} = \$96,000 \div \$120,000$$

$$= \$0.80 \text{ per direct labor dollar}$$

Based on the fact that $38,000 of labor was used in the extraction department (see Event 3), Janis applied $30,400 ($38,000 × $0.80) of overhead to that department. The effects of this application on the company's financial statements follow.

Assets			= Liabilities	+ Equity	Revenue	− Expenses	= Net Income	Cash Flow
Manufacturing Overhead	+	WIP—Extraction						
(30,400)	+	30,400	= NA	+ NA	NA	− NA	= NA	NA

Event 5
Cost of Extract Transferred to
Mixing Department

LO9 Convert partially complete units into equivalent whole units.

The event is an asset exchange transaction. Total assets, net income, and cash flow are not affected.

Janis finished the extraction process for some of the juice and transferred related cost from the Work in Process Inventory account of the extraction department to the Work in Process Inventory account of the mixing department. Based on these events, total product costs in the Work in Process Inventory account for the extraction department amounted to $117,480 ($22,360 beginning balance + $26,720 materials + $38,000 labor + $30,400 overhead). Suppose that beginning inventory had enough fruit to represent 100,000 units of product (cans) and that enough fruit was added to start an additional 485,000 units. Accordingly, the proper amount of fruit has been placed into production to make 585,000 (100,000 + 485,000 units). Furthermore, assume that enough extract has been transferred to the mixing department to make 500,000 cans of juice. Accordingly, 85,000 (585,000 − 500,000) units in ending inventory *have been started but are not complete.* The total $117,480 product cost must be allocated between the 85,000 partially completed units in ending inventory and the 500,000 completed units that have been transferred to the mixing department. To make a rational allocation, we must first convert the 85,000 partially complete units into *equivalent whole units.*

The logic employed to convert partial units into **equivalent whole units** uses simple mathematics. For example, 2 units that are 50 percent complete equal 1 equivalent whole unit ($2 \times 0.5 = 1$). Similarly, 4 units that are 25 percent complete equal 1 equivalent whole unit ($4 \times 0.25 = 1$). Likewise, 100 units that are 30 percent complete equal 30 equivalent whole units ($100 \text{ units} \times 0.30$).

Assume that an engineer estimated the 85,000 partial cans of juice in the extraction department's ending inventory to be 40 percent complete. The amount of equivalent whole units in ending inventory is therefore 34,000 ($85,000 \times 0.4$). The total number of *equivalent units* produced during the period is 534,000 (the 500,000 units that were finished and transferred to the mixing department and the 34,000 equivalent whole units in ending inventory). Based on this information, the **cost per equivalent unit** can now be determined.

Cost per equivalent unit = Total cost ÷ Number of equivalent whole units
Cost per equivalent unit = $117,480 ÷   534,000
               =$0.22 per equivalent unit

The *cost per equivalent unit* can be used to allocate the total cost incurred in the extraction department between the amount to be transferred to the mixing department and the amount to remain in the extraction department's ending Work in Process Inventory account. The allocation is as follows.

	Equivalent Units	×	Cost per Unit	Cost to Be Allocated
Transferred-out costs	500,000	×	$0.22	$110,000
Ending inventory	34,000	×	$0.22	7,480
Total				$117,480

The effects of transferring $110,000 from the extraction department's Work in Process Inventory to the mixing department's Work in Process Inventory follow.

Assets			=	Liabilities	+	Equity	Revenue	−	Expenses	=	Net Income	Cash Flow
WIP—Extraction	+	WIP—Mixing										
(110,000)	+	110,000	=	NA	+	NA	NA	−	NA	=	NA	NA

This event is an asset exchange event. Total assets, net income, and the statement of cash flow are unaffected.

The supporting documentation for the allocation of costs between transferred out and ending inventory is frequently shown in a *cost of production report,* which is usually subdivided into three categories. The first category shows the computation of equivalent units, the second shows the determination of cost per equivalent unit, and the third shows the allocation of total cost between the amount transferred out and the amount remaining in ending inventory. A cost of production report for Janis's allocation of cost for the extraction department is shown in Exhibit 12–8.

The method used here to determine equivalent units is called the **weighted average method**. Note that this method ignores the state of completion of items in beginning inventory. The equivalent unit adjustment is applied *only* to the units in ending inventory. The failure to account for equivalent units in beginning as well as ending inventories can distort the accuracy of the allocation between the cost of goods transferred out and the cost of goods remaining in particular inventory accounts. Managers frequently tolerate some degree of inaccuracy because the weighted average method is relatively easy to implement. However, when accuracy is deemed to be of paramount importance, some companies use a **first-in, first-out (FIFO) method**. This method accounts for the degree of completion of both beginning and ending inventories, but its application is more complicated. Indeed, we believe that a discussion of this method is more appropriate for upper-level accounting courses. Accordingly, the FIFO method will not be covered in this text.

Exhibit 12–8

JANIS JUICE COMPANY
Cost of Production Report
Extraction Department
For the Year Ended December 31, 2003

	Actual		**Equivalent**
Determination of Equivalent Units			
Beginning inventory	100,000		
Units added to production	485,000		
Total	585,000		
Transferred to finished goods	500,000	100% Complete	500,000
Ending inventory	85,000	40% Complete	34,000
Total	585,000		534,000
Determination of Cost per Unit			
Cost Accumulation			
Beginning inventory	$ 22,360		
Materials	26,720		
Labor	38,000		
Overhead	30,400		
Total	$117,480		
Divide by	÷		
Equivalent units	534,000		
Cost per equivalent unit (i.e., per can)	$0.22		
Cost Allocation			
To Work in Process Overhead, Mixing Dept.			
(500,000 × $0.22)	$110,000		
To ending inventory (34,000 × $0.22)	7,480		
Total	$117,480		

Event 6
Additional Raw Materials Used in Mixing Department

Janis mixed (used) $24,400 of additives with the extract obtained from the extraction department. Conceptually, the *transferred-in cost* (juice extract) from the extraction department is a raw material to the mixing department. In addition, the mixing department may obtain and add new materials to the production process. In this case, additives such as sweetener, food coloring, and preservatives are mixed with the juice extract. Although both *transferred-in costs* and *additives* are raw materials, traditional practice classifies them separately in the accounts. Review the mixing department's Work in Process account in Exhibit 12–9 to see how these costs are arranged in the ledger accounts. The effects of using additional materials in the mixing department follow.

Assets			=	Liabilities	+	Equity	Revenue	−	Expenses	=	Net Income	Cash Flow
Raw Material Additives	+	**WIP— Mixing**										
(24,400)	+	24,400	=	NA	+	NA	NA	−	NA	=	NA	NA

This event is an asset exchange event. Total assets, net income, and cash flow are not affected.

Event 7
Production Workers in Mixing Department Paid

Janis paid $48,000 cash to production workers who worked in the mixing department. The effects of this event on the company's financial statements follow.

Assets			=	Liabilities	+	Equity	Revenue	−	Expenses	=	Net Income	Cash Flow
Cash	+	**WIP— Mixing**										
(48,000)	+	48,000	=	NA	+	NA	NA	−	NA	=	NA	(48,000) OA

Exhibit 12–9 *Ledger T-Accounts for Janis Juice Company*

Cash

Bal.	320,000	(1)	84,000
(15)	490,000	(3)	38,000
		(7)	48,000
		(11)	43,000
		(14)	106,330
		(17)	78,200
Bal.	412,470		

Raw Materials—Fruit

Bal.	7,800	(2)	26,720
(1)	25,000		
Bal.	6,080		

Raw Materials—Additives

Bal.	3,100	(6)	24,400
(1)	30,000		
Bal.	8,700		

Raw Materials—Containers

Bal.	9,500	(10)	32,000
(1)	29,000		
Bal.	6,500		

Manufacturing Overhead

(14)	106,330	(4)	30,400
		(8)	38,400
		(12)	34,400
		(18)	3,130
Bal.	0		

Work in Process—Extraction

Bal.	22,360	(5)	110,000
(2)	26,720		
(3)	38,000		
(4)	30,400		
Bal.	7,480		

Work in Process Mixing

Bal.	7,960	(9)	219,300
(5)	110,000		
(6)	24,400		
(7)	48,000		
(8)	38,400		
Bal.	9,460		

Work in Process— Packaging

Bal.	21,130	(13)	331,200
(9)	219,300		
(10)	32,000		
(11)	43,000		
(12)	34,400		
Bal.	18,630		

Finished Goods Inventory

Bal.	20,700	(16)	338,100
(13)	331,200		
Bal.	13,800		

Common Stock

	Bal.	180,000

Retained Earnings

	Bal.	232,550

Revenue

	(15)	490,000

Cost of Goods Sold

(16)	338,100	
(18)	3,130	
Bal.	341,230	

Selling and Admin. Exp.

(17)	78,200	

505

answers to the *curious* accountant

Accountants at Ford Motor Company would have to convert the partially completed units into equivalent whole units to determine the cost per equivalent unit. If we assume that the vehicles move evenly through the production process, it is reasonable to estimate that the ending inventory was 50 percent complete. Under these circumstances, the division would have 5,100 equivalent whole units of product (5,000 completed units plus 100 equivalent whole units in ending inventory [200 partial units × 0.50 percentage of completion]). Cost per equivalent

whole unit could then be computed to be $15,000 ($76,500,000 ÷ 5,100 equivalent units). The portion of the total production cost allocated to the partially completed vehicles is $1,500,000 ($15,000 per unit × 100 equivalent units). This cost would be identified as ending Work in Process Inventory and would be shown on the balance sheet. The amount of work in process inventory could be shown separately or combined with other inventory costs shown on the balance sheet.

This is an asset exchange event. Total assets and net income are not affected. The cash outflow is shown in the operating activities section of the statement of cash flows.

Event 8
Overhead Costs Applied to Mixing Department

Janis applied estimated manufacturing overhead costs to the Work in Process Inventory account in the mixing department. Using the *predetermined overhead* rate established in Event 4, Janis determined that $38,400 ($48,000 labor × 0.80 overhead rate) of overhead costs should be applied to the mixing department's Work in Process Inventory account. The effects of the overhead application on the company's financial statements follow.

Assets			=	Liabilities	+	Equity	Revenue	−	Expenses	=	Net Income	Cash Flow
Manufacturing Overhead	+	WIP— Mixing										
(38,400)	+	38,400	=	NA	+	NA	NA	−	NA	=	NA	NA

The event is an asset exchange transaction. Total assets, net income, and cash flow are not affected.

Event 9
Cost of Mixed Juice Transferred to Packaging Department

Janis finished the mixing process for some of the juice and transferred the related cost from the mixing department's Work in Process Inventory account to the packaging department's Work in Process Inventory account. Based on these events, *total product cost* in the mixing department's Work in Process Inventory account is $228,760 ($7,960 beginning balance + $110,000 transferred-in cost + $24,400 materials + $48,000 labor + $38,400 overhead). An engineer estimated that 510,000 units of mixed juice had been transferred from the mixing department to the packaging department and that 88,000 units of juice remaining in the mixing department were 25 percent complete. Accordingly, the *equivalent whole units* in ending inventory was 22,000 (88,000 × 0.25). The total equivalent whole units produced by the mixing department was 532,000 (510,000 + 22,000). The *cost per equivalent unit* was determined to be $0.43 ($228,760 ÷ 532,000). The allocation between the amount to be transferred out to the packaging department's Work in Process Inventory account and the amount remaining in the mixing department's *ending* Work in Process Inventory account follows.

	Equivalent Units	×	Cost per Unit	Cost to Be Allocated
Transferred-out costs	510,000	×	$0.43	$219,300
Ending inventory	22,000	×	$0.43	9,460
Total				$228,760

The effects of transferring $219,300 from the mixing department's Work in Process Inventory to the packaging department's Work in Process Inventory is as follows.

Assets			=	Liabilities	+	Equity	Revenue	−	Expenses	=	Net Income	Cash Flow
WIP— Mixing	+	WIP— Packaging										
(219,300)	+	219,300	=	NA	+	NA	NA	−	NA	=	NA	NA

This event is an asset exchange event. Total assets, net income, and the statement of cash flows are unaffected. To ensure that you understand the allocation process, find the ending balance in the mixing department's Work in Process Inventory account in Exhibit 12–9. Also find the entry that verifies $219,300 of product cost being transferred from the mixing department's Work in Process Inventory account to the packaging department's Work in Process Inventory account.

Janis added $32,000 of containers and other packaging materials to the work in process in the packaging department. The effects of this event on the financial statements follow:

Event 10
Additional Raw Materials Used in Packaging Department

Assets			= Liabilities + Equity	Revenue − Expenses = Net Income			Cash Flow
Raw Material— Containers	+	WIP— Packaging					
(32,000)	+	32,000 =	NA + NA	NA −	NA =	NA	NA

This event is an asset exchange event. Total assets, net income, and cash flow are not affected.

Janis paid $43,000 cash to production workers who worked in the Packaging Department. The effects of this event on the company's financial statements follow.

Event 11
Production Workers in Packaging Department Paid

Assets			= Liabilities + Equity	Revenue − Expenses = Net Income			Cash Flow
Cash	+	WIP— Packaging					
(43,000)	+	43,000 =	NA + NA	NA −	NA =	NA	(43,000) OA

This is an asset exchange event. Total assets and net income are not affected. The cash outflow is shown in the operating activities section of the statement of cash flows.

Janis applied estimated manufacturing overhead costs to the packaging department's Work in Process Inventory account. Using the *predetermined overhead rate* established in Event 4, Janis determined that $34,400 ($43,000 labor × 0.80 overhead rate) of overhead costs should be applied to the mixing department's Work in Process Inventory account. The effects of the overhead application on the company's financial statements follow.

Event 12
Overhead Costs Applied to Packaging Department

Assets			= Liabilities + Equity	Revenue − Expenses = Net Income			Cash Flow
Manufacturing Overhead	+	WIP— Packaging					
(34,400)	+	34,400 =	NA + NA	NA −	NA =	NA	NA

The event is an asset exchange transaction. Total assets, net income, and cash flow are not affected.

Janis finished the packaging process for some of the juice and transferred the related cost from the packaging department's Work in Process Inventory account to the Finished Goods Inventory account. *Total product cost* in the Work in Process Inventory account for the packaging department is $349,830 ($21,130 beginning balance + $219,300 transfer-in cost + $32,000 materials + $43,000 labor + $34,400 overhead). An engineer estimated that 480,000 units of packaged juice were transferred from the packaging department to the Finished Goods Inventory account. Furthermore, the engineer estimated that 90,000 units of juice remaining in the packaging department were 30 percent complete. Accordingly, the *equivalent whole units* in ending inventory was 27,000 (90,000 × 0.30). The total equivalent whole units produced by the mixing department was 507,000 (480,000 + 27,000). The *cost per equivalent unit* was determined to be $0.69 ($349,830 ÷ 507,000). The allocation between the amount to be transferred out to the Finished Goods Inventory account and the amount remaining in the packaging department's ending Work in Process Inventory account follows.

Event 13
Cost of Goods Manufactured Transferred to Finished Goods Inventory

	Equivalent Units	×	Cost per Unit	Cost to Be Allocated
Transferred-out costs	480,000	×	$0.69	$331,200
Ending inventory	27,000	×	$0.69	18,630
Total				$349,830

The effects of transferring $331,200 from the packaging department's Work in Process Inventory to the Finished Goods Inventory account follow.

Assets			= Liabilities + Equity			Revenue – Expenses = Net Income				Cash Flow
WIP—Packaging	+	Finished Goods								
(331,200)	+	331,200	= NA	+	NA	NA	– NA	=	NA	NA

This event is an asset exchange event. Total assets, net income, and the statement of cash flows are unaffected. To ensure that you understand the allocation process, you should find the ending balance in the packaging department's Work in Process Inventory account. Also find the entry that verifies the transfer of $331,200 of product cost from the packaging department's Work in Process Inventory account to the Finished Goods Inventory account.

Event 14
Cash for Actual Overhead Costs Paid

Janis paid $106,330 cash for actual overhead costs. The effects of this event on the company's financial statements follow.

Assets			= Liabilities + Equity			Revenue – Expenses = Net Income				Cash Flow
Cash	+	Manufacturing Overhead								
(106,330)	+	106,330	= NA	+	NA	NA	– NA	=	NA	(106,330) OA

The incurrence of the *actual overhead costs* is an asset exchange transaction. Total assets and net income are not affected. The cash outflow is shown in the operating activities section of the statement of cash flows.

Event 15
Sales Revenue Recognized

Janis sold 490,000 cans of juice for $1 per can. The effects of this event on the company's financial statements follow.

Assets = Liabilities + Equity			Revenue – Expenses = Net Income			Cash Flow
490,000 =	NA	+ 490,000	490,000 –	NA	= 490,000	490,000 OA

The revenue recognition from the sale of inventory is an asset source event. The asset account, Cash, and the equity account, Retained Earnings, increase, and the recognition of revenue increases the amount of net income shown on the income statement. In addition, the operating activities section of the statement of cash flows reflects an increase.

Event 16
Cost of Goods Sold Recognized

Janis recognized cost of goods sold for the 490,000 cans of juice sold in Event 15. Each finished can of juice cost $0.69 (see Event 13). Accordingly, cost of goods sold was $338,100. The effects of this event on the company's financial statements follow.

Assets = Liabilities + Equity			Revenue – Expenses = Net Income			Cash Flow
(338,100) =	NA	+ (338,100)	NA –	338,100	= (338,100)	NA

The recognition of cost of goods sold is an asset use transaction. It decreases an asset account, Finished Goods Inventory, and an equity account, Retained Earnings. The recognition of the

expense decreases net income. Cash flow is not affected by the recognition of cost of goods sold.

Janis paid $78,200 cash for selling and administrative expenses. The effects of this event on the company's financial statements follow.

Assets	=	Liabilities	+	Equity	Revenue	−	Expenses	=	Net Income	Cash Flow
(78,200)	=	NA	+	(78,200)	NA	−	78,200	=	(78,200)	(78,200) OA

The recognition of selling and administrative expense is an asset use transaction. It decreases an asset account, Cash, and an equity account, Retained Earnings. The recognition of the expense decreases net income. The cash outflow is shown as a decrease in the operating activities section of the statement of cash flows.

Janis closed the Manufacturing Overhead account and increased the Cost of Goods Sold account by $3,130. Actual overhead costs amounted to $106,330 and $103,200 of overhead cost was applied. Accordingly, the overhead has been underapplied by $3,130 ($106,330 − $103,200). This means that too little overhead has been transferred to Work in Process Inventory, Finished Goods Inventory, and Cost of Goods Sold. The amount was assumed to be insignificant and was assigned directly to Cost of Goods Sold. The effects of this event on the company's financial statements follow.

Assets	=	Liabilities	+	Equity	Revenue	−	Expenses	=	Net Income	Cash Flow
(3,130)	=	NA	+	(3,130)	NA	−	3,130	=	(3,130)	NA

Underapplied overhead means that too little estimated cost was transferred from the asset accounts to the Cost of Goods Sold account. The preceding entry corrects this misstatement. The additional $3,130 of overhead costs is assigned to Cost of Goods Sold, thereby decreasing net income. Cash flow is unaffected. After this adjustment, the total increases in the overhead account (actual costs) equal the total decreases (estimated costs). Accordingly, the Manufacturing Overhead account has an ending balance of zero and does not appear on any financial statement.

The ending trial balance for Janis Juice Company is shown in Exhibit 12–10.

Exhibit 12–10

JANIS JUICE COMPANY
Adjusted Trial Balance
As of December 31, 2003

	Debit	Credit
Cash	$412,470	
Raw Materials—Fruit	6,080	
Raw Materials—Additives	8,700	
Raw Materials—Containers	6,500	
Work in Process—Extraction	7,480	
Work in Process—Mixing	9,460	
Work in Process—Packaging	18,630	
Finished Goods	13,800	
Common Stock		$180,000
Retained Earnings		232,550
Revenue		490,000
Cost of Goods Sold	341,230	
Selling and Administrative Expenses	78,200	
Total	$902,550	$902,550

Western Manufacturing Company uses a process cost system. Its products pass through two departments. Beginning inventory in Department I's Work in Process (WIP) account was $5,000. During the month the department added $13,200 of product costs to the WIP account. There were 200 units of product in beginning inventory, and 500 units were started during the month. Ending inventory consisted of 300 units 40 percent complete. Prepare a cost of production report showing the cost of goods transferred from Department I to Department II and the cost of Department I's ending work in process inventory.

Answer

Check Yourself 12–2

Cost of Production Report		
	Actual	Equivalent Units
Determination of Equivalent Units		
Beginning inventory	200	
Units added to production	500	
Total	700	
Transferred to finished goods	400	100% Complete 400
Ending inventory	300	40% Complete 120
Total	700	520
Determination of Cost per Unit		
Cost accumulation		
Beginning inventory	$ 5,000	
Product costs added	13,200	
Total product costs	$18,200	
Divide by	÷	
Equivalent units	520	
Cost per equivalent unit	$ 35	
Cost Allocation		
Transferred to Department II (400 × $35)	$14,000	
Ending WIP Inventory (120 × $35)	4,200	
Total	$18,200	

focus on International Issues

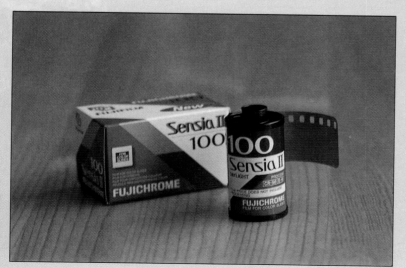

Job-Order, Process, and Hybrid Cost Systems Cross International Borders

Companies throughout the world use job-order, process, and hybrid cost systems. Fuji film, which is made in Japan, is a small, inexpensive, homogeneous product that is suitable to a process cost system. In contrast, the French Concorde is a large, expensive, heterogeneous product that is suited to a job-order cost system.

Job-order and *process cost systems* constitute the two primary methods of accounting for product cost flows in manufacturing companies. Both systems are patterned after the physical flow of products as they move through the production process. Job-order cost systems are best suited to manufacturers that make distinct products or products that are produced in distinct batches. Examples of products suited to job-order systems include buildings, ships, airplanes, and special-order batch items. A job-order cost system accumulates costs for individual products or batches of products. Each product or batch has a job identification number, and its costs are accumulated separately according to the job number. A job-order cost system requires detailed accounting information. While the total cost of all jobs is accumulated in one Work in Process Inventory control account, details regarding the cost of materials, labor, and overhead for each job are kept in subsidiary records called *job-order cost sheets*.

Process cost systems are best suited to manufacturers that make homogeneous products in a continuous production process. Examples of products suited to a process cost system include paint, gasoline, and soft drinks. A process cost system accumulates product costs for each processing department (e.g., cutting, processing, assembling, packaging). Because the units are homogeneous, the cost per unit can be determined by dividing the total processing cost by the number of units (cost averaging). Because some units are partially complete at the end of an accounting period, converting these units into equivalent whole units prior to determining the average cost per unit is necessary. The cost per equivalent whole unit is used to allocate the total processing cost among departments.

a look
back

The remaining two chapters are transitional chapters. Chapter 13 discusses financial statement analysis. Chapter 14 discusses advanced topics regarding the preparation of the statement of cash flows. Some instructors choose to cover these subjects in the financial accounting course, and other instructors cover them in the managerial accounting course. When the subjects are presented in managerial accounting, there is little agreement as to whether they should be introduced at the beginning or the end of the course. Accordingly, it is likely that you have already studied the material in the next two chapters by this point. Under the assumption that this constitutes your last chapter, the author team bids you a fond farewell. We sincerely hope this text has provided you a meaningful learning experience that will serve you well as you progress through your academic training and your ultimate career. Good luck and best wishes!

a look
forward

SELF-STUDY REVIEW PROBLEM 1

Hill Construction Company uses a job-order cost system. The company had three jobs in process at the beginning of the month. The beginning balance in the Work in Process control account was $145,400, made up of $42,400, $65,100, and $37,900 shown on the job cost sheets for Jobs 302, 303, and 304, respectively. During the month, Hill added the following materials and labor costs to each job:

Inventory	Materials	Labor
Job 302	$10,200	$32,000
Job 303	12,400	18,000
Job 304	16,500	10,000
Total	$39,100	$60,000

Overhead cost is applied at the predetermined rate of $0.60 per direct labor dollar. Actual overhead costs for the month were $36,800. Hill completed Job 303 and sold it for $129,000 cash during the month.

Required
a. Determine the balance in the Work in Process account at the end of the month.
b. Explain how the entry to close the Manufacturing Overhead account would affect the Cost of Goods Sold account.
c. Determine the amount of gross margin Hill would report on its income statement for the month.

Solution to Requirement a

Cost accumulated in the Work in Process account:

Inventory	Beg. Bal.	+	Materials	+	Labor	+	Overhead*	=	Total
Job 302	$42,400		$10,200		$32,000		$19,200		$103,800
Job 303	65,100		12,400		18,000		10,800		106,300
Job 304	37,900		16,500		10,000		6,000		70,400

*60% of direct labor cost.

Since Hill has sold Job 303, work in process at the end of the month is the sum of costs assigned to Jobs 302 and 304, $174,200 ($103,800 + $70,400).

Solution to Requirement b

Total applied overhead is $36,000 ($19,200 + $10,800 + $6,000). Since actual overhead is $36,800, overhead is underapplied by $800 ($36,800 − $36,000). Since the overhead is underapplied, cost of goods sold is understated. The entry to close the overhead account would increase the amount of cost of goods sold by $800.

Solution to Requirement c

Sales revenue	$129,000
Cost of goods sold (Job 303, $106,300 + Underapplied Overhead, $800)	(107,100)
Gross margin	$ 21,900

SELF-STUDY REVIEW PROBLEM 2

United Technology Manufacturing Company (UTMC) uses a process cost system. Products pass through two departments. The following information applies to the Assembly Department. Beginning inventory in the department's Work in Process (WIP) account was $18,400. During the month UTMC added $200,273 of product costs to the WIP account. There were 5,700 units of product in the beginning inventory and 45,300 units started during the month. The ending inventory consisted of 4,200 units, which were 30 percent complete.

Required

Prepare a cost of production report for the month.

Solution

Cost of Production Report			
		Actual	Equivalent Units
Determination of Equivalent Units			
Beginning inventory		5,700	
Units added to production		45,300	
Total		51,000	
Transferred to finished goods	100% Complete	46,800	46,800
Ending inventory	30% Complete	4,200	1,260
Total		51,000	48,060
Determination of Cost per Unit			
Cost accumulation			
Beginning inventory		$ 18,400	
Product costs added		200,273	
Total product costs		$218,673	
Divide by		÷	
Equivalent units		48,060	
Cost per equivalent unit		$4.55	
Cost Allocation			
Transferred out (46,800 × $4.55)		$212,940	
Ending WIP Inventory (1,260 × $4.55)		5,733	
Total		$218,673	

KEY TERMS

Cost per equivalent unit *503*
Equivalent whole units *503*
First-in, first-out (FIFO)
   method *503*

Hybrid cost system *492*
Job cost sheet *492*
Job-order cost system *490*

Materials requisition *492*
Process cost system *490*
Transferred-in costs *491*

Weighted average
   method *503*
Work ticket *493*

QUESTIONS

1. To what types of products is a job-order cost system best suited? Provide examples.
2. To what types of products is a process cost system best suited? Provide examples.
3. Why do both job-order and process costing require some form of cost averaging?
4. How is the unit cost of a product determined in a process cost system?
5. Ludwig Company, which normally operates a process cost system to account for the cost of the computers that it produces, has received a special order from a corporate client to produce and sell 5,000 computers. Can Ludwig use a job-order cost system to account for the costs associated with the special order even though it uses a process cost system for its normal operations?
6. Which system, a job-order or a process cost system, requires more documentation?
7. How does a materials requisition form facilitate internal control?
8. In a job-order cost system, what are the Work in Process Inventory subsidiary records called? What information is included in these subsidiary records?
9. How is indirect labor recorded in ledger accounts? How is this labor eventually assigned to the items produced in a job-order cost system?
10. How is depreciation on manufacturing equipment recorded in ledger accounts? How is this depreciation assigned to the items produced in a job-order cost system and in a process cost system?
11. Why is a process cost system not appropriate for companies that produce items that are distinctly different from one another?
12. The president of Videl Corporation tells you that her company has a difficult time determining the cost per unit of product that it makes. It seems that some units are always partially complete. Counting these units as complete understates the cost per unit because all of the units but only part of the cost is included in the unit cost computation. Conversely, ignoring the number of partially completed products overstates the cost per unit because all of the costs are included but some of the number of units are omitted from the per unit computation. How can Videl obtain a more accurate cost per unit figure?
13. Bindon Furniture Manufacturing has completed its monthly inventory count for dining room chairs and recorded the following information for ending inventory: 600 units 100 percent complete, 300 units 60 percent complete, and 100 units 20 percent complete. The company uses a process cost system to determine unit cost. Why would unit cost be inaccurate if 1,000 units were used to determine unit cost?
14. What is the weighted average method of determining equivalent units? Why is it used? What are its weaknesses?
15. What is the purpose of each of the three primary steps in a process cost system? Describe each.
16. In a process cost system, what does the term *transferred-in costs* mean? How is the amount of transferred-in costs determined?
17. The finishing department is the last of four sequential production departments for Kowalski Graphics, Inc. The company's other production departments are design, layout, and printing. The finishing department incurred the following costs in March 2006: direct materials, $40,000; direct labor, $80,000; applied overhead, $90,000; and transferred-in costs, $120,000. Which department incurred the transferred-in costs? In what month were the transferred-in costs incurred?

EXERCISES—SERIES A

EXERCISE 12–1A *Matching Products with Appropriate Cost Systems*   **L.O. 1**

Required
Indicate which cost system (job-order, process, or hybrid) would be most appropriate for the type of product listed in the left-hand column. The first item is shown as an example.

Type of Product	Type of Cost System
a. Boom box	Process
b. House	
c. Custom-made suit	
d. Van with custom features	
e. CPA review course	
f. Shirts	
g. Pots and pans	
h. Apartment building	
i. Automobile	
j. Hollywood movie	
k. Concorde aircraft	
l. Personal computer with special features	
m. Coffee table	
n. Plastic storage containers	
o. TV set	
p. Ship	

L.O. 1 **EXERCISE 12–2A** *Identifying the Appropriate Cost System*

U-Store-It, Inc., makes small aluminum storage bins that it sells through a direct marketing mail-order business. The typical bin measures 6×8 feet. The bins are normally used to store garden tools or other small household items. U-Store-It customizes bins for special-order customers by adding shelving; occasionally, it makes large bins following the unique specifications of commercial customers.

Required

Recommend the type of cost system (job-order, process, or hybrid) that U-Store-It should use. Explain your recommendation.

L.O. 1, 2 **EXERCISE 12–3A** *Job-Order or Process Cost System and a Pricing Decision*

Victor Wong, a tailor in his home country, recently immigrated to the United States. He is interested in starting a business making custom suits for men. Mr. Wong is trying to determine the cost of making a suit so he can set an appropriate selling price. He estimates that his materials cost will range from $50 to $80 per suit. Because he will make the suits himself, he assumes there will be no labor cost. Some suits will require more time than others, but Mr. Wong considers this fact to be irrelevant because he is personally supplying the labor, which costs him nothing. Finally, Mr. Wong knows that he will incur some overhead costs such as rent, utilities, advertising, packaging, delivery, and so on; however, he is uncertain as to the exact cost of these items.

Required

a. Should Mr. Wong use a job-order or a process cost system?
b. How can Mr. Wong determine the cost of suits he makes during the year when he does not know what the total overhead cost will be until the end of the year?
c. Is it appropriate for Mr. Wong to consider labor cost to be zero?
d. With respect to the overhead costs mentioned in the problem, distinguish the *manufacturing overhead* costs from the *selling and administrative* expenses. Comment on whether Mr. Wong should include the selling and administrative expenses in determining the product cost if he uses cost-plus pricing. Comment on whether the selling and administrative expenses should be included in determining the product cost for financial reporting purposes.

L.O. 2, 7 **EXERCISE 12–4A** *Job-Order Costing in a Manufacturing Company*

Liberty at Sea, Inc., builds sailboats. On January 1, 2001, the company had the following account balances: $50,000 for both cash and common stock. Boat 25 was started on February 10 and finished on May 31. To build the boat, Liberty at Sea had incurred cash costs of $6,800 for labor and $5,800 for materials. During the same period, Liberty at Sea paid $8,800 cash for actual manufacturing overhead costs. The company expects to incur $234,000 of indirect overhead cost during 2001. The overhead is allocated to jobs based on direct labor cost. The expected total labor cost for the year is $180,000.

Liberty at Sea uses a just-in-time inventory management system. Consequently, it does not have raw materials inventory. Raw materials purchases are recorded directly in the Work in Process Inventory account.

Required

a. Use the horizontal financial statements model, as illustrated here, to record Liberty at Sea's manufacturing events. In the Cash Flow column, designate the cash flows as operating activities (OA), investing activities (IA), or financing activities (FA). The first row shows beginning balances.

Assets				=	Equity					
Cash	+ Work in Process	+ Finished Goods	+ Manuf. Overhead	=	Com. Stock	+ Ret. Ear.	Rev. − Exp. = Net Inc.			Cash Flow
50,000 +	NA	+ NA	+ NA	=	50,000	+ NA	NA − NA =	NA		NA

b. If Liberty at Sea desires to earn a profit equal to 20 percent of cost, for what price should it sell the boat?

c. If the boat is not sold by year end, what amount would appear in the Work in Process Inventory and Finished Goods Inventory on the balance sheet for Boat 25?

d. Is the amount of inventory you calculated in Requirement c the actual or the estimated cost of the boat?

e. When is it appropriate to use estimated inventory cost on a year-end balance sheet?

EXERCISE 12–5A *Job-Order Costing in a Manufacturing Company*

L.O. 2, 7

Gwan Special Furniture, Inc., makes custom-order furniture to meet the needs of disabled persons. On January 1, 2002, the company had the following account balances: $35,000 for both cash and common stock. In 2002, Gwan worked on three special orders. The relevant direct operating costs follow.

	Direct Labor	Direct Materials
Job 1	$1,500	$2,000
Job 2	900	700
Job 3	3,600	1,800
Total	$6,000	$4,500

Gwan's predetermined manufacturing overhead rate was $0.40 per direct labor dollar. Actual manufacturing costs amounted to $2,379. Gwan paid cash for all costs. The company completed and delivered Jobs 1 and 2 to customers during the year. Job 3 was incomplete at the end of the year. The company sold Job 1 for $6,600 cash and Job 2 for $3,200 cash. Gwan also paid $1,500 cash for selling and administrative expenses for the year.

Gwan uses a just-in-time inventory management system. Consequently, it does not have raw materials inventory. Raw materials purchases are recorded directly in the Work in Process Inventory account.

Required

a. Record the preceding events in a horizontal statements model. In the Cash Flow column, designate the cash flow as operating activities (OA), investing activities (IA), or financing activities (FA). The first row shows beginning balances.

Assets				=	Equity					
Cash	+ Work in Process	+ Finished Goods	+ Manuf. Overhead	=	Com. Stock	+ Ret. Ear.	Rev. − Exp. = Net Inc.			Cash Flow
35,000 +	NA	+ NA	+ NA	=	35,000	+ NA	NA − NA =	NA		NA

b. Record the entry to close the amount of underapplied or overapplied overhead for the year to Cost of Goods Sold (in the expense category) in the horizontal financial statements model.

c. Determine the gross margin for the year.

EXERCISE 12–6A *Job-Order Costing in a Service Company*

L.O. 2, 7

Birchtree Condos, Inc., is a small company owned by John Walters. It leases three condos of differing sizes to customers as vacation facilities. Labor costs for each condo consist of maid service and maintenance cost. Other direct operating costs consist of interest and depreciation. The direct operating costs for each condo follow.

	Direct Labor	Other Direct Operating Costs
Condo 1	$ 9,600	$24,000
Condo 2	12,400	28,000
Condo 3	15,000	38,000
Total	$37,000	$90,000

Indirect operating expenses, which amounted to $27,000, are allocated to the condos in proportion to the amount of other direct operating costs incurred for each.

Required
a. Assuming that the amount of rent revenue from Condo 2 is $64,000, what amount of income did it earn?
b. Based on the preceding information, will the company show finished goods inventory on its balance sheet? If so, what is the amount of this inventory? If not, explain why not.

L.O. 2   EXERCISE 12–7A *Job-Order Cost System*

The following information applies to Job 730 completed by Sommers Manufacturing Company during October 2002. The amount of labor cost for the job was $89,800. Applied overhead amounted to $128,000. The project was completed and delivered to Ludwig Company at a contract price of $380,000. Sommers recognized a gross profit of $68,000 on the project.

Required
Determine the amount of raw materials used to complete Job 730.

L.O. 3   EXERCISE 12–8A *Process Cost System—Determine Equivalent Units*

Royal Furniture Company's cutting department had 400 units in its beginning work in process inventory. During the accounting period it began work on 1,800 units of product and had 550 partially complete units in its ending inventory.

Required
(Each requirement is independent of the others.)
a. Assuming the ending inventory units were 70 percent complete, determine the total number of equivalent whole units (number transferred out plus number in ending inventory) accounted for by the cutting department.
b. Assuming that the total number of equivalent whole units (number transferred out plus number in ending inventory) accounted for by the cutting department was 1,925, what was the ending inventory percentage of completion?

L.O. 3   EXERCISE 12–9A *Cost Allocation in a Process System*

Mori Watches, Inc., makes watches. Its assembly department started the accounting period with a beginning inventory balance of $21,500. During the accounting period, the department incurred $41,000 of transferred-in cost, $19,500 of materials cost, $60,000 of labor cost, and $65,400 of applied overhead cost. The department processed 3,050 total equivalent units of product during the accounting period.

Required
(Each requirement is independent of the others.)
a. Assuming that 600 equivalent units of product were in the ending work in process inventory, determine the amount of cost transferred out of the Work in Process Inventory account of the assembly department to the Finished Goods Inventory account. What was the assembly department's cost of ending work in process inventory?
b. Assuming that 2,800 units of product were transferred out of the assembly department's work in process inventory to finished goods inventory, determine the amount of the assembly department's cost of ending work in process inventory. What was the cost of the finished goods inventory transferred out of the assembly department?

L.O. 3   EXERCISE 12–10A *Process Cost System—Determine Equivalent Units and Allocate Costs*

Alpine Ski Company manufactures snow skis. During the most recent accounting period, the company's finishing department transferred 3,600 sets of skis to finished goods. At the end of the accounting period, 450 sets of skis were estimated to be 60 percent complete. Total product costs for the finishing department amounted to $541,800.

Required
a. Determine the cost per equivalent.
b. Determine the cost of the goods transferred out of the finishing department.
c. Determine the cost of the finishing department's ending work in process inventory.

chose an agreement that provides for a royalty of $0.50 per pound of seed sold. Both agreements have a 10-year term. During 2002, World Agra sold approximately 1,600,000 pounds of the Bio Labs, Inc., seed and 2,400,000 pounds of the Scientific Associates seed. Both types of seed were sold for $1.25 per pound. By the end of 2002, it was apparent that the seed developed by Scientific Associates was superior. Although insect infestation was virtually nonexistent for both types of seed, the seed developed by Scientific Associates produced corn that was sweeter and had consistently higher yields.

World Agra Distributors' chief financial officer, Roger Weatherstone, recently retired. To the astonishment of the annual planning committee, Mr. Weatherstone's replacement, Ray Borrough, adamantly recommended that the marketing department develop a major advertising campaign to promote the seed developed by Bio Labs, Inc. The planning committee reluctantly approved the recommendation. A $100,000 ad campaign was launched; the ads emphasized the ability of the Bio Labs seed to avoid insect infestation. The campaign was silent with respect to taste or crop yield. It did not mention the seed developed by Scientific Associates. World Agra's sales staff was instructed to push the Bio Labs seed and to sell the Scientific Associates seed only on customer demand. Although total sales remained relatively constant during 2003, sales of the Scientific Associates seed fell to approximately 1,300,000 pounds while sales of the Bio Labs, Inc., seed rose to 2,700,000 pounds.

Required

a. Determine the amount of increase or decrease in profitability experienced by World Agra in 2003 as a result of promoting Bio Labs seed. Support your answer with appropriate commentary.

b. Did World Agra's customers in particular and society in general benefit or suffer from the decision to promote the Bio Labs seed?

c. Review the standards of ethical conduct in Exhibit 1–13 of Chapter 1 and comment on whether Mr. Borrough's recommendation violated any of the standards in the code of ethical conduct.

d. Comment on your belief regarding the adequacy of the Standards of Ethical Conduct for Managerial Accountants to direct the conduct of management accountants.

SPREADSHEET ASSIGNMENT *Using Excel* ATC 2–6

Charlie Stork rented a truck for his business on two previous occasions. Since he will soon be renting a truck again, he would like to analyze his bills and determine how the rental fee is calculated. His two bills for truck rental show that on September 1, he drove 1,000 miles and the bill was $1,500, and on December 5, he drove 600 miles and the bill was $1,380.

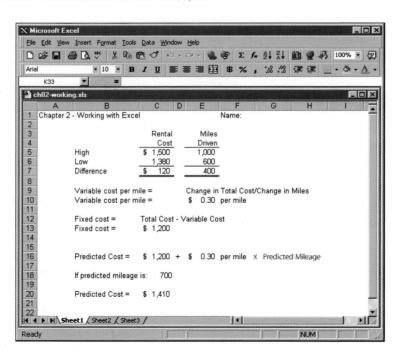

Required

Construct a spreadsheet to calculate the variable and fixed costs of this mixed cost that will allow Mr. Stork to predict his cost if he drives the truck 700 miles. The cells that show as numbers should all be

formulas except C5, C6, E5, E6, and C18. Constructing the spreadsheet in this manner will allow you to change numbers in these five cells to recalculate variable cost, fixed cost, or predicted total cost.

Spreadsheet Tip

1. To format cells to show dollar signs, commas, or both, choose Format, then Cells, then click on the tab titled Numbers, and choose Accounting.

ATC 2–7   SPREADSHEET ASSIGNMENT *Mastering Excel*

Siwa Company makes and sells a decorative ceramic statue. Each statue costs $50 to manufacture and sells for $75. Siwa spends $3 to ship the statue to customers and pays salespersons a $2 commission for each statue sold. The remaining annual expenses of operation are administrative salaries, $70,000; advertising, $20,000; and rent, $30,000. Siwa plans to sell 9,000 statues in the coming year.

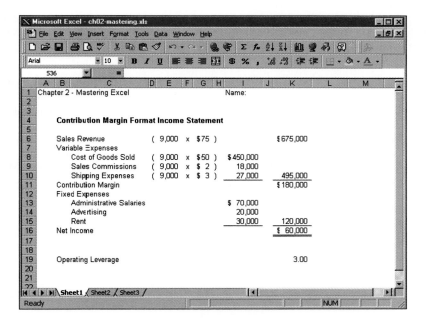

Required

Construct a spreadsheet that shows a contribution margin format income statement and that calculates operating leverage. Place formulas in the spreadsheet to allow changes to any of the preceding information to be automatically reflected in the income statement and operating leverage.

Analysis of Cost, Volume, and Pricing to Increase Profitability

Learning Objectives

After completing this chapter, you should be able to:

1 Determine the sales price of a product using a cost-plus-pricing approach.

2 Use the contribution per unit approach to calculate the break-even point.

3 Use the contribution per unit approach to calculate the sales volume required to attain a target profit.

4 Use the contribution per unit approach to assess the effects of changes in sales price, variable costs, and fixed costs.

5 Understand the concept of target pricing.

6 Consider the ethical considerations associated with misleading advertising.

7 Draw and interpret a cost-volume-profit graph.

8 Calculate the margin of safety in units, dollars, and percentages.

9 Understand how spreadsheet software can be used to conduct sensitivity analysis for cost-volume-profit relationships.

10 Conduct cost-volume-profit analysis using the contribution margin ratio and the equation method.

11 Understand the relationship between operating leverage and the break-even point.

12 Identify the limitations associated with cost-volume-profit analysis.

13 Perform multiple-product break-even analysis.
(Appendix A)

the *curious* accountant

Barbara Malki, owner of Cahaba Cycles, is considering the possibility of establishing a racing team to promote her stores. She plans to sponsor two riders, each of whom will be given a $1,200 bicycle, $200 of decorative clothing, and a $100 racing helmet. In addition, Ms. Malki plans to pay each rider $2,000 to cover the costs of travel and race entry fees. Finally, she plans to spend $5,000 for banners, water bottles, and other promotional items that will be displayed and distributed at races. The average price and costs of bicycles sold at Cahaba Cycles are $900 and $600, respectively. In trying to decide whether she should establish the team, Ms. Malki needs to know how many bicycles her company must sell to cover the costs of the promotional program. Can you provide the information she needs?

Suppose that Ms. Malki finds a bike manufacturer who agrees to cosponsor the bike team by providing free bicycles to the team members. The manufacturer's advertising decals will be displayed on the bikes, and Cahaba's decals will be displayed on the clothing. All other costs remain constant. Under these circumstances, how many bicycles must Cahaba sell to recover the cost of cosponsoring the team?

The president of Bright Day Distributors recently took a managerial accounting course. He was fascinated by the operating leverage concept. His instructor had demonstrated how a small percentage increase in sales volume could produce a significantly higher percentage increase in profitability. Unfortunately, the discussion had been limited to the effects of changes in sales volume. In practice, changes in sales volume are often related to changes in sales price. For example, cutting prices often causes increases in sales volume. Costs as well as sales frequently change. For example, increases in the advertising budget often result in increases in sales volume. Furthermore, higher levels of sales can exceed the relevant range, thereby leading to

*increases in the fixed costs such as the inventory holding costs incurred for warehouse space, personnel, and interest. Indeed, Bright Day's president discovered that increases in sales volume may even affect the company's variable costs. By increasing the size of its inventory purchases, the company could attain volume discounts that would lower its variable cost per unit. Bright Day's president quickly realized that operating leverage represented only one aspect of the business environment. He needed to know more. He needed to understand how changes in prices and costs as well as volume affects profitability. In accounting terms, Bright Day's president is interested in what is commonly called **cost-volume-profit (CVP) analysis.***

LO1 Determine the sales price of a product using a cost-plus-pricing approach.

■ Determining the Contribution Margin per Unit

The contribution margin approach for constructing an income statement introduced in the previous chapter is an extremely useful mechanism for analyzing the relationships between the CVP variables. Recall from Chapter 2 that the *contribution margin* is the difference between sales revenue and variable costs. It is a measure of the amount available to cover fixed costs and thereafter to provide profits for the enterprise. To illustrate, consider the following scenario.

Bright Day Distributors is a medium-size health food sales company. The company distributes nonprescription health food supplements including vitamins, herbs, and natural hormones through a telemarketing program in the northwestern region of the United States. Bright Day recently obtained the rights to distribute the new herb mixture Delatine. A recent research report found that Delatine slowed the aging process in laboratory animals. The research scientists speculated that the substance would have a similar effect on human subjects. Their hypothesis could not be confirmed because of the relatively long span of the human life cycle. The news media picked up the findings of the research report; as stories appeared on network news, talk shows, and in magazine, the demand for Delatine increased.

Delatine costs $24 per bottle. Bright Day uses a **cost-plus-pricing strategy;** it sets prices at cost plus a markup equal to 50 percent of cost. Accordingly, a bottle of Delatine is priced at $36 per bottle ($24 + [0.50 × $24]). The **contribution margin per unit** can be computed as follows:

Sales revenue per unit	$36
Variable cost per unit	24
Contribution margin per unit	$12

For every bottle of Delatine it sells, Bright Day earns a $12 contribution margin. Bright Day's first concern is whether it can sell enough units to produce a total contribution margin sufficient to cover fixed costs. If fixed costs were $120, it would have to sell 10 bottles (10 bottles × $12 per bottle = $120). The president made the point clear when he said, "We don't want to lose money on this product. We have to sell enough units to pay for our fixed costs." After the fixed costs have been covered, the $12 contribution margin represents the amount of dollars added to profits each time a bottle of Delatine is sold. The per unit contribution margin can be used to analyze a variety of cost-volume-profit relationships. Some of the possible applications will be discussed in the following section of this chapter.

■ Determining the Break-even Point

LO2 Use the contribution per unit approach to calculate the break-even point.

Bright Day's management team believes that enthusiasm for the product will diminish rapidly as the attention of the news media shifts to other subjects. The team is concerned about the

capacity of the company's telemarketing department to reach large segments of the population rapidly. The company simply has too few sales operators to enable rapid market penetration. Furthermore, time constraints will not permit the company to employ and train additional sales staff. Bright day needs to reach customers immediately. Accordingly, the managers decided to investigate an immediate television advertising campaign. The company's marketing manager believes that several hundred ads running on various local cable channels would be required to inform customers that they could purchase Delatine through Bright Day. The chief accountant estimates the cost of the proposed campaign to be $60,000. The company president immediately asks, "How many bottles of Delatine would have to be sold to *break even?*"

The **break-even point** is the point where *total revenue equals total costs.* A company neither earns a profit nor incurs a loss at the break-even point. Net income at breakeven is zero. Bright Day's president wants to know what sales volume (i.e., number of bottles of Delatine sold) would be required to *equate sales revenue with total cost.* The cost of the advertising campaign is fixed relative to the level of sales. The cost remains at $60,000 regardless of the number of bottles of Delatine that Bright Day sells. Since Bright Day expects to earn a $12 contribution margin for each bottle it sells, the sales volume required to break even can be calculated by dividing the fixed costs by the contribution margin per unit. The appropriate computations follow.

$$\text{Break-even volume in units} = \frac{\text{Fixed costs}}{\text{Contribution margin per unit}}$$
$$= \frac{\$60,000}{\$12} = 5,000 \text{ units}$$

The break-even point expressed in *sales dollars* can be determined by multiplying the number of units that must be sold to break even by the sales price per unit. Accordingly, the break-even point expressed in dollars is $180,000 (5,000 units $\times$ $36). The following income statement confirms these results.

Sales Revenue (5,000 units $\times$ $36)	$180,000
Total Variable Expenses (5,000 units $\times$ $24)	(120,000)
Total Contribution Margin (5,000 units $\times$ $12)	60,000
Fixed Expenses	(60,000)
Net Income	$ 0

Once fixed costs have been covered (i.e., 5,000 units have been sold), net income will increase by the amount of the *per unit contribution margin* for each additional unit sold. In other words, every bottle of Delatine sold in excess of the break-even point will add $12 to net income. Similarly, each lost sale below the break-even point will reduce the company's net income by $12. Test your comprehension of the effect of the per unit contribution margin on profitability by studying the following income statements.

	Number of Units Sold (a)				
	4,998	4,999	5,000	5,001	5,002
Sales Revenue ($36 per unit $\times$ a)	$179,928	$179,964	$180,000	$180,036	$180,072
Total Variable Expenses ($24 per unit $\times$ a)	(119,952)	(119,976)	(120,000)	(120,024)	(120,048)
Total Contribution Margin ($12 per unit $\times$ a)	$ 59,976	$ 59,988	$ 60,000	$ 60,012	$ 60,024
Fixed Expenses	(60,000)	(60,000)	(60,000)	(60,000)	(60,000)
Net Income	$ (24)	$ (12)	$ 0	$ 12	$ 24

As sales increase from 5,000 to 5,001, net income increases from zero to $12. When sales increase by one additional unit, net income again rises by $12 (i.e., moves from $12 to $24).

Income continues to increase by the $12 per unit contribution margin each time an additional unit is sold. This pattern suggests that beyond the break-even point, the effect of an increase in sales on net income can be computed quickly by multiplying the amount of the change times the contribution margin per unit. Suppose that sales increase from 5,400 to 5,600 units. How will this change affect profitability? Profits will increase by $2,400 ([5,600 − 5,400] × $12). The following comparative income statements illustrate this result.

	Number of Units Sold		200 Unit Difference
	5,400	5,600	
Sales Revenue ($36 per unit)	$194,400	$201,600	$7,200
Total Variable Expenses ($24 per unit)	(129,600)	(134,400)	(4,800)
Total Contribution Margin ($12 per unit)	64,800	67,200	2,400
Fixed Expenses	(60,000)	(60,000)	0
Net Income	$ 4,800	$ 7,200	$2,400

▮ Using the Contribution Approach to Estimate the Sales Volume Necessary to Attain a Target Profit

LO3 Use the contribution per unit approach to calculate the sales volume required to attain a target profit.

After considering Bright Day's usual return on investment target, its president decides that the campaign should produce a $40,000 profit. He asks the accountant to determine the sales volume that would be required to achieve this level of profitability. In this case, the contribution margin must be sufficient to cover the fixed cost and to provide the desired profit. The required sales volume expressed in units can be computed by dividing the amount of the fixed costs plus the desired profit by the contribution margin per unit. The appropriate computations are shown here:

$$\text{Sales volume in units} = \frac{\text{Fixed costs} + \text{Desired profit}}{\text{Contribution margin per unit}}$$
$$= \frac{\$60,000 + \$40,000}{\$12} = 8,333.33 \text{ unit}$$

The required sales volume expressed in sales dollars can be determined by multiplying this number of units by the sales price per unit. Accordingly, the level of required sales expressed in dollars is $300,000 (8,333.33 units × $36). The following income statement confirms these results; all amounts are rounded to the nearest whole dollar.

Sales Revenue (8,333.33 units × $36)	$300,000
Total Variable Expenses (8,333.33 units × $24)	(200,000)
Total Contribution Margin (8,333.33 units × $12)	100,000
Fixed Expenses	(60,000)
Net Income	$ 40,000

In practice, the company does not sell a partial bottle of Delatine. Accordingly, the accountant rounds the 8,333.33 bottles to the nearest whole unit. Recall that we are working with estimated data used for planning and decision making. Accuracy is desirable, but it is not as important as relevance. Accordingly, you should not be concerned when computations do not produce whole numbers. Rounding and approximation are common characteristics of managerial accounting data.

VolTech Company manufactures small engines that it sells for $130 each. Variable costs are $70 per unit. Fixed costs are expected to be $100,000. The management team has established a target profit of $188,000. How many engines must VolTech sell to attain the target profit?

Answer $\dfrac{\text{Sales volume}}{\text{in units}} = \dfrac{\text{Fixed costs + Desired profit}}{\text{Contribution margin per unit}} = \dfrac{\$100,000 + \$188,000}{\$130 - \$70} = 4,800 \text{ units}$

Check Yourself 3–1

Using the Contribution Approach to Estimate the Effects of Changes in Sales Price

After reviewing the accountant's computations, the president turns to the marketing manager and asks, "What are our chances of reaching a sales volume of 8,333 units?" The manager replies, "Slim to none." Indeed, the marketing manager is concerned about the possibility of reaching the 5,000 unit break-even point. She notes that Bright Day has never had a product that sold more than 4,000 bottles during its initial offering. Also, tests conducted by the telemarketing staff indicated that customers are resistant to a $36 per bottle price. The test group included many customers who had heard about the product and expressed an interest in buying it, but when they were told the price, they consistently rejected the offer. Based on similar products, the marketing manager believes that customers would be willing to pay $28 per bottle for Delatine. The company president immediately asks how the change in sales price will affect the sales volume required to produce the $40,000 target profit.

LO4 Use the contribution per unit approach to assess the effects of changes in sales price, variable costs, and fixed costs.

Changing the sales price from $36 to $28 will have a significant effect on the contribution margin. Recall that the original contribution margin was $12 per unit ($36 − $24). The contribution margin will drop to a mere $4 per unit if the sales price is reduced to $28 per bottle ($28 sales price − $24 cost per bottle = $4 contribution margin per bottle). The significant drop in contribution margin per unit will cause a dramatic increase in the sales volume necessary to attain the target profit. The appropriate computations are shown here.

$$\text{Sales volume in units} = \frac{\text{Fixed costs + Desired profit}}{\text{Contribution margin per unit}}$$

$$= \frac{\$60,000 + \$40,000}{\$4} = 25,000 \text{ units}$$

The required sales volume expressed in sales dollars can be determined by multiplying the preceding number of units by the sales price per unit. Accordingly, the requires sales volume *expressed in dollars* is $700,000 (25,000 units × $28). The following income statement confirms these results.

Sales Revenue (25,000 units × $28)	$700,000
Total Variable Expenses (25,000 units × $24)	(600,000)
Total Contribution Margin (25,000 units × $4)	100,000
Fixed Expenses	(60,000)
Net Income	$ 40,000

The marketing manager concludes that it would be impossible to sell 25,000 bottles of Delatine at any price. She suggests that the company drop its cost-plus-pricing strategy and replace it with a new approach called *target pricing*. **Target pricing** begins with the determination of a price at which a product will sell and then focuses on developing that product with a cost structure that will satisfy market demands. Since the target price leads to a

LO5 Understand the concept of target pricing.

o real-world companies use *target pricing?* According to C. Michael Armstrong, CEO of AT&T, target costing is a very real business practice. Indeed, Mr. Armstrong suggests that an unreasonable target price is the chief cause of AT&T's decision to delay the widespread deployment of a new local phone service technology. The new "Project Angel" system uses radio technology to bypass the wires of the Baby Bell phone companies. Unfortunately, the cost of deploying the technology in a test site in Chicago averaged $1,100 per home. Although this cost is prohibitive, AT&T still plans to continue testing the project. According to Mr. Armstrong, "It'll probably take two more cycles of technology" before costs drop to a level that will enable AT&T to offer the system at a competitive price.

Source: Peter Elstrom, "AT&T's Fallen Angel," *Business Week,* April 13, 1998, p. 4.

target cost, this market-based pricing strategy is also called **target costing.** It focuses on the design stage of product development. Given the target price of $28 per bottle, the issue is how to design the product *at a cost* that will enable Bright Day to earn its desired profit of $40,000. Fortunately, the marketing manager had some suggestions.

▋Using the Contribution Approach to Estimate the Effects of Changes in Variable Costs

LO4 Use the contribution per unit approach to assess the effects of changes in sales price, variable costs, and fixed costs.

The manufacturer has agreed to provide Delatine to Bright Day in two additional packaging formats. The current cost is $24 for a bottle containing 100 capsules of 90 milligram (mg) strength. The two new alternatives are (1) a bottle costing $12 that contains 100 capsules of 30 mg strength and (2) a bottle costing $3 that contains 100 capsules of only 5 mg of Delatine mixed with a vitamin C compound. This dosage is the minimum allowable to support a packaging label indicating that the product contains Delatine. The marketing manager observes that both options would enable Bright Day to sell Delatine at a price that customers would be willing to pay.

LO6 Consider the ethical considerations associated with misleading advertising.

The president vehemently rejected the second option. He called the proposal a blatant attempt to deceive customers by suggesting they were buying Delatine when in fact they were getting vitamin C. *He considered the idea to be unethical and dangerous.* He ended his tirade with the statement that he would not be seen on the six o'clock news trying to defend a fast-buck scheme while his company's reputation went up in smoke. After allowing himself a few minutes to calm down, he said that the first option appeared to have some merit. The appropriate dosage for Delatine was uncertain; customers who wanted to take 90 mg per day could take three capsules instead of one. He turned to the accountant and asked, "What's the effect on the bottom line?"

The change in the variable cost (cost per bottle) from $24 to $12 per bottle has a dramatic effect on the level of sales volume required to produce the target profit. The contribution margin per unit shifts from $4 per bottle ($28 sales price − $24 variable cost per bottle) to $16 per bottle ($28 sales price − $12 variable cost per bottle). The significant increase in contribution margin per unit results in a dramatic decrease in the sales volume necessary to attain the target profit. The appropriate computations are shown here.

Healthy people or healthy profits? If you were president of a major drug manufacturing company, which would you choose? Long-term studies for the treatment of high blood pressure suggest that the cheapest medications available (beta blockers and diuretics) are more effective and safer than more expensive ones. Even so, a survey of drug ads in the *New England Journal of Medicine* reveals an advertising program that advocates the use of more expensive medications (calcium-channel blockers and ACE inhibitors). The most aggressively marketed are the high-priced, high-profit calcium-channel blockers. This marketing effort persists despite the fact that studies have linked these drugs to an increased risk of heart attack, cancer, and suicide. Why are the drug companies interested in selling these drugs? Could it have something to do with the fact that calcium-channel blockers have a price of more than three times that of diuretics? The marketing campaign appears to be working. Between 1992 and 1995, sales of calcium-channel blockers increased by approximately 15 percent while that of diuretics dropped by 50 percent. One study suggests that the shift to the more expensive drugs is adding approximately $3 billion in unnecessary expenditures to the national medical bill. Healthy people, or healthy profits? Practicing high ethical standards in business is not always an easy task. Keep in mind, however, that shortcuts to high profitability are filled with booby traps. A class action lawsuit could easily wipe out any benefit attained by unscrupulous business practices. The demise of the silicone breast implant industry stands as a clear example.

Source: Catherine Arnst, "Is Good Marketing Bad Medicine?" *Business Week,* April 13, 1998, p. 62. The opinions regarding the ethical implications are those of the authors of this text.

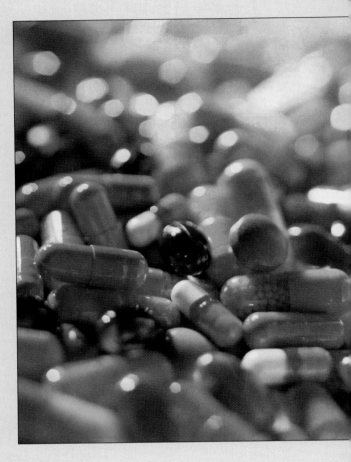

$$\text{Sales volume in units} = \frac{\text{Fixed costs} + \text{Desired profit}}{\text{Contribution margin per unit}}$$

$$= \frac{\$60,000 + \$40,000}{\$16} = 6,250 \text{ units}$$

The required sales volume expressed in sales dollars can be determined by multiplying this number of units by the sales price per unit. Accordingly, the level of sales *expressed in dollars* required to produce the desired profit is $175,000 (6,250 units × $28). The following income statement confirms these amounts.

Sales Revenue (6,250 units × $28)	$175,000
Total Variable Expenses (6,250 units × $12)	(75,000)
Total Contribution Margin (6,250 units × $16)	100,000
Fixed Expenses	(60,000)
Net Income	$ 40,000

Although the drop in required sales from 25,000 units to 6,250 was truly significant, the marketing manager still felt uneasy about the company's ability to sell 6,250 bottles of Delatine. She restated the argument that the company had no other product that produced sales

The number of bikes that must be sold to cover the cost of sponsoring the bike team can be determined by dividing the fixed cost of the promotional campaign by the contribution margin per bike. The contribution margin per bike is $300 ($900 − 600). In the first case, in which Cahaba Cycles acts as the sole sponsor, the number of bikes that must be sold to cover the cost of the promotional campaign is computed as follows:

Bicycle	$1,200
Clothing	200
Helmet	100
Travel and fees	2,000
Cost per biker	$3,500 × 2 = $ 7,000
Promotional items	5,000
Total fixed cost	$12,000 ÷ $300 Contri-bution margin = 40 bikes

If the team is cosponsored, Cahaba will save the fixed cost of two bicycles ($1,200 × 2 = $2,400). Accordingly, total fixed cost will drop to $9,600 ($12,000 − $2,400). Since the price and variable cost of bikes sold to customers do not change, the contribution margin remains constant at $300. The number of bikes that must be sold to cover the new level of fixed costs is as follows:

$$\text{Total fixed cost} = \$9,600 \div \$300 \text{ Contribution margin}$$
$$= 32 \text{ bikes}$$

of that magnitude. The accountant suggested that considerable savings could be obtained by using a series of radio rather than television commercials. While gathering cost data for the TV campaign, the accountant had conferred with account executives of radio companies who had assured him that they could equal the TV audience exposure at about half the cost of the televised ads. Even though the TV ads would likely be more effective, he argued that since radio advertising costs would be half those of TV, the desired profit could be attained at a significantly lower volume of sales. The company president was impressed with the possibilities. He asked the accountant to determine the required sales volume, assuming that advertising costs were cut from $60,000 to $30,000.

▌Using the Contribution Approach to Estimate the Effects of Changes in Fixed Costs

LO4 Use the contribution per unit approach to assess the effects of changes in sales price, variable costs, and fixed costs.

Changing the fixed costs from $60,000 to $30,000 will dramatically affect the sales level required to earn the target profit. Since the contribution margin will cover a lower amount of fixed costs, the sales volume required to reach the desired profit is significantly reduced. The appropriate computations are shown here.

$$\textbf{Sales volume in units} = \frac{\textbf{Fixed costs + Desired profit}}{\textbf{Contribution margin per unit}}$$
$$= \frac{\$30,000 + \$40,000}{\$16} = \textbf{4,375 units}$$

The required sales volume expressed in sales dollars can be determined by multiplying this number of units by the sales price per unit. Accordingly, the level of sales *expressed in dollars* required to produce the desired profit is $122,500 (4,375 units × $28). The following income statement confirms these amounts.

Sales Revenue (4,375 units × $28)	$122,500
Total Variable Expenses (4,375 units × $12)	(52,500)
Total Contribution Margin (4,375 units × $16)	70,000
Fixed Expenses	(30,000)
Net Income	$ 40,000

The marketing manager voiced her approval. Obviously, she could not guarantee any specific sales volume, but she felt confident that sales figures would fall within a range of 4,000 to 5,000 units.

▌Using the Cost-Volume Profit Graph

To further analyze the revised expectations, the accountant had his staff prepare a chart to depict cost-volume-profit (CVP) relationships over the range of sales activity from zero to 6,000 units. The accountant gave his staff the following instructions that were used to produce the CVP graph (sometimes called a *break-even chart*) shown in Exhibit 3–1.

LO7 Draw and interpret a cost-volume-profit graph.

1. *Draw the Axis:* Activity is expressed in units along the horizontal axis and in dollars along the vertical axis.
2. *Draw the Fixed Cost Line:* Fixed costs are constant for all levels of activity. To represent this relationship, a horizontal line is drawn across the graph at the dollar amount of fixed cost. In this case, the horizontal line is drawn at the $30,000 level.
3. *Draw the Total Cost Line:* A diagonal line representing total cost is drawn by selecting some arbitrary level of activity expressed in units and making the following computations. To determine the total variable cost, multiply the selected volume of activity by the variable cost per unit. Add the total variable cost to the total fixed cost. The result is the amount of total cost at the selected level of activity. This point is plotted on the graph. A line starting from the vertical axis at the level of fixed cost is drawn through this point. For example, using a volume of activity of 6,000 units, the total cost amounts to $102,000 ([6,000 units $\times$ $12] + $30,000 fixed cost). A point is plotted at the coordinates of $102,000 and 6,000 units. Another point is plotted at the level of fixed cost and the zero level of activity ($30,000 at zero units). A straight line representing total cost is drawn through these two points.
4. *Draw the Sales Line:* Draw the revenue line by using a procedure similar to that described for drawing the total cost line. Select some arbitrary level of activity expressed in units and multiply that figure by the sales price per unit. Plot the result on the graph and draw a line from the zero origin through this point. For example, using a volume of activity of 6,000 units, the revenue point is $168,000 (6,000 units $\times$ $28). Plot a point at the coordinates of $168,000 and 6,000 units. Drawing a line from the zero origin to the plotted point establishes the revenue line that completes the graph.

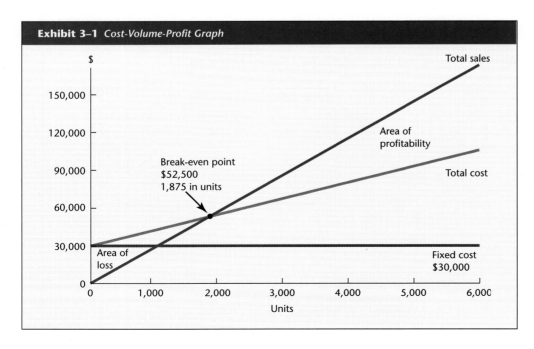

Exhibit 3–1 *Cost-Volume-Profit Graph*

You should trace these procedures to the graph shown in Exhibit 3–1 to ensure your understanding of how to construct a CVP chart.

▌Calculating the Margin of Safety

LO8 Calculate the margin of safety in units, dollars, and percentages.

The final meeting of the management team focused on a discussion of the reliability of the data used to construct the CVP chart. The accountant opened the discussion by calling attention to the sales volume figures under the area of profitability. Recall that 4,375 bottles of Delatine must be sold to earn the company's desired profit. Measured in dollars, budgeted sales amount to $122,500 (4,375 bottles × $28 per bottle). The accountant highlighted the wide gap between this level of budgeted sales and the break-even point. The amount of this gap, called the *margin of safety,* can be measured in number of units or in sales dollars. The appropriate computations are shown here:

	In Units	In Dollars
Budgeted sales	4,375	$122,500
Break-even sales	(1,875)	(52,500)
Margin of safety	2,500	$ 70,000

The **margin of safety** is a measure of the cushion between budgeted sales and the break-even point. Thus, it provides a measure of the extent to which actual sales can fall below budgeted sales before the company reaches its break-even point.

To facilitate comparisons between products or companies of different sizes, the margin of safety can be expressed as a percentage by dividing the margin of safety by the amount of the budgeted sales volume.[1] The appropriate computations are shown here:

$$\text{Margin of safety} = \frac{\text{Budgeted sales} - \text{Break-even sales}}{\text{Budgeted sales}}$$

$$\text{Margin of safety} = \frac{\$122,500 - \$52,500}{\$122,500} \times 100 = 57.14\%$$

This analysis suggests that actual sales would have to fall short of expected sales by more than 57.14 percent before Bright Day would experience a loss. This large a margin of safety suggests that undertaking the proposed radio advertising program for bottles of the 30mg Delatine capsules has minimal risk.

Check Yourself 3–2

Suppose that Bright Day is considering the possibility of selling a protein supplement that will cost Bright Day $5 per bottle. Bright Day believes that it can sell 4,000 bottles of the supplement for $25 per bottle. Fixed costs associated with selling the supplement are expected to be $42,000. Does the supplement have a wider margin of safety than Delatine?

Answer Calculate the break-even point for the protein supplement.

$$\text{Break-even volume in units} = \frac{\text{Fixed costs}}{\text{Contribution margin per unit}} = \frac{\$42,000}{\$25 - \$5} = 2,100 \text{ units}$$

Calculate the margin of safety. Note that the margin of safety expressed as a percentage can be calculated using the number of units or sales dollars. Using either units or dollars yields the same percentage.

$$\text{Margin of safety} = \frac{\text{Budgeted sales} - \text{Break-even sales}}{\text{Budgeted sales}} = \frac{4,000 - 2,100}{4,000} = 47.5\%$$

The margin of safety for Delatine (57.14 percent) exceeds that for the protein supplement (47.5 percent). This suggests that Bright Day is less likely to incur losses selling Delatine than selling the supplement.

[1]The margin of safety percentage can be computed for actual as well as budgeted sales. For example, an analyst may want to compare the margins of safety of two companies under current operating conditions. In this case, actual sales would be substituted for budgeted sales. The formula for computing the margin of safety percentages would be ([Actual sales − Break-even sales] ÷ Actual sales).

Performing Sensitivity Analysis Using Spreadsheet Software

The *margin of safety* focuses on the vulnerability of profits to a decline in sales volume. Other factors could threaten profitability as well. For example, profits decline if costs increase. Safety margins could be determined for fixed and variable costs as well as sales volume. The disadvantage of the margin of safety approach is that is constitutes a unidimensional analysis when profits are subject to multidimensional forces. What happens to profitability if the level of fixed cost is higher than expected but variable costs are lower than expected? What if sales volume is higher than expected as are costs? Fortunately, spreadsheet software is highly efficient for analyzing "what-if" questions such as these. Exhibit 3–2 provides an example of an *Excel* spreadsheet report that permits management to assess the sensitivity of profits to simultaneous changes in fixed cost, variable cost, and sales volume. The report is based on data regarding Bright Day's proposed project for marketing Delatine. Recall that the accountant estimated the cost of the radio campaign to be $30,000. The report provides profitability projections that permit considering conditions in which advertising costs fall to $20,000 or rise to $40,000. Likewise, the effects of potential changes in variable cost and sales volume can be investigated.

The range of scenarios described in the report is impressive, but it represents only a few of the many alternatives that can be analyzed with a few quick keystrokes. The spreadsheet program recalculates profitability figures instantly when one of the variables changes. Suppose that someone asks, "What would happen if we sold 10,000 units?" The accountant merely replaces one of the sales volume figures with the new number, and revised profitability numbers appear instantly. By changing the variables, management can get a real feel for the sensitivity of profits to changes in cost and volume for the project that is under consideration. Investigating a multitude of what-if questions regarding simultaneous changes in fixed cost, variable cost, and volume is called **sensitivity analysis.**

LO9 Understand how spreadsheet software can be used to conduct sensitivity analysis for cost-volume-profit relationships.

Exhibit 3–2 *Spreadsheet Report to Facilitate "What-If" Analysis*

If Fixed Cost Is	While Variable Cost Is	And Sales Volume Is — Then Profitability Will Be				
		2,000	3,000	4,000	5,000	6,000
$20,000	11	14000	31000	48000	65000	82000
20,000	12	12000	28000	44000	60000	76000
20,000	13	10000	25000	40000	55000	70000
30,000	11	4000	21000	38000	55000	72000
30,000	12	2000	18000	34000	50000	66000
30,000	13	0	15000	30000	45000	60000
40,000	11	-6000	11000	28000	45000	62000
40,000	12	-8000	8000	24000	40000	56000
40,000	13	-10000	5000	20000	35000	50000

■ Assessing the Pricing Strategy

After reviewing the spreadsheet report, Bright Day's management team is convinced that it should proceed with the radio campaign for Delatine. Only under the most dire circumstances (i.e., if actual sales fall significantly below expectations while costs increase at rates well above expectations) will the company incur a loss. Indeed, the president feels uneasy because the figures simply look too good to be true. If Bright Day pays $12 per bottle for Delatine and sells it for $28 per bottle as projected, the effective markup on cost would be 133 percent ([$28 − $12] ÷ $12). Recall that the company's normal markup is only 50 percent of cost. The president asks the marketing manager, "Are you sure people will buy this stuff at that price?"

The marketing manager explains that the pricing practice she is advocating is a recognized strategy known as **prestige pricing.** According to this concept, many people are fascinated with new technologies. They are willing to pay a premium to be the first to obtain and use a new product, especially when its introduction receives widespread news media attention, as is the case with Delatine. Similarly, people may be willing to pay more for a product because it carries a prestigious brand name. The marketing manager reminds the president that although the price spread for Delatine is unusually wide, the company has introduced other products at cost-plus margins that were considerably higher than the average 50 percent markup. Indeed, many of its current products sell at above average margins. Certainly, news coverage for Delatine will dissipate, competitors will offer alternatives, and customer interest will wane. That will be the time to reduce prices. The marketing manager is confident that the product will sell initially at the proposed price.

■ Using the Contribution Approach to Assess the Effect of Simultaneous Changes in CVP Variables

LO4 Use the contribution per unit approach to assess the effects of changes in sales price, variable costs, and fixed costs.

In a previous section of this chapter, we discussed the use of sensitivity analysis as a means to analyze the effects of simultaneous changes in CVP variables. On occasion, managers may desire to analyze the impact of simultaneous changes without the availability of computer technology. The contribution approach that has been illustrated to analyze unidimensional CVP relationships can also be used to study the effects of simultaneous changes in CVP variables. The approach offers simple and quick results in a low-technology environment. To illustrate several possible scenarios, assume that Bright Day has developed the following budgeted income statement.

Sales Revenue (4,375 units × $28 sale price)	$122,500
Total Variable Expenses (4,375 units × $12 cost per bottle)	(52,500)
Total Contribution Margin (4,375 units × $16)	70,000
Fixed Expenses	(30,000)
Net Income	$ 40,000

A Decrease in Sales Price Accompanied by an Increase in Sales Volume

Suppose that the marketing manager believes that sales will increase by 625 units if the price per bottle of Delatine is reduced to $25. Under these circumstances, the per unit contribution margin drops to $13 ($25 sales price − $12 cost per bottle). The expected number of units sold increases to 5,000 (4,375 + 625). Should Bright Day reduce the price? To answer this question, compare the profit earned under the existing circumstances with the

profit that will exist under the new circumstances. In this case, the expected profit is computed as follows:

$$\text{Profit} = \text{Contribution margin} - \text{Fixed cost}$$
$$\text{Profit} = (5,000 \times \$13) - \$30,000 = \$35,000$$

Since budgeted income falls from \$40,000 to \$35,000, the suggestion to reduce the sales price should be rejected.

An Increase in Fixed Cost Accompanied by an Increase in Sales Volume

Return to the original data set for the budgeted income statement. In summary, the company expects to sell 4,375 units of Delatine for \$28 per bottle. Variable costs are expected to be \$12 per bottle, and fixed costs are budgeted at \$30,000. Suppose that the management team believes that sales can be increased to 6,000 units if the company pays an additional \$12,000 to advertise its product. The contribution margin per unit will remain unchanged at \$16 (i.e., \$28 − \$12). Should the company incur the additional advertising cost, thereby increasing fixed costs to \$42,000? Based on these figures, the expected profit is as follows:

$$\text{Profit} = \text{Contribution margin} - \text{Fixed cost}$$
$$\text{Profit} = (6,000 \times \$16) - \$42,000 = \$54,000$$

Since budgeted income increases from \$40,000 to \$54,000, Bright Day should seek to increase sales through additional advertising.

A Simultaneous Reduction in Sales Price, Fixed Costs, Variable Costs, and Sales Volume.

Return again to the data set for the original budget. Recall that the company expects to sell 4,375 units of Delatine for \$28 per bottle, and variable cost are expected to be \$12 per bottle. Fixed costs are budgeted at \$30,000. Suppose that Bright Day is able to negotiate a \$4 reduction in the cost of a bottle of Delatine. The management team wants to consider passing on some of the savings to its customers by reducing the sales price to \$25 per bottle. Furthermore, the team believes that advertising costs can be reduced by \$8,000 without seriously affecting sales volume. Sales are expected to fall to 4,200 units because of the reduction in advertising. Additional reductions in demand are not expected, however, because the decrease in the sales price is expected to increase demand by some customers. Should Bright Day proceed with the plan to reduce prices and advertising costs?

Under the revised operating scenario, sales volume would decline to 4,200 units. The contribution margin would increase to \$17 per bottle (\$25 new selling price − \$8 new variable cost per bottle), and fixed cost would fall to \$22,000 (\$30,000 − \$8,000). Based on these figures, the expected profit is as follows.

$$\text{Profit} = \text{Contribution margin} - \text{Fixed cost}$$
$$\text{Profit} = (4,200 \times \$17) - \$22,000 = \$49,400$$

Because budgeted income increases from \$40,000 to \$49,400, Bright Day should proceed with the new operating strategy.

Many other possible scenarios could be considered. However, it should be clear at this point that the contribution approach can be used to analyze independent or simultaneous changes in the CVP variables. Two alternative approaches to CVP analysis, the contribution margin ratio approach and the equation approach, will be introduced in the following sections of this chapter.

▪ Calculating Cost-Volume-Profit (CVP) Analysis Using the Contribution Margin Ratio

LO10 Conduct cost-volume-profit analysis using the contribution margin ratio and the equation method.

When the contribution margin is expressed as a percentage of the sales price, the result is called the **contribution margin ratio.** To illustrate, assume that Bright Day is considering the possibility of selling a new product called Multi Minerals. The expected sales price, variable cost, and contribution margin per unit are shown here:

Sales revenue per unit	$20
Variable cost per unit	12
Contribution margin per unit	$ 8

Based on these data, the *contribution margin ratio* for Multi Minerals is 40 percent ($8 ÷ $20). This ratio suggests that every dollar of sales provides 40 cents ($1 × 0.40) to cover fixed costs. After fixed costs have been covered, each dollar of sales provides 40 cents of profit. Like the *per unit contribution margin,* the *contribution margin ratio* can be used to analyze CVP relationships. The results are identical with the exception that the per unit contribution margin produces a sales volume measured in units while the contribution margin ratio yields a sales volume figure measured in dollars. As such, the two approaches merely represent different means of arriving at the same conclusion. To demonstrate, we calculate the break-even point, assuming that the company expects to incur $24,000 of fixed expenses to market the product. The computations under the alternative approaches follow.

Per Unit Contribution Approach **Break-even in Units**	**Contribution Ratio Approach** **Break-even in Dollars**
$\dfrac{\text{Fixed costs}}{\text{Contribution margin per unit}} = \text{Units}$ $\dfrac{\$24,000}{\$8} = 3,000 \text{ units}$	$\dfrac{\text{Fixed costs}}{\text{Contribution margin ratio}} = \text{Dollars}$ $\dfrac{\$24,000}{40\%} = \$60,000$

Converting the break-even point expressed in units to one expressed in sales dollars demonstrates that the two approaches lead to the same results. Mathematically, 3,000 units × $20 = $60,000. Likewise, the break-even point expressed in sales dollars can be converted to units ($60,000 ÷ $20 = 3,000). Accordingly, it should be clear that the two approaches represent different views of the same data set. The similarities and differences between the two approaches hold when other CVP variables are added or changed. For example, the sales volume necessary to reach a target profit of $8,000 under the two approaches is computed as follows:

Per Unit Contribution Approach **Sales Volume in Units**	**Contribution Ratio Approach** **Sales Volume in Dollars**
$\dfrac{\text{Fixed costs} + \text{Desired profit}}{\text{Contribution margin per unit}} = \text{Units}$ $\dfrac{\$24,000 + \$8,000}{\$8} = 4,000 \text{ units}$	$\dfrac{\text{Fixed costs} + \text{Desired profit}}{\text{Contribution margin ratio}} = \text{Dollars}$ $\dfrac{\$24,000 + \$8,000}{40\%} = \$80,000$

Once again, multiplying the $20 sales price by the sales volume expressed in units equates to the sales volume expressed in dollars ($20 × 4,000 = $80,000). Because both approaches yield the same results, the method to use is a matter of personal preference. However, to ensure your ability to communicate in a variety of potential circumstances, we encourage you to experiment with both approaches. Indeed, you should also master a third alternative, the *equation method,* which is discussed in the following section.

∎ Performing Cost-Volume-Profit Analysis Using the Equation Method

The **equation method** begins with the expression of the break-even point in terms of an algebraic equation. This equation is shown here.[2]

$$\text{Sales} = \text{Variable cost} + \text{Fixed cost}$$

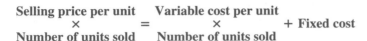

LO10 Conduct cost-volume-profit analysis using the contribution margin ratio and the equation method.

The break-even point expressed in terms of sales volume (i.e., number of units) can be determined by restating the formula as indicated here:

$$\frac{\text{Selling price per unit}}{\text{Number of units sold}} = \frac{\text{Variable cost per unit}}{\text{Number of units sold}} + \text{Fixed cost}$$

Using the Multi Minerals $20 sales price, $12 variable cost, and $24,000 fixed cost, the *break-even point* computed *in number of units* is as follows:

$$\$20 \times \text{Units} = \$12 \times \text{Units} + \$24,000$$
$$\$8 \times \text{Units} = \$24,000$$
$$\text{Units} = 3,000$$

The break-even sales volume expressed in units can be converted into break-even sales volume expressed in dollars by multiplying the sales price per unit by the number of units sold. The *break-even point* for Bright Day expressed *in number of dollars* is as follows.

$$\text{Selling price per unit} \times \text{Number of units sold} = \text{Sales volume in dollars}$$
$$\$20 \quad\quad \times \quad\quad 3,000 \quad\quad = \quad\quad \$60,000$$

The equation method can also be used to analyze additional CVP relationships. For example, the sales volume necessary to attain a target profit of $8,000 can be computed as follows:

$$\frac{\text{Selling price per unit}}{\text{Number of units sold}} = \frac{\text{Variable cost per unit}}{\text{Number of units sold}} + \text{Fixed cost} + \text{Desired profit}$$

The computations are shown here.

$$\$20 \times \text{Units} = \$12 \times \text{Units} + \$24,000 + \$8,000$$
$$\$8 \times \text{Units} = \$32,000$$
$$\text{Units} = 4,000$$

By comparing these results with those determined using the per unit contribution approach and the contribution margin ratio approach, it should be apparent that the equation method is simply another way to achieve the same result. Again, the method you use will depend on your personal preferences and those of the management team you encounter on the job. As a student seeking entry into an unknown work environment, you should familiarize yourself with as many of the alternatives as possible.

---

[2]The equation method results in the same computation as the per unit contribution margin approach. As proof, consider the following. Under the per unit contribution margin approach, the break-even point is determined as follows (X equals the break-even point in units):

$$X = \text{Fixed cost} \div \text{Per unit contribution margin}$$

Under the equation method, the break-even point is determined as follows (X equals the break-even point in units):

$$\text{Unit sales price } (X) = \text{Variable cost per unit } (X) + \text{Fixed cost}$$
$$(\text{Unit sales price} - \text{Variable cost per unit})(X) = \text{Fixed cost}$$
$$\text{Per unit contribution margin } (X) = \text{Fixed cost}$$
$$X = \text{Fixed cost} \div \text{Per unit contribution margin}$$

Check Yourself 3–3

Recall the information presented in Check Yourself 3–1. VolTech Company manufactures small engines that it sells for $130 each, with variable costs of $70 per unit, expected fixed costs of $100,000, and a target profit of $188,000. Use the equation method to calculate the number of engines VolTech must sell to attain the target profit.

Answer

$$\begin{array}{c} \text{Selling price per unit} \\ \times \\ \text{Number of units sold} \end{array} = \begin{array}{c} \text{Variable cost per unit} \\ \times \\ \text{Number of units sold} \end{array} + \text{Fixed cost} + \text{Desired profit}$$

$$\$130 \times \text{Units} = \$70 \times \text{Units} + \$100,000 + \$188,000$$
$$\$60 \times \text{Units} = \$288,000$$
$$\text{Units} = 4,800$$

This is the same result determined in Check Yourself 3–1 exercise. The only difference is in the method used to make the computation.

■ Operating Leverage and the Break-even Point

LO11 Understand the relationship between operating leverage and the break-even point.

From the previous discussion, it should be clear that the contribution margin first covers fixed costs and then provides profit to an enterprise. Until it reaches the break-even point, a company will incur losses because the contribution margin is insufficient to cover the fixed expenses. For example, assume that Bright Day decides to sell Multi Minerals. Recall that the sales price is $20 per bottle, variable cost is $12 per bottle, and fixed costs are $24,000. If Bright Day sells only one bottle, the contribution margin will be $8 ($20 sales price − $12 variable cost). At this point, the company will incur a $23,992 loss ($8 contribution margin − $24,000 fixed cost). With each additional unit sold, losses will decrease by $8. Once sales reach the break-even point, each additional unit sold will contribute $8 to profitability. Accordingly, losses will decline as sales move toward the break-even point and net income will increase as sales move beyond it. These relationships provide useful insight into the behavior of **operating leverage.** Recall that the formula for determining the magnitude of operating leverage is as follows.

$$\text{Operating leverage} = \frac{\text{Total contribution margin}}{\text{Net income (loss)}}$$

The total contribution margin increases proportionally with increases in sales. Accordingly, the numerator increases as the volume of sales increases. The denominator in the equation decreases as sales approach the break-even point and increases thereafter. *This relationship means that the magnitude of operating leverage increases as sales approach the break-even point and decreases thereafter.* To illustrate, review the comparative income statements for Multi Minerals at different levels of sales shown in Exhibit 3–3.

Exhibit 3–3 *Comparative Income Statements*

	Units Sold (a)				
	2,430	2,700	3,000	3,300	3,630
Sales Revenue ($20 × a)	$48,600	$54,000	$60,000	$66,000	$72,600
Variable Cost ($12 × a)	(29,160)	(32,400)	(36,000)	(39,600)	(43,560)
Contribution Margin (b)	19,440	21,600	24,000	26,400	29,040
Fixed Cost	(24,000)	(24,000)	(24,000)	(24,000)	(24,000)
Net Income (c)	$ (4,560)	$ (2,400)	$ 0	$ 2,400	$ 5,040
Magnitude of Operating Leverage (b ÷ c)	4.26	9		11	5.76

When sales increase from 3,300 units to 3,630, the table indicates a 10 percent increase in sales volume (3,630 units − 3,300 units = 330 units ÷ 3,330 units = 10 percent). The 10 percent increase in sales produces a 110 percent increase in net income (10 percent × 11 magnitude = 110 percent). As proof, note that the corresponding $2,640 ($5,040 − $2,400) increase in net income does, in fact, represent a 110 percent increase (i.e., $2,640 ÷ $2,400). An additional 10 percent increase in sales produces only a 57.6 percent increase in net income. You may choose to perform additional validation tests to enhance your understanding.

The magnitude of operating leverage can have a significant impact on the decision-making process. Companies operating at or near the break-even point can increase profitability dramatically by achieving small changes in sales volume. Accordingly, these companies should focus their attention on activities that increase sales, such as training sessions to motivate the sales team, advertising campaigns, and promotional incentives. In contrast, companies operating at levels of activity that are far from the break-even point are not likely to benefit from small changes in sales volume. These companies should not focus on promoting increased sales; instead, they should direct their attention to cost control or new product development. In other words, working smart is just as important as working hard. Developing appropriate priorities is an essential element of learning how to work smart in business practice.

∎ Recognizing Cost-Volume-Profit Limitations

The accuracy of cost-volume-profit analysis is limited because it assumes a strictly linear relationship among the variables. True linearity among actual CVP variables is the exception rather than the norm. For example, suppose that a business receives a volume discount on materials that it purchases. The more material it purchases, the lower its cost per unit. In this case, the cost varies but not in direct proportion to the amount of material purchased. The relationship is not linear. Similarly, fixed costs can change. A supervisor's salary that is thought to be fixed may change if the supervisor receives a raise. Likewise, amounts charged for telephone, rent, insurance, taxes, and so on may increase or decrease. In practice, fixed costs frequently fluctuate. Accordingly, the relationships are not strictly linear.

LO12 Identify the limitations associated with cost-volume-profit analysis.

CVP assumes that factors such as worker efficiency are constant over the range of the activity analyzed. Businesses frequently are able to increase productivity, thereby reducing variable or fixed costs. Indeed, many large consulting companies devote their efforts to improving efficiency and reducing cost (see GE advertisement on the following page). CVP formulas are not constructed to allow for such changes in efficiency.

Finally, the analytical techniques assume that the level of inventory does not change during the period. In other words, sales and production are assumed to be equal. CVP formulas are used to provide the estimated number of units that must be *produced and sold* to attain break-even status or to achieve some designated target profit. Producing or acquiring inventory that is not sold generates costs without producing corresponding revenue. This condition undoubtedly affects the CVP relationships. Accordingly, the assumptions associated with CVP are frequently violated in business practice. Within the relevant range of activity, however, violations of the basic assumptions are normally insignificant. A prudent business manager who exercises good judgment will certainly find the data generated by cost-volume-profit analysis to be useful regardless of its limitations.

Profitability is affected by changes in the sale price, costs, and the volume of activity. The relationship between these variables is known as *cost-volume-profit analysis.* One important variable in the analysis of these relationships is the *contribution margin,* which is determined by subtracting the variable costs from the sales price. The *contribution margin per unit* is the amount from each unit sold available to cover fixed costs. Once fixed costs have been covered, each additional unit sold increases net income by the amount of the per unit contribution margin.

a look
back

Inventory.
The longer it sits, the harder it is to move.

Despite what your balance sheet might tell you, inventory is no longer an asset. Today, big inventories can slow business and even bring it to a screeching halt. But you can keep your profits moving in the right direction by boosting productivity in your supply chain.

GE Information Services can help you shorten cycle times, improve inventory turns and eliminate out-of-stock occurrences. We'll show you how to link suppliers, manufacturers and distributors electronically so that your purchase orders and invoices are easily sent and tracked, auditing is greatly simplified and customer buying trends are instantly identified through point-of-sale data. For one large retailer, that meant reducing stock replenishment cycles from 3 days to 3 hours. Another one of our clients now gets spare parts to overseas distributors up to 10 days sooner.

You'd be surprised how much smoother your business will run after a tune-up by GE Information Services.
Productivity. It's All We Do.™

GE Information Services

For more information, please call 1-800-500-GEIS, or write GE Information Services.
MC07F2, 401 N. Washington St., Rockville, MD 20850. Find us on the Internet at http://www.geis.com.

The *break-even point* (i.e., the point where total revenue equals total cost) in units can be determined by dividing fixed costs by the contribution margin per unit. The break-even point expressed in sales dollars can be determined by multiplying the number of break-even units by the sales price per unit. To determine sales in units to obtain a designated profit, the sum of fixed costs and desired profit is divided by the contribution margin per unit. The contribution margin per unit can also be used to assess the effects of changes in sales price, variable costs, and fixed costs on the company's profitability.

Many methods are available to determine the prices at which products should sell. In *cost-plus pricing,* the sales price per unit is determined by adding a percentage markup to the cost per unit. In contrast *target pricing (target costing)* begins with an estimate of market price that customers would be willing to pay for the product and then develops the product at a cost that will enable the company to earn its desired profit.

A *break-even graph* can be drawn to depict cost-volume-profit relationships for a product over a range of sales activity. Units are expressed along the horizontal axis and sales along the vertical axis. Lines for fixed costs, total costs, and sales can be drawn based on the sales price per unit, variable cost per unit, and fixed costs. The graph can be used to determine the break-even point in units and sales dollars.

The *margin of safety* is the number of units or the amount of sales dollars by which actual sales can fall below expected sales before a loss is incurred. The margin of safety can also be expressed as a percentage to permit comparison among companies of different size. The margin of safety can be computed as a percentage by dividing the difference between budgeted sales and break-even sales by the amount of budgeted sales.

Spreadsheet software as well as the contribution margin approach can be used to conduct sensitivity analysis of cost-volume-profit relationships. *Sensitivity analysis* is used to determine the effect on profitability of different scenarios of fixed costs, variable costs, and sales volumes. The effects of simultaneous changes in all three variables can be assessed.

A *contribution margin ratio* can be used to determine the break-even point in sales dollars. The ratio is a percentage expression determined by dividing the contribution margin per unit by the sales price per unit. Once the contribution ratio has been determined, the break-even volume expressed in dollars can be determined by dividing the total fixed costs by the ratio. Cost-volume-profit relationships can also be examined by using the following algebraic equation:

$$\text{Sales} = \text{Variable cost} + \text{Fixed cost}$$

The magnitude of a company's operating leverage increases as sales approach the break-even point and decreases thereafter. Therefore, companies at or near the break-even point should focus on increases in sales. Companies far from the break-even point obtain little benefit from sales volume changes and should focus on cost control or product development.

Assumptions are made in using cost-volume analysis. The analysis assumes true linearity among the CVP variables, a constant level of worker efficiency, and a constant level of inventory. Violating these assumptions compromises the accuracy of the analysis.

The next chapter will introduce a new concept known as *cost relevance.* Applying the concepts you have learned to real-world business problems can be challenging. Frequently, so much information is available that it is difficult to distinguish the important from the useless. The next chapter will help you learn to identify information that is relevant in a variety of short-term decision-making scenarios including special offers, outsourcing, segment elimination, and asset replacement.

a look
forward

SELF-STUDY REVIEW PROBLEM

Sharp Company makes and sells pencil sharpeners. The variable cost of each sharpener is $20. The sharpeners are sold for $30 each. Fixed operating expenses amount to $40,000.

Required
a. Determine the break-even point in units and sales dollars.
b. Determine the sales volume in units and dollars that is required to attain a profit of $12,000. Verify your answer by preparing an income statement using the contribution margin format.
c. Determine the margin of safety between sales required to attain a profit of $12,000 and break-even sales.
d. Prepare a break-even graph using the cost and price assumptions outlined above.

Solution to Requirement a

Formula for Computing Break-even Point in Units

$$\frac{\text{Fixed cost} + \text{Target profit}}{\text{Contribution margin per unit}} = \frac{\$40,000 + \$0}{\$30 - \$20} = 4,000 \text{ Units}$$

Break-even Point in Sales Dollars

Sales price	$ 30
Times number of units	4,000
Sales volume in no. of dollars	$120,000

Solution to Requirement b

Formula for Computing Unit Sales Required to Attain Desired Profit

$$\frac{\text{Fixed cost} + \text{Target profit}}{\text{Contribution margin per unit}} = \frac{\$40,000 + \$12,000}{\$30 - \$20} = 5,200 \text{ Units}$$

Sales Dollars Required to Attain Desired Profit

Sales price	$ 30
Times number of units	5,200
Sales volume in dollars	$156,000

Income Statement

Sales Volume in Units (a)	5,200
Sales Revenue (a × $30)	$156,000
Variable Costs (a × $20)	(104,000)
Contribution Margin	52,000
Fixed Costs	(40,000)
Net Income	$ 12,000

Solution to Requirement c

Margin of Safety Computations

	Units	Dollars
Budgeted sales	5,200	$156,000
Break-even sales	(4,000)	(120,000)
Margin of safety	1,200	$ 36,000

Percentage Computation

$$\frac{\text{Margin of safety in \$}}{\text{Budgeted sales}} = \frac{\$36,000}{\$156,000} = 23.08\%$$

Solution to Requirement d

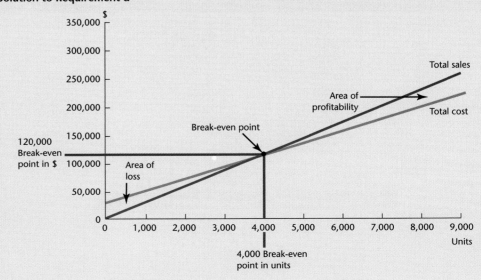

APPENDIX

Multiple-Product Break-even Analysis

When a company analyzes CVP relationships for multiple products that sell simultaneously, the break-even point can be affected by the relative number (i.e., sales mix) of the products sold. For example, suppose that Bright Day decides to run a special sale on its two leading antioxidants, vitamins C and E. The income statements at the break-even point are presented in Exhibit 3–1A.

LO13 Perform multiple-product break-even analysis.

Recall that the break-even point is the point where total sales equal total costs. Accordingly, net income equals zero at that point. The data in Exhibit 3–1A indicate that the budgeted break-even sales volume for the antioxidant special is 2,700 bottles of vitamins with a sales mix consisting of 2,000 bottles of vitamin C and 700 bottles of vitamin E. What happens if the relative sales mix changes? Exhibit 3–2A depicts the expected condition if total sales remain at 2,700 units but the sales mix changes to 2,100 bottles of vitamin C and 600 bottles of vitamin E.

Although the total number of bottles sold remains at 2,700 units, profitability shifts from breaking even to a $280 loss because of the change in the sales mix of the two products, that is, selling more vitamin C than expected and less vitamin E. Because vitamin C has a lower contribution margin (i.e., $1.20 per bottle) than vitamin E (i.e., $4.00 per bottle), selling more of C and less of E reduces profitability. The opposite impact occurs if Bright Day sells more E and less C. Exhibit 3–3A depicts the expected condition if total sales remain at 2,700 units but the sales mix changes to 1,350 bottles each of vitamin C and vitamin E.

Exhibit 3–1A *Budgeted Data for Antioxidant Special*

	Vitamin C			Vitamin E			Total	
	Budgeted Number	Per Unit	Budgeted Amount	Budgeted Number	Per Unit	Budgeted Amount	Budgeted Number	Budgeted Amount
Sales	2,000	7.20 =	$14,400	700	@ 11.00 =	$7,700	2,700	$22,100
Variable cost	2,000	6.00 =	(12,000)	700	@ 7.00 =	(4,900)	2,700	(16,900)
Contribution margin	2,000	1.20 =	2,400	700	@ 4.00 =	2,800	2,700	5,200
Fixed cost			(2,400)			(2,800)		(5,200)
Net income			$ 0			$ 0		$ 0

Exhibit 3–2A *Budgeted Data for Antioxidant Special*

	Vitamin C			Vitamin E			Total	
	Budgeted Number	Per Unit	Budgeted Amount	Budgeted Number	Per Unit	Budgeted Amount	Budgeted Number	Budgeted Amount
Sales	2,100	7.20 =	$15,120	600	@ 11.00 =	$6,600	2,700	$21,720
Variable cost	2,100	6.00 =	(12,600)	600	@ 7.00 =	(4,200)	2,700	(16,800)
Contribution margin	2,100	1.20 =	2,520	600	@ 4.00 =	2,400	2,700	4,920
Fixed cost			(2,400)			(2,800)		(5,200)
Net income			$ 120			$ (400)		$ (280)

Exhibit 3–3A *Budgeted Data for Antioxidant Special*

	Vitamin C			Vitamin E			Total	
	Budgeted Number	Per Unit	Budgeted Amount	Budgeted Number	Per Unit	Budgeted Amount	Budgeted Number	Budgeted Amount
Sales	1,350	7.20 =	$ 9,720	1,350	@ 11.00 =	$14,850	2,700	$24,570
Variable cost	1,350	6.00 =	(8,100)	1,350	@ 7.00 =	(9,450)	2,700	(17,550)
Contribution margin	1,350	1.20 =	1,620	1,350	@ 4.00 =	5,400	2,700	7,020
Fixed cost			(2,400)			(2,800)		(5,200)
Net income			$ (780)			$ 2,600		$ 1,820

Clearly, companies must consider sales mix when they perform break-even analysis for multiproduct business ventures. The multiple product break-even point can be determined using the per unit contribution margin approach. However, it is necessary to use a weighted average to determine the per unit contribution margin. The contribution margin of each product must be weighted by its proportionate share of units sold. For example, in the preceding case, the relative sales mix between the two products is one-half (1,350 units ÷ 2,700 units = 50 percent). What is the break-even point given a relative sales mix of one-half for each product? To answer this question, the companies must first determine the weighted average per unit contribution margin by multiplying the contribution margin of each product by 50 percent. The required computation is shown here.

Analysis of Cost, Volume, and Pricing to Increase Profitability	
Vitamin C ($1.20 × 0.50)	$0.60
Vitamin E ($4.00 × 0.50)	2.00
Weighted average per unit contribution margin	$2.60

The break-even point in total units at a 50/50 sales mix is computed as follows.

Break-even point = Fixed costs ÷ Weighted average per unit contribution margin
Break-even point = $5,200 ÷ $2.60 = 2,000 total units

Next divide the total units to breakeven in proportion to the relative sales mix. In other words, the break-even point occurs at 1,000 bottles of Vitamin C (50 percent of 2,000) and 1,000 bottles of Vitamin E (50 percent of 2,000). The income statements presented in Exhibit 3–4A illustrate these results:

Exhibit 3–4A *Budgeted Data for Antioxidant Special*

	Vitamin C			Vitamin E				Total	
	Budgeted Number	Per Unit	Budgeted Amount	Budgeted Number		Per Unit	Budgeted Amount	Budgeted Number	Budgeted Amount
Sales	1,000	7.20 =	$ 7,200	1,000	@	11.00 =	$11,000	2,000	$18,200
Variable cost	1,000	6.00 =	(6,000)	1,000	@	7.00 =	(7,000)	2,000	(13,000)
Contribution margin	1,000	1.20 =	1,200	1,000	@	4.00 =	4,000	2,000	5,200
Fixed cost			(2,400)				(2,800)		(5,200)
Net income			$ (1,200)				$ 1,200		$ 0

KEY TERMS

Break-even point *101*

Contribution margin per unit *100*

Contribution margin ratio *112*

Cost-plus-pricing strategy *100*

Cost-volume-profit (CVP) analysis *100*

Equation method *113*

Margin of safety *108*

Operating leverage *114*

Prestige pricing *110*

Sensitivity analysis *109*

Target pricing (target costing) *103–104*

QUESTIONS

1. What does the term *breakeven* mean? Name the two ways it can be measured.
2. How does a contribution margin income statement differ from the income statement used in financial reporting?
3. In what three ways can the contribution margin be useful in cost-volume-profit analysis?
4. If Company A has a projected margin of safety of 22 percent while Company B has a margin of safety of 52 percent, which company is at greater risk when actual sales are less than budgeted?
5. What variables affect profitability? Name two methods for determining profitability when simultaneous changes occur in these variables.
6. When would the customer be willing to pay a premium price for a product or service? What pricing strategy would be appropriate under these circumstances?
7. What are three alternative approaches to determine the break-even point? What do the results of these approaches show?

8. What is the equation method for determining breakeven? Explain how the results of this method differ from those of the contribution margin approach.

9. Before the break-even point is reached, what strategy probably would be most effective in increasing profitability and why? After breakeven, what strategies should be considered?

10. If a company is trying to find the break-even point for multiple products that sell simultaneously, what consideration must be taken into account?

11. What assumptions are inherent in cost-volume-profit analysis? Since these assumptions are usually not wholly valid, why do managers still use the analysis in decision making?

12. Mary Hartwell and Jane Jamail, college roommates, are considering the joint purchase of a computer that they can share to prepare class assignments. Ms. Hartwell wants a particular model that costs $2,000; Ms. Jamail prefers a more economical model that costs $1,500. In fact, Ms. Jamail is adamant about her position, refusing to contribute more than $750 toward the purchase. If Ms. Hartwell is also adamant about her position, should she accept Ms. Jamail's $750 offer and apply that amount toward the purchase of the more expensive computer?

13. How would the algebraic formula used to compute the break-even point under the equation method be changed to solve for a desired target profit?

14. Setting the sales price is easy: Enter cost information and desired profit data into one of the cost-volume-profit formulas, and the appropriate sales price can be computed mathematically. Do you agree with this line of reasoning? Explain.

15. What is the relationship between cost-volume-profit analysis and the relevant range?

EXERCISES—SERIES A

EXERCISE 3–1A *Per Unit Contribution Margin Approach*   L.O. 2

Bristol Corporation sells products for $12 each that have variable costs of $9 per unit. Bristol's annual fixed cost is $240,000.

Required
Use the per unit contribution margin approach to determine the break-even point in units and dollars.

EXERCISE 3–2A *Equation Method*   L.O. 2

Yendi Corporation produces products that it sells for $4 each. Variable costs per unit are $2.50, and annual fixed costs are $75,000.

Required
Use the equation method to determine the break-even point in units and dollars.

EXERCISE 3–3A *Contribution Margin Ratio*   L.O. 3

Omega Company incurs annual fixed costs of $90,000. Variable costs for Omega's product are $6 per unit, and the sales price is $10 per unit. Omega desires to earn an annual profit of $30,000.

Required
Use the contribution margin ratio approach to determine the sales volume in dollars and units required to earn the desired profit.

EXERCISE 3–4A *Equation Method*   L.O. 3

Kachi Company produces a product that sells for $27 per unit and has a variable cost of $10 per unit. Kachi incurs annual fixed costs of $150,000. It desires to earn a profit of $37,000.

Required
Use the equation method to determine the sales volume in units and dollars required to earn the desired profit.

EXERCISE 3–5A *Determining Fixed and Variable Cost per Unit*   L.O. 3

Quest Corporation produced and sold 30,000 units of product during October. It earned a contribution margin of $90,000 on sales of $240,000 and determined that cost per unit of product was $7.

Required
Based on this information, determine the variable and fixed cost per unit of product.

L.O. 3   EXERCISE 3–6A *Determining Variable Cost from Incomplete Cost Data*

Barlett Corporation produced 100,000 watches that it sold for $27 each during 2005. The company determined that fixed manufacturing cost per unit was $7 per watch. The company reported a $400,000 gross margin on its 2005 financial statements.

Required

Determine the total variable cost, the variable cost per unit, and the total contribution margin.

L.O. 2, 3   EXERCISE 3–7A *Contribution Margin per Unit Approach for Break-even and Desired Profit*

Information concerning a product produced by Pressler Company appears here.

Sales price per unit	$ 200
Variable cost per unit	110
Total annual fixed manufacturing and operating costs	$630,000

Required

Determine the following:

a. Contribution margin per unit.
b. Number of units that Pressler must sell to break even.
c. Sales level in units that Pressler must reach to earn a profit of $270,000.

L.O. 4   EXERCISE 3–8A *Changing Sales Price*

Stratford Company produces a product that has a variable cost of $3 per unit; the product sells for $8 per unit. The company's annual fixed costs total $300,000; it had net income of $60,000 in the previous year. In an effort to increase the company's market share, management is considering lowering the selling price to $7.50 per unit.

Required

If Stratford desires to maintain net income of $60,000, how many additional units must it sell to justify the price decline?

L.O. 4   EXERCISE 3–9A *Simultaneous Change in Sales Price and Desired Profit*

Use the cost data presented in Exercise 3–8A but assume that in addition to increasing its market share by lowering its selling price to $7.50, Stratford desires to increase its net income by $9,000

Required

Determine the number of units the company must sell to earn the desired income.

L.O. 2, 3, 7   EXERCISE 3–10A *Components of Break-even Graph*

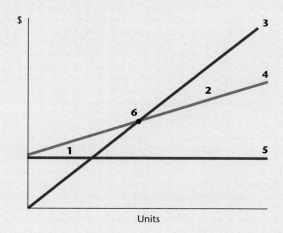

Required

Match the numbers shown in the graph with the following items.

a. Fixed cost line
b. Total cost line
c. Break-even point
d. Area of profit
e. Revenue line
f. Area of loss

EXERCISE 3–11A *Evaluating Simultaneous Changes in Fixed and Variable Costs*

L.O. 4

Nankung Company currently produces and sells 9,000 units annually of a product that has a variable cost of $15 per unit and annual fixed costs of $240,000. The company currently earns a $30,000 annual profit. Assume that Nankung has the opportunity to invest in new labor-saving production equipment that will enable the company to reduce variable costs to $13 per unit. The investment would cause fixed costs to increase by $12,000 because of additional depreciation cost.

Required
a. Use the equation method to determine the sales price per unit under existing conditions (current equipment is used).
b. Prepare a contribution margin income statement, assuming that Nankung invests in the new production equipment. Recommend whether Nankung should invest in the new equipment.

EXERCISE 3–12A *Margin of Safety*

L.O. 8

Haruko Company makes a product that sells for $10 per unit. The company pays $6 per unit for the variable costs of the product and incurs annual fixed costs of $100,000. Haruko expects to sell 32,000 units of product.

Required
Determine Haruko's margin of safety expressed as a percentage.

EXERCISE 3–13A *Cost-Volume-Profit Relationship*

L.O. 2, 3, 4

Joiner, Inc., is a manufacturing company that makes small electric motors it sells for $30 per unit. The variable costs of production are $24 per motor, and annual fixed costs of production are $90,000.

Required
a. How many units of product must Joiner make and sell to break even?
b. How many units of product must Joiner make and sell to earn an $18,000 profit?
c. The marketing manager believes that sales would increase dramatically if the price were reduced to $29 per unit. How many units of product must Joiner make and sell to earn an $18,000 profit, if the sales price is set at $29 per unit?

EXERCISE 3–14A *Understanding of the Global Economy through CVP Relationships*

L.O. 4

An article published in the December 8, 1997, issue of *U.S. News & World Report* summarized several factors likely to support a continuing decline in the rate of inflation over the next decade. Specifically, the article stated that "global competition has . . . fostered an environment of cheap labor, cost cutting, and increased efficiency." The article notes that these developments in the global economy have led to a condition in which "the production of goods is outpacing the number of consumers able to buy them." Even so, the level of production is not likely to decline because factories have been built in developing countries where labor is cheap. The recent decline in the strength of the Asian economies is likely to have a snowballing effect so that within the foreseeable future, there will "be too many goods chasing too few buyers."

Required
a. Identify the production cost factor(s) referred to that exhibit variable cost behavior. Has (have) the cost factor(s) increased or decreased? Explain why the variable costs have increased or decreased.
b. Identify the production cost factor(s) referred to that exhibit fixed cost behavior. Has (have) the cost factor(s) increased or decreased? Explain why the fixed costs have increased or decreased.
c. The article implies that production levels are likely to remain high even though demand is expected to be weak. Explain the logic behind this implication.
d. The article suggests that manufacturers will continue to produce goods even though they may have to sell goods at a price that is below the total cost of production. Considering what you know about fixed and variable costs, speculate on how low manufacturers would permit prices to drop before they would stop production.

L.O. 5　EXERCISE 3–15A *Target Costing*

The marketing manager of NTT Corporation has determined that a market exists for a telephone with a sales price of $29 per unit. The production manager estimates the annual fixed costs of producing between 20,000 and 40,000 telephones would be $180,000.

Required

Assume that NTT desires to earn a $60,000 profit from the phone sales. How much can NTT afford to spend on variable cost per unit if production and sales equal 30,000 phones?

Appendix A

L.O. 13　EXERCISE 3–16A *Multiple Product Break-even Analysis*

Harris Company manufactures two products. The budgeted per unit contribution margin for each product follows.

	Beauty	Grace
Sales price	$50	$90
Variable cost per unit	(30)	(50)
Contribution margin per unit	$20	$40

Harris expects to incur annual fixed costs of $25,000. The relative sales mix of the products is 75 percent for Beauty and 25 percent for Grace.

Required

a. Determine the total number of products (units of Beauty and Grace combined) Harris must sell to break even.

b. How many units each of Beauty and Grace must Harris sell to break even?

PROBLEMS—SERIES A

L.O. 2　PROBLEM 3–17A *Determining the Break-even Point and Preparing a Contribution Margin Income Statement*

Woodfin Manufacturing Company makes a product that it sells for $45 per unit. The company incurs variable manufacturing costs of $21 per unit. Variable selling expenses are $6 per unit, annual fixed manufacturing costs are $100,000, and fixed selling and administrative costs are $80,000 per year.

Required

Determine the break-even point in units and dollars using each of the following approaches.

a. Contribution margin per unit.
b. Equation method.
c. Contribution margin ratio.
d. Confirm your results by preparing a contribution margin income statement for the break-even sales volume.

L.O. 2, 7　PROBLEM 3–18A *Determining the Break-even Point and Preparing a Break-even Graph*

Huckabee Company is considering the production of a new product. The expected variable cost is $15 per unit. Annual fixed costs are expected to be $400,000. The anticipated sales price is $31 each.

Required

Determine the break-even point in units and dollars using each of the following.

a. Contribution margin per unit approach.
b. Equation method.
c. Contribution margin ratio approach.
d. Prepare a break-even graph to illustrate the cost-volume-profit relationships.

PROBLEM 3–19A *Effect of Converting Variable to Fixed Costs* **L.O. 2, 3, 4**

Kuzin Manufacturing Company reported the following data regarding a product it manufactures and sells. The sales price is $32.

Variable costs	
Manufacturing	$15 per unit
Selling	9 per unit
Fixed costs:	
Manufacturing	$160,000 per year
Selling and administrative	40,000 per year

Required
a. Use the per unit contribution margin approach to determine the break-even point in units and dollars.
b. Use the per unit contribution margin approach to determine the level of sales in units and dollars required to obtain a profit of $60,000.
c. Suppose that variable selling costs could be eliminated by employing a salaried sales force. If the company could sell 32,000 units, how much could it pay in salaries for salespeople and still have a profit of $60,000? (*Hint:* Use the equation method.)

PROBLEM 3–20A *Analyzing Change in Sales Price Using the Contribution Margin Ratio* **L.O. 2, 3, 4**

Oglen Company reported the following data regarding the product it sells.

Sales price	$16
Contribution margin ratio	20%
Fixed costs	$360,000

Required
Use the contribution margin ratio approach and consider each requirement separately.
a. What is the break-even point in dollars? In units?
b. To obtain a profit of $80,000, what must the sales be in dollars? In units?
c. If the sales price increases to $20 and variable costs do not change, what is the new break-even point in dollars? In units?

PROBLEM 3–21A *Analyzing Sales Price and Fixed Cost Using the Equation Method* **L.O. 2, 3, 4**

Gemsa Company is considering adding a new product. The cost accountant has provided the following data.

Expected variable cost of manufacturing	$47 per unit
Expected annual fixed manufacturing costs	$78,000

The administrative vice president has provided the following estimates.

Expected sales commission	$3 per unit
Expected annual fixed administrative costs	$42,000

The manager has decided that any new product must at least break even in the first year.

Required
Use the equation method and consider each requirement separately.
a. If the sales price is set at $65, how many units must Gemsa sell to break even?
b. Gemsa estimates that sales will probably be 10,000 units. What sales price per unit will allow the company to break even?
c. Gemsa has decided to advertise the product heavily and has set the sales price at $66. If sales are 9,000 units, how much can the company spend on advertising and still break even?

PROBLEM 3–22A *Margin of Safety and Operating Leverage* **L.O. 8**

Georgi Company is considering the addition of a new product to its cosmetics line. The company has three distinctly different options: a skin cream, a bath oil, or a hair coloring gel. Relevant information and budgeted annual income statements for each of the products follow.

	Relevant Information		
	Skin Cream	**Bath Oil**	**Color Gel**
Budgeted Sales in Units (a)	50,000	90,000	30,000
Expected Sales Price (b)	$7.00	$4.00	$13.00
Variable Costs Per Unit (c)	$4.00	$1.50	$9.00
Income Statements			
Sales Revenue (a × b)	$350,000	$360,000	$390,000
Variable Costs (a × c)	(200,000)	(135,000)	(270,000)
Contribution Margin	$150,000	$225,000	$120,000
Fixed Costs	(120,000)	(210,000)	(104,000)
Net Income	$ 30,000	$ 15,000	$ 16,000

Required
a. Determine the margin of safety as a percentage for each product.
b. Prepare revised income statements for each product, assuming a 20 percent increase in the budgeted sales volume.
c. For each product, determine the percentage change in net income that results from the 20 percent increase in sales. Which product has the highest operating leverage?
d. Assuming that management is pessimistic and risk averse, which product should the company add to its cosmetic line? Explain your answer.
e. Assuming that management is optimistic and risk aggressive, which product should the company add to its cosmetics line? Explain your answer.

L.O. 2, 3, 4, 7, 8   PROBLEM 3–23A *Comprehensive CVP Analysis*

Laredo Company makes and sells products with variable costs of $40 each. Laredo incurs annual fixed costs of $32,000. The current sales price is $60.

Required
The following requirements are interdependent. For example, the $8,000 desired profit introduced in Requirement *c* also applies to subsequent requirements. Likewise, the $50 sales price introduced in Requirement *d* applies to the subsequent requirements.
a. Determine the contribution margin per unit.
b. Determine the break-even point in units and in dollars. Confirm your answer by preparing an income statement using the contribution margin format.
c. Suppose that Laredo desires to earn an $8,000 profit. Determine the sales volume in units and dollars required to earn the desired profit. Confirm your answer by preparing an income statement using the contribution margin format.
d. If the sales price drops to $50 per unit, what level of sales is required to earn the desired profit? Express your answer in units and dollars. Confirm your answer by preparing an income statement using the contribution margin format.
e. If fixed costs drop to $24,000, what level of sales is required to earn the desired profit? Express your answer in units and dollars. Confirm your answer by preparing an income statement using the contribution margin format.
f. If variable cost drops to $30 per unit, what level of sales is required to earn the desired profit? Express your answer in units and dollars. Confirm your answer by preparing an income statement using the contribution margin format.
g. Assume that Laredo concludes that it can sell 1,600 units of product for $50 each. Recall that variable costs are $30 each and fixed costs are $24,000. Compute the margin of safety in units and dollars and as a percentage.
h. Draw a break-even graph using the cost and price assumptions described in Requirement *g*.

L.O. 2, 3, 4, 7, 8   PROBLEM 3–24A *Assessing Simultaneous Changes in CVP Relationships*

Easy Life, Inc. (ELI), sells hammocks; variable costs are $80 each, and the hammocks are sold for $120 each. ELI incurs $190,000 of fixed operating expenses annually.

Required
a. Determine the sales volume in units and dollars required to attain a $50,000 profit. Verify your answer by preparing an income statement using the contribution margin format.

b. ELI is considering implementing a quality improvement program. The program will require a $10 increase in the variable cost per unit. To inform its customers of the quality improvements, the company plans to spend an additional $20,000 for advertising. Assuming that the improvement program will increase sales to a level that is 3,000 units above the amount computed in Requirement a, should ELI proceed with plans to improve product quality? Support your answer by preparing a budgeted income statement.

c. Determine the new break-even point in units and sales dollars as well as the margin of safety percentage, assuming that the quality improvement program is implemented.

d. Prepare a break-even graph using the cost and price assumptions outlined in Requirement b.

Appendix A

PROBLEM 3–25A *Determining the Break-even Point and Margin of Safety for a Company with Multiple Products*

L.O. 13

Chambers Company produces two products. Budgeted annual income statements for the two products are provided here.

	Power			Lite			Total	
	Budgeted Number	Per Unit	Budgeted Amount	Budgeted Number	Per Unit	Budgeted Amount	Budgeted Number	Budgeted Amount
Sales	160	@ $500 =	$80,000	640	@ $450 =	$288,000	800	$368,000
Variable Cost	160	@ $320 =	(51,200)	640	@ $330 =	(211,200)	800	(262,400)
Contribution Margin	160	@ $180 =	$28,800	640	@ $120 =	$ 76,800	800	$105,600
Fixed Costs			(12,000)			(54,000)		(66,000)
Net Income			$16,800			$ 22,800		$ 39,600

Required

a. Based on budgeted sales, determine the relative sales mix between the two products.

b. Determine the weighted-average contribution margin per unit.

c. Calculate the break-even point in total number of units.

d. Determine the number of units of each product Chambers must sell to break even.

e. Verify the break-even point by preparing an income statement for each product as well as an income statement for the combined products.

f. Determine the margin of safety based on the combined sales of the two products.

EXERCISES—SERIES B

EXERCISE 3–1B *Per Unit Contribution Margin Approach*

L.O. 2

Tameron Corporation manufactures products that have variable costs of $6 per unit. Its fixed cost amounts to $75,000. It sells the produce for $9 each.

Required

Use the per unit contribution margin approach to determine the break-even point in units and dollars.

EXERCISE 3–2B *Equation Method*

L.O. 2

Campbell Corporation manufactures products that it sells for $12 each. Variable costs are $7 per unit, and annual fixed costs are $200,000.

Required

Use the equation method to determine the break-even point in units and dollars.

EXERCISE 3–3B *Contribution Margin Ratio*

L.O. 3

Conway Company incurs annual fixed costs of $140,000. Variable costs for Conway's product are $12 per unit, and the sales price is $20 per unit. Conway desires to earn a profit of $40,000.

Required

Use the contribution margin ratio approach to determine the sales volume in dollars and units required to earn the desired profit.

L.O. 3   EXERCISE 3–4B *Equation Method*

Dismukes Company manufactures a product that sells for $30 per unit. It incurs fixed costs of $290,000. Variable cost for its product is $22 per unit. Dismukes desires to earn a target profit is $70,000.

Required

Use the equation method to determine the sales volume in units and dollars required to earn the desired profit.

L.O. 3   EXERCISE 3–5B *Fixed and Variable Cost per Unit*

Vankee Corporation broke even by producing and selling 20,000 units of product during 2005. It earned a contribution margin of $80,000 on sales of $480,000. The company determined that cost per unit of product was $27.

Required

Based on this information, determine the variable and fixed cost per unit of product.

L.O. 3   EXERCISE 3–6B *Determining Variable Cost From Incomplete Data*

Aldrick Corporation produced 60,000 tires and sold them for $70 each during 2007. The company determined that fixed manufacturing cost per unit was $15 per tire. The company reported gross profit of $600,000 on its 2007 financial statements.

Required

Determine the total variable cost, the variable cost per unit, and the total contribution margin.

L.O. 2, 3   EXERCISE 3–7B *Contribution Margin per Unit Approach for Break-even and Desired Profit*

Information concerning a product produced by Lowe Company appears here:

Sales price per unit	$420
Variable cost per unit	270
Total fixed manufacturing and operating costs	$750,000

Required

Determine the following:

a. Contribution margin per unit.
b. Number of units Lowe must sell to break even.
c. Sales level in units that Lowe must reach in order to earn a profit of $150,000.

L.O. 4   EXERCISE 3–8B *Change in Sales Price*

Wang Company manufactures a product that has a variable cost of $7 per unit. The company's fixed costs total $470,000. Wang had net income of $90,000 in the previous year. Its product sells for $15 per unit. In an effort to increase the company's market share, management is considering lowering the product's selling price to $14 per unit.

Required

If Wang desires to maintain net income of $90,000, how many additional units must it sell in order to justify the price decline?

L.O. 4   EXERCISE 3–9B *Simultaneous Change in Sales Price and Desired Profit*

Use the cost data presented in Exercise 3–8B, but assume that in addition to increasing its market share by lowering its selling price to $14, Wang desires to increase its net income by $35,000.

Required

Determine the number of units that Wang must sell to earn the desired income.

L.O. 2, 3, 7   EXERCISE 3–10B *Components of Break-even Graph*

Albert , a 10-year-old boy, wants to sell lemonade on a hot summer day. He hopes to make enough money to buy a new Game Boy. Henry, his elder brother, tries to help him compute his prospect of doing so. The following is the relevant information:

Variable costs	
Lemonade	$0.25 per cup
Paper cup	$0.10 per cup
Fixed costs	
Table and chair	$40.00
Price	$0.75 per cup

The following graph depicts the dollar amount of cost or revenue on the vertical axis and the number of lemonade cups sold on the horizontal axis.

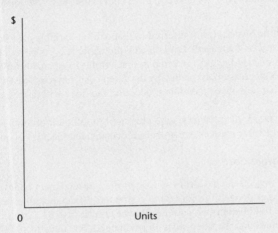

Required
a. Draw a line that depicts the total cost.
b. Draw a line that depicts the total revenue.
c. Identify the break-even point.
d. Identify the area representing profit.
e. Identify the area representing loss.

EXERCISE 3–11B *Evaluating Simultaneous Changes in Fixed and Variable Costs*　　**L.O. 4**

Ashford Company currently produces and sells 10,000 units of a telephone per year that has a variable cost of $13 per unit and a fixed cost of $380,000. The company currently earns a $120,000 annual profit. Assume that Ashford has the opportunity to invest in a new machine that will enable the company to reduce variable costs to $10 per unit. The investment would cause fixed costs to increase by $15,000.

Required
a. Use the equation method to determine the sales price per unit under existing conditions (current machine is used).
b. Prepare a contribution margin income statement assuming Ashford invests in the new technology. Recommend whether Ashford should invest in the new technology.

EXERCISE 3–12B *Margin of Safety*　　**L.O. 8**

Beren Company manufactures scanners that sell for $295 each. The company pays $115 per unit for the variable costs of the product and incurs fixed costs of $1,800,000. Beren expects to sell 20,000 scanners.

Required
Determine Beren's margin of safety expressed as a percentage.

EXERCISE 3–13B *Cost-Volume-Profit Relationship*　　**L.O. 2, 3, 4**

Marino Corporation manufactures faucets. The variable costs of production are $7 per faucet. Fixed costs of production are $81,000. Marino sells the faucets for a price of $25 per unit.

Required
a. How many faucets must Marino make and sell to break even?
b. How many faucets must Marino make and sell to earn a $27,000 profit?

c. The marketing manager believes that sales would increase dramatically if the price were reduced to $22 per unit. How many faucets must Marino make and sell to earn a $27,000 profit, assuming the sales price is set at $22 per unit?

L.O. 4   **EXERCISE 3–14B** *Understanding the Global Economy Through CVP Relationships*

An article published in the April 2, 2001 issue of *Business Week* summarized several factors that had contributed to the economic slowdown that started in the fourth quarter of 2000. Specifically, the article stated, "When companies lowered their demand forecasts, they concluded that they didn't have just a little excess capacity—they had massive excessive capacity, . . ." The article continues to argue that companies with too much capacity have no desire to invest, no matter how low interest rates are.

Required
a. Identify the production cost factor(s) referred to that exhibit variable cost behavior. Has (have) the cost factor(s) increased or decreased? Explain why the variable costs have increased or decreased.
b. Identify the production cost factor(s) referred to that exhibit fixed cost behavior. Has (have) the cost factor(s) increased or decreased? Explain why the fixed costs have increased or decreased.
c. The article argues that new investments in production facilities will decrease. Explain the logic behind this argument.
d. In an economic downturn, manufacturers are pressured to sell their product at low prices. Comment on how low a manufacturer's prices can go before management decides to quit production.

L.O. 5   **EXERCISE 3–15B** *Target Costing*

After substantial marketing research, Carraway Corporation management believes that it can make and sell a new battery with a prolonged life for laptop computers. Management expects the market demand for its new battery to be 10,000 units per year if the battery is priced at $120 per unit. A team of engineers and accountants determines that the fixed costs of producing 8,000 units to 16,000 units is $450,000.

Required
Assume that Carraway desires to earn a $200,000 profit from the battery sales. How much can it afford to spend on variable cost per unit if production and sales equal 10,000 batteries?

Appendix A

L.O. 13   **EXERCISE 3–16B** *Multiple Product Break-even Analysis*

Bessemer Company makes two products. The budgeted per unit contribution margin for each product follows:

	Product M	Product N
Sales price	$32	$60
Variable cost per unit	20	36
Contribution margin per unit	$12	$24

Bessemer expects to incur fixed costs of $28,800. The relative sales mix of the products is 80 percent for Product M and 20 percent for Product N.

Required
a. Determine the total number of products (units of M and N combined) Bessemer must sell to break even.
b. How many units each of Product M and Product N must Bessemer sell to break even?

PROBLEMS—SERIES B

L.O. 2   **PROBLEM 3–17B** *Determining the Break-even Point and Preparing a Contribution Margin Income Statement*

Coleman Company manufactures radio and cassette players and sells them for $100 each. According to the company's records, the variable costs, including direct labor and direct materials, are $50. Factory

depreciation and other fixed manufacturing costs are $192,000 per year. Coleman pays its salespeople a commission of $18 per unit. Annual fixed selling and administrative costs are $128,000.

Required

Determine the break-even point in units and dollars, using each of the following.

a. Contribution margin per unit approach.

b. Equation method.

c. Contribution margin ratio approach.

d. Confirm your results by preparing a contribution margin income statement for the break-even point sales volume.

PROBLEM 3–18B *Determining the Break-even Point and Preparing a Break-even Graph*   **L.O. 2, 7**

Executive officers of Marcus Company are assessing the profitability of a potential new product. They expect that the variable cost of making the product will be $36 per unit and fixed manufacturing cost will be $720,000. The executive officers plan to sell the product for $72 per unit.

Required

Determine the break-even point in units and dollars using each of the following approaches.

a. Contribution margin per unit.

b. Equation method.

c. Contribution margin ratio.

d. Prepare a break-even graph to illustrate the cost-volume-profit relationships.

PROBLEM 3–19B *Effect of Converting Variable to Fixed Costs*   **L.O. 2, 3, 4**

Andrews Company manufactures and sells its own brand of cameras. It sells each camera for $42. The company's accountant prepared the following data:

```
Manufacturing costs
    Variable ................. $18 per unit
    Fixed ................... $150,000 per year

Selling and administrative expenses
    Variable ................. $6 per unit
    Fixed ................... $66,000 per year
```

Required

a. Use the per unit contribution margin approach to determine the break-even point in units and dollars.

b. Use the per unit contribution margin approach to determine the level of sales in units and dollars required to obtain a $126,000 profit.

c. Suppose that variable selling and administrative costs could be eliminated by employing a salaried sales force. If the company could sell 20,000 units, how much could it pay in salaries for the salespeople and still have a profit of $126,000? (*Hint:* Use the equation method.)

PROBLEM 3–20B *Analyzing Change in Sales Price Using the Contribution Margin Ratio*   **L.O. 2, 3, 4**

Willis Company reported the following data regarding the one product it sells.

```
Sales price ........................ $40
Contribution margin ratio ............. 15%
Fixed costs ........................ $144,000 per year
```

Required

Use the contribution margin ratio approach and consider each requirement separately.

a. What is the break-even point in dollars? In units?

b. To obtain a $36,000 profit, what must the sales be in dollars? In units?

c. If the sales price increases to $50 and variable costs do not change, what is the new break-even point in units? In dollars?

PROBLEM 3–21B *Analyzing Sales Price and Fixed Cost Using the Equation Method*   **L.O. 2, 3, 4**

Meridian Company is analyzing whether its new product will be profitable. The following data are provided for analysis.

> Expected variable cost of manufacturing . . . . . . $30 per unit
> Expected fixed manufacturing costs . . . . $48,000 per year
> Expected sales commission . . . . $6 per unit
> Expected fixed administrative costs . . . . $12,000 per year

The company has decided that any new product must at least break even in the first year.

Required
Use the equation method and consider each requirement separately.
a. If the sales price is set at $48, how many units must Meridian sell to break even?
b. Meridian estimates that sales will probably be 6,000 units. What sales price per unit will allow the company to break even?
c. Meridian has decided to advertise the product heavily and has set the sales price at $54. If sales are 9,000 units, how much can the company spend on advertising and still break even?

L.O. 8   **PROBLEM 3–22B** *Margin of Safety and Operating Leverage*

Orkney Company has three distinctly different options available as it considers adding a new product to its automotive division: engine oil, coolant, or windshield washer. Relevant information and budgeted annual income statements for each product follow.

	Relevant Information		
	Engine Oil	**Coolant**	**Windshield Washer**
Budgeted Sales in Units (a)	40,000	60,000	250,000
Expected Sales Price (b)	$2.40	$2.85	$1.15
Variable Costs Per Unit (c)	$1.00	$1.25	$0.35
Income Statements			
Sales Revenue (a × b)	$96,000	$171,000	$287,500
Variable Costs (a × c)	(40,000)	(75,000)	(87,500)
Contribution Margin	$56,000	$ 96,000	$200,000
Fixed Costs	(42,000)	(64,000)	(100,000)
Net Income	$14,000	$ 32,000	$100,000

Required
a. Determine the margin of safety as a percentage for each product.
b. Prepare revised income statements for each product, assuming 20 percent growth in the budgeted sales volume.
c. For each product, determine the percentage change in net income that results from the 20 percent increase in sales. Which product has the highest operating leverage?
d. Assuming that management is pessimistic and risk averse, which product should the company add? Explain your answer.
e. Assuming that management is optimistic and risk aggressive, which product should the company add? Explain your answer.

L.O. 2, 3, 4, 7, 8   **PROBLEM 3–23B** *Comprehensive CVP Analysis*

Surat Company makes a product that it sells for $150. Surat incurs annual fixed costs of $160,000 and variable costs of $100 per unit.

Required
The following requirements are interdependent. For example, the $40,000 desired profit introduced in Requirement *c* also applies to subsequent requirements. Likewise, the $140 sales price introduced in Requirement *d* applies to the subsequent requirements.
a. Determine the contribution margin per unit.
b. Determine the break-even point in units and in dollars. Confirm your answer by preparing an income statement using the contribution margin format.

c. Suppose that Surat desires to earn a $40,000 profit. Determine the sales volume in units and dollars required to earn the desired profit. Confirm your answer by preparing an income statement using the contribution margin format.

d. If the sales price drops to $140 per unit, what level of sales is required to earn the desired profit? Express your answer in units and dollars. Confirm your answer by preparing an income statement using the contribution margin format.

e. If fixed costs drop to $140,000, what level of sales is required to earn the desired profit? Express your answer in units and dollars. Confirm your answer by preparing an income statement using the contribution margin format.

f. If variable costs drop to $80 per unit, what level of sales is required to earn the desired profit? Express your answer in units and dollars. Confirm your answer by preparing an income statement using the contribution margin format.

g. Assume that Surat concludes that it can sell 4,800 units of product for $136 each. Recall that variable costs are $80 each and fixed costs are $140,000. Compute the margin of safety in units and dollars and as a percentage.

h. Draw a break-even graph using the cost and price assumptions described in Requirement g.

PROBLEM 3–24B *Assessing Simultaneous Changes in CVP Relationships*

L.O. 2, 3, 4, 7, 8

Evert Company sells tennis racquets; variable costs for each are $150, and each is sold for $210. Evert incurs $540,000 of fixed operating expenses annually.

Required

a. Determine the sales volume in units and dollars required to attain a $240,000 profit. Verify your answer by preparing an income statement using the contribution margin format.

b. Evert is considering establishing a quality improvement program that will require a $20 increase in the variable cost per unit. To inform its customers of the quality improvements, the company plans to spend an additional $120,000 for advertising. Assuming that the improvement program will increase sales to a level that is 5,000 units above the amount computed in Requirement a, should Evert proceed with plans to improve product quality? Support your answer by preparing a budgeted income statement.

c. Determine the new break-even point and the margin of safety percentage, assuming Evert adopts the quality improvement program.

d. Prepare a break-even graph using the cost and price assumptions outlined in Requirement b.

Appendix A

PROBLEM 3–25B *Determining the Break-even Point and Margin of Safety for a Company with Multiple Products*

L.O. 13

Executive officers of Tompkin Company have prepared the annual budgets for its two products, Washer and Dryer, as follows.

	Washer			Dryer			Total	
	Budgeted Quantity	Per Unit	Budgeted Amount	Budgeted Quantity	Per Unit	Budgeted Amount	Budgeted Quantity	Budgeted Amount
Sales	400	@ $540 =	$216,000	1,200	@ $300 =	$360,000	1,600	$576,000
Variable Cost	400	@ $300 =	(120,000)	1,200	@ $180 =	(216,000)	1,600	(336,000)
Contribution Margin	400	@ $240 =	$ 96,000	1,200	@ $120 =	$144,000	1,600	$240,000
Fixed Costs			(34,000)			(44,000)		(78,000)
Net Income			$ 62,000			$100,000		$162,000

Required

a. Based on the number of units budgeted to be sold, determine the relative sales mix between the two products.

b. Determine the weighted-average contribution margin per unit.

c. Calculate the break-even point in total number of units.

d. Determine the number of units of each product Tompkin must sell to break even.

e. Verify the break-even point by preparing an income statement for each product as well as an income statement for the combined products.

f. Determine the margin of safety based on the combined sales of the two products.

ANALYZE, THINK, COMMUNICATE

ATC 3–1   BUSINESS APPLICATIONS CASE *Sales Required to Achieve a Desired Profit*

Judy Boone just fulfilled a dream as she completed her first season as the owner of a rafting company. Unfortunately, her operation was not profitable. She has enough savings to get her through another season or two, but she realizes that she will have to start making a profit or give up the dream. Her company's income statement for the first year of operation follows.

BOONE RAFTING COMPANY
Income Statement
For the Year Ended December 31, 2003

Revenue	$1,572,000
Rental Cost of Rafts and Camping Equipment	(312,900)
Meals Provided to Rafters	(471,600)
Advertising Expenses	(75,000)
Compensation Paid to Guides	(707,400)
Salary of Office Manager	(24,750)
T-shirts and Hats Provided to Rafters	(47,160)
Office Utility Expense	(5,775)
Net (Loss)	$ (72,585)

Additional Information: Ms. Boone rents equipment on an annual basis. Additional equipment is not available, nor does Ms. Boone provide an allowance for early returns. Guides are paid on a commission basis. Ms. Boone's company served 1,048 rafters during the year.

Required
a. Identify the fixed and variable costs relative to the number of rafters.
b. Reconstruct the income statement using the contribution margin approach.
c. How many rafters are required for Ms. Boone to earn a $75,000 profit?
d. In discussions with her accountant, Ms. Boone was told to expect a 10 percent increase in fixed costs during the following year. She responded with this question, "If these costs are fixed, why are they going to increase?" Assume that you are the accountant; respond to Ms. Boone's question.
e. In addition to the expected increase in fixed costs, the accountant told Ms. Boone to plan for a 20 percent increase in variable costs. Based on these increases, how many rafters must Ms. Boone serve to earn the $75,000 desired profit if the price per rafter remains the same?
f. Assume that Ms. Boone believes it is unlikely that she will attract the number of rafters identified in Part *e*. Explain how she could use *sensitivity analysis* to investigate how to attain a $75,000 profit.

ATC 3–2   GROUP ASSIGNMENT *Effect of Changes in Fixed and Variable Cost on Profitability*

In a month when it sold 200 units of product, Queen Manufacturing Company (QMC) produced the following internal income statement.

Revenue	$8,000
Variable Costs	(4,800)
Contribution Margin	$3,200
Fixed Costs	(2,400)
Net Income	$ 800

QMC has the opportunity to alter its operations in one of the following ways:
1. Increasing fixed advertising costs by $1,600, thereby increasing sales by 120 units.
2. Lowering commissions paid to the sales staff by $8 per unit, thereby reducing sales by 10 units.
3. Decreasing fixed inventory holding cost by $800, thereby decreasing sales by 20 units.

Required
a. The instructor will divide the class into groups and then organize the groups into two sections. For a large class (12 or more groups), four sections may be necessary. At least three groups in each section are needed. Having more groups in one section than another section is acceptable because offsetting advantages and disadvantages exist. Having more groups is advantageous because more people will work on the task but is disadvantageous because having more people complicates communication.

Group Task The sections are to compete with each other to see which section can identify the most profitable alternative in the shortest period of time. No instruction is provided regarding how the sections are to proceed with the task. In other words, each section is required to organize itself with respect to how to accomplish the task of selecting the best alternative. A total quality management (TQM) constraint is imposed that requires zero defects. A section that turns in a wrong answer is disqualified. Once an answer has been submitted to the instructor, it cannot be changed. Sections continue to turn in answers until all sections have submitted a response. The first section to submit the correct answer wins the competition.

b. If any section submits a wrong answer, the instructor or a spokesperson from the winning group should explain how the right answer was determined.

c. Discuss the dynamics of group interaction. How was the work organized? How was leadership established?

RESEARCH ASSIGNMENT *Accuracy Versus Relevance*

ATC 3–3

Frequently, actual fixed and variable cost data are not available. Managerial accountants are required to estimate these costs to facilitate decision making. In the article "Three Significant Digits" in the Winter 1997 edition of the *Journal of Cost Management,* Alfred M. King charged that too many accountants overemphasize reliability and accuracy at the expense of relevance. Read this article and complete the following requirements.

Required

a. The following excerpt is from the King article. "Many management accountants complain that while they are treated as professionals in their chosen field of accounting, they are not invited to sit at the management table when major business decisions are being studied and debated. In short, accountants are not starting players on the management team." Summarize Mr. King's explanation of why this condition exists.

b. Answer the following questions.

  (1) Mr. King notes that "it is better to be approximately right than precisely wrong." He suggests that these words of wisdom are more relevant to managerial accountants than to financial accountants. Explain why Mr. King makes this argument.

  (2) Mr. King charges that the current educational environment leads students to the erroneous conclusion that (1) there is such a thing as the "true" cost of a product and (2) this one "true" cost can be determined accurately and precisely. Why does Mr. King believe this to be an erroneous conclusion?

c. What is the primary weakness associated with the use of the high-low method of estimating cost behavior? What alternative methods can be used to overcome this weakness? (The high-low method is explained in Chapter 2.)

WRITING ASSIGNMENT *Operating Leverage, Margin of Safety, and Cost Behavior*

ATC 3–4

The article "Up Front: More Condensing at the Digest?" in the October 19, 1998, issue of *Business Week* reported that Thomas Ryder, CEO of Reader's Digest Association, was considering a spin-off of Reader's Digest's direct-marketing operations into a joint venture with Time Warner. The article's author, Robert McNatt, noted that the direct marketing of books, music, and videos is a far larger part of the Reader's Digest business than is its namesake magazine. Furthermore, the article stated that 1998 direct-marketing sales of $1.6 billion were down 11 percent from 1997. The decline in revenue caused the division's operating profits to decline 58 percent. The article stated that the contemplated alliance with Time Warner could provide some fast help. Gerald Levin, Time Warner chairman, has said that his company's operations provide customer service and product fulfillment far better than other Web sellers do because of Time Warner's established 250 Web sites.

Required

a. Write a memo explaining how an 11 percent decrease in sales could result in a 58 percent decline in operating profits.

b. Explain briefly how the decline in revenue will affect the company's margin of safety.

c. Explain why a joint venture between Reader's Digest's direct-marketing division and Time Warner could work to the advantage of both companies. (*Hint:* Consider the effects of fixed-cost behavior in formulating your response.)

ETHICAL DILEMMA *Manipulating Reported Earnings*

ATC 3–5

The article "Garbage In, Garbage Out" (*Fortune,* May 25, 1998, pp. 130–38) describes a litany of questionable accounting practices that ultimately led to the demise of Waste Management, Inc. Under

pressure to retain its reputation on Wall Street as a growth company, Waste Management extended its estimates of the lives of its garbage trucks two to four years beyond the standard used in the industry. It also began to use a $25,000 expected salvage value on each truck when the industry standard was to recognize a zero salvage value. Because Waste Management owned approximately 20,000 trucks, these moves had a significant impact on the company's earnings. Extended lives and exaggerated salvage values were also applied to the company's 1.5 million steel dumpsters and its landfill facilities. These accounting practices boosted reported earnings by approximately $110 million per year. The long-term effect on real earnings was disastrous, however; maintenance costs began to soar and the company was forced to spend millions to keep broken-down trucks on the road. Overvalued assets failed to generate expected revenues. The failure to maintain earnings growth ultimately led to the replacement of management. When the new managers discovered the misstated accounting numbers, the company was forced to recognize a pretax charge of $3.54 billion in its 1997 income statement. The stock price plummeted, and the company was ultimately merged out of existence.

Required

a. Did Waste Management manipulate the recognition of fixed or variable costs?

b. Explain how extending the life estimate of an asset increases earnings and the book value of assets.

c. Explain how inflating the salvage value of an asset increases earnings and the book value of assets.

d. Speculate as to what motive would cause executives to manipulate earnings.

e. Review the standards of ethical conduct shown in Exhibit 1–13 of Chapter 1 and comment on whether Waste Management's accounting practices violated any standards.

ATC 3–6   SPREADSHEET ASSIGNMENT *Using Excel*

Bishop Company has provided the estimated data that appear in rows 4 to 8 of the following spreadsheet.

Required

Construct a spreadsheet as follows that would allow you to determine net income, breakeven in units, and operating leverage for the estimates at the top of the spreadsheet, and to see the effects of changes to the estimates. Set up this spreadsheet so that any change in the estimates will automatically be reflected in the calculation of net income, breakeven, and operating leverage.

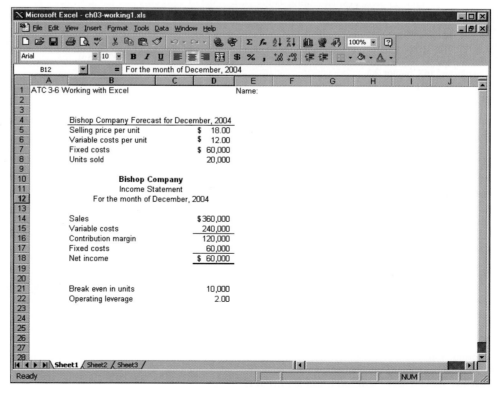

Spreadsheet Tip

1. To center a heading across several columns, such as the Income Statement title, highlight the area to be centered (Columns B, C, and D), choose Format, then choose Cells, and click on the tab titled Alignment. Near the bottom of the alignment window, place a check mark in the box titled Merge cells. The shortcut method to merge cells is to click on the icon near the middle of the top icons that contains an *a* in a box.

SPREADSHEET ASSIGNMENT *Mastering Excel*   ATC 3–7

Required

Build the spreadsheet pictured in Exhibit 3–2. Be sure to use formulas that will automatically calculate profitability if fixed cost, variable cost, or sales volume is changed.

Spreadsheet Tip

1. The shading in column D and in row 6 can be inserted by first highlighting a section to be shaded, choosing Format from the main menu, then Cells, and then clicking on the tab titled Patterns, and then choosing a color for the shading. The shortcut method to accomplish the shading is to click on the fill color icon (it looks like a tipped bucket and is in the upper right area of the screen).

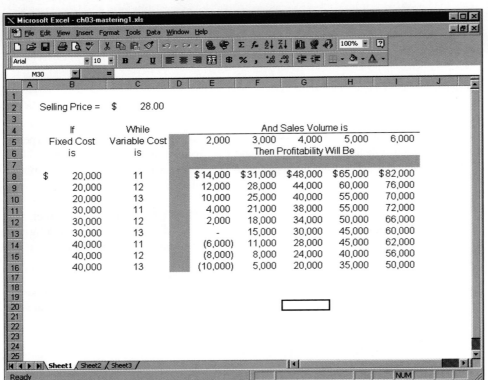

2. Similar to basic math rules, the order of calculation within a formula is multiplication and division before addition and subtraction. Therefore, if you wish to subtract variable cost from selling price and multiply the difference by units sold, the formula must be $= (28 - C8)*E5$.

3. The quickest way to get the correct formulas in the area of E8 to I16 is to place the proper formula in cell E8 and then copy this formula to the entire block of E8:I16. However, the formulas must use the $ around the cell addresses to lock either the row or the column, or both. For example, the formula $= 2*\$B\$8$ can be copied to any other cell and the cell reference will remain B8 because the $ symbol locks the row and column. Likewise, $B8 indicates that only the column is locked, and B$8 indicates that only the row is locked.

Relevant Information for Special Decisions

Learning Objectives

After completing this chapter, you should be able to:

1 Identify the characteristics of relevant information.

2 Recognize sunk costs and understand why these costs are not relevant in decision making.

3 Understand what the term *differential revenue* means.

4 Understand what the terms *avoidable cost* and *differential cost* mean.

5 Distinguish between unit-level, batch-level, product-level, and facility-level costs and understand how these costs are involved in decision making.

6 Understand that relevance is a unique concept and its application is context sensitive.

7 Identify opportunity costs and understand why these costs are relevant in decision making.

8 Distinguish between quantitative versus qualitative characteristics of decision making.

9 Perform analysis leading to appropriate decisions for special order, outsourcing, segment elimination, and asset replacement decisions.

10 Understand the conflict between short- and long-term profitability. (Appendix)

11 Perform the analysis necessary to make decisions regarding the allocation of scarce resources. (Appendix)

the *curious* accountant

U.S. companies have frequently accused companies of other countries of dumping their products in the United States, selling many of these products below cost. Why would a company be willing to sell its products below cost?

Mary Daniels is a partner in a small investment company. Her research has led her to the conclusion that Secor, Inc., is a likely takeover target by a large multinational corporation. She is certain that the price of Secor's stock will appreciate significantly in the immediate future and wants to buy some of the stock. Unfortunately, she is fully invested and short of cash. She thinks to herself, I wish I had known this last week when I bought 1,000 shares of Telstar Communications, Inc., at $24 per share. Telstar had recently launched a series of satellites that promised to enable true international phone service. With a small device not much larger than a thick credit card, customers could send and receive phone calls anywhere in the world. The day after Ms. Daniels bought the stock, Telstar announced technical difficulties with the satellites, and the price of its stock dropped to $20 per share. She told herself, This Telstar stock is going nowhere, but if I sell it now, I'll take a $4,000 loss ([$24 cost − $20 market] × 1,000 shares). Ms. Daniels decided to hold the Telstar stock instead of selling it and buying Secor. The Secor stock appeared to be a sure thing, but she didn't want to incur a loss. Did Ms. Daniels make the right decision? The topics covered in this chapter will help you answer this question.

■ The Decision Environment

The decision environment is exciting and challenging. Decision makers almost always have incomplete information, and they must speculate, estimate, and anticipate because decisions are future oriented. It seems that the right kind of information is never available but useless information is always abundant. The road to the right decision is paved with thousands of useless facts and figures; decision makers need some way to cut to the core to isolate the useful data. Highly successful executives seem to possess an uncanny ability to identify the relevant revenue and cost data. They always seem to make the right choices. It is not merely a matter of luck; the tricks of the trade are revealed in the following pages.

■ Relevant Information

LO1 Identify the characteristics of relevant information.

What distinguishes relevant from useless information? *Relevant information* has two primary characteristics. First, relevant information *indicates differences* between the alternatives. In other words, **relevant information** makes a difference in a decision, but irrelevant information does not. Suppose that you have decided to become a certified public accountant and two prestigious accounting firms have offered you a job. You are now trying to decide which offer to accept. Both offers include identical salaries. Under these circumstances, salary is not a relevant factor in the decision-making process. In other words, because salary does not differ for the alternatives, it cannot be a factor in determining which offer to accept. This does not mean that salary is totally unimportant, but that it is not *relevant* for this specific decision. If you receive a third offer that includes a significantly different salary, salary then becomes relevant because it would enable you to differentiate this offer from the other two. *The point to remember is that relevant information* differs *for the alternatives under consideration.*

A second characteristic of relevant information is that it is *future oriented.* "There is no use in crying over spilt milk." "It's water over the dam." These aphorisms help people avoid the common mistake of trying to change the past. Applying the concept to business decisions, we note that *you cannot avoid a cost that has already been incurred.* To illustrate, return to the case presented in the opening paragraph of this chapter. Recall that Mary Daniels had purchased 1,000 shares of Telstar at $24 per share. She had an opportunity to sell Telstar at $20 per share and invest the proceeds in Secor, the price of which was expected to rise because the company was rumored to be the target of a takeover attempt. She decided to hold the investment in Telstar because she did not want to take a loss. Was the decision to hold the stock a good one?

We cannot say whether Ms. Daniels will make more or less money by deciding to hold the Telstar stock. The price of the stock of either company could go up or down. However, we can say that the decision was based on *irrelevant* data. *Ms. Daniels incurred a loss at the time the price dropped.* She cannot *avoid* a loss that has already occurred. Past mistakes should not affect current decisions. Owning the Telstar stock is equivalent to having $20,000 cash today. The relevant question is whether the $20,000 should be invested in Telstar or Secor. If the answer is Secor, she should sell the Telstar stock and buy Secor stock.

LO2 Recognize sunk costs and understand why these costs are not relevant in decision making.

The investment in the Telstar stock referred to is an example of what accountants call a *sunk cost.* A **sunk cost** is a cost that has been incurred in past transactions; it represents historical facts that cannot be changed by a current decision. *Since* sunk costs *have already been incurred in past transactions, they cannot be avoided and therefore are not relevant for decision-making purposes.*

You may be wondering why we even bother to gather historical information if it is not relevant. Historical information may provide insight into the future. A company that earned $5,000,000 last year is more likely to earn $5,000,000 this year than a company that earned $5,000 last year. Accordingly, the historical information's predictive capacity provides relevance. *Clearly, relevant information must be* future oriented.

Suppose that Ms. Daniels is not naïve, but she fully understands the sunk cost concept and believes that she should sell the Telstar stock. Now let us change the circumstances slightly. Assume that she is an investment counselor and that she purchased the Telstar stock for one of her clients. If she advises her client to sell the stock now, he will know that she gave him bad advice when she told him to buy it. He may lose faith in her abilities and terminate his account. On the other hand, she knows that the client would be better served by knowing the truth. Should she tell him? There is no easy answer to this question. If the client is smart, however, he will appreciate the fact that Ms. Daniels has the courage to admit her mistakes, a person who can do so is in a position to take corrective action. Ms. Daniels hopes that the switch from Telstar to Secor will make money for the client and restore his confidence. Anyway, trying to hide the truth is likely to have its own set of adverse effects. The client will eventually realize that the Telstar investment is not performing and will know that he got bad investment advice. Discovering the condition is truly a matter of when rather than if. In addition, failing to perform at peak level tends to put a person on a cycle of decline; distinguishing what the person truly believes in from what she thinks will serve her immediate interest becomes increasingly more difficult. Gradually, the person loses the ability to think clearly, which impairs performance. In the long term, honesty is not only the right thing but also the most effective strategy for attaining success.

Relevant (Differential) Revenues

As the preceding discussion suggests, *relevant revenues are the expected future revenues that differ for the alternatives under consideration.* Accordingly, they may also be called *differential revenues.* The primary goal of a profit-oriented business is to maximize net income. When evaluating income opportunities, managers choose the option that will maximize revenues and/or minimize costs. All other things being equal, a profit-oriented business seeks to attain all of the revenue that it can. When deciding between two alternative business opportunities, a manager selects the alternative that produces the highest revenue relative to its associated costs. If the two alternatives are expected to produce the same revenue relative to cost, revenue is not relevant because it would not make a *difference* in the amount of net income that could be *obtained in the future.*

LO3 Understand what the term *differential revenue* means.

Relevant (Avoidable) Costs

Profit-oriented businesses seek to minimize cost. In other words, managers try to *avoid* costs whenever possible. Indeed, **relevant costs** are frequently called **avoidable costs;** they are the costs that can be eliminated by taking a specified course of action. For example, suppose that Pecks Department Stores sells men's, women's, and children's clothing and is considering the possibility of discontinuing the children's line. Some of the costs that could be avoided by the elimination include the cost of merchandise; the salaries of the buyers and the sales staff; the cost of interest on debt used to finance the inventory; packaging and transportation; insurance; lost, damaged and stolen merchandise; bad debts; shopping bags; sales slips; price tags; and other supplies. Many other costs could not be avoided, however, and would stay the same regardless of whether the children's line is eliminated. For example, the company president's salary cannot be avoided by closing down the children's line; it does not differ for the

LO4 Understand what the terms *avoidable cost* and *differential cost* mean.

alternatives of keeping the children's line and eliminating it. Either way, the president's salary stays the same. Other examples of costs that cannot be avoided include depreciation on the buildings, rent, property taxes, general advertising, and storewide utilities. *Costs that do not differ for the alternative courses of action are not avoidable and therefore are not relevant to making a decision.*

Revenues as well as expenses are affected by a decision to discontinue the children's clothing line. Obviously, revenues will be less if the clothes are not sold. Before making a decision to eliminate a product line, management must compare the decline in revenue with the avoidable costs. If the avoidable costs (i.e., amount that can be saved) exceed the decline in revenue, the children's line should be eliminated. As discussed later, many qualitative (nonfinancial) factors must be considered when making decisions. From a quantitative perspective, however, the critical factors are the amount of the *relevant* (i.e., differential) *revenue* and the amount of the *relevant* (i.e., differential or avoidable) *cost.*

LO5 Distinguish between unit-level, product-level, and facility-level costs and understand how these costs are related to decision making.

Relationship of Cost Avoidance to a Cost Hierarchy

The identification of avoidable costs can be facilitated by classifying the costs in one of four hierarchical levels.[1] As indicated here, the costs associated with each level can be avoided by eliminating the services or products that compose the level.

1. *Unit-Level Costs.* The costs incurred each time a company generates a product are **unit-level costs.**[2] Examples include the cost of materials, labor, inspections, packaging, shipping, and handling. Incremental (i.e., additional) unit-level costs increase with *each additional unit of product generated. Unit-level costs can be avoided by eliminating the production of a single unit of product.* In other words, the elimination of a single product can avoid the cost of materials, labor, and so on that would have been used to make that product.

2. *Batch-Level Costs.* Products are frequently organized into batches of work rather than in individual units. For example, a heating and air conditioning technician may be assigned to service a batch of air conditioners in an apartment complex. Some costs incurred on the job relate to the entire batch of work, and other costs apply only to individual units. For instance, the labor expended on each air conditioner is classified as a unit-level cost, but the time spent planning the work and setting up the equipment to take to the job site are **batch-level costs.** Similarly, the parts used on each air conditioner are unit-level costs, but the gas used to drive the service truck to the complex is a batch-level cost.

   The classification of costs into unit- versus batch-level categories frequently depends on the context rather than the type of cost. For example, shipping and handling costs to send 200 computers to a university are batch-level costs. In contrast, the shipping and handling cost to deliver a single computer to each of a number of individual customers is a unit-level cost. The elimination of a batch of work can avoid both batch-level and unit-level costs. Similarly, the addition of a batch of work increases batch-level and unit-level costs. Increasing the number of units made or serviced in a particular batch of work increases unit-level but not batch-level costs. Likewise, decreasing the number of units in a batch reduces unit-level costs but not batch-level costs.

3. *Product-Level Costs.* Costs that are incurred to support specific products or services are called **product-level costs.** Examples of product-level costs include quality inspection costs, the costs of engineering efforts necessary to maintain design specifications, the costs of obtaining and protecting patents, the costs of regulatory compliance, and inventory holding costs including interest, insurance, maintenance, and storage. *Product-level costs can*

---

[1]R. Cooper and R. S. Kaplan, *The Design of Cost Management Systems* (Englewood Cliffs, NJ: Prentice-Hall, 1991). Our definitions are broader than those typically presented. Our classifications are designed to encompass service and merchandising companies as well as manufacturing businesses. The original cost hierarchy was developed as a platform for activity-based costing, a topic we will introduce later, but we have found these classifications are equally effective as a tool for identifying avoidable costs.

[2]Recall that we use the term *product* in a generic sense to represent the production of goods or services.

be avoided when a product line is discontinued. For example, suppose that Snapper Company makes the engines used in its lawn mowers. A decision to buy from an outside supplier instead of to make the engines enables Snapper to avoid the associated product-level costs such as the legal cost of patents, the manufacturing supervisory costs of producing the engines, and the maintenance and inventory costs of holding engine parts.

4. *Facility-Level Costs.* **Facility-level costs** are incurred on behalf of the entire company and therefore are not related to any specific product, batch, or unit of production. Because these costs are incurred to maintain the facility as a whole, they are frequently called *facility-sustaining costs.* Examples of these costs include rent, depreciation, personnel administration and training, property and real estate taxes, insurance, maintenance, administrative salaries, selling costs, landscaping, utilities, and security. Total facility-level costs cannot be avoided unless the entire company is dissolved. However, a decision to eliminate a segment of a business (i.e., a division, department, office) may enable the avoidance of some facility-level costs. For example, if a bank eliminates one of its branches, it can avoid the costs of building rental, maintenance, insurance, and so forth associated with the operation of that particular branch. In general, *segment-level facility costs* can be avoided when a segment is eliminated. In contrast, *corporate-level facility costs* cannot be avoided unless the corporation is eliminated.

In practice, the distinctions between the various categories are often blurred. One company may classify sales staff salaries as a facility-level cost while another company may pay commissions that it could trace to product lines or even specific units of a product line. Accordingly, you cannot master the art of cost classification through memorization. Instead, you must exercise judgment when classifying specific cost items into the designated categories.

Relevance Is an Independent Concept

The concept of relevance is independent from the concept of cost behavior. More specifically, a relevant cost can be fixed or variable. To illustrate the independent characteristics of relevant costs, consider the following scenario. Executives of Better Bakery Products are considering the addition of a new product to the company's line of goods. They are trying to decide whether the production of cakes or pies would be more profitable. The following costs have been accumulated for the two options.

LO6 Understand that relevance is a unique concept and its application is context sensitive.

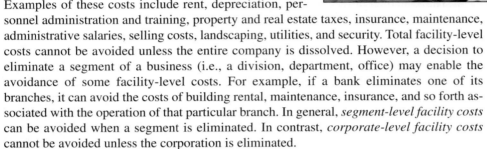

Cost of Cakes		Cost of Pies	
Materials (per unit)	$ 1.50	Materials (per unit)	$ 2.00
Direct labor (per unit)	1.00	Direct labor (per unit)	1.00
Supervisor's salary*	25,000.00	Supervisor's salary*	25,000.00
Franchise fee†	50,000.00	Advertising‡	40,000.00

*It will be necessary to hire a new production supervisor at a cost of $25,000 per year.

†Cakes will be distributed under a nationally advertised label. Better Bakery pays an annual franchise fee for the right to use the product label. Because of the established brand name, Better Bakery will not be required to advertise the product.

‡Better Bakery will market the pies under its own name and will advertise the product in the local market in which the product sells.

Which costs are relevant? Fifty cents per unit of the materials can be avoided by choosing to make cakes instead of pies. A portion of the materials cost is therefore relevant. One dollar per unit of labor will be incurred regardless of whether cakes or pies are made. Accordingly, this cost is not relevant. Notice that although both materials and direct labor are variable costs, one is relevant but the other is not. Since the supervisor's salary will be incurred regardless of

which alternative is selected, it is not relevant. The franchise fee can be avoided if pies are made and advertising costs can be avoided if cakes are made. All three of these costs are fixed, but two are relevant and one is not. Indeed, all of the costs (fixed and variable) could be avoided if the bakery chooses to reject both products. Clearly, whether a cost is fixed or variable has no bearing on its relevance.

Relevancy of Opportunity Costs

LO7 Identify opportunity costs and understand why these costs are relevant in decision making.

Suppose that you pay $50 to acquire a highly desirable ticket to an Olympic event. Just before entering the stadium, someone offers to buy your ticket for $500. If you refuse the offer, how much will it cost you to attend the event? From the perspective of managerial accounting, the answer is $500. The $50 original purchase price is a *sunk cost* and is not relevant to the decision at hand. The decision involves a choice between attending and not attending the Olympic event. The $500 offer differs for the alternatives and is future oriented; it is therefore relevant. If you enter the stadium, you give up the *opportunity* to obtain $500 cash. The sacrifice of a potential benefit associated with a lost opportunity is called an **opportunity cost.**

Suppose that you turn down the first offer to sell your ticket for $500. A few minutes later, another person offers you $600 for the ticket. If you refuse the second offer, does this mean that your opportunity cost has risen to $1,100 (the first $500 offer plus the second $600 offer)? The answer is no; opportunity costs are not cumulative. If you had accepted the first offer, you could not have accepted the second. You may have many opportunities, but the acceptance of one of the alternatives eliminates the possibility of accepting the others. Normally, the opportunity cost is considered to be the highest value of the available alternative courses of action. In this case, the opportunity cost of attending the Olympic event is $600.

Opportunity costs are not recorded in the financial accounting records, but they represent an information factor used in decision making. Remember that financial accounting is historically based, but opportunity costs are future oriented. They affect the decisions that managers make. The financial results of those decisions appear in the financial statements, but the information used to make the decisions does not. The fact that opportunity costs are not recorded does not negate their importance; although they are not a part of the financial accounting system, they are an integral part of management accounting. You would not report the $600 opportunity cost as an expense on the income statement, but it will certainly affect your decision regarding whether you attend the Olympic event. *Opportunity costs are relevant costs.*

Check Yourself 4–1

Aqua, Inc., makes statues for use in fountains. On January 1, 2003, the company paid $13,500 for a mold to make a particular type of statue. The mold had an expected useful life of four years and a salvage value of $1,500. On January 1, 2005, the mold had a market value of $3,000 and a salvage value of $1,200. The expected useful life did not change. What is the relevant cost of using the mold during 2005?

Answer The relevant cost of using the mold in 2005 is the opportunity cost ([market value − salvage value] ÷ remaining useful life), in this case, ($3,000 − $1,200) ÷ 2 = $900. The book value of the asset and associated depreciation is based on a sunk cost that cannot be avoided because it has already been incurred and therefore is not relevant to current decisions. In contrast, Aqua could avoid the opportunity cost (market value) by selling the mold.

Context-Sensitive Relevance

LO6 Understand that relevance is a unique concept and its application is context sensitive.

The very same cost that is classified as relevant in one context may be identified as irrelevant in another context. Consider the salary of a manager of a store that carries men's, women's, and children's clothing. The store manager's salary could not be avoided by the elimination of the children's department, but it could be avoided if the entire store were closed. Accordingly, the salary is not relevant with respect to a decision regarding the elimination of the children's department but is relevant with respect to a decision regarding closing a store. In one context,

the salary is not relevant. In the other context, it is relevant. As this example implies, there is no way to provide a list of all relevant costs. The classification of a particular cost as relevant or irrelevant depends on the unique set of circumstances applicable to the decision at hand. You must focus on understanding the concept rather than trying to memorize some list of relevant costs.

Relationship Between Relevance and Accuracy

Information does not have to be precisely accurate to be relevant. Knowing that the price of a piece of equipment is going to drop can delay a decision to purchase even if you do not know the exact amount of the expected decrease. In other words, you know that part of the cost can be avoided by waiting; you are just not sure of the exact amount. Obviously, the most useful information is highly relevant and precisely accurate. It is equally obvious that information that is totally inaccurate is useless. Likewise, information that is irrelevant is useless regardless of how accurate it may be. What level of accuracy is required for information to be relevant? The degree of accuracy required differs among decision makers and for decisions made by the same person. The balance between accuracy and relevance is one more factor requiring judgment on the part of management accountants.

Quantitative Versus Qualitative Characteristics of Decision Making

Relevant information can have both **quantitative** and **qualitative characteristics.** The previous discussion focused on quantitative data. Now let us consider some qualitative issues. Suppose that you are trying to decide which of two computers to purchase. Computer A costs $300 more than Computer B. Both computers conform to the required performance standards; however, Computer A is housed in a more attractive case. Based on quantitative considerations, an argument could be made for selecting Computer B. You could avoid $300 of cost by purchasing this machine. Even so, the final selection may be affected by the qualitative features. If the machine will be used in instances when clients need to be impressed, appearance may be more important than cost minimization, so Computer A might be purchased even though the quantitative analysis suggested otherwise. Both qualitative and quantitative data are relevant to decision making. Both features must be evaluated to make the choice.

LO8 Distinguish between quantitative versus qualitative characteristics of decision making.

As with quantitative data, *relevant* qualitative features *differ* between the alternatives. If both computers were housed in the same case, attractiveness would not be relevant to a decision regarding the selection of one computer versus the other.

■ Relevant Information and Special Decisions

Five types of special decisions are frequently encountered in business practice: (1) special order, (2) outsourcing, (3) segment elimination, (4) asset replacement, and (5) scarce resource allocation. The following sections discuss the use of relevant information in making the first four types of special decisions. The Appendix to this chapter discusses decisions involving scarce resources.

Special Order Decisions

Occasionally, a company receives an offer to sell its goods at a price significantly below its normal selling price. The company must evaluate this offer carefully before it makes a **special order decision** to accept or reject it. To illustrate, assume that Stoerner Office Products makes three types of office equipment including copy machines, computers, and printers. Stoerner expects to make and sell 2,000 printers in 10 batches containing 200 units per batch during the

LO9 Perform analysis leading to appropriate decisions for special order, outsourcing, segment elimination, and asset replacement decisions.

Exhibit 4–1 *Budgeted Cost for Expected Production of 2,000 Printers*

Unit-level costs		
Materials costs (2,000 units × $90)	$180,000	
Labor costs (2,000 units × $82.50)	165,000	
Overhead (2,000 units × $7.50)	15,000	
Total unit-level costs (2,000 × $180)		$360,000
Batch-level costs		
Assembly setup (10 batches × $1,700)	17,000	
Materials handling (10 batches × $500)	5,000	
Total batch-level costs (10 batches × $2,200)		22,000
Product-level costs		
Engineering design	14,000	
Production manager salary	63,300	
Total product-level costs		77,300
Facility level costs		
Segment-level costs		
Division manager's salary	85,000	
Administrative costs	12,700	
Corporate-level costs		
Company president's salary	43,200	
Depreciation	27,300	
General expenses	31,000	
Total facility-level costs		199,200
Total expected cost		$658,500

Cost per unit: $658,500 ÷ 2,000 = $329.25

coming year. The expected cost of production includes unit-level costs for materials, labor, and overhead. The batch-level costs include assembly setup and materials handling. The company expects to incur product-level costs for engineering design and the salary of a production manager. In addition, facility-level costs associated with the printer division include administrative salaries, depreciation, and general operating expenses. The budgeted costs for the expected production of 2,000 units of product are summarized in Exhibit 4–1.

After adding the normal markup to the total cost per unit, Stoerner set the selling price at $360 per printer. Suppose that Stoerner receives a *special order* for 200 printers that would require production above the expected level of production. In other words, if Stoerner accepts the order, the company's expected sales would increase from 2,000 units to 2,200 printers. It has *excess productive capacity* and is able to make the additional units without disrupting service to its regular customers. Unfortunately, the special order customer is willing to pay only $250 per printer. This price is well below not only Stoerner's normal selling price of $360 but also the company's expected per unit cost of $329.25. Should Stoerner accept or reject the special order? At first glance, it appears that it should reject the special order because the price is below the expected cost per unit. Analyzing relevant costs and revenue leads, however, to a different conclusion.

Analysis of Relevant Costs and Revenues

We begin by considering what happens to existing costs and revenue if Stoerner's accepts the special order. Some of the costs shown in Exhibit 4–1 will not be affected by a decision to accept the special order. Specifically, the product-level and facility-level costs will be incurred even if Stoerner rejects the special order. Because these costs are the same regardless of whether the special order is accepted or rejected, they are not relevant to the decision at hand. The *relevant costs* are the additional costs that will be incurred as a result of accepting the special order. These costs are the *unit-level costs* including materials, labor, and overhead. Furthermore, *batch-level costs* are relevant because the company must produce an additional batch to fill the special order. The unit- and batch-level costs are relevant because they could be avoided if the special offer were rejected. In addition, the amount of revenue will change if Stoerner accepts the special order. Specifically, the amount of revenue will increase by $50,000 ($250 × 200 units) if Stoerner accepts the special order. The relevant information is shown in Exhibit 4–2.

Because differential revenue exceeds the relevant avoidable costs, quantitative factors suggest that Stoerner should accept the offer. As indicated, accepting the offer will increase profitability by $11,800.

Exhibit 4–2 *Relevant Information for Special Order of 200 Printers*

Differential revenue ($250 × 200 units)	$50,000
Avoidable unit-level costs ($180 × 200 units)	(36,000)
Avoidable batch-level costs ($2,200 × 1 batch)	(2,200)
Contribution to income	$11,800

Opportunity Cost Consideration

Suppose that Stoerner has an opportunity to lease the equipment and buildings that constitute its excess capacity for $15,000. This would change the

By this point it should be clear that there is usually a difference between avoidable cost and total cost. When U.S. companies complain that businesses from other countries are selling their products in the United States at a price that is less than cost, they mean full cost (i.e., total cost). Since the avoidable cost may be considerably less than the full cost, products that are sold for less than full cost can still contribute to profitability. This phenomenon explains why products made in Mexico may sell for less in the United States than they sell for in Mexico.

decision to accept the special order. Using the excess capacity to make printers would force Stoerner to give up the opportunity to lease the excess capacity to a third party. The sacrifice of the potential income from the lease is an opportunity cost that will be incurred if the special order is accepted. When the opportunity cost is added to the other relevant costs, the total cost becomes $53,200 ($38,200 unit-level and batch-level costs + $15,000 opportunity cost). Because the avoidable costs would then exceed the differential revenue, the result would be a projected loss of $3,200 ($50,000 differential revenue − $53,200 avoidable costs). Under these circumstances Stoerner should reject the special order but should lease the excess capacity. In other words, the company would be better off to lease the excess capacity than to produce and sell the 200 additional printers.

Relevance and the Decision Context

Return to the assumption that Stoerner does not have the opportunity to lease the excess capacity. Recall that the original data suggested that the company could earn an $11,800 contribution to profit by accepting the special order to sell printers at $250 per unit (see Exhibit 4–2). Because Stoerner can earn a contribution to profit at a price of $250 each, does this mean the company can lower its normal selling price (price charged to existing customers) to this amount? The answer is no. The analysis shown in Exhibit 4–3 illustrates the reason.

Exhibit 4–3 *Projections Based on 2,200 Printers at a Sales Price of $250 per Unit*

Revenue ($250 × 2,200)		$ 550,000
Unit-level supplies and inspection ($180 × 2,200 units)	$396,000	
Batch-level costs ($2,200 × 11 batches)	24,200	
Product-level costs	77,300	
Facility-level costs	199,200	
Total cost		(696,700)
Projected loss		$(146,700)

Clearly, the product-level and facility-level costs cannot be totally ignored. If a company is to be profitable, it must ultimately generate revenue in excess of total costs. Although the facility-level and product-level costs are not relevant to the special order, they are relevant to the operation of the business as a whole.

Qualitative Characteristics

When should a company reject a special order? Obviously, it should reject it if the additional costs are higher than the additional revenues. Furthermore, rejecting a special order may be appropriate even if projected revenues exceed relevant costs. Qualitative characteristics may be even more important than the quantitative factors. If Stoerner's regular customers learn that the company had sold printers to other buyers at $250 per unit, they may demand a similar price for the goods they buy. As demonstrated, Stoerner cannot afford to lower the price for all customers. Accordingly, special order customers should reside outside Stoerner's normal sales territory. In addition, the special order customers should be clearly advised that the special price does not apply to repetitive business. If the special order customer becomes a regular customer, conflicts may occur when Stoerner fills its idle capacity with orders from regular customers. At full capacity, Stoerner should reject special orders at reduced prices because filling those orders reduces its ability to satisfy the regular customers who are willing to pay the higher sales price. Cutting off a special order customer who has been permitted to establish a continuing relationship is likely to lead to ill-feelings and harsh words. A business's reputation can depend on how management handles such relationships.

Outsourcing Decisions

LO9 Perform analysis leading to appropriate decisions for special order, outsourcing, segment elimination, and asset replacement decisions.

For a variety of reasons, one company may produce a product or service for less than another company. Wage rates, economies of scale, specialization, level of bureaucracy, motivation, reward structure, technological competence, degree of automation, and many other cost-related factors differ among companies. As a result, a company may purchase a product or service at a price below its cost to make the product or provide it. This situation explains why automobile companies purchase rather than make many of the parts in their cars. The practice of buying goods and services from other companies is commonly known as **outsourcing.** Determining the relevant cost of buying goods or services is usually an easy task. First, what happens to existing cost if the product or service is outsourced must be determined. Some costs will be unaffected, and other costs will decrease. If the company buys the products, it will not have to pay to have them made. The firm then compares the potential decrease in existing costs with the cost of buying (outsourcing). Cost minimization is achieved by selecting the make-or-buy alternative with the lowest relevant costs.

To illustrate, assume that Stoerner is considering the purchase of the printers that it now makes. A supplier has offered to sell an unlimited supply of printers to Stoerner for $240 each. A quick review of Exhibit 4–1 indicates that Stoerner expects the cost of making printers to be $329.25 per unit. This information suggests that Stoerner could buy the printers for less than it can make them. Analysis of relevant costs proves this conclusion wrong, however.

Analysis of Relevant Costs

What happens to existing costs if Stoerner decides to outsource the printers? Begin by reviewing the information in Exhibit 4–1. A decision to outsource will not affect some costs, for example, the facility-level costs will be incurred regardless of whether Stoerner outsources the printers. Accordingly, these costs are not relevant to the outsourcing decision. In contrast, the relevant costs are those costs that could be avoided if Stoerner purchases the printers. Clearly, purchasing would avoid unit-level and batch-level production costs. If Stoerner purchases the products, it would eliminate the cost of materials, labor, overhead, batch set-up costs, and the materials handling cost. Likewise, it could avoid the product-level costs. Stoerner could eliminate engineering design costs and could lay off the production supervisor, thereby eliminating her salary. Because these costs could be avoided if Stoerner buys the printers, they are relevant to the decision-making process. The relevant (avoidable) costs associated with a decision to outsource the printers are shown in Exhibit 4–4.

Because the relevant cost of production is lower than the purchase price of the printers ($229.65 per unit versus $240.00), the quantitative analysis suggests that Stoerner should continue to make the printers. Indeed, it can expect profitability to decline by $20,700 ($459,300 − [$240 × 2,000]) if the printers are outsourced.

Suppose that Stoerner's accountant identified another cost item that had not been included in the original cost data. The space currently being used to manufacture printers could be converted to warehouse space for finished goods. By using this space for warehouse storage, Stoerner could save $40,000 per year that it currently spends to rent warehouse space. This information would change the decision to continue the production of printers. By using the space to manufacture printers, Stoerner is *forgoing the opportunity* to save $40,000 in warehouse costs. Because the *opportunity cost* can be avoided by purchasing the printers, it is relevant to the outsourcing decision. When the opportunity cost is added to the other relevant costs, the total relevant cost increases to $499,300 ($459,300 + $40,000). Accordingly, the relevant cost per unit becomes $249.65 ($499,300 ÷ 2,000). Because this amount is higher than the purchase price of $240.00, Stoerner should outsource the printers. In other words, it would be better off to buy the printers and use the warehouse space to store the finished goods than to continue producing the printers.

Exhibit 4–4 *Relevant Cost for Expected Production for Outsourcing 2,000 Printers*

Unit-level costs ($180 × 2,000)	$360,000
Batch-level costs ($2,200 × 10)	22,000
Product-level costs	77,300
Total relevant cost	$459,300

Cost per unit: $459,300 ÷ 2,000 = $229.65

Evaluation of the Effect of Growth on the Level of Production

The decision to outsource would change if the level of production increased to 3,000 units. Because some of the avoidable costs are fixed relative to the level of production, cost per unit decreases as volume increases. For example, assume that the product-level costs including the cost of engineering design, the production supervisor's salary, and the opportunity cost are fixed relative to the level of production. Based on these assumptions, relevant cost per unit is computed as shown in Exhibit 4–5.

Exhibit 4–5 *Relevant Cost for Expected Production for Outsourcing 3,000 Printers*

Unit-level costs ($180 × 3,000)	$540,000
Batch-level costs ($2,200 × 15)	33,000
Product-level costs	77,300
Opportunity cost	40,000
Total relevant cost	$690,300

Cost per unit: $690,300 ÷ 3,000 = $230.10

At 3,000 units of production, the relevant cost of making printers is less than the cost of outsourcing ($230.10 versus $240.00). If management believes that the company is likely to experience growth in the near future, it should reject the outsourcing option. This case demonstrates that managers must consider potential growth when making outsourcing decisions.

Qualitative Features

A company that controls the full range of activities from the acquisition of raw materials to the distribution of goods or services is said to use **vertical integration.** Outsourcing reduces the level of vertical integration and thereby forces the company to relinquish its absolute control of the enterprise. Accordingly, the reliability of the supplier is a critical consideration in the outsourcing decision. An unscrupulous supplier may lure an unsuspecting manufacturer into an outsourcing decision through a practice known as **low-ball pricing.** Once the manufacturer comes to depend on the supplier, the supplier raises prices. Problems can also emerge with respect to quality issues and delivery commitments. Poor quality reflects on the seller's reputation. Stoerner's customers will be angry with it if the printers do not work and will not be content with an excuse that blames the supplier. Similarly, if a supplier fails to deliver printers

focus on International Issues

Outsourcing—How Do They Do It in Japan?

Many outsourcing opportunities suffer from a lack of long-term commitment. For example, a supplier may be able to attain economic efficiencies by redesigning its facilities to produce a product needed by a special order customer. Unfortunately, the redesign cost cannot be recovered on a small order quantity. The supplier needs assurances of a long-term relationship to justify a significant investment in the supply relationship. Japanese businesses have resolved this condition through what is sometimes called *obligational contract relationships.* While these contracts are renewable annually, most suppliers expect to form a supply relationship that will last more than five years. Indeed, Japanese custom establishes a commitment between the supplier and the buyer that includes the exchange of sensitive cost information. If deficiencies in price, delivery, or quality conformance occur, the buyer is likely to send production engineers to the offices of the supplier. The buyer's engineers will study the facilities of the supplier and give detailed advice as to how to achieve improved results. In the process of analyzing the supplier's operations, the buyer obtains detailed information regarding the supplier's costs. This

information is used to negotiate prices that ensure reasonable rather than excessive profits for the supplier. Accordingly, costs are controlled for not only the supplier but also the buyer.

Source: Miles B. Gietzmann, "Emerging Practices in Cost Accounting," *Management Accounting (UK),* January 1995, pp. 24–25.

on schedule, Stoerner's customers will blame it, not the supplier, for late deliveries. Stoerner depends on the supplier to deliver quality goods at the designated price, according to a specified schedule. Failures of the supplier become Stoerner's failures.

To protect themselves from unscrupulous or incompetent suppliers, many companies establish a select list of **certified suppliers** with which they strive to develop mutually beneficial relationships. These companies offer incentives such as guarantees to purchase mass quantities with rapid payment schedules. In essence, the companies seek to become the preferred customers of the suppliers, thereby motivating the suppliers to adhere to strict quality standards and delivery schedules. The buyers understand that prices depend on the suppliers' ability to control costs. Accordingly, the buyers and suppliers work together to minimize costs. For example, buyers may share confidential information about their production plans with suppliers if such information would enable the suppliers to better plan their activities to effectively control costs.

Companies must approach the outsourcing decision with caution even when relationships with reliable suppliers are ensured. These companies must direct attention to internal as well as external effects. Outsourcing usually involves employee displacement. Once a trained workforce has been dissolved, it cannot be easily replaced. If conditions with the supplier deteriorate, the reestablishment of internal production capacity will be expensive. Former employees may be reluctant to return to a company that had previously discharged them. Trust and loyalty are difficult to develop but easy to destroy. With this in mind, companies must consider not only the effects on the employees who are discharged but also the morale of those who remain. Increased efficiencies gained through outsourcing are of little benefit if they are acquired at the expense of internal productivity.

Having acknowledged the potential pitfalls associated with outsourcing, we must recognize that the vast majority of U.S. businesses engage in some form of the practice. This widespread acceptance suggests that most companies believe that the benefits available through outsourcing exceed the potential shortcomings.

Check Yourself 4-2

Addison Manufacturing Company pays a production supervisor a salary of $48,000 per year. The supervisor manages the production of sprinkler heads that are used in water irrigation systems. Should the production supervisor's salary be considered a relevant cost to a special order decision? Should the production supervisor's salary be considered a relevant cost to an outsourcing decision?

Answer The production supervisor's salary is not a relevant cost to a special order decision because Addison would pay the salary regardless of whether it accepts or rejects a special order. Since the cost does not differ for the alternatives, it is not relevant. In contrast, the supervisor's salary would be relevant to an outsourcing decision. Addison could dismiss the supervisor if it purchased the sprinkler heads instead of making them. Since the salary could be avoided by purchasing heads instead of making them, the salary is relevant to an outsourcing decision.

Decisions to Eliminate Segments

LO9 Perform analysis leading to appropriate decisions for special order, outsourcing, segment elimination, and asset replacement decisions.

Businesses frequently organize information to facilitate comparisons among different products, departments, or divisions. For example, in addition to a single companywide income statement, J. C. Penney may prepare a separate income statement for each store. It can then evaluate managerial performance by comparing profitability measures among stores. Similarly, Ford Motor Company may prepare income statements for each type of automobile it produces to determine, for example, whether it earned a higher return on its investment in the Taurus or the Explorer line. The component parts of an organization that are designated as reporting entities are called **segments.** *Segment reports* can be prepared for products, services, departments, branches, centers, offices, or divisions. These reports normally consist of revenue and cost data. The primary objective of segment analysis is to determine whether relevant revenues exceed the relevant costs.

Exhibit 4–6 *Projected Revenues and Costs by Segment*

	Copiers	Computers	Printers	Total
Projected revenue	$550,000	$850,000	$780,000	$2,180,000
Projected costs				
Unit-level costs				
Materials costs	(120,000)	(178,000)	(180,000)	(478,000)
Labor costs	(160,000)	(202,000)	(165,000)	(527,000)
Overhead	(30,800)	(20,000)	(15,000)	(65,800)
Batch-level costs				
Assembly setup	(15,000)	(26,000)	(17,000)	(58,000)
Materials-handling	(6,000)	(8,000)	(5,000)	(19,000)
Product-level costs				
Engineering design	(10,000)	(12,000)	(14,000)	(36,000)
Production manager's salary	(52,000)	(55,800)	(63,300)	(171,100)
Facility-level costs				
Segment level				
Division manager's salary	(82,000)	(92,000)	(85,000)	(259,000)
Administrative costs	(12,200)	(13,200)	(12,700)	(38,100)
Allocated—corporate level				
Company president's salary	(34,000)	(46,000)	(43,200)	(123,200)
Depreciation	(19,250)	(29,750)	(27,300)	(76,300)
General expenses	(31,000)	(31,000)	(31,000)	(93,000)
Projected profit (loss)	$ (22,250)	$136,250	$121,500	$ 235,500

When accounting reports indicate that a particular segment is operating at a net loss, management should consider eliminating that segment. However, the decision should not be made hastily. Although it may seem that eliminating the segment would stop the loss, this is not necessarily the case. For example, company-level facility costs that have been allocated to the segment will continue to be incurred even if the segment is eliminated. The subject of *allocation* will be discussed in Chapters 6 and 7. At this point, it is sufficient to note that the term means to divide a total into parts and to assign those parts to certain objects. For example, the $93,000 of general corporate-level facility expenses have been divided equally among the three segments, thereby allocating $31,000 to each segment. Because the $93,000 of cost is incurred at the corporate level, it will continue to be incurred even when the segment is eliminated. In other words, eliminating the segment does not eliminate the corporate-level activities that cause the $93,000 of cost to be incurred. Clearly, the other two corporate-level facility costs (i.e., division manager's salary and depreciation) have not been allocated equally to the three segments. A total cost can be allocated between the three segments in many ways. A full discussion of these alternatives will be provided in the subsequent chapters.

Only the costs that can be avoided by eliminating the segment are relevant to the decision-making process. If the revenue generated by a segment is higher than the avoidable cost, that segment should not be eliminated. To illustrate, we analyze the information in the cost report for Stoerner Office Products that is shown in Exhibit 4–6. As the report indicates, Stoerner divides its operations into three divisions, copiers, computers, and printers.

It appears that Stoerner would be better off by eliminating the copiers segment. You may conclude that by eliminating the segment, the business could avoid the $22,250 loss, thereby increasing overall profitability to $257,750 ($136,250 + $121,500). Analysis of the relevant costs and revenues proves, however, that this conclusion is incorrect.

Analysis of Relevant Costs and Revenue

Begin by asking what happens to existing costs if Stoerner eliminates the copiers division. The allocated portion of corporate-level facility costs would be incurred even if Stoerner stopped making and selling copiers. Further, depreciation cannot be avoided because it is a *sunk cost*. Accordingly, the corporate-level facility costs are not relevant. Many other costs including the

Exhibit 4–7 *Relevant Revenue and Cost Data for Copier Segment*

Projected revenue	$550,000
Projected costs	
Unit-level costs	
Materials costs	(120,000)
Labor costs	(160,000)
Overhead	(30,800)
Batch-level costs	
Assembly setup	(15,000)
Materials handling	(6,000)
Product-level costs	
Engineering design	(10,000)
Production manager's salary	(52,000)
Facility-level costs	
Segment-level	
Division manager's salary	(82,000)
Administrative costs	(12,200)
Projected profit (loss)	$ 62,000

segment-level facility costs, the product-level costs, the batch-level costs, and the unit-level costs could be avoided, however, if the copiers division were eliminated. If the revenue generated from the sale of copiers exceeds these avoidable costs, Stoerner should continue to operate the segment. The relevant revenue and cost items are summarized in Exhibit 4–7.

Because the operation of the segment is contributing $62,000 per year to the store's profitability, Stoerner should continue to operate the copiers division. Indeed, elimination of the segment would cause profitability to decline by $62,000. This point can be verified by reconstructing the revenue and cost data as if the computers and printers divisions were operated without the copiers division. The reconstructed data are shown in Exhibit 4–8. Notice that the projected profit declines by $62,000 ($235,500 − $173,500) without the operation of the copiers segment, verifying the fact that the elimination of the copiers segment would be detrimental to Stoerner's profitability.

Qualitative Considerations in Decisions to Eliminate Segments

As with other special decisions, qualitative factors should be considered when determining whether to eliminate segments. For example, employees will be disrupted; some may be moved into other areas of the company, but others will be discharged. Once a trained workforce is dissolved, reestablishing it is difficult if the company decides to resume the segment's operation later. Furthermore, employees in other segments, suppliers, customers, and investors may believe that the elimination of a segment implies that the company as a whole is experiencing financial difficulty. These individuals may lose faith in the company and seek business contacts with other companies they perceive to be more stable.

Finally, the sales of different product lines are frequently interdependent. Some customers like one-stop shopping; they want to buy all of their office equipment from one supplier. When

Exhibit 4–8 *Projected Revenues and Costs Without Copier Division*

	Computers	Printers	Total
Projected revenue	$850,000	$780,000	$1,630,000
Projected costs			
Unit-level costs			
Materials costs	(178,000)	(180,000)	(358,000)
Labor costs	(202,000)	(165,000)	(367,000)
Overhead	(20,000)	(15,000)	(35,000)
Batch-level costs			
Assembly setup	(26,000)	(17,000)	(43,000)
Materials handling	(8,000)	(5,000)	(13,000)
Product-level costs			
Engineering design	(12,000)	(14,000)	(26,000)
Production manager's salary	(55,800)	(63,300)	(119,100)
Facility-level costs			
Segment level			
Division manager's salary	(92,000)	(85,000)	(177,000)
Administrative costs	(13,200)	(12,700)	(25,900)
Corporate level*			
Company president's salary	(63,000)	(60,200)	(123,200)
Depreciation	(39,375)	(36,925)	(76,300)
General expenses	(46,500)	(46,500)	(93,000)
Projected profit (loss)	$ 94,125	$ 79,375	$ 173,500

*The corporate-level facility costs that were previously *allocated* to the copier division have been reassigned on the basis of one-half to the computer division and one-half to the printer division.

Stoerner no longer sells copiers, customers may stop buying its computers and printers. Accordingly, the elimination of one segment may result in sales losses in other segments.

What will happen to the space that was used to make the copiers has not yet been asked. Suppose that Stoerner Office Products decides to make telephone systems in the space that it previously used for copiers. The contribution to profit associated with the telephone business would be an *opportunity cost* of operating the copier segment. As demonstrated in previous examples, adding the opportunity cost to the avoidable costs of operating the copier segment could change the decision that the previous analysis suggested.

As with outsourcing, changes in the volume can affect elimination decisions. Because many costs associated with operating a segment can be fixed, the cost per unit decreases as production increases. As a result, growth can transform a segment that is currently producing real losses into a segment that produces a real profit. Accordingly, managers must consider growth potential when making elimination decisions.

Capital Corporation is considering eliminating one of its operating segments. Capital employed a real estate broker to determine the marketability of the building that houses the segment. The broker obtained three bids for the building: $250,000, $262,000, and $264,000. The book value of the building is $275,000. Based on this information alone, what is the relevant cost of the building?

Answer The book value of the building is a sunk cost that is not relevant. There are three bids for the building, but only one is relevant because Capital could sell the building only once. The relevant cost of the building is the highest opportunity cost, which in this case is $264,000.

Summary of Relationships Between Avoidable Costs and the Hierarchy of Business Activity

You may have noticed a relationship between the cost hierarchy and the different types of special decisions just discussed. Avoidable costs are drawn from increasingly higher levels of the cost hierarchy as the type of decision moves from special order, to outsourcing, to segment elimination. A special order decision involves making additional units of an existing product. A decision to accept a special order affects unit-level and possibly batch-level costs. In contrast, a decision to outsource a product stops the production of that product. Because no products are made, outsourcing can avoid many product-level as well as unit-level and batch-level costs. Finally, if an entire business division is eliminated, some of the facility-level costs can be avoided. As you move up the scale of the decision hierarchy, more opportunities to avoid costs emerge. Moving to a new category does not mean, however, that all costs associated with the higher level of activity are automatically avoidable. For example, all product-level costs may not be avoidable if a company chooses to outsource a product. The company may incur inventory holding costs regardless of whether it makes or buys the inventory. Under-

LO5 Distinguish between unit-level, product-level, and facility-level costs and understand how these costs are related to decision making.

standing the relationship between decision type and level of cost hierarchy can improve your ability to identify avoidable costs. The relationships to look for are summarized in Exhibit 4–9. For each type of decision, look for avoidable costs in the categories marked with an X. Remember also that sunk costs cannot be avoided.

Exhibit 4–9 *Relationship Between Decision Type and Level of Cost Hierarchy*

Decision Type	Unit Level	Batch Level	Product Level	Facility Level
Special order	X	X		
Outsourcing	X	X	X	
Elimination	X	X	X	X

Equipment Replacement Decisions

Equipment may become technologically deficient long before it deteriorates physically. Accordingly, **equipment replacement decisions** should be determined on the basis of profitability analysis rather than physical deterioration. To illustrate, consider the replacement

analysis performed by the accountant of Stoerner Office Products. Stoerner owns a machine that originally cost $90,000 and is currently being depreciated at the rate of $11,000 per year and has accumulated depreciation of $33,000. The book value of the machine is $57,000 ($90,000 − $33,000). The machine has a remaining estimated useful life of five years and an estimated salvage value of $2,000. Labor costs associated with operating the machine are $9,000 per year. Stoerner has an opportunity to replace the existing equipment with a new machine that offers efficiencies estimated to reduce the labor cost by one-half ($4,500 per year). The old machine can be sold right now for $14,000; the new machine costs $29,000. The expected useful life of the new machine is five years, and its estimated salvage value is $4,000. These facts are summarized here.

Old Machine			New Machine		
Original cost	$90,000		Cost of the new machine	$29,000	
Accumulated depreciation	(33,000)		Salvage value (in 5 years)	4,000	
Book value	$57,000		Operating expense		
			($4,500 × 5 years)	22,500	
Market value (now)	$14,000				
Salvage value (in 5 years)	2,000				
Annual depreciation expense	11,000				
Operating expenses					
($9,000 × 5 years)	45,000				

Analysis of Relevant Costs

The first step in the decision-making process is to determine what relevant costs will be incurred if the old machine is used.

1. The *original cost* ($90,000), *current book value* ($57,000), *accumulated depreciation* ($33,000), and annual *depreciation expense* ($11,000) are different measures of a cost that was incurred in a prior period. As such, they represent sunk costs that are not relevant.
2. The $14,000 market value represents the current sacrifice that must be made to use the existing machine. In other words, if Stoerner does not use the machine, it can sell it for $14,000. From an economic perspective, *forgoing the opportunity* to sell the machine is the same thing as buying it. Accordingly, the *opportunity cost* is relevant to the replacement decision.
3. The salvage value of the old machine reduces the opportunity cost. In other words, Stoerner can sell the old machine today for $14,000 or can use it for five years and then sell it for $2,000. As a result, the opportunity cost of using the old machine for five years is $12,000 ($14,000 − $2,000). Notice that the opportunity cost per year is $2,400 ([$14,000 − $2,000] ÷ 5). This computation is consistent with the computation for straight-line depreciation. Indeed, the annualized opportunity cost can be thought of as opportunity cost depreciation.
4. The $45,000 ($9,000 × 5) of operating expenses will be incurred if the old machine is used but can be avoided if it is replaced. Accordingly, the operating expenses are relevant costs.

Next, determine what relevant costs will be incurred if the new machine is purchased and used.

1. The cost of the new machine represents a future economic sacrifice that must be incurred if the new machine is purchased. Accordingly, it is a relevant cost.
2. The salvage reduces the cost of purchasing the new machine. Although the new machine costs $29,000, part of this amount ($4,000) will be recovered at the end of five years. Accordingly, the relevant cost of purchasing the new machine is $25,000 ($29,000 − $4,000).
3. The $22,500 ($4,500 × 5) of operating expenses will be incurred if the new machine is purchased; it can be avoided if the new machine is not purchased. Accordingly, the operating expenses are relevant costs.

The relevant costs for the two machines are summarized here:

Old Machine		New Machine	
Opportunity cost	$14,000	Cost of the new machine	$29,000
Salvage value	(2,000)	Salvage value	(4,000)
Operating expenses	45,000	Operating expenses	22,500
Total	$57,000	Total	$47,500

The analysis suggests that Stoerner should acquire the new machine because it produces the lowest relevant cost. Stated differently, the $57,000 cost of using the old machine can be *avoided* by incurring the $47,500 cost necessary to acquire and use the new machine. During the five-year period, the company would save $9,500 ($57,000 − $47,500) by purchasing the new machine. Note that the analysis ignores tax considerations and the time value of money. These subjects will be covered in Chapter 10. The present discussion focuses on identifying and using relevant costs in decision making.

Decision making requires managers to make choices between alternative courses of action. Successful decision making depends on a manager's ability to identify and isolate the *relevant information.* Information that is relevant for decision making differs among the alternatives and is future oriented. Relevant revenues are sometimes referred to as *differential revenues* because they are the expected future revenues that differ among the alternatives. Relevant costs are sometimes referred to as *avoidable costs* because they are the future costs that can be eliminated or avoided by taking a specified alternative.

a look **back**

Costs that do not differ among the alternatives are not avoidable and therefore not relevant. *Sunk costs* are not relevant in decision making because they have already been incurred in past transactions and therefore cannot be avoided. *Opportunity costs* are relevant because they represent potential benefits that may or may not be realized, depending on the decision maker's action. In other words, future benefits that differ among the alternatives are relevant. Opportunity costs are not recorded in the financial accounting records.

Classifying costs into one of four hierarchical levels can facilitate the identification of relevant costs. *Unit-level* costs such as materials and labor are the costs incurred each time a single unit of product is made. These costs can be avoided by eliminating the production of a single unit of product. *Batch-level* costs are the costs associated with the production of a group of products. Examples include setup costs and inspection costs related to a batch (group) of work rather than a single unit. Eliminating a batch would avoid both batch-level costs and unit-level costs. *Product-level* costs are incurred to support specific kinds of products or services (design and regulatory compliance costs). Product-level costs can be avoided when a product line is discontinued. *Facility-level* costs are incurred on behalf of the whole company or a segment of the company; the president's salary is an example. In segment elimination decisions, the facility-level costs related to a particular segment being considered for elimination are relevant and avoidable. Those applying to the company as a whole are not avoidable.

Cost behavior (i.e., fixed or variable) is independent from the concept of relevance. Furthermore, a cost that is relevant in one decision context may be irrelevant in another context. Decision making depends on both quantitative as well as qualitative information. *Quantitative information refers to numbers that can be mathematically manipulated. Qualitative information* is nonquantitative information such as personal preferences or opportunities.

The four types of special decisions that are frequently encountered in business include (1) *special orders,* (2) *outsourcing,* (3) *elimination decisions,* and (4) *asset replacement.* The relevant costs in a special order decision are the unit-level and batch-level costs that will be incurred if the special order is accepted. If the differential revenues from the special order exceed the relevant costs, the order should be accepted. Outsourcing decisions must determine whether goods and services should be purchased from other companies. The relevant costs are

the unit-level, batch-level, and product-level costs that could be avoided if the company outsources the product or service. If these costs are more than the cost to buy and the qualitative characteristics are satisfactory, the company should outsource. Segment-related unit-level, batch-level, product-level, and facility-level costs that can be avoided when a segment is eliminated are relevant. If the segment's avoidable costs exceed its differential revenues, it should be eliminated, assuming favorable qualitative features. Asset replacement decisions compare the relevant costs of existing equipment with the relevant costs of new equipment to determine whether replacing the old equipment would be profitable.

a look forward

The next chapter begins a two-chapter investigation of cost measurement. Accountants seek to determine the cost of certain objects. A cost object may be a product, a service, a department, a customer, or any other thing for which the cost is being determined. Some costs can be directly traced to a cost object, others are difficult to trace. Costs that are difficult to trace to cost objects are called *indirect costs* or *overhead*. Indirect costs are assigned to cost objects through a process known as *cost allocation*. The next chapter introduces the basic concepts and procedures associated with cost allocation.

SELF-STUDY REVIEW PROBLEM

Flying High, Inc. (FHI), is a division of The Master Toy Company. FHI makes remote-controlled airplanes. During 2004, FHI incurred the following costs in the process of making 5,000 planes.

Unit-level materials costs (5,000 units @ $80)	$ 400,000
Unit-level labor costs (5,000 units @ $90)	450,000
Unit-level overhead costs (5,000 @ $70)	350,000
Depreciation cost on manufacturing equipment*	50,000
Other manufacturing overhead†	140,000
Inventory holding costs	240,000
Allocated portion of The Master Toy Company's facility-level costs	600,000
Total costs	$2,230,000

*The manufacturing equipment, which originally cost $250,000, has a book value of $200,000, a remaining useful life of four years, and a zero salvage value. If the equipment is not used in the production process, it can be leased for $30,000 per year.

†Includes supervisors' salaries and rent for the manufacturing building.

Required:

a. FHI uses a cost-plus pricing strategy. FHI sets its price at product cost plus $100. Determine the price that FHI should charge for its remote-controlled airplanes.

b. Assume that a potential customer that operates a chain of high-end toy stores has approached FHI. A buyer for this chain has offered to purchase 1,000 planes from FHI at a price of $275 each. Ignoring qualitative considerations, should FHI accept or reject the order?

c. FHI has the opportunity to purchase the planes from Arland Manufacturing Company for $325 each. Arland maintains adequate inventories so that it can supply its customers with planes on demand. Should FHI accept the opportunity to outsource the making of its planes?

d. Use the contribution margin format to prepare an income statement based on historical cost data. Prepare a second income statement that reflects the relevant cost data that Master Toy should consider in a segment elimination decision. Based on a comparison of these two statements, indicate whether Master Toy should eliminate the FHI division.

e. FHI is considering replacing the equipment it currently uses to manufacture its planes. It could purchase replacement equipment for $480,000 that has an expected useful life of four years and a salvage value of $40,000. The new equipment would increase productivity substantially, reducing unit-level labor costs by 20 percent. Assume that FHI would maintain its production and sales at 5,000 planes per year. Prepare a schedule that shows the relevant costs of operating the old equipment versus the costs of operating the new equipment. Should FHI replace the equipment?

Solution to Requirement a.

Product Cost for Remote-Controlled Airplanes	
Unit-level materials costs (5,000 units × $80)	$ 400,000
Unit-level labor costs (5,000 units × $90)	450,000
Unit-level overhead costs (5,000 units × $70)	350,000
Depreciation cost on manufacturing equipment	50,000
Other manufacturing overhead	140,000
Total product cost	$1,390,000

The cost per unit is $278 ($1,390,000 ÷ 5,000 units). The sales price per unit is $378 ($278 + $100). Depreciation expense is included because cost-plus pricing is usually based on historical cost rather than relevant cost. To be profitable in the long run, a company must ultimately recover the amount it paid for the equipment (the historical cost of the equipment).

Solution to Requirement b.
The incremental (relevant) cost of making 1,000 additional airplanes follows. The depreciation expense is not relevant because it represents a sunk cost. The other manufacturing overhead costs are not relevant because they will be incurred regardless of whether FHI makes the additional planes.

Per Unit Relevant Product Cost for Airplanes	
Unit-level materials costs	$ 80
Unit-level labor costs	90
Unit-level overhead costs	70
Total relevant product cost	$240

Since the relevant (incremental) cost of making the planes is less than the incremental revenue, FHI should accept the special order. Accepting the order will increase profits by $35,000 ([$275 incremental revenue − $240 incremental cost] × 1,000 units).

Solution to Requirement c.
Distinguish this decision from the special order opportunity discussed in Requirement b. That special order (Requirement b) decision hinged on the cost of making additional units with the existing production process. In contrast, a make-or-buy decision compares current production with the possibility of making zero units (closing down the entire manufacturing process). If the manufacturing process were shut down, FHI could avoid the unit-level costs, the cost of the lost opportunity to lease the equipment, the other manufacturing overhead costs, and the inventory holding costs. Since the planes can be purchased on demand, there is no need to maintain any inventory. The allocated portion of the facility-level costs is not relevant because it would be incurred regardless of whether FHI manufactured the planes. The relevant cost of making the planes follows.

Relevant Manufacturing Cost for Airplanes	
Unit-level materials costs (5,000 units × $80)	$ 400,000
Unit-level labor costs (5,000 units × $90)	450,000
Unit-level overhead costs (5,000 units × $70)	350,000
Opportunity cost of leasing the equipment	30,000
Other manufacturing overhead costs	140,000
Inventory holding cost	240,000
Total product cost	$1,610,000

The relevant cost per unit is $322 ($1,610,000 ÷ 5,000 units). Since the relevant cost of making the planes ($322) is less than the cost of purchasing them ($325), FHI should continue to make the planes.

Solution to Requirement d.

Income Statements	Historical Cost Data	Relevant Cost Data
Revenue ($378 × 5,000)	$1,890,000	$1,890,000
Less variable costs:		
Unit-level materials costs (5,000 units × $80)	(400,000)	(400,000)
Unit-level labor costs (5,000 units × $90)	(450,000)	(450,000)
Unit-level overhead costs (5,000 units × $70)	(350,000)	(350,000)
Contribution Margin	690,000	690,000
Depreciation cost on manufacturing equipment	(50,000)	
Opportunity cost of leasing manufacturing equipment		(30,000)
Other manufacturing overhead costs	(140,000)	(140,000)
Inventory holding costs	(240,000)	(240,000)
Allocated facility-level administrative costs	(600,000)	
Net Loss	$ (340,000)	
Contribution to Master Toy's Profitability		$ 280,000

Master Toy should not eliminate the segment (FHI). Although it appears to be incurring a loss, the allocated facility-level administrative costs are not relevant because Master Toy would incur these costs regardless of whether it eliminated FHI. Also, the depreciation cost on the manufacturing equipment is not relevant because it is a sunk cost. However, since the company could lease the equipment if the segment were eliminated, the $30,000 potential rental fee represents a relevant opportunity cost. The relevant revenue and cost data show that FHI is contributing $280,000 to the profitability of The Master Toy Company.

Solution to Requirement e.

The relevant costs of using the old equipment versus the new equipment are the costs that differ for the two alternatives. In this case relevant costs include the purchase price of the new equipment, the opportunity cost of the old equipment, and the labor costs. These items are summarized in the following table. The data show the total cost over the four-year useful life of the replacement equipment.

Relevant Cost Comparison	Old Equipment	New Equipment
Opportunity to lease the old equipment ($30,000 × 4 years)	$ 120,000	
Cost of new equipment ($480,000 − $40,000)		$ 440,000
Unit-level labor costs (5,000 units × $90 × 4 years)	1,800,000	
Unit-level labor costs (5,000 units × $90 × 4 years × .80)		1,440,000
Total relevant costs	$1,920,000	$1,880,000

Since the relevant cost of operating the new equipment is less than the cost of operating the old equipment, FHI should replace the equipment.

APPENDIX

Short-Term Versus Long-Term Goals

LO10 Understand the conflict between short- and long-term profitability.

To examine conflicts between short-term versus long-term goals, we return to the equipment replacement decision made by the management team of Stoerner Office Products (see page 155 for details). Suppose that the final equipment replacement decision is made by a departmental supervisor who is under significant pressure to maximize profitability. She is told that if profitability declines, she will lose her job. Under these circumstances, the supervisor may choose to keep the old machine even though it is to the company's advantage to purchase the new one. This occurs because the beneficial impact of the new machine is realized in years 2002 through 2005. Indeed, replacing the equipment will result in more expense/loss recognition in the first year. To illustrate, study the following information.

	2001	2002	2003	2004	2005	Totals
Keep old machine						
Depreciation expense*	$11,000	$11,000	$11,000	$11,000	$11,000	$ 55,000
Operating expense	9,000	9,000	9,000	9,000	9,000	45,000
Total	$20,000	$20,000	$20,000	$20,000	$20,000	$100,000
Replace old machine						
Loss on disposal†	$43,000	$ 0	$ 0	$ 0	$ 0	$43,000
Depreciation expense‡	5,000	5,000	5,000	5,000	5,000	25,000
Operating expense	4,500	4,500	4,500	4,500	4,500	22,500
Total	$52,500	$ 9,500	$ 9,500	$ 9,500	$ 9,500	$90,500

*($57,000 book value − $2,000 salvage) ÷ 5 years = $11,000

†($57,000 book value − $14,000 market value) = $43,000

‡($29,000 cost − $4,000 salvage) ÷ 5 years = $5,000

This analysis verifies fact that total cost at the end of the five-year period is $9,500 less if the equipment is replaced ($100,000 − $90,500). Notice, however, that total costs at the end of the first year are higher by $32,500 ($52,500 − $20,000) if the old machine is replaced. A decision maker under significant pressure to report higher profitability may be willing to sacrifice tomorrow's profits to look better today. By emphasizing short-term profitability, she may secure a promotion before the long-term effects of her decision become apparent. Even if she stays in the same position, her boss may be replaced by someone not so demanding in terms of reported profitability. The department supervisor's intent is to survive the moment and let the future take care of itself. Misguided reward systems can be as detrimental as threats of punishment. For example, a manager may choose short-term profitability to obtain a bonus that is based on reported profitability. It is the responsibility of upper-level management to establish policies and procedures that motivate subordinates to perform in ways that maximize the company's long-term profitability.

Decisions Regarding the Allocation of Scarce Resources

Suppose that Stoerner Office Products makes two types of computers: a high-end network server and an inexpensive personal computer. The relevant sales and variable cost data for each unit follow.

LO11 Perform the analysis necessary to make decisions regarding the allocation of scarce resources.

Network Server		Personal Computer	
Sales price	$4,000	Sales price	$1,500
Less: Variable cost	(3,760)	Less: Variable cost	(1,370)
Contribution margin	$ 240	Contribution margin	$ 130

In many circumstances, variable costs act as proxies for *avoidable costs*. For example, by definition, unit-level costs increase and decrease in direct proportion with the number of units of product made and sold. As previously indicated, unit-level costs are avoidable with respect to many special decision scenarios. To the extent that variable costs are proxies for avoidable costs, the contribution margin can be used as a measure of profitability. Other things being equal, higher contribution margins translate into more profitable products. If Stoerner could sell 1,000 computers, the company would certainly prefer that they be network servers. The contribution to profitability on those machines is almost double the contribution margin on the personal computer.

Even though the contribution margin is higher for network servers, selling personal computers may be more profitable. Why? If Stoerner can sell considerably more of the personal computers, the volume of activity will make up for the lower margin. In other words, selling three personal computers produces more total margin ($3 \times \$130 = \$390$) than selling one network server ($1 \times \$240$). Many factors could limit the sales of one or both of the products. Factors that limit a business's ability to satisfy the demand for its product are called **constraints.** Suppose that warehouse space is limited (i.e., the warehouse is a scarce resource that constrains sales). Accordingly, Stoerner cannot warehouse all of the computers that it needs to satisfy its customer orders. If a network server requires considerably more warehouse space than a personal computer, stocking and selling personal computers may be more profitable than stocking and selling network servers. To illustrate, assume that it requires 5 square feet of warehouse space for a network server and 2 square feet for a personal computer. If only 2,100 square feet of warehouse space are available, which computer should Stoerner stock and sell?

In this case, the warehouse space is considered a scarce resource. The computer that produces the highest contribution margin per unit of scarce resource (i.e., per square foot) is the more profitable product. The per unit computations for each product are shown here.

	Network Server	Personal Computer
Contribution margin per unit (a)	$240	$130
Divide by warehouse space needed to store one unit (b)	5 sq. ft.	2 sq. ft.
Contribution margin per unit of scarce resource (a ÷ b)	$ 48	$ 65

The data suggest that Stoerner should focus on the personal computer. Even though the personal computer produces a lower contribution margin per product, its contribution margin per scarce resource is higher. The effect on total profitability is shown as follows.

	Network Server	Personal Computer
Amount of available warehouse space(a)	2,100	2,100
Divide by warehouse space needed to store one unit (b)	5 sq. ft.	2 sq. ft.
Warehouse capacity in number of units (a ÷ b) = (c)	420	1,050
Times contribution margin per unit (d)	$ 240	$ 130
Total profit potential (c × d)	$100,800	$136,500

Although the quantitative data suggest that Stoerner will maximize profitability by limiting its inventory to personal computers, qualitative considerations may force the company to maintain a reasonable sales mix between the two products. For example, a business that buys several personal computers may also need a network server. A customer who cannot obtain both products from Stoerner may choose to buy nothing at all. Instead, the customer will find a supplier who will satisfy all of his needs. In other words, Stoerner may still need to stock some servers to offer a competitive product line.

The chairman of the board of directors asked Stoerner's president why company sales had remained level while the company's chief competitor had experienced significant increases. The president replied, "You cannot sell what you do not have. Our warehouse is too small. We stop production when we fill up the warehouse. The products sell out rapidly, and then we have to wait around for the next batch of computers to be made. When we are out of stock, our customers turn to the competition. We are constrained by the size of the warehouse." In accounting terms, the warehouse is a **bottleneck.** Its size is limiting the company's ability to sell its products.

Many businesses use a management practice known as the **theory of constraints (TOC)** to increase profitability by managing bottlenecks or constrained resources. TOC's primary objective is to identify the bottlenecks restricting the operations of the business and then to open those bottlenecks through a practice known as **relaxing the constraints.** The effect of applying TOC to the Stoerner case is apparent via contribution margin analysis. According to the preceding computations, a new server and a new personal computer produce a contribution margin of $48 and $65 per square foot of storage space, respectively. So long as additional warehouse space can be purchased for less than these amounts, Stoerner can increase its profitability by acquiring the space.

KEY TERMS

Allocation of scarce resource decisions (Appendix) *159*
Avoidable costs *141*
Batch-level costs *142*
Bottleneck (Appendix) *160*
Certified suppliers *150*
Constraints (Appendix) *159*
Differential costs *141*

Equipment replacement decisions *153*
Facility-level costs *143*
Low-ball pricing *149*
Opportunity costs *144*
Outsourcing *148*
Product-level costs *142*
Qualitative characteristics *145*

Quantitative characteristics *145*
Relaxing the constraints (Appendix) *160*
Relevant costs *141*
Relevant information *140*
Segment *150*

Special order decisions *145*
Sunk costs *140*
Theory of constraints (TOC) (Appendix) *160*
Unit-level costs *142*
Vertical integration *149*

QUESTIONS

1. Identify the primary qualities of revenues and costs that are relevant for decision making.
2. Are variable costs always relevant? Explain.
3. Identify the four hierarchical levels used to classify costs. When can each of these levels of costs be avoided?
4. Describe the relationship between relevance and accuracy.
5. "It all comes down to the bottom line. The numbers never lie." Do you agree with this conclusion? Explain your position.
6. Carmon Company invested $300,000 in the equity securities of Mann Corporation. The current market value of Carmon's investment in Mann is $250,000. Carmon currently needs funds for operating purposes. Although interest rates are high, Carmon's president has decided to borrow the needed funds instead of selling the investment in Mann. He explains that his company cannot afford to take a $50,000 loss on the Mann stock. Evaluate the president's decision based on this information.
7. What is an opportunity cost? How does it differ from a sunk cost?
8. A local bank advertises that it offers a free noninterest-bearing checking account if the depositor maintains a $500 minimum balance in the account. Is the checking account truly free?
9. A manager is faced with deciding whether to replace machine A or machine B. The original cost of machine A was $20,000 and that of machine B was $30,000. Because the two cost figures differ, they are relevant to the manager's decision. Do you agree? Explain your position.
10. Are all fixed costs unavoidable?
11. Identify two qualitative considerations that could be associated with special order decisions.
12. Which of the following would not be relevant to a make-or-buy decision?
    a. Allocated portion of depreciation expense on existing facilities.
    b. Variable cost of labor used to produce products currently purchased from suppliers.
    c. Warehousing costs for inventory of completed products (inventory levels will be constant regardless of whether products are purchased or produced).
    d. Cost of materials used to produce the items currently purchased from suppliers.
    e. Property taxes on the factory building.
13. What two factors should be considered in deciding how to allocate shelf space in a retail establishment?
14. What level(s) of costs is(are) relevant in special order decisions?
15. Why would a company consider outsourcing products or services?
16. Chris Sutter, the production manager of Satellite Computers, insists that the floppy drives used in the company's upper-end computers be outsourced since they can be purchased from a supplier at a lower cost per unit than the company is presently incurring to produce the drives. Jane Meyers, his assistant, insists that if sales growth continues at the current levels, the company will be able to produce the drives in the near future at a lower cost because of the company's predominately fixed cost structure. Does Ms. Meyers have a legitimate argument? Explain.
17. Identify some qualitative factors that should be considered in addition to quantitative costs in deciding whether to outsource.
18. The managers of Wilcox, Inc., are suggesting that the company president eliminate one of the company's segments that is operating at a loss. Why may this be a hasty decision?
19. Why would a supervisor choose to continue using a more costly old machine instead of replacing it with a less costly new machine?
20. Identify some of the constraints that limit a business's ability to satisfy the demand for its products or services.

EXERCISES—SERIES A

EXERCISE 4–1A *Distinction Between Relevance and Cost Behavior*   **L.O. 1**

Susan Cole is trying to decide which of two different kinds of candy to sell in her retail candy store. One type is a name brand candy that will practically sell itself. The other candy is cheaper to purchase but does not carry an identifiable brand name. Ms. Cole believes that she will have to incur significant advertising costs to sell this candy. Several cost items for the two types of candy are as follows:

Brandless Candy		Name Brand Candy	
Cost per box	$ 5.00	Cost per box	$ 6.50
Sales commissions per box	1.00	Sales commissions per box	1.00
Rent of display space	1,500.00	Rent of display space	1,500.00
Advertising	3,000.00	Advertising	2,000.00

Required

Identify each cost as being relevant or irrelevant to Ms. Cole's decision and indicate whether it is fixed or variable relative to the number of boxes sold.

L.O. 1, 2   **EXERCISE 4–2A** *Distinction Between Relevance and Cost Behavior*

Leone Company makes and sells a single product. Leone incurred the following costs in its most recent fiscal year.

Cost Items Appearing on the Income Statement	
Materials Cost ($7 per unit)	Sales Commissions (2% of sales)
Company President's Salary	Salaries of Administrative Personnel
Depreciation on Manufacturing Equipment	Shipping and Handling ($0.25 per unit)
Customer Billing Costs (1% of sales)	Depreciation on Office Furniture
Rental Cost of Manufacturing Facility	Manufacturing Supplies ($0.25 per unit)
Advertising Costs ($250,000 per year)	Production Supervisor's Salary
Labor Cost ($5 per unit)	

Leone could purchase the products that it currently makes. If it purchased the items, the company would continue to sell them using its own logo, advertising program, and sales staff.

Required

Identify each cost as relevant or irrelevant to the outsourcing decision and indicate whether the cost is fixed or variable relative to the number of products manufactured and sold.

L.O. 1   **EXERCISE 4–3A** *Distinction Between Avoidable Costs and Cost Behavior*

Sensation Company makes fine jewelry that it sells to department stores throughout the United States. Sensation is trying to decide which of two bracelets to manufacture. Sensation has a labor contract that prohibits the company from laying off workers freely. Cost data pertaining to the two choices follow.

	Bracelet A	Bracelet B
Cost of materials per unit	$ 26	$ 45
Cost of labor per unit	40	40
Advertising cost per year	8,000	6,000
Annual depreciation on existing equip.	5,000	4,000

Required

a. Identify the fixed costs and determine the amount of fixed cost for each product.
b. Identify the variable costs and determine the amount of variable cost per unit for each product.
c. Identify the avoidable costs and determine the amount of avoidable cost for each product.

L.O. 1, 2, 9   **EXERCISE 4–4A** *Special Order Decision*

Serio Concrete Company pours concrete slabs for single-family dwellings. Taylor Construction Company, which operates outside Serio's normal sales territory, asks Serio to pour 30 slabs for Taylor's new development of homes. Serio has the capacity to build 300 slabs and is presently working on 250 of them. Taylor is willing to pay only $2,500 per slab. Serio estimates the cost of a typical job to include unit-level materials, $1,300; unit-level labor, $900; and an allocated portion of facility-level overhead, $500.

Required

Should Serio accept or reject the special order to pour 30 slabs for $2,500 each? Support your answer with appropriate computations.

EXERCISE 4–5A *Special Order Decision*

L.O. 1, 2, 9

Crawford Company manufactures a personal computer designed for use in schools and markets it under its own label. Crawford has the capacity to produce 20,000 units a year but is currently producing and selling only 15,000 units a year. The computer's normal selling price is $1,600 per unit with no volume discounts. The unit-level costs of the computer's production are $600 for direct materials, $200 for direct labor, and $250 for indirect manufacturing costs. The total product- and facility-level costs incurred by Crawford during the year are expected to be $2,000,000 and $800,000, respectively. Assume that Crawford receives a special order to produce and sell 4,000 computers at $1,200 each.

Required
Should Crawford accept or reject the special order? Support your answer with appropriate computations.

EXERCISE 4–6A *Identifying Qualitative Factors for a Special Order Decision*

L.O. 8

Required
Describe the qualitative factors that Crawford should consider before accepting the special order described in Exercise 4–5A.

EXERCISE 4–7A *Using the Contribution Margin Approach for a Special Order Decision*

L.O. 9

Omega Company, which produces and sells a small digital clock, bases its pricing strategy on a 30 percent markup on total cost. Based on annual production costs for 25,000 units of product, computations for the sales price per clock follow.

Unit-level costs	$200,000
Fixed costs	75,000
Total cost (a)	275,000
Markup (a × 0.30)	82,500
Total sales (b)	$357,500
Sales price per unit (b ÷ 25,000)	$ 14.30

Required
a. Omega has excess capacity and receives a special order for 6,000 clocks for $10 each. Calculate the contribution margin per unit; based on it, should Omega accept the special order?
b. Support your answer by preparing a contribution margin income statement for the special order.

EXERCISE 4–8A *Outsourcing Decision*

L.O. 9

Baja Bicycle Manufacturing Company currently produces the handlebars used in manufacturing its bicycles, which are high-quality racing bikes with limited sales. Baja produces and sells only 4,000 bikes each year. Due to the low volume of activity, Baja is unable to obtain the economies of scale that larger producers achieve. For example, Baja could buy the handlebars for $30 each; they cost $34 each to make. The following is a detailed breakdown of current production costs.

Item	Unit Cost	Total
Unit-level costs		
Materials	$12	$ 48,000
Labor	13	52,000
Overhead	4	16,000
Allocated facility-level costs	5	20,000
Total	$34	$136,000

After seeing these figures, Baja's president remarked that it would be foolish for the company to continue to produce the handlebars at $34 each when it can buy them for $30 each.

Required
Do you agree with the president's conclusion? Support your answer with appropriate computations.

EXERCISE 4–9A *Establishing Price for an Outsourcing Decision*

L.O. 9

Green Lawn, Inc., makes and sells lawn mowers for which it currently makes the engines. It has an opportunity to purchase the engines from a reliable manufacturer. The annual costs of making the engines are shown here.

Cost of materials (24,000 Units $\times$ $15)	$360,000
Labor (24,000 Units $\times$ $20)	480,000
Depreciation on manufacturing equipment*	12,000
Salary of supervisor of engine production	90,000
Rental cost of equipment used to make engines	24,000
Allocated portion of corporate-level facility-sustaining costs	30,000
Total cost to make 24,000 engines	$996,000

*The equipment has a book value of $56,000 but its market value is zero.

Required

a. Determine the maximum price per unit that Green Lawn would be willing to pay for the engines.

b. Would the price computed in Requirement *a* change if production increased to 30,000 units? Support your answer with appropriate computations.

L.O. 8, 9   EXERCISE 4–10A *Outsourcing Decision with Qualitative Factors*

Sound Wave, Inc. (SWI), which makes and sells 20,000 radios annually, currently purchases the radio speakers it uses for $36 each. Each radio uses one speaker. The company has idle capacity and is considering the possibility of making the speakers that it needs. SWI estimates that the cost of materials and labor needed to make speakers would be a total of $35 for each speaker. In addition, the costs of supervisory salaries, rent, and other manufacturing costs would be $75,000. Allocated facility-level costs would be $40,000.

Required

a. Determine the change in net income SWI would experience if it decides to make the speakers.

b. Discuss the qualitative factors that SWI should consider.

L.O. 7, 9   EXERCISE 4–11A *Outsourcing Decision Affected by Opportunity Costs*

Perry Electronics currently produces the shipping containers it uses to deliver the electronics products it sells. The monthly cost of producing 9,000 containers follows.

Unit-level materials	$ 9,000
Unit-level labor	12,000
Unit-level overhead	7,800
Product-level costs*	18,000
Allocated facility-level costs	45,000

*One-third of these costs can be avoided by purchasing the containers.

Trident Container Company has offered to sell comparable containers to Perry for $4.50 each.

Required

a. Should Perry continue to make the containers? Support your answer with appropriate computations.

b. Perry could lease the space it currently uses in the manufacturing process. If leasing would produce $18,000 per month, would your answer to Requirement *a* be different? Explain.

L.O. 7   EXERCISE 4–12A *Opportunity Cost*

Value Truck Lines, Inc., owns a truck that cost $80,000. Currently, the truck's book value is $48,000, and its expected remaining useful life is four years. Value has the opportunity to purchase for $60,000 a replacement truck that is extremely fuel efficient. Fuel cost for the old truck is expected to be $8,000 per year more than fuel cost for the new truck. The old truck is paid for but, in spite of being in good condition, can be sold for only $32,000.

Required

Should Value Truck Lines replace the old truck with the new fuel-efficient model, or should it continue to use the old truck until it wears out? Explain.

L.O. 7, 8   EXERCISE 4–13A *Opportunity Costs*

Kate Nobles owns her own taxi, for which she bought an $18,000 permit to operate two years ago. Ms. Nobles earns $33,000 a year operating as an independent but has the opportunity to sell the taxi and permit

for $60,000 and take a position as dispatcher for Martin Taxi Co. The dispatcher position pays $30,000 a year for a 40-hour week. Driving her own taxi, Ms. Nobles works approximately 55 hours per week. If she sells her business, she will invest the $60,000 and can earn a 10 percent return.

Required
a. Determine the opportunity cost of owning and operating the independent business.
b. Based solely on financial considerations, should Ms. Nobles sell the taxi and accept the position as dispatcher?
c. Discuss the qualitative as well as quantitative factors that Ms. Nobles should consider.

EXERCISE 4–14A *Segment Elimination Decision*   L.O. 9

Dill Company operates three segments. Income statements for the segments imply that profitability could be improved if Segment A were eliminated.

DILL COMPANY
Income Statements
For the Year 2009

Segment	A	B	C
Sales	$162,000	$235,000	$245,000
Cost of Goods Sold	(121,000)	(92,000)	(95,000)
Sales Commissions	(15,000)	(22,000)	(22,000)
Contribution Margin	$ 26,000	$121,000	$128,000
Depreciation and Other General Fixed Overhead Cost	(34,000)	(42,000)	(34,000)
General Fixed Oper. Exp. (allocation of president's salary)	(10,000)	(10,000)	(10,000)
Advertising Expense	(3,000)	(10,000)	0
Net Income	$(21,000)	$ 59,000	$ 84,000

Required
a. Explain the effect on profitability if segment A is eliminated.
b. Prepare comparative income statements for the company as a whole under two alternatives: (1) the retention of Segment A and (2) the elimination of Segment A.

EXERCISE 4–15A *Segment Elimination Decision*   L.O. 9

Galway Transport Company divides its operations into four divisions. A recent income statement for Cahaba Division follows.

GALWAY TRANSPORT COMPANY
Cahaba Division
Income Statement
For the Year 2005

Revenue	$ 500,000
Salaries for Drivers	(350,000)
Fuel Expenses	(50,000)
Insurance	(70,000)
Depreciation Expense (sunk cost)	(50,000)
Division-Level Facility-Sustaining Costs	(40,000)
Companywide Facility-Sustaining Costs	(80,000)
Net Loss	$(140,000)

Required
a. Should Cahaba Division be eliminated? Support your answer by explaining how the division's elimination would affect the net income of the company as a whole. By how much would companywide income increase or decrease?
b. Assume that Cahaba Division is able to increase its revenue to $540,000 by raising its prices. Would this change the decision you made in Requirement *a*? Determine the amount of the increase or decrease that would occur in companywide net income if the segment were eliminated if revenue were $540,000.
c. What is the minimum amount of revenue required to justify continuing the operation of Cahaba Division?

L.O. 4 **EXERCISE 4–16A** *Identifying Avoidable Cost of a Segment*

Moses Corporation is considering the elimination of one of its segments. The segment incurs the following fixed costs. If the segment is eliminated, the building it uses will be sold.

Advertising expense	$120,000
Supervisory salaries	160,000
Allocation of companywide facility-level costs	15,000
Original cost of building	80,000
Book value of building	50,000
Market value of building	60,000
Depreciation on building	10,000
Maintenance costs on equipment	50,000
Real estate taxes on building	4,000

Required
Based on this information, determine the amount of avoidable cost associated with the segment.

L.O. 9 **EXERCISE 4–17A** *Asset Replacement Decision*

A machine purchased three years ago for $130,000 has a current book value using straight-line depreciation of $90,000; its operating expenses are $24,000 per year. A replacement machine would cost $200,000, have a useful life of nine years, and would require $8,000 per year in operating expenses. It has an expected salvage value of $16,000 after nine years. The current disposal value of the old machine is $60,000; if it is kept nine more years, its residual value would be $10,000.

Required
Based on this information, should the old machine be replaced? Support your answer.

L.O. 9 **EXERCISE 4–18A** *Asset Replacement Decision*

Haldman Company is considering replacement of some of its manufacturing equipment. Information regarding the existing equipment and the potential replacement equipment follows.

Existing Equipment		Replacement Equipment	
Cost	$ 70,000	Cost	$80,000
Operating expenses*	100,000	Operating expenses*	16,000
Salvage value	10,000	Salvage value	14,000
Market value	50,000	Useful life	8 years
Book value	32,000		
Remaining useful life	8 years		

*The amounts shown for operating expenses are the cumulative total of all such expected expenses to be incurred over the useful life of the equipment.

Required
Based on this information, recommend whether to replace the equipment. Support your recommendation with appropriate computations.

L.O. 9 **EXERCISE 4–19A** *Asset Replacement Decision*

Odan Company paid $60,000 to purchase a machine on January 1, 2006. During 2008, a technological breakthrough resulted in the development of a new machine that costs $112,500. The old machine costs $36,000 per year to operate, but the new machine could be operated for only $9,000 per year. The new machine, which will be available for delivery on January 1, 2009, has an expected useful life of four years. The old machine is more durable and is expected to have a remaining useful life of four years. The current market value of the old machine is $10,000. The expected salvage value of both machines is zero.

Required

Based on this information, recommend whether to replace the machine. Support your recommendation with appropriate computations.

EXERCISE 4–20A *Annual Versus Cumulative Data for Replacement Decision*

L.O. 7, 9

Because of rapidly advancing technology, Wren Publications, Inc., is considering replacing its existing typesetting machine with leased equipment. The old machine, purchased two years ago, has an expected useful life of six years and is in good condition. Apparently, it will continue to perform as expected for the remaining four years of its expected useful life. A four-year lease for equipment with comparable productivity can be obtained for $12,000 per year. The following data apply to the old machine.

Original cost	$135,000
Accumulated depreciation	45,000
Current market value	67,500
Estimated salvage value	7,500

Required

a. Determine the annual opportunity cost of using the old machine. Based on your computations, recommend whether to replace it.
b. Determine the total cost of the lease over the four-year contract. Based on your computations, recommend whether to replace the old machine.

Appendix

EXERCISE 4–21A *Scarce Resource Decision*

L.O. 11

Gao Funtime Novelties has the capacity to produce either 36,000 corncob pipes or 16,000 cornhusk dolls per year. The pipes cost $3 each to produce and sell for $6 each. The dolls sell for $10 each and cost $4 to produce.

Required

Assuming that Gao Funtime Novelties can sell all it produces of either product, should it produce the corncob pipes or the cornhusk dolls? Show computations to support your answer.

PROBLEMS—SERIES A

PROBLEM 4–22A *Context-Sensitive Relevance*

L.O. 1, 6

Required

Respond to each requirement independently.

a. Describe two decision-making contexts, one in which unit-level materials costs are avoidable, and the other in which they are unavoidable.
b. Describe two decision-making contexts, one in which batch-level setup costs are avoidable, and the other in which they are unavoidable.
c. Describe two decision-making contexts, one in which advertising costs are avoidable, and the other in which they are unavoidable.
d. Describe two decision-making contexts, one in which rent paid for a building is avoidable, and the other in which it is unavoidable.
e. Describe two decision-making contexts, one in which depreciation on manufacturing equipment is avoidable, and the other in which it is unavoidable.

PROBLEM 4–23A *Context-Sensitive Relevance*

L.O. 6

Apricot Construction Company is a building contractor specializing in small commercial buildings. The company has the opportunity to accept one of two jobs; it cannot accept both because they must be performed at the same time and Apricot does not have the necessary labor force for both jobs. Indeed, it will be necessary to hire a new supervisor if either job is accepted. Furthermore, additional insurance will be required if either job is accepted. The revenue and costs associated with each job follow.

Cost Category	Job A	Job B
Contract price	$640,000	$580,000
Unit-level materials	246,000	216,000
Unit-level labor	237,000	242,400
Unit-level overhead	16,400	13,200
Supervisor's salary	72,400	72,400
Rental equipment costs	24,800	28,200
Depreciation on tools (zero market value)	20,000	20,000
Allocated portion of companywide facility-sustaining costs	6,400	5,800
Insurance coverage	16,000	16,000
Cost incurred to obtain and evaluate jobs	4,000	5,000

Required

a. Assume that Apricot has decided to accept one of the two jobs. Identify the information relevant to selecting one job versus the other. Recommend which job to accept and support your answer with appropriate computations.

b. Assume that Job A is no longer available. Apricot's choice is to accept or reject Job B alone. Identify the information relevant to this decision. Recommend whether to accept or reject Job B. Support your answer with appropriate computations.

L.O. 8, 9   PROBLEM 4–24A *Effect of Operating Leverage on Special Order Decision*

Reid Quilting Company makes blankets that it markets through a variety of department stores. It makes the blankets in batches of 800 units. Reid made 20,000 blankets during the prior accounting period. The cost of producing the blankets is summarized here.

Materials cost ($25 per unit × 20,000)	$ 500,000
Labor cost ($30 per unit × 20,000)	600,000
Manufacturing supplies ($3 × 20,000)	60,000
Batch-level costs (25 batches at $4,000 per batch)	100,000
Product-level costs	140,000
Facility-level costs	300,000
Total costs	$1,700,000

Cost per unit = $1,700,000 ÷ 20,000 = $85

Required

a. Comfort Motels has offered to buy a batch of 400 blankets for $65 each. Reid's normal selling price is $100 per unit. Based on the preceding quantitative data, should Reid accept the special order? Support your answer with appropriate computations.

b. Would your answer to Requirement *a* change if Comfort offered to buy a batch of 800 blankets for $65 per unit? Support your answer with appropriate computations.

c. Describe the qualitative factors that Reid Quilting Company should consider before accepting a special order to sell blankets to Comfort Motels.

L.O. 8, 9   PROBLEM 4–25A *Effects of the Level of Production on an Outsourcing Decision*

Aqaba Chemical Company makes a variety of cosmetic products, one of which is a skin cream designed to reduce the signs of aging. Aqaba produces a relatively small amount (10,000 units) of the cream and is considering the purchase of the product from an outside supplier for $4.50 each. If Aqaba purchases from the outside supplier, it would continue to sell and distribute the cream under its own brand name. Aqaba's accountant constructed the following profitability analysis.

Revenue (10,000 units × $10)	$100,000
Unit-level materials costs (10,000 units × $1.40)	(14,000)
Unit-level labor costs (10,000 units × $0.50)	(5,000)
Unit-level overhead costs (10,000 × $0.10)	(1,000)
Unit-level selling expenses (10,000 × $0.25)	(2,500)
Contribution margin	$ 77,500
Skin cream production supervisor's salary	(30,000)
Allocated portion of facility-level costs	(7,500)
Product-level advertising cost	(25,000)
Contribution to companywide income	$ 15,000

Required
a. Identify the cost items relevant to the make-or-outsource decision.
b. Should Aqaba continue to make the product or buy it from the supplier? Support your answer by determining the change in net income if Aqaba buys the cream instead of making it.
c. Suppose that Aqaba is able to increase sales by 5,000 units (sales will increase to 15,000 units). At this level of production, should Aqaba make or buy the cream? Support your answer by explaining how the increase in production affects the cost per unit.
d. Discuss the qualitative factors that Aqaba should consider before deciding to outsource the skin cream. How can Aqaba minimize the risk of establishing a relationship with an unreliable supplier?

PROBLEM 4–26A *Outsourcing Decision Affected by Equipment Replacement*   **L.O. 9**

Alps Bike Company (ABC) makes the frames used to build its bicycles. During 2006, ABC made 20,000 frames; the costs incurred follow.

Unit-level materials costs (20,000 units × $180)	$ 3,600,000
Unit-level labor costs (20,000 units × $210)	4,200,000
Unit-level overhead costs (20,000 × $20)	400,000
Depreciation on manufacturing equipment	100,000
Bike frame production supervisor's salary	80,000
Inventory holding costs	480,000
Allocated portion of facility-level costs	1,200,000
Total costs	$10,060,000

Alps has an opportunity to purchase frames for $390 each.

Additional Information
1. The manufacturing equipment, which originally cost $500,000, has a book value of $400,000, a remaining useful life of four years, and a zero salvage value. If the equipment is not used to produce bicycle frames, it can be leased for $60,000 per year.
2. ABC has the opportunity to purchase for $960,000 new manufacturing equipment that will have an expected useful life of four years and a salvage value of $80,000. This equipment will increase productivity substantially, reducing unit-level labor costs by 15 percent. Assume that ABC will continue to produce and sell 20,000 frames per year in the future.
3. If ABC outsources the frames, the company can eliminate 80 percent of the inventory holding costs.

Required
a. Determine the relevant per unit cost of making the bike frames, assuming the continued use of the existing equipment (the manufacturing costs that could be avoided if the frames were purchased instead of made with the old equipment). Based on the quantitative data, should ABC outsource the bike frames? Support your answer with appropriate computations.
b. Determine the relevant per unit cost of making the bike frames if ABC purchased the new equipment (the manufacturing costs that could be avoided if the frames were purchased instead of made with the new equipment). Based on the cost data computed in Requirements *a* and *b,* should ABC replace the equipment?
c. Should ABC purchase the new equipment and make the frames or should it outsource the frames?
d. Discuss the qualitative factors that ABC should consider before deciding to outsource the bike frames. How can ABC minimize the risk of establishing a relationship with an unreliable supplier?

PROBLEM 4–27A *Eliminating a Segment*   **L.O. 9**

Amarillo Boot Co. sells men's, women's, and children's boots. For each type of boot sold, it operates a separate department that has its own manager. The manager of the men's department has a sales staff of nine employees, the manager of the women's department has six employees, and the manager of the children's department has three employees. All departments are housed in a single store. In recent years, the children's department has operated at a net loss and is expected to continue to do so. Last year's income statements follow.

	Men's Department	Women's Department	Children's Department
Sales	$800,000	$610,000	$268,000
Cost of Goods Sold	(332,000)	(267,000)	(160,000)
Gross Margin	$468,000	$343,000	$108,000
Department Manager's Salary	(48,000)	(42,000)	(28,000)
Sales Commissions	(216,000)	(168,000)	(58,000)
Rent on Store Lease	(25,000)	(25,000)	(25,000)
Store Utilities	(5,000)	(5,000)	(5,000)
Net Income (loss)	$174,000	$103,000	$ (8,000)

Required

a. Determine whether to eliminate the Children's Department.

b. Confirm the conclusion you reached in Requirement *a* by preparing income statements for the company as a whole with and without the Children's Department.

c. Eliminating the Children's Department would increase space available to display men's and women's boots. Suppose management estimates that a wider selection of adult boots would increase the store's net earnings by $32,000. Would this information affect the decision that you made in Requirement *a*? Explain your answer.

L.O. 7, 9   PROBLEM 4–28A *Effect of Activity Level and Opportunity Cost on Segment Elimination Decision*

Tucker Manufacturing Co. produces and sells specialized equipment used in the petroleum industry. The company is organized into three separate operating branches: Division A, which manufactures and sells heavy equipment; Division B, which manufactures and sells hand tools; and Division C, which makes and sells electric motors. Each division is housed in a separate manufacturing facility. Company headquarters is located in a separate building. In recent years, Division B has been operating at a net loss and is expected to continue to do so. Income statements for the three divisions for 2008 follow.

	Division A	Division B	Division C
Sales	$2,500,000	$ 600,000	$3,000,000
Less: Cost of Goods Sold			
Unit-Level Manufacturing Costs	(1,500,000)	(350,000)	(1,850,000)
Rent on Manufacturing Facility	(300,000)	(200,000)	(250,000)
Gross Margin	$ 700,000	$ 50,000	$ 900,000
Less: Operating Expenses			
Unit-Level Selling and Admin. Expenses	(100,000)	(25,000)	(150,000)
Division-Level Fixed Selling and			
Admin. Expenses	(200,000)	(75,000)	(250,000)
Headquarters Facility-Level Costs	(150,000)	(150,000)	(150,000)
Net Income (loss)	$ 250,000	$ (200,000)	$ 350,000

Required

a. Based on the preceding information, recommend whether to eliminate Division B. Support your answer by preparing companywide income statements before and after eliminating Division B.

b. During 2008, Division B produced and sold 20,000 units of hand tools. Would your recommendation in response to Requirement *a* change if sales and production increase to 25,000 units in 2009? Support your answer by comparing differential revenue and avoidable cost for Division B, assuming that it sells 25,000 units.

c. Suppose that Tucker could sublease Division B's manufacturing facility for $225,000. Would you operate the division at a production and sales volume of 25,000 units, or would you close it? Support your answer with appropriate computations.

L.O. 9   PROBLEM 4–29A *Comprehensive Problem Including Special Order, Outsourcing, and Segment Elimination Decisions*

Laramie, Inc., makes and sells state-of-the-art electronics products. One of its segments produces The Math Machine, an inexpensive four-function calculator. The company's chief accountant recently pre-

pared the following income statement showing annual revenues and expenses associated with the segment's operating activities. The relevant range for the production and sale of the calculators is between 30,000 and 60,000 units per year.

Revenue (40,000 units × $8)	$320,000
Unit-Level Variable Costs	
Materials Cost (40,000 × $2)	(80,000)
Labor Cost (40,000 × $1)	(40,000)
Manufacturing Overhead (40,000 × $0.50)	(20,000)
Shipping and Handling (40,000 × $0.25)	(10,000)
Sales Commissions (40,000 × $1)	(40,000)
Contribution Margin	$130,000
Fixed Expenses	
Advertising Costs	(20,000)
Salary of Production Supervisor	(60,000)
Depreciation on Production Equipment (zero market value)	(30,000)
Allocated Companywide Facility-Level Expenses	(50,000)
Net Loss	$ (30,000)

Required (Consider each of the requirements independently.)

a. A large discount store has approached the owner of Laramie about buying 5,000 calculators. It would replace The Math Machine's label with its own logo to avoid affecting Laramie's existing customers. Because the offer was made directly to the owner, no sales commissions on the transaction would be involved, but the discount store is willing to pay only $4.50 per calculator. Based on quantitative factors alone, should Laramie accept the special order? Support your answer with appropriate computations. Specifically, by what amount would the special order increase or decrease profitability?

b. Laramie has an opportunity to buy the 40,000 calculators it currently makes from a reliable competing manufacturer for $4.90 each. The product meets Laramie's quality standards. Laramie could continue to use its own logo, advertising program, and sales force to distribute the products. Should Laramie buy the calculators or continue to make them? Support your answer with appropriate computations. Specifically, how much more or less would it cost to buy the calculators than to make them? Would your answer change if the volume of sales were increased to 60,000 units?

c. Because the calculator division is currently operating at a loss, should it be eliminated from the company's operations? Support your answer with appropriate computations. Specifically, by what amount would the segment's elimination increase or decrease profitability?

Appendix

PROBLEM 4–30A *Allocating Scarce Resources*   **L.O. 11**

The following information applies to the products of Kuerton Company.

	Product A	Product B
Selling price per unit	$52	$48
Variable cost per unit	44	36

Required

Identify the product that should be produced or sold under each of the following constraints. Consider each constraint separately.

a. One unit of Product A requires 2 hours of labor to produce, and one unit of Product B requires 4 hours of labor to produce. Due to labor constraints, demand is higher than the company's capacity to make both products.

b. The products are sold to the public in retail stores. The company has limited floor space and cannot stock as many products as it would like. Display space is available for only one of the two products. Expected sales of Product A are 10,000 units and of Product B are 8,000 units.

c. The maximum number of machine hours available is 40,000. Product A uses 2 machine hours, and Product B uses 5 machine hours. The company can sell all the products it produces.

PROBLEM 4–31A *Conflict Between Short-Term Versus Long-Term Performance*   **L.O. 10**

Tony Preston manages the cutting department of Cantrell Timber Company. He purchased a tree-cutting machine on January 1, 2006, for $400,000. The machine had an estimated useful life of five years and

zero salvage value, and the cost to operate it is $90,000 per year. Technological developments resulted in the development of a more advanced machine available for purchase on January 1, 2007, that would allow a 25 percent reduction in operating costs. The new machine would cost $240,000 and have a four-year useful life and zero salvage value. The current market value of the old machine on January 1, 2007, is $200,000, and its book value is $320,000 on that date. Straight-line depreciation is used for both machines. The company expects to generate $224,000 of revenue per year from the use of either machine.

Required

a. Recommend whether to replace the old machine on January 1, 2007. Support your answer with appropriate computations.

b. Prepare income statements for four years (2007 through 2010) assuming that the old machine is retained.

c. Prepare income statements for four years (2007 through 2010) assuming that the old machine is replaced.

d. Discuss the potential ethical conflicts that could result from the timing of the loss and expense recognition reported in the two income statements.

EXERCISES—SERIES B

L.O. 1 **EXERCISE 4–1B** *Distinction Between Relevance and Cost Behavior*

Tim Sullivan is planning to rent a small shop for a new business. He can sell either sandwiches or donuts. The following costs pertain to the two products.

Sandwiches		Donuts	
Cost per sandwich	$ 1.50	Cost per dozen donuts	$ 1.25
Sales commissions per sandwich	0.05	Sales commissions per dozen donuts	0.07
Monthly shop rental cost	1,000.00	Monthly shop rental cost	1,000.00
Monthly advertising cost	500.00	Monthly advertising cost	300.00

Required

Identify each cost as relevant or irrelevant to Mr. Sullivan's product decision and indicate whether the cost is fixed or variable relative to the number of units sold.

L.O. 1, 2 **EXERCISE 4–2B** *Distinction Between Relevance and Cost Behavior*

Kinkay Company makes and sells a toy plane. Kinkay incurred the following costs in its most recent fiscal year:

Cost Items Reported on Income Statement
Costs of TV Commercials
Labor Costs ($3 per unit)
Sales Commissions (1% of sales)
Sales Manager's Salary
Shipping and Handling Costs ($0.75 per unit)
Cost of Renting the Administrative Building
Utility Costs for the Manufacturing Plant ($0.25 per unit produced)
Manufacturing Plant Manager's Salary
Materials Costs ($4 per unit produced)
Real Estate Taxes on the Manufacturing Plant
Depreciation on Manufacturing Equipment
Packaging Cost ($1 per unit produced)
Wages of the Plant Security Guard

Kinkay could purchase the toy planes from a supplier. If it did, the company would continue to sell them using its own logo, advertising program, and sales staff.

Required

Identify each cost as relevant or irrelevant to the outsourcing decision and indicate whether the cost is fixed or variable relative to the number of toy planes manufactured and sold.

EXERCISE 4–3B *Distinction Between Avoidable Costs and Cost Behavior* L.O. 1

Stuart Phones, Inc., makes telephones that it sells to department stores throughout the United States. Stuart is trying to decide which of two telephone models to manufacture. The company could produce either telephone with its existing machinery. Cost data pertaining to the two choices follow:

	Model 90	Model 30
Materials cost per unit	$ 57	$ 57
Labor cost per unit	46	27
Product design cost	12,000	7,000
Depreciation on existing manufacturing machinery	3,000	3,000

Required
a. Identify the fixed costs and determine the amount of fixed cost for each model.
b. Identify the variable costs and determine the amount of variable cost for each model.
c. Identify the avoidable costs.

EXERCISE 4–4B *Making a Special Order Decision* L.O. 1, 2, 9

Brower Textile Company manufactures high-quality bed sheets and sells them in sets to a well-known retail company for $35 a set. Brower has sufficient capacity to produce 100,000 sets of sheets annually; the retail company currently purchases 80,000 sets each year. Brower's unit-level cost is $20 per set and its fixed cost is $800,000 per year. A motel chain has offered to purchase 10,000 sheet sets from Brower for $27 per set. If Brower accepts the order, the contract will prohibit the motel chain from reselling the bed sheets.

Required
Should Brower accept or reject the special order? Support your answer with appropriate computations.

EXERCISE 4–5B *Making a Special Order Decision* L.O. 1, 2, 9

Sanders Automotive Company manufactures an engine designed for motorcycles and markets the product using its own brand name. Although Sanders has the capacity to produce 28,000 engines annually, it currently produces and sells only 25,000 units per year. The engine normally sells for $400 per unit, with no quantity discounts. The unit-level costs to produce the engine are $150 for direct materials, $100 for direct labor, and $30 for indirect manufacturing costs. Sanders expects total annual product- and facility-level costs to be $500,000 and $750,000, respectively. Assume Sanders receives a special order from a new customer seeking to buy 1,000 engines for $300 each.

Required
Should Sanders accept or reject the special order? Support your answer with appropriate computations.

EXERCISE 4–6B *Identifying Qualitative Factors for a Special Order Decision* L.O. 8

Required
Describe the qualitative factors that Sanders should consider before accepting the special order described in Exercise 4–5B.

EXERCISE 4–7B *Using the Contribution Margin Approach for a Special Order Decision* L.O. 9

Livesy Company produces and sells a food processor that it prices at a 25 percent markup on total cost. Based on data pertaining to producing and selling 40,000 food processors, Livesy computes the sales price per food processor as follows.

Unit-level costs	$ 800,000
Fixed costs	640,000
Total cost (a)	1,440,000
Markup (a $\times$ .25)	360,000
Total sales revenue (b)	$1,800,000
Sales price per unit (b $\div$ 40,000)	$45.00

Required

a. Livesy receives a special order for 7,000 food processors for $19 each. Livesy has excess capacity. Calculate the contribution margin per unit for the special order. Based on the contribution margin per unit, should Livesy accept the special order?

b. Support your answer by preparing a contribution margin income statement for the special order.

L.O. 9   EXERCISE 4–8B *Making an Outsourcing Decision*

Hineburg Boats Company currently produces a battery used in manufacturing its boats. The company annually manufactures and sells 2,000 units of a particular model of fishing boat. Because of the low volume of activity, Hineburg is unable to obtain the economies of scale that larger producers achieve. For example, the costs associated with producing the batteries it uses are almost 40 percent more than the cost of purchasing comparable batteries. Hineburg could buy batteries for $75 each; it costs $105 each to make them. A detailed breakdown of current production costs for the batteries follows:

Item	Unit Cost	Total
Unit-level costs:		
Materials	$ 28	$ 56,000
Labor	20	40,000
Overhead	2	4,000
Allocated facility-level costs	55	110,000
Total	$105	$210,000

Based on these figures, Hineburg's president asserted that it would be foolish for the company to continue to produce the batteries at $105 each when it can buy them for $75 each.

Required

Do you agree with the president's conclusion? Support your answer with appropriate computations.

L.O. 9   EXERCISE 4–9B *Establishing a Price for an Outsourcing Decision*

Happy Kids, Inc., makes and sells skateboards. Happy Kids currently makes the 60,000 wheels used annually in its skateboards but has an opportunity to purchase the wheels from a reliable manufacturer. The costs of making the wheels follow.

Annual Costs Associated with Manufacturing Skateboard Wheels	
Materials (60,000 units × $5)	$300,000
Labor (60,000 units × $3)	180,000
Depreciation on manufacturing equipment*	24,000
Salary of wheel production supervisor	65,000
Rental cost of equipment used to make wheels	55,000
Allocated portion of corporate-level facility-sustaining costs	33,000
Total cost to make 60,000 wheels	$657,000

*The equipment has a book value of $74,000 but its market value is zero.

Required

a. Determine the maximum price per unit that Happy Kids would be willing to pay for the wheels.

b. Would the price computed in Requirement *a* change if production were increased to 80,000 units? Support your answer with appropriate computations.

L.O. 8, 9   EXERCISE 4–10B *Making an Outsourcing Decision with Qualitative Factors Considered*

Legion Computers currently purchases for $8 each keyboard it uses in the 50,000 computers it makes and sells annually. Each computer uses one keyboard. The company has idle capacity and is considering whether to make the keyboards that it needs. Legion estimates that materials and labor costs for making

keyboards would be $5 each. In addition, supervisory salaries, rent, and other manufacturing costs would be $200,000. Allocated facility-level costs would amount to $70,000.

Required
a. Determine the change in net income that Legion would experience if it decides to make the keyboards.
b. Discuss the qualitative factors that Legion should consider.

EXERCISE 4–11B *Outsourcing Decision Affected by Opportunity Costs*   L.O. 7, 9

Shannon Doors Company currently produces the doorknobs for the doors it makes and sells. The monthly cost of producing 2,000 doorknobs is as follows:

Unit-level materials	$2,000
Unit-level labor	2,500
Unit-level overhead	1,600
Product-level costs*	4,000
Allocated facility-level costs	6,000

*Twenty percent of these costs can be avoided if the doorknobs are purchased.

Coleman Company has offered to sell comparable doorknobs to Shannon for $5 each.

Required
a. Should Shannon continue to make the doorknobs? Support you answer with appropriate computations.
b. For $5,000 per month, Shannon could lease the space it currently uses to manufacture doorknobs. Would this potential cash inflow affect your response to Requirement *a*? Explain.

EXERCISE 4–12B *Considering Opportunity Cost*   L.O. 7

Lopez Fishing Tours, Inc., owns a boat that originally cost $80,000. Currently, the boat's net book value is $16,000, and its expected remaining useful life is four years. Lopez has an opportunity to purchase for $64,000 a replacement boat that is extremely fuel efficient. Fuel costs for the old boat are expected to be $12,000 per year more than fuel costs would be for the replacement boat. Lopez could sell the old boat, which is fully paid for and in good condition, for only $30,000.

Required
Should Lopez replace the old boat with the new fuel-efficient model, or should it continue to use the old one until it wears out? Explain.

EXERCISE 4–13B *Considering Opportunity Costs*   L.O. 7, 8

Two years ago, Steve Lanier bought a truck for $22,000 to offer delivery service. Steve earns $32,000 a year operating as an independent trucker. He has an opportunity to sell his truck for $15,000 and take a position as an instructor in a truck driving school. The instructor position pays $25,000 a year for working 40 hours per week. Driving his truck, Steve works approximately 60 hours per week. If Steve sells his truck, he will invest the proceeds of the sale in bonds that pay a 12 percent return.

Required
a. Determine the opportunity cost of owning and operating the independent delivery business.
b. Based solely on financial considerations, should Steve sell his truck and accept the instructor position?
c. Discuss the qualitative as well as quantitative characteristics that Steve should consider.

EXERCISE 4–14B *Segment Elimination Decision*   L.O. 9

The Chilton Company operates three segments. Income statements for the segments imply that Chilton could improve profitability if Segment A were eliminated.

THE CHILTON COMPANY
Income Statement
For the Year 2009

Segment	X	Y	Z
Sales	$ 87,000	$210,000	$200,000
Cost of Goods Sold	(67,000)	(82,000)	(85,000)
Sales Commissions	(14,000)	(22,000)	(20,000)
Contribution Margin	6,000	106,000	95,000
Depreciation and Other General Fixed Overhead Costs	(30,000)	(42,000)	(37,000)
General Fixed Oper. Exp. (allocation of president's salary)	(15,000)	(15,000)	(15,000)
Advertising Expense	(8,000)	(8,000)	0
Net Income	$(47,000)	$ 41,000	$ 43,000

Required

a. Explain the effect on Chilton's profitability if segment X is eliminated.

b. Prepare comparative income statements for the company as a whole under the two alternatives: (1) Segment X is retained or (2) Segment X is eliminated.

L.O. 9   EXERCISE 4–15B *Segment Elimination Decision*

Marion Company divides its operations into six divisions. A recent income statement for the Norwood Division follows:

Income Statement	
Revenue	$750,000
Salaries for Employees	(500,000)
Operating Expenses	(169,000)
Insurance	(37,000)
Depreciation Expense (sunk cost)	(35,000)
Division-Level Facility-Sustaining Costs	(50,000)
Companywide Facility-Sustaining Costs	(58,000)
Net Loss	$(99,000)

Required

a. Should Marion eliminate the Norwood Division? Support your answer by explaining how the division's elimination would affect the net income of the company as a whole. By how much would companywide income increase or decrease?

b. Assume that the Norwood Division could increase its revenue to $770,000 by raising prices. Would this change the decision you made in response to Requirement *a*? Assuming Norwood's revenue becomes $770,000, determine the amount of the increase or decrease that would occur in companywide net income if the segment were eliminated.

c. What is the minimum amount of revenue the Norwood Division must generate to justify its continued operation?

L.O. 4   EXERCISE 4–16B *Identifying Avoidable Cost of a Segment*

The Reich Corporation is considering the elimination of one of its segments. The following fixed costs pertain to the segment. If the segment is eliminated, the building it uses will be sold.

Annual advertising expense	$100,000
Market value of the building	52,000
Annual depreciation on the building	12,000
Annual maintenance costs on equipment	30,000
Annual real estate taxes on the building	7,000
Annual supervisory salaries	70,000
Annual allocation of companywide facility-level costs	12,000
Original cost of the building	67,000
Current book value of the building	41,000

Required

Based on this information, determine the amount of avoidable cost associated with the segment.

EXERCISE 4–17B *Making an Asset Replacement Decision* **L.O. 9**

Rosson Electronics purchased a manufacturing plant four years ago for $7,500,000. The plant costs $2,000,000 per year to operate. Its current book value using straight-line depreciation is $5,500,000. Rosson could purchase a replacement plant for $12,000,000 that would have a useful life of 10 years. Because of new technology, the replacement plant would require only $500,000 per year in operating expenses. It would have an expected salvage value of $1,000,000 after 10 years. The current disposal value of the old plant is $1,400,000, and if Rosson keeps it 10 more years, its residual value would be $500,000.

Required

Based on this information, should Rosson replace the old plant? Support your answer with appropriate computations.

EXERCISE 4–18B *Making an Asset Replacement Decision* **L.O. 9**

Hendrix Company is considering whether to replace some of its manufacturing equipment. Information pertaining to the existing equipment and the potential replacement equipment follows:

Existing Equipment		Replacement Equipment	
Cost	$45,000	Cost	$42,000
Operating expenses*	48,000	Operating expenses*	8,000
Salvage value	8,000	Salvage value	10,000
Market value	16,000	Useful life	10 years
Book value	21,000		
Remaining useful life	10 years		

*The amounts shown for operating expenses are the cumulative total of all such expenses expected to be incurred over the useful life of the equipment.

Required

Based on this information, recommend whether to replace the equipment. Support your recommendation with appropriate computations.

EXERCISE 4–19B *Making an Asset Replacement Decision* **L.O. 9**

Pioline Company, a California-based corporation, paid $57,000 to purchase an air conditioner on January 1, 1995. During 2001, surging energy costs prompted management to consider replacing the air conditioner with a more energy-efficient model. The new air conditioner would cost $80,000. Electricity for the existing air conditioner costs the company $30,000 per year; the new model would cost only $20,000 per year. The new model, which has an expected useful life of 10 years, would be installed on January 1, 2002. Because the old air conditioner is more durable, Pioline estimates it still has a remaining useful life of 10 years even though it has been used. The current market value of the old air conditioner is $27,000. The expected salvage value of both air conditioners is zero.

Required

Based on this information, recommend whether to replace the equipment. Support your recommendation with appropriate computations.

EXERCISE 4–20B *Annual Versus Cumulative Data for Replacement Decision* **L.O. 7, 9**

Because their three adult children have all at last left home, Pedro and Mary Safin recently moved to a smaller house. Pedro owns a riding lawnmower he bought three years ago to take care of the former house's huge yard; it should last another five years. With the new house's smaller yard, Pedro thinks he could hire someone to cut his grass for $400 per year. He wonders if this option is financially sound. Relevant information follows.

Riding Lawn Mower	Amount
Original cost	$2,400
Accumulated depreciation	900
Current market value	1,300
Estimated salvage value	0

Required

a. What is the annual opportunity cost of using the riding mower? Based on your computations, recommend whether Pedro should sell it and hire a lawn service.

b. Determine the total cost of hiring a lawn service for the next five years. Based on your computations, recommend whether Pedro should sell the mower and hire a lawn service.

Appendix

L.O. 11   EXERCISE 4–21B *Scarce Resource Decision*

Microtech has the capacity to annually produce either 50,000 desktop computers or 28,000 laptop computers. Relevant data for each product follow:

	Desktop	Laptop
Sales price	$1,000	$1,800
Variable costs	400	650

Required

Assuming that Microtech can sell all it produces of either product, should the company produce the desktop computers or the laptop computers? Provide computations to support your answer.

PROBLEMS—SERIES B

L.O. 1, 6   PROBLEM 4–22B *Context-Sensitive Relevance*

Required

Respond to each requirement independently.

a. Describe two decision-making contexts, one in which unit-level labor costs are avoidable, and the other in which they are unavoidable.

b. Describe two decision-making contexts, one in which batch-level shipping costs are avoidable, and the other in which they are unavoidable.

c. Describe two decision-making contexts, one in which administrative costs are avoidable, and the other in which they are unavoidable.

d. Describe two decision-making contexts, one in which the insurance premium paid on a building is avoidable, and the other in which it is unavoidable.

e. Describe two decision-making contexts, one in which amortization of a product patent is avoidable, and the other in which it is unavoidable.

L.O. 1, 6   PROBLEM 4–23B *Context-Sensitive Relevance*

Cutlip Machines Company is evaluating two customer orders from which it can accept only one because of capacity limitations. The data associated with each order follow.

Cost Category	Order M	Order N
Contract price	$960,000	$880,000
Unit-level materials	360,000	316,000
Unit-level labor	334,000	344,800
Unit-level overhead	106,000	98,000
Supervisor's salary	80,000	80,000
Rental equipment costs	20,000	24,000
Depreciation on tools (zero market value)	28,000	28,000
Allocated portion of companywide facility-sustaining costs	8,000	7,200
Insurance coverage	54,000	54,000
Cost incurred to obtain and evaluate orders	6,000	4,400

Required

a. Assume that Cutlip has decided to accept one of the two orders. Identify the information relevant to selecting one order versus the other. Recommend which job to accept, and support your answer with appropriate computations.

b. The customer presenting Order M has withdrawn it because of its financial hardship. Under this circumstance, Cutlip's choice is to accept or reject Order N alone. Identify the information relevant to this decision. Recommend whether to accept or reject Order N. Support your answer with appropriate computations.

PROBLEM 4–24B *Effect of Operating Leverage on Special Order Decision* **L.O. 8, 9**

Arnold Company made 200,000 electric drills in batches of 2,000 units each during the prior accounting period. Normally, Arnold markets its products through a variety of hardware stores. The following is the summarized cost to produce electric drills.

Materials cost ($4.50 per unit × 200,000)	$ 900,000
Labor cost ($5.00 per unit × 200,000)	1,000,000
Manufacturing supplies ($0.50 × 200,000)	100,000
Batch-level costs (100 batches at $3,000 per batch)	300,000
Product-level costs	120,000
Facility-level costs	380,000
Total costs	$2,800,000

Cost per unit = $2,800,000 ÷ 200,000 = $14

Required

a. Bypassing Arnold's regular distribution channel, Souter Home Repair and Maintenance, Inc., has offered to buy a batch of 1,200 electric drills for $12 each directly from Arnold. Arnold's normal selling price is $18 per unit. Based on the preceding quantitative data, should Arnold accept the special order? Support your answer with appropriate computations.

b. Would your answer to Requirement *a* change if Souter Home Repair and Maintenance offered to buy a batch of 2,000 electric drills for $12 each? Support your answer with appropriate computations.

c. Describe the qualitative factors that Arnold Company should consider before accepting a special order to sell electric drills to Souter Home Repair and Maintenance.

PROBLEM 4–25B *Effects of the Level of Production on an Outsourcing Decision* **L.O. 8, 9**

One of Bragg Company's major products is a fuel additive designed to improve fuel efficiency and keep engines clean. Bragg, a petrolchemical firm, makes and sells 100,000 units of the fuel additive per year. Its management is evaluating the possibility of having an outside supplier manufacture the product for Bragg for $2 each. Bragg would continue to sell and distribute the fuel additive under its own brand name for either alternative. Bragg's accountant constructed the following profitability analysis.

Revenue (100,000 units × $3.50)	$350,000
Unit-level materials costs (100,000 units × $0.80)	(80,000)
Unit-level labor costs (100,000 units × $0.12)	(12,000)
Unit-level overhead costs (100,000 × $0.38)	(38,000)
Unit-level selling expenses (100,000 × $0.20)	(20,000)
Contribution margin	$200,000
Fuel additive production supervisor's salary	(80,000)
Allocated portion of facility-level costs	(20,000)
Product-level advertising cost	(40,000)
Contribution to companywide income	$ 60,000

Required

a. Identify the cost items relevant to the make-or-outsource decision.

b. Should Bragg continue to make the fuel additive or buy it from the supplier? Support your answer by determining the change in net income if Bragg buys the fuel additive instead of making it.

c. Suppose that Bragg is able to increase sales by 60,000 units (sales will increase to 160,000 units). At this level of sales, should Bragg make or buy the fuel additive? Support your answer by explaining how the increase in production affects the cost per unit.

d. Discuss the qualitative factors that Bragg should consider before deciding to outsource the fuel additive. How can Bragg minimize the risk of establishing a relationship with an unreliable supplier?

L.O. 9   PROBLEM 4–26B *Outsourcing Decision Affected by Equipment Replacement*

During 2007, Spring Toy Company made 10,000 units of Model A, the costs of which follow.

Unit-level materials costs (10,000 units × $10)	$100,000
Unit-level labor costs (10,000 units × $40)	400,000
Unit-level overhead costs (10,000 × $4)	40,000
Depreciation on manufacturing equipment	60,000
Model A production supervisor's salary	60,000
Inventory holding costs	120,000
Allocated portion of facility-level costs	80,000
Total costs	$860,000

An independent contractor has offered to make the same product for Spring for $50 each.

Additional Information:
1. The manufacturing equipment originally cost $420,000 and has a book value of $240,000, a remaining useful life of four years, and a zero salvage value. If the equipment is not used to produce Model A in the production process, it can be leased for $40,000 per year.
2. Spring has the opportunity to purchase for $240,000 new manufacturing equipment that will have an expected useful life of four years and a salvage value of $80,000. This equipment will increase productivity substantially, thereby reducing unit-level labor costs by 20 percent.
3. If Spring discontinues the production of Model A, the company can eliminate 50 percent of its inventory holding cost.

Required
a. Determine the avoidable cost per unit to produce Model A assuming Spring continues to use existing equipment to make the product. Based on the quantitative data, should Spring outsource Model A? Support your answer with appropriate computations.
b. Assuming that the old equipment is replaced, determine the avoidable cost per unit of making Model A using the new equipment. Calculate the impact on profitability if Model A were made using the old versus the new equipment. Based on the per unit cost data computed in Requirements *a* and *b*, should Spring replace the equipment?
c. Assuming that the old equipment has been replaced, should Spring make or outsource Model A?
d. Discuss the qualitative factors that Spring should consider before making a decision to outsource Model A. How can Spring minimize the risk of establishing a relationship with an unreliable supplier?

L.O. 9   PROBLEM 4–27B *Eliminating a Segment*

Park's Grocery Store has three departments, meat, canned food, and produce, each of which has its own manager. All departments are housed in a single store. Recently, the produce department has been suffering a net loss and is expected to continue doing so. Last year's income statements follow.

	Meat Department	Canned Food Department	Produce Department
Sales	$670,000	$600,000	$440,000
Cost of Goods Sold	(270,000)	(330,000)	(260,000)
Gross Margin	$400,000	$270,000	$180,000
Departmental Manager's Salary	(42,000)	(30,000)	(35,000)
Rent on Store Lease	(80,000)	(80,000)	(80,000)
Store Utilities	(20,000)	(20,000)	(20,000)
Other General Expenses	(98,000)	(98,000)	(98,000)
Net Income (loss)	$160,000	$ 42,000	$ (53,000)

Required
a. Determine whether to eliminate the produce department.
b. Confirm the conclusion you reached in Requirement *a* by preparing a before and an after income statement, assuming that the produce department is eliminated.

c. Eliminating the produce department would allow the meat department to expand. It could add seafood to its products. Suppose that management estimates that offering seafood would increase the store's net earnings by $160,000. Would this information affect the decision that you made in Requirement *a*? Explain your answer.

PROBLEM 4–28B *Effect of Activity Level and Opportunity Cost on Segment Elimination Decision*   **L.O. 7, 9**

Tamatsu Company has three separate operating branches: Division X, which manufactures utensils; Division Y, which makes plates; and Division Z, which makes cooking pots. Each division operates its own facility. The company's administrative offices are located in a separate building. In recent years, Division Z has experienced a net loss and is expected to continue to do so. Income statements for 2008 follow.

	Division X	Division Y	Division Z
Sales	$1,800,000	$1,400,000	$1,500,000
Less: Cost of Goods Sold			
Unit-Level Manufacturing Costs	(1,100,000)	(580,000)	(900,000)
Rent on Manufacturing Facility	(240,000)	(220,000)	(360,000)
Gross Margin	$ 460,000	$ 600,000	$ 240,000
Less: Operating Expenses			
Unit-Level Selling and Admin. Expenses	(60,000)	(45,000)	(90,000)
Division-Level Fixed Selling and Admin. Expenses	(140,000)	(125,000)	(180,000)
Administrative Facility-Level Costs	(80,000)	(80,000)	(80,000)
Net Income (loss)	$ 180,000	$ 350,000	$ (110,000)

Required
a. Based on the preceding information, recommend whether to eliminate Division Z. Support your answer by preparing companywide income statements before and after eliminating Division Z.
b. During 2008, Division Z produced and sold 30,000 units of product. Would your recommendation in Requirement *a* change if sales and production increase to 45,000 units in 2009? Support your answer by comparing differential revenue and avoidable cost for Division Z, assuming that 45,000 units are sold.
c. Suppose that Tamatsu could sublease Division Z's manufacturing facility for $740,000. Would you operate the division at a production and sales volume of 45,000 units, or would you close it? Support your answer with appropriate computations.

PROBLEM 4–29B *Comprehensive Problem Including Special Order, Outsourcing, and Segment Elimination Decisions*   **L.O. 9**

Buell Company's electronics division produces a radio/cassette player. The vice president in charge of the division is evaluating the income statement showing annual revenues and expenses associated with the division's operating activities. The relevant range for the production and sale of the radio/cassette player is between 50,000 and 150,000 units per year.

Income Statement	
Revenue (60,000 units × $30)	$1,800,000
Unit-Level Variable Costs	
Materials Cost (60,000 × $15)	(900,000)
Labor Cost (60,000 × $8)	(480,000)
Manufacturing Overhead (60,000 × $1.50)	(90,000)
Shipping and Handling (60,000 × $0.50)	(30,000)
Sales Commissions (60,000 × $2)	(120,000)
Contribution Margin	$ 180,000
Fixed Expenses	
Advertising Costs	(30,000)
Salary of Production Supervisor	(126,000)
Depreciation on Production Equipment (zero market value)	(80,000)
Allocated Companywide Facility-Level Expenses	(120,000)
Net Loss	$ (176,000)

Required (Consider each of the requirements independently.)

a. An international trading firm has approached top management about buying 30,000 radio/cassette players for $26.50 each. It would sell the product in a foreign country, so that Buell's existing customers would not be affected. Because the offer was made directly to top management, no sales commissions on the transaction would be involved. Based on quantitative features alone, should Buell accept the special order? Support your answer with appropriate computations. Specifically, by what amount would profitability increase or decrease if the special order is accepted?

b. Buell has an opportunity to buy the 60,000 radio/cassette players it currently makes from a foreign manufacturer for $26 each. The manufacturer has a good reputation for reliability and quality, and Buell could continue to use its own logo, advertising program, and sales force to distribute the products. Should Buell buy the radio/cassette players or continue to make them? Support your answer with appropriate computations. Specifically, how much more or less would it cost to buy the radio/cassette players than to make them? Would your answer change if the volume of sales were increased to 140,000 units?

c. Because the electronics division is currently operating at a loss, should it be eliminated from the company's operations? Support your answer with appropriate computations. Specifically, by what amount would the segment's elimination increase or decrease profitability?

Appendix

L.O. 11 **PROBLEM 4–30B** *Allocating Scarce Resources*

Steeler Company makes two products, M and N. Product information follows.

	Product M	Product N
Selling price per unit	$69	$84
Variable cost per unit	45	54

Required

Identify the product that should be produced or sold under each of the following constraints. Consider each constraint separately.

a. One unit of Product M requires 3 hours of labor to produce, and one unit of Product N requires 5 hours of labor to produce. Due to labor constraints, demand is higher than the company's capacity to make both products.

b. The products are sold to the public in retail stores. The company has limited floor space and cannot stock as many products as it would like. Display space is available for only one of the two products. Expected sales of Product M are 8,000 units, and expected sales of Product N are 7,000 units.

c. The maximum number of machine hours available is 24,000. Product M uses 4 machine hours, and Product N uses 6 machine hours. The company can sell all the products it produces.

L.O. 10 **PROBLEM 4–31B** *Conflict Between Short-Term Versus Long-Term Performance*

Stones Construction Components, Inc., purchased a machine on January 1, 2001, for $240,000. The chief engineer estimated the machine's useful life to be six years and its salvage value to be zero. The operating cost of this machine is $120,000 per year. By January 1, 2003, a new machine that requires 30 percent less operating cost than the existing machine has become available for $180,000; it would have a four-year useful life with zero salvage. The current market value of the old machine on January 1, 2003, is $100,000, and its book value is $160,000 on that date. Straight-line depreciation is used for both machines. The company expects to generate $320,000 of revenue per year from the use of either machine.

Required

a. Recommend whether to replace the old machine on January 1, 2003. Support your answer with appropriate computations.

b. Prepare income statements for four years (2003 through 2006) assuming that the old machine is retained.

c. Prepare income statements for four years (2003 through 2006) assuming that the old machine is replaced.

d. Discuss the potential ethical conflicts that could result from the timing of the loss and expense recognition reported in the two income statements.

ANALYZE, THINK, COMMUNICATE

BUSINESS APPLICATION CASE *Elimination of a Product Line*

ATC 4–1

The following excerpts were drawn from the article entitled "The Scottish Shogun," published in *U.S. News & World Report,* May 19, 1997, on pages 44 and 45.

The Japanese car maker [Mazda Motor Company] has accumulated nearly a billion dollars in operating losses in three years. Its market share in Japan fell from nearly 8 percent to below 5 percent in the first half of the decade, and its overall car production dropped by a stunning 46 percent. In fact, Mazda has been fighting for its life. To salvage the company, Ford Motor Co., Mazda's biggest shareholder, gambled $430 million [in 1996] and raised its equity stake in Mazda to 33.4 percent, which in practice gave it operating control. The U.S. car maker chose Henry Wallace, a Ford man for 25 years, to spearhead a turnaround. Mr. Wallace is the first foreigner to lead a big Japanese company. While the Japanese have a well-deserved reputation for insularity, they also have a tradition of welcoming foreign guidance when it suits their purposes. In this case, Mr. Wallace has been warmly embraced by the Japanese—both inside and outside Mazda. Wallace's first move was to retrench—cut out product lines, consolidate sales channels, reduce inventory, and in the United States, halt unprofitable fleet and car-rental sales. Wallace also took action to instill a profit motive among the board of directors. Wallace observed, "I don't think previously there was a strong profit motive within the company." Instead, Mazda was a club of engineers who turned out wonderful niche cars—some with exotic styling, others with superb performance—that few consumers wanted to buy. When drivers developed a taste for sport utility vehicles, Mazda's beautiful sedans collected dust on the lots.

Required

a. The article indicated that one action Mr. Wallace took was to cut product lines. Explain which levels (unit, batch, product, and/or facility) of costs could be avoided by eliminating product lines. What sacrifices will Mazda likely have to make to obtain the cost savings associated with eliminating product lines?

b. Suppose that the cost data on the table below apply to three sales channels that were eliminated through the consolidation program.

Additional Information

(1) Sales are expected to drop by 10 percent because of the consolidation program. The remaining sales volume was absorbed by other sales channels.

(2) Half of the sales staff accepted transfers that placed them in positions in other sales channels. The other half left the company.

(3) The supervisor of Channel 1 accepted a job transfer. The other two supervisors left the company.

Annual Costs of Operating Each Sales Channel	Channel 1	Channel 2	Channel 3
Unit-level selling costs			
Selling supplies cost	$ 25,000	$ 18,000	$ 32,000
Sales commissions	285,000	180,000	340,000
Shipping and handling	32,000	19,000	39,000
Miscellaneous	16,000	14,000	23,000
Facility-level selling costs			
Rent	196,000	189,000	192,000
Utilities	32,000	38,000	40,000
Staff salaries	720,000	684,000	870,000
Supervisory salaries	120,000	80,000	136,000
Depreciation on equipment	240,000	246,000	242,000
Allocated companywide facility-level expenses	80,000	80,000	80,000

(4) The combined equipment, with an expected remaining useful life of four years and a $100,000 salvage value, had a market value of $500,000.

(5) The offices operated by the eliminated channels were closed.

Determine the amount of annual costs saved by consolidating the sales channels.

c. How will reducing inventory save costs?

d. Although the cost-cutting measures are impressive, Mr. Wallace was quoted as saying, "Obviously no one is going to succeed in our business just by reducing costs." Speculate as to some other measures that Mr. Wallace could take to improve Mazda's profitability.

ATC 4–2 GROUP ASSIGNMENT *Relevance and Cost Behavior*

Maccoa Soft, a division of Zayer Software Company, produces and distributes an automated payroll software system. A contribution margin format income statement for Maccoa Soft for the past year follows.

Revenue (12,000 units × $1,200)	$14,400,000
Unit-Level Variable Costs	
Product Materials Cost (12,000 × $60)	(720,000)
Installation Labor Cost (12,000 × $200)	(2,400,000)
Manufacturing Overhead (12,000 × $2)	(24,000)
Shipping and Handling (12,000 × $25)	(300,000)
Sales Commissions (12,000 × $300)	(3,600,000)
Nonmanufacturing Miscellaneous Costs (12,000 × $5)	(60,000)
Contribution Margin (12,000 × $608)	$ 7,296,000
Fixed Costs	
Research and Development	(2,700,000)
Legal Fees to Ensure Product Protection	(780,000)
Advertising Costs	(1,200,000)
Rental Cost of Manufacturing Facility	(600,000)
Depreciation on Production Equipment (zero market value)	(300,000)
Other Manufacturing Costs (salaries, utilities, etc.)	(744,000)
Division-Level Facility Sustaining Costs	(1,730,000)
Allocated Companywide Facility-Level Costs	(1,650,000)
Net Loss	$ (2,408,000)

a. Divide the class into groups and then organize the groups into three sections. Assign Task 1 to the first section, Task 2 to the second section, and Task 3 to the third section. Each task should be considered independently of the others.

Group Tasks

(1) Assume that Maccoa has excess capacity. The sales staff has identified a large franchise company with 200 outlets that is interested in Maccoa's software system but is willing to pay only $800 for each system. Ignoring qualitative considerations, should Maccoa accept the special order?

(2) Maccoa has the opportunity to purchase a comparable payroll system from a competing vendor for $600 per system. Ignoring qualitative considerations, should Maccoa outsource producing the software? Maccoa would continue to sell and install the software if the manufacturing activities were outsourced.

(3) Given that Maccoa is generating a loss, should Zayer eliminate it? Would your answer change if Maccoa could increase sales by 1,000 units?

b. Have a representative from each section explain its respective conclusions. Discuss the following:

(1) Representatives from Section 1 should respond to the following: The analysis related to the special order (Task 1) suggests that all variable costs are always relevant. Is this conclusion valid? Explain your answer.

(2) Representatives from Section 2 should respond to the following: With respect to the outsourcing decision, identify a relevant fixed cost and a nonrelevant fixed cost. Discuss the criteria for determining whether a cost is or is not relevant.

(3) Representatives from Section 3 should respond to the following: Why did the segment elimination decision change when the volume of production and sales increased?

ATC 4–3 RESEARCH ASSIGNMENT *Systems Replacement Decision*

The February 1998 issue of *Management Accounting* contains the article "What Automated Expense Reporting Management Can Do for You," written by Dana Bruttig on pages 38–43. The article notes that on average, processing a travel and entertainment report manually costs $25. According to the Hacket Group, a market research and benchmarking firm, shifting to an automated travel and entertainment expense system can reduce the average processing cost to approximately $1.75 per expense report. Some actual results include Libbey-Owens Ford, which reduced it to $1.29; EDS, which reduced it to $2.50; IBM, which expects to reach $4 per report; and American Express, which thinks that the number is $2 per report. Using a conservative estimate of $3 per report for an automated system, a $22 savings ($25 − $3) per report could be achieved by replacing a manual system with an automated system. Read this article and complete the following requirements.

Required
a. Identify three costs that Dana Bruttig believes could be avoided if a company were to install an automated travel and entertainment expense system.
b. Comment on why the cost savings identified in Requirement *a* are difficult to quantify.
c. Suppose that a company's sales staff is already equipped with lap top computers. Comment on whether the cost of computers is relevant to the replacement decision.
d. A sidebar explains that implementing an automated travel and entertainment expense system enabled the EG&G Sealol Company to avoid $37,000 annually in overtime pay. Comment on the qualitative costs associated with this savings (e.g., speculate as to how employee morale is affected).

WRITING ASSIGNMENT *Relevant Versus Full Cost*

ATC 4–4

State law permits the State Department of Revenue to collect taxes for municipal governments that operate within the state's jurisdiction and allows private companies to collect taxes for municipalities. To promote fairness and to ensure the financial well-being of the state, the law dictates that the Department of Revenue must charge municipalities a fee for collection services that is above the cost of providing such services but does not define the term *cost*. Until recently, Department of Revenue officials have included a proportionate share of all departmental costs such as depreciation on buildings and equipment, supervisory salaries, and other facility-level overhead costs when determining the cost of providing collection services, a measurement approach known as *full costing*. The full costing approach has led to a pricing structure that places the Department of Revenue at a competitive disadvantage relative to private collection companies. Indeed, highly efficient private companies have been able to consistently underbid the Revenue Department for municipal customers. As a result, it has lost 30 percent of its municipal collection business over the last two years. The inability to be price competitive led the revenue commissioner to hire a consulting firm to evaluate the current practice of determining the cost to provide collection services.

The consulting firm concluded that the cost to provide collection services should be limited to the relevant costs associated with providing those services, defined as the difference between the costs that would be incurred if the services were provided and the costs that would be incurred if the services were not provided. According to this definition, the costs of depreciation, supervisory salaries, and other facility-level overhead costs are not included because they are the same regardless of whether the Department of Revenue provides collection services to municipalities. The Revenue Department adopted the relevant cost approach and immediately reduced the price it charges municipalities to collect their taxes and rapidly recovered the collection business it had lost. Indeed, several of the private collection companies were forced into bankruptcy. The private companies joined together and filed suit against the Revenue Department, charging that the new definition of cost violates the intent of the law.

Required
a. Assume that you are an accountant hired as a consultant for the private companies. Write a brief memo explaining why it is inappropriate to limit the definition of the costs of providing collection services to relevant costs.
b. Assume that you are an accountant hired as a consultant for the Department of Revenue. Write a brief memo explaining why it is appropriate to limit the definition of the costs of providing collection services to relevant costs.
c. Speculate on how the matter will be resolved.

ETHICAL DILEMMA *Asset Replacement Clouded by Self-Interest*

ATC 4–5

John Dillworth is in charge of buying property used as building sites for branch offices of the National Bank of Commerce. Mr. Dillworth recently paid $110,000 for a site located in a growing section of the city. Shortly after purchasing this lot, Mr. Dillworth had the opportunity to purchase a more desirable lot at a significantly lower price. The traffic count at the new site is virtually twice that of the old site, but the price of the lot is only $80,000. It was immediately apparent that he had overpaid for the previous purchase. The current market value of the purchased property is only $75,000. Mr. Dillworth believes that it would be in the bank's best interest to buy the new lot, but he does not want to report a loss to his boss, Kelly Fullerton. He knows that Ms. Fullerton will severely reprimand him, even though she has made her share of mistakes. In fact, he is aware of a significant bad loan that Ms. Fullerton recently approved. When confronted with the bad debt by the senior vice president in charge of commercial lending, Ms. Fullerton blamed the decision on one of her former subordinates, Ira Sacks. Ms. Fullerton implied that Mr. Sacks had been dismissed for reckless lending decisions when, in fact, he had been an excellent loan officer with an uncanny ability to assess the creditworthiness of his customers. Indeed, Mr. Sacks had voluntarily resigned to accept a better position.

Required

a. Determine the amount of the loss that would be recognized on the sale of the existing branch site.

b. Identify the type of cost represented by the $110,000 original purchase price of the land. Also identify the type of cost represented by its current market value of $75,000. Indicate which cost is relevant to a decision as to whether the original site should be replaced with the new site.

c. Is Mr. Dillworth's conclusion that the old site should be replaced supported by quantitative analysis? If not, what facts do justify his conclusion?

d. Assuming that Mr. Dillworth is a certified management accountant (CMA), do you believe the failure to replace the land violates any of the standards of ethical conduct in Exhibit 1–13 in Chapter 1? If so, which standards would be violated?

e. Discuss the ethical dilemma that Mr. Dillworth faces within the context of Donald Cressey's common features of ethical misconduct that were outlined in Chapter 1.

ATC 4–6　SPREADSHEET ASSIGNMENT *Using Excel*

Dorina Company makes cases of canned dog food in batches of 1,000 cases and sells each case for $15. The plant capacity is 50,000 cases; the company currently makes 40,000 cases. DoggieMart has offered to buy 1,500 cases for $12 per case. Because product-level and facility-level costs are unaffected by a special order, they are omitted.

Required

a. Prepare a spreadsheet like the following one to calculate the contribution to income if the special order is accepted. Construct formulas so that the number of cases or the price could be changed and the new contribution would be automatically calculated.

b. Try different order sizes (such as 2,000) or different prices to see the effect on contribution to profit.

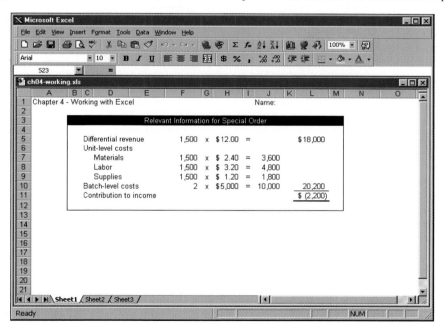

Spreadsheet Tips

1. The numbers in cells F7 to F9 should be formulas that refer to F5. This allows the number of cases to be changed in cell F5 with the other cells changing automatically.

2. The formula in cell F10 uses a function named ROUNDUP to calculate the even number of batches. The formula should be = ROUNDUP(F5/1000,0) where the zero refers to rounding up to the nearest whole number.

SPREADSHEET ASSIGNMENT *Mastering Excel*   ATC 4–7

Refer to Problem 4–30A.

Required

a. Prepare a spreadsheet to solve Requirements *a*, *b*, and *c* in Problem 4–30A.

b. While constructing formulas for Requirement *a* of Problem 4–30A, include a formula to calculate contribution margin per labor hour.

c. While constructing formulas for Requirement *b* of Problem 4–30A, include formulas to calculate total contribution margin for each product.

d. While constructing formulas for Requirement *c* of Problem 4–30A, include formulas to calculate contribution margin per machine hour and total contribution margin for each product.

Chapter

5

Cost Accumulation, Tracing, and Allocation

Learning Objectives

After completing this chapter, you should be able to:

1 Understand the relationships among cost objects, cost drivers, and cost allocation.

2 Distinguish between direct cost versus indirect cost.

3 Appreciate the unique nature of the direct cost concept and understand the context-sensitive nature of cost classification.

4 Understand the mathematical procedures used to make allocations.

5 Select appropriate cost drivers for making allocations under a variety of different circumstances.

6 Understand the implications of cost behavior associated with making allocations.

7 Understand the need to establish cost pools.

8 Understand the allocation of common costs associated with joint products and by-products.

9 Understand the association between cost allocation and relevance.

10 Understand the allocation of service center costs to operating departments under the direct and step methods. (Appendix)

particular department could be avoided if that department were eliminated. Accordingly, both costs are relevant to a segment elimination decision, yet one is classified as direct, and the other is classified as indirect. These examples emphasize the fact that you cannot memorize a list of costs as being direct or indirect, fixed or variable, relevant or not relevant. When trying to identify costs as to type or behavior, you must consider the cost in relation to the context within which it resides.

Allocation of Indirect Costs to Objects

LO4 Understand the mathematical procedures used to make allocations.

Allocation is the process of dividing a total cost into parts and distributing the parts among the relevant cost objects. Accordingly, *cost allocation* is sometimes called **cost distribution.** With respect to ISI, how much of the $38,160 of indirect costs should be allocated to each of the three departments? The first step in the allocation process is to identify the most appropriate cost driver for each cost. To the extent possible, costs should be distributed to reflect the way the departments consume resources. The cost driver enables the accountant to tie the consumption of resources to the cost objects. For example, the store rental fee is related to the size of the store space. Holding other factors constant, the larger the building, the higher the rental fee. In other words, the size of the store is *driving* the rental cost. Based on this rationale, a department that occupies a larger portion of the floor space should be allocated a larger portion of the rental cost. Assume that the store capacity is 23,000 square feet with 12,000, 7,000, and 4,000 square feet being occupied by the women's, men's, and children's departments, respectively. A rational allocation can be accomplished according to the following two-step process.[1]

Step 1. Compute the *allocation rate* by dividing the *total cost to be allocated* ($18,400 rental fee) by the *cost driver* (23,000 square feet of store space). *Since the cost driver is the basis for the allocation process, it is sometimes called the* **allocation base.** The result of the process is called the **allocation rate.** The computation follows.

Total cost to be allocated ÷ Cost driver (i.e., allocation base) = Allocation rate
$18,400 rental fee ÷ 23,000 square feet = $0.80 per square foot

Step 2. Multiply the *allocation rate* by the *weight of the cost driver* (i.e., weight of the base) to determine the allocation *per cost object.* This computation follows.

Cost Object	Allocation Rate	×	Number of Square Feet	=	Allocation per Cost Object
Women's department	$0.80	×	12,000	=	$ 9,600
Men's department	0.80	×	7,000	=	5,600
Children's department	0.80	×	4,000	=	3,200
Total			23,000		$18,400

Cost of utilities can also be logically related to the amount of floor space occupied by each department. The more floor space used, the more heating, lighting, air conditioning, and so on will be consumed. Accordingly, floor space can be considered to be a reasonable cost driver for utility cost. Based on square footage, the cost allocated to each department is computed as follows.

[1]Note that other mathematical approaches can be used to determine the same result. However, to reduce confusion, this text consistently uses the two-step method described here. More specifically, the text consistently follows the practice of determining the amount of an allocation by (1) computing a *rate* and (2) multiplying the *rate* by the *weight of the base* (i.e., cost driver).

reality bytes

How does Southwest Airlines know the cost of flying a passenger from Houston, Texas, to Los Angeles, California? The fact is that Southwest does not know the actual cost of flying particular passengers anywhere. There are many indirect costs associated with flying passengers. Some of these include the cost of planes, fuel, pilots, office buildings, and ground personnel. Indeed, besides insignificant food and beverage costs, there are few costs that could be traced directly to customers. Southwest and other airlines are forced to use allocation and averaging to determine the estimated cost of providing transportation services to customers. Estimated rather than actual cost is used for decision-making purposes.

Step 1. Compute the *allocation rate* by dividing the *total cost to be allocated* ($2,300 utility cost) by the *cost driver* (23,000 square feet of store space). The computation of the allocation rate for utility cost follows.

Total cost to be allocated ÷ Cost driver = Allocation rate

$2,300 utility cost ÷ 23,000 square feet = $0.10 per square foot

Step 2. Multiply the *allocation rate* by the *weight of the cost driver* to determine the allocation *per cost object:*

Cost Object	Allocation Rate	×	Number of Square Feet	=	Allocation per Cost Object
Women's department	$0.10	×	12,000	=	$1,200
Men's department	0.10	×	7,000	=	700
Children's department	0.10	×	4,000	=	400
Total			23,000		$2,300

Check Yourself 5-1

HealthCare, Inc., wants to estimate the cost of operating the three departments (Dermatology, Gynecology, and Pediatrics) that serve patients in its Health Center. Each department performed the following number of patient treatments during the most recent year of operation: Dermatology, 2,600; Gynecology, 3,500; and Pediatrics, 6,200. The annual salary of the Health Center's program administrator is $172,200. How much of the salary cost should HealthCare allocate to the Pediatrics Department?

Answer

Step 1 Compute the *allocation rate.*

Total cost to be allocated ÷ Cost driver (patient treatments) = Allocation rate

$172,200 salary cost ÷ (2,600 + 3,500 + 6,200) = $14 per patient treatment

Step 2 Multiply the *allocation rate* by the *weight of the cost driver* (weight of the base) to determine the allocation per *cost object.*

Cost Object	Allocation Rate	×	No. of Treatments	=	Allocation per Cost Object
Pediatrics Department	$14	×	6,200	=	$86,800

▮Allocation of Joint Costs

Joint costs are common costs incurred in the process of making two or more products. An example is the cost of raw milk (i.e., joint cost) that is used to make cream, whole milk, 2 percent milk, and skim milk. The products derived from joint costs are called **joint products.** Joint costs include not only materials costs but also the costs incurred to transform the materials into finished products. The point in the production process at which products become separate and identifiable is called the **split-off point.** For balance sheet valuation and income determination, all costs incurred up to the split-off point must be allocated to the joint products. Some products require additional processing after the split-off point. These separate and identifiable costs should be assigned to the specific products that cause their incurrence.

LO8 Understand the allocation of common costs associated with joint products and by-products.

To illustrate, assume that Westar Chemical Company uses a joint production process that produces two chemical compounds at the split-off point. The joint cost to produce the two compounds is $48,000, including $27,000 of materials cost and $21,000 of processing cost. The joint products consist of 3,000 gallons of Compound AK and 1,000 gallons of Compound AL. Westar allocates joint costs to the products on the basis of the number of gallons of compound produced. After the split-off point, Compound AL requires further processing before it can be sold. In other words, it has a zero market value at the split-off point. The cost of additional processing is $8,000. The 3,000 gallons of Compound AK sell for $50,000. The 1,000 gallons of Compound AL sell for $13,000. The allocation rate for the *joint cost* is $12 per gallon ($48,000 ÷ 4,000 gallons). At the split-off point, $36,000 ($12 × 3,000 gallons) of the joint cost is allocated to Compound AK and $12,000 ($12 × 1,000) of the joint cost is allocated to Compound AL. The $8,000 of additional processing cost is assigned to Compound AL, resulting in a total cost of $20,000 ($12,000 + $8,000) for that compound. The cost distribution and the determination of gross margin for the two products are shown in Exhibit 5–4.

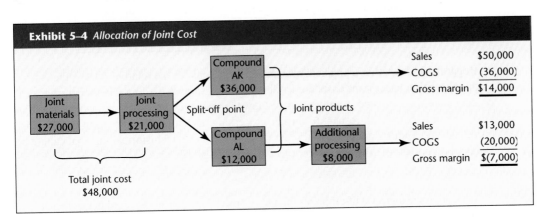

Exhibit 5–4 *Allocation of Joint Cost*

Joint Costs and the Issue of Relevance

The $7,000 loss generated by Compound AL may lead a naive manager to the mistaken conclusion that the $8,000 of additional processing costs should not be incurred to bring this product to market. In fact, this product is contributing $5,000 ($13,000 sales revenue − $8,000 additional processing cost) to the company's overall profitability. The allocated portion of the joint cost ($12,000) is *not relevant* to a decision regarding the further processing of Compound AL. This cost will be incurred regardless of whether Compound AL is processed beyond the split-off point. Because the allocated cost does *not* differ for the alternatives (i.e., process further versus not process further), it is not a relevant cost. To validate this point, we calculate the

LO9 Understand the association between cost allocation and relevance.

total profit for the company under the two alternatives: (1) processing Compound AL beyond the split-off point and (2) not processing Compound AL beyond the split-off point.

	With Additional Processing	Without Additional Processing
Sales	$63,000	$50,000
Cost of goods sold	(56,000)	(48,000)
Gross margin	$ 7,000	$ 2,000

If Compound AL is processed beyond the split-off point, total revenue will equal the sales revenue of Compound AL and Compound AK ($50,000 + $13,000 = $63,000). Total cost equals the joint cost plus the cost of additional processing ($48,000 + $8,000 = $56,000). Without additional processing, Compound AL has a zero market value. Accordingly, total revenue equals the revenue generated by Compound AK ($50,000), and total cost is equal to the joint cost ($48,000).

Relative Sales Value as the Allocation Base

To distribute the earnings more meaningfully over all joint products, many companies allocate joint costs to products on the basis of the relative sales value of each product at the split-off point. In the case of Westar Chemical, all of the joint cost would be allocated to Compound AK because Compound AL has a zero market value at the split-off point. Accordingly, the gross margins of the two products are computed as follows.

	Compound AK	Compound AL
Sales	$50,000	$13,000
Cost of goods sold	(48,000)	(8,000)
Gross margin	$ 2,000	$ 5,000

Regardless of whether a physical measure (e.g., gallons) or the relative sales value is used as the allocation base, joint costs are irrelevant to decisions regarding whether further processing should be pursued. Another way to view the relevance issue is to recognize that joint costs are *sunk costs* with respect to further processing decisions. Because joint costs are incurred before products are processed separately, they represent a historical fact that cannot be changed regardless of whether further processing takes place.

Check Yourself 5–3

What are some logical split-off points for a meat processing company engaged in butchering beef?

Answer The first logical split-off point occurs when processing separates the hide (used to produce leather) from the carcass. Other split-off points occur as further processing produces different cuts of meat (T-bone and New York strip steaks, various roasts, chops, ground chuck, etc.).

By-Product Costs

Like joint products, by-products share common inputs. The difference between a joint product and a by-product is that **by-products** have a relatively insignificant market value relative to the joint products. An example of a by-product is sawdust produced in the process of making lumber. Although the accounting treatment for by-products will not be discussed in this text, you should be aware that the common costs associated with producing them are not relevant with respect to further processing decisions.

Cost Allocation: The Human Factor

Anyone who has tried to divide a candy bar between two children has probably experienced the human side of the allocation process. In practice, allocations frequently have a significant impact on individuals. They may affect performance evaluation and the level of compensation that managers receive. Likewise, allocations may dictate the amount of resources made available to departments, divisions, and other organizational subunits. The manager who has control over resources usually has prestige and the opportunity to affect the organization's operations. The following scenario provides insight into fairness and the emotional aspect of allocation decisions.

LO6 Understand the implications of cost behavior associated with making allocations.

Using Cost Allocation in a Budgeting Decision

A budget is a plan, and Sharon Southport is in dire need of a plan. Dr. Southport is the dean of the School of Business at a major state university. Due to a cutback in state funding, the School of Business has been advised that it will receive a reduction in the funds available for duplicating services. Four departments operate under Dean Southport's control: management, marketing, finance, and accounting. Dean Southport is certain that significant waste exists in the school's use of copy equipment and that some departments are more wasteful than others. She is determined to cut the fat out of the budget rather than simply take proportionate reduction from every department.

In an effort to analyze the situation, Dean Southport reviewed last year's expenditures. She discovered that total copy cost for that year was $36,000. Individual departmental expenditures were $12,000 for management, $10,000 for accounting, $8,000 for finance, and $6,000 for marketing.

Dean Southport wondered how these actual costs would compare to a distribution that divided the total amount of copy cost ($36,000) equally among the four departments. The computations for making the division under this alternative are as follows.

Total copying budget ÷ Number of departments = Amount per department
$36,000 ÷ 4 = $9,000 *per department*

Dividing the total cost equally suggests that each department should have spent $9,000 for copying costs and implies that the management and accounting departments spent too much on copying costs ($3,000 and $1,000 too much, respectively).

Using Cost Drivers to Make Allocations

To ensure a fair allocation, Dean Southport decides to discuss the matter with the chairpersons of the departments. She presents her findings that the management and accounting departments are spending more than an equal share of the total copy cost and opens the discussion by asking whether the chairpersons agree with this conclusion. Dr. Bill Thompson, the chairperson of the management department, protests that an equal allotment is unfair because his department has more faculty members than each of the other three departments. He argues that copy costs are directly related to the size of the faculty; more faculty obviously make more copies. In accounting terms, Dr. Thompson is suggesting that the number of faculty members is an appropriate cost driver for the allocation of copy funds.

Dr. Thompson suggests the following allocation scheme. Because the School of Business has 72 faculty members (29 in management, 16 in accounting, 12 in finance, and 15 in marketing), the allocation should be computed as follows.

Step 1. Compute the *allocation rate*.

Total cost to be allocated $\div$ Cost driver = Allocation rate
$36,000 $\div$ 72 = $500 *per faculty member*

Step 2. Multiply the *rate* by the *weight of the driver* (the number of faculty per department) to determine the allocation *per object* (department).

Department	Allocation Rate	×	Number of Faculty	=	Allocation per Department	Actual Cost, Previous Year
Management	$500	×	29		$14,500	$12,000
Accounting	500	×	16		8,000	10,000
Finance	500	×	12		6,000	8,000
Marketing	500	×	15		7,500	6,000
Total					$36,000	$36,000

Recall that actual copy cost was $12,000 for management, $10,000 for accounting, $8,000 for finance, and $6,000 for marketing. Accordingly, accounting and finance are overspending when cost allocation is based on the size of the faculty. Seeing these figures, Dr. Bob Smethers, chairperson of the accounting department, questions the appropriateness of the use of the number of faculty as the cost driver. Dr. Smethers suggests that the *number of students* rather than the *size of the faculty* drives the cost of copying. He argues that most copying results from the duplication of syllabi, exams, and handouts and that his department teaches mass sections of introductory accounting in which the student/teacher ratio is extremely high. Because his department teaches more students, it should be expected to spend more on copying cost even though it has fewer faculty members. Dr. Smethers demonstrates his point by recomputing the allocation as follows.

Step 1. The allocation rate is computed on the basis of number of students. University records indicate that the School of Business taught 1,200 students during the most recent academic year. Accordingly, she computed the allocation rate (i.e., copy cost per student) as follows.

Total cost to be allocated $\div$ Cost driver = Allocation rate
$36,000 $\div$ 1,200 = $30 *per student*

Step 2. Multiply the *rate* by the *weight of the driver* (number of students served by each department) to determine the allocation *per object* (department).

Department	Allocation Rate	×	Number of Students	=	Allocation per Department	Actual Cost, Previous Year
Management	$30	×	330		$ 9,900	$12,000
Accounting	30	×	360		10,800	10,000
Finance	30	×	290		8,700	8,000
Marketing	30	×	220		6,600	6,000
Total					$36,000	$36,000

Choosing the Best Cost Driver

Given the actual copy cost expenditures of $12,000 for management, $10,000 for accounting, $8,000 for finance, and $6,000 for marketing, the allocation based on the number of students suggests that the management department is overspending on copy cost. Dr. Thompson objects vigorously to the use of the number of students as the cost driver. He continues to argue that the size of the faculty is a more appropriate basis for allocation. The chairs of the finance and marketing departments side with Dr. Smethers, and the dean is forced to settle the dispute.

Dean Southport recognizes that the views of the chairpersons are clouded by self-interest. Clearly, it is to their advantage to identify the management department as the villain of waste. Furthermore, she recognizes that some duplicating costs are in fact related to the size of the faculty. For example, the cost of copying manuscripts that faculty submit for publication relates to faculty size. When more faculty submit articles, the cost of duplication rises. Even so, the dean believes that the number of students, to a significant degree, drives the cost of duplication. Furthermore, she desires to send a signal that encourages faculty to minimize the impact of funding cuts on student services. Accordingly, Dean Southport decides to allocate copying costs on the basis of the number of students served by each department. Dr. Thompson is incensed and storms out of the meeting in anger. The dean proceeds with the development of a budget by assigning the amount of available funds to each department via an allocation based on the number of students.

Controlling Emotions

Dr. Thompson's behavior deserves comment. Expressing anger may relieve frustration but is seldom a sign of clear thinking. Obviously, Dean Southport recognized some merit in Dr. Thompson's contention that copy costs were related to faculty size. Had Dr. Thompson offered a compromise rather than an emotional outburst, he might have been able to increase his department's share of the allocated funds. Perhaps a portion of the funding base could have been allocated using number of faculty members with the other portion being allocated on the basis of number of students. If Dr. Thompson had acted appropriately, all parties might have agreed to the compromise. The technical ability to compute the numbers is of little use without the interpersonal skills necessary to sell ideas. Never forget the human factor.

Managers need to know how much it costs. The "it" could be the cost of products, processes, departments, activities, and so on. The item for which accountants attempt to determine the cost is called a *cost object.* Knowing the cost of specific objects enables management to control costs, evaluate performance, and price products. *Direct costs* can be traced to a cost object in a cost-effective manner. Costs that cannot be easily traced to designated objects are called *indirect costs.*

The same cost can be classified as either a direct or indirect cost, depending on the designation of the cost object. For example, the cost of the salary of a manager of a Burger King restaurant can be directly traced to a particular store but cannot be traced to particular products made and sold in the store. The definitions of direct and indirect are independent of the

definitions of fixed and variable cost behavior; they are also independent of the characteristics that determine relevance. A direct cost could be either fixed or variable or either relevant or nonrelevant, depending on the context within which the cost is used. In summary, one cost can be classified as direct/indirect, fixed/variable, or relevant/not relevant, depending on the designation of the cost object.

Indirect costs are assigned to objects through a process known as *cost allocation.* Allocation is the process of dividing an indirect cost into parts and distributing the parts among the relevant cost objects. Costs are frequently allocated to cost objects in proportion to the factors that cause the cost to be incurred. The factors that cause a cost to be incurred are called *cost drivers.* The first step in the allocation process is to determine the allocation rate by dividing the total cost to be allocated by the chosen cost driver. The next step is to multiply the amount of the cost driver for a particular object by the allocation rate. The result is the amount of the cost to be assigned to the cost object.

More than one driver may be associated with a particular indirect cost. The best cost driver is the one that most accurately reflects the use of the resource by the cost object. Objects that consume the highest resources should be allocated a proportionately higher share of the costs. If no strong cost driver exists, making an arbitrary allocation such as assigning an equal portion of the total cost to each cost object may be necessary.

Allocations have important behavioral implications. Choosing an inappropriate cost driver can distort allocations and motivate managers to act in ways that are detrimental to the company's profitability.

To avoid the time-consuming task of allocating every single indirect cost, managers accumulate many costs into a single total called a *cost pool.* The costs included in the pool should be those that can logically be allocated to the cost object by a single cost driver. A single allocation can then be made for the entire cost pool.

The joint costs that are incurred in the process of making two or more products are allocated between the products at the *split-off point,* which is where the products become separate and identifiable. The allocation base can be the products' relative sales values or some measure of the amount of each product made. If one of the joint products requires additional processing costs to bring it to market, only these additional processing costs are relevant to a decision regarding further processing. The allocated joint costs are not relevant because they will be incurred regardless of whether the by-product is processed after being split off. By-products share common costs with other products but have an insignificant market value relative to their joint products.

The failure to accurately allocate indirect costs to cost objects can result in misinformation that impairs decision making. The next chapter explains how automation has caused distortions in allocations that are determined with traditional approaches. The chapter introduces a new allocation approach known as *activity-based costing* and explains how it can improve efficiency and productivity through a practice known as *activity-based management.* Finally, the chapter introduces a practice known as *total quality management* that seeks to minimize the costs of conforming to a designated standard of quality.

SELF-STUDY REVIEW PROBLEM

New budget constraints have pressured Body Perfect Gym to control costs. The owner of the gym has notified division managers that their job performance evaluations will be highly influenced by their ability to minimize costs. The gym has three divisions, weight lifting, aerobics, and spinning. The owner has formulated a report showing how much it cost to operate each of the three divisions last year. In preparing the report, Mr. Ripple identified several indirect costs that must be allocated among the divisions. These indirect costs are $4,200 of laundry expense, $48,000 of gym supplies, $350,000 of office rent, $50,000 of janitorial services, and $120,000 for administrative salaries. To provide a reasonably accurate cost allocation, Mr. Ripple has identified several potential cost drivers. These drivers and their association with each division follow.

Cost Driver	Weight Lifting	Aerobics	Spinning	Total
Number of participants	26	16	14	56
Number of instructors	10	8	6	24
Square feet of gym space	12,000	6,000	7,000	25,000
Number of staff	2	2	1	5

Required

a. Identify the appropriate cost objects.

b. Identify the most appropriate cost driver for each indirect cost, and compute the allocation rate for assigning each indirect cost to the cost objects.

c. Determine the amount of supplies expense that should be allocated to each of the three divisions.

d. The spinning manager wants to use the number of staff rather than the number of instructors as the allocation base for the supplies expense. Explain why the spinning manager would take this position.

e. Identify two cost drivers other than your choice for Requirement *b* that could be used to allocate the cost of the administrative salaries to the three divisions.

Solution to Requirement a

The objective is to determine the cost of operating each division. Therefore, the cost objects are the three divisions (weight lifting, aerobics, and spinning).

Solution to Requirement b

The costs, appropriate cost drivers, and allocation rates for assigning the costs to the departments follow:

Cost	Base	Computation	Allocation Rate
Laundry expense	Number of participants	$4,200 ÷ 56	$75 per participant
Supplies expense	Number of instructors	$48,000 ÷ 24	$2,000 per instructor
Office rent	Square feet	$350,000 ÷ 25,000	$14 per square foot
Janitorial service	Square feet	$50,000 ÷ 25,000	$2 per square foot
Administrative salaries	Number of divisions	$120,000 ÷ 3	$40,000 per division

There are other logical cost drivers. For example, supplies expense could be allocated based on the number of staff. It is also logical to use a combination of cost drivers. For example, the allocation of supplies expense could be based on the combined number of instructors and staff. For this problem, we assumed that Mr. Ripple chose the number of instructors as the base for allocating supplies expense.

Solution to Requirement c

Department	Cost to Be Allocated	Allocation Rate	×	Weight of Base	=	Amount Allocated
Weight lifting	Supplies expense	$2,000	×	10	=	$20,000
Aerobics	Supplies expense	$2,000	×	8	=	16,000
Spinning	Supplies expense	$2,000	×	6	=	12,000
Total						$48,000

Solution to Requirement d

If the number of staff were used as the allocation base, the allocation rate for supplies expense would be as follows:

$$\$48,000 \div 5 \text{ staff} = \$9,600 \text{ per staff member}$$

Using this rate, the total supplies expense would be allocated among the three divisions as follows:

Department	Cost to Be Allocated	Allocation Rate	×	Weight of Base	=	Amount Allocated
Weight lifting	Supplies expense	$9,600	×	2	=	$19,200
Aerobics	Supplies expense	$9,600	×	2	=	19,200
Spinning	Supplies expense	$9,600	×	1	=	9,600
Total						$48,000

By using the number of staff as the allocation base instead of the number of instructors, the amount of overhead cost allocated to the spinning division falls from $12,000 to $9,600. Since managers are evaluated based on minimizing costs, it is clearly in the spinning manager's self-interest to use the number of staff as the allocation base.

Solution to Requirement e

Among other possibilities, bases for allocating the administrative salaries include the number of participants, the number of lessons, or the number of instructors.

APPENDIX

Allocating Service Center Costs

LO10 Understand the allocation of service center costs to operating departments under the direct and step methods.

Most organizations establish departments responsible for accomplishing specific tasks. Departments that are assigned tasks leading to the accomplishment of the primary objectives of the organization are called **operating departments.** Those that provide support to operating departments are called **service departments.** For example, the department of accounting at a university is classified as an operating department because its faculty perform the university's primary functions of teaching, research, and service. In contrast, the maintenance department is classified as a service department because its employees provide janitorial services that support primary university functions. Professors are more likely to be motivated to perform university functions when facilities are clean, but the university's primary purpose is not to clean buildings. Similarly, the lending department in a bank is an operating department and the personnel department is a service department. The bank is in the business of making loans. Hiring employees is a secondary function that assists the lending activity.

The costs to produce a product (or a service) include both operating and service department costs. Therefore, service department costs must somehow be allocated to the products produced (or services provided). Service department costs are frequently distributed to products through a two-stage allocation process. First-stage allocations involve the distribution of costs from service center cost pools to operating department cost pools. In the second stage, costs in the operating cost pools are allocated to products. Three different approaches can be used to allocate costs in the first stage of the two-stage costing process: the *direct method,* the *step method,* and the *reciprocal method.*

Direct Method

The **direct method** is the simplest allocation approach. It allocates service department costs directly to operating department cost pools. To illustrate, assume that Candler & Associates is a law firm that desires to determine the cost of handling each case. The firm has two operating departments, one that represents clients in civil suits and the other that defends clients in criminal cases. The two operating departments are supported by two service departments, personnel and secretarial support. Candler uses a two-stage allocation system to allocate the service center's costs to the firm's legal cases. In the first stage, the costs to operate each service department are accumulated in separate cost pools. For example, the costs to operate the personnel department are $80,000 in salary, $18,000 in office rental, $12,000 in depreciation, $3,000 in supplies, and $4,000 in miscellaneous costs. These costs are added together in a single services department cost pool amounting to $117,000. Similarly, the costs incurred by the secretarial department are accumulated in a cost pool. We assume that this cost pool contains $156,800 of accumulated costs. The amounts in these cost pools are then allocated to the operating departments' cost pools. The appropriate allocations are described in the following paragraphs.

Assume that Candler's accountant decides that the number of attorneys working in the two operating departments constitutes a rational cost driver for the allocation of the personnel department cost pool and that the number of request forms submitted to the secretarial department constitutes a rational cost driver for the allocation of costs accumulated in the secretarial department cost pool. The total number of attorneys working in the two operating departments is 18, 11 in the civil department and 7 in the criminal department. The secretarial department received 980 work request forms with 380 from the civil department and 600 from the criminal department. Using these cost drivers as the allocation bases, the accountant made the following first-stage allocations.

Determination of Allocation Rates

$$\text{Allocation rate for personel department cost pool} = \frac{\$117,000}{18} = \$6,500 \, per \, attorney$$

$$\text{Allocation rate for secretarial department cost pool} = \frac{\$156,800}{980} = \$160 \, per \, request \, form$$

The accountant then multiplied these rates by the weight of the base to determine the amount of each service cost pool to allocate to each operating department cost pool. The appropriate computations are shown in Exhibit 5–1A.

Exhibit 5–1A *First-Stage Allocations for Candler & Associates—Direct Method*

Allocated Service Department Overhead	Allocation Rate	×	Weight of Base	=	Civil Department	Criminal Department	Total Service Department Cost Pool
Personnel	$6,500	×	11 attorneys	=	$ 71,500		
	6,500	×	7 attorneys	=		$ 45,500	
Total cost of personnel department							$117,000
Secretarial	$160	×	380 requests	=	60,800		
	160	×	600 requests	=		96,000	
Total cost of secretarial department							156,800
Total of cost pools after allocation				=	132,300	141,500	$273,800
Other operating department overhead costs				=	785,100	464,788	
Total of operating department overhead cost pools				=	$917,400	$606,288	

As indicated, the allocated service department costs are pooled with other operating department overhead costs to form the operating department cost pools. In the second stage of the costing process, the costs in the operating department cost pools are allocated to the firm's products (cases). To illustrate second-stage allocations, assume that Candler allocates the operating department overhead cost pools on the basis of billable hours. Furthermore, assume that the civil department expects to bill 30,580 hours to its clients and the criminal department expects to bill 25,262 hours. Based on this information, the following predetermined overhead rates are used to allocate operating department cost pools to particular cases.

$$\text{Predetermined overhead rate for the civil department} = \frac{\$917,400}{30,580} = \$30 \text{ per billable hour}$$

$$\text{Predetermined overhead rate for the criminal department} = \frac{\$606,288}{25,262} = \$24 \text{ per billable hour}$$

These rates are used to calculate the amount of operating department cost pools to include in the determination of the cost to litigate specific cases. For example, a case in the civil department that required 300 billable hours of legal service is allocated $9,000 (300 hours × $30 predetermined overhead rate) of overhead cost. Assuming that the direct costs to litigate the case amounted to $25,000, the total cost of this particular case is $34,000 ($25,000 direct cost + $9,000 allocated overhead). This accumulated cost figure could be used as a guide to determine the charge to the client or the profitability of the case.

Step Method

The direct method of allocating service center costs fails to consider the fact that service departments render assistance to other service departments. A service that is performed by one service department for the benefit of another service department is called an **interdepartmental service.** To illustrate this, we return to the case of Candler & Associates. Suppose that Candler's personnel department works with the employees in the secretarial department as well as the attorneys in the civil and criminal operating departments. Under these circumstances, Candler needs a cost approach that recognizes the interdepartmental service activity. One such approach is known as the **step method.** The primary difference between the direct method and the step method is depicted graphically in Exhibit 5–2A. Focus your attention on the first stage of the allocation process. Notice that the step method includes one additional allocation, specifically from the personnel department cost pool to the secretarial department cost pool. The direct method ignores this interdepartmental service cost allocation. Indeed, the direct method derives its name from the fact that it allocates costs only from service cost pools to operating cost pools.

The fact that the direct method ignores the effect of interdepartmental services may cause distortions in the measurement of cost objects. The primary purpose of the step method is to avoid such distortions, thereby improving the accuracy of product costing. To illustrate this point, consider Candler & Associates. First, note that the interdepartmental portion of the personnel department cost is, in fact, a cost of providing secretarial services. In other words, the personnel service costs could be reduced if the personnel department did not provide service to the secretarial staff. Accordingly, the cost of providing personnel support to the secretarial staff should be included in the secretarial cost pool. Under the direct

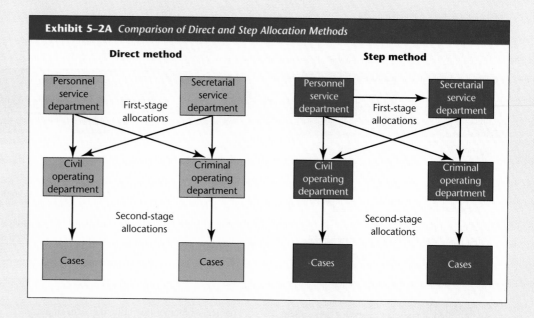

Exhibit 5–2A *Comparison of Direct and Step Allocation Methods*

method, however, the interdepartmental service cost is allocated between the civil and criminal operating departments. This is not a problem in and of itself because the cost of secretarial service is also allocated between the civil and criminal operating departments. Unfortunately, the base used to allocate personnel costs to the operating departments (i.e., number of attorneys) distributes more cost to the civil department than to the criminal department. This is unfortunate because the criminal department uses more secretarial service than the civil department does. In other words, more secretarial cost (i.e., interdepartmental personnel cost) is being allocated to the civil department although the criminal department uses more secretarial services. This means that ultimately the cost to litigate civil cases will be overstated and the cost to litigate criminal cases will be understated.

The step method corrects this distortion by distributing the interdepartmental personnel department cost to the secretarial department cost pool before it is allocated to the operating departments. Because the secretarial cost pool is allocated on the basis of requests for secretarial service, more of the interdepartmental cost will be allocated to the criminal operating division. To validate this result, assume that the personnel department cost pool is allocated to the secretarial department cost pool and the two operating department cost pools on the basis of the number of employees in each department. In addition to the 18 attorneys in the firm, assume that two employees work in the secretarial department. Accordingly, the allocation rate for the personnel cost pool is calculated as follows.

$$\text{Allocation rate for personnel department cost pool} = \frac{\$117,000}{20} = \$5,850 \text{ per employee}$$

Based on this rate, the first step in the allocation process distributes the personnel department cost pool as indicated here.

Personnel Cost Pool Allocated to	Allocation Rate		Weight of Base		Allocated Cost
Secretarial	$5,850	×	2 employees	=	$ 11,700
Civil	5,850	×	11 employees	=	64,350
Criminal	5,850	×	7 employees	=	40,950
Total	5,850	×	20 employees		$117,000

The result of the distribution of personnel department costs is shown as the Step 1 allocation in Exhibit 5–3A. The $11,700 interdepartmental personnel department cost allocated to the secretarial department cost pool is added to the $156,800 existing balance in that cost pool (See Exhibit 5–3A). The result is the accumulation of secretarial cost of $168,500. The second step in the costing process allocates this cost pool to the operating departments. Recall that the secretarial cost pool is allocated on the basis of number of work request forms submitted. Furthermore, recall that 980 request forms were submitted to

the secretarial department (380 from the civil department and 600 from the criminal department). Accordingly, the allocation rate for the secretarial department cost pool is computed as follows.

$$\text{Allocation rate for secretarial department cost pool} = \frac{\$168,500}{980} = \$171.93878 \text{ per request form}$$

Based on this rate, the second step in the allocation process distributes the secretarial cost pool as indicated here.

Secretarial Cost Pool Allocated to	Allocation Rate		Weight of Base		Allocated Cost
Civil	$171.93878	×	380 requests	=	$ 65,337
Criminal	171.93878	×	600 requests	=	103,163
Total	171.93878	×	980 requests		$168,500

The result of this allocation is shown as the Step 2 allocation in Exhibit 5–3A. Notice that the final cost pools for the operating departments reflect the expected shift in the cost distribution between the two departments. Specifically, the cost pool in the criminal department is higher and the cost pool in the civil department is lower than the comparable cost pool amounts computed under the direct method (see Exhibit 5–3A for the appropriate comparison). This distribution of cost is consistent with the fact that more of the interdepartmental service cost should be assigned to the criminal department because it uses more secretarial services than does the civil department. Accordingly, the step method of allocation more accurately reflects the manner in which the two operating departments consume resources.

Exhibit 5–3A *First-Stage Allocations for Candler & Associates—Step Method*

	Personnel Cost Pool		Secretarial Cost Pool		Civil Department		Criminal Department
Cost to be allocated	$117,000		$156,800				
Step 1 allocation	(117,000)	=	11,700	+	$ 64,350	+	$ 40,950
Step 2 allocation			(168,500)	=	65,337	+	103,163
Total in cost pool after allocation	0		0		129,687		144,113
Other operating department overhead costs					785,100		464,788
Total of operating department overhead cost pool					$914,787		$608,901

The preceding illustration considered a simple two-stage allocation process with only two service departments and two operating departments. In large organizations, the costing process may be significantly more complex. Interdepartmental cost allocations may involve several service departments. For example, a personnel department may provide service to a secretarial department that provides service to an engineering department that provides service to the accounting department that provides service to several operating departments. In addition, general overhead costs may be allocated to both service and operating departments before costs are allocated from service to operating departments. For example, general utility costs may be pooled together and allocated to service and operating departments on the basis of square footage of floor space. These allocated utility costs are then redistributed to other service departments and to operating departments in a sequence of step-down allocations. The step-down process usually begins with the cost pool that represents resources used by the largest number of departments. This constitutes the first step in the costing process. The second step proceeds with allocations from the cost pool that represents resources used by the second largest number of departments and so on, until all overhead costs have been allocated to the operating departments. Accordingly, the first stage of a two-stage costing process may include many allocations (steps) before all costs have been distributed to the operating departments. Regardless of how many allocations are included in the first stage, the second stage begins when costs are allocated from the operating departments to the organizations' products.

Reciprocal Method

Note that the step method is limited to one-way interdepartmental relationships. In practice, many departments have two-way working relationships. For example, the personnel department may provide services to the secretarial department and receive services from it. Two-way associations in which departments provide and receive services from one another are called **reciprocal relationships.** Allocations that recognize

reciprocal relationships require complex mathematical manipulation involving the use of simultaneous linear equations. The resultant cost distributions are difficult to interpret. Furthermore, the results attained with the **reciprocal method** are not significantly different from those attained through the step method. As a result, the reciprocal method is rarely used in practice.

KEY TERMS

Allocation *193*
Allocation base *193*
Allocation rate *193*
By-products *204*
Cost *189*
Cost accumulation *190*
Cost allocation *191*
Cost distribution *193*
Cost driver *190*

Cost objects *189*
Cost pool *202*
Cost tracing *191*
Direct cost *192*
Direct method (Appendix) *210*
Indirect cost *192*
Interdepartmental service
(Appendix) *211*

Joint costs *203*
Joint products *203*
Operating departments
(Appendix) *210*
Overhead costs *192*
Predetermined overhead
rate *202*

Reciprocal method
(Appendix) *214*
Reciprocal relationships
(Appendix) *213*
Service departments
(Appendix) *210*
Split-off point *203*
Step method (Appendix) *211*

QUESTIONS

1. What is a cost object? Identify four different cost objects in which an accountant would be interested.
2. Why is cost accumulation imprecise?
3. If the cost object is a manufactured product, what are the three major cost categories to accumulate?
4. What is a direct cost? What criteria are used to determine whether a cost is a direct cost?
5. Why are the terms *direct cost* and *indirect cost* independent of the terms *fixed cost* and *variable cost?* Give an example to illustrate.
6. Give an example of why the statement, "All direct costs are avoidable," is incorrect.
7. What are the important factors in determining the appropriate cost driver to use in allocating a cost?
8. How is an allocation rate determined? How is an allocation made?
9. In a manufacturing environment, which costs are direct and which are indirect in product costing?
10. Why are some manufacturing costs not directly traceable to products?
11. What is the objective of allocating indirect manufacturing overhead costs to the product?
12. On January 31, the managers of Integra, Inc., seek to determine the cost of producing their product during January for product pricing and control purposes. The company can easily determine the costs of direct materials and direct labor used in January production, but many fixed indirect costs are not affected by the level of production activity and have not yet been incurred. The managers can reasonably estimate the overhead costs for the year based on the fixed indirect costs incurred in past periods. Assume the managers decide to allocate an equal amount of these estimated costs to the products produced each month. Explain why this practice may not provide a reasonable estimate of product costs in January.
13. Respond to the following statement: "The allocation base chosen is unimportant. What is important in product costing is that overhead costs be assigned to production in a specific period by an allocation process."
14. Larry Kwang insists that the costs of his school's fund-raising project should be determined after the project is complete. He argues that only after the project is complete can its costs be determined accurately and that it is a waste of time to try to estimate future costs. Georgia Sundum counters that waiting until the project is complete will not provide timely information for planning expenditures. How would you arbitrate this discussion? Explain the trade-offs between accuracy and timeliness.
15. Define the term *cost pool.* How are cost pools important in allocating costs?
16. What are the three methods used for allocating service center costs? How do the methods differ?
17. What is the difference between a joint product and a by-product?

EXERCISES—SERIES A

L.O. 1   **EXERCISE 5–1A** *Allocating Costs Between Divisions*

Sheldon Services Company (SSC) has 40 employees, 28 of whom are assigned to Division A and 12 to Division B. SSC incurred $240,000 of fringe benefits cost during 2004.

Required

Determine the amount of the fringe benefits cost to be allocated to Division A and to Division B.

EXERCISE 5–2A *Allocating to Smooth Cost Over Varying Levels of Production*

L.O. 1

Production workers for Gray Manufacturing Company provided 160 hours of labor in January and 280 hours in February. Gray expects to use 2,400 hours of labor during the year. The rental fee for the manufacturing facility is $4,000 per month.

Required

Explain why allocation is needed. Based on this information, how much of the rental cost should be allocated to the products made in January and to those made in February?

EXERCISE 5–3A *Allocating to Solve a Timing Problem*

L.O. 1

Production workers for Kawasaki Manufacturing Company provided 3,200 hours of labor in January and 2,000 hours in February. The company, whose operation is labor intensive, expects to use 36,000 hours of labor during the year. Kawasaki paid a $45,000 annual premium on July 1 of the prior year for an insurance policy that covers the manufacturing facility for the following 12 months.

Required

Explain why allocation is needed. Based on this information, how much of the insurance cost should be allocated to the products made in January and to those made in February?

EXERCISE 5–4A *Allocating a Fixed Cost*

L.O. 1, 6

Western Air is a large airline company that pays a customer relations representative $3,000 per month. The representative, who processed 900 customer complaints in January and 600 complaints in February, is expected to process 12,000 customer complaints during 2007.

Required

a. Determine the total cost of processing customer complaints in January and in February.
b. Explain why allocating the cost of the customer relations representative would or would not be relevant to decision making.

EXERCISE 5–5A *Allocating Overhead Cost Among Products*

L.O. 1

Sally Hats, Inc., manufactures three different models of hats, Vogue, Beauty, and Deluxe. Sally expects to incur $750,000 of overhead cost during the next fiscal year. Other budget information follows.

	Vogue	Beauty	Deluxe	Total
Direct labor hours	3,000	5,000	4,500	12,500
Machine hours	1,000	1,000	1,000	3,000

Required

a. Use direct labor hours as the cost driver to compute the allocation rate and the budgeted overhead cost for each product.
b. Use machine hours as the cost driver to compute the allocation rate and the budgeted overhead cost for each product.

EXERCISE 5–6A *Allocating Overhead Costs Among Products*

L.O. 1

Norman Company makes three products in its factory: plastic cups, plastic tablecloths, and plastic bottles. The expected overhead costs for the next fiscal year include the following.

Factory manager's salary	$130,000
Factory utility costs	50,000
Factory supplies	20,000
Total overhead costs	$200,000

Norman uses machine hours as the cost driver to allocate overhead costs. Budgeted machine hours for the products are as follows.

Cups	500 Hours
Tablecloths	800
Bottles	1,200
Total machine hours	2,500

Required

Allocate the budgeted overhead costs to the products.

L.O. 1   EXERCISE 5–7A *Allocating Costs Among Products*

Lander Construction Company expects to build three new homes during a specific accounting period. The estimated direct materials and labor costs are as follows.

Expected Costs	Home 1	Home 2	Home 3
Direct labor	$60,000	$ 90,000	$170,000
Direct materials	90,000	130,000	180,000

Assume Lander needs to allocate two major overhead costs ($40,000 of employee fringe benefits and $20,000 of indirect materials costs) among the three jobs.

Required

Choose an appropriate cost driver for each of the overhead costs and determine the total cost of each house.

L.O. 1   EXERCISE 5–8A *Allocating Overhead Cost to Accomplish Smoothing*

Zell Corporation expects to incur indirect overhead costs of $50,000 per month and direct manufacturing costs of $7 per unit. The expected production activity for the first four months of 2003 is as follows.

	January	February	March	April
Estimated production in units	4,000	7,000	3,000	6,000

Required

a. Calculate a predetermined overhead rate based on the number of units of product expected to be made during the first four months of the year.
b. Allocate overhead costs to each month using the overhead rate computed in Requirement *a*.
c. Calculate the total cost per unit for each month using the overhead allocated in Requirement *b*.

L.O. 1   EXERCISE 5–9A *Allocating Overhead for Product Costing*

Sandiego Manufacturing Company produced 600 units of inventory in January 2004. It expects to produce an additional 4,200 units during the remaining 11 months of the year. In other words, total production for 2004 is estimated to be 4,800 units. Direct materials and direct labor costs are $64 and $52 per unit, respectively. Sandiego Company expects to incur the following manufacturing overhead costs during the 2004 accounting period.

Production supplies	$ 2,400
Supervisor salary	96,000
Depreciation on equipment	72,000
Utilities	18,000
Rental fee on manufacturing facilities	48,000
Total	$236,400

Required

a. Determine the cost of the 600 units of product made in January.
b. Is the cost computed in Requirement *a* actual or estimated? Could Sandiego improve accuracy by waiting until December to determine the cost of products? Identify two reasons that a manager would

want to know the cost of products in January. Discuss the relationship between accuracy and relevance as it pertains to this problem.

EXERCISE 5–10A *How the Allocation of Fixed Cost Affects a Pricing Decision*

L.O. 1

Pullman Manufacturing Co. expects to make 24,000 chairs during the 2003 accounting period. The company made 4,000 chairs in January. Materials and labor costs for January were $16,000 and $24,000, respectively. Pullman produced 2,000 chairs in February. Material and labor costs for February were $8,000 and $12,000, respectively. The company paid the $120,000 annual rental fee on its manufacturing facility on January 1, 2003.

Required
Assuming that Pullman desires to sell its chairs for cost plus 40 percent of cost, what price should be charged for the chairs produced in January and February?

EXERCISE 5–11A *Allocating Joint Product Cost*

L.O. 8

Hornback Chemical Company makes three products, B217, K360, and X639, which are joint products from the same materials. In a standard batch of 300,000 pounds of raw materials, the company generates 70,000 pounds of B217, 150,000 pounds of K360, and 80,000 pounds of X639. A standard batch costs $1,800,000 to produce. The sales prices per pound are $4.00, $9.60, and $16.00 for B217, K360, and X639, respectively.

Required
a. Allocate the joint product cost among the three final products using weight as the allocation base.
b. Allocate the joint product cost among the three final products using market value as the allocation base.

Appendix

EXERCISE 5–12A *Allocating a Service Center Cost to Operating Departments*

L.O. 10

Harbert Corporation's computer services department assists two operating departments in using the company's information system effectively. The annual cost of computer services is $400,000. The production department employs 22 employees, and the sales department employs 18 employees. Harbert uses the number of employees as the cost driver for allocating the cost of computer services to operating departments.

Required
Allocate the cost of computer services to operating departments.

EXERCISE 5–13A *Allocating Costs of Service Centers to Operating Departments—*
Step Method

L.O. 10

Brook Health Care Center, Inc., has three clinics servicing the Birmingham metropolitan area. The company's legal services department supports the clinics. Moreover, its computer services department supports all of the clinics and the legal services department. The annual cost of operating the legal services department is $240,000. The annual cost of operating the computer services department is $320,000. The company uses the number of patients served as the cost driver for allocating the cost of legal services and the number of computer workstations as the cost driver for allocating the cost of computer services. Other relevant information follows.

	Number of Patients	Number of Workstations
Hoover clinic	3,000	15
Eastwood clinic	2,100	16
Gardendale clinic	2,900	12
Legal services		7
Computer services		10

Required
a. Allocate the cost of computer services to all of the clinics and the legal services department.
b. After allocating the cost of computer services, allocate the cost of legal services to the three clinics.
c. Compute the total allocated cost of service centers for each clinic.

L.O. 10   EXERCISE 5–14A *Allocating Costs of Service Centers to Operating Departments—Direct Method*

Victoria Trust Corporation has two service departments, actuary and economic analysis. Victoria also has three operating departments, annuity, fund management, and employee benefit services. The annual costs of operating the service departments are $520,000 for actuary and $640,000 for economic analysis. Victoria uses the direct method to allocate service center costs to operating departments. Other relevant data follow.

	Operating Costs*	Revenue
Annuity	$500,000	$ 840,000
Fund management	900,000	1,260,000
Employee benefit services	600,000	1,100,000

*The operating costs are measured before allocating service center costs.

Required

a. Use operating costs as the cost driver for allocating service center costs to operating departments.

b. Use revenue as the cost driver for allocating service center costs to operating departments.

PROBLEMS—SERIES A

L.O. 1, 2, 3, 5   PROBLEM 5–15A *Cost Accumulation and Allocation*

Pinewood Manufacturing Company makes two different products, A and B. The company's two departments are named after the products; for example, Product A is made in Department A. Pinewood's accountant has identified the following annual costs associated with these two products.

Financial data	
Salary of vice president of production division	$ 90,000
Salary of supervisor Department A	38,000
Salary of supervisor Department B	28,000
Direct materials cost Department A	150,000
Direct materials cost Department B	210,000
Direct labor cost Department A	120,000
Direct labor cost Department B	340,000
Direct utilities cost Department A	60,000
Direct utilities cost Department B	12,000
General factorywide utilities	18,000
Production supplies	18,000
Fringe benefits	69,000
Depreciation	360,000
Nonfinancial data	
Machine hours Department A	5,000
Machine hours Department B	1,000

Required

a. Identify the costs that are (1) direct costs of Department A, (2) direct costs of Department B, and (3) indirect costs.

b. Select the appropriate cost drivers for the indirect costs and allocate these costs to Departments A and B.

c. Determine the total estimated cost of the products made in Departments A and B. Assume that Pinewood produced 1,000 units of Product A and 2,000 units of Product B during the year. If Pinewood prices its products at cost plus 40 percent of cost, what price per unit must it charge for Product A and for Product B?

L.O. 1, 5   PROBLEM 5–16A *Selecting an Appropriate Cost Driver (What Is the Base?)*

The Seiler School of Vocational Technology has organized the school training programs into three departments. Each department provides training in a different area as follows: nursing assistant, dental hygiene, and office technology. The school's owner, Angie Seiler, wants to know how much it costs to operate each of the three departments. To accumulate the total cost for each department, the accountant has identified

several indirect costs that must be allocated to each. These costs are $8,400 of phone expense, $1,680 of office supplies, $864,000 of office rent, $96,000 of janitorial services, and $72,000 of salary paid to the dean of students. To provide a reasonably accurate allocation of costs, the accountant has identified several possible cost drivers. These drivers and their association with each department follow.

Cost Driver	Department 1	Department 2	Department 3
Number of telephones	28	32	52
Number of faculty members	20	16	12
Square footage of office space	24,000	14,000	10,000
Number of secretaries	2	2	2

Required
a. Identify the appropriate cost objects.
b. Identify the appropriate cost driver for each indirect cost and compute the allocation rate for assigning each indirect cost to the cost objects.
c. Determine the amount of telephone expense that should be allocated to each of the three departments.
d. Determine the amount of supplies expense that should be allocated to Department 3.
e. Determine the amount of office rent that should be allocated to Department 2.
f. Determine the amount of janitorial services cost that should be allocated to Department 1.
g. Identify two cost drivers not listed here that could be used to allocate the cost of the dean's salary to the three departments.

PROBLEM 5–17A *Cost Allocation in a Service Industry*

L.O. 1, 2

West Airlines is a small airline that occasionally carries overload shipments for the overnight delivery company Never-Fail, Inc. Never-Fail is a multimillion-dollar company started by Peter Never immediately after he failed to finish his first accounting course. The company's motto is "We Never-Fail to Deliver Your Package on Time." When Never-Fail has more freight than it can deliver, it pays West to carry the excess. West contracts with independent pilots to fly its planes on a per trip basis. West recently purchased an airplane that cost the company $5,500,000. The plane has an estimated useful life of 5,000,000 miles and a zero salvage value. During the first week in January, West flew two trips. The first trip was a round trip flight from Chicago to San Francisco, for which West paid $500 for the pilot and $350 for fuel. The second flight was a round trip from Chicago to New York. For this trip, it paid $300 for the pilot and $150 for fuel. The round trip between Chicago and San Francisco is approximately 4,400 miles and the round trip between Chicago and New York is 1,600 miles.

Required
a. Identify the direct and indirect costs that West incurs for each trip.
b. Determine the total cost of each trip.
c. In addition to depreciation, identify three other indirect costs that may need to be allocated to determine the cost of each trip.

PROBLEM 5–18A *Cost Allocation in a Manufacturing Company*

L.O. 1, 5

Gertrude Manufacturing Company makes tents that it sells directly to camping enthusiasts through a mail-order marketing program. The company pays a quality control expert $72,000 per year to inspect completed tents before they are shipped to customers. Assume that the company completed 1,600 tents in January and 1,200 tents in February. For the entire year, the company expects to produce 12,000 tents.

Required
a. Explain how changes in the cost driver (number of tents inspected) affect the total amount of fixed inspection cost.
b. Explain how changes in the cost driver (number of tents inspected) affect the amount of fixed inspection cost per unit.
c. If the cost objective is to determine the cost per tent, is the expert's salary a direct or an indirect cost?
d. How much of the expert's salary should be allocated to tents produced in January and February?

PROBLEM 5–19A *Fairness in the Allocation Process*

L.O. 1, 5

Bellaire Manufacturing Company uses two departments to make its products. Department I is a cutting department that is machine intensive and uses very few employees. Machines cut and form parts and then place the finished parts on a conveyor belt that carries them to Department II where they are

assembled into finished goods. The assembly department is labor intensive and requires many workers to assemble parts into finished goods. The company's manufacturing facility incurs two significant overhead costs, employee fringe benefits and utility costs. The annual costs of fringe benefits are $252,000 and utility costs are $180,000. The typical consumption patterns for the two departments are as follows.

	Department I	Department II	Total
Machine hours used	16,000	4,000	20,000
Direct labor hours used	5,000	13,000	18,000

The supervisor of each department receives a bonus based on how well the department controls costs. The company's current policy requires using a single activity base (machine hours or labor hours) to allocate the total overhead cost of $432,000.

Required

a. Assume that you are the supervisor of Department I. Choose the allocation base that would minimize your department's share of the total overhead cost. Calculate the amount of overhead that would be allocated to both departments using the base that you selected.
b. Assume that you are the supervisor of Department II. Choose the allocation base that would minimize your department's share of the total overhead cost. Calculate the amount of overhead that would be allocated to both departments using the base that you selected.
c. Assume that you are the plant manager and have the authority to change the company's overhead allocation policy. Formulate an overhead allocation policy that would be fair to the supervisors of both Department I and Department II. Compute the overhead allocations for each department using your policy.

L.O. 1   **PROBLEM 5–20A** *Allocation to Accomplish Smoothing*

Edburg Corporation estimated its overhead costs would be $24,000 per month except for January when it pays the $72,000 annual insurance premium on the manufacturing facility. Accordingly, the January overhead costs were expected to be $96,000 ($72,000 + $24,000). The company expected to use 7,000 direct labor hours per month except during July, August, and September when the company expected 9,000 hours of direct labor each month to build inventories for high demand that normally occurs during the Christmas season. The company's actual direct labor hours were the same as the estimated hours. The company made 3,500 units of product in each month except July, August, and September in which it produced 4,500 units each month. Direct labor costs were $24 per unit, and direct materials costs were $10 per unit.

Required

a. Calculate a predetermined overhead rate based on direct labor hours.
b. Determine the total allocated overhead cost for January, March, and August.
c. Determine the cost per unit of product for January, March, and August.
d. Determine the selling price for the product, assuming that the company desires to earn a gross margin of $20 per unit.

L.O. 1, 5   **PROBLEM 5–21A** *Allocating Indirect Costs Between Products*

Chelsea Eadon is considering expanding her business. She plans to hire a salesperson to cover trade shows. Because of compensation, travel expenses, and booth rental, fixed costs for a trade show are expected to be $13,200. The booth will be open 30 hours during the trade show. Ms. Eadon also plans to add a new product line, ProOffice, which will cost $180 per package. She will continue to sell the existing product, EZRecords, which costs $100 per package. Ms. Eadon believes that the salesperson will spend approximately 20 hours selling EZRecords and 10 hours marketing ProOffice.

Required

a. Determine the estimated total cost and cost per unit of each product, assuming that the salesperson is able to sell 80 units of EZRecords and 60 units of ProOffice.
b. Determine the estimated total cost and cost per unit of each product, assuming that the salesperson is able to sell 120 units of EZRecords and 90 units of ProOffice.
c. Explain why the cost per unit figures calculated in Requirement *a* are different from the amounts calculated in Requirement *b*. Also explain how the differences in estimated cost per unit will affect pricing decisions.

PROBLEM 5–22A *Allocating Joint Product Cost*

L.O. 8

Pearson Chicken, Inc., processes and packages chicken for grocery stores. It purchases chickens from farmers and processes them into two different products: chicken drumsticks and chicken steak. From a standard batch of 12,000 pounds of raw chicken that costs $7,000, the company produces two parts: 2,800 pounds of drumsticks and 4,200 pounds of breast for a processing cost of $2,450. The chicken breast is further processed into 3,200 pounds of steak for a processing cost of $2,000. The market price of drumsticks per pound is $1.50 and the market price per pound of chicken steak is $3.40. If Pearson decided to sell chicken breast instead of steak, the price per pound would be $2.00.

Required
a. Allocate the joint product cost between the two final products using weight as the allocation base.
b. Allocate the joint product cost between the two final products using market value as the allocation base.
c. Assume that the company uses market value as the allocation base. Determine the company's gross margin per unit for steak if all chicken breast is processed into steak and sold.

Appendix

PROBLEM 5–23A *Allocating Service Center Costs—Step Method and Direct Method*

L.O. 10

Justin Information Services, Inc., has two service departments, human resources and billing. Justin's operating departments, organized according to the special industry each department serves, are health care, retail, and legal services. The billing department supports only the three operating departments, but the human resources department supports all operating departments and the billing department. Other relevant information follows.

	Human Resources	Billing	Health Care	Retail	Legal Services
Number of employees	20	50	190	140	120
Annual cost*	$900,000	$1,710,000	$6,000,000	$4,800,000	$2,800,000
Annual revenue	—	—	$9,000,000	$6,200,000	$4,800,000

*This is the operating cost before allocating service department costs.

Required
a. Allocate service department costs to operating departments, assuming that Justin adopts the step method. The company uses the number of employees as the base for allocating human resources department costs and department annual revenue as the base for allocating the billing department costs.
b. Allocate service department costs to operating departments, assuming that Justin adopts the direct method. The company uses the number of employees as the base for allocating the human resources department costs and department annual revenue as the base for allocating the billing department costs.
c. Compute the total allocated cost of service centers for each operating department using each allocation method.

EXERCISES—SERIES B

EXERCISE 5–1B *Allocating Costs Between Divisions*

L.O. 1

Jentry and Romero, LLP, has three departments: auditing, tax, and information systems. The departments occupy 2,500 square feet, 1,500 square feet, and 1,000 square feet of office space, respectively. The firm pays $7,500 per month to rent its offices.

Required
How much monthly rent cost should Jentry and Romero allocate to each department?

EXERCISE 5–2B *Allocating Indirect Cost Over Varying Levels of Production*

L.O. 1

Lowder Company's annual factory depreciation is $12,600. Lowder estimated it would operate the factory a total of 1,575 hours this year. The factory operated 160 hours in November and 135 hours in December.

Required

Why would Lowder need to allocate factory depreciation cost? How much depreciation cost should Lowder allocate to products made in November and those made in December?

L.O. 1   EXERCISE 5–3B *Allocating Indirect Cost Over Varying Levels of Production*

On January 1, Loren Corporation paid the annual royalty of $576,000 for rights to use patented technology to make batteries for laptop computers. Loren plans to use the patented technology to produce five different models of batteries. Loren uses machine hours as a common cost driver and plans to operate its machines 48,000 hours in the coming year. The company used 3,000 machine hours in June and 3,600 hours in July.

Required

Why would Loren need to allocate the annual royalty payment rather than simply assign it in total to January production? How much of the royalty cost should Loren allocate to products made in June and those made in July?

L.O. 1, 6   EXERCISE 5–4B *Allocating a Fixed Cost*

Last year, Saline Abdulla bought an automobile for $25,000 to use in his taxi business. He expected to drive the vehicle for 120,000 miles before disposing of it for $1,000. Saline drove 3,200 miles this week and 2,800 miles last week.

Required

a. Determine the total cost of vehicle depreciation this week and last week.

b. Explain why allocating the vehicle cost would or would not be relevant to decision making.

L.O. 1   EXERCISE 5–5B *Allocating Overhead Costs Among Products*

Vilnius, Inc., manufactures three different sizes of automobile sunscreens, Large, Medium, and Small. Vilnius expects to incur $900,000 of overhead costs during the next fiscal year. Other budget information for the coming year follows:

	Large	Medium	Small	Total
Direct labor hours	2,500	5,000	4,500	12,000
Machine hours	700	1,300	1,000	3,000

Required

a. Use direct labor hours as the cost driver to compute the allocation rate and the budgeted overhead cost for each product.

b. Use machine hours as the cost driver to compute the allocation rate and the budgeted overhead cost for each product.

L.O. 1   EXERCISE 5–6B *Allocating Overhead Costs Among Products*

Rowe Company makes three models of computer disks in its factory, Zip100, Zip250, and Zip40. The expected overhead costs for the next fiscal year are as follows:

Payroll for factory managers	$135,000
Factory maintenance costs	55,000
Factory insurance	20,000
Total overhead costs	$210,000

Rowe uses labor hours as the cost driver to allocate overhead cost. Budgeted labor hours for the products are as follows:

Zip100	1,750 hours
Zip250	1,100
Zip40	650
Total labor hours	3,500

Required
Allocate the budgeted overhead costs to the products.

EXERCISE 5–7B *Allocating Costs Among Products*

L.O. 1

Hardin Company makes household plastic bags in three different sizes, Snack, Sandwich, and Storage. The estimated direct materials and direct labor costs are as follows.

Expected Costs	Snack	Sandwich	Storage
Direct materials	$140,000	$235,000	$375,000
Direct labor	75,000	145,000	280,000

Hardin allocates two major overhead costs among the three products: $36,000 of indirect labor cost for workers who move various materials and products to different stations in the factory and $27,500 of employee pension costs.

Required
Determine the total cost of each product.

EXERCISE 5–8B *Allocating Overhead Cost to Accomplish Smoothing*

L.O. 1

In 2003, Pineridge Coast Corporation incurred direct manufacturing costs of $20 per unit and manufacturing overhead costs of $135,000. The production activity for the four quarters of 2003 follows:

	1st Quarter	2nd Quarter	3rd Quarter	4th Quarter
Number of units produced	3,300	2,700	4,500	2,000

Required
a. Calculate a predetermined overhead rate based on the number of units produced during the year.
b. Allocate overhead costs to each quarter using the overhead rate computed in Requirement *a*.
c. Using the overhead allocation determined in Requirement *b*, calculate the total cost per unit for each quarter.

EXERCISE 5–9B *Allocating Overhead for Product Costing*

L.O. 1

Moriarity Manufacturing Company produced 500 units of inventory in January 2002. The company expects to produce an additional 5,900 units of inventory during the remaining 11 months of the year, for total estimated production of 6,400 units in 2002. Direct materials and direct labor costs are $37 and $42 per unit, respectively. Moriarity expects to incur the following manufacturing overhead costs during the 2002 accounting period:

Indirect materials	$ 3,400
Depreciation on equipment	52,000
Utilities cost	14,600
Salaries of plant manager and staff	152,000
Rental fee on manufacturing facilities	42,000
Total	$264,000

Required
a. Determine the estimated cost of the 500 units of product made in January.
b. Is the cost computed in Requirement *a* actual or estimated? Could Moriarity improve accuracy by waiting until December to determine the cost of products? Identify two reasons that a manager would want to know the cost of products in January. Discuss the relationship between accuracy and relevance as it pertains to this problem.

EXERCISE 5–10B *How Fixed Cost Allocation Affects a Pricing Decision*

L.O. 1

McRina Manufacturing Company expects to make 30,000 travel sewing kits during 2002. In January, the company made 1,800 kits. Materials and labor costs for January were $7,200 and $9,000, respectively.

In February, McRina produced 2,200 kits. Material and labor costs for February were $8,800 and $11,000, respectively. The company paid $42,000 for annual factory insurance on January 10, 2002. Ignore other manufacturing overhead costs.

Required

Assuming that McRina desires to sell its sewing kits for cost plus 25 percent of cost, what price should it charge for the kits produced in January and February?

L.O. 8 **EXERCISE 5–11B** *Allocating Joint Product Cost*

Tremain Food Corporation makes two products from soybeans, cooking oil and cattle feed. From a standard batch of 100,000 pounds of soybeans, Tremain produces 20,000 pounds of cooking oil and 80,000 pounds of cattle feed. Producing a standard batch costs $10,000. The sales prices per pound are $1.00 for cooking oil and $0.75 for cattle feed.

Required

a. Allocate the joint product cost to the two products using weight as the allocation base.
b. Allocate the joint product cost to the two products using market value as the allocation base.

Appendix

L.O. 10 **EXERCISE 5–12B** *Allocating a Service Center Cost to Operating Departments*

The administrative department of Pilon Consulting, LLC, provides office administration and professional support to its two operating departments. Annual administrative costs are $450,000. In 2003, the hours chargeable to clients generated by the information services department and the financial planning department were 24,000 and 36,000, respectively. Pilon uses chargeable hours as the cost driver for allocating administrative costs to operating departments.

Required

Allocate the administrative costs to the two operating departments.

L.O. 10 **EXERCISE 5–13B** *Allocating Service Centers' Costs to Operating Departments—Step Method*

Esworthy Consulting, LLP, has three operating departments: tax, estate planning, and small business. The company's internal accounting and maintenance departments support the operating departments. Moreover, the maintenance department also supports the internal accounting department. Other relevant information follows:

	Annual Cost*	Square Feet	Operating Revenue
Tax	$5,000,000	8,000	$8,000,000
Estate planning	2,000,000	2,000	3,500,000
Small business	3,000,000	4,000	6,500,000
Internal accounting	690,000	1,000	0
Maintenance	450,000	1,000	0

*The annual cost figures do not include costs allocated from service departments.

Esworthy allocates its maintenance cost based on the square footage of each department's office space. The firm allocates the internal accounting cost based on each department's operating revenue.

Required

a. Allocate the maintenance cost to the operating and internal accounting departments.
b. After allocating the maintenance cost, allocate the internal accounting cost to the three operating departments.
c. Compute the total allocated cost of the service departments for each operating department.

L.O. 10 **EXERCISE 5–14B** *Allocating Service Centers' Costs to Operating Departments—Direct Method*

Daniels Corporation, a book publisher, has two service departments, editing and typesetting. Daniels also has three operating departments, children's fiction, youth fiction, and adult fiction. The annual costs of operating the editing department are $240,000 and of operating the typesetting department are $420,000. Daniels uses the direct method to allocate service center costs to operating departments. Other relevant data follow.

	Number of Pages	Number of Hours
Children	15,000	5,000
Youth	10,000	8,000
Adult	5,000	7,000

Required

a. Allocate the service center costs to the operating departments using the number of pages as the cost driver.

b. Allocate the service center costs to the operating departments using the number of hours as the cost driver.

PROBLEMS—SERIES B

PROBLEM 5–15B *Cost Accumulation and Allocation*

L.O. 1, 2, 3, 5

Baylor Tools Company has two production departments in its manufacturing facilities. Home tools specializes in hand tools for individual home users, and professional tools makes sophisticated tools for professional maintenance workers. Baylor's accountant has identified the following annual costs associated with these two products:

Financial data	
Salary of vice president of production	$120,000
Salary of manager, home tools	36,000
Salary of manager, professional tools	29,000
Direct materials cost, home tools	200,000
Direct materials cost, professional tools	250,000
Direct labor cost, home tools	224,000
Direct labor cost, professional tools	276,000
Direct utilities cost, home tools	50,000
Direct utilities cost, professional tools	20,000
General factorywide utilities	21,000
Production supplies	27,000
Fringe benefits	75,000
Depreciation	240,000
Nonfinancial data	
Machine hours, home tools	4,000
Machine hours, professional tools	2,000

Required

a. Identify the costs that are the (1) direct costs of home tools, (2) direct costs of professional tools, and (3) indirect costs.

b. Select the appropriate cost drivers and allocate the indirect costs to home tools and to professional tools.

c. Assume that each department makes only a single product. Home tools produces its Deluxe Drill for home use, and professional tools produces the Professional Drill. The company made 30,000 units of Deluxe Drill and 40,000 units of Professional Drill during the year. Determine the total estimated cost of the products made in each department. If Baylor prices its products at cost plus 30 percent of cost, what price per unit must it charge for the Deluxe Drill and the Professional Drill?

PROBLEM 5–16B *Selecting an Appropriate Cost Driver (What Is the Base?)*

L.O. 1, 5

Hsinchu Research Institute has three departments, biology, chemistry, and physics. The institute's controller wants to estimate the cost of operating each department. He has identified several indirect costs that must be allocated to each department including $11,200 of phone expense, $2,400 of office supplies, $1,120,000 of office rent, $140,000 of janitorial services, and $150,000 of salary paid to the director. To provide a reasonably accurate allocation of costs, the controller identified several possible cost drivers. These drivers and their association with each department follow.

Cost Driver	Biology	Chemistry	Physics
Number of telephones	10	14	16
Number of researchers	8	10	12
Square footage of office space	8,000	8,000	12,000
Number of secretaries	1	1	1

Required

a. Identify the appropriate cost objects.

b. Identify the appropriate cost driver for each indirect cost, and compute the allocation rate for assigning each indirect cost to the cost objects.

c. Determine the amount of telephone expense that should be allocated to each of the three departments.

d. Determine the amount of supplies expense that should be allocated to the physics department.

e. Determine the amount of office rent cost that should be allocated to the chemistry department.

f. Determine the amount of janitorial services cost that should be allocated to the biology department.

g. Identify two cost drivers not listed here that could be used to allocate the cost of the director's salary to the three departments.

L.O. 1, 2   PROBLEM 5–17B *Cost Allocation in a Service Industry*

Miller, Lopez, and Associates provides legal services for its local community. In addition to its regular attorneys, the firm hires some part-time attorneys to handle small cases. Two secretaries assist all part-time attorneys exclusively. In 2009, the firm paid $48,000 for the two secretaries who worked a total of 3,200 hours. Moreover, the firm paid Sue Rivera $60 per hour and Tim Gasden $50 per hour for their part-time legal services.

In August 2009, Ms. Rivera completed a case that took her 60 hours. Mr. Gasden finished a case on which he worked 20 hours. The firm also paid a private investigator to uncover relevant facts. The investigation fees cost $1,000 for Ms. Rivera's case and $750 for Mr. Gasden's case. Ms. Rivera used 30 hours of secretarial assistance, and Mr. Gasden used 40 hours.

Required

a. Identify the direct and indirect costs incurred in each case completed in August 2009.

b. Determine the total cost of each case.

c. In addition to secretaries' salaries, identify three other indirect costs that may need to be allocated to determine the cost of the cases.

L.O. 1, 5   PROBLEM 5–18B *Cost Allocation in a Manufacturing Company*

Lawrence's Doors, Inc., makes a particular type of door. The labor cost is $90 per door and the material cost is $160 per door. Lawrence's rents a factory building for $60,000 a month. Lawrence's plans to produce 24,000 doors annually. In March and April, it made 2,000 and 3,000 doors, respectively.

Required

a. Explain how changes in the cost driver (number of doors made) affect the total amount of fixed rental cost.

b. Explain how changes in the cost driver (number of doors made) affect the fixed rental cost per unit.

c. If the cost objective is to determine the cost per door, is the factory rent a direct or an indirect cost?

d. How much of the factory rent should be allocated to doors produced in March and April?

L.O. 1, 5   PROBLEM 5–19B *Fairness in the Allocation Process*

Super Furniture Company has two production departments. The parts department uses automated machinery to make parts; as a result, it uses very few employees. The assembly department is labor intensive because workers manually assemble parts into finished furniture. Employee fringe benefits and utility costs are the two major overhead costs of the company's production division. The fringe benefits and utility costs for the year are $300,000 and $144,000, respectively. The typical consumption patterns for the two departments follow.

	Parts	Assembly	Total
Machine hours used	26,000	4,000	30,000
Direct labor hours used	3,500	20,500	24,000

The supervisor of each department receives a bonus based on how well the department controls costs. The company's current policy requires using a single activity base (machine hours or labor hours) to allocate the total overhead cost of $444,000.

Required

a. Assume that you are the parts department supervisor. Choose the allocation base that would minimize your department's share of the total overhead cost. Calculate the amount of overhead to allocate to both departments using the base that you selected.

b. Assume that you are the assembly department supervisor. Choose the allocation base that would minimize your department's share of the total overhead cost. Calculate the amount of overhead to allocate to both departments using the base that you selected.

c. Assume that you are the plant manager and that you have the authority to change the company's overhead allocation policy. Formulate an overhead allocation policy that would be fair to the supervisors of both the parts and assembly departments. Compute the overhead allocation for each department using your policy.

PROBLEM 5–20B *Allocation to Accomplish Smoothing*

L.O. 1

Andropov Corporation's overhead costs are usually $24,000 per month. However, the company pays $54,000 of real estate tax on the factory facility in March. Thus, the overhead costs for March increase to $78,000. The company normally uses 5,000 direct labor hours per month except for August, September, and October, in which the company requires 9,000 hours of direct labor per month to build inventories for high demand in the Christmas season. Last year, the company's actual direct labor hours were the same as usual. The company made 5,000 units of product in each month except August, September, and October in which it produced 9,000 units per month. Direct labor costs were $8 per unit; direct materials costs were $7 per unit.

Required

a. Calculate a predetermined overhead rate based on direct labor hours.

b. Determine the total allocated overhead cost for the months of March, August, and December.

c. Determine the cost per unit of product for the months of March, August, and December.

d. Determine the selling price for the product, assuming that the company desires to earn a gross margin of $7 per unit.

PROBLEM 5–21B *Allocating Indirect Cost Between Products*

L.O. 1, 5

Bennett Corporation has hired a marketing representative to sell the company's two products, Marvelous and Wonderful. The representative's total salary and fringe benefits are $10,000 monthly. The product cost is $90 per unit for Marvelous and $144 per unit for Wonderful. Bennett expects the representative to spend 48 hours per month marketing Marvelous and 112 hours promoting Wonderful.

Required

a. Determine the estimated total cost and cost per unit, assuming that the representative is able to sell 100 units of Marvelous and 70 units of Wonderful in a month. Allocate indirect cost on the basis of labor hours.

b. Determine the estimated total cost and cost per unit, assuming that the representative is able to sell 250 units of Marvelous and 140 units of Wonderful. Allocate indirect cost on the basis of labor hours.

c. Explain why the cost per unit figures calculated in Requirement *a* differ from the amounts calculated in Requirement *b*. Also explain how the differences in estimated cost per unit will affect pricing decisions.

PROBLEM 5–22B *Allocating Joint Product Cost*

L.O. 8

Cheney Dairy Products, Inc., produces three different products from whole milk: low-fat milk, cream, and butter. Production requires two processing steps. In the first step, the company pasteurizes whole milk and separates it into cream and low-fat milk. In the second step, cream is churned into butter. For a regular batch of 10,000 gallons of whole milk, Cheney pays dairy farmers $4,000. The processing cost of the first step is $3,200. At the end of the first step, the company produces 7,000 gallons of low-fat milk and 2,500 pounds of cream. The weight of 7,000 gallons of low-fat milk is about 57,500 pounds. Cheney sells its low-fat milk for $1.20 per gallon. The cream is churned into 900 pounds of butter. The cost of churning 2,500 pounds of cream is $1,140. The company sells butter for $5.30 per pound. The current market price of cream is $2.40 per pound.

Required

a. Allocate the joint product cost to the cream and low-fat milk products using weight as the allocation base.

b. Allocate the joint product cost to the cream and low-fat milk products using market value as the allocation base.

c. Assume that all cream is further processed to produce butter. Determine the final cost and the market value of butter if market value is used as the allocation base.

Appendix

L.O. 10   **PROBLEM 5–23B** *Allocating Service Center Costs—Step Method and Direct Method*

Payne Corporation has three production departments, forming, assembly, and packaging. The maintenance department supports only the production departments; the computer services department supports all departments including maintenance. Other relevant information follows.

	Forming	Assembly	Packaging	Maintenance	Computer Services
Machine hours	6,000	2,500	1,500	400	
Number of computers	14	20	11	15	8
Annual cost*	$450,000	$800,000	$250,000	$100,000	$90,000

*This is the annual operating cost before allocating service department costs.

Required

a. Allocate service department costs to operating departments, assuming that Payne adopts the step method. The company uses the number of computers as the base for allocating the computer services costs and machine hours as the base for allocating the maintenance costs.

b. Use machine hours as the base for allocating maintenance department costs and the number of computers as the base for allocating computer services cost. Allocate service department costs to operating departments, assuming that Payne adopts the direct method.

c. Compute the total allocated cost of service centers for each operating department using each allocation method.

ANALYZE, THINK, COMMUNICATE

ATC 5–1   **BUSINESS APPLICATIONS CASE** *Allocating Fixed Costs*

Peixoto Company pays $5,000 per month to rent its manufacturing facility. Peixoto estimates total production volume for 2003 to be 12,000 units of product. The company actually produced 800 units of product during January and 900 units in February.

Required

a. For each of the following items, indicate whether the rent charge is a
   (1) Product or general, selling, and administrative (G,S&A) cost.
   (2) Relevant cost with respect to a special order decision.
   (3) Fixed or variable cost relative to the volume of production.
   (4) Direct or indirect if the cost object is the cost of products made in January.

b. With respect to the rent charge, determine the total cost and the cost per unit of products made in January and February.

c. Assuming that actual production in 2003 is 10,000 units, indicate whether the cost of the January production determined in Requirement *b* is over- or understated.

d. Assume that the information computed in Requirement *b* was used to price Peixoto's product in 2003. Furthermore, assume that management used the price estimates to project income and that the income projections were used in public announcements to stock analysts. Finally, assume that actual production was 10,000 units. Indicate whether year-end net income is likely to be higher or lower than management forecasts. Describe the likely impact on Peixoto's stock price and executive stock option incentive program.

GROUP ASSIGNMENT *Selection of the Cost Driver*   ATC 5–2

Vulcan College School of Business is divided into three departments, accounting, marketing, and management. Relevant information for each of the departments follows.

Cost Driver	Accounting	Marketing	Management
Number of students	1,400	800	400
Number of classes per semester	64	36	28
Number of professors	20	24	10

Vulcan is a private school that expects each department to generate a profit. It rewards departments for profitability by assigning 20 percent of each department's profits back to that department. Departments have free rein as to how to use these funds. Some departments have used them to supply professors with computer technology. Others have expanded their travel budgets. The practice has been highly successful in motivating the faculty to control costs. The revenues and direct costs for the year 2004 follow.

	Accounting	Marketing	Management
Revenue	$29,600,000	$16,600,000	$8,300,000
Direct costs	24,600,000	13,800,000	6,600,000

Vulcan allocates to the School of Business $4,492,800 of indirect overhead costs such as administrative salaries and costs of operating the registrar's office and the bookstore.

Required
a. Divide the class into groups and organize the groups into three sections. Assign each section a department. For example, groups in Section 1 should represent the Accounting Department. Groups in Sections 2 and 3 should represent the Marketing Department and Management Department, respectively. Assume that the dean of the school is planning to assign an equal amount of the college overhead to each department. Have the students in each group prepare a response to the dean's plan. Each group should select a spokesperson who is prepared to answer the following questions.
   (1) Is your group in favor of or opposed to the allocation plan suggested by the dean?
   (2) Does the plan suggested by the dean provide a fair allocation? Why?
   The instructor should lead a discussion designed to assess the appropriateness of the dean's proposed allocation plan.
b. Have each group select the cost driver (allocation base) that best serves the self-interest of the department it represents.
c. Consensus on Requirement *c* should be achieved before completing Requirement *d*. Each group should determine the amount of the indirect cost to be allocated to each department using the cost driver that best serves the self-interest of the department it represents. Have a spokesperson from each section go to the board and show the income statement that would result for each department.
d. Discuss the development of a cost driver(s) that would promote fairness rather than self-interest in allocating the indirect costs.

RESEARCH ASSIGNMENT *Allocations Used to Determine Product Cost*   ATC 5–3

The information from the Ann Landers article referenced in the Curious Accountant feature of this chapter was drawn from the article "The Legacy of the $7 Aspirin" by David W. McFadden in the April 1990 issue of *Management Accounting*. Read this article and complete the following requirements.

Required
a. Explain what the term *cost shifting* means.
b. Identify three costs Mr. McFadden discussed that may be shifted to aspirin.
c. Why is aspirin well suited to cost shifting?
d. How does cost shifting increase the cost of medical services?

WRITING ASSIGNMENT *Selection of the Appropriate Cost Driver*   ATC 5–4

Bullions Enterprises, Inc. (BEI), makes gold, silver, and bronze medals used to recognize outstanding athletic performance in regional and national sporting events. The per unit direct costs of producing the medals follows.

	Gold	Silver	Bronze
Direct materials	$300	$130	$ 35
Labor	120	120	120

During 2002, BEI made 1,200 units of each type of medal for a total of 3,600 (1,200 × 3) medals. All medals are created through the same production process, and they are packaged and shipped in identical containers. Indirect overhead costs amounted to $324,000. BEI currently uses the number of units as the cost driver for the allocation of overhead cost. As a result, BEI allocated $90 ($324,000 ÷ 3,600 units) of overhead cost to each medal produced.

Required

The president of the company has questioned the wisdom of assigning the same amount of overhead to each type of medal. He believes that overhead should be assigned on the basis of the cost to produce the medals. In other words, more overhead should be charged to expensive gold medals, less to silver, and even less to bronze. Assume that you are BEI's chief financial officer. Write a memo responding to the president's suggestion.

ATC 5–5   **ETHICAL DILEMMA** *Allocation to Achieve Fairness*

The American Acupuncture Association offers continuing professional education courses for its members at its annual meeting. Instructors are paid a fee for each student attending their courses but are charged a fee for overhead costs that is deducted from their compensation. Overhead costs include fees paid to rent instructional equipment such as overhead projectors, provide supplies to participants, and offer refreshments during coffee breaks. The number of courses offered is used as the allocation base for determining the overhead charge. For example, if overhead costs amount to $5,000 and 25 courses are offered, each course is allocated an overhead charge of $200 ($5,000 ÷ 25 courses). Heidi McCarl, who taught one of the courses, received the following statement with her check in payment for her instructional services.

Instructional fees (20 students × $50 per student)	$1,000
Less: Overhead charge	(200)
Less: Charge of sign language assistant	(240)
Amount due instructor	$ 560

Although Ms. McCarl was well aware that one of her students was deaf and required a sign language assistant, she was surprised to find that she was required to absorb the cost of this service.

Required

a. Given that the Americans with Disabilities Act stipulates that the deaf student cannot be charged for the cost of providing sign language, who should be required to pay the cost of sign language services?

b. Explain how allocation can be used to promote fairness in distributing service costs to the disabled. Describe two ways to treat the $240 cost of providing sign language services that improve fairness.

ATC 5–6   **SPREADSHEET ASSIGNMENT** *Using Excel*

Brook Health Care Center, Inc., has three clinics servicing the Birmingham metropolitan area. The company's legal services department supports the clinics. Moreover, its computer services department supports all of the clinics and the legal services department. The company uses the number of computer workstations as the cost driver for allocating the cost of computer services and the number of patients as the cost driver for allocating cost of legal services. The annual cost of the Department of Legal Services was $340,000, and the annual cost of the Department of Computer Services was $250,000. Other relevant information follows.

	Number of Patients	Number of Workstations
Hoover Clinic	3,100	17
Eastwood Clinic	2,300	13
Gardendale Clinic	2,800	6
Legal Services		14

Required

a. Construct a spreadsheet like the following one to allocate the service costs using the step method.

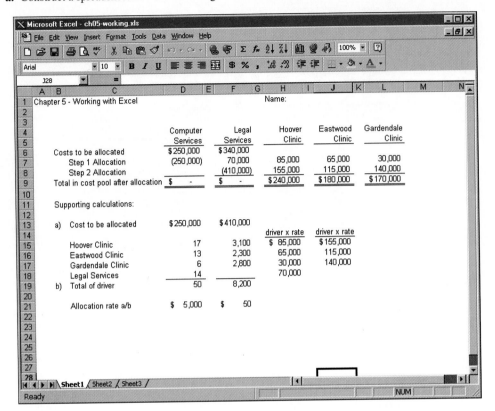

Spreadsheet Tips

1. The headings in rows 4 and 5 are right aligned. To right align text, choose Format, then Cells, and then click on the tab titled Alignment, and set the horizontal alignment to Right. The shortcut method to right align text is to click on the right align icon in the middle of the second tool bar.
2. The supporting calculation section must be completed simultaneously with the allocation table. However, most of the supporting calculations can be completed first. The exception is that the value in cell F13 refers to the sum of cells F6 and F7.

SPREADSHEET ASSIGNMENT *Mastering Excel*

ATC 5–7

Phillips Paints manufactures three types of paint in a joint process: rubberized paint, rust-proofing paint, and aluminum paint. In a standard batch of 250,000 gallons of raw material, the outputs are 120,000 gallons of rubberized paint, 40,000 gallons of rust-proofing paint, and 90,000 gallons of aluminum paint. The production cost of a batch is $2,700,000. The sales prices per gallon are $15, $18, and $20 for rubberized, rust-proofing, and aluminum paint, respectively.

Required

a. Construct a spreadsheet to allocate joint costs to the three products using the number of gallons as the allocation base.
b. Include formulas in your spreadsheet to calculate the gross margin for each paint.

6

Cost Management in an Automated Business Environment
ABC, ABM, and TQM

Learning Objectives

After completing this chapter, you should be able to:

1 Understand the limitations associated with using direct labor hours as a single companywide overhead allocation base.

2 Understand how automation has affected the selection of cost drivers.

3 Distinguish between volume-based and activity-based cost drivers.

4 Identify and use activity cost centers and related cost drivers in an activity-based cost system.

5 Classify activities into one of four hierarchical categories including unit-level, batch-level, product-level, and facility-level activities.

6 Understand the effect that under- or overcosting can have on profitability.

7 Distinguish between manufacturing costs, upstream costs, and downstream costs.

8 Appreciate the limitations of activity-based costing including the effects of employee attitudes and the availability of data.

9 Categorize quality costs into one of four categories including prevention cost, appraisal cost, internal failure cost, and external failure cost.

10 Understand relationships among the components of quality costs.

11 Prepare and interpret information contained in quality cost reports.

other data points. The accountant constructs a second scattergraph to accomplish this objective. This graph is shown in Exhibit 2–26. It is identical to the graph in Exhibit 2–25 except that the straight line is plotted through the center of the entire data set rather than just the high and low points in the data set. The new line is called a **visual fit line.** Although the line is drawn by visual inspection, it should be placed to minimize the total distance between the data points and the line. This usually means that approximately half of the data points appear above and half below the visual fit line. The estimated variable cost per unit is represented by the slope (i.e., steepness) of the visual fit line. The fixed cost is determined by the point (the *intercept*) where the visual fit line crosses the vertical axis (i.e., the total cost line). Therefore, the variable and fixed cost components are determined by the slope and the intercept of the visual fit line.

The intercept shown in Exhibit 2–26 provides an estimate of fixed cost amounting to $100,000. Although the amount of fixed cost is the only item that the company president had asked to see, the variable cost can be easily determined by subtracting the fixed cost from the total cost at any point along the visual fit line. For example, at 15,000 units, total cost amounts to $300,000. Variable cost is determined as follows:

$$\text{Fixed cost} + \text{Variable cost} = \text{Total cost}$$
$$\text{Variable cost} = \text{Total cost} - \text{Fixed cost}$$
$$\text{Variable cost} = \$300,000 - \$100,000$$
$$\text{Variable cost} = \$200,000$$

focus on International Issues

Another Reason Fixed Costs Aren't Always Fixed

Suppose that a company is renting a facility at an annual rental rate that does not change for the next five years *no matter what.* Is this a fixed cost? By now, you are aware that the proper response is to ask fixed in relation to what? Is the rental cost of this facility fixed in relation to the activity at this facility? The answer seems to be yes, but it might be not necessarily.

Consider the Exxon Corporation. If Exxon rents facilities in a country in the eastern hemisphere, Malaysia for example, the annual rental fee may be stated and paid in the local currency. In Malaysia, this is the ringgit. Even though Exxon may be paying the same number of ringgit in rent each year, Exxon's rental cost in U.S. dollars could vary greatly over time. Such potential fluctuations in the dollar amount of what are otherwise fixed costs cause companies to enter very complex arrangements to add stability to transactions that must be paid in foreign currencies.

Exxon was founded and has its headquarters in the United States. It does much business in the United States. Furthermore, Exxon is listed on the New York Stock Exchange and prepares its financial statements in U.S. dollars. However, it does much more business and has many more assets in countries outside the United States. Consider the following table from Exxon's 1996 financial statements.

Before a multinational company can determine whether a cost is fixed, it must determine the applicable currency.

Geographical Area	Earnings*	Percentage of Total	Identifiable Assets*	Percentage of Total
United States	$2,651	35%	$25,161	26%
Other Western Hemisphere	559	7	10,768	11
Eastern Hemisphere	3,932	53	44,821	47
Other	368	5	14,777	16
Totals	$7,510	100%	$95,527	100%

*Amounts in millions.

Variable cost per unit is $13.33, calculated by dividing the total variable cost by the number of units ($200,000 ÷ 15,000 units = $13.33 per unit).

Statistical procedures such as least-squares regression can be used to improve the accuracy of placing the line through the data points. While these procedures are beyond the scope of this text, you may have the opportunity to study them in more advanced courses.

a look back

Cost behavior patterns can play a critically important role in a company's profitability. It is important to understand how different costs behave in relation to changes in the volume of activity. Total *fixed cost* remains constant when activity changes. Fixed cost per unit decreases with increases in activity and increases with decreases in activity. In contrast, total *variable cost* increases proportionately with increases in activity and decreases proportionately with decreases in activity. Variable cost per unit remains constant regardless of how activity changes. The definitions of fixed and variable costs have meaning only within the context of a specified range of activity (i.e., the relevant range) for a defined period of time. In addition, cost behavior depends on the measure of volume being considered (e.g., a store manager's salary is fixed relative to the number of customers visiting a particular store but is variable relative to the number of stores operated). A mixed cost contains a mixture of fixed and variable cost components.

Fixed costs allow companies to take advantage of *operating leverage*. With operating leverage, each additional sale decreases the cost per unit. This principle allows a small percentage change in volume of revenue to have a significantly larger percentage change on profits. The *magnitude of operating leverage* can be determined by dividing the contribution margin by net income. When revenues have covered fixed costs and all costs are fixed, each dollar of revenue represents pure profit. Having a fixed cost structure (i.e., operating leverage) has risks and rewards for a company. If the volume of sales is increasing, costs do not increase, allowing profits to soar. Alternatively, if the volume of sales is decreasing, costs do not decrease and profits decline significantly more than revenues. Companies with high variable costs in relation to fixed costs do not experience as great a level of operating leverage. Their costs increase or decrease in proportion to increases in revenue. These companies experience less risk but fail to reap disproportionately higher profits when volume soars.

Under the contribution margin approach, variable costs are subtracted from revenue to determine the amount of *contribution margin*. Fixed costs are then subtracted from the contribution margin to determine the amount of net income. Accordingly, the contribution margin represents the amount available to pay fixed costs and provide a profit. This format is used for internal reporting purposes.

Cost per unit is an average cost that is easier to compute than the actual cost of each unit and is more relevant to decision making than the actual cost. Computation of the average cost per unit must consider the span of time from which data are drawn. Distortions can result from the use of long as well as short time spans.

Fixed and variable costs can be estimated by using methods such as the *high-low method* and *scattergraphs*. The high-low method and scattergraphs are easy to use and provide a reasonable degree of accuracy.

a look forward

The next chapter will show you how changes in cost, volume, and pricing affect profitability. You will learn to determine the number of units of product that must be produced and sold in order to break even (i.e., the number of units that will produce an amount of revenue that is exactly equal to total cost). You will learn to establish the price of a product using a cost-plus-pricing approach and to establish the cost of a product using a target-pricing approach. Finally, the chapter will show you how to use a break-even chart to examine potential profitability over a range of operating activity and how to use a technique known as *sensitivity analysis* to examine how simultaneous changes in sales price, volume, fixed costs, and variable costs affect profitability.

SELF-STUDY REVIEW PROBLEM

Mensa Mountaineering Company (MMC) provides guided mountain climbing expeditions in the Rocky Mountains. Its only major expense is guide salaries; it pays each guide $4,800 per climbing expedition. MMC charges its customers $1,500 per expedition and expects to take five climbers on each expedition.

Part 1

Base your answers on the preceding information.

Required

a. Determine the total cost of guide salaries and the cost of guide salaries per climber assuming that four, five, or six climbers are included in a trip. Relative to the number of climbers in a single expedition, is the cost of guides a fixed or a variable cost?

b. Relative to the number of expeditions, is the cost of guides a fixed or a variable cost?

c. Determine the profit of an expedition assuming that five climbers are included in the trip.

d. Determine the profit assuming a 20 percent increase (six climbers total) in expedition revenue. What is the percentage change in profitability?

e. Determine the profit assuming a 20 percent decrease (four climbers total) in expedition revenue. What is the percentage change in profitability?

f. Explain why a 20 percent shift in revenue produces more than a 20 percent shift in profitability. What term describes this phenomenon?

Part 2

Assume that the guides offer to make the climbs for a percentage of expedition fees. Specifically, MMC will pay guides $960 per climber on the expedition. Assume also that the expedition fee charged to climbers remains at $1,500 per climber.

Required

g. Determine the total cost of guide salaries and the cost of guide salaries per climber assuming that four, five, or six climbers are included in a trip. Relative to the number of climbers in a single expedition, is the cost of guides a fixed or a variable cost?

h. Relative to the number of expeditions, is the cost of guides a fixed or a variable cost?

i. Determine the profit of an expedition assuming that five climbers are included in the trip.

j. Determine the profit assuming a 20 percent increase (six climbers total) in expedition revenue. What is the percentage change in profitability?

k. Determine the profit assuming a 20 percent decrease (four climbers total) in expedition revenue. What is the percentage change in profitability?

l. Explain why a 20 percent shift in revenue does not produce more than a 20 percent shift in profitability.

Solution to Part 1, Requirement a

Number of climbers (a)	4	5	6
Total cost of guide salaries (b)	$4,800	$4,800	$4,800
Cost per climber (b ÷ a)	1,200	960	800

Since the total cost remains constant (fixed) regardless of the number of climbers on a particular expedition, the cost is classified as fixed. Note that the cost per climber decreases as the number of climbers increases. This is the *per unit* behavior pattern of a fixed cost.

Solution to Part 1, Requirement b

Since the total cost of guide salaries changes proportionately each time the number of expeditions increases or decreases, the cost of salaries is variable relative to the number of expeditions.

Solution to Part 1, Requirements c, d, and e

Number of Climbers	4	Percentage Change	5	Percentage Change	6
Revenue ($1,500 per climber)	$6,000	⇐(20%) ⇐	$7,500	⇒+20% ⇒	$9,000
Cost of guide salaries (fixed)	4,800		4,800		4,800
Profit	$1,200	⇐(55.6%) ⇐	$2,700	⇒+55.6% ⇒	$4,200

Percentage change in revenue: $\pm\$1,500 \div \$7,500 = \pm20\%$
Percentage change in profit: $\pm\$1,500 \div \$2,700 = \pm55.6\%$

Solution to Part 1, Requirement f
Since the cost of guide salaries remains fixed while volume (number of climbers) changes, the change in net income, measured in absolute dollars, exactly matches the change in revenue. More specifically, each time MMC increases the number of climbers by one, revenue and net income increase by $1,500. Since the base figure for net income ($2,700) is lower than the base figure for revenue ($7,500), the percentage change in net income ($1,500 ÷ $2,700 = 55.6%) is higher than percentage change in revenue ($1,500 ÷ $7,500). This phenomenon is called *operating leverage.*

Solution for Part 2, Requirement g

Number of climbers (a)	4	5	6
Per climber cost of guide salaries (b)	$ 960	$ 960	$ 960
Cost per climber (b × a)	3,840	4,800	5,760

Since the total cost changes in proportion to changes in the number of climbers, the cost is classified as variable. Note that the cost per climber remains constant (stays the same) as the number of climbers increases or decreases. This is the *per unit* behavior pattern of a variable cost.

Solution for Part 2, Requirement h
Since the total cost of guide salaries changes proportionately with changes in the number of expeditions, the cost of salaries is also variable relative to the number of expeditions.

Solution for Part 2, Requirements i, j, and k

Number of Climbers	4	Percentage Change	5	Percentage Change	6
Revenue ($1,500 per climber)	$6,000	⇐ (20%) ⇐	$7,500	⇒+20% ⇒	$9,000
Cost of guide salaries (variable)	3,840		4,800		5,760
Profit	$2,160	⇐ (20%) ⇐	$2,700	⇒+20% ⇒	$3,240

Percentage change in revenue: $\pm\$1,500 \div \$7,500 = \pm20\%$
Percentage change in profit: $\pm\$540 \div \$2,700 = \pm20\%$

Solution for Part 2, Requirement l
Since the cost of guide salaries changes when volume (number of climbers) changes, the change in net income is proportionate to the change in revenue. More specifically, each time the number of climbers increases by one, revenue increases by $1,500 and net income increases by $540 ($1,500 − $960). Accordingly, the percentage change in net income will always equal the percentage change in revenue. This means that there is no operating leverage when all costs are variable.

KEY TERMS

Activity base *62*
Contribution margin *57*
Cost averaging *62*
Cost behavior *60*

Cost structure *56*
Economies of scale *54*
Fixed cost *51*
High-low method *65*

Mixed costs (semivariable costs) *64*
Operating leverage *53*
Relevant range *61*

Scattergraph *66*
Variable cost *52*
Visual fit line *67*

QUESTIONS

1. Define *fixed cost* and *variable cost* and give an example of each.
2. How can knowing cost behavior relative to volume fluctuations affect decision making?
3. Define the term *operating leverage* and explain how it affects profits.
4. How is operating leverage calculated?
5. Explain the limitations of using operating leverage to predict profitability.
6. If volume is increasing, would a company benefit more from a pure variable or a pure fixed cost structure? Which cost structure would be advantageous if volume is decreasing?
7. When are economies of scale possible? In what types of businesses would you most likely find economies of scale?
8. Explain the risk and rewards to a company that result from having fixed costs.
9. Are companies with predominately fixed cost structures likely to be most profitable?
10. How is the relevant range of activity related to fixed and variable cost? Give an example of how the definitions of these costs become invalid when volume is outside the relevant range.
11. Sam's Garage is trying to determine the cost of providing an oil change. Why would the average cost of this service be more relevant information than the actual cost for each customer?
12. When would the high-low method be appropriate for estimating variable and fixed costs? When would least-squares regression be the most desirable?
13. Which cost structure has the greater risk? Explain.
14. The president of Bright Corporation tells you that he sees a dim future for his company. He feels that his hands are tied because fixed costs are too high. He says that fixed costs do not change and therefore the situation is hopeless. Do you agree? Explain.
15. All costs are variable because if a business ceases operations, its costs fall to zero. Do you agree with the statement? Explain.
16. Because of seasonal fluctuations, Norel Corporation has a problem determining the unit cost of the products it produces. For example, high heating costs during the winter months causes per unit cost to be higher than per unit cost in the summer months even when the same number of units of product is produced. Suggest several ways that Norel can improve the computation of per unit costs.
17. Verna Salsbury tells you that she thinks the terms fixed cost and variable cost are confusing. She notes that fixed cost per unit changes when the number of units changes. Furthermore, variable cost per unit remains fixed regardless of how many units are produced. She concludes that the terminology seems to be backward. Explain why the terminology appears to be contradictory.

EXERCISES—SERIES A

EXERCISE 2–1A *Identifying Cost Behavior*

L.O. 1

Sally's Kitchen, a fast-food restaurant company, operates a chain of restaurants across the nation. Each restaurant employs eight people; one is a manager paid a salary plus a bonus equal to 3 percent of sales. Other employees, two cooks, one dishwasher, and four waitresses, are paid salaries. Each manager is budgeted $2,000 per month for advertising cost.

Required
Classify each of the following costs incurred by Sally's Kitchen as fixed, variable, or mixed.
a. Manager's compensation relative to the number of customers.
b. Waitresses' salaries relative to the number of restaurants.
c. Advertising costs relative to the number of customers for a particular restaurant.
d. Rental costs relative to the number of restaurants.
e. Cooks' salaries at a particular location relative to the number of customers.
f. Cost of supplies (cups, plates, spoons, etc.) relative to the number of customers.

L.O. 1 **EXERCISE 2–2A** *Identifying Cost Behavior*

At the various activity levels shown, Wathen Company incurred the following costs.

Units sold		50	100	150	200	250
a.	Total salary cost	$2,200.00	$ 3,400.00	$ 4,600.00	$ 5,800.00	$ 7,000.00
b.	Total cost of goods sold	5,000.00	10,000.00	15,000.00	20,000.00	25,000.00
c.	Depreciation cost per unit	180.00	90.00	60.00	45.00	36.00
d.	Total rent cost	4,500.00	4,500.00	4,500.00	4,500.00	4,500.00
e.	Total cost of shopping bags	5.00	10.00	15.00	20.00	25.00
f.	Cost per unit of merchandise sold	50.00	50.00	50.00	50.00	50.00
g.	Rental cost per unit of merchandise sold	45.00	22.50	15.00	11.25	9.00
h.	Total phone expense	125.00	225.00	325.00	425.00	525.00
i.	Cost per unit of supplies	1.00	1.00	1.00	1.00	1.00
j.	Total insurance cost	1,000.00	1,000.00	1,000.00	1,000.00	1,000.00

Required
Identify each of these costs as fixed, variable, or mixed.

L.O. 1 **EXERCISE 2–3A** *Determining Fixed Cost per Unit*

Sheppard Corporation incurs the following annual fixed costs:

Item	Cost
Depreciation	$110,000
Officers' salaries	240,000
Long-term lease	60,000
Property taxes	20,000

Required
Determine the total fixed cost per unit of production, assuming that Sheppard produces 25,000, 30,000, or 35,000 units. (Round your answer to the nearest cent.)

L.O. 1 **EXERCISE 2–4A** *Determining Total Variable Cost*

The following variable production costs apply to goods made by Granger Manufacturing Corporation.

Item	Cost per Unit
Materials	$4.00
Labor	3.60
Variable overhead	0.80
Total	$8.40

Required
Determine the total variable production cost, assuming that Granger makes 20,000, 24,000, or 28,000 units.

EXERCISE 2–5A *Fixed Versus Variable Cost Behavior*

L.O. 1

Enzo Company's cost and production data for two recent months included the following:

	January	February
Production (units)	50	100
Rent	$2,000	$2,000
Utilities	$ 800	$1,600

Required

a. Separately calculate the rental cost per unit and the utilities cost per unit for both January and February.

b. Based on both total and per unit amounts, identify which cost is variable and which is fixed. Explain your answer.

EXERCISE 2–6A *Fixed Versus Variable Cost Behavior*

L.O. 1

Dillon Trophies makes and sells trophies it distributes to little league ballplayers. The company normally produces and sells between 10,000 and 13,000 trophies per year. The following cost data apply to various activity levels.

Number of trophies	10,000	11,000	12,000	13,000
Total costs incurred				
Fixed	$ 44,000			
Variable	96,000			
Total costs	$140,000			
Cost per unit				
Fixed	$ 4.40			
Variable	9.60			
Total cost per trophy	$14.00			

Required

a. Complete the preceding table by filling in the missing amounts for the levels of activity shown in the first row of the table. Round all cost per unit figures to the nearest whole penny.

b. Explain why the total cost per trophy decreases as the number of trophies increases.

EXERCISE 2–7A *Fixed Versus Variable Cost Behavior*

L.O. 1

Kirston Entertainment sponsors rock concerts. The company is considering a contract to hire a band at a cost of $50,000 per concert.

Required

a. What are the total band cost and the cost per person if concert attendance is 2,000, 2,500, 3,000, 3,500, or 4,000?

b. Is the cost of hiring the band a fixed or a variable cost?

c. Draw a graph and plot total cost and cost per unit if attendance is 2,000, 2,500, 3,000, 3,500, or 4,000.

d. Identify Kirston's major business risks and explain how they can be minimized.

EXERCISE 2–8A *Fixed Versus Variable Cost Behavior*

L.O. 1

Kirston Entertainment sells souvenir T-shirts at each rock concert that it sponsors. The shirts cost $10 each. Any excess shirts can be returned to the manufacturer for a full refund of the purchase price. The sales price is $15 per shirt.

Required

a. What are the total cost of shirts and cost per shirt if sales amount to 2,000, 2,500, 3,000, 3,500, or 4,000?

b. Is the cost of T-shirts a fixed or a variable cost?

c. Draw a graph and plot total cost and cost per shirt if sales amount to 2,000, 2,500, 3,000, 3,500, or 4,000.

d. Comment on Kirston's likelihood of incurring a loss due to its operating activities.

L.O. 1 **EXERCISE 2–9A** *Graphing Fixed Cost Behavior*

The following graphs depict the dollar amount of fixed cost on the vertical axes and the level of activity on the horizontal axes.

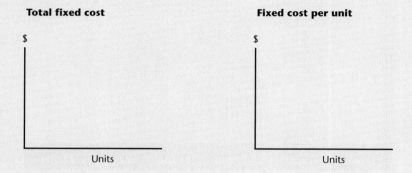

Required

a. Draw a line that depicts the relationship between total fixed cost and the level of activity.

b. Draw a line that depicts the relationship between fixed cost per unit and the level of activity.

L.O. 1 **EXERCISE 2–10A** *Graphing Variable Cost Behavior*

The following graphs depict the dollar amount of variable cost on the vertical axes and the level of activity on the horizontal axes.

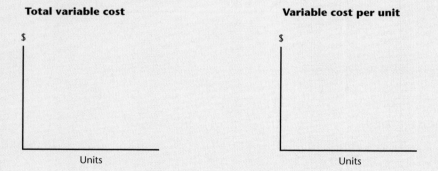

Required

a. Draw a line that depicts the relationship between total variable cost and the level of activity.

b. Draw a line that depicts the relationship between variable cost per unit and the level of activity.

L.O. 1 **EXERCISE 2–11A** *Mixed Cost at Different Levels of Activity*

Gagliano Corporation paid one of its sales representatives $4,300 during the month of March. The rep is paid a base salary plus $15 per unit of product sold. During March, the rep sold 200 units.

Required

Calculate the total monthly cost of the sales representative's salary for each of the following months.

Month	April	May	June	July
Number of units sold	240	160	250	160
Total variable cost				
Total fixed cost				
Total salary cost				

EXERCISE 2–12A *Using Fixed Cost as a Competitive Business Strategy*

L.O. 1, 2, 3, 6

The following income statements illustrate different cost structures for two competing companies.

Income Statements		
	Company Name	
	East	**West**
Number of Customers (a)	100	100
Sales Revenue (a × $500)	$50,000	$50,000
Variable Cost (a × $400)	NA	(40,000)
Variable Cost (a × $0)	0	NA
Contribution Margin	50,000	10,000
Fixed Cost	(40,000)	0
Net Income	$10,000	$10,000

Required
a. Reconstruct East's income statement, assuming that it serves 200 customers when it lures 100 customers away from West by lowering the sales price to $300 per customer.
b. Reconstruct West's income statement, assuming that it serves 200 customers when it lures 100 customers away from East by lowering the sales price to $300 per customer.
c. Explain why the price-cutting strategy increased East Company's profits but caused a net loss for West Company.

EXERCISE 2–13A *Using Contribution Margin Format Income Statement to Measure the Magnitude of Operating Leverage*

L.O. 4, 5

The following income statement was drawn from the records of Fairbank Company, a merchandising firm.

FAIRBANK COMPANY Income Statement For the Year Ended December 31, 2004	
Sales Revenue (4,000 units × $150)	$600,000
Cost of Goods Sold (4,000 units × $80)	(320,000)
Gross Margin	280,000
Sales Commissions (10% of sales)	(60,000)
Administrative Salaries Expense	(90,000)
Advertising Expense	(40,000)
Depreciation Expense	(50,000)
Shipping and Handling Expenses (4,000 units × $1)	(4,000)
Net Income	$ 36,000

Required

a. Reconstruct the income statement using the contribution margin format.
b. Calculate the magnitude of operating leverage.
c. Use the measure of operating leverage to determine the amount of net income Fairbank will earn if sales increase by 10 percent.

L.O. 5   EXERCISE 2–14A *Assessing the Magnitude of Operating Leverage*

The following income statement applies to Melvin Company for the current year:

Income Statement	
Sales Revenue (500 units $\times$ $40)	$20,000
Variable Cost (500 units $\times$ $22)	(11,000)
Contribution Margin	9,000
Fixed Costs	(6,000)
Net Income	$ 3,000

Required

a. Use the contribution margin approach to calculate the magnitude of operating leverage.
b. Use the operating leverage measure computed in Requirement *a* to determine the amount of net income that Melvin Company will earn if it experiences a 15 percent increase in revenue. The sales price per unit is not affected.
c. Verify your answer to Requirement *b* by constructing an income statement based on a 15 percent increase in sales revenue. The sales price is not affected. Calculate the percentage change in net income for the two income statements.

L.O. 8   EXERCISE 2–15A *Averaging Costs*

Julio Camps, Inc., leases the land on which it builds camp sites. Julio is considering opening a new site on land that requires $2,000 of rental payment per month. The variable cost of providing service is expected to be $4 per camper. The following chart shows the number of campers Julio expects for the first year of operation of the new site.

Jan.	Feb.	Mar.	Apr.	May	June	July	Aug.	Sept.	Oct.	Nov.	Dec.	Total
200	100	300	300	400	600	800	800	500	300	200	300	4,800

Required

Assuming that Julio wants to earn $10 per camper, determine the price it should charge for a camp site in February and August.

L.O. 10   EXERCISE 2–16A *Estimating Fixed and Variable Costs Using the High-Low Method*

Rangoon Boat Company makes inexpensive aluminum fishing boats. Production is seasonal, with considerable activity occurring in the spring and summer. Sales and production tend to decline in the fall and winter months. During 2005, the high point in activity occurred in April when it produced 200 boats at a total cost of $140,000. The low point in production occurred in December when it produced 40 boats at a total cost of $44,000.

Required

Use the high-low method to estimate the amount of fixed cost incurred each month by Rangoon Boat Company.

PROBLEM 2–17A *Identifying Cost Behavior*   L.O. 1

Required

Identify the following costs as fixed or variable.

Costs related to plane trips between Atlanta, Georgia, and Seattle, Washington, follow. Pilots are paid on a per trip basis.

a. Cost of a maintenance check relative to the number of passengers on a particular trip.
b. Fuel costs relative to the number of trips.
c. Pilots' salaries relative to the number of trips flown.
d. Depreciation relative to the number of planes in service.
e. Cost of refreshments relative to the number of passengers.
f. Pilots' salaries relative to the number of passengers on a particular trip.

First Federal Bank operates several branch offices in grocery stores. Each branch employs a supervisor and two tellers.

g. Supervisors' salaries relative to the number of branches operated.
h. Supervisors' salaries relative to the number of customers served in a particular branch.
i. Facility rental costs relative to the size of customer deposits.
j. Tellers' salaries relative to the number of tellers in a particular district.
k. Supplies cost relative to the number of transactions processed in a particular branch.
l. Tellers' salaries relative to the number of customers served at a particular branch.

Costs related to operating a fast-food restaurant follow.

m. Depreciation of equipment relative to the number of customers served at a particular restaurant.
n. Depreciation of equipment relative to the number of restaurants.
o. Building rental cost relative to the number of customers served in a particular restaurant.
p. Manager's salary of a particular store relative to the number of employees.
q. Food cost relative to the number of customers.
r. Utility cost relative to the number of restaurants in operation.
s. Company president's salary relative to the number of restaurants in operation.
t. Land costs relative to the number of hamburgers sold at a particular restaurant.

PROBLEM 2–18A *Cost Behavior and Averaging*   L.O. 1

May Lin has decided to start Lin Cleaning, a residential housecleaning service company. She is able to rent cleaning equipment at a cost of $750 per month. Labor costs are expected to be $75 per house cleaned and supplies are expected to cost $6 per house.

Required

a. Determine the total expected cost of equipment rental and the average expected cost of equipment rental per house cleaned, assuming that Lin Cleaning cleans 10, 20, or 30 houses during one month. Is the cost of equipment a fixed or a variable cost?
b. Determine the total expected cost of labor and the average expected cost of labor per house cleaned, assuming that Lin Cleaning cleans 10, 20, or 30 houses during one month. Is the cost of labor a fixed or a variable cost?
c. Determine the total expected cost of supplies and the average expected cost of supplies per house cleaned, assuming that Lin Cleaning cleans 10, 20, or 30 houses during one month. Is the cost of supplies a fixed or a variable cost?
d. Determine the total expected cost of cleaning houses, assuming that Lin Cleaning cleans 10, 20, or 30 houses during one month.
e. Determine the average expected cost per house, assuming that Lin Cleaning cleans 10, 20, or 30 houses during one month. Why does the cost per unit decrease as the number of houses increases?
f. If Ms. Lin tells you that she prices her services at 20 percent above cost, would you assume that she means average or actual cost? Why?

PROBLEM 2–19A *Context-Sensitive Nature of Cost Behavior Classifications*   L.O. 1

Champion Bank's start-up division establishes new branch banks. Each branch opens with three tellers. Total teller cost per branch is $90,000 per year. The three tellers combined can process up to 90,000 customer transactions per year. If a branch does not attain a volume of at least 60,000 transactions during its first year of operations, it is closed. If the demand for services exceeds 90,000 transactions, an additional teller is hired, and the branch is transferred from the start-up division to regular operations.

Required
a. What is the relevant range of activity for new branch banks?
b. Determine the amount of teller cost in total and the average teller cost per transaction for a branch that processes 60,000, 70,000, 80,000, or 90,000 transactions. In this case (the activity base is the number of transactions for a specific branch), is the teller cost a fixed or a variable cost?
c. Determine the amount of teller cost in total and the average teller cost per branch for Champion Bank, assuming that the start-up division operates 10, 15, 20, or 25 branches. In this case (the activity base is the number of branches), is the teller cost a fixed or a variable cost?

L.O. 1 **PROBLEM 2–20A** *Context-Sensitive Nature of Cost Behavior Classifications*

Cindy Zeller operates a sales booth in computer software trade shows, selling an accounting software package, *EZRecords*. She purchases the package from a software manufacturer for $100 each. Booth space at the convention hall costs $8,000 per show.

Required
a. Sales at past trade shows have ranged between 100 and 300 software packages per show. Determine the average cost of sales per unit if Ms. Zeller sells 100, 150, 200, 250, or 300 units of *EZRecords* at a trade show. Use the following chart to organize your answer. Is the cost of booth space fixed or variable?

	Sales Volume in Units (a)				
	100	150	200	250	300
Total cost of software (a × $100)	$10,000				
Total cost of booth rental	8,000				
Total cost of sales (b)	$18,000				
Average cost per unit (b ÷ a)	$180.00				

b. If Ms. Zeller wants to earn a $40 profit on each package of software she sells at a trade show, what price must she charge at sales volumes of 100, 150, 200, 250, or 300 units?
c. Record the total cost of booth space if Ms. Zeller attends one, two, three, four, or five trade shows. Record your answers in the following chart. Is the cost of booth space fixed or variable relative to the number of shows attended?

	Number of Trade Shows Attended				
	1	2	3	4	5
Total cost of booth rental	$8,000				

d. Ms. Zeller provides decorative shopping bags to customers who purchase software packages. Some customers take the bags; others do not. Some customers stuff more than one software package into a single bag. The number of bags varies in relation to the number of units sold, but the relationship is not proportional. Assume that Ms. Zeller uses $40 of bags for every 50 software packages sold. What is the additional cost per unit sold? Is the cost fixed or variable?

L.O. 2 **PROBLEM 2–21A** *Effects of Operating Leverage on Profitability*

Master Training Services (MTS) provides instruction on the use of computer software for the employees of its corporate clients. It offers courses in the clients' offices on the clients' equipment. The only major expense MTS incurs is instructor salaries; it pays instructors $5,000 per course taught. MTS recently agreed to offer a course of instruction to the employees of Oliver Incorporated at a price of $400 per student. Oliver estimated that 20 students would attend the course.

Base your answer on the preceding information.

Part 1:
Required
a. Relative to the number of students in a single course, is the cost of instruction a fixed or a variable cost?
b. Determine the profit, assuming that 20 students attend the course.
c. Determine the profit, assuming a 10 percent increase in enrollment (i.e., enrollment increases to 22 students). What is the percentage change in profitability?
d. Determine the profit, assuming a 10 percent decrease in enrollment (i.e., enrollment decreases to 18 students). What is the percentage change in profitability?
e. Explain why a 10 percent shift in enrollment produces more than a 10 percent shift in profitability. Use the term that identifies this phenomenon.

Part 2:
The instructor has offered to teach the course for a percentage of tuition fees. Specifically, she wants $250 per person attending the class. Assume that the tuition fee remains at $400 per student.

Required
a. Is the cost of instruction a fixed or a variable cost?
b. Determine the profit, assuming that 20 students take the course.
c. Determine the profit, assuming a 10 percent increase in enrollment (i.e., enrollment increases to 22 students). What is the percentage change in profitability?
d. Determine the profit, assuming a 10 percent decrease in enrollment (i.e., enrollment decreases to 18 students). What is the percentage change in profitability?
e. Explain why a 10 percent shift in enrollment produces a proportional 10 percent shift in profitability.

Part 3:
MTS sells a workbook with printed material unique to each course to each student who attends the course. Any workbooks that are not sold must be destroyed. Prior to the first class, MTS printed 20 copies of the books based on the client's estimate of the number of people who would attend the course. Each workbook costs $25 and is sold to course participants for $40. This cost includes a royalty fee paid to the author and the cost of duplication.

Required
a. Calculate the workbook cost in total and per student, assuming that 18, 20, or 22 students attend the course.
b. Classify the cost of workbooks as fixed or variable relative to the number of students attending the course.
c. Discuss the risk of holding inventory as it applies to the workbooks.
d. Explain how a just-in-time inventory system can reduce the cost and risk of holding inventory.

PROBLEM 2–22A *Effects of Fixed and Variable Cost Behavior on the Risk and Rewards of Business Opportunities*

L.O. 2, 3, 6

Northern and Southern Universities offer executive training courses to corporate clients. Northern pays its instructors $8,000 per course taught. Southern pays its instructors $320 per student enrolled in the class. Both universities charge executives a $480 tuition fee per course attended.

Required
a. Prepare income statements for Northern and Southern, assuming that 25 students attend a course.
b. Northern University embarks on a strategy to entice students from Southern University by lowering its tuition to $240 per course. Prepare an income statement for Northern, assuming that the university is successful and enrolls 50 students in its course.
c. Southern University embarks on a strategy to entice students from Northern University by lowering its tuition to $240 per course. Prepare an income statement for Southern, assuming that the university is successful and enrolls 50 students in its course.
d. Explain why the strategy described in Part *b* produced a profit but the same strategy described in Part *c* produced a loss.
e. Prepare income statements for Northern and Southern Universities, assuming that 15 students attend a course.
f. It is always better to have fixed than variable cost. Explain why this statement is false.
g. It is always better to have variable than fixed cost. Explain why this statement is false.

PROBLEM 2–23A *Analyzing Operating Leverage*

L.O. 5

James Swindle is a venture capitalist facing two alternative investment opportunities. He intends to invest $1 million in a start-up firm. He is nervous, however, about future economic volatility. He asks you to analyze the following financial data for the past year's operations of the two firms he is considering and give him some business advice.

	Company Name	
	Dawson	Travis
Variable cost per unit (a)	$12	$6
Sales revenue (10,000 units × $16)	$160,000	$160,000
Variable cost (10,000 units × a)	(120,000)	(60,000)
Contribution margin	$ 40,000	$100,000
Fixed cost	(20,000)	(80,000)
Net income	$ 20,000	$ 20,000

Required

a. Use the contribution margin approach to compute the operating leverage for each firm.

b. If the economy expands in coming years, Dawson and Travis will both enjoy a 10 percent per year increase in sales, assuming that the selling price remains unchanged. Compute the change in net income for each firm in dollar amount and in percentage. (Note: Since the number of units increases, both revenue and variable cost will increase.)

c. If the economy contracts in coming years, Dawson and Travis will both suffer a 10 percent decrease in sales volume, assuming that the selling price remains unchanged. Compute the change in net income for each firm in dollar amount and in percentage. (Note: Since the number of units decreases, both total revenue and total variable cost will decrease.)

d. Write a memo to James Swindle with your analyses and advice.

L.O. 8   PROBLEM 2–24A *Selecting the Appropriate Time Period for Cost Averaging*

Excite Movies is considering a contract to rent a movie for $1,200 per day. The contract requires a minimum one-week rental period. Estimated attendance is as follows:

Monday	Tuesday	Wednesday	Thursday	Friday	Saturday	Sunday
500	400	100	500	900	1,000	600

Required

a. Determine the average cost per person of the movie rental contract separately for each day.

b. Suppose that Excite chooses to price movie tickets at cost as computed in Part *a* plus $2.50. What price would it charge per ticket on each day of the week?

c. Use weekly averaging to determine a reasonable price to charge for movie tickets.

d. Comment on why weekly averaging may be more useful to business managers than daily averaging.

L.O. 8   PROBLEM 2–25A *Identifying Relevant Issues for Cost Averaging*

Climax, Inc., offers mountain-climbing expeditions for its customers, providing food, equipment, and guides. Climbs normally require one week to complete. The company's accountant is reviewing historical cost data to establish a pricing strategy for the coming year. The accountant has prepared the following table showing cost data for the most recent climb, the company's average cost per year, and the five-year average cost.

	Span of Time		
	Recent Climb	One Year	Five Years
Total cost of climbs (a)	$8,000	$506,540	$1,550,000
Number of climbers (b)	10	620	2,500
Cost per climber (a ÷ b)	$800	$817	$620

Required

Write a memo that explains the potential advantages and disadvantages of using each of the per unit cost figures as a basis for establishing a price to charge climbers during the coming year. What other factors must be considered in developing a pricing strategy?

PROBLEM 2–26A *Estimating Fixed and Variable Cost*   **L.O. 10**

Vestavia Computer Services, Inc., has been in business for six months. The following are basic operating data for that period.

	Month					
	July	**Aug.**	**Sept.**	**Oct.**	**Nov.**	**Dec.**
Service hours	120	136	260	420	320	330
Revenue	$6,000	$6,800	$13,000	$21,000	$16,000	$16,500
Operating costs	$4,200	$5,200	$ 7,000	$11,100	$ 9,000	$10,500

Required

a. What is the average service revenue per hour for the six-month time period?

b. Use the high-low method to estimate the total monthly fixed cost and the variable cost per hour.

c. Determine the average contribution margin per hour.

d. Use the scattergraph method to estimate the total monthly fixed cost and the variable cost per hour.

e. Compare the results of the two methods and comment on the difference.

PROBLEM 2–27A *Estimating Fixed and Variable Cost*   **L.O. 10**

Hanson Handcrafts, Inc. manufactures "antique" wooden cabinets to house modern radio and CD players. HHI began operations in January of last year. Melissa Kennedy, the owner, asks for your assistance. She believes that she needs to better understand the cost of the cabinets for pricing purposes. You have collected the following data concerning actual production over the past year:

Month	Number of Cabinets Produced	Total Cost
January	800	$21,000
February	3,600	32,500
March	1,960	29,500
April	600	18,600
May	1,600	29,000
June	1,300	27,000
July	1,100	25,600
August	1,800	31,000
September	2,280	32,000
October	2,940	31,500
November	3,280	32,000
December	400	16,500

Required

a. To understand the department's cost behavior, you decide to plot the points on graph paper and sketch a total cost line.

   (1) Enter the number of units and their costs in increasing order.

   (2) Plot the points on the graph.

   (3) Sketch a graph so the line "splits" all of the points (half of the points appear above and half below the line).

b. Using the line you just sketched, visually estimate the total cost to produce 2,000 units.

c. Using the high-low method, compute the total cost equation for the preceding data.

   (1) Compute the variable cost per unit.

   (2) Compute total fixed costs.

   (3) Assemble the total cost equation.

   (4) Sketch a line between the high and low points on your graph.

d. Using the high-low method, estimate the total cost to produce 2,000 units.

e. After discussing the results with your teammates, decide which method you believe is better.

EXERCISES—SERIES B

L.O. 1   EXERCISE 2–1B *Identifying Cost Behavior*

Kango Copies, Inc., provides professional copying services to customers through the 20 copy stores it operates in the southwestern United States. Each store employs a manager and four assistants. The manager earns $3,500 per month plus a bonus of 3 percent of sales. The assistants earn hourly wages. Each copy store costs $3,000 per month to lease. The company spends $5,000 per month on corporate-level advertising and promotion.

Required

Classify each of the following costs incurred by Kango Copies as fixed, variable, or mixed.
a. Store manager's salary relative to the number of copies made for customers.
b. Cost of paper relative to the number of copies made for customers.
c. Lease cost relative to the number of stores.
d. Advertising and promotion costs relative to the number of copies a particular store makes.
e. Lease cost relative to the number of copies made for customers.
f. Assistants' wages relative to the number of copies made for customers.

L.O. 1   EXERCISE 2–2B *Identifying Cost Behavior*

At the various sales levels shown, Bombay Company incurred the following costs.

	Units sold	50	100	150	200	250
a.	Total cost of goods sold	$4,000.00	$8,000.00	$12,000.00	$16,000.00	$20,000.00
b.	Depreciation cost per unit	30.00	15.00	10.00	7.50	6.00
c.	Total rent cost	600.00	600.00	600.00	600.00	600.00
d.	Total shipping cost	40.00	80.00	120.00	160.00	200.00
e.	Rent cost per unit of merchandise sold	12.00	6.00	4.00	3.00	2.40
f.	Total utility cost	200.00	300.00	400.00	500.00	600.00
g.	Supplies cost per unit	4.00	4.00	4.00	4.00	4.00
h.	Total insurance cost	500.00	500.00	500.00	500.00	500.00
i.	Total salary cost	1,500.00	2,000.00	2,500.00	3,000.00	3,500.00
j.	Cost per unit of merchandise sold	8.00	8.00	8.00	8.00	8.00

Required

Identify each of these costs as fixed, variable, or mixed.

L.O. 1   EXERCISE 2–3B *Determining Fixed Cost per Unit*

Manan Corporation incurs the following annual fixed production costs:

Item	Cost
Insurance cost	$ 75,000
Patent amortization cost	1,000,000
Depreciation cost	500,000
Property tax cost	60,000

Required

Determine the total fixed production cost per unit if Manan produces 10,000, 20,000, or 50,000 units

L.O. 1   EXERCISE 2–4B *Determining Total Variable Cost*

The following variable manufacturing costs apply to goods produced by Kyomoto Manufacturing Corporation.

Item	Cost per Unit
Materials	$4.00
Labor	2.50
Variable overhead	1.00
Total	$7.50

Required

Determine the total variable manufacturing cost if Kyomoto produces 4,000, 6,000, or 8,000 units.

EXERCISE 2–5B *Fixed Versus Variable Cost Behavior* L.O. 1

Firstech Company's production and total cost data for two recent months follow.

	January	February
Units produced	500	1,000
Total depreciation cost	$4,000	$4,000
Total factory supplies cost	$2,000	$4,000

Required

a. Separately calculate the depreciation cost per unit and the factory supplies cost per unit for both January and February.

b. Based on total and per unit amounts, identify which cost is variable and which is fixed. Explain your answer.

EXERCISE 2–6B *Fixed Versus Variable Cost Behavior* L.O. 1

General Chairs Corporation produces ergonomically designed chairs favored by architects. The company normally produces and sells from 10,000 to 16,000 chairs per year. The following cost data apply to various production activity levels.

Number of Chairs	10,000	12,000	14,000	16,000
Total costs incurred				
Fixed	$ 84,000			
Variable	60,000			
Total costs	$144,000			
Per unit chair cost				
Fixed	$ 8.40			
Variable	6.00			
Total cost per chair	$ 14.40			

Required

a. Complete the preceding table by filling in the missing amounts for the levels of activity shown in the first row of the table.

b. Explain why the total cost per chair decreases as the number of chairs increases.

EXERCISE 2–7B *Fixed Versus Variable Cost Behavior* L.O. 1

Johnny Comb needs extra money quickly because his mother's sudden hospitalization has resulted in unexpected medical bills. Mr. Comb has learned fortune-telling skills through his long friendship with Vince Vantz, who tells fortunes during the day at the city market. Mr. Vantz has agreed to let Mr. Comb use his booth to tell fortunes during the evening for a rent of $50 per night.

Required
a. What is the booth rental cost both in total and per customer if the number of customers is 5, 10, 15, 20, or 25?
b. Is the cost of renting the fortune-telling booth fixed or variable relative to the number of customers?
c. Draw two graphs. On one, plot total booth rental cost for 5, 10, 15, 20, and 25 customers; on the other, plot booth rental cost per customer for 5, 10, 15, 20, or 25 customers.
d. Mr. Comb has little money. What major business risks would he take by renting the fortune-telling booth? How could he minimize those risks?

L.O. 1   EXERCISE 2–8B *Fixed Versus Variable Cost Behavior*

In the evenings, Johnny Comb works telling fortunes using his friend Vince Vantz's booth at the city market. Mr. Vantz pays the booth rental, so Mr. Comb has no rental cost. As a courtesy, Mr. Comb provides each customer a soft drink. The drinks cost him $0.50 per customer.

Required
a. What is the soft drink cost both in total and per customer if the number of customers is 5, 10, 15, 20, or 25?
b. Is the soft drink cost fixed or variable?
c. Draw two graphs. On one, plot total soft drink cost for 5, 10, 15, 20, and 25 customers; on the other, plot soft drink cost per customer for 5, 10, 15, 20, and 25 customers.
d. Comment on the likelihood that Mr. Comb will incur a loss on this business venture.

L.O. 1   EXERCISE 2–9B *Graphing Fixed Cost Behavior*

Rudolf Computers leases space in a mall at a monthly rental cost of $2,000. The following graphs depict rental cost on the vertical axes and activity level on the horizontal axes.

Total monthly rental cost   **Rental cost per computer**

$ $

Number of computers sold   Number of computers sold

Required
a. Draw a line that depicts the relationship between the total monthly rental cost and the number of computers sold.
b. Draw a line that depicts the relationship between rental cost per computer and the number of computers sold.

L.O. 1   EXERCISE 2–10B *Graphing Variable Cost Behavior*

Rudolf Computers purchases computers from a manufacturer for $1,000 per computer. The following graphs depict product cost on the vertical axes and activity level on the horizontal axes.

Total product cost   **Product cost per computer**

$ $

Number of computers sold   Number of computers sold

Required
a. Draw a line that depicts the relationship between total product cost and the number of computers sold.
b. Draw a line that depicts the relationship between cost per computer and the number of computers sold.

EXERCISE 2–11B *Mixed Cost at Different Levels of Activity*   L.O. 1

Java Hats Corporation uses workers in Indonesia to manually weave straw hats. The company pays the workers a daily base wage plus $0.10 per completed hat. On Monday, workers produced 100 hats for which the company paid wages of $60.

Required
Calculate the total cost of the workers' wages for each of the following days.

Day	Monday	Tuesday	Wednesday	Thursday
Number of hats woven	100	120	160	80
Total variable cost				
Total fixed cost				
Total wages cost				

EXERCISE 2–12B *Effect of Cost Structure on Projected Profits*   L.O. 1, 2, 3, 6

Century and Millenium compete in the same market. The following budgeted income statements illustrate their cost structures.

Income Statements		
	Company	
	Century	Millenium
Number of Customers (a)	120	120
Sales Revenue (a × $100)	$12,000	$12,000
Variable Cost (a × $70)	NA	(8,400)
Contribution Margin	12,000	3,600
Fixed Cost	(8,400)	NA, 0
Net Income	$ 3,600	$ 3,600

Required
a. Assume that Century can lure all 120 customers away from Millenium by lowering its sales price to $60 per customer. Reconstruct Century's income statement based on 240 customers.
b. Assume that Millenium can lure all 120 customers away from Century by lowering its sales price to $60 per customer. Reconstruct Millenium's income statement based on 240 customers.
c. Why does the price-cutting strategy increase Century's profits but result in a net loss for Millenium?

EXERCISE 2–13B *Using a Contribution Margin Format Income Statement to Measure the*   L.O. 4, 5
                Magnitude of Operating Leverage

Calera Company, a merchandising firm, reported the following operating results.

Income Statement	
Sales Revenue (8,000 units × $100)	$800,000
Cost of Goods Sold (8,000 units × $60)	(480,000)
Gross Margin	320,000
Sales Commissions (10% of sales revenue)	(80,000)
Administrative Salaries Expense	(60,000)
Advertising Expense	(75,000)
Depreciation Expense	(68,000)
Shipping and Handling Expense (8,000 units × $1)	(8,000)
Net Income	$29,000

Required

a. Reconstruct the income statement using the contribution margin format.

b. Calculate the magnitude of operating leverage.

c. Use the measure of operating leverage to determine the amount of net income that Calera will earn if sales revenue increases by 10 percent.

L.O. 5   **EXERCISE 2–14B** *Assessing the Magnitude of Operating Leverage*

The following budgeted income statement applies to Massey Company:

Income Statement	
Sales Revenue (750 units × $40)	$30,000
Variable Cost (750 units × $28)	(21,000)
Contribution Margin	9,000
Fixed Cost	(7,000)
Net Income	$ 2,000

Required

a. Use the contribution margin approach to calculate the magnitude of operating leverage.

b. Use the operating leverage measure computed in Requirement *a* to determine the amount of net income that Massey Company will earn if sales volume increases by 10 percent. Assume the sales price per unit remains unchanged at $40.

c. Verify your answer to Requirement *b* by constructing an alternative income statement based on a 10 percent increase in sales volume. The sales price per unit remains unchanged at $40. Calculate the percentage change in net income for the two income statements.

L.O. 8   **EXERCISE 2–15B** *Averaging Costs*

Thompson Entertainment, Inc., operates a movie theater that has monthly fixed expenses of $5,000. In addition, the company pays film distributors $2 per ticket sold. The following chart shows the number of tickets Thompson expects to sell in the coming year:

Jan.	Feb.	Mar.	Apr.	May	June	July	Aug.	Sept.	Oct.	Nov.	Dec.	Total
2,000	1,600	3,200	3,400	3,200	4,200	5,100	4,000	5,000	3,100	3,000	2,200	40,000

Required

Assume that Thompson wants to earn $3 per movie patron. What price should it charge for a ticket in January and in September?

EXERCISE 2–16B *Estimating Fixed and Variable Costs Using the High-Low Method*   **L.O. 10**

Greenville Ice Cream Company produces various ice cream products for which demand is highly seasonal. The company sells more ice cream in warmer months and less in colder ones. Last year, the high point in production activity occurred in August when Greenville produced 20,000 gallons of ice cream at a total cost of $18,000. The low point in production activity occurred in February when the company produced 10,000 gallons of ice cream at a total cost of $14,000.

Required
Use the high-low method to estimate the amount of fixed cost per month incurred by Greenville Ice Cream Company.

PROBLEMS—SERIES B

PROBLEM 2–17B *Identifying Cost Behavior*   **L.O. 1**

Required
Identify the following costs as fixed or variable.

Costs related to operating a retail gasoline company.
 a. Utility cost relative to the number of stations in operation.
 b. The company's cost of national TV commercials relative to the number of stations in operation.
 c. Depreciation of equipment relative to the number of customers served at a station.
 d. Property and real estate taxes relative to the amount of gasoline sold at a particular station.
 e. Depreciation of equipment relative to the number of stations.
 f. Cashiers' wages relative to the number of customers served in a station.
 g. Salary of a manager of a particular station relative to the number of employees.
 h. Gasoline cost relative to the number of customers.

Costs related to shuttle bus trips between Houston Intercontinental Airport and downtown Houston. Each bus driver receives a specific salary per month. A manager schedules bus trips and supervises drivers, and a secretary receives phone calls.

 i. A driver's salary relative to the number of passengers on a particular trip.
 j. Fuel costs relative to the number of trips.
 k. Fuel costs relative to the number of passengers on a particular trip.
 l. Drivers' salaries relative to the number of trips driven.
 m. Office staff salaries relative to the number of passengers on a particular trip.
 n. Depreciation relative to the number of buses in service.

Susie's Barbershop operates several stores in shopping centers. Each store employs a supervisor and three barbers. Each barber receives a specific salary per month plus a 10 percent commission based on the service revenues he or she has generated.

 o. Barbers' salaries relative to the number of barbers in a particular district.
 p. Supplies cost relative to the number of hair services provided in a particular store.
 q. Barbers' salaries relative to the number of customers served at a particular store.
 r. Store rental costs relative to the number of customers.
 s. Barbers' commissions relative to the number of customers.
 t. Supervisory salaries relative to the number of customers served in a particular store.

PROBLEM 2–18B *Cost Behavior and Averaging*   **L.O. 1**

Ginger Grant asks you to analyze the operating cost of her lawn services business. She has bought the needed equipment with a cash payment of $18,000. Upon your recommendation, she agrees to adopt straight-line depreciation. The equipment has an expected life of three years and no salvage value. Ms. Grant pays her workers $20 per lawn service. Material costs, including fertilizer, pesticide, and supplies, are expected to be $5 per lawn service.

Required
 a. Determine the total cost of equipment depreciation and the average cost of equipment depreciation per lawn service, assuming that Ms. Grant provides 20, 25, or 30 lawn services during one month. Is the cost of equipment a fixed or a variable cost?

b. Determine the total expected cost of labor and the average expected cost of labor per lawn service, assuming that Ms. Grant provides 20, 25, or 30 lawn services during one month. Is the cost of labor a fixed or a variable cost?

c. Determine the total expected cost of materials and the average expected cost of materials per lawn service, assuming that Ms. Grant provides 20, 25, or 30 lawn services during one month. Is the cost of fertilizer, pesticide, and supplies a fixed or a variable cost?

d. Determine the total expected cost per lawn service, assuming that Ms. Grant provides 20, 25, or 30 lawn services during one month.

e. Determine the average expected cost per lawn service, assuming that Ms. Grant provides 20, 25, or 30 lawn services during one month. Why does the cost per unit decrease as the number of lawn services increases?

f. If Ms. Grant tells you that she prices her services at 30 percent above cost, would you assume that she means average or actual cost? Why?

L.O. 1   **PROBLEM 2–19B** *Context-Sensitive Nature of Cost Behavior Classifications*

Rica and Hull Tax Services' Development Department is responsible for establishing new community branches. Each branch opens with two tax accountants. Total cost of payroll per branch is $80,000 per year. Together the two accountants can process up to 2,500 simple tax returns per year. The firm's policy requires closing branches that do not reach the quota of 1,500 tax returns per year. On the other hand, the firm hires an additional accountant for a branch and elevates it to the status of a regular operation if the customer demand for services exceeds 2,500 tax returns.

Required

a. What is the relevant range of activity for a new branch established by the Development Department?

b. Determine the amount of payroll cost in total and the average payroll cost per transaction for a branch that processes 1,500, 2,000, or 2,500 tax returns. In this case (the activity base is the number of tax returns for a specific branch), is the payroll cost a fixed or a variable cost?

c. Determine the amount of payroll cost in total and the average payroll cost per branch for Rica and Hull Tax Services, assuming that the Development Department operates 20, 30, or 40 branches. In this case (the activity base is the number of branches), is the payroll cost a fixed or a variable cost?

L.O. 1

PROBLEM 2–20B *Context-Sensitive Nature of Cost Behavior Classifications*

Tom Wendall sells a newly developed camera, Delicate Image. He purchases the cameras from the manufacturer for $200 each and rents a store in a shopping mall for $4,000 per month.

Required

a. Determine the average cost of sales per unit if Mr. Wendall sells 100, 200, 300, 400, or 500 units of Delicate Image per month. Use the following chart to organize your answer.

	Sales Volume in Units (a)				
	100	200	300	400	500
Total cost of cameras (a × $200)	$20,000				
Total cost of store rental	4,000				
Total cost of sales (b)	$ 24,000				
Average cost per unit (b ÷ a)	$240.00				

b. If Mr. Wendall wants to make a gross profit of $35 on each camera he sells, what price should he charge at sales volumes of 100, 200, 300, 400, or 500 units?

c. Record the total cost of store rental if Mr. Wendall opens a camera store at one, two, three, four, or five shopping malls. Record your answers in the following chart. Is the cost of store rental fixed or variable relative to the number of stores opened?

	Shopping Malls				
	1	2	3	4	5
Total cost of store rental	$4,000				

d. Mr. Wendall provides decorative ornaments to customers who purchase cameras. Some customers take the ornaments, others do not, and some take more than one. The number of ornaments varies in relation to the number of cameras sold, but the relationship is not proportional. Assume that, on average, Mr. Wendall gives away $100 worth of ornaments for every 100 cameras sold. What is the additional cost per camera sold? Is the cost fixed or variable?

PROBLEM 2–21B *Effects of Operating Leverage on Profitability*

L.O. 2

Become CPA, Inc., conducts CPA review courses. Public universities that permit free use of a classroom support the classes. The only major expense incurred by Become CPA is the salary of instructors, which is $7,500 per course taught. The company recently planned to offer a review course in Boston for $400 per candidate; it estimated that 50 candidates would attend the course.

Complete these requirements based on the preceding information.

Part 1
Required
a. Relative to the number of CPA candidates in a single course, is the cost of instruction a fixed or a variable cost?
b. Determine the profit, assuming that 50 candidates attend the course.
c. Determine the profit, assuming a 10 percent increase in enrollment (i.e., enrollment increases to 55 students). What is the percentage change in profitability?
d. Determine the profit, assuming a 10 percent decrease in enrollment (i.e., enrollment decreases to 45 students). What is the percentage change in profitability?
e. Explain why a 10 percent shift in enrollment produces more than a 10 percent shift in profitability. Use the term that identifies this phenomenon.

Part 2
The instructor has offered to teach the course for a percentage of tuition fees. Specifically, he wants $150 per candidate attending the class. Assume that the tuition fee remains at $400 per candidate.

Required
f. Is the cost of instruction a fixed or a variable cost?
g. Determine the profit, assuming that 50 candidates take the course.
h. Determine the profit, assuming a 10 percent increase in enrollment (i.e., enrollment increases to 55 students). What is the percentage change in profitability?
i. Determine the profit, assuming a 10 percent decrease in enrollment (i.e., enrollment decreases to 45 students). What is the percentage change in profitability?
j. Explain why a 10 percent shift in enrollment produces a proportional 10 percent shift in profitability.

Part 3
Become CPA sells a workbook to each student who attends the course. The workbook contains printed material unique to each course. Workbooks that are not sold must be destroyed. Prior to the first class, Become CPA printed 50 copies of the books based on the estimated number of people who would attend the course. Each workbook costs $40 and is sold for $50. This cost includes a royalty fee paid to the author and the cost of duplication.

Required
k. Calculate the total cost and the cost per candidate of the workbooks, assuming that 45, 50, or 55 candidates attend the course.
l. Classify the cost of workbooks as fixed or variable relative to the number of candidates attending the course.
m. Discuss the risk of holding inventory as it applies to the workbooks.
n. Explain how a just-in-time inventory system can reduce the cost and risk of holding inventory.

PROBLEM 2–22B *Effects of Fixed and Variable Cost Behavior on the Risk and Rewards of Business Opportunities*

L.O. 2, 3, 6

Country Club and Suburb Club are competing health and recreation clubs in Columbus. They both offer tennis training clinics to adults. Country pays its coaches $5,000 per season. Suburb pays its coaches $200 per student enrolled in the clinic per season. Both clubs charge a tuition fee of $300 per season.

Required

a. Prepare income statements for Country and Suburb, assuming that 25 students per season attend each clinic.

b. The ambitious new director of Country Club tries to increase his market share by reducing the club's tuition per student to $180 per clinic. Prepare an income statement for Country, assuming that the club attracts all of Suburb's customers and therefore is able to enroll 50 students in its clinics.

c. Independent of Part *b*, Suburb Club tries to lure Country's students by lowering its price to $180 per student. Prepare an income statement for Suburb, assuming that the club succeeds in enrolling 50 students in its clinics.

d. Explain why the strategy described in Part *b* produced a profit while the same strategy described in Part *c* produced a loss.

e. Prepare an income statement for Country Club and Suburb Club, assuming that 15 students attend a clinic at the original $300 tuition price.

f. It is always better to have fixed rather than variable cost. Explain why this statement is false.

g. It is always better to have variable rather than fixed cost. Explain why this statement is false.

L.O. 7,8 **PROBLEM 2–23B** *Analysis of Operating Leverage*

Sharon Baker has invested in two start-up companies. At the end of the first year, she asks you to evaluate their operating performance. The following operating data apply to the first year.

	Company Name	
	Yala	**Tumu**
Variable cost per unit (a)	$24	$12
Sales revenue (25,000 units × $32)	$800,000	$800,000
Variable cost (25,000 units × a)	(600,000)	(300,000)
Contribution margin	$200,000	$500,000
Fixed cost	(100,000)	(400,000)
Net income	$100,000	$100,000

Required

a. Use the contribution margin approach to compute the operating leverage for each firm.

b. If the economy expands in the coming year, Yala and Tumu will both enjoy a 10 percent per year increase in sales volume, assuming that the selling price remains unchanged. (*Note:* Since the number of units increases, both revenue and variable cost will increase.) Compute the change in net income for each firm in dollar amount and in percentage.

c. If the economy contracts in the following year, Yala and Tumu will both suffer a 10 percent decrease in sales volume, assuming that the selling price remains unchanged. (*Note:* Since the number of units decreases, both revenue and variable cost decrease.) Compute the change in net income for each firm in both dollar amount and percentage.

d. Write a memo to Sharon Baker with your evaluation and recommendations.

L.O. 8 **PROBLEM 2–24B** *Selecting the Appropriate Time Period for Cost Averaging*

The City Fairground Commission is considering signing a contract to hire a circus at a cost of $3,000 per day. The contract requires a minimum performance period of one week. Estimated circus attendance is as follows:

Monday	Tuesday	Wednesday	Thursday	Friday	Saturday	Sunday
800	600	400	860	1,440	1,860	1,540

Required
a. For each day, determine the average cost of the circus contract per person attending.
b. Suppose that the commission prices circus tickets at cost as computed in Part *a* plus $2.00. What would be the price per ticket charged on each day of the week?
c. Use weekly averaging to determine a reasonable price to charge for the circus tickets.
d. Comment on why weekly averaging may be more useful to business managers than daily averaging.

PROBLEM 2–25B *Identifying Relevant Issues for Cost Averaging*

L.O. 7

Gobi Tours, Inc., organizes adventure tours for people interested in visiting a desert environment. A desert tour generally lasts three days. Gobi provides food, equipment, and guides. Tyler Summers, the president of Gobi Tours, needs to set prices for the coming year. He has available the company's past cost data in the following table.

	Span of Time		
	Recent Tour	**One Year**	**Ten Years**
Total cost of tours (a)	$9,600	$465,000	$2,880,000
Number of tourists (b)	32	1,500	12,000
Cost per tourist (a ÷ b)	$300	$310	$240

Required
Write a memo to Mr. Summers explaining the potential advantages and disadvantages of using each of the different per tourist cost figures as a basis for establishing a price to charge tourists during the coming year. What other factors must Mr. Summers consider in developing a pricing strategy?

PROBLEM 2–26B *Estimating Fixed and Variable Costs*

L.O. 10

Newsome Legal Services provides legal advice to clients. The following data apply to the first six months of operation.

	Month					
	Jan.	**Feb.**	**Mar.**	**Apr.**	**May**	**June**
Service hours	80	102	135	156	186	170
Revenue	$4,800	$6,120	$8,100	$9,360	$11,160	$10,200
Operating costs	6,800	7,520	8,000	8,050	8,814	8,800

Required
a. What is the average service revenue per hour for the six-month time period?
b. Use the high-low method to estimate the total monthly fixed cost and the variable cost per hour.
c. Determine the average contribution margin per hour.
d. Use the scattergraph method to estimate the total monthly fixed cost and the variable cost per hour.
e. Compare the results of the two methods and comment on any differences.

PROBLEM 2–27B *Estimating Fixed and Variable Cost*

L.O. 10

Perfect Frames, Inc. (PFI), which manufactures ornate frames for original art work, began operations in January 2001. Justin Jamail, the owner, asks for your assistance. He believes that he needs to better understand the cost of the cabinets for pricing purposes. You have collected the following data concerning actual production over the past year:

Month	Number of Frames Produced	Total Cost
January	1,600	$42,000
February	7,200	65,000
March	3,920	59,000
April	1,200	37,200
May	3,200	58,000
June	2,600	54,000
July	2,200	51,200
August	3,600	62,000
September	4,560	64,000
October	5,880	63,000
November	6,560	64,000
December	800	33,000

Required

a. To understand the department's cost behavior, you decide to plot the points on graph paper and sketch a total cost line.
   (1) Enter the number of units and their costs in increasing order.
   (2) Plot the points on the graph.
   (3) Sketch a graph so the line "splits" all of the points (half of the points appear above and half appear below the line).
b. Using the line you just sketched, visually estimate the total cost to produce 4,000 units.
c. Using the high-low method, compute the total cost equation for the preceding data.
   (1) Compute the variable cost per unit.
   (2) Compute total fixed costs.
   (3) Assemble the total cost equation.
   (4) Sketch a line between the high and low points on your graph.
d. Using the high-low method, estimate the total cost to produce 4,000 units.
e. After discussing the results with your teammates, decide which method you believe is better.

ANALYZE, THINK, COMMUNICATE

ATC 2–1 BUSINESS APPLICATIONS CASE *Operating Leverage*

The following information comes from recent annual reports of the Boeing Company and JCPenney Company, Inc.

Description of Business for Boeing Company

The Boeing Company, together with its subsidiaries (herein referred to as the "Company"), is one of the world's major aerospace firms. The Company operates in two principal industries: commercial aircraft, and information, space and defense systems. Commercial aircraft operations—conducted through Boeing Commercial Airplane Group—involve development, production and marketing of commercial jet aircraft and providing related support services, principally to the commercial airline industry worldwide. Information, space and defense systems operations—conducted through Boeing Information, Space and Defense Systems Group—involve research, development, production, modification and support of the following products and related systems: military aircraft, including fighter, transport and attack aircraft; helicopters; space and missile systems; satellite launching vehicles; rocket engines; and specialized information services. . . .

Operating revenues and income for two years are as follows (in millions):

	1996	1995
Operating revenues	$22,681	$19,515
Operating income	1,354	902

Description of Business for JCPenney Company, Inc.

JCPenney Company, Inc. ("Company") was founded by James Cash Penney in 1902. Incorporated in Delaware in 1924, the Company has grown to be a major retailer. The major portion of the

Company's business consists of providing merchandise and services to consumers through department stores that include catalog departments. The Company markets predominantly family apparel, jewelry, shoes, accessories, and home furnishings. In addition, the Company, through its wholly-owned subsidiary, Eckerd Corporation ("Eckerd"), operates a chain of approximately 2,780 drugstores located throughout the northeast, southeast, and Sunbelt regions of the United States. The Company also has several direct marketing insurance subsidiaries, the principal of which is JCPenney Life Insurance Company, which markets life, health, accident and credit insurance as well as a growing portfolio of non-insurance products.

Operating revenues and income for two recent years are as follows (for retail sales business in millions):

	1997	1996
Operating revenues	$29,618	$22,653
Operating income	1,783	1,333

Required
a. Which company has the higher operating leverage?
b. Write a brief paragraph explaining why one of the companies would have a higher level of operating leverage than the other company.
c. If revenues for both companies declined, which company would most likely experience the greatest decline in operating income? Explain your answer.

GROUP ASSIGNMENT *Operating Leverage*

ATC 2–2

The Parent Teacher Association (PTA) of Meadow High School is planning a fund-raising campaign. The PTA is considering the possibility of hiring Eric Logan, a world-renowned investment counselor, to address the public. Tickets would sell for $28 each. The school has agreed to let the PTA use Harville Auditorium at no cost. Mr. Logan is willing to accept one of two compensation arrangements. He will sign an agreement to receive a fixed fee of $10,000 regardless of the number of tickets sold. Alternatively, he will accept payment of $20 per ticket sold. In communities similar to that in which Meadow is located, Mr. Logan has drawn an audience of approximately 500 people.

Required
a. In front of the class, present a statement showing the expected net income assuming 500 people buy tickets.
b. The instructor will divide the class into groups and then organize the groups into four sections. The instructor will assign one of the following tasks to each section of groups.

Group Tasks
(1) Assume the PTA pays Mr. Logan a fixed fee of $10,000. Determine the amount of net income that the PTA will earn if ticket sales are 10 percent higher than expected. Calculate the percentage change in net income.
(2) Assume that the PTA pays Mr. Logan a fixed fee of $10,000. Determine the amount of net income that the PTA will earn if ticket sales are 10 percent lower than expected. Calculate the percentage change in net income.
(3) Assume that the PTA pays Mr. Logan $20 per ticket sold. Determine the amount of net income that the PTA will earn if ticket sales are 10 percent higher than expected. Calculate the percentage change in net income.
(4) Assume that the PTA pays Mr. Logan $20 per ticket sold. Determine the amount of net income that the PTA will earn if ticket sales are 10 percent lower than expected. Calculate the percentage change in net income.

c. Have each group select a spokesperson. Have one of the spokespersons in each section of groups go to the board and present the results of the analysis conducted in Part *b*. Resolve any discrepancies in the computations presented at the board and those developed by the other groups.
d. Draw conclusions regarding the risks and rewards associated with operating leverage. At a minimum, answer the following questions.
(1) Which type of cost structure (fixed or variable) produces the higher growth potential in profitability for a company?
(2) Which type of cost structure (fixed or variable) faces the higher risk of declining profitability for a company?
(3) Under what circumstances should a company seek to establish a fixed cost structure?
(4) Under what circumstances should a company seek to establish a variable cost structure?

ATC 2–3 RESEARCH ASSIGNMENT *Fixed Versus Variable Cost*

Economies of scale result in lower per unit costs. Economies of scale are achieved when productive capacity (size or scale) increase without proportionate increases in cost. For example, using megaships has lowered freight costs. These large vessels permit significantly larger loads of cargo to be delivered without proportionate increases in investment, marketing, fuel, and administration costs. On page 131 of the September 21, 1998, issue of *Business Week* is the article "Seeking a Deep Harbor." Read this article and complete the following requirements.

Required

a. Identify some costs that would be fixed regardless of the amount of cargo carried when using a giant cargo vessel to transport merchandise.

b. Identify some costs that would be variable with respect to the amount of cargo carried when using a giant cargo vessel to transport merchandise.

c. Relative to the number of ships that will use the New York channel, is the expected $732 million cost of dredging a fixed or a variable cost?

d. How can economies of scale be achieved when larger ships cost more to make than smaller ones? More specifically, since larger ships cost more, how can the depreciation charge per unit of cargo be less?

e. Explain how the president of a New York trucking business could benefit from ideas in this article.

ATC 2–4 WRITING ASSIGNMENT *Cost Averaging*

Candice Sterling is a veterinarian. She has always been concerned for the pets of low-income families. These families love their pets but frequently do not have the means to provide them proper veterinary care. Dr. Sterling decides to open a part-time veterinary practice in a low-income neighborhood. She plans to volunteer her services free of charge two days per week. Clients will be charged only for the actual costs of materials and overhead. Dr. Sterling leases a small space for $300 per month. Utilities and other miscellaneous costs are expected to be approximately $180 per month. She estimates the variable cost of materials to be approximately $10 per pet served. A friend of Dr. Sterling who runs a similar type of clinic in another area of town indicates that she should expect to treat the following number of pets during her first year of operation.

Jan.	Feb.	Mar.	Apr.	May	June	July	Aug.	Sept.	Oct.	Nov.	Dec.
18	26	28	36	42	54	63	82	42	24	20	15

Dr. Sterling's friend has noticed that visits increase significantly in the summer because children who are out of school tend to bring their pets to the vet more often. Business tapers off during the winter and reaches a low point in December when people spend what little money they have on Christmas presents for their children. After looking at the data, Dr. Sterling becomes concerned that the people in the neighborhood will not be able to afford pet care during some months of operation even if it is offered at cost. For example, the cost of providing services in December would be approximately $42 per pet treated ($480 overhead ÷ 15 pets = $32 per pet, plus $10 materials cost). She is willing to provide her services free of charge, but she realizes that she cannot afford to subsidize the practice further by personally paying for the costs of materials and overhead in the months of low activity. She decides to discuss the matter with her accountant to find a way to cut costs even more. Her accountant tells her that her problem is cost *measurement* rather than cost *cutting*.

Required

Assume that you are Dr. Sterling's accountant. Write a memo describing a pricing strategy that resolves the apparent problem of high costs during months of low volume. Recommend in your memo the price to charge per pet treated during the month of December.

ATC 2–5 ETHICAL DILEMMA *Profitability Versus Social Conscience (Effects of Cost Behavior)*

Advances in biological technology have enabled two research companies, Bio Labs, Inc. and Scientific Associates, to develop an insect-resistant corn seed. Neither company is financially strong enough to develop the distribution channels necessary to bring the product to world markets. World Agra Distributors, Inc., has negotiated contracts with both companies for the exclusive right to market their seed. Bio Labs signed an agreement to receive an annual royalty of $1,000,000. In contrast, Scientific Associates

the *curious* accountant

Microsoft Corporation plans to spend $500 million over 18 months to market its new XBOX game machine. Suppose that Bill Gates has asked you to determine the unit cost of making an XBOX machine. Would you consider the promotion costs as part of the cost of the machine? Assume that Microsoft prices its products at cost plus a designated markup above the cost. Would you consider the promotion costs in determining the appropriate sales price?

Andy Grove, president and CEO of Intel Corporation, is credited with the motto "Only the paranoid survive." Mr. Grove describes a wide variety of concerns that make him paranoid. Specifically, he states the following:

> *I worry about products getting screwed up, and I worry about products getting introduced prematurely. I worry about factories not performing well, and I worry about having too many factories. I worry about hiring the right people, and I worry about morale slacking off. And, of course, I worry about competitors. I worry about other people figuring out how to do what we do better or cheaper, and displacing us with our customers. But these worries pale in comparison to how I feel about what I call strategic inflection points.[1]*

Mr. Grove describes strategic inflection points as "a time in the life of a business when its fundamentals are about to change."[2] The forces of change can be so powerful that they transform the very essence of conducting business. Consider the ways the airplane changed the transportation industry, television affected radio, satellites altered television programming, fast-food restaurants altered the food-processing industry, automated tellers changed the banking

[1]Andrew S. Grove, *Only the Paranoid Survive* (New York: Bantam Doubleday Dell, 1996), p. 3.
[2]Ibid, p. 3.

industry, plastic debit cards affected check printers, super stores affected the small retail industry, and the Internet is changing the communications industry.

Most students have completed an introductory financial accounting course prior to reading this text. Considering what you have learned about financial accounting, do Intel's financial statements contain the information Mr. Grove needs to address his worries? Clearly, the historical-based financial information contained in the income statement, balance sheet, statement of stockholders' equity, and statement of cash flows is insufficient to effectively manage a business. **Financial accounting** *is not designed to satisfy the full range of needs of business managers. Its scope is limited to the needs of external users including creditors, investors, government agencies, financial analysts, news reporters, and so on. The field of accounting that is designed to satisfy the information needs of managers and other individuals working inside the business is called* **managerial accounting.** *This text is designed to introduce you to the fundamental concepts associated with accounting information that is useful in managing the operations of a business.*

▌Differences Between Managerial and Financial Accounting

LO1 Distinguish between managerial and financial accounting.

Clearly, the information needs of internal and external users overlap. For example, both investors and managers are affected by strategic inflection points. Even so, the information needed to operate a business can be quite different from the information necessary to evaluate its investment potential. Some of the distinguishing characteristics of management accounting are discussed in the following section.

Users

As indicated, financial accounting provides information that is primarily used by investors, creditors, and others who work *outside* the business. In contrast, managerial accounting focuses on information that is used by executives, managers, and operators who work *inside* the business. The two user groups need different types of information.

Level of Aggregation

Investors and creditors frequently use general economic indicators as well as company-specific financial information when making their investment and credit decisions. For example, an investor considering the purchase of stock versus bond securities might be interested in the government's monetary policy, the growth rate of the gross domestic product, changes in the level of disposable income, tax policy, and the trend of corporate profits. In addition to general economic data, investors also use company-specific financial statement information. With respect to company-specific financial data, investors generally desire *global information* that reflects the performance of the company as a whole. They are much less interested in data regarding the performance of specific subunits such as particular divisions, stores, or departments. For example, an investor is not so much interested in the performance of a particular Sears store as she is in the performance of Sears Roebuck Company versus the performance of JC Penney Company.

Internal users need information that facilitates the decision making necessary to *plan, direct,* and *control* the operations of a particular enterprise. The type of information needed by internal personnel is related to their job level in the organizational hierarchy. At the base level of a business organization, workers need information that is useful in making products or delivering services to customers. For example, the manager of the children's department of a particular JC Penney store needs to know how many pairs of blue jeans to have available for a back-to-school sale. When preparing the work schedule, the departmental manager might need information regarding the availability of staff and the company policy regarding overtime pay. Other considerations include the availability of supplies such as shopping bags, cash register tapes, sales tags, and so forth. Indeed, the vast majority of information used at the operating level is nonfinancial.

As you move up the organizational ladder, financial information becomes increasingly important. Middle managers need information regarding the financial as well as the operating performance of their responsibility centers. For example, the manager of a JC Penney store is likely to be held responsible for achieving growth in the store's revenue and for controlling its expenses. The store manager is also interested in nonfinancial data such as operating hours, the types of merchandise sold, the store layout, the image created by advertising campaigns, customer return policies, and employee training.

Senior executives make extensive use of the company's financial statements. Top executives use financial data when comparing the performance of their companies against that of their competitors. Financial information is also important in communicating companywide goals, objectives, and accomplishments to stockholders and in providing information necessary to obtain financing from creditors. Executives also use financial information in making strategic decisions regarding mergers and acquisitions, as well as for decisions regarding the sale of subsidiaries, divisions, or product lines. To a lesser degree, executives might also use economic indicators and operating information. However, even these data are normally presented in summary form, which enables executive-level managers to assess the condition of the overall organization. Exhibit 1–1 summarizes the information needs of different user groups.

In summary, the financial accounting system is a component of the managerial accounting system. The managerial accounting system provides a much richer data set that includes economic and nonfinancial data as well as financial statement data. Information provided to insiders becomes increasingly disaggregated and nonfinancial as you move down the organizational hierarchy.

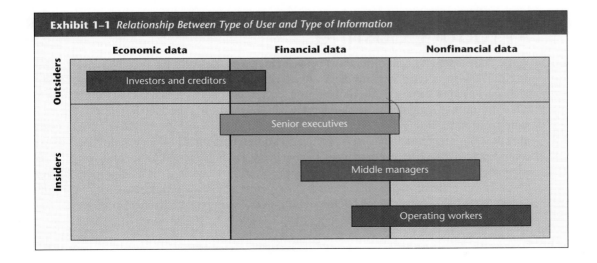

Exhibit 1–1 *Relationship Between Type of User and Type of Information*

Regulation

Financial accounting is designed to generate information for the general public. In an effort to protect the public interest, Congress established the **Securities and Exchange Commission (SEC)** and gave it authority to regulate public financial reporting practices. The SEC has delegated much of its authority for developing accounting rules to the **Financial Accounting Standards Board (FASB).** The FASB supports a broad base of pronouncements and practices known as **generally accepted accounting principles (GAAP).** GAAP severely restricts the accounting procedures and practices that can be applied to the preparation of published financial statements. Beyond financial statement data, much of the information generated in management accounting systems is proprietary information that is not made available to the public. Since this information is not distributed to the public, regulation designed to protect the public interest is not needed. Indeed, management accounting is restricted only by the **value-added principle.** Management accountants are free to engage in any information-gathering and reporting activity so long as the activity adds value in excess of its cost. For example, management accountants are free to make forecasts that enable managers to set production schedules to be able to satisfy customer demand. In contrast, financial accounting as prescribed by GAAP does not permit forecasting.

Characteristics of Information

Management's responsibilities include planning, directing, and controlling the operations of the business. Meeting these responsibilities requires future as well as historical information. Predicting the future frequently requires subjective judgment. While financial accounting is characterized by its objectivity, reliability, consistency, and historical nature, managerial accounting is more concerned with relevance and timeliness. Managerial accounting includes more estimates and fewer facts than does financial accounting. Financial accounting reports what happened yesterday; managerial accounting reports what is expected to happen tomorrow.

Time Horizon

Financial information is reported on a delayed basis for a specified time period. The normal accounting period is one year. This reporting time frame is acceptable for historical reports, but it is inadequate for operating purposes. Management cannot wait until the end of the year to discover problems. Planning, controlling, and directing must be continual. Accordingly, managerial accounting information is necessarily captured and delivered in a more timely fashion than financial accounting information. Exhibit 1–2 summarizes the critical differences between financial and managerial accounting.

▌Product Costing

While there are significant differences between managerial and financial accounting, the two disciplines also overlap in many areas. One such area is that of estimating **product cost.**[3] Managers need to know the cost of their products for a variety of reasons. Cost information is often useful in pricing decisions; knowing what you paid for a product certainly influences your decision regarding the price at which you are willing to sell that product. Indeed, **cost-plus pricing** is a common business practice.[4] **Product costing** is also an essential part of the control process. To effectively manage the business, executives must know how actual costs compare to budgeted costs. Are costs higher or lower than expected? Who is responsible for the variances between expected and actual costs? What action can be taken to control the variances? These questions cannot be answered unless executives understand product costing practices and procedures.

[3]This text uses the term *product* in a generic sense to mean both goods and services.
[4]Other pricing strategies will be introduced in subsequent chapters.

Exhibit 1–2 *Comparative Features of Managerial Versus Financial Accounting Information*

Features	Managerial Accounting	Financial Accounting
Users	Insiders including executives, managers, and operators	Outsiders including investors, creditors, government agencies, analysts, and reporters
Level of aggregation	Local information on subunits of the organization	Global information on the company as a whole
Information type	Economic and physical data as well as financial data	Financial data
Regulation	No regulation, limited only by the value-added principle	Regulation by SEC, FASB, and other determinors of GAAP
Information characteristics	Estimates that promote relevance and enable timeliness	Factual information that is characterized by objectivity, reliability, consistency, and accuracy
Time horizon	Past, present, and future	Past only, historically based
Reporting frequency	Continuous reporting	Delayed with emphasis on annual reports

Product costing also affects financial reporting. For example, the cost of merchandise is accumulated in an inventory account before it is expensed as cost of goods sold. Accordingly, expense recognition is delayed until the point of sale. As a result, the classification of costs as inventory or expense can affect the amount of assets shown on the balance sheet and the amount of net income shown on the income statement. Since product costing affects financial reporting, it can influence investors, creditors, and taxing authorities as well as managers.

▌Product Costs in Manufacturing Companies

LO2 Identify the components of product cost for a manufacturing entity.

To this point, your experience with product costing is likely limited to merchandising businesses. Determining the amount of product cost for these businesses is a relatively simple matter. The cost of the product is usually the price paid plus some adjustment for transportation costs incurred to acquire the goods. Manufacturing companies are more complex; instead of buying their products, they make them. The cost of making products includes the cost of materials, labor, and other resources (i.e., overhead) that are used in the production process. This means that some of the costs you are accustomed to treating as expenses will now be treated as assets. To understand the accountant's distinctions between a cost and an expense, consider the case of Tabor Manufacturing Company.

Tabor Manufacturing Company

Tabor Manufacturing Company was organized for the purpose of manufacturing wooden tables. The company spent $1,000 to build four tables; the cost included $390 for materials, $470 for work performed by a carpenter, and $140 for tools used in making the tables. What is the amount of expense incurred by Tabor? The answer is zero. The costs of materials, labor, and overhead (i.e., tools) are *product costs*. The $1,000 cash has been transformed into products (i.e., four tables). Accordingly, the payments of cash for materials, labor, and tools were *asset exchange* transactions. One asset (cash) decreased while another asset (tables) increased. An expense will not be recognized until the tables are used (sold); in the meantime, the cost of the tables will be shown in an inventory (asset) account known as **Finished Goods.** Exhibit 1–3 provides a graphical image of the way cash is transformed into inventory.

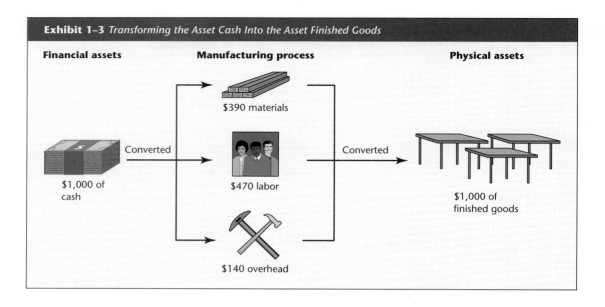

Exhibit 1–3 *Transforming the Asset Cash Into the Asset Finished Goods*

Financial assets — **Manufacturing process** — **Physical assets**

$1,000 of cash → Converted → $390 materials / $470 labor / $140 overhead → Converted → $1,000 of finished goods

Cost per Unit

LO3 Understand the need to determine the average cost per unit of a product.

How much did each table made by Tabor Manufacturing cost? The actual cost for each of the four tables is different. The carpenter probably spent a little more time on some of the tables than others. Likewise, the tools were used in different proportions on each table. Finally, mistakes were likely made on some of the tables that were not made on others. Accordingly, more materials were probably used to make some of the tables. Determining the exact cost of each table requires an unreasonable amount of record keeping; indeed, it is virtually impossible. Minute details such as a millisecond of labor cannot be effectively measured. Even if we could determine the exact cost of each table, the information would be of little use. Minor differences in the cost per unit would make no difference in terms of pricing or other decisions that management needs to make. For these reasons, accountants normally calculate cost per unit as an average. In the case of Tabor Manufacturing, the **average cost** per table is $250 (i.e., $1,000 ÷ 4 units). Unless stated otherwise, you should assume that the term *cost per unit* means *average cost per unit.*

Check Yourself 1–1

All boxes of General Mills' Total Raisin Bran cereal are priced at exactly the same amount in your local grocery store. Does this mean that the actual cost of making each box of cereal was exactly the same price?

Answer No, making each box would not cost exactly the same amount. For example, some boxes contain slightly more or less cereal than other boxes. Accordingly, some boxes cost slightly more or less to make than others do. General Mills uses average cost rather than actual cost to develop its pricing strategy.

Costs Can Be Assets or Expenses

LO4 Understand the difference between a cost and an expense.

It might seem odd that wages paid to production workers are included in an inventory account instead of being expensed on the income statement. Remember, however, that an expense is incurred when an asset *is used* in the process of earning revenue. Notice that the cash paid to production workers was not used to produce revenue. Instead, the cash was used to produce inventory. The revenue will be earned when the inventory is used (sold). So long as the inventory remains on hand, the amount of production wages and other product costs (i.e., materials and overhead) should remain in an inventory account. This means that at the end of an accounting period, some portion of the *product cost* could be on the balance sheet in an asset account (i.e., inventory) while the other portion could be shown as an expense (i.e., cost of goods sold) on the income statement. Costs that are not classified as product costs are normally expensed in the period in which the economic sacrifice is incurred. These costs include *general operating costs, selling and administrative costs, interest costs, and the cost of taxes.* To illustrate, return to the example of Tabor Manufacturing. Recall that Tabor made four tables at an average cost per unit of $250. Assume that Tabor pays an employee a $200 sales commission to sell three of the tables. The sales commission is expensed immediately. The total product cost for the three tables sold is $750 (i.e., 3 tables × $250 each). This cost (i.e., $750) is expensed on the income statement as cost of goods sold. The portion of the total product cost remaining in inventory is $250 (1 table × $250). Exhibit 1–4 shows the relationship between the costs incurred and the expenses recognized for Tabor Manufacturing Company.

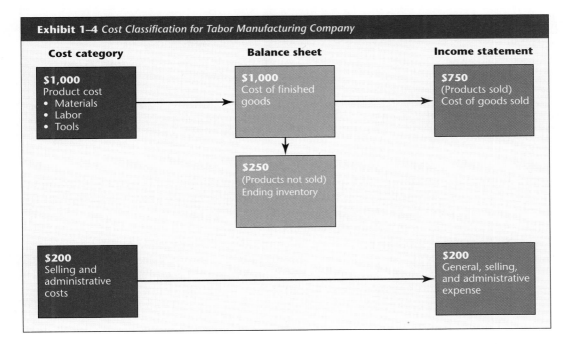

Exhibit 1–4 *Cost Classification for Tabor Manufacturing Company*

Effect of Product Costs on Financial Statements

To illustrate the unique features of accounting for product costs in manufacturing companies, assume that Patillo Manufacturing Company was started on January 1, 2004. Patillo experienced the following accounting events during its first year of operations. *Assume that all transactions are cash transactions.*[5]

LO5 Explain how product versus G, S, & A costs affect financial statements.

1. Acquired $15,000 cash by issuing common stock.
2. Paid $2,000 for the materials that were used to make its products. All products started were completed during the period.
3. Paid $1,200 for salaries of selling and administrative employees.
4. Paid $3,000 for wages of production workers.
5. Paid $2,800 for furniture used in selling and administrative offices.

[5]The illustration assumes that all inventory started during the period was completed during the period. Accordingly, Patillo has only one inventory account entitled Finished Goods Inventory. Many manufacturing companies normally have three levels of inventory at the end of an accounting period including Raw Materials Inventory, Work in Process Inventory (i.e., inventory of partially completed units), and Finished Goods Inventory. A detailed discussion of these inventory items is included in Chapter 11.

Exhibit 1–5 *Effect of Product Versus Selling and Administrative Costs on Financial Statements*

Event No.	Assets					Equity						Cash Flow†	
	Cash	+ Inventory	+ Office Furn.*	+ Manuf. Equip.*	=	Com. Stk.	+ Ret. Ear.	Rev.	− Exp.	= Net Inc.			
1	15,000					15,000						15,000	FA
2	(2,000)	2,000										(2,000)	OA
3	(1,200)						(1,200)		− 1,200	(1,200)		(1,200)	OA
4	(3,000)	3,000										(3,000)	OA
5	(2,800)		2,800									(2,800)	IA
6			(600)				(600)		− 600	(600)			
7	(4,500)			4,500								(4,500)	IA
8		1,000		(1,000)									
9	7,500						7,500	7,500		7,500		7,500	OA
10		(4,000)					(4,000)		− 4,000	(4,000)			
Totals	9,000 +	2,000	+ 2,200	+ 3,500	=	15,000 +	1,700	7,500	− 5,800	= 1,700		9,000	NC

*Negative amounts in these columns represent accumulated depreciation.

†The letters in the far right-hand column of Exhibit 1–5 designate different types of cash flow activities. The letters FA represent financing activities, IA represents investing activities, and OA represents operating activities. The letters NC on the bottom row represent the net change in cash. If you have not studied the statement of cash flows, we recommend that you study the information in the Appendix at the end of this chapter prior to continuing your study. Alternatively, your instructor might prefer to cover cash flow effects later in the course. In this case, you can ignore the information in the Cash Flow column.

6. Recognized depreciation expense on office furniture purchased in Event 5. The furniture acquired on January 1 had a $400 estimated salvage value and a four-year useful life. The annual depreciation charge is $600 (i.e. [$2,800 − $400] ÷ 4).
7. Paid $4,500 for manufacturing equipment.
8. Recognized depreciation expense on equipment purchased in Event 7. The equipment was acquired on January 1. It had a $1,500 estimated salvage value and a three-year useful life. The annual depreciation charge is $1,000 (i.e. [$4,500 − $1,500) ÷ 3).
9. Sold inventory to customers for $7,500 cash.
10. The inventory sold in Event 9 cost $4,000 to make.

The effects of these transactions on the balance sheet, income statement, and statement of cash flows are shown in Exhibit 1–5. Study this exhibit carefully. Pay particular attention to the fact that similar costs such as wages for production workers and salaries for administrative personnel can have radically different effects on the financial statements.

Material Costs

The purchase price of materials used in the manufacturing process is a *product cost.* Materials used to make products are normally called **raw materials.** The cost of raw materials is accumulated in an asset account (i.e., inventory) until the time the products are sold. Remember that materials cost is only one component of total manufacturing costs. When goods are sold, the cost of materials, labor and overhead is expensed as *cost of goods sold.* The costs of materials that can be easily and conveniently traced to products are called **direct raw materials** costs.

Labor Costs

Notice that the salaries paid to selling and administrative employees and the wages paid to production workers are treated differently (i.e., Event 3 versus Event 4). Salaries paid to selling and administrative employees are expensed immediately, but the cost of wages of production workers is added to an inventory account. These wages are expensed as part of cost of goods sold at the time the goods are sold. Prior to the point of sale, labor costs of production employees remain on the balance sheet in an inventory account. Labor costs that can be easily and conveniently traced to products are called **direct labor** costs. The cost flow of wages for production employees versus salaries for selling and administrative personnel is shown in Exhibit 1–6.

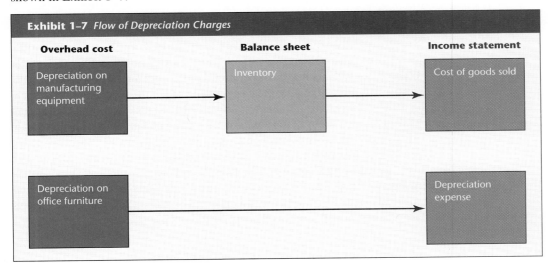

Exhibit 1–6 *Flow of Labor Costs*

Labor costs	Balance sheet	Income statement
Production wages	Inventory	Cost of goods sold
Selling and administrative salaries		Salary expense

Overhead Costs

Although the cost of depreciation totaled $1,600 ($600 on office furniture and $1,000 on manufacturing equipment), only the $600 of depreciation on office furniture appears directly on the income statement. The depreciation on manufacturing equipment is split between the income statement (i.e., cost of goods sold) and the balance sheet (i.e, inventory). The cost flow associated with the depreciation of the manufacturing equipment versus office furniture is shown in Exhibit 1–7.

Exhibit 1–7 *Flow of Depreciation Charges*

Overhead cost	Balance sheet	Income statement
Depreciation on manufacturing equipment	Inventory	Cost of goods sold
Depreciation on office furniture		Depreciation expense

Total Product Cost. A summary of the total product cost incurred by Patillo Manufacturing is shown in Exhibit 1–8.

Exhibit 1–8 *Schedule of Inventory Costs*

Materials	$2,000
Labor	3,000
Manufacturing overhead*	1,000
Total product costs	6,000
Less: Cost of goods sold	(4,000)
Ending inventory balance	$2,000

*Depreciation ([$4,500 − $1,500] ÷ 3)

Exhibit 1–9

PATILLO MANUFACTURING COMPANY
Financial Statements
December 31, 2004

Income Statement

Revenue	$7,500
Cost of Goods Sold	(4,000)
Gross Margin	3,500
G, S, & A Expenses	
Salaries Expense	(1,200)
Depreciation Expense—Office Furniture	(600)
Net Income	$1,700

Balance Sheet

Cash	$ 9,000
Finished Goods Inventory	2,000
Office Furniture	2,800
Accumulated Depreciation	(600)
Manufacturing Equipment	4,500
Accumulated Depreciation	(1,000)
Total Assets	$16,700
Equity	
Common Stock	$15,000
Retained Earnings	1,700
Total Equity	$16,700

Statement of Cash Flows

Operating Activities	
Inflow from Revenue	$ 7,500
Outflow for Inventory	(5,000)
Outflow for S&A Salaries	(1,200)
Net Inflow from Operating Activities	1,300
Investing Activities	
Outflow for Equipment and Furniture	(7,300)
Financing Activities	
Inflow from Capital Acquisitions	15,000
Net Change in Cash	9,000
Beginning Cash Balance	-0-
Ending Cash Balance	$ 9,000

General, Selling, and Administrative Costs

The **general, selling, and administrative costs** (G, S, & A) are normally expensed *in the period* in which the associated economic sacrifice is made. Accordingly, the salary expense for selling and administrative employees and the depreciation on office furniture are shown on the income statement. Because of this recognition pattern, nonproduct expenses are sometimes called **period costs.** The income statement, balance sheet, and statement of cash flows for Patillo Manufacturing is shown in Exhibit 1–9.

The $4,000 of cost of goods sold shown on the income statement includes a portion of the materials, labor, and overhead costs. Similarly, the $2,000 of finished goods inventory on the balance sheet is composed of materials, labor, and overhead. These product costs will be recognized as expense in the next accounting period when the goods have been sold. Accordingly, classifying a cost as a product cost could delay, but not eliminate, its recognition as an expense. All product costs are ultimately recognized as expense. Notice that cost classification does not affect cash flow. Cash inflows and outflows are recognized in the period that cash is collected or paid regardless of whether the cost is recorded in an asset account or is expensed on the income statement.

Overhead Costs: A Closer Look

Costs such as depreciation on manufacturing equipment cannot be easily traced to products. Suppose that Patillo Manufacturing makes both chairs and tables. What part of the depreciation is caused by manufacturing tables versus manufacturing chairs? Similarly, suppose that a production supervisor oversees the labor of employees who work on both tables and chairs. How much of the supervisor's salary should be assigned to tables and how much to chairs? Remember that the supervisor did not work directly on either product line. Likewise, the cost of glue used in the production department would be difficult to trace to tables versus chairs. You could count the drops of glue used on each product, but the information would not be useful enough to merit the time and money spent collecting the data. Costs that cannot be traced to products and services in a *cost-effective* manner are called **indirect costs.** The indirect costs required to make products are called **manufacturing overhead.** Some of the items commonly included in manufacturing overhead are indirect materials, indirect labor, factory utilities, rent of manufacturing facilities, depreciation on manufacturing assets, and production planning and setup costs.

Check
Yourself
1–2

Lawson Manufacturing Company paid production workers wages of $100,000. It incurred materials costs of $120,000 and manufacturing overhead costs of $160,000. Selling and administrative salaries were $80,000. Lawson started and completed 1,000 units of product and sold 800 of these units. The company sets sales prices at $220 above the average per unit production cost. Based on this information alone, determine the amount of gross margin and net income. What is Lawson's pricing strategy called?

Answer Total product cost is $380,000 ($100,000 labor + $120,000 materials + $160,000 overhead). Cost per unit is $380 ($380,000 ÷ 1,000 units). The sales price per unit is $600 ($380 + $220). Cost of goods sold is $304,000 ($380 × 800 units). Sales revenue is $480,000 ($600 × 800 units). Gross margin is $176,000 ($480,000 revenue − $304,000 cost of goods sold). Net income is $96,000 ($176,000 gross margin − $80,000 selling and administrative salaries). Lawson's pricing strategy is called *cost-plus* pricing.

Since indirect costs cannot be effectively traced to products, they are normally distributed to products through a process known as **cost allocation,** which is the process of dividing a total cost into parts and assigning the parts to relevant objects. To illustrate, suppose that production workers spend an eight-hour day making a chair and a table. The chair requires two hours to complete and the table requires six hours. Now suppose that $120 of utilities is consumed during the day. How much of the $120 should be assigned to each piece of furniture? The utility cost cannot be directly traced to each specific piece of furniture, but the piece of furniture that required more labor also likely consumed a larger part of the utility cost. Using this line of reasoning, it is rational to distribute the utility cost to the two pieces of furniture on the basis of *direct labor hours.* Specifically, the utility cost could be allocated at a rate of $15 per hour ($120 ÷ 8 hours). The chair would be assigned $30 of the total cost ($15 per hour × 2 hours). The remaining $90 of cost ($15 × 6 hours) would be assigned to the table. The allocation of the utility cost is shown visually in Exhibit 1–10.

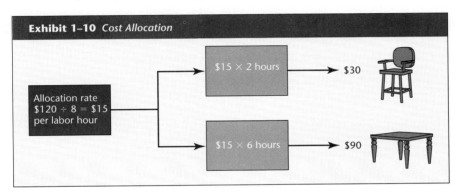

Exhibit 1–10 *Cost Allocation*

We will discuss the details of cost allocation in Chapter 5, but at this stage you should understand that overhead costs are normally allocated to products rather than being traced directly to them.

Manufacturing Product Cost Summary

As indicated, the cost of a product made by a manufacturing company is normally composed of three categories: direct materials, direct labor, and manufacturing overhead. The relevant information regarding these three cost components is summarized in Exhibit 1–11.

■ Importance of Cost Classification

Who cares whether a cost is classified as an asset or an expense? To answer this question, begin by considering how cost classification affects financial statements. Accumulating costs in asset accounts as opposed to recognizing them as expenses produces, at least in the short term, more favorable financial statements. Specifically, *the amount of total assets and net income is higher if a cost is classified as an asset than if it is expensed.* As a result, anyone who has an interest in a company's financial statements is concerned with how costs are classified. For example, managers who are given bonuses based on net income are motivated to classify costs as assets rather than expenses. Similarly, a company that is trying to show a favorable financial position to issue stock or borrow money is motivated to delay expense recognition. In contrast, a company trying to avoid taxes tries to expense costs rather than classify them as assets.

LO6 Understand how cost classification affects financial statements and managerial decisions.

Marion Manufacturing Company

To illustrate some of the practical implications of cost classification, assume that Marion Manufacturing Company (MMC) was started when it acquired $12,000 from the issue of common stock. During its first year of operation, the company incurred specifically identifiable product

Exhibit 1–11 *Components of Manufacturing Product Cost*

Component 1—Direct Materials
Sometimes called *raw materials.* In addition to basic resources such as wood or metals, it can include manufactured parts. For example, engines, glass, and car tires can be considered as raw materials for an automotive manufacturer. If the amount of a material in a product is known, it can usually be classified as a direct material. The cost of direct materials can be easily traced to specific products.

Component 2—Direct Labor
The cost of wages paid to factory workers involved in "hands-on" contact with the products being manufactured. If the amount of time employees worked on a product can be determined, this cost can usually be classified as direct labor. Like direct materials, labor costs must be easily traced to a specific product in order to be classified as a direct cost.

Component 3—Manufacturing Overhead
Costs that cannot be easily traced to specific products. Accordingly, these costs are called *indirect costs.* They can include but are not limited to the following:

1. Indirect materials such as glue, nails, paper, and oil. Indeed, note that indirect materials used in the production process may not appear in the finished product. An example is a chemical solvent used to clean products during the production process but is not a component material found in the final product.
2. Indirect labor such as the cost of salaries paid to production supervisors, inspectors, and maintenance personnel.
3. Rental cost for manufacturing facilities and equipment.
4. Utility costs.
5. Depreciation.
6. Security.
7. The cost of preparing equipment for the manufacturing process (i.e., setup costs).
8. Maintenance cost for the manufacturing facility and equipment.

Exhibit 1–12 *Financial Statements Under Alternative Cost Classification Scenarios*

Income Statements	Scenario 1	Scenario 2
Revenue (700 × $18)	$12,600	$12,600
Cost of Goods Sold	(5,600)	(8,400)
Gross Margin	7,000	4,200
Selling and Administrative Expense	(4,000)	0
Net Income	$ 3,000	$ 4,200

Balance Sheets		
Assets		
Cash	$12,600	$12,600
Inventory	2,400	3,600
Total Assets	$15,000	$16,200
Equity		
Common Stock	$12,000	$12,000
Retained Earnings	3,000	4,200
Total Equity	$15,000	$16,200

Statements of Cash Flows		
Operating Activities		
Inflow from Customers	$12,600	$12,600
Outflow for Inventory	(8,000)	(12,000)
Outflow for S&A	(4,000)	0
Net Inflow from Operating Activities	600	600
Investing Activities	0	0
Financing Activities		
Acquisition of Capital	12,000	12,000
Net Change in Cash	12,600	12,600
Beginning Cash Balance	0	0
Ending Cash Balance	$12,600	$12,600

costs (i.e., materials, labor and overhead) amounting to $8,000. MMC also incurred $4,000 of costs to design the product and plan the manufacturing process. During the accounting period, MMC made 1,000 units of product and sold 700 units at a price of $18 each. All transactions were cash transactions.

Exhibit 1–12 shows financial statements for MMC under two alternative scenarios. The first scenario treats the $4,000 of design and planning costs as selling and administrative expenses. In contrast, the second scenario treats the $4,000 of design and planning costs as product costs; accordingly, these costs are accumulated in the inventory account and expensed when the goods are sold.

Statement Differences

The first difference between the income statements is the amount of cost of goods sold. Under Scenario 1, the total product cost is $8,000, which results in a cost per unit of $8 each (i.e., $8,000 ÷ 1,000 units). Since 700 units were sold, the cost of goods sold amounts to $5,600 ($8 × 700). In contrast, total product cost under Scenario 2 is $12,000 ($8,000 specifically identifiable product costs + $4,000 of design and planning costs classified as product cost). Accordingly, the cost per unit becomes $12 ($12,000 ÷ 1,000 units), and the cost of goods sold becomes $8,400 ($12 × 700 units).

The second difference between the income statements is the amount of selling and administrative expense. Under Scenario 1, the $4,000 of design and planning costs is classified as selling and administrative expense. In contrast, Scenario 2 has no selling and administrative expense because the $4,000 of design and planning costs is classified as a product cost. Under Scenario 2, the design and planning costs constitute $4 per unit ($4,000 ÷ 1,000 units) of the total product cost. As a result, only $2,800 ($4 × 700) of the total design and planning costs are expensed because they are included in cost of goods sold. Therefore, a $2,800 difference exists between the amounts of cost of goods sold under the two scenarios (i.e., $8,400 − $5,600). The remaining $1,200 (i.e., $4 × 300) of the design and planning costs is contained in an inventory account under Scenario 2. This explains the $1,200 difference in the amounts of inventory reported under the two scenarios ($3,600 − $2,400). Since net income is larger under Scenario 2, retained earnings is also higher under that scenario.

Clearly, the Scenario 2 income statement and balance sheet provide a more favorable portrayal of business operations. Notice, however, that cash flow is not affected by the classification of cost. The same amount of cash was collected and paid under both scenarios. Since cost of goods sold and selling and administrative expense are both considered to be operating items, no difference exists in the amount of cash flow from operating activities regardless of whether the $4,000 of design and planning costs is classified as a product cost or a selling and administrative expense.

Practical Implications

The financial statement differences shown in Exhibit 1–12 are merely *timing differences.* Indeed, when the remaining inventory is sold, the $1,200 portion of the design and planning costs included in inventory under Scenario 2 will be expensed through cost of goods sold. In other words, once all of the inventory is sold, total expenses and retained earnings will be the same under both scenarios. The accumulation of cost in an inventory account acts only to delay the ultimate expense recognition. Even so, the temporary effects on the financial statements can have important implications with respect to the (1) availability of financing, (2) motivations of management, and (3) payment of income taxes.

Availability of Financing

The willingness of creditors and investors to provide capital to a business is influenced by their expectations of the business's future financial performance. If a business is able to generate sufficient cash flows, it will be able to make interest payments and to repay the principal balance of its liabilities. Investors are interested in future earnings because they will share in the wealth. Because creditors and investors use financial statement data to predict future performance, their credit and investment decisions can be influenced by the way costs are classified (i.e., asset versus expense). In general, more favorable financial statements enhance a company's ability to obtain financing from creditors or investors.

The **efficient markets hypothesis** supports the argument that creditors and investors look to the substance of business events regardless of the way the transactions are reported in financial statements; therefore, the credit and investment markets are efficient. Whether creditors and investors are deceived by spurious reporting practices is a matter of unresolved debate.[6] Even if we assume that markets are efficient, we must acknowledge the fact that many restrictive covenants[7] in credit agreements use financial statement data. Executive compensation also can be influenced by financial statement data. Accordingly, financial statement data

---

[6]There is widespread acceptance of the weak and semistrong forms of the efficient markets hypothesis. These forms relate to efficient assimilation of public information. There is considerable controversy regarding the strong form, which suggests efficiency with respect to insider information.

[7]A restrictive covenant is an agreement or clause in a debt contract that provides assurance to creditors regarding the payment of principal and interest. Such agreements frequently involve restrictions that are measured by financial ratios. These ratios are based on financial statement data.

might affect the type of executive talent that a company is able to attract. As a result, financial reporting practices can have real economic consequences that impact investment and credit decisions regardless of whether the market is efficient. In other words, classifying costs as assets rather than expensing them might affect the willingness of creditors and investors to provide capital to a business.

Management Motivation

As suggested, financial statement data might affect executive compensation. For example, assume that Marion Manufacturing has a management incentive plan that provides a bonus pool equal to 10 percent of net income. Under Scenario 1, managers would receive $300 ($3,000 $\times$ 0.10). In contrast, managers would receive $420 ($4,200 $\times$ 0.10) under Scenario 2. Do not be deceived by the relatively small numbers. We could illustrate with hundreds of thousands of dollars just as well as hundreds of dollars; the amounts in the illustrations are small to facilitate communication. Under these circumstances, managers would clearly favor Scenario 2. Indeed, managers might be tempted to misclassify costs to manipulate the content of financial statements.

Since accumulating costs in asset accounts merely delays expense recognition, why would a manager be tempted to misclassify costs? After all, isn't the benefit only temporary? Not necessarily. A manager who repeats the practice year after year can maintain a continual delay. In other words, even as the old costs reach the point of expense recognition, new costs are being added to asset accounts. Accordingly, a new delay replaces the old delay. The delay can be maintained so long as the practice continues. It is also important to recognize that even temporary delays can make a difference. Suppose that the manager classifies costs in a manner that provides him a compensation bonus in 2005 and then changes jobs in 2006. Under these circumstances, the manager receives a bonus that he otherwise would not have obtained. Even if the delay of expense recognition serves only to benefit the manager by allowing him to receive a bonus in 2005 that he will otherwise obtain in 2006, the manager will gain a *time value of money* benefit. In other words, receiving the bonus early has a value. At a minimum, the manager could invest the bonus money and earn interest during the time of the delay.

To reduce the temptations of statement manipulation, many companies tie bonus plans to the company's stock price rather than to its financial statements. To the extent that the market is efficient, it rewards performance that adds value to the company by bidding up the company's stock price. An efficient market is not deceived by accounting practices designed solely to manipulate financial statements. The growing number of companies using stock options in their incentive programs might suggest that today's business organizations believe that stock prices are better indicators of performance than are financial statements.

Income Tax Considerations

Since income taxes are determined by taking a designated percentage of taxable income, managers seek to minimize taxes by reporting the minimum amount of taxable income. Accordingly, Scenario 1 in Exhibit 1–12 depicts the most favorable tax condition. In other words, with respect to taxes, managers prefer to classify costs as expenses rather than assets. Obviously, the Internal Revenue Service prefers the opposite treatment. Disagreements between the Internal Revenue Service and taxpayers are ultimately settled in federal courts.

LO7 Appreciate the need for a code of ethical conduct.

■ Ethical Considerations

The preceding discussion provides a glimmer of insight into the conflicts of interest that management accountants face in the course of performing their duties. Accountants hold positions of trust within their organizations and the business community. The information they generate is used to make decisions that can have a significant financial impact on many individuals. Accordingly, management accountants must be prepared not only to make hard choices between legitimate alternatives but also to face conflicts of a more sinister nature. Some of the more common conflicts that accountants might encounter include requests or pressure to

1. Perform duties for which they have not been trained to perform competently.
2. Disclose confidential information.
3. Compromise their integrity through falsification, embezzlement, bribery, and so on.
4. Distort objectivity by issuing misleading or incomplete reports.

Yielding to such temptations can have disastrous consequences. The primary job of a management accountant is to provide information that is useful in making decisions. Information is worthless if its provider cannot be trusted. Accordingly, accountants have an obligation to themselves, their organizations, and the public to maintain high standards of ethical conduct. In recognition of this obligation, the Institute of Management Accountants (IMA)[8] has issued a statement entitled *Standards of Ethical Conduct for Management Accountants,* which is summarized in Exhibit 1–13. In addition to these professional standards, management accountants are frequently required to abide by organizational codes of ethics. The failure to perform in accordance with professional and organizational ethical standards can lead to personal disgrace and loss of employment.

Accountants are placed in positions of trust that foster the temptation to violate criminal laws. Misleading investors and creditors through deliberate misrepresentations in financial reports is an act of criminal fraud that is ultimately punishable by incarceration. Likewise, taking money or other assets in violation of trust constitutes criminal embezzlement. By the very nature of their work, accountants are presented with disproportionate opportunities for criminal misconduct. Make no mistake about it: Ethical and criminal misconduct is a serious matter in business practice.

Exhibit 1–13 *Standards of Ethical Conduct for Management Accountants*

Competence Management accountants have a responsibility to
- Maintain an appropriate level of professional competence by ongoing development of their knowledge and skills.
- Perform their professional duties in accordance with relevant laws, regulations, and technical standards.
- Prepare complete and clear reports and recommendations after appropriate analysis of relevant and reliable information.

Confidentiality Management accountants have a responsibility to
- Refrain from disclosing confidential information acquired in the course of their work except when authorized, unless legally obligated to do so.
- Inform subordinates as appropriate regarding the confidentiality of information acquired in the course of their work and monitor their activities to ensure the maintenance of the confidentiality.
- Refrain from using or appearing to use confidential information acquired in the course of their work for unethical or illegal advantage either personally or through third parties.

Integrity Management accountants have a responsibility to
- Avoid actual or apparent conflicts of interest and advise all appropriate parties of any potential conflict.
- Refrain from engaging in any activity that would prejudice their ability to carry out their duties ethically.
- Refuse any gift, favor, or hospitality that would influence or would appear to influence their actions.
- Refrain from either actively or passively subverting the attainment of the organization's legitimate and ethical objectives.
- Recognize and communicate professional limitations or other constraints that would preclude responsible judgment or successful performance of an activity.
- Communicate unfavorable as well as favorable information and professional judgments or opinions.
- Refrain from engaging in or supporting any activity that would discredit the profession.

Objectivity Management accountants have a responsibility to
- Communicate information fairly and objectively.
- Disclose fully all relevant information that could reasonably be expected to influence an intended user's understanding of the reports, comments, and recommendations presented.

---

[8]The Institute of Management Accountants is the largest professional organization of management accountants in the United States. The organization has conducted and reported on many research studies pertaining to management accounting subjects. The Institute issues a series of standards designed to influence the conduct of management accountants. The IMA publishes the monthly journal *Management Accounting.* For additional information on the Institute, visit its web site at *http://www.imanet.org.*

Jeffrey Wigand is famous for whistleblowing on the tobacco industry. Assume that Mr. Wigand was an active member of IMA. Assume further that he had obtained his information in the course of completing his duties as a management accountant of the tobacco company. Under these circumstances, would Mr. Wigands's whistleblowing disclosures conform to the code of ethical conduct advocated by the IMA? The answer is no. According to IMA standards (*SMA Number 1C,* 1983), a management accountant who is unable to satisfactorily resolve an ethical conflict between himself and his employer is required to resign from the organization and to submit an informative memorandum to an appropriate representative of the organization. The communication of such conflicts to authorities outside the organization is a breach of confidentiality that is inappropriate unless required by law.

Source: G. Rechtschaffen and J. A. Yardley, "Whistleblowing and the Law," *Management Accounting,* March 1995, p. 40.

▌Common Features of Criminal and Ethical Misconduct

People who become involved in unethical or criminal behavior usually do so unexpectedly. They start with small indiscretions that evolve gradually into more serious violations of trust. Accordingly, *awareness* constitutes a key ingredient for the avoidance of unethical or illegal conduct. In a effort to increase awareness, Donald Cressey studied hundreds of criminal cases to identify the primary factors that lead to trust violations.[9] He found these three factors were common to all cases:

- The existence of a secret problem.
- The presence of an opportunity.
- The capacity for rationalization.

It is important to note that individuals have different ideas about what they think must be kept secret. Consider two responses to the problem of an imminent business failure. One person might feel so ashamed that she cannot discuss the problem with anyone. Another person in the same situation might want to talk to anyone, even a stranger, in the hope of getting help. Cressey's findings suggest that the person who is inclined toward secrecy is more likely to accept an unethical or illegal solution. In other words, secrecy increases vulnerability.

Few individuals like to think of themselves as evil. Accordingly, they develop rationalizations to justify their misconduct. Cressey found a significant number of embezzlers who contended that they were only "borrowing the money" even after being convicted and sentenced to jail. Some of the more common rationalizations include peer pressure, loyalty to unscrupulous superiors, family needs, revenge, and personal vices such as drug addiction, gambling, and promiscuity. To avoid involvement in ethical misconduct, accountants must develop a strong sense of personal responsibility. They cannot allow themselves to blame other people or unfair circumstances for their problems. They must learn to hold themselves personally accountable for their actions.

[9]D. R. Cressey, *Other People's Money* (Montclair, NJ: Patterson Smith, 1973).

Ethical misconduct is a serious offense in the accounting profession. Accountants must realize that in this arena, their careers are vulnerable to a single mistake. A person caught in white-collar crime loses the opportunity to hold a white-collar job. Second chances are rarely granted to them. Given this condition, it is extremely important that you learn how to recognize and avoid the common features of ethical misconduct. To help you prepare for the real-world ethical dilemmas that you are likely to encounter, we have included an ethics case at the end of each chapter. When working with these cases, you should attempt to identify the effects of (1) secrecy, (2) opportunity, and (3) rationalization.

■ Upstream and Downstream Costs

Product costing as described thus far pertains to the measurement of cost for financial reporting purposes. In other words, we have been interested in deciding which costs go on the balance sheet versus the income statement. Product costing for financial reporting focuses on the measurement of costs incurred during the manufacturing process. Most companies incur product-related costs before and after, as well as during, the manufacturing process. For example, Ford Motor Company incurs significant research and development costs prior to starting to mass produce a new model car. These **upstream costs** occur before the manufacturing process begins. Similarly, companies normally incur significant costs after the manufacturing process is complete. Examples of **downstream costs** include the costs of transportation, advertising, sales commissions, and bad debts.

LO8 Distinguish product costs from upstream and downstream costs.

Profitability analysis requires attention to upstream and downstream costs as well as manufacturing product costs. To be profitable, a company must recover the total cost of developing, producing, and delivering its products to its customers. To illustrate, assume that Pearson Electronics incurs $30,000,000 in research and development costs leading to the production of a new computer-processing chip. Manufacturing costs including materials, labor, and overhead costs are expected to be approximately $150 per chip. Furthermore, the company expects to pay a sales commission of $25 per chip to its sales staff. The company expects to produce and sell 1,500,000 chips before the processor becomes technologically obsolete. Assuming that the company desires to earn a profit margin equal to 20 percent of cost, what price should it charge per processor? To answer this question, we must first determine what is meant by *20 percent of cost*. More specifically, what is cost? Do we mean manufacturing product cost (i.e., $150), or do we mean the total of all costs associated with the product, which amounts to $195 ($150 manufacturing cost + upstream research and development of $20 [$30,000,000 ÷ 1,500,000 units] + downstream sales commissions of $25)?

If the sales price is based solely on manufacturing product cost, the sales price is $180 ($150 + [150 × 20%]). A $180 sales price is insufficient to cover the $195 total cost per unit of developing, manufacturing, and selling the product. Clearly, the pricing decision must include *all* costs associated with the product. The manufacturing product cost is only a subset of the total cost that must be considered in the pricing decision. Indeed, the effective management of a business organization requires careful analysis of the costs of all activities that it performs.

■ Product Costs in Service Companies

Service companies differ from manufacturing companies in that they provide assistance rather than goods to their customers. For example, a doctor prescribes a treatment to help the patient to get well. Similarly, AT&T provides a communication system that permits conversations

LO9 Understand how products provided by service companies differ from products made by manufacturing companies.

between individuals who are separated by a distance that would otherwise prohibit interaction. Likewise, an airline provides transportation service, and a bank aids customers with financial transactions. Service businesses differ from manufacturing entities in that they have no inventory. How does product costing relate to a service company that has no tangible output? In other words, how can a company have product costs when it has no inventory?

First, cost accumulation is not restricted to tangible output. Clearly it costs money to provide medical advice, just as it costs money to make pharmaceutical products. Indeed, *service companies, like manufacturing companies, incur materials, labor, and overhead costs* in the process of providing services to their customers. For example, a hospital providing medical service to a patient incurs costs for medical supplies (materials), salaries of doctors and nurses (labor), and depreciation, utilities, insurance, and so on (overhead).

The *primary difference between manufacturing entities and service companies is that the products provided by service companies are consumed immediately.* In contrast, products made by manufacturing companies can be retained in the form of inventory prior to being purchased by customers. Like their counterparts in manufacturing, managers of service companies are under increasing pressure to lower costs, improve quality, and increase productivity. Information regarding product costing is useful in the accomplishment of these goals regardless of whether the consumption of the product is immediate or delayed. Although service companies might not report product costs in the form of inventory on their financial statements, they certainly segregate and analyze product costs for internal decision-making purposes.

Check Yourself 1–3

The cost of making a Burger King hamburger includes the cost of materials, labor, and overhead. Does this mean that Burger King is a manufacturing company?

Answer No, Burger King is not a manufacturing company. It is a service company because its products are consumed immediately. In contrast, there may be a considerable delay between the time the product of a manufacturing company is made and the time it is consumed. For example, it could be several months between the time Ford Motor Company makes an Explorer and the time the Explorer is ultimately sold to a customer. The primary difference between service and manufacturing companies is that manufacturing companies have inventories of products and service companies do not.

▌Cost Measurement in Managerial Reports

Your background in financial accounting might mislead you with respect to the way that cost data are likely to appear in managerial reports. Financial accounting suggests that costs are used solely to develop a single set of financial statements. This is not true with respect to managerial reporting. Managers are interested not only in the profitability of the business as a whole but also in the profitability of its various subcomponents. For example, managers might be interested in the profitability of particular products, customers, departments, equipment purchases, and business strategies. Because managers analyze different subcomponents of a business, the same cost might be viewed from different perspectives. For instance, although research and development costs are usually included in general, selling, and administrative expenses for the purpose of financial reports, these costs might be considered a component of product cost for the purpose of making a pricing decision. In addition, research and development could be considered a departmental cost if management were trying to assess the effectiveness of the research department. Likewise, the same research and development costs might be included in a social responsibility report when the president of the company is trying to convince consumers that the company is concerned with the development of environmentally safe products. Be prepared to broaden your perspective regarding the measurement and use of cost data. You must *interpret* cost data in a variety of different contexts. Accordingly, *thinking* will serve you more effectively than *memorizing.*

Emerging Trends in Managerial Accounting

Many factors are contributing to the development of a *global economy.* Satellites enable worldwide communication; super ships move vast supplies of merchandise swiftly and efficiently across oceans. Delivery companies such as Federal Express and United Parcel Service guarantee overnight delivery to virtually every corner of the world. Executives move across international boundaries in supersonic aircraft. Trade agreements reduce or eliminate tariffs, quotas, and other barriers to free trade. As a result, many companies face worldwide competition. The new competitive environment has forced these companies to reengineer their production and delivery systems to eliminate waste, reduce errors, and minimize costs.

LO10 Explain how emerging trends are affecting the managerial accounting discipline.

One of the key ingredients to successful **reengineering** is a practice known as *benchmarking.* **Benchmarking** involves the identification of the **best practices** used by world-class competitors. By studying and mimicking these practices, a company uses benchmarking to implement the most effective methods of accomplishing various tasks. Four widely recognized *best practices* identified by world-class companies include total quality management (TQM), activity-based management (ABM), value-added assessment, and just-in-time inventory (JIT).

Total Quality Management

To promote effective operations, many companies have implemented **total quality management (TQM)** programs. TQM is a two-dimensional management philosophy that includes (1) a systematic problem-solving philosophy that encourages front-line workers to achieve *zero defects* and (2) an organizational commitment to achieving *customer satisfaction.* A key component of TQM is **continuous improvement,** which refers to an ongoing process through which employees learn to eliminate waste, reduce response time, minimize defects, and simplify the design and delivery of products and services to customers.

focus on International Issues

Where in the World Do New Managerial Accounting Practices Come From?

Many of the emerging practices in managerial accounting have their foundations in Asian companies. These companies established employee relationships that achieve continuous improvement by encouraging employees to participate in the design as well as the execution of their work. Employee empowerment through the practice known as *kaizen management* recognizes gradual, continuous improvement as the ultimate key to cost reduction and quality control. Employees are encouraged to identify and eliminate nonvalue-added activities, idle time, and waste. The response is overwhelming when employee suggestions are taken seriously. For example, the Toyota Motor Corporation reported the receipt of approximately two million employee suggestions in one year alone.

Source: Takao Tanaka, "Kaizen Budgeting: Toyota's Cost Control System Under TQC," *Journal of Cost Management,* Winter 1996, p. 62.

Activity-Based Management

Andy Grove's strategic inflection points discussed at the beginning of this chapter are frequently based on simple changes in perspective. For example, imagine how the realization that the world is round instead of flat changed people's approach to travel. A developing strategic inflection point for management accounting stems from realizing that an organization cannot manage *costs*. Instead, it manages the *activities* that cause costs to be incurred. **Activities** are the actions taken by an organization to accomplish its mission. The primary mission of all organizations is to provide products (i.e., goods and services) that their customers *value*. Accordingly, the sequence of activities through which an organization provides products to its customers is called a **value chain. Activity-based management** seeks to manage the value chain to create new or to refine existing **value-added activities** and to eliminate or reduce *nonvalue-added activities*. As its name implies, a value-added activity is any unit of work that contributes to a product's ability to satisfy customer needs. Cooking adds value to food served to a hungry customer. **Nonvalue-added** activities are tasks undertaken that do not contribute to a product's ability to satisfy customer needs. Waiting for the oven to preheat so that food can be cooked does not add value. Most customers value cooked food, but they do not value waiting for it.

Value-Added Assessment

Activity-based management requires a critical assessment of the full range of activities that cause the customers of a business to *value* its products. To illustrate, consider the value-added activities associated with a pizza restaurant. Begin with a customer who is hungry for pizza; certain activities must be performed to satisfy that hunger. These activities are outlined in Exhibit 1–14. At a minimum, the restaurant must conduct some type of research and development (obtain a recipe), obtain the raw materials (gather the ingredients), manufacture the product (mix and cook the ingredients), market the product (i.e., advise the consumer of its availability), and deliver the product (transfer the pizza to the customer).

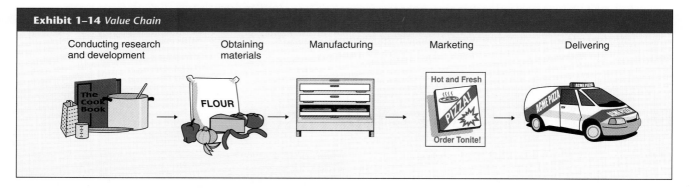

Exhibit 1–14 *Value Chain*

Conducting research and development → Obtaining materials → Manufacturing → Marketing → Delivering

Businesses are able to gain competitive advantages by adding activities that effectively satisfy customer needs. For example, Domino's Pizza grew rapidly as a result of its recognition of the value customers placed on the convenience of having a pizza delivered to their homes. Alternatively, Little Caesar's has been highly successful at satisfying the value customers place on low prices. Other restaurateurs might seek to satisfy customer values pertaining to taste, ambiance, or location. Businesses can also gain competitive advantages by identifying and eliminating nonvalue-added activities. By eliminating nonvalue-added activities, a business can provide products of equal quality at a lower cost than its competitors. Some of the more common nonvalue-added activities and approaches taken to eliminate them are discussed in the next section of this text.

Just-in-Time Inventory

A common nonvalue-added activity found in many types of business organizations is maintaining excess amounts of inventory. Consumers want inventory to be available when they need it, but they do not benefit when more inventory is stored than is necessary to meet their

At Ford Motor Company's plant in Valencia, Spain, suppliers feed parts such as these bumpers just in time and in the right order directly to the assembly line.

demands. Indeed, the customer could suffer from excessive inventory holdings because some of the cost of inventory maintenance is passed on in the form of higher prices. Many businesses have been able to simultaneously reduce their inventory holding costs and increase customer satisfaction by making inventory available **just in time (JIT)** for customer consumption. For example, hamburgers that are made to order are fresher and more individualized than those that are made in advance and stored until a customer places an order. Many fast-food restaurants have discovered that JIT systems lead not only to greater customer satisfaction but also to reduced costs through the elimination of waste.

Traditionally, manufacturing companies have maintained large amounts of inventory to avoid production disruptions. Large supplies of raw materials are maintained to ensure their availability in case suppliers are unable to provide the materials when they are needed. Large numbers of finished goods also are maintained to ensure the ability to meet unexpected customer demands. Some companies even maintain inventories of partially completed goods as a buffer against the possibility of internal disruptions such as strikes or mechanical failures. For example, the entire production process of Ford Motor Company could be halted if employees working in the brake factory went out on strike. This potential disaster can be avoided if Ford maintains a large enough supply of brakes to provide a cushion of time before a strike can be settled.

Unfortunately, maintaining large amounts of inventory is expensive. Many **inventory holding costs** are obvious: financing, warehouse space, supervision, theft, damage, and obsolescence. Other costs are hidden: diminished motivation, sloppy work, inattentive attitudes, and increased production time. Employees are less concerned with avoiding problems that create shortages if they feel there is an ample supply of inventory available to cover unanticipated shortfalls. For example, a purchasing agent was overheard making the comment, "I'm not sure if the clerk got that order right. Anyway, it doesn't really matter. If they send us the wrong stuff, we have a large enough supply of parts on hand that we have time to send back the wrong parts and reorder the right ones." The agent failed to consider the cost of processing a new order. Someone must be paid to inspect the goods when they arrive. If the order is wrong, someone must repackage the merchandise and return it to the supplier. Someone must spend time reordering the right parts. These costs could be avoided if the supply of inventory were low enough to motivate the purchasing agent to get the order right in the first place.

To increase efficiency and profitability, many managers are asking whether the value added by inventory buffers is sufficient to justify the costs incurred. It could cost less to solve the problems that create the need for inventory than it costs to maintain the inventory. For example, avoiding a strike could cost less than maintaining enough inventory to wait out its settlement. Similarly, establishing **most-favored customer status** with reliable suppliers could ensure a steady supply of raw materials even when shortages exist for other customers. Such assurances can eliminate the need for maintaining raw materials inventories. Likewise, proper mechanical maintenance can reduce the likelihood of mechanical disruptions, thereby reducing the need for inventories of partially completed goods. Furthermore, communication and commitments from customers can stabilize demand and minimize the need for finished goods inventories. Under ideal conditions, materials and finished products are made available *just in time* to satisfy manufacturing and customer needs, thereby eliminating the requirement for inventories. Few companies have been able to reach the JIT ideal of zero inventory, but many have reduced the size of their inventories and the holding costs associated with them.

Check Yourself 1–4

A strike at a General Motors brake plant caused an almost immediate shutdown of many of the company's assembly plants. What could have caused such a rapid and widespread shutdown?

Answer A rapid and widespread shutdown could have occurred because General Motors uses a just-in-time inventory system. With a just-in-time inventory system, there is no stockpile of inventory to draw on when strikes or other forces disrupt inventory deliveries. This illustrates a potential negative effect of using a just-in-time inventory system.

Just-in-Time Illustration

To illustrate the benefits of a JIT system, consider the case of Paula Elliot, a student at a large urban university. She helps support herself by selling flowers on a street corner. In the late afternoon, she purchases flowers from a florist, drives them to a downtown location, and sells them to people who are on their way home from work. She pays $2 for a single stem rose and sells each rose for $3. She purchases 25 roses per day and works three days per week. Some days she does not have enough flowers to meet customer demand. On other days, she must throw away one or two flowers. She believes that quality is important and refuses to sell flowers that are not fresh. During the month of May, she purchased 300 roses and sold 280. She calculated her driving cost to be $45. Her income statement for the month is shown in Exhibit 1–15.

Exhibit 1–15 *Income Statement*

Sales Revenue (280 units × $3 per unit)	$840
Cost of Goods Sold (300 units × $2 per unit)	(600)
Gross Margin	240
Driving Expense	(45)
Net Income	$195

Exhibit 1–16 *Income Statement*

Sales Revenue (310 units × $3 per unit)	$930
Cost of Goods Sold (310 units × $2 per unit)	(620)
Gross Margin	310
Driving Expense	0
Net Income	$310

After studying just-in-time inventory systems in her managerial accounting class, Paula was convinced that she could apply the concepts to increase the profitability of her own small business. She began by *reengineering* her distribution system. Specifically, she began purchasing her flowers from a florist located within walking distance of her sales location. She had considered purchasing from this florist earlier but had rejected the idea because the florist's normal selling price was $2.25 per rose. That price was too high considering her current cost of $2.00 per rose. After learning about *most-favored customer status,* however, she decided to discuss the matter with the prospective florist. By guaranteeing the new florist that she would buy at least 30 roses per week, she was able to convince him to match her current cost of $2.00 per rose. The florist agreed that she could make purchases in batches of any size so long as the total amounted to at least 30 per week. Under this arrangement, Paula was able to buy roses *just in time* to meet customer demand. Each day she purchased a small number of flowers. When she ran out, she simply returned to the florist for additional ones.

The JIT system also enabled her to eliminate the *nonvalue-added activities* associated with driving to the old florist, thereby eliminating the driving expense. Customer satisfaction actually improved because no one was ever turned away because of the lack of inventory. In June, Paula was able to buy and sell 310 roses with no waste and no driving expense. The June income statement is shown in Exhibit 1–16.

Paula was ecstatic about the $115 increase in profitability (i.e., $310 in June − $195 May = $115 increase), but she was puzzled as to exactly what had caused the change. Clearly, she had saved $40 by avoiding waste (20 flowers × $2 each). She had also eliminated $45 of driving expenses. However, these two factors explained only $85 ($40 waste + $45 driving expense) of the $115 total. What had caused the remaining $30 ($115 − $85) increase in profitability? Paula decided to ask her accounting professor to help her understand the remaining $30 difference.

The professor explained that the May sales had suffered from *lost opportunities.* Recall that under the old inventory system, Paula had to turn away some prospective customers because she sold out of flowers before all customers were served. Notice that sales increased from 280 roses in May to 310 roses in June. The most logical explanation for the 30 unit difference (310 − 280) is that customers who would have purchased flowers in May were unable to do so because of a lack of availability. Accordingly, May's sales suffered from a lost opportunity to earn a gross margin of $1 per flower on 30 roses. In accounting terms, May's profitability suffered from a $30 **opportunity cost.** This cost provides the missing link in explaining the difference in the profitability between May and June. The total $115 difference is composed of (1) savings of $40 from the elimination of waste, (2) driving expense of $45, and (3) opportunity cost of $30.

In summary, companies that carry inventory incur two types of cost. The first category is explicit holding cost that includes financing charges, warehouse space, personnel, and lost, damaged, stolen, or otherwise wasted inventory. The second is the hidden cost of lost opportunities such as lost sales or employee inefficiency. Just-in-time inventory systems eliminate or diminish these costs by managing resources so that they are consumed immediately, thereby eliminating the need for inventories. The subject of opportunity cost has widespread application and will be discussed in more depth in subsequent chapters of the text.

Value Chain Analysis Across Companies

Comprehensive value chain analysis extends from obtaining raw materials to the ultimate disposal of finished products. It encompasses the activities performed not only by a particular organization but also by that organization's suppliers and those who service its finished products. For example, PepsiCo must be concerned with the activities of the company that supplies the containers that hold its soda as well as the retail companies that sell its products. If cans of Pepsi fail to open properly, the customer is likely to blame PepsiCo rather than the supplier of the cans. Likewise, a customer who receives a bad glass of Pepsi in a restaurant may conclude that the soda brand is distasteful rather than blaming the restaurateur for failing to properly mix carbonated water with the soft drink syrup. Comprehensive value chain analysis can lead to the identification and elimination of nonvalue-added activities that occur between companies. For example, container companies could be encouraged to build manufacturing facilities near Pepsi's bottling factories, thereby eliminating nonvalue-added activities associated with transporting empty containers from the manufacturer to the bottling facility. The result is a cost saving that benefits the customer by lowering costs without affecting quality.

Managerial accounting focuses on the information needs of *internal* users, while *financial accounting* focuses on the information needs of *external* users. Managerial accounting uses a wider range of information such as economic, operating, nonfinancial, and financial data. Managerial accounting information is local (i.e., pertains to the company's subunits), is limited by cost/benefit considerations, is more concerned with relevance and timeliness, and is future oriented. Financial accounting information, on the other hand, is more global than managerial accounting information. In other words, it supplies information that applies to the whole company. Financial accounting is regulated by numerous authorities, is characterized by objectivity, is focused on reliability and accuracy, and is historical in nature.

a look
back

Both managerial and financial accounting are concerned with product costing. Financial accountants need product cost information to determine the amount of inventory shown on the balance sheet and the amount of cost of goods sold shown on the income statement. Managerial accountants need to know the cost of products for pricing decisions and for control and evaluation purposes. When determining the unit cost of products, managers use the average cost per unit. The actual cost of each product requires an unreasonable amount of time and record keeping and makes no difference in product pricing and product costs control decisions.

Product costs are the costs incurred in the process of making products. They include the costs of direct labor, direct materials, and overhead. *Overhead costs* are product costs that cannot be cost effectively traced to the product; therefore, they are assigned to products through a process known as *cost allocation.* Examples of overhead include indirect materials, indirect labor, depreciation, rent, and utilities on manufacturing facilities. Product costs are first accumulated in an asset account (inventory). They are expensed as cost of goods sold in the period the inventory is sold. The difference between the sales revenue and cost of goods sold is called *gross margin.*

General, selling, and administrative costs are classified separately from product costs. They are subtracted from the gross margin to determine net income. General, selling, and administrative costs can be divided into two categories. The costs that occur before the manufacturing process begins (e.g., research and development costs) are called *upstream costs.* The costs that incur after manufacturing is complete (e.g., transportation) are called *downstream costs.*

Service companies, like manufacturing companies, incur materials, labor, and overhead costs, but the products provided by service companies are consumed immediately. Therefore, service company product costs are not accumulated in an inventory account.

A *code of ethical conduct* is needed in the accounting profession because accountants hold positions of trust and face conflicts of interest. In recognition of the temptations that accountants face, the IMA has issued the statement *Standard of Ethical Conduct for Management Accountants,* which provides accountants guidance in resisting temptations and in making difficult decisions.

Emerging trends such as *just-in-time inventory* and *activity-based management* are methods that many companies have used to reengineer their production and delivery systems to eliminate waste, reduce errors, and minimize costs. Activity-based management seeks to eliminate or reduce *nonvalue-added activities* and to create new *value-added activities.* Just-in-time inventory seeks to reduce inventory holding costs and to lower prices for customers by making inventory available just in time for customer consumption.

a look forward

Now that you have gained an appreciation for one type of cost classification (i.e., product versus G, S, & A), you are ready to see how other classifications can be used to facilitate managerial decision making. In the next chapter, you will learn how to classify costs according to the *behavior* costs exhibited when the number of units of product increases or decreases (i.e., volume of activity changes). More specifically, you will learn to distinguish between costs that vary with activity volume changes versus costs that remain fixed with activity volume changes. You will learn not only to recognize *cost behavior* but also how such recognition can facilitate the evaluation of business risk and opportunity.

SELF-STUDY REVIEW PROBLEM

Tuscan Manufacturing Company makes a unique headset for use with mobile phones. During 2003, its first year of operations, Tuscan experienced the following accounting events. Other than the adjusting entries for depreciation, assume that all transactions are cash transactions.

1. Acquired $850,000 cash from the issue of common stock.
2. Paid $50,000 of research and development costs to develop the headset.
3. Paid $140,000 for the materials used to make headsets, all of which were started and completed during the year.
4. Paid salaries of $82,200 to selling and administrative employees.
5. Paid wages of $224,000 to production workers.

6. Paid $48,000 to purchase furniture used in selling and administrative offices.
7. Recognized depreciation on the office furniture. The furniture, acquired January 1, had an $8,000 estimated salvage value and a four-year useful life. The amount of depreciation is computed as ([cost − salvage] ÷ useful life). Specifically, ([$48,000 − $8,000] ÷ 4 = $10,000).
8. Paid $65,000 to purchase manufacturing equipment.
9. Recognized depreciation on the manufacturing equipment. The equipment, acquired January 1, had a $5,000 estimated salvage value and a three-year useful life. The amount of depreciation is computed as ([cost − salvage] ÷ useful life). Specifically, ([$65,000 − $5,000] ÷ 3 = $20,000).
10. Paid $136,000 for rent and utility costs on the manufacturing facility.
11. Paid $41,000 for inventory holding expenses for completed headsets (rental of warehouse space, salaries of warehouse personnel, and other general storage costs).
12. Tuscan started and completed 20,000 headset units during 2003. The company sold 18,400 headsets at a price of $38 per unit.
13. Compute the average product cost per unit and recognize the appropriate amount of cost of goods sold.

Required
a. Show how these events affect the balance sheet, income statement, and statement of cash flows by recording them in a horizontal financial statements model.
b. Explain why Tuscan's recognition of cost of goods sold expense had no impact on cash flow.
c. Prepare a formal income statement for the year.
d. Distinguish between the product costs and the upstream and downstream costs that Tuscan incurred.
e. The company president believes that Tuscan could save money by buying the inventory that it currently makes. The warehouse supervisor said that would not be possible because the purchase price of $27 per unit was above the $26 average cost per unit of making the product. Assuming that the purchased inventory would be available on demand, explain how the company president could be correct and why the warehouse supervisor could be biased in his assessment of the option to buy the inventory.

Solution to Requirement a

Event No.	Assets				=	Equity						
	Cash	+ Inventory +	Office Furn.* +	Manuf. Equip*. =		Com. Stk. +	Ret. Ear.	Rev. −	Exp. =	Net Inc.	Cash Flow	
1	850,000					850,000					850,000	FA
2	(50,000)						(50,000)		− 50,000	(50,000)	(50,000)	OA
3	(140,000)	140,000									(140,000)	OA
4	(82,200)						(82,200)		− 82,200	(82,200)	(82,200)	OA
5	(224,000)	224,000									(224,000)	OA
6	(48,000)		48,000								(48,000)	IA
7			(10,000)				(10,000)		− 10,000	(10,000)		
8	(65,000)			65,000							(65,000)	IA
9		20,000		(20,000)								
10	(136,000)	136,000									(136,000)	OA
11	(41,000)						(41,000)		− 41,000	(41,000)	(41,000)	OA
12	699,200						699,200	699,200		699,200	699,200	OA
13		(478,400)					(478,400)		− 478,400	(478,400)		
Totals	763,000 +	41,600 +	38,000 +	45,000 =		850,000 +	37,600	699,200 −	661,600 =	37,600	763,200	NC

*Negative amounts in these columns represent accumulated depreciation.

The average cost per unit of product is determined by dividing the total product cost by the number of headsets produced. Specifically, ($140,000 + $224,000 + $20,000 + $136,000) ÷ 20,000 = $26. Cost of goods sold is $478,400 ($26 × 18,400).

Solution to Requirement b
The impact on cash flow occurs when Tuscan pays for various product costs. In this case, cash outflows occurred when Tuscan paid for materials, labor, and overhead. The cash flow consequences of these transactions were recognized before the cost of goods sold expense was recognized.

Solution to Requirement c

TUSCAN MANUFACTURING COMPANY
Income Statement
For the Year Ended December 31, 2003

Sales Revenue (18,400 units × $38)	$699,200
Cost of Goods Sold (18,400 × $26)	(478,400)
Gross Margin	220,800
R & D Expenses	(50,000)
Selling and Admin. Salary Expense	(82,200)
Admin. Depreciation Expense	(10,000)
Inventory Holding Expense	(41,000)
Net Income	$ 37,600

Solution to Requirement d

Inventory product costs for manufacturing companies focus on the costs necessary to make the product. The cost of research and development (Event 2) occurs before the inventory is made and is therefore an upstream cost, not an inventory (product) cost. The inventory holding costs (Event 11) are incurred after the inventory has been made and are therefore downstream costs, not product costs. Selling costs (included in Events 4 and 7) are normally incurred after products have been made and are therefore usually classified as downstream costs. Administrative costs (also included in Events 4 and 7) are not related to making products and are therefore not classified as product costs. Administrative costs may be incurred before, during, or after products are made, so they may be classified as either upstream or downstream costs. Only the costs of materials, labor, and overhead that are actually incurred for the purpose of making goods (Events 3, 5, 9, and 10) are classified as product costs.

Solution to Requirement e

Since the merchandise would be available on demand, Tuscan could operate a just-in-time inventory system thereby eliminating the inventory holding expense. Since the additional cost to purchase is $1 per unit ($27 − $26), it would cost Tuscan an additional $20,000 ($1 × 20,000 units) to purchase its product. However, the company would save $41,000 of inventory holding expense. The warehouse supervisor could be biased by the fact that his job would be lost if the company purchased its products and thereby could eliminate the need for warehousing inventory. If Tuscan does not maintain inventory, it would not need a warehouse supervisor.

APPENDIX

The **statement of cash flows** explains how a company obtained and used *cash* during the accounting period (usually one year). The sources of cash are called *cash inflows,* and the uses are known as *cash outflows.* The statement classifies cash receipts (inflows) and payments (outflows) into three categories: operating activities, investing activities, and financing activities. The **operating activities** section of the statement of cash flows reports the cash received from revenue and the cash paid for expenses.

The **investing activities** section of the statement of cash flows includes cash received from the sales of or the amount paid for productive assets. **Productive assets** are assets used to operate the business. They are sometimes called *long-term* assets because they are normally used for more than one accounting period. For example, cash outflows for the purchase of land or cash inflows from the sale of a building would be reported in the investing activities section of the statement of cash flows. In contrast, cash spent for the purchase of supplies would be reported in the operating activities section because supplies represent short-term assets that would generally be consumed within a single accounting period.

The **financing activities** section of the statement of cash flows reports the cash transactions associated with the resource providers (owners and creditors). More specifically, financing activities include cash obtained from or paid to owners, including dividends. Also, cash borrowed from or principal repaid to creditors would be reported in the financing activities section. However, note that interest paid to creditors is treated as an expense and is reported in the operating activities section of the

Exhibit 1–17A *Classification Scheme Statement of Cash Flows*

Cash flows from operating activities:
Cash receipts (inflows) from revenue
Cash payments (outflows) for expenses (including interest)

Cash flows from investing activities:
Cash receipts (inflows) from the sale of long-term assets
Cash payments (outflows) for the purchase of long-term assets

Cash flows from financing activities:
Cash receipts (inflows) from borrowed funds
Cash receipts (inflows) from issuing common stock
Cash payments (outflows) to repay borrowed funds
Cash payments (outflows) for dividends

statement of cash flows. The primary cash inflows and outflows associated with each type of business activity are shown in Exhibit 1–17A; the list of items in the exhibit is not comprehensive. More detailed coverage of the statement of cash flows is presented in Chapter 14.

KEY TERMS

Activities *22*
Activity-based management (ABM) *22*
Average cost *8*
Benchmarking *21*
Best practices *21*
Continuous improvement *21*
Cost allocation *13*
Cost-plus pricing *6*
Direct labor *11*
Direct raw materials *10*
Downstream costs *19*
Efficient markets hypothesis *15*

Financial accounting *4*
Financial Accounting Standards Board (FASB) *6*
Financing activities (Appendix) *28*
Finished goods *7*
General, selling, and administrative costs *12*
Generally accepted accounting principles (GAAP) *6*
Indirect costs *12*
Investing activities (Appendix) *28*
Just in time (JIT) *23*

Managerial accounting *4*
Manufacturing overhead *12*
Most-favored customer status *24*
Nonvalue-added activities *22*
Operating activities (Appendix) *28*
Opportunity cost *25*
Overhead *11*
Period costs *12*
Product costs *6*
Product costing *6*
Productive assets *28*
Raw materials *10*

Reengineering *21*
Securities and Exchange Commission (SEC) *6*
Statement of cash flows *28*
Total Quality Management (TQM) *21*
Upstream costs *19*
Value-added activity *22*
Value chain *22*
Value-added principle *6*

QUESTIONS

1. What are some differences between financial and managerial accounting?
2. What does the value-added principle mean as it applies to managerial accounting information? Give an example of value-added information that may be included in managerial accounting reports but is not shown in publicly reported financial statements.
3. What are the two dimensions of a total quality management (TQM) program? Why is TQM being used in business practice?
4. How does product costing used in financial accounting differ from product costing used in managerial accounting?
5. What does the statement "costs can be assets or expenses" mean?
6. Why are the salaries of production workers accumulated in an inventory account instead of being expensed on the income statement?
7. How do product costs affect the financial statements?
8. What is an indirect cost? Provide examples of product costs that would be classified as indirect.
9. How does a product cost differ from a general, selling, and administrative cost? Give examples of each.
10. Why is cost classification important to managers?
11. What does the term *reengineering* mean? Name some reengineering practices.
12. What is cost allocation? Give an example of a cost that needs to be allocated.
13. How has the Institute of Management Accountants responded to the need for high standards of ethical conduct in the accounting profession?
14. What are some of the common ethical conflicts that accountants encounter?
15. What costs should be considered in determining the sales price of a product?
16. What does the term *activity-based costing* mean?
17. What is a value chain?
18. What do the terms *value-added activity* and *nonvalue-added activity* mean? Provide an example of each type of activity.
19. What is a just-in-time (JIT) inventory system? Name some inventory costs that can be eliminated or reduced by its use.

EXERCISES—SERIES A

EXERCISE 1–1A *Identifying Financial Versus Managerial Accounting Items* L.O. 1

Required
Indicate whether each of the following items is representative of managerial or of financial accounting.
a. Information is regulated by the SEC, FASB, and other sources of GAAP.
b. Information is based on estimates that are bounded by relevance and timeliness.

c. Information is historically based and usually reported annually.
d. Information is local and pertains to subunits of the organization.
e. Information includes economic and nonfinancial data as well as financial data.
f. Information is global and pertains to the company as a whole.
g. Information is provided to insiders including executives, managers, and operators.
h. Information is factual and is characterized by objectivity, reliability, consistency, and accuracy.
i. Information is reported continuously and has a current or future orientation.
j. Information is provided to outsiders including investors, creditors, government agencies, analysts, and reporters.

L.O. 5   EXERCISE 1–2A *Identifying Product Versus General, Selling, and Administrative Costs*

Required

Indicate whether each of the following costs should be classified as a product cost or as a general, selling, and administrative cost.

a. Salaries of employees working in the accounting department.
b. Commissions paid to sales staff.
c. Interest on the mortgage for the company's corporate headquarters.
d. Indirect labor used to manufacture inventory.
e. Attorney's fees paid to protect the company from frivolous lawsuits.
f. Research and development costs incurred to create new drugs for a pharmaceutical company.
g. The cost of secretarial supplies used in a doctor's office.
h. Depreciation on the office furniture of the company president.
i. Direct materials used in a manufacturing company.
j. Indirect materials used in a manufacturing company.

L.O. 5   EXERCISE 1–3A *Classifying Costs: Product or GS&A/Asset or Expense*

Required

Use the following format to classify each cost as a product cost or a general, selling, and administrative (G, S, & A) cost. Also indicate whether the cost would be recorded as an asset or an expense. The first item is shown as an example.

Cost Category	Product/ G, S, & A	Asset/ Expense
Research and development costs	G, S, & A	Expense
Cost to set up manufacturing equipment		
Utilities used in factory		
Cars for sales staff		
Distributions to stockholders		
General office supplies		
Raw materials used in the manufacturing process		
Cost to rest office equipment		
Wages of production workers		
Advertising costs		
Promotion costs		
Production supplies		
Depreciation on administration building		
Depreciation on manufacturing equipment		

L.O. 5   EXERCISE 1–4A *Identifying Effect of Product Versus General, Selling, and Administrative Costs on Financial Statements*

Required

Graffeo Industries recognized accrued compensation cost. Use the following model to show how this event would affect the company's financial statement under the following two assumptions: (1) the compensation is for office personnel and (2) the compensation is for production workers. Use pluses or minuses to show the effect on each element. If an element is not affected, indicate so by placing the letters NA under the appropriate heading.

	Assets = Liab. + Equity	Rev. − Exp. = Net Inc.	Cash Flow
1.			
2.			

EXERCISE 1–5A *Identify Effect of Product Versus General, Selling, and Administrative Costs on Financial Statements* **L.O. 5**

Required

Smyth Industries recognized the annual cost of depreciation on December 31, 2006. Using the following horizontal financial statement model, indicate how this event affected the company's financial statements under the following two assumptions: (1) the depreciation was on office furniture and (2) the depreciation was on manufacturing equipment. Indicate whether the event increases (I), decreases (D), or has no affect (NA) on each element of the financial statements. Also, in the Cash column, indicate whether the cash flow is associated with operating activities (OA), investing activities (IA), or financing activities (FA). (Note: Show accumulated depreciation as a decrease in the book value of the appropriate asset account.)

Event No.	Assets				Equity		Rev. − Exp. = Net Inc.	Cash Flow
	Cash + Inventory +	Manuf. Equip. +	Office Furn. =		Com. Stk. +	Ret. Ear.		
1.								
2.								

EXERCISE 1–6A *Identifying Product Costs in a Manufacturing Company* **L.O. 2**

Lydia Giles was talking to another accounting student, Todd Crawford. Upon discovering that the accounting department offered an upper-level course in cost measurement, Lydia remarked to Todd, "How difficult can it be? My parents own a toy store. All you have to do to figure out how much something costs is look at the invoice. Surely you don't need an entire course to teach you how to read an invoice."

Required
a. Identify the three main components of product cost for a manufacturing entity.
b. Explain why measuring product cost for a manufacturing entity is more complex than measuring product cost for a retail toy store.
c. Assume that Lydia's parents rent a store for $6,000 per month. Different types of toys use different amounts of store space. For example, displaying a bicycle requires more store space than displaying a deck of cards. Also, some toys remain on the shelf longer than others. Fad toys sell rapidly, but traditional toys sell more slowly. Under these circumstances, how would you determine the amount of rental cost required to display each type of toy? Identify two other costs incurred by a toy store that may be difficult to allocate to individual toys.

EXERCISE 1–7A *Identifying Product Versus General, Selling, and Administrative Costs* **L.O. 5**

A review of the accounting records of Obert Manufacturing indicated that the company incurred the following payroll costs during the month of June.
1. Salary of the company president—$32,000.
2. Salary of the vice president of manufacturing—$16,000.
3. Salary of the chief financial officer—$18,800.
4. Salary of the vice president of marketing—$15,600.
5. Salaries of middle managers (department heads, production supervisors) in manufacturing plant—$196,000.
6. Wages of production workers—$938,000.
7. Salaries of administrative secretaries—$112,000.
8. Salaries of engineers and other personnel responsible for maintaining production equipment—$178,000.
9. Commissions paid to sales staff—$252,000.

Required
a. What amount of payroll cost would be classified as general, selling, and administrative expense?

b. Assuming that Obert made 4,000 units of product and sold 3,600 of them during the month of June, determine the amount of payroll cost that would be included in cost of goods sold.

L.O. 2, 4, 5   **EXERCISE 1–8A** *Recording Product Versus General, Selling, and Administrative Costs in a Financial Statements Model*

Milster Manufacturing experienced the following events during its first accounting period.
1. Recognized depreciation on manufacturing equipment.
2. Recognized depreciation on office furniture.
3. Recognized revenue from cash sale of products.
4. Recognized cost of goods sold from sale referenced in Event 3.
5. Acquired cash by issuing common stock.
6. Paid cash to purchase raw materials that were used to make products.
7. Paid wages to production workers.
8. Paid salaries to administrative staff.

Required

Use a horizontal financial statements model to show how each event affects the balance sheet, income statement, and statement of cash flows. Indicate whether the event increases (I), decreases (D), or has no effect (NA) on each element of the financial statements. In the Cash Flow column, indicate whether the cash flow is associated with operating activities (OA), investing activities (IA), or financing activities (FA). The first transaction has been recorded as an example. (*Note:* Show accumulated depreciation as a decrease in the book value of the appropriate asset account.)

Event No.			Assets				Equity					
	Cash +	Inventory +	Manuf. Equip. +	Office Furn. =	Com. Stk. +	Ret. Ear.	Rev.	− Exp.	= Net Inc.		Cash Flow
1	NA	I	D	NA	NA	NA	NA	NA	NA		NA

L.O. 2, 3, 4   **EXERCISE 1–9A** *Allocating Product Costs Between Ending Inventory and Cost of Goods Sold*

Zarzour Manufacturing Company began operations on January 1. During the year, it started and completed 4,000 units of product. The company incurred the following costs.
1. Raw materials purchased and used—$4,000.
2. Wages of production workers—$6,000.
3. Salaries of administrative and sales personnel—$2,400.
4. Depreciation on manufacturing equipment—$7,200.
5. Depreciation on administrative equipment—$2,800.

Zarzour sold 3,000 units of product.

Required

a. Determine the total product cost for the year.
b. Determine the total cost of the ending inventory.
c. Determine the total of cost of goods sold.

L.O. 4 & 5   **EXERCISE 1–10A** *Financial Statement Effects for Manufacturing Versus Service Organizations*

The following financial statements model shows the effects of recognizing depreciation in two different circumstances. One circumstance represents recognizing depreciation on a machine used in a manufacturing company. The other circumstance recognizes depreciation on X-ray equipment used in a doctor's office. The effects of each event have been recorded using the letter (I) to represent increase, (D) for decrease, and (NA) for no effect.

Event No.			Assets			Equity					
	Cash +	Inventory +	Equip. =	Com. Stk. +	Ret. Ear.	Rev.	− Exp.	= Net Inc.		Cash Flow
1	NA	NA	D	NA	D	NA	I	D		NA
2	NA	I	D	NA	NA	NA	NA	NA		NA

Required
a. Identify the event that represents depreciation on the X-ray equipment.
b. Explain why recognizing depreciation on equipment used in a manufacturing company affects financial statements differently from recognizing depreciation on equipment used in a service organization.

EXERCISE 1–11A *Identifying the Effect of Product Versus General, Selling, and Administrative Cost on the Income Statement and Statement of Cash Flows*   **L.O. 5**

Required
Each of the following events describes acquiring an asset that requires a year-end adjusting entry. Explain how acquiring the asset and making the adjusting entry affect the amount of net income and the cash flow shown on the year-end financial statements. Also, in the Cash Flow column, indicate whether the cash flow is associated with operating activities (OA), investing activities (IA), or financing activities (FA). Use (NA) for no effect. Assume a December 31 annual closing date. The first event has been recorded as an example. Assume that any products that have been made have not been sold.

Event No.	Net Income Amount of Change	Cash Flow Amount of Change
1. Purchase of computer equipment	NA	($7,000) IA
1. Make adjusting entry	($1,500)	NA

1. Paid $7,000 cash on January 1 to purchase computer equipment to be used for administrative purposes. The equipment had an estimated expected useful life of four years and a $1,000 salvage value.
2. Paid $7,000 cash on January 1 to purchase manufacturing equipment. The equipment had an estimated expected useful life of four years and a $1,000 salvage value.
3. Paid $6,000 cash in advance on May 1 for a one-year rental contract on administrative offices.
4. Paid $6,000 cash in advance on May 1 for a one-year rental contract on manufacturing facilities.
5. Paid $1,000 cash to purchase supplies to be used by the marketing department. At the end of the year, $200 of supplies was still on hand.
6. Paid $1,000 cash to purchase supplies to be used in the manufacturing process. At the end of the year, $200 of supplies was still on hand.

EXERCISE 1–12A *Upstream and Downstream Costs*   **L.O. 8**

During 2007, Linn Manufacturing Company incurred $90,000,000 of research and development (R&D) costs to create a long-life battery to use in computers. In accordance with FASB standards, the entire R&D cost was recognized as an expense in 2007. Manufacturing costs (direct materials, direct labor, and overhead) are expected to be $260 per unit. Packaging, shipping, and sales commissions are expected to be $50 per unit. Linn expects to sell 2,000,000 batteries before new research renders the battery design technologically obsolete. During 2007, Linn made 440,000 batteries and sold 400,000 of them.

Required
a. Identify the upstream and downstream costs.
b. Determine the 2007 amount of cost of goods sold and the ending inventory balance.
c. Determine the sales price assuming that Linn desires to earn a profit margin that is equal to 25 percent of the *total cost* of developing, making, and distributing the batteries.
d. Prepare an income statement for 2007. Use the sales price developed in Part c.
e. Why would Linn price the batteries at a level that would generate a loss for the 2007 accounting period?

EXERCISE 1–13A *Value Chain Analysis*   **L.O. 10**

Sonic Speaker Company (SSC) manufactures and sells high-quality audio speakers. The speakers are encased in solid walnut cabinets supplied by Cranston Cabinet, Inc. Cranston packages the speakers in durable moisture-proof boxes and ships them by truck to SSC's manufacturing facility, which is located 50 miles from the cabinet factory.

Required
Identify the nonvalue-added activities that occur between the companies described in the preceding scenario. Provide a logical explanation as to how these nonvalue-added activities could be eliminated.

L.O. 10 **EXERCISE 1–14A** *Identify the Effect of a Just-in-Time Inventory System on Financial Statements*

After reviewing the financial statements of ASIPCO, Jim Aultry concluded that the company was a service company. Mr. Aultry based his conclusion on the fact that ASIPCO's financial statements displayed no inventory accounts.

Required
Explain how ASIPCO's implementation of a 100 percent effective just-in-time inventory system could have led Mr. Aultry to a false conclusion regarding the nature of ASIPCO's business.

L.O. 10 **EXERCISE 1–15A** *Using JIT to Minimize Waste and Lost Opportunity*

Ken Hand, a teacher at Grove Middle School, is in charge of ordering the T-shirts to be sold for the school's annual fund-raising project. The T-shirts are printed with a special Grove School logo. In some years, the supply of T-shirts has been insufficient to satisfy the number of sales orders. In other years, T-shirts have been left over. Excess T-shirts are normally donated to some charitable organization. T-shirts cost the school $4 each and are normally sold for $6 each. Mr. Hand has decided to order 500 shirts.

Required
a. If the school receives actual sales orders for 450 shirts, what amount of profit will the school earn? What is the cost of waste due to excess inventory?
b. If the school receives actual sales orders for 550 shirts, what amount of profit will the school earn? What amount of opportunity cost will the school incur?
c. Explain how a JIT inventory system could maximize profitability by eliminating waste and opportunity cost.

L.O. 10 **EXERCISE 1–16A** *Using JIT to Minimize Holding Costs*

Nico's Pet Supplies purchases its inventory from a variety of suppliers, some of which require a six-week lead time before delivering the goods. To ensure that she has a sufficient supply of goods on hand, Ms. Chen, the owner, must maintain a large supply of inventory. The cost of this inventory averages $20,000. She usually finances the purchase of inventory and pays a 10 percent annual finance charge. Ms. Chen's accountant has suggested that she establish a relationship with a single large distributor who can satisfy all of her orders within a two-week time period. Given this quick turnaround time, she will be able to reduce her average inventory balance to $5,000. Ms. Chen also believes that she could save $3,000 per year by reducing phone bills, insurance, and warehouse rental space costs associated with ordering and maintaining the larger level of inventory.

Required
a. Is the new inventory system available to Ms. Chen a pure or approximate just-in-time system?
b. Based on the information provided, how much of Ms. Chen's inventory holding cost could be eliminated by taking the accountant's advice?

PROBLEMS—SERIES A

L.O. 2, 3, 4, 5, 6 **PROBLEM 1–17A** *Product Versus General, Selling, and Administrative Costs*

Ashton Manufacturing Company was started on January 1, 2004, when it acquired $90,000 cash by issuing common stock. Ashton immediately purchased office furniture and manufacturing equipment costing $10,000 and $28,000, respectively. The office furniture had a five-year useful life and a zero salvage value. The manufacturing equipment had a $4,000 salvage value and an expected useful life of three years. The company paid $12,000 for salaries of administrative personnel and $16,000 for wages to production personnel. Finally, the company paid $18,000 for raw materials that were used to make inventory. All inventory was started and completed during the year. Ashton completed production on 5,000 units of product and sold 4,000 units at a price of $12 each in 2004. (Assume that all transactions are cash transactions.)

Required
a. Determine the total product cost and the average cost per unit of the inventory produced in 2004.
b. Determine the amount of cost of goods sold that would appear on the 2004 income statement.
c. Determine the amount of the ending inventory balance that would appear on the December 31, 2004, balance sheet.

d. Determine the amount of net income that would appear on the 2004 income statement.

e. Determine the amount of retained earnings that would appear on the December 31, 2004, balance sheet.

f. Determine the amount of total assets that would appear on the December 31, 2004 balance sheet.

g. Determine the amount of net cash flow from operating activities that would appear on the 2004 statement of cash flows.

h. Determine the amount of net cash flow from investing activities that would appear on the 2004 statement of cash flows.

PROBLEM 1–18A *Effect of Product Versus Period Costs on Financial Statements*   **L.O. 2, 4, 5**

Mantooth Manufacturing Company experienced the following accounting events during its first year of operation. With the exception of the adjusting entries for depreciation, assume that all transactions are cash transactions.

1. Acquired $50,000 cash by issuing common stock.

2. Paid $8,000 for the materials used to make its products, all of which were started and completed during the year.

3. Paid salaries of $4,400 to selling and administrative employees.

4. Paid wages of $7,000 to production workers.

5. Paid $9,600 for furniture used in selling and administrative offices. The furniture was acquired on January 1. It had a $1,600 estimated salvage value and a four-year useful life.

6. Paid $13,000 for manufacturing equipment. The equipment was acquired on January 1. It had a $1,000 estimated salvage value and a three-year useful life.

7. Sold inventory to customers for $25,000 that had cost $14,000 to make.

Required

Explain how these events would affect the balance sheet, income statement, and statement of cash flows by recording them in a horizontal financial statements model as indicated here. The first event is recorded as an example. In the Cash Flow column, indicate whether the amounts represent financing activities (FA), investing activities (IA), or operating activities (OA).

Financial Statements Model											
	Assets				Equity						
Event No.	Cash	+ Inventory +	Manuf. Equip.* +	Office Furn.* =	Com. Stk.	+ Ret. Ear.		Rev. – Exp. = Net Inc.			Cash Flow
1	50,000				50,000						50,000 FA

*Record accumulated depreciation as negative amounts in these columns.

PROBLEM 1–19A *Product Versus General, Selling, and Administrative Costs*   **L.O. 2, 3, 4, 5**

The following transactions pertain to 2006, the first year operations of Bartlett Company. All inventory was started and completed during 2006. Assume that all transactions are cash transactions.

1. Acquired $2,000 cash by issuing common stock.

2. Paid $400 for materials used to produce inventory.

3. Paid $600 to production workers.

4. Paid $200 rental fee for production equipment.

5. Paid $160 to administrative employees.

6. Paid $80 rental fee for administrative office equipment.

7. Produced 300 units of inventory of which 200 units were sold at a price of $7.00 each.

Required

Prepare an income statement, balance sheet, and statement of cash flows.

PROBLEM 1–20A *Service Versus Manufacturing Companies*   **L.O. 2, 3, 4, 5**

Decker Company began operations on January 1, 2005, by issuing common stock for $30,000 cash. During 2005, Decker received $40,000 cash from revenue and incurred costs that required $60,000 of cash payments.

Required

Prepare an income statement, balance sheet, and statement of cash flows for Decker Company for 2005, under each of the following independent scenarios.

a. Decker is a promoter of rock concerts. The $60,000 was paid to provide a rock concert that produced the revenue.
b. Decker is in the car rental business. The $60,000 was paid to purchase automobiles. The automobiles were purchased on January 1, 2005, have four-year useful lives, with no expected salvage value. Decker uses straight-line depreciation. The revenue was generated by leasing the automobiles.
c. Decker is a manufacturing company. The $60,000 was paid to purchase the following items:
   (1) Paid $8,000 cash to purchase materials that were used to make products during the year.
   (2) Paid $20,000 cash for wages of factory workers who made products during the year.
   (3) Paid $2,000 cash for salaries of sales and administrative employees.
   (4) Paid $30,000 cash to purchase manufacturing equipment. The equipment was used solely to make products. It had a three-year life and a $6,000 salvage value. The company uses straight-line depreciation.
   (5) During 2005, Decker started and completed 2,000 units of product. The revenue was earned when Decker sold 1,500 units of product to its customers.
d. Refer to Part *c*. Could Decker determine the actual cost of making the 907th unit of product? How likely is it that the actual cost of the 907th product was exactly the same as the cost of producing the 908th unit of product? Explain why management may be more interested in average cost than in actual cost.

L.O. 2, 3, 4, 5, 6

PROBLEM 1–21A *Importance of Cost Classification*

Obert Manufacturing Company (OMC) was started when it acquired $40,000 by issuing common stock. During the first year of operations, the company incurred specifically identifiable product costs (materials, labor, and overhead) amounting to $24,000. OMC also incurred $16,000 of engineering design and planning costs. There was a debate regarding how the design and planning costs should be classified. Advocates of Option 1 believe that the costs should be classified as general, selling, and administrative costs. Advocates of Option 2 believe it is more appropriate to classify the design and planning costs as product costs. During the year, OMC made 4,000 units of product and sold 3,000 units at a price of $14 each. All transactions were cash transactions.

Required
a. Prepare an income statement, balance sheet, and statement of cash flows under each of the two options.
b. Identify the option that results in financial statements that are more likely to leave a favorable impression on investors and creditors.
c. Assume that OMC provides an incentive bonus to the company president equal to 10 percent of net income. Compute the amount of the bonus under each of the two options. Identify the option that provides the president with the higher bonus.
d. Assume a 35 percent income tax rate. Determine the amount of income tax expense under each of the two options. Identify the option that minimizes the amount of the company's income tax expense.
e. Comment on the conflict of interest between the company president as determined in Part *c* and the owners of the company as indicated in Part *d*. Describe an incentive compensation plan that would avoid a conflict of interest between the president and the owners.

L.O. 10

PROBLEM 1–22A *Value Chain Analysis*

Haley Company invented a new process for manufacturing ice cream. The ingredients are mixed in high-tech machinery that forms the product into small round beads. Like a bag of balls, the ice cream beads are surrounded by air pockets in packages. This design has numerous advantages. First, each bite of ice cream melts rapidly when placed in a person's mouth, creating a more flavorful sensation when compared to ordinary ice cream. Also, the air pockets mean that a typical serving includes a smaller amount of ice cream. This not only reduces materials cost but also provides the consumer with a low-calorie snack. A cup appears full of ice cream, but it is really half full of air. The consumer eats only half the ingredients that are contained in a typical cup of blended ice cream. Finally, the texture of the ice cream makes scooping it out of a large container a very easy task. The frustration of trying to get a spoon into a rock-solid package of blended ice cream has been eliminated. Haley Company named the new product Sonic Cream.

Like many other ice cream producers, Haley Company purchases its raw materials from a food wholesaler. The ingredients are mixed in Haley's manufacturing plant. The packages of finished product are distributed to privately owned franchise ice cream shops that sell Sonic Cream directly to the public.

Haley provides national advertising and is responsible for all research and development costs associated with making new flavors of Sonic Cream.

Required
a. Based on the information provided, draw a comprehensive value chain for Haley Company that includes its suppliers and customers.
b. Identify the place in the chain where Haley Company is exercising its opportunity to create added value beyond that currently being provided by its competitors.

PROBLEM 1–23A *Using JIT to Reduce Inventory Holding Costs*

L.O. 10

Steed Manufacturing Company obtains its raw materials from a variety of suppliers. Steed's strategy is to obtain the best price by letting the suppliers know that it buys from the lowest bidder. Approximately four years ago, unexpected increased demand resulted in materials shortages. Steed was unable to find the materials it needed even though it was willing to pay premium prices. Because of the lack of raw materials, Steed was forced to close its manufacturing facility for two weeks. Its president vowed that her company would never again be at the mercy of its suppliers. She immediately ordered her purchasing agent to perpetually maintain a one-month supply of raw materials. Compliance with the president's orders resulted in a raw materials inventory amounting to approximately $2,000,000. Warehouse rental and personnel costs to maintain the inventory amounted to $10,000 per month. Steed has a line of credit with a local bank that calls for a 12 percent annual rate of interest. Assume that Steed finances the raw materials inventory with the line of credit.

Required
a. Based on the information provided, determine the annual holding cost of the raw materials inventory.
b. Explain how a JIT system could reduce Steed's inventory holding cost.
c. Explain how most-favored customer status could enable Steed to establish a JIT inventory system without risking the raw materials shortages experienced in the past.

PROBLEM 1–24A *Using JIT to Minimize Waste and Lost Opportunity*

L.O. 10

Exam Success, Inc., provides review courses twice each year for students studying to take the CPA exam. The cost of textbooks is included in the registration fee. Text material requires constant updating and is useful for only one course. To minimize printing costs and ensure availability of books on the first day of class, ESI has books printed and delivered to its offices two weeks in advance of the first class. To ensure that enough books are available, ESI normally orders 10 percent more than expected enrollment. Usually there is an oversupply of books that is thrown away. However, demand occasionally exceeds expectations by more than 10 percent and there are too few books available for student use. ESI had been forced to turn away students because of a lack of textbooks. ESI expects to enroll approximately 100 students per course. The tuition fee is $800 per student. The cost of teachers is $25,000 per course, textbooks cost $60 each, and other operating expenses are estimated to be $35,000 per course.

Required
a. Prepare an income statement, assuming that 95 students enroll in a course. Determine the cost of waste associated with unused books.
b. Prepare an income statement, assuming that 115 students attempt to enroll in the course. Note that five students are turned away because of too few textbooks. Determine the amount of lost profit resulting from the inability to serve the five additional students.
c. Suppose that textbooks can be produced through a high-speed copying process that permits delivery *just in time* for class to start. The cost of books made using this process, however, is $65 each. Assume that all books must be made using the same production process. In other words, ESI cannot order some of the books using the regular copy process and the rest using the high-speed process. Prepare an income statement under the JIT system assuming that 95 students enroll in a course. Compare the income statement under JIT with the income statement prepared in Requirement *a*. Comment on how the JIT system would affect profitability.
d. Assume the same facts as in Requirement *c* with respect to a JIT system that enables immediate delivery of books at a cost of $65 each. Prepare an income statement under the JIT system, assuming that 115 students enroll in a course. Compare the income statement under JIT with the income statement prepared in Requirement *b*. Comment on how the JIT system would affect profitability.
e. Discuss the possible effect of the JIT system on the level of customer satisfaction.

EXERCISES—SERIES B

L.O. 1   **EXERCISE 1–1B** *Financial Versus Managerial Accounting Items*

Required

Indicate whether each of the following items is representative of financial or managerial accounting.

a. Condensed financial information sent to current investors at the end of each quarter.
b. Audited financial statements submitted to bankers when applying for a line of credit.
c. A weekly cash budget used by the treasurer to determine whether cash on hand is excessive.
d. Monthly sales reports used by the vice president of marketing to help allocate funds.
e. Divisional profit reports used by the company president to determine bonuses for divisional vice presidents.
f. Financial results used by stockbrokers to evaluate a company's profitability.
g. Quarterly budgets used by management to determine future borrowing needs.
h. Financial statements prepared in accordance with generally accepted accounting principles.
i. Annual financial reports submitted to the SEC in compliance with federal securities laws.
j. Projected budget information used to make logistical decisions.

L.O. 5   **EXERCISE 1–2B** *Identifying Product Versus General, Selling, and Administrative Costs*

Required

Indicate whether each of the following costs should be classified as a product cost or as a general, selling, and administrative cost.

a. The salary of the company president.
b. The salary of the cell phone manufacturing plant manager.
c. The depreciation on administrative buildings.
d. The depreciation on the company treasurer's computer.
e. The fabric used in making a customized sofa for a customer.
f. The salary of an engineer who maintains all manufacturing plant equipment.
g. Wages paid to workers in a manufacturing plant.
h. The salary of the receptionist working in the sales department.
i. Supplies used in the sales department.
j. Wages of janitors who clean the factory floor.

L.O. 5   **EXERCISE 1–3B** *Classifying Costs: Product or Period/Asset or Expense*

Required

Use the following format to classify each cost as a product cost or a general, selling, and administrative (G,S,&A) cost. Also indicate whether the cost would be recorded as an asset or an expense. The first cost item is shown as an example.

Cost Category	Product/ G,S&A	Asset/ Expense
Raw material used to make products	Product	Asset
Natural gas used in the factory		
Cost of television commercials		
Wages of factory workers		
Paper and ink cartridges used in the cashier's office		
Lubricant used to maintain factory equipment		
Cost of a delivery truck		
Cash dividend to stockholders		
Cost of merchandise shipped to customers		
Depreciation on vehicles used by salespeople		
Wages of administrative building security guards		
Supplies used in the plant manager's office		
Computers for the accounting department		
Depreciation on computers used in factory		

EXERCISE 1–4B *Effect of Product Versus General, Selling, and Administrative Costs on Financial Statements*

L.O. 5

Required

Crumpton Plastics Company accrued a tax liability. Use the following horizontal financial statements model to show the effect of this accrual under the following two assumptions: (1) the tax is on administrative buildings or (2) the tax is on production equipment. Use plus signs and/or minus signs to show the effect on each element. If an element is not affected, indicate so by placing the letters NA under the appropriate heading.

	Assets	=	Liab.	+	Equity	Rev.	−	Exp.	=	Net Inc.	Cash Flow
1.											
2.											

EXERCISE 1–5B *Effect of Product Versus General, Selling, and Administrative Cost on Financial Statements*

L.O. 5

Required

Monya Corporation recognized the annual expiration of insurance on December 31, 2008. Using the following horizontal financial statements model shown, indicate how this event affected the company's financial statements under the following two assumptions: (1) the insurance was for office equipment or (2) the insurance was for manufacturing equipment. Indicate whether the event increases (I), decreases (D), or does not affect (NA) each element of the financial statements. In the Cash Flow column, indicate whether the cash flow is associated with operating activities (OA), investing activities (IA), or financing activities (FA).

Event No.	Assets						Equity				Rev.	−	Exp.	=	Net Inc.	Cash Flow
	Cash	+	Prepaid Insurance	+	Inventory	=	Com. Stk.	+	Ret. Ear.							
1.																
2.																

EXERCISE 1–6B *Product Costs in a Manufacturing Company*

L.O. 2

Because friends and neighbors frequently praise her baking skills, Angelica Angilini plans to start a new business baking cakes for customers. She wonders how to determine the cost of her cakes.

Required
a. Identify and give examples of the three components of product cost incurred in producing cakes.
b. Explain why measuring product cost for a bakery is more complex than measuring product cost for a retail store.
c. Assume that Angelica decides to bake cakes for her customers at her home. Consequently, she will avoid the cost of renting a bakery. However, her home utility bills will increase. She also plans to offer different types of cakes for which baking time will vary. Cakes mixed with ice cream will require freezing, and other cakes will need refrigeration. Some can cool at room temperature. Under these circumstances, how can Angelica estimate the amount of utility cost required to produce a given cake? Identify two costs other than utility cost that she will incur that could be difficult to measure.

EXERCISE 1–7B *Product Versus General, Selling, and Administrative Costs*

L.O. 5

In reviewing Gemni Company's September accounting records, Jose Giralda, the chief accountant, noted the following depreciation costs.
1. Factory buildings — $25,000.
2. Computers used in manufacturing — $4,000.
3. A building used to display finished products — $8,000.
4. Trucks used to deliver merchandise to customers — $14,000.
5. Forklifts used in the factory — $22,000.
6. Furniture used in the president's office — $9,000.
7. Elevators in administrative buildings — $6,000.
8. Factory machinery — $9,000.

Required

a. What amount of depreciation cost would be classified as general, selling, and administrative expense?

b. Assume that Gemni manufactured 3,000 units of product and sold 2,000 units of product during the month of September. Determine the amount of depreciation cost that would be included in cost of goods sold.

L.O. 2, 4, 5 **EXERCISE 1–8B** *Recording Product Versus General, Selling, and Administrative Costs in a Financial Statements Model*

Yamamoto Electronics Company experienced the following events during its first accounting period.

1. Received $100,000 cash by issuing common stock.
2. Paid $15,000 cash for wages to production workers.
3. Paid $10,000 for salaries to administrative staff.
4. Purchased for cash and used $9,000 of raw materials.
5. Recognized $1,000 of depreciation on administrative offices.
6. Recognized $1,500 of depreciation on manufacturing equipment.
7. Recognized $48,000 of sales revenue from cash sales of products.
8. Recognized $30,000 of cost of goods sold from the sale referenced in Event 7.

Required

Use a horizontal financial statements model to show how each event affects the balance sheet, income statement, and statement of cash flows. Indicate whether the event increases (I), decreases (D), or does not affect (NA) each element of the financial statements. In the Cash Flow column, indicate whether the cash flow is associated with operating activities (OA), investing activities (IA), or financing activities (FA). The first transaction is shown as an example. (*Note:* Show accumulated depreciation as a decrease in the book value of the appropriate asset account.)

Event No.		Assets				Equity						
	Cash +	Inventory +	Manuf. Equip. +	Adm. Offices =	Com. Stk. +	Ret. Ear.	Rev. −	Exp. =	Net Inc.	Cash Flow		
1	I	NA	NA	NA	I	NA	NA	NA	NA	I FA		

L.O. 2, 3, 4 **EXERCISE 1–9B** *Allocating Product Costs Between Ending Inventory and Cost of Goods Sold*

Sun Moon Manufacturing Company began operations on January 1. During January, it started and completed 2,000 units of product. The company incurred the following costs:

1. Raw materials purchased and used — $2,500.
2. Wages of production workers — $2,000.
3. Salaries of administrative and sales personnel — $1,000.
4. Depreciation on manufacturing equipment — $1,500.
5. Depreciation on administrative equipment — $1,200.

Sun Moon sold 1,600 units of product.

Required

a. Determine the total product cost.

b. Determine the total cost of the ending inventory.

c. Determine the total of cost of goods sold.

L.O. 4 & 5 **EXERCISE 1–10B** *Financial Statement Effects for Manufacturing Versus Service Organizations*

The following horizontal financial statements model shows the effects of recording the expiration of insurance in two different circumstances. One circumstance represents the expiration of insurance on a factory building. The other circumstance represents the expiration of insurance on an administrative building. The cash flow effects are shown using (I) for increase, (D) for decrease, and (NA) for no effect.

Event No.		Assets			Equity					
	Cash +	Prepaid Insurance +	Inventory =	Com. Stk. +	Ret. Ear.	Rev. −	Exp. =	Net Inc.	Cash Flow	
1	NA	D	I	NA	NA	NA	NA	NA	NA	
2	NA	D	NA	NA	D	NA	I	D	NA	

Required

a. Identify the event that represents the expiration of insurance on the factory building.

b. Explain why recognizing the expiration of insurance on a factory building affects financial statements differently than recognizing the expiration of insurance on an administrative building.

EXERCISE 1–11B *Effect of Product Versus General, Selling, and Administrative Cost on the Income Statement and Statement of Cash Flows*

L.O. 5

Each of the following asset acquisitions requires a year-end adjusting entry.

	Net Income	Cash Flow
Event No.	Amount of Change	Amount of Change
1. Purchased franchise	NA	($50,000) IA
1. Adjusting Entry	($5,000)	NA

1. Paid $50,000 cash on January 1 to purchase a hamburger franchise that had an estimated expected useful life of 10 years and no salvage value.
2. Paid $50,000 cash on January 1 to purchase a patent to manufacture a special product. The patent had an estimated expected useful life of 10 years.
3. Paid $3,600 cash on April 1 for a one-year insurance policy on the administrative building.
4. Paid $3,600 cash on April 1 for a one-year insurance policy on the manufacturing building.
5. Paid $1,200 cash to purchase office supplies for the accounting department. At the end of the year, $300 of office supplies was still on hand.
6. Paid $1,200 cash to purchase factory supplies. At the end of the year, $300 of factory supplies was still on hand.

Required

Explain how both acquiring the asset and recording the adjusting entry affect the amount of net income and the cash flow reported in the annual financial statements. In the Cash Flow Column, indicate whether the cash flow is associated with operating activities (OA), investing activities (IA), financing activities (FA). Assume a December 31 annual closing date. The first event is shown as an example. Assume that any products that have been made have not been sold.

EXERCISE 1–12B *Upstream and Downstream Costs*

L.O. 8

During 2007 Jocelyn Pharmaceutical Company incurred $50,000,000 of research and development (R&D) costs to develop a new hay fever drug called Allergone. In accordance with FASB standards, the entire R&D cost was recognized as expense in 2007. Manufacturing costs (direct materials, direct labor, and overhead) to produce Allergone are expected to be $40 per unit. Packaging, shipping, and sales commissions are expected to be $5 per unit. Jocelyn expects to sell 5,000,000 units of Allergone before developing a new drug to replace it in the market. During 2007, Jocelyn produced 800,000 units of Allergone and sold 500,000 of them.

Required

a. Identify the upstream and downstream costs.

b. Determine the 2007 amount of cost of goods sold and the December 31, 2007, ending inventory balance.

c. Determine the unit sales price Jocelyn should establish assuming it desires to earn a profit margin equal to 40 percent of the *total cost* of developing, manufacturing, and distributing Allergone.

d. Prepare an income statement for 2007 using the sales price from Part *c*.

e. Why would Jocelyn price Allergone at a level that would generate a loss for 2007?

EXERCISE 1–13B *Value Chain Analysis*

L.O. 10

Fastidious Vincent washed his hair at home and then went to a barbershop for a haircut. The barber explained that shop policy is to shampoo each customer's hair before cutting, regardless of how recently it had been washed. Somewhat annoyed, Vincent submitted to the shampoo, after which the barber cut his hair with great skill. After the haircut, the barber dried his hair and complimented Vincent on his appearance. He added, "That will be $18, $3 for the shampoo and $15 for the cut and dry." Vincent did not tip the barber.

Required

Identify the nonvalue-added activity described. How could the barber modify this nonvalue-added activity?

L.O. 10   **EXERCISE 1–14B** *Effect of a Just-in-Time Inventory System on Financial Statements*

In reviewing Tannihill Company's financial statements for the past two years, Kent Yerling, a bank loan officer, noticed that the company's inventory level had increased significantly while sales revenue had remained constant. Such a trend typically indicates increasing inventory carrying costs and slowing cash inflows. Mr. Yerling concluded that the bank should deny Tannihill's credit line application.

Required

Explain how implementing an effective just-in-time inventory system would affect Tannihill's financial statements and possibly reverse Mr. Yerling's decision about its credit line application.

L.O. 10   **EXERCISE 1–15B** *Using JIT to Minimize Waste and Lost Opportunity*

Pedro Estradas is the editor-in-chief of his school's yearbook. The school has 750 students and 50 faculty and staff members. The firm engaged to print copies of the yearbook charges the school $10 per book and requires a 10-day lead time for delivery. Pedro and his editors plan to order 600 copies to sell at the school fair for $15 each.

Required

a. If the school sells 550 yearbooks, what amount of profit will it earn? What is the cost of waste due to excess inventory?

b. If 150 buyers are turned away after all yearbooks have been sold, what amount of profit will the school earn? What amount of opportunity cost will the school incur?

c. How could Pedro use a JIT inventory system to maximize profits by eliminating waste and opportunity cost?

L.O. 10   **EXERCISE 1–16B** *Using JIT to Minimize Holding Costs*

Maggie's Beauty Salon purchases inventory supplies from a variety of vendors, some of which require a four-week lead time before delivering inventory purchases. To ensure that she will not run out of supplies, Maggie McGee, the owner, maintains a large inventory. The average cost of inventory on hand is $9,000. Ms. McGee usually finances inventory purchases with a line of credit that has a 12 percent annual interest charge. Her accountant has suggested that she purchase all inventory from a single large distributor that can satisfy all of her orders within a three-day period. With such prompt delivery, Ms. McGee would be able to reduce her average inventory balance to $2,000. She also believes that she could save $1,000 per year through reduced phone bills, insurance costs, and warehouse rental costs associated with ordering and maintaining the higher level of inventory.

Required

a. Is the inventory system the accountant suggested to Ms. McGee a pure or approximate just-in-time system?

b. Based on the information provided, how much inventory holding cost could Ms. McGee eliminate by taking the accountant's advice?

PROBLEMS—SERIES B

L.O. 2, 3, 4, 5, 6   **PROBLEM 1–17B** *Product Versus General, Selling, and Administrative Costs*

Sain Manufacturing Company was started on January 1, 2007, when it acquired $134,000 cash by issuing common stock. Sain immediately purchased office furniture and manufacturing equipment costing $20,000 and $38,000, respectively. The office furniture had a four-year useful life and a zero salvage value. The manufacturing equipment had a $2,000 salvage value and an expected useful life of six years. The company paid $14,000 for salaries of administrative personnel and $18,000 for wages of production personnel. Finally, the company paid $24,000 for raw materials that were used to make inventory. All inventory was started and completed during the year. Sain completed production on 8,000 units of product and sold 6,000 units at a price of $14 each in 2007. (Assume that all transactions are cash transactions.)

Required

a. Determine the total product cost and the average cost per unit of the inventory produced in 2007.

b. Determine the amount of cost of goods sold that would appear on the 2007 income statement.
c. Determine the amount of the ending inventory balance that would appear on the December 31, 2007, balance sheet.
d. Determine the amount of net income that would appear on the 2007 income statement.
e. Determine the amount of retained earnings that would appear on the December 31, 2007, balance sheet.
f. Determine the amount of total assets that would appear on the December 31, 2007, balance sheet.
g. Determine the amount of net cash flow from operating activities that would appear on the 2007 statement of cash flows.
h. Determine the amount of net cash flow from investing activities that would appear on the 2007 statement of cash flows.

PROBLEM 1–18B *Effect of Product Versus General, Selling, and Administrative Costs on Financial Statements*

L.O. 2, 4, 5

Abbot Company experienced the following accounting events during its first year of operation. With the exception of the adjusting entries for depreciation, all transactions were cash transactions.
1. Acquired $80,000 cash by issuing common stock.
2. Paid $15,000 for the materials used to make its products. All products started were completed during the period.
3. Paid salaries of $6,000 to selling and administrative employees.
4. Paid wages of $9,000 to production workers.
5. Paid $12,000 for furniture used in selling and administrative offices. The furniture was acquired on January 1. It had a $1,500 estimated salvage value and a seven-year useful life.
6. Paid $22,000 for manufacturing equipment. The equipment was acquired on January 1. It had a $2,000 estimated salvage value and a five-year useful life.
7. Sold inventory to customers for $43,000 that had cost $25,000 to make.

Required
Explain how these events would affect the balance sheet, income statement, and statement of cash flows by recording them in a horizontal financial statements model as indicated here. The first event is recorded as an example. In the Cash Flow column, indicate whether the amounts represent financing activities (FA), investing activities (IA), or operating activities (OA).

Financial Statements Model									
	Assets					Equity			
Event No.	Cash	+ Inventory	+ Manuf. Equip.*	+ Office Furn.*	=	Com. Stk.	+ Ret. Ear.	Rev. – Exp. = Net Inc.	Cash Flow
1	80,000					80,000			80,000 FA

*Record accumulated depreciation as negative amounts in these columns.

PROBLEM 1–19B *Product Versus General, Selling, and Administrative Costs*

L.O. 2, 3, 4, 5

The following transactions pertain to 2008, the first year of operations of Galon Company. All inventory was started and completed during the accounting period. All transactions were cash transactions.
1. Acquired $56,000 of contributed capital from its owners.
2. Paid $9,600 for materials used to produce inventory.
3. Paid $4,400 to production workers.
4. Paid $5,000 rental fee for production equipment.
5. Paid $1,500 to administrative employees.
6. Paid $3,200 rental fee for administrative office equipment.
7. Produced 1,900 units of inventory of which 1,500 units were sold at a price of $17.40 each.

Required
Prepare an income statement, balance sheet, and statement of cash flows.

PROBLEM 1–20B *Service Versus Manufacturing Companies*

L.O. 2, 3, 4, 5

Foshee Company began operations on January 1, 2005, by issuing common stock for $94,000 cash. During 2005, Foshee received $77,000 cash from revenue and incurred costs that required $90,000 of cash payments.

Required

Prepare an income statement, balance sheet, and statement of cash flows for Foshee Company for 2005, under each of the following independent scenarios.

a. Foshee is an employment agency. The $90,000 was paid for employee salaries and advertising.

b. Foshee is a trucking company. The $90,000 was paid to purchase two trucks. The trucks were purchased on January 1, 2005, had five-year useful lives and no expected salvage value. Foshee uses straight-line depreciation.

c. Foshee is a manufacturing company. The $90,000 was paid to purchase the following items:

　(1) Paid $18,000 cash to purchase materials used to make products during the year.

　(2) Paid $28,000 cash for wages to production workers who make products during the year.

　(3) Paid $4,000 cash for salaries of sales and administrative employees.

　(4) Paid $40,000 cash to purchase manufacturing equipment. The equipment was used solely for the purpose of making products. It had a six-year life and a $4,000 salvage value. The company uses straight-line depreciation.

　(5) During 2005, Foshee started and completed 2,600 units of product. The revenue was earned when Foshee sold 2,200 units of product to its customers.

d. Refer to Part *c*. Could Foshee determine the actual cost of making the 500th unit of product? How likely is it that the actual cost of the 500th unit of product was exactly the same as the cost of producing the 501st unit of product? Explain why management may be more interested in average cost than in actual cost.

L.O. 2, 3, 4, 5, 6　　**PROBLEM 1–21B** *Importance of Cost Classification*

Shunnarah Company was started when it acquired $70,000 by issuing common stock. During the first year of operations, the company incurred specifically identifiable product costs (materials, labor, and overhead) amounting to $40,000. Shunnarah also incurred $20,000 of product development costs. There was a debate regarding how the product development costs should be classified. Advocates of Option 1 believed that the costs should be included in the general, selling, and administrative cost category. Advocates of Option 2 believed it would be more appropriate to classify the product development costs as product costs. During the first year, Shunnarah made 10,000 units of product and sold 8,000 units at a price of $14 each. All transactions were cash transactions.

Required

a. Prepare an income statement, balance sheet, and statement of cash flows under each of the two options.

b. Identify the option that results in financial statements that are more likely to leave a favorable impression on investors and creditors.

c. Assume that Shunnarah provides an incentive bonus to the company president that is equal to 8 percent of net income. Compute the amount of the bonus under each of the two options. Identify the option that provides the president with the higher bonus.

d. Assume a 35 percent income tax rate. Determine the amount of income tax expense under each of the two options. Identify the option that minimizes the amount of the company's income tax expense.

e. Comment on the conflict of interest between the company president as determined in Part *c* and the stockholders of the company as indicated in Part *d*. Describe an incentive compensation plan that would avoid conflicts between the interests of the president and the owners.

L.O. 10　　**PROBLEM 1–22B** *Value Chain Analysis*

Chris Huggins visited her personal physician for treatment of flu symptoms. She was greeted by the receptionist, who gave her personal history and insurance forms to complete. She needed no instructions; she completed these same forms every time she visited the doctor. After completing the forms, Ms. Huggins waited for 30 minutes before being ushered into the patient room. After waiting there for an additional 15 minutes, Dr. Watson entered the room. The doctor ushered Ms. Huggins into the hallway where he weighed her and called her weight out to the nurse for recording. Ms. Huggins had gained 10 pounds since her last visit, and the doctor suggested that she consider going on a diet. Dr. Watson then took her temperature and asked her to return to the patient room. Ten minutes later, he returned to take a throat culture and draw blood. She waited another 15 minutes for the test results. Finally, the doctor returned and told Ms. Huggins that she had strep throat and bronchitis. Dr. Watson prescribed an antibiotic and told her to get at least two days of bed rest. Ms. Huggins was then ushered to the accounting department to settle her bill. The accounting clerk asked her several questions; the answers to most of them were on the forms that she had completed when she first arrived at the office. Finally, Ms. Huggins paid her required copayment and left the office. Three weeks later, she received a bill indicating that she had not paid the copayment. She called the accounting department, and, after a search of the records, the clerk verified that the bill had, in fact, been paid. The clerk apologized for the inconvenience and inquired as to whether Ms. Huggins' health had improved.

Required
a. Identify at least three value-added and three nonvalue-added activities suggested in this scenario.
b. Provide logical suggestions for how to eliminate the nonvalue-added activities.

PROBLEM 1–23B *Using JIT to Reduce Inventory Holding Costs*

L.O. 10

Kane Automobile Dealership, Inc. (KAD), buys and sells a variety of cars made by Goal Motor Corporation. KAD maintains about 30 new cars in its parking lot for customers' selection; the cost of this inventory is approximately $320,000. Additionally, KAD hires security guards to protect the inventory from theft and a maintenance crew to keep the facilities attractive. The total payroll cost for the guards and maintenance crew amounts to $80,000 per year. KAD has a line of credit with a local bank that calls for a 15 percent annual rate of interest. Recently, Jason Caldwell, the president of KAD, learned that a competitor in town, Swann Dealership, has been attracting some of KAD's usual customers because Swann could offer them lower prices. Mr. Caldwell also discovered that Swann carries no inventory at all but shows customers a catalog of cars as well as pertinent information from on-line computer databases. Swann promises to deliver any car that a customer identifies within three working days.

Required
a. Based on the information provided, determine KAD's annual inventory holding cost.
b. Name the inventory system that Swann uses and explain how the system enables Swann to sell at reduced prices.

PROBLEM 1–24 B *Using JIT to Minimize Waste and Lost Opportunity*

L.O. 10

Susan's Hamburger is a small fast-food shop in a busy shopping center that operates only during lunch hours. Susan Khan, the owner and manager of the shop, is confused. On some days, she does not have enough hamburgers to satisfy customer demand. On other days, she has more hamburgers than she can sell. When she has excess hamburgers, she has no choice but to dump them. Usually, Ms. Kahn prepares about 160 hamburgers before the busy lunch hour. The product cost per hamburger is approximately $0.75; the sales price is $2.50 each. Ms. Khan pays general, selling, and administrative expenses that include daily rent of $50 and daily wages of $40.

Required
a. Prepare an income statement based on sales of 100 hamburgers per day. Determine the cost of wasted hamburgers if 160 hamburgers were prepared in advance.
b. Prepare an income statement assuming that 200 customers attempt to buy a hamburger. Since Ms. Kahn has prepared only 160 hamburgers, she must reject 40 customer orders because of insufficient supply. Determine the amount of lost profit.
c. Suppose that hamburgers can be prepared quickly after each customer orders. However, Ms. Kahn must hire an additional part-time employee at a cost of approximately $20 per day. The per unit cost of each hamburger remains at $0.75. Prepare an income statement under the JIT system assuming that 100 hamburgers are sold. Compare the income statement under JIT with the income statement prepared in Requirement *a*. Comment on how the JIT system would affect profitability.
d. Assume the same facts as in Requirement *c* with respect to a JIT system that requires additional labor costing $20 per day. Prepare an income statement under the JIT system, assuming that 200 hamburgers are sold. Compare the income statement under JIT with the income statement prepared in Requirement *b*. Comment on how the JIT system would affect profitability.
e. Explain how the JIT system might be able to improve customer satisfaction as well as profitability.

ANALYZE, THINK, COMMUNICATE

BUSINESS APPLICATIONS CASE *Financial Versus Managerial Accounting*

ATC 1–1

In the July 20, 1998, edition of *Business Week* magazine, Harold Ruttenberg, founder and CEO of Just For Feet, Inc., referred to some information that highlighted his company's success. When comparing his "big box stores" to his mall-based rivals, he noted that the size of a typical Just For Feet store is between 15,000 and 25,000 square feet, while rival stores such as Foot Locker and Footaction USA, Inc., average between 4,000 and 6,000. Ruttenberg noted that the larger size lets Just For Feet buy in bulk and negotiate discounts of between 15 percent and 20 percent. These discounts are passed on to customers in each store's Combat Zone, where discounts can reach 70 percent. Such discounting has enabled Just For Feet to retain a highly competitive pricing advantage. Ruttenberg also highlighted the company's selection and training programs that have produced employees whose performance far outpaces the competition. The average Just For Feet store produces sales of $650 per square foot; the typical mall store produces only $250 per square foot. On the down side, Ruttenberg noted that Just For Feet experienced a sharp increase in inventory holding costs until an information system was installed to help bring the inventory stock level down. It fell 22 percent, from $152 of inventory per square foot in 1996 to $119 of inventory per square foot in 1997.

Required

a. Indicate whether the information described in this narrative would be best described as financial or managerial accounting information. Support your answer with appropriate commentary.

b. Provide some additional examples of managerial and financial accounting information that could apply to Just For Feet, Inc.

c. Explain why the manager of a Just For Feet store needs different kinds of information than investors or creditors need. Give an example of information that would be useful to a store manager but irrelevant to an investor or creditor.

ATC 1–2   GROUP ASSIGNMENT *Product Versus Upstream and Downstream Costs*

Victor Holt, the accounting manager of Sexton Inc., gathered the following information for 2006. Some of it can be used to construct an income statement for 2006. Ignore items that do not appear on an income statement. Some computation may be required. For example, the cost of manufacturing equipment would not appear on the income statement. However, the cost of manufacturing equipment is needed to compute the amount of depreciation. All units of product were started and completed in 2006.

1. Issued $864,000 of common stock.
2. Paid engineers in the product design department $10,000 for salaries that were accrued at the end of the previous year.
3. Incurred advertising expenses of $70,000.
4. Paid $720,000 for materials used to manufacture the company's product.
5. Incurred utility costs of $160,000. These costs were allocated to different departments on the basis of square footage of floor space. Mr. Holt identified three departments and determined the square footage of floor space for each department to be as shown in the table to the right.

Department	Square Footage
Research and development	10,000
Manufacturing	60,000
Selling and administrative	30,000
Total	100,000

6. Paid $880,000 for wages of production workers.
7. Paid cash of $658,000 for salaries of administrative personnel. There was $16,000 of accrued salaries owed to administrative personnel at the end of 2006. There was no beginning balance in the Salaries Payable account for administrative personnel.
8. Purchased manufacturing equipment two years ago at a cost of $10,000,000. The equipment had an eight-year useful life and a $2,000,000 salvage value.
9. Paid $390,000 cash to engineers in the product design department.
10. Paid a $258,000 cash dividend to owners.
11. Paid $80,000 to set up manufacturing equipment for production.
12. Paid a one-time $186,000 restructuring cost to redesign the production process to implement a just-in-time inventory system.
13. Prepaid the premium on a new insurance policy covering nonmanufacturing employees. The policy cost $72,000 and had a one-year term with an effective starting date of May 1. Four employees work in the research and development department and eight employees in the selling and administrative department. Assume a December 31 closing date.
14. Made 69,400 units of product and sold 60,000 units at a price of $70 each.

Required

a. Divide the class into groups of four or five students per group, and then organize the groups into three sections. Assign Task 1 to the first section of groups, Task 2 to the second section of groups, and Task 3 to the third section of groups.

Group Tasks

(1) Identify the items that are classified as product costs and determine the amount of cost of goods sold reported on the 2006 income statement.

(2) Identify the items that are classified as upstream costs and determine the amount of upstream cost expensed on the 2006 income statement.

(3) Identify the items that are classified as downstream costs and determine the amount of downstream cost expensed on the 2006 income statement.

b. Have the class construct an income statement in the following manner. Select a member of one of the groups assigned the first group task identifying the product costs. Have that person go to the board and list the costs included in the determination of cost of goods sold. Anyone in the other groups who disagrees with one of the classifications provided by the person at the board should voice an objection and explain why the item should be classified differently. The instructor should lead the class to a consensus on the disputed items. After the amount of cost of goods sold is determined, the student at the board constructs the part of the income statement showing the determination of gross margin. The exercise continues in a similar fashion with representatives from the other sections explaining the composition of the upstream and downstream costs. These items are added to the income statement started by the first group representative. The final result is a completed income statement.

RESEARCH ASSIGNMENT *Financial Versus Managerial Accounting*

ATC 1–3

Starting on page 26 of the September 21, 1998, issue of *Business Week* is an article entitled "Billboards Aren't Boring Anymore." Read this article and complete the following requirements.

Required
a. Identify information in this article that is associated with financial accounting.
b. Identify information in this article that is associated with managerial accounting.
c. Explain how the president of Delta Airlines could use the information in this article to improve the profitability of his company.
d. Explain how an investor could use the information in this article to improve the average return on her investment portfolio.
e. Comment on the usefulness of the article to the manager of the kitchen of a Pizza Hut restaurant.

WRITING ASSIGNMENT *Emerging Practices in Managerial Accounting*

ATC 1–4

The 1998 annual report of the Maytag Corporation contained the following excerpt:

During the first quarter of 1996, the Company announced the restructuring of its major appliance operations in an effort to strengthen its position in the industry and to deliver improved performance to both customers and shareowners. This included the consolidation of two separate organizational units into a single operation responsible for all activities associated with the manufacture and distribution of the Company's brands of major appliances and the closing of a cooking products plant in Indianapolis, Indiana, with transfer of that production to an existing plant in Cleveland, Tennessee.

The restructuring cost Maytag $40 million and disrupted the lives of many of the company's employees.

Required
Assume that you are Maytag's vice president of human relations. Write a letter to the employees who are affected by the restructuring. The letter should explain why it was necessary for the company to undertake the restructuring. Your explanation should refer to the ideas discussed in the section "Emerging Trends in Managerial Accounting" of this chapter.

ETHICAL DILEMMA *Product Cost Versus Selling and Administrative Expense*

ATC 1–5

Eddie Emerson is a proud woman with a problem. Her daughter has been accepted into a prestigious law school. While Ms. Emerson beams with pride, she is worried sick about how to pay for the school; she is a single parent who has worked hard to support herself and her three children. She had to go heavily into debt to finance her own education. Even though she now has a good job, family needs have continued to outpace her income and her debt burden is staggering. She knows she will be unable to borrow the money needed for her daughter's law school.

Ms. Emerson is the controller of a small manufacturing company. She has just accepted a new job offer. Indeed, she has not yet told her employer that she will be leaving in a month. She is concerned that her year-end incentive bonus may be affected if her boss learns of her plans to leave. She plans to inform the company immediately after receiving the bonus. She knows her behavior is less than honorable, but she believes that she has been underpaid for a long time. Her boss, a relative of the company's owner, makes twice what she makes and does half the work. Why should she care about leaving with a little extra cash? Indeed, she is considering an opportunity to boost the bonus.

Ms. Emerson's bonus is based on a percentage of net income. Her company recently introduced a new product line that required substantial production start-up costs. Ms. Emerson is fully aware that GAAP requires these costs to be expensed in the current accounting period, but no one else in the company has the technical expertise to know exactly how the costs should be treated. She is considering misclassifying the start-up costs as product costs. If the costs are misclassified, net income will be significantly higher, resulting in a nice boost in her incentive bonus. By the time the auditors discover the misclassification, Ms. Emerson will have moved on to her new job. If the matter is brought to the attention of her new employer, she will simply plead ignorance. Considering her daughter's needs, Ms. Emerson decides to classify the start-up costs as product costs.

Required

a. Based on this information, indicate whether Ms. Emerson believes the number of units of product sold will be equal to, less than, or greater than, the number of units made. Write a brief paragraph explaining the logic that supports your answer.

b. Explain how the misclassification could mislead an investor or creditor regarding the company's financial condition.

c. Explain how the misclassification could affect income taxes.

d. Identify the factors that contributed to the breach of ethical conduct. When constructing your answer, you may want to refer to the section "Common Features of Criminal and Ethical Misconduct" of this chapter.

e. Review the standards of ethical conduct shown in Exhibit 1–13 and identify at least two standards that Ms. Emerson's misclassification of the start-up costs violated.

ATC 1–6   SPREADSHEET ASSIGNMENT *Using Excel*

The following transactions pertain to 2006, the first year operations of the Barlett Company. All inventory was started and completed during 2006. Assume that all transactions are cash transactions.

1. Acquired $2,000 cash by issuing common stock.
2. Paid $400 for materials used to produce inventory.
3. Paid $600 to production workers.
4. Paid $200 rental fee for production equipment.
5. Paid $160 to administrative employees.
6. Paid $80 rental fee for administrative office equipment.
7. Produced 300 units of inventory of which 200 units were sold at a price of $7.00 each.

Required

Construct a spreadsheet that includes the income statement, balance sheet, and statement of cash flows.

ATC 1–7   SPREADSHEET ASSIGNMENT *Mastering Excel*

Mantooth Manufacturing Company experienced the following accounting events during its first year of operation. With the exception of the adjusting entries for depreciation, assume that all transactions are cash transactions.

1. Acquired $50,000 by issuing common stock.
2. Paid $8,000 for the materials used to make its products, all of which were started and completed during the year.
3. Paid salaries of $4,400 to selling and administrative employees.
4. Paid wages of $7,000 to production workers.
5. Paid $9,600 for furniture used in selling and administrative offices. The furniture was acquired on January 1. It had a $1,600 estimated salvage value and a four-year useful life.
6. Paid $13,000 for manufacturing equipment. The equipment was acquired on January 1. It had a $1,000 estimated salvage value and a three-year useful life.
7. Sold inventory to customers for $25,000 that had cost $14,000 to make.

Construct a spreadsheet of the financial statements model as shown here:

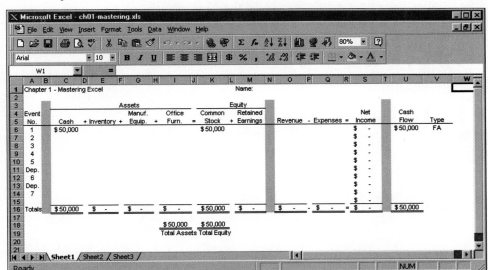

Required

Place formulas in row 16 to automatically add the columns. Also add formulas in column S to calculate net income after each event, and add formulas in row 18 to compute total assets and equity. Notice that you must enter the events since only the first one is shown as an example.

Spreadsheet Tips

1. The column widths are set by choosing Format, then Column, and then Width.
2. The shading in columns B, N, and T is added by highlighting a column and choosing Format, then Cells, and then clicking on the tab titled Patterns and choosing a color.
3. The sum function is an easy way to add a column or row. For example, the formula in cell C16 is =SUM(C6:C15).
4. As an example of the formulas in column S (net income), the formula in cell S7 is =S6+O7−Q7.
5. If you find that some of the columns are too far to the right to appear on your screen, you can set the zoom level to show the entire spreadsheet. The zoom is set by choosing View, then Zoom, and then clicking on Custom and typing 100 percent in the box. The shortcut method to set the zoom is to click in the box on the right side of the top tool bar that appears immediately below the menu.

Chapter

2

Cost Behavior, Operating Leverage, and Profitability Analysis

Learning Objectives

After completing this chapter, you should be able to:

1 Distinguish between fixed and variable cost behavior.

2 Understand how operating leverage affects profitability.

3 Understand how cost behavior affects profitability.

4 Prepare an income statement under a contribution margin approach.

5 Calculate the magnitude of operating leverage.

6 Use cost behavior to create a competitive operating advantage.

7 Understand how cost behavior is affected by the relevant range and the decision-making context.

8 Select an appropriate time period for the calculation of the average cost per unit.

9 Define the term *mixed costs*.

10 Use the high-low method and scattergraphs to estimate fixed and variable costs.

the *curious* accountant

Most people would expect an increase in a company's revenues to cause an increase in its profits, but they may be surprised that a small percentage of change in revenue can generate a dramatic difference in profits. Consider the following data for Texaco.

Year	Revenues (in millions)	Percentage Increase From Previous Year	Operating Income Before Taxes (in millions)	Percentage Increase From Previous Year
2000	$50,100	43.5	$4,218	137.1
1999	34,925	13.0	1,779	153.8
1998	30,910	N/A	701	N/A

Note that the profitability numbers shown are for *operating income before taxes;* they do not include any unusual items that may have occurred at Texaco. Considering this, what could possibly explain how a relatively small increase in revenue (13%) could result in such a large increase in operating income (153.8%)?

*Three college students have decided to take a short vacation. They are considering inviting a fourth person to join them. One student remarks that they will all save money if the fourth person goes along because many of the costs necessary to make the trip will be the same regardless of whether three or four people go. For example, the cost of the hotel room is $90 per night. If three people stay in the room, the cost per person is $30 ($90 ÷ 3 = $30). If four people stay in the room, the cost is only $22.50 per person ($90 ÷ 4 = $22.50). In accounting terms, the cost of the hotel room is a **fixed cost.** In other words, the total cost is fixed at $90 even if the number of people staying in the room changes. Other costs vary, depending on how many people participate. Food costs will likely be more for four people than for three. The*

51

*food cost is an example of **variable cost**. If the fixed costs are high in relation to the variable costs, adding additional participants will significantly reduce the cost per person. Indeed, the differential could be so significant that it would influence a person's decision as to whether to make the trip. Accordingly, the way a cost behaves (i.e., is fixed or variable) can have a significant impact on decision making.*

LO1 Distinguish between fixed and variable cost behavior.

▌Fixed Cost Behavior

This chapter examines the effect of cost behavior on the risks and rewards of operating a business. Just as fixed and variable cost behavior can impact personal choices, it can also affect business decisions such as these. How much more will it cost to send one more employee to a sales meeting? If more people buy our products, can we charge less? If sales increase by 10 percent, how will profits be affected? Managers seeking answers to such questions must consider the relationships between costs and activities. Examples of activity measures include the number of people attending a training program, the amount of goods sold, the number of clients served, the number of orders processed, the number of sales calls made, the number of products made, and the number of patients treated. Knowing how costs behave in relation to a given level of business activity enables management to maximize profitability through more effective planning and control. To illustrate, consider the case of Star Productions, Inc. (SPI).

SPI is an entertainment company that specializes in promoting rock concerts. The company is considering paying a band $48,000 to play a concert. Obviously, SPI must sell enough tickets to cover this cost. In this case, the relevant activity base is the number of tickets sold. The cost of the band is a *fixed cost* because it does not change with the number of tickets sold. Exhibit 2–1 demonstrates fixed cost behavior patterns by showing the *total cost* and the *cost per unit* at three different levels of activity.

Exhibit 2–1 *Fixed Cost Behavior*			
Number of tickets sold (a)	2,700	3,000	3,300
Total cost of band (b)	$48,000	$48,000	$48,000
Cost per ticket sold (b ÷ a)	$17.78	$16.00	$14.55

Notice that fixed cost in *total* and fixed cost *per unit* exhibit distinctly different behavior patterns. The total cost of the band remains constant (i.e., fixed) at $48,000 regardless of the number of tickets sold. Accordingly, there is logical consistency between the term *fixed cost* and the cost behavior pattern with respect to *total cost*. In other words, *total fixed cost remains constant (i.e., fixed) when activity changes.* In contrast, *fixed cost per unit* changes inversely each time the number of tickets sold changes. As the number of tickets sold increases, the fixed cost per ticket decreases. As ticket sales decrease, fixed cost per ticket increases. This means that there is a contradiction between the term *fixed cost per unit* and the behavior pattern that is implied in the terminology. Specifically, *fixed cost per unit* is *not fixed.* Instead, it changes each time the number of tickets changes. This contradiction in terminology can cause untold confusion. We highly recommend that you carefully study the behavior patterns shown in Exhibit 2–2 before proceeding with your reading assignment.

Clearly, the fixed cost data shown in Exhibit 2–1 are useful in helping management decide whether to sponsor the concert. For example, the information could be used to examine potential pricing scenarios. The per unit cost data represent the minimum ticket prices required to cover the fixed cost at various levels of activity. These data could be compared to the prices

Exhibit 2–2 *Fixed Cost Behavior*		
When Activity	**Increases**	**Decreases**
Total fixed cost	Remains constant	Remains constant
Fixed cost **per unit**	Decreases	Increases

of other events that would compete for the customer's business (movie prices, prices of sporting events, prices of theater tickets, etc.). If the concert prices are not competitive, sales will not materialize and the business venture will lose money. Similarly, management must assess the likelihood of being able to sell the various numbers of tickets. How do these data compare with the band's track record for ticket sales at other

W ho cares if costs exhibit fixed or variable behavior? Andrew Farkas cares. Mr. Farkas has used the concept of fixed cost to establish a successful real estate property management company, Insignia Financial Group. Mr. Farkas's stake in Insignia is reported to be worth approximately $160 million. Property management companies existed before Mr. Farkas started Insignia, but the property management business was considered to have a relatively low profit potential because the costs of operating such companies were high relative to the level of revenue they were able to generate. Mr. Farkas spent millions of dollars to develop a standardized computer management process. The investment was substantial, and the cost was basically fixed. When Mr. Farkas implemented an aggressive plan to expand Insignia's client base, revenues soared but costs remained relatively stable. The result was a highly profitable business that earned Mr. Farkas recognition as the "first new real-estate mogul in a decade."

Source: Fred Vogelstein, "A Real-Estate Tycoon for the '90s," *U.S. News & World Report,* May 19, 1997, p. 52.

concerts? Although decision making always involves uncertainty, applying appropriate analytical techniques such as those discussed in this chapter can reduce risk.

■ Operating Leverage

You probably know that large objects can be moved with little effort when *physical leverage* is properly applied. In business, managers apply **operating leverage** to convert small changes in revenue into dramatic changes in profitability. Fixed costs constitute the *lever* that managers use to accomplish the disproportionate changes between revenue and profitability. The leverage relationships between revenue, fixed costs, and profitability are depicted in Exhibit 2–3.

LO2 Understand how operating leverage affects profitability.

When *all costs are fixed,* every additional sales dollar contributes one dollar toward the potential profitability of a project. In other words, once fixed costs have been covered, each sales dollar represents pure profit. As a result, a small change in the volume of sales can have a significant effect on profitability. To illustrate, assume that SPI estimates that it will sell 3,000 tickets for $18 each. Given this starting point, a 10 percent difference in actual versus estimated sales volume will produce a 90 percent difference in profitability. This fact can be verified by examining the data shown in Exhibit 2–4.

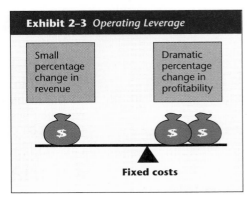

Exhibit 2–3 *Operating Leverage*

Exhibit 2–4 *Effect of Operating Leverage on Profitability*					
Number of tickets sold	2,700	⇐−10% ⇐	3,000	⇒+10% ⇒	3,300
Sales revenue ($18 per ticket)	$48,600		$54,000		$59,400
Cost of band (fixed cost)	(48,000)		(48,000)		(48,000)
Gross profit	$ 600	⇐−90% ⇐	$ 6,000	⇒+90% ⇒	$11,400

Calculating Percentages

The percentages shown in Exhibit 2–4 are computed by comparing a base measure with one of the alternative measures. To illustrate, we compute the percentage change in the gross profit at 3,000 units (i.e., base measure) with the gross profit at 3,300 units (i.e., the alternative measure). The percentage change is computed in two steps. First, subtract the gross profit at the base measure ($6,000) from the gross profit at the alternative ($11,400). The difference is $5,400 ($11,400 − $6,000). Next, divide the difference by the base measure of gross profit. The result is a 90 percent increase in profitability ($5,400 ÷ $6,000 = 0.90). The percentage decline in profitability is computed in a similar manner. First, determine the difference in the base measure of gross profit and the alternative measure of gross profit ($600 − $6,000 = −$5,400). Divide the difference by the base (−$5,400 ÷ $6,000 = −0.90). The minus sign indicates that profitability *declined* by 90 percent. The general formula for the computation of the percentage change is as follows:

$$[(\text{Alternative measure} - \text{Base measure}) \div \text{Base measure}] \times 100 = \% \text{ change}$$

Students frequently miscalculate percentages because they do not carefully consider the identification of the base measure versus the alternative measures. It may help to think of the base measure as the starting point and the alternative measure as the final destination. In the preceding example, the starting point (base measure) was the data set at estimated sales of 3,000 units. The alternative measures were the data sets if actual sales ended up being either 2,700 units or 3,300 units. You should force yourself to distinguish between the *base measure* and the *alternative measures* before you make any computations. Rushing into the calculations can lead to errors. Your motto should always be *think before you calculate.*

Economies of Scale

The concept of operating leverage is consistent with what economists call the **economies of scale.** This concept recognizes that *the cost per unit can be reduced by taking advantage of opportunities that become available when the size of an operation increases.* In SPI's case, the cost per ticket decreases as the number of tickets sold increases. Since the level of sales affects the cost per ticket, it affects pricing and profitability as well. Clearly, SPI can charge less if 3,000 people buy tickets than if only 2,700 do so. Lower prices may, in turn, spark higher levels of customer demand, which then lowers unit cost even further. Accordingly, managers must pay careful attention to the expected behavior patterns as well as the amounts of the cost components of a particular business venture. The relationship between fixed cost and the level of expected activity is a significant factor in many managerial decisions.

Risk and Reward Assessment

Risk refers to the possibility that sacrifices may exceed benefits. Once incurred, a fixed cost is an unalterable economic sacrifice. As such, it represents the ultimate risk associated with a particular business project. If SPI pays the band but nobody buys a ticket, the company will lose $48,000. SPI can avoid this risk by converting the *fixed cost* into a *variable cost.*

▌Variable Cost Behavior

LO2 Understand how operating leverage affects profitability.

To illustrate variable cost behavior, assume that SPI is able to convince the band to play for compensation equal to $16 per ticket sold. Exhibit 2–5 shows the total cost of hiring the band and the cost per ticket sold at three different levels of activity.

Since the band is paid $16 for each ticket sold, the *total variable cost* increases in direct proportion to the number of tickets sold. A total cost of $16 will be incurred if SPI sells one ticket (1 × $16); the total cost if two tickets are sold is $32 (2 × $16); ticket sales of three results in

Exhibit 2–5 *Variable Cost Behavior*

Number of tickets sold (a)	2,700	3,000	3,300
Total cost of band (b)	$43,200	$48,000	$52,800
Cost per ticket sold (b ÷ a)	$16	$16	$16

total cost of $48 (3 × $16), and so on. This explains why the total cost of the band increases proportionally as ticket sales move from 2,700 to 3,000 to 3,300. The *variable cost per ticket* remains at $16, however, regardless of whether the number of tickets sold is 1,

Exhibit 2–6 *Variable Cost Behavior*

When Activity	Increases	Decreases
Total variable cost	Increases proportionately	Decreases proportionately
Variable cost **per unit**	Remains constant	Remains constant

2, 3, or 3,000. Notice that variable cost per unit behaves in a manner that is contradictory to the behavior implied in the terminology. Specifically, *variable cost* per unit *remains constant* regardless of how many tickets are sold. Here also you should carefully study the behavior patterns of a variable cost that are shown in Exhibit 2–6 before proceeding with your reading assignment.

Notice that shifting the cost structure from fixed to variable has enabled SPI to avoid the fixed cost risk. If no one buys a ticket, SPI loses nothing because the company incurs no cost. If only one person buys a ticket at the $18 ticket price, SPI earns a $2 profit ($18 sales revenue − $16 cost of band). Does this mean that managers should avoid fixed costs whenever possible? Not necessarily. Shifting the cost structure from fixed to variable reduces not only the level of risk but also the potential for profits. In other words, managers cannot avoid the downside risk of a fixed cost operating structure without also losing the upside benefit. Exhibit 2–7 shows that when the cost structure is variable, the relationship between sales and profitability is proportional. A 10 percent increase in sales results in a 10 percent increase in profitability. Likewise, a 10 percent decline in sales produces a corresponding 10 percent decline in profitability. Variable costs do not provide opportunities for operating leverage.

Exhibit 2–7 *Variable Cost Eliminates Operating Leverage*

Number of tickets sold	2,700	⇐−10% ⇐	3,000	⇒+10% ⇒	3,300
Sales revenue ($18 per ticket)	$48,600		$54,000		$59,400
Cost of band (variable cost)	(43,200)		(48,000)		(52,800)
Gross profit	$ 5,400	⇐−10% ⇐	$ 6,000	⇒+10% ⇒	$ 6,600

Suppose that you are sponsoring a political rally at which Ralph Nader will speak. You estimate that approximately 2,000 people will buy tickets to hear Mr. Nader's speech. The tickets are expected to be priced at $12 each. Would you prefer a contract that agrees to pay Mr. Nader $10,000 or one that agrees to pay him $5 per ticket purchased?

Answer Your answer would depend on how certain you are that 2,000 people will purchase tickets. If it were likely that many more than 2,000 tickets would be sold, you would be better off with a fixed cost structure, agreeing to pay Mr. Nader a flat fee of $10,000. If attendance numbers are highly uncertain, you would be better off with a variable cost structure thereby guaranteeing a lower cost if fewer people buy tickets.

Check Yourself 2–1

Relationship Between Cost Behavior and Revenue

Exhibit 2–8 compares the relationship between revenue and total fixed cost with the relationship between revenue and total variable cost. Clearly, a pure fixed cost structure offers greater risk and higher potential rewards. A company will incur a loss until it has generated enough revenue to cover its fixed cost. Thereafter, every dollar of revenue represents pure profit. As volume increases, income becomes disproportionately larger than total costs. In contrast, a pure variable cost structure offers security (a profit is earned at any level of sales). Unfortunately, costs increase proportionately with increases in revenue, thereby eliminating disproportionate growth in profitability.

LO1 Distinguish between fixed and variable cost behavior.

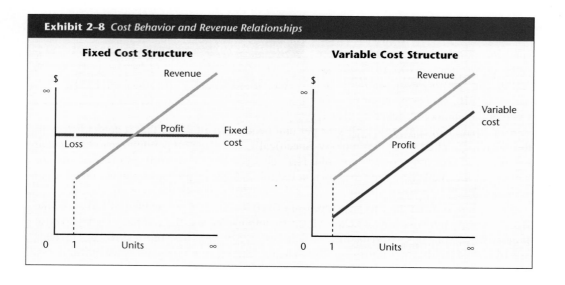

Exhibit 2–8 *Cost Behavior and Revenue Relationships*

∎ Effect of Cost Structure on Profit Stability

LO3 Understand how cost behavior affects profitability.

The preceding discussion suggests that companies with higher levels of fixed costs are more likely to experience earnings volatility. To further illustrate this point, consider the following scenario. Suppose that three companies produce and sell the same product. Each company sells 10 units for $10 each. Furthermore, each company incurs $60 of cost in the process of making and selling its products. Despite these similarities, the companies operate under radically different **cost structures.** The entire $60 of cost incurred by Company A is fixed. Company B incurs $30 of fixed cost and $30 of variable cost ($3 per unit). All $60 of cost incurred by Company C is variable ($6 per unit). The income statements of the three companies are shown in Exhibit 2–9.

When sales change, the size of the corresponding change in net income is directly related to the company's cost structure. The more fixed cost, the higher the fluctuation in net income. To illustrate, assume that sales increase by one unit; the resulting income statements are shown in Exhibit 2–10.

Company A, which has the highest level of fixed costs, experienced a $10 ($50 − $40) increase in profitability; Company C, which has the lowest level of fixed cost (zero), had only a $4 ($44 − $40) increase in profitability. Company B, which had a 50/50 mixture of fixed and variable cost, had a mid-range $7 ($47 − $40) increase in net income. The effect of fixed cost on volatility holds for decreases as well as increases in sales volume. To illustrate, assume that sales decrease by one unit (from 10 to 9 units). The resulting income statements are shown in Exhibit 2–11.

Here, also, Company A experiences the largest variance in earnings ($10 decrease). Company B had a moderate decline of $7, and Company C had the least volatility with only a $4 decline. Clearly, the stability of earnings is directly related to a company's cost structure. So what is the best structure? If given a choice, should a manager select fixed or variable costs? There is no definitive answer to this question. How-

Exhibit 2–9 *Income Statements*

	Company Name		
	A	**B**	**C**
Variable Cost per Unit (a)	$0	$3	$6
Sales Revenue (10 units × $10)	$100	$100	$100
Variable Cost (10 units × a)	0	(30)	(60)
Fixed Cost	(60)	(30)	0
Net Income	$ 40	$ 40	$ 40

Exhibit 2–10 *Income Statements*

	Company Name		
	A	**B**	**C**
Variable Cost per Unit (a)	$0	$3	$6
Sales Revenue (11 units × $10)	$110	$110	$110
Variable Cost (11 units × a)	0	(33)	(66)
Fixed Cost	(60)	(30)	0
Net Income	$ 50	$ 47	$ 44

After reading the preceding material, you should understand that Texaco's dramatic growth in net income was due in part to operating leverage. You now know that a company's cost structure affects the relationship between changes in its revenues and changes in its profits. Companies with relatively high fixed costs have relatively high operating leverage. More specifically, a given percentage change in revenues can cause a much larger change in its profits. Petroleum companies have many fixed costs. For example, the costs of the refineries and oil tankers (depreciation) stay constant (fixed) regardless of the amount of gasoline produced. Other assets that are likely to result in fixed depreciation charges include the cost of computer systems,

office furniture, fuel trucks, and other equipment. Indeed, Texaco's fixed assets and the resultant depreciation charges between 1998 and 2000 remained relatively constant (see the following data from Texaco's annual reports).

Year	Property, Plant & Equipment (in millions)	Percentage Change From Previous Year
2000	$15,681	0.78
1999	15,560	5.42
1998	14,761	N/A

ever, rational responses can be given for specific sets of circumstances. Highly leveraged companies (those with high levels of fixed cost) experience higher profits when sales increase and higher losses when sales decline. Companies with low leverage have more stable earnings. Revenue changes trigger corresponding increases and decreases in net income, but the magnitude of those swings is lower if the degree of operating leverage is low. A manager who believes that revenues are likely to increase should create a highly leveraged cost structure. If the manager locks costs in, when sales grow she will reap significant rewards. On the other hand, if there is a great deal of uncertainty about earnings growth or if the manager believes that revenue is likely to decline, it would be wise to develop a low leverage cost structure.

Exhibit 2–11 *Income Statements*

	Company Name		
	A	B	C
Variable Cost per Unit (a)	$0	$3	$6
Sales Revenue (9 units × $10)	$90	$90	$90
Variable Cost (9 units × a)	0	(27)	(54)
Fixed Cost	(60)	(30)	0
Net Income	$30	$33	$36

If both Kroger Food Stores and Delta Airlines were to experience a 5 percent increase in revenues, which company would be more likely to experience a higher percentage increase in net income?

Answer Delta would be more likely to experience a higher percentage increase in net income because a large portion of its cost (e.g., employee salaries and depreciation) is fixed cost, while a large portion of Kroger's cost is variable (e.g., cost of goods sold).

Check Yourself 2–2

■ Determination of the Contribution Margin

The relationships between cost structure and profitability are so important that managerial accountants frequently construct income statements in which costs are categorized according to their behavior patterns. The first step under this approach is to subtract variable costs from revenue; the result is called the **contribution margin.** This margin represents the amount that is available to pay fixed expenses and thereafter to provide profits to the enterprise. The amount of net income is computed by subtracting the fixed costs from the contribution margin. The contribution margin approach is not acceptable for public reporting (i.e., GAAP prohibits its use in external financial reports), but it is widely used for internal reporting purposes.

LO4 Prepare an income statement under the contribution margin approach.

57

Measurement of Operating Leverage Using Contribution Margin

LO5 Calculate the magnitude of operating leverage.

The contribution margin approach has many applications that will be discussed in later chapters of this text. One application that is pertinent to the material in this chapter is the measurement of operating leverage. To illustrate, assume that the comparative income statements shown in Exhibit 2–12 are available for Bragg Company and Biltmore Company. The formula for determining the magnitude of the operating leverage is as follows:

$$\text{Operating leverage} = \frac{\text{Contribution margin}}{\text{Net income}}$$

Applying this formula to the income statement data reported for Bragg and Biltmore produces the following measures.

Bragg Company

$$\text{Operating leverage} = \frac{\$140}{\$20} = 7$$

Biltmore Company

$$\text{Operating leverage} = \frac{\$80}{\$20} = 4$$

Exhibit 2–12 *Income Statements*

	Company Name	
	Bragg	**Biltmore**
Variable Cost per Unit (a)	$6	$12
Sales Revenue (10 units × $20)	$200	$200
Variable Cost (10 units × a)	(60)	(120)
Contribution Margin	140	80
Fixed Cost	(120)	(60)
Net Income	$ 20	$ 20

Exhibit 2–13 *Comparative Income Statements for Bragg Company*

Units (a)	10		11
Sales Revenue ($20 × a)	$200	⇒+10% ⇒	$220
Variable Cost ($6 × a)	(60)		(66)
Contribution Margin	140		154
Fixed Cost	(120)		(120)
Net Income	$ 20	⇒+70% ⇒	$ 34

Exhibit 2–14 *Comparative Income Statements for Biltmore Company*

Units (a)	10		11
Sales Revenue ($20 × a)	$200	⇒+10% ⇒	$220
Variable Cost ($12 × a)	(120)		(132)
Contribution Margin	80		88
Fixed Cost	(60)		(60)
Net Income	$ 20	⇒+40% ⇒	$ 28

The computations indicate that Bragg is more highly leveraged than Biltmore. Given a percentage change in revenue, Bragg's corresponding change in profitability is seven times greater than the change in revenue. In contrast, Biltmore's profits change only at the rate of four times the percentage change in revenue. More specifically, a 10 percent increase in revenue produces a 70 percent increase (10 percent × 7) in profitability for Bragg Company and 40 percent increase (10 percent × 4) in profitability for Biltmore Company. This condition is verified by the income statements shown in Exhibits 2–13 and 2–14.

As previously indicated, operating leverage is neither good nor bad; it is a condition that can work to a company's advantage or disadvantage, depending on how it is used. The following section explains how operating leverage can be used to create a competitive advantage in business practice.

Check Yourself 2–3

Boeing Company's 2001 10K annual report filed with the Securities and Exchange Commission refers to "higher commercial airlines segment margins." Is Boeing referring to gross margins or contribution margins?

Answer Since the data come from the company's external annual report, the reference must be to gross margins (revenue − cost of goods sold), a product cost measure. The contribution margin (revenue − variable cost) is a measure used in internal reporting.

Use of Fixed Cost to Provide a Competitive Operating Advantage

Mary MaHall and John Strike have established tutoring services companies to support themselves while they are attending college. Both Ms. MaHall and Mr. Strike act as business managers and hire other students to provide the tutoring services offered by their companies. Ms. MaHall pays her tutors salaries; her labor costs are fixed at $16,000 per year regardless of the number of hours of tutoring performed. Mr. Strike pays his employees $8 per hour; accordingly, his labor is a variable cost. Both currently provide 2,000 hours of tutoring services at the price of $11 per hour. As indicated in Exhibit 2–15, both companies currently produce the same profit.

LO6 Use cost behavior to create a competitive operating advantage.

Exhibit 2–15 Comparative Profitability at 2,000 Hours of Tutoring				
		MaHall		**Strike**
Number of hours of tutoring provided		2,000		2,000
Service revenue ($11 per hour)		$22,000		$22,000
Cost of tutors	Fixed	(16,000)	Variable ($8 × 2,000)	(16,000)
Net income		$ 6,000		$ 6,000

Suppose that each company adopts a strategy to take over the other company's customers by reducing the price of tutoring services to $7 per hour. First consider what happens to Ms. MaHall if she successfully implements this strategy. Then consider what happens to Mr. Strike if he successfully implements this strategy. Look at each case independently. In other words, what happens if Ms. MaHall's company takes over Mr. Strike's customers, thereby raising its services to 4,000 hours? Next, what happens to Mr. Strike if he takes over Ms. MaHall's customers (i.e., he provides 4,000 hours of tutoring)? The profitability for each scenario is shown in Exhibit 2–16.

Exhibit 2–16 Comparative Profitability at 4,000 Hours of Tutoring				
		MaHall		**Strike**
Number of hours of tutoring provided		4,000		4,000
Service revenue ($7 per hour)		$28,000		$28,000
Cost of tutors	Fixed	(16,000)	Variable ($8 × 4,000)	(32,000)
Net income (loss)		$12,000		$(4,000)

Ms. MaHall's fixed cost structure enables her company to operate at significantly higher levels of activity without increasing the cost of providing services. Unfortunately for him, Mr. Strike's costs increase proportionally with increases in sales volume. This situation places MaHall at a competitive advantage when activity increases. However, do not forget that operating leverage works both ways. Suppose that a new computer-assisted tutoring services company enters the market. The new service is more expensive, but it is technologically superior to the services that Ms. MaHall and Mr. Strike provide. Accordingly, some of their customers choose to spend the extra money necessary to obtain the computer-assisted instruction. Ms. MaHall and Mr. Strike can continue to provide services at the original price of $11 per hour. However, total demand falls to 1,000 hours. Even if Ms. MaHall could capture the entire market, her operations would produce a loss as indicated in Exhibit 2–17. On the other hand, Mr. Strike can produce a profit at any number of hours from one to infinity. This fact is demonstrated by showing his profit picture at 1,000 hours in Exhibit 2–17.

No absolute rules exist as to whether a company should operate with fixed versus variable costs. Management accountants are required to exercise judgment in performing their duties;

Exhibit 2–17 *Comparative Profitability at 1,000 Hours of Tutoring*

		MaHall		Strike
Number of hours of tutoring provided		1,000		1,000
Service revenue ($11 per hour)		$11,000		$11,000
Cost of tutors	Fixed	(16,000)	Variable ($8 × 1,000)	(8,000)
Net income (loss)		$ (5,000)		$ 3,000

they must understand how **cost behavior** can affect profitability under different operating scenarios. They must also make predictions as to the business conditions that are likely to prevail once their operating strategy is implemented.

■ Cost Behavior Summarized

The previous illustrations introduced the terms *fixed* and *variable costs*. These terms will be used repeatedly throughout this textbook. It is critically important that you gain a thorough understanding of the behavior patterns of these two cost categories. The following section provides a graphical presentation and a summary chart that highlight the differences between fixed and variable costs. You should study these graphs and the summary chart carefully before proceeding with your course of study.

With respect to fixed costs, the term *fixed* refers to the behavior of *total cost*. The *cost per unit* of a fixed cost *varies inversely* with changes in the level of activity. As activity increases, fixed cost per unit decreases. As activity decreases, fixed cost per unit increases. These relationships are shown graphically in Exhibit 2–18.

LO1 Distinguish between fixed and variable cost behavior.

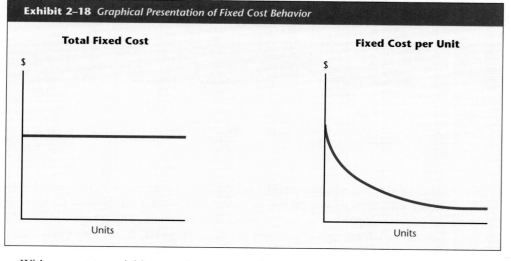

Exhibit 2–18 *Graphical Presentation of Fixed Cost Behavior*

With respect to variable cost, the term *variable* refers to the behavior of *total cost*. Total variable cost increases or decreases proportionally with changes in the volume of activity. In contrast, *variable cost per unit remains fixed* at all levels of activity. These relationships are shown graphically in Exhibit 2–19.

The relationships between fixed and variable costs are summarized in the chart in Exhibit 2–20. Again, we urge you to study these relationships carefully.

LO7 Understand how cost behavior is affected by the relevant range and the decision-making context.

The Relevant Range

Suppose that SPI is required to rent a concert hall at a cost of $5,000. The facility has a capacity to seat 4,000 people. Is the cost of the concert hall a fixed or variable cost? Since total

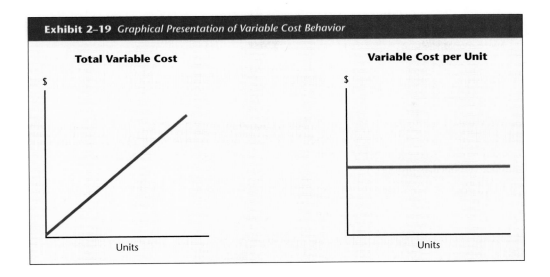

Exhibit 2–19 *Graphical Presentation of Variable Cost Behavior*

Total Variable Cost   **Variable Cost per Unit**

Exhibit 2–20 *Fixed and Variable Cost Behavior*

When Activity Level Changes	Total Cost	Cost per Unit
Fixed costs	Remains constant	Changes *inversely*
Variable costs	Changes in *direct* proportion	Remains constant

cost remains the same regardless of whether one ticket, 4,000 tickets, or any number in between is sold, the cost is a fixed cost relative to ticket sales. However, what happens if significantly more than 4,000 people desire to attend the concert? Under these circumstances, SPI may choose to rent a larger facility at a higher cost. In other words, *the cost is fixed only for a designated range of activity.*

A similar condition exists for many variable costs. Suppose that SPI is purchasing 1,800 T-shirts at a cost of $12 each. The supplier may offer a discount to buyers who purchase more than 2,000 units. In this case, the company's variable cost per unit would decrease if it increased its order size to exceed 2,000 units. The point to remember is that cost behavior applies to a specified range of activity. The range of activity over which the definitions of fixed and variable costs apply is commonly called the **relevant range.** Also notice that the definitions of fixed and variable are bound by a specified period of time. With respect to the concert hall, the time period is one day. If the time period is changed from one to two days, the total cost of rental is no longer fixed. Instead, it moves from $5,000 to $10,000. It is fixed at $5,000 for one day only. As this discussion implies, *the classification of fixed versus variable can have meaning only within the context of a specified relevant range of activity for a defined period of time.*

Context-Sensitive Definitions of Fixed and Variable

The behavior pattern of a particular cost may change from fixed to variable or vice versa, depending on the context in which the cost is considered. For example, the cost of the band was considered to be fixed at $48,000 when STI was considering hiring it to play at a single concert. Regardless of how many tickets it sells, the total cost remains fixed at $48,000. However, a variable behavior pattern occurs if SPI decides to use the band to perform at a series of concerts. The total cost and the cost per concert if the band plays one, two, three, four, or five concerts at a cost of $48,000 per concert are shown in Exhibit 2–21.

Within this context, the total cost of hiring the band increases proportionally with the number of concerts while cost per concert remains constant. Accordingly, the cost is a variable cost. Clearly, the same cost can behave as a fixed cost or as a variable cost, depending on the

LO7 Understand how cost behavior is affected by the relevant range and the decision-making context.

Exhibit 2-21 *Cost Behavior Relative to Number of Concerts*					
Number of concerts (a)	1	2	3	4	5
Cost per concert (b)	$48,000	$48,000	$ 48,000	$ 48,000	$ 48,000
Total cost (a × b)	$48,000	$96,000	$144,000	$192,000	$240,000

activity base used to define the cost. When trying to identify a cost as fixed or variable, you must first ask yourself, *"fixed or variable" relative to what activity base?* The cost of the band is fixed *relative* to the number of tickets sold for a specific concert; it is variable *relative* to the number of concerts produced.

Check Yourself 2–4

Is the compensation cost for managers of Pizza Hut Restaurants a fixed cost or a variable cost?

Answer The answer depends on the context. For example, since a store manager's salary remains unchanged regardless of how many customers enter a particular restaurant, it can be classified as a fixed cost relative to the number of customers at a particular restaurant. However, the more restaurants that Pizza Hut operates, the higher the total managers' compensation cost will be. Accordingly, managers' salary cost would be classified as a variable cost relative to the number of restaurants opened.

▌Cost Averaging

LO8 Select an appropriate time period for the calculation of the average cost per unit.

Lake Resorts, Inc. (LRI), provides water skiing lessons for its guests. Since the demand for lessons is seasonal (there is more demand in July than in December), LRI has decided to rent equipment (boat, skis, ropes, life jackets, etc.) on an as-needed basis. LRI's accountant has collected the following data regarding the expected cost of providing ski lessons:

1. The daily rental fee for equipment is $80.
2. Instructors are paid $15 per hour.
3. Fuel costs amount to $2 per hour of operation.
4. Each lesson requires one hour of time. Ten hours of effective ski time are available each day.

Suppose that management wants to know the cost per lesson if 2, 5, or 10 lessons are provided per day. The appropriate computations are shown in Exhibit 2–22.

It is important to recognize that the cost per lesson shown in Exhibit 2–22 is an *average cost.* Accountants focus on average costs because they are relatively easy to compute and are frequently more relevant to decision making than are actual costs. Consider some of the difficulties that would be encountered in trying to determine the actual cost of each individual lesson. Because the cost of equipment rental covers any number of lessons within the relevant range, it cannot be identified as an actual cost of any particular lesson. Because some skiers weigh more than others, pulling them behind the boat requires the use of more gas. Likewise, wind conditions, water currents, the number of times a skier falls, and the presence of other boats affect cost factors such as the actual time required to administer a lesson, the use of equipment, and the consumption of fuel. Determining the exact amount of each resource used for each lesson is an impossible task.

Even if the actual cost per lesson could be computed, the information would be of little value. What could be gained by

Exhibit 2-22 *Analysis of Total and Unit Cost*			
Number of Lessons (a)	**2**	**5**	**10**
Cost of equipment rental	$ 80	$ 80	$ 80
Cost of instruction (a × $15)	30	75	150
Cost of fuel (a × $2)	4	10	20
Total cost (b)	$114	$165	$250
Cost per lesson (b ÷ a)	$ 57	$ 33	$ 25

Natasha Bell is a business student who works part-time to help pay for her college expenses. She is currently taking her first accounting course. Natasha often hears managers at her employer's company refer to depreciation as a *fixed cost*. The instructor in her accounting course requires students to study the financial statements of several real-world companies, including those of America Online (AOL). While reviewing AOL's income statement, Natasha noticed that the company's depreciation did not appear to be fixed. In fact, it went from $2.8 million in 1994 to $12.3 million in 1995 to $33.4 million in 1996. What could possibly explain why this *fixed cost changed* so radically over a three-year period?

When an accountant says a cost is fixed, remember that it can stay the same (i.e., be fixed) in relation to one factor but change (i.e., be variable) in relation to other factors. Also, fixed costs are fixed only within a relevant range. The depreciation cost for a single network server is fixed for a certain range of activity, but the capacity of each server is limited. AOL's client base has been growing so rapidly that the top end of server capacity (i.e., the upper end of the relevant range) is exceeded regularly. To provide service to a rapidly expanding customer base, AOL purchased many new servers and other depreciable assets from 1994 to 1996. The balance of property, plant, and equipment at AOL for these three years follows:

Year	Property, Plant, and Equipment
1994	$ 20,306,000
1995	70,919,000
1996	101,277,000

Clearly, depreciation charges can be expected to increase as the investment in depreciable assets increases. In this case, *fixed* means "stays the same" relative to a certain number of customers. When the number of customers exceeds the relevant range, additional investments and corresponding depreciation charges increase.

knowing that on a day when 10 lessons were administered, it cost a little more or less to administer the fifth lesson than the sixth? Customers are accustomed to standardized pricing. They do not want pricing that depends on which way the wind is blowing, even if the direction of the wind affects the actual cost of a ski lesson. Also, customers need price data to help them make decisions. They need to know how much the company will charge them before they decide whether to take a lesson. They do not want to wait until after the lesson for someone to determine the exact cost. Accordingly, average cost data may be more useful than actual cost information for pricing decisions.

Average cost data are also useful for performance evaluation and for control. Knowing whether an instructor spent a few minutes more or less on a particular lesson is of little use. Knowing, however, that an instructor averages 10 extra minutes on virtually every lesson taught signals the need for corrective action. Knowing what happens *on average* is more useful than knowing what happened in one particular instance.

Computing the average cost per unit requires considering the span of time from which data are drawn. Suppose that during one day in the 2007 season, an instructor administered 10 lessons for a total cost of $250. During the 2006 season, LRI administered a total of 589 lessons at a cost of $19,437. Furthermore, assume that the records indicate that during the last five seasons, LRI administered 2,500 lessons at a total cost of $55,000. What is the average cost per lesson for the day, the year, and the five-year period? The answers are provided in Exhibit 2–23.

Exhibit 2–23 *Cost per Lesson*

	Span of Time		
	One Day	**One Year**	**Five Years**
Total cost of lessons (a)	$250	$19,437	$55,000
Number of lessons (b)	10	589	2,500
Cost per lesson (a ÷ b)	$25	$33	$22

Assuming that management has decided to price ski lessons at $5 above the average cost per lesson, which of the cost per lesson figures should be used to establish the price? Should the price be $30 ($25 + $5), $38 ($33 + $5) or $27 ($22 + $5)?[1] The shorter interval (i.e., one day) represents the most current information, but it may also be the least relevant. Suppose that the one-day average cost was computed on a Sunday when demand for ski lessons was extremely high. This would explain why the daily cost per lesson figure is lower than the yearly amount. The fixed cost of equipment rental is spread over a large number of lessons, making the cost per lesson small. Unfortunately, the Sunday average has little relevance for setting Monday's prices. This is true because customer demand drops sharply on Monday when many weekend vacationers return to work.

An average based on yearly data is probably more appropriate. If last year's season is a good predictor of this year's demand, pricing lessons at $38 provides a return that approximates the $5 average that management desires to earn. On days when demand is high, cost per unit will be low, and the resort will earn more than $5 per lesson. On days when demand is low, it will earn less than $5. However, on average, it will earn the desired return. Distortions can also result from the use of long as well as short time spans. For example, data drawn from the five seasons may not reflect current costs or recent changes in customer demand. For example, equipment rental cost was probably less five years ago than it is today. As this discussion implies, the selection of the most appropriate time span requires considerable judgment. *A good management accountant provides much more than number crunching.*

■ Use of Estimates in Real-World Problems

LO9 Define the term *mixed costs.*

Identifying fixed and variable costs in real-world contexts normally requires the use of estimated rather than actual costs. Imagine the difficulty of trying to classify all of the different costs incurred by a large company such as Delta Airlines as fixed or variable. Record keeping would be horrendous. The volume of the work required would be complicated by the fact that some costs are neither purely fixed nor variable. Instead, they contain a mixture of fixed and variable components. These costs are called **mixed costs** or **semivariable costs.** Consider, for example, the charges for cellular phone service. Customers are typically charged a flat rate plus an amount for each minute that they use the phone. The flat rate stays the same no matter how long the phone is used. Even if no calls are made, the customer must pay the flat rate fee. This portion of the phone cost behaves as a fixed cost. However, the total bill increases for each minute that the phone is in use. The more the phone is used, the higher the bill. With respect to this portion of the bill, the cost behavior is variable.

Dividing a mixed cost into its respective fixed and variable components may be difficult if many phones are in use simultaneously. For example, suppose that the annual phone expense for a multinational sales company is $1,280,000. The company uses thousands of phones that are serviced by a variety of cellular companies that charge different rates for phone usage. Dividing the total expense into fixed and variable components would require the analysis of thousands of separate phone bills. Fortunately, this tedious task usually is unnecessary because a company may find estimated rather than actual costs to be adequate for decision making. The next section describes a method of dividing total cost into estimated fixed and variable components.

[1]The cost plus method is only one of several possible pricing strategies. Other pricing practices will be discussed in subsequent chapters.

High-Low Method of Estimating Fixed and Variable Costs

Suppose that Rainy Day Books is interested in expanding its operations by opening a new store. The company president, who is attempting to evaluate the risk of opening it, wants to know the level of fixed cost likely to be incurred. To satisfy the president's request, the accountant gathered the data shown in Exhibit 2–24 regarding the sales volume and cost history of an existing store. Assuming that the new store can operate with approximately the same cost structure, the data can be used to estimate the amount of fixed cost likely to be incurred by the new store. The procedures used to make the estimate will be discussed in the following paragraphs.

LO10 Use the high-low method and scattergraphs to estimate fixed and variable costs.

The first step is to identify the high and low activity points in the data set. Indeed, the procedure used is called the **high-low method.** The total cost of operating the store *depends* on the number of books sold (i.e., the more books sold, the higher the total cost). Accordingly, the number of books sold is called the *independent variable,* and the total cost is called the *dependent variable.*

Applying the high-low method begins with identifying the highest and lowest activity points in the data set. Notice that the lowest point expressed in units sold does not correspond to the lowest point for total cost. The lowest point in units sold occurred in May; the lowest total cost occurred in March. Which should be classified as the low point? The answer is the low point for the number of units sold. The determining factor is the independent variable. Since cost depends on sales volume, we must focus our attention on the number of units sold. The high point in sales volume occurred in December. The relevant number and cost data for the December and May high and low points follow:

Exhibit 2–24 *Cost Data*		
Month	**Units Sold**	**Total Cost**
January	30,000	$450,000
February	14,000	300,000
March	12,000	150,000
April	25,000	440,000
May	10,000	180,000
June	11,000	240,000
July	20,000	350,000
August	18,000	400,000
September	17,000	360,000
October	16,000	320,000
November	27,000	490,000
December	34,000	540,000

The variable cost per unit is determined by dividing the difference in the total cost by the difference in the number of units sold, as follows:

	Units Sold	**Total Cost**
High (December)	34,000	$540,000
Low (May)	10,000	$180,000

$$\frac{\text{Variable cost}}{\text{per unit}} = \frac{\text{Difference in total cost}}{\text{Difference in volume}} = \frac{(\$540,000 - \$180,000)}{(34,000 - 10,000)} = \frac{\$360,000}{24,000} = \$15$$

The fixed cost component can now be determined by subtracting the variable cost from the total cost. The computation can use the high point or the low point. Either reference point yields the same result. Computations using the high point are as follows:

$$\text{Fixed Cost} + \text{Variable cost} = \text{Total cost}$$
$$\text{Fixed cost} = \text{Total cost} - \text{Variable cost}$$
$$\text{Fixed cost} = \$540,000 - (\$15.00 \times 34,000 \text{ units})$$
$$\text{Fixed cost} = \$30,000$$

The high-low method is easy to use, but it is vulnerable to inaccuracies. Notice that although the data set has 12 data points, only 2 of them are used to develop the fixed and variable cost estimates. If either or both of these points are not representative of the true relationship between fixed and variable costs, the estimates produced by the high-low method will be inaccurate. Accordingly, *the chief advantage of the high-low method is simplicity of use; its chief disadvantage is vulnerability to inaccuracy.* Rainy Day's accountant decides to use a scattergraph to test the accuracy of the high-low method.

▌Scattergraph Method of Estimating Fixed and Variable Costs

Lo10 Use the high-low method and scattergraphs to estimate fixed and variable costs.

Scattergraphs are sometimes used as an estimation technique for dividing total cost into fixed and variable cost components. In this case, Rainy Day's accountant constructs a **scattergraph** by recording the number of books sold along the horizontal axis. Cost data are recorded along the vertical axis. The 12 data points are then plotted on the graph, and a line is drawn through the high and low points in the data set. The result is shown in Exhibit 2–25.

After viewing the scattergraph in Exhibit 2–25, the accountant is certain that the high and low points are not representative of the data set. Notice that most of the data points are above the high-low line. The line should be shifted upward to reflect the influence of the

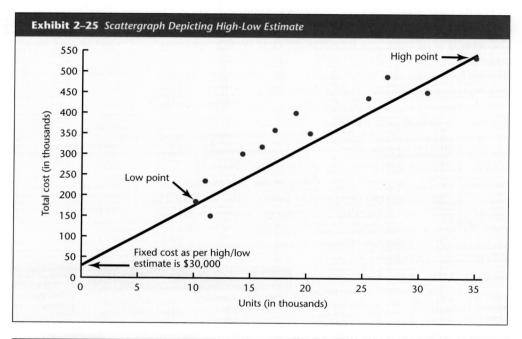

Exhibit 2–25 *Scattergraph Depicting High-Low Estimate*

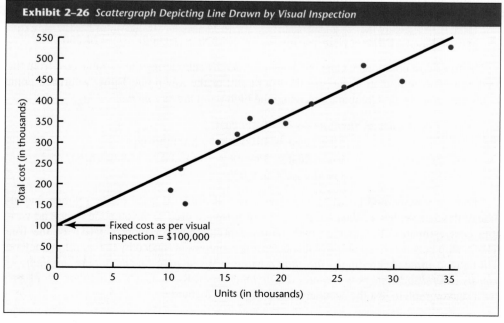

Exhibit 2–26 *Scattergraph Depicting Line Drawn by Visual Inspection*